MICROECONOMICS

SECOND EDITION

UPDATED EDITION

MICROECONOMICS

SECOND EDITION

MICHAEL PARKIN

UNIVERSITY
OF
WESTERN ONTARIO

**ADDISON-WESLEY
PUBLISHING COMPANY**

READING, MASSACHUSETTS ◆ MENLO PARK, CALIFORNIA ◆ NEW YORK
DON MILLS, ONTARIO ◆ WOKINGHAM, ENGLAND ◆ AMSTERDAM
BONN ◆ SYDNEY ◆ SINGAPORE ◆ TOKYO
MADRID ◆ SAN JUAN ◆ MILAN ◆ PARIS

Library of Congress Cataloging-in-Publication Data

Parkin, Michael, 1939–
    Microeconomics / Michael Parkin.—Updated 2nd ed.
      p.   cm.
    Includes index.
    ISBN 0-201-50032-9
    1. Microeconomics.   I. Title.
HB172.P24   1994
338.5—dc20   93-45830
                                  CIP

Executive Editor:	**Barbara Rifkind**
Senior Sponsoring Editor:	**Marjorie Williams**
Senior Development Editor:	**Marilyn R. Freedman**
Production Supervisor:	**Loren Hilgenhurst Stevens**
Managing Editor:	**Kazia Navas**
Cover Design Director:	**Peter M. Blaiwas**
Cover Design Associate:	**Eileen R. Hoff**
Cover and Interior Designer:	**Karen Gourley-Lehman**
Art and Design Coordinator:	**Meredith Nightingale**
Art Development Editor:	**Kelley Hersey, Focus Design**
Technical Art Supervisor:	**Joseph Vetere**
Technical Art Consultants:	**Loretta Bailey and Dick Morton**
Art Coordinators:	**Janice Alden Mello and Connie Hulse**
Illustrators:	**TSI Graphics**
Electronic Vignettes:	**Frank Mazzola, Jr., Raffaele Delicata Design, and Thomas Vanin-Bishop, Ampersand Studios**
Photo Researchers:	**Pembroke Herbert and Sandi Rygiel, Picture Research Consultants**
Prepress Services Manager:	**Sarah McCracken**
Assistant Editor:	**Kari Heen**
Special Project Manager:	**Cindy Johnson**
Copyeditor:	**Barbara Willette**
Production Services:	**Jane Hoover, Lifland et al., Bookmakers, and Sarah Hallet Corey**
Layout Artists:	**Jane Hoover and Karen Gourley-Lehman**
Permissions Editor:	**Mary Dyer**
Indexer:	**Alexandra Nickerson**
Manufacturing Supervisor:	**Roy Logan**
Senior Marketing Manager:	**David Theisen**
Creative Services Manager:	**Eileen Spingler**
Compositor:	**Black Dot Graphics**
Color Separator:	**Black Dot Graphics**
Printer:	**R. R. Donnelley & Sons Company**

Printed in the United States of America.
1 2 3 4 5 6 7 8 9-DO-97969594

To Robin

About Michael Parkin

Michael Parkin received his training as an economist at the Universities of Leicester and Essex in England. Currently in the Department of Economics at the University of Western Ontario, Canada, Professor Parkin has held faculty appointments at Brown University, the University of Manchester, and the University of Essex. He has served on the editorial boards of the *American Economic Review* and the *Journal of Monetary Economics* and as managing editor of the *Canadian Journal of Economics*. He is the author of *Macroeconomics* (Prentice-Hall). Professor Parkin's research on macroeconomics, monetary economics, and international economics has resulted in 160 publications in journals and edited volumes, including the *American Economic Review*, the *Journal of Political Economy*, the *Review of Economic Studies*, the *Journal of Monetary Economics*, and the *Journal of Money, Credit and Banking*. It became most visible to the

public with his work on inflation that discredited the use of wage and price controls. Michael Parkin also spearheaded the movement toward European monetary union. Professor Parkin is an experienced and dedicated teacher of introductory economics.

PREFACE

O CHANGE THE WAY STUDENTS SEE THE world—this is my purpose in teaching economics and has remained my goal in preparing this revision. There is no greater satisfaction for a teacher than sharing the joy of students who have come to understand the powerful lessons of the economic approach. But these lessons are not easy to master. Every day in my classroom, I relearn the challenges of gaining the insights that we call the economist's way of thinking and recall my own early struggles to master this discipline. In preparing this revision, I have been able to draw on the experiences not only of my own students, but also of hundreds of users of the first edition, both instructors and their students.

Three assumptions have guided the choices that faced me in writing this book. First, students are eager to learn, but they are overwhelmed by the seemingly endless claims on their time and energy. Therefore they want to know why they are being asked to study a particular body of material and require demonstration of its relevance to their own everyday experience. Second, students expect thoughtful and straightforward explanations, so they can begin to apply the principles they are learning. Third, today's students are more interested in the present and the future than in the past. They want to learn the economics of the 1990s so that, as they enter the twenty-first century, they will be equipped with the principles that will help them understand apparently unpredictable events.

Approach

The core of the principles course has been around for more than 100 years, and other important elements, especially parts of the theory of the firm and Keynesian macroeconomics, have been with us for more than 50 years. But economics has also been developing and changing rapidly during the past few decades. All principles texts pay some attention to these more recent developments, but none has succeeded in integrating the new and traditional. My goal has been to incorporate new ideas—game theory, the modern theory of the firm, information, and public choice—into the body of timeless principles.

The presence of modern topics does not translate into "high level"; nor does it translate into "bias." At every point, I have striven to make recent developments accessible to beginning students. Where these theories are controversial, alternative approaches are presented, evaluated, and compared.

But this book does have a point of view. It is that economics is a serious, lively, and evolving science—a science that seeks to develop a body of theory powerful enough to explain the economic world around us and that pursues its task by building, testing, and rejecting economic models. Where matters are settled, I present what we know; where controversy persists, I present the alternative viewpoints.

The Second Edition Update

Consistent with my desire to keep pace with rapid change in the economic landscape, I have made many changes to bring this special updated edition closer to the student's "real time." For instance, four of the second edition's "Reading Between the Lines" features have been replaced. Statistics have been updated through 1992. And the Clinton administration's first steps in formulating policy have been included.

Microeconomics and Changes in the Second Edition

The structure of the microeconomics presentation remains consistent with the first edition, but I have made many important changes. I have simplified but vastly increased the range of application of the demand and supply model (Chapter 6) to deal with such issues as who pays a sales tax and trading in prohibited goods. I have expanded the treatment of the marginal utility theory of consumer choice (Chapter 7) to give a stronger graphical derivation of consumer equilibrium and the demand curve. The modern theory of the firm, including principal and agent issues, is given a much simplified treatment in Chapter 9, and isoquants are covered in the appendix to Chapter 10. My presentation of the game theory approach to understanding oligopoly has been

well received for its simple yet serious treatment. In revising the oligopoly chapter (Chapter 13), I recognized that students can gain additional insights from the traditional oligopoly models and included these. A completely new chapter (Chapter 17) deals with the issues arising from uncertainty and incomplete information and illustrates these issues with examples drawn from markets for used cars, insurance, credit, and risky assets. My approach in this chapter is the same as in the rest of the book—to explain a difficult (and in this case relatively new) topic in a clear and accessible way that fits naturally into the core principles sequence. Finally, the discussion of income distribution issues in Chapter 18 now contains a much expanded treatment of income redistribution policies, including the negative income tax.

Special Features

This second edition, like its predecessor, is packed with special features designed to enhance the learning process.

Art Program

A highly successful innovation in the first edition was the outstanding art program. The art not only was visually attractive and engaging but also communicated the economic principles unambiguously and clearly. We received enormously positive feedback on the art program, confirming our belief that one of the most important tools for economists is graphical analysis and also that this is precisely an area that gives many students much difficulty. In the second edition, we have further refined the data-based art by deriving a style that clearly reveals the data and trends. In addition, diagrams that illustrate economic processes now consistently distinguish key economic players (firms, households, governments, and markets).

Our goal is to show clearly "where the economic action is." To achieve this, we observe a consistent protocol in style, notation, and use of color, including:

◆ Highlighting shifted curves, points of equilibrium, and the most important features in red

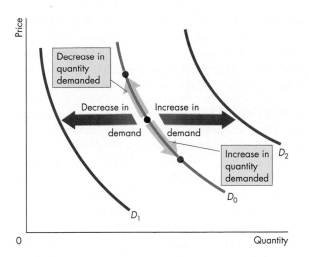

- Using arrows in conjunction with color to lend directional movement to what are usually static presentations
- Pairing graphs with data tables from which the curves have been plotted
- Using color consistently to underscore the content and referring to such use of color in the text and captions
- Labeling key pieces of information in graphs with boxed notes
- Rendering each piece electronically so that precision is achieved

The entire art program has been developed with the study and review needs of the student in mind. We have retained the following features:

- Marking the most important figures and tables with a red key ◆ and listing them at the end of the chapter under "Key Figures and Tables"
- Using complete, informative captions that encapsulate major points in the graph so that students can preview or review the chapter by skimming through the art

The Interviews

Substantive interviews with famous economists constituted another popular feature in the first edition. I am continuing the tradition and have included all new interviews—nine in total—each with an economist who has contributed significantly to advancing the thinking and practice in our discipline. Three of the interviews are with Nobel laureates: Kenneth Arrow, Ronald H. Coase, and Robert Solow. The

interviews encourage students to participate in the conversations as the economists discuss their areas of specialization, their unique contributions to economics, and also their general insights that are relevant to beginning students.

Each interview opens one of the book's nine parts and has been carefully edited to be self-contained. Since each interview discusses topics that are introduced formally in the subsequent chapters, students can use it as a preview to some of the terminology and theory they are about to encounter. A more careful reading afterwards will give students a fuller appreciation of the discussion. Finally, the whole series of interviews can be approached as an informal symposium on the subject matter of economics as it is practiced today.

Reading Between the Lines

Another feature of the previous edition that was well received was "Reading Between the Lines." These news article spreads help students to build critical thinking skills and to interpret daily news events (and their coverage in the media) using economic principles. I have updated all of the news articles in this edition and have selected topics that appeal to students, such as falling SAT scores, Nintendo rentals, and the environmental debate over the spotted owl. Each "Reading Between the Lines" spread contains three passes at a story. It begins with a facsimile (usually abbreviated) of an actual newspaper or magazine article. It then presents a digest of the article's essential points. Finally, it provides an economic analysis of the article, based on the economic methods presented in that chapter.

Our Advancing Knowledge

The fully revised "Our Advancing Knowledge" features help students trace the evolution of pathbreaking economic ideas and recognize the universality of their application, not only to the past but to the present. For example, Adam Smith's powerful ideas about the division of labor apply to the creation of a computer chip as well as to the pin factory of the eighteenth century. And Dionysius Lardner's 1850s application of demand and supply theory to railroad pricing applies equally to airline pricing today. A new visual design brings excitement and vitality to these inserts, much in the way that the ideas have brought excitement and vitality to economics.

Learning Aids

We have refined our careful pedagogical plan to ensure that this book complements and reinforces classroom learning. Each chapter contains the following pedagogical elements:

Objectives   Each chapter opens with a list of objectives that enable students to set their goals as they begin the chapter.

Chapter Openers   Intriguing puzzles, paradoxes, or metaphors frame the important questions that are unraveled and resolved as the chapter progresses.

Highlighted In-Text Reviews   Succinct summaries for review are interspersed throughout the chapter at the ends of sections.

Key Terms   Highlighted within the text, these concepts form the first part of a three-tiered review of economic vocabulary. These terms are repeated with page references at chapter ends and compiled in the end-of-book glossary.

Key Figures and Tables   The most important figures and tables are identified with the red key and listed at chapter end. ◆

End-of-Chapter Study Material   Chapters conclude with summaries organized around major headings, lists of key terms with page references, lists of key figures and tables with page references, review questions, and problems. In the second edition, we have added many new problems.

Flexibility

I have tried to accommodate a wide range of teaching approaches by building flexibility and optionality into the book. There are several optional sections, which are indicated by footnote. These may be omitted with no loss of continuity.

The Teaching and Learning Package

Our fully integrated text and supplements package provides students and professors with a seamless teaching and learning experience. The authors of the components are outstanding educators and scholars and have brought their own human capital (and that of their students!) to the job of improving the quality and value of the ancillaries for the second edition.

Study Guide   Now available in microeconomics and macroeconomics split versions, the revised Study Guide was prepared by David Spencer of Brigham Young University. Carefully coordinated with the main textbook, each chapter of the Study Guide contains: Chapter in Perspective; Learning Objectives; Helpful Hints; Self-Test (concepts review, true/false, multiple-choice, and short-answer questions, and problems) and Answers to Self-Test; and Key Figures and Tables.

Economics in the News with Video Selections
Updated with all new articles, this unique workbook extends the "Reading Between the Lines" feature of the textbook. Prepared by Saul Pleeter (U.S. Department of Defense) and Philip Way of the University of Cincinnati, the supplement includes eighty-five recent news articles organized according to the topical outline of the textbook. An introductory paragraph, learning objectives, and preview precede a facsimile of each article, which is accompanied by analytical questions that give students practice in developing their ability to think like economists. In this edition we have also incorporated ten video excerpts from the MacNeil-Lehrer Business Reports. Just as for the print articles, Pleeter and Way provide a series of probing questions to help students dissect the economic principles that underlie the issues illustrated in the video news clips.

Instructor's Manual for Economics in the News   The solutions to questions and problems in Economics in the News are available to instructors upon request from the Business and Economics Group at Addison-Wesley.

Test Item File   Thoroughly revised test items were prepared by David Denslow of the University of Florida and Barbara Haney Martinez of the Center for Economic Education at the University of Alaska, Fairbanks. The file includes over 4,000 multiple choice questions, about half of which are new to this edition. All questions have been reviewed carefully for accuracy by Robert Horn and Sharon O'Hare at James Madison University. Each chapter includes a section of questions that are directly from the Study Guide and a section of questions that parallel those in the Study Guide.

Computerized Test Item File   Testing software with graphics capability for IBM-PC and compatible microcomputers or Macintosh microcomputers is available to qualified adopters.

Instructor's Manual   A brand new Instructor's Manual has been prepared by Mark Rush of the University of Florida. It includes detailed chapter outlines and teaching suggestions; cross-references to the color acetates, videos, and software; answers to all review questions and problems in the textbook; additional discussion questions; information on material new to the second edition; explanations of how each chapter relates to the rest of the book; and a flexibility guide for different course sequences.

Acetates and Overlays   Key figures from the text are rendered in full color on the acetates. There are 180 acetates, of which 70 have overlays. The acetates are available to qualified adopters of the textbook (contact your Addison-Wesley sales representative).

MacNeil-Lehrer Business Reports Videos   An exclusive from Addison-Wesley, these videos illustrate economic principles in action via highly topical news stories. Ten video selections, split evenly between macroeconomic and microeconomic concepts, can be used in conjunction with either the textbook or the Economics in the News supplement. The videos are free to adopters.

Video Guide to MacNeil-Lehrer Business Reports
Helpful teaching notes and discussion questions for using videos in the classroom, as well as relevant graphics prepared as transparency masters, are provided free to adopters.

"Economics in Action" Software   New to this edition is truly interactive tutorial software available for both IBM-compatible and Macintosh computers. This software was created specifically for this text by Douglas McTaggart (co-author of the Australian edition of this book) and David Gould of Bond University, Paul Davies of the University of Melbourne, and myself, with a great deal of help from the many people thanked below. The software includes modules on core concepts such as graphing,

production possibilities and opportunity cost, demand and supply, elasticity, utility and demand, product curves and cost curves, perfect competition, monopoly, macroeconomic performance, aggregate demand and aggregate supply, expenditure multipliers, money and banking, and international trade.

Three interactive modes take full advantage of the computer's capability to facilitate critical thinking skills. First, a tutorial mode walks students through the central concepts. Second, a quiz mode enables guided self-testing. Third, a free mode allows students and professors to interact with economic models by changing parameters and observing the effects on the graphs. For professors, a special disk is available that extends this capability to generating electronic transparencies for dynamic use in the classroom.

In addition to its emphasis on interaction, the software is also closely integrated with the text. The art style is the same, the terminology is consistent, and supporting material in the text is cross-referenced in the software.

The software has its own authoring language that enables professors to customize tutorials, quizzes, and graphs to fit their own course material. The software has been fully tested and reviewed for accuracy. An Economics in Action Instructor's Guide is available.

Acknowledgments

The endeavor of creating a principles textbook involves the creative collaboration and contribution of many individuals. Although the extent of my debts cannot be fully acknowledged here, it is nevertheless a joy to record my gratitude to the many people who have helped, some without realizing just how helpful they were.

I want to thank those of my colleagues at the University of Western Ontario who have taught me a great deal that can be found in these pages: Jim Davies, Jeremy Greenwood, Ig Horstmann, Peter Howitt, Greg Huffman, David Laidler, Phil Reny, Chris Robinson, John Whalley, and Ron Wonnacott.

I want to extend a special thanks to Glenn MacDonald, who worked well beyond the call of duty discussing this project with me from its outset, helping me develop many of the pedagogical features and reading and commenting in detail on all the micro chapters. Special thanks also go to Doug McTaggart of Bond University and Christopher Findlay of the University of Adelaide, co-authors of the Australian edition, and David King, co-author of the European edition. Their suggestions arising from their adaptations of the first edition have been extremely helpful in fine-tuning this edition. More than that, Doug and I worked together on the early drafts of the new chapter on uncertainty and information in the perfect Queensland winter of 1991.

I also want to acknowledge my debt to those who have had a profound influence on my whole view of and approach to economics and whose influence I can see in these pages. Although I never sat in their classrooms, they are in a very real sense my teachers. I am especially grateful to John Carlson (Purdue University), Carl Christ (Johns Hopkins University), Robert Clower (University of South Carolina), Ed Feige (University of Wisconsin at Madison), Herschel Grossman (Brown University), and Sam Wu (University of Iowa). I also want to place on record my enormous debt to the late Karl Brunner. The energy, drive, and entrepreneurship of this outstanding economist provided me and my generation of economists with incredible opportunities to interact and learn from each other in a wide variety of conference settings, in both the United States and Europe.

It is also a pleasure to acknowledge my debt to the several thousand students to whom I have been privileged to teach introductory economics. The instant feedback that comes from the look of puzzlement or enlightenment has taught me, more than anything else, how to teach economics.

Producing a text such as this is a team effort, and the members of the Addison-Wesley "Parkin Team" are genuine co-producers of this book. I am especially grateful to and have been truly inspired by Barbara Rifkind, an extraordinary editor who, as executive editor, created and directed the team with whom it has been a privilege to work. I am also deeply indebted to my development editor, Marilyn Freedman. The personal dedication and professional skill that she brought to the task of crafting the book's broad thrust and fine details and her commit-

ment to making the book as interesting, effective, and error-free as possible were extraordinary. High praise and great thanks go to Loren Hilgenhurst Stevens, who, as production supervisor, coordinated the entire production process, coping calmly and decisively with the cascading crises that daily crossed her desk as she brought all the many complex elements together. Sincere thanks also to Marjorie Williams, who, as senior economics editor, managed and coordinated all the interviews and devised the weekly workload memo that kept my nose pointed firmly in the desired direction; Dave Theisen, business and economics marketing manager, who devised and managed the marketing plan; Kari Heen, assistant editor, whose cheery voice and friendly faxes lifted the sagging spirits in just the right way at just the right time; and especially Cindy Johnson, project manager of the supplements, whose outstanding editorial and managerial skills and personal commitment have brought together a state-of-the-art teaching and learning package. Great thanks go to Loretta Bailey, Janice Mello, Sherry Berg, Sharon Cogdill, Phyllis Coyne, Kelley Hersey, Jane Hoover, Karen Lehman, Stephanie Magean, Dick Morton, Kazia Navas, Meredith Nightingale, and Barbara Willette.

I also wish to express my gratitude to Bob McGough, a superb financial and economics journalist, who provided a thorough and creative edit of an early draft of the first edition and who taught me a great deal about how to write more clearly and effectively. Mark Rush, David Denslow, Barbara Haney Martinez, David Spencer, Saul Pleeter, Phillip Way, Paul Davis, and David Gould were the primary authors of the supplements package and graciously shared their professional insights and teaching expertise with me. I also want to thank my secretary, Barbara Craig, who helped at various stages of this book, typing and retyping its countless drafts and redrafts.

I have left until last four people to whom I want to give special thanks. First, my wife, colleague, best friend, and co-author of the Canadian edition, Robin Bade, has been almost a co-author of this work. She has read every word that I have written, commented in detail on every draft, and helped manage the project from its conception to its conclusion. Without the anticipation of her help and its availability, I could not have contemplated embarking on this project. Finally, I want to acknowledge the help and inspiration of my children, Catherine, Richard, and Ann. Through the years when I was developing and writing the first edition, they were going through various stages of high school and college. They forced me to craft a book that they could understand and found interesting. In preparing this edition, I have been especially helped by Richard, who became a Harvard Graphics wizard and created the entire art manuscript.

The empirical test of this textbook's value continues to be made in the classroom. I would appreciate hearing from instructors and students about how I might continue to improve the book in future editions.

Michael Parkin
Department of Economics
University of Western Ontario
London, Ontario N6A 5C2

Reviewers

Update Reviews

Gerald McDonald, Southeast Missouri State University
Mark Rush, University of Flordia

Manuscript Reviews

Ronald M. Ayers, University of Texas at San Antonio
Mohsen Bahmani-Oskooee, University of Wisconsin–Milwaukee
Charles L. Ballard, Michigan State University
Vanessa Craft, Bentley College
Ronald E. Crowe, University of Central Flordia
Shirley J. Gedeon, The University of Vermont
James Robert Gillette, Texas A&M University
John W. Graham, Rutgers—The State University of New Jersey, Newark Campus
James H. Holcomb, The University of Texas at El Paso
Robert N. Horn, James Madison University
Noreen E. Lephardt, Marquette University
Steven J. Matusz, Michigan State University
J. M. Pogodzinski, San Jose State University
James E. Price, Syracuse University
Jonathan B. Pritchett, Tulane University
Christine Rider, St. John's University
Richard Rosenberg, Pennsylvania State University
Peter Rupert, State University of New York at Buffalo

Planning Reviews

Mary E. Allender, University of Portland
Philip J. Grossman, Wayne State University
Bruce Herrick and members of the Department of Economics, Washington and Lee University
Andrew Kliman, New York Institute of Technology

M. L. Livingston, University of Northern Colorado
Nan Maxwell, California State University–Hayward
Henry McCarl, University of Alabama at Birmingham
Augustus Shackelford, El Camino College
Eleanor T. von Ende, Texas Tech University
Larry Wimmer, Brigham Young University
Gary Zinn, East Carolina University

Accuracy Reviews

William Aldridge, Shelton State Community College
Donald H. Dutkowsky, Syracuse University
Mark Rush, University of Florida
David Spencer, Brigham Young University

Telephone Interviews

David Abel, Mankato State University
Richard Adelstein, Wesleyan University
Marjorie Baldwin, East Carolina University
Maurice Ballabon, City University of New York, Bernard M. Baruch College
Scott Benson, Jr., Idaho State University
Steven Berry, Yale University
Scott Bloom, North Dakota State University
Mary O. Borg, University of North Florida
Michael Boyd, University of Vermont
Jim Bradley, University of South Carolina
Habtu Braha, Coppin State College
Michael Brun, Illinois State University
Gregory Bush, Suffolk County Community College
Rupert Caine, Onondaga Community College
Fred Carstensen, University of Connecticut
Shirley Cassing, University of Pittsburgh
Cleveland A. Chandler, Sr., Howard University
Larry Chenault, Miami University
Edward Christ, Cabrini College

Donald Coffin, Indiana University
Walter Coleman, Shaw University
James Perry Cover, University of Alabama
Anthony Davies, State University of New York at Albany
Edward A. Day, University of Central Florida
Larry DeBrock, University of Illinois at Urbana-Champaign
David Denslow, University of Florida
Johan Deprez, Texas Tech University
Frances Durbin, University of Delaware
John Eastwood, Northern Arizona University
David H. Feldman, College of William and Mary
David Ferrell, Central College
Warren Ford, North Shore Community College
Joseph Fosu, Western Illinois University
Alwyn Fraser, Atlantic Union College
Arthur Friedberg, Mohawk Valley Community College
Joseph Fuhrig, Golden Gate University
Ena Garland, Babson College
Gasper Garofalo, University of Akron
Maria Giuili, Diablo Valley College
Marsha Goldfarb, University of Maryland, Baltimore County
Mary Goldschmid, College of Mount Saint Vincent
Lawrence Gwinn, Wittenberg University
Anthony Gyapong, Wayne State University
Ahsan Habib, Adrian College
Steven Henson, Western Washington University
Carter Hill, Louisiana State University
Basawaraj Hiremath, Fisk University
Chris W. Holmes, Bainbridge College
Soloman Honig, Montclair State College
Esmail Hossein-zadeh, Drake University
Sheng Hu, Purdue University
M. G. Inaba, Hofstra University
Wasfy B. Iskander, Rhodes College
Rebecca Janski, Indiana State University
Nancy Jianakoplos, Colorado State University
Holorin Jones, Empire State College
Allen Kelly, Duke University
Jyoti Khanna, Cleveland State University
Shin Kim, Chicago State University
John J. Klein, Georgia State University
Ghanbar Kooti, Albany State College
Julia Lane, American University

Stanley J. Lawson, St. John's University
Dennis Patrick Leyden, University of North Carolina
Y. Joseph Lin, University of California–Riverside
Colin Linsley, St. John Fisher College
Ashley Lyman, University of Idaho
Kathryn Marshall, Ohio University
Robert Marshall, Duke University
Therese McCarty, Union College
David Mirza, Loyola University
Richard Moss, Ricks College
Archontis Pantsios, State University of New York at Binghamton
Sanjay Paul, State University of New York at Buffalo
Richard Payne, Boise State University
Pegg Pelt, Gulf Coast Community College
Robert Pugh, Surry Community College
Jack Railey, Illinois Central College
Victor Rieck, Miami Dade Community College
Debra Rose, Gordon College
Gary Santoni, Ball State University
Phillip Sarver, University of Southern Colorado
George Sawdy, Providence College
Ralph Scott, Hendrix College
Chiqurupati Rama Seshu, State University of New York at New Paltz
Michael Sesnowitz, Kent State University
Larry G. Sgontz, University of Iowa
Steve Shapiro, University of North Florida
B. Ted Stecker, North Hennepin Community College
Andrew Stern, California State University–Long Beach
Gerard Stockhauser, Creighton University
Sue Stockly, University of Texas at Austin
Michael Stoller, State University of New York at Plattsburgh
Scot Stradley, University of North Dakota
Fredrick Tiffany, Wittenberg University
James Vincent, University of St. Thomas
Arthur Welsh, Pennsylvania State University
Bert Wheeler, Liberty University
Chuck Whiteman, University of Iowa
Peter Wilanoski, University of Portland
Patricia Wiswell, Columbia-Greene Community College
Craig Witt, University of Louisville

PART 1: Robert Solow (pp. 1–4), © L. Barry Hetherington.

CHAPTER 1: Pin factory (p. 22), **Culver Pictures.** Woman holding silicon wafer (p. 23), **Tony Stone Worldwide.** Adam Smith (p. 23), **The Bettmann Archive.**

CHAPTER 4: The railroad suspension bridge near Niagara Falls, anonymous (p. 86), **gift of Maxim Karolik for the M. and M. Karolik Collection of American Paintings, 1815–1865; courtesy Museum of Fine Arts, Boston.** Crowded airport (p. 87), **Steve Proehl/The Image Bank.** Antoine-Augustin Cournot (p. 87), **Historical Pictures/Stock Montage.** Alfred Marshall (p. 87), **Historical Pictures/Stock Montage.**

PART 2: Herbert Stein (pp. 97–100), **American Enterprise Institute for Public Policy Research.**

CHAPTER 6: Boston tea party (p. 136), **American Antiquarian Society.** Gas pump (p. 137), **Lightstream.** Fleeming Jenkins (p. 137), **Mary Evans Picture Library.**

PART 3: Richard Easterlin (pp. 152–154), Irene Fertik/USC Periodicals.

CHAPTER 7: Women workers canning peaches (p. 172), **Keystone-Mast Collection, California Museum of Photography, University of California at Riverside.** Modern businesswoman (p. 173), **Richard Wood/The Picture Cube.** Jeremy Bentham (p. 173), **Mary Evans Picture Library.** William Stanley Jevons (p. 173), **MacMillan Press.**

PART 4: Ronald H. Coase (pp. 203–204), **David Joel, Randy Tunnell/The University of Chicago.**

CHAPTER 10: Ford assembly line (p. 256), **Brown Brothers.** Michael Dell (p. 257), **Will Van Overbeek.** Jacob Viner (p. 257), **Seeley G. Mudd Library, Princeton University.** Ronald H. Coase (p. 257), **David Joel/The University of Chicago.**

PART 5: Kenneth Arrow (pp. 274–277), **Stanford University.**

CHAPTER 12: Puck monopoly cartoon (p. 322), **Culver Pictures.** Cable TV worker (p. 323), © 1992 John Lidington, Continental Cablevision. Joan Robinson (p. 323), **Ramsey & Muspratt Archives.**

PART 6: Claudia Goldin (pp. 372–375), **Jane Reed/Harvard University.**

CHAPTER 14: Chicago city scene (p. 398), **Chicago Historical Society.** Cartoon of stacked cars (p. 399), *The Economist,* 9/14/91; reprinted by permission of Robert Hunt. Harold Hotelling (p. 399), **photography by Wootten-Moulio.** Thomas Robert Malthus (p. 399), **The Bettmann Archive.**

PART 7: Anthony Atkinson (pp. 454–457), **Carlo Faulds/Cambridge University.**

CHAPTER 18: Homeless man on Fifth Avenue (p. 506), **AP/Wide World Photos.** Frankfurt crowd (p. 507), **Mike Mazzaschi/Stock Boston.** Simon Kuznets (p. 507), **Harvard University News Office.**

PART 8: Anne Friedlaender (pp. 512–515), © L. Barry Hetherington.

CHAPTER 19: Great Lakes pollution (p. 530), **Jim Baron/© 1992 Image Finders.** Lake Erie fishing boat (p. 531), **Pat Mullen.** James Buchanan (p. 531), **George Mason University, photo by Carl Zitzman.** Arthur Pigou (p. 531), **Y. H. Mottram/National Portrait Gallery, London.**

PART 9: Jeffrey Sachs (pp. 577–579), **Hank Morgan.**

CHAPTER 22: Nineteenth-century clipper ship card (p. 592), **Museum of the City of New York.** Container ship (p. 593), **Sea-Land Corporation.** David Ricardo (p. 593), **Historical Pictures/Stock Montage.**

CHAPTER 23: Chinese peasant farmers (p. 616), **Mark Riboud/Magnum.** Affluent contemporary Chinese couple (p. 617), **Owen Franken/Stock Boston.** Karl Marx (p. 617), **The Bettmann Archive.**

BRIEF CONTENTS

PART 1   INTRODUCTION   1

Chapter 1   What Is Economics?   **5**
Chapter 2   Making and Using Graphs   **27**
Chapter 3   Production, Specialization, and Exchange   **49**
Chapter 4   Demand and Supply   **71**

PART 2   HOW MARKETS WORK   97

Chapter 5   Elasticity   **101**
Chapter 6   Markets in Action   **124**

PART 3   HOUSEHOLDS' CHOICES   152

Chapter 7   Utility and Demand   **156**
Chapter 8   Possibilities, Preferences, and Choices   **178**

PART 4   FIRMS' CHOICES   203

Chapter 9   Organizing Production   **207**
Chapter 10   Output and Costs   **231**

PART 5   MARKETS FOR GOODS AND SERVICES   274

Chapter 11   Competition   **278**
Chapter 12   Monopoly   **312**
Chapter 13   Monopolistic Competition and Oligopoly   **340**

PART 6   MARKETS FOR FACTORS OF PRODUCTION   327

Chapter 14   Pricing and Allocating Factors of Production   **376**
Chapter 15   Labor Markets   **406**
Chapter 16   Capital and Natural Resource Markets   **427**

PART 7   MARKETS, UNCERTAINTY, AND DISTRIBUTION   454

Chapter 17   Uncertainty and Information   **458**
Chapter 18   The Distribution of Income and Wealth   **484**

PART 8   MARKETS AND GOVERNMENT   512

Chapter 19   Market Failure   **516**
Chapter 20   Public Choice   **536**
Chapter 21   Regulation and Antitrust Law   **557**

PART 9   INTERNATIONAL ECONOMICS   577

Chapter 22   Trading with the World   **581**
Chapter 23   Economic Systems in Transition   **608**

CONTENTS

PART 1

INTRODUCTION
TALKING WITH ROBERT SOLOW **1**

CHAPTER 1 What Is Economics? **5**

Choice and Change **6**
Wages and Earnings **7**
Government, Environment, and Economic Systems **7**
Unemployment **7**
Inflation **8**
International Trade **8**
Wealth and Poverty **8**

Scarcity **9**
Economic Activity **9**
Choice **10**
Opportunity Cost **10**
Competition and Cooperation **11**

The Economy **12**
What Is the Economy? **12**
Decision Makers **13**
Markets **14**
Decisions **14**
Coordination Mechanisms **14**
The Global Economy **16**

Economic Science **17**
What Is and What Ought To Be **17**
Observation and Measurement **18**
Economic Theory **18**
Economic Model **18**
Microeconomic and Macroeconomic Models **20**
Model, Theory, and Reality **21**

OUR ADVANCING KNOWLEDGE
UNDERSTANDING THE SOURCES OF ECONOMIC WEALTH **22**

Summary **24**
Key Elements **25**
Review Questions **25**
Problems **26**

CHAPTER 2 Making and Using Graphs **27**

Three Kinds of Lies **28**

Graphing Data 29
  Two-Variable Graphs **29**
  Scatter Diagrams **30**
  Time-Series Graphs **32**

Graphs Used in Economic Models 38
  Things That Go Up and Down Together **38**
  Things That Move in Opposite Directions **38**
  Things That Have a Maximum and a Minimum
    40
  Things That Are Independent **41**

The Slope of a Relationship 42
  Calculating Slope of a Straight Line **42**
  Calculating Slope of a Curved Line **43**

**Graphing Relationships among More Than Two
  Variables 44**
  Other Things Being Equal **44**

READING BETWEEN THE LINES
GRAPHS IN ACTION 36

Summary **46**
Key Elements **46**
Review Questions **47**
Problems **47**

CHAPTER 3 Production, Specialization,
                and Exchange **49**

Making the Most of It **50**

The Production Possibility Frontier 51
  A Model Economy **51**
  Jane's Preferences **53**

Opportunity Cost 54
  The Best Alternative Forgone **54**
  Measuring Opportunity Cost **54**
  Increasing Opportunity Cost **54**
  The Shape of the Frontier **54**
  Everything Has an Increasing Opportunity Cost
    54
  Production Possibilities in the Real World **56**

Economic Growth 57
  The Cost of Economic Growth **57**
  Capital Accumulation and Technological Change
    57
  Economic Growth in the Real World **59**

Gains from Trade 60
  Comparative Advantage: Jane Meets Joe **60**
  Achieving the Gains from Trade **61**
  Productivity and Absolute Advantage **62**

Exchange in the Real World 63
  Property Rights **63**
  Money **66**

READING BETWEEN THE LINES
THE GAINS FROM SPECIALIZATION AND EXCHANGE
    64

Summary **67**
Key Elements **68**
Review Questions **68**
Problems **69**

CHAPTER 4   Demand and Supply **71**

Slide, Rocket, and Roller Coaster **72**

Demand **73**
- What Determines Buying Plans? **73**
- The Law of Demand **73**
- Demand Schedule and Demand Curve **74**
- Willingness to Pay **74**
- A Change in Demand **75**
- Movement along the Demand Curve versus a Shift in the Curve **76**

Supply **78**
- What Determines Selling Plans? **78**
- The Law of Supply **78**
- Supply Schedule and Supply Curve **79**
- Minimum Supply Price **79**
- A Change in Supply **79**
- Movement along the Supply Curve versus a Shift in the Curve **81**

Price Determination **82**
- Price as a Regulator **82**
- Equilibrium **83**

Predicting Changes in Price and Quantity **85**
- A Change in Demand **85**
- A Change in Supply **88**
- Changes in Both Supply and Demand **89**
- Walkmans, Apartments, and Coffee **92**

OUR ADVANCING KNOWLEDGE
DISCOVERING THE LAWS OF DEMAND AND SUPPLY **86**

READING BETWEEN THE LINES
DEMAND AND SUPPLY IN ACTION **90**

Summary **93**
Key Elements **94**
Review Questions **95**
Problems **95**

CHAPTER 5   Elasticity **101**

OPEC's Dilemma **102**

Elasticity of Demand **103**
- Two Possible Scenarios **103**
- Slope Depends on Units of Measurement **104**
- Calculating Elasticity **104**
- Minus Sign and Elasticity **105**
- Why Average Price and Quantity? **105**
- Percentages and Proportions **106**
- Elastic and Inelastic Demand **106**
- Elasticity along a Straight-Line Demand Curve **107**
- Why Elasticity Is Smaller at Lower Prices **107**
- Constant Elasticity Demand Curves **108**
- Real-World Elasticities **108**
- Substitutability **109**
- Proportion of Income Spent on a Good **109**
- Time Frame for Demand **110**

Elasticity, Revenue, and Expenditure **111**

More Demand Elasticities **112**
- Income Elasticity of Demand **112**
- Real-World Income Elasticities of Demand **114**
- Cross Elasticity of Demand **114**

Elasticity of Supply **118**
- Technological Conditions **118**
- Time Frame for Supply **118**

READING BETWEEN THE LINES
ELASTICITY IN ACTION **116**

Summary **120**
Key Elements **121**
Review Questions **121**
Problems **122**

PART 3

HOUSEHOLDS' CHOICES
TALKING WITH RICHARD EASTERLIN **152**

CHAPTER 6 Markers in Action **124**

Turbulent Times **125**

Housing Markets and Rent Ceilings 126
The Market Response to an Earthquake **126**
After the Earthquake **128**
Long-Run Adjustments **128**
A Regulated Housing Market **128**
Search Activity **129**
Black Markets **130**
Rent Ceilings in Practice **130**

The Labor Market and Minimum Wage Regulation 131
The Minimum Wage **134**
The Minimum Wage in Reality **135**

Taxes 136
Who Pays a Sales Tax? **136**
Tax Division and Elasticity of Supply **137**
Tax Division and Elasticity of Demand **138**

Markets for Prohibited Goods 142
A Reminder about the Limits of Economics **142**
A Free Market for Drugs **142**
Prohibition on Drugs **142**
Legalizing and Taxing Drugs **143**

Stabilizing Farm Revenue 144
No Stabilization Program **144**
Speculative Markets in Inventories **146**
Stabilizing Farm Revenue **147**

OUR ADVANCING KNOWLEDGE
WHO PAYS THE TAXES? **136**

READING BETWEEN THE LINES
TAXES AT WORK **140**

Summary **147**
Key Elements **149**
Review Questions **149**
Problems **150**

CHAPTER 7 Utility and Demand **156**

Water, Water, Everywhere **157**

Individual Demand and Market Demand 158

Household Consumption Choices 159
Constraints **159**
Preferences **159**
Temperature—An Analogy **159**
Total Utility and Consumption **160**
Marginal Utility **160**
Utility Maximization **162**
The Utility-Maximizing Choice **162**
Equalizing Marginal Utility per Dollar Spent **162**
Units of Utility **164**

Predictions of Marginal Utility Theory 164
A Fall in the Price of Movies **164**
A Rise in the Price of Soda **165**
The Effects of a Rise in Income **167**
Marginal Utility and the Real World **167**

Criticisms of Marginal Utility Theory 170
Utility Can't Be Observed or Measured **170**
"People Aren't That Smart" **170**

Some Implications of Marginal Utility Theory 171
Consumer Surplus and the Gains from Trade **171**
Calculating Consumer Surplus **171**
The Paradox of Value **174**

READING BETWEEN THE LINES
MARGINAL UTILITY THEORY IN ACTION **168**

OUR ADVANCING KNOWLEDGE
UNDERSTANDING HUMAN BEHAVIOR **172**

Summary **174**
Key Elements **175**
Review Questions **176**
Problems **176**

PART 4

FIRMS' CHOICES
TALKING WITH RONALD H. COASE **203**

CHAPTER 8 Possibilities, Preferences, and Choices **178**

Subterranean Movements **179**

Consumption Possibilities **180**
  Constraint **180**
  Divisible and Indivisible Goods **181**
  The Budget Equation **181**
  Changes in Prices and Income **182**

Preferences **184**
  A Preference Map **185**
  Indifference Curves and Preferences **186**
  Degree of Substitutability **188**

Choice **189**
  Properties of the Best Affordable Point **190**

Predicting Consumer Behavior **191**
  A Change in Price **191**
  The Demand Curve **192**
  A Change in Income **192**
  A Change in Price: Income and Substitution Effects **192**

Model, Theory, and Reality **195**
  The Model **195**
  The Theory **196**
  Back to the Facts **196**

Other Household Choices **196**
  Work Hours and Labor Supply **196**
  Saving **197**

READING BETWEEN THE LINES
HOUSEHOLD CHOICE THEORY IN ACTION **198**

Summary **200**
Key Elements **201**
Review Questions **201**
Problems **202**

CHAPTER 9 Organizing Production **207**

An Apple a Day **208**

The Firm and Its Economic Problem **209**
  What Is a Firm? **209**
  Principal-Agent Relationships **209**
  The Firm's Decisions **209**
  The Forms of Business Organization **210**
  The Relative Importance of Different Types of Firms **211**
  The Pros and Cons of Different Types of Firms **211**

Business Finance **212**
  How Firms Raise Capital **212**
  Financing Decisions and Stock Prices **214**

Cost and Profit **218**
  Pay Now, Use Later **218**
  Buildings, Plant, and Machinery Costs **218**
  Inventory Costs **220**
  Inputs Not Paid For **220**
  The Bottom Line **220**

Economic Efficiency **222**

Firms and Markets **224**
  Why Firms? **224**

READING BETWEEN THE LINES
ORGANIZING PRODUCTION OF COMPUTERS **226**

Summary **228**
Key Elements **229**
Review Questions **229**
Problems **229**

CHAPTER 10 Output and Costs 231

Survival of the Fittest 232

Firms' Objectives and Constraints 233
The Objective: Profit Maximization 233
Constraints 233
The Short Run and the Long Run 234

Short-Run Technology Constraint 234
Total Product 234
Marginal Product 235
Average Product 237
Relationship Between Marginal and Average
Values 238
The Shapes of the Product Curves 238

Short-Run Cost 240
Total Cost 240
Marginal Cost 242
Average Cost 242
Short-Run Cost Curves 242
Why the Average Total Cost Curve Is U-Shaped
243
Cost Curves and the Technology Constraint 244
Real-World Short-Run Costs 245

Plant Size, Cost, and Capacity 248
The Capacity Utilization Puzzle 248
Short-Run Cost and Long-Run Cost 248
The Production Function 249
Diminishing Returns 250
Returns to Scale 250

Plant Size and Cost 251
Four Different Plants 251
The Long-Run Average Cost Curve 251
Shifts in Cost Curves 255

Returns to Scale in Reality 255
Excess Capacity 258
Operating Flat Out 258

READING BETWEEN THE LINES
AUTO PLANT COST CURVES 246

OUR ADVANCING KNOWLEDGE
FIRMS AND COSTS 256

Summary 259
Key Elements 261
Review Questions 261
Problems 262

Appendix: Producing at Least Cost 263
Input Substitution 263
The Substitutability of Capital and Labor 264
Isoquants 265
Isocost Lines 266
The Least-Cost Technique 268
Marginal Product and Marginal Cost 271

PART 5

MARKETS FOR GOODS AND SERVICES
TALKING WITH KENNETH ARROW **274**

CHAPTER 11   Competition **278**

Hot Rivalry in Ice Cream **279**

Perfect Competition 280
  When a Firm Can't Influence Price **280**
  Elasticity of Industry and Firm Demand **280**
  Competition in Everyday Life **281**

Firms' Choices in Perfect Competition 282
  Profit and Revenue **282**
  Profit-Maximizing Output **284**
  Profit in the Short Run **285**
  The Firm's Supply Curve **289**

Output, Price, and Profit in the Short Run 290
  Short-Run Industry Supply Curve **290**
  Short-Run Competitive Equilibrium **292**

Output, Price, and Profit in the Long Run 292
  Entry and Exit **293**
  Changes in Plant Size **295**

Responding to Changing Tastes and Advancing Technology 296
  A Permanent Decrease in Demand **296**
  A Permanent Increase in Demand **297**
  External Economies and Diseconomies **299**
  Technological Change **302**
  Farms in Distress **304**

Competition and Efficiency 305
  Allocative Efficiency **305**
  The Invisible Hand **307**
  Obstacles to Efficiency **307**

READING BETWEEN THE LINES
COMPETITION IN ACTION **300**

Summary **308**
Key Elements **309**
Review Questions **310**
Problems **310**

CHAPTER 12   Monopoly **312**

The Profits of Generosity **313**

How Monopoly Arises 314
  Barriers to Entry **314**

Single-Price Monopoly 315
  Demand and Revenue **315**
  Revenue and Elasticity **316**
  Price and Output Decision **318**
  No Monopoly Supply Curve **321**

Price Discrimination 321
  Price Discrimination and Total Revenue **324**
  Price Discrimination and Consumer Surplus **324**
  Price and Output Decisions with Price
    Discrimination **325**
  Perfect Price Discrimination **327**
  Discrimination among Groups **328**
  Limits to Price Discrimination **328**

Comparing Monopoly and Competition 328
  Price and Output **329**
  Allocative Efficiency **330**
  Redistribution **331**
  Rent Seeking **331**
  Gains from Monopoly **335**

OUR ADVANCING KNOWLEDGE
UNDERSTANDING MONOPOLY POWER **322**

READING BETWEEN THE LINES
THE END OF A SWEET ARRANGEMENT **332**

Summary **337**
Key Elements **338**
Review Questions **338**
Problems   **339**

CHAPTER 13 Monopolistic Competition
and Oligopoly **340**

Fliers and War Games **341**

Varieties of Market Structure 342
Measures of Concentration **342**
Concentration in the U.S. Economy **343**
Limitations of Measures of Concentration **344**
Market Types in the U.S. Economy **345**

Monopolistic Competition 346
Price and Output in Monopolistic Competition **346**
Excess Capacity **347**
Efficiency of Monopolistic Competition **350**
Product Innovation **350**
Advertising **350**

Oliogopoly 351

Traditional Models of Oligopoly 351
The Kinked Demand Curve Model **351**
Dominant Firm Oligopoly **352**

Oligopoly and Game Theory 354
Familiar Games: What They Have in Common **354**
Rules of the Oligopoly Game **354**
Strategies in the Oligopoly Game **354**
Payoffs in the Oligopoly Game **355**
The Prisoners' Dilemma **355**

A Duopoly Game 357
Cost and Demand Conditions **357**
Colluding to Maximize Profit **358**
Cheating on a Collusive Agreement **359**
The Payoff Matrix and Equilibrium **362**
Repeated Games **363**
Uncertainty **364**

Games and Price Wars 365
The Incredible Electrical Conspiracy **365**
Preserving Secrecy **366**

Other Strategic Variables 366
An R & D Game in the Disposable Diaper Industry **366**

READING BETWEEN THE LINES
MONOPOLISTIC COMPETITION IN ACTION **348**

Summary **368**
Key Elements **370**
Review Questions **370**
Problems **371**

CHAPTER 14 Pricing and Allocating
Factors of Production **376**

Many Happy Returns **377**

Factor Prices and Incomes **378**
  An Overview **378**

Demand for Factors **380**
  Profit Maximization **381**
  Marginal Revenue Product and Factor Price **381**
  The Firm's Demand for Labor **381**
  Market Demand **386**
  Elasticity of Demand for Labor **386**

Supply of Factors **387**
  Supply of Labor **388**
  Supply of Capital **390**
  Supply of Land **391**

Competitive Equilibrium **392**
  Labor Market Equilibrium **392**
  Capital Market Equilibrium **393**
  Land Market Equilibrium **397**

Economic Rent and Transfer Earnings **400**

READING BETWEEN THE LINES
THE MARKET FOR CEOs **394**

OUR ADVANCING KNOWLEDGE
RUNNING OUT OF SPACE? **398**

Summary **402**
Key Elements **403**
Review Questions **404**
Problems **404**

CHAPTER 15 Labor Markets **406**

The Sweat of Our Brows **407**

Skill Differentials **408**
  The Demand for Skilled and Unskilled Labor **408**
  The Supply of Skilled and Unskilled Labor **408**
  Wage Rates of Skilled and Unskilled Labor **409**
  Do Education and Training Pay? **410**

Union-Nonunion Wage Differentials **410**
  Unions' Objectives and Constraints **412**
  Unions in a Competitive Labor Market **413**
  Monopsony **414**
  Monopsony, Minimum Wage, and Unions **415**
  The Scale of Union-Nonunion Wage Differentials
    418

Wage Differentials Between Sexes and Races **419**
  Discrimination **419**
  Human Capital Differences **421**
  Degrees of Specialization **421**

Comparable-Worth Laws **422**

READING BETWEEN THE LINES
WAGE LAWS VERSUS LAWS OF SUPPLY AND
  DEMAND **416**

Summary **424**
Key Elements **425**
Review Questions **425**
Problems **426**

PART 7
MARKETS, UNCERTAINTY, AND DISTRIBUTION
TALKING WITH TONY ATKINSON 454

CHAPTER 16 Capital and Natural Resource Markets 427

Boom and Bust 428

Capital, Investment, and Saving 429
Financial Assets and Physical Assets 429
Capital and Investment 430
Saving and Portfolio Choice 430

Capital Markets in the United States Today 431
The Nation's Balance Sheet 432

Demand for Capital 434
Net Present Value of Investment 434
Demand Curve for Capital 436
Changes in the Demand for Capital 437

The Supply of Capital 438
Interest Rate 438
Supply Curve of Capital 439
Changes in the Supply of Capital 439

Interest Rates and Asset Prices 440
Two Sides of the Same Coin 440
Equilibrium Interest Rate 440
Stock Market Value of a Firm 441
Price-Earnings Ratio 441
Stock Market Volume and Prices 444
Takeovers and Mergers 444

Natural Resource Markets 445
Supply and Demand in a Natural Resource Market 446
Price of a Natural Resource 447
Equilibrium Stock and Flow 447
Unexpected Price Changes 449
Conservation and Doomsday 450

READING BETWEEN THE LINES
THE GLOBAL CAPITAL MARKET 442

Summary 451
Key Elements 452
Review Questions 453
Problems 453

CHAPTER 17 Uncertainty and Information 458

Lotteries and Lemons 459

Coping with Uncertainty 460
Uncertainty and Risk 460
Utility of Wealth 460
Measuring the Cost of Risk 461
Risk Aversion and Risk Neutrality 462

Insurance 463
Insurance Industry in the United States 463
How Insurance Works 464
Why It Pays to Insure 464

Information 466
Searching for Price Information 466
Advertising 468

Private Information 469
Markets for Cars 469
Markets for Credit 472
Markets for Insurance 475

Managing Risk in Financial Markets 475
Diversification to Lower Risk 476
Forward and Futures Markets 477
Rational Expectations 478

READING BETWEEN THE LINES
PROFITING FROM INFORMATION 470

Summary 481
Key Elements 482
Review Questions 483
Problems 483

CHAPTER 18   The Distribution of Income
and Wealth 484

Riches and Rags 485

Distributions of Income and Wealth in the United
    States Today 486
    Lorenz Curves 487
    Inequality over Time 488
    Who Are the Rich and the Poor? 488
    Poverty 489
    Extreme Wealth 492

Income Redistribution 492
    Income Taxes 492
    Income Maintenance Programs 492
    Provision of Goods and Services below Cost 493
    The Scale of Income Redistribution 493
    Problems and Reform Proposals 494

Comparing Like with Like 496
    Wealth versus Income 496
    Human Capital 497
    Human and Nonhuman Capital 497
    Annual or Lifetime Income and Wealth 498

Factor Prices and Endowments 500
    Labor Markets and Wages 500
    Distribution of Endowments 501

Choices and the Distribution of Income and Wealth
    502
    Wages and the Supply of Labor 502
    Choices Skew the Distribution of Income 503
    Savings and Bequests 504

Ideas about Fairness 505
    End-State Theories 505
    How Much Inequality Is Consistent with End-
        State Theories? 505
    The Big Tradeoff 508
    The Process View of Justice 508

READING BETWEEN THE LINES
BLACK INEQUALITY 490

OUR ADVANCING KNOWLEDGE
UNCERTAINTY AND THE DISTRIBUTION OF INCOME
    AND WEALTH 506

Summary 509
Key Elements 510
Review Questions 510
Problems 511

PART 8

MARKETS AND GOVERNMENT

TALKING WITH ANN FRIEDLAENDER **512**

CHAPTER 19 Market Failure **516**

Government—The Solution or the Problem? **517**

The Government Sector **518**
  The Structure and Scale of Government **518**
  The Scale and Growth of Government **518**
  Economic Theory of Government **519**
  Market Failure **519**
  Redistribution **519**
  Public Interest and Public Choice **519**

Public Goods **520**
  Private Goods and Public Goods **520**
  Free Riding **521**
  Benefits and Costs **521**
  Private Provision **523**
  Public Provision **523**

Externalities **525**
  Private Property Rights and Externalities **528**
  Taxes and External Costs **528**
  Subsidies and External Benefits **529**

READING BETWEEN THE LINES
A GLOBAL EXTERNALITY **526**

OUR ADVANCING KNOWLEDGE
UNDERSTANDING EXTERNALITIES **530**

Summary **532**
Key Elements **533**
Review Questions **534**
Problems **534**

CHAPTER 20 Public Choice **536**

Rhetoric and Reality **537**

The Political Marketplace **538**
  The Behavior of Politicians and Voters **539**
  Externalities **540**
  Interest Groups and Redistribution **541**
  Voting for Income Redistribution **543**
  Model and Reality **544**
  The Behavior of Bureaucrats **545**
  Voter Ignorance and Well-Informed Interest
    Groups **546**

Taxes and Subsidies **547**
  Excise Taxes **547**
  Why Do Tax Rates Vary? **548**

READING BETWEEN THE LINES
THE POLITICAL MARKET IN SUBSIDIES **552**

Summary **554**
Key Elements **555**
Review Questions **555**
Problems **556**

CHAPTER 21 Regulation and Antitrust Law **557**

Public Interest or Special Interests? **558**

Market Intervention 559
Regulation **559**
Antitrust Law **559**
Surpluses and Their Distribution **559**

Economic Theory of Regulation 560
Demand for Regulation **560**
The Supply of Regulation **560**
Equilibrium **561**

Regulation and Deregulation 562
The Scope of Regulation **562**
The Regulatory Process **563**
Regulation of Natural Monopoly **564**
Public Interest or Capture? **567**
Regulation of Cartels **567**
Making Predictions **569**

Antitrust Law 570
Landmark Antitrust Cases **570**
Public or Special Interest? **574**

READING BETWEEN THE LINES
LIMITING COMPETITION IN CHIPS **572**

Summary **574**
Key Elements **575**
Review Questions **576**
Problems **576**

CHAPTER 22 Trading with the World **581**

Silk Routes and Rust Belts **582**

Patterns and Trends in International Trade 583
U.S. International Trade **583**
Trends in Trade **584**

Opportunity Cost and Comparative Advantage 586
Opportunity Cost in Pioneerland **586**
Opportunity Cost in Magic Empire **586**
Comparative Advantage **587**

The Gains from Trade 587
Reaping the Gains from Trade **587**
Balanced Trade **588**
Changes in Production and Consumption **588**
Calculating the Gains from Trade **590**
Gains for All **590**
Absolute Advantage **590**
Gains from Trade in Reality **591**
Trade in Similar Goods **591**

Trade Restrictions 595
The History of Tariffs **595**
How Tariffs Work **596**
Nontariff Barriers **600**
How Quotas and VERs Work **601**
Why Quotas and VERs Might Be Preferred to Tariffs **602**
Dumping and Countervailing Duties **603**
Why Is International Trade Restricted? **603**
Compensating Losers **604**
Political Outcome **604**

OUR ADVANCING KNOWLEDGE
UNDERSTANDING THE GAINS FROM INTERNATIONAL TRADE **592**

READING BETWEEN THE LINES
THE GAINS FROM TRADE IN ACTION **598**

Summary **605**
Key Elements **606**
Review Questions **606**

CHAPTER 23   Economic Systems in
Transition **608**

The Market Bandwagon **609**

**The Economic Problem and Its Alternative Solutions
610**
Alternative Economic Systems **610**
Alternative Systems Compared **612**

Economic Change in the Former Soviet Union 615
Economic History of the Soviet Union **615**
Soviet-Style Central Planning **618**
The Market Sector **619**
Money in the Soviet Union **619**
Soviet Economic Decline **619**
Living Standards in the Late 1980s **621**
Market Economy Reforms **621**
Transition Problems **621**

Economic Transition in Eastern Europe 625
East Germany **625**
Czech Republic, Slovakia, Hungary, and Poland
626

Economic Transition in China 627
The Great Leap Forward **627**
The 1978 Reforms **628**
China's Success **629**
Growing Out of the Plan **630**

The Transition from Central Plan to Market 631
Styles of Market Economy **631**
The Sequence of Reform **632**
The Speed of Reform **633**

OUR ADVANCING KNOWLEDGE
UNDERSTANDING THE LIMITS OF CENTRAL
PLANNING **616**

READING BETWEEN THE LINES
THE MARKET COMES TO MOSCOW **622**

Summary **633**
Key Elements **635**
Review Questions **635**

INDEX 645

GLOSSARY 636

TABLE 656

MICROECONOMICS
SECOND EDITION

INTRODUCTION

Talking with Robert Solow

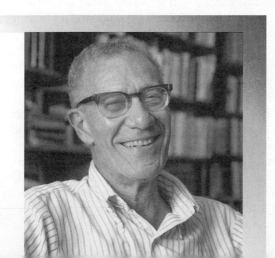

obert M. Solow was born in New York City in 1924. He was an undergraduate and graduate student at Harvard University, where he obtained his Ph.D. in 1951. Professor Solow is an Institute Professor at MIT and has received all the honors possible for his outstanding contributions, including the John Bates Clark Medal (awarded to the best economist under 40) in 1961, President of the Econometrics Society, and President of the American Economics Association. In 1987, he was awarded the Nobel Memorial Prize in Economics. Professor Solow has studied a wide range of problems, including the links between unemployment and inflation, the theory of long-run economic growth, and the role of nonrenewable natural resources. Michael Parkin talked with Professor Solow about some of these issues and the economic landscape of the 1990s.

Professor Solow, why and how did you get into economics?

I grew up during the Depression of the 1930s and went to college in 1940 just before the outbreak of the Second World War. Our economy and our society were functioning badly, so it was hard *not* to be interested in economics. As a freshman and sophomore, I studied a little of all the social sciences. Then I joined the Army. When I came back to the university, I had to choose an area of study. I chose economics because it combined analytical precision with a focus on what seemed the central social problems.

Today there is a lot of anxiety about the prospects for income growth in the United States in the 1990s. Is the anxiety justified?

There is plenty of reason to be anxious about income growth in the 1990s. You only have to look at the 1970s and 1980s to understand why. So far nothing has happened to suggest that the near stagnation of the past two decades will give way to something better. There are no signs of greater investment and no partic-

1

> "**I**t is a fantasy . . . that a handful of space-age engineers simply have to apply themselves . . . to revolutionize civilian technology."

ular reasons to expect the rate of technological progress to improve. Perhaps we will be able to release much of the first-class science and engineering talent that has been used in weapons systems and divert it to advancing civilian technology. But that hasn't happened yet; and when it does happen, there will not be some instantaneous golden age. Good people will eventually produce good results, but it is a fantasy to believe that a handful of space-age engineers simply have to apply themselves in order to revolutionize civilian technology. They will have some old habits to unlearn and new ones to acquire. My guess is that we will scrape along in the 1990s.

Does the same prediction hold true for jobs in the 1990s?

Jobs present an altogether more complicated question. An economy can grow slowly and generate plenty of jobs, and I expect that our economy will do so. There is a lot of talk about whether it will produce "good" jobs. In a sense, the answer is no, if by good jobs one means jobs with good wages and rising wages. On average, incomes will follow productivity. For example, if productivity rises only very slowly, then incomes

will also rise only very slowly on the average. I doubt that the range of unemployment rates will be very different from the recent past. So there will be about the usual number of jobs, paying about what productivity will permit.

Remember that it is not quite right to speak of "jobs" as if they are all the same. In the 1980s, Americans with good education and advanced skills did well, even if not quite as well as earlier. It is the uneducated with limited skills who find themselves falling behind, forced to compete with low-wage labor elsewhere.

Does creating jobs inevitably create more inflation? Or can we have steady growth *and* stable prices?

We can probably have reasonably steady growth and reasonably stable prices. The harder question is whether we can do it with a low unemployment rate. I am something of a pessimist here. It seems to me that no one has yet found a way to achieve price stability in an economy that runs along with very little unemployment and excess industrial capacity. Japan may be an exception, but I don't pretend to understand how the Japanese economy works in this respect. Anyway, there is no guar-

antee that the Japanese secret, if there is one, could be transferred elsewhere. The tendency of modern macroeconomics is to define the problem away, I fear: "low unemployment" *is* whatever is compatible with stable prices. To my mind, the "natural rate of unemployment" is an analytically and empirically flimsy concept. There is room for different models of the way the labor market works, with quite different implications for the understanding of inflation. This is an active subject of research right now.

How should we view international competition from Japan?

I think there are two sides to the Japan problem. The important thing to keep in mind is that no one is forced to buy a Japanese car or VCR. Many Americans do so because they prefer the combination of price and quality. North American manufacturing can get a lot better. It has already started to do so. From that point of view, competition from Japan and Europe is a good thing. Eliminate it and there is danger that our own producers will backslide. Between exchange rate movements and productivity improvements at home, we will come to an equilibrium.

I also think that evidence suggests that the Japanese do not play completely by the free-trade rules. I suspect that Japanese institutions, policies, and habits contribute to the large Japanese trade surplus. Of course, a country that saves a lot more than it can invest at home is bound to have a current-account surplus. We should keep pressuring Japan, hard, to abide by the norms. But we should not kid ourselves: the main part of the problem and its solution lie at home.

Has the federal government deficit got in the way of using tax cuts to stimulate our economy?

It certainly has. You can make a case that the Reagan administration intended the massive tax cuts of 1981–1983 to do just that, to leave the federal government without the resources to undertake any positive action at all. There is no doubt that the Congress today feels that there is no elbow room. Some may think that was a good idea. I have no doubt that micromanagement by government is a loser. But I think that passive macroeconomic policy will occasionally get us what we have now—three years of stagnation, apparently to be followed by a period of weak growth.

What is an appropriate goal of macroeconomic policy?

Prolonged budget deficits that persist even when the economy is doing well present a real problem. They are a drain on the national saving, and they imply some combination of low investment and large current-account deficits. So it should be a goal of macroeconomic policy to move toward budget balance or even a surplus, depending on how much we value investment and growth compared with current consumption. But when the economy is weak, when there is plenty of idle labor and capacity, the situation is different. There is no need for investment to displace consumption. There is room for both, and consumption spending stimulates investment. Both fiscal and monetary policy stimuli would be a good thing, even at the expense of a temporary increase in the deficit.

Are there any limits to economic growth? Are we going to run Spaceship Earth out of fuel?

Finding a route to sustainable growth or sustainable development or even to a sustainable state will not be easy. First of all, I think the various scenarios in which the world economy runs

"It may be a mistake
to think in terms
of Great Unsolved
Problems and
Sensational
Breakthroughs."

out of resources and then falls into a tailspin are neither valid nor helpful. My reading is that they are poor science and poor economics. We are more likely to experience rising costs of fuel and materials than to run out. We simply cannot know what tastes and technology will be like 50 or 100 years from now.

There are, however, plenty of things that people and policy should be concerned with now. Ensure that full environmental costs are reckoned into economic decision making. Impose the taxes or regulations that are needed for efficient long-run use of fish stocks and other renewable resources. Subsidize scientific and technological research that can find or create new materials and energy sources. Help and induce poor countries to control their populations. I really don't think that Doomsday scenarios move us in these directions.

What are the most important economic questions that have not been answered and that the next generation of economists will work on and possibly solve?

It may be a mistake to think in terms of Great Unsolved Problems and Sensational Breakthroughs. Instead, the next generation of economists would be wise to direct themselves toward slowly coming to understand the way the economy works. I have already mentioned the behavior of the labor market as a fertile field for research: flows into and out of employment, how they and the stocks of employed and unemployed workers relate to the level of wages. Those are traditional questions. But more and more data accumu-

late, and models are improved. A lot of purely technical finger exercises get done on the way.

Another, less traditional, set of questions emerges from growth theory. Once upon a time, it was customary to treat technological change as exogenous. No one believed that, of course, but economics seemed to have little to say about the pace and direction of invention and innovation. It is now fashionable to go a step further and try to understand the allocation of resources to research and development and the payoff to resources invested. It is far from clear that this work will get very far. But it is obviously important, so the effort has to be made.

How would you advise a student to prepare for a career in economics today? What subjects are the most important to study while an undergraduate? Math? History? Politics?

Certainly an undergraduate interested in economics has no choice but to learn a little mathematics. Better to get it done before graduate school. Then some probability, statistics, and econometrics. Those are indispensable research tools. Then what? Almost anything, I would say. These days you meet too many economists who don't seem to know anything else—not history, not literature, not anything. I think anyone would be a better economist for knowing that there are other things in the world. My own favorite, I will admit, is history, especially social history and economic history. What I am hoping for is some grasp of the many ways in which people have managed to organize themselves and their societies, to give some insight into our own.

CHAPTER 1

WHAT IS ECONOMICS?

After studying this chapter, you will be able to:

- ◆ State the kinds of questions that economics tries to answer

- ◆ Explain why all economic questions and economic activity arise from scarcity

- ◆ Explain why scarcity forces people to make choices

- ◆ Define opportunity cost

- ◆ Describe the function and the working parts of an economy

- ◆ Distinguish between positive and normative statements

- ◆ Explain what is meant by an economic theory and how economic theories are developed by building and testing economic models

F YOU WANTED TO WATCH A MOVIE IN YOUR HOME IN 1975, you had to rent a movie projector and screen—as well as the movie itself. The cost of such entertainment was as high as that incurred by a theater showing the same movie to several hundred people. Only the rich chose to watch movies in the comfort of their own homes. ◆ ◆ In 1976, the video cassette recorder (VCR) became available to consumers. Its typical price tag was $2,000 ($4,000 in today's dollars). Even at such a high price, the VCR slashed the cost of home movie watching. Since that time, the price of VCRs has steadily fallen so that today you can buy a reliable machine for $200. A video can be rented for a dollar a day and can be bought for less than $30. In just a few years, watching a movie at home changed from a luxury available to the richest few to an event enjoyed by millions.

Choice and Change

◆ ◆ Advances in technology affect the way we consume. We now watch far more movies at home than we did a decade ago because new technologies have lowered the cost. ◆ ◆ We hear a great deal these days about lasers. Their most dramatic use is in weapons systems such as those used in "Desert Storm" in 1991. They are also used to guide the machines that bore tunnels and lay pipelines and to align the jigs that build the wings and bodies of modern jet aircraft. But lasers affect us every day. They scan prices at the supermarket checkout. They create holograms on credit cards, making them harder to forge. Neurosurgeons and eye surgeons use them in our hospitals. These advances in technology affect the way we produce.

Ever-changing technology raises the first big economic question:

How do people choose what to consume and how to produce and how are these choices affected by the discovery of new technologies?

Wages and Earnings

On a crisp, bright winter day on the ski slopes at Aspen, a bronzed 23-year-old instructs some beginning skiers in the snowplow turn. For this pleasant and uncomplicated work, the young man, who quit school after eleventh grade, is paid $10 an hour.

In a lawyer's office in the center of a busy city, a 23-year-old secretary handles a large volume of correspondence, filing, scheduling, and meetings. She arrives home most evenings exhausted. She has a bachelor's degree in English and has taken night courses in computer science and word processing. She receives $8 an hour for her work.

On September 12, 1993, Pete Sampras and Cedric Pioline played a superb tennis match in the men's final of the U.S. Open. At the end of the hard-fought match, the winner—Sampras—received $500,000; Pioline collected only half that amount. A similar phenomenon can be seen in the headquarters of large corporations. Chief executive officers who work no harder (and in some cases even less hard) than the people immediately beneath them receive far higher salaries than their subordinates.

Situations like these raise the second big economic question:

What determines people's incomes and why do some people receive much larger rewards than others whose efforts appear to be similar?

Government, Environment, and Economic Systems

The federal government has grown. At the beginning of this century, it provided law and order and national defense. Today, it provides education, interstate highways, and social security; it regulates the production of food, drugs, and nuclear energy; and it puts satellites into orbit. Tomorrow, if President Clinton is able to implement one of his major campaign promises, it will expand its role even further to provide affordable health care for everyone.

The environment is fragile. Chlorofluorocarbons (CFCs), used as coolants in refrigerators and air conditioners and as cleaning solvents for computer circuits, are believed to damage the atmosphere's protective ozone layer. The burning of coal and oil adds carbon dioxide and other gases to the atmosphere, which prevent infrared radiation from escaping and result in a gradual warming of the planet— the greenhouse effect. The long-term consequences of these two processes might be devastating.

The global economic order is changing dramatically. In Russia and the other countries of Eastern Europe, governments have abandoned central economic planning and begun to sell off or give away state-owned farms and factories. At the same time, these countries have introduced democratic forms of government. The immediate result of these changes was economic chaos. Production and employment fell, and prices increased rapidly. But the goal and hope of these countries is to establish an open and democratic system of government and a type of economic system similar to what we have in the United States.

These facts about government, the environment, and the dramatic changes taking place in Eastern Europe raise the third big economic question:

What is the most effective role for government in economic life and can government help us protect our environment and do as effective a job as private enterprise at producing goods and services?

Unemployment

During the Great Depression, the four years from 1929 to 1933, unemployment afflicted almost one fifth of the labor force in the industrial world. For months and in some cases years on end, many families had no income other than meager payments from the government or from private charities. In the 1950s and 1960s, unemployment rates stayed below 5 percent in most countries and, in some, below 2 percent. During the 1970s and early 1980s, unemployment steadily increased so that by late 1982 and early 1983 almost 11 percent of the U.S. labor force was looking for work. But in 1989, the U.S. unemployment rate had fallen to 5 percent.

Unemployment hurts different groups unequally. When the average unemployment rate in the United States was 7 percent—as it was in 1992—the unemployment rate among young people 16 to 19 years old was 19 percent. But for young black males it was 36 percent. These facts raise the fourth big economic question:

What are the causes of unemployment and why are some groups more severely affected than others?

Inflation

Between August 1945 and July 1946, prices in Hungary rose by an average of 20,000 percent per month. In the worst month, July 1946, they rose 419 quadrillion percent (a quadrillion is the number 1 followed by 15 zeros).

In 1992, the cost of living in Brazil rose by 1,000 percent. This meant that in downtown Rio de Janiero a sandwich that cost 25,000 cruzeiros on January 1 cost 250,000 cruzeiros by the end of the year. That same year, prices rose only 3 percent in the United States. But in the late 1970s, prices in the United States were rising at a rate well in excess of 10 percent a year. These facts raise the fifth economic question:

Why do prices rise and why do some countries sometimes experience rapid price increases while others have stable prices?

International Trade

In the 1960s, almost all the cars and trucks on the highways of the United States were Fords, Chevrolets, and Chryslers. By the 1980s, Toyotas, Hondas, Volkswagens, and BMWs were a common sight on these same highways. As a matter of fact, in 1990, more than one third of all new cars sold in the United States were imported; in 1950, less than 1 percent were.

Cars are not exceptional. The same can be said of television sets, clothing, and computers.

Governments regulate international trade in cars and in most other commodities. They impose taxes on imports, called tariffs, and also establish quotas, which restrict the quantities that may be imported. These facts raise the sixth big economic question:

What determines the pattern and the volume of trade between nations and what are the effects of tariffs and quotas on international trade?

Wealth and Poverty

At the mouth of the Canton River in southeast China is a small rocky peninsula and a group of islands with virtually no natural resources. But this bare land supports more than five million people who, though not excessively rich, live in rapidly growing abundance. They produce much of the world's fashion goods and electronic components. They are the people of Hong Kong.

On the eastern edge of Africa, bordering the Red Sea, a tract of land a thousand times larger supports a population of 34 million people—only seven times that of Hong Kong. Its people suffer such abject poverty that in 1985 rock singers from Europe and North America organized one of the most spectacular worldwide fund-raising efforts ever seen—Live Aid—to help them. These are the desperate and dying people of Ethiopia.

Hong Kong and Ethiopia, two extremes in income and wealth, are not isolated examples. The poorest two thirds of the world's population consumes less than one fifth of all the things produced. A middle income group accounts for almost one fifth of the world's population and consumes almost one fifth of the world's output. A further one fifth of the world's population—living in rich countries such as the United States, Canada, Western Europe, Japan, Australia, and New Zealand—consumes two thirds of the world's output.

These facts raise the seventh big economic question:

What causes differences in wealth among nations, making the people in some countries rich and those in other countries poor?

These seven big questions provide an overview of economics. They are *big* questions for two reasons. First, they have an enormous influence on the quality of human life. Second, they are hard questions to answer. They generate passionate argument and debate, and just about everybody has an opinion about them. One of the hardest things for students of economics, whether beginners or seasoned practitioners, is to stand clear of the passion and emotion and to approach their work with the detachment, rigor, and objectivity of a scientist.

Later in this chapter, we'll explain how economists try to find answers to economic questions. But before doing that, let's go back to the big questions.

What do these questions have in common? What makes them *economic* questions? What distinguishes them from non-economic questions?

Scarcity

All economic questions arise from a single and inescapable fact: you can't always get what you want. We live in a world of scarcity. An economist defines **scarcity** to mean that wants always exceed the resources available to satisfy them. A child wants a 75¢ can of soft drink and a 50¢ pack of gum but has only $1.00 in her pocket. She experiences scarcity. A student wants to go to a party on Saturday night but also wants to spend that same night catching up on late assignments. He also experiences scarcity. The rich and the poor alike face scarcity. The U.S. government with its $1.4 trillion budget faces scarcity. The total amount that the federal government wants to spend on defense, health, education, welfare, and other services exceeds what it collects in taxes. Even parrots face scarcity—there just aren't enough crackers to go around.

Wants do not simply exceed resources; they are unlimited. People want good health and a long life, material comfort, security, physical and mental recreation, and, finally, an awareness and understanding of themselves and their environment.

None of these wants are satisfied for everyone; and everyone has some unsatisfied wants. While many Americans have all the material comfort they want, many do not. No one feels entirely satisfied with his or her state of health and length of life. No one feels entirely secure, even in this post–Cold War era, and no one—not even the wealthiest person—has the time to enjoy all the travel, vacations, and art that he or she would like. Not even the wisest and most knowledgeable philosopher or scientist knows as much as he or she would like to know.

We can imagine a world that satisfies people's wants for material comfort and perhaps even security. But we cannot imagine a world in which people live as long and in as good a state of health as they would like. Nor can we imagine people having all the time, energy, and resources to enjoy all the sports, travel, vacations, and art that they would like. Natural resources and human resources—in the form of time, muscle-power, and brain-power—as well as all the dams, highways, buildings, machinery, tools, and other equipment that have been built by past human efforts amount to an enormous heritage, but they are limited. Our unlimited wants will always outstrip the limited resources available to satisfy them.

Economic Activity

The confrontation of unlimited wants with limited resources results in economic activity. **Economic activity** is what people do to cope with scarcity. And **economics** is the study of how people use their limited resources to try to satisfy unlimited wants. Defined in this way, economic activity and economics deal with a wide range of issues and problems. The seven big questions posed earlier are examples of the more important problems that economists study. Let's see how those questions could not arise if resources were infinitely abundant and scarcity did not exist.

With unlimited resources there would be no need to devise better ways of producing more goods. Studying how we all spend our time and effort would not be interesting because we would simply do what we enjoyed without restriction. We would do only the things that we enjoyed because there would be enough goods and services to satisfy everyone without effort. Unemployment would not be an issue because no one would work—except for people who wanted to work simply for the pleasure that it gave them. There would be no wages. Inflation—rising prices—would not be a problem because no

"Not only do I want a cracker—we all want a cracker!"

Drawing by Modell; © 1985 The New Yorker Magazine, Inc.

one would care about prices. Questions about government intervention in economic life would not arise because there would be no need for government-provided goods and no taxes. We would simply take whatever we wanted from the infinite resources available. There would be no international trade since, with complete abundance, it would be pointless to transport things from one place to another. Finally, differences in wealth among nations would not arise because we would all have as much as we wanted. There would be no such thing as rich and poor countries—all countries would be infinitely wealthy.

You can see that this science fiction world of complete abundance would have no economic questions. It is the universal fact of scarcity that produces economic questions.

Choice

Faced with scarcity, people must make *choices*. When we cannot have everything that we want, we have to choose among the available alternatives. Because scarcity forces us to choose, economics is sometimes called the science of choice—the science that explains the choices that people make and predicts how changes in circumstances affect their choices.

To make a choice, we balance the benefits of having more of one thing against the costs of having less of something else. The process of balancing benefits against costs and doing the best within the limits of what is possible is called **optimizing**. There is another word that has a similar meaning—*economizing*. **Economizing** is making the best use of the resources available. Once people have made a choice and have optimized, they cannot have more of *everything*. To get more of one thing means having less of something else. Expressed in another way: in making choices, we face costs. Whatever we choose to do, we could always have chosen to do something else instead.

Opportunity Cost

Economists use the term *opportunity cost* to emphasize that making choices in the face of scarcity implies a cost. The **opportunity cost** of any action is the best alternative forgone. If you cannot have everything that you want, then you have to choose among the alternatives. The best thing that you

choose not to do—the forgone alternative—is the cost of the thing that you choose to do.

Dollar Cost We often express opportunity cost in terms of dollars. But this is just a convenient unit of measure. The dollars spent on a book are not available for spending on a CD. The opportunity cost of the book is not the dollars spent on it, but the CD forgone.

Time Cost The opportunity cost of a good includes the value of the time spent obtaining it. If it takes an hour to visit your dentist, the value of that hour must be added to the amount you paid your dentist. We can convert time into a dollar cost by using a person's hourly wage rate. If you take an hour off work to visit your dentist, the opportunity cost of that visit (expressed in units of dollars) is the amount that you paid to your dentist plus the wages that you lost by not being at work. Again, it's important to keep reminding yourself that the opportunity cost is not the dollars involved but the goods that you could have bought with those dollars.

External Cost Not all of the opportunity costs that you incur are the result of your own choices. Sometimes others make choices that impose opportunity costs on you. And your own choices can impose opportunity costs on others. For example, when you enjoy a cold drink from your refrigerator, part of its opportunity cost (borne by others) is the increased carbon dioxide in the atmosphere resulting from burning coal to generate the electricity that powers the refrigerator.

Best Alternative Forgone In measuring opportunity cost, we value only the *best* alternative forgone. To make this clear, consider the following example. You are supposed to attend a lecture at 8:30 on a Monday morning. There are two alternatives to attending this lecture: stay in bed for an hour or go jogging for an hour. You cannot stay in bed *and* go jogging for that same hour. The opportunity cost of attending the lecture is not the cost of an hour in bed *and* the cost of jogging for an hour. If these are the only two alternatives that you would contemplate, then you have to decide which one you would do if you did not go to the lecture. The opportunity cost of attending a lecture for a jogger is an hour of exercise; the opportunity cost of attending a lecture for a late sleeper is an hour in bed.

Scarcity implies cost—opportunity cost. It also implies one other fundamental feature of human life—competition.

Competition and Cooperation

Competition If wants exceed resources, wants must compete against each other for what is available. **Competition** is a contest for command over scarce resources. In the case of the child with $1.00 in pocket money who wants a soft drink and gum that add up to $1.25, the soft drink and gum compete for the $1.00 in her pocket. For the student who has allowed assignments to accumulate, the party and the assignments compete with each other for Saturday night. For the government, defense and social services compete with each other for limited tax dollars.

Scarcity also implies competition between people. Because it is not possible to have everything that you want, you must compete with others for what is available. In modern societies, competition has been organized within a framework of almost universally accepted rules that have evolved. This evolution of rules is itself a direct response to the problem of scarcity. Not all societies, even modern societies, employ identical rules to govern competition. For example, the way in which economic life is organized in the United States differs greatly from that in the former Soviet Union. In the final chapter, we examine these differences and compare alternative economic systems. For now, we'll focus on the rules that govern competition in the United States.

A key rule of economic competition in the United States is that people own what they have acquired through voluntary exchange. People can compete with each other by offering more favorable exchanges—for example, selling something for a lower price or buying something for a higher price. But they cannot compete with each other by simply taking something from someone else.

Cooperation Perhaps you are thinking that scarcity does not make competition inevitable and that cooperation would better solve economic problems. **Cooperation** means working with others to achieve a common end. If instead of competing with each other we cooperated, wouldn't that solve our economic problems? Unfortunately, cooperation does not eliminate economic problems, because it does not eliminate economic scarcity. But cooperation is part of the solution to scarcity. We cooperate, for example, when we agree to rules of the game that limit competition to avoid violence and when we agree to participate in an economic system based on the rule of law and voluntary exchange.

Other examples of solving economic problems through cooperation abound. Marriage partners cooperate. Most forms of business also entail cooperation. Workers cooperate with each other on the production line; members of a management team cooperate with each other to design, produce, and market their products; management and workers cooperate; business partners cooperate.

Common as it is, cooperative behavior neither solves the economic problem nor eliminates competition. Almost all cooperative behavior implies some prior competition to find the best individuals with whom to cooperate. Marriage provides a good example. Although marriage is a cooperative affair, unmarried people compete intensely to find a marriage partner. Similarly, although workers and management cooperate with each other, firms compete for the best workers and workers compete for the best employers. Professionals such as lawyers and doctors compete with each other for the best business partners.

Competition does not end when a partner has been found. Groups of people who cooperate together compete with other groups. For example, although a group of lawyers may have formed a partnership and may work together, they will be in competition with other lawyers.

R E V I E W

Scarcity is the confrontation of unlimited wants with limited resources. Scarcity forces people to make choices. To make choices, people evaluate the costs of alternative actions. We call these opportunity costs, to emphasize that doing one thing removes the opportunity to do something else. Scarcity also implies that people must compete with each other. Economics studies the activities arising from scarcity. ◆

You now know the types of questions that economists try to answer and that all economic questions and economic activity arise from scarcity. In the following chapters, we are going to study economic activity and discover how a modern economy such as that of the United States works. But before we do that, we need to stand back and take an overview of the economy.

The Economy

What do we mean by "the economy"? How does an economy work? Rather than trying to answer these questions directly, let's begin by asking similar questions about a more familiar subject. What is an airplane? How does an airplane work?

Without delving into the detail that would satisfy an aeronautical engineer, most of us could take a shot at answering these two questions. We would describe an airplane as a flying machine that transports people and cargo. To explain how an airplane works, we would describe its key components—fuselage (or body), wings, and engines, and also perhaps its flaps, rudder, and control and navigation systems. We would also explain that as powerful engines move the machine forward, its wings create an imbalance in air pressure that lifts it into the air.

This example nicely illustrates four things. First, it is hard to explain what something is without saying what it does. To say that an airplane is a machine does not tell us much. We have to go beyond that and say what the machine is for and how it works.

Second, it is hard to explain how something works without being able to divide it up into components. Once we have described something in terms of its components, we can explain how those components work and how they interact with each other.

Third, it is hard to explain how something works without leaving out some details. Notice that we did not describe an airplane in all its detail. Instead, we isolated the most important parts in order to explain how the whole works. We did not mention the in-flight movie system, the seat belts, or the color of the paint on the wings. We supposed that these things were irrelevant to an explanation of how an airplane works.

Fourth, and finally, there are different levels of understanding how something works. We gave a superficial account of how an airplane works. An aeronautical engineer would have given a deeper explanation, and experts in the individual components—engines, navigation systems, control system, and so on—would have given even more detailed and precise explanations than a general engineer.

Now let's return to questions about the economy. What is the economy? How does it work?

What Is the Economy?

The **economy** is a mechanism that allocates scarce resources among competing uses. This mechanism achieves three things:

◆ What
◆ How
◆ For whom

1. *What* goods and services will be produced and in *what* quantities? Will more VCRs be made or will more movie theaters be built? Will young professionals vacation in Europe or live in large houses? Will more high-performance sports cars or more trucks and station wagons be built?

2. *How* will the various goods and services be produced? Will a supermarket operate with three checkout lines and clerks using laser scanners or six checkout lines and clerks keying in prices by hand? Will workers weld station wagons by hand or will robots do the job? Will farmers keep track of their livestock feeding schedules and inventories by using paper and pencil records or personal computers? Will credit card companies use computers to read charge slips in New York or ship paper records to Barbados for hand processing?

3. *For whom* will the various goods and services be produced? The distribution of economic benefits depends on the distribution of income. People with high incomes are able to consume more goods and services than people with low incomes. Who gets to consume what thus depends on income. Will the ski instructor consume more than the lawyer's secretary? Will the people of Hong Kong consume more than the people of Ethiopia?

FIGURE **1.1**

A Picture of the Economy

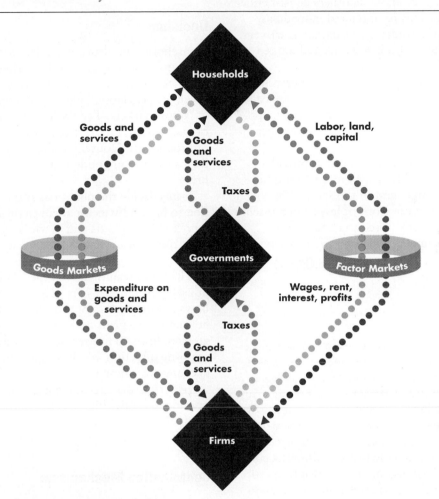

Households, firms, and governments make economic decisions. Households decide how much of their labor, land, and capital to supply in exchange for wages, rent, interest, and profits. They also decide how much of their income to spend on the various types of goods and services available. Firms decide how much labor, land, and capital to hire and how much of the various types of goods and services to pro-

duce. Governments decide which goods and services they will provide and the taxes that households and firms will pay.

These decisions by households, firms, and governments are coordinated in markets—the goods markets and factor markets. In these markets, prices constantly adjust to keep buying and selling plans consistent.

To understand how an economy achieves its objectives, we must identify its main components and then study the way in which these components interact with each other. Figure 1.1 shows a picture of the economy. It contains two types of components:

◆ Decision makers
◆ Markets

Decision Makers

Decision makers are the economic actors. They make the economizing choices. Figure 1.1 identifies three types of decision makers:

1. Households
2. Firms
3. Governments

A **household** is any group of people living together as a decision-making unit. Every individual in the economy belongs to a household. Some households consist of a single person, while others consist either of families or of groups of unrelated individuals, such as two or three students sharing an apartment. Each household has unlimited wants and limited resources.

A **firm** is an organization that uses resources to produce goods and services. All producers are called firms, no matter how big they are or what they produce. Car makers, farmers, banks, and insurance companies are all firms.

A **government** is an organization that provides goods and services and redistributes income and wealth. The most important of the services provided by government is a framework of laws and a mechanism for their enforcement (courts and police forces). But governments also provide such services as national defense, public health, transportation, and education.

Markets

In ordinary speech, the word *market* means a place where people buy and sell goods such as fish, meat, fruits, and vegetables. In economics, *market* has a more general meaning. A **market** is any arrangement that facilitates buying and selling. An example is the market in which oil is bought and sold—the world oil market. The world oil market is not a place. It is the arena in which the many firms—oil producers, oil users, wholesalers, and brokers—who buy and sell oil interact. In this market, decision makers do not meet physically. They make deals by telephone, fax, and direct computer link.

Figure 1.1 identifies two types of market: goods markets and factor markets. **Goods markets** are those in which goods and services are bought and sold. **Factor markets** are those in which factors of production are bought and sold.

Factors of production are the economy's productive resources. They are classified under three headings:

1. Labor
2. Land
3. Capital

Labor is the brain-power and muscle-power of human beings; **land** includes natural resources of all

kinds; **capital** is all the equipment, buildings, tools, and other manufactured goods that can be used in production.

Decisions

Households and firms make decisions that result in the transactions in the goods markets and factor markets shown in Fig. 1.1. Households decide how much of their labor, land, and capital to sell or rent in factor markets. They receive incomes in the form of wages, rent, interest, and profit from these factors of production. Households also decide how to spend their incomes on goods and services produced by firms.

Firms decide the quantities of factors of production to hire, how to use them to produce goods and services, what goods and services to produce, and in what quantities. They sell their output in goods markets.

The flows resulting from these decisions by households and firms are shown in Fig. 1.1. The red flows are the factors of production that go from households to firms and the goods and services that go from firms to households. The green flows in the opposite direction are the payments made in exchange for these items.

Governments decide what goods and services to provide to households and firms, as well as the rates of taxes that create the funds to pay for them. These actions by governments are also shown in Fig. 1.1.

Coordination Mechanisms

Perhaps the most striking thing about the choices made by households, firms, and governments is that they surely must come into conflict with each other. For example, households choose how much work to do and what type of work to specialize in, but firms choose the type and quantity of labor to employ in the production of various goods and services. In other words, households choose the types and quantities of labor to sell, and firms choose the types and quantities of labor to buy. Similarly, in markets for goods and services, households choose the types and quantities of goods and services to buy, while firms choose the types and quantities to sell. Government choices regarding taxes and the provision of goods and services also enter the picture. Taxes taken by the government affect the amount of income that households and firms have available for spending. Also, decisions by firms and households depend on the types and quantities of goods and services that governments make available. For example, if the government provides excellent highways but a dilapidated railroad system, households will allocate more of their income to buying motor vehicles and less to buying train rides.

How is it possible for the millions of individual decisions made by households, firms, and governments to be consistent with each other? What makes households want to sell the same types and quantities of labor that firms want to buy? What happens if the number of households wanting to work as economics professors exceeds the number that universities want to hire? How do firms know what to produce so that households will buy their output? What happens if firms want to sell more hamburgers than households want to buy?

Markets Coordinate Decisions   Markets coordinate individual decisions through price adjustments. To see how, think about the market for hamburgers in your local area. Suppose that the quantity of hamburgers being offered for sale is less than the quantity that people would like to buy. Some people who want to buy hamburgers will not be able to do so. To make the choices of buyers and sellers compatible, buyers will have to scale down their appetites and more hamburgers will have to be offered for sale. An increase in the price of hamburgers will produce this outcome. A higher price will encourage producers to offer more hamburgers for sale. It will also curb the appetite for hamburgers and change some lunch plans. Fewer people will buy hamburgers and more will buy hot dogs (or some other alternative to hamburgers). More hamburgers (and more hot dogs) will be offered for sale.

Now imagine the opposite situation. More hamburgers are available than people want to buy. In this case, the price is too high. A lower price will discourage the production and sale of hamburgers and encourage their purchase and consumption. Decisions to produce and sell, and to buy and consume, are continuously adjusted and kept in balance with each other by adjustments in prices.

In some cases, prices get stuck or fixed. When this happens, some other adjustment has to make the plans and choices of individuals consistent. Customers waiting in lines and inventories of goods operate as a temporary safety valve when the market price is stuck. If people want to buy more than the quantity that firms have decided to sell, and if the price is temporarily stuck, then one of two things can happen. Sometimes, firms wind up selling more than they would like and their inventories shrink. At other times, lines of customers develop and only those who get to the head of the line before the goods run out are able to make a purchase. The longer the line or the bigger the decline in inventories, the more prices adjust to keep buying and selling decisions in balance.

We have now seen how the market solves the question of *what* quantity to produce—how many hamburgers to make. The market also solves the question of *how* to produce in similar fashion. For example, hamburger producers can use gas, electric power, or charcoal to cook their hamburgers. Which fuel is used depends in part on the flavor that the producer wants to achieve and on the cost of the different fuels. If a fuel becomes very expensive, as did oil in the 1970s, less of it is used and more of other fuels are used in its place. By substituting one fuel for another as the costs of the different fuels change, the market solves the question of how to produce.

Finally, the market helps solve the question of *for whom* to produce. Skills, talents, and resources that are in very short supply command a higher price than those in greater abundance. The owners of rare resources and skills obtain a larger share of the output of the economy than the owners of resources that are in abundant supply.

Alternative Coordination Mechanisms   The market is one of two alternative coordination mechanisms. The other is a command mechanism. A **command mechanism** is a method of determining *what, how,* and *for whom* goods and services are produced, using an hierarchical organization structure in which people carry out the instructions given to them. The best example of an hierarchical organization structure is the military. Commanders make decisions requiring actions that are passed down a chain of command. Soldiers and marines on the front line take the actions they are ordered to take.

An economy that relies on a command mechanism is called a **command economy**. Examples of command economies in today's world are China, North Korea, Vietnam, and Cambodia. Before they embarked on programs of reform in the late 1980s, the former Soviet Union and other countries of Eastern Europe also had command economies.

In a command economy, a central planning bureau makes decisions about *what, how,* and *for whom* goods and services are to be produced. We will study command economies and compare them with other types of economies at the end of our study of economics, in the last chapter.

An economy that determines *what, how,* and *for whom* goods and services are produced by coordinating individual choices through markets is called a **market economy.** But most real-world economies use both markets and commands to coordinate economic activity. An economy that relies on both markets and command mechanisms is called a **mixed economy.**

The U.S. economy relies extensively on the market as a mechanism for coordinating the decisions of individual households and firms. But the U.S. economy also uses command mechanisms. The economy of the armed forces is a command economy. Command mechanisms are also employed in other government organizations and also within large firms. There is also a command element in our legal system. By enacting laws and establishing regulations and agencies to monitor the market economy, governments influence the economic decisions of households and firms and change our economic course.

Thus *what, how,* and *for whom* goods and services are produced in the United States depends mainly on the market mechanism, but also partly on a command mechanism, so the U.S. economy is a mixed economy.

The Global Economy

A **closed economy** is one that has no links with any other economy. The only closed economy is that of the entire world. The U.S. economy is an **open economy,** an economy that has economic links with other economies.

The economic links between the U.S. economy and the rest of the world are illustrated in Fig. 1.2. Firms in the open U.S. economy sell some of their production to the rest of the world. These sales are U.S. exports of goods and services. Also, firms, households, and governments in the United States buy goods and services from firms in other countries. These purchases are U.S. imports of goods and services. Both types of transactions take place in world goods markets and are illustrated in the figure.

FIGURE 1.2

International Linkages

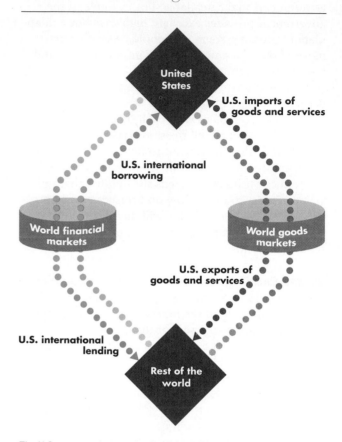

The U.S. economy buys and sells goods and services in world goods markets. What it buys are U.S. imports, and what it sells are U.S. exports. The U.S. economy also borrows from and lends to the rest of the world. These transactions take place in the world financial markets.

The total values of exports and imports are not necessarily equal to each other. When U.S. exports exceed U.S. imports, we have a surplus. When U.S. imports exceed U.S. exports, we have a deficit. A country with a surplus lends to the rest of the world, and a country with a deficit borrows from the rest of the world. These international lending and borrowing transactions take place in the world financial markets and are also illustrated in Fig. 1.2.

The United States has had an international deficit in recent years. As a consequence, by the mid-1980s, foreigners had larger investments in the United States than we had in the rest of the world. Other countries, notably those of the European Community and Japan, have international surpluses and are using those surpluses to invest in businesses in the United States.

During the 1980s, the global economy became a highly integrated mechanism for allocating scarce resources and deciding *what* will be produced, *how* it will be produced, and *for whom* it will be produced. It is also a mechanism deciding *where* the various goods and services will be produced and consumed.

REVIEW

An economy is a mechanism that determines what is produced, how it is produced, and for whom it is produced. Choices are made by households, firms, and government, that are coordinated through markets—markets for goods and services and markets for factors of production—or by command mechanisms. The U.S. economy relies mainly on markets but to a degree on command mechanisms. The U.S. economy and the global economy became highly integrated during the 1980s. ◆

We have now described an economy in about as much detail as we described an airplane. But we're about to become the economic equivalent of aeronautical engineers! We're going to build economies that fly! To do that, we have to understand the principles of economics as thoroughly as aeronautical engineers understand the principles of flight. To discover these principles, economists approach their work with the rigor and objectivity of natural scientists—they do economic science.

Economic Science

Economic science, like the natural sciences (such as physics and biology) and the other social sciences (such as political science, psychology, and sociology), is an at-

tempt to find a body of laws. All sciences have two components:

1. Careful and systematic observation and measurement
2. Development of a body of theory to direct and interpret observations

All sciences are careful to distinguish between two types of statements:

◆ Statements about what *is*
◆ Statements about what *ought* to be

What Is and What Ought To Be

Statements about what *is* are **positive statements.** Statements about what *ought* to be are **normative statements.** Let's illustrate the distinction between positive and normative statements with two examples.

First, consider the controversy over global warming. Some scientists believe that the burning of coal and oil is increasing the carbon dioxide content of the earth's atmosphere and leading to higher temperatures that eventually will have devastating consequences for life on this planet. "Our planet is warming because of an increased carbon dioxide buildup in the atmosphere" is a positive statement. "We ought to cut back on our use of carbon-based fuels such as coal and oil" is a normative statement. Second, consider the economic controversy over tax cuts and cutbacks on social programs. "Lower taxes and less generous social programs will make people work harder" is a positive statement. "Taxes and social programs should be cut" is a normative statement.

Positive statements may be true or false. It is the task of science—whether natural, social, or economic—to discover and catalog positive statements that are true, that is, consistent with what we observe in the world. Normative statements are matters of opinion. You agree or disagree with them. Science is silent on normative questions. It is not that such questions are unimportant. On the contrary, they are often the most important questions of all. Nor is it that scientists as people do not have opinions on such questions. It is simply that the activity of doing science cannot settle a normative matter, and the possession of scientific knowledge does not equip a person with superior morals or norms. A difference of opinion on a positive matter can ultimately be settled by careful observation and measurement. A difference of opinion on a normative matter cannot be settled in that way. In fact, there are no well-defined rules for settling a normative dispute, and sometimes reasonable people simply have to agree to disagree. When they cannot, political and judicial institutions intervene so that decisions can be made. We settle normative disagreements in the political, not the scientific, arena. The scientific community can, and often does, contribute to the normative debates of political life. But science is a distinct activity. Even though scientists have opinions about what ought to be, those opinions have no part in science itself.

Now let's see how economists attempt to discover and catalog positive statements that are consistent with their observations and that enable them to answer economic questions.

Observation and Measurement

Economic phenomena can be observed and measured in great detail. We can catalog the amounts and locations of natural and human resources. We can describe who does what kind of work, for how many hours, and how they are paid. We can catalog the things that people produce, consume, and store and their prices. We can describe in detail who borrows and who lends and at what interest rates. We can also catalog the things that government taxes and at what rates, the programs it finances and at what cost.

These are examples of the array of things that economists can describe through careful observation and measurement of economic activity.

In today's world, computers have given us access to an enormous volume of economic description. Government agencies around the world, national statistical bureaus, private economic consultants, banks, investment advisors, and research economists working in universities generate an astonishing amount of information about economic behavior.

But economists do more than observe and measure economic activity, crucial as that is. Describing something is not the same as understanding it. You can describe your digital watch in great detail, but that does not mean you can explain what makes it work. Understanding what makes things work requires the discovery of laws. That is the main task of economists—the discovery of laws governing economic behavior. How do economists go about this task?

Economic Theory

We can describe in great detail the ups and downs, or cycles, in unemployment, but can we explain *why* unemployment fluctuates? We can describe the fall in the price of a VCR or a pocket calculator and the dramatic increase in its use, but can we explain the low price and popularity of such items? Did the fall in the price lead more people to use pocket calculators, or did their popularity lower the costs of production and make it possible to lower the price? Or did something else cause both the fall in the price and the increase in use?

Questions like these can be answered only by developing a body of economic theory. An **economic theory** is a general rule or principle that enables us to understand and predict the economic choices that people make. We develop economic theories by building and testing economic models. What is an economic model?

Economic Model

You have just seen an economic model. To answer the question "What is an economy and how does it work?" we built a model of an economy. We did not describe in all their detail all the economic actions that take place in the United States. We concentrated our attention only on those features that seemed important for understanding economic choices, and we ignored everything else. You will perhaps better appreciate what we mean by an economic model if you think about more familiar models.

We have all seen model trains, cars, and airplanes. Although we do not usually call dolls and stuffed animals "models," we can think of them in this way. Architects make models of buildings, and biologists make models of DNA (the double helix carrier of the genetic code).

A model is usually smaller than the real thing that it represents. But models are not always smaller in scale (think of a biologist's model of the components of cells), and in any case, the scale of a model is not its most important feature. A model also shows less detail than its counterpart in reality. For example, all the models that we have mentioned resemble the real thing in *appearance,* but they are not usually made of the same substance, nor do they work like the real thing that they represent. The architect's model of a new high-rise shows us what the building will look like and how it will conform with the buildings around it—but it does not contain plumbing, telephone cables, elevator shafts, air conditioning plants, and other interior workings.

All the models that we have discussed (including those that are typically used as toys) represent something that is real, but they lack some key features and deliberately so. The model abstracts from the detail of the real thing. It includes only those features that are needed for the purpose at hand. It leaves out the inessential or unnecessary. What a model includes and leaves out is not arbitrary; it results from a conscious and careful decision.

The models that we have just considered are all physical models. We can see the real thing and we can see the model. Indeed, the purpose of those models is to enable us to visualize the real thing. Some models, including economic models, are not physical. We cannot look at the real thing and look at the model and simply decide whether the model is a good or bad representation of the real thing. But the idea of a model as an abstraction from reality still applies to an economic model.

An economic model has two components:

1. Assumptions
2. Implications

Assumptions form the foundation on which a model is built. They are propositions about what is important and what can be ignored. **Implications** are the outcome of a model. The link between a model's assumptions and its implications is a process of logical deduction.

Let's illustrate these components of a model by building a simple model of your daily journey to school. The model has three assumptions:

1. You want to be in class when it begins at 9:00 A.M.
2. The bus ride to school takes 30 minutes.
3. The walk from the bus to class takes 5 minutes.

The implication of this model is that you will be on the bus no later than 8:25 A.M. With knowledge of the bus timetable, we could use this model to predict the bus that you would catch to school.

The assumptions of a model depend on the model's purpose. The purpose of an economic model is to understand how households, firms, and governments make choices in the face of scarcity. Thus in building an economic model, we abstract from the rich detail of human life and focus only on behavior

that is relevant for coping with scarcity. Everything else is ignored. Economists know that people fall in love and form deep friendships, that they experience great joy and security or great pain and anxiety. But economists assume that in seeking to understand economic behavior, they may build models that ignore many aspects of life. They focus on one and only one feature of the world: people have wants that exceed their resources and so, by their choices, have to make the best of things.

Assumptions of an Economic Model Economic models are based on four key assumptions:

1. *People have preferences.* Economists use the term **preferences** to denote likes and dislikes and the intensity of those likes and dislikes. People can judge whether one situation is better, worse, or just as good as another one. For example, you can judge whether, for you, one loaf of bread and no cheese is better, worse, or just as good as a half a loaf of bread and four ounces of cheese.

2. *People are endowed with a fixed amount of resources and a technology that can transform those resources into goods and services.* Economists use the term **endowment** to refer to the resources that people have and the term **technology** to describe the methods of converting those endowments into goods and services.

3. *People economize.* People choose how to use their endowments and technologies in order to make themselves as well-off as possible. Such a choice is called a rational choice. A **rational choice** is one which, among all possible choices, best achieves the goals of the person making the choice. Each choice, no matter what it is or how foolish it may seem to an observer, is interpreted, in an economic model, as a rational choice. Choices are made on the basis of the information available. With hindsight, and with more information, people may well feel that some of their past choices were bad ones. This fact does not make such choices irrational. Again, a rational choice is the best possible course of action, from the point of view of the person making the choice, given that person's preferences and *given the information available when the choice is made.*

4. *People's choices are coordinated.* One person's choice to buy something must be matched by another person's choice to sell that same thing.

One person's choice to work at a particular job must be matched by another person's choice to hire someone to do that job. The coordination of individual choices is made by either a market mechanism or a command mechanism.

Implications of an Economic Model   The implications of an economic model are the equilibrium values of various prices and quantities. An **equilibrium** is a situation in which everyone has economized—that is, all individuals have made the best possible choices in the light of their own preferences and given their endowments, technologies and information—and in which those choices have been coordinated and made compatible with the choices of everyone else. Equilibrium is the solution or outcome of an economic model.

The term *equilibrium* conjures up the picture of a balance of opposing forces. For example, a balance scale can be said to be in equilibrium if a pound of butter is placed on one side of the balance and a one-pound weight is placed on the other side. The two weights exactly equal each other and so offset each other, leaving the balance arm horizontal. A soap bubble provides another excellent physical illustration of equilibrium. The delicate spherical film of soap is held in place by a balance of forces of the air inside the sphere and the air outside it.

This second physical analogy illustrates a further important feature of an equilibrium. An equilibrium is not necessarily static but may be dynamic—constantly changing. By squeezing or stretching the bubble, you can change its shape, but its shape is always determined by the balance of the forces acting upon it (including the forces that you exert upon it).

An economic equilibrium has a great deal in common with that of the soap bubble. First, it is in a constant state of motion. At each point in time, each person makes the best possible choice, given the endowments and actions of others. But changing circumstances alter those choices. For example, on a busy day in Manhattan, there are more cars looking for parking spaces than the number of spaces available. But people do get to park. Individual cars are leaving and arriving at a steady pace. As soon as one car vacates a parking space, another instantly fills it. In this situation, the equilibrium number of free spaces is zero. But being in equilibrium does not mean that everyone gets to park instantly. There is an equilibrium amount of time spent finding a

"And now a traffic update: A parking space has become available on Sixty-fifth Street between Second and Third. Hold it! A bulletin has just been handed me. That space has been taken."

Drawing by H. Martin; © 1987 The New Yorker Magazine, Inc.

vacant space. People hunting for a space are frustrated and experience rising blood pressure and increased anger. But there is still an equilibrium in the hunt for available parking spaces.

Similarly, an economic equilibrium does not mean that everyone is experiencing economic prosperity. The constraints may be such that some people are very poor. Nevertheless, given their preferences, their endowments, the available technologies, and the actions of everyone else, each person has made the best possible choice and sees no advantage in modifying his or her current action.

Microeconomic and Macroeconomic Models

Economic models fall into two categories: microeconomic and macroeconomic. **Microeconomics** is the branch of economics that studies the decisions of individual households and firms. Microeconomics also studies the way in which individual markets work and the detailed way in which regulation and taxes affect the allocation of labor and of goods and services.

Macroeconomics is the branch of economics that studies the economy as a whole. It seeks to understand the big picture rather than the detailed individual choices. In particular, it studies the determination of the overall level of economic activity—of unemployment, aggregate income, average prices, and inflation.

Of the seven big economic questions, those dealing with technological change, production and consumption, and wages and earnings are microeconomic. Those dealing with unemployment, inflation, and differences in wealth among nations are macroeconomic.

Model, Theory, and Reality

People who build models often get carried away and start talking as if their model *is* the real world—as if their model is reality. No matter how useful it is, there is no sense in which a model can be said to be reality.

A model is abstract. It lists assumptions and their implications. When economists talk about people who have made themselves as well-off as possible, they are not talking about real people. They are talking about artificial people in an economic model. Do not lose sight of this important but easily misunderstood fact.

Economic theory is the bridge between economic models and the real world. Economic theory is a catalog of models that seem to work—that seem to enable us to understand and interpret the past and to predict some aspects of the future. Economic theory evolves from a process of building and testing economic models.

To test an economic model, its implications are matched against actual events in the real world. That is, the model is used to make predictions about the real world. The model's predictions may correspond to or be in conflict with the facts. It is by comparing the model's predictions with the facts that we are able to test a model. The process of developing economic theories by using models is illustrated in Fig. 1.3. We begin by building a model. The model's implications are used to generate predictions about the world. These predictions and their test form the basis of a theory. When predictions are in conflict with the facts, either a theory is discarded in favor of a superior alternative or we return to the model-building stage, modifying our assumptions and creating a new model. Economics itself provides guidance on how we might discover a better model. It prompts us to look for some aspect

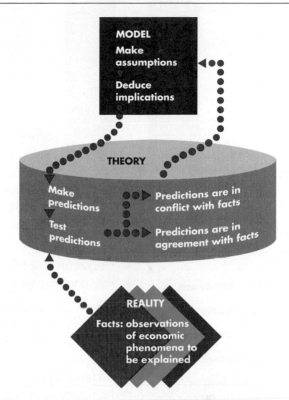

FIGURE **1.3**

How Theories Are Developed

Economic theories are developed by building and testing economic models. An economic model is a set of *assumptions* about what is important and what can be ignored and the *implications* of those assumptions. The implications of a model form the basis of *predictions* about the world. These predictions are tested by being checked against the facts. If the predictions are in conflict with the facts, the model-building process begins again with new assumptions. Only when the predictions are in agreement with the facts has a useful theory been developed.

of preferences, endowments, technology, or the coordination mechanism that has been overlooked.

Economics is a young science and a long way from having achieved its goal of explaining and understanding economic activity. Its birth can be dated fairly precisely in the eighteenth century with the publication of Adam Smith's *The Wealth of Nations* (see Our Advancing Knowledge, pp. 22–23). In the closing years of the twentieth century, economic science has managed to discover a sizable

UNDERSTANDING
the Sources of
ECONOMIC WEALTH

In 1776, new technologies were being invented and applied to the manufacture of cotton and wool, iron, transportation, and agriculture in what came to be called the "Industrial Revolution."

Adam Smith was keenly interested in these events. He wanted to understand the sources of economic wealth, and he brought his acute powers of observation and abstraction to bear on this question. His answer:

◆ The division of labor
◆ Free domestic and international markets

Smith identified the division of labor as the source of "the greatest improvement in the productive powers of labor." The division of labor became even more productive when applied to creating new technologies. Scientists and engineers, trained in extremely narrow fields, became specialists at inventing. Their powerful skills speeded the advance of technology so that by the 1850s we could make machines that could make consumer goods and other machines by performing repetitive operations faster, more accurately, and for longer than people.

But, said Smith, the fruits of the division of labor are limited by the extent of the market. To make the market as large as possible, there must be no impediments to free trade both within a country and among countries. Smith argued that when each person makes the best possible economic choice based on self-interest, that choice leads as if by "an invisible hand" to the best outcome for society as a whole.

> "It is not from the benevolence of the butcher, the brewer, or the baker, that we expect our dinner, but from their regard to their own interest."
>
> ADAM SMITH
> *The Wealth of Nations*

Adam Smith speculated that one person, working hard, using the hand tools available in the 1770s, might possibly make 20 pins a day. Yet by using those same hand tools but breaking the process into a number of individually small operations in which people specialize—by the division of labor—he observed that ten people could make a staggering 48,000 pins a day. One draws out the wire, another straightens it, a third cuts it, a fourth points it, a fifth grinds it. Three specialists make the head and a fourth attaches it. Finally, the pin is polished and wrapped in paper.

Memory chips give your computer its instant-recall ability, logic chips provide its number-crunching power, and custom chips make your camera idiot-proof. The computer chip is an extraordinary example of the productivity of the division of labor. Designers, using computers (made from microchips), create the chip's intricate circuits. Machines print the design on paper and photograph it on glass plates called masks that work like stencils. Workers prepare silicon wafers on which the circuits are printed. Some slice the wafers, others polish them, others bake them, and yet others coat them with a light-sensitive chemical. Technicians put masks and wafers into a machine that shines light through the mask, imprinting a copy of the circuit onto the wafer. Chemicals eat the unexposed portion of the wafer. A further series of passes through gas-filled ovens deposits atoms that act as transistors. Aluminum is deposited on the wafer to connect the transistors. Finally, a diamond saw or laser separates the hundreds of chips on the wafer.

Adam Smith, born in 1723 in Kirkcaldy, a small fishing town near Edinburgh, Scotland, and only child of the town's customs officer (who died before his son was born), was a giant of a scholar who made extraordinary contributions in ethics and jurisprudence as well as economics.

His first academic appointment, at age 28, was as Professor of Logic at the University of Glasgow. He subsequently became tutor to a wealthy Scottish duke whom he accompanied on a two-year European grand tour, following which he received a pension of £300 a year—ten times the average income at that time.

ADAM SMITH AND THE *Wealth of Nations*

With the financial security of his pension, Smith devoted ten years to writing the treatise that founded economic science, *An Inquiry into the Nature and Causes of The Wealth of Nations*, which was published to great acclaim in 1776.

Many had written on economic issues before Adam Smith, but it was he who made economics a science. His account of what was then known was so broad and authoritative that no subsequent writer on economics could advance his own ideas while ignoring the state of general knowledge.

number of useful generalizations. In many areas, however, we are still going around the circle— changing assumptions, performing new logical deductions, generating new predictions, and getting wrong answers yet again. The gradual accumulation of correct answers gives most practitioners some faith that their methods will eventually provide usable answers to the big economic questions.

As we make progress, though, more and more things become clearer and seem to fit together. Theoretical advances lead to deeper understanding. This feature of economics is shared with scientists in all fields. As Albert Einstein, the great physicist, said, "Creating a new theory is not like destroying an old barn and erecting a skyscraper in its place. It is rather like climbing a mountain, gaining new and wider views, discovering new connections between

our starting point and its rich environment. But the point from which we started still exists and can be seen, although it appears smaller and forms a tiny part of our broad view gained by the mastery of the obstacles on our adventurous way up."[1]

◆ ◆ ◆ ◆ In the next chapter, we will study some of the tools that economists use to build economic models. Then, in Chapter 3, we will build an economic model and use that model to understand the world around us and to start to answer some of the seven big economic questions.

_____

[1] These words are attributed to Einstein in a letter by Oliver Sacks to *The Listener,* 88, No. 2279, November 30, 1972, 756.

S U M M A R Y

Scarcity

All economic questions arise from the fundamental fact of scarcity. Scarcity means that wants exceed resources. Human wants are effectively unlimited, but the resources available to satisfy them are finite.

Economic activity is what people do to cope with scarcity. Scarcity forces people to make choices. Making the best choice possible from what is available is called optimizing or economizing. To make the best possible choice, a person weighs the costs and benefits of the alternatives—optimizes.

Opportunity cost is the cost of one choice in terms of the best forgone alternative. The opportunity cost of any action is the best alternative action that could have been undertaken in its place. Attending class instead of staying in bed has an opportunity cost—the cost of one hour of rest.

Scarcity forces people to compete with each other for scarce resources. People may cooperate in certain areas, but all economic activity ultimately results in competition among individuals acting alone or in groups. (pp. 9–11)

The Economy

People have unlimited wants but limited resources or factors of production—labor, land, and capital. The economy is a mechanism that allocates scarce

resources among competing uses, determining *what, how,* and *for whom* the various goods and services will be produced.

The economy's two key components are decision makers and markets. Economic decision makers are households, firms, and governments. Households decide how much of their labor, land, and capital to sell or rent and how much of the various goods and services to buy. Firms decide what factors of production to hire and which goods and services to produce. Governments decide what goods and services to provide to households and firms and how much to raise in taxes.

The decisions of households, firms, and governments are coordinated through markets in which prices adjust to keep buying plans and selling plans consistent. Alternatively, coordination can be achieved by a command mechanism. The U.S. economy relies mainly on markets, but there is a command element in the actions taken by governments that also influences the allocation of scarce resources. The U.S. economy is therefore a mixed economy. (pp. 12–17)

Economic Science

Economic science, like the natural sciences and the other social sciences, attempts to find a body of laws. Economic science makes only *positive* statements—statements about what is. It does not make *normative* statements—statements about what ought to be. Economists try to find economic laws by developing a body of economic theory, and economic theory, in turn, is developed by building and testing economic models. Economic models are abstract, logical constructions that contain two components: assumptions and implications. An economic model has four key assumptions:

1. People have preferences.

2. People have a given endowment of resources and technology.
3. People economize.
4. People's choices are coordinated through market or command mechanisms.

The implications of an economic model are the equilibrium values of various prices and quantities that result from each individual doing the best that is possible, given the individual's preferences, endowments, information, and technology and given the coordination mechanism. (pp. 17–24)

KEY ELEMENTS

Key Terms

Assumptions, 19
Capital, 14
Closed economy, 16
Command economy, 15
Command mechanism, 15
Competition, 11
Cooperation, 11
Economic activity, 9
Economic theory, 18
Economics, 9
Economizing, 10
Economy, 12
Endowment, 19
Equilibrium, 20
Factor market, 14
Factors of production, 14
Firm, 14
Goods market, 14
Government, 14
Household, 14

Implications, 19
Labor, 14
Land, 14
Macroeconomics, 20
Market, 14
Market economy, 16
Microeconomics, 20
Mixed economy, 16
Normative statement, 17
Open economy, 16
Opportunity cost, 10
Optimizing, 10
Positive statement, 17
Preferences, 19
Rational choice, 19
Scarcity, 9
Technology, 19

Key Figure

Figure 1.1   A Picture of the Economy, 13

REVIEW QUESTIONS

1 Give two examples, different from those in the chapter, that illustrate each of the seven big economic questions.

2 Why does scarcity force us to make choices?

3 What do we mean by "rational choice"? Give examples of rational and irrational choices.

4 Why does scarcity force us to economize?

5 Why does optimization require us to calculate costs?

6 Why does scarcity imply competition?

7 Why can't we solve economic problems by cooperating with each other?

8 Name the main economic decision makers.

9 List the economic decisions made by households, firms, and governments.

10 What is the difference between a command mechanism and a market?

11 Distinguish between positive and normative statements by listing three examples of each type of statement.

12 What are the four key assumptions of an economic model?

13 Explain the difference between a model and a theory.

P R O B L E M S

1 You plan to go to school this summer. If you do, you won't be able to take your usual job that pays $6,000 for the summer and you won't be able to live at home for free. The cost of your tuition will be $2,000, textbooks $200, and living expenses $1,400. What is the opportunity cost of going to summer school?

2 On Valentine's Day, Bernie and Catherine exchanged gifts: Bernie sent Catherine red roses and Catherine bought Bernie a box of chocolate. They each spent $15. They also spent $50 on dinner and split the cost evenly. Did either Bernie or Catherine incur any opportunity costs? If so, what were they? Explain your answer.

3 Nancy asks Beth to be her maid-of-honor at her wedding. Beth accepts. Which of the following are part of her opportunity cost of being Nancy's maid-of-honor? Explain why they are or are not.

a The $200 Beth spent on a new outfit for the occasion

b The $50 she spent on a party for Nancy's friends

c The money she spent on a haircut a week before the wedding

d The weekend visit she missed for her grandmother's 75th birthday—the same weekend as the wedding

e The $10 she spent on lunch on the way to the wedding

4 The local mall has free parking, but the mall is always very busy, and it usually takes 30 minutes to find a parking space. Today when you found a vacant spot, Harry also wanted it. Is parking really free at this mall? If not, what did it cost you to park today? When you parked your car today, did you impose any costs on Harry? Explain your answers.

5 Which of the following statements are positive and which are normative?

a A cut in wages will reduce the number of people willing to work.

b High interest rates prohibit many young people from buying their first home.

c No family ought to pay more than 25 percent of its income in taxes.

d The government should reduce the number of minorities in the military and increase the number of whites.

e The government ought to supply a medical insurance scheme for everyone free of charge.

6 You have been hired by Soundtrend, a company that makes and markets tapes, records, and compact discs (CDs). Your employer is going to start selling these products in a new region that has a population of 10 million people. A survey has indicated that 50 percent of people buy only popular music, 10 percent buy only classical music, and no one buys both types of music. Another survey suggests that the average income of a pop music fan is $10,000 a year and that of a classical fan is $50,000 a year. Based on a third survey, it appears that, on the average, people with low incomes spend one quarter of 1 percent of their income on tapes, records, and CDs, while people with high incomes spend 2 percent of their income on these products.

Build a model to enable Soundtrend to predict how much will be spent on pop music and classical music in this region in one year. In doing so:

a List your assumptions.

b Work out the implications of your assumptions.

c Highlight the potential sources of errors in your predictions.

CHAPTER 2

MAKING
AND
USING
GRAPHS

After studying this chapter, you will be able to:

◆ Make and interpret a scatter diagram and a time-series graph

◆ Distinguish between linear and nonlinear relationships and relationships that have a maximum and a minimum

◆ Define and calculate the slope of a line

◆ Graph relationships among more than two variables

BENJAMIN DISRAELI, BRITISH PRIME MINISTER IN THE LATE nineteenth century, is reputed to have said that there are three kinds of lies: lies, damned lies, and statistics. One of the most powerful ways of conveying statistical information is in the form of a picture—a graph. Thus graphs, too, like statistics, can tell lies. But the right graph does not lie. Indeed, it reveals data and helps its viewer to see and think about relationships that would otherwise be obscure. ◆ ◆ Graphs are a surprisingly modern invention. The first graphs appeared in the late eighteenth century, long after the discovery of mathematically sophisticated ideas such as logarithms and calculus. But today, especially in the age of the personal computer and the video display, graphs have become almost more important than words. The ability to make and use graphs is as important as the ability to read and write. ◆ ◆ How do economists use graphs? What are the different types of graphs that

Three Kinds of Lies

economists use? What do economic graphs reveal and what can they hide? What are the main pitfalls that can result in a graph that lies? ◆ ◆ The seven big questions that you studied in Chapter 1—the problems that economics seeks to solve—are difficult ones. They involve relationships among a large number of variables. Hardly anything in economics has a single cause. Instead, a large number of variables interact with each other. It is often said that in economics, everything depends on everything else. Well, maybe not everything else, but lots of things. Variations in the quantity of ice cream consumed are caused not merely by variations in the air temperature or in the price of cream, but by at least these two factors and probably several others as well. How can we draw graphs of relationships that involve several variables, all of which vary simultaneously? How can we interpret such relationships?

◆ ◆ ◆ ◆ In this chapter, we are going to look at the different kinds of graphs that are used in economics. We are going to learn how to make them and read them. We are going to look at examples of useful graphs as well as misleading graphs. We are also going to study how we can calculate the strength of the effect of one variable on another.

◆ ◆ There are no graphs or techniques used in this book that are more complicated than those explained and described in this chapter. If you are already familiar with graphs, you may want to skip or at least only skim this chapter. Whether you study this chapter thoroughly or give it a quick pass, you should regard it as a handy reference chapter to which you can return if you feel that you need additional help understanding the graphs that you encounter in your study of economics.

Graphing Data

G raphs represent a quantity as a distance. Figure 2.1 gives two examples. Part (a) shows temperature, measured in degrees Fahrenheit, as the distance on a scale. Movements from left to right represent increases in temperature. Movements from right to left represent decreases in temperature. The point marked 0 represents zero degrees Fahrenheit. To the right of zero, the temperatures are positive. To the left of zero, the temperatures are negative (as indicated by the minus sign in front of the numbers).

Figure 2.1(b) provides another example. This time altitude, or height, is measured in thousands of feet above sea level. The point marked 0 represents sea level. Points to the right of zero represent feet above sea level. Points to the left of zero (indicated by a minus sign) represent depths below sea level. There are no rigid rules about the scale for a graph. The scale is determined by the range of the variable being graphed and the space available for the graph.

FIGURE 2.1

Graphing a Single Variable

(a) Temperature

(b) Height

All graphs have a scale that measures a quantity as a distance. The two scales here measure temperature and height. Numbers to the right of zero are positive. Numbers to the left of zero are negative.

The two graphs in Fig. 2.1 show just a single variable. Marking a point on either of the two scales indicates a particular temperature or a particular height. Thus the point marked *a* represents 32°F, the freezing point of water. The point marked *b* represents 20,320 feet, the height of Mount McKinley, the highest mountain in North America.

Graphing a single variable as we have done does not usually reveal much. Graphs become powerful when they show how two variables are related to each other.

Two-Variable Graphs

To construct a two-variable graph, we set two scales perpendicular to each other. Let's continue to use the same two variables as those in Fig. 2.1. We will measure temperature in exactly the same way, but we will turn the height scale to a vertical position. Thus temperature is measured exactly as it was before, but height is now represented by movements up and down a vertical scale.

The two scale lines in Fig. 2.2 are called **axes.** The vertical line is called the ***y*-axis,** and the horizontal line is called the ***x*-axis.** The letters *x* and *y* appear on the axes of Fig. 2.2. Each axis has a zero point that is shared by the two axes. The zero point, common to both axes, is called the **origin.**

FIGURE **2.2**

Graphing Two Variables

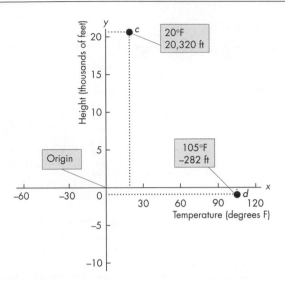

The relationship between two variables is graphed by drawing two axes perpendicular to each other. Height is measured here on the *y*-axis and temperature on the *x*-axis. Point *c* represents the top of Mt. McKinley, 20,320 feet above sea level (measured on the *y*-axis), with a temperature of 20°F (measured on the *x*-axis). Point *d* represents Death Valley, 282 feet below sea level, with a temperature of 105°F.

To represent something in a two-variable graph, we need two pieces of information. For example, Mount McKinley is 20,320 feet high and, on a particular day, the temperature at its peak is 20°F. We can represent this information in Fig. 2.2 by marking the height of the mountain on the *y*-axis at 20,320 feet and the temperature on the *x*-axis at 20°F. We can now identify the values of the two variables that appear on the axes by marking point *c*.

Two lines, called coordinates, can be drawn from point *c*. **Coordinates** are lines running from a point on a graph perpendicularly to an axis. The line running from *c* to the *x*-axis is the **y-coordinate**, because its length is the same as the value marked off on the *y*-axis. Similarly, the line running from *c* to the vertical axis is the **x-coordinate**, because its length is the same as the value marked off on the *x*-axis.

Now let's leave the top of Mount McKinley, at 20,320 feet and 20°F, and go to Death Valley in the

Mojave Desert, the lowest point in the United States at 282 feet *below* sea level. Death Valley is represented by point *d*, which shows that we are 282 feet below sea level (the *y*-coordinate) and the temperature is 105°F (the *x*-coordinate).

Economists use graphs similar to this one in a variety of ways. Let's look at two examples.

Scatter Diagrams

Economists use graphs to reveal and describe the relationship between two economic variables. The most important type of graph used for these purposes is the scatter diagram, an example of which is shown in Fig. 2.3. A **scatter diagram** plots the value of one economic variable associated with the value

FIGURE **2.3**

A Scatter Diagram: Consumption and Income

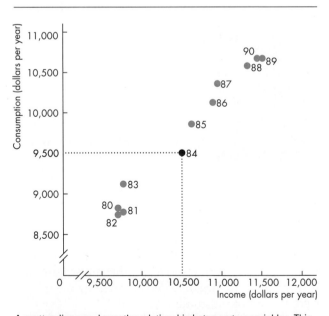

A scatter diagram shows the relationship between two variables. This scatter diagram shows the relationship between average consumption and average income during the years 1980 to 1990. Each point shows the values of the two variables in a specific year, and the year is identified by the two-digit number. For example, in 1984 average consumption was $9,500 and average income was $10,500. The pattern formed by the points shows that as income increases, so does consumption.

of another. It measures one of the variables on the *x*-axis and the other variable on the *y*-axis.

The Relationship Between Consumption and Income

Figure 2.3 uses a scatter diagram to show the relationship between consumption and income. The *x*-axis measures average income, and the *y*-axis measures average consumption. Each point represents average consumption and average income in the United States in a given year between 1980 and 1990. The points for all eleven years are "scattered" within the graph. Each point is labeled with a two-digit number that tells us its year. For example, the point marked 84 tells us that in 1984, average consumption was $9,500 and average income was $10,500.

This graph reveals that a relationship *does* exist between average income and average consumption. The pattern formed by the points in Fig. 2.3 tells us that when income increases, consumption also increases.

Breaks in the Axes

Notice that each axis in Fig. 2.3 has a break in it—illustrated by the small gaps. The breaks indicate that there are jumps from the origin, 0, to the first values recorded. The breaks are used because in the period covered by the graph average consumption was never less than $8,500 and average income was never less than $9,500. With no breaks in the axes of this graph, there would be a lot of empty space, all the points would be crowded into the top right corner, and we would not be able to see whether a relationship existed between these two variables. By using axis breaks, we are able to bring the relationship into view. In effect, we use a zoom lens to bring the relationship into the center of the graph and magnify it so that it fills the graph.

The range of the variables plotted on the axes of a graph are an important feature of a graph, and it is a good idea to get into the habit of always looking closely at the axis values—and labels—before you start to interpret a graph.

Other Relationships

Figure 2.4 shows two other scatter diagrams. In part (a), the *x*-axis shows the percentage of households owning a video cassette recorder, and the *y*-axis shows its average price. Each point with its two-digit number represents a year. Thus the point marked 81 tells us that the

More Scatter Diagrams

(a) VCR ownership and price

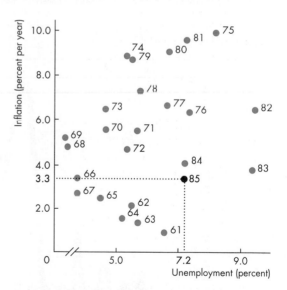

(b) Unemployment and inflation

Part (a) is a scatter diagram showing the relationship between the percentage of households owning a VCR and the average price of a VCR. It shows that as the price of a VCR has fallen, the percentage of households owning a VCR has increased. Part (b) is a scatter diagram showing inflation and unemployment. It shows that there is no clear relationship between these two variables.

average price of a VCR in 1981 was $600 and that VCRs were owned by 20 percent of all households. The pattern formed by the points in part (a) tells us that as the price of a VCR falls, a larger percentage of households own one.

In part (b), the *x*-axis measures unemployment in the United States, and the *y*-axis measures inflation. Again, each point with its two-digit number represents a year. The point marked 85 tells us that in 1985 unemployment was 7.2 percent and inflation was 3.3 percent. The pattern formed by the points in part (b) does not reveal a clear relationship between the two variables. The graph thus informs us, by its lack of a distinct pattern, that there is no relationship between these two variables.

A scatter diagram enables us to see the relationship between two economic variables. But it does not give us a clear picture of how those variables evolve over time. To see the evolution of economic variables, we use a different but common kind of graph—the time-series graph.

Time-Series Graphs

A **time-series graph** measures time (for example, years or months) on the *x*-axis and the variable or variables in which we are interested on the *y*-axis.

Figure 2.5 illustrates a time-series graph. Time is measured in years on the *x*-axis. The variable that we are interested in—the U.S. unemployment rate (the percentage of the labor force unemployed)—is measured on the *y*-axis. The time-series graph conveys an enormous amount of information quickly and easily:

1. It tells us the *level* of the unemployment rate—when it is *high* and *low*. When the line is a long way from the *x*-axis, the unemployment rate is high. When the line is close to the *x*-axis, the unemployment rate is low.

2. It tells us how the unemployment rate *changes*—whether it *rises* or *falls*. When the line slopes upward, as in the early 1930s, the unemployment rate is rising. When the line slopes downward,

---

FIGURE 2.5

A Time-Series Graph

A time-series graph plots the level of a variable on the *y*-axis against time (day, week, month, or year) on the *x*-axis. This graph shows the

U.S. unemployment rate each year from 1900 to 1990.
Source: Economic Report of the President.

as in the early 1940s, the unemployment rate is falling.

3. It tells us the *speed* with which the unemployment rate is *changing*—whether it is rising or falling *quickly* or *slowly*. If the line rises or falls very steeply, then unemployment is changing quickly. If the line is not steep, unemployment is rising or falling slowly. For example, unemployment rose very quickly between 1930 and 1932. Unemployment went up again in 1933 but more slowly. Similarly, when unemployment was falling in the early 1950s, it fell quickly between 1950 and 1951, but then it began to fall much more slowly in 1952 and 1953.

A time-series graph can also be used to depict a trend. A **trend** is a general tendency for a variable to rise or fall. You can see that unemployment had a general tendency to rise from the mid-1940s to the mid-1980s. That is, although there were ups and downs in the unemployment rate, there was an upward trend.

Graphs also allow us to compare different periods quickly. It is apparent, for example, that the 1930s were different from any other period in the twentieth century because of exceptionally high unemployment. You can also see that unemployment fluctuated more violently in the years before 1920 than it did in the years after 1950. The sawtooth pattern is more jagged in the period from 1900 to 1930 than it is in the period after 1950.

Thus we can see that Fig. 2.5 conveys a wealth of information, and it does so in much less space than we have used to describe only some of its features.

Misleading Time-Series Graphs   Although time-series graphs are powerful devices for conveying a large amount of information, they can also be used to distort data and to create a misleading picture. The two most commonly used ways of distorting data are stretching and squeezing the scales on the *y*-axis and omitting the origin—the zero point—on the *y*-axis.

Figure 2.6 illustrates the first of these devices. It contains exactly the same information as Fig. 2.5, but the information is packaged in a different way. In part (a) the scale on the *y*-axis has been compressed; in part (b) it has been expanded. When we look at these two parts as a whole, they suggest that unemployment was pretty stable during the first half of this century, but that it has trended upward dramatically in the last 40 years or so.

You might think that this graphical way of distorting data is so outrageous that no one would ever

---

FIGURE 2.6

Misleading Graphs: Squeezing and Stretching Scales

(a) 1900–1944

(b) 1945–1990

Graphs can mislead by squeezing and stretching the scales. These two graphs show exactly the same thing as Fig. 2.5—U.S. unemployment from 1900 to 1990. Part (a) has squeezed the *y*-axis, while part (b) has stretched that axis. The result appears to be a low and stable unemployment rate before 1945 and a rising, highly volatile unemployment rate after that date. Contrast the lie of Fig. 2.6 with the truth of Fig. 2.5.

attempt to use it. If you scrutinize the graphs that you see in newspapers and magazines, you will be surprised how common this device is.

Figure 2.7 illustrates the effect of omitting the origin on the y-axis. Sometimes, omitting the origin is precisely the correct thing to do, as it enables the

graph to reveal its information. But there are also times when omitting the origin is misleading. In parts (a) and (b), you can see a graph of the unemployment rate between 1970 and 1990. Part (a) includes the origin, and part (b) does not. The graph in part (a) provides a clear account of what hap-

---

FIGURE **2.7**

Omitting the Origin

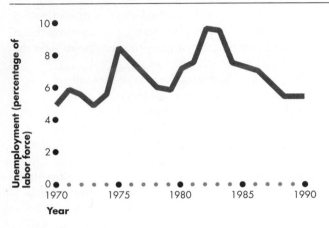

(a) Revealing graph with origin

(b) Misleading graph with origin omitted

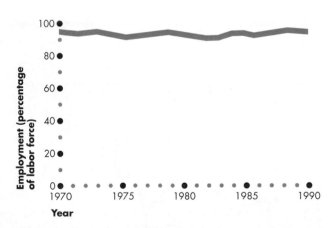

(c) Uninformative graph with origin

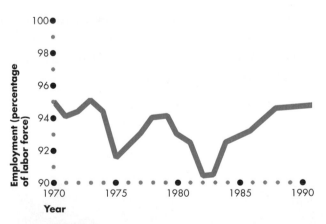

(d) Revealing graph with origin omitted

Sometimes the origin is omitted from a graph. This practice can be either revealing or misleading, depending on how it is used. Parts (a) and (b) graph the U.S. unemployment rate between 1970 and 1990. Part (a) is graphed with the origin on the y-axis, and part (b) without it. Part (a) reveals a large amount of information about the level and changes in the unemployment rate over this time period. Part (b) overdramatizes the rises and falls in unemployment and gives no direct visual information about its level.

Parts (c) and (d) graph the employment rate. Part (c) contains an origin on the y-axis, and part (d) does not. In this case the graph in part (c) with the origin on the y-axis is uninformative and shows virtually no variation in the employment rate. The graph in part (d) gives a clear picture of fluctuations in the employment rate and is more informative than part (c) about those fluctuations.

pened to unemployment over the time period in question. You can use that graph in the same way that we used Fig. 2.5 to describe all the features of unemployment during that time period. But the graph in part (b) is less revealing and distorts the picture. It fails to reveal the *level* of unemployment. It focuses only on, and exaggerates, the magnitude of the increases and decreases in the unemployment rate. In particular, the increases in the unemployment rate in 1974–1975 and in 1981–1982 look enormous when compared with the increases that appear in part (a). With the origin omitted, small percentage changes in unemployment look like many hundredfold changes. Another example of this device is shown in Reading Between the Lines, on pp. 36–37.

Parts (c) and (d) of Fig. 2.7 graph the employment rate—the percentage of the labor force employed. Part (c) includes the origin, and part (d) omits it. As you can see, the graph in part (c) reveals very little about movements in the employment rate. It seems to suggest that the employment rate was pretty constant and lying between 90 and 95 per cent. The main feature of part (c) is an enormous amount of empty space and an inefficient use of the space available. Part (d) shows the same information but with the origin omitted. The scale begins at 90 percent. In this case, we can see very clearly the ups and downs in the employment rate. This graph does not provide a visual impression of the level of employment, but it does provide a clear picture of variations in its rate.

The decision about whether to include or exclude the origin of the graph depends on what the graph is designed to reveal. To convey information about the level of employment and unemployment and variations in their rates, the graphs in parts (a) and (d) of Fig. 2.7 are almost equally revealing. By comparison, the graphs in parts (b) and (c) convey almost no information.

Comparing Two Time Series   Sometimes we want to use a time-series graph to compare two different variables. For example, suppose you wanted to know how the balance of the government's budget—its surplus or deficit—fluctuated and how those fluctuations compared with fluctuations in the unemployment rate. You can examine two such series by drawing a graph of each of them in the manner shown in Fig. 2.8(a). The scale for the unemployment rate appears on the left side of the figure, and

Time-Series Relationships

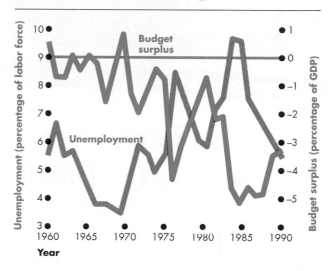

(a) Unemployment and budget surplus

(b) Unemployment and budget deficit

A time-series graph can be used to reveal relationships between two variables. These two graphs show the unemployment rate and the balance of the government's budget between 1960 and 1990. The unemployment line is identical in the two parts. In part (a), the budget balance is shown measuring surpluses upward and deficits downward (as negative numbers) on the right scale. It looks as if the budget goes into a bigger deficit when unemployment rises, but not much else is shown by part (a). Part (b) inverts the scale on which the budget is measured. Now a deficit is measured in the up direction and a surplus in the down direction on the right scale. The relationship between the budget deficit and unemployment is now easier to see.

Graphs in Action

The Wall Street Journal, August 27, 1991

Concern Goes Up as SAT Scores Go Down

By Gary Putka

Scholastic Aptitude Test scores declined despite increased course loads and higher grades in U.S. high schools, suggesting that efforts to reform education are being hampered by falling academic standards. . . .

The average composite score on the SAT, the most-taken college-admissions test, fell to 896 from 900 out of a maximum 1,600. The average score has fallen four years in a row and is at its lowest point since 1983's 893. The verbal score, which fell two points to 422, is the lowest on record at the College Board, the New York organization that gives the test on behalf of U.S. colleges. The score in mathematics, the test's other part, slipped two points to 474, also the lowest since 1984. . . .

Need for a New Strategy

"You either have to say it's too early and reforms haven't been in place long enough, or all the things we put in the schools were wrong and we need a radical new strategy," said Albert Shanker, president of the American Federation of Teachers. "My own view is the latter is the case." . . .

Mr. Shanker said that his analysis of federal test scores indicate that only 4% of high-school graduates "really know algebra," although 96% of those who took the SAT reported taking an algebra class. Ninety-three percent took geometry. Yet on the math section of the SAT, which is largely a test of algebra and geometry, students got an average of only 26 of 60 questions correct. . . .

Not all of the SAT data pointed to educational setbacks. The total number of test takers, which stayed about flat at one million, represented 42% of this year's high-school graduates, up from 40% in 1990 and an indication of rising educational aspirations. . . .

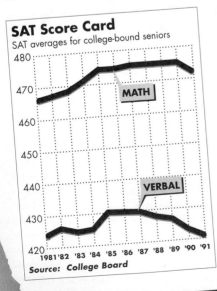

SAT Score Card
SAT averages for college-bound seniors
Source: College Board

The average composite SAT score has fallen for four years in a row.

The verbal score in 1991 was the lowest on record, and the mathematics score in 1991 was at its lowest level since 1984.

The 1980s have been years of major reforms in education and of large increases in expenditure on education.

Many people read these facts as a sign of "falling academic standards" and of the failure of the reforms.

The percentage of high school graduates taking the SAT increased from 40 percent in 1990 to 42 percent in 1991.

This last fact is seen as a sign of "rising educational aspirations."

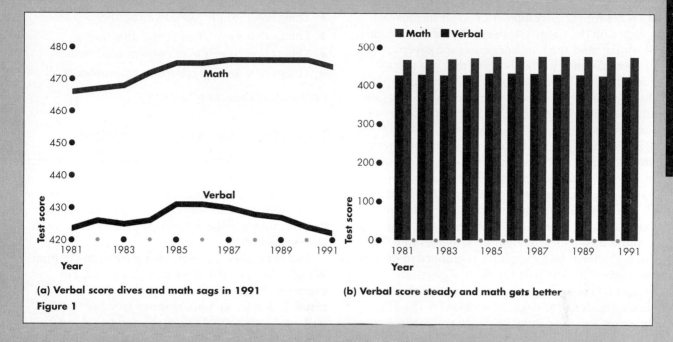

(a) Verbal score dives and math sags in 1991

(b) Verbal score steady and math gets better

Figure 1

Background and Analysis

A 2 percent fall in the SAT verbal score is shown in both parts of Fig. 1, but the false impression of a large fall is created in part (a)—as in the news story—by omitting the origin.

During the 1980s, the number of students taking the SAT increased and the college entry age population decreased. The percentage of the college entry age population taking the SAT increased from 23 percent in 1981 to 29 percent in 1991.

Other things being equal, the larger the percentage of the population taking *any* test, the lower the average score.

Figure 2 gives a third view of the falling SAT scores that shows the relationship between the SAT scores and the percentage of the college entry age population taking the test.

Despite the increased percentage taking the test, the math score increased throughout the 1980s and dipped only in 1991. These facts suggest remarkable improvements in mathematical achievement.

The verbal score increased between 1981 and 1985 but declined as the percentage taking the test increased after 1985. It continued to decline in 1990 and 1991, even though the percentage of the population taking the test stabilized.

(a) SAT math score and percentage taking test

Figure 2

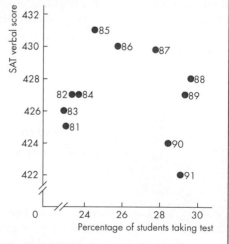

(b) SAT verbal score and percentage taking test

the scale for the government's budget surplus appears on the right. The purple line shows unemployment, and the blue line shows the government's budget. You will probably agree that it is pretty hard work figuring out from Fig. 2.8(a) just what the relationship is between the unemployment rate and the government's budget. But it does look as if there is a tendency for the budget to go into a bigger deficit (blue line goes downward) when the unemployment rate increases (purple line goes upward). In other words, it seems as if these two variables have a tendency to move in opposite directions.

In a situation such as this, it is often more revealing to flip the scale of one of the variables over and graph it upside-down. Figure 2.8(b) does this. The unemployment rate in part (b) is graphed in exactly the same way as in part (a). But the government's budget has been flipped over. Now, instead of measuring the deficit (a negative number) in the down direction and the surplus (a positive number) in the up direction, we measure the deficit upward and the surplus downward. You can now "see" very clearly the relationship between these two variables. There is indeed a tendency for the government's deficit to get bigger when the unemployment rate gets higher. But the relationship is by no means an exact one. There are significant periods, clearly revealed in the graph, when the deficit and the unemployment rate move apart. You can "see" these periods as those in which the gap between the two lines widens.

Now that we have seen how we can use graphs in economics to represent economic data and to show the relationship between variables, let us examine how economists use graphs in a more abstract way to construct and analyze economic models.

Graphs Used in Economic Models

Although you will encounter many different kinds of graphs in economics, there are some patterns that, once you have learned to recognize them, will instantly convey to you the meaning of a graph. There are graphs that show each of the following:

- Things that go up and down together
- Things that move in opposite directions
- Things that have a maximum or a minimum
- Things that are not related to each other at all

Let's look at these four cases.

Things That Go Up and Down Together

Graphs that show the relationship between two variables that move up and down together are shown in Fig. 2.9. The relationship between two variables that move in the same direction is called a **positive relationship**. Such a relationship is shown by a line that slopes upward.

Part (a) shows the relationship between the number of miles traveled in 5 hours and speed. For example, the point marked *a* tells us that we will travel 200 miles in 5 hours if our speed is 40 miles an hour. If we double our speed and travel at 80 miles an hour, we will cover a distance of 400 miles in 5 hours. The relationship between the number of miles traveled in 5 hours and speed is represented by an upward-sloping straight line. A relationship depicted by a straight line is called a **linear relationship**.

Part (b) shows the relationship between distance sprinted and exhaustion (exhaustion being measured by the time it takes the heart rate to return to normal). This relationship is an upward-sloping one depicted by a curved line that starts out with a gentle slope but then becomes steeper as we move along the curve away from the origin.

Part (c) shows the relationship between the number of problems worked by a student and the amount of study time. This relationship is illustrated by an upward-sloping curved line that starts out with a steep slope but then becomes more gentle as we move away from the origin.

There are three types of upward-sloping lines in the graphs in Fig. 2.9: one straight and two curved. But they are all called curves. Any line on a graph—no matter whether it is straight or curved—is called a **curve**.

Things That Move in Opposite Directions

Figure 2.10 shows relationships between things that move in opposite directions. A relationship between variables that move in opposite directions is called a **negative relationship**.

FIGURE **2.9**

Positive Relationships

(a) Positive constant slope

(b) Positive increasing slope

(c) Positive decreasing slope

Each part of this figure shows a positive relationship between two variables. That is, as the value of the variable measured on the x-axis increases, so does the value of the variable measured on the y-axis. Part (a) illustrates a linear relationship—a relationship whose slope is constant as we move along the curve. Part (b) illustrates a positive relationship whose slope becomes steeper as we move along the curve away from the origin. It is a positive relationship with an increasing slope. Part (c) shows a positive relationship whose slope becomes flatter as we move away from the origin. It is a positive relationship with a decreasing slope.

FIGURE **2.10**

Negative Relationships

(a) Negative constant slope

(b) Negative decreasing slope

(c) Negative increasing slope

Each part of this figure shows a negative relationship between two variables. Part (a) shows a linear relationship—a relationship whose slope is constant as we travel along the curve. Part (b) shows a negative relationship of decreasing slope. That is, the slope of the relationship gets less steep as we travel along the curve from left to right. Part (c) shows a negative relationship of increasing slope. That is, the slope becomes steeper as we travel along the curve from left to right.

Part (a) shows the relationship between the number of hours available for playing squash and the number of hours for playing tennis. One extra hour spent playing tennis means one hour less playing squash and vice versa. This relationship is negative and linear.

Part (b) shows the relationship between the cost per mile traveled and the length of a journey. The longer the journey, the lower is the cost per mile. But as the journey length increases, the cost per mile decreases at a decreasing rate. This feature of the relationship is illustrated by the fact that the curve slopes downward, starting out steep at a short journey length and then becoming flatter as the journey length increases.

Part (c) shows the relationship between the amount of leisure time and the number of problems worked by a student. If the student takes no leisure, 25 problems can be worked. If the student takes 5 hours of leisure, only 20 problems can be worked (point *a*). Increasing leisure time beyond 5 hours produces a large reduction in the number of problems worked, and if the student takes 10 hours of leisure a day, no problems get worked. This relationship is a negative one that starts out with a gentle slope at a low number of leisure hours and becomes increasingly steep as leisure hours increase.

Things That Have a Maximum and a Minimum

Economics is about optimizing, or doing the best with limited resources. Examples of optimizing include making the highest possible profits and achieving the lowest possible costs of production. Economists make frequent use of graphs depicting relationships that have a maximum or a minimum. Figure 2.11 illustrates such relationships.

Part (a) shows the relationship between rainfall and wheat yield. When there is no rainfall, wheat will not grow, so the yield is zero. As the rainfall increases up to 10 days a month, the wheat yield also increases. With 10 rainy days each month, the wheat yield reaches its maximum at 40 bushels an acre (point *a*). Rain in excess of 10 days a month starts to lower the yield of wheat. If every day is rainy, the wheat suffers from a lack of sunshine and the yield falls back almost to zero. This relationship

FIGURE **2.11**

Maximum and Minimum Points

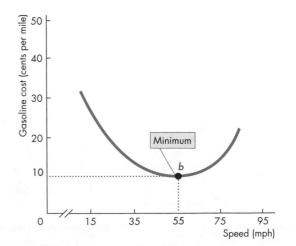

(a) Maximum

Part (a) shows a relationship that has a maximum point, *a*. The curve rises at first, reaches its highest point, and then falls. Part (b) shows a

(b) Minimum

relationship with a minimum point, *b*. The curve falls to its minimum and then rises.

is one that starts out positive, reaches a maximum, and then becomes negative.

Part (b) shows the reverse case—a relationship that begins with a negative slope, falls to a minimum, and then becomes positive. An example of such a relationship is the gasoline cost per mile as the speed of travel varies. At low speeds, the car is creeping along in a traffic snarl-up. The number of miles per gallon is low, so the gasoline cost per mile is high. At very high speeds, the car is operated beyond its most efficient rate, and again the number of miles per gallon is low and the gasoline cost per mile is high. At a speed of 55 miles an hour, the gasoline cost per mile traveled is at its minimum (point *b*).

Things That Are Independent

There are many situations in which one variable is independent of another. No matter what happens to the value of one variable, the other variable remains constant. Sometimes we want to show the indepen-

dence between two variables in a graph. Figure 2.12 shows two ways of achieving this. In part (a), your grade in economics is shown on the vertical axis against the price of bananas on the horizontal axis. Your grade (75 percent in this example) does not depend on the price of bananas. The relationship between these two variables is shown by a horizontal straight line. In part (b), the output of French wine is shown on the horizontal axis and the number of rainy days a month in California is shown on the vertical axis. Again, the output of French wine (3 billion gallons a year in this example) does not change when the number of rainy days in California changes. The relationship between these two variables is shown by a vertical straight line.

Figures 2.9 through 2.12 illustrate ten different shapes of graphs that we will encounter in economic models. In describing these graphs, we have talked about curves that slope upward or slope downward and slopes that are steep or gentle. The concept of slope is an important one. Let's spend a little time discussing exactly what we mean by slope.

FIGURE 2.12

Variables with No Relationship

(a) Unrelated: horizontal

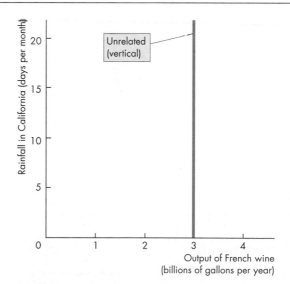

(b) Unrelated: vertical

This figure shows how we can graph two variables that are unrelated to each other. In part (a), a student's grade in economics is plotted at 75 percent regardless of the price of bananas on the *x*-axis. In part (b), the output of the vineyards of France does not vary with the rainfall in California.

The Slope of a Relationship

The **slope** of a relationship is the change in the value of the variable measured on the y-axis divided by the change in the value of the variable measured on the x-axis. We use the Greek letter Δ to represent "change in." Thus Δy means the change in the value of the variable measured on the y-axis, and Δx means the change in the value of the variable measured on the x-axis. Therefore the slope of the relationship is

$$\Delta y / \Delta x.$$

If a large change in the variable measured on the y-axis (Δy) is associated with a small change in the variable measured on the x-axis (Δx), the slope is large and the curve is steep. If a small change in the variable measured on the y-axis (Δy) is associated with a large change in the variable measured on the x-axis (Δx), the slope is small and the curve is flat.

We can make the idea of slope sharper by doing some calculations.

Calculating Slope of a Straight Line

The slope of a straight line is the same regardless of where on the line you calculate it. Thus the slope of a straight line is constant. Let's calculate the slopes of the lines in Fig. 2.13. In part (a), when x increases from 2 to 6, y increases from 3 to 6. The change in x is +4—that is, Δx is 4. The change in y is +3—that is, Δy is 3. The slope of that line is

$$\frac{\Delta y}{\Delta x} = \frac{3}{4}.$$

FIGURE **2.13**

The Slope of a Straight Line

(a) Positive slope

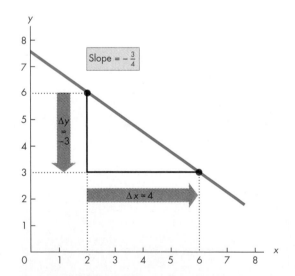

(b) Negative slope

To calculate the slope of a straight line, we divide the change in the value of the variable measured on the y-axis by the change in the value of the variable measured on the x-axis. Part (a) shows the calculation of a positive slope (when x goes up, y goes up). When x goes up from 2 to 6, the change in x is 4—that is, Δx equals 4. That change in x brings about an increase in y from 3 to 6, so Δy equals 3. The slope ($\Delta y / \Delta x$) equals ¾. Part (b) shows a negative slope (when x goes up, y goes down). When x goes up from 2 to 6, Δx equals 4. That change in x brings about a decrease in y from 6 to 3, so Δy equals –3. The slope ($\Delta y / \Delta x$) equals –¾.

In part (b), when *x* increases from 2 to 6, *y* decreases from 6 to 3. The change in *y* is *minus* 3—that is, Δy is –3. The change in *x* is *plus* 4—that is, Δx is +4. The slope of the curve is

$$\frac{\Delta y}{\Delta x} = \frac{-3}{4}.$$

Notice that the two slopes have the same magnitude (3/4), but the slope of the line in part (a) is positive (+3/+4 = 3/4), while that in part (b) is negative (–3/+4 = –3/4). The slope of a positive relationship is positive; the slope of a negative relationship is negative.

Calculating Slope of a Curved Line

Calculating the slope of a curved line is trickier. The slope of a curved line is not constant. Its slope depends on where on the line we calculate it. There are two ways to calculate the slope of a curved line: you can calculate the slope at a point on the line, or you can calculate the slope across an arc of the line. Let's look at the two alternatives.

Slope at a Point   To calculate the slope at a point on a curved line, you need to construct a straight line that has the same slope as the curve at the point in question. Figure 2.14 shows how such a calculation is made. Suppose you want to calculate the

---

The Slope of a Curve

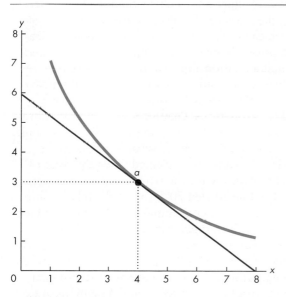

(a) Slope at a point

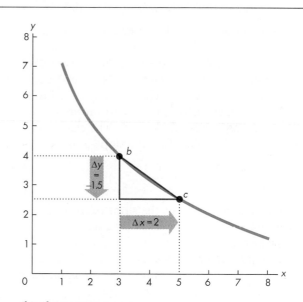

(b) Slope across an arc

The slope of a curve can be calculated either at a point, as in part (a), or across an arc, as in part (b). The slope at a point is calculated by finding the slope of a straight line that touches the curve only at one point. One such straight line touches the curve at point *a*. The slope of that straight line is calculated by dividing the change in *y* by the change in *x*. When *x* increases from 0 to 8, Δx equals 8. That change in *x* is associated with a fall in *y* from 6 to 0, so Δy equals –6. The slope of the line is –6/8, or –3/4.

To calculate the slope across an arc, we place a straight line across the curve from one point to another and then calculate the slope of that straight line. One such line is that from *b* to *c* in part (b). The slope of the straight line *bc* is calculated by dividing the change in *y* by the change in *x*. In moving from *b* to *c*, *x* goes up by 2, Δx equals 2, and *y* goes down by 1½, Δy equals –1½. The slope of the line *bc* is –1½ divided by 2, or –3/4.

slope of the curve at the point marked *a*. Place a ruler on the graph so that it touches point *a* and no other point on the curve; then draw a straight line along the edge of the ruler. The straight red line in part (a) is such a line. If the ruler touches the curve only at point *a*, then the slope of the curve at point *a* must be the same as the slope of the edge of the ruler. If the curve and the ruler do not have the same slope, the line along the edge of the ruler will cut the curve instead of just touching it.

Having now found a straight line with the same slope as the curve at point *a*, you can calculate the slope of the curve at point *a* by calculating the slope of the straight line. We already know how to calculate the slope of a straight line, so the task is straightforward. In this case, as *x* increases from 0 to 8 ($\Delta x = 8$), *y* decreases from 6 to 0 ($\Delta y = -6$). Therefore the slope of the straight line is

$$\frac{\Delta y}{\Delta x} = \frac{-6}{8} = \frac{-3}{4}.$$

Thus the slope of the curve at point *a* is −3/4.

Slope across an Arc   Calculating a slope across an arc is similar to calculating an average slope. In Fig. 2.14(b), we are looking at the same curve as in part (a), but instead of calculating the slope at point *a*, we calculate the slope for a change in *x* from 3 to 5. As *x* increases from 3 to 5, *y* decreases from 4 to 2½. The change in *x* is +2 ($\Delta x = 2$). The change in *y* is −1½ ($\Delta y = -1½$). Therefore the slope of the line is

$$\frac{\Delta y}{\Delta x} = \frac{-1½}{2} = \frac{-3}{4}.$$

This calculation gives us the slope of the line between points *b* and *c*. In this particular example, the slope of the arc *bc* is identical to the slope of the curve at point *a* in part (a). Calculating the slope does not always work out so neatly. You might have some fun constructing counterexamples.

Graphing Relationships among More Than Two Variables

We have seen that we can graph a single variable as a point on a

straight line and we can graph the relationship between two variables as a point formed by the *x*- and *y*-coordinates in a two-dimensional graph. You might be suspecting that although a two-dimensional graph is informative, most of the things in which you are likely to be interested involve relationships among many variables, not just two.

Examples of relationships among more than two variables abound. For example, consider the relationship between the price of ice cream, the air temperature, and the amount of ice cream eaten. If ice cream is expensive and the temperature is low, people eat much less ice cream than when ice cream is inexpensive and the temperature is high. For any given price of ice cream, the quantity consumed varies with the temperature; for any given temperature, the quantity of ice cream consumed varies with its price.

Other Things Being Equal

Figure 2.15 illustrates such a situation. The table shows the number of gallons of ice cream that will be eaten each day at various temperatures and ice cream prices. How can we graph all these numbers? To graph a relationship that involves more than two variables, we consider what happens if all but two of the variables are held constant. This device is called ceteris paribus. **Ceteris paribus** is a Latin phrase that means "other things being equal." For example, in Fig. 2.15(a), you can see what happens to the quantity of ice cream consumed when the price of ice cream varies while the temperature is held constant. The line labeled 70°F shows the relationship between ice cream consumption and the price of ice cream when the temperature stays at 70°F. The numbers used to plot that line are those in the third column of the table in Fig. 2.15. For example, when the temperature is 70°F, 18 gallons are consumed when the price is 30¢ a scoop and 13 gallons are consumed when the price is 45¢. The curve labeled 90°F shows the consumption of ice cream when the price varies and the temperature is 90°F.

Alternatively, we can show the relationship between ice cream consumption and temperature while holding the price of ice cream constant, as is shown in Fig. 2.15(b). The curve labeled 30¢ shows how the consumption of ice cream varies with the temperature when ice cream costs 30¢, and a second curve shows the relationship when ice cream costs 15¢. For example, at 30¢ a scoop, 12 gallons are

FIGURE **2.15**

Graphing a Relationship among Three Variables

(a) Price and consumption at a given temperature

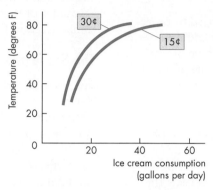

(b) Temperature and consumption at a given price

(c) Temperature and price at a given consumption

Price (cents per scoop)	Ice cream consumption (gallons per day)			
	30°F	50°F	70°F	90°F
15	12	18	25	50
30	10	12	18	37
45	7	10	13	27
60	5	7	10	20
75	3	5	7	14
90	2	3	5	10
105	1	2	3	6

The quantity of ice cream consumed (one variable) depends on its price (a second variable) and the air temperature (a third variable). The table provides some hypothetical numbers that tell us how many gallons of ice cream are consumed each day at different prices and different temperatures. For example, if the price is 45¢ per scoop and the temperature is 50°F, 10 gallons of ice cream will be consumed. To graph a relationship among three variables, the value of one variable must be held constant.

Part (a) shows the relationship between price and consumption, holding temperature constant. One curve holds temperature constant at 90°F and the other at 70°F. Part (b) shows the relationship between temperature and consumption, holding price constant. One curve holds the price at 30¢ and the other at 15¢. Part (c) shows the relationship between temperature and price, holding consumption constant. One curve holds consumption constant at 10 gallons and the other at 7 gallons.

consumed when the temperature is 50°F and 18 gallons when the temperature is 70°F.

Figure 2.15(c) shows the combinations of temperature and price that result in a constant consumption of ice cream. One curve shows the combination that results in 10 gallons a day being consumed, and the other shows the combination that results in 7 gallons a day being consumed. A high price and a high temperature lead to the same consumption as a

lower price and lower temperature. For example, 7 gallons are consumed at 30°F and 45 cents per scoop and at 70°F and 75 cents per scoop.

◆ ◆ ◆ ◆ With what you have now learned about graphs, you can move forward with your study of economics. There are no graphs in this book that are more complicated than those that have been explained here.

S U M M A R Y

Graphing Data

There are two main types of graphs used to represent economic data: scatter diagrams and time-series graphs. A scatter diagram plots the value of one economic variable associated with the value of another. Such a diagram reveals whether or not there is a relationship between two variables and, if there is a relationship, its nature.

A time-series graph plots the value of one or more economic variables on the vertical axis (*y*-axis) and time on the horizontal axis (*x*-axis). A well-constructed time-series graph quickly reveals the level, direction of change, and speed of change of a variable. It also reveals trends. Graphs sometimes mislead, especially when the origin is omitted or when the scale is stretched or squeezed to exaggerate or understate a variation. (pp. 29–38)

Graphs Used in Economic Models

Graphs are used in economic models to illustrate relationships between variables. There are four cases: positive relationships, negative relationships, relationships that have a maximum or a minimum, and variables that are not related to each other. Examples of these different types of relationships are summarized in Figs. 2.9 through 2.12. (pp. 38–41)

The Slope of a Relationship

The slope of a relationship is calculated as the change in the value of the variable measured on the *y*-axis divided by the change in the value of the variable measured on the *x*-axis, that is, $\Delta y/\Delta x$. A straight line has a constant slope, but a curved line has a varying slope. To calculate the slope of a curved line, we calculate the slope either at a point or across an arc. (pp. 42–44)

Graphing Relationships among More Than Two Variables

To graph a relationship among more than two variables, we hold constant the values of all the variables except two. We then plot the value of one of the variables against the value of another. Holding constant all the variables but two is called the ceteris paribus assumption—the assumption of other things being equal. (pp. 44–45)

K E Y   E L E M E N T S

Key Terms

Axes, 29
Ceteris paribus, 44
Coordinates, 30
Curve, 38
Linear relationship, 38
Negative relationship, 38
Origin, 29
Positive relationship, 38
Scatter diagram, 30
Slope, 42
Time-series graph, 32
Trend, 33
x-axis, 29

x-coordinate, 30
y-axis, 29
y-coordinate, 30

Key Figures

Figure 2.9   Positive Relationships, 39
Figure 2.10   Negative Relationships, 39
Figure 2.11   Maximum and Minimum Points, 40
Figure 2.12   Variables with No Relationship, 41
Figure 2.13   The Slope of a Straight Line, 42
Figure 2.14   The Slope of a Curve, 43
Figure 2.15   Graphing a Relationship among Three
              Variables, 45

REVIEW QUESTIONS

1 Why do we use graphs?

2 What are the two scale lines on a graph called?

3 What is the origin on a graph?

4 What do we mean by the *y*-coordinate and the *x*-coordinate?

5 What is a scatter diagram?

6 What is a time-series graph?

7 List three things that a time-series graph shows quickly and easily.

8 What do we mean by trend?

9 Sketch some graphs to illustrate the following:

a Two variables that move up and down together

b Two variables that move in opposite directions

c A relationship between two variables that has a maximum

d A relationship between two variables that has a minimum

10 Which of the relationships in question 9 is a positive relationship and which a negative relationship?

11 What is the definition of the slope of a relationship?

12 What are the two ways of calculating the slope of a curved line?

13 How do we graph relationships among more than two variables?

PROBLEMS

1 The inflation rate in the United States between 1970 and 1990 was as follows:

Year	Inflation rate (percent per year)
1970	5.7
1971	4.4
1972	3.2
1973	6.2
1974	11.0
1975	9.1
1976	5.8
1977	6.5
1978	7.6
1979	11.3
1980	13.5
1981	10.3
1982	6.2
1983	3.2
1984	4.3
1985	3.6
1986	1.9

Year	Inflation rate (percent per year)
1987	3.6
1988	4.1
1989	4.8
1990	5.4

Draw a time-series graph of these data, and use your graph to answer the following questions:

a In which year was inflation highest?

b In which year was inflation lowest?

c In which years did inflation rise?

d In which years did inflation fall?

e In which year did inflation rise/fall the fastest?

f In which year did inflation rise/fall the slowest?

g What have been the main trends in inflation?

2 Interest rates on treasury bills in the United States between 1970 and 1990 were as follows:

Year	Interest rate (percent per year)
1970	6.5
1971	4.3

Year	Interest rate (percent per year)
1972	4.1
1973	7.0
1974	7.9
1975	5.8
1976	5.0
1977	5.3
1978	7.2
1979	10.0
1980	11.5
1981	14.0
1982	10.7
1983	8.6
1984	9.6
1985	7.5
1986	6.0
1987	5.8
1988	6.7
1989	8.1
1990	7.5

Use these data together with those in problem 1 to draw a scatter diagram showing the relationship between inflation and the interest rate. Use this diagram to determine whether there is a relationship between inflation and the interest rate and whether it is positive or negative.

3 Use the following information to draw a graph showing the relationship between two variables x and y:

x	0	1	2	3	4	5	6	7	8
y	0	1	4	9	16	25	36	49	64

a Is the relationship between x and y positive or negative?

b Does the slope of the relationship rise or fall as the value of x rises?

4 Using the data in problem 3:

a Calculate the slope of the relationship between x and y when x equals 4.

b Calculate the slope of the arc when x rises from 3 to 4.

c Calculate the slope of the arc when x rises from 4 to 5.

d Calculate the slope of the arc when x rises from 3 to 5.

e What do you notice that is interesting about your answers to (b), (c), and (d) compared with your answer to (a)?

5 Calculate the slopes of the following two relationships between two variables x and y:

a

x	0	2	4	6	8	10
y	20	16	12	8	4	0

b

x	0	2	4	6	8	10
y	0	8	16	24	32	40

6 Draw a graph showing the following relationship between two variables x and y:

x	0	1	2	3	4	5	6	7	8	9
y	0	2	4	6	8	10	8	6	4	2

a Is the slope positive or negative when x is less than 5?

b Is the slope positive or negative when x is greater than 5?

c What is the slope of this relationship when x equals 5?

d Is y at a maximum or at a minimum when x equals 5?

7 Draw a graph showing the following relationship between two variables x and y:

x	0	1	2	3	4	5	6	7	8	9
y	10	8	6	4	2	0	2	4	6	8

a Is the slope positive or negative when x is less than 5?

b Is the slope positive or negative when x is greater than 5?

c What is the slope of this relationship when x equals 5?

d Is y at a maximum or at a minimum when x equals 5?

CHAPTER 3

PRODUCTION, SPECIALIZATION, AND EXCHANGE

After studying this chapter, you will be able to:

- ◆ Define the production possibility frontier

- ◆ Calculate opportunity cost

- ◆ Explain why economic growth and technological change do not provide free gifts

- ◆ Explain comparative advantage

- ◆ Explain why people specialize and how they gain from trade

- ◆ Explain why property rights and money have evolved

WE LIVE IN A STYLE THAT MOST OF OUR GRANDPARENTS could not even have imagined. Advances in medicine have cured diseases that terrified them. Most of us live in better and more spacious homes. We eat more, we grow taller, we are even born larger than they were. Our parents are amazed at the matter-of-fact way in which we handle computers. We casually use products—microwave ovens, graphite tennis rackets, digital watches—that didn't exist in their youth. Economic growth has made us richer than our parents and grandparents. ◆ ◆ But economic growth and technological change, and the wealth they bestow, have not liberated us from scarcity. Why not? Why, despite our immense wealth, do we still have to face costs? Why are there no "free lunches"? ◆ ◆ We see an incredible amount of specialization and trading in the modern world. Each one of us specializes in a particular job—as lawyer, car maker, homemaker. Countries and regions also specialize—Florida in orange juice, Idaho in potatoes, Detroit in cars,

Making the Most of It

and the Silicon Valley in computer-related products. We have become so specialized that one farm worker can feed 100 people. Only one in five of us works in manufacturing. More than half of us work in wholesale and retail trade, banking and finance, other services, and government. Why do we specialize? How do we benefit from specialization and exchange? ◆ ◆ Over many centuries, institutions and social arrangements have evolved that today we take for granted. One of them is private property rights, together with the legal system that protects them. Another is money. Why have these institutions evolved? And how do they extend our ability to specialize and increase production?

◆ ◆ ◆ ◆ These are the questions that we tackle in this chapter. We will begin by making the idea of scarcity more precise. Then we will go on to see how we can measure opportunity cost. We will also see how, when each individual tries to get the most out of scarce resources, specialization and exchange occur. That is, people specialize in doing what they do best and exchange their products with other specialists. We are also going to see why such institutions as private property and money exist and how they arise from people's attempts to make the most of their limited resources.

The Production Possibility Frontier

What do we mean by production? **Production** is the conversion of land, labor, and capital into goods and services. We defined the factors of production in Chapter 1. Let's briefly recall what they are.

Land is all the gifts of nature. It includes the air, the water, and the land surface, as well as the minerals that lie beneath the surface of the earth. *Labor* is all the muscle-power and brain-power of human beings. The voices and artistry of singers and actors, the strength and coordination of athletes, the daring of astronauts, the political skill of diplomats, as well as the physical and mental skills of the many millions of people who make cars and cola, gum and glue, wallpaper and watering cans are included in this category.

Capital is all the goods that have been produced and can now be used in the production of other goods and services. Examples include the interstate highway system, the fine buildings of great cities, dams and power projects, airports and jumbo jets, car production lines, shirt factories, and cookie shops. A special kind of capital is called human capital. **Human capital** is the accumulated skill and knowledge of human beings, which arise from their training and education.

Goods and services are all the valuable things that people produce. Goods are tangible—cars, spoons, VCRs, and bread. Services are intangible—haircuts, amusement park rides, and telephone calls. There

are two types of goods: capital goods and consumption goods. **Capital goods** are goods that are used in the production process and can be used many times before they eventually wear out. Examples of capital goods are buildings, computers, automobiles, and telephones. **Consumption goods** are goods that can be used just once. Examples are dill pickles and toothpaste. **Consumption** is the process of using up goods and services.

Our limited resources and the technologies available for transforming those resources into goods and services limit what can be produced. That limit is described by the production possibility frontier. The **production possibility frontier** (PPF) marks the boundary between those combinations of goods and services that can be produced and those that cannot. It is important to understand the production possibility frontier in the real world, but to achieve that goal more easily, we will first study an economy that is simpler than the one in which we live—a model economy.

A Model Economy

Instead of looking at the real-world economy with all its complexity and detail, we will build a model of an economy. The model will have features that are essential to understanding the real economy, but we will ignore most of reality's immense detail. Our model economy will be simpler in three important ways:

1. Everything that is produced is also consumed so that in our model, capital resources neither grow nor shrink. (Later we will examine what happens if we consume less than we produce and add to capital resources.)

2. There are only two goods, corn and cloth. (In the real world we use our scarce resources to produce countless goods and services.)

3. There is only one person, Jane, who lives on a deserted island and has no dealings with other people. (Later we will see what happens when Jane's island economy has links with another economy. Also, we'll extend our view to the real world with its five billion people.)

Jane uses all the resources of her island economy to produce corn and cloth. She works 10 hours each day. The amount of corn and cloth that Jane produces depends on how many hours she devotes to

---

TABLE 3.1

Jane's Production Possibilities

Hours worked (per day)		Corn grown (pounds per month)		Cloth produced (yards per month)
0	either	0	or	0
2	either	6	or	1
4	either	11	or	2
6	either	15	or	3
8	either	18	or	4
10	either	20	or	5

If Jane does no work, she produces no corn or cloth. If she works for 2 hours per day and spends the entire amount of time on corn production, she produces 6 pounds of corn per month. If that same time is used for cloth production, 1 yard of cloth is produced but no corn. The last four rows of the table show the amounts of corn or cloth that can be produced per month as more hours are devoted to each activity.

---

producing them. Table 3.1 sets out Jane's production possibilities for corn and cloth. If she does no work, she produces nothing. Two hours a day devoted to corn farming produces 6 pounds of corn per month. Devoting more hours to corn increases the output of corn, but there is a decline in the extra amount of corn that comes from extra effort. The reason for this decline is that Jane has to use increasingly unsuitable land for growing corn. At first, she plants corn on a lush, flat plain. Eventually, when she has used all the arable land, she has to start planting on the rocky hills and the edge of the beach. The numbers in the second column of the table show how the output of corn rises as the number of hours devoted to cultivating it rises.

To produce cloth, Jane gathers wool from sheep that live on the island. As she devotes more hours to collecting wool and making cloth, her output rises. The numbers in the third column of Table 3.1 show how the output of cloth rises as the number of hours devoted to this activity rises.

If Jane devotes all her time to growing corn, she can produce 20 pounds of corn in a month. In that

case, however, she cannot produce any cloth. Conversely, if she devotes all her time to making cloth, she can produce 5 yards a month but will have no time left for growing corn. Jane can devote some of her time to corn and some to cloth but not more than 10 hours a day total. Thus she can spend 2 hours growing corn and 8 hours making cloth or 6 hours on one and 4 hours on the other (or any other combination of hours that add up to 10 hours).

We have defined the production possibility frontier as the boundary between what is attainable and what is not attainable. You can calculate Jane's production possibility frontier by using the information in Table 3.1. These calculations are summarized in the table in Fig. 3.1 and graphed in that figure as Jane's production possibility frontier. To see how we calculated that frontier, let's concentrate first on the table in Fig. 3.1.

Possibility *a* shows Jane devoting no time to cloth and her entire 10-hour working day to corn. In this case, she can produce 20 pounds of corn per month and no cloth. For possibility *b*, she spends 2 hours a day making cloth and 8 hours growing corn, to produce a total of 18 pounds of corn and 1 yard of cloth a month. The pattern continues on to possibility *f*, where she devotes 10 hours a day to cloth and no time to corn. These same numbers are plotted in the graph shown in Fig. 3.1. Yards of cloth are measured on the horizontal axis and pounds of corn on the vertical axis. Points *a*, *b*, *c*, *d*, *e*, and *f* represent the numbers in the corresponding row of the table.

Of course, Jane does not have to work in blocks of 2 hours, as in our example. She can work 1 hour or 1 hour and 10 minutes growing corn and devote the rest of her time to making cloth. All other feasible allocations of Jane's 10 hours enable her to produce the combinations of corn and cloth described by the line that joins points *a*, *b*, *c*, *d*, *e*, and *f*. This line shows Jane's production possibility frontier. She can produce at any point on the frontier or inside it, within the orange area. These are attainable points. Points outside the frontier are unattainable. To produce at points beyond the frontier, Jane needs more time than she has—more than 10 hours a day. By working 10 hours a day producing both corn and cloth, Jane can choose any point she wishes on the frontier. And by working less than 10 hours a day, or by not putting her resources to their best possible use—by wasting some of her resources—she can produce at a point inside the frontier.

FIGURE **3.1**

Jane's Production Possibility Frontier

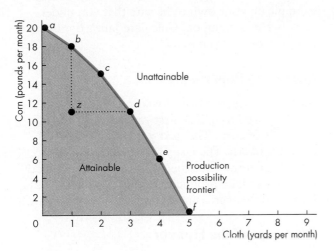

Possibility	Corn (pounds per month)		Cloth (yards per month)
a	20	and	0
b	18	and	1
c	15	and	2
d	11	and	3
e	6	and	4
f	0	and	5

The table lists six points on Jane's production possibility frontier. Row *e* tells us that if Jane produces 6 pounds of corn, the maximum cloth production that is possible is 4 yards. These same points are graphed as points *a, b, c, d, e,* and *f* in the figure. The line passing through these points is Jane's production possibility frontier, which separates the attainable from the unattainable. The attainable orange area contains all the possible production points. Jane can produce anywhere inside this area or on the production possibility frontier. Points outside the frontier are unattainable. Jane prefers points on the frontier to any point inside. She prefers points between *b* and *d* on the frontier to point *z* inside the frontier because they give her more of both goods.

Jane's Preferences

Jane produces corn and cloth not for the fun of it, but so that she can eat and keep warm. She wants much more corn and cloth than she can produce, and the more of each she has, the better she likes it. Because Jane wants as much as possible of both corn and cloth, the best she can do is to produce—and therefore consume—at a point *on* her production possibility frontier. To see why, consider a point such as *z* in the attainable region. At point *z*, Jane is wasting resources. She may be taking time off work, but leisure time on the island is not worth anything to Jane. Or she may not be using her sheep and her cornfields as effectively as possible. Jane can improve her situation at *z* by moving to a point such as *b* or *d* or to a point on the frontier between *b* and *d*, such as point *c*. Jane can have more of both goods on the frontier than at points inside it. At point *b*, she can consume more corn and no less cloth than at point *z*. At point *d*, she can consume more cloth and no less corn than at point *z*. At point *c*, she can consume more corn and more cloth than at point *z*. Jane will never choose points such as *z* because preferred points, such as *b, c,* and *d*, are available to her. That is, Jane prefers some point on the frontier to a point inside it.

We have just seen that Jane wants to produce at some point on her production possibility frontier, but she is still faced with the problem of choosing her preferred point. In choosing between one point and another, Jane is confronted with opportunity costs. At point *c*, for example, she has less cloth and more corn than at point *d*. If she chooses point *d*, she does so because she figures that the extra cloth is worth the corn forgone. Let's go on to explore opportunity cost more closely and see how we can measure it.

R E V I E W

The production possibility frontier is the boundary between the attainable and the unattainable. There is always a point on the frontier that is preferred to any point inside it. But moving from one point on the frontier to another involves an opportunity cost—having less of one good to get more of another. ◆

Opportunity Cost

We've defined opportunity cost as the best alternative forgone: for a late sleeper, the opportunity cost of attending an early morning class is an hour in bed; for a jogger, it is an hour of exercise. The concept of opportunity cost can be made more precise by using a production possibility frontier such as the one shown in Fig. 3.1. Let's see what that curve tells us.

The Best Alternative Forgone

The production possibility frontier in Fig. 3.1 traces the boundary between attainable and unattainable combinations of corn and cloth. Since there are only two goods, there is no difficulty in working out what is the best alternative forgone. More corn can be grown only by paying the price of having less cloth, and more cloth can be made only by bearing the cost of having less corn. Thus the opportunity cost of an additional yard of cloth is the amount of corn forgone, and the opportunity cost of producing an additional pound of corn is the amount of cloth forgone. Let's put numerical values on the opportunity costs of corn and cloth.

Measuring Opportunity Cost

We are going to measure opportunity cost by using Jane's production possibility frontier. We will calculate how much cloth she has to give up to get more corn and how much corn she has to give up to get more cloth.

If all Jane's time is used to produce corn, she produces 20 pounds of corn and no cloth. If she decides to produce 1 yard of cloth, how much corn does she have to give up? You can see the answer in Fig. 3.2. To produce 1 yard of cloth, Jane moves from a to b and gives up 2 pounds of corn. Thus the opportunity cost of the first yard of cloth is 2 pounds of corn. If she decides to produce an additional yard of cloth, how much corn does she give up? This time, Jane moves from b to c and gives up 3 pounds of corn to produce the second yard of cloth.

These opportunity costs are set out in the table of Fig. 3.2. The first two rows set out the opportunity costs that we have just calculated. The table also lists the opportunity costs of moving between points c, d, e, and f on Jane's production possibility frontier of Fig. 3.1. You might want to work out another example on your own to be sure that you understand what is going on. Calculate Jane's opportunity cost of moving from e to f.

Increasing Opportunity Cost

As you can see, opportunity cost varies with the quantity produced. The first yard of cloth costs 2 pounds of corn. The next yard of cloth costs 3 pounds of corn. The last yard of cloth costs 6 pounds of corn. Thus the opportunity cost of cloth increases as Jane produces more cloth. Figure 3.2(a) illustrates the increasing opportunity cost of cloth.

The Shape of the Frontier

Pay special attention to the shape of the production possibility frontier in Fig. 3.1. When a large amount of corn and not much cloth is produced—between points a and b—the frontier has a gentle slope. When a large amount of cloth and not much corn is produced—between points e and f—the frontier is steep. The whole frontier bows outward. These features of the production possibility frontier are a reflection of increasing opportunity cost. You can see the connection between increasing opportunity cost and the shape of the production possibility frontier in Fig. 3.2(b). Between points a and b, 1 yard of cloth can be obtained by giving up a small amount of corn. Here the opportunity cost of cloth is low, and the opportunity cost of corn is high. Between points e and f, a large amount of corn must be given up to produce 1 extra yard of cloth. In this region, the opportunity cost of cloth is high, and the opportunity cost of corn is low.

Everything Has an Increasing Opportunity Cost

We've just worked out the opportunity cost of cloth. But what about the opportunity cost of corn? Does it also increase as more of it is produced? You can see the answer in Fig. 3.2. By giving up 1 yard of

FIGURE **3.2**
Jane's Opportunity Costs of Corn and Cloth

The table records Jane's opportunity cost of cloth. The first yard of cloth costs 2 pounds of corn. The next yard of cloth costs 3 pounds of corn. The opportunity cost of cloth rises as Jane produces more cloth, with the last yard of cloth costing 6 pounds of corn. Part (a) of the figure shows the increasing opportunity cost of cloth, and part (b) shows increasing opportunity cost as Jane moves along her outward-bowed production possibility frontier, increasing her production of cloth and decreasing her production of corn.

As Jane increases her cloth production:
First **1** yard of cloth costs **2** pounds of corn
Next **1** yard of cloth costs **3** pounds of corn
Next **1** yard of cloth costs **4** pounds of corn
Next **1** yard of cloth costs **5** pounds of corn
Last yard of cloth costs **6** pounds of corn

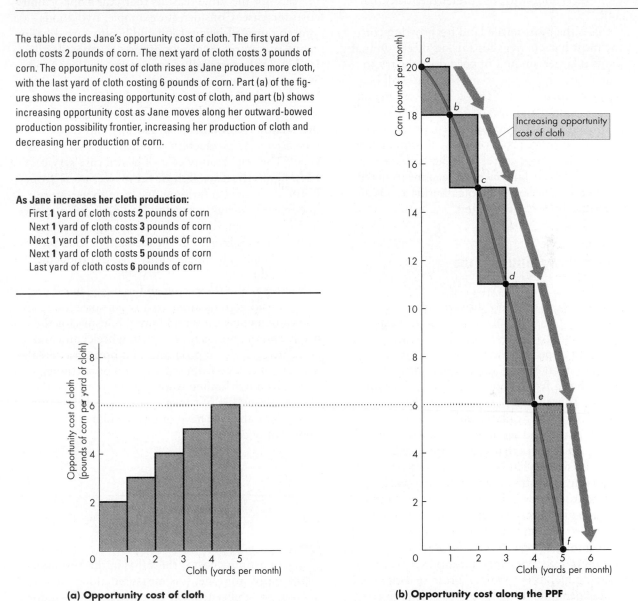

(a) Opportunity cost of cloth

(b) Opportunity cost along the PPF

cloth to produce some corn, Jane moves from *f* to *e* and produces 6 pounds of corn. Thus the opportunity cost of the first 6 pounds of corn is 1 yard of cloth. Moving from *e* to *d*, you can see that the next 5 pounds of corn cost 1 yard of cloth. Thus the

opportunity cost of corn also increases as Jane makes more corn.

Increasing opportunity cost and the outward bow of the production possibility frontier arise from the fact that scarce resources are not equally useful in all activities. For instance, some of the land on Jane's island is extremely fertile and produces a high crop yield, while other land is rocky and barren. The sheep on the island, however, prefer the rocky, barren land.

Jane uses the most fertile land for growing corn and the most barren areas for raising sheep. Only if she wants a larger amount of corn does she try to cultivate relatively barren areas. If she uses all her time to grow corn, she has to use some very unsuitable, low-yielding land. Devoting some time to making cloth, and reducing the time spent growing corn by the same amount, produces a small drop in corn production but a large increase in the output of cloth. Conversely, if Jane uses all her time to make cloth, a small reduction in woolgathering yields a large increase of corn production.

Production Possibilities in the Real World

Jane's island is dramatically different from the world that we live in. The fundamental lesson it teaches us, however, applies to the real world. The world has a fixed number of people endowed with a given amount of human capital and limited time. The world also has a fixed amount of land and capital equipment. These limited resources can be employed, using the available but limited technology to produce goods and services. But there is a limit to the goods and services that can be produced, a boundary between what is attainable and what is not attainable. That boundary is the real-world economy's production possibility frontier. On that frontier, producing more of any one good requires producing less of some other good or goods.

For example, a presidential candidate who promises better welfare and education services must at the same time, to be credible, promise either cuts in defense spending or higher taxes. Higher taxes mean less money left over for vacations and other consumption goods and services. The cost of better welfare and educational services is less of other goods. On a smaller scale but equally important, each time you decide to rent a video, you decide not to use your limited income to buy soda, popcorn, or some other good. The cost of one more video is one less of something else.

On Jane's island, we saw that the opportunity cost of a good increased as the output of the good increased. Opportunity costs in the real world increase for the same reasons that Jane's opportunity costs increase. Consider, for example, two goods vital to our well-being: food and health care. In allocating our scarce resources, we use the most fertile land and the most skillful farmers to produce food. We use the best doctors and the least fertile land for health care. If we shift fertile land and tractors away from farming and ask farmers to do surgery, the production of food drops drastically and the increase in the production of health care services is small. The opportunity cost of health care services rises. Similarly, if we shift our resources away from health care toward farming, we have to use more doctors and nurses as farmers and more hospitals as hydroponic tomato factories. The drop in health care services is large, but the increase in food production small. The opportunity cost of producing more food rises.

This example is extreme and unlikely, but these same considerations apply to any pair of goods that you can imagine: guns and butter, housing for the needy and diamonds for the rich, wheelchairs and golf carts, television programs and breakfast cereals. We cannot escape from scarcity and opportunity cost. Given our limited resources, more of one thing always means less of something else, and the more of anything that we have or do, the higher is its opportunity cost.

REVIEW

Opportunity cost is the value of the best alternative forgone. It is measured along the production possibility frontier by calculating the number of units of one good that must be given up to obtain one more unit of the other good. The production possibility frontier is bowed outward because not all resources are equally useful for producing all goods. The most useful resources are employed first. Because the frontier is bowed outward, the opportunity cost of each good increases as more of it is produced. ◆

Economic Growth

Although the production possibility frontier defines the boundary between what is attainable and what is unattainable, that boundary is not static. It is constantly changing. Sometimes the production possibility frontier shifts *inward*, reducing our production possibilities. For example, droughts or other extreme climatic conditions shift the frontier inward. Sometimes the frontier moves outward. For example, excellent growing and harvest conditions have this effect. Sometimes the frontier shifts outward because we get a new idea. It suddenly occurs to us that there is a better way of doing something that we never before imagined possible—we invent the wheel.

Over the years, our production possibilities have undergone enormous expansion. The expansion of our production possibilities is called **economic growth**. As a consequence of economic growth, we can now produce much more than we could a hundred years ago and quite a bit more than even ten years ago. By the late 1990s, if the same pace of growth continues, our production possibilities will be even greater. By pushing out the frontier, can we avoid the constraints imposed on us by our limited resources? That is, can we get our free lunch after all?

The Cost of Economic Growth

We are going to discover that although we can and do increase our production possibilities, we cannot have economic growth without incurring costs. The faster the pace of economic growth, the less we can consume at the present time. Let's investigate the costs of growth by examining why economies grow and prosper.

Two key activities generate economic growth: capital accumulation and technological progress. **Capital accumulation** is the growth of capital resources. **Technological progress** is the development of new and better ways of producing goods and services. As a consequence of capital accumulation and

technological progress, we have an enormous quantity of cars and airplanes that enable us to produce more transportation than when we had only horses and carriages; we have satellites that make transcontinental communications possible on a scale much larger than that produced by the earlier cable technology. But accumulating capital and developing new technology are costly. To see why, let's go back to Jane's island economy.

Capital Accumulation and Technological Change

So far, we've assumed that Jane's island economy can produce only two goods, corn and cloth. But let's now suppose that while pursuing some of the sheep, Jane stumbles upon an outcrop of flint stone and a forest that she had not known about before. She realizes that she can now make some flint tools and start building fences around the corn and sheep, thereby increasing production of both of these goods. But to make tools and build fences, Jane has to devote time to these activities. Let's continue to suppose that there are only 10 hours of working time available each day. Time spent making tools and building fences is time that could have been spent growing corn and making cloth. Thus to expand her future production, Jane must produce less corn and cloth today so that some of her time can be devoted to making tools and building fences. The decrease in her output of corn and cloth today is the opportunity cost of expanding her production of these two goods in the future.

Figure 3.3 provides a concrete example. The table sets out Jane's production possibilities for producing capital—tools and fences—as well as current consumption goods—corn and cloth. If she devotes all her working hours to corn and cloth production (row *e*), she produces no capital—no tools or fences. If she devotes enough time to producing one unit of capital each month (row *d*), her corn and cloth production is cut back to 90 percent of its maximum possible level. She can devote still more time to capital accumulation, and as she does so, her corn and cloth production falls by successively larger amounts.

The numbers in the table are graphed in Fig. 3.3. Each point, *a* through *e*, represents a row of the

FIGURE **3.3**

Economic Growth on Jane's Island

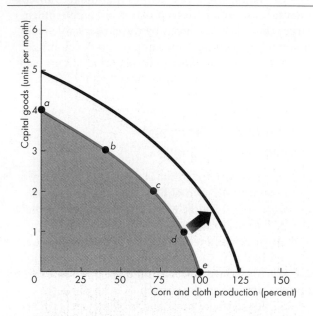

Possibility	Capital (units per month)	Corn and cloth production (percent)
a	4	0
b	3	40
c	2	70
d	1	90
e	0	100

If Jane devotes all her time to corn and cloth production, she produces no capital equipment (row *e* of the table). If she devotes more time to capital accumulation, she produces successively smaller amounts of corn and cloth. The curve *abcde* is Jane's production possibility frontier for capital and consumption goods (tools and fence versus corn and cloth). If Jane produces no capital (point *e*), her production possibility frontier remains fixed at *abcde*. If she cuts her current production of corn and cloth and produces one unit of capital (point *d*), her future production possibility frontier lies outside her current frontier. The more time Jane devotes to accumulating capital and the less to producing corn and cloth, the farther out her frontier shifts. The decreased output of corn and cloth is the opportunity cost of increased future production possibilities.

table. Notice the similarity between Fig. 3.3 and Fig. 3.1. Each shows a production possibility frontier. In the case of Fig. 3.3, the frontier is that between producing capital equipment—tools and fences—and producing current consumption goods—corn and cloth. If Jane produces at point *e* in Fig. 3.3, she produces no capital goods and remains stuck on the production possibility frontier for corn and cloth shown in Fig. 3.1. But if she moves to point *d* in Fig. 3.3, she can produce one unit of capital each month. To do so, Jane reduces her current production of corn and cloth to 90 percent of what she can produce if all her time is devoted to those activities. In terms of Fig. 3.1, Jane's current production possibility frontier for corn and cloth shifts to the left as less time is devoted to corn and cloth production and some of her time is devoted to producing capital goods.

By decreasing her production of corn and cloth and producing tools and building fences, Jane is able to increase her future production possibilities. An increasing stock of tools and fences makes her more productive at growing corn and producing cloth. She can even use tools to make better tools. As a consequence, Jane's production possibility frontier shifts outward as shown by the shift arrow. Jane experiences economic growth.

But the amount by which Jane's production possibility frontier shifts out depends on how much time she devotes to accumulating capital. If she devotes no time to this activity, the frontier remains at *abcde*—the original production possibility frontier. If she cuts back on current production of corn and cloth and produces one unit of capital each month (point *d*), her frontier moves out in the future to the position shown by the red curve in Fig. 3.3. The less time she devotes to corn and cloth production and the more time to capital accumulation, the farther out the frontier shifts.

But economic growth is not a free gift for Jane. To make it happen, she has to devote more time to producing tools and building fences and less to producing corn and cloth. Economic growth is no magic formula for abolishing scarcity.

Economic Growth in the Real World

The ideas that we have explored in the setting of Jane's island also apply to our real-world economy. If we devote all our resources to producing food, clothing, housing, vacations, and the many other consumer goods that we enjoy and none to research, development, and accumulating capital, we will have no more capital and no better technologies in the future than we have at present. Our production possibilities in the future will be exactly the same as those we have today. If we are to expand our pro-

duction possibilities in the future, we must produce fewer consumption goods today. The resources that we free up today will enable us to accumulate capital and to develop better technologies for producing consumption goods in the future. The cut in the output of consumption goods today is the opportunity cost of economic growth.

The recent experience of the United States and Japan provides a striking example of the effects of our choices on the rate of economic growth. In 1965, the production possibilities per person in the United States were much larger than those in Japan (see Fig. 3.4). The United States devoted one fifth of its resources to producing capital goods and the other four fifths to producing consumption goods, as illustrated by point *a* in Fig. 3.4(a). But Japan devoted one third of its resources to producing capital goods and only two thirds to producing consumption goods, as illustrated by point *a* in Fig. 3.4(b). Both countries experienced economic growth, but the growth in Japan was much more

---

FIGURE 3.4

Economic Growth in the United States and Japan

(a) United States

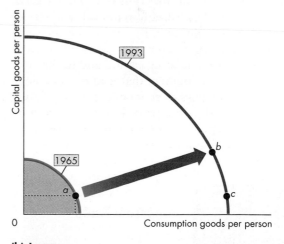

(b) Japan

In 1965, the production possibilities per person in the United States, part (a), were much larger than those in Japan, part (b). But Japan devoted one third of its resources to producing capital goods, while the United States devoted only one fifth—point *a* in each part of the figure. Japan's more rapid increase in capital resources resulted in its production possibility frontier shifting out more quickly than that of the

United States. The two production possibilities per person in 1993 are similar. If Japan produces at point *b* on its 1993 frontier, it will continue to grow more quickly than the United States. If Japan increases consumption and produces at point *c* on its 1993 frontier, its growth rate will slow down to that of the United States.

rapid than the growth in the United States. Because Japan devoted a bigger fraction of its resources to producing capital goods, its stock of capital equipment grew more quickly than ours, and its production possibilities expanded more quickly. As a result, Japanese production possibilities per person are now so close to those in the United States that it is hard to say which country has the larger per person production possibilities. If Japan continues to devote a third of its resources to producing capital goods (at point *b* on its 1993 production possibility frontier), it will continue to grow much more rapidly than the United States, and its frontier will move out beyond our own. If Japan increases its production of consumption goods and reduces its production of capital goods (moving to point *c* on its 1993 production possibility frontier), then its rate of economic expansion will slow down to that of our own.

REVIEW

E conomic growth results from the accumulation of capital and the development of better technologies. To reap the fruits of economic growth, we must incur the cost of fewer goods and services for current consumption. By cutting the current output of consumption goods, we can devote more resources to accumulating capital and to the research and development that lead to technological change—the engines of economic growth. Thus economic growth does not provide a free lunch. It has an opportunity cost—the fall in the current output of consumption goods. ◆

Gains from Trade

N o one excels at everything. One person is more athletic than another; another person has a quicker mind or a better memory. What one person does with ease, someone else finds difficult.

Comparative Advantage: Jane Meets Joe

Differences in individual abilities mean that there are also differences in individual opportunity costs of producing various goods. Such differences give rise to **comparative advantage**—we say that a person has a comparative advantage in producing a particular good if that person can produce the good at a lower opportunity cost than anyone else.

People can produce for themselves all the goods that they consume, or they can concentrate on producing one good (or perhaps a few goods) and then exchange some of their own products for the output of others. Concentrating on the production of only one good or a few goods is called **specialization**. We are going to discover how people can gain by specializing in the good at which they have a comparative advantage and trading their output with others.

Let's return again to our island economy. Suppose that Jane has discovered another island very close to her own and that it too has only one inhabitant—Joe. Jane and Joe each have access to a simple boat that is adequate for transporting themselves and their goods between the two islands.

Joe's island, too, can produce only corn and cloth, but its terrain differs from that on Jane's island. While Jane's island has a lot of fertile corn-growing land and a small sheep population, Joe's island has little fertile corn-growing land and plenty of hilly land and sheep. This important difference between the two islands means that Joe's production possibility frontier is different from Jane's. Figure 3.5 illustrates these production possibility frontiers. Jane's frontier is labeled "Jane's PPF," and Joe's frontier is labeled "Joe's PPF."

Jane and Joe can be self-sufficient in corn and cloth. **Self-sufficiency** is a situation in which people produce only enough for their own consumption. Suppose that Jane and Joe are each self-sufficient. Jane chooses to produce and consume 3 yards of cloth and 11 pounds of corn a month, point *d*. Joe chooses to produce and consume 2 yards of cloth and 7 pounds of corn a month, point *b'*. These choices are identified on their respective production possibility frontiers in Fig. 3.5. (Each could have chosen any other point on his or her own production possibility frontier.) Total production of corn and cloth is the sum of Jane's and Joe's production: 18 pounds of corn and 5 yards of cloth. Point *n* in the figure represents this total production.

FIGURE **3.5**

The Gains from Specialization and Exchange

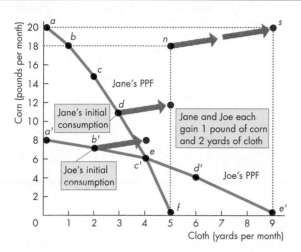

When Jane and Joe are each self-sufficient, Joe consumes 7 pounds of corn and 2 yards of cloth (point *b′*), and Jane consumes 11 pounds of corn and 3 yards of cloth (point *d*). Their total production is 18 pounds of corn and 5 yards of cloth (point *n*). Joe and Jane can do better by specialization and exchange. Jane, whose comparative advantage is in corn production, specializes in that activity, producing 20 pounds a month (point *a*). Joe, whose comparative advantage is in cloth production, specializes in that activity, producing 9 yards of cloth a month (point *e′*). Total production is then 20 pounds of corn and 9 yards of cloth (point *s*). If Jane gives Joe 8 pounds of corn in exchange for 5 yards of cloth, they each enjoy increased consumption of both corn and cloth. They each gain from specialization and exchange.

Jane's Comparative Advantage   In which of the two goods does Jane have a comparative advantage? We have defined comparative advantage as a situation in which one person's opportunity cost of producing a good is lower than another person's opportunity cost of producing that same good. Jane, then, has a comparative advantage in producing whichever good she produces at a lower opportunity cost than Joe. What is that good?

You can answer the question by looking at the production possibility frontiers for Jane and Joe in Fig. 3.5. At the points at which they are producing and consuming, Jane's production possibility frontier is much steeper than Joe's. To produce one more

pound of corn, Jane gives up less cloth than Joe. Hence Jane's opportunity cost of a pound of corn is lower than Joe's. This means that Jane has a comparative advantage in producing corn.

Joe's Comparative Advantage   Joe's comparative advantage is in producing cloth. His production possibility frontier at his consumption point is flatter than Jane's. This means that Joe has to give up less corn to produce one more yard of cloth than Jane does. Joe's opportunity cost of a yard of cloth is lower than Jane's, so Joe has a comparative advantage in cloth production.

Achieving the Gains from Trade

Can Jane and Joe do better than be self-sufficient? In particular, what would happen if each were to specialize in producing the good at which each has a comparative advantage and then trade with the other?

If Jane, who has a comparative advantage in corn production, puts all her time into growing corn, she can grow 20 pounds. If Joe, who has a comparative advantage in cloth production, puts all his time into making cloth, he can make 9 yards. By specializing, Jane and Joe together can produce 20 pounds of corn and 9 yards of cloth (the amount labeled *s* in the figure). Point *s* shows the production of 20 pounds of corn (all produced by Jane) and 9 yards of cloth (all produced by Joe). Clearly, Jane and Joe produce more cloth and corn at point *s* than they were producing at point *n*, when each took care of only his or her own requirements. Jane and Joe prefer point *s* to point *n* because, between them, they have more of both corn and cloth at point *s* than at point *n*. They have an additional 2 pounds of corn and 4 yards of cloth.

To obtain the gains from trade, Jane and Joe must do more than specialize in producing the good at which each has a comparative advantage. They must exchange the fruits of their specialized production. Suppose that Jane and Joe agree to exchange 5 yards of cloth for 8 pounds of corn. Jane has 20 pounds of corn, and Joe has 9 yards of cloth before any exchange takes place. After the exchange takes place, Joe consumes 8 pounds of corn and Jane 12 pounds of corn; Joe consumes 4 yards of cloth and Jane 5 yards of cloth. Compared to the time when they were each self-sufficient, Jane now has 1 extra pound of corn and 2 extra yards of cloth, and Joe has 1 extra pound of corn and 2 extra yards of cloth. The gains from trade are represented by the increase in consumption of both goods that each obtains. Each consumes at a point outside their individual production possibility frontier.

Productivity and Absolute Advantage

Productivity is defined as the amount of output produced per unit of inputs used to produce it. For example, Jane's productivity in making cloth is measured as the amount of cloth she makes per hour of work. If one person has greater productivity than another in the production of all goods, that person is said to have an **absolute advantage**. In our example, neither Jane nor Joe has an absolute advantage. Jane is more productive than Joe in growing corn, and Joe is more productive than Jane in making cloth.

It is often suggested that people and countries that have an absolute advantage can outcompete others in the production of all goods. For example, it is often suggested that the United States cannot compete with Japan because the Japanese are more productive than we are. This conclusion is wrong, as you are just about to discover. To see why, let's look again at Jane and Joe.

Suppose that a volcano engulfs Jane's island, forcing her to search for a new one. And suppose further that this disaster leads to good fortune. Jane stumbles onto a new island that is much more productive than the original one, enabling her to produce twice as much of either corn or cloth with each hour of her labor. Jane's new production possibilities appear in Table 3.2. Notice that she now has an absolute advantage.

We have already worked out that the gains from trade arise when each person specializes in producing the good in which he or she has a comparative advantage. Recall that a person has a comparative advantage in producing a particular good if that person can produce it at a lower opportunity cost than anyone else. Joe's opportunity costs remain exactly the same as they were before. What has happened to Jane's opportunity costs now that she has become twice as productive?

You can work out Jane's opportunity costs by using exactly the same calculation that was used in the table of Fig. 3.2. Start by looking at Jane's

TABLE 3.2

Jane's New Production Possibilities

Possibility	Corn (pounds per month)		Cloth (yards per month)
a	40	and	0
b	36	and	2
c	30	and	4
d	22	and	6
e	12	and	8
f	0	and	10

opportunity cost of corn. The first 12 pounds of corn that Jane grows cost her 2 yards of cloth. So the opportunity cost of 1 pound of corn is ⅙ of a yard of cloth—the same as Jane's original opportunity cost of corn. If you calculate the opportunity costs for Jane's production possibilities *a* through *f*, you will discover that each of them has remained the same.

Since the opportunity cost of cloth is the inverse of the opportunity cost of corn, Jane's opportunity costs of cloth also have remained unchanged. Let's work through one example. If Jane moves from *a* to *b* to make 2 yards of cloth, she will have to reduce her corn production by 4 pounds—from 40 to 36 pounds. Thus the first 2 yards of cloth cost 4 pounds of corn. The cost of 1 yard of cloth is therefore 2 pounds of corn—exactly the same as before.

When Jane becomes twice as productive as before, each hour of her time produces more output, but her opportunity costs remain the same. One more unit of corn costs the same in terms of cloth forgone as it did previously. Since Jane's opportunity costs have not changed and Joe's have not changed, Joe continues to have a comparative advantage in producing cloth. Both Jane and Joe can have more of both goods if Jane specializes in corn production and Joe in cloth production.

The key point to recognize is that it is *not* possible for a person having an absolute advantage to have a comparative advantage in everything.

Gains from trade come from comparative advantage. A person has a comparative advantage in producing a good if that person can produce the good at a lower opportunity cost than anyone else. Thus differences in opportunity cost are the source of gains from specialization and exchange. Each person specializes in producing the good in which he or she has a comparative advantage and then exchanges some of that output for the goods produced by others. ◆ ◆ If a person can produce a good with fewer inputs than someone else—is more productive—that person has an absolute advantage but not necessarily a comparative advantage. Even a person with an absolute advantage gains from specialization and exchange. ◆

Exchange in the Real World

In the real world, countries can gain by specializing in the production of those goods and services in which they have a comparative advantage. An example is given in Reading Between the Lines on pp. 64–65. But to obtain the gains from trade in the real world, where billions of people specialize in millions of different activities, trade has to be organized. To organize trade, we have evolved rules of conduct and mechanisms for enforcing those rules. One such mechanism is private property rights. Another is the institution of money. In the island economy of Jane and Joe, direct exchange of one good with another is feasible. In the real-world economy, direct exchange of one good for another would be very cumbersome. To lubricate the wheels of exchange, societies have created money—a medium that enables indirect exchange of goods for money and money for goods. Let's examine these two aspects of exchange arrangements in more detail.

Property Rights

Property rights are social arrangements that govern the ownership, use, and disposal of property. **Property** is anything of value: it includes land and buildings—the things that we call property in ordinary speech; it also includes stocks and bonds, durable goods, and plant and equipment; it also includes intellectual property. **Intellectual property** is the intangible product of creative effort, protected by copyrights and patents. This type of property includes books, music, computer programs, and inventions of all kinds.

What if property rights did not exist? What would such a social science fiction world be like?

A World Without Property Rights   Without property rights, people could take possession of whatever they had the strength to obtain for themselves. In such a world, people would have to devote a good deal of their time, energy, and resources to protecting what they had produced or acquired.

In a world without property rights, it would not be possible to reap all the gains from specialization and exchange. People would have little incentive to specialize in producing those goods at which they each had a comparative advantage. In fact, the more of a particular good someone produced, the bigger the chance that others would simply help themselves to it. Also, if a person could take the goods of others without giving up something in exchange, then there would be no point to specializing in producing something for exchange. In a world without property rights, no one would enjoy the gains from specialization and exchange, and everyone would specialize only in unproductive acts of piracy.

It is to overcome the problems that we have just described that property rights have evolved. Let's examine these property rights as they operate to govern economic life in the United States today.

Property Rights in Private Enterprise Capitalism
The U.S. economy operates for the most part on the principles of private enterprise capitalism. **Private enterprise** is an economic system that permits individuals to decide on their own economic activities. **Capitalism** is an economic system that permits private individuals to own the capital resources used in production.

The Gains from Special- ization and Exchange

The New York Times, February 21, 1991

Bush Asserts Need for Foreign Oil

BY MATTHEW L. WALD

Saying he was committed to "the power of the marketplace," President Bush presented an energy policy today that he asserted would save energy, increase domestic production of fuels and improve the environment without new taxes or harsh Government edicts. . . .

The plan gives considerable attention to oil. In contrast to the energy policy initiatives undertaken by Presidents Richard Nixon and Jimmy Carter in the oil crises that occurred during their terms, the Bush proposal asserts that the United States will have to live with a high level of dependence on foreign oil. . . .

The Energy Secretary, James D. Watkins, defended the policy's approach to energy efficiency, saying that its critics "want Government control of how you run your life."

FORTUNE, DECEMBER 31, 1990

America's Hottest Export: Pop Culture

BY JOHN HUEY

Industrial hard guys like Henry Ford, Andrew Carnegie, and George Westinghouse probably wouldn't take much heart from what we're about to report, but there is good news for the U.S. these days on the export front. Around the globe, folks just can't get enough of America. They may not want our *hardware* any

more—our cars, steel, or television sets. But when they want a jolt of popular culture—and they want more all the time—they increasingly turn to American *software*—our movies, music, TV programming, and home video, which together now account for an annual trade surplus of some $8 billion. Only aerospace—aircraft

and related equipment—outranks pop culture as an export.

Like it or not, Mickey Mouse, Michael Jackson, and Madonna—her overseas sales are 2½ times her domestic numbers—prop up what's left of our balance of trade. Radio Free Europe and Radio Moscow are out; international broadcasts of CNN and MTV are in.

Essence of the Stories

The Bush Administration energy policy is one that relies on a large amount of oil imports from other countries.

The Energy Secretary claims this approach delivers energy efficiently.

One of the major U.S. exports is pop culture—movies, music, TV programming, and home videos.

Only aerospace equipment outranks pop culture as an export.

Madonna's overseas sales are 2½ times her domestic sales.

Background and Analysis

Holding the production of all other goods and services constant, the United States can produce pop culture and oil along the production possibility frontier, U.S. PPF in the figure.

With no specialization and exchange, we could consume 3 million hours of pop culture and 6 billion barrels of oil a day at point *a* in the figure (the numbers are hypothetical).

By specializing in the production of pop culture and cutting back our domestic production of oil, we can produce 8 million hours of fun a day and 3 billion barrels of oil at point *b* in the figure.

We can exchange pop culture for oil with the rest of the world along the red line in the figure. This line shows our international trading possibilities.

At point *b*, our opportunity cost of producing oil—the hours of fun we must give up to produce one more barrel—exceeds its opportunity cost in the rest of the world—the amount of fun we must give up to get one more barrel of foreign oil. By specializing in pop culture and selling it to the rest of the world in exchange for oil, we can increase our consumption of both pop culture and oil and consume at point *c* in the figure.

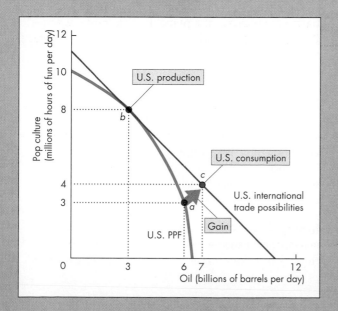

65

Under the property rights in such an economic system, individuals own what they have made, what they have acquired in a voluntary exchange with others, or what they have been given. Any attempt to remove someone's property against that person's will is considered theft, a crime that is punished by a sufficiently severe penalty to deter most people from becoming thieves.

It is easy to see that property rights based on these ideas can generate gainful trade: people can specialize in producing those goods that, for them, have the least opportunity cost. Some people will specialize in enforcing and maintaining property rights (for example, politicians, judges, and police officers), and all individuals will have the incentive to trade with each other, offering the good in which they have a comparative advantage in exchange for the goods produced by others.

The U.S. economic system is based on private property rights and voluntary exchange. But there are important ways in which private property rights are modified in our country.

Taxes Modify Private Property Rights   Taxes on expenditure, income, and wealth transfer property from individuals to governments. Such transfers limit people's efforts to create more property and reduce their gains from specialization and exchange. But the taxes themselves are not arbitrary. Everyone faces the same rules and can calculate the effects of their own actions on the taxes for which they will be liable.

Regulation Modifies Private Property Rights   Some voluntary exchanges are prohibited or regulated. For example, food and drug manufacturers cannot place a product on the market without first obtaining approval from a government agency. The government controls or prohibits the sale of many types of drugs and also restricts trading in human beings and their component parts—that is, it prohibits the selling of slaves, children, and human organs.

These restrictions on the extent of private property and on the legitimacy of voluntary exchange, though important, do not, for the most part, seriously impede specialization and gainful trade. Most people take the view that the benefits of regulation—for example, prohibiting the sale of dangerous drugs—far outweigh the costs imposed on the sellers.

Let's now turn to the other social institution that permits specialization and exchange—the development of an efficient means of exchange.

Money

We have seen that well-defined property rights based on voluntary exchange allow individuals to specialize and exchange their output with each other. In our island economy, we studied only two people and two goods. Exchange in such a situation was a simple matter. In the real world, however, how can billions of people exchange the millions of goods that are the fruits of their specialized labor?

Barter   Goods can be simply exchanged for other goods. The direct exchange of one good for another is known as **barter**. However, barter severely limits the amount of trading that can take place. Imagine that you have roosters but you want to get roses. First, you must look for someone with roses who wants roosters. Economists call this a **double coincidence of wants**—when person A wants to sell exactly what person B wants to buy, and person B wants to sell exactly what person A wants to buy. As the term implies, such occurrences are coincidences and will not arise frequently. A second way of trading by barter is to undertake a sequence of exchanges. If you have oranges and you want apples, you might have to trade oranges for plums, plums for pomegranates, pomegranates for pineapples, and then eventually pineapples for apples.

Cumbersome though it is, quite a large amount of barter trade does take place. For example, when British rock star Rod Stewart played in Budapest, Hungary, in 1986, he received part of his $30,000 compensation in Hungarian sound equipment, electrical cable, and the use of a forklift truck. And before the recent changes in Eastern Europe, hairdressers in Warsaw, Poland, obtained their barbershop equipment from England in exchange for hair clippings that they supplied to London wigmakers.

Although barter exchange does occur, it is an inefficient means of exchanging goods. Fortunately, a better alternative has been invented.

Monetary Exchange   An alternative to barter is **monetary exchange**—a system in which some commodity or token serves as the medium of exchange.

A **medium of exchange** is anything that is generally acceptable in exchange for goods and services. **Money** can also be defined as a medium of exchange—something that can be passed on to others in exchange for goods and services.

Money lowers the cost of transacting and makes millions of transactions possible that simply would not be worth undertaking by barter. Can you imagine the chain of barter transactions you'd have to go through every day to get your coffee, Coke, textbooks, professor's time, video, and all the other goods and services you consume? In a monetary exchange system, you exchange your time and effort for money and use that money to buy the goods and services you consume, cutting out the incredible hassle you'd face each day in a world of barter.

Metals such as gold, silver, and copper have long served as money. Most commonly, they serve as money by being stamped as coins. Primitive societies have traditionally used various commodities, such as seashells, as money. During the Civil War and for several years after, people used postage stamps as money. Prisoners of war in German camps in World War II used cigarettes as money. Using cigarettes as a medium of exchange should not be confused with barter. When cigarettes play the role of money, people buy and sell goods by using cigarettes as a medium of exchange.

In modern societies, governments provide paper money. The banking system also provides money in the form of checking accounts. Checking accounts can be used for settling debts simply by writing an instruction—writing a check—to the bank requesting that funds be transferred to another checking account. Electronic links between bank accounts, now becoming widespread, enable direct transfers between different accounts without any checks being written.

◆ ◆ ◆ ◆ You have now begun to see how economists go about the job of trying to answer some important questions. The simple fact of scarcity and the associated concept of opportunity cost allow us to understand why people specialize, why they trade with each other, why they have social conventions that define and enforce private property rights, and why they use money. One simple idea—scarcity and its direct implication, opportunity cost—explains so much!

S U M M A R Y

The Production Possibility Frontier

The production possibility frontier is the boundary between what is attainable and what is not attainable. Production can take place at any point inside or on the production possibility frontier, but it is not possible to produce outside the frontier. There is always a point on the production possibility frontier that is better than a point inside it. (pp. 51–53)

Opportunity Cost

The opportunity cost of any action is the best alternative action forgone. The opportunity cost of acquiring one good is equivalent to the amount of another good that must be given up. The opportunity cost of a good increases as the quantity of it produced increases. (pp. 54–56)

Economic Growth

Although the production possibility frontier marks the boundary between the attainable and the unattainable, that boundary does not remain fixed. It changes over time, partly because of natural forces (for example, changes in climate and the accumulation of ideas about better ways of producing) and partly because of the choices that we make (choices about consumption and saving). If we use some of today's resources to produce capital goods and for research and development, we will be able to produce more goods and services in the future. The economy will grow. But growth cannot take place without incurring costs. The opportunity cost of more goods and services in the future is consuming fewer goods and services today. (pp. 57–60)

Gains from Trade

A person has a comparative advantage in producing a good if that person can produce the good at a lower opportunity cost than anyone else. People can gain from trade if each specializes in the activity at which he or she has a comparative advantage. Each person produces the good for which his or her opportunity cost is lower than everyone else's. They then exchange part of their output with each other. By this activity, each person is able to consume at a point *outside* his or her individual production possibility frontier.

When a person is more productive than another person—is able to produce more output from fewer inputs—that person has an absolute advantage. But having an absolute advantage does not mean that there are no gains from trade. Even if someone is more productive than other people in all activities,

as long as the other person has a lower opportunity cost of some good, then gains from specialization and exchange are available. (pp. 60–63)

Exchange in the Real World

Exchange in the real world involves the specialization of billions of people in millions of different activities. To make it worthwhile for each individual to specialize and to enable societies to reap the gains from trade, institutions and mechanisms have evolved. The most important of these are private property rights, with a political and legal system to enforce them, and a system of monetary exchange. These institutions enable people to specialize, exchanging their labor for money and their money for goods, thereby reaping the gains from trade. (pp. 63–67)

K E Y   E L E M E N T S

Key Terms

Absolute advantage, 62
Barter, 66
Capital accumulation, 57
Capital goods, 51
Capitalism, 63
Comparative advantage, 60
Consumption, 51
Consumption goods, 51
Double coincidence of wants, 66
Economic growth, 57
Goods and services, 51
Human capital, 51
Intellectual property, 63
Medium of exchange, 67
Monetary exchange, 66
Money, 67

Private enterprise, 63
Production, 51
Production possibility frontier, 51
Productivity, 62
Property, 63
Property rights, 63
Self-sufficiency, 60
Specialization, 60
Technological progress, 57

Key Figures

Figure 3.1 Jane's Production Possibility Frontier, 53
Figure 3.2 Jane's Opportunity Costs of Corn and Cloth, 55
Figure 3.3 Economic Growth on Jane's Island, 58

R E V I E W   Q U E S T I O N S

1 How does the production possibility frontier illustrate scarcity?

2 How does the production possibility frontier illustrate opportunity cost?

3 Explain what shifts the production possibility frontier outward and what shifts it inward.

4 Explain how our choices influence economic growth. What is the cost of economic growth?

5 Why does it pay people to specialize and trade with each other?

6 What are the gains from trade? How do they arise?

7 Why do social contracts such as property rights and money become necessary?

8 What is money? Give some examples of money. In the late 1980s, people in Rumania could use Kent cigarettes to buy almost anything. Was this monetary exchange or barter? Explain your answer.

9 What are the advantages of monetary exchange over barter?

P R O B L E M S

1 Suppose that there is a change in the weather conditions on Jane's island that makes the corn yields much higher. This enables Jane to produce the following amounts of corn:

Hours worked (per day)	Corn (pounds per month)
0	0
2	60
4	100
6	120
8	130
10	140

Her cloth production possibilities are the same as those that appeared in Table 3.1.

a What are six points on Jane's new production possibility frontier?

b What are Jane's opportunity costs of corn and cloth? List them at each of the five levels of output.

c Compare Jane's opportunity cost of cloth with that in the table in Fig. 3.2. Has her opportunity cost of cloth gone up, gone down, or remained the same? Explain why.

2 Amy lives with her parents and attends the local college. The college is operated by the state government, and tuition is free. Jobs that pay $7 an hour are available to high school graduates in the town. Amy's mother, a high school graduate, takes a part-time job so that Amy can go to school. Amy's textbooks cost $280, and Amy gets an allowance of $140 a month from her mother. List the items that make up the opportunity cost of Amy attending college.

3 Suppose that Leisureland produces only two goods—food and suntan oil. Its production possibilities are

Food (pounds per month)		Suntan oil (gallons per month)
300	and	0
200	and	50
100	and	100
0	and	150

Busyland also produces only food and suntan oil, and its production possibilities are

Food (pounds per month)		Suntan oil (gallons per month)
150	and	0
100	and	100
50	and	200
0	and	300

a What are the opportunity costs of food and suntan oil in Leisureland? List them at each output given in the table.

b Why are the opportunity costs the same at each output level?

c What are the opportunity costs of food and suntan oil in Busyland? List them at each output given in the table.

4 Suppose that in problem 3 Leisureland and Busyland do not specialize and trade with each other—each country is self-sufficient. Leisureland produces and consumes 50 pounds of food and 125 gallons of suntan oil per month. Busyland produces and consumes 150 pounds of food per month and no suntan oil. The countries then begin to trade with each other.

a   Which good does Leisureland export, and which good does it import?

b   Which good does Busyland export, and which good does it import?

c   What is the maximum quantity of food and suntan oil that the two countries can produce if each country specializes in the activity at which it has the lower opportunity cost?

5 Suppose that Busyland becomes three times as productive as in problem 3.

a   Show, on a graph, the effect of the increased productivity on Busyland's production possibility frontier.

b   Does Busyland now have an absolute advantage in producing both goods?

c   Can Busyland gain from specialization and trade with Leisureland now that it is twice as productive? If so, what will it produce?

d   What are the total gains from trade? What do these gains depend on?

6 Andy and Bob work at Mario's Pizza Palace. In an 8-hour day, Andy can make 240 pizzas or 100 ice cream sundaes, and Bob can make 80 pizzas or 80 ice cream sundaes. Who does Mario get to make the ice cream sundaes? Who makes the pizzas? Explain your answer.

CHAPTER 4

DEMAND
AND
SUPPLY

After studying this chapter, you will be able to:

- ◆ Construct a demand schedule and a demand curve

- ◆ Construct a supply schedule and a supply curve

- ◆ Explain how prices are determined

- ◆ Explain how quantities bought and sold are determined

- ◆ Explain why some prices rise, some fall, and some fluctuate

- ◆ Make predictions about price changes using the demand and supply model

SLIDE, ROCKET, AND ROLLER COASTER—DISNEYLAND rides? No. Commonly used descriptions of the behavior of prices. There are lots of examples of price slides. One particular example is probably very familiar to you. In 1979, Sony began to market a pocket-sized cassette player that delivered its sound through tiny earphones. Sony named its new product the Walkman and gave it a price tag of around $300—more than $500 in today's money. Today Sony has been joined by many other producers of Walkman clones, and you can buy a Walkman (or its equivalent) that's even better than the 1979 prototype for less than one tenth of the original price. During the time that the Walkman has been with us, the quantity bought has increased steadily each year. Why has there been a long and steady slide in the price of the Walkman? Why hasn't the increase in the quantity bought kept its price high? ◆ ◆ Rocket-

ing prices are also a familiar phenomenon. An important recent example is that of rents paid for apartments and houses, especially in central locations in big cities. Huge increases in rents and house prices have not deterred people from living in the centers of cities—on the contrary, their numbers have increased slightly in recent years. Why do people continue to seek housing in city centers when rents have rocketed so sharply? ◆ ◆ There are lots of price roller coasters—cases in which prices rise and fall from season to season or year to year. Prices of coffee, strawberries, and many other agricultural commodities fit this pattern. Why does the price of coffee roller-coaster even when people's taste for coffee hardly changes at all? ◆ ◆ Though amusement park rides provide a vivid description of the behavior of prices, many of the things that we buy have remarkably steady prices. The audiocassette tapes that we play in a Walkman are an example. The price of a tape has barely changed over the past ten years. Nevertheless, the number of tapes bought has risen steadily year after year. Why do firms sell more and more tapes, even though they're not able to get higher prices for them, and why do people willingly buy more tapes, even though their price is no lower than it was a decade ago?

◆ ◆ ◆ ◆ We will discover the answers to these and similar questions by studying the theory of demand and supply. This powerful theory enables us to analyze many important economic events that affect our lives. It even enables us to make predictions about future prices.

Demand

T he **quantity demanded** of a good or service is the amount that consumers plan to buy in a given period of time at a particular price. Demands are different from wants. **Wants** are the unlimited desires or wishes that people have for goods and services. How many times have you thought that you would like something "if only you could afford it" or "if it weren't so expensive"? Scarcity guarantees that many—perhaps most—of our wants will never be satisfied. Demand reflects a decision about which wants to satisfy. If you demand something, then you've made a plan to buy it.

The quantity demanded is not necessarily the same amount as the quantity actually bought. Sometimes the quantity demanded is greater than the amount of goods available, so the quantity bought is less than the quantity demanded.

The quantity demanded is measured as an amount per unit of time. For example, suppose a person consumes one cup of coffee a day. The quantity of coffee demanded by that person can be

expressed as 1 cup per day or 7 cups per week or 365 cups per year. Without a time dimension, we cannot tell whether a particular quantity demanded is large or small.

What Determines Buying Plans?

The amount that consumers plan to buy of any particular good or service depends on many factors. Among the more important ones are

◆ The price of the good
◆ The prices of related goods
◆ Income
◆ Expected future prices
◆ Population
◆ Preferences

The theory of demand and supply makes predictions about prices and quantities bought and sold. Let's begin by focusing on the relationship between the quantity demanded and the price of a good. To study this relationship, we hold constant all other influences on consumers' planned purchases. We can then ask: how does the quantity demanded of the good vary as its price varies?

The Law of Demand

The law of demand states:

Other things being equal, the higher the price of a good, the lower is the quantity demanded.

Why does a higher price reduce the quantity demanded? The key to the answer lies in *other things being equal.* Because other things are being held constant, when the price of a good rises, it rises *relative* to the prices of all other goods. Although each good is unique, it has substitutes—other goods that serve almost as well. As the price of a good climbs higher, relative to the prices of its substitutes, people buy less of that good and more of its substitutes.

Let's consider an example—blank audiocassette tapes, which we'll refer to as "tapes." Many different goods provide a service similar to that of a tape; for example, records, compact discs, prerecorded tapes, radio and television broadcasts, and live concerts. Tapes sell for about $3 each. If the price of a tape doubles to $6 while the prices of all the other goods remain constant, the quantity of tapes demanded will fall. People will buy more compact discs and prerecorded tapes and fewer blank tapes. If the price of a tape falls to $1 while the prices of all the other goods stay constant, the quantity of tapes demanded will rise, and the demand for compact discs and prerecorded tapes will fall.

Demand Schedule and Demand Curve

A **demand schedule** lists the quantities demanded at each different price when all the other influences on consumers' planned purchases—such as the prices of related goods, income, expected future prices, population, and preferences—are held constant.

The table in Fig. 4.1 sets out a demand schedule for tapes. For example, if the price of a tape is $1, the quantity demanded is 9 million tapes a week. If the price of a tape is $5, the quantity demanded is 2 million tapes a week. The other rows of the table show us the quantities demanded at prices between $2 and $4.

A demand schedule can be illustrated by drawing a demand curve. A **demand curve** graphs the relationship between the quantity demanded of a good and its price, holding constant all other influences on consumers' planned purchases. The graph in Fig. 4.1 illustrates the demand curve for tapes. By convention, the quantity demanded is always measured on the horizontal axis, and the price is measured on the vertical axis. The points on the demand curve labeled *a* through *e* represent the rows of the demand schedule. For example, point *a* on the graph represents a quantity demanded of 9 million tapes a week at a price of $1 a tape.

Willingness to Pay

There is another way of looking at the demand curve: it shows the highest price that people are willing to pay for the last unit bought. If a large quantity is available, that price is low; but if only a small quantity is available, that price is high. For example, if 9 million tapes are available each week, the highest price that consumers are willing to pay for the 9 millionth tape is $1. But if only 2 million tapes are available each week, consumers are willing to pay $5 for the last tape available.

FIGURE 4.1

The Demand Curve and the Demand Schedule

	Price (dollars per tape)	Quantity (millions of tapes per week)
a	1	9
b	2	6
c	3	4
d	4	3
e	5	2

The table shows a demand schedule listing the quantity of tapes demanded at each price if all other influences on buyers' plans are held constant. At a price of $1 a tape, 9 million tapes a week are demanded; at a price of $3 a tape, 4 million tapes a week are demanded. The demand curve shows the relationship between quantity demanded and price, holding everything else constant. The demand curve slopes downward: as price decreases, the quantity demanded increases. The demand curve can be read two ways. For a given price, it tells us the quantity that people plan to buy. For example, at a price of $3 a tape, the quantity demanded is 4 million tapes a week. For a given quantity, the demand curve tells us the maximum price that consumers are willing to pay for the last tape bought. For example, the maximum price that consumers will pay for the 6 millionth tape is $2.

This view of the demand curve may become clearer if you think about your own demand for tapes. If you are given a list of possible prices of tapes, you can write down alongside each price your planned weekly purchase of tapes—your demand schedule for tapes. Alternatively, if you are told that there is just one tape available each week, you can say how much you are willing to pay for it. If you are then told that there is one more tape available, you can say the maximum price that you will be willing to pay for that second tape. This process can continue—you are told that there is one more tape available, and you say how much you are willing to pay for each extra tape. The schedule of prices and quantities arrived at is your demand schedule.

A Change in Demand

The term **demand** refers to the entire relationship between the quantity demanded and the price of a good. The demand for tapes is described by both the demand schedule and the demand curve in Fig. 4.1. To construct a demand schedule and demand curve, we hold constant all the other influences on consumers' buying plans. But what are the effects of each of those other influences?

1. Prices of Related Goods   The quantity of tapes that consumers plan to buy does not depend only on the price of tapes. It also depends in part on the prices of related goods. These related goods fall into two categories: substitutes and complements.

A **substitute** is a good that can be used in place of another good. For example, a bus ride substitutes for a train ride; a hamburger substitutes for a hot dog; a pear substitutes for an apple. As we have seen, tapes have many substitutes—records, prerecorded tapes, compact discs, radio and television broadcasts, and live concerts. If the price of one of these substitutes increases, people economize on its use and buy more tapes. For example, if the price of compact discs doubles, fewer compact discs are bought, and the demand for tapes increases—there is much more taping of other people's compact discs. Conversely, if the price of one of these substitutes decreases, people use the now cheaper good in larger quantities, and they buy fewer tapes. For example, if the price of prerecorded tapes decreases, people play more of these tapes and make fewer of their own tapes—the demand for blank tapes falls.

The effects of a change in the price of a substitute occur no matter what the price of a tape. Whether tapes have a high or a low price, a change in the price of a substitute encourages people to make the substitutions that we've just reviewed. As a consequence, a change in the price of a substitute changes the entire demand schedule for tapes and shifts the demand curve.

A **complement** is a good that is used in conjunction with another good. Some examples of complements are hamburgers and french fries, party snacks and drinks, spaghetti and meat sauce, running shoes and jogging pants. Tapes also have their complements: Walkmans, tape recorders, and stereo tape decks. If the price of one of these complements increases, people buy fewer tapes. For example, if the price of a Walkman doubles, fewer Walkmans are bought and, as a consequence, fewer people are interested in buying tapes—the demand for tapes decreases. Conversely, if the price of one of these complements decreases, people buy more tapes. For example, if the price of the Walkman halves, more Walkmans are bought, and a larger number of people buy tapes—the demand for tapes increases.

2. Income   Another influence on demand is consumer income. Other things remaining the same, when income increases, consumers buy more of most goods, and when income decreases, they buy less of most goods. Consumers with higher incomes demand more of most goods. Consumers with lower incomes demand less of most goods. Rich people consume more food, clothing, housing, art, vacations, and entertainment than do poor people.

Although an increase in income leads to an increase in the demand for most goods, it does not lead to an increase in the demand for all goods. Goods that do increase in demand as income increases are called **normal goods.** Goods that decrease in demand when income increases are called **inferior goods.** Examples of inferior goods are rice and potatoes. These two goods are a major part of the diet of people with very low incomes. As incomes increase, the demand for these goods declines as more expensive meat and dairy products are substituted for them.

3. Expected Future Prices   If the price of a good is expected to rise, it makes sense to buy more of the good today and less in the future, when its price is higher. Similarly, if its price is expected to fall, it pays to cut back on today's purchases and buy more later, when the price is expected to be lower. Thus the higher the expected future price of a good, the larger is today's demand for the good.

4. Population Demand also depends on the size of the population. Other things being equal, the larger the population, the greater is the demand for all goods and services, and the smaller the population, the smaller is the demand for all goods and services.

5. Preferences Finally, demand depends on preferences. *Preferences* are an individual's attitudes toward goods and services. For example, a rock music fanatic has a much greater preference for tapes than does a tone-deaf workaholic. As a consequence, even if they have the same incomes, their demands for tapes will be very different.

There is, however, a fundamental difference between preferences and all the other influences on demand. Preferences cannot be directly observed. We can observe today's price of a good and the prices of its substitutes and complements. We can observe income and population size. We can observe economic forecasts of future prices. But we cannot observe people's preferences. Economists assume that *changes* in preferences occur only slowly and so are not an important influence on *changes* in demand.

A summary of influences on demand and the direction of those influences is presented in Table 4.1.

Movement along the Demand Curve versus a Shift in the Curve

Changes in the influences on buyers' plans cause either a movement along the demand curve or a shift in it. Let's discuss each case in turn.

Movement along the Demand Curve If the price of a good changes but everything else remains the same, there is a movement along the demand curve. For example, if the price of a tape changes from $3

TABLE 4.1

The Demand for Tapes

THE LAW OF DEMAND

The quantity of tapes demanded

Decreases if:	*Increases if:*
◆ The price of a tape rises	◆ The price of a tape falls

CHANGES IN DEMAND

The demand for tapes

Decreases if:	*Increases if:*
◆ The price of a substitute falls	◆ The price of a substitute rises
◆ The price of a complement rises	◆ The price of a complement falls
◆ Income falls*	◆ Income rises*
◆ The price of a tape is expected to fall in the future	◆ The price of a tape is expected to rise in the future
◆ The population decreases	◆ The population increases

*A tape is a normal good

---

to $5, the result is a movement along the demand curve, from point *c* to point *e* in Fig. 4.1.

A Shift in the Demand Curve If the price of a good remains constant but some other influence on buyers' plans changes, we say that there is a change in demand for that good. We illustrate the change in demand as a shift in the demand curve. For example, a fall in the price of the Walkman—a complement of tapes—increases the demand for tapes. We illustrate this increase in demand for tapes with a new demand schedule and a new demand curve. Consumers demand a larger quantity of tapes at each and every price.

The table in Fig. 4.2 provides some hypothetical numbers that illustrate such a shift. The table sets out the original demand schedule when the price of a Walkman is $200 and the new demand schedule when the price of a Walkman is $50. These numbers record the change in demand. The graph in Fig. 4.2 illustrates the corresponding shift in the demand

FIGURE 4.2

A Change in the Demand Schedule and a Shift in the Demand Curve

	Original demand schedule (Walkman $200)			New demand schedule (Walkman $50)	
	Price (dollars per tape)	Quantity (millions of tapes per week)		Price (dollars per tape)	Quantity (millions of tapes per week)
a	1	9	a´	1	13
b	2	6	b´	2	10
c	3	4	c´	3	8
d	4	3	d´	4	7
e	5	2	e´	5	6

A change in any influence on buyers other than the price of the good itself results in a new demand schedule and a shift in the demand curve. Here, a fall in the price of a Walkman—a complement of tapes—increases the demand for tapes. At a price of $3 a tape (row c of table), 4 million tapes a week are demanded when the Walkman costs $200 and 8 million tapes a week are demanded when the Walkman costs only $50. A fall in the price of a Walkman increases the demand for tapes. The demand curve shifts to the right, as shown by the shift arrow and the resulting red curve.

curve. When the price of the Walkman falls, the demand curve for tapes shifts to the right.

A Change in Demand versus a Change in Quantity Demanded A point on the demand curve shows the quantity demanded at a given price. A movement along the demand curve shows a **change in the quantity demanded**. The entire demand curve shows demand. A shift in the demand curve shows a **change in demand**.

Figure 4.3 illustrates and summarizes these distinctions. If the price of a good falls but nothing else

FIGURE 4.3

A Change in Demand versus a Change in the Quantity Demanded

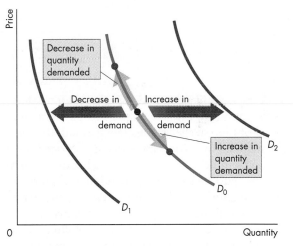

When the price of a good changes, there is a movement along the demand curve and a *change in the quantity of the good demanded*. For example, if the demand curve is D_0, a rise in the price of the good produces a decrease in the quantity demanded and a fall in the price of the good produces an increase in the quantity demanded. The blue arrows on demand curve D_0 represent these movements along the demand curve. If some other influence on demand changes, which increases the quantity that people plan to buy, there is a shift in the demand curve to the right (from D_0 to D_2) and an *increase in demand*. If some other influence on demand changes, which reduces the quantity people plan to buy, there is a shift in the demand curve to the left (from D_0 to D_1) and a *decrease in demand*.

changes, then there is an increase in the quantity demanded of that good (a movement down the demand curve D_0). If the price rises but nothing else changes, then there is a decrease in the quantity demanded (a movement up the demand curve D_0). When any other influence on buyers' planned purchases changes, the demand curve shifts and there is a *change* (an increase or a decrease) *in demand*. A rise in income (for a normal good), in population, in the price of a substitute, or in the expected future price of the good or a fall in the price of a complement shifts the demand curve to the right (to the red demand curve D_2). This represents an *increase in demand*. A fall in income (for a normal good), in population, in the price of a substitute, or in the expected future price of the good or a rise in the price of a complement shifts the demand curve to the left (to the red demand curve D_1). This represents a *decrease in demand*. For an inferior good, the effects of changes in income are in the opposite direction to those described above.

REVIEW

The quantity demanded is the amount of a good that consumers plan to buy in a given period of time. Other things being equal, the quantity demanded of a good increases if its price falls. Demand can be represented by a schedule or curve that sets out the quantity demanded at each price. Demand describes the quantity that consumers plan to buy at each possible price. Demand also describes the highest price that consumers are willing to pay for the last unit bought. Demand increases if the price of a substitute rises, if the price of a complement falls, if income rises (for a normal good), or if the population increases; demand decreases if the price of a substitute falls, if the price of a complement rises, if income falls (for a normal good), or if the population decreases. ◆ ◆ If the price of a good changes but all other influences on buyers' plans are held constant, there is a change in the quantity demanded and a movement along the demand curve. All other influences on consumers' planned purchases shift the demand curve. ◆

Supply

The **quantity supplied** of a good is the amount that producers plan to sell in a given period of time at a particular price. The quantity supplied is not the amount a firm would like to sell but the amount it definitely plans to sell. However, the quantity supplied is not necessarily the same as the quantity actually sold. If consumers do not want to buy the quantity a firm plans to sell, the firm's sales plans will be frustrated. Like quantity demanded, the quantity supplied is expressed as an amount per unit of time.

What Determines Selling Plans?

The amount that firms plan to sell of any particular good or service depends on many factors. Among the more important ones are

◆ The price of the good
◆ The prices of factors of production
◆ The prices of related goods
◆ Expected future prices
◆ The number of suppliers
◆ Technology

Because the theory of demand and supply makes predictions about prices and quantities bought and sold, we focus first on the relationship between the price of a good and the quantity supplied. To study this relationship, we hold constant all the other influences on the quantity supplied. We ask: how does the quantity supplied of a good vary as its price varies?

The Law of Supply

The law of supply states:

Other things being equal, the higher the price of a good, the greater is the quantity supplied.

Why does a higher price lead to a greater quantity supplied of a good? It is because the cost of producing an additional unit of the good increases (at least eventually) as the quantity produced increases. To induce them to incur a higher cost and increase production, firms must be compensated with a higher price.

Supply Schedule and Supply Curve

A **supply schedule** lists the quantities supplied at each different price when all other influences on the amount firms plan to sell are held constant. Let's construct a supply schedule. To do so, we examine how the quantity supplied of a good varies as its price varies, holding constant the prices of other goods, the prices of factors of production used to produce it, expected future prices, and the state of technology.

The table in Fig. 4.4 sets out a supply schedule for tapes. It shows the quantity of tapes supplied at each possible price. For example, if the price of a tape is $1, no tapes are supplied. If the price of a tape is $4, 5 million tapes are supplied each week.

A supply schedule can be illustrated by drawing a supply curve. A **supply curve** graphs the relationship between the quantity supplied and the price of a good, holding everything else constant. Using the numbers listed in the table, the graph in Fig. 4.4 illustrates the supply curve for tapes. For example, point *d* represents a quantity supplied of 5 million tapes a week at a price of $4 a tape.

Minimum Supply Price

Just as the demand curve has two interpretations, so too does the supply curve. So far we have thought about the supply curve and the supply schedule as showing the quantity that firms will supply at each possible price. But we can also think about the supply curve as showing the minimum price at which the last unit will be supplied. Looking at the supply schedule in this way, we ask: what is the minimum price that brings forth a supply of a given quantity? For firms to supply the 3 millionth tape each week, the price has to be at least $2 a tape. For firms to supply the 5 millionth tape each week, they have to get at least $4 a tape.

A Change in Supply

The term **supply** refers to the entire relationship between the quantity supplied of a good and its

FIGURE 4.4

The Supply Curve and the Supply Schedule

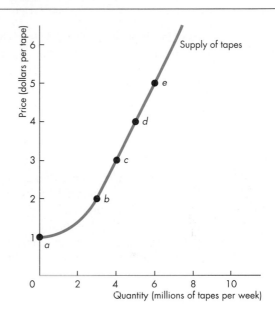

	Price (dollars per tape)	Quantity (millions of tapes per week)
a	1	0
b	2	3
c	3	4
d	4	5
e	5	6

The table shows the supply schedule of tapes. For example, at $2 a tape, 3 million tapes a week are supplied; at $5 a tape, 6 million tapes a week are supplied. The supply curve shows the relationship between the quantity supplied and price, holding everything else constant. The supply curve usually slopes upward: as the price of a good increases, so does the quantity supplied. A supply curve can be read in two ways. For a given price, it tells us the quantity that producers plan to sell. For example, at a price of $3 a tape, producers plan to sell 4 million tapes a week. The supply curve also tells us the minimum acceptable price at which a given quantity will be offered for sale. For example, the minimum acceptable price that will bring forth a supply of 4 million tapes a week is $3 a tape.

price. The supply of tapes is described by both the supply schedule and the supply curve in Fig. 4.4. To construct a supply schedule and supply curve, we hold constant all the other influences on suppliers' plans. Let's now consider these other influences.

1. Prices of Factors of Production

The prices of the factors of production used to produce a good exert an important influence on its supply. For example, an increase in the prices of the labor and the capital equipment used to produce tapes increases the cost of producing tapes, so the supply of tapes decreases.

2. Prices of Related Goods

The supply of a good can be influenced by the prices of related goods. For example, if an automobile assembly line can produce either sports cars or sedans, the quantity of sedans produced will depend on the price of sports cars and the quantity of sports cars produced will depend on the price of sedans. These two goods are *substitutes in production*. An increase in the price of a substitute in production lowers the supply of the good. Goods can also be complements in production. *Complements in production* arise when two things are, of necessity, produced together. For example, extracting chemicals from coal produces coke, coal tar, and nylon. An increase in the price of any one of these by-products of coal increases the supply of the other by-products.

Tapes have no obvious complements in production, but they do have substitutes in production: prerecorded tapes. Suppliers of tapes can produce blank tapes and prerecorded tapes. An increase in the price of prerecorded tapes encourages producers to increase the supply of prerecorded tapes and decrease the supply of blank tapes.

3. Expected Future Prices

If the price of a good is expected to rise, it makes sense to sell less of the good today and more in the future, when its price is higher. Similarly, if its price is expected to fall, it pays to expand today's supply and sell less later, when the price is expected to be lower. Thus, other things being equal, the higher the expected future price of a good, the smaller is today's supply of the good.

4. The Number of Suppliers

Other things being equal, the larger the number of firms supplying a good, the larger is the supply of the good.

5. Technology

New technologies that enable producers to use fewer factors of production will lower the cost of production and increase supply. For example, the development of a new technology for tape production by companies such as Sony and Minnesota Mining and Manufacturing (3M) has lowered the cost of producing tapes and increased their supply.

A summary of influences on supply and the directions of those influences is presented in Table 4.2. Over the long term, changes in technology are the most important influence on supply.

T A B L E 4.2

The Supply of Tapes

THE LAW OF SUPPLY

The quantity of tapes supplied

Decreases if:	*Increases if:*
◆ The price of a tape falls	◆ The price of a tape rises

CHANGES IN SUPPLY

The supply of tapes

Decreases if:	*Increases if:*
◆ The price of a factor of production used to produce tapes increases	◆ The price of a factor of production used to produce tapes decreases
◆ The price of a substitute in production rises	◆ The price of a substitute in production falls
◆ The price of a complement in production falls	◆ The price of a complement in production rises
◆ The price of a tape is expected to rise in the future	◆ The price of a tape is expected to fall in the future
◆ The number of firms supplying tapes decreases	◆ The number of firms supplying tapes increases
	◆ More efficient technologies for producing tapes are discovered

Movement along the Supply Curve versus a Shift in the Curve

Changes in the influences on producers cause either a movement along the supply curve or a shift in it.

Movement along the Supply Curve   If the price of a good changes but everything else influencing suppliers' planned sales remains constant, there is a movement along the supply curve. For example, if the price of tapes increases from $3 to $5 a tape, there will be a movement along the supply curve from point *c* (4 million tapes a week) to point *e* (6 million tapes a week) in Fig. 4.4.

A Shift in the Supply Curve   If the price of a good remains constant but another influence on suppliers' planned sales changes, then there is a change in supply and a shift in the supply curve. For example, as we have already noted, technological advances lower the cost of producing tapes and increase their supply. As a result, the supply schedule changes. The table in Fig. 4.5 provides some hypothetical numbers that illustrate such a change. The table contains two supply schedules: the original, based on "old" technology, and one based on "new" technology. With the new technology, more tapes are supplied at each price. The graph in Fig. 4.5 illustrates the resulting shift in the supply curve. When tape-producing technology improves, the supply curve of tapes shifts to the right, as shown by the shift arrow and the red supply curve.

A Change in Supply versus a Change in Quantity Supplied   A point on the supply curve shows the quantity supplied at a given price. A movement along the supply curve shows a **change in the quantity supplied**. The entire supply curve shows supply. A shift in the supply curve shows a **change in supply**.

Figure 4.6 illustrates and summarizes these distinctions. If the price of a good falls but nothing else changes, then there is a decrease in the quantity supplied of that good (a movement down the supply curve S_0). If the price of a good rises but nothing else changes, there is an increase in the quantity supplied (a movement up the supply curve S_0). When any other influence on sellers changes, the supply curve

FIGURE 4.5

A Change in the Supply Schedule and a Shift in the Supply Curve

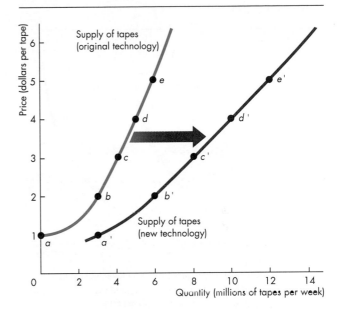

	Original technology			New technology	
	Price (dollars per tape)	Quantity (millions of tapes per week)		Price (dollars per tape)	Quantity (millions of tapes per week)
a	1	0	*a′*	1	3
b	2	3	*b′*	2	6
c	3	4	*c′*	3	8
d	4	5	*d′*	4	10
e	5	6	*e′*	5	12

If the price of a good remains constant but another influence on its supply changes, there will be a new supply schedule and the supply curve will shift. For example, if Sony and 3M invent a new, cost-saving technology for producing tapes, the supply schedule changes, as shown in the table. At $3 a tape, producers plan to sell 4 million tapes a week with the old technology and 8 million tapes a week with the new technology. Improved technology increases the supply of tapes and shifts the supply curve for tapes to the right.

FIGURE 4.6

A Change in Supply
versus a Change in the
Quantity Supplied

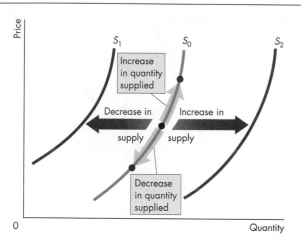

When the price of a good changes, there is a movement along the supply curve and a *change in the quantity of the good supplied*. For example, if the supply curve is S_0, a rise in the price of the good produces an increase in the quantity supplied, and a fall in the price produces a decrease in the quantity supplied. The blue arrows on curve S_0 represent these movements along the supply curve. If some other influence on supply changes, increasing the quantity that producers plan to sell, there is a shift in the supply curve to the right (from S_0 to S_2) and an *increase in supply*. If some other influence on supply changes, reducing the quantity the producers plan to sell, there is a shift to the left in the supply curve (from S_0 to S_1) and a *decrease in supply*.

shifts and there is a *change in supply*. If the supply curve is S_0 and there is, say, a technological change that reduces the amounts of the factors of production needed to produce the good, then supply increases and the supply curve shifts to the red supply curve S_2. If production costs rise, supply decreases and the supply curve shifts to the red supply curve S_1.

REVIEW

T he quantity supplied is the amount of a good that producers plan to sell in a given period

of time. Other things being equal, the quantity supplied of a good increases if its price rises. Supply can be represented by a schedule or a curve that shows the relationship between the quantity supplied of a good and its price. Supply describes the quantity that will be supplied at each possible price. Supply also describes the lowest price at which producers will supply the last unit. Supply increases if the prices of the factors of production used to produce the good fall, the prices of substitutes in production fall, the prices of complements in production rise, the expected future price of the good falls, or technological advances lower the cost of production. If the price of a good changes but all other influences on producers' plans are held constant, there is a change in the quantity supplied and a movement along the supply curve but *no change in supply*. A change in any other influence on producers' plans changes supply and shifts the supply curve. Changes in the prices of factors of production, in the prices of substitutes in production and complements in production, in expected future prices, or in technology shift the supply curve and are said to change supply. ◆

Let's now bring the two concepts of demand and supply together and see how prices are determined.

Price Determination

W e have seen that when the price of a good rises, the quantity demanded decreases and the quantity supplied increases. We are now going to see how adjustments in price coordinate the choices of buyers and sellers.

Price as a Regulator

The price of a good regulates the quantities demanded and supplied. If the price is too high, the quantity supplied exceeds the quantity demanded. If the price is too low, the quantity demanded exceeds the quantity supplied. There is one price, and only one price, at which the quantity demanded equals the quantity supplied. We are going to work out what that price is. We are also going to discover that natural forces operating in a market move the price toward the level that makes the quantity demanded equal the quantity supplied.

The demand schedule shown in the table in Fig. 4.1 and the supply schedule shown in the table in Fig. 4.4 appear together in the table in Fig. 4.7. If the price of a tape is $1, the quantity demanded is 9 million tapes a week, but no tapes are supplied. The quantity demanded exceeds the quantity supplied by 9 million tapes a week. In other words, at a price of $1 a tape, there is a shortage of 9 million tapes a week. This shortage is shown in the final column of the table. At a price of $2 a tape, there is still a shortage but only of 3 million tapes a week. If the price of a tape is $5, the quantity supplied exceeds the quantity demanded. The quantity supplied is 6 million tapes a week, but the quantity demanded is only 2 million. There is a surplus of 4 million tapes a week. There is one price and only one price at which there is neither a shortage nor a surplus. That price is $3 a tape. At that price the quantity demanded is equal to the quantity supplied—4 million tapes a week.

The market for tapes is illustrated in the graph in Fig. 4.7. The graph shows both the demand curve of Fig. 4.1 and the supply curve of Fig. 4.4. The demand curve and the supply curve intersect when the price is $3 a tape. At that price, the quantity demanded and supplied is 4 million tapes a week. At each price *above* $3 a tape, the quantity supplied exceeds the quantity demanded. There is a surplus of tapes. For example, at $4 a tape, the surplus is 2 million tapes a week, as shown by the blue arrow in the figure. At each price *below* $3 a tape, the quantity demanded exceeds the quantity supplied. There is a shortage of tapes. For example, at $2 a tape, the shortage is 3 million tapes a week, as shown by the red arrow in the figure.

Equilibrium

We defined *equilibrium* in Chapter 1 as a situation in which opposing forces balance each other and in which no one is able to make a better choice given the available resources and actions of others. In an equilibrium, the price is such that opposing forces exactly balance each other. The **equilibrium price** is the price at which the quantity demanded equals the

FIGURE 4.7

Equilibrium

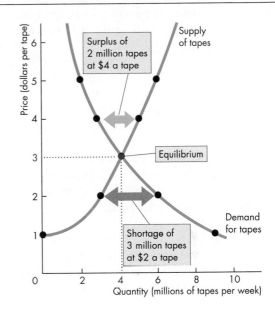

Price (dollars per tape)	Quantity demanded (millions of tapes per week)	Quantity supplied (millions of tapes per week)	Shortage (–) or surplus (+) (millions of tapes per week)
1	9	0	−9
2	6	3	−3
3	4	4	0
4	3	5	+2
5	2	6	+4

The table lists the quantities demanded and quantities supplied as well as the shortage or surplus of tapes at each price. If the price of a tape is $2, 6 million tapes a week are demanded and 3 million are supplied. There is a shortage of 3 million tapes a week, and the price rises. If the price of a tape is $4, 3 million tapes a week are demanded but 5 million are supplied. There is a surplus of 2 million tapes a week, and the price falls. If the price of a tape is $3, 4 million tapes a week are demanded and 4 million are supplied. There is neither a shortage nor a surplus. Neither buyers nor sellers have any incentive to change the price. The price at which the quantity demanded equals the quantity supplied is the equilibrium price.

quantity supplied. The **equilibrium quantity** is the quantity bought and sold at the equilibrium price. To see why equilibrium occurs where the quantity demanded equals the quantity supplied, we need to examine the behavior of buyers and sellers a bit more closely. First, let's look at the behavior of buyers.

The Demand Curve and the Willingness to Pay

Suppose the price of a tape is $2. In such a situation, producers plan to sell 3 million tapes a week. Consumers cannot force producers to sell more than they want to sell, so the quantity sold is also 3 million tapes a week. What is the highest price that buyers are willing to pay for the 3 millionth tape each week? The answer can be found on the demand curve in Fig. 4.7—it is $4 a tape.

If the price remains at $2 a tape, the quantity of tapes demanded is 6 million tapes a week—3 million tapes more than are available. In such a situation, the price of a tape does not remain at $2. Because people want more tapes than are available at that price and because they are willing to pay up to $4 a tape, the price rises. If the quantity supplied stays at 3 million tapes a week, the price rises all the way to $4 a tape.

In fact, the price doesn't have to rise by such a large amount because at higher prices, the quantity supplied increases. The price will rise from $2 a tape to $3 a tape. At that price, the quantity supplied is 4 million tapes a week, and $3 a tape is the highest price that consumers are willing to pay. At $3 a tape, buyers are able to make their planned purchases and producers are able to make their planned sales. Therefore no buyer has an incentive to bid the price higher.

The Supply Curve and the Minimum Supply Price

Suppose that the price of a tape is $4. In such a situation, the quantity demanded is 3 million tapes a week. Producers cannot force consumers to buy more than they want, so the quantity bought is 3 million tapes a week. Producers are willing to sell 3 million tapes a week for a price lower than $4 a tape. In fact, you can see on the supply curve in Fig. 4.7 that suppliers are willing to sell the 3 millionth tape each week at a price of $2. At $4 a tape, they would like to sell 5 million tapes each week. Because they want to sell more than 3 million tapes a week at $4 a tape, and because they are willing to sell the 3 millionth tape for as little as $2, they will continu-

ously undercut each other to get a bigger share of the market. They will cut their price all the way to $2 a tape if only 3 million tapes a week can be sold.

In fact, producers don't have to cut their price to $2 a tape because the lower price brings forth an increase in the quantity demanded. When the price falls to $3, the quantity demanded is 4 million tapes a week, which is exactly the quantity that producers want to sell at that price. So when the price reaches $3 a tape, producers have no incentive to cut the price any further.

The Best Deal Available for Buyers and Sellers   Both situations that we have just examined result in price changes. In the first case, the price starts out at $2 and is bid upward. In the second case, the price starts out at $4 and producers undercut each other. In both cases, prices change until they hit the price of $3 a tape. At that price, the quantity demanded and the quantity supplied are equal, and no one has any incentive to do business at a different price. Consumers are paying the highest acceptable price and producers are selling at the lowest acceptable price.

When people can freely make bids and offers and when they seek to buy at the lowest price and sell at the highest price, the price at which they trade is the equilibrium price—the quantity demanded equals the quantity supplied.

R E V I E W

T he equilibrium price is the price at which the plans of buyers and sellers match each other —the price at which the quantity demanded equals the quantity supplied. If the price is below equilibrium, the quantity demanded exceeds the quantity supplied, buyers offer higher prices, sellers ask for higher prices, and the price rises. If the price is above equilibrium, the quantity supplied exceeds the quantity demanded, buyers offer lower prices, sellers ask for lower prices, and the price falls. Only when the price is such that the quantity demanded and the quantity supplied are equal are there no forces acting on the price to make it change. Therefore that price is the equilibrium price. At that price, the quantity actually bought and sold is also equal to the quantity demanded and the quantity supplied. ◆

The theory of demand and supply that you have just studied is now a central part of economics. But that was not always so. Only 100 years ago, the best economists of the day were quite confused about these matters, which today even students in introductory courses find relatively easy to get right (see Our Advancing Knowledge on pp. 86–87).

As you'll discover in the rest of this chapter, the theory of demand and supply enables us to understand and make predictions about changes in prices —including the price slides, rockets, and roller coasters described in the chapter opener.

Predicting Changes in Price and Quantity

The theory we have just studied provides us with a powerful way of analyzing influences on prices and the quantities bought and sold. According to the theory, a change in price stems from either a change in demand or a change in supply, or a change in both. Let's look first at the effects of a change in demand.

A Change in Demand

What happens to the price and quantity of tapes if demand for tapes increases? We can answer this question with a specific example. If the price of a Walkman falls from $200 to $50, the demand for tapes will increase as is shown in the table in Fig. 4.8. The original demand schedule and the new one are set out in the first three columns of the table. The table also shows the supply schedule.

The original equilibrium price was $3 a tape. At that price, 4 million tapes a week were demanded and supplied. When demand increases, the price that makes the quantity demanded equal the quantity supplied is $5 a tape. At this price, 6 million tapes are bought and sold each week. When demand increases, both the price and the quantity increase.

We can illustrate these changes in the graph in Fig. 4.8. The graph shows the original demand for and supply of tapes. The original equilibrium price is $3 a tape and the quantity is 4 million tapes a week. When demand increases, the demand curve shifts to the right. The equilibrium price rises to $5 a

FIGURE **4.8**

The Effect of a Change in Demand

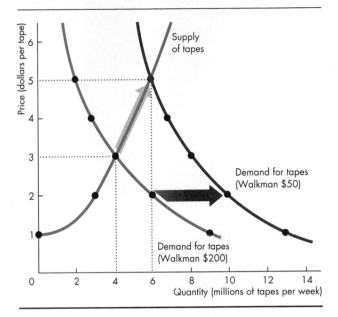

Price (dollars per tape)	Quantity demanded (millions of tapes per week)		Quantity supplied (millions of tapes per week)
	Walkman $200	Walkman $50	
1	9	13	0
2	6	10	3
3	4	8	4
4	3	7	5
5	2	6	6

With the price of a Walkman at $200, the demand for tapes is the blue curve. The equilibrium price is $3 a tape and the equilibrium quantity is 4 million tapes a week. When the price of a Walkman falls from $200 to $50, there is an increase in the demand for tapes and the demand curve shifts to the right—the red curve. At $3 a tape, there is now a shortage of 4 million tapes a week. The quantities of tapes demanded and supplied are equal at a price of $5 a tape. The price rises to this level and the quantity supplied increases. But there is no change in supply. The increase in demand increases the equilibrium price to $5 and increases the equilibrium quantity to 6 million tapes a week.

tape and the quantity supplied increases to 6 million tapes a week, as is highlighted in the figure. There is an increase in the quantity supplied but *no change in supply*.

DISCOVERING the Laws of DEMAND AND SUPPLY

Railroads in the 1850s were as close to the cutting edge of technology as airlines are today. Railroad investment was profitable, but as in the airline industry today, competition was fierce.

The theory of demand and supply was being developed at the same time as the railroads were expanding, and it was their economic problems that gave the newly emerging theory its first practical applications.

In France, Jules Dupuit worked out how to use demand theory to calculate the value of railroad bridges. His work was the forerunner of what is today called *cost-benefit analysis*. Working with the very same principles invented by Dupuit, economists today calculate the costs and benefits of highways, airports, dams, and power stations.

In England, Dionysius Lardner showed railroad companies how they could increase their profits by cutting rates on long-distance business, where competition was fiercest, and raising rates on short-haul business, where they had less to fear from other suppliers. The principles first worked out by Lardner in the 1850s are used by economists working for the major airline companies today to work out the freight rates and passenger fares that will give the airline the largest possible profit. And the rates that result have a lot in common with those railroad rates of the nineteenth century. The airlines have local routes that feed like the spokes of a wheel into a hub on which there is little competition and on which they charge high fares (per mile), and they have long-distance routes between hubs on which they compete fiercely with other airlines and on which fares per mile are lowest.

> "When demand and supply are in stable equilibrium, if any accident should move the scale of production from its equilibrium position, there will be instantly brought into play forces tending to push it back to that position; just as, if a stone hanging by a string is displaced from its equilibrium position, the force of gravity will at once tend to bring it back to its equilibrium position."
>
> ALFRED MARSHALL
> *Principles of Economics*

Dupuit used the law of demand to determine whether a bridge or canal would be valued enough by its users to justify the cost of building it, and Lardner first worked out the relationship between the cost of production and supply and used demand and supply theory to explain the costs, prices, and profits of railroad operations and to discover ways of increasing revenue by raising rates on short-haul business and lowering them on long-distance freight.

The law of demand was discovered by Antoine-Augustin Cournot (1801–1877), pictured right, professor of mathematics at the University of Lyon, France, and it was he who drew the first demand curve in the 1830s. The first practical application of demand theory, by Jules Dupuit (1804–1866), a French engineer/economist, was the calculation of the benefits from building a bridge—and, given that a bridge had been built, of the correct toll to charge for its use.

The laws of demand *and* supply and the connection between the costs of production and supply were first worked out by Dionysius Lardner (1793–1859), an Irish professor of philosophy at the University of London. Known satirically among scientists of the day as "Dionysius Diddler," Lardner worked on an amazing range of problems from astronomy to railway engineering to economics. A colorful character, he would have been a regular guest of Arsenio Hall, Phil Donahue, and Oprah Winfrey if their talk shows had been around in the 1850s. He visited the École des Ponts et Chaussées (the School of Bridges and Roads) in Paris and must have learned a great deal from Dupuit, who was doing his major work on economics at the time.

Many others had a hand in refining the theory of demand and supply, but the first thorough and complete statement of the theory as we know it today was that of Alfred Marshall (1842–1924), pictured left, professor of political economy at the University of Cambridge, who, in 1890, published a monumental treatise—*Principles of Economics*—a work that became *the* textbook on economics for almost half a century. Marshall was an outstanding mathematician, but he kept mathematics and even diagrams in the background. His own supply and demand diagram (reproduced here at its original size) appears only in a footnote.

THE DISCOVERERS OF

THE Laws of Demand and Supply

The exercise that we've just conducted can easily be reversed. If we start at a price of $5 a tape, trading 6 million tapes a week, we can then work out what happens if demand falls back to its original level. You can see that the fall in demand decreases the equilibrium price to $3 a tape and decreases the equilibrium quantity to 4 million tapes a week. Such a fall in demand could arise from a decrease in the price of compact discs or of CD players.

We can now make our first two predictions. Holding everything else constant:

◆ When demand increases, both the price and the quantity increase.

◆ When demand decreases, both the price and the quantity decrease.

A Change in Supply

Suppose that Sony and 3M have just introduced a new cost-saving technology in their tape-production plants. The new technology changes the supply. The new supply schedule (the same one that was shown in Fig. 4.5) is presented in the table in Fig. 4.9. What is the new equilibrium price and quantity? The answer is highlighted in the table: the price falls to $2 a tape and the quantity rises to 6 million a week. You can see why by looking at the quantities demanded and supplied at the old price of $3 a tape. The quantity supplied at that price is now 8 million tapes a week, and there is a surplus of tapes. The price falls. Only when the price is $2 a tape does the quantity supplied equal the quantity demanded.

Figure 4.9 illustrates the effect of an increase in supply. It shows the demand curve for tapes and the original and new supply curves. The initial equilibrium price is $3 a tape and the original quantity is 4 million tapes a week. When the supply increases, the supply curve shifts to the right. The equilibrium price falls to $2 a tape and the quantity demanded increases to 6 million tapes a week, highlighted in the figure. There is an increase in the quantity demanded but *no change in demand*.

The exercise that we've just conducted can easily be reversed. If we start out at a price of $2 a tape with 6 million tapes a week being bought and sold, we can work out what happens if the supply curve shifts back to its original position. You can see that the fall in supply increases the equilibrium price to $3 a tape and decreases the equilibrium quantity to

FIGURE 4.9

The Effect of a Change in Supply

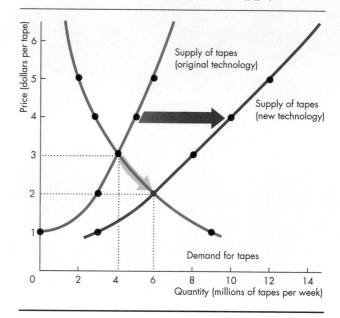

With the original technology, the supply of tapes is shown by the blue curve. The equilibrium price is $3 a tape and the equilibrium quantity is 4 million tapes a week. When the new technology is adopted, there is an increase in the supply of tapes. The supply curve shifts to the right—the red curve. At $3 a tape, there is now a surplus of 4 million tapes a week. The quantities of tapes demanded and supplied are equal at a price of $2 a tape. The price falls to this level and the quantity demanded increases. But there is no change in demand. The increase in supply lowers the price of tapes to $2 and increases the quantity to 6 million tapes a week.

Price (dollars per tape)	Quantity demanded (millions of tapes per week)	Quantity supplied (millions of tapes per week)	
		Original technology	New technology
1	9	0	3
2	6	3	6
3	4	4	8
4	3	5	10
5	2	3	12

4 million tapes a week. Such a fall in supply could arise from an increase in the cost of labor and raw materials.

We can now make two more predictions. Holding everything else constant:

◆ When supply increases, the quantity increases and the price falls.

◆ When supply decreases, the quantity decreases and the price rises.

Reading Between the Lines on pp. 90–91 shows the effects of the floods in the Midwest in the spring and summer of 1993 on the supply of crops.

Changes in Both Supply and Demand

In the above exercises, either demand or supply changed, but only one at a time. If just one of these changes, we can predict the direction of change of the price and the quantity. If both demand and supply change, we cannot always say what will happen to both the price and the quantity. For example, if both demand and supply increase, we know that the quantity increases, but we cannot predict whether the price rises or falls. To make such a prediction, we need to know the relative magnitude of the increase in demand and supply. If demand increases and supply decreases, we know that the price rises, but we cannot predict whether the quantity increases or decreases. Again, to be able to make a prediction about the change in the quantity, we need to know the relative magnitudes of the changes in demand and supply.

As an example of a change in both supply and demand, let's take one final look at the market for tapes. We've seen how demand and supply determine the price and quantity of tapes, how an increase in demand resulting from a fall in the price of a Walkman both raises the price of tapes and increases the quantity bought and sold, and how an increase in the supply of tapes resulting from an improved technology lowers the price of tapes and increases the quantity bought and sold. Let's now examine what happens when both of these changes —a fall in the price of a Walkman (which increases the demand for tapes) and an improved production technology (which increases the supply of tapes)— occur together.

The table in Fig. 4.10 brings together the numbers that describe the original quantities demanded and supplied and the new quantities demanded and supplied after the fall in the price of the Walkman and the improved tape production technology. These

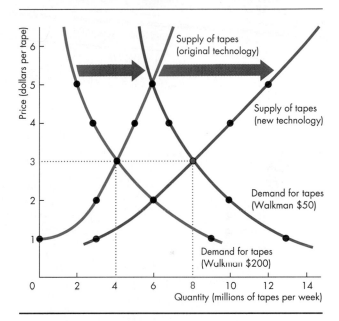

FIGURE 4.10

The Effect of a Change in Both Demand and Supply

	Original quantities (millions of tapes per week)		New quantities (millions of tapes per week)	
Price (dollars per tape)	Quantity demanded (Walkman $200)	Quantity supplied (original technology)	Quantity demanded (Walkman $50)	Quantity supplied (new technology
1	9	0	13	3
2	6	3	10	6
3	4	4	8	8
4	3	5	7	10
5	2	6	6	12

When a Walkman costs $200, the price of a tape is $3 and the equilibrium quantity is 4 million tapes a week. A fall in the price of a Walkman increases the demand for tapes, and improved technology increases the supply of tapes. The new technology supply curve intersects the higher demand curve at $3, the same price as before, but the quantity increases to 8 million tapes a week. The increase in both demand and supply increases the quantity but leaves the price unchanged.

same numbers are illustrated in the graph. The original demand and supply curves intersect at a price of $3 a tape and a quantity of 4 million tapes a week.

Demand and Supply in Action

The Essence of the Story

THE KANSAS CITY STAR, SATURDAY, JULY 10, 1993

Flood Isn't Likely to Jolt Food Prices

BY GENE MEYER

So far, the flooding of Midwestern farm fields is not likely to float food prices out of sight, agricultural authorities say.

But if weather hurts crops about three weeks from now, grocery budgets will be in big trouble, the experts warn.

That's because in agriculture, as in other endeavors in life, timing is everything.

For farmers, "the extent of flooding is simply beyond belief," said Mark Bogner, agricultural meteorologist at WeatherData Services Inc. in Wichita.

Rain or floods this spring and summer have devastated crops in much of Kansas, most of northern Missouri, all of Iowa, and a great deal of Minnesota, Wisconsin, and Illinois.

Very simply, this may be the biggest natural calamity farmers in those states have faced since the droughts of 1983 and 1988, Bogner said.

However, federal food price forecasters are sticking by earlier predictions that food prices this year will rise no more than 2 percent to 3 percent, which would be the second smallest increase in about a decade.

Some foods, notably meat, are even apt to drop in price, at least temporarily, said Ralph Parlett of the U.S. Department of Agriculture's Economic Research Service.

That's because when floods or droughts raise prices for livestock feed too sharply, farmers often must sell more cattle or hogs than they might have planned.

"Of course, we pay for it the following year, when meat production drops and prices rise," Parlett said.

Analysts outside government see little reason to dispute the official view.

"Production will be down a bit more than expected and prices will be higher, but you won't see them run up the way they did early in the 1980s," said Sid Love, senior grains analyst with Bill Helming Consulting Services in Lenexa.

. . . The world has changed since the last time widespread meteorological mayhem hit the Midwest.

Economies overseas are shakier, competing farm production is greater, and "the world just does not need as large a U.S. crop as it did 10 or 15 years ago," [Alan] Barkema [a senior economist at the Federal Reserve bank of Kansas City] said.

So, even though some authorities fear that rain and flooding may be a more than $1 billion blow to the national food chain, the price increases consumers will pay because of the flood "will be a few tenths of a percent at most," Barkema estimated. . . .

Rain and floods in the spring and summer of 1993 devastated crops in Kansas, Missouri, Iowa, Minnesota, Wisconsin, and Illinois and created a calamity for farmers in those states.

Despite the floods, food prices were expected to rise by only 2–3 percent in 1993—the second smallest annual increase in a decade.

Meat prices were expected to fall in 1993 and then rise in 1994. The reason is that, when floods raise the prices for livestock feed too sharply, farmers often must sell more cattle or hogs than they might have planned.

Background and Analysis

Figure 1 shows the market for non-meat food in the United States in 1993. The demand curve is D. The world price of non-meat food is P_0. Because large quantities of most food items are available from the rest of the world at the current price, the world supply is S_W. The quantity of non-meat food is Q_0.

Before the floods, the supply of non-meat food by U.S. farmers is the curve labeled S_0 in Fig. 1. The quantity of such food produced in the United States is U_0.

The floods decrease U.S. farm production, and the supply curve shifts leftward to S_1. Food from the rest of the world fills the gap, and the price does not rise. But U.S. farm sales fall to U_1, and farm revenue falls by the amount shown by the red rectangle to the amount shown by the blue rectangle.

Figure 2 shows the market for animal feed. Before the floods, the supply curve is S_0, the price is P_0, and the quantity is Q_0. The floods decrease supply to S_1, and the price rises to P_1.

Figure 3 shows the effects of the change in the price of animal feed on the market for meat. Before the floods, the supply curve is S_0, the price is P_0, and the quantity is Q_0. With higher feed prices, farmers slaughter more animals and the supply of meat increases to S_1. The price of meat falls to P_1. But the following year, with fewer animals, farmers decrease the supply of meat to S_2 and the price rises to P_2.

Figure 1

Figure 2

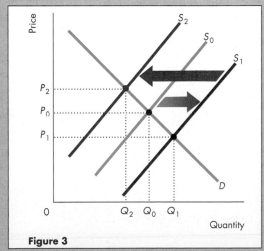

Figure 3

The new supply and demand curves also intersect at a price of $3 a tape but at a quantity of 8 million tapes a week. In this example, the increases in demand and supply are such that the rise in price brought about by an increase in demand is offset by the fall in price brought about by an increase in supply—so the price does not change. An increase in either demand or supply increases the quantity. Therefore when both demand and supply increase, so does quantity. Note that if demand had increased slightly more than shown in the figure, the price would have risen. If supply had increased by slightly more than shown in the figure, the price would have fallen. But in both cases, the quantity would have increased.

Walkmans, Apartments, and Coffee

At the beginning of this chapter, we looked at some facts about prices and quantities of Walkmans, apartments, and coffee. Let's use the theory of demand and supply to explain the movements in the prices and the quantities of those goods. Figure 4.11 illustrates the analysis.

FIGURE **4.11**

More Changes in Supply and Demand

(a) Walkmans

(b) Apartments

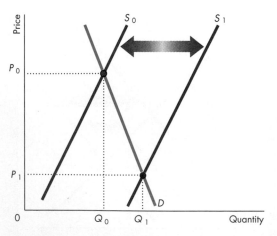

(c) Coffee

A large increase in the supply of Walkmans, from S_0 to S_1, combined with a small increase in demand, from D_0 to D_1, results in a fall in the price of the Walkman, from P_0 to P_1, and an increase in the quantity, from Q_0 to Q_1 (part a). An increase in the demand for apartments produces a large increase in the price, from P_0 to P_1, but only a small increase in the quantity, from Q_0 to Q_1 (part b). Variations in the weather and in growing conditions lead to fluctuations in the supply of coffee, between S_0 and S_1, which produce fluctuations in the price of coffee, between P_0 and P_1, and in the quantity, between Q_0 and Q_1 (part c).

First, let's consider the Walkman, shown in part (a). In 1980, using the original technology, the supply of Walkmans is described by the supply curve S_0. The 1980 demand curve is D_0. The quantities supplied and demanded in 1980 are equal at Q_0, and the price is P_0. Advances in technology and the building of additional production plants increase supply and shift the supply curve from S_0 to S_1. At the same time, increasing incomes increase the demand for Walkmans but not by nearly as much as the increase in supply. The demand curve shifts from D_0 to D_1. With the new demand curve D_1 and supply curve S_1, the equilibrium price is P_1 and the quantity is Q_1. The large increase in supply combined with a smaller increase in demand results in an increase in the quantity of Walkmans and a dramatic fall in their price.

Next, let's consider apartments in the center of the city, as in part (b). The supply of apartments is described by supply curve S. The supply curve is steep, reflecting the fact that there is a fixed number of apartment buildings. As the number of young urban professionals increases and the number of two-income families increases, the demand for city apartments increases sharply. The demand curve shifts from D_0 to D_1. As a result, the price increases from P_0 to P_1 and the quantity also increases, but not as much as the price.

Finally, let's consider the market for coffee, shown in part (c). The demand for coffee is described by curve D. The supply of coffee fluctuates between S_0 and S_1. When growing conditions are good, the supply curve is S_1. When there are adverse growing conditions such as frost, the supply decreases and the supply curve is S_0. As a consequence of fluctuations in supply, the price of coffee fluctuates between P_0 (the maximum price) and P_1 (the minimum price). The quantity fluctuates between Q_0 and Q_1.

◆ ◆ ◆ ◆ By using the theory of demand and supply, you will be able to explain past fluctuations in prices and quantities and also make predictions about future fluctuations. But you will want to do more than predict whether prices are going to rise or fall. In your study of microeconomics, you will learn to predict *by how much* they will change. In your study of macroeconomics you will learn to explain fluctuations in the economy as a whole. In fact, the theory of demand and supply can help answer almost every economic question.

S U M M A R Y

Demand

The quantity demanded of a good or service is the amount that consumers plan to buy in a given period of time at a particular price. Demands are different from wants. Wants are unlimited, whereas demands reflect decisions to satisfy specific wants. The quantity that consumers plan to buy of any good depends on:

◆ The price of the good
◆ The prices of related goods—substitutes and complements
◆ Income
◆ Expected future prices
◆ Population
◆ Preferences

Other things being equal, the higher the price of a good, the smaller is the quantity of that good demanded. The relationship between the quantity demanded and price, holding constant all other influences on consumers' planned purchases, is illustrated by the demand schedule or demand curve. A change in the price of a good produces movement along the demand curve for that good. Such a movement is called a change in the quantity demanded.

Changes in all other influences on buying plans are said to change demand. When demand changes, there is a new demand schedule and the demand curve shifts. When there is an increase in demand, the demand curve shifts to the right; when there is a decrease in demand, the demand curve shifts to the left. (pp. 73–78)

Supply

The quantity supplied of a good or service is the amount that producers plan to sell in a given period of time. The quantity that producers plan to sell of any good or service depends on:

◆ The price of the good
◆ The prices of factors of production
◆ The prices of related goods
◆ Expected future prices
◆ The number of suppliers
◆ Technology

Other things being equal, the higher the price of a good, the larger is the quantity of that good supplied. The relationship between the quantity supplied and price, holding constant all other influences on firms' planned sales, is illustrated by the supply schedule or supply curve. A change in the price of a good produces movement along the supply curve for that good. Such a movement is called a change in the quantity supplied.

Changes in all other influences on selling plans are said to change supply. When supply changes, there is a new supply schedule and the supply curve shifts. When there is an increase in supply, the supply curve shifts to the right; when there is a decrease in supply, the supply curve shifts to the left. (pp. 78–82)

Price Determination

Price regulates the quantities supplied and demanded. The higher the price, the greater is the quantity supplied and the smaller is the quantity demanded. At high prices, there is a surplus—an excess of the quantity supplied over the quantity demanded. At low prices, there is a shortage—an excess of the quantity demanded over the quantity supplied. There is one price and only one price at which the quantity demanded equals the quantity supplied. That price is the equilibrium price. At that price, buyers have no incentive to offer a higher price and suppliers have no incentive to sell at a lower price. (pp. 82–84)

Predicting Changes in Price and Quantity

Changes in demand and supply lead to changes in price and in the quantity bought and sold. An increase in demand leads to a rise in price and to an increase in quantity. A decrease in demand leads to a fall in price and to a decrease in quantity. An increase in supply leads to an increase in quantity and to a fall in price. A decrease in supply leads to a decrease in quantity and to a rise in price. A simultaneous increase in demand and supply increases the quantity bought and sold but can raise or lower the price. If the increase in demand is larger than the increase in supply, the price rises. If the increase in demand is smaller than the increase in supply, the price falls. (pp. 85–93)

K E Y   E L E M E N T S

Key Terms

Change in demand, 77
Change in supply, 81
Change in the quantity demanded, 77
Change in the quantity supplied, 81
Complement, 75
Demand, 75
Demand curve, 74
Demand schedule, 74
Equilibrium price, 83
Equilibrium quantity, 84
Inferior good, 75
Normal good, 75

Quantity demanded, 73
Quantity supplied, 78
Substitute, 75
Supply, 79
Supply curve, 79
Supply schedule, 79
Wants, 73

Key Figures and Tables

Figure 4.1   The Demand Curve and the Demand
             Schedule, 74
Figure 4.3   A Change in Demand versus a Change
             in the Quantity Demanded, 77

Figure 4.4   The Supply Curve and the Supply Schedule, 79

Figure 4.6   A Change in Supply versus a Change in the Quantity Supplied, 82

Figure 4.7   Equilibrium, 83

Table 4.1   The Demand for Tapes, 76

Table 4.2   The Supply of Tapes, 80

REVIEW QUESTIONS

1 Define the quantity demanded of a good or service.

2 Define the quantity supplied of a good or service.

3 List the more important factors that influence the amount that consumers plan to buy and say whether an increase in each factor increases or decreases consumers' planned purchases.

4 List the more important factors that influence the amount that firms plan to sell and say whether an increase in each factor increases or decreases firms' planned sales.

5 State the law of demand and the law of supply.

6 If a fixed amount of a good is available, what does the demand curve tell us about the price that consumers are willing to pay for that fixed quantity?

7 If consumers are willing to buy only a certain fixed quantity, what does the supply curve tell us about the price at which firms will supply that quantity?

8 Distinguish between:

a A change in demand and a change in the quantity demanded

b A change in supply and a change in the quantity supplied

9 Why is the price at which the quantity demanded equals the quantity supplied the equilibrium price?

10 Describe what happens to the price of a tape and the quantity of tapes sold if:

a The price of CDs increases.

b The price of a Walkman increases.

c The supply of live concerts increases.

d Consumers' incomes increase and firms producing tapes switch to new cost-saving technology.

e The prices of the factors of production used to make tapes increase.

f A new good comes onto the market that makes tapes obsolete.

PROBLEMS

1 Suppose that one of the following events occurs:

a The price of gasoline rises.

b The price of gasoline falls.

c All speed limits on highways are abolished.

d A new fuel-effective engine that runs on cheap alcohol is invented.

e The population doubles.

f Robotic production plants lower the cost of producing cars.

g A law banning car imports from Japan is passed.

h The rates for auto insurance double.

i The minimum age for drivers is increased to 19 years.

j A massive and high-grade oil supply is discovered in Mexico.

k The environmental lobby succeeds in closing down all nuclear power stations.

l The price of cars rises.

m The price of cars falls.

n The summer temperature is 10 degrees lower than normal, and the winter temperature is 10 degrees higher than normal.

State which of the above events will produce:
1 A movement along the demand curve for gasoline
2 A shift of the demand curve for gasoline to the right
3 A shift of the demand curve for gasoline to the left
4 A movement along the supply curve of gasoline
5 A shift of the supply curve of gasoline to the right
6 A shift of the supply curve of gasoline to the left
7 A movement along the demand curve for cars
8 A movement along the supply curve of cars
9 A shift of the demand curve for cars to the right
10 A shift of the demand curve for cars to the left
11 A shift of the supply curve of cars to the right
12 A shift of the supply curve of cars to the left
13 An increase in the price of gasoline
14 A decrease in the quantity of oil bought and sold

2 The demand and supply schedules for gum are as follows:

Price (cents per pack)	Quantity demanded	Quantity supplied
	(millions of packs per week)	
10	200	0
20	180	30
30	160	60
40	140	90
50	120	120
60	100	140
70	80	160
80	60	180
90	40	200

a What is the equilibrium price of gum?
b How much gum is bought and sold each week?

Suppose that a huge fire destroys one half of the gum-producing factories. Supply decreases to one half of the amount shown in the above supply schedule.
c What is the new equilibrium price of gum?
d How much gum is now bought and sold each week?
e Has there been a shift in or a movement along the supply curve of gum?
f Has there been a shift in or a movement along the demand curve for gum?
g As the gum factories destroyed by fire are rebuilt and gradually resume gum production, what will happen to:
(1) The price of gum
(2) The quantity of gum bought
(3) The demand curve for gum
(4) The supply curve of gum

3 Suppose the demand and supply schedules for gum are those in problem 2. An increase in the teenage population increases the demand for gum by 40 million packs per week.
a Write out the new demand schedule for gum.
b What is the new quantity of gum bought and sold each week?
c What is the new equilibrium price of gum?
d Has there been a shift in or a movement along the demand curve for gum?
e Has there been a shift in or a movement along the supply curve of gum?

4 Suppose the demand and supply schedules for gum are those in problem 2. An increase in the teenage population increases the demand for gum by 40 million packs per week, and simultaneously the fire described in problem 2 occurs, wiping out one half of the gum-producing factories.
a Draw a graph of the original and new demand and supply curves.
b What is the new quantity of gum bought and sold each week?
c What is the new equilibrium price of gum?

PART 2

HOW MARKETS WORK

**Talking
with
Herbert
Stein**

Herbert Stein was born in Detroit in 1916. He obtained his A.B. degree from Williams College in 1935 and his Ph.D. from the University of Chicago in 1958. Herbert Stein has made a profession of analyzing and advising on national economic policy and has spent his entire career in Washington. He was Chairman of the Council of Economic Advisors to President Nixon from 1972 to 1974 and is currently a Senior Fellow at the American Enterprise Institute in Washington. He is a regular contributor to the national public debate on economic policy through his many writings and especially through his regular columns in the *Wall Street Journal.* His latest book, written with Murray Foss, is *An Illustrated Guide to the American Economy,* published in 1992 by the American Enterprise Institute.

Dr. Stein, what attracted you to economics?

I was in college during the Great Depression. That experience surely focused my attention on economics. But there were other, more direct factors at work. As a student, my two best subjects were English and economics. But I could not see how I would make a living out of English. Moreover, at my college there was a $500 prize for an essay in the field of economics. The prize had been awarded only about four times in the previous 50 years, but still it was there as an incentive. And indeed, I won it.

Yours has been an unusual career path for an economist. Why did you choose a Washington-based policy advisory role over the opportunity to teach or do economic research?

In 1938, while still working toward my Ph.D. at the University of Chicago, I went to work in Washington, D.C. From 1940 to 1945, during World War II, many economists moved to Washington. During this period, I learned that I was good at, and that I enjoyed, applying a little list

9 7

"**T**he best economists . . . keep foremost in their minds . . . that economic actions have important indirect and long-run effects."

of economic principles to a body of data in order to produce a policy statement or options paper that the educated public could understand. There have always been other economists who would be better teachers or writers of journal articles than I, but few who would be better at what I did. This comparative advantage provided me with employment opportunities superior in many respects to what I could have obtained in a university. By the way, it wasn't until 1958 that I finished my dissertation, but by then it no longer had a major impact on my career.

You are reported to have said that economists don't know very much but that politicians know even less. What do economists know that politicians don't know?

I did say that economists know more about economics than politicians do. But that may not have been a precise statement. The difference is probably less in knowledge than in objectives. What the best economists, unlike most politicians, keep foremost in their minds is that economic actions have important indirect and long-run effects. Most of the more specific things economists

know—about markets, for example—are really specific cases of these indirect and long-run effects. Of course, politicians are capable of obtaining whatever knowledge they need, but in general they do not find this specialized knowledge of economists very useful.

We usually think of economic policy as being either pro-business and conservative or pro-labor and liberal. Is this the right distinction?

I do not find these terms—"conservative," "liberal," "pro-business," and "pro-labor"—useful any more, if they ever have been. Fifteen years ago, conservatism included support for strong defense against communism, resistance to inflation, and fiscal prudence. But the communist threat has evaporated; inflation, at least for the time, is not an issue; and practicing conservatives have given up their claim to being champions of fiscal prudence.

No one can be unflinchingly pro-labor any more, in the sense of pro–labor-union, because the union movement is withering away. At the same time, everyone has to be at least somewhat pro-labor, because labor is the great affluent American middle class.

> " **E**veryone has to be at least somewhat pro-labor, because labor is the great affluent American middle-class."

Similarly, neither can anyone be totally pro- or anti-business. Some have adopted a position that they call pro-business but that I prefer to call "pro-businesses." They want to promote particular industries and businesses that the government would select. That is, they want to supplant or supplement the operation of market forces in determining the direction of investment, research, and production by adopting policies that are favorable to chosen businesses. In principle, conservatives object to this approach as inefficient and as unnecessary expansions of the government's power. The difference between conservatives and liberals in devotion to market processes is unlikely to become a major issue. Neither side will be either pure in adherence to the market or thoroughgoing in rejecting it. Therefore, as conditions change and as distinctions blur, such shorthand labels are more and more uninformative and misleading.

Why are so many politicians, whether conservative or liberal, so anti-market?

Politicians in general are not anti-market. They are just not devoted to it. The benefits from interfering with the market generally are prompt, clear, and evident to the beneficiaries. The costs are diffused and perhaps delayed.

The classic case of anti-market economic policy is interference with international trade through tariffs, quotas, voluntary agreements, and similar devices. In the short run, these measures benefit certain protected industries. The U.S. auto industry, for example, benefited from the Japanese agreement to limit auto exports to the United States. Likewise, American textile producers benefited from an international textile agreement limiting exports to the United States. Voters accepted such arrangements because those who were injured, either by higher prices for the products that might have been obtained more cheaply abroad or because their own export sales were hurt, did not fully realize what was happening to them. Still, government interference with foreign trade has diminished greatly over the past sixty years, which is some evidence that people are becoming more aware of the damage that such interference does to particular sectors and to the country in general.

> " **P**oliticians in general are not anti-market. They are just not devoted to it."

> " It's possible that the market may result in a distribution of income that society legitimately considers inappropriate."

Is it possible to be too pro-market?

No. Now, it's possible that the market may result in a distribution of income that the society legitimately considers inappropriate. And calculations of private market participants may exclude some social costs or benefits that are important, as in the case of pollution. The problem is to try to make an objective assessment of the claims that the market is not yielding the best solution and that some government action would be superior. The proper role of economists is to be skeptical about such claims but not dogmatically to deny the possibility that they may be justified in some cases.

What are the sorts of issues that the Council of Economic Advisors addresses, and what in your opinion is the appropriate role for economic advisors?

In the past 46 years or so since the Council of Economic Advisors to the President was established, it has concentrated on two main issues. The first, which was dominant in the early period, was the problem of economic stabilization—avoiding large-scale unemployment and inflation. Economic advice in this area followed the trend of thinking in the profession. Initially very committed to active, fine-tuning fiscal policy, the Council later gave more weight to monetary policy and, still later, became much more reserved about activism and more concerned with the long-run consequences of short-run stabilization measures. The second major problem addressed by the Council was the evaluation of the performance of markets and of the possible effects of proposed interventions in markets. The whole arsenal of microeconomic theory has been brought to bear on these issues, and that has been a valuable contribution.

On most subjects, what is called for from advisors is not a recommendation but an option paper evaluating the likely consequences of the different policy choices that are available. That is psychologically difficult to produce because it requires an objective appraisal of one's own preferences. I wish more economists were trained in writing such papers.

What advice would you give to a student embarking on the study of economics today?

I assume that an economics student will be fully exposed to economic analysis, both micro and macro. I would suggest that economics students try to add three other subject to their studies.

First, become familiar with some body of economic data, such as national income data or international economic data, to learn about the problems in creating and using statistical representations of the real world. Second, study some economic history for a more realistic understanding of the applicability of economics to policy. And third, learn about other social sciences—notably political science and sociology—since the lines between them and economics are increasingly blurring.

CHAPTER 5

ELASTICITY

After studying this chapter, you will be able to:

◆ Define and calculate the price elasticity of demand

◆ Explain what determines the elasticity of demand

◆ Distinguish between short-run demand and long-run demand

◆ Use elasticity to determine whether a price change will increase or decrease revenue

◆ Define and calculate other elasticities of demand

◆ Define and calculate the elasticity of supply

◆ Distinguish among momentary supply, long-run supply, and short-run supply

F THE SUPPLY OF A GOOD DECREASES, ITS PRICE RISES.
But by how much? To answer this question, you will
have to don a flowing caftan: you have just been
named chief economic strategist for OPEC—the
Organization of Petroleum Exporting Countries. You
want to bring more money into OPEC. Would you
restrict the supply of oil to raise prices? Or would
you produce more oil? ◆ ◆   You know that a higher price will bring in more
dollars per barrel, but lower production means that fewer barrels will be sold.
Will the price rise high enough to offset the smaller quantity that OPEC will sell?
◆ ◆   As OPEC's economic strategist, you need to know about the demand for
oil in great detail. For example, as the world economy grows, how will that

growth translate into an increasing demand for oil?
What about substitutes for oil? Will we discover inexpensive methods to convert coal and tar sands into
usable fuel? Will nuclear energy become safe and

OPEC's Dilemma

cheap enough to compete with oil? ◆ ◆   A bumper grape crop is good news
for wine consumers. It brings plentiful supplies at lower prices. But is it good
news for grape growers? Do they make a bigger income? Or does the lower price
more than wipe out their gains from larger quantities sold? ◆ ◆   Looking for
greater tax revenues, the government decides to increase the tax rates on tobacco
and alcohol. Does the higher tax rate bring in more tax revenue? Or do people
switch to substitutes for tobacco and alcohol on such a massive scale that the
higher tax rate brings in less tax revenue?

◆ ◆ ◆ ◆ In this chapter you will learn how to tackle questions such as the ones just posed. You will learn how we can measure in a precise way the responsiveness of the quantities bought and sold to changes in prices and other influences on buyers or sellers.

Elasticity of Demand

Let's begin by looking a bit more closely at your task as OPEC's economic strategist. You are trying to decide whether to advise a cut in output to shift the supply curve and raise the price of oil. To make this decision, you need to know how the quantity of oil demanded responds to a change in price. You also need some way to measure that response.

Two Possible Scenarios

To understand the importance of the responsiveness of the quantity of oil demanded to a change in its price, let's compare two possible scenarios in the oil industry, shown in Fig. 5.1. In the two parts of the figure, the supply curves are identical, but the demand curves differ.

The supply curve labeled S_0 in each part of the figure shows the initial supply. It intersects the demand curve, in both cases, at a price of $10 a barrel and a quantity of 40 million barrels a day. Suppose that you contemplate a cut in supply that shifts the supply curve from S_0 to S_1. In part (a), the new supply curve S_1 intersects the demand curve D_a at a price of $30 a barrel and a quantity of 23 million barrels a day. In part (b), with demand curve D_b, the same supply curve shift increases the price to $15 a barrel and decreases the quantity to 15 million barrels a day.

You can see that in part (a) the price increases by more and the quantity decreases by less than it does in part (b). What happens to the revenue of the oil producers in these two cases? The revenue from the sale of a good equals the price of the good multiplied by the quantity sold. An increase in price has

FIGURE **5.1**

Demand, Supply, and Revenue

(a) More revenue

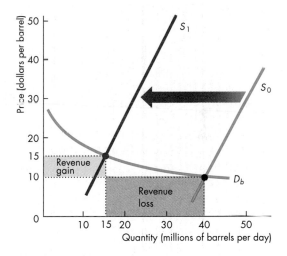

(b) Less revenue

If supply is cut from S_0 to S_1, the price rises and the quantity bought decreases. In part (a), revenue—the quantity multiplied by price—increases from $400 million to $690 million a day. The increase in revenue from a higher price (blue area) exceeds the decrease in revenue from lower sales (red area). In part (b), revenue decreases from $400 million to $225 million a day. The increase in revenue from a higher price (blue area) is smaller than the decrease in revenue from lower sales (red area). These two different responses in revenue arise from different responses of the quantity demanded to a change in price.

two opposing effects on revenue. The higher price brings in more revenue on each unit sold (blue area) but also leads to a decrease in the quantity sold, which in turn results in less revenue (red area). In case (a), the first effect is larger (blue area exceeds red area), so revenue increases. In case (b), the second effect is larger (red area exceeds blue area), so revenue decreases.

You can confirm these results by calculating the original and new revenues and comparing them. In both cases, the original revenue was $400 million a day ($10 a barrel multiplied by 40 million barrels a day). In case (a), revenue increases to $690 million a day ($30 a barrel multiplied by 23 million barrels a day). In case (b), revenue decreases to $225 million a day ($15 a barrel multiplied by 15 million barrels a day).

Slope Depends on Units of Measurement

The difference between these two cases is the responsiveness of the quantity demanded to a change in price. Demand curve D_a is steeper than demand curve D_b. But we can't compare two demand curves simply by their slopes, because the slope of a demand curve depends on the units in which we measure the price and quantity.

Also, we often need to compare the demand curves for different goods and services. For example, when deciding by how much to change tax rates, the government needs to compare the demand for oil and the demand for tobacco. Which is more responsive to price? Which can be taxed at an even higher rate without decreasing the tax revenue? Comparing the slopes of these two demand curves has no meaning, since oil is measured in gallons and tobacco in pounds—completely unrelated units.

To overcome these problems, we need a measure of response that is independent of the units of measurement of prices and quantities. Elasticity is such a measure.

Calculating Elasticity

The **price elasticity of demand** measures the responsiveness of the quantity demanded of a good to a change in its price. It is calculated by using the formula

$$\text{Price elasticity of demand} = \frac{\text{Percentage change in quantity demanded}}{\text{Percentage change in price}}$$

To use this formula to calculate the elasticity of demand, we need to know the quantities demanded at different prices, holding constant all the other influences on consumers' buying plans. As an example, let's assume that we have the relevant data on prices and quantities demanded of oil and calculate the elasticity of demand for oil. The calculations are illustrated in Fig. 5.2 and summarized in Table 5.1.

At $9.50 a barrel, 41 million barrels a day are sold. If the price increases to $10.50 a barrel, the quantity demanded decreases to 39 million barrels a day. When the price increases by $1 a barrel, the quantity demanded decreases by 2 million barrels a day. To calculate the elasticity of demand, we have to express changes in price and quantity demanded as percentage changes. But there are two prices and two quantities—the original and the new. Which price and which quantity do we use for calculating the percentage change? By convention, we use the *average price* and the *average quantity*. By using the average price and average quantity, we are actually

---

Calculating the Elasticity of Demand

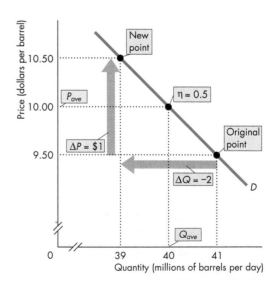

The elasticity of demand (η) is calculated midway between the original price-quantity point and the new price-quantity point as $(\Delta Q/Q_{ave})/(\Delta P/P_{ave})$. This calculation measures the elasticity at an average price of $10 per barrel and an average quantity of 40 million barrels.

calculating elasticity at a point on the demand curve midway between the original price-quantity point and the new price-quantity point, as shown in Fig. 5.2. The original price was $9.50 and the new price is $10.50, so the average price is $10. A $1 price change is 10 percent of the average price. The original quantity was 41 million barrels and the new quantity is 39 million barrels, so the average quantity demanded is 40 million barrels. A change in quantity of –2 million barrels a day is –5 percent of the average quantity.

The price elasticity of demand is

$$\frac{-5\%}{10\%} = -0.5$$

Minus Sign and Elasticity

When the price of a good *increases* along a demand curve, the quantity demanded *decreases*. Because a *positive* price change results in a *negative* change in the quantity demanded, the price elasticity of demand is negative. But it is the *absolute value* of the price elasticity of demand that tells us how responsive—how elastic—demand is. To make it easier to compare elasticities, we drop the minus sign and use the term **elasticity of demand** to mean the *absolute value* of the *price* elasticity of demand, and we denote it by the Greek letter *eta* (η). In this example, the elasticity of demand (η) is 0.5.

Why Average Price and Quantity?

We use the *average* price and *average* quantity to avoid having two values for the elasticity of demand, depending on whether the price increases or decreases. A price increase of $1 is 10.5 percent of $9.50, and 2 million barrels is 4.9 percent of 41 million barrels. If we use these numbers to calculate the elasticity, we get 0.47. A price decrease of $1 is 9.5 percent of $10.50, and 2 million barrels is 5.1

TABLE 5.1

Calculating the Elasticity of Demand

	Numbers	Symbols and formulas*
Prices (dollars per barrel)		
Original price	$ 9.50	P_0
New price	$10.50	P_1
Change in price	$ 1.00	$\Delta P = P_1 - P_0$
Average price	$10.00	$P_{ave} = (P_0 + P_1)/2$
Percentage change in price	10%	$(\Delta P/P_{ave}) \times 100$
Quantities (millions of barrels per day)		
Original quantity demanded	41	Q_0
New quantity demanded	39	Q_1
Change in quantity demanded	–2	$\Delta Q = Q_1 - Q_0$
Average quantity demanded	40	$Q_{ave} = (Q_0 + Q_1)/2$
Percentage change in quantity demanded	–5%	$(\Delta Q/Q_{ave}) \times 100$
Percentage change in quantity demanded divided by the percentage change in price	–0.5	$[(\Delta Q/Q_{ave}) \times 100]/[(\Delta P/P_{ave}) \times 100]$ $= (\Delta Q/Q_{ave})/(\Delta P/P_{ave})$
Elasticity of demand	0.5	η

*The Greek letter *delta* (Δ) stands for "change in."

percent of 39 million barrels. Using these numbers to calculate the elasticity, we get 0.54. If we use the average price and average quantity demanded, the elasticity is 0.5 regardless of whether the price increases or decreases.

Percentages and Proportions

Although elasticity is the ratio of the *percentage* change in the quantity demanded to the *percentage* change in the price, it is also, equivalently, the *proportionate* change in the quantity demanded divided by the *proportionate* change in the price. In Table 5.1, notice that although the formula multiplies both the proportionate change in price ($\Delta P/P_{ave}$) and the proportionate change in quantity demanded ($\Delta Q/Q_{ave}$) by 100 to create the percentage change, those hundreds cancel when we divide.

Elastic and Inelastic Demand

The elasticity that we have just calculated is 0.5. Is that a large or a small elasticity? The elasticity of demand can range between zero and infinity. The elasticity of demand is zero if the quantity demanded does not change when the price changes. An example of a good that has a very low elasticity of demand (perhaps zero) is insulin. This commodity is of such importance to many diabetics that they will buy the quantity that keeps them healthy at almost any price.

If a price rise causes a decrease in the quantity demanded, the elasticity is greater than zero. When the percentage change in the quantity demanded is less than the percentage change in price, the elasticity is less than 1 (the example that we calculated in

Table 5.1 is such a case). If the percentage change in the quantity demanded equals the percentage change in price, the elasticity of demand is 1. If the percentage change in the quantity demanded exceeds the percentage change in price, the elasticity is greater than 1.

In an extreme case, the quantity demanded may be infinitely sensitive to price changes. At a particular price, people demand any quantity of a good, but if the price rises by 1¢, then the quantity demanded drops to zero. In this case, an almost zero percentage change in the price produces an infinite percentage change in the quantity demanded, so the elasticity of demand is infinity. An example of a good that has a very high elasticity of demand (almost infinite) is marker pens at the campus bookstore. If the price of marker pens increases at the campus bookstore, while all other prices, including the price of marker pens at the local supermarket, remain constant, there will be a large decrease in the quantity of marker pens bought at the campus bookstore. Marker pens at the local supermarket are almost perfect substitutes for marker pens at the campus bookstore.

For elasticities between zero and 1, demand is called **inelastic;** for elasticities greater than 1, demand is called **elastic.** The dividing line between inelastic and elastic demand is called **unit elastic demand.** When elasticity is equal to infinity, demand is called **perfectly elastic;** when elasticity is equal to zero, demand is called **perfectly inelastic.**

Table 5.2 shows examples of inelastic, unit elastic, and elastic demands. We can see in this table the changes in quantities demanded for a 10 percent change in price. The first row simply reproduces the calculations that you worked through in Table 5.1.

TABLE **5.2**

Elastic and Inelastic Demand

Effects of a 10 percent price change

	Original quantity demanded	New quantity demanded	Average quantity demanded	Change in quantity demanded	Percentage change in quantity demanded	Elasticity of demand
Inelastic demand	41	39	40	−2	−5	0.5
Unit elastic demand	42	38	40	−4	−10	1.0
Elastic demand	50	30	40	−20	−50	5.0

The second row shows the case of a unit elastic demand. The initial quantity demanded was 42 million barrels a day, and the new quantity demanded is 38. Thus the average quantity demanded is 40, and the change in the quantity demanded is –4. The percentage change in the quantity demanded is –10 percent. Therefore the elasticity of demand is 1. The final case is one in which the original quantity demanded was 50 and the new quantity demanded is 30. The average quantity demanded is still 40, but the change in quantity demanded is now –20. The percentage change in the quantity demanded is –50 percent. In this case, the elasticity is 5.

Elasticity along a Straight-Line Demand Curve

Elasticity is not the same as slope, but the two are related. To understand how they are related, let's look at elasticity along a straight-line demand curve—a demand curve that has a constant slope.

Figure 5.3 illustrates the calculation of elasticity along such a demand curve. Let's start with a price of $50 a barrel. What is the elasticity if we lower the price from $50 to $40? The change in the price is –$10 and the average price is $45 (average of $50 and $40), which means that the proportionate change in price is

$$\frac{\Delta P}{P_{ave}} = \frac{-10}{45}$$

The original quantity demanded is zero and the new quantity demanded is 10 million barrels a day, so the change in the quantity demanded is 10 million barrels a day and the average quantity is 5 million barrels a day (the average of 10 million and zero). Thus the proportionate change in the quantity demanded is

$$\frac{\Delta Q}{Q_{ave}} = \frac{10}{5}.$$

Dividing the proportionate change in the quantity demanded by the proportionate change in the price gives

$$\frac{\Delta Q/Q_{ave}}{\Delta P/P_{ave}} = \frac{10/5}{-10/45} = -9.$$

Then taking the absolute value gives us the elasticity of demand:

$$\eta = 9.$$

FIGURE 5.3

Elasticity along a Straight-Line Demand Curve

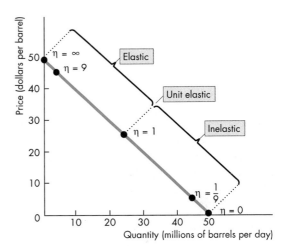

On a straight-line demand curve, elasticity decreases as the price falls and the quantity demanded increases. Demand is unit elastic at the midpoint of the demand curve (elasticity is 1). Above the midpoint, demand is elastic (elasticity is greater than 1); below the midpoint, demand is inelastic (elasticity is less than 1).

Using this same method, we can calculate the elasticity of demand when the price of a barrel is cut repeatedly by $10—from $45 to $35, from $40 to $30, from $35 to $25, and so on. You can verify the elasticity of demand at other points on the demand curve in Fig. 5.3. On a straight-line demand curve, the elasticity decreases as the price falls.

At the midpoint of the demand curve, where the price is $25 a barrel and the quantity demanded is 25 million barrels a day, elasticity is exactly 1. Above the midpoint, the elasticity is greater than 1 and it increases as the price rises. Below the midpoint, the elasticity is less than 1 and it decreases as the price falls. Elasticity is infinity when the price is $50 a barrel and the quantity demanded is zero, and elasticity is zero when the quantity demanded is 50 million barrels a day and the price is zero.

Why Elasticity Is Smaller at Lower Prices

Why is elasticity smaller at lower prices along a straight-line demand curve? It is because the *levels* of price and quantity demanded affect their *percentage* changes. For a given change in price, the percentage change is small at a high price and large at a low price. Similarly, for a given change in quantity demanded, the percentage change is small at a large quantity and large at a small quantity. So for a given change in price, the lower the initial price, the larger is the percentage change in price, the smaller is the percentage change in the quantity demanded, and the smaller is the elasticity.

Constant Elasticity Demand Curves

A demand curve can have a constant elasticity. A perfectly inelastic demand curve has a constant elasticity of zero ($\eta = 0$) and is vertical. A perfectly elastic demand curve has a constant elasticity of infinity ($\eta = \infty$) and is horizontal. Other constant elasticity demand curves are *curved*. Figure 5.4 illustrates three constant elasticity demand curves—the cases of zero, unity, and infinity.

The example that we gave earlier, of a good with very low elasticity of demand (shown as zero in part a of the figure) is insulin. Regardless of the price, the quantity demanded remains constant in part (a). An example of a good whose elasticity is close to 1 (part b) is electricity. As its price increases, the quantity

demanded decreases by the same percentage amount. The example that we gave of a good whose elasticity is (almost) infinite (part c) is marker pens at the campus bookstore. Marker pens are bought from the campus bookstore only if their price doesn't exceed that of marker pens at the local supermarket. If the price of marker pens at the campus bookstore exceeds the price at the local supermarket, the quantity of marker pens bought from the bookstore is zero. If the price of marker pens at the local supermarket exceeds that at the campus bookstore, marker pens are bought only from the bookstore. When the prices are equal, there is no unique quantity demanded.

Real-World Elasticities

Actual values of elasticities of demand have been estimated from the average spending patterns of consumers, and some examples are set out in Table 5.3. But elasticity is not just a number calculated by economists. Whether demand is elastic or inelastic is of enormous importance to each of us. In the 1970s, when OPEC did in fact cut back on the supply of oil, Americans discovered that their demand for oil was inelastic. Despite the smaller supplies, we still demanded a lot of oil and gasoline, which led to cuts

---

FIGURE **5.4**

Demand Curves with Constant Elasticity

(a) Zero elasticity   **(b) Unit elasticity**   **(c) Infinite elasticity**

Each demand curve shown here has a constant elasticity. The demand curve in part (a) has zero elasticity. The demand curve in part (b) has unit elasticity. The demand curve in part (c) has infinite elasticity.

T A B L E **5.3**

Some Price Elasticities in the U.S. Economy

Industry	Elasticity
Elastic demand	
Metals	1.52
Electrical engineering products	1.39
Mechanical engineering products	1.30
Furniture	1.26
Motor vehicles	1.14
Instrument engineering products	1.10
Professional services	1.09
Transportation services	1.03
Inelastic demand	
Gas, electricity, and water	0.92
Oil	0.91
Chemicals	0.89
Beverages (all types)	0.78
Tobacco	0.61
Food	0.58
Banking and insurance services	0.56
Housing services	0.55
Clothing	0.49
Agricultural and fish products	0.42
Books, magazines, and newspapers	0.34
Coal	0.32

Source: Ahsan Mansur and John Whalley, "Numerical Specification of Applied General Equilibrium Models: Estimation, Calibration, and Data," in *Applied General Equilibrium Analysis,* eds. Herbert E. Scarf and John B. Shoven (New York: Cambridge University Press, 1984), 109.

in spending on other things—people took fewer vacations; vast companies were thrown into a panic as they tried to adjust; schools had to cut the salaries of teachers so that they could pay for heating oil; speed restrictions were imposed; and angry car own-

ers had to face the premature obsolescence of their gas guzzlers.

What makes the demand for some goods elastic and the demand for others inelastic? Elasticity depends on:

◆ The ease with which one good can be substituted for another
◆ The proportion of income spent on the good
◆ The amount of time elapsed since the price change

Substitutability

Substitutability depends on the nature of the good itself. For example, oil, a good with an inelastic demand, certainly has substitutes but none that are very close (imagine a steam-driven, coal-fueled car or a nuclear-powered jetliner). On the other hand, metals, a group of goods with elastic demands, have very good substitutes in the form of plastics.

The degree of substitutability between two goods depends on how narrowly (or broadly) we define them. For example, even though oil does not have a close substitute, different types of oil substitute for each other without much difficulty. Oils from different parts of the world differ in weight and chemical composition. Let's consider a particular kind of oil—called Saudi Arabian Light. Its elasticity will be relevant if you happen to be the economic advisor to Saudi Arabia (as well as the OPEC economic strategist!). Suppose Saudi Arabia is contemplating a unilateral price rise, which means that prices of other types of oil will stay the same. Although Saudi Arabian Light has unique characteristics, other oils can easily substitute for it, and most buyers will be very sensitive to its price relative to the prices of other types of oil. Demand in this case is highly elastic.

This example, which distinguishes between oil in general and different types of oil, has broad applications. For example, the elasticity of demand for meat is low, but the elasticity of demand for beef, lamb, or pork is high. The elasticity of demand for personal computers is low, but the elasticity of demand for an IBM, Zenith, or Apple is high.

Proportion of Income Spent on a Good

Other things being equal, the higher the proportion of income spent on a good, the higher is the elasticity. If only a small fraction of income is spent on a good, then a change in its price will have little impact on the consumer's overall budget. In contrast, even a small rise in the price of a good that commands a large part of a consumer's budget will induce the consumer to undertake a radical reappraisal of expenditures.

To appreciate the importance of the proportion of income spent on a good, consider your own elasticity of demand for textbooks and chewing gum. If the price of textbooks doubles (increases 100 percent), there will be an enormous decrease in the quantity of textbooks bought. There will be an increase in sharing and in illegal photocopying. If the price of chewing gum doubles (also a 100 percent increase), there will be almost no change in the quantity of gum demanded. Why the difference? Textbooks take a large proportion of your budget, while gum takes only a tiny portion. You don't like either price increase, but you hardly notice the effects of the increased price of gum, while the increased price of textbooks blows you away!

Time Frame for Demand

Elasticity also depends on the amount of time that has elapsed since a price change. In general, the greater the lapse of time, the higher the elasticity of demand. The reason is related to substitutability. The greater the passage of time, the more it becomes possible to develop substitutes for a good whose price has increased. Thus at the moment of a price increase, the consumer often has little choice but to continue consuming similar quantities of a good. However, given enough time, the consumer finds alternatives or cheaper substitutes and gradually lowers the rate of purchase of items that have become more expensive. To take account of the importance of time on the elasticity of demand, we distinguish between two time frames for demand:

1. Short-run demand
2. Long-run demand

Short-Run Demand   The **short-run demand curve** describes the initial response of buyers to a change in the price of a good. The short-run response depends on whether the price change is seen as permanent (or at least long-lasting) or temporary. A price change that is believed to be temporary produces a highly elastic buyer response. Why would you pay a higher price now if you believe you can

get the same thing for a lower price a few days from now? And if the price is temporarily low, why wouldn't you take advantage of it and buy a lot before the price goes up again?

For example, you can make telephone calls at lower rates on weekends than during the week. The fall in price on Saturday and the rise in price on Monday produce a large change in the quantity demanded—demand is highly elastic. Of course, many calls are made during normal business hours, but the lower price on the weekend induces a large switch from business day calling to weekend calling. Other examples are seasonal variations in the price of travel and of certain fresh fruits and vegetables.

When a price change is believed to be permanent, the quantity bought does not change much in the short run. That is, short-run demand is inelastic. The reason is that people find it hard to change their buying habits. More importantly, they often have to adjust their consumption of other complementary goods, an expensive and time-consuming undertaking.

An example of a permanent, or at least a long-lasting, price change occurred in the market for oil in the early 1970s. At the end of 1973 and the beginning of 1974, the price of oil increased fourfold, leading in turn to a sharp rise in the costs of home heating and of gasoline. Initially, consumers had little choice but to accept the price increases and maintain consumption at more or less their original levels. Home heating equipment and cars might not have been very energy-efficient, but nothing else was available. Drivers could lower their average speed and economize on gasoline. Thermostats could be turned down, but that too imposed costs—costs of discomfort. As a consequence, there were severe limits on the extent to which people felt it worthwhile to cut back on their consumption of the now much more costly fuel. The short-run buyer response in the face of this sharp price increase was inelastic.

Long-Run Demand   The **long-run demand curve** describes the response of buyers to a change in price after all possible adjustments have been made. Long-run demand is more elastic than short-run demand. The 1974 rise in the price of oil and gasoline produced a clear demonstration of the distinction between long-run and short-run demand. Initially, buyers responded to higher gasoline and oil prices by using their existing capital equipment—furnaces and gas guzzlers—in a way that economized on the more expensive fuel. With a longer time to respond, people bought more energy-efficient capital equipment. Cars became smaller and more fuel-efficient, and car engines also became more efficient.

Two Demand Curves   The short-run and long-run demand curves for oil in 1974 looked like those in Fig. 5.1. Look back at that figure and refresh your memory about the two demand curves in parts (a) and (b). The short-run demand curve is D_a, and the long-run demand curve is D_b. The price of a barrel of oil in 1974 was $10, and 40 million barrels a day were bought and sold. At that price and quantity, long-run demand, D_b, is much more elastic than short-run demand, D_a.

R E V I E W

T he elasticity of demand is a measure of the response of a change in the quantity demanded to a change in price that is independent of the units of measurement. It is calculated as the absolute value of the percentage change in the quantity demanded divided by the percentage change in price. The elasticity of demand ranges between zero and infinity. Goods that have a high elasticity of demand are those that have close substitutes and on which a large proportion of income is spent. Goods that have a low elasticity of demand are those that do not have good substitutes and on which a small portion of income is spent. Elasticity is also higher the longer the time lapse since a price change. ◆

Elasticity, Revenue, and Expenditure

R evenue is the price of a good multiplied by the quantity *sold*. Expenditure is the price of a good multiplied by the quantity *bought*. Thus revenue and expenditure are two sides of the same coin—revenue is the receipts of the sellers, while expenditure is the outlays of the buyers. When the price of a good rises along a demand curve, the quantity sold decreases. What happens to revenue (and expenditure) depends on the extent to which the quantity sold decreases as the price rises. If a 1 percent rise in the price reduces the quantity sold by less than 1 percent, revenue increases. If a 1 percent rise in price reduces the quantity sold by more than 1 percent, revenue decreases. If a 1 percent rise in price reduces the quantity sold by 1 percent, the price rise and the quantity decrease just offset each other and revenue stays constant. But we now have a precise way of linking the percent change of the quantity sold to the percent change in price—the elasticity of demand. When the price of a good rises, the size of the elasticity of demand determines whether revenue increases or decreases. Table 5.4 gives some examples based on the three cases in Table 5.2.

In case *a*, the elasticity of demand is 0.5. When the price rises from $9.50 to $10.50, the quantity sold decreases from 41 million to 39 million barrels a day. Revenue, which is equal to price multiplied by quantity sold, was originally $9.50 multiplied by 41 million, which is $389.50 million a day. After the price rises, revenue increases to $409.50 million a day. Thus a rise in the price leads to an *increase* in revenue of $20 million a day.

In case *b*, the elasticity of demand is 1. The quantity sold decreases from 42 million to 38 million barrels a day as the price rises from $9.50 to $10.50. Revenue in this case is the same at each price, $399 million a day. Thus when the price changes and the elasticity of demand is 1, revenue *does not change*.

In case *c*, the elasticity of demand is 5. When the price rises from $9.50 to $10.50, the quantity sold decreases from 50 million to 30 million barrels a day. The original revenue was $475 million a day, but the new revenue is $315 million a day. Thus in this case, a rise in the price leads to a *decrease* in revenue of $160 million a day.

Elasticity and revenue are closely connected. When the elasticity of demand is greater than 1, the percentage decrease in the quantity demanded exceeds the percentage rise in price and therefore revenue decreases. When the elasticity of demand is less than 1, the percentage decrease in the quantity demanded is less than the percentage rise in price and therefore revenue increases. When the elasticity of demand is 1, the percentage decrease in the quantity demanded equals the percentage rise in price and revenue remains constant. The extra revenue from a higher price is exactly offset by the loss in revenue from the smaller quantities sold.

TABLE 5.4

Elasticity of Demand, Revenue, and Expenditure

| | Elasticity | Price (dollars per barrel) | | Quantity demanded (millions of barrels per day) | | Revenue/expenditure (millions of dollars per day) | | |
		Original	New	Original	New	Original	New	Change
a	0.5	9.50	10.50	41	39	389.50	409.50	+20
b	1.0	9.50	10.50	42	38	399.00	399.00	0
c	5.0	9.50	10.50	50	30	475.00	315.00	−160

As we have seen, long-run demand curves are more elastic than short-run demand curves. It is possible, therefore, that an increase in price will result in an increase in revenue in the short run but not in the long run. If the short-run elasticity is less than 1 but the long-run elasticity is greater than 1, this outcome will occur. Reading Between the Lines on pp. 116–117 is a practical application of the relationship between the elasticity of demand and revenue in the timber industry.

So far, we've studied the most important elasticity—the price elasticity of demand. But there are other useful elasticities. Let's see what they are.

More Demand Elasticities

The quantity demanded of any good (or service or factor of production) is influenced by many things other than its price. It depends on, among other things, incomes and the prices of other goods. We can calculate elasticities of demand with respect to these other variables as well. Let's now examine some of these additional elasticities.

Income Elasticity of Demand

As income grows, how will the demand for a particular good change? The answer depends on the income elasticity of demand for the good. The **income elasticity of demand** is the percentage change in the quantity demanded divided by the percentage change in income. It is represented by η_y. That is,

$$\eta_y = \frac{\text{Percentage change in quantity demanded}}{\text{Percentage change in income}}.$$

Income elasticities of demand can be positive or negative; however, there are three interesting ranges for the income elasticity of demand:

1. Greater than 1 (income elastic)
2. Between zero and 1 (income inelastic)
3. Less than zero (negative income elasticity)

These three cases are illustrated in Fig. 5.5, and some real-world examples are shown in Table 5.5. Part (a) of the figure shows an income elasticity of demand that is greater than 1. As income increases, the quantity demanded increases, but the quantity demanded increases faster than income. The curve slopes upward and has an increasing slope. Goods that fall into this category include ocean cruises, custom clothing, international travel, jewelry, and works of art.

Part (b) shows an income elasticity of demand that is between zero and 1. In this case, the quantity demanded increases as income increases, but income increases faster than the quantity demanded. The curve slopes upward, but the slope declines as income increases. Goods that fall into this category include food, clothing, furniture, newspapers, and magazines.

Part (c) illustrates a third category of goods that is a bit more complicated. For these goods, as income increases, the quantity demanded increases until it reaches a maximum at income m. Beyond that point, as income continues to increase, the

F I G U R E **5.5**

Income Elasticity of Demand

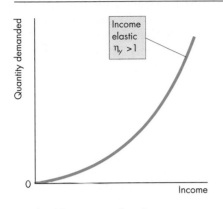

(a) Elasticity greater than 1

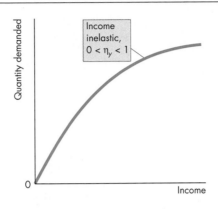

(b) Elasticity between zero and 1

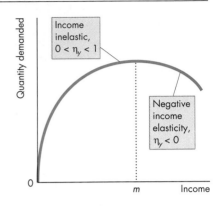

(c) Elasticity less than 1 and becomes negative

There are three ranges of values for income elasticity of demand. In part (a), income elasticity of demand is greater than 1. In this case, as income increases, the quantity demanded increases but by a bigger percentage than the increase in income. In part (b), income elasticity of demand is between zero and 1. In this case, as income increases, the quantity demanded increases but by a smaller percentage than the increase in income. In part (c), the income elasticity of demand is positive at low incomes but becomes negative as income increases above level m. Maximum consumption occurs at the income m.

T A B L E **5.5**

Some Income Elasticities of Demand

Industry	Elasticity	Industry	Elasticity
Elastic demand		**Unit Elastic demand**	
Airline travel	5.82	Dentists' services	1.00
Movies	3.41		
Foreign travel	3.08	**Inelastic demand**	
Housing services	2.45		
Electricity	1.94	Shoes and other footwear	0.94
Restaurant meals	1.61	Tobacco	0.86
Local buses and trains	1.38	Alcoholic beverages	0.62
Gasoline and oil	1.36	Water	0.59
Haircutting	1.36	Clothing	0.51
Cars	1.07	Newspapers and magazines	0.38
		Telephone	0.32

Source: H. S. Houthakker and Lester D. Taylor, *Consumer Demand in the United States* (Cambridge, Mass.: Harvard University Press, 1970).

quantity demanded declines. The elasticity of demand is positive but less than 1 up to income *m*. Beyond income *m*, the income elasticity of demand is negative. Examples of goods in this category include one-speed bicycles, small motorbikes, potatoes, and rice. Low income consumers buy most of these goods. At low-income levels, the demand for such goods increases as income increases. Eventually, income reaches a level (at point *m*) at which consumers replace these goods with superior alternatives. For example, a small car replaces the motorbike, and fruit, vegetables, and meat begin to appear in a diet that was heavy in rice or potatoes.

Goods whose income elasticities of demand are positive are called *normal goods*. Goods whose income elasticities of demand are negative are called *inferior goods*.

Real-World Income Elasticities of Demand

Estimates of income elasticities of demand in the United States are shown in Table 5.5. By using estimates of income elasticity of demand, we can translate projections of average income growth rates into growth rates of demand for particular goods and services. For example, if average incomes grow by 3 percent a year, the demand for gasoline and oil will grow by 4 percent a year (3 percent multiplied by the income elasticity of demand for gasoline and oil, which, as shown in Table 5.5, is 1.36).

Cross Elasticity of Demand

The quantity of any good demanded depends on the prices of its substitutes and complements. The responsiveness of the quantity demanded of a particular good to the prices of its substitutes and complements is measured by cross elasticity of demand, which is represented by η_x. The **cross elasticity of demand** is calculated as the percentage change in the quantity demanded of one good divided by the percentage change in the price of another good (a substitute or a complement). That is,

$$\eta_x = \frac{\text{Percentage change in quantity demanded of one good}}{\text{Percentage change in the price of another good}}.$$

The cross elasticity of demand with respect to the price of a substitute is positive. The cross elasticity of demand with respect to the price of a complement is negative. Figure 5.6 makes it clear why. In part (a), when the price of coal (a substitute for oil) rises, the demand for oil increases. In part (b), when the price of cars (a complement of oil) rises, the demand for oil decreases. The more easily two goods substitute for or complement each other, the larger is the magnitude of their cross elasticity.

Table 5.6 provides a compact summary of all the different kinds of demand elasticities you've just studied.

FIGURE **5.6**

Cross Elasticities: Substitutes and Complements

(a) Substitutes

(b) Complements

Part (a) shows the cross elasticity of demand with respect to the price of a substitute. When the price of coal increases, the quantity of oil demanded also increases. Part (b) shows the cross elasticity of demand with respect to the price of a complement. When the price of cars increases, the quantity of oil demanded decreases.

TABLE **5.6**

A Compact Glossary of Elasticities of Demand

Price elasticities (η)

A relationship is described as:	When η is:	Which means that:
Perfectly elastic or infinitely elastic	**Infinity**	The smallest possible increase (decrease) in price causes an infinitely large decrease (increase) in the quantity demanded
Elastic	**Less than infinity but greater than 1**	The percentage decrease (increase) in the quantity demanded exceeds the percentage increase (decrease) in price
Unit elastic	**1**	The percentage decrease (increase) in the quantity demanded equals the percentage increase (decrease) in price
Inelastic	**Greater than zero but less than 1**	The percentage decrease (increase) in the quantity demanded is less than the percentage increase (decrease) in price
Perfectly inelastic or completely inelastic	**Zero**	The quantity demanded is the same at all prices

Income elasticities (η_y)

A relationship is described as:	When η_y is:	Which means that:
Income elastic (normal good)	**Greater than 1**	The percentage increase (decrease) in the quantity demanded is greater than the percentage increase (decrease) in income
Income inelastic (normal good)	**Less than 1 but greater than zero**	The percentage increase (decrease) in the quantity demanded is less than the percentage increase (decrease) in income
Negative income-elastic (inferior good)	**Less than zero**	When income increases (decreases), quantity demanded decreases (increases)

Cross elasticities (η_x)

A relationship is described as:	When η_x is:	Which means that:
Perfect substitutes	**Infinity**	The smallest possible increase (decrease) in the price of one good causes an infinitely large increase (decrease) in the quantity demanded of the other good
Substitutes	**Positive, less than infinity**	If the price of one good increases (decreases), the quantity demanded of the other good also increases (decreases)
Independent	**Zero**	The quantity demanded of one good remains constant regardless of the price of the other good.
Complements	**Less than zero (negative)**	The quantity demanded of one good decreases (increases) when the price of the other good increases (decreases)

Elasticity in Action

THE WASHINGTON POST, AUGUST 4, 1991

The Owl's Golden Egg

Environmentalism Could Boost Lumber Profits and Prices

BY JOHN M. BERRY

It is sometimes hard to tell the winners and the losers, and why each is winning or losing, in the war over timber cutting on federal land in the Pacific Northwest.

The regional timber industry has sought to portray itself as a clear loser if environmentalists get their way and the timber harvest is sharply curtailed to protect recreational uses, scenic vistas, water quality, fisheries and wildlife such as the officially endangered spotted owl.

Nevertheless, a few weeks ago Mark S. Rogers, a wood industry analyst at Prudential Securities Inc. in New York, declared in a headline on a research paper, "What's Good for the Spotted Owl Is Great for the Wood-Products Industry."

"No tonic could be better for the depressed wood-products industry than a decrease in capacity coinciding with an increase in demand," Rogers wrote. "Thanks to the controversy over the spotted owl, industry capacity is almost certain to be cut just as the housing recovery begins to stimulate demand."

Rogers said the lumber industry has been plagued for more than a decade with too much production capacity, a condition that has kept profits low. Reduced harvests in this region will lead to a cut in industry capacity of 5 percent to 10 percent and a rebound in profits, he predicted.

This follows a decade in which national lumber production surged, rising from 31.8 billion board feet in 1981 to 49 billion board feet in 1989, as construction boomed around the country.

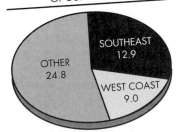

LUMBER PRODUCTION
1990 ESTIMATES, IN BILLIONS OF BOARD FEET

OTHER 24.8

SOUTHEAST 12.9

WEST COAST 9.0

SOURCE: American Forest Council

The Essence
of the Story

The timber industry has experienced a large increase in production during the 1980s, but its profits have been low.

The demand for timber products is predicted to increase, and so are industry profits.

Environmentalists are seeking cuts in timber production in the Pacific Northwest.

Regional timber producers believe that they will lose from these cuts.

A timber industry analyst believes that the industry's profits will increase as a result of lower production in the Northwest.

Figure 1

Figure 2

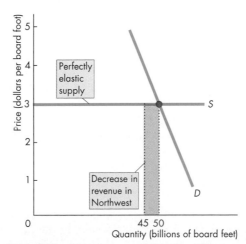

Figure 3

Background
and Analysis

Timber is bought and sold on an unregulated national and international market in which the price is determined by demand and supply as shown in Fig. 1.

Timber has substitutes, but in the short run, none of them are very close and the demand for timber is inelastic.

Because the demand for timber is inelastic, a decrease in supply will increase price and increase industry revenue, as shown in Fig. 2. Mark S. Rogers predicts this outcome as the consequence of cutting Northwest production.

But Northwest timber has perfect substitutes on the production side—timber from the Southeast, other regions, and other parts of the world—and the supply of timber is possibly perfectly elastic.

If the supply of timber is perfectly elastic, a decrease in production in the Northwest will be offset by an increase in production in other places—as shown in Fig. 3. The price of timber will be unchanged by the lower production in the Northwest, and the Northwest producers will lose, as they predict and fear.

Let's now turn our attention to the supply curve and study the elasticity of supply.

Elasticity of Supply

We've seen how the concept of elasticity of demand may be used to determine the extent of a change in the quantity demanded when there is a change in price. As Fig. 5.1 illustrates, such changes result from a change in supply that shifts the supply curve and leads to a movement along a demand curve. There is a change in the quantity demanded but no change in demand.

But suppose we want to predict the effects on price and quantity of a change in demand. A change in demand shifts the demand curve and leads to a movement along the supply curve. To make such a prediction, we need to know how responsive the quantity supplied is to the price of a good. That is, we need to know the elasticity of supply.

The **elasticity of supply** is the percentage change in the quantity supplied of a good divided by the percentage change in its price. It is represented by η_s. That is,

$$\eta_s = \frac{\text{Percentage change in quantity supplied}}{\text{Percentage change in price}}.$$

The supply curves that we have considered in this chapter (and those in Chapter 4) all slope upward. When the price increases, the quantity supplied increases. Upward-sloping supply curves have a positive elasticity.

There are two interesting cases of the elasticity of supply. If the quantity supplied is fixed regardless of the price, the supply curve is vertical. In this case, the elasticity of supply is zero. An increase in price leads to no change in the quantity supplied. Supply is perfectly inelastic. If there is a price below which nothing will be supplied but at which suppliers are willing to sell any quantity demanded, the supply curve is horizontal. In this case, the elasticity of supply is infinite. The small fall in price reduces the quantity supplied from an indefinitely large amount to zero. Supply is perfectly elastic.

The magnitude of the elasticity of supply depends on:

- The technological conditions governing production
- The amount of time elapsed since the price change

Technological Conditions

The importance of technological conditions can be illustrated by considering two extreme examples. Some goods, such as a painting by Georgia O'Keeffe, are unique. There is just one of each of her paintings. Its supply curve is vertical, and its elasticity of supply is zero. At the other extreme, a good such as sand for making silicon chips is available in indefinitely large quantities at a virtually constant cost of production. Its supply curve is horizontal, and its elasticity of supply is infinity. The supply of internationally produced goods to an individual country—even a large country such as the United States—is also highly elastic. An example of such a good is timber, the market for which is featured in Reading Between the Lines on pp. 116–117.

The supply of most goods and services lies between the two extremes. The quantity produced can be increased, but only by incurring a higher cost. If a higher price is offered, the quantity supplied increases. Such goods and services have an elasticity of supply between zero and infinity.

Time Frame for Supply

To study the influence of the length of time elapsed since a price change, we distinguish three time frames for supply:

1. Momentary supply
2. Short-run supply
3. Long-run supply

Momentary Supply   When the price of a good rises or falls in a sudden, unforeseen way, we use the momentary supply curve to describe the initial change in the quantity supplied. The **momentary supply curve** shows the response of the quantity supplied immediately following a price change.

Some goods, such as fruits and vegetables, have a perfectly inelastic momentary supply—which means that the supply curve is vertical. The quantities supplied depend on the crop-planting decisions made earlier. In the case of oranges, for example, planting decisions have to be made many years in advance of the crop being available.

Other goods, an example of which is electric power, have an elastic momentary supply. When we all turn on our TV sets and air conditioners simultaneously, there is a big surge in the demand for electricity and the quantity bought increases, but the price remains constant. Electricity producers usually anticipate fluctuations in demand and bring more generators into operation to ensure that the quantity supplied equals the quantity demanded without raising the price.

Long-Run Supply   The **long-run supply curve** shows the response of the quantity supplied to a change in price after all the technologically possible ways of adjusting supply have been exploited. In the case of oranges, the long run is the time it takes new plantings to grow to full maturity—about 15 years. In some cases, the long-run adjustment occurs only after a completely new production plant has been built and workers have been trained to operate it—typically a process that may take several years.

Short-Run Supply   The **short-run supply curve** shows how the quantity supplied responds to a price change when only *some* of the technologically possible adjustments to production have been made. The first adjustment that is usually made is in the amount of labor employed. To increase output in the short run, firms work their labor force overtime and perhaps hire additional workers. To decrease their output in the short run, firms lay off workers or reduce their hours of work. With the passage of more time, firms can make additional adjustments, perhaps training additional workers or buying additional tools and other equipment. The short-run response to a price change, unlike the momentary and long-run responses, is not a unique response but a sequence of adjustments.

Three Supply Curves   Three supply curves corresponding to the three time frames are illustrated in Fig. 5.7. They are the supply curves in the world market for coal in a year in which the price is $70 a ton and the quantity of coal produced is 3 billion tons. The three supply curves all pass through that point. Momentary supply is perfectly inelastic at 3 billion tons, as shown by the light blue curve labeled *MS*. Long-run supply, as shown by the dark blue curve labeled *LS*, is the most elastic of the three supplies. Short-run supply, as shown by the curve labeled *SS*, lies between the other two. In fact, there is a series of short-run supply curves between the

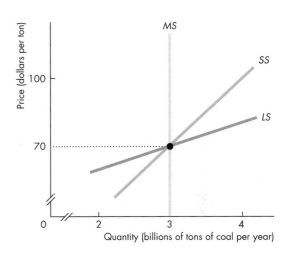

FIGURE 5.7

Supply: Momentary, Short-Run, and Long-Run

The momentary supply curve (*MS*) shows how quantity supplied responds to a price change the moment that it occurs. The very light blue momentary supply curve shown here is perfectly inelastic. The medium blue short-run supply curve (*SS*) shows how the quantity supplied responds to a price change after some adjustments to production have been made. The dark blue long-run supply curve (*LS*) shows how the quantity supplied responds to a price change when all the technologically possible adjustments to the production process have been made.

momentary and long-run curves. Each supply is successively more elastic. As more time elapses following a price change, more changes can be made in the method of production to increase output. The short-run supply curve *SS* shown in Fig. 5.7 is an example of one of these short-run supply curves.

The momentary supply curve (*MS*) is vertical because, at a given moment in time, no matter what the price of coal, producers cannot change their output. They have a certain labor force and a certain amount of coal-mining equipment in place, and there is a given amount of output that can be produced. But as time elapses, coal-producing companies can increase their capacity. They can hire and train more miners and buy more equipment. In the long run, they can sink new mines, discover more accessible coal deposits, and increase the quantity supplied even more in response to a given price rise.

◆ ◆ ◆ ◆ You have now studied the theory of demand and supply, and you have learned how to measure the responsiveness of the quantities demanded to changes in prices and income. You have also learned how to measure the responsiveness of the quantity supplied to a change in the price. In the next chapters we are going to use what we have learned about demand, supply, and elasticity to study the ways in which some real-world markets work—markets in action.

S U M M A R Y

Elasticity of Demand

Elasticity of demand is a measure of the responsiveness of the quantity demanded of a good to a change in its price. It enables us to calculate the effect of a change in supply on price, quantity bought, and revenue. Elasticity of demand (η) is the absolute value of the percentage change in the quantity demanded divided by the percentage change in price.

The larger the elasticity, the greater is the responsiveness of the quantity demanded to a given change in price. When the percentage change in the quantity demanded is smaller than the percentage change in price, elasticity is between zero and 1 and demand is inelastic. When the percentage change in the quantity demanded equals the percentage change in price, elasticity is 1 and demand is unit elastic. When the percentage change in the quantity demanded is larger than the percentage change in price, elasticity is greater than 1 and demand is elastic.

Along a straight-line demand curve, elasticity declines as the price falls and the quantity demanded increases.

The size of the elasticity depends on how easily one good may serve as a substitute for another, on the proportion of income spent on the good, and on the time that has elapsed since the price change.

We use two time frames to analyze demand: short-run and long-run. Short-run demand describes the initial response of buyers to a price change. Long-run demand describes the response of buyers to a price change after all possible adjustments have been made. Short-run demand is usually less elastic than long-run demand. (pp. 103–111)

Elasticity, Revenue, and Expenditure

If the elasticity of demand is less than 1, a decrease in supply leads to an increase in revenue—the percentage increase in price is greater than the percentage decrease in the quantity bought. If the elasticity of demand is greater than 1, a decrease in supply leads to a decrease in revenue—the percentage increase in price is less than the percentage decrease in the quantity bought. (pp. 111–112)

More Demand Elasticities

Income elasticity of demand measures the responsiveness of demand to a change in income. Income elasticity of demand is calculated as the percentage change in the quantity bought divided by the percentage change in income. The larger the income elasticity of demand, the greater is the responsiveness of the quantity bought to a given change in income. When income elasticity is between zero and 1, demand is income inelastic. In this case, as income increases, the quantity bought increases but the percentage of income spent on a good decreases. When income elasticity is greater than 1, demand is income elastic. In this case, as income increases, the quantity bought increases and the percentage of income spent on the good also increases. When income elasticity is less than zero, demand is negative income-elastic. In this case, as income increases, the quantity bought decreases. Income elasticities are greater than 1 for items that are typically consumed by the rich; they are positive but less than 1 for more basic consumption items. Income elasticities are less than zero for inferior goods—goods that are consumed only at low incomes and that disappear as budgets increase.

Cross elasticity of demand measures the responsiveness of demand for one good to a change in the price of another good (a substitute or a complement). Cross elasticity of demand is calculated as the percentage change in the quantity demanded of one good divided by the percentage change in the price of another good. The cross elasticity of demand with respect to the price of a substitute is positive. The cross elasticity of demand with respect to the price of a complement is negative. (pp. 112–118)

Elasticity of Supply

The elasticity of supply measures the responsiveness of the quantity supplied to a change in price. Elasticity of supply is calculated as the percentage change in the quantity supplied of a good divided by the percentage change in its price. Supply elasticities are usually positive but range between zero (vertical supply curve) and infinity (horizontal supply curve).

We classify supply according to three different time frames: momentary, long-run, and short-run.

Momentary supply refers to the response of suppliers to a price change at the instant that it happens. Long-run supply refers to the response of suppliers to a price change when all the technologically feasible adjustments in production have been made. Short-run supply refers to the response of suppliers to a price change after some adjustments in production have been made. For many goods, momentary supply is perfectly inelastic. Supply becomes more elastic as suppliers have more time to respond to price changes. (pp. 118–119)

KEY ELEMENTS

Key Terms

Cross elasticity of demand, 114
Elastic demand, 106
Elasticity of demand, 105
Elasticity of supply, 118
Income elasticity of demand, 112
Inelastic demand, 106
Long-run demand curve, 110
Long-run supply curve, 119
Momentary supply curve, 118
Perfectly elastic demand, 106
Perfectly inelastic demand, 106
Price elasticity of demand, 104
Short-run demand curve, 110
Short-run supply curve, 118
Unit elastic demand, 106

Key Figures and Tables

Figure 5.2   Calculating the Elasticity of Demand, 104
Figure 5.3   Elasticity along a Straight-Line Demand Curve, 107
Figure 5.4   Demand Curves with Constant Elasticity, 108
Figure 5.5   Income Elasticity of Demand, 113
Table 5.1   Calculating the Elasticity of Demand, 105
Table 5.6   A Compact Glossary of Elasticities of Demand, 115

REVIEW QUESTIONS

1 Define the price elasticity of demand.

2 Why is elasticity a more useful measure of responsiveness than slope?

3 Draw a graph of, or describe the shape of, a demand curve that along its whole length has an elasticity of:

a   Infinity
b   Zero
c   Unity

4 What three factors determine the size of the elasticity of demand?

5 What do we mean by short-run demand and long-run demand?

6 Explain why the short-run demand curve is usually less elastic than the long-run demand curve.

7 What is the connection between elasticity and revenue? If the elasticity of demand is 1, by how much does a 10 percent price increase change revenue?

8 Define the income elasticity of demand.

9 Give an example of a good whose income elasticity is

a   Greater than 1
b   Positive but less than 1
c   Less than zero

10 Define the cross elasticity of demand. Is the cross elasticity of demand positive or negative?

11 Define the elasticity of supply. Is the elasticity of supply positive or negative?

12 Give an example of a good whose elasticity of supply is

a   Zero
b   Greater than zero but less than infinity
c   Infinity

13 What do we mean by momentary, short-run, and long-run supply?

14 Why is momentary supply perfectly inelastic for many goods?

15 Why is long-run supply more elastic than short-run supply?

P R O B L E M S

1 The demand schedule for videotape rentals is

Price (dollars per videotape)	Quantity demanded (videotapes per day)
0	150
1	125
2	100
3	75
4	50
5	25
6	0

a   At what price is the elasticity of demand equal to:
  (1) 1
  (2) Infinity
  (3) Zero
b   What price brings in the most revenue per day?
c   Calculate the elasticity of demand for a rise in price from $4 to $5.

2 Assume that the demand for videotape rentals in problem 1 increases by 10 percent at each price.
a   Draw the old and new demand curves.
b   Calculate the elasticity of demand for a rise in the rental price from $4 to $5. Compare your answer with that of problem 1(c).

3 Which item in each of the following pairs has the larger price elasticity of demand?
a   *People* magazine or all magazines
b   Vacations in Florida or vacations in North America
c   Broccoli or vegetables

4 You have been hired as an economic consultant by OPEC and given the following schedule showing the world demand for oil:

Price (dollars per barrel)	Quantity demanded (millions of barrels per day)
10	60,000
20	50,000
30	40,000
40	30,000
50	20,000

Your advice is needed on the following questions:

a   If the supply of oil is cut back so that the price rises from $20 to $30 a barrel, will the revenue from oil sales increase or decrease?
b   What will happen to revenue if the supply of oil is cut back further and the price rises to $40 a barrel?
c   What is the price that will achieve the highest revenue?
d   What quantity of oil will be sold at the price that answers part (c)?
e   What are the values of the price elasticity of demand for price changes of $10 a barrel at average prices of $15, $25, $35, and $45 a barrel?
f   What is the elasticity of demand at the price that maximizes revenue?
g   Over what price range is the demand of oil inelastic?

5 State the sign (positive or negative) and, where possible, the range (less than 1, 1, greater than 1) of the following elasticities:

a The elasticity of demand for ice cream at the point of maximum revenue

b The cross elasticity of demand for ice cream with respect to the price of frozen yogurt

c The income elasticity of demand for Caribbean cruises

d The income elasticity of demand for toothpaste

e The elasticity of supply of Irish salmon

f The cross elasticity of demand for corn ready to be popped with respect to the price of popcorn machines

6 The following table gives some data on the demand for chocolate chip cookies:

Price (cents per cookie)	Quantity demanded (thousands per day)	
	Short-run	Long-run
10	700	1,000
20	500	500
30	300	0

At a price of 20¢ a cookie:

a Calculate the elasticity of short-run demand.

b Calculate the elasticity of long-run demand.

c Is the demand for cookies more elastic in the short run or the long run?

7 The following table gives some data on the supply of chocolate chip cookies:

Price (cents per cookie)	Quantity supplied (thousands per day)		
	Momentary	Short-run	Long-run
10	500	300	0
20	500	500	500
30	500	700	1,000

At a price of 20¢ a cookie, calculate the elasticity of:

a Momentary supply

b Short-run supply

c Long-run supply

8 In problem 7, which supply is most elastic and which is most inelastic? Compare the elasticities of supply when the average price of a cookie is 15¢. Compare them when the average price of a cookie is 25¢.

CHAPTER 6

MARKETS IN ACTION

After studying this chapter, you will be able to:

- Explain the short-run and long-run effects of a change in supply on price and the quantity bought and sold

- Explain the short-run and long-run effects of a change in demand on price and the quantity bought and sold

- Explain the effects of price controls

- Explain why price controls can lead to black markets

- Explain how sales taxes affect prices

- Explain how the prohibition of a good affects its price and quantity consumed

- Explain why farm prices and revenues fluctuate

- Explain how inventories and speculation limit price fluctuations

N 1906, SAN FRANCISCO SUFFERED A DEVASTATING earthquake that destroyed countless buildings but killed very few people. The population somehow had to fit into a vastly smaller number of houses and apartments. How did the San Francisco housing market cope? What happened to rents and to the quantity of housing services available? Did rents have to be controlled to keep housing affordable? ◆ ◆ Robots now make cars, and people build and maintain the robots—increasing our productivity. But the tasks performed by the least skilled workers are the ones mechanized, so technological change brings a decrease in the demand for unskilled workers. And ever more sophisticated equipment needs ever more sophisticated management and maintenance and brings a steady increase in the demand for skilled workers. How do labor markets cope with these changes in the demand for labor?

Turbulent Times

Does falling demand lower the wages of the unskilled? Can minimum wage laws help the unskilled? ◆ ◆ Most things we buy are taxed. And if President Clinton's plan to reduce the federal deficit succeeds, more taxes will be introduced. How do taxes affect the prices and quantities of the things we buy? Do buyers pay the full amount of the tax? ◆ ◆ Trading in some goods—such as drugs and human organs—is prohibited. How does the prohibition of trade affect the amounts of prohibited goods consumed? How does it affect the prices paid by those who trade illegally? ◆ ◆ Grain yields in 1991 were high, but those in 1988 were extremely low because crops were devastated by drought. How do farm prices and revenues react to such output fluctuations? How do the actions of speculators influence farm revenues?

◆ ◆ ◆ ◆ In this chapter, we use the theory of demand and supply (of Chapter 4) and the concept of elasticity (of Chapter 5) to answer questions such as those that we have just posed. Let's begin by studying how a market responds to a severe supply shock.

Housing Markets and Rent Ceilings

To see how an unregulated market copes with a massive supply shock, let's transport ourselves to the city of San Francisco in April 1906, as the city is facing the effects of its massive earthquake and fire. You can sense the enormity of San Francisco's problems by reading some headlines from the *New York Times* about the first days of the crisis. On April 19, 1906:

Over 500 Dead, $200,000,000 Lost in San Francisco Earthquake
Nearly Half the City Is in Ruins and 50,000 Are Homeless

On April 20, 1906:

Army of Homeless Fleeing from Devastated City 200,000 Without Shelter and Facing Famine

And again on April 21, 1906:

San Francisco's New Peril; Gale Drives Fire Ferryward
Fighting Famine and Disease Among the 200,000 Refugees
San Francisco Multitudes Camped Out Shelterless and in Want

The commander of federal troops in charge of the emergency described the magnitude of the problem:

> Not a hotel of note or importance was left standing. The great apartment houses had vanished . . . two hundred and twenty-five thousand people were . . . homeless.[1]

Almost overnight, more than half the people in a city of 400,000 had lost their homes. Temporary shelters and camps alleviated some of the problem, but it was also necessary to utilize the apartment buildings and houses left standing. As a consequence, they had to accommodate 40 percent more people than they had before the earthquake.

The *San Francisco Chronicle* was not published for more than a month after the earthquake. When the newspaper reappeared on May 24, 1906, the city's housing shortage—what would seem like a major news item that would still be of grave importance—was not mentioned. Milton Friedman and George Stigler describe the situation:

> *There is not a single mention of a housing shortage!* The classified advertisements listed sixty-four offers of flats and houses for rent, and nineteen of houses for sale, against five advertisements of flats or houses wanted. Then and thereafter a considerable number of all types of accommodation except hotel rooms were offered for rent.[2]

How did San Francisco cope with such a devastating reduction in the supply of housing?

The Market Response to an Earthquake

We can work out how the unregulated San Francisco housing market responded to the earthquake of 1906 by using the theory of demand and supply that we studied in Chapters 4 and 5. Figure 6.1 analyzes this market. Part (a) shows the situation before the earthquake and parts (b) and (c), after the earthquake. The horizontal axis of each part measures the quantity of housing units, and the vertical axis measures the monthly rent of a unit of housing.

Look first at the situation before the earthquake (part a). The demand curve for housing is *D*. There are two supply curves: the short-run supply curve, which is labeled *SS*, and the long-run supply curve, which is labeled *LS*. The short-run supply curve shows how the quantity of housing supplied varies as the price (rent) varies, while the number of houses and apartment buildings remains constant. This supply response arises from a variation in the intensity with which existing buildings are used. The quantity

---

[1]Reported in Milton Friedman and George J. Stigler, "Roofs or Ceilings? The Current Housing Problem," in *Popular Essays on Current Problems,* vol. 1, no. 2 (New York: Foundation for Economic Education, 1946), 3–15.

[2]Ibid., 3.

FIGURE **6.1**

The San Francisco Housing Market in 1906

(a) Before earthquake

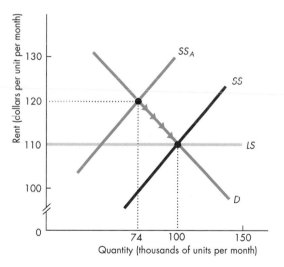

(c) Long-run adjustment

Before the earthquake, the San Francisco housing market is in equilibrium; 100,000 housing units are traded each month at an average rent of $110 a month. This equilibrium is at the intersection of demand curve *D*, short-run supply curve *SS*, and long-run supply curve *LS* (part a). After the earthquake, the short-run supply curve shifts from *SS* to *SS_A* (part b). The equilibrium rent rises to $120 a month and the number of housing units available falls to 74,000 a month. The rent rises because only 44,000 units of housing will be supplied at the old rent of $110 a month, and the price that demanders will willingly pay for the 44 thousandth unit is $130 a month. With rents at $120 a month, there is profit in building new apartments and houses. As the building program proceeds, the short-run supply curve shifts to the right. As it does so (part c), rents gradually fall back to $110 a month and the number of housing units available increases gradually to 100,000. Note that we use a special arrowed line to indicate such gradual movements along a curve.

of housing supplied increases as families rent out rooms or parts of their houses and apartments to others, and the quantity supplied decreases as families occupy a larger number of the rooms that are under their control.

The long-run supply curve shows how the quantity supplied varies after enough time has elapsed for new apartment buildings and houses to be erected or existing buildings to be destroyed. The long-run supply curve is shown as being perfectly elastic. We do not actually know that the long-run supply curve is perfectly elastic, but it is a reasonable assumption. It implies that the cost of building an apartment is pretty much the same regardless of whether there are 50,000, 100,000, or 150,000 apartments in existence.

The equilibrium price and quantity traded are determined at the point of intersection of the short-run supply curve and the demand curve. Before the earthquake, that equilibrium rent is $110 a month, and the quantity of housing units traded is 100,000 as shown in Fig. 6.1(a). In addition (for simplicity), the housing market is on its long-run supply curve, *LS*. Let's now look at the situation immediately after the earthquake.

After the Earthquake

After the earthquake and the subsequent fires, housing for 56 percent of the population is destroyed. Figure 6.1(b) reflects the new situation by shifting the short-run supply curve *SS* to the left by 56,000 units to become the short-run supply curve *SS*$_A$ (*A* for after the earthquake). If people use the remaining housing units with the same intensity as before the earthquake and if the rent remains at $110 a month, only 44,000 units of housing are available.

But rents do not remain at $110. With only 44,000 units of housing available, the maximum rent that will willingly be paid for the last available apartment is $130 a month. Since people value the available housing more highly than the long-run price of $110 a month, they offer to pay higher rents. At higher rents, people with accommodations economize on their use of space and make their spare rooms, attics, and basements available to others. Thus the quantity of housing units offered increases. The market achieves a new, short-run equilibrium at a rent of $120 a month, where 74,000 units of housing are available. In this new short-run equilibrium, approximately 20 percent of the population has left the city and a further 6 percent has been housed in temporary camps.[3]

You've now seen how the housing market reacts, almost overnight, to a devastating shock. When supply decreases, the intersection point of the new short-run supply curve and the demand curve determines the price and the quantity bought and sold. The price rises; people who are willing to pay the higher price find housing, and those who have housing are willing to economize on its use. People who are unwilling or unable to pay the higher rents either leave the city or are housed in temporary shelters.

[3]Ibid., 3.

Long-Run Adjustments

The new equilibrium depicted in Fig. 6.1(b) is not the end of the story. The long-run supply curve tells us that with sufficient time for new apartment buildings and houses to be constructed, housing will be supplied at a rent of $110 a month. Since the current rent of $120 a month is higher than the long-run supply price of housing, there will be a rush to build and supply new apartments and houses. As time passes, more apartments and houses are built, and the short-run supply curve starts moving back gradually to the right.

Figure 6.1(c) illustrates the long-run adjustment. As the short-run supply curve shifts back to the right, it intersects the demand curve at lower rents and higher quantities. The market follows the arrows down the demand curve. The process ends when there is no further profit in building new housing units. Such a situation occurs at the original rent of $110 a month and the original quantity of 100,000 units of housing.

REVIEW

An earthquake reduces the short-run supply, raising rents and lowering the quantity traded. Higher rents immediately bring forth an increase in the quantity of housing supplied as people economize on their own use of space and make rooms available for rent to others. High rents also lead to increased building activity, which causes the short-run supply curve to shift gradually back to the right. As this process continues, the price of housing falls and the quantity rises. The original (pre-earthquake) equilibrium eventually is restored (because nothing has happened in the meantime to shift the long-run supply curve or the demand curve). ◆

A Regulated Housing Market

We've just seen how the housing market of San Francisco coped with a massive supply shock. One of the things that happened was that rents increased sharply. Let's now suppose that the San Francisco city government imposed a rent ceiling. A **rent ceiling** is a regulation making it illegal to charge a rent higher than a specified level. What would have happened if a rent ceiling of $110 a month—the rent before the earthquake—had been imposed? This question is answered in Fig. 6.2.

First, let's work out what will happen to the quantities supplied and demanded. The quantity supplied at the controlled rent of $110 a month is 44,000 units. The quantity demanded at that rent is 100,000 units. When the quantity demanded exceeds the quantity supplied, what determines the quantity actually bought and sold? The answer is the smaller of the quantities demanded and supplied. At a monthly rent of $110, the suppliers of housing want to supply only 44,000 units. They cannot be forced to supply more. The demanders would like to rent 100,000 units at that price, but they cannot do so. The difference between the quantity demanded and the quantity supplied is called the excess quantity demanded.

When a rent ceiling of $110 a month is imposed, the quantity of housing available falls to 44,000 units, but the quantity demanded remains constant at 100,000 units. There is an excess demand of 56,000 units. Is that the end of the story? Is this situation an equilibrium? To answer this question, we need to explore a bit more closely what the demanders are doing.

If the rent really is $110 a month, a lot of people who would like to rent more housing will not be able to do so. Moreover, some people would be willing to pay much more than $110 a month to get an apartment. To understand why, recall that there are two ways of interpreting a demand curve. One interpretation is that the curve tells us the quantities demanded at each price. But the demand curve also tells us the highest price that demanders will pay for the last unit available. What is the highest price that people will pay for the last apartment available? The answer, which can be read from the demand curve, is $130 a month. Since the people who are not able to find housing are willing to pay more than the rent ceiling, the situation that we have just described is not an equilibrium. Two mechanisms come into play in an unbalanced situation such as this one to achieve equilibrium. They are search activity and black markets.

Search Activity

Even when the quantity demanded exceeds the quantity supplied, some suppliers have goods available. But many are sold out. In these circumstances, buyers spend time looking for a supplier with whom they can do business. The time and effort spent in searching for someone with whom to do business is called **search activity**. Even in markets in which prices are permitted to fluctuate to bring equality between the quantities demanded and supplied, search activity takes place. But when price is regulated, search activity increases.

The time spent searching for available supplies imposes costs on buyers. Adjustments in the time spent searching bring about an equilibrium. You can see why by thinking about the total amount that the demanders are willing to pay for the last unit of housing available. With only 44,000 housing units available, demanders are willing to pay $130 a month. But the rent is restricted to $110. How does the buyer spend another $20? The answer is by

FIGURE 6.2

A Rent Ceiling

If there had been a rent ceiling of $110 a month after the earthquake, the quantity of housing supplied would have been stuck at 44,000 units. People would willingly pay $130 a month for the 44 thousandth unit. The difference between the rent ceiling and the maximum price that will willingly be paid is the value of the time used up in searching for an available apartment. The individuals doing the searching are those with the lowest opportunity cost of time. Those whose value of time is high avoid search costs by buying on an illegal black market.

using $20 worth of time in the business of searching for an available apartment. That is, the total cost of housing—the price actually paid for housing obtained—is equal to the rent paid to the owner plus the opportunity cost of time spent searching for the available supply.

Black Markets

Opportunity cost (the value of the best opportunity forgone) enables us to predict *who* will search for available housing. Some people earn high wages, and others earn low wages. If it takes one hour to find an apartment, the total price paid is higher for a high-wage earner than for a low-wage earner. Therefore the lowest-paid people will be those who devote the most time to searching out available supplies. High-wage earners will devote time to search activity only if they place a much higher value on the good than do low-wage earners.

A person with a high opportunity cost of time has another way of obtaining a good—buying it from someone whose opportunity cost of time is lower. The person with a low wage can devote time to searching out the available supplies and then resell to someone whose opportunity cost of searching is higher. Buying goods in this way is illegal and creates what is known as a black market. A **black market** is an illegal trading arrangement in which buyers and sellers do business at a price that is higher than the legally imposed price ceiling. The functioning of a black market depends on how tightly the government polices its price regulations, on the chances of being caught violating them, and on the scale of the penalties imposed for violations.

At one extreme, the chance of being caught violating a rent ceiling is small. In this case, the black market will function similarly to an unregulated market, and the black market rent and quantity bought and sold will be close to the unregulated equilibrium. At the other extreme, policing is highly effective and large penalties are imposed on violators. In this case, the rent ceiling will restrict the quantity bought and sold to 44,000 units. The small number of black marketeers operating in the market will buy at the controlled rent of $110 a month and sell at $130 a month. The government will constantly try to detect and punish such people. The equilibrium in the black market will be such that anyone

can obtain an apartment for $130 a month, and the profit for the black marketeer is just sufficient compensation for the risk of being caught and punished.

There are many examples of markets other than housing markets that are regulated in some way and in which economic forces result in black market trading. The best recent examples were in Russia and the other Eastern European countries before the collapse of central planning.

We've just looked at what would have happened in a hypothetical situation if there had been rent ceilings after the San Francisco earthquake. But San Francisco actually did have rent ceilings 45 years later—after World War II—so we can see how rent ceilings operated in practice. Let's take a look at that episode in the history of the San Francisco housing market.

Rent Ceilings in Practice

By 1940, the population of San Francisco had increased to 635,000. At that time, only 93 percent of the city's houses and apartments were occupied. The situation stayed much the same throughout World War II. Then, after the war, the population increased by 30 percent, but the number of houses and apartments increased by only 20 percent. As a result, each dwelling unit had to house 10 percent more people in 1946 than one year earlier. The housing problems that San Francisco suffered in 1946 were only a quarter of the magnitude of the problems that followed the earthquake in 1906. Yet the 1946 housing shortage was a major political problem:

> On January 8 [1946] the California State Legislature was convened, and the Governor listed the housing shortage as "the most critical problem facing California." During the first five days of the year there were altogether only four advertisements offering houses or apartments for rent . . . [and] . . . there were thirty advertisements per day by persons wanting to rent houses or apartments.[4]

The key difference between San Francisco in 1906 and in 1946 was the way in which scarce

---
[4]Ibid., 4.

housing was rationed. In 1906, the scarce housing was allocated by an unregulated market. Rent increases achieved an equilibrium between the quantity of housing supplied and the quantity demanded and resulted in a steady increase in the quantity of housing available. In 1946, rent ceilings were in place. Scarce housing was allocated by people devoting time and effort to searching out and advertising for available houses and apartments. The actual cost of housing—taking account of the frustration and effort involved in finding accommodation—exceeded the controlled rent level and even exceeded the rents that would have prevailed in an unregulated market.

We've now studied the way in which a market responds, in both the short run and the long run, to a change in supply and how a regulated market would work in the face of such a supply shock. Let's now study how a market responds, in both the short run and the long run, to a change in demand. We'll study how an unregulated market handles such a shock and the effects of government intervention to limit price movements.

The Labor Market and Minimum Wage Regulation

Labor-saving technology is constantly being invented, and as a result, the demand for certain types of labor, usually the least skilled types, is constantly decreasing. How does the labor market cope with this continuous decrease in the demand for unskilled labor? Doesn't it mean that the wages of the unskilled will constantly be falling? To study this question, let's examine the market for unskilled labor.

Figure 6.3(a) shows this market. The quantity of labor (millions of hours per year) is measured on the horizontal axis and the wage rate (dollars per hour) on the vertical axis. The demand curve for unskilled labor is D. There are two supply curves for unskilled labor: the upward-sloping short-run supply curve SS and the horizontal long-run supply curve LS.

The short-run supply curve shows how the hours of labor supplied by a given number of workers vary as the wage rate varies. To get workers to work longer hours, firms have to offer higher wages, so the short-run supply curve is upward sloping.

The long-run supply curve shows the relationship between the quantity of labor supplied and the wage rate after enough time has passed for people to have acquired new skills and moved to new types of jobs. The number of people in the unskilled labor market depends on the wage in this market compared with other opportunities. If the wage is high enough, people will enter this market. If the wage is too low, people will leave it and seek training to enter the skilled labor market. Because people can freely enter and leave the unskilled labor market, the long-run supply curve is highly elastic. Here (for simplicity) it is assumed to be perfectly elastic (horizontal).

The labor market is initially in equilibrium at a wage rate of $4 an hour and with 30 million hours of labor being supplied. We're now going to analyze what happens in the labor market if the demand for this particular type of labor falls as a result of the invention of some labor-saving technology. Figure 6.3(b) shows the short-run effects of such a change. The demand curve before the new technology is introduced is D. After the introduction of the new technology, the demand curve shifts to the left, to D_A. The wage rate falls to $3 an hour and the quantity of labor employed falls to 20 million hours. This short-run effect on wages and employment is not the end of the story.

People who are now earning only $3 an hour look around for other opportunities. They see, for example, that the new labor-saving equipment doesn't always work properly, and when it breaks down, it is maintained by more highly paid, highly skilled workers. There are many other jobs (in markets for other types of skills) paying higher wages than $3 an hour. One by one, workers decide to quit this particular market for unskilled labor. They go back to school, or they take jobs that pay less but offer on-the-job training. As a result of these decisions, the short-run supply curve begins to shift to the left.

Figure 6.3(c) shows the long-run adjustment. As the short-run supply curve shifts to the left, it intersects the demand curve D_A at higher wage rates and lower levels of employment. In the long run, the

FIGURE **6.3**

A Market for Unskilled Labor

(a) Before invention

(b) After invention

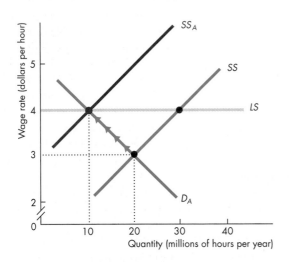

(c) Long-run adjustment

A market for unskilled labor is in equilibrium (part a) at a wage rate of $3 an hour with 30 million hours of labor a year being traded. The short-run supply curve (SS) slopes upward because employers have to pay a higher wage to get more hours out of a given number of workers. The long-run supply curve (LS) is perfectly elastic because workers will eventually enter this labor market if the wage rate is above $3 an hour or leave it if the wage rate is below $3 an hour. The invention of a labor-saving machine shifts the demand curve from D to D_A (part b). The wage rate falls to $2 an hour, and employment falls to 20 million hours a year. With the lower wage, workers begin to leave this market to undertake training for other types of work. As they do so, the short-run supply curve shifts to SS_A (part c). As the supply curve shifts, the wage rate gradually increases, and the employment level decreases. Ultimately, wages return to $3 an hour, and employment falls to 10 million hours a year.

short-run supply curve will have shifted all the way to SS_A. At this point, the wage has returned to $4 an hour, and the level of employment has fallen to 10 million hours.

Sometimes, the adjustment process that we have just described will take place quickly. At other times, it will be a long drawn-out affair. If the adjustment process is long and drawn out and wages remain low for a prolonged period, there will be a temptation on the part of government to intervene in the market, setting a minimum wage to protect the incomes of the lowest-paid workers. What are the effects of imposing a minimum wage?

The Minimum Wage

Suppose that when the demand for labor decreases from D to D_A, as illustrated in Fig. 6.3(b), and the wage falls to $3 an hour, the government passes a minimum wage law. A **minimum wage law** is a regulation that makes trading labor below a specified wage illegal. In particular, suppose that the government declares that the minimum wage is $4 an hour. What are the effects of this law? The answer can be found by studying Fig. 6.4. In that figure, the minimum wage is shown as the horizontal red line labeled "Minimum wage." At the minimum wage, only 10 million hours of labor are demanded (point *a*). But 30 million hours of labor are available at that wage (point *b*). Because the number of hours demanded is less than the number of hours supplied, 20 million hours of available labor go unemployed.

What are the workers doing with their unemployed hours? They are looking for work. It pays to spend a lot of time searching for work. With only 10 million hours of labor being employed, there are many people willing to supply their labor for wages

much lower than the minimum wage. In fact, the 10 millionth hour of labor will be supplied for as little as $2.

How do we know that there are people willing to work for as little as $2 an hour? Look again at Fig. 6.4. As you can see, when only 10 million hours of work are available, the lowest wage at which workers will supply that 10 millionth hour—read off from the supply curve—is $2. Someone who manages to find a job will earn $4 an hour—$2 an hour more than the lowest wage at which someone is willing to work. It pays the unemployed, therefore, to spend a considerable amount of time and effort looking for work. Even though only 10 million hours of labor actually find employment, each person will spend time and effort searching for one of the scarce jobs.

The severity of the unemployment generated by a minimum wage depends on the demand for and supply of labor. You can see that if the supply curve were farther to the left, unemployment would be less. In fact, if the supply curve cut the demand curve at point *a*, the minimum wage would be the same as the unregulated wage. In such a situation, there would be no unemployment. Also, the farther to the right the demand for labor, the smaller is the amount of unemployment. If the demand curve cut the supply curve at point *b*, then, again, the minimum wage would be the same as the unregulated wage, and there would be no unemployment.

The Minimum Wage in Reality

The **Fair Labor Standards Act** makes it illegal to hire an adult worker for less than $4.25 an hour. Economists are not in agreement on the effects of the minimum wage or on how much unemployment it causes. However, they do agree that minimum wages bite hardest on the unskilled. Since there is a preponderance of unskilled workers among the young—the young have had less opportunity to obtain work experience and acquire skills—we would expect the minimum wage to cause more unemployment among young workers than among older workers. That is exactly what happens. The unemployment rate for teenagers is more than twice the average. Although many factors other than the minimum wage influence unemployment among young people, it is almost certain that part of the higher unemployment among the young arises from the impact of minimum wage laws.

FIGURE 6.4

The Minimum Wage and Unemployment

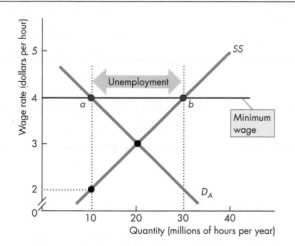

The demand curve for labor is D_A and the supply curve is *SS*. In an unregulated market, the wage rate is $3 an hour and 20 million hours of labor a year are employed. If a minimum wage of $4 an hour is imposed, only 10 million hours of labor are hired, but 30 million hours are available. This results in unemployment—*ab*—of 20 million hours of labor a year. With only 10 million hours of labor being demanded, workers will willingly supply that ten millionth hour for $2. It will pay such suppliers to spend the difference between the minimum wage and the wage for which they are willing to work—$2 an hour—in time and effort looking for a job.

REVIEW

G overnments intend minimum wages to protect the incomes of the lowest paid. But a minimum wage lowers the quantity of labor demanded and hired. Some people will want to work, but they will be unemployed and will spend time searching for work. The young and the unskilled are hit hardest by the minimum wage. ◆

We've now seen how price ceilings and minimum wages affect prices and the quantities produced and consumed. Taxes are another important influence on markets. Let's look at their effects.

Taxes

O ne reason the demand and supply model was developed in the nineteenth century was to enable predictions to be made about the effects of taxes on prices and on the quantities produced and consumed. (See Our Advancing Knowledge, pp. 136–137.) Here, we'll look at the effects of sales taxes.

Do the prices of the goods and services that you buy increase by the full amount of a sales tax? Sales tax is added to the price of a good or service when you pay for it at the cash register, so isn't it obvious that *you* pay the entire tax? Isn't the price higher than it otherwise would be by an amount equal to the tax? It can be, but usually it isn't. And it is even possible that you, the consumer, actually pay none of the sales tax, forcing the seller to pay it for you. Let's see how we can make sense of these apparently absurd statements.

Who Pays a Sales Tax?

To study the effect of a sales tax, we need to start by looking at a market in which there is no such tax. We'll then introduce a sales tax and see the changes it brings.

The market for CD players is shown in Fig. 6.5. The demand curve is *D*, and the supply curve is *S*.

FIGURE 6.5

A Sales Tax

The demand curve for CD players is *D* and the supply curve is *S*. With no taxes, the price is $100 per player and 5,000 players a week are bought and sold. Imposing a sales tax increases the minimum price that sellers are willing to accept. The curve *S + tax* shows the terms on which sellers will make CD players available. The vertical distance between the supply curve *S* and the new supply curve *S + tax* equals the tax—$10 a player. The new equilibrium is at a price of $105 with 4,000 CD players a week bought and sold. The sales tax increases the price by less than the tax, decreases the price received by the supplier, and decreases the quantity bought and sold. It brings in revenue to the government equal to the blue area.

With no sales tax, the equilibrium occurs at a price of $100 per player and 5,000 players a week bought and sold.

A sales tax of $10 a player is now imposed. When a CD player is sold, the $10 tax must be added to its price. Does the price increase by $10 from $100 to $110? It doesn't, because at a price of $110 the quantity of CD players demanded decreases to 3,000 a week, a quantity smaller than that supplied.

When a sales tax is imposed on a good, it is offered for sale at a higher price than in a no-tax situation. To determine that higher price, we must add the tax to the minimum price that suppliers are willing to accept for each quantity sold. To do this, we construct the new curve $S + tax$. The vertical distance between the supply curve S and the curve $S + tax$ equals the tax. The curve $S + tax$ describes the terms on which the good is available to buyers. A new equilibrium is determined where this new supply curve intersects the demand curve. This equilibrium is at a price of $105 and a quantity of 4,000 CD players a week.

The $10 sales tax has increased the price paid by the consumer by less than $10 and has decreased the price received by the supplier. The $10 tax paid is made up of the higher price to the buyer and the lower price to the seller.

The tax brings in tax revenue to the government equal to the tax per item multiplied by the items sold. It is illustrated by the blue area in the figure. The $10 tax on CD players brings in a tax revenue of $40,000 a week.

In this example, the buyer and the seller split the tax equally; the buyer pays $5 a player, and so does the seller. This equal sharing of the tax is a special case and does not usually occur. But some split of the tax between the buyer and seller is usual. And cases in which either the buyer or the seller pays the entire tax can occur. Let's look at these.

Tax Division and Elasticity of Supply

The division of the burden of a tax between buyers and sellers depends, in part, on the elasticity of supply. There are two extreme cases:

◆ Perfectly inelastic supply—seller pays
◆ Perfectly elastic supply—buyer pays

Perfectly Inelastic Supply Figure 6.6(a) shows the market for water from a mineral spring that flows at

---

FIGURE **6.6**

Sales Tax and the Elasticity of Supply

(a) Inelastic supply

(b) Elastic supply

Part (a) shows the market for water from a mineral spring. Supply is perfectly inelastic and the supply curve is S_I. The demand curve is D. With no tax, the price is 50¢ a bottle. A sales tax of 5¢ decreases the price received by sellers, but the price remains at 50¢ a bottle and the number of bottles bought remains the same. Suppliers pay the entire tax.

Part (b) shows the market for sand from which silicon is extracted.

Supply is perfectly elastic at a price of 10¢ a pound. The supply curve is S_E and the demand curve is D. With no tax, the price is 10¢ a pound and 5,000 pounds a week are bought. A sales tax of 1¢ a pound increases the minimum price at which sellers are willing to supply to 11¢ a pound. The supply curve shifts to $S_E + tax$. The price increases to 11¢ a pound, the quantity decreases to 3,000 pounds a week, and buyers pay the entire tax.

WHO Pays the TAXES?

Taxes increase the price paid by the buyer and decrease the price received by the seller. As a result, they decrease the quantities bought and sold and inflict costs on both buyers and sellers. These costs must be weighed against the benefits of the things on which the government spends the taxes it collects.

In the late nineteenth century, economists worked out how to measure the costs of taxes and to determine who bears those costs. At this time, most of the taxes were those on international trade—like the taxes we impose on imported Japanese automobiles today. It was discovered that a critical factor determining the effects of taxes is what we now call the *elasticity of demand*. Taxing goods that have an inelastic demand has a bigger effect on the price than on the quantity and brings in a large tax revenue. The smaller the effect of a tax on the quantity bought, the less the tax decreases consumption and the lower is its cost. So it pays to tax items—sometimes luxuries such as boats and expensive cars and sometimes necessities such as gasoline—that have an inelastic demand.

It was also discovered that the *elasticity of supply* plays an important role in determining the effects of taxes. Taxing goods that have an inelastic supply lowers the price received by the seller but has a small effect on the quantity sold and brings in a large tax revenue. The smaller the effect of a tax on the quantity sold, the less the tax decreases consumption and the lower is its cost. So it also pays to tax items that have an inelastic supply. This explains why land is a common item to tax.

"Thus, although the French may tax our goods, and so inflict a loss on themselves and on us, this is no reason for our inflicting an additional loss on the two communities by taxing the import of their goods."

FLEEMING JENKIN
"On the Principles which Regulate the Incidence of Taxes"

Taxes are the revenue source that enables governments to provide a wide range of valuable public services. But taxes also impose a burden on those who pay them. When those who pay get none of the benefits, the seeds of a tax revolt are sown. Such was the situation in 1773 when the British Parliament imposed a tea tax on its American colonists. Rather than buy tea and pay this tax, the colonists held a tea party of a different kind, dumping valuable cargoes of British tea into the waters of Boston harbor.

Every time you buy a gallon of gas, the government collects part of what you pay as a tax. And these taxes are large. They average 17½ cents a gallon. Even the lowest rate, in Georgia, is 7½ cents a gallon and the highest rate, in Rhode Island, is 26 cents a gallon. Who really pays these high gas taxes? Do the buyers pay? Does the seller pay? Or do the buyer and seller share the burden of the tax? If they share it, in what proportions?

FLEEMING JENKIN:

An *Engineer's Contribution to Economics*

Fleeming Jenkin (1833–1885) was a distinguished engineer who put his clear mind to work on a wide range of problems. Jenkin was not a famous economist in his own day, and his contributions to economic science were subsequently rediscovered by others. But he was a remarkable person who made a remarkable contribution to economics.

Jenkin worked on submarine cables, electrical standards, urban sanitation, and developing an electrical monorail transportation system. Between all these engineering projects, he was one of the first people to work out the laws of supply and demand and to put them to work on practical questions. One of these questions was: Who pays the taxes imposed on the sale of goods and services—the buyer or the seller or a combination of the two? The answer he came up with is the right one and is explained in this chapter.

a constant rate that can't be controlled. The quantity supplied is 100,000 bottles a week, regardless of the price. The supply is perfectly inelastic and the supply curve is S_I. The demand curve for the water from this spring is D. With no tax, the price is 50¢ a bottle and the 100,000 bottles that flow from the spring are bought at that price.

If this spring water is taxed at 5¢ a bottle, we must add the tax to the minimum price at which the spring owners are willing to sell the water to determine the terms on which this water will be available to consumers. But the spring owners are able to supply only one quantity—100,000 bottles a week—at any price (greater than zero). Consumers, on the other hand, are willing to buy the 100,000 bottles available each week only if the price is 50¢ a bottle. So the price remains at 50¢ a bottle, and the suppliers pay the entire tax. A sales tax of 5¢ a bottle reduces the price received by suppliers to 45¢ a bottle.

Perfectly Elastic Supply   Figure 6.6(b) shows the market for sand from which computer-chip makers extract silicon. There is a virtually unlimited quantity of this sand available, and its owners are willing to supply any quantity at a price of 10¢ a pound. The supply is perfectly elastic and the supply curve is S_E. The demand curve for sand is D in Fig. 6.6(b). With no tax, the price is 10¢ a pound and 5,000 pounds a week are bought at that price.

If this sand is taxed at 1¢ a pound, we must add the tax to the minimum price at which the owners are willing to sell the sand to determine the terms on which this sand will be available to computer-chip makers. Since without the tax the suppliers of sand are willing to supply any quantity at 10¢ a pound, with the 1¢ tax they are willing to supply any quantity at 11¢ a pound along the curve $S_E + tax$. A new equilibrium is determined where this new supply curve intersects the demand curve. This equilibrium is at a price of 11¢ a pound and 3,000 pounds a week are bought and sold. The sales tax has increased the price paid by consumers by the full amount of the tax—1¢ a pound—and has decreased the quantity sold.

We've seen that when supply is perfectly inelastic, the seller pays the tax, and when supply is perfectly elastic, the buyer pays it. In the usual case, supply is neither perfectly inelastic nor perfectly elastic, and the tax is split between the seller and the buyer. But the division depends on the elasticity of supply. The more elastic the supply, the larger is the portion of the tax paid by the buyer.

Tax Division and Elasticity of Demand

The division of the burden of a tax between buyers and sellers also depends on the elasticity of demand. Again, there are two extreme cases:

◆ Perfectly inelastic demand—buyer pays
◆ Perfectly elastic demand—seller pays

Perfectly Inelastic Demand   Figure 6.7(a) shows the market for insulin, a vital daily medication of diabetics. The quantity demanded is 100,000 doses a day, regardless of the price. That is, a diabetic would sacrifice almost all other goods and services rather than not consume the insulin dose that provides good health and survival. The demand for insulin reflects this fact and is perfectly inelastic. It is shown by the vertical curve D. The supply curve of insulin is S. With no tax, the price is $2 a dose, and the 100,000 doses a day that keep the population of diabetics healthy are bought.

If insulin is taxed at 20¢ a dose, we must add the tax to the minimum price at which the drug companies are willing to sell insulin to determine the terms on which it will be available to consumers. The result is a new supply curve $S + tax$. The new equilibrium occurs at a price of $2.20 a dose, but the quantity bought does not change. The buyer pays the entire sales tax of 20¢ a dose.

Perfectly Elastic Demand   Figure 6.7(b) shows the market for pink marker pens. Aside from a few pink freaks, people don't care whether they use a pink, blue, yellow, or green marker pen. If pink markers are less expensive than the others, everyone will use pink. If pink markers are more expensive than the others, no one will use them. The demand for pink marker pens is perfectly elastic at the price of other colored marker pens—$1 a pen in Fig. 6.7(b). The demand curve for pink markers is the horizontal curve D. The supply curve is S. With no tax, the price of a pink marker is $1 and 4,000 a week are bought at that price.

If a sales tax of 10¢ a pen is levied on pink—and only pink—marker pens, we must add the tax to the minimum price at which suppliers are willing to sell them to determine the terms on which pink marker

FIGURE **6.7**

Sales Tax and the Elasticity of Demand

(a) Inelastic demand

Part (a) shows the market for insulin. The demand for insulin is perfectly inelastic, as shown by the curve *D*. The supply curve of insulin is *S*. With no tax, the price is $2 a dose and 100,000 doses a day are bought. A sales tax of 20¢ a dose increases the price at which sellers are willing to make insulin available and shifts the supply curve to *S + tax*. The price rises to $2.20 a dose, but the quantity bought does not change, and buyers pay the entire tax.

(b) Elastic demand

Part (b) shows the market for pink marker pens. The demand for pink marker pens is perfectly elastic at the price of other colored marker pens—$1 a pen. The demand curve is *D* and the supply curve is *S*. With no tax, the price of a pink marker pen is $1 and 4,000 a week are bought. A sales tax of 10¢ a pink pen decreases the supply of pink marker pens, shifting the supply curve to *S + tax*. The price remains at $1 a pen and the quantity of pink markers sold decreases to 1,000 a week. Suppliers pay the entire tax.

pens will be available to consumers. The new supply curve is *S + tax*. The new equilibrium is at a price of $1 a pen, the same as before, and the quantity of pink markers sold decreases to 1,000 a week. The 10¢ sales tax has left the price paid by the consumer unchanged but has decreased the amount received by the supplier by the full amount of the sales tax— 10¢ a pen. As a result, sellers decrease the quantity offered for sale. (In the case of pink marker pens, it is likely that once sellers have run down their inventories, supply will also be perfectly elastic. In this case, pink marker pens will disappear!)

We've seen how the amount of tax paid, as well as its division between the buyer and the seller, depends on the elasticities of supply and demand. You can use this analysis of the effects of taxes to work out what is happening in many real-world

markets. One such market is that for travel, and some effects of travel taxes are explored in Reading Between the Lines, pp. 140–141.

REVIEW

The effect of a sales tax depends on the elasticities of supply and demand. The more elastic the supply, the larger is the price increase, the larger is the quantity decrease, and the larger is the portion of the tax paid by the buyer. The less elastic the demand, the larger is the price increase, the smaller is the quantity decrease, and the larger is the portion of the tax paid by the buyer. ◆

Taxes
at Work

USA TODAY, JANUARY 6, 1993

Travel taxes targeted by industry

BY CATHY LYNN GROSSMAN

Higher taxes on airfares and hotel rooms are pinching the travel industry, which Tuesday launched a major effort to curtail such costs.

Travelers paid $47 billion in such taxes during 1992—up 75% from five years ago, The American Society of Travel Agents says.

And a new study by the American Economics Group finds that "a 10% increase in the cost of a trip will reduce demand by 7.6%," says Robert Hazard of Choice Hotels.

Some travel consumer costs:

● A typical 3-day trip to Chicago from Washington, D.C., includes $173.45 in taxes—10% on the airline ticket, 14.9% on the hotel room and 18% on the rental car, says ASTA. Taxes account for more than 12% of the $1,424 overall tab.

● A spot check on hotel room taxes in six popular destinations range from 21.25% per night in New York City to 10% in Orlando. In-between are Chicago at 14.9%, Washington at 12.5% and San Francisco and New Orleans both at 11%—though New Orleans adds a $1 to $3 surcharge depending on the size of the hotel.

● Air passengers pay 10% on all tickets and, depending on destination, may owe $12 more in passenger facility charges at airports, a $6 international departure tax, a $5 customs fee, a $5 immigration fee and a $2 agricultural fee. . . .

The Essence of the Story

■n 1992, taxes on travel costs were $47 billion, up 75 percent from 1987, according to The American Society of Travel Agents.

▲ study by the American Economics Group found that a 10 percent increase in the cost of a trip reduces demand by 7.6 percent.

▲ typical three-day trip to Chicago from Washington, D.C. costs $1,424, which includes $173.45, or 12 percent, in taxes.

■otel room taxes are 21.25 percent in New York City, 14.9 percent in Chicago, 12.5 percent in Washington, 11 percent in San Francisco, 11 percent plus a surcharge in New Orleans, and 10 percent in Orlando.

▲irline passengers pay 10 percent on all tickets and other charges that depend on their destination.

Background and Analysis

A change in the cost of a trip, other things remaining the same, brings a movement along the demand curve for trips and a *change in the quantity of trips demanded.* Thus the study by the American Economics Group, which found that "a 10% increase in the cost of a trip will reduce demand by 7.6%," actually found that a 10 percent increase in the cost of a trip will decrease *the quantity demanded* by 7.6 percent.

The estimate by the American Economics Group translates into an estimate of the elasticity of demand (see Chapter 5, pp. 104–105) of 0.76. The demand curve for trips, curve *D* in the figure, is based on this estimate. With no travel taxes, the supply curve is *S* in the figure. The number of trips is 420 million a year, and the (average) cost of a trip is $920.

With taxes of 12 percent, the supply curve shifts to *S + tax.* The cost of a trip rises to $1,000, and the number of trips decreases to 390 million a year.

The tax per trip is $120, and total taxes are $47 billion ($120 × 390 million = $46.8 billion).

The traveler (demander) now pays $1,000 for a trip that previously cost $920 and so pays $80 of the tax ($1,000 − $920 = $80). The supplier receives only $880, compared with $920 previously and so pays $40 of the tax ($920 − $880 = $40).

The division of the tax results from the assumption in the figure about the *elasticity of supply.* Only if supply is *perfectly elastic,* which is unlikely, does the traveler pay the entire tax and the supplier pay nothing.

The travel industry is concerned because taxes decrease the amount of travel and leave the suppliers paying part of the tax bill.

141

Markets for Prohibited Goods

The markets for many goods and services are regulated, and buying or selling some goods is prohibited—the goods and services are illegal. The best-known example of such goods is illegal drugs.

Despite the fact that drugs are illegal, trade in drugs does take place. In fact, it is a multibillion-dollar business. Such trade can be understood by using the same economic models and principles that explain trading in markets for legal goods and services. Also, economic models can help us to understand the debate about drugs. They can help to answer questions such as: What would happen if drugs are legalized? Would they become less expensive? Would their consumption increase?

A Reminder about the Limits of Economics

Before we begin to study the market for drugs, let's remind ourselves that economics is a science that tries to answer questions about how the economic world works. It neither condones nor condemns the activities that it seeks to explain. It is vital that as a well-informed citizen, you have an opinion about drugs and about public policy toward them. What you learn about the economics of markets for illegal goods is one input into developing your opinion. But it is not a substitute for your moral judgments and does not help you to develop those judgments. What follows contains no moral judgments. It is a value-free analysis of how markets for prohibited goods work, not an argument about how they ought to be regulated and controlled.

To study the market for prohibited goods, we're first going to examine the prices and quantities that would prevail if these goods were not prohibited. Next, we'll see how prohibition works. Then we'll see how a tax might be used to limit the consumption of these goods.

A Free Market for Drugs

The demand for drugs is determined by the same forces that determine the demand for other goods.

Other things being equal, the lower the price of drugs, the larger is the quantity of drugs demanded. The demand curve for drugs, D, is shown in Fig. 6.8. The supply of drugs is also determined in a similar way to the supply of other goods and is shown as the supply curve S in the figure. If drugs were not prohibited, the quantity bought and sold would be Q_c and the price would be P_c.

Prohibition on Drugs

When trading in a good is prohibited, the cost of undertaking such trading increases. By how much

---

FIGURE 6.8

The Market for a Prohibited Good

The demand curve for drugs is D, and the supply curve is S. With no prohibition on drugs, the quantity consumed is Q_c at a price P_c—point c. If selling drugs is illegal, the cost of breaking the law by selling drugs (CBL) is added to the other costs, and supply decreases to $S + CBL$. The price rises and the quantity consumed decreases—point a. If buying drugs is illegal, the cost of breaking the law is subtracted from the maximum price that buyers are willing to pay, and demand decreases to $D - CBL$. The price falls and the quantity consumed decreases—point b. If both buying and selling are illegal, both the supply curve and the demand curve shift, and the quantity consumed decreases even more, but (in this example) the price remains at its unregulated level—point d.

the cost increases and on whom the cost falls depend on the penalties for violating the law and the effectiveness with which the law is enforced. The larger the penalties for violation and the more effective the policing, the higher are the costs. Penalties may be imposed on sellers, buyers, or both.

Penalties on Sellers   When sellers of illegal goods such as drugs are penalized, the cost of selling increases. Supply decreases and the supply curve shifts. In Fig. 6.8, the cost of breaking the law by selling drugs (*CBL*) is added to the other costs, and the supply decreases, shifting the supply curve to *S + CBL*. If penalties are imposed only on sellers, the market moves from point *c* to point *a*. The price increases and the quantity bought decreases.

Penalties on Buyers   When buyers of illegal goods are penalized, the goods have less value to buyers. The cost of breaking the law must be subtracted from the value of the good to determine the maximum price that buyers are willing to pay. Demand decreases and the demand curve shifts. In Fig. 6.8, the demand curve shifts to *D − CBL*. If penalties are imposed only on buyers, the market moves from point *c* to point *b*. The price and the quantity bought decrease.

Penalties on Both Sellers and Buyers   If penalties are imposed on sellers *and* buyers, both supply and demand decrease, and both the supply curve and demand curve shift. If the costs of breaking the law are the same for both buyers and sellers, both curves shift by the same amounts. This is the case in Fig. 6.8. The market moves to point *d*. The price remains at the competitive market price, but the quantity bought decreases to Q_p. But other distributions of penalties are possible. The larger the penalty and greater the degree of law enforcement, the larger is the decrease in demand and/or supply and the greater the shift of the demand and/or supply curve.

With high enough penalties and effective law enforcement, it is possible to decrease demand and supply to the point at which the quantity bought is zero. But in reality, such an outcome is unusual. It does not happen in the case of illegal drugs. The key reason is the high cost of law enforcement and insufficient resources for the police to achieve effective enforcement. Because of this situation, some people suggest that drugs (and other illegal goods) should be legalized and sold openly but should also be

taxed at a high rate in the same way that legal drugs such as alcohol are taxed. How would such an arrangement work?

Legalizing and Taxing Drugs

If drugs were legalized, there would be no costs of law breaking. With no taxes on drugs, the quantity Q_c in Fig. 6.8 would be consumed. But suppose that drugs were taxed at a high rate. Figure 6.9 shows the effects of such an arrangement. Here, the tax rate has been chosen to make the quantity bought the same as with a prohibition. The tax added to the supply price shifts the supply curve to *S + tax*. Equilibrium occurs at a quantity of Q_p. The price paid by consumers increases to P_b and the price received by suppliers decreases to P_s. The government collects a tax revenue equal to the blue area in the figure.

FIGURE **6.9**

Legalizing and Taxing Drugs

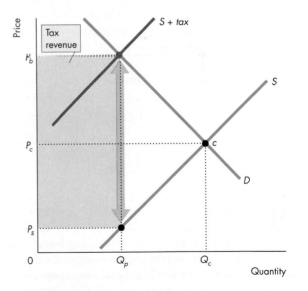

Drugs are legalized but taxed at a high rate. The tax added to the supply price shifts the supply curve from *S* to *S + tax*. The quantity bought decreases to Q_p, the price paid by consumers increases to P_b, and the price received by suppliers decreases to P_s. The government collects a tax revenue equal to the blue area.

Illegal Trading to Evade the Tax   It is likely that an extremely high tax rate would be needed to cut drug consumption to the level that would prevail with a prohibition. It is also likely that many drug dealers and consumers would try to cover up their activities to evade the tax. If they did act in this way, they would face the cost of breaking the law—the tax law. If the penalty for tax law violation was as severe and as effectively policed as drug dealing laws, the analysis that we've already conducted would also apply to this case. The quantity of drugs consumed would remain at Q_p. But to the extent that the tax was successfully evaded, the tax revenue would fall short of the area highlighted in Fig. 6.9.

Some Pros and Cons of Taxes versus Prohibition   So which works more effectively, prohibition or taxing? The comparison we've just made suggests that the two methods can be made to be equivalent if the taxes and penalties are set at the appropriate levels. But there are some differences. In favor of taxes and against prohibition is the fact that the tax revenue can be used to make law enforcement more effective. It can also be used to run a more effective education campaign against drugs. In favor of prohibition and against taxes is the fact that a prohibition sends a signal that may influence preferences, decreasing the demand for drugs. Also, some people intensely dislike the idea of the government profiting from trade in harmful substances.

REVIEW

P enalizing dealers for the sale of an illegal good increases the cost of selling the good and decreases the supply of it. Penalizing buyers for the consumption of an illegal good decreases the willingness to pay for the good and decreases the demand for it. The quantity bought decreases and the price increases if penalties for selling are higher than those for buying, and the price decreases if penalties for buying are higher than those for selling. Taxing a good at a sufficiently high rate can achieve the same consumption level as prohibition. ◆

Stabilizing Farm Revenue

F arm revenue fluctuates a great deal because of variations in harvests and prices. Sometimes, the combination of rainfall, sunshine, and temperature throughout the growing and harvesting seasons is all wrong, resulting in low crop yields. Sometimes the climate is ideal, resulting in bumper harvests. At other times the climate is average, resulting in normal crop yields. How do variations in crop yields affect farm revenue? And how might those revenues be stabilized?

No Stabilization Program

Figure 6.10 illustrates the market for wheat. In both parts, the demand curve for wheat is D. Once farmers have harvested their crop, they have no control over the quantity supplied and supply is inelastic along a *momentary supply curve*. In normal climate conditions, the momentary supply curve is MS_0 (in both parts of the figure).

The price is determined at the point of intersection of the momentary supply curve and the demand curve. In normal conditions, the price is $3 a bushel. The quantity of wheat produced is 16 billion bushels, and farm revenue is $48 billion. Suppose the opportunity cost to farmers of producing wheat is also $48 billion. Then in normal conditions, farmers just cover their opportunity cost.

Poor Harvest   Suppose there is a bad growing season, resulting in a poor harvest. What happens to the price of wheat and the revenue of farmers? These questions are answered in Fig. 6.10(a). Supply decreases to 14 billion bushels and the momentary supply curve shifts to the left to MS_1. With a decrease in supply, the price increases to $4 a bushel.

What happens to total farm revenue? It *increases* to $56 billion. A decrease in supply has brought an increase in price and an increase in farm revenue. The reason is that the demand for wheat is *inelastic*. The percentage decrease in the quantity demanded is

FIGURE **6.10**

Harvests, Farm Prices, and Farm Revenue

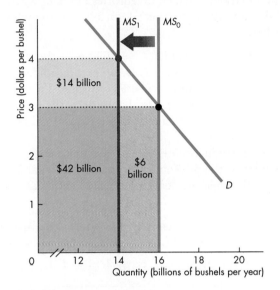

(a) Poor harvest: revenue increases

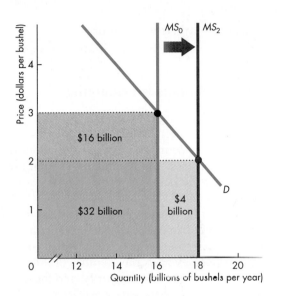

(b) Bumper harvest: revenue decreases

In both parts, the demand curve for wheat is *D*, in normal times the momentary supply curve is MS_0, and 16 billion bushels are sold for $3 a bushel. In part (a), a poor growing season decreases supply, shifting the momentary supply curve to MS_1. The price increases to $4 a bushel, and farm revenue *increases* from $48 billion to $56 billion—the increase in revenue from the higher price ($14 billion light blue area)

exceeds the decrease in revenue from the smaller quantity ($6 billion red area). In part (b), a bumper harvest increases supply, shifting the momentary supply curve to MS_2. The price decreases to $2 a bushel, and farm revenue *decreases* to $36 billion—the decrease in revenue from the lower price ($16 billion red area) exceeds the increase in revenue from the increase in the quantity sold ($4 billion light blue area).

less than the percentage increase in price. You can verify this fact by noticing in Fig. 6.10(a) that the increase in revenue from the higher price ($14 billion light blue area) exceeds the decrease in revenue from the smaller quantity ($6 billion red area). Farmers are now making a profit in excess of their opportunity cost.

Although total farm revenue increases when there is a poor harvest, some farmers, whose entire crop is wiped out, suffer a fall in revenue. Others, whose crop is unaffected, make an enormous gain.

Bumper Harvest   Figure 6.10(b) shows what happens in the opposite situation, when there is a bumper harvest. Now supply increases to 18 billion bushels and the momentary supply curve shifts to

the right to MS_2. With the increased quantity supplied, the price falls to $2 a bushel. Farm revenues also decline—to $36 billion. They do so because the demand for wheat is inelastic. To see this fact, notice in Fig. 6.10(b) that the decrease in revenue from the lower price ($16 billion red area) exceeds the increase in revenue from the increase in the quantity sold ($4 billion light blue area). Farmers are now not covering their opportunity cost.

Elasticity of Demand   In the example we've just worked through, demand is inelastic. If demand is elastic, the price fluctuations go in the same directions as those we've worked out, but revenues fluctuate in the opposite directions. Bumper harvests increase revenue, and poor harvests decrease it. But the demand for most agricultural products is inelastic, and the case we've studied is the relevant one.

Because farm revenues fluctuate, institutions have evolved to stabilize them. There are two types of institutions:

◆ Speculative markets in inventories
◆ Farm price and revenue stabilization agencies

Speculative Markets in Inventories

Many goods, including a wide variety of agricultural products, can be stored. These inventories provide a cushion between production and consumption. If production decreases, goods can be sold from inventory; if production increases, goods can be put into inventory.

In a market that has inventories, we must distinguish production from supply. The quantity produced is not the same as the quantity supplied. The quantity supplied exceeds the quantity produced when goods are sold from inventory, and the quantity supplied is less than the quantity produced when goods are put into inventory. The supply curve therefore depends on the behavior of inventory holders. Let's see how they behave.

The Behavior of Inventory Holders Inventory holders speculate. They buy at a low price and sell at a high price. That is, they buy goods and put them into inventory when the price is low and sell them from inventory when the price is high. They make a profit equal to the difference between their buying price and selling price, minus the cost of storage.[5]

But how do inventory holders know when to buy and when to sell? How do they know whether the price is high or low? To decide whether a price is high or low, inventory holders make their best forecast of future prices.[6] If the price is above its expected future level, they sell goods from inventory. If the price is below its expected future level, they buy goods to put into inventory. Even if the price is just a penny above or below the inventory holder's expected price, goods are supplied from or put into

inventory. This behavior by inventory holders makes the supply curve perfectly elastic at the price expected by inventory holders.

Let's work out what happens to price and quantity in a market in which inventories are held when production fluctuates. Let's look again at the wheat market.

Fluctuations in Production In Fig. 6.11 the demand curve for wheat is D. Inventory holders expect the future price to be $3 a bushel. The supply curve is S—supply is perfectly elastic at the future price expected by inventory holders. Production fluctuates between Q_1 and Q_2.

When production fluctuates and there are no inventories, the price and the quantity fluctuate. Price falls when production increases and rises when

---

[5]We will suppose that the cost of storage is so small that we can ignore it. This assumption, though not essential, enables us to see more sharply the effects of inventory holders' decisions on prices.

[6]The process of making the best possible forecast—a *rational expectation*—is explained in Chapter 17, pp. 478–479.

FIGURE **6.11**

How Inventories Limit Price Changes

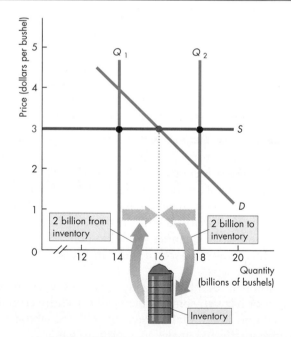

Inventory holders supply from inventory if the price rises above $3 a bushel and take wheat into inventory if the price falls below $3 a bushel, making supply perfectly elastic along the supply curve S. When production decreases to Q_1, 2 billion bushels are supplied from inventory; when production increases to Q_2, 2 billion bushels are added to inventory. The price remains constant at $3 a bushel.

production decreases. We saw this result in Fig. 6.10. But if there are inventories, the price does not fluctuate. When production is low, at Q_1 or 14 billion bushels, inventory holders sell 2 billion bushels from inventory and the quantity bought by consumers is 16 billion bushels. The price remains at $3 a bushel. When production is high, at Q_2 or 18 billion bushels, inventory holders buy 2 billion bushels and consumers continue to buy 16 billion bushels. Again, the price remains at $3 a bushel.

Inventories in Reality   The model of a market with inventories that we've just reviewed is the simplest possible. But it shows how inventories and inventory holders' expectations about future prices reduce price fluctuations. In the above example, the price fluctuations are entirely eliminated. When there are costs of carrying inventories and when inventories become almost depleted, some price fluctuations do occur, but these fluctuations are smaller than those occurring in a market without inventories.

Farm Revenue   Even if inventory speculation succeeds in stabilizing prices, it does not stabilize farm revenue. With the price stabilized, farm revenue fluctuates as production fluctuates. But the direction in which revenue fluctuates is now reversed. Bumper harvests bring larger revenues than poor harvests. The reason is that now farmers, in effect, face a perfectly elastic demand curve for their output.

Stabilizing Farm Revenue

Every country has regulatory agencies that intervene in agricultural markets. The most extensive such agencies are in the European Community. But they are also present in the United States, where they stabilize the prices of many agricultural products, such as grains, dairy products, tobacco, rice, peanuts, and cotton.

These agencies operate at an enormous cost to taxpayers. Usually, they set price floors—similar to the minimum wage that we studied earlier—above the production cost of efficient farms. The result is persistent excess supply, which the stabilization agency must mop up. The stabilization agency buys more than it sells and winds up with a large inventory. Such has been the outcome in Europe, where agencies have mountains of butter and lakes of wine! The cost of buying and storing the inventory falls on taxpayers, and the main gainers are the large, efficient farms.

R E V I E W

T he demand for most farm products is inelastic. With no inventory, a poor harvest (a decrease in supply) increases price and increases farm revenue, and a bumper harvest (an increase in supply) decreases price and decreases farm revenue. Inventory holders speculate, buying at a low price and selling at a high price, reducing price fluctuations. Farm stabilization agencies also limit price fluctuations but usually create surpluses.   ◆

◆ ◆ ◆ We've now completed our study of demand and supply and its applications. You've seen how this powerful model enables us to make predictions about prices and quantities traded and also how it enables us to understand a wide variety of markets and situations.   ◆ ◆   We're now going to start digging a bit more deeply into people's economic choices. In the next part we'll study the economic choices of households.

S U M M A R Y

Housing Markets and Rent Ceilings

A sudden decrease in the supply of housing shifts the short-run supply curve to the left. Rents increase. In the short run, higher rents bring forth an increase in the quantity of housing supplied as people econo- mize on the available space. In the long run, the higher rents stimulate building activity, resulting in a shift to the right in the short-run supply curve. Through this process, rents gradually decrease, and the quantity of housing available gradually increases.

If a rent ceiling prevents rents from increasing, the quantity of housing supplied is lower, in both the short run and the long run, than it would be in an unregulated market. There is no inducement to economize on space in the short run and no incentive to build new houses and apartments in the long run. Equilibrium is achieved by people spending time searching for housing and by the development of a black market. The total cost of housing, including the value of the time spent searching, exceeds the cost in an unregulated market. (pp. 126–131)

The Labor Market and Minimum Wage Regulation

A decrease in the demand for unskilled labor lowers wages and reduces employment in the short run. Low wages encourage people to quit a particular market and to acquire skills and seek different, more highly paid work. As they do so, the short-run supply curve for unskilled labor shifts to the left. As it does so, it intersects the demand curve at higher wages and lower levels of employment. Eventually, the wage will return to its previous level but at a much lower employment level.

If the government imposes a minimum wage, a decrease in the demand for labor will result in an increase in unemployment and an increase in the amount of time spent searching for a job. Minimum wages bite hardest on people having the fewest skills, and such workers tend to be young people. The unemployment rate among such people is more than twice the average rate. (pp. 131–134)

Taxes

When a sales tax is imposed on a good or service, the item in question is offered for sale at a higher price than in a no-tax situation. Usually, the quantity traded decreases, and the price of the good increases but by less than the amount of the tax. The tax is borne partly by the buyer and partly by the seller. The division of the burden of a tax between buyers and sellers depends on the elasticity of supply and the elasticity of demand. There are four extreme cases:

1. If supply is perfectly inelastic, the quantity and price remain constant, and the seller pays the entire tax.

2. If supply is perfectly elastic, the quantity decreases, the price increases by the full amount of the tax, and the buyer pays the entire tax.

3. If demand is perfectly inelastic, the quantity remains constant, the price increases by the full amount of the tax, and the buyer pays the entire tax.

4. If demand is perfectly elastic, the quantity decreases, the price remains constant, and the seller pays the entire tax.

The more elastic the supply and the less elastic the demand, the greater is the price increase, the smaller is the quantity decrease, and the larger is the portion of the tax paid by the buyer. (pp. 134–139)

Markets for Prohibited Goods

Other things being equal, the lower the price of drugs, the larger is the quantity of drugs demanded, and the higher the price, the larger is the quantity of drugs supplied. Penalties for selling an illegal good increase the cost of selling it and decrease its supply. Penalties on buyers decrease their willingness to pay and decrease the demand for the good. The higher the penalties and the more effective the law enforcement, the smaller is the quantity bought. The price is higher or lower than the unregulated price, depending on whether penalties for sellers or buyers are higher. Effective law enforcement and high enough penalties will decrease demand and supply to the point at which the good disappears.

A tax set at a sufficiently high rate will also decrease the quantity of drug consumption, but there will be a tendency for the tax to be evaded. If the penalty for tax law violation is as severe and as effectively policed as drug dealing laws, the quantity of drugs consumed will remain at the prohibition level but the tax revenue will be lower. Tax revenue from a drug tax could be used to make law enforcement more effective and to pay for a campaign against drugs. But prohibiting drugs sends a signal that may influence preferences, decreasing the demand for drugs. (pp. 142–144)

Stabilizing Farm Revenue

Farm revenues fluctuate because climatic conditions bring fluctuations in crop yields. The demand for most farm products is inelastic, so a decrease in supply brings an increase in price and an increase in farm revenue, and a bumper harvest brings a decrease in price and a decrease in farm revenues. Inventory holders and official agencies act to stabilize farm prices and revenues.

Inventory holders speculate, buying at a low price and selling at a high price. As a consequence (and ignoring storage costs), the supply curve is perfectly elastic at the future price expected by inventory holders. When production is low, inventory holders sell from inventory, preventing the price from rising. When production is high, inventory holders buy, preventing the price from falling.

Farm stabilization agencies set minimum prices that create persistent surpluses. (pp. 144–147)

K E Y   E L E M E N T S

Key Terms

Black market, 130
Fair Labor Standards Act, 133
Minimum wage law, 132
Rent ceiling, 128
Search activity, 129

Key Figures

Figure 6.1   The San Francisco Housing Market in 1906, 127
Figure 6.2   A Rent Ceiling, 129
Figure 6.3   A Market for Unskilled Labor, 132
Figure 6.4   The Minimum Wage and Unemployment, 133
Figure 6.5   A Sales Tax, 134
Figure 6.8   The Market for a Prohibited Good, 142

R E V I E W   Q U E S T I O N S

1 Describe what happens to the rent and to the quantity of housing available if an earthquake suddenly and unexpectedly reduces the supply of housing. Trace the evolution of the rent and the quantity traded over time.

2 In the situation described in question 1, how will things be different if a rent ceiling is imposed?

3 Describe what happens to the price and quantity bought and sold in a market in which there is a sudden and unforeseen increase in supply. Trace the evolution of the price and quantity bought and sold in the market over time.

4 Describe what happens to the price and quantity bought and sold in a market in which there is a sudden and unforeseen increase in demand. Trace the evolution of the price and quantity bought and sold in the market over time.

5 Describe what happens to the wage rate and quantity of labor employed when there is a sudden and unforeseen decrease in demand for labor. Trace the evolution of the wage rate and employment over time.

6 In the situation described in question 5, how are things different if a minimum wage is introduced?

7 Why does a minimum wage create unemployment?

8 When a government regulation prevents a price from changing, what forces come into operation to achieve an equilibrium?

9 How does the imposition of a sales tax on a good influence the supply of and demand for that good? How does it influence the price of the good and the quantity bought?

10 How does a prohibition of the sale of a good affect the demand for and supply of the good? How does it affect the price of the good and the quantity bought?

11 How does a prohibition of the consumption of a good affect the demand for and supply of the good? How does it affect the price of the good and the quantity bought?

12 Explain the alternative ways in which the consumption of harmful drugs can be controlled. What are the arguments for and against each method?

13 Why do farm revenues fluctuate?

14 Do farm revenues increase or decrease when there is a bumper crop and there are no inventories? Why?

15 Explain why speculation can stabilize the price of a storable commodity but does not stabilize the revenues of the producers of such a commodity.

16 How can an official agency stabilize farm revenues? Is such stabilization profitable?

P R O B L E M S

You will find it easier to answer these problems by drawing the supply and demand curves on graph paper.

1 You have been given the following information about the market for rental housing in your town:

Rent (dollars per month)	Quantity demanded	Quantity supplied
100	20,000	0
150	15,000	5,000
200	10,000	10,000
250	5,000	15,000
300	2,500	20,000
350	1,500	25,000

a What is the equilibrium rent?

b What is the equilibrium quantity of housing bought and sold?

2 Now suppose that a rent ceiling of $150 a month is imposed in the housing market described in problem 1.

a What is the quantity of housing demanded?

b What is the quantity of housing supplied?

c What is the excess quantity of housing demanded?

d What is the maximum price that demanders will be willing to pay for the last unit available?

e Suppose that the average wage rate is $10 per hour. How many hours a month will a person spend looking for housing?

3 The demand for and supply of teenage labor are as follows:

Wage rate (dollars per hour)	Hours demanded	Hours supplied
2	3,000	1,000
3	2,500	1,500
4	2,000	2,000
5	1,500	2,500
6	1,000	3,000

a What is the equilibrium wage rate?

b What is the level of employment?

c What is the level of unemployment?

d If the government imposes a minimum wage of $3 an hour for teenagers, how many hours do teenagers work?

e If the government imposes a minimum wage of $5 an hour for teenagers, what are the employment and unemployment levels?

f If there is a minimum wage of $5 an hour and demand increases by 500 hours, what is the level of unemployment?

4 The following table illustrates three supply curves for train travel:

Price (cents per passenger mile)	Quantity supplied (billions of passenger miles)		
	Momentary	Short-run	Long-run
10	500	300	100
20	500	350	200
30	500	400	300
40	500	450	400
50	500	500	500
60	500	550	600

Price (cents per passenger mile)	Quantity supplied (billions of passenger miles)		
	Momentary	Short-run	Long-run
70	500	600	700
80	500	650	800
90	500	700	900
100	500	750	1,000

a If the price is 50¢ per passenger mile, what is the quantity supplied in
  (1) The long run
  (2) The short run
b Suppose that the price is initially 50¢ but that it then rises to 70¢. What will be the quantity supplied
  (1) Immediately following the price rise
  (2) In the short run
  (3) In the long run

5 Suppose that the supply of train travel is the same as in problem 4. The following table gives two demand schedules—original and new:

Price (cents per passenger mile)	Quantity demanded (billions of passenger miles)	
	Original	New
10	10,000	10,300
20	5,000	5,300
30	2,000	2,300
40	1,000	1,300
50	500	800
60	400	700
70	300	600
80	200	500
90	100	400
100	0	300

a What is the original equilibrium price and quantity?
b After the increase in demand has occurred, what is
  (1) The momentary equilibrium price and quantity
  (2) The short-run equilibrium price and quantity
  (3) The long-run equilibrium price and quantity
6 The short-run and long-run demand for train travel are as follows:

Price (cents per passenger mile)	Quantity demanded (billions of passenger miles)	
	Short-run	Long-run
10	700	10,000
20	650	5,000
30	600	2,000
40	550	1,000
50	500	500
60	450	400
70	400	300
80	350	200
90	300	100
100	250	0

The supply of train travel is as given in problem 4.
a What is the long-run equilibrium price and quantity of train travel?
b Serious floods destroy one fifth of the trains and train tracks. Supply falls by 100 billion passenger miles. What happens to the price and the quantity of train travel in:
  (1) The short run
  (2) The long run
7 The following are the demand and supply schedules for chocolate brownies:

Price (cents per brownie)	Quantity demanded (millions per day)	Quantity supplied (millions per day)
90	1	7
80	2	6
70	3	5
60	4	4
50	5	3
40	6	2

a If there is no tax on brownies, what is their price and how many are produced and consumed?
b If a tax of 20¢ per brownie is introduced, what happens to the price of a brownie and the number produced and consumed?
c How much tax does the government collect and who pays it?

8 Calculate the elasticity of demand in Fig. 6.10 when the price of wheat changes from $2 to $4 a bushel. Does its magnitude imply that farm revenues fluctuate in the same direction as price fluctuations or in the opposite direction?

PART 3

HOUSEHOLDS' CHOICES

Talking

with

Richard

Easterlin

Born in Ridgefield Park, New Jersey, in 1926, Richard Easterlin received his first degree from the Stevens Institute of Technology in Philadelphia. He followed that with graduate work at the University of Pennsylvania, where he obtained his Ph.D. in 1953. Professor Easterlin spent most of his career at the University of Pennsylvania but moved to the University of Southern California in 1982. Professor Easterlin's work has been at the interface of economics and demography, studying the implications of the choices that people make about marriage and children for the evolution of populations as a whole.

What attracted you to economics?

My first encounter with an economics course was in the graduate MBA curriculum at the University of Pennsylvania. There was a great air of excitement in the field at that time, the late 1940s. The Keynesian revolution was afoot, and the use of fiscal policy as a tool for avoiding another Great Depression had powerful appeal. Methodologically, I found economics appealing because it involved problem-solving techniques much like those of engineering, which was my undergraduate major. The difference was that the problems economics was dealing with were great social concerns.

What attracted you to questions of demography?

The truth is, I was not initially attracted to demography. My view of population was unfortunately like that of many graduate economics students today, that it is not a proper subject for economic analysis. But I was invited to join an empirical research project on population redistribution and economic growth in the United States. Although my work

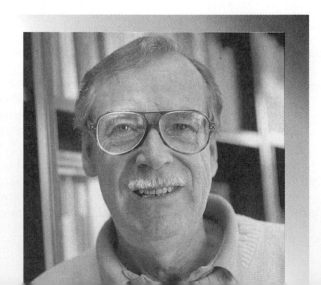

related to economic aspects of the project—estimating trends in income, agriculture, and manufacturing—some demography started to rub off on me. I never had any formal demographic training, but I benefited from frequent contact with collaborators in demographic economics and sociology. I soon developed a fairly good grip on the subject matter and techniques of the field.

What is special about the way *economists* study demographic issues?

Economists bring to bear a systematic theoretical framework of great potential value in a field where emphasis on statistical techniques and measurement has dominated. Unfortunately, however, economists too often have little knowledge of the field of demography and little respect for non-economists. Early in my career, I was prone to the latter shortcoming and wrote a draft of an arrogant article about the American baby boom, demeaning the work of demographers. I received feedback that it was a good article but had benefited enormously from prior work by demographers. I was asked,

"Why put them down?" Ever since, I've tried to have a more balanced appreciation of demographers and their work and, more generally, that of disciplines other than economics.

At the University of Pennsylvania in the 1970s, you were the intellectual leader of what came to be called the "Pennsylvania School." Was there in fact such a school? What were the principal views that characterized it?

The Pennsylvania School comprised a fairly small group of scholars who, at least in the area of childbearing behavior, were willing to expand the limits of economic theory to take into account systematic changes in preferences and the real-world existence of natural fertility (the latter came to be called "supply-side" considerations in fertility behavior). In contrast, the opposing Chicago School more or less adamantly pursued a demand theory that focused on prices and income alone. In considering sources of demand change, they ignored the possibility of preference change due to differences among generations in their socialization experience.

> " The question is whether this fertility upswing will resume once the current recession ends."

What were the intellectual roots of your Pennsylvania School perspective?

I had found economic theory to be useful in understanding demographic behavior. Indeed, early on, when Gary Becker (who is closely associated with the Chicago School) and I were fellow researchers at the National Bureau of Economic Research in New York, we had many fruitful discussions. But while Becker tended to put theory first (though not without concern for its value in interpreting real-world problems), I tended to put real-world problems first and see economic theory as merely one tool for understanding them.

My foremost concern at the time was the causes of the post–World War II American baby boom and subsequent baby bust. As I studied the data, I increasingly felt that economic theory as usually applied failed to supply an answer. Like most economists, I was reluctant to consider the effect of changing tastes or preferences as a possible causal influence. Eventually, however, I changed my views, as I came to see the relevance of what sociologists call socialization and reference group theory to the determination of preferences. This changed view of tastes was also influenced by demographers' empirical work on childbearing preferences. Later, when I started working on the transition from high to low fertility in less developed countries, I benefited greatly from demographers' empirical work on natural fertility. This means fertility is not deliberately regulated, a concept many economists, especially those of the Chicago School, find hard to swallow.

Has there been a convergence of the Pennsylvania and Chicago Schools, or do sharp differences remain between them?

There has been some convergence. With regard to the demand for children, Becker's work on child endowments is a step in the direction of recognizing how one's home environment may influence behavior. But it still carefully avoids the idea of preference change. There has also been limited recognition by Chicago School economists of what are called supply-side constraints on fertility, but in the Chicago view, these remain purely biological, for example, subfertility or infertility.

How can these differences be resolved?

On the theoretical side, I'm afraid there is unlikely to be much further convergence. Chicago-trained economists are distinctive in their preference for what I consider to be a fairly narrow theoretical paradigm. Their approach means either rejecting or rewriting the theoretical contributions of other disciplines, such as sociology. It also means rejecting much of the survey evidence on attitudes collected by demographers.

In a broader sense, time will help resolve the differences between the two views. For example, so far as I'm aware, Chicago theorists see the future of American fertility and that of developed countries generally as one of continued fertility decline. The Pennsylvania School is more prone to accept the likelihood of longer-term fertility swings—up and down. The 1990s should be of special interest in this regard.

> "**D**emographic policies are not important or appropriate ways to promote economic growth in either developed or less developed countries."

American fertility moved up sharply from 1986 to 1990, contrary to what Chicago-type theory would lead one to expect. The question is whether this fertility upswing will resume once the current recession ends. If it continues, it would have direct bearing on the relative merits of the Chicago and Pennsylvania School theories.

Two of the world's biggest countries, China and India, are struggling under the burden of huge and rapidly growing populations. How can economics help design effective population programs for countries such as these?

I'm not a population alarmist. Rapid population growth in less developed countries is due to dramatic mortality decline. Hand in hand with mortality decline goes major health improvement, which in turn means more vigorous labor and less labor time lost due to the debilitating effects of disease. There is no empirical evidence that rapid population growth has caused significantly slower economic growth. Moreover, historical experience—and, I might add, the theory of the Pennsylvania School—shows that the phase of rapid population growth is a temporary one. Fer-

tility decline follows mortality decline, and this is currently going on in both China and India.

In the 1970s, I was a member of a United Nations team that visited India to study its family planning program. I saw first-hand the harmful effects of family planning programs being pushed by both Indians and Americans who feared population explosion. The worst effect of their programs was disregard of basic human rights. I feel that the case for family planning programs should rest not on unfounded population explosion theories but on concern for maternal, child, and family welfare. If programs are concerned with this goal, then economists could usefully contribute to them via cost-benefit analysis, a notion that is frequently absent in these programs.

Some populations decline. Currently, there are concerns about possible adverse effects of declining population growth in a number of countries, such as Canada, the United States, and those in Western and Northern Europe. Why does population growth decline, and is it a problem?

I am also not an alarmist about the problems of declining population growth in developed coun-

tries. This development reflects the long-term shift in fertility from high to low, which, as I previously mentioned, lags a corresponding movement in mortality. Neither historical experience nor a properly conceived theory of economic growth warrants concern that declining population growth will seriously impede economic growth. Prospective population changes in the developed countries are not greatly out of line with historical experience. The policies needed to raise the rate of economic growth are those relating to stimulation of aggregate demand, promotion of international trade and monetary cooperation, and the design of appropriate education, science, research, and development programs. Demographic policies are not important or appropriate ways to promote economic growth, in either developed or less developed countries.

What are the central principles of economics that you find most useful in your work as an economic demographer?

The traditional micro and macro principles of economic theory. But, as I indicated, economic theory is not enough. The incorporation of sociological theory, especially on reference groups and socialization, is important, as are contributions from a variety of other social and natural science disciplines. Economic theory needs to be informed by the wide range of survey evidence generated by researchers in other disciplines. In my experience, training in economics is a good starting point for the study of human behavior, but no more than that.

CHAPTER 7

UTILITY
AND
DEMAND

After studying this chapter, you will be able to:

◆ Explain the connection between individual demand and market demand

◆ Define total utility and marginal utility

◆ Explain the marginal utility theory of consumer choice

◆ Use the marginal utility theory to predict the effects of changing prices

◆ Use the marginal utility theory to predict the effects of changing income

◆ Define and calculate consumer surplus

◆ Explain the paradox of value

WE NEED WATER TO LIVE. WE DON'T NEED DIAMONDS FOR much besides decoration. If the benefits of water far outweigh the benefits of diamonds, why, then, does water cost practically nothing while diamonds are terribly expensive? ◆ ◆ When OPEC restricted its sale of oil in 1973, it created a dramatic rise in price, but people continued to use almost as much oil as they had before. Our demand for oil was inelastic. But why? ◆ ◆ When Sony introduced the Walkman in 1979, it cost about $300, and consumers didn't buy very many. Since then, the price has decreased dramatically, and people are buying Walkmans in enormous quantities. Our demand for portable audio headsets is elastic. What makes the demand for some things elastic while the demand for others is inelastic? ◆ ◆ Over the past 15 years, after removing the effects of inflation, incomes have increased by 40 percent. Over that same period, expenditure on electricity has increased by 66 percent, while expenditure on transportation has increased by only 18 percent. Thus the proportion of income spent on electricity has increased while the proportion spent on transportation has decreased. Why, as incomes rise, does the proportion of income spent on some goods rise and that spent on others fall?

Water, Water, Everywhere

◆ ◆ ◆ ◆ In the last three chapters, we've seen that demand has an important effect on the price of a good. But we have not analyzed what exactly shapes a person's demand. This chapter explains why demand is elastic for some goods and inelastic for others. It also explains why the prices of some things, such as diamonds and water, are so out of proportion to their benefits.

Individual Demand and Market Demand

T he relationship between the total quantity of a good demanded and its price is called **market demand.** But goods and services are demanded by individuals. The relationship between the quantity of a good demanded by a single individual and its price is called **individual demand.** Market demand is the sum of all individual demands.

The table in Fig. 7.1 illustrates the relationship between individual demand and market demand. In this example, Lisa and Chuck are the only people. The market demand is the total demand of Lisa and Chuck. At $3 a movie, Lisa demands 5 movies and Chuck demands 2, so the total quantity demanded by the market is 7 movies. Figure 7.1 illustrates the relationship between individual and market demand curves. Lisa's demand curve for movies in part (a) and Chuck's in part (b) sum *horizontally* to the market demand curve in part (c).

The market demand curve is the horizontal sum of the individual demand curves and is formed by adding the quantities demanded by each individual at each price.

FIGURE **7.1**

Individual and Market Demand Curves

(a) Lisa's demand   **(b) Chuck's demand**   **(c) Market demand**

Price of a movie (dollars)	Quantity of movies demanded		
	Lisa	Chuck	Market
7	1	0	1
6	2	0	2
5	3	0	3
4	4	1	5
3	5	2	7
2	6	3	9

The table and diagram illustrate how the quantity of movies demanded varies as the price of a movie varies. In the table, the market demand is the sum of the individual demands. For example, at a price of $3, Lisa demands 5 movies and Chuck demands 2 movies, so the total quantity demanded in the market is 7 movies. In the diagram, the market demand curve is the horizontal sum of the individual demand curves. Thus when the price is $3, the market demand curve shows that the quantity demanded is 7 movies, the sum of the quantities demanded by Lisa and Chuck.

Let's investigate an individual demand curve by studying how a household makes its consumption choices.

Household Consumption Choices

A household's consumption choice is determined by two factors:

◆ Constraints
◆ Preferences

Constraints

A household's choices are constrained by its income and the prices of the goods and services that it buys. Marginal utility theory assumes that the household has a given income to spend and that it can't influence the prices of the goods and services that it buys.

To study marginal utility theory, we'll examine Lisa's consumption choices. Lisa has a monthly income of $30 and spends it on only two goods—movies and soda. Movies cost $6 each, and soda costs 50¢ a can or $3 for a six-pack. Figure 7.2 illustrates Lisa's possible consumption levels of movies and soda. Rows *a* through *f* in the table show six possible ways of allocating $30 to these two goods. For example, Lisa can buy 2 movies for $12 and 6 six-packs for $18 (row *c*). The same possibilities are represented by the points *a* through *f* in the figure. The line passing through those points is a boundary between what Lisa can afford and cannot afford. Her choices must lie inside the orange area or along the line *af*.

Preferences

How does Lisa divide her $30 between these two goods? The answer depends on her likes and dislikes—on her *preferences*. Marginal utility theory uses the concept of utility to describe preferences. The benefit or satisfaction that a person gets from the consumption of a good or service is called **utility**. But what exactly is utility and in what units can we measure it? Utility is an abstract concept, and the units of utility are chosen arbitrarily.

FIGURE 7.2

Consumption Possibilities

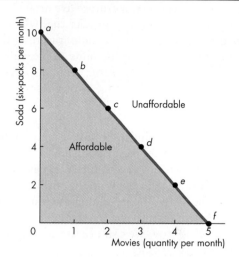

Six possible ways of allocating $30 to movies and soda are shown as rows *a* through *f* in the table. For example, Lisa can buy 2 movies and 6 six-packs (row *c*). Each row shows a combination of movies and soda that costs $30. These possibilities are points *a* through *f* in the figure. The line through those points is a boundary between what Lisa can and cannot afford. Her choices must lie inside the orange area or along the line *af*.

	Movies	Expenditure	Soda	
Possibility	Quantity	Expenditure (dollars)	Six-packs	Expenditure (dollars)
a	0	0	10	30
b	1	6	8	24
c	2	12	6	18
d	3	18	4	12
e	4	24	2	6
f	5	30	0	0

Temperature—An Analogy

Temperature is an abstract concept, and the units of temperature are chosen arbitrarily. You know when you feel hot, and you know when you feel cold. But you can't *observe* temperature. You can observe water turning to steam if it is hot enough or turning to ice if it is cold enough. You can construct an instrument, called a thermometer, that will predict when such changes will occur. The scale on the thermometer is what we call temperature. But the units in which we measure temperature are arbitrary. For example, we can accurately predict that when a Celsius thermometer shows a temperature of 0°, water will turn to ice. But the units of measurement do not matter because this same event also occurs when a Fahrenheit thermometer shows a temperature of 32°.

The concept of utility helps us make predictions about consumption choices in much the same way that the concept of temperature helps us make predictions about physical phenomena. It has to be admitted, though, that the marginal utility theory is not as precise as the theory that enables us to predict when water will turn to ice or steam.

Let's now see how we can use the concept of utility to describe preferences.

Total Utility and Consumption

Total utility is the total benefit or satisfaction that a person gets from the consumption of goods and services. Total utility depends on the person's level of consumption—more consumption gives more total utility. Table 7.1 shows Lisa's total utility from consuming different quantities of movies and soda. If she sees no movies, she gets no utility from movies. If she sees 1 movie in a month, she gets 50 units of utility. As the number of movies she sees in a month increases, her total utility increases, so if she sees 10 movies a month, she gets 250 units of total utility. The other part of the table shows Lisa's total utility from soda. If she drinks no soda, she gets no utility. As the amount of soda she drinks rises, her total utility increases.

Marginal Utility

Marginal utility is the change in total utility resulting from a one-unit increase in the quantity of a good consumed. The table in Fig. 7.3 shows the calculation of Lisa's marginal utility of movies. When her consumption of movies increases from 4 to 5 movies a month, her total utility from movies increases from 150 units to 175 units. Thus for Lisa, the marginal utility of seeing a fifth movie each month is 25 units. Notice that marginal utility appears midway between the quantities of consumption. It does so

TABLE 7.1

Lisa's Total Utility from Movies and Soda

Movies		Soda	
Quantity per month	Total utility	Six-packs per month	Total utility
0	0	0	0
1	50	1	75
2	88	2	117
3	121	3	153
4	150	4	181
5	175	5	206
6	196	6	225
7	214	7	243
8	229	8	260
9	241	9	276
10	250	10	291

because the *change* in consumption from 4 to 5 movies is what produces the *marginal* utility of 25 units. The table displays calculations of marginal utility for each level of movie consumption.

Figure 7.3(a) illustrates the total utility that Lisa gets from movies. As you can see, the more movies Lisa sees in a month, the more total utility she gets. Part (b) illustrates her marginal utility. This graph tells us that as Lisa sees more movies, the marginal utility she gets from watching movies decreases. For example, her marginal utility from the first movie is 50 units, from the second, 38 units, and from the third, 33 units. We call this decrease in marginal utility as the consumption of a good increases the principle of **diminishing marginal utility**.

Marginal utility is positive but diminishes as the consumption of a good increases. Why does marginal utility have these two features? In Lisa's case, she likes movies, and the more she sees, the better. That's why marginal utility is positive. The benefit that Lisa gets from the last movie seen is its marginal utility. To see why marginal utility diminishes, think about how you'd feel in the following two sit

FIGURE 7.3

Total Utility and Marginal Utility

Quantity	Total utility	Marginal utility
0	0	
		50
1	50	
		38
2	88	
		33
3	121	
		29
4	150	
		25
5	175	
		21
6	196	
		18
7	214	
		15
8	229	
		12
9	241	
		9
10	250	

(a) Total utility

(b) Marginal utility

The table shows that as Lisa's consumption of movies increases, so does the utility she derives from movies. For example, 4 movies give 150 units of utility, while 5 movies give 175 units. The table also shows her marginal utility—the change in utility resulting from the last movie seen. Marginal utility declines as consumption increases. For example,

the marginal utility from the fourth movie is 29 units, while that from the fifth movie is 25 units. Lisa's utility and marginal utility from movies are graphed in the figure. Part (a) shows the extra utility gained from each additional movie as a bar. Part (b) shows the marginal utility of each new movie as a declining series of steps.

uations. In one, you've just been studying for 29 evenings in a row. An opportunity arises to see a movie. The utility you get from that movie is the marginal utility from seeing one movie in a month. In the second situation, you've been on a movie binge. For the past 29 nights, you have not even

seen an assignment or test. You are up to your eyeballs in movies. You are happy enough to go to a movie on yet one more night. But the thrill that you get out of that thirtieth movie in 30 days is not very large. It is the marginal utility of the thirtieth movie in a month.

REVIEW

L isa divides her income of $30 a month between movies that cost $6 each and soda that costs $3 a six-pack. Lisa's preferences are described by using the concept of utility: the more movies Lisa sees in a given month, the more total utility she gets; the more cans of soda she drinks in a month, the more total utility she gets. The increase in total utility that results from the last unit of a good consumed is called marginal utility. As the quantity of a good consumed increases, marginal utility decreases. ◆

Utility Maximization

Utility maximization is the attainment of the greatest possible utility. A household's income and the prices that it faces limit the utility that it can obtain. We assume that a household consumes in a way that maximizes its total utility, taking into consideration its income and the prices that it faces. In Lisa's case, we examine how she allocates her spending between movies and soda to maximize her total utility, assuming that movies cost $6 each, soda costs $3 a six-pack, and Lisa has only $30 a month to spend.

The Utility-Maximizing Choice

Let's calculate how Lisa spends her money to maximize her total utility by constructing a table. Table 7.2 considers the same affordable combinations of movies and soda that are shown in Fig. 7.2. It records three things: first, the number of movies consumed and the total utility derived from them (the left side of the table); second, the number of six-packs of soda consumed and the total utility derived from them (the right side of the table); and third, the total utility derived from both movies and soda (the middle column of the table).

Consider, for example, the first row of Table 7.2. It shows Lisa watching no movies, getting no utility from them, but getting 291 units of total utility from drinking 10 six-packs of soda. Her total utility from movies and soda is 291 units. The rest of the table is constructed in exactly the same way.

The consumption of movies and soda that maximizes Lisa's total utility is highlighted in the table.

TABLE 7.2

Lisa's Utility-Maximizing Combinations of Movies and Soda

Movies		Total utility from movies and soda	Soda	
Quantity	Total utility		Total utility	Six-packs
0	0	291	291	10
1	50	310	260	8
2	88	313	225	6
3	121	302	181	4
4	150	267	117	2
5	175	175	0	0

When Lisa consumes 2 movies and 6 six-packs of soda, she gets 313 units of total utility. This is the best Lisa can do, given that she has only $30 to spend and given the prices of movies and six-packs. If she buys 8 six-packs of soda, she can see only 1 movie and gets 310 units of total utility, 3 less than the maximum attainable. If she sees 3 movies and drinks only 4 six-packs, she gets 302 units of total utility, 11 less than the maximum attainable.

We've just described a consumer equilibrium. A **consumer equilibrium** is a situation in which a consumer has allocated his or her income in the way that maximizes total utility.

In finding Lisa's consumer equilibrium, we measured her total utility from the consumption of movies and soda. There is a better way of determining a consumer equilibrium that does not involve measuring total utility at all. Let's look at this alternative.

Equalizing Marginal Utility per Dollar Spent

Another way to find out the allocation that maximizes a consumer's total utility is to make the marginal utility per dollar spent on each good equal for all goods. The **marginal utility per dollar spent** is the marginal utility obtained from the last unit of a good consumed divided by the price of the good. For example, Lisa's marginal utility from consuming the first movie is 50 units of utility. The price of a movie is $6, which means that the marginal utility per dollar spent on movies is 50 units divided by $6, or 8.33 units of utility per dollar.

Total utility is maximized when all the consumer's income is spent and when the marginal utility per dollar spent is equal for all goods.

Lisa maximizes total utility when she spends all her income and consumes movies and soda such that

$$\frac{\text{Marginal utility from movies}}{\text{Price of movies}} = \frac{\text{Marginal utility from soda}}{\text{Price of soda}}.$$

Call the marginal utility from movies MU_m, the marginal utility from soda MU_s, the price of movies P_m, and the price of soda P_s. Then Lisa's utility is maximized when she spends all her income and when

$$\frac{MU_m}{P_m} = \frac{MU_s}{P_s}.$$

Let's use this formula to find Lisa's utility-maximizing allocation of her income.

Table 7.3 sets out Lisa's marginal utilities per dollar spent for both movies and soda. For example, in row b, Lisa's marginal utility from movies is 50 units and, since movies cost $6 each, her marginal

utility per dollar spent on movies is 8.33 units per dollar (50 units divided by $6). Each row contains an allocation of Lisa's income that uses up her $30. You can see that Lisa's marginal utility per dollar spent on each good, like marginal utility itself, decreases as consumption of the good increases.

Total utility is maximized when the marginal utility per dollar spent on movies is equal to the marginal utility per dollar spent on soda—possibility c, with Lisa consuming 2 movies and 6 six-packs—the same allocation as we calculated in Table 7.2.

Figure 7.4 shows why the rule "equalize marginal utility per dollar spent on all goods" works. Suppose that instead of consuming 2 movies and 6 six-packs

TABLE 7.3

Maximizing Utility by Equalizing Marginal Utilities per Dollar Spent

	Movies ($6 each)			Soda ($3 per six-pack)		
	Quantity	Marginal utility	Marginal utility per dollar spent	Six-packs	Marginal utility	Marginal utility per dollar spent
a	0	0		10	15	5.00
b	1	50	8.33	8	17	5.67
c	2	38	6.33	6	19	6.33
d	3	33	5.50	4	28	9.33
e	4	29	4.83	2	42	14.00
f	5	25	4.17	0	0	

FIGURE 7.4

Equalizing Marginal Utility per Dollar Spent

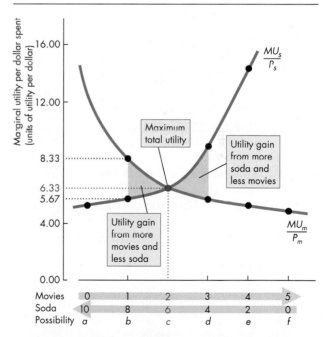

If Lisa consumes 1 movie and 8 six-packs of soda (possibility *b*), she gets 8.33 units of utility from the last dollar spent on movies and 5.67 units of utility from the last dollar spent on soda. She can get more total utility by buying one more movie. If she consumes 4 six-packs and 3 movies (possibility *d*), she gets 5.50 units of utility from the last dollar spent on movies and 9.33 units of utility from the last dollar spent on soda. She can get more total utility by buying one fewer movie. When Lisa's marginal utility per dollar spent on both goods is equal, her total utility is maximized.

(possibility *c*), Lisa consumes 1 movie and 8 six-packs (possibility *b*). She then gets 8.33 units of utility from the last dollar spent on movies and 5.67 units from the last dollar spent on soda. In this situation, it pays Lisa to spend less on soda and more on movies. If she spends a dollar less on soda and a dollar more on movies, her total utility from soda decreases by 5.67 units and her total utility from movies increases by 8.33 units. Lisa's total utility increases if she spends less on soda and more on movies.

Or suppose that Lisa consumes 3 movies and 4 six-packs (possibility *d*). In this situation, her marginal utility per dollar spent on movies is less than her marginal utility per dollar spent on soda. Lisa can now get more total utility by cutting her spending on movies and increasing her spending on soda. When Lisa's marginal utility per dollar spent on both goods is equal, she cannot get more total utility by spending differently. Her total utility is maximized.

Units of Utility

In calculating the utility-maximizing allocation of income in Table 7.3 and Fig. 7.4, we have not used the concept of total utility at all. All the calculations have been performed by using marginal utility and price. By making the marginal utility per dollar spent equal for both goods, we know that Lisa has maximized her total utility.

This way of viewing maximum utility is important; it means that the units in which utility is measured do not matter. We could double or halve all the numbers measuring utility, or multiply them by any other positive number, or square them, or take their square roots. None of these transformations of the units used to measure utility make any difference to the outcome. It is in this respect that utility is analogous to temperature. Our prediction about the freezing of water does not depend on the temperature scale; our prediction about maximizing utility does not depend on the units of utility.

R E V I E W

A consumer allocates his or her income to maximize total utility by making the marginal

utility per dollar spent on each good equal. Once the marginal utilities per dollar spent are equal, the consumer cannot reallocate spending to get more total utility from a given income. The units in which utility is measured are irrelevant—all that matters is that the marginal utility per dollar spent is equal for all goods. ◆

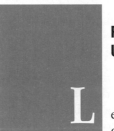

Predictions of Marginal Utility Theory

Let's now use marginal utility theory to make some predictions. What happens to Lisa's consumption of movies and soda when their prices change and when her income changes?

A Fall in the Price of Movies

To determine the effect of a change in price on consumption requires three steps. First, determine the combinations of movies and soda that can be bought at the new prices. Second, calculate the new marginal utilities per dollar spent. Third, determine the consumption of each good that makes the marginal utility per dollar spent on each good equal and that just exhausts the money available for spending.

Table 7.4 shows the combinations of movies and soda that exactly exhaust Lisa's $30 of income when movies cost $3 each and soda costs $3 a six-pack. Lisa's preferences do not change when prices change, so her utility schedule remains the same as that in Table 7.1. But now we divide her marginal utility from movies by $3, the new price of a movie, to get the marginal utility per dollar spent on movies.

What is the effect of the fall in the price of a movie on Lisa's consumption? You can find the answer by comparing her new utility-maximizing allocation (Table 7.4) with her original allocation (Table 7.3). Lisa responds to a fall in the price of a movie by watching more movies (up from 2 to 5 a month) and drinking less soda (down from 6 to 5 six-packs a month). That is, Lisa substitutes movies for soda when the price of a movie falls. Figure 7.5

TABLE 7.4

How a Change in the Price of Movies Affects Lisa's Choices

Movies ($3 each)		Soda ($3 per six-pack)	
Quantity	Marginal utility per dollar spent	Six-packs	Marginal utility per dollar spent
0		10	5.00
1	16.67	9	5.33
2	12.67	8	5.67
3	11.00	7	6.00
4	9.67	6	6.33
5	8.33	5	8.33
6	7.00	4	9.33
7	6.00	3	12.00
8	5.00	2	14.00
9	4.00	1	25.00
10	3.00	0	

FIGURE 7.5

A Fall in the Price of Movies

(a) Movies

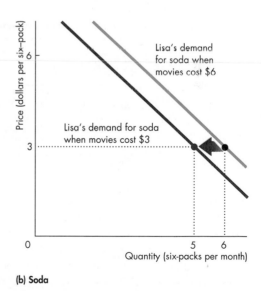

(b) Soda

When the price of movies falls and the price of soda remains constant, the quantity of movies demanded by Lisa increases and, in part (a), Lisa moves along her demand curve for movies. Also, Lisa's demand for soda decreases and, in part (b), her demand curve for soda shifts to the left.

illustrates these effects. In part (a), a fall in the price of movies produces a movement along Lisa's demand curve for movies, and in part (b), it shifts her demand curve for soda.

A Rise in the Price of Soda

Table 7.5 shows the combinations of movies and soda that exactly exhaust Lisa's $30 of income when movies cost $3 each and soda costs $6 a six-pack. Now we divide her marginal utility from soda by $6, the new price of a six-pack, to get the marginal utility per dollar spent on soda.

The effect of the rise in the price of soda on Lisa's consumption is seen by comparing her new utility-maximizing allocation (Table 7.5) with her previous allocation (Table 7.4). Lisa responds to a rise in the price of soda by drinking less soda (down from 5 to 2 six-packs a month) and watching more movies (up from 5 to 6 a month). That is, Lisa substitutes

TABLE 7.5

How a Change in the Price of Soda Affects Lisa's Choices

Movies ($3 each)		Soda ($6 per six-pack)	
Quantity	Marginal utility per dollar spent	Six-packs	Marginal utility per dollar spent
0		5	4.17
2	12.67	4	4.67
4	9.67	3	6.00
6	7.00	2	7.00
8	5.00	1	12.50
10	3.00	0	

movies for soda when the price of soda rises. Figure 7.6 illustrates these effects. In part (a), a rise in the price of soda produces a movement along Lisa's demand curve for soda, and in part (b), it shifts her demand curve for movies.

REVIEW

When the price of a movie falls but the price of soda stays constant, Lisa increases her consumption of movies and reduces her consumption of soda. There is a movement along her demand curve for movies and a shift in her demand for soda. When the price of a movie stays constant but the price of soda increases, Lisa reduces her consumption of soda and increases her consumption of movies. There is a movement along her demand curve for soda and a shift in her demand for movies.

FIGURE 7.6

A Rise in the Price of Soda

(a) Soda

(b) Movies

When the price of soda rises and the price of movies remains constant, the quantity of soda demanded by Lisa decreases and, in part (a), Lisa moves along her demand curve for movies. Also, Lisa's demand for movies increases and, in part (b), her demand curve for movies shifts to the right.

When the price of a movie falls or the price of soda rises, and Lisa does not change her consumption, her marginal utility per dollar spent on movies exceeds that spent on soda. To restore the equality of the marginal utility per dollar spent on each good, she must increase her consumption of movies and decrease her consumption of soda. ◆

Marginal utility theory predicts these two results: when the price of a good rises, the quantity demanded of that good decreases; if the price of one good rises, the demand for another good that can serve as a substitute increases. Does this sound familiar? It should. These predictions of marginal utility theory correspond to the assumptions that we made about consumer demand in Chapter 4. There we *assumed* that the demand curve for a good sloped downward, and we *assumed* that a rise in the price of a substitute increased demand. Marginal utility theory predicts these responses to price changes. In doing so, it makes four assumptions: first, consumers have a given income and face given prices; second, they maximize total utility; third, they get more utility as they consume more of a good; fourth, as consumption increases, marginal utility declines.

Next let's see the effects of a change in income on consumption.

The Effects of a Rise in Income

Let's suppose that Lisa's income increases to $42 a month and that movies cost $3 each and a six-pack costs $3 (as in Table 7.4). We saw, in Table 7.4, that with these prices and with an income of $30 a month, Lisa consumes 5 movies and 5 six-packs a month. We want to compare this consumption of movies and soda with Lisa's consumption at an income of $42. The calculations for the comparison are shown in Table 7.6. With $42, Lisa can buy 14 movies a month and no soda, or 14 six-packs a month and no movies, or any combination of the two goods as shown in the rows of the table. We calculate the marginal utility per dollar spent in exactly the same way as we did before and find the quantities at which the marginal utilities per dollar spent on movies and on soda are equal. With an income of $42, the marginal utility per dollar spent on each good is equal when Lisa watches 7 movies and drinks 7 six-packs of soda a month.

TABLE 7.6

Lisa's Choices with an Income of $42 a Month

Movies ($3 each)		Soda ($3 per six-pack)	
Quantity	Marginal utility per dollar spent	Six-packs	Marginal utility per dollar spent
0		14	
1	16.67	13	
2	12.67	12	
3	11.00	11	
4	9.67	10	5.00
5	8.33	9	5.33
6	7.00	8	5.67
7	6.00	7	6.00
8	5.00	6	6.33
9	4.00	5	8.33
10	3.00	4	9.33
11		3	12.00
12		2	14.00
13		1	25.00
14		0	

By comparing this situation with that in Table 7.4, we see that with an additional $12 a month, Lisa consumes 2 more six-packs and 2 more movies. This response arises from Lisa's preferences, as described by her marginal utilities. Different preferences produce different quantitative responses. But, for normal goods, a higher income always brings a larger consumption of all goods. For Lisa, soda and movies are normal goods. When her income increases, Lisa buys more of both goods.

Marginal Utility and the Real World

The marginal utility theory is summarized in Table 7.7. This theory can be used to answer a wide range of questions about the real world. An example, described in Reading Between the Lines on pp. 168–169, is its ability to explain the fluctuations in

Marginal
Utility Theory
in Action

~The New York Times, July 7, 1991

Wood Makes a Baseball Comeback

BY ERIC N. BERG

LOUISVILLE, KY.—As recently as 1985, the wooden baseball bat seemed doomed in all but professional leagues, done in by aluminum bats that not only were far more durable but also seemed to contain more base hits.

Never mind that no fan ever preferred the ping of aluminum striking the ball to the resounding crack of a wooden bat. Or that every great slugger has made his name using wood.

But now wooden bats are making a comeback, to the joy of everyone who insists that baseball is meant to be played on grass instead of a rug, with an organist instead of recorded disco tunes, while fans eat peanuts and hot dogs instead of taco chips and frozen yogurt.

Aluminum bats still outsell wooden ones, but sales of wooden bats are up 50 percent in the last two years, bat companies say.

Behind the comeback are several factors, including thrift, changes in retailing, a growth in the memorabilia business and wishful thinking about a career in Major League Baseball.

There is no debate that aluminum bats are far more durable—almost impossible to break. But they cost at least twice as much as wooden bats, sometimes far more. At discount stores, aluminum bats start at $20, while the best sell for up to $70; wooden bats, for children and adults, sell for $10 to $15. Some parents have decided they would rather buy the less expensive wooden bat and take their chances on its breaking. Bats are unlikely to snap in the relatively tame games of young children. . . .

Other parents, stars in their eyes, say they buy wooden bats to give their children a better chance at the long odds of becoming professional players. . . .

Of all the reasons for the return of the wooden bat, perhaps the most important is the growth of discount chains. Before a new Wal-Mart opens, bat makers say, it will be stocked with hundreds of bats, both aluminum and wood. The same is true at other rapidly growing discounters, like K Mart and Target Stores. . . .

The growing appetite for players' autographs, baseball cards and souvenirs has also helped wooden bat makers. Some Major League players order 100 to 1,000 bats each, which they autograph and then sell at baseball memorabilia shows.

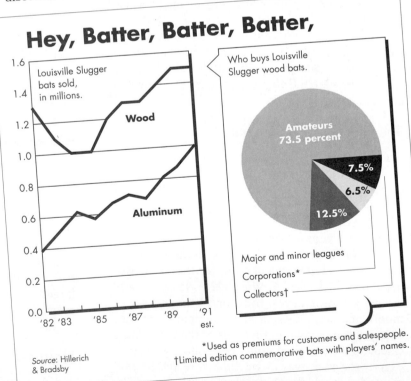

Hey, Batter, Batter, Batter,

Louisville Slugger bats sold, in millions.

Wood

Aluminum

Who buys Louisville Slugger wood bats.

Amateurs 73.5 percent

7.5%

6.5%

12.5%

Major and minor leagues

Corporations*

Collectors†

*Used as premiums for customers and salespeople.
†Limited edition commemorative bats with players' names.

Source: Hillerich & Bradsby

The Essence of the Story

Aluminum baseball bats outsell wood ones.

But sales of wood bats, after falling for many years, are growing again.

Reasons for increased sales include:

◆ Thrift
◆ Changes in retailing
◆ Growth in the memorabilia business
◆ Wishful thinking about a career in Major League Baseball

Aluminum bats are unbreakable but cost $20 to $70; wooden bats are breakable but not by small children and cost $10 to $15.

Major League players buy wooden bats, which they autograph and sell at baseball memorabilia shows.

Discount chains such as Wal-Mart, Kmart, and Target Stores are well stocked with both aluminum and wooden bats.

Wooden bats give children a better chance at the long odds of becoming professional players.

Background and Analysis

Consumers make the marginal utility per dollar spent equal across all goods—including wooden and aluminum baseball bats.

Call the marginal utility of wooden bats MU_w, the marginal utility of aluminum bats MU_a, the price of wooden bats P_w, and the price of aluminum bats P_a. Total utility is maximized when

$$\frac{MU_w}{P_w} = \frac{MU_a}{P_a}.$$

The quantity of wooden bats bought has increased rapidly, but so has the quantity of aluminum bats bought.

The data in the story (and in Fig. 1) show that sales of aluminum Louisville Sluggers grew from 25 percent to 40 percent of total sales between 1982 and 1991—a fact that is different from the impression given by the story.

The proportion of wooden Louisville Sluggers increased between 1985 and 1988 but declined after 1988—another fact that is different from the impression given by the story.

The prices of aluminum bats increased in relation to the prices of wooden bats from 1985 to 1988 and decreased after 1988—see Fig. 1.

The movements in the prices and quantities shown in Fig. 1 are consistent with the marginal utility theory. When the price of aluminum bats increases relative to the price of wooden bats, the percentage of bats that are aluminum decreases; when the price of aluminum bats decreases relative to the price of wooden bats, the percentage of bats that are aluminum increases.

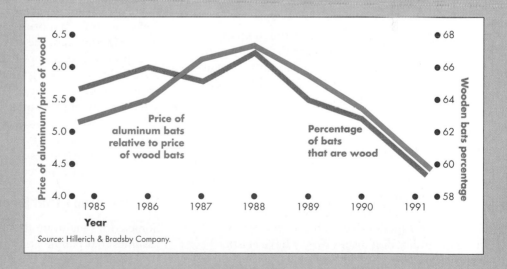

Source: Hillerich & Bradsby Company.

TABLE 7.7

Marginal Utility Theory

Assumptions

(a)   A consumer has a given income and faces given prices.

(b)   A consumer derives utility from the goods consumed.

(c)   Each additional unit of consumption yields additional utility; marginal utility is positive.

(d)   As the quantity of a good consumed increases, marginal utility decreases.

Implication

Utility is maximized when the marginal utility per dollar spent is equal for all goods and all income is spent.

Predictions

(a)   Other things being equal, the higher the price of a good, the lower is the quantity bought (the law of demand).

(b)   The higher the price of a good, the higher is the consumption of substitutes for that good.

(c)   The higher the consumer's income, the greater is the quantity demanded of normal goods.

the relative popularity of wooden and aluminum baseball bats. Other examples are the ability of the theory to answer the questions posed at the beginning of this chapter: why is the demand for audio headsets elastic and the demand for oil inelastic; and why, as income increases, does the proportion of income spent on electricity increase while the proportion spent on transportation decreases? These patterns in our spending result from the speed with which our marginal utility for each good diminishes as its consumption is increased. Goods whose marginal utility diminishes rapidly have inelastic demands and small income effects; goods whose marginal utility diminishes slowly have elastic demands and large income effects.

But the marginal utility theory can do much more than explain households' consumption choices. It can be used to explain *all* household choices. One of these choices, the allocation of time between work

in the home, office, or factory and leisure is the theme of Our Advancing Knowledge on pp. 172–173.

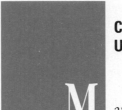

Criticisms of Marginal Utility Theory

Marginal utility theory helps us to understand the choices people make, but there are some criticisms of this theory. Let's look at them.

Utility Can't Be Observed or Measured

Agreed—we can't observe utility. But we don't need to observe it to use it. We can and do observe the quantities of goods and services that people consume, the prices of those goods and services, and people's incomes. Our goal is to understand the consumption choices that people make and to predict the effects of changes in prices and incomes on these choices. To make such predictions, we *assume* that people derive utility from their consumption, that more consumption yields more utility, and that marginal utility diminishes. From these assumptions, we make predictions about the directions of change in consumption when prices and incomes change. As we've already seen, the actual numbers that we use to express utility do not matter. Consumers maximize utility by making the marginal utility per dollar spent on each good equal. As long as we use the same scale to express utility for all goods, we'll get the same answer regardless of the units on our scale. In this regard, utility is similar to temperature—water freezes when it's cold enough, and that occurs independently of the temperature scale used.

"People Aren't That Smart"

Some critics maintain that marginal utility theory assumes that people are supercomputers. It requires people to look at the marginal utility of every good at every different quantity they might consume, divide those numbers by the prices of the goods, and then calculate the quantities so as to equalize the marginal utility of each good divided by its price.

Such criticism of marginal utility theory confuses the actions of people in the real world with those of people in a model economy. A model economy is no more an actual economy than a model railway is an actual railway. The people in the model economy perform the calculations that we have just described. People in the real world just consume. We observe their consumption choices, not their mental gymnastics. The marginal utility theory proposes that the consumption patterns that we observe in the real world are similar to those implied by the model economy in which people do compute the quantities of goods that maximize utility. We test how closely the marginal utility model resembles reality by checking the predictions of the model against observed consumption choices.

Marginal utility theory also has some broader implications that provide an interesting way of testing its usefulness. Let's examine two of these.

Some Implications of Marginal Utility Theory

We all love bargains—paying less for something than its usual price. One implication of the marginal utility theory is that we almost *always* get a bargain when we buy something. That is, we place a higher total value on the things we buy than on the amount they cost us. Let's see why.

Consumer Surplus and the Gains from Trade

In Chapter 3, we saw how people can gain by specializing in the things at which they have a comparative advantage and then trading with each other. Marginal utility theory provides a precise way of measuring the gains from trade.

When Lisa buys movies and soda, she exchanges her income for them. Does Lisa profit from this exchange? Are the dollars she has to give up worth more or less than the movies and soda are worth to her? As we are about to discover, the principle of diminishing marginal utility guarantees that Lisa,

and everyone else, gets more value from the things they buy than the amount of money they give up in exchange.

Calculating Consumer Surplus

The **value** that a consumer places on a good is the maximum amount that person would be willing to pay for it. The amount actually paid for a good is its price. **Consumer surplus** is the difference between the value of a good and its price. Diminishing marginal utility guarantees that a consumer always makes some consumer surplus. To understand why, let's look again at Lisa's consumption choices.

As before, let's assume that Lisa has $30 a month to spend, that movies cost $3 each, and that she watches 5 movies each month. Now let's look at Lisa's demand curve for movies, shown in Fig. 7.7. We can see from Lisa's demand curve that if she were able to watch only 1 movie a month, she

FIGURE 7.7

Consumer Surplus

Lisa is willing to pay $7 to watch her first movie, $6 to watch her second, $5 to watch her third, and $4 to watch her fourth. She actually has to pay only $3 for each movie. At that price, she sees 5 movies. She has a consumer surplus on the first four movies equal to $10—the difference between the highest price she is willing to pay and the price actually paid ($4 + $3 + $2 + $1).

UNDERSTANDING
Human
BEHAVIOR

The economic analysis of human behavior, in the workplace, in the markets for goods and services, in the markets for labor services, in financial markets, and in transactions with each other in social as well as economic situations, is based on the idea that our behavior can be understood as a response to scarcity. Everything we do can be understood as a choice that maximizes utility subject to the constraints imposed by our limited resources and technology. If people's preferences are stable in the face of changing constraints, then we have a chance of predicting how they will respond to an evolving environment.

The incredible change that has occurred over the past 100 years in the way women allocate their time can be explained as the consequence of changing constraints. Technological advances have equipped the nation's factories with machines that have increased the productivity of both women and men, thereby raising the wages they can earn. The increasingly technological world has increased the return to education for both women and men and has led to a large increase in the number of high-school and college graduates of both sexes. And equipped with a wide array of gadgets and machines that cut the time of household jobs, women have increasingly allocated their time to work outside the home.

This economic view might not be correct, but it is a powerful one. And if it is correct, the changing attitudes toward women are a consequence, not a cause, of their economic advancement.

> "Economy is the art of making the most of life."
>
> GEORGE BERNARD SHAW
> *"Man and Superman"*

Economists explain people's actions as the consequence of choices that maximize utility subject to constraints. In the 1890s, fewer than 5 percent of women chose paid employment and most of those who did had low-paying and unattractive jobs. The other 95 percent of women chose unpaid work in the home. What were the constraints that led to these choices?

Many economists have contributed to our understanding of human behavior, but three stand out from the rest. They are Jeremy Bentham (1748–1832), pictured left, William Stanley Jevons (1835–1882), pictured right, and Gary Becker (1930–).

Bentham, who lived in London (and whose embalmed body is preserved to this day in a glass cabinet in the University of London), was the first to use the concept of utility to explain and prescribe human choices. The distinction between explanation and prescription was not a sharp one in Bentham's day. He was a founder of social security and advocated guaranteed employment, minimum wages, and social benefits such as free education and free medical care.

Jevons' main claim to fame in his own day was his proposal—wrong as it turned out—that economic fluctuations are caused by sun spots. He was a co-discoverer of the concept of *marginal utility,* and it was he who devel-

BENTHAM, JEVONS, & BECKER:

UNDERSTANDING
People's Choices

oped the theory explained in this chapter.

Gary Becker teaches both economics and sociology at the University of Chicago. He has used the ideas of Bentham and

Jevons to explain a wide range of human choices, including the choices made by women about how many children to bear and how much and what type of work to do.

would be willing to pay $7 to see it. She would be willing to pay $6 to see a second movie, $5 to see a third, and so on.

Luckily for Lisa, she has to pay only $3 for each movie she sees—the market price of a movie. Although she values the first movie she sees in a month at $7, she pays only $3, which is $4 less than she would be willing to pay. The second movie she sees in a month is worth $6 to her. The difference between the value that she places on the movie and what she has to pay is $3. The third movie she sees in a month is worth $5 to her, which is $2 more than she has to pay for it, and the fourth movie is worth $4, which is $1 more than she has to pay for it. You can see this progression in Fig. 7.7, which highlights the difference between the price she pays ($3) and the higher value she places on the first, second, third, and fourth movies. These differences are a gain to Lisa. Let's calculate her total gain.

The total amount that Lisa is willing to pay for the 5 movies she sees is $25 (the sum of $7, $6, $5, $4, and $3). She actually pays $15 (5 movies multiplied by $3). The extra value that she receives from the movies is therefore $10. This amount is the value of Lisa's consumer surplus. From watching 5 movies a month, she gets $10 worth of value in excess of what she has to spend to see them.

Let's now look at another implication of the marginal utility theory.

The Paradox of Value

More than 200 years ago, Adam Smith posed a paradox that we also raised at the start of this chapter. Water, which is essential to life itself, costs little, but diamonds, which are useless in comparison to water, are expensive. Why? Adam Smith could not solve the paradox. Not until the theory of marginal utility had been invented could anyone give a satisfactory answer.

You can solve Adam Smith's puzzle by distinguishing between total utility and marginal utility. The total utility that we get from water is enormous. But remember, the more we consume of something, the smaller is its marginal utility. We use so much water that the marginal utility—the benefit we get from one more glass of water—diminishes to a tiny value. Diamonds, on the other hand, have a small total utility relative to water, but because we buy few diamonds, they have a high marginal utility.

Our theory also tells us that consumers spend their income in a way that makes the marginal utility from each good divided by its price equal for all goods. This also holds true for their spending on diamonds and water: diamonds have a high marginal utility divided by a high price, while water has a low marginal utility divided by a low price. In each case, the marginal utility per dollar spent is the same.

◆ ◆ ◆ ◆ We've now completed our study of the marginal utility theory of consumption. We've used that theory to examine how Lisa allocates her income between the two goods that she consumes—movies and soda. We've also seen how the theory can be used to resolve the paradox of value. Furthermore, we've seen how the theory can be used to explain our real-world consumption choices.
◆ ◆ In the next chapter, we're going to study an alternative theory of household behavior. To help you see the connection between the marginal utility theory of this chapter and the more modern theory of consumer behavior of the next chapter, we'll continue with the same example. We'll meet Lisa again and discover another way of understanding how she gets the most out of her $30 a month.

SUMMARY

Individual Demand and Market Demand

Individual demand represents the relationship between the price of a good and the quantity demanded by a single individual. Market demand is the sum of all individual demands. (pp. 158–159)

Household Consumption Choices

The marginal utility theory explains how people divide their spending between goods and services. The theory is based on a model that assumes certain characteristics about the consumer. The consumer has a given income and faces given prices. The consumer derives utility from the goods consumed, and the consumer's total utility increases as consumption of the good increases. The change in total utility resulting from a one-unit increase in the consumption of a good is called marginal utility. Marginal utility declines as consumption increases. The consumer's goal is to maximize total utility, which occurs when the marginal utility per dollar spent on each good is equal and all income is spent. (pp. 159–164)

Predictions of Marginal Utility Theory

Marginal utility theory predicts how prices and income affect the amounts of each good consumed. First, it predicts the law of demand. That is, other things being equal, the higher the price of a good, the lower is the quantity demanded of that good. Second, it predicts that, other things being equal, the higher the consumer's income, the greater is the consumption of all normal goods. (pp. 164–170)

Criticisms of Marginal Utility Theory

Some people criticize marginal utility theory because utility cannot be observed or measured. However, the size of the units of measurement of utility does not matter. All that matters is that the ratio of the marginal utility from each good to its price is equal for all goods. Any units of measure that are consistently applied will do. The concept of utility is analogous to the concept of temperature—it cannot be directly observed, but it can be used to make predictions about events that are observable.

Another criticism of marginal utility theory is that consumers can't be as smart as the theory implies. In fact, the theory makes no predictions about the thought processes of consumers. It makes predictions only about their actions and assumes that people spend their income in what seems to them to be the best possible way. (pp. 170–171)

Some Implications of Marginal Utility Theory

Marginal utility theory implies that every time we buy goods and services, we get more value for our expenditure than the money we spend. We benefit from consumer surplus, which is equal to the difference between the maximum amount that we are willing to pay for a good and the price that we actually pay.

Marginal utility theory resolves the paradox of value: water is extremely valuable but cheap, while diamonds are less valuable though expensive. When we talk loosely about value, we are thinking of total utility. The total utility of water is higher than the total utility of diamonds. But, at the quantities consumed, the marginal utility of water is lower than the marginal utility of diamonds. People choose the amounts of water and diamonds to consume so as to maximize total utility. In maximizing total utility, they make the marginal utility per dollar spent the same for water as for diamonds. (pp. 171–174)

KEY ELEMENTS

Key Terms

Consumer equilibrium, 162
Consumer surplus, 171
Diminishing marginal utility, 160
Individual demand, 158
Marginal utility, 160
Marginal utility per dollar spent, 162
Market demand, 158
Total utility, 160
Utility, 159
Utility maximization, 162
Value, 171

Key Figures and Tables

Figure 7.1 Individual and Market Demand Curves, 158
Figure 7.2 Consumption Possibilities, 159
Figure 7.3 Total Utility and Marginal Utility, 161
Figure 7.4 Equalizing the Marginal Utility per Dollar Spent, 163
Figure 7.5 A Fall in the Price of Movies, 165
Figure 7.6 A Rise in the Price of Soda, 166
Figure 7.7 Consumer Surplus, 171
Table 7.7 Marginal Utility Theory, 170

R E V I E W   Q U E S T I O N S

1 What is the relationship between individual demand and market demand?

2 How do we construct a market demand curve from individual demand curves?

3 What do we mean by utility?

4 Distinguish between total utility and marginal utility.

5 How does marginal utility change as the level of consumption of a good changes?

6 Susan is a consumer. When is Susan's utility maximized?

a When she has spent all her income

b When she has spent all her income and marginal utility is equal for all goods

c When she has spent all her income and the marginal utility per dollar spent is equal for all goods

Explain your answer.

7 What does the marginal utility theory predict about the effect of a change in price on the quantity of a good consumed?

8 What does the marginal utility theory predict about the effect of a change in the price of one good on the consumption of another good?

9 What does the marginal utility theory predict about the effect of a change in income on consumption of a good?

10 How would you answer someone who says that the marginal utility theory is useless because utility cannot be observed?

11 How would you respond to someone who tells you that the marginal utility theory is useless because people aren't smart enough to compute a consumer equilibrium in which the marginal utility per dollar spent is equal for all goods?

12 What is consumer surplus? How is consumer surplus calculated?

13 What is the paradox of value? How does the marginal utility theory resolve it?

P R O B L E M S

1 Shirley's demand for yogurt is given by the following:

Price (dollars per pound)	Quantity (cartons per week)
1	12
2	9
3	6
4	3
5	1

a Draw a graph of Shirley's demand for yogurt.

Dan also likes yogurt. His demand for yogurt is given by the following:

Price (dollars per pound)	Quantity (cartons per week)
1	6
2	5
3	4
4	3
5	2

b Draw a graph of Dan's demand curve.

c If Shirley and Dan are the only two individuals, construct the market demand schedule for yogurt.

Draw a graph of the market demand for yogurt.

e Draw a graph to show that the market demand curve is the horizontal sum of Shirley's demand curve and Dan's demand curve.

2 Calculate Lisa's marginal utility from soda from the numbers given in Table 7.1. Draw two graphs, one of her total utility and the other of her marginal utility from soda. Make your graphs look similar to those in Fig. 7.3.

3 Max enjoys windsurfing and snorkeling. He obtains the following utility from each of these sports:

Half-hours per month	Utility from windsurfing	Utility from snorkeling
1	60	20
2	110	38
3	150	53
4	180	64
5	200	70
6	206	75
7	211	79
8	215	82
9	218	84

a Draw graphs showing Max's utility from windsurfing and from snorkeling.
b Compare the two utility graphs. Can you say anything about Max's preferences?
c Draw graphs showing Max's marginal utility from windsurfing and from snorkeling.
d Compare the two marginal utility graphs. Can you say anything about Max's preferences?

4 Max has $35 to spend. Equipment for windsurfing rents for $10 a half-hour, while snorkeling equipment rents for $5 a half-hour. Use this information together with that given in problem 3 to answer the following questions.
a What is the marginal utility per dollar spent on snorkeling if Max snorkels for:
(1) Half an hour
(2) One and a half hours

b What is the marginal utility per dollar spent on windsurfing if Max windsurfs for:
(1) Half an hour
(2) One hour
c How long can Max afford to snorkel if he windsurfs for:
(1) Half an hour
(2) One hour
(3) One and a half hours
d Will Max choose to snorkel for one hour and windsurf for one and a half hours?
e Will he windsurf for more or less than one and a half hours?
f How long will Max choose to windsurf and to snorkel?

5 Max's sister gives him $20 to spend on his leisure pursuits, so he now has $55 to spend. How long will Max now windsurf and snorkel?

6 If Max has only $55 to spend and the rent on windsurfing equipment halves to $5 a half-hour, how will Max now spend his time windsurfing and snorkeling?

7 Does Max's demand curve for windsurfing slope downward or upward?

8 Max takes a Club Med holiday, the cost of which includes unlimited sports activities—including windsurfing, snorkeling, and tennis. There is no extra charge for any equipment. Max decides to spend three hours each day on both windsurfing and snorkeling. How long does he windsurf? How long does he snorkel?

9 Sara's demand for windsurfing is given by:

Price (dollars per half-hour)	Time windsurfing (half-hours per month)
12.50	8
15.00	6
17.50	4
20.00	2

a If windsurfing costs $17.50 a half-hour, what is Sara's consumer surplus?
b If windsurfing costs $12.50 a half-hour, what is Sara's consumer surplus?

CHAPTER 8

POSSIBILITIES, PREFERENCES, AND CHOICES

After studying this chapter, you will be able to:

◆ Calculate and graph a household's budget line

◆ Work out how the budget line changes when prices and income change

◆ Make a map of preferences by using indifference curves

◆ Calculate a household's optimal consumption plan

◆ Predict the effects of price and income changes on the pattern of consumption

◆ Explain why the workweek gets shorter as wages rise

◆ Explain how budget lines and indifference curves can be used to understand all household choices

L IKE THE CONTINENTS FLOATING ON THE EARTH'S

mantle, our spending patterns change steadily over

time. On such subterranean movements, business

empires rise and fall. Goods such as home videos and

microwave popcorn now appear on our shopping

lists, while Davy Crockett coonskin caps and horse-

drawn carriages have disappeared. Miniskirts

appear, disappear, and reappear in cycles of fashion. ◆ ◆ But the glittering

surface of our consumption obscures deeper and slower changes in how we

spend. In the last few years, we've seen a proliferation of gourmet food shops and

designer clothing boutiques. Yet we spend a smaller percentage of our income

today on food and clothing than we did in 1950. Despite the growth of jet travel

and interstate highways, we spend about the same

percentage of our income on transportation today as

we did 40 years ago. At the same time, the percent-

age of our income spent on fuel, housing, and med-

Subterranean Movements

ical care has grown steadily. Why does consumer spending change over the years?

How do people react to changes in income and changes in the prices of the things

they buy? ◆ ◆ Similar subterranean movements govern the way we spend our

time. For example, the workweek has fallen steadily from 70 hours a week in the

nineteenth century down to 35 hours a week today. Why has the average work-

week declined? Similarly, there have been trends in fertility, marriage, education,

crime, and social interactions. Why do the habits and social mores of one genera-

tion become the old-fashioned ideas of another?

◆ ◆ ◆ ◆ We're going to study a model of household choice that predicts the effects of changes in prices and incomes on what people buy, on how much work they do, on how much they borrow and lend, and even on how many children they have and how much crime they commit.

Consumption Possibilities

How does a household divide its income among the goods and services available? We are going to study a model of household choice that can answer this question and that predicts how consumption patterns change when income and prices change. Our first step is to examine the constraint on the household's possible choices.

Constraint

A household's consumption choices are constrained by the household's income and by the prices of the goods and services available. We're going to study a household that has a given amount of income to spend and that cannot influence the prices of the goods and services it buys. It has to take those prices as given.

The limits to a household's consumption choices are described by its **budget line.** To make the concept of the household's budget line as clear as possible, we'll consider the example of Lisa, who has an income of $30 a month to spend.[1] She buys two goods—movies and soda. Movies cost $6 each; soda costs $3 for a six-pack. If Lisa spends all of her income, she will reach the limits to her consumption of movies and soda.

In Fig. 8.1, each row of the table shows an affordable way for Lisa to consume movies and

soda. Row *a* indicates that she can buy 10 six-packs of soda and see no movies. You can see that this combination of movies and soda exhausts her monthly income of $30. Now look at row *f*. It says

[1]If you have read the preceding chapter on marginal utility theory, you have already met Lisa. This tale of her thirst for soda and zeal for movies will sound familiar to you—up to a point. But in this chapter, we're going to use a different method for representing preferences—one that does not require us to resort to the idea of utility.

FIGURE 8.1
The Budget Line

Consumption possibility	Movies (per month)	Soda (six-packs per month)
a	0	10
b	1	8
c	2	6
d	3	4
e	4	2
f	5	0

Lisa's budget line shows the boundary between what Lisa can and cannot afford. The table lists Lisa's affordable combinations of movies and soda when she has an income of $30 and when soda costs $3 a six-pack and movies cost $6 each. For example, row *a* tells us that Lisa can buy 10 six-packs and see no movies—a combination that exhausts her $30 income. The figure graphs Lisa's budget line. Points *a* through *f* on the graph represent rows of the table. For divisible goods, the budget line is the continuous line *af*.

that Lisa can watch 5 movies and drink no soda—another combination that exhausts the $30 available. Each of the other rows in the table also exhausts Lisa's income. (Check that each of the other rows costs exactly $30.) The numbers in the table define Lisa's consumption possibilities. We can graph Lisa's consumption possibilities as points *a* through *f* in Fig. 8.1.

Divisible and Indivisible Goods

Some goods can be bought in any quantity desired. Such goods are called divisible. Examples of divisible goods are gasoline and electricity, both of which can be bought in almost any quantity at all. Other goods—called indivisible goods—can be bought only in whole units. Movies are an example of an indivisible good. Although you can watch a fraction of a movie (as presumably you've done when you've picked a loser), you can buy movies only in whole units.

We can best understand the model of household choice that we're about to study if we suppose that all goods and services are divisible. In this case, the consumption possibilities are not just the points *a* through *f* shown in Fig. 8.1, but those points plus all the intermediate points that form a continuous straight line running from *a* to *f*. Such a line is a budget line. Thus, for example, if instead of movies and soda, we measure gallons of gasoline on the vertical axis and yards of cloth on the horizontal axis, Lisa can buy at any point along the line, consuming any fraction of a gallon or a yard.

Though Lisa can consume at only one of the six points represented by the rows of the table in our example, we'll develop the model so that it can deal with the case in which goods are divisible into any desired units.

Lisa's budget line is a constraint on her choices. It marks the boundary between what is affordable and what is unaffordable. She can afford all the points on the line and inside it. She cannot afford points outside the line. The constraint on her consumption depends on prices and on her income, and the constraint changes when prices and her income change.

The Budget Equation

To discover how the constraint on consumption changes when prices and income change, we need to describe the budget line in the form of an equation.

Such an equation is called the budget equation. The **budget equation** states the limits to consumption for a given income and for given prices. We're going to work out such an equation and, to keep things tidy, we'll summarize our calculations in Table 8.1.

The left side of the table works out the budget equation by using symbols that apply to any consumer; the right side of the table works out the equation by using numbers that describe Lisa's situation. The first section of the table lists the variables that affect a household's budget. Those variables are income, the prices of the goods consumed, and the quantities consumed. To make our calculations clear, we have assigned symbols to each of these variables. In Lisa's case, her income is $30, the prices are $6 for movies and $3 for soda, and Lisa will choose the quantities of movies and soda to consume.

The consumer's budget is set out in the second section of the table. It states that expenditure (on the

---

TABLE **8.1**

Calculating the Budget Equation

In general		In Lisa's case
1. The variables		
Income $\quad = y$		$y \;=\; \$30$
Price of movies $\quad = P_m$		$P_m \;=\; \$6$
Price of soda $\quad = P_s$		$P_s \;=\; \$3$
Quantity of movies $\;=\; Q_m$		$Q_m \;=\;$ **Lisa's choice**
Quantity of soda $\;=\; Q_s$		$Q_s \;=\;$ **Lisa's choice**

2. The budget

$$P_s Q_s + P_m Q_m = y \qquad\qquad (\$3)Q_s + (\$6)Q_m = \$30$$

3. Calculating the budget equation

◆ **Divide by** P_s **to obtain**

$$Q_s + \frac{P_m}{P_s} Q_m = \frac{y}{P_s}.$$

◆ **Subtract** $(P_m/P_s)Q_m$ **from both sides to obtain**

$$Q_s = \frac{y}{P_s} - \frac{P_m}{P_s} Q_m.$$

◆ **Divide by** $\$3$ **to obtain**

$$Q_s + 2Q_m = 10.$$

◆ **Subtract** $2Q_m$ **from both sides to obtain**

$$Q_s = 10 - 2Q_m.$$

left side of the equation) equals income (on the right side of the equation). Look at the elements of expenditure. Expenditure is equal to the sum of the expenditures on each of the goods. Expenditure on any one good equals its price multiplied by the quantity consumed. In Lisa's case, income (on the right side) is $30, and the most that she can spend (on the left side of the equation) is the amount of soda consumed (Q_s) multiplied by the price of a soda ($3) plus the number of movies consumed (Q_m) multiplied by their price ($6).

The third section of the table shows you how to derive the budget equation from the consumer's budget equation. There are just two steps. First, divide both sides by the price of soda. Second, subtract $(P_m/P_s)Q_m$ from both sides of the resulting equation. The result is the budget equation shown in the last line of the table. The budget equation is

$$Q_s = \frac{y}{P_s} - \frac{P_m}{P_s} Q_m.$$

This equation tells us how the consumption level of one good varies as consumption of the other good varies. To interpret the equation, let's go back to the budget line of Fig. 8.1.

Let's first check that the budget equation that we have derived in Table 8.1 delivers the graph of the budget in Fig. 8.1. Begin by setting Q_m equal to zero. In this case, the budget equation tells us that Q_s will be 10. This combination of Q_s and Q_m is the same as that shown in row *a* of the table in Fig. 8.1. Setting Q_m equal to 5 makes Q_s equal to zero (row *f* of the table in Fig. 8.1). Check that you can derive the other rows of the table in Fig. 8.1.

The budget equation contains two variables under the control of the individual (Q_m and Q_s) and two numbers outside the individual's control. Let's look more closely at the two numbers outside the individual's control (y/P_s and P_m/P_s).

The first number, y/P_s, or 10 in Lisa's case, is the maximum number of six-packs that can be bought. It is called real income in terms of soda. **Real income** is income expressed in units of goods. Real income in terms of a particular good is income divided by the price of that good. In Lisa's case, her real income is 10 six-packs. In Fig. 8.1, the budget line intersects the vertical axis at Lisa's real income in terms of soda. That is, if Lisa spends all her income on soda, she can buy 10 six-packs.

Let's now look at the second number in the budget equation that is outside the consumer's control, P_m/P_s, or 2 in Lisa's case. This number shows the relative price of the two goods. A **relative price** is the price of one good divided by the price of another good. In the equation, P_m/P_s is the relative price of movies in terms of soda. For Lisa, that relative price is 2. That is, in order to see one more movie, she has to give up 2 six-packs.

You can see the relative price of movies to soda in Fig. 8.1 as the magnitude of the slope of the budget line. To calculate the slope of the budget line, recall the formula for slope that was introduced in Chapter 2: the slope of a line equals the change in the variable measured on the *y*-axis divided by the change in the variable measured on the *x*-axis as we move along the line. In this case, the variable measured on the *y*-axis is the quantity of soda, and the variable measured on the *x*-axis is the quantity of movies. Along Lisa's budget line, as soda decreases from 10 to 0, movies increase from 0 to 5. Therefore the slope of the budget line is $-10/5$, or -2. The flatter the budget line, the less expensive is the good measured on the horizontal axis relative to the good measured on the vertical axis. The steeper the line, the more expensive is the good measured on the horizontal axis relative to the one on the vertical axis. In other words, the slope of the budget line is the relative price of the good whose quantity appears on the horizontal axis.

The relative price of one good in terms of another is the opportunity cost of the first good in terms of the second. In Lisa's case, the opportunity cost of 1 movie is 2 six-packs of soda. Equivalently, the opportunity cost of 2 six-packs of soda is 1 movie.

Changes in Prices and Income

Let's now work out what happens to the budget line when prices and income change. We'll begin with a change in the price of one good.

A Change in the Price of Movies   Suppose that the price of movies rises. What happens to Lisa's budget line? To make things vivid, let's suppose that the price of movies falls to $3 a movie. By working through the calculations in Table 8.1, you can work out Lisa's budget line with the new price of movies. Recall that the budget equation is

$$Q_s = \frac{y}{P_s} - \frac{P_m}{P_s} Q_m.$$

Nothing has happened to income (y) or the price of soda (P_s). Lisa's real income in terms of soda remains 10. But the price of movies has fallen and is now equal to the price of soda. Therefore the relative price of movies (P_m/P_s) has decreased to 1. Lisa's new budget equation is

$$Q_s = 10 - Q_m.$$

Let's check that this new budget equation works. With movies costing $3 each, Lisa can see as many as 10 movies with her income. Using Lisa's new budget equation, you will see that substituting 10 for Q_m results in zero for Q_s. We know that this answer is correct because if Lisa sees 10 movies, she spends all her income on movies and has nothing left to spend on soda.

Figure 8.2(a) shows how the fall in the price of movies affects the budget line. Because the price of movies has gone down, the new budget line is flatter than budget line af. But notice that point a has not changed. If Lisa spends all her income on soda, she can still buy 10 six-packs. In other words, Lisa's real

income in terms of soda has not changed. Only the price of movies has changed. Movies have become cheaper in terms of soda. Previously, 1 movie was worth 2 six-packs. In the new situation, the relative price or opportunity cost of 1 movie is 1 six-pack.

Let's see what happens to the budget line when the price of soda changes.

A Change in the Price of Soda   Let's go back to the original situation in which movies cost $6 each and soda $3 a six-pack. What happens to Lisa's budget line if the price of a six-pack rises? Let's suppose that the price goes up from $3 to $6. If Lisa spends all her income on soda, she can buy 5 six-packs. Her real income in terms of soda has gone down. Since movies cost $6 each and soda costs $6 a six-pack, the relative price of movies is 1, the same as in the previous example. The opportunity cost of 1 movie is 1 six-pack of soda. We can work out the new budget line by using the budget equation:

$$Q_s = \frac{y}{P_s} - \frac{P_m}{P_s}Q_m.$$

FIGURE 8.2

Prices, Income, and the Budget Line

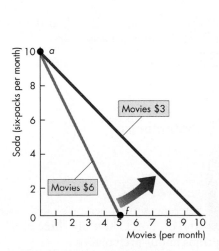

(a) A fall in the price of movies

(b) A rise in the price of soda

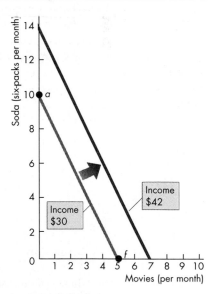

(c) A rise in income

In part (a), the price of a movie falls from $6 to $3. In part (b), the price of a six-pack of soda increases from $3 to $6. In part (c), income

increases from $30 to $42, but prices remain constant. The arrow in each part indicates the shift in the budget line.

The price of a soda (P_s) is now $6. Lisa's income is still $30, and the price of a movie is still $6. So Lisa's budget equation is

$$Q_s = \frac{30}{6} - \frac{6}{6} Q_m,$$

or

$$Q_s = 5 - Q_m.$$

Figure 8.2(b) shows the new budget line. Notice this time that point f has not moved. If Lisa spends all her income on movies, she can still see only 5 movies. Her real income in terms of movies has not changed.

Look at the new budget lines in parts (a) and (b) of Fig. 8.2. In part (a), both movies and soda cost $3; in part (b), they both cost $6. Lisa earns $30 in both cases. Therefore in part (b), she can consume less of everything than in part (a), but movies have the same opportunity cost in the two cases—to see 1 more movie, she must give up 1 six-pack of soda. Notice that the new budget line in part (b) has the same slope as the new budget line in part (a).

Let's now see what happens to the budget line when income changes.

A Change in Income   If prices remain constant and income increases, a person can then consume more of all goods. Go back to the initial situation in which Lisa had an income of $30, movies cost $6 each, and a six-pack costs $3. Keeping the prices of the two goods constant, let's work out what happens if Lisa's income goes up from $30 to $42. Again, recall the budget equation:

$$Q_s = \frac{y}{P_s} - \frac{P_m}{P_s} Q_m.$$

Let's put into this equation the numbers for prices and for the new income. The price of soda (P_s) is $3, and the price of movies (P_m) is $6. Income ($y$) is $42. Putting these numbers into the equation gives

$$Q_s = \frac{42}{3} - \frac{6}{3} Q_m,$$

or

$$Q_s = 14 - 2Q_m.$$

Lisa's real income has gone up because her income has gone up, while the prices of movies and soda have stayed the same. Her real income in terms of soda has gone up from 10 to 14. That is, if she spends all her income on soda, she can now buy 14 six-packs. Her real income in terms of movies has

also gone up. If she spends all her income on movies, she can see 7 movies.

The shift in Lisa's budget line is shown in Fig. 8.2(c). The initial budget line is the same one we began with in parts (a) and (b), when Lisa's income was $30. The new budget line shows Lisa able to consume more of each good. The new line is parallel to the old one but farther out. The two budget lines are parallel, or have the same slope, because the relative price is the same in both cases. With movies costing $6 each and a six-pack costing $3, Lisa must give up 2 six-packs to see 1 movie. The new budget line is farther out than the initial one because her real income has increased.

R E V I E W

T he budget line describes the maximum amounts of consumption that a household can undertake, given its income and the prices of the goods it buys. A change in the price of one good changes the slope of the budget line. If the price of the good measured on the horizontal axis rises, the budget line gets steeper. A change in income makes the budget line shift, but its slope does not change. ◆

Let's now leave the budget line and look at the second ingredient in the model of household choice—preferences.

Preferences

P references are a person's likes and dislikes. There are three fundamental assumptions about preferences:

◆ Preferences do not depend on the prices of goods.

◆ Preferences do not depend on income.

◆ More of any good is preferred to less of that good.

The first two assumptions amount to the proposition that people's likes and dislikes do not depend on what they can afford to buy. This assumption does *not* mean that people's preferences do not change over time. Nor does it mean that their preferences are not influenced by the things that they have consumed and experienced. It *does* mean that just because income increases or the price of a good decreases, people do not, *for one of those reasons*, suddenly decide that they like a particular good more than they did before.

The third assumption—more of any good is preferred to less of that good—is just a different way of saying that wants are unlimited. Of course, in reality, you can imagine having enough of any one good to want no more of it, but there will always be something that you will prefer to have more of.

We are going to discover in this section a very neat idea—that of drawing a map of a person's preferences.

A Preference Map

Let's see how we can draw a map of a person's preferences by constructing a map of Lisa's preferences for movies and soda. This map, which appears in Fig. 8.3, measures the number of movies seen on the horizontal axis and the number of six-packs consumed on the vertical axis. Let's start with Fig. 8.3(a) and focus on point *c*, where Lisa sees 2 movies and consumes 6 six-packs of soda. We will use this point as a reference and ask how Lisa likes all the other points in relation to point *c*.

Figure 8.3(b) takes us to the next step. It is divided into four areas. The area shaded yellow has, at each point, more movies and more soda than at point *c*. Lisa prefers all the points in this area to point *c*. The area shaded gray has, at each point, fewer movies and less soda than at point *c*. She prefers point *c* to all the points in this area. Points in the two white areas have either more movies and

---

FIGURE **8.3**

Mapping Preferences

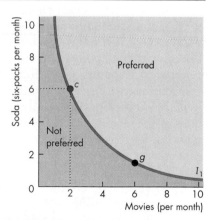

(a) A consumption point   **(b) Preference relations**   **(c) Indifference curve**

If Lisa consumes 6 six-packs of soda and 2 movies, she consumes at point *c* in part (a). Lisa prefers more goods to fewer goods. This fact is illustrated in part (b). She prefers any point at which she consumes more of both soda and movies to point *c* (all the points in the yellow area). She prefers point *c* to any point at which fewer movies and six-packs are consumed (all the points in the gray area). Whether she prefers seeing more movies but having less soda than at point *c* depends on how many more movies and how much less soda she has. Similarly, if she consumes more soda and sees fewer movies than at

point *c*, whether she prefers that situation to *c* depends on how much more soda and how many fewer movies she has. The boundary between points that she prefers to point *c* and those to which *c* is preferred is shown in part (c). That boundary is called an indifference curve. Lisa is indifferent between points such as *g* and *c* on the indifference curve. She prefers any point above the indifference curve (yellow area) to any point on it, and she prefers any point on the indifference curve to any point below it (gray area).

less soda than point c or more soda and fewer movies than point c. How does Lisa rank points in these areas against point c? To answer this question, we need to take the final step in constructing a map of Lisa's preferences.

Figure 8.3(c) takes the final step. It contains a line—I_1—passing through point c and through what were the two white areas. That line defines the boundary between points that Lisa prefers to point c and points she regards as inferior to point c. Lisa is indifferent between point c and the other points on the line I_1, such as point g. The line is called an indifference curve. An **indifference curve** is a line that shows all combinations of two goods that give the consumer equal satisfaction. The indifference curve in Fig. 8.3(c) shows all the combinations of movies and soda that give Lisa equal satisfaction.

The indifference curve shown in Fig. 8.3(c) is just one of a whole family of such curves. This indifference curve appears again in Fig. 8.4. It is labeled I_1 and passes through points c and g. Two other indifference curves are I_0 and I_2. Lisa prefers any point on indifference curve I_2 to those on indifference curve I_1, and she prefers any point on I_1 to those on I_0. We refer to I_2 as being a higher indifference curve than I_1 and I_1 as higher than I_0.

Indifference curves never intersect each other. To see why, consider indifference curves I_1 and I_2 in Fig. 8.4. We know that point j is preferred to point c. We also know that all points on indifference curve I_2 are preferred to all points on indifference curve I_1. If these indifference curves did intersect, the consumer would be indifferent between the combination of goods at the intersection point and combinations c and j. But we know that j is preferred to c, so such a point cannot exist. Thus the indifference curves never intersect.

A preference map consists of a series of indifference curves. The indifference curves shown in Fig. 8.4 are only a part of Lisa's preference map. Her entire map consists of an infinite number of indifference curves, all of them sloping downward and none of them intersecting. They resemble the contour lines on a map measuring the height of mountains. An indifference curve joins points representing combinations of goods among which a consumer is indifferent in much the same way that contour lines on a map join points of equal height above sea level. By looking at the shape of the contour lines on a map, we can draw conclusions about the terrain. In

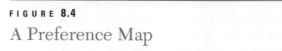

FIGURE 8.4

A Preference Map

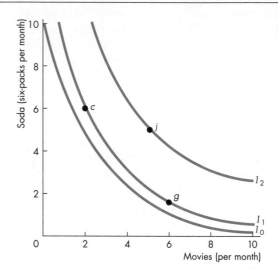

A preference map consists of an infinite number of indifference curves. Here, we show just three—I_0, I_1, and I_2—that are part of Lisa's preference map. Each indifference curve shows points among which Lisa is indifferent. For example, she is indifferent between point c and point g on indifference curve I_1. But points on a higher indifference curve are preferred to points on a lower indifference curve. For example, Lisa prefers all the points on indifference curve I_2 to all the points on indifference curve I_1; she prefers point j to points c or g.

the same way, by looking at the shape of a person's indifference curves, we can draw conclusions about preferences. But interpreting a preference map requires a bit of work. It also requires some way of describing the shape of the indifference curves. In the next two sections, we'll learn how to "read" a preference map.

Indifference Curves and Preferences

We use the concept of the marginal rate of substitution to describe the shape of an indifference curve. The **marginal rate of substitution** (or MRS) is the rate at which a person will give up good y in order to get more of good x and at the same time remain indifferent. The marginal rate of substitution is measured from the slope of an indifference curve. If the indifference curve is steep, the marginal rate of substitution is high. The person is willing to give up a large quantity of good y (the good measured on the y-axis) in exchange for a small quantity of good x (the good measured on the x-axis) while remaining indifferent. If the indifference curve is flat, the marginal rate of substitution is low. The person is willing to give up only a small amount of good y and must be compensated with a large amount of good x to remain indifferent.

Let's work out the marginal rate of substitution in two cases, both illustrated in Fig. 8.5. The curve labeled I_1 is one of Lisa's indifference curves. Suppose that Lisa drinks 6 six-packs of soda and watches 2 movies (point c in the figure). What is her marginal rate of substitution at this point? It is calculated by measuring the magnitude of the slope of the indifference curve at that point. To measure the slope, place a straight line against, or tangential to, the indifference curve at that point. The slope of that line is the change in the quantity of soda divided by the change in the quantity of movies as we move along the line. As soda consumption decreases

by 10 six-packs, movie consumption increases by 5. The slope of the line is –2. Thus when Lisa is consuming 2 movies and 6 six-packs of soda, her marginal rate of substitution is 2.

Now, suppose that Lisa is consuming 6 movies and 1½ six-packs (point g in Fig. 8.5). What is her marginal rate of substitution at this point? The answer is found by calculating the slope of the indifference curve at that point. That slope is the same as the slope of the straight line that is drawn tangential to the point. Here, as soda consumption decreases by 4½ six-packs, movie consumption increases by 9. Hence the slope equals –½. Her marginal rate of substitution is ½. Thus when Lisa sees 6 movies and consumes 1½ six-packs of soda a month, she is willing to substitute movies for soda at the rate of half a six-pack per movie while remaining indifferent.

Notice that if Lisa drinks a lot of soda and does not see many movies, her marginal rate of substitution is high. If she watches a lot of movies and does not drink much soda, her marginal rate of substitution is low. This feature of the marginal rate of substitution is the central assumption of the theory of consumer behavior and is referred to as the diminishing marginal rate of substitution. The assumption of **diminishing marginal rate of substitution** is a general tendency for the marginal rate of substitution to diminish as the consumer moves along an indifference curve, increasing consumption of good x and decreasing consumption of good y.

You may be able to appreciate why we assume the principle of a diminishing marginal rate of substitution by thinking about your own preferences. Imagine two situations: in one, you are watching 3 movies a night but have no soda; in the other, you have 6 six-packs of soda and no movies. In the first situation, you will probably willingly give up seeing 1 movie if you can get just a small amount of soda in exchange. In the second situation, you will probably be willing to give up quite a lot of soda to watch just 1 movie. Your preferences satisfy the principle of diminishing marginal rate of substitution.

The shape of the indifference curves incorporates the principle of the diminishing marginal rate of substitution because the curves are bowed toward the origin. The tightness of the bend of an indifference curve tells us how willing a person is to substitute one good for another while remaining indifferent. Let's look at some examples that will clarify this point.

FIGURE 8.5

The Marginal Rate of Substitution

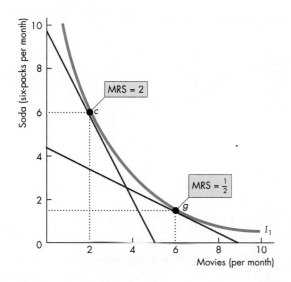

The magnitude of the slope of an indifference curve is called the marginal rate of substitution, or MRS. The marginal rate of substitution tells us how much of one good a person is willing to give up to gain more of another good while remaining indifferent. The marginal rate of substitution at point c is 2; at point g it is ½.

Degree of Substitutability

Most of us would not regard movies and soda as being close substitutes for each other. We probably have some fairly clear ideas about how many movies we want to see each month and how many cans of soda we want to drink. Nevertheless, to some degree, we are willing to substitute between these two goods. No matter how big a soda freak you are, there is surely some increase in the number of movies you can see that will compensate you for being deprived of a can of soda. Similarly, no matter how addicted you are to the movies, surely some number of cans of soda will compensate you for being deprived of seeing one movie. A person's indifference curves for movies and soda might look something like those shown in Fig. 8.6(a).

Close Substitutes Some goods substitute so easily for each other that most of us do not even notice which we are consuming. A good example concerns different brands of personal computers. Zenith, Leading Edge, and Tandy are all clones of the IBM

PC, but most of us can't tell the difference between the three clones and indeed the IBM machine itself. The same holds true for marker pens. Most of us don't care whether we use a marker pen from the campus bookstore or the local supermarket. When two goods are perfect substitutes for each other, their indifference curves are straight lines that slope downward, as illustrated in Fig. 8.6(b). The marginal rate of substitution between perfect substitutes is constant.

Complements Some goods cannot substitute for each other at all. Instead, they are complements. The complements in Fig. 8.6(c) are left and right running shoes. Indifference curves of perfect complements are L-shaped. One left running shoe and one right running shoe are as good as one left shoe and two right ones. Two of each is preferred to one of each, but two of one and one of the other is no better than one of each.

The extreme cases of perfect substitutes and perfect complements shown here don't often happen in

---

FIGURE **8.6**

The Degree of Substitutability

(a) Ordinary goods

(b) Perfect substitutes

(c) Perfect complements

The shape of the indifference curves reveals the degree of substitutability between two goods. Part (a) shows the indifference curves for two ordinary goods: movies and soda. To remain indifferent as less soda is consumed, one must see more movies. The number of movies that compensates for a reduction in soda increases as less soda is consumed. Part (b) shows the indifference curves for two perfect substitutes. For the consumer to remain indifferent, one fewer marker pen from the local supermarket must be replaced by one extra marker pen from the campus bookstore. Part (c) shows two perfect complements—goods that cannot be substituted for each other at all. Two left running shoes with one right running shoe is no better than one of each. But two of each is preferred to one of each.

"With the pork I'd recommend an Alsatian white or a Coke."

Drawing by Weber; © 1988 The New Yorker Magazine, Inc.

reality. They do, however, illustrate that the shape of the indifference curve shows the degree of substitutability between two goods. The more perfectly substitutable the two goods, the more nearly are their indifference curves straight lines and the less quickly does the marginal rate of substitution fall. Poor substitutes for each other have tightly curved indifference curves, approaching the shape of those shown in Fig. 8.6(c).

As you can see in the cartoon, according to the waiter's preferences, Coke and Alsatian white wine are perfect substitutes for each other and each is a complement with pork. We hope the customers agree with him.

R E V I E W

A person's preferences can be represented by a preference map. A preference map consists of a series of indifference curves. Indifference curves slope downward, bow toward the origin, and do not intersect each other. The magnitude of the slope of an indifference curve is called the marginal rate of substitution. The marginal rate of substitution falls as a person consumes less of the good measured on the y-axis and more of the good measured on the x-axis. The tightness of an indifference curve tells us how well two goods substitute for each other.

Indifference curves that are almost straight lines indicate that the goods are close substitutes. Indifference curves that are tightly curved and that approach an L-shape indicate that the two goods complement each other. ◆

The two components of the model of household choice are now in place: the budget line and the preference map. We will now use these two components to work out the consumer's choice.

Choice

Recall that Lisa has $30 to spend and she buys only two goods: movies (at $6 each) and soda (at $3 a six-pack). We've learned how to construct Lisa's budget line, which summarizes what she can buy, given her income and the prices of movies and soda (Fig. 8.1). We've also learned how to characterize Lisa's preferences in terms of her indifference curves (Fig. 8.4). We are now going to bring Lisa's budget line and indifference curves together and discover her best affordable way of consuming movies and soda.

The analysis is summarized in Fig. 8.7. You can see in that figure the budget line from Fig. 8.1 and the indifference curves from Fig. 8.4. Let's first focus on point h on indifference curve I_0. That point is on Lisa's budget line, so we know that she can afford it. But does she prefer this combination of movies and soda over all the other affordable combinations? The answer is no, she does not. To see why not, consider point c, at which she consumes 2 movies and 6 six-packs. Point c is also on Lisa's budget line, so we know that she can afford to consume at this point. But point c is on indifference curve I_1, a higher indifference curve than I_0. Therefore we know that Lisa prefers point c to point h.

Are there any affordable points that Lisa prefers to point c? The answer is that there are not. All Lisa's other affordable consumption points—all the other points on or below her budget line—lie on indifference curves that are below I_1. Indifference curve I_1 is the highest indifference curve on which Lisa can afford to consume.

FIGURE 8.7

The Best Affordable Point

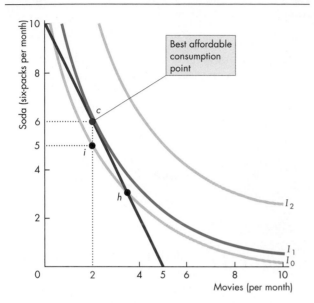

Lisa's best affordable consumption point is *c*. At that point, she is on her budget line and so spends her entire income on the two goods. She is also on the highest attainable indifference curve. Higher indifference curves (such as I_2) do not touch her budget line, and so she cannot afford any point on them. At point *c*, the marginal rate of substitution (the magnitude of the slope of the indifference curve) equals the relative price of movies (the magnitude of the slope of the budget line). A point such as *h* on the budget line is not Lisa's best affordable consumption point because at that point she is willing to give up more movies in exchange for soda than she has to. She can move to a point such as *i*, which she regards as being just as good as point *h* and which allows her to still have some income left over. She can spend that income and move to *c*, a point that she prefers to point *i*.

Let's look more closely at Lisa's best affordable choice.

Properties of the Best Affordable Point

The best affordable point—point *c* in this example—has two properties. It is *on:*

◆ The budget line
◆ The highest attainable indifference curve

On the Budget Line   The best affordable point is *on* the budget line. If Lisa consumes at a point inside her budget line, there are affordable points on the

budget line at which she can consume more of both goods. Lisa prefers any of these points to the one inside the budget line. The best affordable point cannot be outside the budget line because Lisa cannot afford such a point.

On the Highest Attainable Indifference Curve   The chosen point is *on* the highest attainable indifference curve where that curve has the same slope as the budget line. Stated another way, the marginal rate of substitution between the two goods (the magnitude of the slope of the indifference curve) equals their relative price (the magnitude of the slope of the budget line).

To see why this condition describes the best affordable point, consider point *h*, which Lisa regards as inferior to point *c*. At point *h*, Lisa's marginal rate of substitution is less than the relative price—indifference curve I_0 is flatter than Lisa's budget line. As Lisa gives up movies for soda and moves up indifference curve I_0, she moves inside her budget line and has some money left over. She can move to point *i*, for example, where she consumes 2 movies and 5 six-packs and has $3 to spare. She is indifferent between the combination of goods at point *i* and that at point *h*. But she prefers point *c* to point *i*, since at *c* she has more soda than at *i* and sees the same number of movies.

By moving along her budget line from point *h* toward point *c*, Lisa passes through a whole array of indifference curves (not shown in the figure) located between indifference curves I_0 and I_1. All of these indifference curves are higher than I_0, and therefore any point on them is preferred to point *h*. Once she gets to point *c*, Lisa has reached the highest attainable indifference curve. If she keeps moving along the budget line, she will start to encounter indifference curves that are lower than I_1.

REVIEW

The consumer has a given income and faces fixed prices. The consumer's problem is to allocate that fixed income in the best possible way. Affordable combinations of goods are described by the consumer's budget line. The consumer's preferences are represented by indifference curves. The consumer's best allocation of income occurs when all income is spent (on the budget line) and when the marginal rate of substitution (the magnitude of the slope of the indifference curve) equals the relative price (the magnitude of the slope of the budget line). ◆

We will now use this model of household choice to make some predictions about changes in consumption patterns when income and prices change.

Predicting Consumer Behavior

L et's examine how consumers respond to changes in prices and income. We'll start by looking at the effect of a change in price. By studying the effect of a change in price on a consumer's choice, holding all other effects constant, we are able to derive a consumer's demand curve.

A Change in Price

The effect of a change in price on the quantity of a good consumed is called the **price effect**. We will use Fig. 8.8(a) to work out the price effect of a fall in the price of movies. We start with movies costing $6 each, soda costing $3 a six-pack, and Lisa's income at $30 a month. In this situation, she consumes at point *c*, where her budget line is tangential to her highest attainable indifference curve, I_1. She consumes 6 six-packs and 2 movies a month.

Now suppose that the price of a movie falls to $3. We've already seen how a change in price (in Fig. 8.2a) affects the budget line. With a lower price of movies, the budget line moves outward and becomes less steep. The new budget line is the dark red one in Fig. 8.8(a). Lisa's best affordable point is *j*, at which she consumes 5 movies and 5 six-packs of soda. As you can see, Lisa drinks less soda and watches more movies now that movies cost less. She reduces her soda consumption from 6 to 5 six-packs and increases her movie consumption from 2 to 5. Lisa substitutes movies for soda when the price of movies falls and the price of soda and her income remain constant.

FIGURE **8.8**

Price Effect and Demand Curve

(a) Price effect

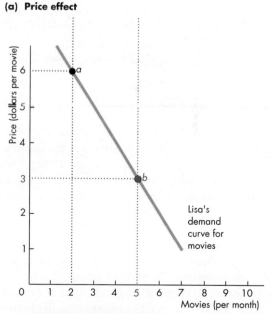

(b) Demand curve

Initially, Lisa consumes at point *c* (part a). If the price of a movie falls from $6 to $3, she consumes at point *j*. The increase in the consumption of movies from 2 to 5 per month is the price effect. When the price of a movie falls, Lisa consumes more movies. She also consumes less soda. Lisa's demand curve for movies is shown in part (b). When the price of movies is $6, she consumes 2 a month, at point *a*. When the price of movies falls to $3, she consumes 5 a month, at point *b*. The demand curve is traced by varying the price of movies and calculating Lisa's best affordable consumption of movies for each different price.

The Demand Curve

This analysis of the effect of a change in the price of movies enables us to derive Lisa's demand curve for movies. Recall that the demand curve graphs the relationship between the quantity demanded of a good and its price, holding constant all other influences on the quantity demanded. We can derive Lisa's demand curve for movies by gradually lowering the price of movies and working out how many movies she sees by finding her best affordable point at each different price. Figure 8.8(b) highlights just two prices and two points that lie on Lisa's demand curve for movies. When the price of movies is $6, Lisa consumes 2 movies a month at point *a*. When the price falls to $3, she increases her consumption to 5 movies a month at point *b*. The entire demand curve is made up of these two points plus all the other points that tell us Lisa's best affordable consumption of movies at each price—more than $6, between $6 and $3, and less than $3—given the price of soda and Lisa's income. As you can see, Lisa's demand curve for movies slopes downward— the lower the price of a movie, the more she watches each month. This is the law of demand.

Next, let's examine what happens when Lisa's income changes.

A Change in Income

The effect of a change in income on consumption is called the **income effect**. Let's work out the income effect by examining how consumption changes when income changes with constant prices. We've already seen, earlier in this chapter, how a change in income shifts the budget line. We worked out and illustrated (in Fig. 8.2c) that an increase in income shifts the budget line outward, with its slope unchanged.

It will be clear to you that, as income increases, a person can consume more of all goods. But being able to consume more of all goods does not mean that a person will do so. Goods are classified into two groups: normal goods and inferior goods. *Normal goods* are goods whose income effect is positive—consumption increases as income increases. *Inferior goods* are goods whose income effect is negative—consumption decreases as income increases.

As the name implies, most goods are normal goods. But a few are inferior goods. Rice and potatoes are perhaps the most obvious. People with low incomes have a heavy rice or potato component to their diet. As incomes increase, people substitute

chicken and beef for rice and potatoes. Thus as income increases, the consumption of chicken and beef increases but that of rice and potatoes decreases. Therefore chicken and beef are normal goods, while rice and potatoes are inferior goods.

Figure 8.9 illustrates the two types of income effect. Part (a) shows the income effect for normal goods, using Lisa's consumption as an example. With an income of $30 and with movies costing $6 each and soda costing $3 for a six-pack, she consumes at point *c*—2 movies and 6 six-packs. If her income goes up to $42, she consumes at point *k*— consuming 3 movies and 8 six-packs. Thus with a higher income, Lisa consumes more of both goods. These income effects are marked on the axes of Fig. 8.9(a). As you can see, both income effects are positive. In Lisa's case, as her income increases, she consumes more movies and more soda. For Lisa, both movies and soda are normal goods.

Figure 8.9(b) shows the income effect for an inferior good—rice. At the initial income level, the household consumes at point *a*—2 ounces of chicken and 6 ounces of rice a day. When income increases, chicken consumption increases to 6 ounces a day, but rice consumption decreases to 4 ounces a day, at point *b*. The income effect for an inferior good is negative.

A Change in Price: Income and Substitution Effects

We've now worked out the effects of a change in the price of movies and the effects of a change in Lisa's income on the consumption of movies and soda. We've discovered that when her income increases, she increases her consumption of both goods. Movies and soda are *normal goods*. When the price of movies falls, Lisa increases her consumption of movies and decreases her consumption of soda. A fall in the price of a normal good leads to an increase in the consumption of that good, as well as to a decrease in the consumption of the substitutes for that good. In this example, a fall in the price of movies leads to an increase in the consumption of movies and to a decrease in the consumption of soda, a substitute for movies. To see why these changes in spending patterns occur when there is a change in price, we separate the effect of the change into two parts. One part is called the substitution effect; the other part is called the income effect. The price effect and its separation into a substitution

FIGURE 8.9

The Income Effect

(a) Normal goods

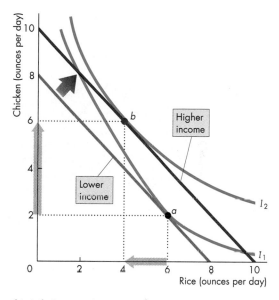

(b) Inferior good

An increase in income increases the consumption of most goods. These goods are normal goods. In part (a), Lisa consumes more of both soda and movies (as shown by the orange arrows) as her income increases. Soda and movies are normal goods, but some goods are

inferior goods. The consumption of inferior goods decreases as income increases. In part (b), as income increases, the consumption of rice decreases and more chicken is consumed (again shown by orange arrows). For this consumer, rice is an inferior good.

effect and an income effect are illustrated in Fig. 8.10. Part (a) shows the price effect we've already worked out in Fig. 8.8. Let's see how that price effect comes about, first by isolating the substitution effect.

The Substitution Effect   The **substitution effect** is the effect of a change in price on the quantities consumed when the consumer (hypothetically) remains indifferent between the original and the new combinations of goods consumed. To work out Lisa's substitution effect, we have to imagine that when the price of movies falls, Lisa's income also decreases by an amount that is just enough to leave her on the same indifference curve as before.

The substitution effect is illustrated in Fig. 8.10(b). When the price of movies falls from $6 to

$3, let's suppose (hypothetically) that Lisa's income decreases to $21. What's special about $21? It is the income that is just enough, at the new price of movies, to keep Lisa's best affordable point on the same indifference curve as her initial consumption point *c*. Lisa's budget line in this situation is the light red line shown in Fig. 8.10(b). With the new price of movies and the new lower income, Lisa's best affordable point is *l* on indifference curve I_1. The move from *c* to *l* isolates the substitution effect of a price change. The substitution effect of the fall in the price of movies is an increase in the consumption of movies from 2 to 4 and a decrease in the consumption of soda from 6 to 3 six-packs. The direction of the substitution effect never varies: when the relative price of a good falls, the consumer substitutes more of that good for the other good.

FIGURE **8.10**

Price Effect, Substitution Effect, and Income Effect

(a) Price effect

(b) Substitution effect

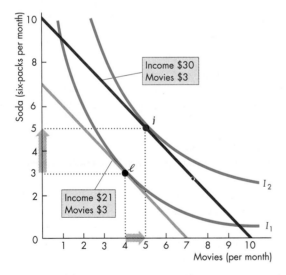

(c) Income effect

The price effect can be separated into a substitution effect and an income effect. The price effect is shown in part (a) and is the same as that in Fig. 8.8(a).

The substitution effect in part (b) is calculated by imagining that Lisa's income decreases at the same time as the fall in the price of a movie, so that when she chooses her best affordable point, she is indifferent between that and the original situation. The move from c to l is the substitution effect. The substitution effect of a price change always results in more consumption of the good whose price has fallen. The orange arrows show the changes in consumption.

The income effect (part c) is calculated by reversing the imaginary pay cut. Income is increased by holding prices constant at their new level. The budget line moves outward and more of both goods is consumed, as shown by the orange arrows. The move from l to j is the income effect.

Income Effect   To calculate the substitution effect, we gave Lisa a $9 pay cut. Now let's give Lisa her money back. This means shifting Lisa's budget line, as shown in Fig. 8.10(c). That move does not involve any change in prices. The budget line moves outward, but its slope does not change. This change in the budget is similar to the one that occurs in Fig.

8.9, where we studied the effect of income on consumption. As Lisa's budget line shifts outward, her consumption possibilities expand, and her best affordable point becomes j on indifference curve I_2. The move from l to j isolates the income effect of a price change. The increase in income increases the consumption of both movies and soda; they are normal goods.

Price Effect   As Fig. 8.10 illustrates, we have separated the effect of a change in price, shown in part (a), into two parts: part (b) keeps the consumer indifferent between the two situations (by making a hypothetical income change at the same time) and looks at the substitution effect of the price change; part (c) keeps prices constant and (hypothetically) restores the original income. It looks at the income effect. The substitution effect always works in the same direction—the consumer slides along an indifference curve, buying more of the good whose price has fallen. The direction of the income effect depends on whether the good is normal or inferior. By definition, normal goods are ones whose consumption increases as income increases. In our example, movies and soda are normal goods because the income effect increases their consumption. Both the income effect and the substitution effect increase Lisa's consumption of movies.

The substitution and income effects of a price change are marked off on the axes in parts (b) and (c) of Fig. 8.10. The move from point c to point l is the substitution effect, and the move from point l to point j is the income effect. For movies, the income effect reinforces the substitution effect, with the result that Lisa's consumption of movies increases. For soda, the substitution effect and the income effect work in opposite directions, with the result that Lisa's consumption of soda decreases.

The example that we have just studied is that of a change in the price of a normal good. For an inferior good—a good whose consumption decreases as income increases—the income effect is negative. Thus for an inferior good, it is not always the case that a lower price leads to an increase in the quantity demanded of the good. The lower price has a substitution effect that tends to increase the quantity demanded. But the lower price also has a negative income effect, which reduces the demand for the inferior good. Thus the income effect offsets the substitution effect to some degree.[2]

---

[2]It has been suggested that the negative income effect for some goods is so large that it dominates the substitution effect. As a result, a lower price leads to a decrease in the quantity demanded for such a good. Goods of this type are called "Giffen goods," named after Sir Robert Giffen, an Irish economist. During a potato famine in Ireland in the nineteenth century, Giffen noticed that when the price of potatoes increased, the quantity of potatoes consumed also increased. Potatoes made up such a large part of the diets of these impoverished people that when the price of potatoes rose, consumers couldn't afford to buy meat or other substitutes, which were all even more expensive.

Model, Theory, and Reality

We have built a model of household choice that makes predictions about consumption choices and how those choices are affected by changes in income and prices. This model leads to a theory of household choice that helps us to understand past spending patterns and to predict future ones. Let's summarize this model.

The Model

All models begin with assumptions. By using logic, we work out the implications of those assumptions. Let's look at the assumptions and implications in the model of household choice.

Assumptions   The assumptions of the model of household choice are as follows:

◆ A household has a fixed income to allocate among various goods.
◆ The prices of goods cannot be influenced by the household.
◆ The household has preferences and can compare alternative combinations of goods as preferred, not preferred, or indifferent.
◆ Preferences can be represented by indifference curves.
◆ Indifference curves bow toward the origin—the marginal rate of substitution falls as consumption of the good measured on the x-axis increases and consumption of the good measured on the y-axis decreases.
◆ The household chooses its best affordable combination of goods.
◆ Preferences do not change when prices and incomes change. *Choices* change, but the new choices result from given preferences and changed constraints.

Implications   The implications of the model of household choice are as follows:

◆ The chosen consumption point is affordable and is *on* the budget line.

◆ The chosen consumption point is on the highest attainable indifference curve.

◆ At the chosen consumption point, the slope of the indifference curve equals the slope of the budget line. Expressed in another way, the marginal rate of substitution equals the relative price of the two goods.

◆ For normal goods, an increase in income increases demand.

◆ For inferior goods, an increase in income decreases demand.

◆ For any good, a rise in its price has a substitution effect that decreases the quantity demanded of it.

◆ For a normal good, a rise in its price decreases the quantity demanded of it—the income effect and the substitution effect reinforce each other. This is the law of demand.

The above is, in a nutshell, the model of household choice we have studied in this chapter. That model provides a basis for developing a theory that explains the patterns of consumption.

The Theory

The theory of consumer choice can be summarized as follows:

◆ The choices made by real people resemble the choices made by the artificial people in the model economy.

◆ Spending patterns in the model look like the actual spending patterns in the real world.

What the Theory Is Not The theory of consumer choice does *not* say that people compute marginal rates of substitution and then set them equal to relative prices to decide how much of each good to buy. Economists do not have a theory about the mental processes that people use to arrive at their choices.

Back to the Facts

We started this chapter by observing how consumer spending has changed over the years. The theory of consumption choice studied in this chapter can be used to explain those changes. Spending patterns are interpreted as being the best choices that households can make, given their preferences and incomes and given the prices of the goods they consume. Changes

in prices and in income lead to changes in the best possible choice—changes in consumption patterns.

Models based on the same ideas you've studied here are used to explain the actual changes that occur and to measure the response of consumption to changes in prices and in income—the price and income elasticities of demand. You met some measures of these elasticities in Chapter 5. Most of those elasticities were measured by using models of exactly the same type that we've studied here (but models that have more than two goods).

But the model of household choice can do much more than explain consumption choices. It can be used to explain a wide range of other household choices. Let's look at some of these.

Other Household Choices

Households make many choices other than those about how to spend their income on the various goods and services available. But we can use the model of consumer choice to understand many other household choices. Some of these are discussed in Our Advancing Knowledge on pp. 172–173. Here, we'll study the two key choices that households make. They are

◆ How many hours to work
◆ How much to save

Work Hours and Labor Supply

Every day, we have to allocate our 24 hours among leisure, working for ourselves, and working for someone else. When we work for someone else, we are supplying labor.

We can understand our labor supply decisions by using the theory of household choice. Supplying more labor is exactly the same thing as consuming less leisure. Leisure is a good, just like movies and soda. Other things being equal, a situation that has more leisure is preferred to one that has less leisure. We have indifference curves for leisure and consumption goods that are similar to those we've already studied. For example, we can relabel the axes of Fig. 8.4 so that instead of soda, we measure all consumption goods on the *y*-axis, and instead of movies, we measure leisure on the *x*-axis.

We can't have as much leisure and consumption as we'd like. Our choices are constrained by the wages that we can earn. For a given hourly wage rate, increasing our consumption of goods and services is possible only if we decrease our leisure time and increase our supply of labor. The wage rate that we can earn determines how much extra consumption we can undertake by giving up an extra hour of leisure. The magnitude of the slope of our indifference curve tells us the marginal rate of substitution—the rate at which we will be willing to give up consumption of goods and services to get one more hour of leisure while remaining indifferent. Our best choice of consumption and leisure has exactly the same properties as our best choice of movies and soda. We get onto the highest possible indifference curve by making the marginal rate of substitution between consumption and leisure equal to the wage rate relative to the price of consumption goods.

Changes in wages affect our choice of consumption and leisure in a similar way to that in which a change in the price of movies affects our consumption of movies and soda. A higher wage rate makes leisure more expensive. There is a substitution effect encouraging us to take less leisure and work longer hours, thereby consuming more goods and services. But a higher wage rate also has an income effect. A higher wage leads to a higher income, and with a higher income, we consume more of all normal goods. Leisure is a normal good. Other things being equal, the higher the income, the more leisure we take. In Reading Between the Lines, pp. 198–199, Elizabeth Cook's high income has perhaps encouraged her to take more leisure.

People who can earn only a very low hourly wage rate tend to work fewer hours, or perhaps not at all. As the wage rate increases, the substitution effect encourages less leisure and more work to be undertaken. But as the wage rate keeps on increasing, the income effect eventually comes to dominate the substitution effect. The higher wage leads to higher consumption of goods and services and to additional leisure. It is the ultimately dominant role of the income effect that has resulted in a steadily shorter workweek despite the fact that wages have increased.

Saving

We don't have to spend all our income here and now. Nor are we constrained to consuming only our current income. We can consume less than our current income, saving the difference for future consumption. Or we can consume more than our current income, borrowing the difference and repaying our loan by consuming less later. Choosing when to consume, how much to save, and how much to borrow can also be understood by using the same theory of household choice that explained Lisa's allocation of her income to movies and soda.

Other things being equal, more consumption today is preferred to less. Also, other things being equal, more consumption in the future is preferred to less. As a consequence, we have indifference curves for consumption now and in the future that are similar to our indifference curves for any pair of goods. Of course, we cannot consume as much as we'd like to today or in the future. Our choices are constrained. The constraint on our choices depends on our income and the interest rate that we can earn on our savings or that we have to pay on our borrowing. The interest rate is a relative price—the relative price of consumption today versus consumption in the future. We choose the timing of consumption (and the amount of saving or borrowing to undertake) by making the marginal rate of substitution between current and future consumption equal to the interest rate. Thus high interest rates will discourage borrowing and lead to lower current consumption and higher future consumption.

◆ ◆ ◆ ◆ We've now completed our study of household choices. We've seen how we can derive the law of demand from a model of household choice. We've also seen how that same model can be applied to a wide range of other choices, including the demand for leisure and the supply of labor. ◆ ◆ In Part 4, we're going to study the choices made by firms. We'll see how, in the pursuit of profit, firms make choices governing the supply of goods and services and the demand for factors of production (inputs). ◆ ◆ After completing these chapters, we'll then bring the analysis of households and firms back together again, studying their interactions in markets for goods and services and factors of production.

The Wall Street Journal, August 5, 1991

Trading Fat Paychecks for Free Time

By Carol Hymowitz

What's the point of a six-figure salary with no time to enjoy it?

That's what Elizabeth Cook asked herself recently before she quit her Manhattan law job just to unwind. She traveled to Maine, where she learned how to make goat cheese.

"My life consisted of going to work and coming home for a few hours to catch some sleep," says Ms. Cook, a 33-year-old attorney, who routinely put in 14-hour days. "Friends stopped calling because I was always canceling on them at the last moment. And I began to realize if I didn't get off this treadmill, at 50 I'd be in the same spot, in the office at midnight faxing documents." Ms. Cook hopes to find a new job in September, but not one that requires such long hours—no matter how high the pay.

In companies around the country, a growing number of managers and professionals are balking at schedules that don't reflect their true priorities and values. They're admitting that the emphasis they have placed on career success and making lots of money hasn't made them very happy. Instead, they want time for family, friends and fun—even at a sizable income loss.

"Leisure time—not money—is becoming the status symbol of the 1990s," says John P. Robinson, who directs the Americans' Use of Time

Project at the University of Maryland. "A large segment of Americans say they feel a significant time crunch— and the more time needy they feel, the stronger their desire to take time off."

So Much to Do, So Little Time
Americans' attitudes about their goals and the time pressures in their lives.

GOALS FOR THE 1990s

77% Spend time with family and friends.

74% Improve yourself Intellectually, emotionally or physically.

72% Save money.

66% Have free time to spend any way you please.

61% Make money.

59% Pursue personal experiences such as traveling and hobbies.

Illustration by Chris Demarest

The Essence of the Story

According to John P. Robinson, director of a time-use research project, a large number of people are placing more emphasis on leisure time and less on money in the 1990s.

One such person is Elizabeth Cook, a former Manhattan attorney, who quit a job with long hours to unwind and hopes to find a new job with shorter hours —no matter how high the pay.

Managers and professionals in growing numbers say that making lots of money hasn't made them happy, and they want more time for family, friends, and fun—even at a sizable income loss.

Background and Analysis

People value both leisure time and consumption goods and prefer more of both to less of both. The amount of leisure that is willingly given up to get more consumption goods (measured in dollars) is described by an indifference curve such as I_0 in Fig. 1.

An unskilled worker whose wage is low has the budget line in Fig. 1 and makes the best choice possible by working 8 hours, taking 16 hours of leisure, and earning $40 a day.

An attorney whose wage is high has the budget line in Fig. 2 and makes the best choice possible by working 14 hours, taking 10 hours of leisure, and earning $1,400 a day.

An attorney who has been earning $1,400 a day for 10 years may have saved a large part of that income and is earning a large amount of interest on the saving. The interest income shifts the attorney's budget line rightward, as shown in Fig. 3. Now the best choice possible is to work only 8 hours and take 16 hours of leisure.

Much of the concern about leisure time is a reflection of the fact that we are becoming more wealthy and can afford more free time.

But high wages have an income effect—inducing more leisure and less work —and a substitution effect —inducing more work and less leisure. Each individual balances these forces and chooses her or his own best possible time allocation.

Figure 1

Figure 2

Figure 3

SUMMARY

Consumption Possibilities

A household's budget line shows the limits to consumption given the household's income and the prices of goods. The budget line is the boundary between what the consumer can and cannot afford.

Changes in prices and changes in income produce changes in the budget line. The magnitude of the slope of the budget line equals the relative price of the two goods. The point at which the budget line intersects each axis marks the consumer's real income in terms of the good measured on that axis. (pp. 180–184)

Preferences

A consumer's preferences can be represented by indifference curves. An indifference curve joins all the combinations of goods among which the consumer is indifferent. A consumer prefers points above an indifference curve to the points on it and prefers points on an indifference curve to all points below it. Indifference curves bow toward the origin.

The magnitude of the slope of an indifference curve is called the marginal rate of substitution. A key assumption is that of a diminishing marginal rate of substitution. In other words, the marginal rate of substitution diminishes as consumption of the good measured on the y-axis decreases and consumption of the good measured on the x-axis increases. The more perfectly two goods substitute for each other, the straighter are the indifference curves. The less easily they substitute, the more tightly curved are the indifference curves. Goods that are always consumed together are complements and have L-shaped indifference curves. (pp. 184–189)

Choice

A household consumes at the best affordable point. Such a point is on the budget line and on the highest attainable indifference curve. At that point, the indifference curve and the budget line have the same slope—the marginal rate of substitution equals the relative price. (pp. 189–191)

Predicting Consumer Behavior

Goods are classified into two groups: normal goods and inferior goods. Most goods are normal. When income increases, a consumer buys more normal goods and fewer inferior goods. If prices are held constant, the change in consumption resulting from a change in income is called the income effect.

The change in consumption resulting from a change in the price of a good is called the price effect. The price effect can be divided into a substitution effect and an income effect. The substitution effect is calculated as the change in consumption resulting from the change in price accompanied by a (hypothetical) change in income that leaves the consumer indifferent between the initial situation and the new situation. The substitution effect of a price change always results in an increase in consumption of the good whose price has decreased. The income effect of a price change is the effect of (hypothetically) restoring the consumer's original income but keeping the price of the good constant at its new level. For a normal good, the income effect reinforces the substitution effect. For an inferior good, the income effect offsets the substitution effect. (pp. 191–195)

Model, Theory, and Reality

A model of household choice is based on the assumption that households' preferences can be represented by indifference curves that bow toward the origin (that have a diminishing marginal rate of substitution). The model has the implication that the household will choose to consume on its budget line at a point at which the marginal rate of substitution and relative price are equal. A change in price leads to a new choice that corresponds to the law of demand: when the price of a good falls, the quantity consumed increases; when income increases, the demand for (normal) goods increases.

The theory of household choice based on this model is that the choices made in the real world correspond to choices made in the model economy. Such a model is used to measure the response of consumption to changes in price and income—the price and income elasticities of demand that appeared in Chapter 5. (pp. 195–196)

Other Household Choices

The model of household choice also enables us to understand households' choices regarding the allocation of time between leisure and work, the allocation of consumption over time, and decisions regarding borrowing and saving. (pp. 196–199)

K E Y   E L E M E N T S

Key Terms

Budget equation, 181
Budget line, 180
Diminishing marginal rate of substitution, 187
Income effect, 192
Indifference curve, 186
Marginal rate of substitution, 186
Price effect, 191
Real income, 182
Relative price, 182
Substitution effect, 193

Key Figures and Tables

Figure 8.1   The Budget Line, 180
Figure 8.3   Mapping Preferences, 185
Figure 8.4   A Preference Map, 186
Figure 8.7   The Best Affordable Point, 190
Table 8.1   Calculating the Budget Equation, 181

R E V I E W   Q U E S T I O N S

1 What determines the limits to a household's consumption choices?

2 What is the budget line?

3 What determines the intercept of the budget line on the y-axis?

4 What determines the intercept of the budget line on the x-axis?

5 What determines the slope of the budget line?

6 What do all the points on an indifference curve have in common?

7 What is the marginal rate of substitution?

8 How can you tell how closely two goods substitute for each other according to the preferences of a consumer by looking at the consumer's indifference curves?

9 What two conditions are satisfied when a consumer makes the best possible consumption choice?

10 What is the effect of a change in income on consumption?

11 What is the effect of a change in price on consumption?

12 Define and distinguish between the income effect and the substitution effect of a price change.

P R O B L E M S

1 Sara has an income of $9 a week. Popcorn costs $1 a bag, and cola costs $1.50 a can.

a What is Sara's real income in terms of cola?

b What is her real income in terms of popcorn?

c What is the relative price of cola in terms of popcorn?

d What is the opportunity cost of a can of cola?

e What is Sara's budget equation?

f Calculate the equation for Sara's budget line (placing cans of cola on the left side).

g Draw a graph of Sara's budget line with popcorn on the *x*-axis.

h In part (g), what is the slope of Sara's budget line? What is it equal to?

2 Suppose that with the same income and prices as in problem 1, Sara chooses to consume 4 cans of cola and 3 bags of popcorn each week.

a Is Sara on her budget line?

b What is her marginal rate of substitution of cola for popcorn?

3 Now suppose that the price of cola doubles to $3 a can and the price of popcorn doubles to $2 a bag. At the same time, Sara's income doubles to $18 a week.

a Can Sara still buy the same quantities of cola and popcorn as before if she wants to?

b What is Sara's real income now? What is the relative price? Describe how Sara's budget line has changed.

4 In problem 3, what are your answers if only:

a The price of cola changed

b The price of popcorn changed

c Sara's income changed

5 Jerry buys cookies that cost $1 each and comic books that cost $2 each. Each month, Jerry buys 20 cookies and 10 comic books. He spends all of his income. Next month, the price of cookies will fall to 50¢, but the price of a comic book will rise to $3.

a Will Jerry be able to buy 20 cookies and 10 comic books next month?

b Will he want to?

c If he changes his consumption, which good will he buy more of and which less of?

d Which situation does Jerry prefer—cookies at $1 and comic books at $2 or cookies at 50¢ and comic books at $3?

e When the prices change next month, will there be an income effect and a substitution effect at work or just one of them? If there is only one effect at work, which one will it be?

6 Now suppose that the prices of cookies and comic books are at their original levels—$1 and $2, respectively. Jerry gets a pay raise of $10 a month. He now buys 16 comic books and 18 cookies. For Jerry, are cookies and comic books normal goods or inferior goods?

PART 4

FIRMS' CHOICES

Talking with Ronald H. Coase

Ronald H. Coase was born in England in 1910. He obtained his B.Com. from the University of London in 1932. After holding positions at the Dundee School of Economics, the University of Liverpool, and the London School of Economics, Professor Coase migrated to the United States in 1951 and has held positions at the University of Buffalo, the University of Virginia, and, since 1964, the Law School at the University of Chicago. Professor Coase was awarded the Nobel Memorial Prize in Economics in 1991 for pioneering work, some of which was conceived before he received his bachelor's degree (see Our Advancing Knowledge, pp. 256–257).

When, why, and how did you start thinking about economic questions?

When I was an undergraduate at the London School of Economics, I did not take courses in economic theory. Most of my courses, such as those in accounting, statistics, and law, had nothing to do with economics. Arnold Plant had been appointed Professor of Commerce at the London School of Economics in 1930. Only five months before the final examinations in 1931, I took a seminar of his. It was a revelation to me to hear Plant explain Adam Smith's Invisible Hand and how the whole economic system was coordinated by a pricing mechanism that led producers to produce things that consumers valued most highly and to produce at the lowest cost. I was no doubt also influenced by the fact that I was very friendly with a number of fellow students who were economics specialists and we often talked about economics. The London School of Economics at that time was a very active place, and all sorts of ideas were being developed, such as the opportunity cost approach. While Plant's seminar got me going, it got me going in a place where economics

"**W**e should begin by taking a walk into the street and studying the real problems of the economic system."

was very much in the air. Even though I wasn't taking economics courses, I still talked about economics with other people. It was in this rather indirect way that I got interested in economics.

How did Plant's seminars shape your interest in the place of the firm and help lead to the incredible insights that provided the explanation of why firms exist?

Plant left me with a puzzle. It was the time of the Great Depression. Unemployment was everywhere, and people were producing all sorts of schemes for economic planning and coordinating the economic system. Plant was very much opposed to all these schemes for economic planning, and he pointed out that if you want coordination, the pricing mechanism acting through competition would give all the coordination necessary. This was a puzzle to me. If pricing did it all, why do we have management—the function of which is to coordinate? You must realize it seems a simpler question now that we know the answer than it was at that time.

So you had this puzzle, and you answered the puzzle. But how did such a young, untrained person come to have the insights that you had concerning the fundamental theory of the firm?

In fact, it is only an untrained person who could. If you receive thorough training in economics, you're trained in thinking in a particular way, and that means there are things you do not think about. After all, when did economists start taking an interest in the firm? Most still haven't. And yet most resources are employed within the firm. Certain questions never arise in their minds because they supposedly have all the answers.

There was one other important contributing factor. I went to the London School of Economics as a student in 1929, and I finished in 1931. The Russian Revolution had started in 1917, but it wasn't until 1928 that Stalin came to power and they had the first five-year plan. There was a lot of discussion going on at the time I was a student about planning in a communist society, with almost no experience of what it would be. Some economists in the West said that it was impossible to have a centrally planned economy. Lenin had said that the Russian economic system would be run as one big factory. Since we had factories in the West, some extremely large, why was it that you can't run society as one large factory? Anyway, those thoughts were flitting through my mind. It must be remembered that I was a socialist at that time.

You are on record as favoring plain English for the most part as the tool of analysis rather than mathematical and formal methods in economics. What is the place of those methods versus careful verbal, logical reasoning? And what do you think of the way we are training young economists today?

I've certainly been very critical of the way in which mathematics has been used in economics. I've been critical, for example, of how some economists develop very elaborate systems of analysis that are difficult to learn and use in order to study imaginary systems. I have no doubt at all that if ever we start to analyze the *actual* economic system, about which we currently know very little, then ultimately a mathematical approach will be needed. Just as in the natural sciences, interrelations in the economic system are so complex that mathematical analysis will be essential to understand them. But at the moment, we turn economic analysis into a game. Unable or unwilling to analyze the real economic system, we invent imaginary ones that we can study with the techniques we have at our disposal. There is no end to the work that can be done along these lines, but it's useless.

We start our work as economists by studying the work of other economists. Instead, we should begin by taking a walk into the street and studying the real problems of the economic system. When students focus their learning on what economists have said and are trained in the techniques of what economists do, they come out very well trained in certain techniques of analysis, and they then want to apply them. For example, nothing is bigger at the moment than game theory. Well, I think at present it's largely useless. People say, "Ah, but it must apply somewhere!" Maybe eventually we'll find that in certain areas and for certain problems the game theoretic techniques that have been developed are just what we need. But it's no good starting off with your techniques and then looking around for a problem to use them on.

Okay, let's take a walk into the street, so to speak, and discuss a major real-world problem: the way in which we allocate that scarce resource, the frequency spectrum. You wrote about this problem many years ago, and of course the frequency spectrum is an even more valuable resource today than it was then. What was behind your thinking on this issue?

What I suggested over 30 years ago was that instead of allocating use of the radiofrequency spectrum by means of administrative decisions—which are carried out in the United States in a very imperfect and inefficient way—we should use pricing. But pricing requires one to discuss what the highest bidder would actually purchase, and that led me to a discussion of the rationale of a property rights system.

The interesting thing is that these ideas that I put forward over 30 years ago are now being treated seriously. I know that they are being discussed within the

"**B**ut it's no good starting off with your techniques and then looking around for a problem to use them on."

> **"I** don't start with the idea that there is an economic solution."

Federal Communications Commission, for example. I've also learned that there are similar discussions going forward in France. There is no doubt work going on elsewhere that I don't know about.

Let's take a problem with a bigger global externality, such as the warming of the planet and increased carbon dioxide buildup. Do you see an economic solution to the problem of global warming based on your ideas about property rights?

Well, the answer is that I don't ever have an economic solution. That's what economists always have—that price should equal marginal cost, and things like that.

Many people think human beings have certain rights. That is not my position. The rights for me follow after you've discovered which ones promote the best sort of society. I try to look at the problem, make sure that it's correctly stated, ask what the real alternative institutional arrangements are for handling it, and then discuss which seems on the whole best. So I don't start with the idea that there is an economic solution. Rather, there's a choice among institutional arrangements.

But in a fundamental sense, that is economics, is it not?

It's what I'd like economics to be. One of the problems with economics is that we're so close to public policy, and the closer we are to public policy, the less solid the analysis tends to be. People are trying to promote certain

solutions, and therefore they are less concerned with finding the truth than with producing studies that support their conclusions. Nowhere is it clearer to me that this happens than in subjects like global warming or the effects of radiation. Yet, it is very difficult to formulate or critique policy recommendations without first establishing the basic facts. The basic scientific facts about global warming are not at all clear. For example, the variation in temperature historically has been extremely great, ranging from Ice Ages to conditions that produce tropical forests. It's not clear whether that is due to something happening in the sun or some other cause. One of the difficulties in dealing with public policy questions is that the data are often so contaminated by the desire to promote certain positions that it is extraordinarily difficult to know what the basic facts really are.

What advice do you have for today's students of economics?

To look at the world and find problems they'd like to work on. I think the way to start is to look for problems, things for which we don't have a decent answer.

What tools of reasoning and what tools of analysis do you recommend they bring to bear on the problems?

The ones necessary to solve it! Don't bother too much about learning the methods of analysis, but start by trying to frame the problem well and then learn along the way what techniques of analysis you will need to know to solve it.

> **"S**tart by trying to frame the problem well and then learn along the way what techniques of analysis you will need to know to solve it."

CHAPTER 9

ORGANIZING
PRODUCTION

After studying this chapter, you will be able to:

◆ Explain what a firm is and
  describe the economic problems
  that *all* firms face

◆ Describe and distinguish between
  different forms of business
  organization

◆ Explain how firms raise the
  money to finance their operations

◆ Calculate and distinguish between
  a firm's historical costs and its
  opportunity costs

◆ Define technological efficiency
  and economic efficiency and
  distinguish between them

◆ Explain why firms solve some
  economic problems and markets
  solve others

ON A JULY DAY IN 1977, A TINY NEW FIRM WAS BORN that grew into a giant—Apple Computer. But that day was not unusual. Every day a new successful firm is born. Apple began its life when Steven Jobs and Stephen Wozniak, two Stanford University students working out of a garage, bought a few components and produced the world's first commercially successful personal computer. From that modest start, Apple Computer has grown into a giant. Apple Computer is one of some 20 million firms that operate in the United States today. They range from multinational giants, such as IBM and Sony, to small family restaurants and corner stores. Three quarters of all firms are operated by their owners, as Apple once was. But corporations (like Apple today) account for 90 percent of all business sales. What are the different forms a firm can take?

An Apple a Day

Why do some firms remain small, while others become giants? Why are most firms owner-operated, while most business is undertaken by corporations? ◆ ◆ Firms spend billions of dollars on buildings and production lines and on developing and marketing new products. How does a firm get the finances needed to pay for all these activities? What do investors expect in return when they put money into a firm? And how do we measure a firm's economic health? ◆ ◆ The market is an amazing mechanism for coordinating the economic actions of millions of individuals. Firms are another type of coordination mechanism. Why do firms coordinate some activities and markets others? Why don't people simply buy everything they need from each other in markets?

◆ ◆ ◆ ◆ In this chapter we are going to learn about the many different types of firms, but we'll understand better the behavior of all firms if we focus first on the things they have in common.

The Firm and Its Economic Problem

The 20 million firms in the United States differ enormously in size and in what they do. What do they have in common? What is the distinguishing characteristic of a firm? What are the different ways in which firms are organized? Why are there different forms of organization? These are the questions we'll tackle first.

What Is a Firm?

A **firm** is an institution that hires factors of production and *organizes* them to produce and sell goods and services. To organize production, a firm enters into a wide range of relationships with a large number of individuals and other firms.

One of these relationships is that between the firm and its owner (or owners), since a firm has a separate legal identity from the individuals who own it. For example, if you buy a share in the stock of the Bank of America, you are a part owner of that company. You have a relationship with the company that defines your obligations if the company cannot meet its debts and that defines your rights to a share in the company's profits.

Other relationships are those between a firm and its managers and other workers. For example, if you get a job at the Bank of America as a teller, you are an employee of the company. You have a relationship with the company that defines your obligations to perform certain tasks in exchange for a compensation and benefits package.

A firm also has relationships with other firms. For example, if you run a window-cleaning company and get a contract with the Bank of America to clean its office windows, you have a relationship with the bank that defines your agreement to perform a specific service for a specific price.

Principal-Agent Relationships

The relationships between a firm and its owners, managers, and workers and between a firm and other firms are called **agency relationships.** In an agency relationship an *agent* undertakes an action that affects a *principal*. An **agent** is a person (or firm) hired by a firm (or another person) to do a specified job. A **principal** is a firm (or person) that hires a person (or firm) to undertake a specified job. For example, as a stockholder of the Bank of America, you are a principal and the managers are your agents. Your profit depends on how good a job the managers do. As a teller, your manager is a principal and you are an agent. Your performance determines whether the bank gains a new valued customer, helping the manager to meet her operating targets. As the window cleaner, you are also an agent and the bank is the principal. The bank wants clean windows, but the quality of your work determines whether it gets them.

The Firm's Decisions

Firms exist because of scarcity. They enable us to get more out of our scarce resources than would be possible if we didn't use the rich array of relationships that they embody. But each firm has to solve its own economic problem. That is, each firm has to get the most it can out of the scarce resources under its control. To do so, a firm has to decide on the following:

◆ Which goods and services to produce and in what quantities
◆ Which of its inputs to produce itself and which to buy from other firms
◆ Which techniques of production to use
◆ Which factors of production to employ and in what quantities
◆ How to organize its management structure
◆ How to compensate its factors of production and suppliers

A firm's receipts from the sale of goods and services are called *revenue*. The total payment that a firm makes for the services of factors of production is called *cost*. The difference between a firm's revenue and cost is its *profit* (if revenue exceeds cost) or its *loss* (if cost exceeds revenue). A firm's revenue, cost, and profits (or losses) are obviously affected by the choices it makes to solve its economic problem.

The goal of a firm's owners is to make the largest possible profit. But running a firm is not just a matter of giving orders and getting them obeyed. In most firms, it isn't possible for the shareholders to monitor the managers or even for the managers to monitor the workers and the other firms who supply it with goods and services. To achieve their goal, the firm's owners (principals) must induce its managers (agents) to pursue the maximum possible profit. And the managers (principals) must induce the workers and other firms (agents) to work efficiently. Each principal attempts to do this by creating incentives that induce each agent to work in the interests of the firm. For example, managers often share in a firm's profits, and workers get bonuses for meeting production targets.

But the perfect incentive scheme does not exist. Managers pursue their own goals, and so do workers. Nonetheless, firms constantly strive to find ways of improving performance and increasing profits.

Although all firms face common problems, they do not solve their problems in the same way. In particular, the management structure and the arrangements for compensating factors of production vary from firm to firm and lead to different forms of business organization. Let's look at these different forms.

The Forms of Business Organization

There are three main forms of business organization:

◆ Proprietorship
◆ Partnership
◆ Corporation

Which form a firm takes influences its management structure, how it compensates factors of production, how much tax its owners pay, and who receives its profits and is liable for its debts if it goes out of business.

Proprietorship   A **proprietorship** is a firm with a single owner—a proprietor—who has unlimited liability. *Unlimited liability* is the legal responsibility for all the debts of a firm up to an amount equal to the entire wealth of the owner. If a proprietorship cannot pay its debts, the personal property of the owner can be claimed by those to whom the firm owes

money. Corner stores, computer programmers, professional athletes, and artists are all examples of proprietorships.

The proprietor makes the management decisions and is the firm's sole residual claimant. A firm's *residual claimant* is the person who receives the firm's profits and is responsible for its losses.

The profits of a proprietorship are part of the income of the proprietor. They are added to any other income that the proprietor has and are taxed as personal income.

Partnership   A **partnership** is a firm with two or more owners who have unlimited liability. Partners must agree on an appropriate management structure and on how to divide the firm's profits among themselves. As in a proprietorship, the profits of a partnership are taxed as the personal income of the owners. But each partner is legally liable for all the debts of the partnership (only limited by the wealth of an individual partner). Liability for the full debts of the partnership is called *joint unlimited liability.* Most law firms and accounting firms are partnerships.

Corporation   A **corporation** is a firm owned by one or more limited liability stockholders. *Limited liability* means the owners have legal liability only for the value of their initial investment. The stock of a corporation is divided into shares. A *share* is a fraction of the stock of a corporation. Shares in most corporations can be bought and sold on stock markets such as the New York Stock Exchange.

Some corporations, no bigger than a proprietorship, have just one effective owner and are managed in the same way as a proprietorship. Large corporations have elaborate management structures headed by a chief executive officer and senior vice-presidents responsible for such areas as production, finance, marketing, and research. These senior executives are in turn served by a series of specialists. Each layer in the management structure knows enough about what happens in the layer below to exercise control, but the entire management consists of specialists who concentrate on a narrow aspect of the corporation's activities.

The corporation receives its financial resources from its owners (the stockholders) and by issuing bonds (loans on which it pays a fixed interest rate).

If a corporation makes a profit, the residual claimants to that profit are the stockholders. If a corporation incurs a loss on such a scale that it becomes bankrupt, the residual loss is absorbed by the banks and other corporations to which the troubled corporation is in debt. The stockholders themselves, by virtue of their limited liability, are responsible for the debt of the corporation only up to the value of their initial investment.

The profits of a corporation are taxed independently of the incomes of its stockholders, so corporate profits are, in effect, taxed twice. After the corporation has paid tax on its profits, the stockholders themselves pay taxes on their dividend income.

The Relative Importance of Different Types of Firms

Figure 9.1(a) shows the relative importance of the three main types of firms for the economy as a whole. The figure also shows that the revenue of corporations is much larger than that of the other two types of firms. Although only 20 percent of all firms are corporations, they generate 90 percent of revenue.

Figure 9.1(b) shows the percentage of total revenue accounted for by the different types of firms in various industries. Proprietorships account for a large percentage of revenue in agriculture, forestry, and fishing and in the service sector. They also account for a large percentage in construction and retail trades. Partnerships are more prominent in agriculture, forestry and fishing, services, mining, and finance, insurance, and real estate than in other sectors of the economy. Corporations are important in all sectors and have the manufacturing field almost to themselves.

Why do corporations dominate the business scene? Why do the other forms of business survive? And why are proprietorships and partnerships more prominent in some sectors? The answer to these questions lies in the pros and cons of the various different forms of business organization.

The Pros and Cons of Different Types of Firms

Since each of the three main types of firms exists in large numbers, each type obviously has advantages in particular situations. Each type also has its disadvantages, which explains why it has not driven out the other two. These pros and cons of each type of firm are summarized in Table 9.1.

FIGURE **9.1**

The Relative Importance of the Three Main Types of Firms

(a) Number of firms and total revenue

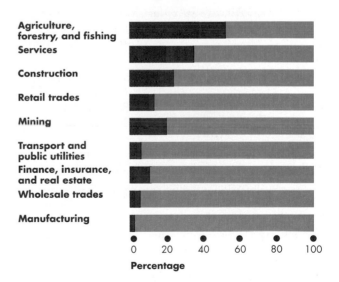

(b) Total revenue in various industries

Three quarters of all firms are proprietorships, a fifth are corporations, and only a twentieth are partnerships. Corporations account for 90 percent of business revenue (part a). But proprietorships and partnerships account for a significant percentage of business revenue in some industries (part b). These types of firms are especially significant in agriculture and services.

Source: U.S. Bureau of the Census, *Statistical Abstract of the United States: 1990,* 110th ed. (Washington, D.C.: 1990): 521, 641.

TABLE 9.1

The Pros and Cons of Different Types of Firms

Type of firm	Pros	Cons
Proprietorship	◆ Easy to set up ◆ Simple decision making ◆ Profits taxed only once as owner's income	◆ Bad decisions not checked by need for consensus ◆ Owner's entire wealth at risk ◆ Firm dies with owner ◆ Capital is expensive ◆ Labor is expensive
Partnership	◆ Easy to set up ◆ Diversified decision making ◆ Can survive withdrawal of partner ◆ Profits taxed only once as owners' incomes	◆ Achieving consensus may be slow and expensive ◆ Owners' entire wealth at risk ◆ Withdrawal of partner may create capital shortage ◆ Capital is expensive
Corporation	◆ Owners have limited liability ◆ Large-scale, low-cost capital available ◆ Professional management not restricted by ability of owners ◆ Perpetual life ◆ Long-term labor contracts cut labor costs	◆ Complex management structure can make decisions slow and expensive ◆ Profits bear corporation tax and dividends are taxed as income of stockholders

REVIEW

A firm is an institution that enters into a wide range of relationships—agency relationships—with owners, managers, workers, and other firms to organize the production of goods and services. Each main type of firm—proprietorship, partnership, and corporation—has its advantages and each plays a role in every sector of the economy. ◆

Business Finance

Every year firms raise billions of dollars to enable them to buy buildings, plant, and equipment and to finance their inventory holdings. Let's see how they do it.

How Firms Raise Capital

All firms get some of their capital from their owners. The owner's stake in a business is called **equity** or **equity capital**. Proprietorships and partnerships raise additional money by borrowing from the bank or from friends. This limits the amount of money that they can raise. Corporations raise much more money than partnerships and proprietorships. For example, an airline may raise hundreds of millions of dollars to buy a bigger fleet of jets. A steel manufacturer may raise hundreds of millions of dollars to build a new plant. The more permanent structure of corporations gives them two important ways of raising large sums of money that are not generally available to households and unincorporated businesses. They are

◆ Selling bonds
◆ Issuing stock

Let's look at these two ways in which corporations raise billions of dollars each year.

Selling Bonds   A **bond** is a legally enforceable obligation to pay specified sums of money at specified future dates. Usually a corporate bond specifies that a certain sum of money called the *redemption value* of the bond will be paid at a certain future date called the *maturity date*. In addition, another sum will be paid each year between the date of issue of the bond and the maturity date. The sum of money paid each year is called the *coupon payment*.

An example of bond financing is shown in Fig. 9.2. On June 25, 1987, the General Cinema Corporation raised more than $100 million by selling bonds. On that day, General Cinema obligated

FIGURE **9.2**

Selling Bonds

This announcement is neither an offer to sell nor a solicitation of offers to buy any of these securities.
The offering is made only by the Prospectus and the related Prospectus Supplement.

NEW ISSUE   June 25, 1987

$125,000,000

General Cinema Corporation

9⅜% Subordinated Notes Due 1997

Price 99.25%
plus accrued interest, if any, from July 1, 1987

Copies of the Prospectus and the related Prospectus Supplement may be obtained in any State in which this announcement is circulated only from such of the undersigned as may legally offer these securities in such State.

The First Boston Corporation   **Salomon Brothers Inc**

Shearson Lehman Brothers Inc.   Goldman, Sachs & Co.   Merrill Lynch Capital Markets

Morgan Stanley & Co.   PaineWebber Incorporated
   Incorporated

Donaldson, Lufkin & Jenrette   Bear, Stearns & Co. Inc.   Alex. Brown & Sons
   Securities Corporation   Incorporated

Dillon, Read & Co. Inc.   Drexel Burnham Lambert   E. F. Hutton & Company Inc.
                                     Incorporated

Kidder, Peabody & Co.   Cyrus J. Lawrence   Lazard Frères & Co.
   Incorporated   Incorporated

Oppenheimer & Co., Inc.   Prudential-Bache Capital Funding   L. F. Rothschild & Co.
                                                                    Incorporated

Smith Barney, Harris Upham & Co.   Wertheim Schroder & Co.   Dean Witter Reynolds Inc.
   Incorporated

                              First Manhattan Co.

A bond is an obligation to make coupon payments and a redemption payment. General Cinema issued bonds promising to pay 9⅜ percent each year as a coupon payment. For each $100 of redemption value, General Cinema received $99.25.

itself to make a payment on the maturity date, July 1, 1997, of $125 million plus the interest then owing. It also committed itself to making a coupon payment of 9⅜ percent on July 1 each year. General Cinema did not get $125 million on July 1, 1987. The bonds were sold for 99¼ percent of the redemption value. That is, General Cinema received $99.25 for every $100 that it promised to pay back.

Issuing Stock   The second major way in which corporations raise money is by issuing stock. Money raised in this way is the corporation's *equity capital* because the stockholders of a corporation are its owners. They have bought shares of the corporation's stock.

There are three types of corporate stock:

◆ Common stock

◆ Preferred stock

◆ Convertible stock

Common stock entitles its holder to vote at stockholders' meetings and to participate in the election of directors. The holder of common stock is entitled to claim a dividend only if the directors vote to pay one. Such a dividend is paid at a variable rate, determined by the directors and varying according to the firm's profits.

Preferred stock gives no voting rights but gives a prior claim on dividends at a fixed rate, regardless of the profit level. If the corporation cannot meet all its obligations, preferred stockholders are paid before common stockholders but after bondholders.

Convertible stock entitles its holder to a fixed coupon payment together with the privilege of being able to convert the stock into a fixed number of shares of common stock. Thus convertible stock is not quite a bond and not quite a stock.

Corporations issue billions of shares of their stock, and these shares regularly trade on stock exchanges. A **stock exchange** is an organized market for trading in stock. The most important stock exchanges in the United States are the New York Stock Exchange (NYSE) and the American Stock Exchange (ASE) in New York City. Although only the NYSE is physically located on Wall Street, in the parlance of finance they are both "on Wall Street." Other major U.S. stock exchanges are in Boston, Philadelphia, Chicago, and San Francisco.

FIGURE **9.3**

Issuing Stock

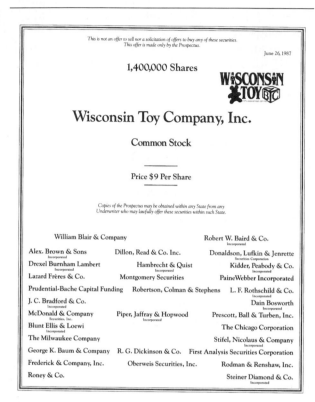

Common stock is stock in a company that entitles its holder to vote at stockholders' meetings, to participate in the election of directors, and to receive a dividend (if the directors vote to pay one). Wisconsin Toy issued 1,400,000 shares of common stock at $9 a share, thereby raising $12,600,000 of additional capital.

An example of a firm raising capital by issuing stock is illustrated in Fig. 9.3. In June 1987, Wisconsin Toy Company, Inc. sold 1.4 million shares of common stock for $9 a share, thereby raising $12.6 million. Unlike the case of a bond, there is no obligation to make payments to stockholders. But there is an expectation of such payments—otherwise no one would buy the shares.

Financing Decisions and Stock Prices

A firm's financing decision has an important influence on its profits. Let's see how by looking a bit more closely at General Cinema and Wisconsin Toy.

Was the bond issue a good deal for General Cinema? And did Wisconsin Toy get the right price for its stock?

Bond Sales and Cash Flows   When General Cinema sold its bonds in 1987, it received $124 million (99.25 percent of $125 million). But it was then committed to making coupon payments of almost $11.7 million (9⅜ percent of $125 million) each year through 1996. Also, it is obliged to pay another $11.7 million (the final coupon payment) plus $125 million (the redemption value) in 1997. At that time, General Cinema will have paid out a total of $242 million, $118 million more than it received in 1987.

On the face of it, this appears to be a terrible way of doing business. Why would General Cinema find that a worthwhile deal? To answer this question, we need to understand a fundamental principle of business (and personal) finance.

Discounting and Present Value   When a firm raises capital by selling a bond, it takes on an obligation to make a series of *future* payments. Cash flows into General Cinema in 1987 and out in 1988 through 1997.

If you are given a choice between a dollar today and a dollar a year from today, you will choose a dollar today. The same is true for General Cinema. A dollar in 1987 is worth more to General Cinema than that same dollar in 1988 and even more still than that same dollar in 1997. A dollar today is worth more than a dollar in the future because today's dollar can be invested to earn interest.

To compare an amount of money in the future with an amount of money today, we must calculate today's value—the present value—of the future amount of money. The **present value** of a future amount of money is the amount that, if invested today, will grow as large as that future amount, taking into account the interest that it will earn. Let's express this idea with an equation:

$$\text{Future amount} = \text{Present value} \times (1 + r).$$

If you have $100 today and the interest rate (r) is 10 percent a year ($r = 0.1$), one year from today you will have $110. Check that the above formula delivers that answer. One hundred dollars multiplied by 1.1 equals $110.

The formula that we have just used calculates a future amount from the present value and an interest rate. To calculate the present value, we just have to work backward. Instead of multiplying the present value by $(1 + r)$, we divide the future amount by $(1 + r)$. That is,

$$\text{Present value} = \frac{\text{Future amount}}{(1 + r)}.$$

You can use this formula to calculate present value. Calculating present value is called discounting. **Discounting** is the conversion of a future amount of money to its present value. Let's check that we can use the present value formula by calculating the present value of $110 one year from now if the interest rate is 10 percent a year. You'll be able to guess that the answer is $100 because we just calculated that $100 invested today at 10 percent a year becomes $110 in one year. Thus it follows immediately that the present value of $110 in one year's time is $100. But let's use the formula. Putting the numbers into the above formula, we have

$$\text{Present value} = \frac{\$110}{(1 + 0.1)}$$

$$= \frac{\$110}{(1.1)}$$

$$= \$100.$$

Calculating the present value of an amount of money one year from now is the easiest case. But we can also calculate the present value of an amount any number of years in the future. As an example, let's see how we calculate the present value of an amount of money available two years from now.

Suppose that you invest $100 today for two years at an interest rate of 10 percent a year. The money will earn $10 in the first year, which means that by the end of the first year you will have $110. If the interest of $10 is invested, then the interest earned in the second year will be a further $10 on the original $100 plus $1 on the $10 interest. Thus the total interest earned in the second year will be $11. The total interest earned overall will be $21 ($10 in the first year and $11 in the second year). After two years, you will have $121. From the definition of present value, you can see that the present value of $121 two years hence is $100. That is, $100 is the present amount that, if invested at 10 percent interest, will grow to $121 two years from now.

To calculate the present value of an amount of money two years in the future, we use the formula

$$\text{Present value} = \frac{\begin{array}{c}\text{Amount of money} \\ \text{two years in future}\end{array}}{(1 + r)^2}$$

Let's see if the formula works by calculating the present value of $121 two years in the future if the rate of interest is 10 percent a year. Putting these numbers into the above formula gives

$$\text{Present value} = \frac{\$121}{(1 + 0.1)^2}$$

$$= \frac{\$121}{(1.1)^2}$$

$$= \frac{\$121}{1.21}$$

$$= \$100.$$

We can calculate the present value of an amount of money any number of years in the future by using a formula based on the two that we've already used. The general formula is

$$\text{Present value} = \frac{\begin{array}{c}\text{Amount of money} \\ \text{available } n \text{ years in future}\end{array}}{(1 + r)^n}$$

For example, if the rate of interest is 10 percent a year, $100 received 10 years from now will have a present value of $38.55. That is, if $38.55 is invested today at an interest rate of 10 percent, it will accumulate to $100 in 10 years. (You may want to check that calculation on your pocket calculator.)

Let's now return to the main question: why does it pay General Cinema to borrow $124 million in 1987 and pay out $242 million over the next 10 years?

The Present Value of a Bond   First, General Cinema isn't planning to pay out $242 million on a $124 million loan just for fun. It plans to use the money for its business. Let's suppose that General Cinema plans to build $124 million worth of movie theaters in college towns across the country. It doesn't have $124 million in its pocket to spare. It can borrow the money from the bank at 9.5 percent interest. Alternatively, it can sell the bonds that we have just been describing. Let's suppose it sells the bonds.

You know from what you have learned about discounting that a sum of money paid two or five or 10 years in the future is worth a smaller sum today. Discounting tells you that the money General Cinema pays in future years to its bondholders is worth less today. How much less? To find out, let's calculate the present value of the bond payments.

We will use the formulas that we have just learned. To begin, we need to list the cash that General Cinema is going to receive and to pay out. Such a list appears in Table 9.2, in the column headed "Cash flow." A plus sign (+) means that money flows into General Cinema, and a minus sign (–) means that money flows out from General Cinema. In 1987, General Cinema receives $99.25 on each $100 worth of bonds. Between 1988 and 1996, the company makes coupon payments of $9.375. In 1997, the company makes a final coupon payment of $9.375 and redeems each bond for $100, so it makes a total payment of $109.375. To calculate the present value of this stream of receipts and pay-

TABLE 9.2

General Cinema Corporation Bonds: Cash Flow per $100 of Redemption Value

Year	Cash flow (dollars)	Present value at 9½% (dollars)
1987	+99.250	+99.250
1988	–9.375	–8.562
1989	–9.375	–7.819
1990	–9.375	–7.141
1991	–9.375	–6.521
1992	–9.375	–5.955
1993	–9.375	–5.439
1994	–9.375	–4.967
1995	–9.375	–4.536
1996	–9.375	–4.141
1997	–109.375	–44.134
Net	–94.500	0.035

ments, we divide each item by $(1 + r)^n$. The variable n is the number of years in the future that the money is paid, and r is the interest rate. Since General Cinema could have borrowed the money that it needs from the bank for 9.5 percent, that is the interest rate we will use for calculating the present value of a bond. The interest rate (r) is 0.095.

The results of our calculations are set out in Table 9.2 in the column headed "Present value." The present value of a sum of money today is the sum itself. So for 1987, the present value of the cash flow is $99.25. The present value of $9.375 one year hence is $8.562. How did we arrive at that figure? We used our formula:

$$\text{Present value} = \frac{\$9.375}{(1 + 0.095)}$$

$$= \frac{\$9.375}{1.095}$$

$$= \$8.562.$$

You can use your pocket calculator to verify this calculation. The further out we go into the future, the smaller are the present values. In the final year, when General Cinema makes a $100 payment to redeem the bond plus the coupon payment of $9.375 for the last year, the present value of that payment is $44.134.

The sum of the present values is called the net present value. The **net present value** of a stream of future payments is the sum of the present values of the payments in each year. As you can see, the net present value per $100 worth of bonds is $0.035 (or 3.5 cents) when the interest rate is 9.5 percent a year. The net present value of General Cinema's entire bond issue of $124,000,000 is $43,400 ($124,000,000 multiplied by $0.035 divided by $100). That is, the present value of the payments is $43,400 less than the amount received in the first place.

Now you can see that General Cinema was not so crazy to take in $124 million in 1987 and pay out $242 million over the next 10 years. The present value of its future payments is far smaller than $242 million. In our example, we used an interest rate of 9.5 percent to calculate the present value. Using other interest rates will yield different results. But if a bank loan at an interest rate of 9.5 percent is the alternative, issuing the bond is better than borrowing from the bank. The wisdom of borrowing at all will finally depend on the profits of the new college town movie theaters. General Cinema will want the theaters to earn enough profits to meet the payments on the bonds.

The Price of a Share of Stock   We've seen how one firm, General Cinema, lowered the cost of raising capital by selling bonds. But often firms issue new stock, such as the Wisconsin Toy Company did in 1987. That company raised $12.6 million by issuing 1.4 million shares of common stock for $9 a share. What determined the price for the shares of Wisconsin Toy's common stock? Why couldn't it get $10 a share? Why were people willing to pay more than $8 a share?

To answer these questions, we need to examine common stock as an investment. The holder of a share receives a dividend each year. Suppose that a corporation is expected to pay a dividend of $110 a share one year from now and nothing thereafter. What will such a share be worth? You probably guessed it: the share will be worth the present value of $110 one year from now. If the interest rate is 10 percent a year, the present value of $110 one year from now is $100. People will be willing to pay $100 for the share today. If the share sells for less than $100, there will be a strong demand for it, since the expected return on the share will exceed 10 percent, the prevailing interest rate. For example, if you can buy the stock for $90, and you receive $110 next year, you will have earned $20, or 22 percent, on your initial $90 investment. If someone tries to sell the share for more than $100, no one will buy it. No one will pay more than $100 for a claim to $110 one year from now if the interest rate is 10 percent. You will do better by simply putting $100 in the bank and collecting $110 in one year's time.

In general, the price of a share is the present value of its expected future dividends. To drive this fact home, let's consider another example. Suppose that investors expect a corporation to pay a dividend of $10 a share each and every year into the indefinite future. Suppose also that the interest rate is 10 percent a year. What will that corporate share be worth? The answer is $100. An investment of $100 in the share will produce $10 a year, or a return of 10 percent a year. That is the same as the interest rate available on other investments. The net present value of $10 a year forever, discounted at a 10 percent interest rate, is $100.[1]

Investors can estimate future dividends, but they cannot know them for sure, and their estimates can change. These changing expectations cause share prices to fluctuate dramatically. Because corporations pay dividends out of their profits, news about a corporation's profitability can change investors' expectations of future dividends.

One number that investors pay attention to is called the price-earnings ratio. The *price-earnings ratio* is the current price of a share divided by the current profit per share. A high price-earnings ratio means that investors are willing to pay a high price for a share compared to the profits that the share is currently earning. Such a situation arises when the firm's future profits are expected to be high relative to its current profits. A low price-earnings ratio means that investors are willing to pay only a low price for a share relative to its current earnings. This situation arises when future profits are expected to be low compared with current profits.

In this example, we have worked out how the price of a share of common stock is determined. The prices of preferred stock and convertible stock are determined in a similar manner and depend on the expected future stream of payments that will be made to the holders of those stocks.

---

[1] If you like algebra, you might find the following demonstration of this result helpful. First, write out the formula for the present value of $10 forever, at an interest rate of 10 percent (0.1):

$$PV = \frac{\$10}{1.1} + \frac{\$10}{(1.1)^2} + \cdots + \frac{\$10}{(1.1)^n} + \cdots.$$

The dots stand for the years between year 2 and year n and the years beyond year n. Next, divide this equation by 1.1 to give

$$\frac{PV}{1.1} = \frac{\$10}{(1.1)^2} + \cdots + \frac{\$10}{(1.1)^n} + \cdots.$$

Now subtract the second equation from the first to give

$$PV - \frac{PV}{1.1} = \frac{\$10}{(1.1)}.$$

Multiply both sides of this equation by 1.1 to give

$$(1.1)\,PV - PV = \$10, \quad \text{or} \quad (0.1)\,PV = \$10.$$

Finally, divide both sides of the last equation by 0.1 to give

$$PV = \frac{\$10}{0.1} = \$100.$$

So the present value of $10 forever at an interest rate of 10 percent is $100.

REVIEW

Firms finance purchases of buildings, plant, and equipment by selling bonds (promises of a fixed income independent of the firm's profit) and issuing stock (opportunities to share in the firm's profit). Firms borrow if doing so increases the net present value of their cash flow. The stock market value of a firm is equal to the present value of its expected future profits. ◆

Let's now turn to another aspect of a firm's finances—the measurement of its costs and profits.

Cost and Profit

Cost is the total payment made by a firm for the services of factors of production. There are two ways of measuring cost—the accountant's way and the economist's way.

Accountants measure historical cost. **Historical cost** values factors of production at the prices actually paid for them. Economists measure opportunity cost. *Opportunity cost* is the best alternative forgone. For example, the opportunity cost of an hour in the classroom is an hour of swimming if that is the best alternative forgone.

Although opportunity cost is a real alternative forgone, it is convenient, when measuring the costs of firms, to express opportunity cost in dollars. But don't lose sight of the fact that this measure is just a convenience. When we calculate the opportunity cost of producing something, we state what was given up to produce the good.

Historical cost sometimes equals opportunity cost. It does so when a firm pays for a factor of production at the same time as it uses it. The historical cost is the amount paid for the factor of production. But this same amount could have been spent on goods, so it is also the opportunity cost (expressed in dollars) of using this factor of production. For example, if a pizza restaurant hires a waiter, the wages paid are both the historical cost and the op-

portunity cost of the waiter—the firm pays the waiter at the same time as it uses the waiter. Labor is the most important factor of production whose historical cost typically equals its opportunity cost.

Historical cost and opportunity cost diverge when a firm pays for a factor of production and uses it some time later and when it uses a factor of production that it does not pay for.

Pay Now, Use Later

Factors of production that are not entirely used up in a single production period are called **durable inputs.** When a firm uses a durable input, it usually pays for the input long before it finishes using it. For example, GM buys an assembly line and then uses it over a period of a few years. Similarly, a firm may carry inventories of raw materials and semifinished products that it uses over a prolonged period. For example, GM keeps an inventory of steel sheets from which it presses car bodies. It may use sheets in production that it bought a year earlier. What is the opportunity cost of using equipment bought several years earlier? What is the opportunity cost of taking items from inventory?

Buildings, Plant, and Machinery Costs

The cost of buildings, plant, and machinery has two components:

◆ Depreciation
◆ Interest

Depreciation   The fall in the value of a durable input over a given period of time is **depreciation.** Accountants assess this fall in value by applying a conventional depreciation rate to the original purchase price. For buildings, a conventional depreciation allowance is 5 percent a year. Thus, if a firm builds a factory for $100,000, the accountant regards 5 percent of that amount, $5,000, as a cost of production in the first year. At the end of the first year, the accountant records the value of the building as $95,000 (the original cost minus the 5 percent depreciation). In the next year, the accountant regards $4,750 as a cost of production (5 percent of the remaining $95,000 value of the building), and so on. The accountant uses different depreciation rates for different types of inputs. Fifteen percent is a common rate for plant and equipment.

Interest   If a firm borrows money to buy a building, plant, or equipment, the accountant counts the interest on the borrowing as a cost of production. So, in this case, if the firm borrows the entire $100,000 and if the interest rate is 10 percent a year, the accountant treats the $10,000 interest payment as a cost of production. If the firm has not borrowed anything to build the factory but has instead used its own previously earned profits, the accountant regards the interest cost incurred in production as zero.

Next, let's see how economists determine these costs. Like accountants, economists also look at depreciation and interest costs to assess the cost of buildings, plant, and machinery, but economists calculate both as opportunity cost.

Economic Depreciation   The change in the market price of a durable input over a given period is **economic depreciation**. For example, economic depreciation over a year is calculated as the market price of the input at the beginning of the year minus its market price at the end of the year. That amount is part of the implicit cost of using the input. The original cost of the equipment is not directly relevant to this calculation. The equipment could have been sold at the beginning of the year for the market price then prevailing. The opportunity cost of hanging onto the equipment, therefore, is the value lost by not selling it. If a firm has kept the equipment for a year and used it, the difference between its market prices at the beginning of the year and at the end of the year tells us how much of its value has been used up in production.

Sunk Costs   A situation sometimes arises in which a firm has bought some equipment and the equipment is in place, functioning well, but has no resale value. The historical cost of buying that equipment is called a sunk cost. A **sunk cost** is the historical cost of buying plant and machinery that have no current resale value. The opportunity cost of using such equipment is zero.

Interest Costs   The other cost of using durable inputs is interest. Whether a firm borrows to buy its buildings, plant, and equipment or uses previously earned profits to pay for them, it makes no difference to the opportunity cost of the funds tied up in the productive assets. If a firm borrowed the money, then the company made an interest payment. (That's the payment the accountant picks up using the historical cost method.) If the firm uses its own funds, then the opportunity cost is the amount that could have been earned by using those funds for something else. The firm could have sold the equipment at the beginning of the year and used the funds from the sale for some other purpose. At the very least, the firm could have put the money in the bank and earned interest. The interest passed up is the opportunity cost of the funds tied up in equipment, regardless of whether that money is borrowed or not. So the economist's measure of the interest cost of a durable resource—its opportunity cost—is the value of the input at the beginning of the year multiplied by the current year's interest rate.

Inflation   Inflation complicates the calculation of opportunity cost. A change in prices that results purely from inflation—a rise in all prices—does not affect opportunity cost. To avoid being misled by inflation, we measure opportunity cost in terms of the prices prevailing in a single year. As a result of the high inflation rates experienced in the 1970s and early 1980s, accountants also have begun to pay attention to the distortions that inflation can cause in measuring historical cost and comparing costs between one year and another.

Implicit Rental Rate   To measure the opportunity cost of using buildings, plant, and equipment, we calculate the sum of economic depreciation and interest costs. Another way of looking at this opportunity cost is as the income that the firm forgoes by not renting out its assets to another firm and instead renting the assets to itself. When a firm rents assets to itself, it pays an **implicit rental rate** for their use. You are familiar with the idea of renting equipment. People commonly rent houses, apartments, cars, televisions, VCRs, and videotapes; firms commonly rent earth-moving equipment, satellite launching services, and so on. When someone rents a piece of equipment, that person pays an *explicit* rent. When an owner uses a piece of equipment rather than renting it out, the economist notes that the owner could have rented the equipment out instead. By not doing so, owners *implicitly* rent from themselves. Another term that is sometimes used to describe an implicit cost or rent is an imputed cost. An **imputed cost** is an opportunity cost that does not require an actual expenditure of cash.

Next, let's examine inventory costs.

Inventory Costs

Inventories are stocks of raw materials, semifinished goods, and finished goods held by firms. Some firms have small inventories or inventories that turn over very quickly. In such cases, the accountant's historical cost and the economist's opportunity cost are the same. When a production process requires inventories to be held for a long time, the two measurements differ and possibly in important ways.

Historical Cost Measures   To measure the cost of using inventories, accountants use a historical cost method called FIFO, which stands for "First In, First Out." This method of pricing the use of inventories assumes, as a convenient fiction, that the first item placed into the inventory is literally the first one out. An alternative accountant's measure that is used in some cases is called LIFO, which stands for "Last In, First Out." This measure, though not quite opportunity cost, is sometimes close to it, since it measures the cost of an inventory item at the price most recently paid. If prices are constant, the price most recently paid is the same as the price that will have to be paid to replace the used item and therefore is precisely its opportunity cost. But so is FIFO. When prices are changing, LIFO gets closer to the opportunity cost than FIFO.

Opportunity Cost Measures   The opportunity cost of using an item from inventory is its current replacement cost. If an item is taken out of inventory, it will have to be replaced by a new item. The cost of that new item is the opportunity cost of using the item taken from inventory.

Inputs Not Paid For

A firm's owner often uses her or his own factors of production, and the firm doesn't directly pay for these factors. But they do have opportunity costs. Let's see what they are.

Owners' Wages   The owner of a firm often puts a great deal of time and effort into working for the firm but rarely takes an explicit wage payment for this work. Instead, the owner withdraws cash from the business to meet living expenses. Accountants regard such withdrawals of cash as part of the owner's profit from the business rather than as a measure of the cost of the owner's time. But the owner could have worked at some other activity and earned a wage. The opportunity cost of the owner's time is the income forgone by the owner by not working in the best alternative job.

Patents, Trademarks, and Names   Many firms have patents, trademarks, or a name that has come to be associated with reliability, service, or some other desirable characteristic. Sometimes firms have acquired these things by their own past efforts. In other cases, they have bought them. A firm always has the option of selling its patents, trademarks, or name to other firms.

In calculating historical cost, these items are ignored unless the firm actually bought them. But they have an opportunity cost regardless of whether they were bought. The opportunity cost of a firm's patents, trademarks, or name used in this year's production is the change in their market value—the change in the best price for which they could be sold. If their value falls over the year, there is an additional opportunity cost of production. If their value rises, there is a negative opportunity cost, or a reduction in the opportunity cost of production.

The Bottom Line

What does all this add up to? Is the historical measure of cost higher or lower than the opportunity cost measure? And what about the bottom line—the profit or loss of the firm? Does the accountant come up with the same answer as the economist, or is there a difference in the measurement of profit as well?

Profit is the difference between revenue and cost. There is no difference in the accountant's measure and the economist's measure of a firm's receipts or revenue. However, the two measures of cost generally differ. Opportunity cost generally includes more things than historical cost, so the historical measure of cost understates the opportunity cost of production. Thus profit as measured by economists is generally less than profit as measured by accountants. Profit as measured by economists is called economic profit. **Economic profit** is revenue minus costs, when the opportunity costs of production are included in costs.

To see how this works out, let's look at an example. Rocky owns a shop that sells bikes. His revenue, costs, and profit appear in Table 9.3. The historical view is on the left side, and the economic view on the right side.

TABLE **9.3**

Rocky's Mountain Bikes' Revenue, Cost, and Profit Statement

The accountant		The economist	
Item	Amount	Item	Amount
Sales revenue	$300,000	Sales revenue	$300,000
Costs:		Costs:	
Wholesale cost of bikes	150,000	Wholesale cost of bikes	150,000
Utilities and other services	20,000	Utilities and other services	20,000
Wages	50,000	Wages	50,000
		Rocky's wages (imputed)*	40,000
Depreciation 10%	22,000	Fall in market value of assets†	10,000
Bank interest	12,000	Bank interest	12,000
		Interest on Rocky's money‡	
		invested in firm (imputed)	11,500
Total costs	$254,000	Total costs	$293,500
Profit	$46,000	Profit	$6,500

*Rocky could have worked elsewhere for $40 an hour, but he worked 1,000 hours on the firm's business, which means that the opportunity cost of his time is $40,000.

†The fall in the market value of the assets of the firm gives the opportunity cost of not selling them one year ago. That is part of the opportunity cost of using them for the year.

‡Rocky has invested $115,000 in the firm. If the current rate of interest is 10 percent a year, the opportunity cost of those funds is $11,500.

Rocky sold $300,000 worth of bikes during the year. This amount appears as his revenue. The wholesale cost of bikes was $150,000, he bought $20,000 worth of utilities and other services, and he paid out $50,000 in wages to his mechanic and sales clerk. Rocky also paid $12,000 in interest to the bank. All of the items just mentioned appear in both the accountant's and the economist's statement. The remaining items differ between the two statements; some notes at the foot of the table explain the differences.

The only additional cost taken into account by the accountant is depreciation, which the accountant calculates as a fixed percentage of Rocky's assets. The economist imputes a cost to Rocky's time and money invested in the firm and also calculates economic depreciation. The historical cost method puts Rocky's cost at $254,000 and his profit at $46,000. In contrast, the opportunity cost of Rocky's year in business was $293,500 and his economic profit was $6,500.

REVIEW

A firm's economic profit is the difference between its revenue and the opportunity cost of production. Opportunity cost differs from historical cost. Historical cost measures cost as the dollars spent to buy inputs. Opportunity cost measures cost as the value of the best alternative forgone. The most important differences between the two measures arise when assessing the cost of durable inputs and of inputs that the firm does not directly buy, such as the labor of the owner. ◆

We are interested in measuring the opportunity cost of production, not for its own sake, but so that we can compare the efficiency of alternative methods of production. What do we mean by efficiency?

Economic Efficiency

How does a firm choose among alternative methods of production? What is the most efficient way of producing? There are two concepts of efficiency: technological efficiency and economic efficiency. **Technological efficiency** occurs when it is not possible to increase output without increasing inputs. **Economic efficiency** occurs when the cost of producing a given output is as low as possible.

Technological efficiency is an engineering matter. Given what is technologically feasible, something can or cannot be done. Economic efficiency depends on the prices of the factors of production. Something that is technologically efficient is not necessarily economically efficient. But something that is economically efficient is always technologically efficient. Let's study technological efficiency and economic efficiency by looking at an example.

Suppose that there are four methods of making TV sets:

a. *Robot production.* One person monitors the entire computer-driven process.

b. *Production line.* Workers specialize in a small part of the job as the emerging TV set passes them on a production line.

c. *Human production.* Workers specialize in a small part of the job but walk from bench to bench to perform their tasks.

d. *Hand-tool production.* A single worker uses a few hand tools to make a TV set.

Table 9.4 sets out the amount of labor and capital required to make 10 TV sets a day by each of these four methods. Are all of these alternative methods technologically efficient? By inspecting the table you will be able to see that method *c* is not technologically efficient. It requires 100 workers and 10 units of capital to produce 10 TV sets. Those same 10 TV sets can be produced by method *b* with 10 workers and the same 10 units of capital. Therefore method *c* is not technologically efficient.

TABLE 9.4

Four Ways of Making 10 TV Sets a Day

Method	Quantities of inputs	
	Labor	Capital
a **Robot production**	1	1,000
b **Production line**	10	10
c **Human production**	100	10
d **Hand-tool production**	1,000	1

Of the four ways of making 10 TV sets a day shown here, only three are technologically efficient—methods *a*, *b*, and *d*. Method *c* is technologically inefficient because it uses the same amount of capital as method *b* but more labor.

Are any of the other methods not technologically efficient? The answer is no: each of the other three methods is technologically efficient. Method *a* uses less labor and more capital than method *b*, and method *d* uses more labor and less capital than method *b*.

What about economic efficiency? Are all three methods economically efficient? To answer that question, we need to know the labor and capital costs. Let's suppose that labor costs $75 per person-day and that capital costs $250 per machine-day. Recall that economic efficiency occurs with the least expensive production process. Table 9.5 calculates the costs of using the four different methods of production. As you can see, the least expensive method of producing a TV set is *b*. Method *a* uses less labor but more capital. The combination of labor and capital needed for method *a* winds up costing much more than that for method *b*. Method *d*, the other technologically efficient method, uses much more labor and hardly any capital. Like method *a*, it winds up costing far more to make a TV set using method *d* than method *b*.

Method *c* is technologically inefficient. It uses the same amount of capital as method *b* but 10 times as

TABLE 9.5

The Costs of Four Ways of Making 10 TV Sets a Day

Method	Labor cost ($75 per day)		Capital cost ($250 per day)		Total cost	Cost per TV set
a	$75	+	$250,000	=	$250,075	$25,007.50
b	750	+	2,500	=	3,250	325.00
c	7,500	+	2,500	=	10,000	1,000.00
d	75,000	+	250	=	75,250	7,525.00

much labor. It is interesting to notice that although method c is technologically inefficient, it costs less to produce a TV set using method c than it does using methods a and d. But method b dominates method c. Because method c is not technologically efficient, there is always a lower cost-method available. That is, a technologically inefficient method is never economically efficient.

Although b is the economically efficient method in this example, method a or d could be economically efficient in other circumstances. Let's see when.

First, suppose that labor costs $150 a person-day and capital only $1 a machine-day. Table 9.6 now shows the costs of making a TV set. In this case, method a is economically efficient. Capital is now sufficiently cheap relative to labor that the method using the most capital is the economically efficient method. Firms substitute capital for labor to take advantage of the low cost of capital.

Now, suppose that labor costs only $1 a day while capital costs $1,000 a day. Table 9.7 shows the costs in this case. As you can see, method d, which uses a lot of labor and little capital, is now the economically efficient method. Firms now substitute labor for capital.

A firm that does not use the economically efficient method of production makes a smaller profit. Natural selection favors firms that choose the economically efficient method of production and goes against firms that do not. In extreme cases, an inefficient firm may go bankrupt or be taken over by another firm that can see the possibilities for lower cost and greater profit. Efficient firms will be stronger and better able to survive temporary adversity than inefficient ones.

TABLE 9.6

The Costs of Three Ways of Making 10 TV Sets: High Labor Costs

Method	Labor cost ($150 per day)		Capital cost ($1 per day)		Total cost	Cost per TV set
a	$150	+	$1,000	=	$1,150	$115.00
b	1,500	+	10	=	1,510	151.00
d	150,000	+	1	=	150,001	15,000.10

TABLE 9.7

The Costs of Three Ways of Making 10 TV Sets: High Capital Costs

Method	Labor cost ($1 per day)		Capital cost ($1,000 per day)		Total cost	Cost per TV set
a	$1	+	$1,000,000	=	$1,000,001	$100,000.10
b	10	+	10,000	=	10,010	1,001.00
d	1,000	+	1,000	=	2,000	200.00

Firms and Markets

At the beginning of this chapter, we defined a firm as an institution that buys or hires factors of production and organizes these resources to produce and sell goods and services. In organizing production, firms coordinate the economic activities of many individuals. But a firm is not the only institution that coordinates economic activity. Coordination can also be achieved by using the market. In Chapter 1, we defined the market as a mechanism for coordinating people's buying and selling plans. By buying inputs and services in many individual markets, each one of us can organize the production of the goods and services that we consume. Consider, for example, two ways in which you might get your creaking car fixed:

◆ *Firm coordination.* You take the car to the garage. Parts and tools as well as the mechanic's time are coordinated by the garage owner, and your car gets fixed. You pay one bill for the entire job.

◆ *Market coordination.* You hire a mechanic who diagnoses the problems and makes a list of the parts and tools needed to fix them. You buy the parts from the local wrecker's yard and rent the tools from ABC Rentals. You hire the

mechanic again to fix the problems. You return the tools and pay your bills—wages to the mechanic, rental to ABC, and the cost of the parts used to the wrecker.

What determines the method that you use? The answer is cost. Taking account of the opportunity cost of your own time as well as the costs of the other inputs that you'd have to buy, you will use the method that costs least. In other words, you will use the economically efficient method.

Firms coordinate economic activity when they can perform a task more efficiently than markets. In such a situation, it will pay someone to set up a firm. If markets can perform a task more efficiently than a firm, people will use markets and any attempt to set up a firm to replace such market coordination will be doomed to failure.

Why Firms?

There are three key reasons why, in many instances, firms are more efficient than markets as coordinators of economic activity. Firms achieve:

◆ Lower transactions costs
◆ Economies of scale
◆ Economies of team production

Transactions Costs   The idea that firms exist because there are activities in which they are more efficient than markets was first suggested by Nobel Prize–winning University of Chicago economist

Ronald Coase.[2] Coase focused on the firm's ability to reduce or eliminate transactions costs. **Transactions costs** are the costs arising from finding someone with whom to do business, of reaching an agreement about the price and other aspects of the exchange, and of ensuring that the terms of the agreement are fulfilled. *Market* transactions require buyers and sellers to get together and negotiate the terms and conditions of their trading. Sometimes lawyers have to be hired to draw up contracts. A broken contract leads to still more expenses. A *firm* can lower such transactions costs by reducing the number of individual transactions undertaken.

Consider, for example, the two ways of getting your car fixed that we've just described. The first method requires that you undertake only one transaction with one firm. It's true that the firm has to undertake several transactions—hiring the labor and buying the parts and tools required to do the job. But the firm doesn't have to undertake those transactions simply to fix your car. One set of such transactions enables the firm to fix hundreds of cars. Thus there is an enormous reduction in the number of individual transactions that take place if people get their cars fixed at the garage rather than going through the elaborate sequence of market transactions that we described above.

Economies of Scale   When the cost of producing a unit of a good falls as its output rate increases, **economies of scale** exist. Many industries experience economies of scale, and automobile and television manufacturing are two examples. Economies of scale can be reaped only by a large organization; thus they give rise to firm coordination rather than market coordination.

Team Production   A production process in which individuals work in a group and each individual specializes in mutually supportive tasks is **team production**. Sport provides the best example of team activity. Some team members specialize in pitching and some in batting, some in defense and some in offense. The production of goods and services offers many examples of team activity. For example, pro-

duction lines in automobile and TV manufacturing plants work most efficiently when individual activity is organized in teams, each specializing in a small task. You can also think of an entire firm as being a team. The team has buyers of raw material and other inputs, production workers, and salespeople. There are even specialists within these various groups. Each individual member of the team specializes, but the value of the output of the team and the profit earned depend on the coordinated activities of all the team's members.

The idea that firms arise as a consequence of the economies of team production was first suggested by Armen Alchian and Harold Demsetz of the University of California at Los Angeles.[3]

Because firms can economize on transactions costs, reap economies of scale, and organize efficient team production, it is firms rather than markets that coordinate most of our economic activity. There are, however, limits to the economic efficiency of firms. If firms become too big or too diversified in the things they seek to do, the cost of management and monitoring per unit of output begins to rise, and, at some point, the market becomes more efficient at coordinating the use of resources—see Reading Between the Lines, pp. 226–227.

Sometimes firms enter into long-term relationships with each other that effectively cut out ordinary market transactions and make it difficult to see where one firm ends and another begins. For example, GM has long-term relationships with suppliers of windows, tires, and other parts. Such relationships make transactions costs lower than they would be if the firms went shopping on the open market each time they wanted new supplies. At the same time, a firm avoids diseconomies of scale that can arise if it becomes too big and its management becomes unresponsive to changing conditions.

◆ ◆ ◆ ◆ In the next chapter, we are going to study the choices of firms. We will study their production decisions, how they minimize costs, and how they choose the amounts of the various inputs to employ.

[2]Ronald H. Coase, "The Nature of the Firm," *Economica* (November 1937): 386–405.

[3]Armen Alchian and Harold Demsetz, "Production, Information Costs, and Economic Organization," *American Economic Review* 57, 5 (December 1972): 777–795.

Organizing
Production
of Computers

The Essence
of the Story

❚BM is a large firm that organizes the production of mainframes and minicomputers, personal computers, notebook computers, and work stations.

❚BM is looking at ways of breaking up into a number of smaller companies that specialize in different types of computers and that are more rapidly responsive to developments in the marketplace.

Possibilities include selling parts of the firm's operations to partners or to the public, with IBM owning a majority or minority interest in the newly created companies.

The New York Times, November 27, 1991

I.B.M. Will Change in Effort to Keep Market Dominance

BY JOHN MARKOFF

In a sweeping overhaul of the way it does business, I.B.M., long one of the world's most admired and successful companies, said yesterday that it would become a federation of smaller, nimbler companies able to respond more quickly to the demands of the marketplace.

John F. Akers, the company's chairman, said in a telephone interview yesterday that I.B.M., the world's largest computer maker, was examining a number of ways to do this, including selling major portions of its operations to partners or even the public. The company's hope is to bring new life to stagnating product lines.

Industry executives said that the move to a family of loosely affiliated subsidiaries would have been unthinkable a few years ago, when the company was often viewed as a juggernaut and referred to as "battleship I.B.M."

'Destroyers,' Not 'Battleship'

Now a radically different enterprise is envisioned, one where quick-moving "destroyers" can be more competitive and where a unit's managers may be accountable directly to a different set of shareholders than the parent corporation's. . . .

Mr. Akers said that in the future I.B.M. might own a majority stake—or even only a minority interest—in some of the newly created companies that it hopes will ignite new growth in businesses like personal computers, notebook computers and work stations. In the past, these product lines have frequently been hamstrung because they have been forced to share the overhead of I.B.M.'s older and slower-moving businesses, notably mainframes and minicomputers. . . .

Background and Analysis

Economic activity can be coordinated by markets or by firms, with both coordination mechanisms playing a key role in the production of all goods and services.

IBM has used command mechanisms and a large hierarchical organization to coordinate the production and marketing of a wide variety of types of computers, in competition with a number of smaller firms, many of them specialists in niches of the larger market. This organization is illustrated in Fig. 1.

IBM's plan is to rely more on market coordination and less on command coordination, as shown in Fig. 2.

Instead of being coordinated by a large and costly organization ("Big Blue"), the separate "baby blues," as they are known, will interact directly with computer users. They plan to become more sensitive and responsive to the demands of those users, thereby increasing IBM's market share and restoring its profitability. The baby blues are depicted as the five shapes at the base of Fig. 2.

It is possible, however, that nothing will save IBM in the competitive marketplace of the 1990s and that only new firms will have the dynamism needed to succeed.

Figure 1

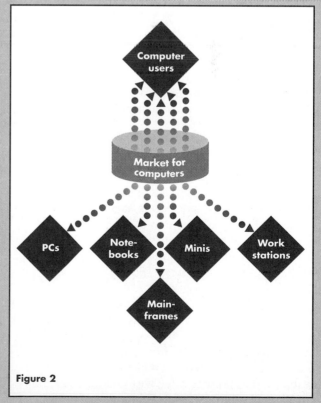

Figure 2

S U M M A R Y

The Firm and Its Economic Problem

A firm is an institution that enters into a wide range of agency relationships to hire factors of production that it organizes to produce and sell goods and services. In an agency relationship an agent undertakes an action that affects a principal and the principal sets the terms of the relationship to best achieve her or his ends. Firms decide what to produce and in what quantities, the techniques of production to use, the quantities of each factor of production to employ, the organization and management structure, and the arrangements for compensating the factors of production.

There are three main forms of business organization: proprietorship, partnership, and corporation. Each has its advantages and disadvantages. Proprietorships are easy to set up and face lower taxes than corporations, but they are risky and face higher costs of capital and labor. Partnerships can draw on diversified expertise, but they can also involve decision conflicts. Corporations have limited liability, so they can obtain large-scale capital at relatively low cost. They can hire professional management, but complex management structures can slow down decisions. Corporations pay taxes on profits, and their stockholders pay taxes on dividends. Proprietorships are the most common form of business organization, but corporations account for most of the economy's production. (pp. 209–212)

Business Finance

Firms raise money to finance their purchases of plant and equipment by selling bonds and issuing stock. When a firm sells bonds, it promises its bondholders a fixed payment that is independent of the firm's profit. When a firm issues stock, it offers stockholders an opportunity to become part owners of the firm but with limited liability for the firm's debts.

Firms take actions that are expected to increase the net present value of their cash flow. In deciding whether to raise money by issuing bonds, firms calculate the present value of the payments that they will obligate themselves to make to bondholders and compare that present value with that of some alternative method of financing. The value of a firm's

stock is determined on the stock market by the present value of the expected future stream of dividends that the firm will pay from its profits. The value of a firm's stock is *not* determined by its *current profit*, although, to the extent that current profit is an indicator of future profit, it is a relevant factor. For this reason, the price-earnings ratios of firms vary considerably. (pp. 212–218)

Cost and Profit

Business profit is calculated as the difference between revenue and cost. Accountants and economists measure cost in different ways. Accountants measure historical cost; economists measure opportunity cost. Opportunity cost usually exceeds historical cost because it includes imputed costs that are not counted as part of historical cost. The different measures of cost lead to different measures of profit. Economic profit equals revenue minus opportunity cost. (pp. 218–221)

Economic Efficiency

There are two concepts of efficiency: technological efficiency and economic efficiency. A method of production is technologically efficient when, to produce a given output, it is not possible to use less of one factor of production without at the same time using more of another. A method of production is economically efficient when the cost of producing a given output is as low as possible. Economic efficiency requires technological efficiency. Economic efficiency also takes into account the relative prices of inputs. Economically efficient firms have a better chance of surviving than do inefficient ones. (pp. 222–224)

Firms and Markets

Firms coordinate economic activities when they are able to achieve lower costs than coordination through markets. Firms are able to economize on transactions costs and to achieve the benefits of economies of scale and of team production. (pp. 224–227)

Key Terms

Agency relationship, 209
Agent, 209
Bond, 213
Corporation, 210
Depreciation, 218
Discounting, 215
Durable input, 218
Economic depreciation, 219
Economic efficiency, 222
Economic profit, 220
Economies of scale, 225
Equity, 212
Equity capital, 212
Firm, 209
Historical cost, 218
Implicit rental rate, 219
Imputed cost, 219
Inventories, 220
Net present value, 216

Partnership, 210
Present value, 214
Principal, 209
Proprietorship, 210
Stock exchange, 213
Sunk costs, 219
Team production, 225
Technological efficiency, 222
Transactions costs, 225

Key Figures and Tables

Figure 9.1   The Relative Importance of the Three
              Main Types of Firms, 211
Table 9.1   The Pros and Cons of Different Types of
              Firms, 212
Table 9.3   Rocky's Mountain Bikes' Revenue,
              Cost, and Profit Statement, 221
Table 9.4   Four Ways of Making 10 TV Sets a
              Day, 222

REVIEW QUESTIONS

1 What is a firm?

2 What are the economic problems that all firms face? List the main forms of business organization and the advantages and disadvantages of each.

3 What are the main ways in which firms can raise money?

4 What is a bond?

5 What is a stock?

6 What do we mean by net present value?

7 What determines the value of a bond?

8 What determines the value of a stock?

9 Distinguish between historical cost and opportunity cost. What are the main items of opportunity cost that don't get counted as part of historical cost?

10 Define economic efficiency.

11 Distinguish between economic efficiency and technological efficiency.

12 Why do firms, rather than markets, coordinate such a large amount of economic activity?

PROBLEMS

1 Soap Bubbles, Inc. has a bank loan of $1 million on which it is paying an interest rate of 10 percent a year. The firm's financial advisor suggests paying off the loan by selling bonds. Soap Bubbles, Inc.

has to offer bonds with a redemption value two years in the future of $1,050,000 and with a coupon payment of 9 percent to raise $1 million.

a Does it pay Soap Bubbles to sell the bonds to repay the bank loan?

b What is the present value of the profit or loss that would result from repaying the bank loan and selling the bonds?

2 One year ago, Jack and Jill set up a vinegar bottling firm (called JJVB).

◆ Jack and Jill put $50,000 of their own money into the firm.

◆ They bought equipment for $30,000 and an inventory of bottles and vinegar for $15,000.

◆ They hired one employee to help them for an annual wage of $20,000.

◆ JJVB's sales for the year were $100,000.

◆ Jack gave up his previous job, at which he earned $30,000, and spent all his time working for JJVB.

◆ Jill kept her old job, which paid $30 an hour, but gave up 10 hours of leisure each week (for 50 weeks) to work for JJVB.

◆ The cash expenses of JJVB were $10,000 for the year.

◆ The inventory at the end of the year was worth $20,000.

◆ The market value of the equipment at the end of the year was $28,000.

◆ JJVB's accountant depreciated the equipment by 20 percent a year.

a Construct JJVB's profit and loss account as recorded by its accountant.

b Construct JJVB's profit and loss account based on opportunity cost rather than historical cost concepts.

3 There are three methods you can use for doing your tax return: a personal computer, a pocket calculator, or a pencil and paper. With a PC, you complete the job in an hour; with a pocket calculator, it takes 12 hours; and with a pencil and paper, it takes two days. The PC and its software cost $1,000, the pocket calculator costs $10, and the pencil and paper cost $1. Assume there is no depreciation.

a Which, if any, of the above methods are technologically efficient?

b Suppose that your wage rate is $5 an hour. Which of the above methods is economically efficient?

c Suppose that your wage rate is $50 an hour. Which of the above methods is economically efficient?

d Suppose that your wage rate is $500 an hour. Which of the above methods is economically efficient?

CHAPTER **10**

After studying this chapter, you will be able to:

◆ Explain the objective of a firm

◆ Explain what limits a firm's profitability

◆ Explain the relationship between a firm's output and its costs

◆ Derive a firm's short-run cost curves

◆ Explain how cost changes when a firm's plant size changes

◆ Derive a firm's long-run average cost curve

◆ Explain why some firms operate with excess capacity and others overutilize their plants

SIZE DOES NOT GUARANTEE SURVIVAL IN BUSINESS. OF the 100 largest companies in the United States in 1917, only 22 still remained in that league in 1991. But remaining small does not guarantee survival either. Every year, millions of small businesses close down. Call a random selection of restaurants and fashion boutiques from *last* year's yellow pages and see how many have vanished. What does a firm have to do to be one of the survivors? ◆ ◆ Firms differ in lots of ways—from Mom-and-Pop's convenience store to multinational giants producing hi-tech goods. But regardless of their size or what they produce, all firms must decide what to produce, how much to produce, and how to produce it. How do firms make these decisions? ◆ ◆ Most auto makers in the United States can produce far more cars than they can sell. Why do auto makers have expensive equipment lying around that isn't fully used? Many electric utilities in the United States

Survival of the Fittest

don't have enough production equipment on hand to meet demand on the coldest and hottest days and have to buy power from other producers. Why don't such firms have a bigger production plant and supply the market themselves?

◆ ◆ ◆ ◆ We are going to answer these questions in this chapter. To do so, we are going to study the economic decisions of a small, imaginary firm—Swanky, Inc., a producer of knitted sweaters. The firm is owned and operated by Sidney. By studying Swanky's economic problems and the way Sidney solves them, we will be able to get a clear view of the problems that face all firms—small ones like Swanky as well as the giants.

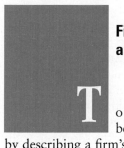

Firms' Objectives and Constraints

To understand and predict the behavior of firms, we will start by describing a firm's objectives—what it is trying to achieve.

The Objective: Profit Maximization

The firm that we will study has a single objective: profit maximization. **Profit maximization** is striving for the largest possible profit. As you know, the fundamental problem from which all economic activity springs is scarcity. Profit maximization is a direct consequence of scarcity. Seeking to make the best possible use of scarce resources is the same thing as trying to make the highest possible profit. A firm that tries to maximize profit has the best chance of surviving in a competitive environment and of avoiding being the target of a successful takeover by another firm.

Sidney is constantly striving to make the highest possible profits, but there are limits to, or constraints on, the profits that a firm can make. What are they?

Constraints

There are two types of constraints that limit the profits a firm can make. They are

◆ Market constraints
◆ Technology constraint

Market Constraints   A firm's **market constraints** are the conditions under which it can buy its inputs and sell its output. On the output side, people have a limited demand for each good or service and will buy additional quantities only at lower prices. Firms have to recognize this constraint on how much they can sell. A small firm competing with many other firms in a large market has no choice but to sell its output at the same price as everyone else. It cannot, through its own actions, influence the market price. A large firm that dominates the market for a particular good can manipulate the price to its own advantage. But in so doing, it has to accept the fact that at higher prices it will sell lower quantities.

On the input side, people have a limited supply of the factors of production that they own and will supply additional quantities only at higher prices. Most firms, even large ones, compete with many other firms in the markets for factors of production and have no choice but to buy their inputs at the same prices as everyone else. Except in rare circumstances, firms cannot manipulate the market prices of their factors of production through their own actions.

We will study the output market constraints on firms more thoroughly in Chapters 11 through 13 and the input market constraints in Chapters 14 through 16. Swanky, the firm that we will study in this chapter, is small and cannot influence the prices at which it sells its sweaters or at which it buys the inputs used to make them.

Technology Constraint   Firms use inputs to produce outputs. Any feasible way in which inputs can be converted into output is called a **technique.** For example, one technique that Swanky can adopt to produce sweaters uses workers equipped with knitting needles. A second technique uses labor and hand-operated knitting machines. A third technique uses automated knitting machines that require a small amount of labor to set them going and to reset them for different sizes and styles of sweaters. A fourth technique uses robotic knitting machines controlled by computers that automatically adjust the size, type, and color of the sweaters with human intervention only at the point of programming the computer. These different techniques use different amounts of labor and capital. But they are all capable of producing the same total output.

Some techniques are capital-intensive and some are labor-intensive. A **capital-intensive technique** uses a relatively large amount of capital and a relatively small amount of labor. A computer-controlled automated knitting machine is an example of a capital-intensive technique. A **labor-intensive technique** uses a relatively large amount of labor and a relatively small amount of capital. Knitting sweaters by hand—where the only capital equipment used is knitting needles—is an example of a labor-intensive technique.

To maximize profit, a firm will choose a technologically efficient production method. Recall the definition of technological efficiency that you encountered in Chapter 9—a state in which no more output can be produced without using more inputs.

Technological efficiency does not necessarily require the use of up-to-date or sophisticated equipment. When knitters are working flat out, even if they are using only needles, sweaters are being produced in a technologically efficient way. To produce more sweaters will require more knitters. No resources are being wasted. Similarly, when a computerized automated knitting plant is operating flat out, sweaters are also being produced in a technologically efficient way.

A firm can do no better than use a technologically efficient technique. But it must determine which technique to employ, since not all technologically efficient methods of production are economically efficient. Furthermore, the possibilities that are open to the firm will depend on the length of the planning period over which the firm is making its decisions. A firm that wants to change its output rate overnight has far fewer options than one that can plan ahead and change its output rate several months in the future. In studying the way a firm's technology constrains its actions, we distinguish between two planning horizons—the short run and the long run.

The Short Run and the Long Run

The **short run** is a period of time in which the quantity of at least one input is fixed and the quantities of the other inputs can be varied. The **long run** is a period of time in which the quantities of all inputs can be varied. Inputs whose quantity can be varied in the short run are called **variable inputs**. Inputs whose quantity cannot be varied in the short run are called **fixed inputs**.

There is no fixed time that can be marked on the calendar to separate the short run from the long run. The short-run and long-run distinction varies from one industry to another. For example, if an electric power company decides that it needs a bigger production plant, it will take several years to implement its decision. If United Airlines decides that it needs 100 additional Boeing 767s, it will take a few years for Boeing to turn out the new planes needed to accommodate United's demand. The short run for these firms is several years in length. At the other extreme, a laundromat or a copying service has a short run of just a month or two. New premises can be acquired and new machines installed and made operational quickly.

Swanky has a fixed amount of capital equipment in the form of knitting machines, and to vary its output in the short run, it has to vary the quantity of labor that it uses. For Swanky, labor is the variable input. The quantity of knitting machinery is fixed in the short run, and this equipment is Swanky's fixed input. In the long run, Swanky can vary the quantity of both knitting machines and labor employed.

Let's look a bit more closely at the short-run technology constraint.

Short-Run Technology Constraint

To increase output in the short run, a firm must increase the quantity of a variable input[1]. The firm's short-run technology constraint determines how much additional variable input is needed to produce a given amount of additional output. A firm's short-run technology constraint is described by using three related curves that show the relationship between the quantity of a variable input and:

◆ Total product

◆ Marginal product

◆ Average product

Total Product

The total quantity produced is called **total product**. The **total product curve** shows the maximum output attainable with a given amount of capital as the amount of labor employed is varied. Equivalently, the relationship between total product and the amount of labor employed can be described by a schedule that lists the amounts of labor required to produce given amounts of output. Swanky's total product schedule and curve are shown in Fig. 10.1.

---

[1]If you are anxious to move more quickly to a study of costs, you may omit this section and jump immediately to the section entitled "Short-Run Cost."

FIGURE **10.1**

Total Product

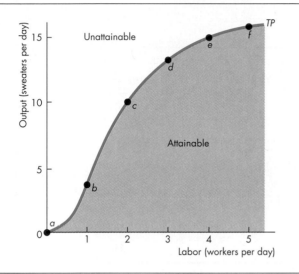

	Labor (workers per day)	Output (sweaters per day)
a	0	0
b	1	4
c	2	10
d	3	13
e	4	15
f	5	16

The numbers in the table show how, with one knitting machine, Swanky can vary the total output of sweaters by varying the amount of labor it employs. For example, 1 worker (row *b*) produces 4 sweaters a day; 2 workers (row *c*) produce 10 sweaters a day. The short-run production function is graphed here as the total product curve *TP*. Points *a* through *f* on the curve correspond to the rows of the table. The total product curve separates the attainable output from the unattainable.

As you can see, when employment is zero, no sweaters are knitted. As employment increases, so does the number of sweaters knitted. The total product curve for Swanky, labeled *TP*, is based on the schedule in the figure. Points *a* through *f* on the curve correspond to the same rows in the table.

The total product curve has a lot in common with the *production possibility frontier* you met in Chapter 3. It separates the attainable output levels from those that are unattainable. All the points that lie above the curve are unattainable. Points that lie below the curve, in the orange area, are attainable. But they are technologically inefficient—they use more labor than is necessary to produce a given output. Only the points *on* the total product curve are technologically efficient.

Marginal Product

The **marginal product** of any input is the increase in total product resulting from an increase of one unit of that input. The **marginal product of labor** is the change in total product resulting from a one-unit increase in the quantity of labor employed, holding the quantity of capital constant. It is calculated as the change in output divided by the change in the quantity of labor employed. In Swanky's case, the marginal product of labor is the additional number of sweaters knitted each day that results from hiring one additional worker each day. The magnitude of that marginal product depends on how many workers Swanky is employing. Swanky's marginal product of labor is calculated in the table of Fig. 10.2. The first two columns of the table are the same as the table in Fig. 10.1. The last column shows the calculation of marginal product. For example, when the quantity of labor increases from 1 to 2 workers, total product increases from 4 to 10 sweaters. The change in total product—6 sweaters—is the marginal product of the second worker.

Swanky's marginal product of labor is illustrated in the two parts of Fig. 10.2. Part (a) reproduces the total product curve that you met in Fig. 10.1. Part (b) shows the marginal product curve (labeled *MP*). In part (a), the marginal product of labor is illustrated by the orange bars. The height of each bar measures marginal product. Marginal product is also measured by the slope of the total product curve. Recall that the slope of a curve is the change in *y*—output—divided by the change in *x*—labor input—as we move along the curve. A 1-unit increase in labor input, from 1 to 2 workers, increases output from 4 to 10 sweaters, so the slope from point *b* to point *c* is 6, exactly the same as the marginal product that we've just calculated.

FIGURE **10.2**

Total Product and Marginal Product

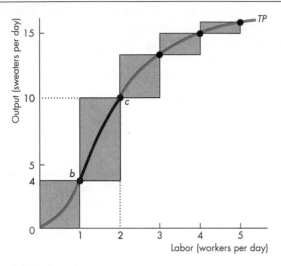

(a) Total product

	Labor (workers per day)	Output (sweaters per day)	Marginal product (sweaters per worker)
a	0	0	
			 4
b	1	4	
			 6
c	2	10	
			 3
d	3	13	
			 2
e	4	15	
			 1
f	5	16	

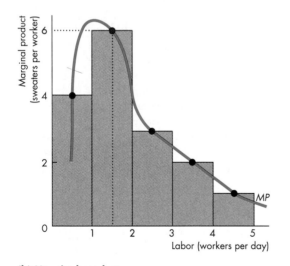

(b) Marginal product

The table calculates marginal product as the change in total product resulting from a 1-unit increase in labor input. For example, when labor increases from 1 to 2 workers a day (row *b* to row *c*), total product increases from 4 to 10 sweaters a day. The marginal product of the second worker is 6 sweaters. (Marginal product is shown midway between the rows to emphasize that it is the result of *changing* inputs—moving from one row to the next.)

Marginal product is illustrated in both parts of the figure by the orange bars. The height of a bar indicates the size of the marginal product. For example, when labor increases from 1 to 2, marginal product is the orange bar whose height is 6 sweaters (visible in each part of the figure). The steeper the slope of the total product curve (*TP*) in part (a), the higher is marginal product (*MP*) in part (b). Marginal product increases to a maximum (when 1 worker is employed in this example) and then declines—diminishing marginal product.

Notice the relationship between the total and marginal product curves. The steeper the *slope* of the total product curve, the higher is the *level* of the marginal product curve. The total product curve in part (a) of Fig. 10.2 shows that an increase in employment from 1 to 2 workers increases output from 4 to 10 sweaters (an increase of 6). The increase in output of 6 sweaters appears on the ver-

tical axis of part (b) as the marginal product of the second worker. We plot that marginal product at the midpoint between 1 and 2 workers per day. Notice that marginal product shown in Fig. 10.2(b) reaches a peak at 1 unit of labor and at that point marginal product is more than 6. The peak occurs at 1 unit of labor because the total product curve is steepest at 1 unit of labor.

FIGURE **10.3**

Total Product, Marginal Product, and Average Product

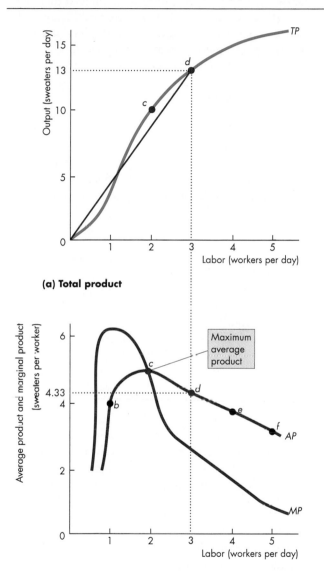

(a) Total product

(b) Marginal product and average product

	Labor (workers per day)	Output (sweaters per day)	Average product (sweaters per worker)
b	1	4	4.00
c	2	10	5.00
d	3	13	4.33
e	4	15	3.75
f	5	16	3.20

Average product—total product per unit of labor—is calculated in the table by dividing total product by the quantity of labor employed. For example, in a day, 3 workers produce 13 sweaters, so the average product of 3 workers is 4.33 sweaters per worker.

The two parts of the figure show two ways of representing average product on a graph. In part (a), average product is measured as the slope of a straight line from the origin to a point on the total product curve. The straight line to point *d* is such a line. The slope of that line is 4.33 (13 sweaters divided by 3 workers). Part (b) graphs average product. Points *b* through *f* on the average product curve, *AP*, correspond to the rows of the table. Part (b) also shows the connection between the average product and marginal product curves. When marginal product exceeds average product, average product is increasing. When marginal product is less than average product, average product is decreasing. When marginal product and average product are equal, average product is at its maximum. Part (b) shows that marginal product increases from 0 to 1 worker and decreases thereafter and that average product increases from 0 to 2 workers and decreases thereafter.

Average Product

Total product per unit of variable input is called **average product**. In Swanky's case, average product is the total number of sweaters produced each day, divided by the number of workers employed each day. Swanky's average product is calculated in the table in Fig. 10.3. For example, 3 workers can knit

13 sweaters a day, so the average product is 13 divided by 3, which is 4.33 sweaters per worker.

Average product is illustrated in the two parts of Fig. 10.3. First, average product can be measured in part (a) as the slope of a line from the origin to a point on the total product curve. For example, at point *d*, 3 workers knit 13 sweaters. The slope of the line from the origin to point *d* is equal to the output—13 sweaters—divided by the quantity of labor used—3 workers. The result is an average product for 3 workers of 4.33 sweaters per worker. You can use this method of calculating average product to check that point *c* is the point of maximum average product. The steepest line from the origin that touches the total product curve touches only at *c*. Place a ruler on the curve and check that. Since the slope of such a line measures average product and this line is steepest when 2 workers are employed, average product is at a maximum at that point.

Part (b) graphs the average product curve, *AP*, and also shows the relationship between average product and marginal product. Points *b* through *f* on the average product curve correspond to those same rows in the table. Average product increases from 1 to 2 workers (its maximum value at point *c*) but then decreases as yet more workers are employed. Notice also that the highest average product occurs where average and marginal product are equal to each other. That is, the marginal product curve cuts the average product curve at the point of maximum average product. When marginal product exceeds average product, average product is increasing. When marginal product is less than average product, average product is decreasing.

Why does Swanky care about marginal product and average product? Because they have an important influence on the costs of producing sweaters and the way those costs vary as the production rate varies. We will examine these matters soon, but first we will take one more look at how marginal product and average product are related. You will meet this type of relationship many times in your study of economics and in your everyday life.

Relationship Between Marginal and Average Values

We have seen, in Fig. 10.3, that when marginal product exceeds average product, average product is increasing, and when marginal product is less than average product, average product is decreasing. We have also seen that when marginal product equals average product, average product is neither increasing nor decreasing—it is at its maximum and is constant. These relationships between the average and marginal product curves are a general feature of the relationship between the average and marginal values of any variable. Let's look at a familiar example.

Sidney (the owner of Swanky) attends an introductory economics class with his friends Steve and Sam. Each receives a grade of 70 percent in the course the first semester, but each achieved this in a different way. Table 10.1 illustrates how. They took four tests, each worth a quarter of the final mark. Sidney, preoccupied with managing Swanky, started out disastrously with 55 percent but then steadily improved. Steve started out brilliantly but then nosedived, while Sam scored 70 percent on every test.

We can calculate the average and the marginal scores of these three students. The average score is simply the total marks obtained divided by the number of tests written. After two tests, Sidney has an aggregate score of 55 percent plus 65 percent, which is 120 percent, so his average score is 60 percent. A student's marginal score is the score on the last test written. After two tests, Sidney's marginal score was 65 percent.

Over the four tests, Sidney's marginal score rises, Steve's falls, and Sam's is constant. But notice what the average scores are doing. For Sidney, the average is rising. His marginal score is higher than his average score, and his average rises. For Steve, the marginal score falls. So, too, does his average. Steve's marginal score is always below his average score and pulls his average down. Sam's marginal score equals his average score, so his average stays constant.

These examples of an everyday relationship between marginal and average values agree with the relationship between marginal and average products that we have just discovered. Average product increases when marginal product exceeds average product (Sidney). Average product decreases when marginal product is below average product (Steve). Average product is at a maximum and constant (it neither rises nor falls) when marginal product equals average product (Sam).

The Shapes of the Product Curves

Now let's get back to studying production. The total, marginal, and average product curves are different for different firms and different types of goods. Ford Motor Company's production function is different from that of Jim's Burger Stand, which in turn is different from that of Sidney's sweater factory. But the shapes of the product curves are similar, because almost every production process incorporates two features:

TABLE 10.1

Average and Marginal Test Scores

	Test	Test score	Aggregate score	Average score	Marginal score
Sidney					
	1	55	55	55	
					 65
	2	65	120	60	
					 75
	3	75	195	65	
					 85
	4	85	280	70	
Steve					
	1	85	85	85	
					 75
	2	75	160	80	
					 65
	3	65	225	75	
					 55
	4	55	280	70	
Sam					
	1	70	70	70	
					 70
	2	70	140	70	
					 70
	3	70	210	70	
					 70
	4	70	280	70	

On the second test, Sidney scores 65 percent. After the first two tests, he has an average score of 60 percent. On the third test, Sidney scores 75 percent. His marginal score is the change in his aggregate score as the result of doing one more test. The marginal score after three tests is 75 percent. This score is located midway between the scores for the second and third tests to emphasize that it is associated with doing one more test. His marginal score now exceeds his previous average (60 percent), so his average after three tests is higher (65 percent). Steve's marginal score is below his average score, so his average falls. Sam's marginal score equals his average score, so his average remains constant.

◆ Increasing marginal returns initially
◆ Diminishing marginal returns eventually

Increasing Marginal Returns   **Increasing marginal returns** occur when the marginal product of an additional worker exceeds the marginal product of the previous worker. If Sidney employs just one worker at Swanky, that person has to learn all the different aspects of sweater production—running the knitting machines, fixing breakdowns, packaging and mailing sweaters, buying and checking the type and color of the wool. All of these tasks have to be done by that one person. If Sidney hires a second person, the two workers can specialize in different parts of the production process. As a result, two workers produce more than twice as much as one. This is the range over which marginal returns are increasing.

Diminishing Marginal Returns   *Increasing* marginal returns do not always occur, but all production processes eventually reach a point of *diminishing* marginal returns. **Diminishing marginal returns** occur when the marginal product of an additional worker is less than the marginal product of the previous worker. If Sidney hires a third worker, output increases but not by as much as it did when he added the second worker. With a third worker, the factory produces more sweaters, but the equipment is being operated closer to its limits. Furthermore, there are times when the third worker has nothing to do because the plant is running without the need for further attention. Adding yet more and more workers continues to increase output but by successively smaller amounts. This is the range over which marginal returns are diminishing. This phenomenon is such a pervasive one that it is called "the law of diminishing returns." The **law of diminishing returns** states that:

As a firm uses more of a variable input, with the quantity of fixed inputs constant, its marginal product eventually diminishes.

Because marginal product eventually diminishes, so does average product. Recall that average product decreases when marginal product is less than average product. If marginal product is diminishing, it must eventually become less than average product, and when it does so, average product declines.

The product and technology concepts we've just studied are summarized in a compact glossary in Table 10.2.

TABLE 10.2

A Compact Glossary on Product

Term	Symbol	Equation	Definition
Fixed input			An input whose quantity used cannot be varied in the short run
Variable input	*L*		An input (labor in our examples) whose quantity used can be varied in the short run
Total product	*TP*		Output produced
Marginal product	*MP*	$MP = \Delta TP \div \Delta L$	Change in total product resulting from a one-unit rise in variable input (equals change in total product divided by change in variable factor)
Average product	*AP*	$AP = TP \div L$	Total product per unit of variable input (equals total product divided by number of units of variable factor)
Point of maximum average product			Output rate above which average product diminishes
Point of maximum marginal product			Output rate above which marginal product diminishes

R E V I E W

Three curves—total product, marginal product, and average product—show how the output rate of a given plant varies as the input of labor is varied. Initially, as the amount of labor increases, average product and marginal product increase. But eventually, average product and marginal product decline. When marginal product exceeds average product, average product increases. When marginal product is below average product, average product decreases. When marginal product and average product are equal, average product is at its maximum. ◆

Short-Run Cost

To produce more output in the short run, a firm must employ more labor. But if it employs more labor, its costs increase. Thus, to produce more output, a firm must increase its costs. We're going to examine how a firm's costs vary as it varies its output by studying Swanky's costs.

Swanky cannot influence the prices of its inputs and has to pay the market price for them. Given the prices of its inputs, Swanky's lowest attainable cost of production for each output level is determined by its technology. Let's see how.

Total Cost

A firm's **total cost** is the sum of the costs of all the inputs it uses in production. It includes the cost of renting land, buildings, and equipment and the wages paid to the firm's work force. Total cost is divided into two categories: fixed cost and variable cost. A **fixed cost** is a cost that is independent of the output level. A **variable cost** is a cost that varies with the output level. **Total fixed cost** is the cost of the fixed inputs. **Total variable cost** is the cost of the variable inputs. We call total cost *TC*, total fixed cost *TFC*, and total variable cost *TVC*.

Swanky's total cost and its division into total fixed cost and total variable cost appear in the table of Fig. 10.4. Swanky has one knitting machine, and

FIGURE **10.4**
Short-Run Costs

(a) Total costs

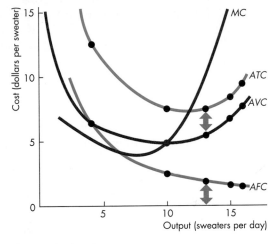

(b) Marginal and average costs

Labor (workers per day)	Output (sweaters per day)	Total fixed cost (TFC)	Total variable cost (TVC)	Total cost (TC)	Marginal cost (change in dollars per change in output) (MC)	Average fixed cost (AFC)	Average variable cost (AVC)	Average total cost (ATC)
			(dollars per day)				(dollars per sweater)	
0	0	25	0	25		—	—	—
					. . . . 6.25			
1	4	25	25	50		6.25	6.25	12.50
					. . . . 4.17			
2	10	25	50	75		2.50	5.00	7.50
					. . . . 8.33			
3	13	25	75	100		1.92	5.77	7.69
					. . . . 12.50			
4	15	25	100	125		1.67	6.67	8.33
					. . . . 25.00			
5	16	25	125	150		1.56	7.81	9.38

Short-run costs are calculated in the table and illustrated in the graphs. At each level of employment and output in the table, total variable cost (TVC) is added to total fixed cost (TFC) to give total cost (TC). The change in total cost per unit change in output gives marginal cost (MC). Average costs are calculated by dividing the total costs by output.

The firm's total cost curves are shown in part (a). Total cost (TC) increases as output increases. Total fixed cost (TFC) is constant—it graphs as a horizontal line—and total variable cost (TVC) increases in a similar way to total cost. The vertical distance between the TC and

TVC curves equals total fixed cost (TFC).

The average and marginal cost curves are shown in part (b). Average fixed cost (AFC) decreases as the constant total fixed cost is divided by ever higher output levels. The curves showing average total cost (ATC) and average variable cost (AVC) are U-shaped. The vertical distance between them is equal to average fixed cost, which becomes smaller as output increases. The marginal cost curve (MC) is also U-shaped. It cuts the average variable cost curve and the average total cost curve at their minimum points.

this is its fixed input. To produce more sweaters, Sidney must hire more labor, and the first two columns of the table show how many sweaters can be produced at each level of employment. This is Swanky's technology constraint.

Let's suppose that Swanky rents its knitting machine for $25 a day. This amount is Swanky's total fixed cost. Let's suppose that Swanky can hire workers at a wage rate of $25 a day. Total variable cost depends on the quantity of labor hired. For example, when Swanky employs 3 workers, total variable cost is $75 (3 multiplied by $25). Total cost is the sum of total fixed cost and total variable cost. For example, when Swanky employs 3 workers, total variable cost is $75, total fixed cost is $25, and total cost is $100.

Marginal Cost

A firm's **marginal cost** is the increase in total cost resulting from a one-unit increase in output. To calculate marginal cost, we find the change in total cost and divide it by the change in output. For example, when output increases from 4 to 10 sweaters, total cost increases from $50 to $75. The change in output is 6 sweaters, and the change in total cost is $25. The marginal cost of one of those 6 sweaters is $4.17 ($25 divided by 6).

Notice that when Swanky hires a second worker, marginal cost decreases from $6.25 for the first worker to $4.17 for the second worker. But when a third, fourth, and fifth worker are employed, marginal cost successively increases. Marginal cost increases because each additional worker produces a successively smaller addition to output—*the law of diminishing returns*.

Average Cost

Average cost is the cost per unit of output. There are three average costs:

1. Average fixed cost
2. Average variable cost
3. Average total cost

Average fixed cost (*AFC*) is total fixed cost per unit of output. **Average variable cost** (*AVC*) is total variable cost per unit of output. **Average total cost** (*ATC*) is total cost per unit output. Average fixed cost plus

average variable cost equals average total cost. For example, in the table in Fig. 10.4, when output is 10 sweaters, average fixed cost is $2.50 ($25 divided by 10), average variable cost is $5.00 ($50 divided by 10), and average total cost is $7.50 ($75 divided by 10 or, equivalently, $2.50 average fixed cost plus $5.00 average variable cost).

Short-Run Cost Curves

We can illustrate Swanky's short-run costs as short-run cost curves (Fig. 10.4a). Total fixed cost is a constant $25. It appears in the figure as the horizontal green curve labeled *TFC*. Total variable cost and total cost both increase with output. They are graphed in the figure as the purple total variable cost curve (*TVC*) and the blue total cost curve (*TC*). The vertical distance between those two curves is equal to total fixed cost—as indicated by the green arrows.

The average cost curves appear in Fig. 10.4(b). The green average fixed cost curve (*AFC*) slopes downward. As output increases, the same constant fixed cost is spread over a larger output: when Swanky produces only 4 sweaters, average fixed cost is $6.25; when it produces 16 sweaters, average fixed cost is $1.56.

The blue average total cost curve (*ATC*) and the purple average variable cost curve (*AVC*) are U-shaped curves. The vertical distance between the average total cost and average variable cost curves is equal to average fixed cost—as indicated by the green arrows. That distance shrinks as output increases, since average fixed cost declines with increasing output.

Figure 10.4(b) also illustrates the marginal cost curve. It is the red curve labeled *MC*. That curve is also U-shaped. It cuts the average variable cost curve and the average total cost curve at their minimum points. That is, when marginal cost exceeds average cost, average cost is increasing, and when marginal cost is less than average cost, average cost is decreasing. This relationship holds for both the *ATC* and the *AVC* curves. You might wonder why the marginal cost curve cuts both the average total cost curve and the average variable cost curve at their minimum points. It does so because the source of the change in total cost, from which we calculate marginal cost, is variable cost. For average variable cost to decrease, marginal cost must be less than average variable cost, and for average variable cost to increase, marginal cost must exceed average variable cost. Similarly, for average total cost to decrease, marginal cost must be less than average total cost, and for average total cost to increase, marginal cost must exceed average total cost. This is exactly the same relationship we found when studying students' grades in Table 10.1.

Why the Average Total Cost Curve Is U-Shaped

The U-shape of the average total cost curve arises from the influence of two opposing forces:

◆ Decreasing average fixed cost

◆ Eventually increasing average variable cost

Because total fixed cost is constant, as output increases, average fixed cost decreases—the average

fixed cost curve is downward sloping. But at low output levels the average fixed cost curve is steep, while at high output levels it is relatively flat. Because of diminishing returns, average variable cost eventually increases—the average variable cost curve eventually slopes upward and gets steeper.

Since average total cost is the sum of average fixed cost and average variable cost, the average total cost curve combines these two effects. At first the average total cost curve slopes downward because the effect of spreading fixed costs over larger output levels is the dominant influence on average total cost. But as output increases, diminishing returns bring ever higher average variable cost, and the average total cost curve slopes upward. At the point at which these two opposing influences on average total cost are balanced, average total cost is at its minimum.

The cost concepts we've just studied are summarized in a compact glossary in Table 10.3.

TABLE 10.3

A Compact Glossary on Cost

Term	Symbol	Equation	Definition
Fixed cost			Cost that is independent of the output level
Variable cost			Cost that varies with the output level
Total fixed cost	TFC		Cost of the fixed inputs (equals their number times their unit price)
Total variable cost	TVC		Cost of the variable inputs (equals their number times their unit price)
Total cost	TC	$TC = TFC + TVC$	Cost of all inputs (equals fixed costs plus variable costs)
Marginal cost	MC	$MC = \Delta TC \div \Delta TP$	Change in total cost resulting from a one-unit rise in total product (*TP*) (equals the change in total cost divided by the change in total product)
Average fixed cost	AFC	$AFC = TFC \div TP$	Total fixed cost per unit of output (equals total fixed cost divided by total product)
Average variable cost	AVC	$AVC = TVC \div TP$	Total variable cost per unit of output (equals total variable cost divided by total product)
Average total cost	ATC	$ATC = AFC + AVC$	Total cost per unit of output (equals average fixed cost plus average variable cost)

Cost Curves and the Technology Constraint[2]

The shapes of a firm's cost curves are determined by its technology, and there are some interesting relationships between its cost curves and its product curves.

First, there is a relationship between the total variable cost curve in Fig. 10.4(a) and the total product curve in Fig. 10.1. They both slope upward, but look closely at their shapes. Initially, as more labor is employed, the total product curve gets steeper and the total variable cost curve gets less steep. This is the range over which marginal product is increasing. Once diminishing returns set in, as more labor is employed, the total variable cost curve gets steeper and the total product curve gets less steep.

Second, there is a relationship between the marginal product curve in Fig. 10.2 and the marginal

cost curve in Fig. 10.4(b). The marginal cost curve is like the flip side of the marginal product curve. Marginal cost is at a minimum at the same output at which marginal product is at a maximum. The output range over which marginal cost is decreasing is the same as that over which marginal product is increasing. Similarly, the output range over which marginal cost is increasing is the same as that over which marginal product is decreasing—the range of diminishing marginal product.

Third, there is a relationship between the average product curve in Fig. 10.3(b) and the average cost curve in Fig. 10.4(b). It is similar to the relationship between the marginal curves that we've just described. The average cost curve is like the flip side of the average product curve. Average variable cost is at a minimum at the same output at which average product is at a maximum (10 sweaters). The output range over which average variable cost is decreasing is the same as that over which average product is increasing. Similarly, the output range over which average variable cost is increasing is the same as that over which average product is decreasing.

---

[2]If you skipped the section entitled "Short-Run Technology Constraint," you will also want to skip this short section.

FIGURE 10.5

NEPOOL's Output and Cost

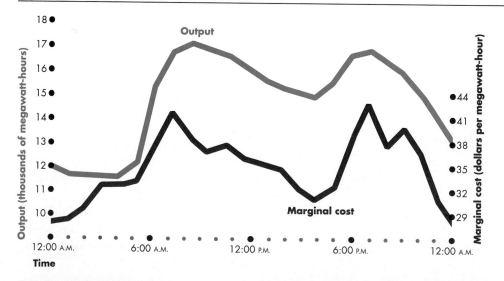

During a 24-hour period, electric power production fluctuated between 11,500 and 17,000 megawatt-hours. Over the same period, marginal cost fluctuated between $29 and $44 per megawatt-hour. The empirical relationship between output and marginal cost is not exact because of maintenance scheduling and uncontrollable factors such as plant breakdowns.

Real-World Short-Run Costs

Swanky's costs are a lot like the costs of a real-world firm. Let's confirm this fact by looking at the costs of a group of real firms, the New England Power Pool (NEPOOL). NEPOOL is an association of 92 electric power companies serving more than 5 million customers in the six New England states.

NEPOOL's production fluctuates between 11,500 and 17,000 megawatt-hours, depending partly on the time of day, partly on the day of the week, and partly on the temperature. To vary their output in the short run, the power producers vary the amount of fuel that they use. Fuel is the variable input of a power producer. The power source with the lowest fuel cost in the New England system is nuclear. Large coal-burning and oil-burning generators come next. The power sources with the highest fuel cost are small gas-turbine generators that use the same kind of fuel as jet aircraft.

On a cold winter day, the hour-by-hour output of the NEPOOL producers and the marginal cost per 1,000 megawatt-hours fluctuated in the manner shown in Fig. 10.5. As you can see, there are two cycles over a 24-hour period in electric power production. From 1:00 A.M. to 6:00 A.M., output (shown by the blue curve) is between 11,500 and 12,000 megawatt-hours. Then between 6:00 A.M. and 7:00 A.M., output increases as we all turn on morning TV shows, toasters, and coffeemakers. Output reaches a peak at 9:00 A.M. and then falls off slightly during the day to a low point at 4:00 P.M. In the early evening, there is another TV viewing and meal-preparation peak and then a gradual fall through to midnight as people go to bed. The marginal cost of production follows a similar cycle and fluctuates between $29 a megawatt-hour at the trough and $44 a megawatt-hour at the peak.

The relationship between output and marginal cost is not perfect because mechanical failure and maintenance shutdowns make it impossible always to use the generator with the lowest marginal cost. But it is pretty close, as Fig. 10.6 shows. Here, each point represents the marginal cost and output at a particular hour. For example, you can see in Fig. 10.5 that, between 10:00 P.M. and 11:00 P.M., 14,000 megawatt-hours were produced at a marginal cost of $32 a megawatt-hour. That output and marginal cost generate point *a* in Fig. 10.6. The continuous red curve labeled *MC* is the marginal cost curve for NEPOOL.

FIGURE 10.6

NEPOOL's Marginal Cost Curve

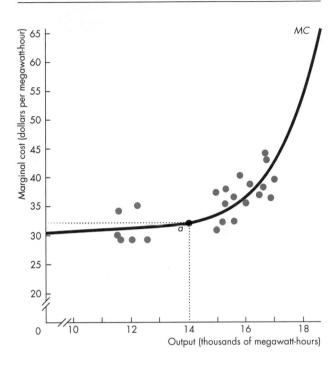

Each point in the figure represents marginal cost at a particular hour on a particular day. For example, point *a* represents a marginal cost of $32 per megawatt-hour and an output rate of 14,000 megawatt-hours. The marginal cost curve for electric power in New England rises steeply as output approaches the physical limits of the generating plant.

Notice the similarity between the marginal cost curves for NEPOOL and Swanky. All production processes experience diminishing returns and have marginal cost curves that (eventually) slope upward.

Swanky adjusts its rate of sweater production by varying the amount of labor it employs and varying the extent to which it utilizes its fixed amount of knitting machinery—its physical plant. NEPOOL meets fluctuations in the production of electric power by varying the fuel input and varying the output of a fixed physical generating plant. All types of firms face cost curves such as the ones you've just studied. Another example—that of General Motors' cost curves—is given in Reading Between the Lines on pp. 246–247.

Auto Plant Cost Curves

The New York Times, July 3, 1991

G.M.'s Plan for a Nearly Nonstop Auto Plant

BY DORON P. LEVIN

DETROIT   The General Motors Corporation and a local chapter of the United Automobile Workers union have tentatively agreed to begin near-nonstop assembly operations at G.M.'s Lordstown, Ohio, plant starting next summer. The step would enable G.M. to effectively produce as many cars at one plant as the company can now assemble in two.

The move represents a growing trend among American auto makers to cut costs by wringing more use from existing plants. The Chrysler Corporation, for example, has an agreement with the U.A.W. to step up mini-van production, if needed, by using three shifts instead of the usual two. . . .

Under the G.M. and union proposal for Lordstown, the plant would operate with two 10-hour shifts Monday through Friday, one 10-hour shift on Saturday and one 10-hour shift on Sunday, for a total of 120 hours of production weekly.

G.M.'s push to trim production and labor costs at its Baltimore plant, which makes midsized vans, precipitated a strike last week because workers complained that the faster pace was causing too many accidents. . . .

Beyond the pace of work, some manufacturing experts are concerned that near-nonstop assembly operations do not allow enough time for routine maintenance and repairs. . . .

Although G.M. declined to comment on its production capacity at Lordstown, [Bill] Alli [the U.A.W. shop chairman] said the company had told him that the plant would be able to build 480,000 cars annually. A G.M. spokesman said that in the latest year the plant produced 360,000 cars on two shifts, plus overtime.

In the new Lordstown arrangement, three crews of workers would each work four days a week, 10 hours a day. Two crews would receive 44 hours of pay for a 40-hour workweek. The third crew, working Friday though Monday, would receive 48 hours of pay.

General Motors and the United Automobile Workers union have tentatively agreed to operate G.M.'s Lordstown, Ohio, plant for twelve 10-hour shifts—120 hours—each week.

Under the deal, weekday workers receive 44 hours of pay for a 40-hour workweek and weekend workers receive 48 hours of pay for a 40-hour workweek.

The plant will be able to build 480,000 cars annually compared with 360,000 cars under the previous arrangement of two 8-hour shifts plus overtime.

The deal is part of a trend to cut costs by squeezing more from existing plants.

Workers say that the faster pace causes too many accidents, and experts say that near-nonstop operations do not allow enough time for maintenance and repairs.

Background and Analysis

By increasing output, auto producers are able to spread their fixed cost over a larger quantity produced and lower their average fixed cost (*AFC*)—for example, from *A* to *B* in Fig. 1.

But with two 8-hour shifts plus overtime, the cost of the additional labor that is needed to increase output increases average variable cost by more than the decrease in average fixed cost. As a result, average total cost (*ATC*) increases—for example, from *C* to *D* in Fig. 1.

By introducing 10-hour shifts, the cost of the first 80 crew hours—Monday through Thursday crews—increases to 88 crew hours of pay—a 10 percent increase on the cost with 8-hour shifts. But the next 40 crew hours—Friday through Sunday crews—cost only 48 crew hours of pay, a lower amount than the overtime wage rate.

Figure 1

Figure 2

Because the 10-hour shift arrangement *increases* the cost of the first 80 crew hours but *decreases* the cost of the next 40 crew hours, it increases *ATC* at low outputs but decreases *ATC* at high outputs, as shown in Fig. 2. With 8-hour shifts plus overtime, the average total cost curve is ATC_0, and with 10-hour shifts it is ATC_1.

With the output rate of 360,000 cars per year, it does not pay to switch to 10-hour shifts because average total cost is higher. But with the higher output rate of 480,000 cars per year, average total cost is lower with 10-hour shifts.

Figure 2 shows the average total cost of producing 480,000 cars with a 10-hour shift to be the same as that of producing 360,000 cars with 8-hour shifts—*C* dollars per car. We do not know from the article whether this assumption is correct. It is possible, because of the faster and more intense pace of plant operation, that higher maintenance costs reduce the benefits of the 10-hour shift arrangement.

As the demand grows, firms such as Swanky, electric power utilities, and auto makers install new plant and equipment. When does it pay Swanky to install new knitting machines, the New England power producers to install new and larger generators, and GM to install new assembly lines? Let's now answer these questions.

Plant Size, Cost, and Capacity

We have studied how the cost of production varies for a given sweater plant when different quantities of labor are used. The output rate at which a plant's average total cost is at a minimum is called the **capacity** of the plant. If a plant's output is below the point of minimum average total cost—that is, if it produces a lower amount than its capacity—it is said to have **excess capacity**. If a plant's output is above the point of minimum average total cost—that is, if it produces a higher amount than its capacity—it is said to have **overutilized capacity**.

The economist's use of the word *capacity* differs from the everyday use. It seems more natural to talk about a plant operating at capacity when it cannot produce any more. However, when we want to refer to the maximum output that a plant can produce, we call that output the **physical limits** of the plant.

The cost curves that were shown in Fig. 10.4 apply to a plant size of one knitting machine that has a fixed cost of $25. There is a set of short-run cost curves like those shown in Fig. 10.4 for each different plant size. In the short run, a firm will be economically efficient if it produces at a point on the short-run cost curve for its given plant. In the long run, though, the firm can do better. It can choose its plant size and therefore can create a different short-run cost curve on which it will operate.

The Capacity Utilization Puzzle

NEPOOL sometimes operates its plants at outputs above capacity and close to their physical limits. This situation is not uncommon. High-quality gardeners, plumbers, electricians, painters, and other suppliers of services often work so hard that they produce at an average total cost that is higher than their minimum average cost. To get the work done, they have to hire extra help at overtime wage rates and work evenings and weekends, thereby incurring a high average cost of production.

Operating with increasing average total cost looks uneconomic. Why don't such firms buy more capital equipment and increase the scale of their business to meet the obvious high demand for their output? Is there an economic reason why they don't?

In contrast, it is not uncommon in many industries to have an almost permanent excess capacity. Steel production is an example. Excess capacity also occurs in the auto industry, in many mining operations, and in a host of other industries. These producers claim that they could increase their output if the demand for their product was higher and, as a result, could produce at a lower average total cost.

It sounds as if these firms have invested in too big a production plant. It seems as if the steel producers and auto makers would be better off if they had smaller plants so that they could produce closer to the point of minimum average total cost. Is this in fact the case? Or is there some economic explanation for why firms in such industries persistently have excess capacity? This section provides a large part of the answers to these questions.

You have already studied how a firm's costs change when it varies its use of labor while holding constant the size of its production plant. This cost behavior is described by the firm's short-run cost curves. Now we are going to study how a firm's costs vary when all its inputs vary—labor and the scale of the production plant. These variations in costs are described by the firm's long-run cost curves.

Although we want to understand the behavior of real firms, we will, as before, spend most of our time studying the long-run costs of our imaginary firm—Swanky, Inc. We will then use the insights that we get from this sweater factory to make sense of the behavior of real firms.

Short-Run Cost and Long-Run Cost

Short-run cost is made up of the fixed cost of a fixed plant and the variable cost of labor. The behavior of short-run cost depends on the short-run production function. **Long-run cost** is the cost of production when a firm uses the economically efficient plant size. The behavior of long-run cost depends on the firm's production function. A **production function** is the relationship between the maximum output attainable and the quantities of inputs used.

The Production Function

Swanky's production function is shown in Fig. 10.7. In the table, we look at four different plant sizes and five different quantities of labor input. Perhaps you will recognize the numbers in the column for a plant size of one knitting machine. This is the sweater factory whose short-run product and cost curves we have just studied. With one knitting machine, output varies as the labor input is varied, as described by the numbers in that column. The table also shows three other plant sizes: two, three, and four times

the size of the original one. If Sidney doubles the plant size (to 2 knitting machines), the various amounts of labor can produce the outputs shown in the second column of the table. The other two columns show the outputs of yet larger plants. Each of the columns of the table is a short-run production function. The production function itself is just the collection of all the short-run production functions.

The total product curves for these four different plant sizes appear in Fig. 10.7. As you can see, each total product curve has the same basic shape, but the bigger the sweater plant, the larger is the number of sweaters knitted each day by a given number of workers. One of the fundamental technological facts reflected in the shape of a total product curve is the law of diminishing returns.

FIGURE **10.7**

The Production Function

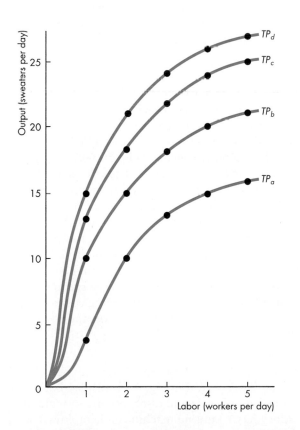

Labor (workers per day)	Output (sweaters per day)			
	Plant *a*	Plant *b*	Plant *c*	Plant *d*
1	4	10	13	15
2	10	15	18	21
3	13	18	22	24
4	15	20	24	26
5	16	21	25	27
Knitting machines (number)	1	2	3	4

The table shows four short-run production functions for four plant sizes. These production functions are plotted in the graph and are labeled TP_a (1 knitting machine), TP_b (2 knitting machines), TP_c (3 knitting machines), and TP_d (4 knitting machines). Each total product curve displays diminishing marginal product. The bigger the plant, the higher is the total product for any given amount of labor employed. The highlighted numbers in the table show what happens as the firm changes its scale of production. Doubling the scale from 1 machine and 1 worker to 2 machines and 2 workers more than doubles the output—increasing returns to scale. Increasing the scale again from 2 workers and 2 machines to 3 workers and 3 machines and to 4 workers and 4 machines increases output by a smaller percentage than the increase in inputs—decreasing returns to scale.

Diminishing Returns

Diminishing returns occur in all four plants as the labor input increases. You can check that fact by doing calculations for the larger plants similar to those done in Fig. 10.2. Regardless of the size of the plant, the larger the labor input, the lower (eventually) is its marginal product.

Just as we can calculate the marginal product of labor for each plant size, we can also calculate the marginal product of capital for each quantity of labor. The **marginal product of capital** is the change in total product resulting from a one-unit increase in the quantity of capital employed, holding the quantity of labor constant. It is calculated in a similar way to the marginal product of labor. Also, it behaves in a similar way to the marginal product of labor. That is, if the labor input is held constant as the capital input is increased, the marginal product of capital diminishes.

The law of diminishing returns tells us what happens to output when a firm changes one input, either labor or capital, and holds the other input constant. What happens to output if a firm changes both labor and equipment?

Returns to Scale

A change in scale occurs when there is an equal percentage change in the use of all the firm's inputs. For example, if Swanky has been employing one worker and has one knitting machine and then doubles its use of both inputs (to use two workers and two knitting machines), the scale of the firm will double. **Returns to scale** are the increases in output that result from increasing all inputs by the same percentage. There are three possible cases:

◆ Constant returns to scale
◆ Increasing returns to scale
◆ Decreasing returns to scale

Constant Returns to Scale   **Constant returns to scale** occur when the percentage increase in a firm's output is equal to the percentage increase in its inputs. If constant returns to scale are present, when a firm doubles all its inputs, its output exactly doubles. Constant returns to scale occur if an increase in output is achieved by replicating the original production process. For example, General Motors can double its production of Cavaliers by doubling its production facility for those cars. It can build an identical production line and hire an identical number of workers. With the two identical production lines, GM will produce exactly twice as many cars.

Increasing Returns to Scale   **Increasing returns to scale** (also called **economies of scale**) occur when the percentage increase in output exceeds the percentage increase in inputs. If economies of scale are present when a firm doubles all its inputs, its output more than doubles. Economies of scale occur in production processes in which increased output enables a firm to use a more productive technology. For example, if GM produces only 100 cars a week, it will not pay to install an automated assembly line. The cost per car will be lower if instead GM uses skilled, but expensive, workers equipped only with inexpensive hand tools. But at an output rate of a few thousand cars a week, it will pay GM to install an automated assembly line. Each worker will specialize in a small number of tasks and will become highly proficient in them. General Motors may use 100 times more capital and labor, but the number of cars it can make will increase much more than a hundredfold. It will experience increasing returns to scale.

Decreasing Returns to Scale   **Decreasing returns to scale** (also called **diseconomies of scale**) occur when the percentage increase in output is less than the percentage change in inputs. For example, if inputs double and output increases by 50 percent, diseconomies of scale are present. Diseconomies of scale occur in all production processes at some output rate, but perhaps at a very high one. The most common source of diseconomies of scale is the increasingly complex management and organizational structure required to control a large firm. The larger the organization, the larger are the number of layers in the management pyramid and the greater are the costs of monitoring and maintaining control of all the various stages in the production and marketing process.

Scale Economies at Swanky   Swanky's production possibilities, set out in Fig. 10.7, display both economies of scale and diseconomies of scale. If Sidney has 1 knitting machine and employs 1 worker, his factory will produce 4 sweaters a day. If he doubles the firm's inputs to 2 knitting machines and 2 workers, the factory's output increases almost fourfold to 15 sweaters a day. If he increases his inputs another 50 percent to 3 knitting machines and 3 workers, output increases to 22 sweaters a day—an increase of less than 50 percent. Doubling the scale of Swanky from 1 to 2 units of each input gives rise to economies of scale, but the further increase from 2 to 3 units of each input gives rise to diseconomies of scale.

Whether a firm experiences increasing, constant, or decreasing returns to scale has an important effect on its long-run costs. Let's see how.

Plant Size and Cost

Earlier in this chapter, we worked out Swanky's short-run costs when it has a fixed amount of capital—one knitting machine—and a variable number of workers. We can also work out the short-run costs of different plant sizes. It takes longer to change the size of the production plant than to change the size of the plant's work force. That is why we speak of a short run for each different plant size. But Sidney can buy another knitting machine and put it into his existing factory. He will then have a different size of plant. He can vary the amount of labor employed in that plant, and as he does so, we can trace the short-run cost curves associated with those different levels of variable input.

Let's look at the short-run costs for different plants and see how plant size itself affects the short-run cost curves.

Four Different Plants

We've already studied the costs of a plant with 1 knitting machine. We'll call that Plant a. The table in Fig. 10.8 sets out the costs for Plant a and for three other plants—what we will call Plants b, c, and d. Plant b has 2 knitting machines; Plant c has 3 knitting machines; and Plant d has 4 knitting machines.

The average total cost curves associated with the original plant and these three larger plants appear in Fig. 10.8(a). The average total cost curve for each of the four plant sizes has the same basic U-shape. Which of these cost curves Swanky operates on depends on its plant size. For example, if Swanky has Plant a, then its average total cost curve will be ATC_a and it will cost $7.69 per sweater to knit 13 sweaters a day. But Swanky can produce 13 sweaters a day with any of these four different plant sizes. If it uses Plant b, the average total cost curve is ATC_b and the average total cost of a sweater will be $6.80. And if it uses Plant d, the average total cost of a sweater will be $9.50. If Swanky wants to produce 13 sweaters a day, the economically efficient plant is Plant b—the one with the lowest average total cost of production.

The Long-Run Average Cost Curve

The **long-run average cost curve** traces the relationship between the lowest attainable average total cost and output when both capital and labor inputs can be varied. This curve is illustrated in Fig. 10.8(b) as $LRAC$. The curve is derived directly from the four short-run average total cost curves that we have just reviewed in Fig. 10.8(a). As you can see, from either part (a) or part (b), Plant a has the lowest average total cost for all output rates up to 10 sweaters a day. Plant b has the lowest average total cost for output rates between 10 and 18 sweaters a day. Between output rates of 18 and 24 sweaters a day, Plant c has the lowest average total cost. Finally, for output rates above 24 sweaters a day, Plant d has the lowest average total cost. The segments of the four average total cost curves for which each plant has the lowest average total cost are highlighted in Fig. 10.8(b). The scallop-shaped curve made up of these four segments is the long-run average cost curve.

Swanky will be on its long-run average cost curve if it does the following: to produce up to 10 sweaters a day, it uses 1 machine; to produce between 11 and 18 sweaters a day, it uses 2 machines; to produce between and 19 and 24 sweaters, it uses 3 machines; and, finally, to produce more than 24 sweaters, it uses 4 machines. Within these ranges, it varies its output by varying the amount of labor employed.

FIGURE **10.8**

Short-Run and Long-Run Costs

(a) Short-run average cost

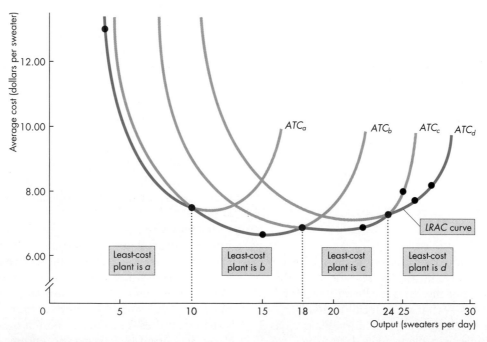

(b) Long-run average cost

Labor (workers per day)	Output (sweaters per day)	Total fixed cost	Total variable cost	Total cost	Average total cost (dollars per sweater)
			(dollars per day)		

Plant *a*: 1 unit of capital—total cost of capital = $25

1	4	25	25	50	12.50
2	10	25	50	75	7.50
3	13	25	75	100	7.69
4	15	25	100	125	8.33
5	16	25	125	150	9.38

Plant *b*: 2 units of capital—total cost of capital = $50

1	10	50	25	75	7.50
2	15	50	50	100	6.67
3	18	50	75	125	6.94
4	20	50	100	150	7.50
5	21	50	125	175	8.33

Plant *c*: 3 units of capital—total cost of capital = $75

1	13	75	25	100	7.69
2	18	75	50	125	6.94
3	22	75	75	150	6.82
4	24	75	100	175	7.29
5	25	75	125	200	8.00

Plant *d*: 4 units of capital—total cost of capital = $100

1	15	100	25	125	8.33
2	21	100	50	150	7.14
3	24	100	75	175	7.29
4	26	100	100	200	7.69
5	27	100	125	225	8.33

The table shows the short-run costs of four different plants. Each plant has a different fixed cost. Plant *a* has 1 knitting machine and a fixed cost of $25; Plant *b* has 2 knitting machines and a fixed cost of $50; Plant *c* has 3 knitting machines and a fixed cost of $75; and Plant *d* has 4 knitting machines and a fixed cost of $100. The short-run average total cost curve for each plant is graphed in part (a). Part (b) illustrates the construction of the long-run average cost curve. The curve traces the lowest attainable costs of production at each output when both capital and labor inputs are varied. On the long-run average cost curve, Swanky uses Plant *a* to produce up to 10 sweaters a day, Plant *b* to produce between 11 and 18 sweaters a day, Plant *c* to produce between 19 and 24 sweaters a day, and Plant *d* to produce more than 24 sweaters a day.

Long-Run Cost and Returns to Scale There is a connection between the long-run average cost curve and returns to scale. Figure 10.9 shows this connection. When long-run average cost is decreasing, there are increasing returns to scale (or economies of scale). When long-run average cost is increasing, there are decreasing returns to scale (or diseconomies of scale). At outputs up to 15 sweaters a day, Swanky experiences economies of scale; at 15 sweaters a day, long-run average cost is at a minimum. When output increases above 15 sweaters a day, Swanky experiences diseconomies of scale.

The long-run average cost curve that we have derived for Swanky has two special features that will not always be found in a firm's long-run cost curve. First, Swanky is able to adjust its plant size only in big jumps. In contrast, we can imagine varying the plant size in tiny increments so that there is an infinite number of plant sizes. In such a situation, there is an infinite number of short-run average total cost curves, one for each plant. Second, Swanky's long-run average cost curve is U-shaped—it slopes either

downward (economies of scale) or upward (diseconomies of scale). In contrast, many production processes have constant returns to scale over some intermediate range of output, and long-run average cost is constant. The long-run average cost curve is horizontal.

Figure 10.10 illustrates this situation. Here, there is an infinite number of plant sizes, so the long-run average cost curve is smooth, not scalloped like Swanky's. For outputs up to Q_1, there are increasing returns to scale and long-run average cost is decreasing. For outputs between Q_1 and Q_2, there are constant returns to scale and long-run average cost is constant. And for outputs that exceed Q_2, there are decreasing returns to scale and long-run average cost is increasing.

To keep the figure clear, only one of the infinite number of short-run average total cost curves, labeled *SRAC*, is shown. Each short-run average total cost curve touches the long-run average cost curve, *LRAC*, at a single point (1 output). Thus, for each output, there is a unique, economically efficient

FIGURE 10.9

Returns to Scale

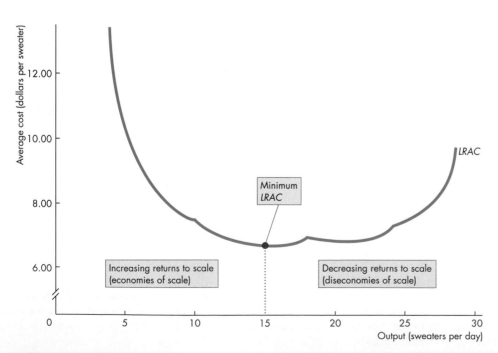

When the long-run average cost curve (*LRAC*) slopes downward, there are increasing returns to scale (or economies of scale). When the long-run average cost curve slopes upward, there are decreasing returns to scale (or diseconomies of scale).

FIGURE **10.10**

Short-Run and Long-Run Average Costs

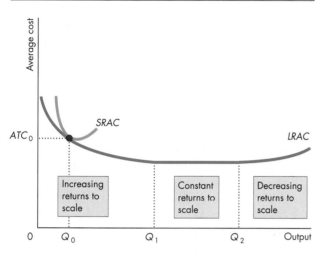

If capital can be varied in small units, there are an infinitely large number of plant sizes and an infinitely large number of short-run average
total cost curves. Each short-run average total cost curve touches the
long-run average cost curve at a single point. For example, the short-
run average total cost curve (*SRAC*) touches the long-run average cost
curve (*LRAC*) at the output rate Q_0 and average total cost ATC_0. The
short-run average total cost curve shown is representative of the infinite number of others, each with only one point touching the long-run
average cost curve. For outputs up to Q_1, there are increasing returns
to scale; for outputs between Q_1 and Q_2, there are constant returns to
scale; and for outputs greater than Q_2, there are decreasing returns to
scale.

plant size. The short-run average total cost curve
shown in Fig. 10.10 is for the plant that can produce
output rate Q_0 at minimum average total cost,
ATC_0.

The first time the long-run average cost curve
appeared in print, it was drawn incorrectly. Take a
look at Our Advancing Knowledge (pp. 256–257) to
see why. You will understand the connection
between short-run and long-run average cost
curves more thoroughly after you have studied this
material.

Long-Run Costs Are Total Costs   When we examine
short-run costs, we distinguish between fixed, variable, and total costs. We make no such distinctions

for long-run costs. All inputs vary in the long run, so
there are no long-run fixed costs. Since there are no
long-run fixed costs, long-run total cost and long-
run variable cost are the same thing. The long-run
average variable cost is the long-run average cost.

There is a long-run marginal cost curve that goes
with the long-run average cost curve. The relationship between the long-run average cost curve and
the long-run marginal cost curve is similar to that
between the short-run average cost curve and the
short-run marginal cost curve. When long-run average cost is decreasing, long-run marginal cost is less
than long-run average cost. When long-run average
cost is increasing, long-run marginal cost exceeds
long-run average cost, and when long-run average
cost is constant, long-run marginal cost is equal to
long-run average cost.

Shifts in Cost Curves

Both short-run and long-run cost curves depend on
two things: the production function and input
prices. A change in technology shifts the production
function and thus shifts the cost curves. Technological advances increase the output that can be produced from given inputs. They also shift the total
product curve as well as the average and the marginal product curves upward, and they shift the cost
curves downward. For example, advances in genetic
engineering are making it possible to increase the
milk production of a cow without increasing the
amount of food that it eats—a technological
advance that lowers the cost of milk production.

Resource or input prices also affect the cost
curves. If the price of an input increases, it directly
increases cost and shifts the cost curves upward.

Returns to Scale in Reality

L et's close this chapter by looking
at some real-world examples and
see why there is a great deal of excess capacity in
some industries while in others firms are operating
flat out.

FIRMS and COSTS

Why do firms exist? Ronald H. Coase was the first to ask and answer this question. Firms exist, he said, because they enable us to avoid costs arising from market transactions. Without firms, each individual would have to find the best way of selling her or his own resources in a wide range of markets. The time cost of these activities would be extremely large. With firms, each person sells her or his resources to just one firm—the one offering the highest price—and managers direct the resources hired by the firm to their highest-value uses.

How are firm's costs related to their output? Jacob Viner answered this question, showing how a firm's short-run and long-run cost curves are related to each other. But he didn't get it quite right, and his mistake can reinforce your understanding of the short-run average cost curve (*SRAC*) and the long-run average cost curve (*LRAC*). (Viner's mistake is contained in an article that has been reprinted many times. One of its most accessible sources is in Kenneth E. Boulding and George J. Stigler (eds.), *Readings in Price Theory* (Chicago: Richard D. Irwin, 1952), 198–232. The article was first published in *Zeitschrift für National-konomie*, vol. III (1931): 23–46.)

Viner asked his drafts-man to draw a long-run average cost curve that satisfied two conditions:

◆ Not rise above any *SRAC* curve at any point
◆ Pass through the minimum point of each *SRAC* curve

The *SRAC* curve in Fig. 1 is never below the *LRAC* and thus satisfies Viner's first condition—that the *LRAC* not rise above any *SRAC* at any point. But it does not satisfy the second—that the *LRAC* pass through the minimum points of each *SRAC*. Viner's wrong version of a long-run average cost curve is shown in Fig. 2. That curve does pass through the minimum points of the *SRAC* curves and so satisfies the second condition but not the first.

It is not possible to draw a curve that satisfies both of Viner's conditions (except when there are constant returns to scale and *LRAC* is horizontal). The curve in Fig. 1 is a long-run average cost curve, and Viner's curve in Fig. 2 is not.

Figure 1 Long-run average cost curve

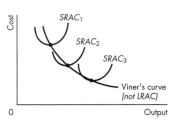

Figure 2 Viner's error

Factories employing hundreds of workers using specialized machinery became common in the industrial revolution of the eighteenth century. By organizing production on a large scale and by allocating resources directly rather than indirectly through markets, firms were able to cut the costs of production. This process saw a further advance with the development of the production line method in the automobile industry of the 1920s.

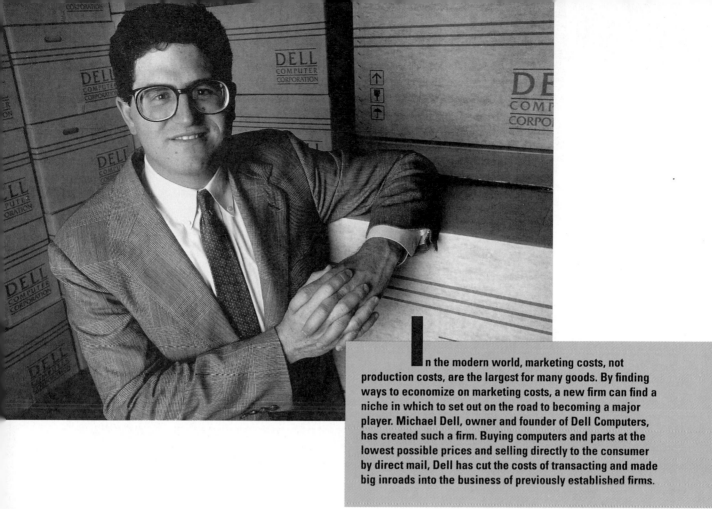

In the modern world, marketing costs, not production costs, are the largest for many goods. By finding ways to economize on marketing costs, a new firm can find a niche in which to set out on the road to becoming a major player. Michael Dell, owner and founder of Dell Computers, has created such a firm. Buying computers and parts at the lowest possible prices and selling directly to the consumer by direct mail, Dell has cut the costs of transacting and made big inroads into the business of previously established firms.

Our understanding of the working of firms was developed in the 1930s, and many economists contributed to our advancing knowledge. Two important contributers were Ronald H. Coase (1910–), pictured right, and Jacob Viner (1892–1970), pictured left.

Coase was born in England but has lived in the United States since 1951, which he first visited as a 20-year-old on a traveling scholarship during the depths of the Great Depression. It was on that visit, and before he had completed his bachelor's degree, that he conceived the ideas for his paper, "The Nature of the Firm," cited 60 years later by the Swedish Academy of Sciences as his main contribution to economics when awarding him the Nobel Prize for Economic Science.

Viner was born in Montreal, Canada, the son of a poor immigrant family from Eastern Europe. He was educated at McGill and Harvard Universities and taught at Chicago and Princeton. Viner's main contribution was to explain the nature of a firm's costs, and it was he who first described the firm's cost curves that are explained in this chapter.

RONALD COASE & JACOB VINER:

UNDERSTANDING
How
Firms
Work

Excess Capacity

It has been estimated that one vacuum cleaner factory can produce a quarter of all the vacuum cleaners produced in the United States before its long-run average cost reaches its minimum.[3] But there are more than four vacuum cleaner factories in the United States, so each factory is operating at an output rate below that at which long-run average cost is at a minimum. The situation also holds for TV picture tubes and for steel, cars, and petroleum refining. Economies of scale also exist in the market for typewriters, cigarettes, semiconductors, and matches.

Figure 10.11 illustrates the situation that prevails in those industries that can lower their average production costs if the market is big enough to permit them to expand to their most efficient scale. Output, limited by the extent of the market, is Q_0. The firm is producing efficiently at an average total cost of ATC_0. But the firm has excess capacity. It can lower its costs to ATC_{min} even with its existing plant if output can be increased to Q_c, and it can lower its costs even more by switching to a bigger plant. But the firm can't sell more than Q_0. So, even when it is operating as efficiently as possible, the firm has excess capacity. The production of vacuum cleaners, TV picture tubes, steel, cars, and the other products mentioned above are examples of industries in which the situation shown in Fig. 10.11 prevails.

[3]James V. Koch, *Industrial Organization and Prices*, 2nd ed. (Englewood Cliffs, N.J.: Prentice-Hall, 1980), 123–134.

FIGURE **10.11**

Excess Capacity

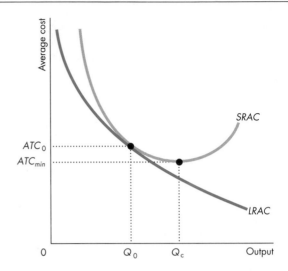

The size of the market limits a firm's output to Q_0. At output Q_0, the long-run average cost curve is downward sloping—there are economies of scale. To produce Q_0 at least cost, the firm installs a plant with a capacity of Q_c and operates the plant below capacity. This situation prevails in many industries, including those manufacturing vacuum cleaners, TV picture tubes, steel, cars, refined petroleum, typewriters, cigarettes, semiconductors, and matches.

Operating Flat Out

When we examined the short-run marginal cost of NEPOOL, we discovered that its marginal cost increases as it produces more power. As we saw in Fig. 10.6, NEPOOL's marginal cost curve slopes upward and becomes extremely steep at output rates in excess of 17,000 megawatt-hours. Why don't the companies in NEPOOL build additional plants? We can answer this question by applying the lessons that you've just learned about the relationship between short-run and long-run costs.

Figure 10.12 shows NEPOOL's short-run marginal cost curve (*MC*) as well as its short-run average total cost curve (*ATC*). Two points are marked on the *x*-axis. Point *C* is NEPOOL's capacity. (The word *capacity* is being used here in its economic sense as the output rate that minimizes average total cost.) The other point marked is *L*, the physical limits of the output of the existing plant.

NEPOOL's marginal cost curve slopes upward very steeply because as its output approaches its physical limits, generators are brought into operation that use very expensive fuel (similar to that used by jet aircraft). But the average total cost curve has a much more gentle slope. Why? Because the bulk of NEPOOL's costs are not variable fuel costs at all but fixed costs. NEPOOL's fixed resources—equipment and skilled labor—cannot be varied to meet hourly shifts in demand for power. The great proportion of total costs coming from these fixed resources smooths out NEPOOL's average total cost. NEPOOL's output fluctuates between 11,500 and 17,000 megawatt-hours (see Fig. 10.6), a range over which the marginal cost curve is upward sloping but the average total cost curve is downward sloping.

Overutilizing Capacity

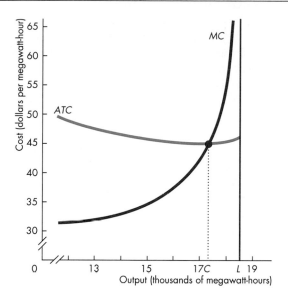

Although NEPOOL faces a steeply increasing marginal cost, its average total cost declines up to output *C*. The capacity (minimum cost) of NEPOOL's plant is output *C*. Output *L* is the physical limit of its plant. Between *C* and *L*, average total cost rises. When demand increases so that NEPOOL is producing in the range between *C* and *L* for a significant amount of time, it will be efficient to increase plant size to meet the additional demand. It will not be efficient to build a bigger plant to meet current demand even though at peak demand NEPOOL is operating flat out. Although marginal cost can be lowered with a larger plant, average total cost will rise.

Occasionally, output increases above capacity and therefore moves into the range in which average total cost is increasing. But such cases are rare—occurring only at the peak of demand for the year.

As the demand for electric power gradually increases, the NEPOOL producers will be able to achieve greater economic efficiency by increasing their plant size. Currently, output fluctuates between 11,500 megawatt-hours and 17,000 megawatt-hours. If demand fluctuates between 17,000 and 19,000 megawatt-hours, production will be taking place on the upward-sloping part of the short-run average total cost curve, and on some occasions, it will be necessary for NEPOOL to operate flat out—at its physical limits—and to import power from neighboring power pools to meet the demand. It will pay NEPOOL producers to increase their production capacity to meet the additional demand.

It does not pay to increase capacity to meet demand fluctuations in the range currently being experienced. An increased plant will increase the fixed costs and shift the average total cost curve upward. The new average total cost curve will be below the current one only at higher outputs than can be sold. Thus it pays the NEPOOL power companies to stick with their existing plants and operate them flat out to meet the peak demand.

◆ ◆ ◆ ◆ We've now studied the way in which a firm's costs vary as it varies its inputs and output rate. We've seen how the fact that marginal product eventually diminishes gives rise to eventually increasing average and marginal cost. We've also seen how long-run cost curves take their shape from economies and diseconomies of scale—long-run average cost decreasing as output increases with economies of scale and long-run average cost increasing as output increases with diseconomies of scale. ◆ ◆ Our next task is to study the interactions of firms and households in markets for goods and services and see how prices, output levels, and profits are determined.

S U M M A R Y

Firms' Objectives and Constraints

Firms aim to maximize profit. Profit maximization stems directly from scarcity. Only firms that maximize profits can survive in a competitive environment.

Constraints are imposed on profit maximization by the market and by technology. Some firms operate in such competitive markets that they have no choice but to sell their output at the going price. In other cases the firm can choose the price of its output. However, at higher prices, it will sell less. Most firms are unable to influence the markets for their inputs and have to buy them at the going prices. Technology limits the production process of firms. If firms are technologically efficient, then they can increase their output only by using more inputs.

In the short run, some inputs cannot be changed. In most cases, the capital input is fixed in the short run while labor can be varied. (pp. 233–234)

Short-Run Technology Constraint

The short-run production function describes the limits to output as a firm changes the quantity of a variable input such as labor. The short-run production function is described by the total, marginal, and average product curves. Total product is the output produced in a given period. Average product is total product per unit of variable input. Marginal product is the change in total product resulting from a one-unit increase in the variable input. As the variable input is increased, marginal product increases at first until it reaches a peak, and thereafter it declines—diminishing returns begin. When marginal product exceeds average product, average product is increasing. When marginal product is less than average product, average product is decreasing. When marginal product equals average product, average product is at its maximum. (pp. 234–240)

Short-Run Cost

Total cost is divided into total fixed cost and total variable cost. As output increases, total cost increases because total variable cost increases. Marginal cost is the additional cost of producing one more unit of output. Average total cost is total cost per unit of output.

Costs depend on how much a firm produces. Average fixed cost decreases as output increases. Average variable cost and average total cost are U-shaped curves. Marginal cost is also U-shaped. When marginal cost is less than average cost, average cost is decreasing, and when marginal cost exceeds average cost, average cost is increasing. When average product is at a maximum, average variable cost is at a minimum. When average product is increasing, average variable cost is decreasing, and when average product is decreasing, average variable cost is increasing. (pp. 240–248)

Plant Size, Cost, and Capacity

Plant capacity is the output rate with the lowest average total cost. Firms that produce a smaller amount than their capacity are said to have excess capacity; those that produce a larger amount than their capacity are said to have overutilized their capacity. Firms choose their plant size to minimize long-run cost.

Long-run cost is the cost of production when all inputs—labor as well as plant and equipment—have been adjusted to their economically efficient levels. The behavior of long-run cost depends on the firm's production function. As a firm uses more labor while holding capital constant, it eventually experiences diminishing returns. When it uses more capital while holding labor constant, it also experiences diminishing returns. When it varies all its inputs in equal proportions, it experiences returns to scale. Returns to scale can be constant, increasing, or decreasing. (pp. 248–251)

Plant Size and Cost

There is a set of short-run cost curves for each different plant size. There is one least-cost plant for each output. The higher the output, the larger is the plant that will minimize average total cost.

The long-run average cost curve traces out the relationship between the lowest attainable average total cost and output when both capital and labor inputs can be varied. With increasing returns to scale, the long-run average cost curve slopes downward. With decreasing returns to scale, the long-run average cost curve slopes upward.

There is no distinction between fixed cost and variable cost in the long run. Since all inputs are variable, all costs are also variable.

Short-run and long-run cost curves shift when either input prices or technology changes. An improvement in technology increases the output from a given set of inputs and shifts the cost curves downward. A rise in input prices shifts the cost curves upward. (pp. 251–255)

Returns to Scale in Reality

Some firms, including those that make vacuum cleaners, TV picture tubes, and cars, have increasing returns to scale (economies of scale). Usually economies of scale exist when the total market is too small to allow the efficient scale of production. In such industries, firms operate efficiently with excess capacity.

Some firms overutilize their plants, operating them at an output rate that exceeds capacity. NEPOOL is a good example. Though the marginal cost of electric power increases as output increases, only rarely does NEPOOL produce so much power that it is operating on the upward-sloping section of its short-run average total cost curve. Only if a firm persistently operates on the upward-sloping part of its short-run average total cost curve will it be efficient to increase its plant size. (pp. 255–259)

KEY ELEMENTS

Key Terms

Average fixed cost, 242
Average product, 237
Average total cost, 242
Average variable cost, 242
Capacity, 248
Capital-intensive technique, 233
Constant returns to scale, 250
Decreasing returns to scale, 250
Diminishing marginal returns, 239
Diseconomies of scale, 250
Economies of scale, 250
Excess capacity, 248
Fixed cost, 240
Fixed inputs, 234
Increasing marginal returns, 239
Increasing returns to scale, 250
Labor-intensive technique, 233
Law of diminishing returns, 239
Long run, 234
Long-run average cost curve, 251
Long-run cost, 248
Marginal cost, 242
Marginal product, 235
Marginal product of capital, 250
Marginal product of labor, 235

Market constraints, 233
Overutilized capacity, 248
Physical limits, 248
Production function, 249
Profit maximization, 233
Returns to scale, 250
Short run, 234
Technique, 233
Total cost, 240
Total fixed cost, 240
Total product, 234
Total product curve, 234
Total variable cost, 240
Variable cost, 240
Variable inputs, 234

Key Figures and Tables

Figure 10.2   Total Product and Marginal Product, 236
Figure 10.3   Total Product, Marginal Product, and Average Product, 237
Figure 10.4   Short-Run Costs, 241
Figure 10.8   Short-Run and Long-Run Costs, 252
Figure 10.9   Returns to Scale, 254
Table 10.2   A Compact Glossary on Product, 240
Table 10.3   A Compact Glossary on Cost, 243

REVIEW QUESTIONS

1 Why do we assume that firms maximize profit?

2 What are the main constraints on a firm's ability to maximize profit?

3 Distinguish between the short run and the long run.

4 Define total product, average product, and marginal product. Explain the relationships between a total product curve, average product curve, and marginal product curve.

5 State the law of diminishing returns. What does this law imply about the shapes of the total, marginal, and average product curves?

6 Define total cost, total fixed cost, total variable cost, average total cost, average fixed cost, average variable cost, and marginal cost.

7 What is the relationship between the average total cost curve, the average variable cost curve, and the marginal cost curve?

8 Define the long-run average cost curve. What is the relationship between the long-run average cost curve and the short-run average total cost curve?

9 What does the long-run average cost curve tell us?

10 Define economies of scale. What effects do economies of scale have on the shape of the long-run average cost curve?

11 When does the long-run average cost curve touch the minimum point of a short-run average total cost curve?

12 When does the long-run average cost curve touch a point on the short-run average total cost curve to the left of its minimum point?

13 When does the long-run average cost curve touch a point on the short-run average total cost curve to the right of its minimum point?

14 Why might long-run average cost decline? Why might long-run average cost increase?

15 What makes the short-run cost curves shift

a upward   **b** downward

P R O B L E M S

1 The total product schedule of Rubber Duckies, Inc., a firm making rubber boats, is described by the following:

Labor (number of workers employed per week)	Output (rubber boats per week)
1	1
2	3
3	6
4	10
5	15
6	21
7	26
8	30
9	33
10	35

a Draw the total product curve.

b Calculate average product and draw the average product curve.

c Calculate marginal product and draw the marginal product curve.

d What is the relationship between average product and marginal product at output rates below 30 boats a week? Why?

e What is the relationship between average product and marginal product at outputs above 30 boats a week? Why?

2 Suppose that the price of labor is $400 a week, the total fixed cost is $10,000 a week, and the total product schedule is the same as in problem 1.

a Calculate the firm's total cost, total variable cost, and total fixed costs for each of the outputs given.

b Draw the total cost, total variable cost, and total fixed cost curves.

c Calculate the firm's average total cost, average fixed cost, average variable cost, and marginal cost at each of the outputs given.

d Draw the following cost curves: average total cost, average variable cost, average fixed cost, and marginal cost.

3 Suppose that total fixed cost increases to $11,000 a week. How will this affect the firm's average total cost, average fixed cost, average variable cost, and marginal cost curves in problem 2?

4 Suppose that total fixed cost remains at $10,000 a week but that the price of labor increases to $450 a week. Using these new costs, rework problems 2(a) and 2(b) and draw the new cost curves.

APPENDIX

TO

CHAPTER 10

◆

PRODUCING

AT

LEAST

COST

Input Substitution

Y ou would be hard-pressed to think of many goods that can be produced in only one way. Just about every good and service can be produced by using a capital-intensive technique or a labor-intensive technique. For example, cars can be made with computer-controlled robotic assembly lines that use enormous amounts of capital and hardly any labor, a capital-intensive technique, or they can be built by skilled labor using only hand tools, a labor-intensive technique.

The firm's technically feasible range of production possibilities is described by its production function. For example, Swanky, Inc.'s production function tells us the maximum daily output of sweaters that can be produced by using different combinations of labor and capital. Figure A10.1 shows Swanky's production function. It tells us, for example, that when Sidney hires 2 workers a day and rents 2 machines, the output produced is 15 sweaters a day. The figure highlights that Swanky can use three different techniques to produce 15 sweaters a day and two different techniques to produce 10 and 21 sweaters a day.

The production function in Fig. A10.1 can be used to calculate the marginal product of labor and the marginal product of capital. The *marginal product of labor* is the change in total product per unit change of labor, holding the amount of capital constant. We've already learned how to calculate the marginal product of labor, so we'll not repeat the calculations here. The marginal product of capital is the change in total product per unit change in capital, holding the amount of labor constant. Although we have not calculated the marginal product of capital, it is done in exactly the same way as the calculation of the marginal product of labor. Furthermore, the law of diminishing returns applies to capital just as it does to labor. That is, holding labor input constant, the marginal product of capital diminishes as the capital input increases.

It's easy to see why the law of diminishing returns applies to capital by imagining this scene in Swanky's knitting factory. Suppose that there is 1 worker with 1 machine. Output (as shown in Fig. A10.1) is 4 sweaters a day. If an extra machine is installed, the 1 worker can still easily handle the 2 machines. One machine can be set to knit blue sweaters and the other, red sweaters. There's no need to stop the machines to change the wool color. Output more than doubles to 10 sweaters a day. But if a third machine is added, a single worker finds it hard to cope with the increasingly complex factory. For example, there are now three times as many

FIGURE **A10.1**

Swanky's Production Function

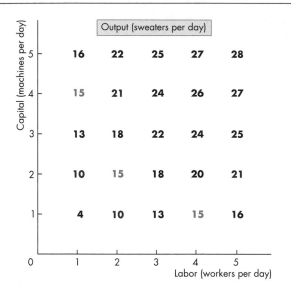

The figure shows how many sweaters can be produced per day by various combinations of labor and capital inputs. For example, by using 1 worker and 2 knitting machines, Swanky can produce 10 sweaters a day; and by using 4 workers and 2 machines, Swanky can produce 20 sweaters.

TABLE **A10.1**

Substituting Between Capital and Labor to Produce 15 Sweaters a Day

Method	Capital (K)	Labor (L)	Fall in capital (−ΔK)	Rise in labor (ΔL)	Marginal rate of substitution of labor for capital (−ΔK/ΔL)
a	4	1			
			2	1	2
b	2	2			
			1	2	½
c	1	4			

Switching from method *a* to method *b* involves cutting capital (−ΔK) by 2 machines and raising labor (ΔL) by 1 worker. The marginal rate of substitution of labor for capital—which is the ratio of the fall in capital (−ΔK) to the rise in labor (ΔL)—is 2. Switching from method *b* to method *c* involves cutting capital by 1 machine and raising labor by 2 workers, which means that the marginal rate of substitution of labor for capital is ½.

breakdowns as there were with just one machine. The worker has to spend an increasing amount of time fixing problems. Output increases to only 13 sweaters a day.

Although all goods and services can be produced by using a variety of alternative methods of production, the ease with which capital and labor can be substituted for each other varies from industry to industry. The production function reflects the ease with which inputs can be substituted for each other. Also, the production function can be used to calculate the degree of substitutability between inputs. Such a calculation involves a new concept—that of the marginal rate of substitution of capital for labor.

The Substitutability of Capital and Labor

The **marginal rate of substitution of labor for capital** is the decrease in capital needed per unit increase in labor that keeps output constant. Table A10.1 illustrates

how to calculate the marginal rate of substitution of labor for capital. As we saw in Fig. A10.1, an output of 15 sweaters a day can be produced with 4 knitting machines and 1 worker, 2 units of each input, or 1 knitting machine and 4 workers. Let's call those methods *a*, *b*, and *c*.

We can calculate the marginal rate of substitution of labor for capital by changing the method of producing 15 sweaters a day and calculating the ratio of the fall in capital to the rise in labor. Switching the method from *a* to *b* reduces the capital input by 2 machines and increases the labor input by 1 worker. The marginal rate of substitution is 2. Switching from method *b* to *c* reduces capital by 1 machine and increases labor by 2 workers. The marginal rate of substitution is ½.

The marginal rates of substitution we've just calculated obey the **law of diminishing marginal rate of substitution,** which states that:

The marginal rate of substitution of labor for capital falls as the amount of capital decreases and the amount of labor increases.

You can see that the law of diminishing marginal rate of substitution makes sense by considering Swanky's sweater factory. With 1 worker racing among 4 knitting machines, desperately trying to keep them all operating, coping with breakdowns, and keeping the wool from tangling, output can be held constant at 15 sweaters a day by getting rid of 1 machine and hiring only a small additional amount of labor. The marginal rate of substitution is high. At the other extreme, 4 workers are falling over each other to operate 1 machine. In this situation, output can be kept constant at 15 sweaters a day by laying off 2 workers and installing 1 additional machine. The marginal rate of substitution is low. The principle of the diminishing marginal rate of substitution applies to (almost) all production processes.

Isoquants

A graph of the different combinations of labor and capital that produce 15 sweaters a day is called an isoquant. An **isoquant** is a curve that shows the different combinations of labor and capital required to produce a given quantity of output. The word *isoquant* means "equal quantity"—*iso* meaning equal and *quant* meaning quantity. There is an isoquant for each output level. The series of isoquants is called an **isoquant map**. Figure A10.2 shows an isoquant map. It has three isoquants: one for 10 sweaters, one for 15 sweaters, and one for 21 sweaters. Each isoquant shown is based on the production function presented in Fig. A10.1. But Fig. A10.2 does not show all the isoquants. For example, Swanky's isoquant for 10 sweaters shows all the techniques of production—the combinations of workers and knitting machines—that can produce 10 sweaters a day. Isoquants for larger outputs are farther from the origin. That is because for any given capital input, to produce more output Swanky needs more labor, and for any given labor input, to produce more output Swanky needs more capital. For example, if Sidney hires 1 worker and rents 2 machines (point *a*), Swanky's output is 10 sweaters a day. But if Sidney rents 2 more machines (point *b*), Swanky's output

FIGURE **A10.2**

An Isoquant Map

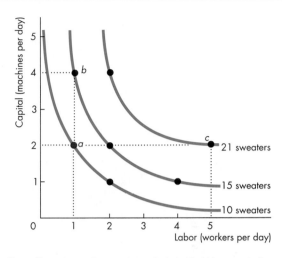

The figure illustrates an isoquant map, but one that shows only three isoquants—those for 10, 15, and 21 sweaters a day. These curves correspond to the production function shown in Fig. A10.1. If Swanky uses 2 machines and 1 worker (point *a*), it produces 10 sweaters. If it uses 4 machines and 1 worker (point *b*), it produces 15 sweaters. And if it uses 2 machines and 5 workers, it produces 21 sweaters.

increases to 15 sweaters a day. Or if Sidney hires 4 more workers (point *c*), Swanky's output increases to 21 sweaters a day.

Marginal Rate of Substitution

The marginal rate of substitution equals the magnitude of the slope of the isoquant. Figure A10.3 illustrates this relationship. The figure shows the isoquant for 13 sweaters a day. Pick any point on this isoquant and imagine increasing labor by the smallest conceivable amount and decreasing capital by the amount necessary to keep output constant at 13 sweaters. As we reduce the capital input and increase the labor input, we travel along the isoquant. If the isoquant is steep (as at point *a*), the capital input decreases by a large amount relative to the increase in the labor input. The marginal rate of substitution is high. But if the isoquant has a gentle slope (as at point *b*), the capital input decreases by a small amount relative to the increase in labor, and the marginal rate of substitution is small.

FIGURE **A10.3**

The Marginal Rate of Substitution

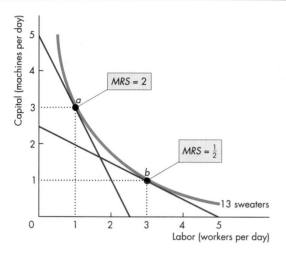

The marginal rate of substitution is measured by the magnitude of the slope of the isoquant. To calculate the marginal rate of substitution at point *a*, use the red line that is tangential to the isoquant at point *a*. Calculate the slope of that line to find the slope of the isoquant at point *a*. The magnitude of the slope at point *a* is 2. Thus at a point *a*, the marginal rate of substitution of labor for capital is 2. The marginal rate of substitution at point *b* is found from the slope of the line tangential to the isoquant at that point. That slope is ½. Thus the marginal rate of substitution of labor for capital at point *b* is ½.

The marginal rate of substitution at point *a* is the magnitude of the slope of the straight red line that is tangent to the isoquant at point *a*. The slope of the isoquant at point *a* is the same as the slope of the line. To calculate that slope, let's move along the red line from 5 knitting machines and no workers to 2.5 workers and no knitting machines. Capital decreases by 5 knitting machines, and labor increases by 2.5 workers. The magnitude of the slope is 5 divided by 2.5, which equals 2. Thus at point *a*, the marginal rate of substitution of labor for capital is 2.

The marginal rate of substitution at point *b* is the magnitude of the slope of the straight red line that is tangent to the isoquant at point *b*. This line has the same slope as the isoquant at point *b*. Along this red line, if capital falls by 2.5 knitting machines, labor increases by 5 workers. The magnitude of the slope is 2.5 knitting machines divided by 5 workers,

which equals ½. Thus at point *b*, the marginal rate of substitution of labor for capital is ½.

You can now see that the law of diminishing marginal rate of substitution is embedded in the shape of the isoquant. When the capital input is large and the labor input is small, the isoquant is steep. As the capital input decreases and the labor input increases, the slope of the isoquant diminishes. Only curves that are bowed toward the origin have this feature; thus isoquants are always bowed toward the origin.

Isoquants are very nice, but what do we do with them? The answer is that we use them to work out a firm's least-cost technique of production. But to do so, we need to illustrate the firm's costs in the same sort of diagram that contains the isoquants.

Isocost Lines

An **isocost line** shows all the combinations of capital and labor that can be bought for a given total cost. To make the concept of the isocost line as clear as possible, we'll consider the following example. Swanky is going to spend a total of $100 a day producing sweaters. Knitting-machine operators can be hired for $25 a day, and knitting machines can be rented for $25 a day. The points *a*, *b*, *c*, *d*, and *e* in Fig. A10.4 show five possible combinations of labor and capital that Swanky can employ for a total cost of $100. For example, point *b* shows that Swanky can use 3 machines (costing $75) and 1 worker (costing $25). If Swanky can employ workers and machines for fractions of a day, then any of the combinations along the line *ae* can be employed for a total cost of $100. This line is Swanky's isocost line for a total cost of $100.

The Isocost Equation

The isocost line can be described by an isocost equation. An **isocost equation** states the relationship between the quantities of inputs that can be hired for a given total cost. We'll work out the isocost

Swanky's Input Possibilities

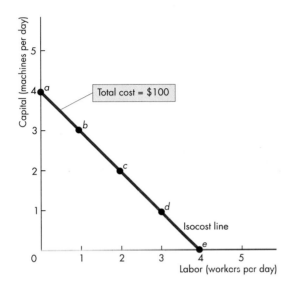

For a given total cost, Swanky's input possibilities depend on input prices. If labor and capital cost $25 a day each, for a total cost of $100 Swanky can employ the combinations of capital and labor shown by the points a through e. The line passing through these points is an iso-cost line. It shows the combinations of capital and labor, when each costs $25 a day, that have a total cost of $100.

equation by using symbols that apply to any firm and numbers that describe Swanky's situation.

The variables that affect the firm's total cost (TC) are the prices of the inputs—the price of labor (P_L) and the price of capital (P_K)—and the quantities of the inputs employed—labor (L) and capital (K). In Swanky's case, we're going to look at the amount of labor and capital that can be employed when each input costs $25 a day and when total cost is $100. The cost of the labor employed ($P_L \times L$) plus the cost of the capital employed ($P_K \times K$) is the firm's total cost (TC). That is,

$$P_L L + P_K K = TC,$$

and, in Swanky's case,

$$25L + 25K = 100.$$

To calculate the isocost equation, divide the firm's total cost by the price of capital and then subtract $(P_L/P_K)L$ from both sides of the resulting equation. The isocost equation is

$$K = TC/P_K - (P_L/P_K)L.$$

It tells us how the capital input varies as the labor input varies, holding total cost constant. Swanky's isocost equation is

$$K = 4 - L.$$

This equation corresponds to the isocost line in Fig. A10.4.

The Effect of Input Prices

Along the isocost line that we have just calculated, capital and labor cost $25 a day each. Because these input prices are the same, in order to increase labor by 1 unit, capital must be decreased by 1 unit. The magnitude of the slope of the isocost line shown in Fig. A10.4 is 1. The slope tells us that 1 unit of labor costs 1 unit of capital.

Next, let's consider some different prices, as shown in the table for Fig. A10.5. If the daily wage rate is $50 and the daily rental rate for knitting machines remains at $25, then 1 worker costs the same as 2 machines. Holding total cost constant at $100, to use 1 more worker now requires using 2 fewer machines. With the wage rate double that of the machine rental rate, the isocost line is line B in Fig. A10.5(a), and the magnitude of its slope is 2. That is, in order to hire 1 more worker and keep total cost constant, Swanky must give up 2 knitting machines.

If the daily wage rate remains at $25 and the daily rental rate of a knitting machine rises to $50, then 2 workers cost the same as 1 machine. In this case, in order to hire 1 more worker and keep total cost constant, Swanky must give up only half a knitting machine. The magnitude of the slope of the isocost line is now ½, as shown by line C in Fig. A10.5(b).

The higher the relative price of labor, the steeper is the isocost line. The magnitude of the slope of the isocost line measures the relative price of labor in terms of capital—that is, the price of labor divided by the price of capital.

FIGURE **A10.5**

Input Prices and the Isocost Line

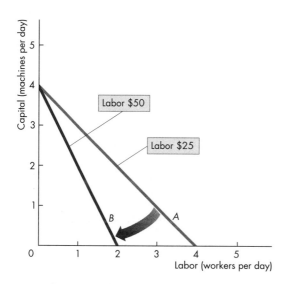

(a) **An increase in the price of labor**

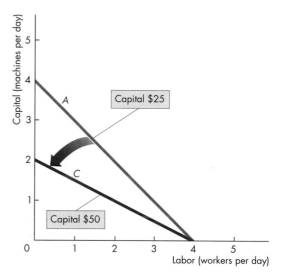

(b) **An increase in the price of capital**

Isocost line	Price of capital (rental rate per day)	Price of labor (wage per day)	Isocost equation for $TC = \$100$
A	$25	$25	$K = 4 - L$
B	$25	$50	$K = 4 - 2L$
C	$50	$25	$K = 2 - (\tfrac{1}{2})L$

The slope of the isocost line depends on the relative input prices. Three cases are set out in the table (each for a total cost of $100). In case *A*, both labor and capital have a price of $25 a day and the isocost line is that labeled *A*. In case *B*, the price of labor rises to $50 but the price of capital remains $25 and the isocost line becomes that labeled *B*. Its slope is twice that of *A*. In case *C* the price of capital rises to $50 and the price of labor remains constant at $25 and the isocost line becomes that labeled *C*. Its slope is half that of *A*.

The Isocost Map

An **isocost map** shows a series of isocost lines, each for a different level of total cost. The larger the total cost, the larger are the quantities of all inputs that can be employed. Figure A10.6 illustrates an isocost map. In that figure, the middle isocost line is the original one that appears in Fig. A10.4. It is the isocost line for a total cost of $100 when both capital and labor cost $25 a day each. The other two isocost lines in Fig. A10.6 are for a total cost of $125 and $75, holding the prices of the inputs constant at $25 each.

The Least-Cost Technique

The **least-cost technique** is the combination of inputs that minimizes total cost of producing a given output. Let's suppose that Swanky wants to produce 15 sweaters a day. What is the least-cost way of doing this? The answer can be seen in Fig. A10.7. The isoquant for 15

FIGURE **A10.6**

An Isocost Map

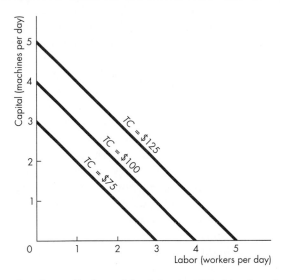

There is an isocost line for each level of cost, and the lines shown here are just a sample. This isocost map shows three isocost lines: one for a total cost of $75, one for $100, and one for $125. For each isocost line, the prices of capital and labor are $25 each. The magnitude of the slope of the lines in an isocost map is determined by the relative price of the two inputs—the price of labor divided by the price of capital. The higher the total cost, the further is the isocost line from the origin.

FIGURE **A10.7**

The Least-Cost Technique of Production

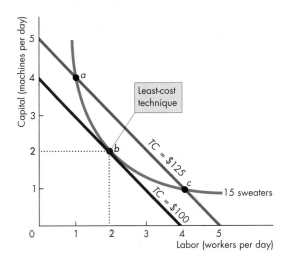

The least-cost technique of producing 15 sweaters occurs when 2 machines and 2 workers are employed at point *b*. An output of 15 sweaters can be produced with the technique illustrated by point *a* (4 machines and 1 worker) or with the technique illustrated by point *c* (1 machine and 4 workers). With either of these techniques, the total cost is $125 and exceeds the total cost at *b* of $100. At *b*, the isoquant for 15 sweaters is tangential to the isocost line for $100. The isocost line and the isoquant have the same slope. If the isoquant intersects the isocost line—for example at *a* and *c*—the least-cost technique has not been found. With the least-cost technique, the marginal rate of substitution (the magnitude of the slope of isoquant) equals the relative price of the inputs (the magnitude of the slope of isocost line).

sweaters is shown, and the three points on that isoquant (marked *a*, *b*, and *c*) illustrate the three techniques of producing 15 sweaters that were shown earlier in Fig. A10.1. The figure also contains two isocost lines—each drawn for a price of capital and a price of labor of $25. One isocost line is for a total cost of $125, and the other is for a total cost of $100.

First, consider point *a*, which is on the isoquant for 15 sweaters and also on the isocost line with a total cost of $125. Swanky can produce 15 sweaters at point *a* by using 1 worker and 4 machines. The total cost, using this technique of production, is $125. Point *c*, which uses 4 workers and 1 machine, is similar to point *a*, except that it shows another technique by which the firm can produce 15 sweaters for a cost of $125.

Next look at point *b*. At this point, Swanky uses 2 machines and 2 workers to produce 15 sweaters at

a total cost of $100. Point *b* is the *least-cost technique,* or the *economically efficient technique,* for producing 15 sweaters when knitting machines and workers each cost $25 a day. At those input prices, there is no way that Swanky can produce 15 sweaters for less than $100.

There is an important feature of point *b*, the least-cost technique. At that point, the isoquant on which Swanky is producing (the isoquant for 15 sweaters) has a slope equal to that of the isocost line. The isocost line (for a total cost of $100) is tangential to the isoquant (for 15 sweaters).

Notice that although there is only one way that Swanky can produce 15 sweaters for $100, there are several ways of producing 15 sweaters for more than $100. Techniques shown by points *a* and *c* are two examples. All the points between *a* and *b* and all the points between *b* and *c* are also ways of producing 15 sweaters for a cost that exceeds $100 but is less than $125. That is, there are isocost lines between those shown, for total costs falling between $100 and $125. Those isocost lines cut the isoquant for 15 sweaters at the points between *a* and *b* and between *b* and *c*. Swanky can also produce 15 sweaters for a cost that even exceeds $125. That is, the firm can change its technique of production by moving to a point on the isoquant higher than point *a* and using a more capital-intensive technique than at point *a*. Or the firm could move to a point on the isoquant lower than point *c* and use a more labor-intensive technique than at point *c*. All of these ways of producing 15 sweaters are economically inefficient.

You can see that Swanky cannot produce 15 sweaters for less than $100 by imagining the isocost line for $99. That isocost line will not touch the isoquant for 15 sweaters. That is, the firm cannot produce 15 sweaters for $99. At $25 for a unit of each input, $99 will not buy the inputs required to produce 15 sweaters.

Marginal Rate of Substitution Equals Relative Input Price

When a firm is using the least-cost technique of production, the marginal rate of substitution between the inputs equals their relative price. Recall that the marginal rate of substitution is the magnitude of the slope of an isoquant. Relative input prices are measured by the magnitude of the slope of the isocost line. We've just seen that producing at least cost means producing at a point where the isocost line is tangential to the isoquant. Since the two curves are tangential, their slopes are equal. Hence the marginal rate of substitution (the magnitude of the slope of isoquant) equals the relative input price (the magnitude of the slope of isocost line).

You will perhaps better appreciate the importance of relative input prices if we examine what happens to the least-cost technique when those prices change.

Changes in Input Prices

The least-cost technique of production depends in an important way on the relative prices of the inputs. The case that we've just studied is one in which capital and labor cost $25 a day each. Let's look at two other cases: one in which capital costs twice as much as labor and another in which labor costs twice as much as capital.

If knitting machines cost $25 a day and a worker is paid $50 a day, the isocost line becomes twice as steep as the one in Fig. A10.7. That is, to hire one more worker while holding total cost constant, Swanky has to operate two fewer knitting machines. Let's see how this change in input prices changes the least-cost production technique. Figure A10.8(a) illustrates this. You can see in that figure the isoquant for 15 sweaters a day and the initial inputs of 2 knitting machines and 2 workers. When wages are $50 a day and knitting machines cost $25 a day, the isocost line becomes steeper. Also, to continue producing 15 sweaters a day, total cost has to rise. That is, the minimum total cost for producing 15 sweaters is higher than originally. The new, steeper isocost line in the figure is that for the minimum cost at which 15 sweaters can be produced at the new input prices. Along that isocost line, Swanky is spending $140. This is the least-cost method of producing 15 sweaters a day; it is achieved by using 3 machines and 1.3 workers a day. (These inputs cost $140: 3 machines × $25 = $75 and 1.3 workers × $50 = $65.)

Next, let's see what happens if wages stay constant but the cost of a machine increases. In particular, suppose that knitting machines cost $50 a day while wages stay at $25 a day. In this case, the isocost line becomes less steep. Swanky now has to give up only half a worker-day to get one more machine. The effect of this change on the least-cost technique is illustrated in Fig. A10.8(b). Again, the initial isocost line and least-cost technique are shown in the figure. When the cost of capital increases, the isocost line flattens. The least-cost method of producing 15 sweaters a day now uses 1.3 machines and 3 workers a day. This combination again costs Swanky $140 a day, but it is the least-cost method of producing 15 sweaters a day when machines cost $50 and labor $25 a day.

A change in input prices leads to input substitution. Less of the input whose price has increased and more of the other input are used to produce a given output level. The size of this substitution depends on the technology itself. If the inputs are very close substitutes for each other, the isoquants will be almost straight lines and substitution will be large. If the

Changes in Input Prices

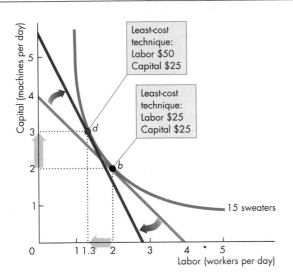

(a) An increase in wages

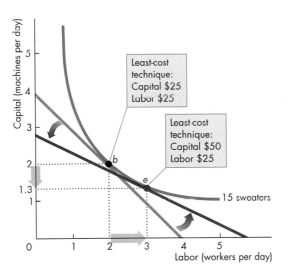

(b) An increase in the price of capital

If the price of labor doubles while the price of capital is held constant, the isocost line becomes twice as steep (part a). The least-cost method of producing 15 sweaters a day changes from point *b* to point *d* (using 1 more machine and 0.7 fewer workers per day). If the price of capital doubles while the price of labor is held constant, the isocost line becomes half as steep (part b). The least-cost method of producing 15 sweaters a day now changes from point *b* to point *e*. One additional worker is hired, and 0.7 fewer machines are used.

inputs are not close substitutes for each other, the isoquants will be curved very tightly and quite large changes in input prices will lead to only small substitution effects.

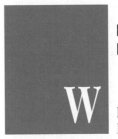

Marginal Product and Marginal Cost

When we studied short-run and long-run cost in the chapter, we learned about the connection between the marginal product curve of a variable input and the marginal cost curve. In the output range over which marginal product increases, marginal cost decreases; in the output range over which marginal product decreases, marginal cost increases. We also learned in the chapter that it pays a firm to change its plant size if a different plant can produce the firm's desired output at a lower short-run cost than the existing plant. In this appendix, we learned how to calculate the firm's cost-minimizing combination of capital (plant) and labor. Thus our discussion of product curves and cost curves in the chapter and of isocost lines, isoquants, and least-cost techniques of production in this appendix are both dealing with the same problem. But they're looking at the problem from different viewpoints. Let's examine the connection between these two approaches to the firm's cost minimization problem.

First, we're going to learn about the relationship between the marginal rate of substitution and marginal products.

Marginal Rate of Substitution and Marginal Products

The marginal rate of substitution and the marginal products are linked together in a simple formula:

The marginal rate of substitution of labor for capital equals the marginal product of labor divided by the marginal product of capital.

A few steps of reasoning are needed to establish this fact. First, we know that output changes when a firm changes the amount of labor and capital employed. Furthermore, we know that the effect on output of a change in one of the inputs is determined by the marginal product of the input. That is,

$$\text{Change in output} = MP_L \times \Delta L + MP_K \times \Delta K.$$

That is, the change in output is equal to the change in the labor input multiplied by its marginal product plus the change in the capital input multiplied by its marginal product.

Suppose now that the firm wants to remain on an isoquant—that is, Swanky wants to produce the same number of sweaters when it changes its labor and capital inputs. To remain on an isoquant, the change in output must be zero. We can make the change of output zero in the above equation, and doing so yields the equation

$$MP_L \times \Delta L = -MP_K \times \Delta K.$$

This equation tells us what must happen to the capital and labor inputs for Swanky to stay on an isoquant. If the labor input increases, the capital input must decrease, or, equivalently, if the labor input decreases, the capital input must increase. Thus we can write this equation in a slightly different way:

$$MP_L \times \Delta L = MP_K \times -\Delta K.$$

If we divide both sides of the above equation by the increase in the labor input (ΔL) and also divide both sides by the marginal product of capital (MP_K), we get

$$-\Delta K/\Delta L = MP_L/MP_K.$$

This equation tells us that when Swanky remains on an isoquant, the decrease in its capital input ($-\Delta K$) divided by the increase in its labor input (ΔL) is equal to the marginal product of labor (MP_L) divided by the marginal product of capital (MP_K). But we have defined the marginal rate of substitution of labor for capital as the decrease in capital divided by the increase in labor when we remain on a given isoquant. What we have discovered, then, is that the marginal rate of substitution of labor for capital is the ratio of the marginal product of labor to the marginal product of capital.

Marginal Cost

We can use the fact that we have just discovered—that the marginal rate of substitution of labor for capital equals the ratio of the marginal product of

labor to the marginal product of capital—to work out an important implication of cost minimization. A few steps are needed, and Table A10.2 provides a guide to those steps.

Part (a) defines some symbols. Part (b) reminds us that the marginal rate of substitution of labor for capital is the slope of the isoquant, which in turn equals the ratio of the marginal product of labor (MP_L) to the marginal product of capital (MP_K). Part (b) also reminds us that the magnitude of the slope of the isocost line equals the ratio of the price of labor (P_L) to the price of capital (P_K). Part (c) of the table summarizes some propositions about a firm that is using the least-cost technique of production.

TABLE A10.2

The Least-Cost Technique

(a) Symbols

Marginal rate of substitution of labor for capital	MRS
Marginal product of labor	MP_L
Marginal product of capital	MP_K
Price of labor	P_L
Price of capital	P_K

(b) Definitions

The magnitude of the slope of the isoquant (MRS)	MP_L/MP_K
The magnitude of the slope of the isocost line	P_L/P_K

(c) The least-cost technique

Slope of the isoquant = Slope of the isocost line

Therefore:	$MP_L/MP_K = P_L/P_K$
Equivalently:	$MP_L/P_L = MP_K/P_K$

That is,

Total cost is minimized when the marginal product per dollar spent on labor equals the marginal product per dollar spent on capital.

Equivalently, flipping the last equation over:	$P_L/MP_L = P_K/MP_K$

That is,

When total cost is minimized, marginal cost with fixed capital and a change in labor input equals marginal cost with fixed labor and a change in capital input.

The first of these propositions is that when the least-cost technique is employed, the slope of the isoquant and the isocost line are the same. That is,

$$MP_L/MP_K = P_L/P_K.$$

The second proposition is that total cost is minimized when the marginal product per dollar spent on labor equals the marginal product per dollar spent on capital. To see why, just rearrange the above equation in the following way. First, multiply both sides by the marginal product of capital and then divide both sides by the price of labor. We then get

$$MP_L/P_L = MP_K/P_K.$$

This equation says that the marginal product of labor per dollar spent on labor is equal to the marginal product of capital per dollar spent on capital. In other words, the extra output from the last dollar spent on labor equals the extra output from the last dollar spent on capital. This makes sense. If the extra output from the last dollar spent on labor exceeds the extra output from the last dollar spent on capital, it will pay the firm to use less capital and use more labor. By doing so, the firm can produce the same output at a lower total cost. Conversely, if the extra output from the last dollar spent on capital exceeds the extra output from the last dollar spent on labor, it will pay the firm to use less labor and use more capital. Again, by doing so, the firm lowers the cost of producing a given output. A firm achieves the least-cost technique of production only when the extra output from the last dollar spent on all the inputs is the same.

The third proposition is that with the least-cost technique for producing a given output, marginal cost with fixed capital and variable labor equals marginal cost with fixed labor and variable capital. To see this proposition, simply flip the last equation over and write it as

$$P_L/MP_L = P_K/MP_K.$$

Expressed in words, this equation says that the price of labor divided by its marginal product must equal the price of capital divided by its marginal product. But what is the price of an input divided by its marginal product? The price of labor divided by the marginal product of labor is marginal cost when the capital input is held constant. To see why this is so, first recall the definition of marginal cost: *marginal cost* is the change in total cost resulting from a unit increase in output. If output increases because one more unit of labor is employed, total cost rises by the cost of the extra labor and output increases by the marginal product of the labor. So marginal cost is the price of labor divided by the marginal product of labor. For example, if labor costs $25 a day and if the marginal product of labor is 2 sweaters, then the marginal cost of a sweater is $12.50 ($25 divided by 2).

The price of capital divided by the marginal product of capital has a similar interpretation. The price of capital divided by the marginal product of capital is marginal cost when the labor input is constant. As you can see from the above equation, with the least-cost technique of production, marginal cost is the same regardless of whether the capital input is constant and more labor is used or the labor input is constant and more capital is used.

PART 5

MARKETS FOR GOODS AND SERVICES

Talking

with

Kenneth

Arrow

Kenneth Arrow was born in New York City in 1921. He was an undergraduate at City College and a graduate student at Columbia, where he obtained his Ph.D. in 1951. He has been a professor at Harvard University but since 1979 has been at Stanford University. Professor Arrow has made fundamental contributions to economic theory, especially in areas dealing with uncertainty, information, and organization. He was awarded the Nobel Prize for Economic Science in 1972.

Professor Arrow, what drew you to economics?

My path into economics exemplifies one of my guiding observations on life—that it is highly uncertain. Being brought up during the Great Depression in a family not immune to it, I was deeply concerned about economic conditions. My main bent was clearly for mathematics, but I did take an unusual number of courses in history and some in economics at college. Largely on my own, I became fascinated with mathematical statistics, a field that was undergoing rapid development at the time. In retrospect, my strongest interest was in the foundations of statistical inference. When I entered graduate study in mathematics at Columbia University, I wanted to study statistics with Harold Hotelling, who was actually in the Department of Economics. Under his influence, I eventually enrolled in economics. Hotelling taught a course in mathematical economics, which excited me intensely—though a recent review of my lecture notes leaves me somewhat puzzled as to the basis of my enthusiasm. The course covered only the theory of the firm and of the household.

What did your study of economics involve?

Columbia in the early 1940s was dominated by an institutionalist heritage and a dislike of formal theory. There was no general course in economic theory, but instead a year-long course in the history of economic theory. It crowded the whole curriculum, apart from statistics, into a single year. I also read a good deal on my own, notably American economic history, which I enjoyed greatly, and economic theory, mostly on the then-fashionable topic of imperfect competition and on the exciting work of Hicks and Samuelson, as well as Hotelling's important papers on natural resource economics and general welfare. Looking back, I consider the fact that I did most of my learning on my own to have been a great advantage.

What's your view of the role of mathematics in economics?

Mathematics is a tool that has turned out to be very useful in economics. While there are many issues in economics for which verbal reasoning enables one to see through the issues, there are many others, particularly those which emphasize complex interactions, that can be understood only with the aid of mathematics. This is equally true whether one is trying to get a theoretical understanding or seeking a basis for empirical analysis. An undergraduate who aspires to further study in economics should certainly study calculus with many variables and linear algebra, some elements at least of differential equations, and, if possible, real analysis. Beyond that, quantity is more important than specialization. It is practice at mathematics that counts rather than specific courses.

You are known for your work in general equilibrium theory. Why is this branch of economics important?

In many ways, general equilibrium theory is the underlying premise of all economic reasoning, even when it is not explicitly invoked. Briefly, it emphasizes the interconnection of markets. The demand for any one product depends not only on the price of that product but also on the prices of the other products that the consumer buys, as well as on the prices of the products that he

275

or she sells—labor, capital, or whatever. Similarly, the output of a product by a firm depends not only on the price for that product but also on the prices of the other products the firm might sell and on the prices of the firm's inputs.

A tenet of economic theory is that markets clear, at least over time. That is, prices are such that the supply of cotton cloth will equal the demand. But both supply and demand depend not only on the price of cotton cloth but also on wages, interest rates, and the prices of other goods bought by consumers or used by firms. Hence the condition of market clearing has to be interpreted as a large number of equations—each saying supply equals demand in some markets—which *simultaneously* determine a large number of unknowns, such as the prices in each of the markets.

General equilibrium theory as now developed has many limitations. It assumes perfect competition, although there are obvious departures from competition in many parts of the economy. Further, many economists argue that the economy overall does not tend toward equilibrium. But I would contend that that line of reasoning argues for developing general equilibrium theory further. Analysis of individual parts

of the economy can never be complete without understanding the wider implications and feedbacks.

Can you give an example of how general equilibrium theory has given a useful description of real events?

The sharp increases in oil prices in 1973 and 1979 and the accompanying decrease in supplies gave rise to great public fears, usually motivated by failure to understand that the economy will react by changing behavior in many industries. Industrial users of oil for heating found ways of conserving, industries that used oil contracted, automobiles were redesigned to reduce gasoline consumption, and the search for oil and oil substitutes, especially natural gas, was intensified. Hence the system as a whole, not just the oil market, reacted in ways that could be understood only when the economy as a whole was considered, not merely the oil market.

> " **W**e have made great progress in developing tools of analysis but much less in understanding how to interpret them in the real world."

Why do we spend so much time in the principles course studying perfect competition and the other extreme case of monopoly?

Competition is important to study because it does occur in many markets and because it serves as a useful guideline. Pure monopoly is very rare. But in fact the theory of the intermediate cases of monopolistic competition and oligopoly is much less understood than that of monopoly, so at least some picture, some insight, can be obtained from the study of monopoly.

Have we at least made some progress in understanding oligopoly?

There has been a good deal of study, especially through the development of game theory. But the very foundations of this theory are still not understood. What in fact are the strategies available to the oligopolists? Do they choose prices, or do they choose quantities? More progress has been made on competition in other dimensions, such as quality. In short, we have made great progress in developing tools of analysis but much less in understanding how to interpret them in the real world.

What do you regard as the place of theory in the science of economics?

Most empirical analysis in applied fields today starts with a theoretically inspired model and then fits theory to the real world by econometrics. It is also true that good policymaking depends on some theoretical understanding of the economy. Economic theory is very limited in its ability to predict accurately and in some cases is misleading. But it provides the basis for both empirical analysis and policy formation, even if events in the real world move in a different direction.

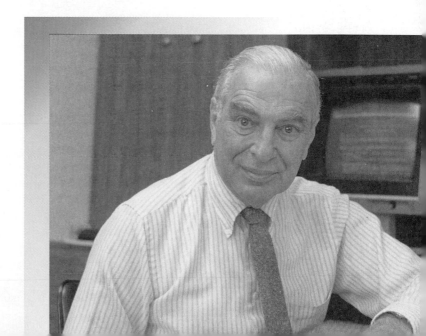

CHAPTER 11

COMPETITION

After studying this chapter, you will be able to:

♦ Define perfect competition

♦ Explain why a perfectly competitive firm cannot influence the market price

♦ Explain how a competitive industry's output changes when price changes

♦ Explain why firms sometimes shut down temporarily and lay off workers

♦ Explain why firms enter and leave an industry

♦ Predict the effects on an industry and on a typical firm of a change in demand and of a technological advance

♦ Explain why farmers have had such a bad time in recent years

♦ Explain why perfect competition is efficient

CE CREAM IS BIG BUSINESS. IN 1988, CLOSE TO 1 BILLION gallons were bought—an average of four gallons per person—at a cost of more than $7 billion. Competition in the ice cream industry is fierce. National names, such as Häagen-Dazs and Frusen Glädjé, are competing with other national, regional, and local brands. Ben and Jerry's, Bart's, and Annabel's are all battling for a place in a crowded market. ◆ ◆ In this fiercely competitive environment, new firms are entering and trying their luck while other firms are being squeezed out of the business. Some are growing and disappearing in a matter of months. One example is Steve's Homemade Ice Cream, Inc. of Bloomfield, New Jersey. After growing 56 percent in 1987, sales became stagnant in 1988. Steve's moved into microwave sundaes and other products. Many other ice cream producers have moved into frozen yogurt. How does competi-

Hot Rivalry in Ice Cream

tion affect prices and profits? What causes some firms to leave an industry and others to enter it? What are the effects on profits and prices of new firms entering and old firms leaving an industry? ◆ ◆ In 1990 and 1991, more than 10 million people were unemployed. Of these, 6 million were unemployed because they had been laid off by firms seeking to trim their costs and avoid bankruptcy. Ice cream producers, computer manufacturers, and firms in almost every sector of the economy laid off workers on a massive scale. Those years were unusually harsh ones, but even in a typical year, more than 3 million people are laid off. Why do firms lay off workers? When will a firm temporarily shut down, laying off its workers? ◆ ◆ Over the past few years, there has been a dramatic fall in the prices of all kinds of consumer goods, such as

VCRs, Walkmans, and personal computers. What exactly goes on in an industry when the price of its output falls dramatically? What happens to the profits of the firms producing such goods? ◆ ◆ American farms have been in the news a great deal in recent years. Most farmers have fallen on very hard times. Many of them have gone out of business. What is happening in the farm sector that is creating such serious problems?

◆ ◆ ◆ ◆ To tackle the questions just posed, we have to look beyond the individual firm standing in isolation and think about how firms interact with each other. Most goods are produced by more than one firm, so the firms compete with each other. Each firm tries to outdo its rivals by producing at a lower cost and by selling a larger output, thereby making the biggest possible profit. In this chapter we'll study markets in which firms are locked together in such stiff competition that the best a firm can do is to match its rivals in terms of quality and price.

Perfect Competition

In order to study competitive markets, we are going to build a model of a market in which competition is as fierce and extreme as possible. Economists call the most extreme form of competition perfect competition. **Perfect competition** occurs in a market in which:

◆ There are many firms, each selling an identical product.

◆ There are many buyers.

◆ There are no restrictions on entry into the industry.

◆ Firms in the industry have no advantage over potential new entrants.

◆ Firms and buyers are completely informed about the prices of the products of each firm in the industry.

Therefore in perfect competition, no single firm can exert a significant influence on the market price of a good. Firms in such markets are said to be price takers. A **price taker** is a firm that cannot influence the price of its product.

Perfect competition does not occur frequently in the real world, but in many industries, competition is so fierce that the model of perfect competition we're about to study is of enormous help in predicting the behavior of the firms in these industries. Ice cream making and retailing, farming, fishing, wood pulping and paper milling, the manufacture of paper cups and plastic shopping bags, grocery retailing, photo finishing, lawn service, plumbing, painting, and dry cleaning and the provision of laundry services are all examples of industries that are highly competitive.

When a Firm Can't Influence Price

Perfectly competitive or, equivalently, price-taking behavior occurs in markets in which a single firm produces a small fraction of the total output of a particular good. Imagine for a moment that you are a wheat farmer in Kansas. You have a thousand acres under cultivation—which sounds like a lot. But then you go on a drive, first heading west. The flat lands turn into rolling hills as you head toward the Rocky Mountains, but everywhere you look you see thousands and thousands of acres of wheat. The sun goes down in the west behind millions of acres of golden plants. The next morning, it rises in the east above the same scene. Driving to Colorado, Oklahoma, Texas, and back up to Nebraska and the Dakotas reveals similar vistas. You also find unbroken stretches of wheat in Canada, Argentina, Australia, and the former Soviet Union. Your thousand acres is a drop in the bucket.

You are a price taker. Nothing makes your wheat any better than any other farmer's. If everybody else sells their wheat for $3 a bushel, and you want $3.10, why would people buy from you? They can simply go to the next farmer, and the one after that, and the next and buy all they need for $3.

Elasticity of Industry and Firm Demand

A price-taking firm faces a demand curve that is perfectly elastic. To see why this is so, let's consider an example. Suppose that there are 1,000 firms of equal size producing a good. Even if one firm doubles its output (a big change for an individual firm), industry output will rise by only 0.1 percent (one thousandth is 0.1 percent). If the elasticity of industry demand for the good is 0.5, then this increase in industry output results in a 0.2 percent fall in price. To put things in perspective, a price change of this magnitude is $1 on a $500 television set, 10¢ on a $50 dress, or 1¢ on a $5 movie ticket. But these price changes, although small, are much larger than the ones that result from changes in output of a magnitude that a firm might actually make. Therefore when a firm changes its output rate, the effect of that change on price is tiny and the firm ignores it. The firm behaves as if its own actions have no effect on the market price.

Table 11.1 works through a real-world example—the market for fish—and shows the relationship between the elasticity of demand facing an individual competitive fishery and the fish market as a whole. The elasticity of the market demand for fish is 0.42, but the elasticity of an individual producer's demand is almost 40,000.

When we studied the concept of elasticity in Chapter 5, we discovered that a horizontal demand curve has an elasticity of infinity. An elasticity of 40,000 is not quite infinity, but it is very large. A firm whose demand has such an elasticity has, for all practical purposes, an infinitely elastic demand. Such a firm's demand curve is horizontal. The firm is a price taker.

Competition in Everyday Life

We have defined perfect competition as a market in which a firm has no choice but to be a price taker. Even massive percentage changes in a firm's own output have only a negligible effect on the market price. In such a situation, there is little point in a firm attempting to set its own price at a level different from the market. If a firm tries to charge a higher price, no one will buy its output; if it offers its goods for a lower price, it will sell them, but it can sell them for the market price, so there is no point in price cutting.

The inability of a perfectly competitive firm to compete by price cutting makes it seem as if a perfectly competitive market is not, in fact, very competitive at all. If firms don't compete on price, in what sense are they competing with each other?

Firms compete with each other in much the same way as athletes or football teams do. Firms try to

---

TABLE 11.1

A Fishery's Elasticity of Demand

(a) Data

- ◆ World output of fish is 169 billion pounds a year.
- ◆ The average U.S. fishery produces 1.8 million pounds a year.
- ◆ The average price of fish is 37.5¢ a pound.
- ◆ The elasticity of demand for fish and fish products (η_m) is 0.42.

(b) Effect on world price

- ◆ If an average U.S. fishery raises output by 100 percent, world output rises by 1.8 million pounds—0.00107 percent.
- ◆ To calculate change in world price, use the formula

$$\eta_m = \frac{\text{Percentage change in quantity}}{\text{Percentage change in price}},$$

  which means that

$$\text{Percentage change in price} = \frac{\text{Percentage change in quantity}}{\eta_m}.$$

- ◆ To find the fall in price, use the formula

$$\text{Percentage change in price} = \frac{0.00107}{0.42}$$
$$= 0.00254 \text{ percent}$$

  So a price fall of 0.00254 percent is a fall of 0.00095¢.

- ◆ When a firm doubles its output, the price falls by 0.00095¢.

(c) Elasticity of a fishery's demand

- ◆ The elasticity of a firm's demand (η_f) is given by

$$\eta_f = \frac{\text{Percentage change in firm's output sold}}{\text{Percentage change in price}}$$
$$= \frac{100}{0.00254}$$
$$= 39,370$$

Part (a) provides some data about the market for fish. Most fish is sold frozen, and the market for fish is a worldwide market. Part (b) calculates the effects on the world market price of fish if one U.S. fishery doubles its output. If one fishery doubles its output, world output will rise by 1.8 million pounds, or change by approximately 0.001 percent. As a result of this increase in output, the world price of fish falls by 0.00254 percent, or 0.00095¢ a pound. Part (c) calculates the elasticity of the individual producer's demand, η_f. That elasticity is almost 40,000!

find new tricks that will give them the edge over their competitors and enable them to win. Sometimes, though, the competition that they face is so stiff that they are left with little room to maneuver. This happens in sporting events, too. For example, when two wrestlers are closely matched, they compete with each other, but neither of them has much room to maneuver. They are locked in such fierce competition that the best they can do is to match each other's moves, try not to make a mistake, and accept the inevitable—that the outcome will be close and may even be a tie.

Like evenly matched athletes, firms in perfect competition are locked in such a fierce competitive struggle with each other that they have no choice but to mimic each other's actions and put up with an outcome analogous to a tie. They produce comparable quality goods at comparable prices.

Let's now study the behavior of a perfectly competitive industry, beginning with an examination of the choices made by a typical firm in such an industry.

Firms' Choices in Perfect Competition

A perfectly competitive firm has to make three key decisions:

◆ Whether to stay in the industry or to leave it
◆ If the decision is to stay in the industry, whether to produce or to temporarily shut down
◆ If the decision is to produce, how much to produce

In studying the competitive firm's choices, we will continue to look at a model firm whose single objective is to maximize its profit. We'll first consider a situation in which a firm decides to produce. We will then look at the other cases—firms that decide to shut down production temporarily or to leave the industry altogether.

Profit and Revenue

Profit is the difference between a firm's total revenue and total cost. We defined and studied the behavior

of total cost in the last two chapters. But what is total revenue? Let's begin by looking at the concepts of revenue.

Total revenue is the value of a firm's sales. It equals the price of the firm's output multiplied by the number of units of output sold (price × quantity). **Average revenue** is total revenue divided by the total quantity sold—revenue per unit sold. Since total revenue is price times quantity sold, average revenue (total revenue divided by quantity sold) equals price. **Marginal revenue** is the change in total revenue resulting from a one-unit increase in the quantity sold. Since, in the case of perfect competition, the price remains constant when the quantity sold changes, the change in total revenue is equal to price multiplied by the change in quantity. Therefore in perfect competition, marginal revenue equals price.

An example of these revenue concepts is set out for Swanky, Inc. in Fig. 11.1. The table shows three different quantities of sweaters sold. For a price taker, as the quantity sold varies, the price stays constant—in this example at $25. Total revenue is equal to price multiplied by quantity. For example, if Swanky sells 8 sweaters, total revenue is 8 times $25, which equals $200. Average revenue is total revenue divided by quantity. Again, if Swanky sells 8 sweaters, average revenue is total revenue ($200) divided by quantity (8), which equals $25. Marginal revenue is the change in total revenue resulting from a one-unit change in quantity. For example, when the quantity sold rises from 7 to 8, total revenue rises from $175 to $200, so marginal revenue is $25. (Notice that in the table, marginal revenue appears *between* the lines for the quantities sold. This arrangement presents a visual reminder that marginal revenue results from the *change* in the quantity sold.)

Suppose that Swanky is one of a thousand similar small producers of sweaters. The demand and supply curves for the entire sweater industry are shown in Fig. 11.1(a). Demand curve *D* intersects supply curve *S* at a price of $25 and a quantity of 7,000 sweaters. Figure 11.1(b) shows Swanky's demand curve. Since the firm is a price taker, its demand curve is perfectly elastic—the horizontal line at $25. The figure also illustrates Swanky's total, average, and marginal revenues, calculated in the table. The average revenue curve and marginal revenue curve are the same as the firm's demand curve. That is, the

FIGURE **11.1**

Demand, Price, and Revenue in Perfect Competition

(a) Sweater industry

(b) Swanky's demand, average revenue, and marginal revenue

(c) Swanky's total revenue

Quantity sold (Q) (sweaters per day)	Price (P) (dollars per sweater)	Total revenue (TR = P × Q) (dollars)	Average revenue (AR = TR/Q) (dollars per sweater)	Marginal revenue (MR = ΔTR/ΔQ) (dollars per sweater)
7	25	175	25	
8	25	200	25	25
9	25	225	25	25

In perfect competition, price is determined where the industry demand and supply curves intersect. Such an equilibrium is illustrated in part (a), where the price is $25 and 7,000 sweaters are bought and sold. Swanky, a perfectly competitive firm, faces a fixed price, $25 in this example, regardless of the quantity it produces. The table calculates Swanky's total, average, and marginal revenues. For example, when 7 sweaters are sold, total revenue is $175, and average revenue is $25. When sales increase from 7 sweaters to 8 sweaters, marginal revenue equals $25. The demand curve faced by Swanky is perfectly elastic at the market price and is shown in part (b) of the figure. Swanky's demand curve is also its average revenue curve and marginal revenue curve (AR = MR). Swanky's total revenue curve (TR) is shown in part (c). Point *a* on the total revenue curve corresponds to the first row of the table.

firm's demand curve tells us the revenue per sweater sold and the change in total revenue that results from selling one more sweater. Swanky's total revenue curve (part c) shows the total revenue for each quantity sold. For example, when Swanky sells 7 sweaters, total revenue is $175 (point *a*). Since each additional sweater sold brings in a constant amount—in this case $25—the total revenue curve is an upward-sloping straight line with a constant slope equal to the price of a sweater.

R E V I E W

A firm in a perfectly competitive market is a price taker. The firm's demand curve is perfectly elastic at the market price. The firm's average revenue and marginal revenue are each equal to price, so the marginal revenue and average revenue curves are the same as the firm's demand curve. Total revenue rises as the quantity sold rises. ◆

Profit-Maximizing Output

Profit is the difference between a firm's total revenue and total cost. Maximizing profit is the same thing as maximizing the difference between total revenue and total cost. Even though a perfectly competitive firm cannot influence its price, it can influence its profit by choosing its level of output. As we have just seen, a perfectly competitive firm's total revenue changes when its output changes. Also, as we discovered in Chapter 10, a firm's total cost varies as its output varies. By changing its inputs and its output, a firm can change its total cost. In the *short run*, a firm can change its output by changing its variable inputs and by changing the intensity with which it operates its fixed inputs. In the *long run*, a firm can vary all its inputs. Let's work out how a firm maximizes profit in the short run.

Total Revenue, Total Cost, and Profit Figure 11.2 shows Swanky's total revenue, total cost, and profit both as numbers (in the table) and as curves (in the graphs). Part (a) of the figure shows Swanky's total revenue and total cost curves. These curves are graphs of the numbers shown in the first three columns of the table. The total revenue curve (*TR*) is the same as that in Fig. 11.1(c). The total cost curve (*TC*) is similar to the one that you met in Chapter 10. Notice that Swanky's total cost is $25 when output is zero. This amount is Swanky's fixed cost—the cost that is incurred even if nothing is produced and sold. As output increases, so does total cost.

The difference between total revenue and total cost is profit. As you can see in Fig. 11.2(b), Swanky will make a profit at any output above 4 and below 12 sweaters a day. At outputs below 4 sweaters, Swanky makes a loss. A loss is also made if output exceeds 12 sweaters a day. At outputs of 4 sweaters and 12 sweaters, total cost equals total revenue. Swanky makes zero profit. An output at which total cost equals total revenue is called a **break-even point**.

Swanky's profit, calculated in the final column of the table, is graphed in part (b) of the figure. Notice the relationship between the total revenue, total cost, and profit curves. Profit is measured by the vertical distance between the total revenue and total cost curves. When the total revenue curve in part (a) is above the total cost curve, between 4 and 12 sweaters, the firm is making a profit and the profit curve in part (b) is above the horizontal axis. At the break-even point, where the total cost and total revenue curves intersect, the profit curve cuts the horizontal axis.

When the profit curve is at its highest, the distance between *TR* and *TC* is greatest. In this example, profit maximization occurs at an output of 9 sweaters a day. At this output, profit is $40 a day.

Marginal Calculations In working out Swanky's profit-maximizing output, we examined its cost and revenue schedules and, from all the possibilities, picked out the point at which profit is at a maximum. There is a quicker, neater, and more powerful way of figuring out the profit-maximizing output. All Swanky has to do is to calculate its marginal cost and marginal revenue and compare the two. If marginal revenue exceeds marginal cost, it pays to produce more. If marginal revenue is less than marginal cost, it pays to produce less. When marginal revenue and marginal cost are equal, profit is maximized. Let's convince ourselves that this rule works.

Look at the table in Fig. 11.3. It records Swanky's marginal revenue and marginal cost. Recall that marginal revenue is the change in revenue per unit change in the quantity sold and is, for a perfectly competitive firm, the same as its price. In this case, marginal revenue is $25. Marginal cost is the change in total cost per unit change in output. For example, when output rises from 8 to 9 sweaters, total cost rises from $163 to $185, a rise of $22, which is the marginal cost of changing the output rate from 8 to 9 sweaters a day. The marginal revenue and marginal cost curves corresponding to the table appear in Fig. 11.3.

Now focus on the highlighted row of the table. When output rises from 8 to 9 sweaters, marginal cost is $22. Since marginal revenue is $25, the rise in total revenue exceeds the rise in total cost. Profit goes up by the difference—$3. By looking at the last column of the table, you can see that profit does indeed rise by $3. Because marginal revenue exceeds marginal cost, it pays to expand output from 8 to 9 sweaters. At 8 sweaters a day profit is $37, and at 9 sweaters a day it is $40—$3 more.

Suppose that output is expanded yet further to 10 sweaters a day. Marginal revenue is still $25, but marginal cost is now $27. Marginal cost exceeds marginal revenue by $2. So expanding output to 10 sweaters increases total cost by $2 more than total revenue, and profit falls by $2. So, to maximize

FIGURE **11.2**

Total Revenue, Total Cost, and Profit

(a) Revenue and cost

(b) Profit and loss

Quantity (Q) (sweaters per day)	Total revenue (TR) (dollars)	Total cost (TC) (dollars)	Profit (TR − TC) (dollars)
0	0	25	−25
1	25	49	−24
2	50	69	−19
3	75	86	−11
4	100	100	0
5	125	114	11
6	150	128	22
7	175	144	31
8	200	163	37
9	225	185	40
10	250	212	38
11	275	246	29
12	300	300	0
13	325	360	−35

The table lists Swanky's total revenue, total cost, and profit. Part (a) graphs the total revenue and total cost curves. Profit is seen in part (a) as the blue area between the total cost and total revenue curves. The maximum profit, $40 a day, occurs when 9 sweaters are produced—where the vertical distance between the total revenue and total cost curves is at its largest. At outputs of 4 sweaters a day and 12 sweaters a day, Swanky makes zero profit—these are break-even points. At outputs below 4 sweaters a day and above 12 sweaters a day, Swanky makes a loss. Part (b) of the figure shows Swanky's profit curve. The profit curve is at its highest when profit is at a maximum and cuts the horizontal axis at the break-even points.

profit, all Swanky has to do is to compare marginal cost and marginal revenue. As long as marginal revenue exceeds marginal cost, it pays to increase output. Swanky keeps increasing output until the cost of producing one more sweater equals the price at which the sweater can be sold. At that point, it is making maximum profit. If Swanky makes one more

sweater, that sweater will cost more to produce than the revenue it will bring in, so Swanky will not produce it.

Profit in the Short Run

We've just seen that we can calculate a firm's profit-maximizing output by comparing marginal revenue

FIGURE **11.3**

Marginal Revenue, Marginal Cost, and Profit-Maximizing Output

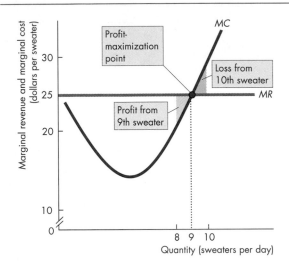

Quantity (Q) (sweaters per day)	Total revenue (TR) (dollars)	Marginal revenue (MR) (dollars per sweater)	Total cost (TC) (dollars)	Marginal cost (MC) (dollars per sweater)	Profit (TR − TC) (dollars)
0	0		25		−25
		25		24	
1	25		49		−24
		25		20	
2	50		69		−19
		25		17	
3	75		86		−11
		25		14	
4	100		100		0
		25		14	
5	125		114		11
		25		14	
6	150		128		22
		25		16	
7	175		144		31
		25		19	
8	200		163		37
		25		22	
9	225		185		40
		25		27	
10	250		212		38
		25		34	
11	275		246		29
		25		54	
12	300		300		0
		25		60	
13	325		360		−35

Another way of finding the profit-maximizing output is to determine the output at which marginal revenue equals marginal cost. The table shows that if output rises from 8 to 9 sweaters, marginal cost is $22, which is less than the marginal revenue of $25. If output rises from 9 to 10 sweaters, marginal cost is $27, which exceeds the marginal revenue of $25. The figure shows that marginal cost and marginal revenue are equal when Swanky produces 9 sweaters a day. If marginal revenue exceeds marginal cost, an increase in output increases profit. If marginal revenue is less than marginal cost, an increase in output lowers profit. If marginal revenue equals marginal cost, profit is maximized.

with marginal cost. But maximizing profit is not the same thing as *making* a profit. Maximizing profit can mean minimizing loss. We cannot tell whether a firm is actually making a profit only by comparing the marginal revenue and marginal cost curves. To check whether a firm is making a profit, we need to look at total revenue and total cost, as we did before, or we need to compare average total cost with price. When a firm makes a profit, average total cost is lower than price. If average total cost exceeds price, the firm makes a loss. When average total cost equals price, the firm breaks even.

Three Possible Profit Outcomes The three possible profit outcomes in the short run are illustrated in Fig. 11.4. In part (a), Swanky is making an econom-

ic profit. At a price of $25, marginal revenue equals marginal cost at an output of 9 sweaters a day. That is, the profit-maximizing output is 9 sweaters a day. Average total cost is lower than the market price, and economic profit is represented by the blue rectangle. The height of that rectangle is the gap between price and average total cost, or economic profit per sweater. Its length shows the quantity of sweaters produced. So the rectangle's area measures Swanky's economic profit: profit per sweater (the rectangle's height—$4.44 a sweater) multiplied by the number of sweaters produced (its length—9 sweaters) equals total profit (its area—$40).

In part (b), Swanky breaks even. At a price of $20, Swanky's profit-maximizing output is 8 sweaters. The average total cost of producing this

FIGURE 11.4

Three Possible Profit Outcomes in the Short Run

(a) Economic profit   **(b) Zero economic profit**   **(c) Economic loss**

In the short run, a firm's economic profit may be positive, zero (break even), or negative (a loss). If the market price is greater than the average total cost of producing the profit-maximizing output, the firm makes a profit (part a). If price equals minimum average total cost, the firm breaks even (part b). If the price is below minimum average total cost, the firm makes a loss (part c). The firm's profit is shown as the blue rectangle, and the firm's loss is the red rectangle.

output level is $20, the same as its price. It is also the minimum average total cost. The economic profit that Swanky makes in this case is zero.

In part (c), Swanky incurs an economic loss. At a price of $17, the profit-maximizing output is 7 sweaters. At that output, average total cost is $20.57, so the firm is losing $3.57 a sweater and incurring a total loss of $25.

Temporary Plant Shutdown   There are some situations in which a firm's profit-maximizing decision is to shut down temporarily, lay off its workers, and produce nothing. A firm's **shutdown point** is the level of output and price at which the firm is just covering its total *variable* cost. If the price is so low that total revenue is not enough to cover total variable cost, the firm shuts down.

A firm cannot escape its fixed costs. These costs are incurred even at zero output. A firm that shuts down and produces no output makes a loss equal to its total fixed cost. If the price just equals average variable cost, total revenue equals total variable cost and the firm's loss equals its total fixed cost. But if price is below average variable cost, total revenue

does not cover total variable cost, and if the firm produces just one unit of output, its loss exceeds total fixed cost. It is in such a situation that the firm minimizes its loss by shutting down. Its loss then equals total fixed cost.

The shutdown point is reached when the market price falls to a level equal to the minimum average variable cost. Table 11.2 illustrates what happens at the shutdown point. The table has two parts: part (a) shows a case in which it just pays the firm to keep producing, and part (b) shows a case in which it just pays the firm to shut down. The table shows Swanky's total fixed cost, total variable cost, and total cost of producing 6, 7, and 8 sweaters. It also shows the average variable cost and marginal cost. The cost data are the same in both parts (a) and (b) of the table.

Next let's look at the revenue. In part (a), the price of a sweater is $17. To find Swanky's total revenue, multiply the price by the quantity sold. We calculate the profit or loss (and they are all losses in this case) by subtracting total cost from total revenue. For example, if Swanky sells 7 sweaters at $17 each, then total revenue is $119. Total cost is $144,

TABLE **11.2**

The Shutdown Point

(a) *Swanky keeps on producing*

Output (sweaters per day)	Total fixed cost (dollars)	Total variable cost (dollars)	Total cost (dollars)	Average variable cost (dollars per sweater)	Marginal cost (dollars per sweater)	Price (dollars per sweater)	Total revenue (dollars)	Marginal revenue (dollars per sweater)	Profit (+) or loss (−) (dollars)
6	25	103	128	17.17		17	102		−26
					.16			17	
7	25	119	144	17.00		17	119		−25
					.19			17	
8	25	138	163	17.25		17	136		−27

(b) *Swanky shuts down*

Output (sweaters per day)	Total fixed cost (dollars)	Total variable cost (dollars)	Total cost (dollars)	Average variable cost (dollars per sweater)	Marginal cost (dollars per sweater)	Price (dollars per sweater)	Total revenue (dollars)	Marginal revenue (dollars per sweater)	Profit (+) or loss (−) (dollars)
6	25	103	128	17.17		16.99	101.94		−26.06
					.16			........16.99	
7	25	119	144	17.00		16.99	118.93		−25.07
					.19			........16.99	
8	25	138	163	17.25		16.99	135.92		−27.08

The shutdown point occurs at the point of minimum average variable cost. If price equals minimum average variable cost, Swanky is indifferent between producing at the shutdown point and producing nothing. If price falls below minimum average variable cost, Swanky produces nothing. Minimum average variable cost is $17 and occurs at 7 units of output. If the price is $17 and Swanky produces 7 sweaters, its loss equals its total fixed cost of $25 (part a). If the price falls to $16.99, even when it produces at the point of minimum average variable cost, the firm makes a loss that is bigger than its total fixed cost, and so it shuts down (part b).

so the loss equals $144 minus $119, which is $25. We calculate the loss from producing 6 sweaters or 8 sweaters in a similar way.

The minimum loss occurs when 7 sweaters are produced. You can see that fact directly by looking at the profit or loss column. You can also check that the loss is minimized by looking at marginal cost and marginal revenue. Increasing output from 6 to 7 sweaters has a marginal cost of $16 but a marginal revenue of $17, so total revenue rises by more than total cost. Increasing output still further, from 7 to 8 sweaters, has a marginal cost of $19, which exceeds marginal revenue, so profit falls (loss rises).

Swanky's loss when producing 7 sweaters exactly equals its total fixed costs—$25. Alternatively, if Swanky produces nothing, it will also lose its $25 of total fixed cost. So, at a price of $17, Swanky is indifferent between producing and shutting down—it makes a loss equal to its fixed cost.

In part (b), the price is $16.99—a lower price but by just a penny. Costs are unchanged. We calculate total revenue and profit in the same way as before. The output that maximizes profit (minimizes loss) is still 7 sweaters, but in this case the minimum possible loss is $25.07. Swanky loses 7¢ more than it would if it produced nothing at all. The firm will shut down. Its minimum average variable cost is $17. At $17 it just pays to produce, and at $16.99 it just pays to shut down. The minimum output that Swanky produces is 7 sweaters.

Real-World Shutdowns   Shutdowns occur in the real world either because of a fall in price or because of a rise in costs. Shutdowns occur most frequently in raw material–producing sectors as a result of fluctuating prices. For example, if the price of gold falls, gold mines temporarily stop producing. If the price of nickel falls, nickel mines shut down. Shutdowns also occur in many industries—such as those producing ice cream, cars, and transportation services.

A famous example of an airline shutdown occurred in 1982. Braniff, a Dallas-based airline, had grown rapidly following the deregulation of the airline business in 1978. When 1,000 new domestic routes became available, Braniff's aggressive chairman, Harding Lawrence, applied for 624 of them, spreading over the Southwest and the Southeast. The company also added routes to Asia, Europe, and the Middle East. If airfares had remained stable, the company's expansion plans would have been highly profitable. But the airlines became embroiled in a fare cutting orgy, and at a time when fuel prices were rising sharply. Braniff, vastly overextended, lost more than $40 million in 1979, and by 1981 it was losing $160 million. In May 1982, after 54 years in the airline business, Braniff laid off all its workers and stopped flying. Because the firm was losing more than its total variable cost and because it saw no prospect of the situation improving, it shut down.

REVIEW

I n perfect competition, a firm's marginal revenue equals its price. A firm maximizes profit by producing the output at which marginal cost equals marginal revenue (equals price). The lowest output a firm will produce is that at which average variable cost is at a minimum. If price falls below the minimum of average variable cost, the best a firm can do is to stop producing and make a loss equal to its total fixed cost. Maximizing profit is not the same thing as making a profit. In the short run, a firm can make a profit, break even, or make a loss. The maximum loss that a firm will make is equal to its total fixed cost. ◆

The Firm's Supply Curve

A **perfectly competitive firm's supply curve** shows how a firm's profit-maximizing output varies as the market price varies, other things remaining constant. We are now going to derive Swanky's supply curve. Actually, we have already calculated three points on Swanky's supply curve. We discovered that when the price is $25, Swanky produces 9 sweaters a day; when the price is $20, Swanky produces 8 sweaters a day; and when the price is $17, Swanky is indifferent between producing 7 sweaters a day and shutting down. We are now going to derive Swanky's entire supply curve. Figure 11.5 illustrates the analysis.

Figure 11.5(a) shows Swanky's marginal cost and average variable cost curves, and Fig. 11.5(b) shows its supply curve. There is a direct connection between the marginal cost and average variable cost curves and the supply curve. Let's see what that connection is.

The smallest quantity that Swanky will supply is at the shutdown point. When the price is equal to the minimum average variable cost, the marginal revenue curve is MR_0 and the firm produces the output at its shutdown point—point s in the figure. If the price falls below minimum average variable cost, Swanky produces nothing. As the price rises above its minimum average variable cost, Swanky's output rises. Since Swanky maximizes profit by producing the output at which marginal cost equals price, we can determine from its marginal cost curve how much the firm produces at each price. At a price of $25, the marginal revenue curve is MR_1. Swanky maximizes profit by producing 9 sweaters. At a price of $31, the marginal revenue curve is MR_2 and Swanky produces 10 sweaters. The supply curve, shown in Fig. 11.5(b), has two separate parts. First, in the range of prices that exceed the minimum of average variable cost, the supply curve is the same as the marginal cost curve—above the shutdown point (s). Second, at prices below minimum average variable cost, Swanky shuts down and produces nothing, and its supply curve runs along the vertical axis.

FIGURE **11.5**

Swanky's Supply Curve

(a) Marginal cost and average variable cost

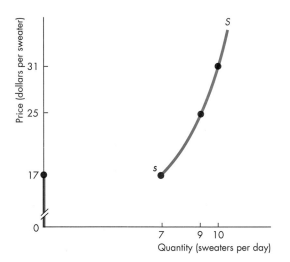

(b) Firm's supply curve

Part (a) shows Swanky's profit-maximizing output at each market price. At $25 a sweater, Swanky produces 9 sweaters. At $17 a sweater, Swanky produces 7 sweaters. At any price below $17 a sweater, Swanky produces nothing. Swanky's shutdown point is *s*. Part (b) shows Swanky's supply curve—the number of sweaters Swanky will produce at each price. Swanky's supply curve is made up of its marginal cost curve (part a) at all points above the average variable cost curve and the vertical axis at all prices below minimum average variable cost.

So far, we have studied a single firm in isolation. We have seen that the firm's profit-maximizing actions depend on the market price—which the firm takes as given. The higher the price, the larger is the quantity that the firm will choose to produce—the firm's supply curve is upward sloping. But how is the market price determined? To answer this question, we need to study not one firm in isolation but the market as a whole.

Output, Price, and Profit in the Short Run

Market price is determined by industry demand and industry supply. It is the price that makes the quantity demanded equal the quantity supplied. But the quantity supplied depends on the supply decisions of all the individual firms in the industry. Those supply decisions, in turn, depend on the market price.

A short-run equilibrium prevails in a competitive market when each firm operates its plant to produce the profit-maximizing output level and when the total quantity produced by all the firms in the market equals the quantity demanded at that price. To find the short-run equilibrium, we first need to construct the short-run industry supply curve.

Short-Run Industry Supply Curve

The **short-run industry supply curve** shows how the total quantity supplied in the short run by all firms in an industry varies as the market price varies. The quantity supplied in the short run by the industry at a given price is the sum of the quantities supplied in the short run by all firms in the industry at that price. To construct the industry supply curve, we sum horizontally the supply curves of the individual firms. Let's see how we do that.

Suppose that the competitive sweater industry consists of 1,000 firms exactly like Swanky. The relationship between a firm's supply curve and the industry supply curve for this case is illustrated in Fig. 11.6. Each of the 1,000 firms in the industry has a supply schedule like Swanky's, set out in the table.

At a price below $17, every firm in the industry will shut down production so that the industry will supply nothing. At $17, each firm is indifferent between shutting down and producing 7 sweaters. Since each firm is indifferent, some firms will produce and others will shut down. Industry supply can be anything between 0 (all firms shut down) and 7,000 (all firms producing 7 sweaters a day each). Thus at $17, the industry supply curve is horizontal—it is perfectly elastic. As the price rises above $17, each firm increases its quantity supplied and the industry quantity supplied also increases, but by 1,000 times that of each individual firm.

The supply schedules set out in the table form the basis of the supply curves that are graphed in Fig.

11.6. Swanky and every other firm has the supply curve S_F shown in Fig. 11.6(a); the industry supply curve S_I is shown in Fig. 11.6(b). Look carefully at the units on the horizontal axes of parts (a) and (b), and note that in part (a) the units are individual sweaters while in part (b) they are thousands of sweaters. There are two important differences. First, at each price, the quantity supplied by the industry is 1,000 times the quantity supplied by a single firm. Second, at a price of $17, the firm supplies either nothing or 7 sweaters a day. There is no individual firm supply curve between those two numbers. But for the industry, any quantity between zero and 7,000 will be produced, so the industry supply curve is perfectly elastic over that range.

FIGURE 11.6

Firm and Industry Supply Curves

(a) Swanky, Inc.

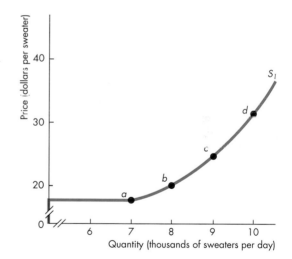

(b) Sweater industry

The industry supply schedule is the sum of the supply schedules of all individual firms. An industry that consists of 1,000 identical firms has a supply schedule similar to that of the individual firm. But the quantity supplied by the industry is 1,000 times as large as that of the individual firm (see the table). At the shutdown price, the firm produces either 0 or 7 sweaters per day. The industry supply curve is perfectly elastic at the shutdown price. Part (a) shows Swanky's supply curve, S_F, and part (b) shows the sweater industry supply curve, S_I. Points a, b, c, and d correspond to the rows of the table. Note that the unit of measurement on the horizontal axis for the industry supply curve is 1,000 times the unit for Swanky.

	Price (dollars per sweater)	Quantity supplied by Swanky, Inc. (sweaters per day)	Quantity supplied by industry (sweaters per day)
a	17	0 or 7	0 to 7,000
b	20	8	8,000
c	25	9	9,000
d	31	10	10,000

Short-Run Competitive Equilibrium

Price and industry output are determined by industry demand and supply. Three different possible short-run competitive equilibrium positions are shown in Fig. 11.7. The supply curve (S) is the same as S_I, which we derived in Fig. 11.6. If the demand curve is D_1, the equilibrium price is $25 and industry output is 9,000 sweaters a day. If the demand curve is D_2, the price is $20 and industry output is 8,000 sweaters a day. If the demand curve is D_3, the price is $17 and industry output is 7,000 sweaters a day.

To see what is happening to each individual firm and its profit in these three situations, you need to check back to Fig. 11.4. With demand curve D_1, the price is $25 a sweater, each firm produces 9 sweaters a day and makes a profit as shown in Fig. 11.4(a); if

the demand curve is D_2, the price is $20 a sweater, each firm produces 8 sweaters a day and makes a zero profit, as shown in Fig. 11.4(b); and if the demand curve is D_3, the price is $17 a sweater, each firm is indifferent between producing 7 sweaters a day and shutting down and, in either event, is making a loss equal to total fixed cost, as shown in Fig. 11.4(c). If the demand curve shifts farther to the left than D_3, the price will remain constant at $17, since the industry supply curve is horizontal at that price. Some firms will continue to produce 7 sweaters a day, and others will shut down. Firms will be indifferent between these two activities and, whichever they choose, will make a loss equal to their total fixed cost. The number of firms continuing to produce will just be enough to satisfy the market demand at a price of $17.

FIGURE 11.7

Three Short-Run Equilibrium Positions for a Competitive Industry

The competitive sweater industry's supply curve is S. If demand is D_1, the price is $25 and the industry produces 9,000 sweaters. If demand is D_2, the price is $20 and industry output is 8,000 sweaters. If demand is D_3, the price is $17 and industry output is 7,000 sweaters. To see what is happening to the individual firms, look back at Fig. 11.4. When the price is $25, the firms are making a profit; when the price is $20, they are breaking even (making zero profit); and when the price is $17, they are incurring a loss. Even when they make a loss, the firms are maximizing profit (minimizing loss).

REVIEW

In a competitive industry, the price and quantity sold are determined by industry supply and industry demand. Industry supply is the sum of the supplies of all the individual firms. The price determined by industry demand and industry supply cannot be influenced by the actions of any one individual firm. Each firm takes the market price and, given that price, maximizes profit. The firm maximizes its profit by producing the output at which marginal cost equals marginal revenue (equals price), as long as price is not lower than minimum average variable cost. If the price falls below minimum average variable cost, the firm shuts down and incurs a loss equal to its total fixed cost. ◆

Output, Price, and Profit in the Long Run

We have seen that in short-run equilibrium a firm might make a profit, make a loss, or break even. Though each of these three situations is a short-run equilibrium, only one of them is a long-run equilibrium. To see why, we need to examine the dynamic forces at work in a competitive industry. An industry adjusts over time in two ways. First, the number of firms in the industry changes; second, the existing firms change the scale of their plants, thereby shifting their short-run cost curves. Let's study the effects of these two dynamic forces in a competitive industry.

Entry and Exit

Entry is the act of setting up a new firm in an industry. **Exit** is the act of closing down a firm and leaving an industry. When will a new firm enter an industry or an existing one leave? How do entry and exit affect the market price, profit, and output in an industry? Let's first look at the causes of entry and exit.

Profits and Losses as Signals
What triggers entry and exit? The prospect of profit triggers entry, and the prospect of continuing losses triggers exit. Temporary profits and temporary losses that are

purely random, like the winnings and losings at a casino, do not trigger entry or exit, but the prospect of profits or losses for some foreseeable future period does. An industry making economic profits attracts new entrants; one making economic losses induces exits; and an industry in which neither economic losses nor economic profits are being made stimulates neither entry nor exit. Thus profits and losses are the signals to which firms respond in making entry and exit decisions.

What are the effects of entry and exit on price and profits?

Effects of Entry and Exit on Price and Profits
The immediate effect of entry and exit is to shift the industry supply curve. If more firms enter an industry, the industry supply curve shifts to the right: supply increases. If firms exit an industry, the industry supply curve shifts to the left: supply falls. The effects of entry and exit on price and on the total quantity sold in the sweater industry are shown in Fig. 11.8.

FIGURE 11.8

Entry and Exit

(a) Effect of entry

(b) Effect of exit

When new firms enter the sweater industry, the industry supply curve shifts to the right, from S_1 to S_2 (part a). The equilibrium price falls from $25 to $20, and the quantity sold increases from 9,000 to 10,000 sweaters. When firms exit the sweater industry, the industry supply

curve shifts to the left, from S_3 to S_4 (part b). The equilibrium price rises from $17 to $20, and the quantity sold decreases from 7,000 to 6,000 sweaters.

Entry   First, let's look at what happens when new firms enter an industry. Suppose that the demand curve for sweaters is D_1 and the industry supply curve is S_1, so sweaters sell for $25 and 9,000 sweaters are being bought and sold. Now suppose that some new firms enter the industry. As they do so, the industry supply curve shifts to the right to become S_2. With the higher supply and unchanged demand, the price falls from $25 to $20 a sweater and the quantity increases from 9,000 to 10,000.

As the price falls, Swanky and the other firms in the industry will react by lowering their output. That is, for each existing firm in the industry, its profit-maximizing output falls. Since the price falls, and since each firm sells less, profit falls for each firm. You can see this reduction of profit by glancing back at Fig. 11.4. Initially, when the price is $25, each firm makes a profit and is in the situation shown in Fig. 11.4(a). When the price falls to $20, the firm's profit disappears and the firm is in the situation shown in Fig. 11.4(b).

You have just discovered an important result:

As new firms enter an industry, the price falls and the profit of each existing firm falls.

A good example of this process has occurred in the last few years in the personal computer industry. When IBM introduced its first personal computer in the early 1980s, the price of PCs gave IBM a big profit. Very quickly thereafter, new firms such as Compaq, Zenith, Leading Edge, and a host of others entered the industry with machines technologically identical to the IBM. In fact, they were so similar that they came to be called "clones." The massive wave of entry into the personal computer industry shifted the supply curve to the right and lowered the price and the profits for all firms.

Exit   Let's see what happens when firms leave an industry. Again, the impact of a firm leaving is to shift the industry supply curve, but this time to the left. Figure 11.8(b) illustrates. Suppose that initially the demand curve is D_3 with an industry supply curve S_3, so the market price is $17 and 7,000 sweaters are being sold. As firms leave the industry, the supply curve shifts to the left and becomes S_4. With the fall in supply, industry output falls from 7,000 to 6,000 sweaters and the price rises from $17 to $20.

To see what is happening to Swanky, go back again to Fig. 11.4. With the demand curve D_3 and a price of $17, Swanky is in a situation like that illustrated in Fig. 11.4(c). Price is lower than average total cost, and Swanky is making a loss. Some firms exit, and Swanky (and some others) hang in. As firms exit, the price rises from $17 to $20, so the firms that remain increase their output, and their losses vanish. They are then back in a situation like that illustrated in Fig. 11.4(b).

You have just worked out the second important result:

As firms leave an industry, the price rises and so do the profits of the remaining firms.

An example of a firm leaving an industry is International Harvester, a manufacturer of farm equipment. For decades, people associated the name "International Harvester" with tractors, combines, and other farm machines. But International Harvester wasn't the only maker of farm equipment. The industry became intensely competitive, and the firm began losing money. Now the company has a new name, Navistar International, and it doesn't make tractors anymore. After years of losses and shrinking revenues, it got out of the farm business in 1985. Now it makes trucks. Another example is Singer sewing machines. The name "Singer" still means sewing machines to millions of people, but Singer no longer makes these machines. It makes electronic equipment for jet aircraft and the like.

Both Singer and International Harvester exited because they were losing money on their operations. Their exits lowered supply and made it possible for the remaining firms in those two industries to break even.

Long-Run Equilibrium   We've seen that the prospect of profit triggers entry and the prospect of continuing loss triggers exit. We have also seen that entry into an industry lowers the profits of the existing firms and that exit from an industry increases the profits of the remaining firms. Long-run equilibrium results from the interaction of profits and losses as signals to entry and exit and the effects of entry and exit on profits and losses.

Long-run equilibrium occurs in a competitive industry when economic profits are zero. If an industry makes economic profits, firms enter the industry and the supply curve shifts to the right. As a result, the market price falls and so do profits. Firms continue to enter and profits continue to fall as long as the industry is earning positive economic profits.

In an industry with economic losses, some firms will exit. As those firms leave the industry, the supply curve shifts to the left and the market price rises. As the price rises, the industry's losses shrink. As long as losses continue, some firms will leave the industry. Only when losses have been eliminated and zero economic profits are being made will firms stop exiting.

Let's now examine the second way in which the competitive industry adjusts in the long run—by existing firms changing their plant size.

Changes in Plant Size

A firm will change its plant size whenever it can increase its profit by doing so. A situation in which a firm can profitably expand its output by increasing its plant is illustrated in Fig. 11.9. In that figure the price (and marginal revenue) is $20. With its current plant, Swanky's marginal and average total cost—its short-run costs—are shown by the curves *SRMC* and *SRAC*. Swanky maximizes profit by producing 8 sweaters a day, but with its existing plant, Swanky makes zero economic profit.

Swanky's long-run average cost curve is *LRAC*. By installing more knitting machines—increasing its plant size—Swanky can lower its costs and operate at a positive economic profit. For example, if Swanky increases its plant size so that it operates at point *m*, the minimum of its long-run average cost, it lowers its average cost from $20 to $14 and makes a profit of $6 a sweater. Since Swanky is a price taker, expanding output from 8 to 12 sweaters does not lower the market price and so would be a profitable thing for Swanky to do. Because it takes time to change the production plant, the short-run equilibrium prevails. Nevertheless, over time, the firm will gradually expand its plant.

As firms expand their plants, the short-run industry supply curve starts to shift to the right. (Recall that the industry supply curve is the sum of the supply curves of all the individual firms.) With increases in supply and a given demand, the price gradually falls. As the price falls, so do profits. It will pay firms to expand as long as expansion increases prof-

FIGURE **11.9**

Changes in Plant Size

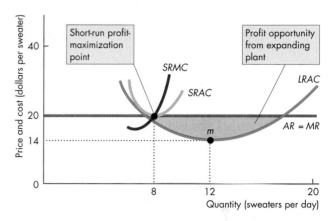

Swanky has a plant whose short-run cost curves are *SRMC* and *SRAC*. The price of a sweater is $20, so average revenue and marginal revenue (*AR – MR*) are $20. The profit-maximizing short-run output is 8 sweaters a day. Swanky's long-run costs are described by the long-run average cost curve (*LRAC*). The firm will want to expand its plant to take advantage of lower average costs and make a bigger profit—it will want to move into the blue area. As firms expand, the industry supply increases and the price falls.

its. Only when no economic profits are being made will firms stick with their existing plant size. There is only one possible plant size that is consistent with long-run equilibrium in a competitive industry, and that is the one associated with the minimum long-run average cost (point *m* in Fig. 11.9).

Figure 11.10 illustrates the long-run competitive equilibrium. It occurs at a price of $14 with each firm producing 12 sweaters a day. Each firm in the industry has the plant size such that its marginal cost and average total cost curves are *SRMC* and *SRAC*. Each firm produces the output at which its short-run marginal cost equals price. No firm can change its output in the short run and make more profit. As each firm is producing at minimum long-run average cost (point *m* on *LRAC*), no firm has an incentive to expand or contract its production plant—a bigger plant or a smaller plant will lead to a higher long-run average cost and an economic loss. Finally, no firm has an incentive to leave the industry or to enter it.

FIGURE **11.10**

The Long-Run Equilibrium of a Firm

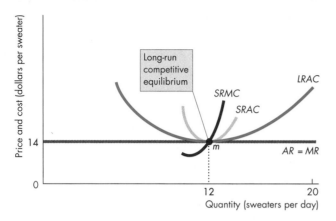

As firms expand their plants, industry supply increases and the price falls. Long-run equilibrium occurs when the price equals $14 and each firm is producing at point *m*, its point of minimum long-run average cost.

R E V I E W

Long-run competitive equilibrium is described by three conditions:

◆ Firms maximize short-run profit, so marginal cost equals marginal revenue (equals price).

◆ Economic profits are zero, so no firm has an incentive to enter or to leave the industry.

◆ Long-run average cost is at a minimum, so no firm has an incentive to expand or to contract its plant. ◆

Responding to Changing Tastes and Advancing Technology

Increased awareness of the health hazards of smoking has caused a decrease in the demand for tobacco and cigarettes.

The development of inexpensive car and air transportation has caused a huge decrease in the demand for long-distance trains and buses. Solid-state electronics have caused a large decrease in the demand for TV and radio repair. There has been a decrease in the demand for American-made cars as a result of high-quality alternatives from Japan. What happens in a competitive industry when there is a permanent decrease in the demand for its products?

The development of the microwave oven has produced an enormous increase in the demand for paper, glass, and plastic cooking utensils and for plastic wrap. The demand for almost all products is steadily increasing as a result of increasing population and increasing incomes. What happens in a competitive industry when the demand for its product increases?

Advances in technology are constantly lowering the costs of production. New biotechnologies have dramatically lowered the costs of many food and pharmaceutical products. New electronics technologies have lowered the cost of producing just about every good and service. What happens in a competitive industry when technological change lowers its production costs?

Let's use the theory of perfect competition to answer these questions.

A Permanent Decrease in Demand

Suppose that an industry starts out in long-run competitive equilibrium, shown in Fig. 11.11(a). The demand curve labeled D_0 and the supply curve labeled S_0 represent the initial demand and supply in the market. The price initially is P_0, and the total industry output is Q_0. A single firm is shown in Fig. 11.11(b). Initially, it produces the quantity q_0 and makes zero economic profit.

Now suppose that demand decreases to D_1, as shown in part (a). This decrease in demand causes the price to drop to P_1. At this lower price, each firm produces a smaller output (q_1), and the quantity supplied by the industry decreases from Q_0 to Q_1 as the industry slides down its short-run supply curve (S_0). The industry is now in short-run equilibrium but not long-run equilibrium. It is in short-run equilibrium because each firm is maximizing profit. But it is not in long-run equilibrium because each firm is making an economic loss—its average total cost exceeds the price.

FIGURE **11.11**

A Decrease in Demand

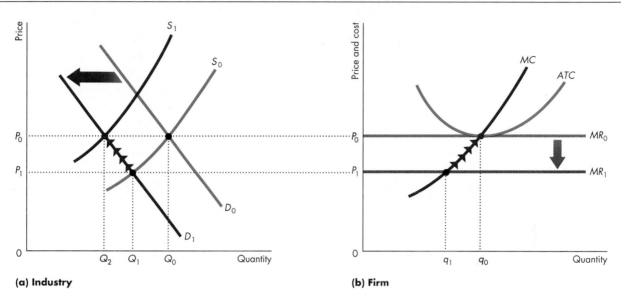

(a) Industry

(b) Firm

An industry starts out in long-run competitive equilibrium. Part (a) shows the industry demand curve D_0 and the industry supply curve S_0, the equilibrium quantity Q_0, and the market price P_0. Each firm sells at price P_0, so its marginal revenue curve is MR_0 in part (b). Each firm produces q_0 and makes a zero profit. Demand decreases from D_0 to D_1 (part a). The equilibrium price falls to P_1, each firm lowers its output to q_1 (part b), and industry output falls to Q_1. In this new situation, firms are making losses and some firms will leave the industry. As they do

so, the industry supply curve gradually shifts to the left, from S_0 to S_1. This shift gradually raises the industry price from P_1 back to P_0. While the price is below P_0, firms are making losses and some are leaving the industry. Once the price has returned to P_0, the smaller number of firms whose supply curves add up to the industry supply curve (S_1) will each be making a zero profit. There will be no further incentive for any firm to leave the industry. Each firm produces q_0, and industry output is Q_2.

In this situation, firms will leave the industry. As they do so, the industry supply curve starts shifting to the left, the quantity supplied shrinks, and the price gradually rises. At each higher price, the profit-maximizing output is higher, so the firms remaining in the industry raise their output as the price rises. Each slides up its marginal cost or supply curve (part b). Eventually, enough firms will have left the industry for the supply curve to have shifted to S_1 (part a). When that has happened, the price will have returned to its original level (P_0). At that price, the firms remaining in the industry will produce the same amount as they did before the fall in demand (q_0). No firms will want to leave the industry because of losses, and none will want to enter. The industry supply curve settles down at S_1, and total

industry output is Q_2. The industry is again in long-run equilibrium.

In the long-run equilibrium following a permanent decrease in demand, fewer firms remain in the industry. Each remaining firm produces the same output in the new long-run equilibrium as it did initially. While moving from the original equilibrium to the new one, firms that remain in the industry suffer losses. But they keep their losses to a minimum because they adjust their output to keep price equal to marginal cost.

A Permanent Increase in Demand

What happens in a competitive industry when the demand for its product increases? Let's begin the story again in long-run equilibrium, as shown in Fig. 11.12(a). With demand curve D_0 and supply curve S_0, the market price is P_0 and quantity Q_0 is sold by the industry. Figure 11.12(b) shows a single firm. At price P_0, the firm is making zero economic profit and producing an output of q_0. Now suppose that the demand for the industry's output increases from D_0 to D_1. The increased demand raises the price to P_1. The quantity supplied by the industry rises from Q_0 to Q_1 as each firm increases its output from q_0 to q_1 (part b). At price P_1 and quantity Q_1, the industry is in short-run equilibrium but not in long-run equilibrium. Firms in the industry are making economic profits. These economic profits will attract new firms into the industry.

As new firms enter, the industry supply curve starts shifting to the right, and as it does so, it intersects the demand curve at lower and lower prices

and higher and higher quantities. Firms in the industry react to the falling price by cutting their output. That is, in Fig. 11.12(b) each firm slides back down its marginal cost curve in order to maximize profit at each successively lower price. Eventually, enough new firms enter the industry to shift the industry supply curve all the way to S_1. By that time, the market price falls to P_0, the original price, and the industry output is Q_2. At a price of P_0, each firm cuts its output back to its original level, q_0. Each firm is again making zero economic profit, and no firms enter or exit the industry. This new situation is a long-run equilibrium. During the adjustment process from the initial long-run equilibrium to the new one, all firms—both those firms that were in the industry originally and those that entered—make economic profits.

The process that we've just described goes on in

FIGURE **11.12**

An Increase in Demand

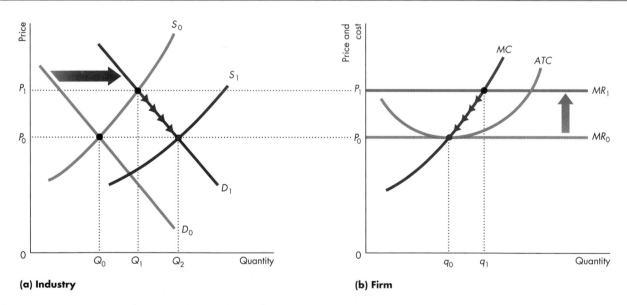

(a) Industry

(b) Firm

A competitive industry is in long-run equilibrium. The demand curve is D_0, and the supply curve is S_0 (part a). The industry's output is Q_0, and the market price is P_0. Each firm faces the marginal revenue curve MR_0 and maximizes profit by producing q_0 (part b). Demand increases from D_0 to D_1. The price rises to P_1, and industry output increases to Q_1. Each firm increases its output to q_1. In this situation, firms are making a profit (price is greater than average total cost). New firms will enter the industry, and as they do so, the industry supply curve shifts to the right. As the supply curve shifts to the right, the price gradually falls and

each individual firm gradually cuts its output from q_1 back to q_0. Since firms are entering the industry, total industry output increases even though each firm's output is cut back. The new equilibrium occurs when enough firms have entered the industry for the supply curve to have moved to S_1 with the price restored to its original level, P_0, and with each firm making zero profit. At this point, industry output is at Q_2. Since each firm is making a zero profit, there is no further tendency for new firms to enter the industry, so the supply curve remains stationary at S_1.

many real-world markets. An example is the market for pizza, which experienced strong expansion throughout the 1980s—see Reading Between the Lines, pp. 300–301.

External Economies and Diseconomies

One feature of the predictions that we have just generated seems odd: in the long run, regardless of whether demand increases or decreases, the price returns to its original level. Is that outcome inevitable? In fact, it is not. It is possible for the long-run equilibrium price to rise, fall, or stay the same. Figure 11.13 illustrates these three cases. In part (a), the long-run supply curve (LS_A) is perfectly elastic. In this case, an increase in demand from D_0 to D_1 (or a decrease in demand from D_1 to D_0) results in a change in the quantity sold but an

---

FIGURE **11.13**

Long-Run Changes in Price and Quantity

(a) Constant cost industry

(b) Increasing cost industry

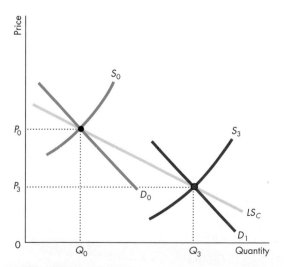

(c) Decreasing cost industry

Three possible long-run changes in price and quantity are illustrated. When demand increases from D_0 to D_1, entry occurs and the industry supply curve shifts from S_0 to S_1. In part (a), the long-run supply curve, LS_A, is horizontal. The quantity increases from Q_0 to Q_1, and the price remains constant at P_0. In part (b), the long-run supply curve is LS_B; the price increases to P_2, and the quantity increases to Q_2. This case occurs in industries with external diseconomies. In part (c), the long-run supply curve is LS_C; the price decreases to P_3, and the quantity increases to Q_3. This case occurs in an industry with external economies.

Competition in Action

THE POST-STANDARD, JULY 8, 1991

The Pizza War Mushrooms

As Big Chains Battle, Little Shops Fight for Slice of the Pie

BY ELIZABETH DORAN

When the pizza shops battle over who gets the biggest slice of the pie, they bring out their heavy artillery.

Their weapons include pepperoni, mushrooms and extra cheese, two-for-one deals and deep discounts. Toss in the ultimate ingredient—home delivery—and the pizza wars are cooking.

Local pizza chains are following the national trend—each one trying to better the other with mouth-watering deals.

The Big Three—Pizza Hut Inc., Domino's Pizza Inc. and Little Caesar's Pizza—are waging the war on the front lines, but the foot soldiers, from regional chains down to the neighborhood ma-and-pa pizzerias, also are in the thick of the battle.

Healthy competition, however, may not bode well for the smaller pizza shops.

"There's an old saying: 'When the elephants fight, the ants take a beating,' " Correll added. "When the Big Three do war, they trample on the little guys who are competing in the same arena. If they're healthy, they survive. If they're marginal, they sink."

The Big Three's passion for promotions has driven the price of pizza down. To stay afloat, the little guy may have to follow suit, however reluctantly.

Ronald Ross, owner of two of the Twin Trees restaurants in Syracuse, finds himself in that position. Although he'd rather avoid it, Ross said he's had to issue coupons "a bit more than we want to" to stay competitive, even though it lowers the company's profits. . . .

"We're a small company, and so it's tough to compete with the big chains," he said. . . .

. . . There are more than 130 establishments listed under "pizza" in the 1991–1992 Syracuse Yellow Pages, compared with just under 70 in the 1981–1982 telephone book.

Other small shops which have opened in recent years, such as Severino's in Fayetteville, match their competitors' prices. Severino's does that in part by accepting coupons from both Pizza Hut and Domino's, said Jim Harriger, assistant manager. . . .

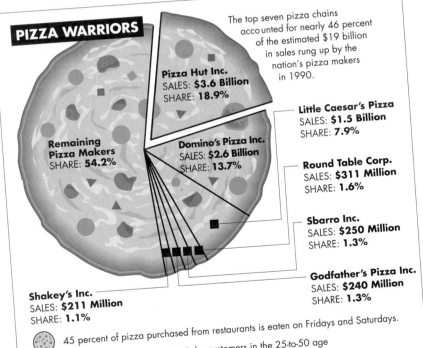

PIZZA WARRIORS

The top seven pizza chains accounted for nearly 46 percent of the estimated $19 billion in sales rung up by the nation's pizza makers in 1990.

Pizza Hut Inc.
SALES: **$3.6 Billion**
SHARE: **18.9%**

Remaining Pizza Makers
SHARE: **54.2%**

Domino's Pizza Inc.
SALES: **$2.6 Billion**
SHARE: **13.7%**

Little Caesar's Pizza
SALES: **$1.5 Billion**
SHARE: **7.9%**

Round Table Corp.
SALES: **$311 Million**
SHARE: **1.6%**

Sbarro Inc.
SALES: **$250 Million**
SHARE: **1.3%**

Godfather's Pizza Inc.
SALES: **$240 Million**
SHARE: **1.3%**

Shakey's Inc.
SALES: **$211 Million**
SHARE: **1.1%**

45 percent of pizza purchased from restaurants is eaten on Fridays and Saturdays.

Almost half of all pizza eaten is by customers in the 25-to-50 age bracket. Customers over 50 are least likely to order pizza, while teenagers prefer pizza two-to-one over restaurant food.

Source: Nation's Restaurant News; National Restaurant Association CREST survey

The Post-Standard

The Essence of the Story

More than 130 establishments produce pizza in the area covered by the Syracuse Yellow Pages in 1991–1992, compared with under 70 a decade earlier.

The Big Three pizza chains—Pizza Hut Inc., Domino's Pizza Inc., and Little Caesar's Pizza—and the smaller regional and local pizza producers are locked in a fierce competitive battle.

The competition is especially tough for the smaller pizza shops. They must match the prices and quality of the big producers. Only the healthy survive; the marginal ones fail.

Background and Analysis

The pizza market in large cities can be explained by the model of perfect competition. Some pizza producers are large, and some are small. But no firm is large enough to control the price of pizza.

In 1980, the demand for pizza was D_0 and the supply was S_0 (see Fig. 1a). Competition among a large number of suppliers keeps the price at its equilibrium level, which in 1980 was P_0. The quantity sold was Q_0.

The demand for pizza increased through the 1980s and by 1991 was D_1. Increased demand brought profits that induced the entry of new firms and the expansion of existing ones. As a result, supply increased and by 1991 was S_1. The price decreased to

P_1, and the quantity of pizza sold increased to Q_1.

Some pizza producers have lower average costs than others. The Big Three are low-cost producers. But so are many of the smaller firms. A low-cost producer's average total cost curve, ATC_L, and marginal cost curve, MC_L, are shown in Fig. 1(b).

The demand curve facing a low-cost producer is perfectly elastic at the market-determined price, P_1. The profit-maximizing output is q_L, the quantity that makes marginal cost equal to price, as shown in Fig. 1(b). The firm makes an economic profit shown by the blue rectangle. Such firms enter and expand as long as profit opportunities exist.

Some producers—most likely small ones and firms in a poor location—have high average costs, shown by the average total cost

curve ATC_M in Fig. 1(c). Such a firm's marginal cost curve is MC_M, and it maximizes profit by producing q_M, the quantity at which marginal cost equals the market-determined price.

The firm shown makes zero economic profit and is a marginal producer. Firms with average costs higher than those shown in Fig. 1(c) have gone out of business. The firm in Fig. 1(c) will go out of business as low-cost firms enter and expand, increasing supply and lowering the price below P_1.

As the demand for pizza increased throughout the 1980s, the forces we have described shifted the supply curve of pizza in Fig. 1(a) to the right, keeping prices low and bringing new resources into the pizza industry in response to changing consumer demands.

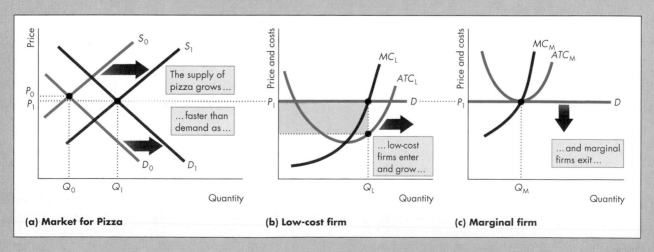

(a) Market for Pizza   (b) Low-cost firm   (c) Marginal firm unchanged price. This is the case that we have just analyzed. In part (b), the long-run supply curve (LS_B) slopes upward. In this case, when demand increases from D_0 to D_1, the price increases, and when demand decreases from D_1 to D_0, the price decreases. Finally, part (c) shows a case in which the long-run supply curve (LS_C) slopes downward. In this case, an increase in demand from D_0 to D_1 results in a fall in the price in the long run. A decrease in demand from D_1 to D_0 results in a higher price in the long run.

Which outcome occurs depends on external economies and external diseconomies. **External economies** are factors beyond the control of an individual firm that lower its average total cost as industry output rises. **External diseconomies** are factors outside the control of a firm that raise its average total cost as industry output rises. There are many examples of external economies and diseconomies.

One of the best examples of external economies is the growth of specialist support services for an industry as it expands. As farm output increased in the nineteenth and early twentieth centuries, the services available to farmers expanded and their costs fell. Farm machinery, fertilizers, transportation networks, storage, and marketing facilities all improved—lowering farm costs. Farms enjoyed the benefits of external economies. As a consequence, as the demand for farm products increased, the quantity produced increased but the price fell (as in Fig. 11.13c).

One of the best examples of external diseconomies is congestion. The airline industry provides a good illustration. With bigger airline industry output, there is greater congestion of both airports and airspace, which results in longer delays and extra waiting time for passengers and airplanes. These external diseconomies mean that as the demand for air transportation continues to increase, eventually (in the absence of further technological change), prices will rise (as in Fig. 11.13b).

Technological Change

Industries are constantly discovering lower-cost techniques of production. Most cost-saving production techniques cannot be implemented, however, without investing in new plant and equipment. As a consequence, it takes time for a technological

advance to spread through an industry. Some firms whose plants are on the verge of being replaced will be quick to adopt the new technology, while other firms whose plants have recently been replaced will continue to operate with older technology until they can no longer cover their average variable cost. Once average variable cost cannot be covered, it pays a firm to scrap even a relatively new plant (embodying the original technology) in favor of a plant with the new technology.

Let's work out exactly what happens to the output and profit of each firm in an industry reshaped by a new technology. Figure 11.14(a) shows the demand curve for an industry (D) and an initial supply curve (S_0). The price is P_0, and the quantity is Q_0. Initially, there are only original technology firms in existence (Fig. 11.14b). Each firm has a marginal cost curve MC_O and an average total cost curve ATC_O. At the market price (P_0), each firm faces a marginal revenue curve MR_0, produces an output q_0^O, and makes zero economic profit. The industry is in long-run competitive equilibrium.

New technology allows firms to produce at substantially lower cost than with the existing technology. The cost curves of firms with the new technology are shown in Fig. 11.14(c). Suppose that one firm with the new technology enters the industry. Since the industry is competitive, this one firm will be a negligible part of the total industry and will hardly affect the industry supply, so the supply curve remains at S_0. The price remains at P_0, and the new technology firm produces a profit-maximizing output of q_0^N and makes a positive economic profit.

Gradually, more new technology firms enter the industry, and after a period, enough have entered to shift the industry supply curve to S_1 in part (a). By this time, the market price has fallen to P_1 and the industry output has risen to Q_1. Each firm takes the price P_1 and maximizes its profit. Each new technology firm, in part (c), maximizes profit by producing the output q_1^N and continues to make a positive economic profit. Each original technology firm, in part (b), minimizes its loss by producing the output q_1^O.

More new technology firms will continue to enter, since the new technology is profitable. Original technology firms will begin to leave the industry or switch to the new technology because the original technology is unprofitable. Eventually, all the firms in the industry will be new technology firms, and by this time, the industry supply curve will have moved

Technological Change in a Competitive Industry

(a) Industry **(b) Original technology firms** **(c) New technology firms**

Initially, the industry supply curve is S_0 and the demand curve is D, so the equilibrium price is P_0, and quantity Q_0 is traded (part a). Each individual firm, shown in part (b), produces q_0^0 and makes a zero profit. A new technology is developed. The costs associated with the new technology (ATC_N and MC_N) are shown in part (c) and are lower than those for the original technology. A new technology firm, faced with the price P_0, produces a profit-maximizing output of q_0^N and makes a profit. Since the new technology is profitable, more and more firms will use it. As they do so, the industry supply curve begins to shift to the right, from S_0 to S_1. With an increase in industry supply, industry output increases to Q_1, but the price falls to P_1. As a result, new technology firms will cut their output from q_0^N to q_1^N, but they will still be making a profit. Original

technology firms will cut their output from q_0^0 to q_1^0. They will be making losses. As firms with the original technology begin to close down and more new technology firms enter the industry, the industry supply curve continues to shift to the right, from S_1 to S_2. At S_2, the price is P_2 and industry output is Q_2. Each new technology firm is now producing q_2 and making a zero profit, and there are no firms using the original technology.

The effect of the introduction of the new technology has been to increase industry output and lower price. In the process, firms that adopted the new technology early made profits, while firms that stuck with the original technology for too long incurred losses.

to S_2. The supply curve S_2 is based on the marginal cost curves of the new technology firms. The supply curve S_0 is based on the marginal cost curves of the original technology firms. The supply curve S_1 is based on the marginal cost curves for both original technology and new technology firms. With supply curve S_2, the market price is P_2 and the industry output is Q_2. At price P_2, the new technology firms produce a profit-maximizing output of q_2, making zero profits. The industry long-run equilibrium price is P_2.

The process that we have just analyzed is one in which some firms experience economic profits and others experience economic losses. It is a period of dynamic change for an industry. Some firms do well,

and others do badly. Often a change of the kind that we have just examined will have a geographical dimension to it. For example, the new technology firms might be located in a new industrial region of a country, while the original technology firms might be located in a traditional industrial region. Alternatively, the new technology firms might be in a foreign country, while the original technology firms are in the domestic economy. The struggles of the American textile industry to keep up with the fierce competition from Hong Kong and Taiwan is a good example of this phenomenon. Another example is the dairy industry, which is undergoing a major technological change arising from the use of hormones.

When the demand for a competitive industry's product declines, firms begin to incur losses and leave the industry. Exiting firms decrease supply, and the price begins to increase. Eventually, enough firms exit, and the remaining firms just cover their costs. When the demand for a competitive industry's product increases, firms make profits and new firms enter. Entry increases the industry supply, and the price begins to fall. Eventually, enough firms enter to compete away all the economic profit. ◆ ◆ When a new technology lowers costs, the industry supply increases and price falls. Firms that adopt the new technology make a profit, and those sticking with the old technology incur a loss. Old technology firms either adopt the new technology or exit. Eventually, all firms remaining in the industry have adopted the new technology and are just covering their costs. ◆

Farms in Distress

In 1981, there were 2.4 million farms in the United States. The average farm had 425 acres. The population of farms has steadily declined over the years. In the five years between 1976 and 1981, that decline was close to 1 percent a year. But in the five years between 1981 and 1986, 220,000 farms (9 percent of the total) disappeared—more than three times the number that went out of business in the preceding five years. At the same time, the average size of farms increased by 7 percent to 455 acres. Through the early to mid-1980s, there were many indications of financial distress in the farm sector. By 1985, more than 5 percent of farms were unable to meet their bank loan repayment schedules; almost 40 percent had borrowed up to their loan limits; close to 5 percent a year were going out of business; and close to 4 percent were in bankruptcy. Why have American farms gone through a period of such tremendous financial distress? Why have so many farms gone out of business? Why, after such a shakeout, is the remaining farm larger, on the average?

The farm problem is a complex one. In fact, there is no single "farm problem" but many individual problems, varying from region to region and from crop to crop. But there is a single, common problem that affected all farmers to some degree during the early 1980s. It's on this problem that we'll focus.

Although some farmers are wealthy, many are not. They have to buy their land and farm buildings and equipment by borrowing from the bank. In the early 1980s, the cost of bank borrowing increased on an unprecedented scale. Bank loans that in the 1970s had cost an average of 7 or 8 percent a year suddenly were costing an average of 13 percent and climbed briefly to 20 percent in 1981. The cost remained high at 15 percent a year through 1982. This massive increase in the cost of borrowing represented an increase in the fixed costs of a farm. Recall that fixed costs are those incurred independently of the volume of output. Even if a farm produces nothing, it has to pay the bank the interest on its loans.

We can analyze the effects of an increase in fixed costs in the farm sector by using the model of a perfectly competitive industry that we've just been studying. Figure 11.15 shows you what happens. In part (a), a farm's average total cost curve is ATC and its marginal cost curve is MC. The market price is P_0, and the farm's marginal revenue curve is MR. The farm's profit-maximizing output is q_0. The initial situation shown in part (a) is a long-run equilibrium with the farm making zero economic profit.

An increase in total fixed cost shifts the average total cost curve upward but does not change the marginal cost curve. (Recall that marginal cost is the cost of producing one additional unit of output. Since the increase in interest charges increases fixed cost but not variable cost, marginal cost is unchanged.) Suppose that the increased fixed cost shifts the average total cost curve to ATC'. If the price remains P_0, the farm's profit-maximizing output remains at q_0. But the farm is now losing money. In Fig. 11.15(a), the loss is equal to the red rectangle.

The size of a farm's loss depends on its financial situation. Farms with large debts make the largest losses. During the 1980s, 9 percent of farms had loans that exceeded 70 percent of the value of their land and buildings. It is these farms that incur the largest losses. These are the farms that will begin to leave the industry. As farms go out of business, the supply curve for farm products starts to shift to the left and the price of farm products begins to increase. Figure 11.15(b) shows what happens in the long run. When enough farms have left the industry, the price will have increased from P_0 to P_1. At the

FIGURE 11.15

The Effects of High Interest Rates on Farm Profits and Prices

(a) High interest rates cause losses

(b) Exit raises prices—eventually

Initially, an individual farm has an average total cost curve *ATC*, and at a price of P_0 its profit-maximizing output is q_0 (part a). Fixed costs increase, shifting the average total cost curve upward to *ATC'*. Marginal cost and price remain constant, and so does the profit-maximizing output. Farms now make a loss shown by the red rectangle. As

some farms exit, the industry supply curve shifts to the left and the price begins to rise from P_0 to P_1. The profit-maximizing output increases from q_0 to q_1 (part b). The process of adjustment is not instantaneous, and farms make losses for a prolonged period.

higher price, farm output increases from q_0 to q_1 and farms are no longer losing money. Individual farm outputs are now bigger than before, which means that the average farm uses more inputs—more labor, machines, and land.

But the situation shown in part (b) takes a long time to come about. The price does not rise quickly from P_0 to P_1. The main factor slowing the rise in price is the fact that even with a large exit of U.S. farms, these farms produce but a small fraction of the world supply of most agricultural products. As a consequence, farms make losses for a prolonged period of time, during which the adjustment process takes place.

You've now studied how a competitive market works and have used the model of perfect competition to interpret and explain a variety of aspects of real-world economic behavior. The last topic that we'll study in this chapter is the efficiency of perfect competition.

Competition and Efficiency

In perfect competition, freedom of entry ensures that firms produce at the least possible cost. Also, the fact that each firm is a price taker, facing a perfectly elastic demand curve, results in firms producing a quantity such that marginal cost equals price. These features of a perfectly competitive market have important implications for the efficiency of such a market.

Allocative Efficiency

Allocative efficiency occurs when no resources are wasted—when no one can be made better off without someone else being made worse off. If someone can be made better off without making someone else worse off, a more efficient allocation of resources can be achieved. Three conditions must be satisfied to achieve allocative efficiency:

♦ Economic efficiency
♦ Consumer efficiency
♦ Equality of marginal social cost and marginal social benefit

We defined economic efficiency in Chapter 9 as a situation in which the cost of producing a given output is minimized. Economic efficiency involves technological efficiency—producing the maximum possible output from given inputs—as well as using inputs in their cost-minimizing proportions. Economic efficiency occurs whenever firms maximize profit. Since firms in perfect competition maximize profit, perfect competition is economically efficient.

Consumer efficiency occurs when consumers cannot make themselves better off by reallocating their budgets. A consumer's best possible budget allocation is summarized in the consumer's demand curves. That is, a demand curve tells us the quantity demanded at a given price when the consumer has made the best possible use of a given budget. Thus when the quantity bought at a given price is a point on the demand curve, the allocation satisfies consumer efficiency.

The third condition occurs in perfect competition if there are no external costs and benefits. **External costs** are those costs not borne by the producer but borne by other members of society. Examples of such costs are the costs of pollution and congestion. **External benefits** are those benefits accruing to people other than the buyer of a good. Examples of such benefits are the pleasure we get from well-designed buildings and beautiful works of art. As long as *someone* buys these things, *everyone* can enjoy them.

Marginal social cost is the cost of producing one additional unit of output, including external costs. **Marginal social benefit** is the dollar value of the benefit from one additional unit of consumption, including any external benefits. Allocative efficiency occurs when marginal social cost equals marginal social benefit. Figure 11.16 illustrates such a situation. The marginal social benefit curve is MSB, and the marginal social cost curve is MSC. Allocative efficiency occurs at a quantity Q^* and a price P^*. In this situa-

FIGURE **11.16**

Allocative Efficiency

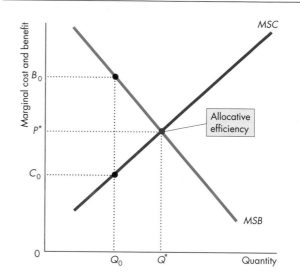

Allocative efficiency, which occurs when no resources are wasted, requires that marginal social cost (MSC) be equal to marginal social benefit (MSB). Allocative efficiency occurs at output Q^*. If output is Q_0, marginal social cost (C_0) will be less than marginal social benefit (B_0). The benefit from one additional unit of output exceeds its cost. A perfectly competitive market delivers allocative efficiency when there are no external costs and benefits. In such a situation, the marginal social cost curve is the industry supply curve and the marginal social benefit curve is the industry demand curve. The price is P^*, and the quantity traded is Q^*.

tion, there is no waste. No one can be made better off without someone else being made worse off. If output is above Q^*, marginal social cost will exceed marginal social benefit. The cost of producing the last unit will exceed its benefit. If output is below Q^*, marginal social benefit will exceed marginal social cost. Producing one more unit will bring more benefit than it costs.

There are some circumstances in which perfect competition delivers allocative efficiency, as shown in Fig. 11.16. Those circumstances are ones in which there are no external costs and benefits. In such a case, all the benefits accrue to the buyers of a good and the costs are borne by its producer. In that case, the marginal social benefit curve is the same as the industry demand curve. Also, the marginal social cost curve is the industry supply curve. With perfect competition, price and quantity are determined at the point of intersection of the demand and supply curves. Hence a perfectly competitive market produces an output Q^* at a price P^*. Perfect competition delivers allocative efficiency.

To check that in this situation no resources are being wasted—no one can be made better off without someone being made worse off—consider what will happen if output is restricted to Q_0. At that output, marginal social cost is C_0 but marginal social benefit is B_0. Everyone can be made better off by increasing output. Producers will willingly supply more of the good for a price higher than C_0. Consumers will willingly buy more of the good for a price lower than B_0. Everyone would like to trade more. But once output has increased to Q^*, there are no further available gains from increasing the output of this good. The benefit to the consumer of the last unit produced exactly equals the cost to the producer of the last unit.

The Invisible Hand

The founder of economic science, Adam Smith, suggested that a competitive market acts like an invisible hand to guide buyers and sellers to achieve the best possible social outcome. Each participant in a competitive market is, according to Smith, "led by an invisible hand to promote an end which was no part of his intention." You can see the invisible hand at work in the cartoon. Adam Smith was not able to work out his conclusion with the clarity and precision with which we are able to do so today. It is the work of Léon Walras and Vilfredo Pareto and, more recently, of Nobel Prize–winning American economists Kenneth Arrow and Gérard Debreu that demonstrated the precise conditions under which perfect competition and maximum social welfare coincide.

Obstacles to Efficiency

There are two main obstacles to allocative efficiency:

◆ External costs and external benefits
◆ Monopoly

External costs and external benefits mean that many goods cannot be efficiently produced even in perfectly competitive markets. Such goods as national defense, the enforcement of law and order, the provision of clean drinking water, and the disposal

Drawing by M. Twohy; © 1985 The New Yorker Magazine, Inc.

of sewage and garbage are all examples of goods in which there are enormous external benefits. Left to competitive markets, we would have too small a production of such goods. There are also many examples of goods that impose high external costs. The production of steel and chemicals generates air and water pollution. Perfect competition will result in an overproduction of such goods. One of the key functions of government is to modify the outcome of competitive markets in cases such as these. Government institutions (which we study in Chapters 19 through 21) arise, in part, because of external costs and benefits.

Another obstacle to allocative efficiency is the existence of monopoly. Monopoly, which we study in the next chapter, results in the restriction of output below its competitive level in order to increase price and make a larger profit. Precisely how monopoly achieves this outcome is the subject of the next chapter.

◆ ◆ ◆ ◆ We have now completed our study of perfect competition. We have seen how a firm in a perfectly competitive market chooses its profit-maximizing output. We have seen how the actions of all the firms in a market combine to determine the market supply curve and how the market supply and demand curves determine the price and quantity. We have seen how a competitive industry operates in the short run, and we have studied the dynamic forces that move such a market to a long-run equilibrium. We have used the model of perfect competition to understand several important features of real-world markets. Finally, we have seen that under some specific circumstances, perfect competition delivers an economically efficient allocation of resources.

◆ ◆ Although many markets approximate the model of perfect competition, many do not. Our next task, in Chapters 12 and 13, is to study markets that depart from perfect competition. When we have completed this study, we'll have a toolkit of alternative models of markets that will enable us to study all the possible situations that arise in the real world. We begin, in the next chapter, by going to the opposite extreme of perfect competition—pure monopoly. Then, in Chapter 13, we'll study the markets between perfect competition and pure monopoly—monopolistic competition and oligopoly (competition among a few producers).

S U M M A R Y

Perfect Competition

Perfect competition occurs in a market in which a large number of firms produce an identical good, there are many buyers, firms face competition from potential new entrants, and all firms and buyers are fully informed about the prices charged by each firm. In perfect competition, each firm sells its good for the same price and no single firm can influence the market price. Even if one firm doubles its output, the industry output will change by a tiny percentage and the market price will hardly be affected at all. (pp. 280–282)

Firms' Choices in Perfect Competition

A competitive firm takes the market price and has to choose how much to produce, when to temporarily shut down, and when to permanently leave an industry. The firm's choices are motivated by its desire to maximize profit. Firms maximize profit by producing the output that makes marginal cost equal to marginal revenue.

A firm's maximum profit is not necessarily a positive profit. If price is above average total cost, the firm makes a profit. If price equals average total cost, the firm breaks even. If price is below average total cost, the firm makes a loss. If price is low enough, the firm maximizes profit by temporarily shutting down and laying off its workers. It pays to shut down production if price is below minimum average variable cost. When price equals minimum average variable cost, the firm makes a loss equal to its total fixed costs whether it produces the profit-maximizing output or shuts down.

The firm's supply curve is the upward-sloping part of its marginal cost curve at all points above the point of minimum average variable cost and runs along the vertical axis at all prices below minimum average variable cost. (pp. 282–290)

Output, Price, and Profit in the Short Run

The short-run industry supply curve shows how the total quantity supplied in the short run by all the firms in an industry varies as the market price varies.

The market price occurs where the quantity supplied and the quantity demanded are equal. Each firm takes the market price as given and chooses the output that maximizes profit. In short-run equilibrium, each firm can make an economic profit, make an economic loss, or break even. (pp. 290–292)

Output, Price, and Profit in the Long Run

If the firms in an industry make positive economic profits, existing firms will expand and new firms will enter the industry. If the firms in an industry make economic losses, some firms will leave the industry and the remaining firms will produce less. Entry and exit shift the industry supply curve. As firms enter, the industry supply curve shifts to the right. As firms leave, the industry supply curve shifts to the left. Entry causes profits of existing firms to fall, and exit causes profits of existing firms to rise (or losses to fall). In long-run equilibrium, firms make zero economic profit. No firm wants to enter or leave the industry, and no firm wants to expand or contract its production plant. Long-run competitive equilibrium occurs when each firm maximizes its short-run profit, economic profit is zero so there is no entry or exit, and each firm produces at the point of minimum long-run average cost, so it has no incentive to change its plant size. (pp. 292–296)

Responding to Changing Tastes and Advancing Technology

In a perfectly competitive market, a permanent decrease in demand leads to a lower industry output and a smaller number of firms in the industry. A permanent increase in demand leads to a rise in industry output and an increase in the number of firms in the industry. If there are no external economies or diseconomies, the market price remains constant in the long run as demand changes. If there are external economies, price falls in the long run as demand increases. If there are external diseconomies, price rises in the long run as demand increases.

New technology increases the industry supply, and in the long run the market price falls and the quantity sold increases. The number of firms in the industry falls. Firms that are slow to change to the new technology will make losses and eventually will go out of business. Firms that are quick to adopt the new technology will make economic profits initially, but in the long run they will make zero economic profit.

The farm problem of the 1980s can be interpreted by using the model of perfect competition. A large increase in interest rates—a fixed cost—increased average total cost and brought losses. These losses, in turn, forced many farms out of business. As the number of farms declines, the supply curve of farm products shifts to the left and prices increase. But this process takes time—time during which persistent losses occur in the farm sector. Eventually, after the adjustment process is complete, a smaller number of farms will break even. (pp. 296–305)

Competition and Efficiency

Allocative efficiency occurs when no one can be made better off without making someone else worse off. Three conditions for allocative efficiency—economic efficiency, consumer efficiency, and equality of marginal social cost and marginal social benefit—occur in perfect competition when there are no external costs and benefits. It is this situation that Adam Smith was describing when he talked of the economy being led by an "invisible hand."

There are two main obstacles to the achievement of allocative efficiency—the existence of external costs and external benefits and the existence of monopoly. (pp. 305–308)

KEY ELEMENTS

Key Terms

Allocative efficiency, 305
Average revenue, 282
Break-even point, 284
Entry, 293
Exit, 293
External benefits, 306
External costs, 306
External diseconomies, 302

External economies, 302
Marginal revenue, 282
Marginal social benefit, 306
Marginal social cost, 306
Perfect competition, 280
Perfectly competitive firm's supply curve, 289
Price taker, 280
Short-run industry supply curve, 290
Shutdown point, 287

Key Figures

Figure 11.2   Total Revenue, Total Cost, and Profit, 285

Figure 11.3   Marginal Revenue, Marginal Cost, and Profit-Maximizing Output, 286

Figure 11.5   Swanky's Supply Curve, 290

Figure 11.6   Firm and Industry Supply Curves, 291

Figure 11.13   Long-Run Changes in Price and Quantity, 299

Figure 11.16   Allocative Efficiency, 306

REVIEW QUESTIONS

1 What are the main features of a perfectly competitive industry?

2 Why can't a perfectly competitive firm influence the industry price?

3 List the three key decisions that a firm in a perfectly competitive industry has to make in order to maximize profit.

4 Why is marginal revenue equal to price in a perfectly competitive industry?

5 When will a perfectly competitive firm temporarily stop producing?

6 What is the connection between a competitive firm's supply curve and its marginal cost curve?

7 What is the relationship between a firm's supply curve and the short-run industry supply curve in a perfectly competitive industry?

8 Why do firms enter an industry?

9 What happens to the short-run industry supply curve when firms enter a competitive industry?

10 What is the effect of entry on the price and quantity produced?

11 What is the effect of entry on profit?

12 Trace the effects of a permanent increase in demand on price, quantity sold, number of firms, and profit.

13 Trace the effects of a permanent decrease in demand on price, quantity sold, number of firms, and profit.

14 Under what circumstances will a perfectly competitive industry have:

a A perfectly elastic long-run supply curve

b An upward-sloping long-run supply curve

c A downward-sloping long-run supply curve

15 Use the model of a perfectly competitive industry to explain why such a large number of farms went out of business in the 1980s.

16 What is allocative efficiency and under what circumstances does it arise?

PROBLEMS

1 Suppose that a firm produces one hundredth of an industry's output. The elasticity of the industry's demand is 4. What is the elasticity of the firm's demand?

2 Why have the prices of pocket calculators and VCRs fallen?

3 What has been the effect of a rise in world population on the wheat market and the individual wheat farmer?

4 Pat's Pizza Kitchen is a price taker. It has the following hourly costs:

Output (pizzas per hour)	Total cost (dollars per hour)
0	10
1	21
2	30
3	41
4	54
5	69
6	86

a If pizzas sell for $14, what is Pat's profit-maximizing output per hour? What is his profit?

b   What is Pat's shutdown point?

c   Derive Pat's supply curve.

d   What price will cause Pat to leave the pizza industry?

e   What price will cause other firms with costs identical to Pat's to enter the industry?

f   What is the long-run equilibrium price of pizzas?

5 How has the diaper service industry been affected by the fall in the U.S. birth rate and the development of disposable diapers?

6 The market demand schedule for record albums is as follows:

Price (dollars per album)	Quantity demanded (albums per week)
3.65	500,000
4.40	475,000
5.20	450,000
6.00	425,000
6.80	400,000
7.60	375,000
8.40	350,000
9.20	325,000
10.00	300,000
10.80	275,000
11.60	250,000
12.40	225,000
13.20	200,000
14.00	175,000
14.80	150,000

The market is perfectly competitive, and each firm has the same cost structure, described by the following table:

Output (albums per week)	Marginal cost (dollars per album)	Average variable cost (dollars per album)	Average total cost (dollars per album)
150	6.00	8.80	15.47
200	6.40	7.80	12.80
250	7.00	7.00	11.00
300	7.65	7.10	10.43
350	8.40	7.20	10.06
400	10.00	7.50	10.00
450	12.40	8.00	10.22
500	12.70	9.00	11.00

There are 1,000 firms in the industry.

a   What is the industry price?

b   What is the industry's output?

c   What is the output of each firm?

d   What is the economic profit of each firm?

e   What is the shutdown point?

f   What is the long-run equilibrium price?

g   What is the number of firms in the long run?

7 The same demand conditions as those in problem 6 prevail and there are still 1,000 firms in the industry, but fixed costs increase by $980.

a   What is the short-run profit-maximizing output for each firm?

b   Do firms enter or exit the industry in the long run?

c   What is the new long-run equilibrium price?

d   What is the new long-run equilibrium number of firms in the industry?

8 The same cost conditions as those in problem 6 prevail and there are 1,000 firms in the industry, but the falling price of compact discs decreases the demand for record albums and the demand schedule becomes as follows:

Price (dollars per album)	Quantity demanded (albums per week)
2.95	500,000
3.54	475,000
4.13	450,000
4.71	425,000
5.30	400,000
5.89	375,000
6.48	350,000
7.06	325,000
7.65	300,000
8.24	275,000
8.83	250,000
9.41	225,000
10.00	200,000
10.59	175,000
11.18	150,000

a   What is the short-run profit-maximizing output for each firm?

b   Do firms enter or exit the industry in the long run?

c   What is the new long-run equilibrium price?

d   What is the new long-run equilibrium number of firms in the industry?

CHAPTER 12

MONOPOLY

After studying this chapter, you will be able to:

- ◆ Define monopoly

- ◆ Explain the conditions under which monopoly arises

- ◆ Distinguish between legal monopoly and natural monopoly

- ◆ Explain how a monopoly determines its price and output

- ◆ Define price discrimination

- ◆ Explain why price discrimination leads to a bigger profit

- ◆ Compare the performance of a competitive and a monopolistic industry

- ◆ Define rent seeking and explain why it arises

- ◆ Explain the conditions under which monopoly is more efficient than competition

YOU HAVE BEEN READING A LOT IN THIS BOOK ABOUT firms that want to maximize profit. But perhaps you've been looking around at some of the places where you do business and wondering whether they are really so intent on profit. After all, don't you get a student's discount when you get a haircut? Don't museums and movie theaters give discounts to students, too? And what about the airline that gives a discount for buying a ticket in advance? Are your barber and movie theater owner, as well as the museum and airline operators, simply generous folks to whom the model of profit-maximizing firms does not apply? Aren't they simply throwing profit away by cutting ticket prices and offering discounts? ◆ ◆ When you want a phone line installed, you really have only one choice—you have to call the local phone company. If you live in New York City and want to buy cable TV service, you have only one option: buy from Manhattan Cable. Regardless of where

The Profits of Generosity

you live, you have no choice about the supplier of your local phone service, gas, electricity, or water. If you want to mail a letter, there is only one producer of letter-carrying services (aside from expensive couriers), the U.S. Postal Service. These are all examples of a single producer of a good or service controlling its supply. Such firms are obviously not like firms in perfectly competitive industries. They don't face a market-determined price. They can choose their own price. How do such firms behave? How do they choose the quantity to produce and the price at which to sell it? How does their behavior compare with that of firms in perfectly competitive industries? Do such firms charge prices that are too high and that damage the interests of consumers? And do such firms bring any benefits?

◆ ◆ ◆ ◆ In this chapter we study markets in which individual firms can influence the quantity of goods supplied and, as a consequence, exert an influence on price. We analyze the price and quantity decisions of such firms when they sell all their output at the same price to all their customers. After that, we study markets in which a firm can charge a higher price to some customers than others. We also compare the performance of a firm in such an industry with that of a competitive firm and examine whether monopoly is as efficient as competition.

How Monopoly Arises

A monopoly is an industry in which there is one supplier of a good, service, or resource that has no close substitutes and in which there is a barrier preventing the entry of new firms. The supply of local phone services, gas, electricity, and water are examples of local monopolies—monopolies restricted to a given location. The U.S. Postal Service is an example of a national monopoly—a sole supplier of letter-carrying service.

Barriers to Entry

The key feature of a monopoly is the existence of barriers preventing the entry of new firms. **Barriers to entry** are legal or natural impediments protecting a firm from competition from potential new entrants.

Legal Barriers to Entry   Legal barriers to entry give rise to legal monopoly. **Legal monopoly** occurs when a law, license, or patent restricts competition by preventing entry.

The first type of legal barrier to entry is a public franchise. A **public franchise** is an exclusive right granted to a firm to supply a good or service. An example of a public franchise is the U.S. Postal Service, which has the exclusive right to carry first-class mail. Another common form of public franchise occurs on freeways and turnpikes where particular firms are given exclusive rights to sell gasoline and food services.

A second legal barrier is a government license. A **government license** controls entry into particular occupations, professions, and industries. Government licensing in the professions is the most important example of this type of barrier to entry. For example, a license is required to practice medicine, law, dentistry, schoolteaching, architecture, and a variety of other professional services and industries. Licensing does not create monopoly, but it does restrict competition.

A third legal restriction on entry is a patent. A **patent** is an exclusive right granted by the government to the inventor of a product or service. A patent is valid for a limited time period that varies from country to country. In the United States, a patent is valid for 17 years. Patents protect inventors by creating a property right and thereby encourage invention by preventing others from copying an invention until sufficient time has elapsed for the inventor to have reaped some benefits. They also stimulate *innovation*—the use of new inventions—by increasing the incentives for inventors to publicize their discoveries and offer them for use under license.

Natural Barriers to Entry   Natural barriers to entry give rise to natural monopoly. **Natural monopoly** occurs when there is a unique source of supply of a raw material or when one firm can supply the entire market at a lower price than two or more firms can. As the definition of natural monopoly implies, natural barriers to entry take two forms. First, a single firm may own and control the entire supply of a mineral or natural resource. This type of monopoly occurs in the production of particular types of mineral water for which there is just a single, unique source and for some raw materials such as diamonds and chromium. De Beers, a South African company, for example, owns and controls four fifths of the world's diamond mines. Also, all the sources of chromium, again concentrated in southern Africa, are controlled by a small number of producers.

Natural monopoly can also arise because of economies of scale. When a single producer can supply the entire market at a lower average total cost of production than can two or more firms, then only a single firm can survive in the industry. Examples of natural monopoly arising from economies of scale are public utilities, such as the distribution of electricity, natural gas, and water.

Most monopolies in the real world, whether legal or natural, are regulated in some way by government or by government agencies. We will study such regulation in Chapter 21. Here we will consider an unregulated monopoly for two important reasons. First, we can better understand why governments regulate monopolies and the effects of regulation if we also know how an unregulated monopoly would behave. Second, even in industries with more than one producer, firms often have a degree of monopoly power, arising from locational advantages or from important differences in product quality protected by patents. The theory of monopoly sheds important light on the behavior of such firms and industries.

We will begin by studying the behavior of a single-price monopoly. A **single-price monopoly** is a monopoly that charges the same price for each and every unit of its output. How does a single-price monopoly determine the quantity to produce and the price to charge for its output?

Single-Price Monopoly

The starting point for understanding how a single-price monopoly chooses its price and output is to work out the relationship between the demand for the good produced by the monopoly and the monopoly's revenue.

Demand and Revenue

Since in a monopoly there is only one firm, the demand curve facing that firm is the industry demand curve. Let's look at an example—Bobbie's Barbershop, the sole supplier of haircuts in Cairo, Nebraska. The demand schedule that Bobbie faces is set out in Table 12.1. At a price of $20, Bobbie sells no haircuts. The lower the price, the more haircuts per hour Bobbie is able to sell. For example, at a price of $12, consumers demand 4 haircuts per hour (row *e*), and at a price of $4, they demand 8 haircuts per hour (row *i*).

Total revenue (*TR*) is the price (*P*) multiplied by the quantity sold (*Q*). For example, in row *d*, Bobbie sells 3 haircuts at $14 each, so total revenue is $42. *Marginal revenue* (*MR*) is the change in total revenue (ΔTR) resulting from a one-unit rise in the quantity sold. For example, if the price falls from $18 (row *b*) to $16 (row *c*), the quantity sold rises from 1 to 2 haircuts. Total revenue rises from $18 to

TABLE 12.1

Single-Price Monopoly's Revenue

	Price (*P*) (dollars per haircut)	Quantity demanded (*Q*) (haircuts per hour)	Total revenue (*TR* = *P* × *Q*) (dollars)	Marginal revenue (*MR* = $\Delta TR/\Delta Q$) (dollars per haircut)
a	20	0	0	
				18
b	18	1	18	
				14
c	16	2	32	
				10
d	14	3	42	
				6
e	12	4	48	
				2
f	10	5	50	
				−2
g	8	6	48	
				−6
h	6	7	42	
				−10
i	4	8	32	
				−14
j	2	9	18	
				−18
k	0	10	0	

The table shows Bobbie's demand schedule—the number of haircuts demanded per hour at each price. Total revenue (*TR*) is price multiplied by quantity sold. For example, row *c* shows that when the price is $16 a haircut, two haircuts are sold for a total revenue of $32. Marginal revenue (*MR*) is the change in total revenue resulting from a one-unit increase in the quantity sold. For example, when the price falls from $16 to $14 a haircut, the quantity sold increases from 2 to 3 haircuts and total revenue increases by $10. The marginal revenue from the third haircut is $10. Total revenue rises through row *f*, where 5 haircuts are sold for $10, and it falls thereafter. In the output range over which total revenue is increasing, marginal revenue is positive; in the output range over which total revenue is decreasing, marginal revenue is negative.

$32, so the change in total revenue is $14. Since the quantity sold rises by 1 haircut, marginal revenue equals the change in total revenue and is $14. When recording marginal revenue, we write it between two rows to emphasize that marginal revenue relates to the *change* in the quantity sold.

Figure 12.1 shows Bobbie's demand curve (*D*). Each row of Table 12.1 corresponds to a point on the demand curve. For example, row *d* in the table and point *d* on the demand curve tell us that at a price of $14, Bobbie sells 3 haircuts. The figure also

FIGURE **12.1**

Demand and Marginal Revenue for a Single-Price Monopoly

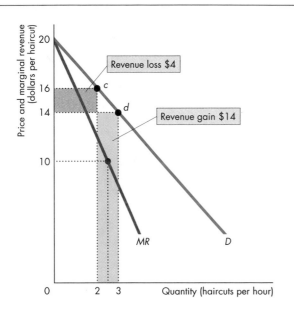

The monopoly demand curve (*D*) is based on the numbers in Table 12.1. At a price of $16 a haircut, Bobbie sells 2 haircuts an hour. If she lowers the price to $14, she sells 3 haircuts an hour. The sale of the third haircut brings a revenue gain of $14 (the price charged for the third haircut). But there is a revenue loss of $4 ($2 per haircut) on the 2 haircuts that she could have sold for $16 each. The marginal revenue (extra total revenue) from the third haircut is the difference between the revenue gain and the revenue loss—$10. The marginal revenue curve (*MR*) shows the marginal revenue at each level of sales. Marginal revenue is lower than price.

shows Bobbie's marginal revenue curve (*MR*). Notice that the marginal revenue curve is below the demand curve. That is, at each level of output, marginal revenue is less than price. Why is marginal revenue less than price? It is because when the price is lowered to sell one more unit, there are two opposing effects on total revenue. The lower price results in a revenue loss, and the increased quantity sold results in a revenue gain. For example, at a price of $16, Bobbie sells 2 haircuts (point *c*). If she reduces the price to $14, she sells 3 haircuts and has a revenue gain of $14 on the third haircut. But she receives only $14 on the first two as well—$2 less than before—so her revenue loss on the first 2 haircuts is $4. She has to deduct this amount from the

revenue gain of $14. Marginal revenue—the difference between the revenue gain and the revenue loss—is $10.

Figure 12.2 shows Bobbie's demand curve (*D*), marginal revenue curve (*MR*), and total revenue curve (*TR*) and illustrates the connections between them. Again, each row in Table 12.1 corresponds to a point on the curves. For example, row *d* in the table and point *d* on the graphs tell us that when 3 haircuts are sold for $14 each (part a), total revenue is $42 (part b). Notice that as the quantity sold rises, total revenue rises to a peak of $50 (point *f*) and then declines. To understand the behavior of total revenue, notice what happens to marginal revenue as the quantity sold increases. Over the range 0 to 5 haircuts, marginal revenue is positive. When more than 5 haircuts are sold, marginal revenue becomes negative. The output range over which marginal revenue is positive is the same as that over which total revenue is rising. The output range over which marginal revenue is negative is the same as that over which total revenue declines. When marginal revenue is zero, total revenue is at a maximum.

Revenue and Elasticity

When we studied elasticity in Chapter 5, we discovered a connection between the elasticity of demand and the effect of a change in price on total expenditure or total revenue. Let's refresh our memories of that connection.

Recall that the elasticity of demand is the percentage change in the quantity demanded divided by the percentage change in price. If a 1 percent decrease in price results in a greater than 1 percent increase in the quantity demanded, the elasticity of demand is greater than 1 and demand is *elastic*. If a 1 percent decrease in price results in a less than 1 percent increase in the quantity demanded, the elasticity of demand is less than 1 and demand is *inelastic*. If a 1 percent decrease in price results in a 1 percent increase in the quantity demanded, the elasticity of demand is 1 and demand is *unit elastic*.

The elasticity of demand influences the change in total revenue. If demand is elastic, total revenue increases when the price decreases; if demand is inelastic, total revenue decreases when the price decreases; and if demand is unit elastic, total revenue does not change when the price changes.

The output range over which total revenue increases when the price decreases is the same as

FIGURE 12.2

A Single-Price Monopoly's Revenue Curves

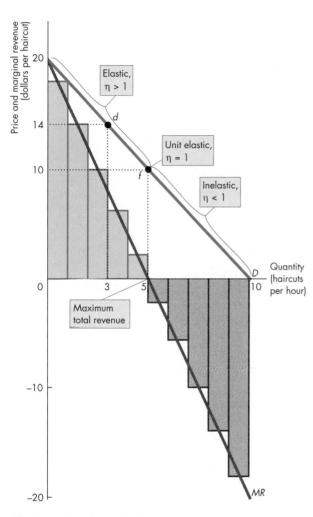

(a) Demand and marginal revenue curves

(b) Total revenue curve

Bobbie's demand curve (*D*) and marginal revenue curve (*MR*), shown in part (a), and total revenue curve (*TR*), shown in part (b), are based on the numbers in Table 12.1. For example, at a price of $14, Bobbie sells 3 haircuts an hour (point *d* in part a) for a total revenue of $42 (point *d* in part b). Over the range 0 to 5 haircuts an hour, total revenue is increasing and marginal revenue is positive, as shown by the blue bars. Over the range 5 to 10 haircuts an hour, total revenue declines—marginal revenue is negative, as shown by the red bars. Over the output range for which marginal revenue is positive, demand is elastic. Over the output range for which marginal revenue is negative, demand is inelastic. At the output at which marginal revenue is zero, demand is unit elastic.

that over which marginal revenue is positive—shown in Fig. 12.2. Thus the output range over which marginal revenue is positive is also the output range over which demand is elastic—over which the elasticity of demand is greater than 1. The output range over which total revenue decreases when price decreases is the same as that over which marginal revenue is negative. Thus the output range over which marginal revenue is negative is also the output range over which demand is inelastic—over which the elasticity of demand is less than 1. The output at which total revenue remains constant when price decreases is that at which marginal revenue is zero. Thus the output at which marginal revenue is zero is also the output at which demand is unit elastic—at which the elasticity of demand is 1.

The relationship that you have just discovered has an important implication: a profit-maximizing monopoly never produces an output in the inelastic range of its demand curve. If it did so, marginal revenue would be negative—each additional unit sold would lower total revenue. In such a situation, it always pays to charge a higher price and sell a smaller quantity. But exactly what price and quantity does a profit-maximizing monopoly firm choose?

Price and Output Decision

Profit is the difference between total revenue and total cost. To determine the output level and price that maximize a monopoly's profit, we need to study the behavior of both revenue and costs as output varies.

A monopoly faces the same types of technology and cost constraints as a competitive firm. The monopoly has a production function that is subject to diminishing returns. The monopoly buys its inputs in competition with other firms at prices that it cannot influence. The sole difference between the monopoly that we'll study here and a perfectly competitive firm lies in the market constraint for the output that each firm faces. The competitive firm is a price taker, whereas the monopoly supplies the entire market. Because the monopoly supplies the entire market, its output decision affects the price at which that output is sold. It is this fact that gives rise to the difference between the decisions faced by these two types of firm.

We have already looked at Bobbie's revenue in Table 12.1 and Figs. 12.1 and 12.2. The revenue information contained in Fig. 12.3 is extracted from

FIGURE **12.3**

A Monopoly's Output and Price

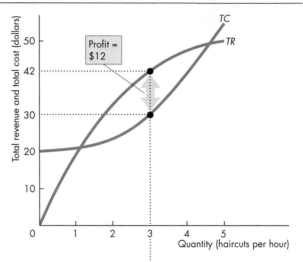

(a) Total revenue and total cost curves

(b) Total profit curve

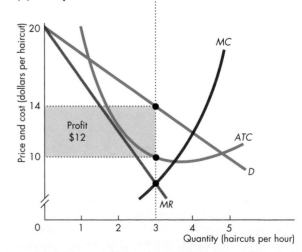

(c) Demand and marginal revenue and cost curves

FIGURE **12.3 (continued)**

Price (P) (dollars per haircut)	Quantity demanded (Q) (haircuts per hour)	Total revenue ($TR = P \times Q$) (dollars)	Marginal revenue ($MR = \Delta TR/\Delta Q$) (dollars per haircut)	Total cost (TC) (dollars)	Marginal cost ($MC = \Delta TC/\Delta Q$) (dollars per haircut)	Profit ($TR - TC$) (dollars)
20	0	0		20		−20
			18		1	
18	1	18		21		−3
			14		3	
16	2	32		24		+8
			10		6	
14	3	42		30		+12
			6		10	
12	4	48		40		+8
			2		15	
10	5	50		55		−5

The table adds information about total cost (*TC*), marginal cost (*MC*), and profit (*TR − TC*) to the information on demand and revenue in Table 12.1. For example, at a price of $16, 2 haircuts will be sold for a total revenue of $32. The total cost of producing 2 haircuts is $24, so profit equals $8 ($32 − $24). Profit is at a maximum in the row highlighted in red in the table.

The numbers in the table are graphed in the three parts of the figure. The total cost and total revenue curves appear in part (a). The vertical distance between total revenue (*TR*) and total cost (*TC*) equals total profit. Maximum profit occurs at 3 haircuts an hour. Part (b) shows the total profit curve. This curve reaches a maximum at 3 haircuts an

hour. The total profit curve is at a maximum (part b) when the vertical distance between the total revenue and total cost curves is also at a maximum (part a). Where total revenue equals total cost (in part a), the total profit curve cuts the horizontal axis (in part b). Part (c) shows that at the profit-maximizing output of 3 haircuts, marginal cost (*MC*) equals marginal revenue (*MR*). The monopoly sells the output for the maximum possible price as determined by its demand curve. In this case, that price is $14. The monopoly's profit is illustrated in part (c) by the blue rectangle. That profit is $12—the profit per haircut ($4) multiplied by 3 haircuts.

Table 12.1. The figure also contains information on Bobbie's costs and profit.

Total cost (*TC*) rises as output increases, and so does total revenue (*TR*). Profit equals total revenue minus total cost. As you can see in the table in Fig. 12.3, the maximum profit ($12) occurs when Bobbie sells 3 haircuts for $14 each. If she sells 2 haircuts for $16 each or 4 haircuts for $12 each, her profit will be only $8.

You can see why 3 haircuts is the profit-maximizing output by looking at the marginal revenue and marginal cost columns. When Bobbie increases output from 2 to 3 haircuts, she generates a marginal revenue of $10 and incurs a marginal cost of $6. Profit increases by the difference—$4. If Bobbie increases output yet further, from 3 to 4 haircuts, she generates a marginal revenue of $6 and a marginal cost of $10. In this case, marginal cost exceeds marginal revenue by $4, so profit falls by $4. It always pays to produce more if marginal revenue

exceeds marginal cost and to produce less if marginal cost exceeds marginal revenue. It pays to produce neither more nor less when marginal cost and marginal revenue are equal to each other. Thus the profit-maximizing output occurs when marginal revenue equals marginal cost.

The information set out in the table is shown graphically in Fig. 12.3. Part (a) shows Bobbie's total revenue curve (*TR*) and total cost curve (*TC*). Profit is the vertical distance between *TR* and *TC*. Bobbie maximizes her profit at 3 haircuts an hour—profit is $42 minus $30, or $12. Part (b) shows how her profit varies with the number of haircuts sold.

Figure 12.3(c) shows the demand curve (*D*) and the marginal revenue curve (*MR*) along with the marginal cost curve (*MC*) and average total cost curve (*ATC*). The profit-maximizing output is 3 haircuts, where marginal cost equals marginal revenue. The price charged is found by reading from the demand curve the highest price at which 3 haircuts can be sold. That price is $14. When Bobbie produces 3 haircuts, average total cost is $10 (read from the *ATC* curve). Her profit per haircut is $4 ($14 minus $10). Bobbie's total profit is indicated by the blue rectangle, which equals the profit per haircut ($4) multiplied by the number of haircuts (3), for a total profit of $12. Since price always *exceeds* marginal revenue and, at the profit-maximizing output, marginal revenue equals marginal cost, price always exceeds marginal cost. (The theory of monopoly price determination shown in Fig. 12.3c was first worked out by the brilliant Joan Robinson—see Our Advancing Knowledge on pp. 322–323.)

Bobbie makes a positive profit. But there is nothing to guarantee that a monopoly will be able to make a profit. A monopoly can make a zero profit or even, in the short run, a loss. Figure 12.4 shows the conditions under which these other two outcomes will occur.

If Bobbie's average total cost is ATC_a, as shown in Fig. 12.4(a), then the profit-maximizing output, where marginal revenue equals marginal cost, will

be 3 haircuts. At this output, average cost just equals price, so both the profit per haircut and total profit are zero. If Bobbie's average total cost curve is ATC_b, as shown in Fig. 12.4(b), then marginal cost equals marginal revenue at 3 haircuts and average total cost is $16. But 3 haircuts can only be sold for $14 each, so Bobbie makes a loss of $2 a haircut. That loss, however, is the minimum possible loss, so Bobbie is still maximizing profit. A monopoly that makes a loss will do so only in the short run. If the situation shown in Fig. 12.3(b) were permanent, Bobbie would go out of business.

When we studied a competitive firm, we checked to see whether price was higher or lower than average variable cost. With a price below average variable cost, it pays a firm to shut down temporarily and produce nothing. It makes a loss equal to total fixed cost. Like a competitive firm, Bobbie also needs to check average variable cost to see whether it pays to shut down temporarily. There is no point in any firm—competitor or monopoly—making a loss that exceeds total fixed cost.

FIGURE **12.4**

Short-Run Profit, Costs, and Demand

(a) Zero profit

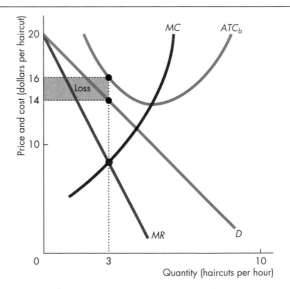

(b) Loss

In the short run, a monopoly can make zero profit or even a loss. Part (a) shows a monopoly making zero profit. At the profit-maximizing output—3 haircuts an hour—average total cost and price are $14 each. Part (b) shows a monopoly making a short-run loss. In this case, at the

profit-maximizing output (again 3 haircuts an hour), average total cost is $16 and price is $14, so the firm incurs a loss of $6. The loss is represented by the red rectangle.

If firms in a perfectly competitive industry are making a positive economic profit, new firms enter. That does not happen in a monopoly industry. Barriers to entry prevent new firms from entering. So a firm can make a positive economic profit and continue to do so indefinitely in a monopoly industry. Sometimes that profit is large, as in the cable TV industry.

No Monopoly Supply Curve

Unlike a perfectly competitive firm, a monopoly does not have a supply curve. Recall that a supply curve shows the quantity supplied at each price. A change in demand in a competitive industry results in the industry moving along its supply curve and each firm moving along its marginal cost curve. A change in demand in a monopoly also produces a change in price and quantity, but the monopoly does not slide along a supply curve. Instead, given the new demand conditions, the monopoly picks the combination of output and price that maximizes profit, given its cost curves. As in competitive conditions, the monopoly chooses to sell a quantity such that marginal revenue equals marginal cost. But the relationship between price and marginal revenue, and that between price and marginal cost, depends on the shape of the demand curve. For a given profit-maximizing quantity, the steeper the demand curve, the higher is the price at which that quantity is sold. It is for this reason that there is no unique relationship between the monopoly's profit-maximizing quantity and price and therefore no such thing as a monopoly's supply curve.

A single-price monopoly maximizes profit by producing an output at which marginal cost equals marginal revenue. At that output, the monopoly charges the highest price that consumers are willing to pay. Since a monopoly's price exceeds its marginal revenue, its price also exceeds its marginal cost. But there is no guarantee that a monopoly will make a profit in the short run. Depending on its cost curves and the demand for its output, the monopoly might make a positive economic profit, make a zero profit, or incur a loss. But a monopoly can make a positive economic profit even in the long run, since

there are barriers to the entry of new firms. There is no unique relationship between the quantity that a monopoly produces and its price—there is no monopoly supply curve. ◆

Price Discrimination

Price discrimination is the practice of charging some customers a higher price than others for an identical good or of charging an individual customer a higher price on a small purchase than on a large one. An example of price discrimination is the practice of charging children or students a lower price than adults to see a movie. Another example is the common practice of barbers and hairdressers giving discounts to senior citizens and students. Price discrimination can be practiced in varying degrees. **Perfect price discrimination** occurs when a firm charges a different price for each unit sold and charges each consumer the maximum price that he or she is willing to pay for each unit. Though perfect price discrimination does not happen in the real world, it shows the limit to which price discrimination can be taken.

Not all price *differences* imply price *discrimination*. In many situations, goods that are similar but not identical have different costs and sell for different prices *because* they have different costs. For example, we saw in Chapter 10 that the marginal cost of producing electricity depends on the time of day. If an electric power company charges a higher price for consumption between 7:00 and 9:00 in the morning and between 4:00 and 7:00 in the evening than it does at other times of the day, this practice is not called price discrimination. Price discrimination charges varying prices to consumers, not because of differences in the cost of producing the good but because different consumers have different demands for the good.

At first sight, it appears that price discrimination contradicts the assumption of profit maximization. Why would a movie operator charge children half price? Why would a hairdresser or barber charge students and senior citizens less? Aren't these producers losing profit by being nice guys?

UNDERSTANDING
Monopoly
POWER

Monopolies may well be greedy, but are they able to convert their greed into higher prices than those charged by competitive firms? If so, to what extent? And being big, are monopolies able to exploit their workers and suppliers, paying lower wages and prices than smaller firms must pay?

These questions puzzled generations of economists. Adam Smith said, "The price of a monopoly is upon every occasion the highest which can be got." But Smith was wrong. The questions were first answered correctly by Antoine-August Cournot, although his answer was not appreciated until almost a century later when Joan Robinson explained how monopolies behave.

Questions about monopoly behavior took on an urgent and practical tone during the 1870s, a time when rapid technological change and falling transportation costs enabled huge monopolies to emerge in the United States. Monopolies dominated oil, steel, railroads, tobacco, and even sugar, and industrial empires grew ever larger.

The success of the nineteenth-century monopolies led to the creation of our antitrust laws—laws that limit the use of monopoly power. Those laws have been used to prevent monopolies from being set up and to break up existing monopolies. They were used in the 1960s to break up a conspiracy between General Electric and Westinghouse when they colluded to fix their prices instead of competing against each other. The laws were also used in the 1980s to bring greater competition in long-distance telecommunications. But in spite of antitrust laws, monopolies still exist. One of the most prominent is cable television. Like their notorious forerunners, the cable television companies use their monopoly power and make large profits.

> "People in the same trade seldom meet together, even for merriment and diversion, but the conversation ends in . . . some contrivance to raise prices."
>
> **ADAM SMITH**
> *The Wealth of Nations*

Ruthless greed, exploitation of both workers and customers—these are the traditional images of monopolies and the effects of their power. And these images appeared to be an accurate description in the 1880s, when monopolies were at their peak of power and influence. One monopolist, John D. Rockefeller, Sr., had built his giant Standard Oil Company, which, by 1879, was refining 90 percent of the nation's oil and controlling its entire pipeline capacity.

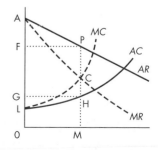

In spite of antitrust laws that regulate monopolies, they still exist. One of the most prominent is that in cable television. In most cities, one firm decides which channels viewers will receive and the price they will pay. During the 1980s, with the advent of satellite technology and specialist cable program producers such as CNN and HBO, the cable companies expanded their offerings. At the same time, they steadily increased prices and their businesses became very profitable. Are the local cable companies exploiting their customers? What would happen to their prices if they were regulated? And what would happen to the number of channels and to the quality and variety of the programs they offered?

At the age of thirty, Joan Robinson (1903–1983) published *The Economics of Imperfect Competition*, a book that revolutionized industrial economics, introduced *marginal revenue* into the economics vocabulary, and originated the modern diagram of monopoly price, output, and profit. (Compare the figure with Figure 12.3c.)

JOAN ROBINSON: DISCOVERING *the Limits to Monopoly Power*

Robinson was a formidable debater and reveled in verbal battles, a notable one of which was with the famous MIT economist Paul Samuelson. Anxious to make a point on the blackboard, Samuelson asked Robinson for the chalk. Monopolizing the chalk and board, the unyielding Robinson snapped, "Say it in words, young man."

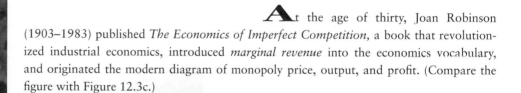

This story illustrates Joan Robinson's approach to economics: work out the answers to economic problems using the most powerful methods of logic available, but then "say it in words." Don't be satisfied with a formal argument if you don't *understand* it.

323

Deeper investigation shows that far from losing profit, price discriminators actually make a bigger profit than they would otherwise. Thus a monopoly has an incentive to try to find ways of discriminating among groups of consumers and charging each group the highest possible price. Some people may pay less with price discrimination, but others pay more. How does price discrimination bring in more total revenue?

Price Discrimination and Total Revenue

The total revenue received by a single-price monopoly equals the quantity sold multiplied by the single price charged. That revenue is illustrated in Fig. 12.5(a). Suppose that Bobbie sells 4 haircuts for a single price of $12 each. Bobbie's total revenue, $48, is the area of the blue rectangle—the quantity sold, 4 haircuts, multiplied by the price, $12.

Now suppose that Bobbie can sell some haircuts for one price and some for another, higher price. Figure 12.5(b) illustrates this case. The first 2 haircuts are sold for $16 each, and then two more are

sold for the original price, $12. In this case, Bobbie has greater total revenue than when she charges a single price. The extra revenue earned on the first 2 haircuts sold has to be added to the original revenue. Total revenue, the blue area shown in part (b), is $56 (2 at $12 plus 2 at $16).

What will happen if Bobbie can perfectly price discriminate? The answer is shown in Fig. 12.5(c). Each haircut is sold for the maximum possible price. The first haircut sells for $18, the next for $16, the third for $14, and the fourth for $12. Total revenue, the blue area in part (c), is $60.

Price Discrimination and Consumer Surplus

Demand curves slope down because the value that an individual places on a good falls as the quantity consumed of that good rises. When all the units consumed can be bought for a single price, consumers benefit. We call this benefit *consumer surplus*. (If you need to refresh your understanding of consumer

---

FIGURE 12.5

Total Revenue and Price Discrimination

(a) One price

(b) Two prices

(c) Many prices

If Bobbie sells 4 haircuts for the same price—$12 each—her total revenue is $48, as shown by the blue rectangle in part (a). If she charges two prices—$16 each for the first 2 haircuts and $12 each for the next 2—her total revenue will be $56, as shown by the blue area in part (b). If Bobbie charges four different prices—$18 for the first haircut, $16 for

the second haircut, $14 for the third haircut, and $12 for the fourth haircut—her total revenue will be $60, as shown by the blue area in part (c). The more finely a monopoly can discriminate, the larger is the total revenue from a given level of sales.

surplus, flip back to Chapter 7, p. 171.) Price discrimination can be seen as an attempt by a monopoly to capture the consumer surplus (or as much of the surplus as possible) for itself.

Discriminating among Units of a Good   One form of price discrimination charges each single buyer a different price on each unit of a good bought. An example of this type of discrimination is a discount for bulk buying. The larger the order, the larger is the discount—and the lower is the price. This type of price discrimination works because each individual's demand curve slopes downward. For example, suppose that Lisa is willing to pay $7 to see one movie a month, $6 to see two, and $5 to see three. If movies cost $5, she sees three and pays $5 for each. But the value to her of the first movie is $7—$2 more than she pays for it. And the value to her of the second movie is $6—$1 more than she pays for it. Lisa's consumer surplus is $3.

Now imagine that a movie theater offers the following monthly subscription. For $7, you can see one movie a month; for $13, you can see two movies a month; for $18, you can see three movies a month. If Lisa opts for the three-movie package, the movie theater extracts from Lisa her entire consumer surplus. But to extract every dollar of consumer surplus from every buyer, the monopolist would have to offer each individual customer a separate contract based on that customer's own demand curve. Clearly, such price discrimination cannot be carried out in practice because a firm does not have sufficient information about each individual consumer's demand curve to be able to do the necessary calculations. But by making arrangements of the type just described that extract most of the consumer surplus of a typical customer, firms can move somewhere toward perfect price discrimination.

Discriminating among Individuals   Even when it is not possible to charge each individual a different price for each unit bought, it might still be possible to discriminate among individuals. This possibility arises from the fact that some people place a higher value on consuming one more unit of a good than do other individuals. By charging such an individual a higher price, the producer can obtain some of the consumer surplus that would otherwise accrue to its customers.

Let's look a bit more closely at the price and output decisions of a monopoly that practices price discrimination.

Price and Output Decisions with Price Discrimination

Price discrimination often takes the form of discriminating between different groups of consumers on the basis of age, employment status, or other easily distinguished characteristics. Price discrimination works only if each group has a different price elasticity of demand for the product. If one group has a high elasticity and the other a low elasticity, then a firm can increase profit by charging a lower price to the group with the high elasticity and a higher price to the group with a low elasticity.

Let's stick with the example of haircuts. Bobbie suspects that the students and the elderly of Cairo have a higher elasticity of demand for haircuts than do other people—they do not seem to care as much about getting a bit shaggy as do the business people and homemakers. Let's see how Bobbie exploits these differences in demand and raises her profit by price discriminating. Until now, Bobbie has sold 3 haircuts an hour at $14 a haircut, for a total revenue of $42. With a total cost of $30 an hour, Bobbie makes an hourly profit of $12. Bobbie's costs, revenues, and profit are shown in the table in Fig. 12.3.

Bobbie has noticed that students and elderly customers come in less frequently than other clients. In fact, of the 3 haircuts she does each hour, 2 are for business people or homemakers and only 1 for an elderly customer or a student. Bobbie also suspects that the business people and homemakers will still turn up for haircuts at the rate of 2 an hour even if she charges them a higher price. She knows that to get more students and seniors, she has to lower the price she charges them. Bobbie decides to try price discriminating between the two groups. But she has to figure out what price to charge each group to maximize her profit.

Table 12.2 sets out the calculations that Bobbie performs. It shows Bobbie's estimates of the demand schedules for her two groups of customers. It also shows the total revenue and marginal revenue calculations for the two separate groups. Bobbie's marginal costs are the same for both groups—hair is hair, whether it belongs to a student or a homemaker. But marginal revenue differs between the two

TABLE 12.2

Profiting from Price Discrimination

Price (P) (dollars per haircut)	Students and the elderly				Others			
	Quantity demanded (Q) (haircuts per hour)	Total revenue (TR) (dollars)	Marginal revenue (MR) (dollars per haircut)		Quantity demanded (Q) (haircuts per hour)	Total revenue (TR) (dollars)	Marginal revenue (MR) (dollars per haircut)	
20	0	0			0	0		
			0				18	
18	0	0			1	18		
			0				14	
16	0	0			2	32		
			14				−4	
14	1	14			2	28		
			10				−4	
12	2	24			2	24		
			6				−4	
10	3	30			2	20		

Profit calculation:

Profit = *TR* − *TC* = ($12 × 2) + ($16 × 2) − $40 = $16.

As a single-price monopoly, Bobbie sells 3 haircuts an hour for $14 each and makes a maximum profit of $12, as was shown in Fig. 12.3. By discriminating between two groups of customers—the first group consisting of students and the elderly and the second group consisting of all other customers—Bobbie is able to make a bigger profit. She raises the price of regular haircuts to $16 and lowers the price for students and the elderly to $12. Her sales increase to 4 haircuts an hour, and her profit rises to $16.

groups of customers. For example, when the price falls from $18 to $16, the marginal revenue from students and the elderly is zero, while for others it is $14. When the price falls from $16 to $14, the marginal revenue from students and the elderly is $14, while that from others is *minus* $4.

Bobbie calculates her profit-maximizing prices and output in the following way. She knows that the marginal cost of the third haircut is $6. (To see this, look back at the table for Fig. 12.3.) If her output increases, the marginal cost of the fourth haircut is $10. She looks at her marginal revenues and compares them with this $10 marginal cost. She notices that if she charges her business and homemaking customers $16, this group buys 2 haircuts an hour for a marginal revenue of $14. If she charges her students and elderly customers $12, that group buys 2 haircuts an hour and brings in a marginal revenue of $10. Thus when she sells a total of 4 haircuts (2 to students and elderly and 2 to other customers), the marginal revenue from the students and elderly, $10, equals the marginal cost of the fourth haircut.

But she can see that if she lowers the price to either group, marginal revenue will fall short of marginal cost. Marginal cost will climb to $15 for a fifth haircut, and marginal revenue will fall to $6 if an extra haircut is sold to students and the elderly. Other customers have an inelastic demand curve and will not buy any more than 2 haircuts, so marginal revenue from lowering the price to that group is negative. Thus Bobbie can make no more profit than that arising from charging students and the elderly $12 and other customers $16 and producing 4 haircuts an hour. The profit from such price discrimination is $16. (The calculation is set out at the foot of Table 12.2.)

Perfect Price Discrimination

Suppose that Bobbie is able to devise a means of being a perfect price discriminator. How much profit can she make in this case? Bobbie's demand and cost curves are shown in Fig. 12.6. As a single-price monopoly, she produces 3 haircuts, sells them for $14 each, and makes a profit of $12—the light blue

FIGURE **12.6**

Output and Profit with Perfect Price Discrimination

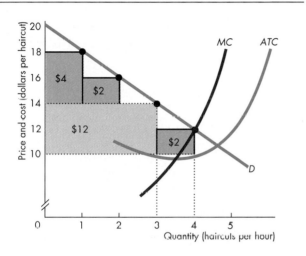

Maximum profit with single price:		$12	Quantity: 3 haircuts
add	extra profit from 1st haircut	+4	
add	extra profit from 2nd haircut	+2	
add	extra profit from 4th haircut (extra revenue is $12 and the marginal cost is $10)	+2	
equals	maximum profit with price discrimination	$20	Quantity: 4 haircuts

Bobbie's profit as a single-price monopoly, shown by the light blue area, is $12. With perfect price discrimination, Bobbie charges $18 for the first haircut, $16 for the second, $14 for the third, and $12 for the fourth. Marginal revenue equals price in each case because, with perfect price discrimination, the marginal revenue curve is the same as the demand curve. Profit is maximized when the demand curve intersects the marginal cost curve. It does not pay Bobbie to sell a fifth haircut because its marginal revenue (price) is less than its marginal cost. Bobbie's additional profit as a perfect price discriminator, shown by the dark blue areas, is $8. Her maximum total profit with perfect price discrimination is $20. The calculation is summarized in the table.

rectangle. (Refresh your memory if necessary by referring back to Fig. 12.3c.) If Bobbie can get each of her customers to pay the maximum price that each is willing to pay for a haircut, then she can sell the first haircut for $18. She makes an extra profit of $4 ($18 minus $14) from that first haircut sold. She can sell the second haircut for $16, $2 more than before. She will still sell the third for $14, since that is the maximum price that the third customer is willing to pay for a haircut. If Bobbie continues to produce 3 haircuts, her profit rises to $18, an increase of $6.

But Bobbie will not stop at 3 haircuts an hour. To see why, consider the marginal revenue from selling a fourth haircut and the marginal cost of producing it. The fourth haircut can be sold for $12. The marginal cost of the fourth haircut, from the table in Fig. 12.3, is only $10. So by producing a fourth haircut and selling it for $12, Bobbie makes a further $2 profit. The maximum profit with perfect price discrimination occurs when Bobbie sells 4 haircuts, each for the maximum price that the consumers are willing to pay. That profit is $20. It is illustrated in the figure as the sum of the light blue and the three dark blue rectangles. The table in Fig. 12.6 summarizes this calculation.

When a firm practices perfect price discrimination, its output exceeds that of a single-price monopoly. It produces up to the point at which the marginal cost curve cuts the demand curve. The less perfect the price discrimination, the smaller is the additional output produced.

R E V I E W

Price discrimination increases a monopoly's profit by increasing its total revenue. By charging the highest price for each unit of the good that each person is willing to pay, a monopoly perfectly price discriminates and captures all of the consumer surplus. Much price discrimination takes the form of discriminating among different groups of customers, charging a higher price to some and a lower price to others. Such price discrimination increases total revenue and profit, but it is possible only if the two groups have different elasticities of demand. A price-discriminating monopoly produces a larger output than a single-price monopoly. ◆

Discrimination among Groups

You can now see why it pays to price discriminate. The sign in Bobbie's window—"Haircuts $16: special for students and seniors, only $12"—is no generous gesture. It is profit-maximizing behavior. The model of price discrimination that you have just studied explains a wide variety of familiar pricing practices, even by firms that are not pure monopolies. For example, airlines offer lower fares for advance-purchase tickets than for last-minute travel. Last-minute travelers usually have a low elasticity of demand, while vacation travelers who can plan ahead have a higher elasticity of demand. Retail stores of all kinds hold seasonal "sales" when they reduce their prices, often by substantial amounts. These sales are a form of price discrimination. Each season, the newest fashions carry a high price tag, but retailers do not expect to sell all their stock at such high prices. At the end of the season, they sell off what is left at a discount. Thus such stores discriminate between buyers who have an inelastic demand (for example, those who want to be instantly fashionable) and buyers who have an elastic demand (for example, those who pay less attention to up-to-the-minute fashion and more attention to price).

Limits to Price Discrimination

Since price discrimination is profitable, why don't more firms do it? Why don't we see senior citizen discounts on speeding tickets? What are the limits to price discrimination?

Profitable price discrimination can take place only under certain conditions. First, it is possible to price discriminate only if the good cannot be resold.

If a good can be resold, then customers who get the good for the low price can resell it to someone willing to pay a higher price. Price discrimination breaks down. It is for this reason that price discrimination usually occurs in markets for services rather than in markets for storable goods. One major exception, price discrimination in the sale of fashion clothes, works because at the end of the season when the clothes go on sale, the fashion plates are looking for next season's fashions. People buying on sale have no one to whom they can resell the clothes at a higher price.

Second, a price-discriminating monopoly must be able to identify groups with different elasticities of demand. The characteristics used for discrimination must also be within the law. These requirements usually limit price discrimination to cases based either on age or employment status or on the timing of the purchase.

Despite these limitations, there are some ingenious criteria used for discriminating. For example, American Airlines Inc. discriminates among many different passenger groups on many of its international flights. Five economy class alternatives between New York and London in March 1992 were

- $2,084—no restrictions
- $918—no stopovers, mid-week only
- $599—21-day advance purchase, mid-week only
- $439—14-day advance purchase, no refund
- $379—21-day advance purchase, mid-week only, no refund

These different prices discriminate between different groups of customers with different elasticities of demand.

"Yoo-hoo! My husband gets the senior-citizen discount! Yoo-hoo, Officer, yoo-hoo!"

Drawing by Booth; © 1989 The New Yorker Magazine, Inc.

Comparing Monopoly and Competition

We have now studied a variety of ways in which firms and households interact in markets for goods and services. In Chapter 11, we saw how perfectly competitive firms behave and discovered the price and output at which they operate. In this chapter, we have studied the price and output of a single-price monopoly and a monopoly that price discriminates. How do the quantities produced, prices, and profits of these different types of firms compare with each other?

To answer this question, let's imagine an industry made up of a large number of identical competitive firms. We will work out what the price charged and quantity produced will be in that industry. Then we will imagine that a single firm buys out all the individual firms and creates a monopoly. We will then work out the price charged and quantity produced by the monopoly, first when it charges a single price and second when it price discriminates.

Price and Output

We will conduct the analysis by using Fig. 12.7. The industry demand curve is D, and the industry supply curve is S. In perfect competition, the market equilibrium occurs where the supply curve and the demand curve intersect. The quantity produced by the industry is Q_C, and the price is P_C.

Each firm takes the price P_C and maximizes its profit by producing the output at which its own marginal cost equals the price. Since each firm is a small part of the total industry, there is no incentive for any firm to try to manipulate the price by varying its output.

Now suppose that this industry is taken over by a single firm. No changes in production techniques occur, so the new combined firm has costs identical to those of the original separate firms. The new single firm recognizes that by varying output, it can influence price. It also recognizes that its marginal revenue curve is MR. To maximize profit, the firm chooses an output at which marginal revenue equals marginal cost. But what is the monopoly's marginal cost curve? To answer this question, you need to recall the relationship between the marginal cost curve and the supply curve of a competitive firm. The supply curve of an individual competitive firm is its marginal cost curve. The supply curve of a competitive industry is the sum of the supply curves of individual firms. The industry supply curve tells us how the sum of the quantities supplied by each firm varies as the price varies. Thus the industry supply curve is also the industry's marginal cost curve. (The supply curve has also been labeled MC to remind you of this fact.) Therefore, when the industry is taken over by a single firm, that firm's marginal cost

FIGURE 12.7

Monopoly and Competition Compared

A competitive industry has a demand curve D and a supply curve S. Equilibrium occurs where the quantity demanded equals the quantity supplied at quantity Q_C and price P_C. If all the firms in the industry are taken over by a single producer that sells the profit-maximizing output for a single price, marginal revenue is MR and the supply curve of the competitive industry (S) becomes the monopoly's marginal cost curve (MC). The monopoly produces the output at which marginal revenue equals marginal cost. A single-price monopoly produces Q_M and sells that output for the price P_M. A perfectly price-discriminating monopoly produces Q_C and charges a different price for each unit sold. The prices charged range from P_A to P_C.

Monopoly restricts output and raises the price. But the more perfectly a monopoly can price discriminate, the closer its output gets to the competitive output.

curve is the same as what used to be the competitive industry's supply curve.

We have seen that a competitive industry always operates at the point of intersection of its supply and demand curves. In Fig. 12.7, this is the point at which price is P_C and the industry produces the quantity Q_C. In contrast, the single-price monopoly maximizes profit by restricting output to Q_M, so that marginal revenue equals marginal cost. Since the marginal revenue curve is below the demand curve, output Q_M will always be smaller than output Q_C. The monopoly charges the highest price for which output Q_M can be sold, and that price is P_M.

If the monopoly can perfectly price discriminate, it will charge a different price on each unit sold and increase output to Q_C. The highest price charged is P_A, and the lowest price charged is P_C, the price in a competitive market. The price P_A is the highest that is charged because at yet higher prices, nothing can be sold. The price P_C is the lowest charged because when a monopoly perfectly price discriminates, its marginal revenue curve is the same as the demand curve and at prices below P_C marginal cost exceeds marginal revenue.

The key price and output differences between competition and monopoly are the following:

◆ Monopoly price exceeds the competitive price.

◆ Monopoly output is less than competitive output.

◆ The more perfectly the monopoly can price discriminate, the closer its output gets to the competitive output.

Allocative Efficiency

Monopoly is less efficient than competition. It prevents some of the gains from trade from being achieved. To see why, look at Fig. 12.8. The maximum price that consumers are willing to pay for each unit is shown by the demand curve. The difference between the maximum price that they are willing to pay for each unit bought and the price that they do pay is *consumer surplus*. Under perfect competition (part a), consumers have to pay only P_C for each unit bought and obtain a consumer surplus represented by the green triangle.

A single-price monopoly (part b) restricts output to Q_M and sells that output for P_M. Consumer surplus is reduced to the smaller green triangle. Consumers lose partly by having to pay more for what is available and partly by getting less of the good. But is the consumers' loss equal to the monopoly's gain? Is there simply a redistribution of the gains from trade? A closer look at Fig. 12.8(b) will convince you that there is a reduction in the gains from trade. It is true that some of the loss in consumer surplus does accrue to the monopoly—the monopoly gets the difference between the higher price (P_M) and P_C on the quantity sold (Q_M). So the monopoly has taken the blue rectangle part of the consumer surplus.

What, though, has become of the rest of the consumer surplus? The answer is that because output has been restricted, it is lost. But more than that has

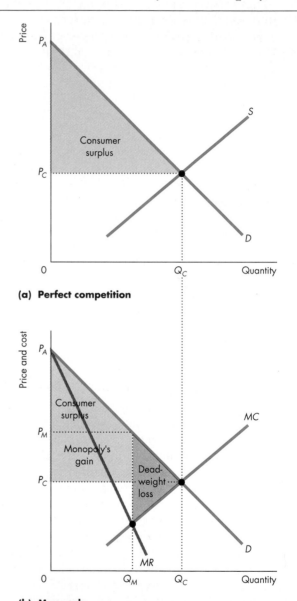

F I G U R E 12.8

Allocative Inefficiency of Monopoly

(a) Perfect competition

(b) Monopoly

In perfect competition (part a), demand curve *D* intersects supply curve *S* at quantity Q_C and price P_C. Consumer surplus is represented by the green triangle. With free entry, firms' profits in long-run equilibrium are zero. Consumer surplus is maximized. Under a single-price monopoly (part b), output is restricted to Q_M and the price increases to P_M. Consumer surplus is reduced to the smaller green triangle. The monopoly takes the blue rectangle for itself, but the gray triangle is a deadweight loss. Part of the deadweight loss (above P_C) is a loss of consumer surplus, and part of it (below P_C) is a loss of producer surplus.

been lost. The total loss resulting from the lower monopoly output (Q_M) is the gray triangle in Fig. 12.8(b). The part of the gray triangle above P_C is the loss of consumer surplus, and the part of the triangle below P_C is a loss to the producer—a loss of producer surplus. **Producer surplus** is the difference between a producer's revenue and the opportunity cost of production. It is calculated as the sum of the differences between price and the marginal cost of producing each unit of output. Under competitive conditions, the producer sells the output between Q_M and Q_C for a price of P_C. The marginal cost of producing each extra unit of output through that range is shown by the marginal cost (supply) curve. Thus the vertical distance between the marginal cost curve and the price represents a producer surplus. Part of the producer surplus is lost when a monopoly restricts output below its competitive level.

The gray triangle, which measures the total loss of both consumer and producer surplus, is called the deadweight loss. **Deadweight loss** measures allocative inefficiency as the reduction in consumer and producer surplus resulting from a restriction of output below its efficient level. The combination of a monopoly's reduced output and higher price results in the monopoly capturing some of the consumer surplus. It also results in the elimination of the producer surplus and the consumer surplus on the output that a competitive industry would have produced but that the monopoly does not.

We have seen that a single-price monopoly creates a deadweight loss by restricting output. What is the deadweight loss if the monopoly practices perfect price discrimination? The answer is zero. A perfect price discriminator produces the same output as the competitive industry. The last item sold costs P_C, the same as its marginal cost. Thus from the point of view of allocative efficiency, a perfect price-discriminating monopoly achieves the same result as perfect competition.

Redistribution

Under perfect competition, the consumer surplus is the green triangle in Fig. 12.8(a). With free entry, the long-run equilibrium economic profit of each perfectly competitive firm is zero. We've just seen that the creation of monopoly reduces consumer surplus. Further, in the case of a single-price monopoly, a deadweight loss arises. But what happens to the distribution of surpluses between producers and con-

sumers? The answer is that the monopoly always wins. In the case of a single-price monopoly (Fig. 12.8b), the monopoly gains the blue rectangle at the expense of the consumer. It has to offset against that gain its loss of producer surplus—its share of the deadweight loss. But there is always a net positive gain for the monopoly and a net loss for the consumer. We also know that because there is a deadweight loss, the consumer loses more than the monopoly gains.

In the case of a perfect price-discriminating monopoly, there is no deadweight loss but there is an even larger redistribution away from consumers to the monopoly. In this case, the monopoly captures the entire consumer surplus, the green triangle in Fig. 12.8(a).

An example of these possible effects of monopoly is given in Reading Between the Lines on pp. 332–333, which looks at the market for low-calorie sweeteners.

REVIEW

The creation of a monopoly results in a redistribution of economic gains away from consumers to the monopoly producer. If the monopoly can perfectly price discriminate, it produces the same output as a competitive industry and achieves allocative efficiency but captures the entire consumer surplus. If the monopoly cannot perfectly price discriminate, it restricts output below the level that a competitive industry would produce and creates a deadweight loss. The monopoly gains and the consumer loses, but the loss of the consumer exceeds the gain of the monopoly. In this case, monopoly creates allocative inefficiency. ◆

Rent Seeking

Operating a monopoly is more profitable than operating a firm in a perfectly competitive industry. Economic profit can be made in a competitive industry in the short run but not in the long run. Freedom of entry brings new firms into a profitable industry and results in economic profit being competed away. Barriers to entry prevent this process in a monopoly industry, so a monopoly can enjoy economic profit even in the long run. Because monopoly is more

The End of a Sweet Arrangement

THE CHICAGO TRIBUNE, JULY 28, 1991

As NutraSweet patent expires, consumers may benefit most

BY NANCY RYAN

As NutraSweet Co. celebrated a decade of unprecedented growth and brand-name recognition on its 10th anniversary this month, the aspartame producer faces a not-so-sweet competitive environment in the next 10 years.

Its exclusive patent on the sugar substitute, which helped revolutionize the diet-soda industry, expires in December 1992—a milestone most experts agree will dramatically change the carbonated beverage industry and the Deerfield, Ill.-based manufacturer.

But "the winner in all of this is going to be the consumer," said Jesse Meyers, publisher of Beverage Digest newsletter. "We're going to have the technology of Monsanto (NutraSweet's parent company) and its competitors giving the consumers better products at lower retail prices."

Several businesses are expected to attempt to sell aspartame as a generic commodity or under their own brand names, and several major manufacturers have come up with other sweeteners that may end up replacing aspartame for some products.

"Over the next two to five years, as the FDA approves more products, there will be better and improved sweeteners," said Tom Pirko, head of BevMark, a Los Angeles-based consultant to the beverage industry.

Johnson & Johnson's McNeil Specialty Products is awaiting Food and Drug Administration approval of its sucralose, which can be used in baked goods and other foods currently off limits to NutraSweet, and the government agency already has approved acesulfame-k, made by the German manufacturer Hoechst Celanese, for limited use.

FDA approvals for Pfizer Inc.'s alitame and NutraSweet's Sweetener 2000, which is 10,000 times sweeter than sugar, also are pending.

"They will chip away at NutraSweet as companies try out new blends. But NutraSweet is going to hang around for a long time," Pirko said. "It's part of the landscape."

No other food ingredient has gained the kind of brand identity that NutraSweet has. Its trademark red swirl has helped make the name known to almost 98 percent of Americans, according to NutraSweet's president and chief operating officer, Lauren S. Williams.

Though NutraSweet, which is part of Monsanto's G. D. Searle division, also produces the tabletop sweetener Equal and is included in foods and other beverages, Coke and Pepsi make up some two-thirds of the company's sales.

The Essence of the Story

NutraSweet Co., a subsidiary of Monsanto Company, makes NutraSweet, the brand name of the aspartame used to sweeten diet sodas, and Equal, a table sweetener.

The NutraSweet used in Coke and Pepsi makes up two thirds of the company's sales and is protected by a patent that expires in 1992.

When the NutraSweet patent expires, several firms are expected to offer aspartame as a generic commodity or under their own brand names.

Other firms have developed substitutes for aspartame. One is sucralose, made by McNeil Specialty Products, a subsidiary of Johnson & Johnson. This sweetener can be used in baked goods and other foods for which NutraSweet is unsuitable.

Other substitutes are acesulfame-k, made by the German manufacturer Hoechst Celanese; alitame, made by Pfizer Inc.; and Sweetener 2000—a sweetener that is 10,000 times sweeter than sugar—made by NutraSweet.

Background and Analysis

NutraSweet Co. produces aspartame in three large plants in Augusta, Georgia; Harbor Beach, Michigan; and University Park, Illinois. In 1990, its sales were $933 million and its profit was $183 million.

The average total cost curve ATC and marginal cost curve MC of a typical plant are illustrated in Fig. 1(a).

To expand output, NutraSweet can add plants like the one in Fig. 1(a). It can increase output by q, the capacity of a plant, at a marginal cost of C, so marginal cost for the firm and the industry that it controls is the horizontal line shown in Fig. 1(b).

Protected by a patent, NutraSweet is the sole supplier of aspartame, which it markets under the brand name NutraSweet. The demand curve for NutraSweet is D shown in Fig. 1(b).

If NutraSweet Co. sells aspartame for a single price, its marginal revenue curve is MR and it maximizes profit by producing an output of Q_M and selling it for P_M per unit. Its economic profit is shown by the blue rectangle. The gray triangle shows the resulting deadweight loss, and the green triangle shows the consumer surplus.

If NutraSweet price discriminates—and it probably does—its output exceeds Q_M and the deadweight loss is smaller than that shown in Fig. 1(b).

When patent protection expires at the end of 1992 and there is free entry into the sweetener industry, competition will drive the price down to its competitive level.

If perfect competition arises, the price will be driven down to equal minimum average total cost, P_C, as shown in Fig. 2(a). Industry output increases to Q_C, and consumer surplus also increases, as shown in Fig. 2(b).

Each individual plant produces its least-cost output of q, but the number of plants (of both NutraSweet Co. and its competitors) increases to produce the larger total output.

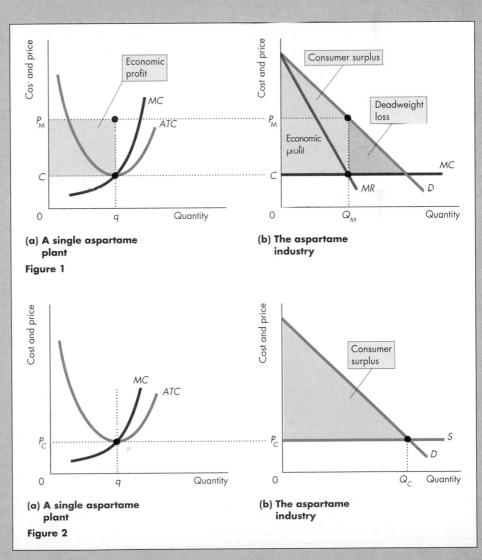

(a) A single aspartame plant

Figure 1

(b) The aspartame industry

(a) A single aspartame plant

Figure 2

(b) The aspartame industry

profitable than perfect competition, there is an incentive to attempt to create monopoly. The activity of creating monopoly is called **rent seeking**. The name *rent seeking* arises from the fact that another name for consumer surplus and producer surplus is *rent*. We've just seen that a monopoly makes its profit by diverting part of the consumer surplus to itself. Thus pursuing maximum monopoly profit is the same thing as diverting consumer surplus, or rent seeking.

Rent seeking is not a costless activity. To obtain a monopoly right, resources have to be used. Furthermore, everyone has an incentive to seek monopoly power, so there will be competition for monopoly rights. There are two ways in which people compete for monopoly rights—they buy an existing right or they create a new one. But existing monopoly rights had to be created at some time, so, ultimately, competition for monopoly rights is a process that uses productive resources to establish a monopoly right. What is the value of the resources that a person will use to obtain a monopoly right? The answer is any amount up to the monopoly's profit. If the value of resources spent trying to acquire a monopoly exceeds the monopoly's profit, the net result is an economic loss. But as long as the value of the resources used to acquire a monopoly falls short of the monopoly's profit, there is a profit to be earned. If there is no barrier to entry, the value of the resources used up in rent seeking will, in equilibrium, equal the monopoly's profit.

Because of rent seeking, monopoly imposes costs that exceed the deadweight loss that we calculated earlier. To calculate that cost, we must add to the deadweight loss the value of resources used in rent seeking. That amount equals the entire monopoly profit, since that is the value of the resources that it pays to use in rent seeking. Thus the cost of monopoly is the deadweight loss plus monopoly profit.

What exactly are the resources used in rent seeking? What do rent seekers do? One form of rent seeking is the searching out of existing monopoly rights that can be bought for a lower price than the monopoly's economic profit—that is, seeking to acquire existing monopoly rights. This form of rent seeking results in a market price for monopoly rights that is close to the economic profit. There are many real-world examples of this type of rent-seeking activity. One that is well known is the purchase of taxicab licenses. In most cities, taxicabs are regulated. The city restricts both the fares and the number

of taxis that are permitted to operate. Operating a taxi is profitable—resulting in economic profit or rent being earned by the operator. A person who wants to operate a taxi has to buy the right to do so from someone who already has that right. Competition for that right leads to a price sufficiently high to eliminate long-run economic profit. For example, in New York City, the price that has to be paid for the right to operate a taxi is close to $100,000.[1]

Rent seeking is also big business among airlines. In 1986, United Airlines bought the rights to all the international air routes across the Pacific Ocean that had previously been owned and operated by Pan American Airlines. United paid Pan Am $500 million for the exclusive rights to these routes. Pan Am had originated these Pacific routes, and other U.S. airlines were prohibited from competing on them by an international air transportation agreement entered into by the United States and other governments. To acquire these routes, United had to pay Pan Am a price that provided as much profit as Pan Am would have made by hanging onto the rights and operating the routes itself. Competition for these rights among airlines resulted in the most efficient potential operator buying them, because that operator was willing to offer the highest price.

By 1991, Pan Am was in deep trouble and its entire assets went on the block. An incredible bidding war broke out for its domestic shuttle, European, and Latin American routes and equipment. At one point in the battle, four airlines—American, Delta, Northwest, and TWA—were competing with bids exceeding $300 billion for these valuable monopoly rights.

Although a great deal of rent-seeking activity involves searching out existing monopoly rights that can be profitably bought, much of it is devoted to the creation of monopoly. This type of rent-seeking activity takes the form of lobbying and seeking to influence the political process. Such influence is sometimes sought by making campaign contributions in exchange for legislative support or by indirectly seeking to influence political outcomes through publicity in the media or more direct contacts with politicians and bureaucrats. (This type of rent seeking is discussed and explained more fully in Chapters 20 and 21.)

---

[1]Taxis do not earn $100,000 in a single year. The $100,000 price tag is the *present value* of the expected future profits—see Chapter 9, pp. 214–217.

REVIEW

W hen rent seeking is taken into account, there are no guaranteed long-run profits, even from monopoly. Competition for monopoly rights results in the use of resources to acquire those rights that are equal in value to the potential monopoly profit. As a consequence, monopoly imposes costs equal to the deadweight loss plus the monopoly's economic profit. ◆

Gains from Monopoly

In our comparison of monopoly and competition, monopoly comes out in a pretty bad light. If monopoly is so bad, why do we put up with it? Why don't we have laws that crack down on monopoly so hard that it never rears its head? As we'll see in Chapter 21, we do indeed have laws that limit monopoly power. We also have laws that regulate those monopolies that exist. But monopoly is not all bad. Let's look at its potential advantages and some of the reasons for its existence.

The main reasons for the existence of monopoly are

◆ Economies of scale and economies of scope
◆ Incentive to innovate

Economies of Scale and Scope   You met economies of scale in Chapters 9 and 10. There we defined *economies of scale* as decreases in average total cost resulting from increasing a firm's scale. The scale of a firm increases when it increases all its inputs—capital, labor, and materials—in the same proportions. For example, if all inputs double, total cost also doubles. If output more than doubles, average total cost declines or, equivalently, the firm has economies of scale.

Economies of scope are decreases in average total cost made possible by increasing the number of different goods produced. Economies of scope are important when highly specialized (and expensive) technical inputs can be shared by different goods. For example, McDonald's can produce both hamburgers and french fries at an average total cost that is lower than what it would cost two separate firms to produce the same goods. McDonald's can do so because the hamburgers and fries share the use of specialized food storage and preparation facilities.

Firms producing a wide range of products can hire specialist computer programmers, designers, and marketing experts whose skills can be used across the product range, thereby spreading their costs and lowering the cost of production of each of the goods.

Large-scale firms that have control over supply and can influence price—and that therefore behave like the monopoly firm we've been studying in this chapter—can reap these economies of scale and scope. Small, competitive firms cannot. As a consequence, there are situations in which the comparison of monopoly and competition that we made earlier in this chapter is not a valid one. Recall that we imagined the takeover of a large number of competitive firms by a single monopoly firm. But we also assumed that the monopoly would use exactly the same technology as the small firms and have the same costs. But if one large firm can reap economies of scale and scope, its marginal cost curve will lie below the supply curve of a competitive industry made up of thousands of small firms. It is possible for such economies of scale and scope to be so large as to result in a higher output and lower price under monopoly than a competitive industry would achieve.

Figure 12.9 illustrates such a situation. Here the demand curve and the marginal revenue curve are the same regardless of whether the industry is a competitive one or a monopoly. With a competitive industry, the supply curve is S, the quantity produced is Q_C, and the price is P_C. With a monopoly that can exploit economies of scale and scope, the marginal cost curve is MC_M. The monopoly maximizes profit by producing the output (Q_M) at which marginal revenue equals marginal cost. The price that maximizes profit is P_M. By exploiting a superior technology not available to each of the large number of small firms, the monopoly is able to achieve a higher output and lower price than the competitive industry.

There are many examples of industries in which economies of scale are so important that they lead to an outcome similar to that shown in Fig. 12.9. Public utilities such as gas, electric power, water, and local telephone service are all such cases. There are also many examples of industries in which a combination of economies of scale and economies of scope is important. Examples are the brewing of beer, the manufacture of refrigerators and other household appliances, the production of pharmaceuticals, and the refining of petroleum.

FIGURE 12.9

When Economies of Scale and Scope Make Monopoly More Efficient

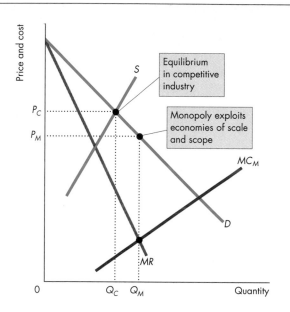

In some industries, economies of scale and economies of scope result in the monopoly's marginal cost curve (MC_M) lying below the competitive industry supply curve (S). In such a case, it is possible that the single-price monopoly output (Q_M) exceeds the competitive output (Q_C) and that the monopoly price (P_M) is below the competitive price (P_C).

Innovation   Innovation is the first-time application of new knowledge in the production process. Innovation may take the form of developing a new product or a lower-cost way of making an existing product. Controversy has raged among economists over whether large firms with monopoly power or small competitive firms lacking such monopoly power are the most innovative. It is clear that some temporary monopoly power arises from innovation. A firm that develops a new product or process and patents it obtains exclusive right to that product or process for the term of the patent.

But does the granting of a monopoly, even a temporary one, to an innovator increase the pace of innovation? One line of reasoning suggests that it does. With no protection, an innovator is not able to enjoy the profits from innovation for very long. Thus the incentive to innovate is weakened. A contrary argument is that monopolies can afford to be

lazy while competitive firms cannot. Competitive firms must strive to innovate and cut costs even though they know that they cannot hang onto the benefits of their innovation for long. But that knowledge spurs them on to greater and faster innovation.

A matter such as this one cannot be resolved by listing arguments and counterarguments. It requires a careful empirical investigation. Many such investigations have been conducted. But the evidence that they bring to bear on this question is mixed. They show that large firms do much more research and development than do small firms. They also show that large firms are significantly more prominent at the development end of the research and development process. But measuring research and development is measuring the volume of inputs into the process of innovation. What matters is not input but output. Two measures of the output of research and development are the number of patents and the rate of productivity growth. On these measures, there is no clear evidence that big is best. But there is a clear pattern in the process of diffusion of technological knowledge. After innovation, a new process or product spreads gradually through the industry. Whether an innovator is a small firm or a large firm, large firms jump on the bandwagon more quickly than do small firms. Thus large firms are important in speeding the process of diffusion of technological advances.

In determining public policy toward monopoly (matters discussed in Chapter 21), laws and regulations are designed that balance these positive aspects of monopoly (economies of scale and scope and innovation) against the deadweight loss and redistribution that they also generate.

◆ ◆ ◆ ◆ We've now studied two models of market structure—perfect competition and monopoly. We've used these two models to make predictions about allocative efficiency and the effects on prices and quantities of changing cost and demand conditions. ◆ ◆ Although there are examples of markets in the U.S. economy that are highly competitive or highly monopolistic, the markets for most goods and services lie somewhere between these two extremes. In the next chapter, we're going to study this middle ground between monopoly and competition. We're going to discover that many of the lessons we have learned from these two extreme models are still relevant and useful in understanding behavior in real-world markets.

SUMMARY

How Monopoly Arises

Monopoly arises because of barriers to entry that prevent competition. Barriers to the entry of new firms may be legal or natural. Legal barriers take the form of public franchise, government license, or patent. Natural barriers exist when a single firm possesses total control of a mineral or natural resource or when economies of scale are so large that a single firm can supply an entire market at a lower average total cost than can several firms. (pp. 314–315)

Single-Price Monopoly

A monopoly is an industry in which there is a single supplier of a good, service, or resource. A single-price monopoly is a firm that charges the same price for each unit of output. The monopoly's demand curve is the market demand curve for the good. For a single-price monopoly, marginal revenue is less than price. Total revenue rises at first, but above some output level it begins to decline. When total revenue is rising, marginal revenue is positive. When total revenue is falling, marginal revenue is negative. When marginal revenue is positive (total revenue rising), the elasticity of demand is greater than 1. The elasticity of demand equals 1 when total revenue is at a maximum.

A monopoly's technology and costs behave in a way similar to those of any other type of firm. The monopoly maximizes profit by producing the output that makes marginal revenue equal to marginal cost and by charging the maximum price that consumers are willing to pay for that output. The price charged always exceeds marginal cost. A monopoly has no supply curve. (pp. 315–321)

Price Discrimination

Price discrimination is the practice of charging some consumers a higher price than others for an identical item or charging an individual customer a higher price on a small purchase than on a large one. Price discrimination is an attempt by the monopoly to convert consumer surplus into profit. Perfect price discrimination extracts all the consumer surplus. Such a monopoly charges a different price for each unit sold and obtains the maximum price that each consumer is willing to pay for each unit bought. With perfect price discrimination, the monopoly's marginal revenue curve is the same as its demand curve and the monopoly produces the same output as would a perfectly competitive industry.

A monopoly can discriminate between different groups of customers on the basis of age, employment status, or other distinguishable characteristics. Such price discrimination increases the monopoly's profit if each group has a different elasticity of demand for the product. To maximize profit with price discrimination, the monopoly produces an output such that marginal cost equals marginal revenue but then charges each group the maximum price that it is willing to pay.

Price discrimination can be practiced only when it is impossible for a buyer to resell the good and when consumers with different elasticities can be identified. (pp. 321–328)

Comparing Monopoly and Competition

If a monopoly takes over all the firms in a perfectly competitive industry and if the technology and input prices in the industry remain unchanged, the monopoly charges a higher price and produces a lower quantity than would prevail in a perfectly competitive industry. If the monopoly can perfectly price discriminate, it produces the competitive quantity and sells the last unit for the competitive price.

Monopoly is less efficient than competition because it prevents some of the gains from trade from being achieved. A monopoly captures some part of the consumer surplus. But to do so, it restricts output and creates a deadweight loss. The more a monopoly is able to price discriminate, the smaller is the deadweight loss but the larger is the monopoly profit and the smaller is the consumer surplus.

Monopoly always redistributes the gains from trade away from consumers toward the producer. The more perfectly a monopoly can price discriminate, the smaller is the deadweight loss but the larger is the reallocation of surpluses from consumers to the producer.

Monopoly imposes costs that equal its deadweight loss plus the cost of the resources devoted to rent seeking—searching out profitable monopoly opportunities. It pays to use resources that are equal in value to the entire monopoly profit that might be attained. As a result, the cost of monopoly equals its deadweight loss plus the entire monopoly profit.

There are some industries in which a monopoly is more efficient than a large number of perfectly competitive firms. Such industries are those in which economies of scale and scope are so large that the monopoly's output is higher and its price is lower than those that would arise if the industry had a large number of firms. There are also situations in which monopoly may be more innovative than competition, resulting in a faster pace of technological change. (pp. 328–336)

K E Y E L E M E N T S

Key Terms

Barriers to entry, 314
Deadweight loss, 331
Economies of scope, 335
Government license, 314
Legal monopoly, 314
Monopoly, 314
Natural monopoly, 314
Patent, 314
Perfect price discrimination, 321
Price discrimination, 321
Producer surplus, 331
Public franchise, 314

Rent seeking, 334
Single-price monopoly, 315

Key Figures

Figure 12.1 Demand and Marginal Revenue for a Single-Price Monopoly, 316
Figure 12.2 A Single-Price Monopoly's Revenue Curves, 317
Figure 12.3 A Monopoly's Output and Price, 318
Figure 12.7 Monopoly and Competition Compared, 329

R E V I E W Q U E S T I O N S

1 What is a monopoly? What are some examples of monopoly in your state?

2 How does monopoly arise?

3 Distinguish between a legal monopoly and a natural monopoly. Give examples of each type.

4 Explain why marginal revenue is always less than average revenue for a single-price monopoly.

5 Why does a monopoly's profit increase as output rises initially but eventually decrease when output gets too big?

6 Explain how a monopoly chooses its output and price.

7 Does a monopoly operate on the inelastic part of its demand curve? Explain why it does or does not.

8 Explain why a monopoly produces a smaller output than an equivalent competitive industry.

9 Is monopoly as efficient as competition?

10 What is deadweight loss?

11 Can any monopoly price discriminate? If yes, why? If no, why not?

12 Show graphically the deadweight loss under perfect price discrimination.

13 As far as allocative efficiency is concerned, is single-price monopoly better or worse than perfect price discrimination? Why?

14 Explain why people indulge in rent-seeking activities.

15 When taking account of the cost of rent seeking, what is the social cost of monopoly?

16 What are economies of scale and economies of scope? What effects, if any, do they have on the allocative efficiency of monopoly?

17 Explain why the consumer loses more under perfect price discrimination than under single-price monopoly.

PROBLEMS

1 Minnie's Mineral Springs, a single-price monopoly, has the following demand schedule and total cost for bottled mineral water:

Quantity (bottles)	Price (dollars per bottle)	Total cost (dollars)
0	10	1
1	8	3
2	6	7
3	4	13
4	2	21
5	0	31

a   Calculate Minnie's total revenue schedule.
b   Calculate its marginal revenue schedule.
c   At what price is the elasticity of demand equal to 1?

2 Calculate Minnie's profit-maximizing levels of:

a   Output   d   Marginal revenue
b   Price   e   Profit
c   Marginal cost

3 Suppose that Minnie's can perfectly price discriminate. What is its profit-maximizing:

a   Output   c   Profit
b   Total revenue

4 How much would someone be willing to pay Minnie's for a license to operate its mineral spring?

5 Two demand schedules for round-trip flights between New York and Los Angeles are set out below.

Weekday travelers		Weekend travelers	
Price (dollars per round-trip)	Quantity demanded (thousands of round-trips)	Price (dollars per round-trip)	Quantity demanded (thousands of round-trips)
1,500	0	500	0
1,000	10	250	10
500	20	125	20
250	30	0	30
125	40		
0	50		

The schedule for weekday travelers is for those making round-trips on weekdays and returning within the same week. The schedule for weekend travelers is for those who stay through the weekend. (The former tend to be business travelers, and the latter tend to be vacation and pleasure travelers.) The marginal cost of a round-trip is a constant $125. If a single-price monopoly airline controls the New York–Los Angeles route, use a graph to find out the following:

a   What price is charged?
b   How many passengers travel?
c   What is the consumer surplus?

6 If the airline in problem 5 discriminates between round-trips within a week and round-trips through the weekend:

a   What is the price for the round-trip within the week?
b   What is the price of the airline ticket with a weekend stay?
c   What is the consumer surplus?

7 Barbara runs a truck stop on the prairie, miles from anywhere. She has a monopoly and faces the following demand schedule for meals:

Price (dollars per meal)	Quantity demanded (meals per week)
1.00	160
1.50	140
2.00	120
2.50	100
3.00	80
3.50	60
4.00	40
4.50	20
5.00	10

Barbara's marginal cost and average total cost are a constant $2 per meal.

a   If Barbara charges all customers the same price for a meal, what price is it?
b   What is the consumer surplus of all the customers who buy a meal from Barbara?
c   What is the producer surplus?
d   What is the deadweight loss?

CHAPTER 13

MONOPOLISTIC COMPETITION AND OLIGOPOLY

After studying this chapter, you will be able to:

- ◆ Describe and distinguish among market structures that lie between perfect competition and monopoly

- ◆ Define monopolistic competition and oligopoly

- ◆ Explain how price and output are determined in a monopolistically competitive industry

- ◆ Explain why the price may be sticky in an oligopolistic industry

- ◆ Explain how price and output are determined when there is one dominant firm and several small firms in an industry

- ◆ Explain duopoly and oligopoly as games that firms play

- ◆ Predict the price and output behavior of duopolists

- ◆ Make predictions about price wars and competition among small numbers of firms

EVERY WEEK, WE RECEIVE A NEWSPAPER STUFFED WITH supermarket fliers describing this week's "specials," providing coupons and other enticements, all designed to grab our attention and persuade us that A&P, Kroger, Safeway, Alpha Beta, Winn Dixie, Stop & Shop, Shop 'n' Save, and H.E.B.'s have the best deals in town. One claims the lowest price, another the best brands, yet another the best value for the money even if its prices are not the lowest. How do firms locked in fierce competition with other firms set their prices, pick their products, and choose the quantities to produce? How are the profits of such firms affected by the actions of other firms? ◆ ◆ Suddenly, in 1973, the prices that people paid for gasoline, heating oil, and other petroleum products depended on the whims of the Organization of Petroleum Exporting Countries (OPEC). In

Fliers and War Games

that year, OPEC raised the price of oil from $3 to $12 a barrel. And it kept on increasing prices to $35 a barrel by 1982. Then, equally suddenly and to the surprise of millions of people, OPEC fell apart. By 1986 the price of oil had collapsed to one half of its 1982 level. Headlines screamed, "The Price War Is Here" and "Frenzied Gas Wars Push Down Pump Prices." How did OPEC increase the price of oil in the 1970s? And why did OPEC's stranglehold on oil prices disappear?

◆ ◆ ◆ ◆ The theories of monopoly and perfect competition do not predict the kind of behavior that we've just described. There are no fliers and coupons, best brands, or price wars in perfect competition because each firm produces an identical product and is a price taker. And there are none in monopoly because each monopoly firm has the entire market to itself. To understand coupons, fliers, and price wars, we need richer models of the behavior of firms in markets than those of perfect competition and monopoly. This chapter presents such models. But before turning to these models, we are going to describe the characteristics of different types of markets so that we can identify those to which each model applies.

Varieties of Market Structure

We have studied two types of market structure—perfect competition and monopoly. In perfect competition, a large number of firms produce identical goods and there are no barriers to the entry of new firms into the industry. In this situation, each firm is a price taker and, in the long run, there is no economic profit. In monopoly, there is one firm that is protected by barriers preventing the entry of new firms. The firm sets its price to maximize profit and enjoys economic profit even in the long run.

Many real-world industries are not well described by the models of perfect competition and monopoly. They lie somewhere between these two cases. There are many situations in which firms are in fierce competition with a large number of other firms but they do have some power to set prices. There are other cases in which the industry consists of very few firms and each firm has considerable power in price determination.

Measures of Concentration

In order to tell how close to the competitive or monopolistic extreme an industry comes, economists have developed measures of industrial concentration. These measures are designed to indicate the degree of control that a small number of firms have over a market.

The most commonly used measure of concentration is called the four-firm concentration ratio. The **four-firm concentration ratio** is the percentage of the value of sales accounted for by the largest four firms in an industry. (Concentration ratios are also defined and measured for the largest 8, 20, and 50 firms in an industry.) Table 13.1 sets out two hypothetical concentration ratio calculations, one for tires and one for printing. In this example, there are 14 firms in the tire industry. The biggest four have 80 percent

TABLE **13.1**

Concentration Ratio Calculations

Tiremakers		Printers	
Firm	Sales (millions of dollars)	Firm	Sales (millions of dollars)
Top, Inc.	200	Fran's	2.5
ABC, Inc.	250	Ned's	2.0
Big, Inc.	150	Tom's	1.8
XYZ, Inc.	100	Jill's	1.7
Top 4 sales	700	Top 4 sales	8.0
Other 10 firms	175	Other 1,000 firms	1,592.0
Industry sales	875	Industry sales	1,600.0

Four-firm concentration ratios:

Tiremakers: 700/875 = 80%   Printers: 8/1,600 = 0.5%

of the sales of the industry, so the four-firm concentration ratio for that industry is 80 percent. In the printing industry, with 1004 firms, the top four firms account for only 0.5 percent of total industry sales. In that case, the four-firm concentration ratio is 0.5 percent.

Another commonly used measure of concentration is the Herfindahl-Hirschman (H-H) Index. The **Herfindahl-Hirschman Index** is calculated as the square of market share (percentage) of each firm summed over the largest 50 firms (or summed over all the

firms if there are fewer than 50) in a market. For example, if a market is shared equally by two firms, the H-H Index is equal to $50^2 + 50^2 = 5,000$. If each of the largest 50 firms has a market share of 0.5 percent, the H-H Index is equal to $0.5^2 \times 50 = 12.5$.

Concentration in the U.S. Economy

The Department of Commerce uses data on individual firms' sales to calculate concentration ratios for a large number of industry groups. A selection of their calculations is shown in Fig. 13.1. As you can

---

FIGURE **13.1**

Some Concentration Measures in the United States

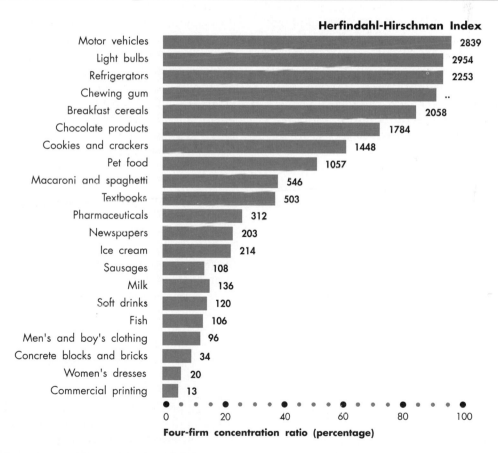

Measured by the four-firm concentration ratio and the Herfindahl-Hirschman Index, the industries producing motor vehicles, light bulbs, and refrigerators are highly concentrated, while the commercial printing, women's dresses, and concrete blocks and bricks industries are highly competitive. The industries producing macaroni, spaghetti, and textbooks have an intermediate degree of concentration.

Source: U.S. Department of Commerce, *Concentration Ratios in Manufacturing*, MC82-S-7, Washington D.C., 1986.

see, some industries—from pharmaceuticals to commercial printing and including ice cream and soft drinks—have low concentration ratios. These industries are highly competitive. At the other extreme are industries with a high concentration ratio, such as motor vehicles, light bulbs, refrigerators, chewing gum, and breakfast cereals. These are industries in which there is competition but among a small number of firms, each of which has considerable control over its price. Medium concentration ratios are found for such products as pet foods and textbooks.

Limitations of Measures of Concentration

The idea behind calculating concentration ratios is to provide information about the degree of competitiveness of a market. A low concentration ratio indicates a high degree of competition, and a high concentration ratio indicates an absence of competition. In the extreme case of monopoly, the four-firm concentration ratio is 100—the largest (and only) firm makes the entire industry sales. But there are problems with concentration ratios as measures of competitiveness. Although the ratios themselves are useful, they have to be supplemented by other information. There are three key problems.

1. Geographical Scope of the Market   Concentration ratio data are based on a national view of the market. Many goods are indeed sold in a national market, but some are sold in a regional market and some in a global one. The newspaper industry is a good example of one in which the local market is more important than the national market. Thus, although the concentration ratio for newspapers is not high, there is nevertheless a high degree of concentration in the newspaper industry in most cities. The automobile industry is an example of one for which there is a global market. Thus, although the biggest four U.S. car producers account for 92 percent of all cars sold by U.S. producers, they account for a much smaller percentage of the total U.S. car market (including imports) and an even smaller percentage of the global market for cars.

2. Barriers to Entry and Turnover   Measures of concentration do not tell us how severe are the barriers

to entry in an industry. Some industries, for example, are highly concentrated but have virtually free entry and experience an enormous amount of turnover of firms. A good example is the market in local restaurants. Many small towns have few restaurants. But there are no restrictions on entering the restaurant industry, and indeed firms do enter and exit with great regularity.

3. Market and Industry   The classifications used to calculate concentration ratios allocate every firm in the U.S. economy to a particular industry. But markets for particular goods do not always correspond exactly to particular industries. For example, Westinghouse is classified by the Department of Commerce as being in the electrical goods and equipment industry. That is indeed the main product line of Westinghouse. But Westinghouse also produces, among other things, gas-fired incinerators and plywood. Thus this one firm operates in three quite separate markets. Furthermore, the market or markets in which a firm operates depend on the profit opportunities that exist. There are many spectacular examples of firms that have built their initial organization on one product but then diversified into a wide variety of others.

Nevertheless, concentration ratios combined with information about the geographical scope of the market, barriers to entry, and the extent to which large, multiproduct firms straddle a variety of markets do provide the basis for classifying industries. The less concentrated an industry and the lower its barriers to entry, the more closely it approximates the perfect competition case. The more concentrated an industry and the higher the barriers to entry, the more it approximates the monopoly case.

But there is a great deal of space between perfect competition and monopoly. That space is occupied by two other market types. The first of these is monopolistic competition. **Monopolistic competition** is a market type in which a large number of firms compete with each other by making similar but slightly different products. Making a product slightly different from the product of a competing firm is called **product differentiation**. Because of product differentiation, a monopolistically competitive firm has an element of monopoly power. The firm is the sole producer of the particular version of the good in question. For example, in the market for microwave popcorn, only Nabisco makes Planters Premium Select. Only General Mills makes Pop Secret. And only American Popcorn makes Jolly Time. Each of these firms has a monopoly on a particular brand of microwave popcorn. Differentiated products are not necessarily different in an objective sense. For example, the different brands of microwave popcorn might actually be only different ways of packaging an identical commodity. What matters is that consumers perceive products to be differentiated. In fact, there are claims that the different brands of microwave popcorn are different in ways other than their packaging—for example, in "popability."

Oligopoly is a market type in which a small number of producers compete with each other. There are hundreds of examples of oligopolistic industries. Oil and gasoline production, the manufacture of electrical equipment, and international air transportation are but a few. In some oligopolistic industries, each firm produces an almost identical product, while in others, products are differentiated. For example, oil and gasoline are essentially the same whether they are produced by Texaco or Exxon. But Chrysler's Acclaim is a differentiated commodity from Chevrolet's Lumina and Ford's Mercury Topaz.

Table 13.2 summarizes the characteristics of the two market types that we're going to study in this chapter, monopolistic competition and oligopoly, along with those of perfect competition and monopoly.

Market Types in the U.S. Economy

Three quarters of the value of goods and services bought and sold in the United States is traded in markets that are essentially competitive—markets that have almost perfect competition or monopolistic competition. Monopoly is rare—accounting for less than 3 percent of the value of goods and services in the United States—and is found mainly in public utilities and public transportation. A similarly small number of markets—accounting for less than 3 percent of the value of sales—are dominated by one or two firms but are not monopolies. These, too, are in the public utilities and transportation sectors. Oligopoly, found mainly in manufacturing, accounts for about 18 percent of sales.

Over the years, the U.S. economy has become increasingly competitive. This trend and the percentages of each market type are shown in Fig. 13.2.

T A B L E **13.2**

Market Structure

Characteristics	Perfect competition	Monopolistic competition	Oligopoly	Monopoly
Number of firms in industry	Many	Many	Few	One
Product	Identical	Differentiated	Either identical or differentiated	No close substitutes
Barriers to entry	None	Some	Scale and scope economies	Scale and scope economies or legal barriers
Firm's control over price	None	Some	Considerable	Considerable or regulated
Concentration ratio (0 to 100)	0	Low	High	100
Examples	Wheat, corn	Food, clothing	Automobiles, cereals	Local phone service, electric and gas utilities

FIGURE **13.2**

The Market Structure of the U.S. Economy

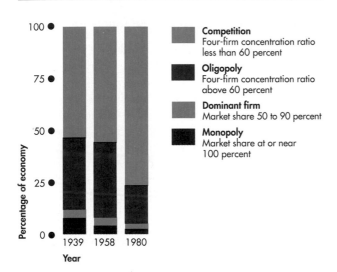

Three quarters of the U.S. economy is effectively competitive (perfect competition or monopolistic competition), one fifth is oligopolistic, and the rest is dominated by a few firms or is monopolistic. The economy has been getting more competitive over the years.

Source: William G. Shepherd, "Causes of Increased Competition in the U.S. Economy, 1939–1980," *Review of Economics and Statistics,* November, 1982, pp. 613–626.

Monopolistic Competition

Three conditions define a monopolistically competitive industry:

◆ Each firm faces a downward-sloping demand curve.

◆ There is free entry.

◆ There are a large number of firms in the industry.

Because each firm faces a downward-sloping demand curve, it has to choose its price as well as its output. Also the firm's marginal revenue curve is different from its demand curve. These features of

monopolistic competition are also present in monopoly. The important difference between monopoly and monopolistic competition lies in free entry.

In monopoly, there is no entry. In monopolistic competition, there is free entry. As a consequence, though monopolistic competition enables economic profits to occur in the short run, they cannot persist forever. When profits are available, new firms will enter the industry. Such entry will result in lower prices and lower profits. When losses are being incurred, firms will leave the industry. Such exit will increase prices and increase profits. In long-run equilibrium, firms will neither enter nor leave the industry, and firms will be making a zero economic profit.

Because the industry consists of a large number of firms, no one firm can effectively influence what other firms will do. That is, if one firm changes its price, that firm is such a small part of the total industry that it will have no effect on the actions of the other firms in the industry.

Price and Output in Monopolistic Competition

To see how price and output are determined by a firm in a monopolistically competitive industry, let's look at Fig. 13.3. Part (a) deals with the short run, and part (b) with the long run. To keep things simple, we will suppose that the industry consists of a large number of firms with a differentiated product and that all firms in the industry have identical demand and cost curves. Let's concentrate initially on the short run. The demand curve D is the demand curve for the firm's own variety of the product. For example, it is the demand for Bayer aspirin rather than for painkillers in general or for McDonald's hamburgers rather than for hamburgers in general. The curve MR is the marginal revenue curve associated with the demand curve. The firm's average total cost (ATC) and marginal cost (MC) are also shown in the figure. A firm maximizes profit in the short run by producing output Q_S, where marginal revenue equals marginal cost, and charging the price P_S. The firm's average total cost is C_S, and the firm makes a short-run profit, as measured by the blue rectangle.

So far, the monopolistically competitive firm looks just like a monopoly. It produces the quantity at which marginal revenue equals marginal cost and then charges the highest possible price for that quan-

FIGURE **13.3**

Monopolistic Competition

(a) Short run

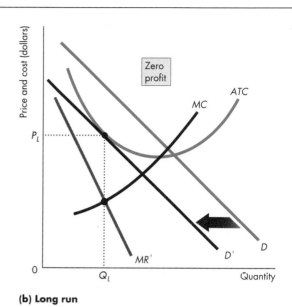

(b) Long run

Under monopolistic competition, a firm faces a downward-sloping demand curve and so has to choose its price and the quantity to produce. Profit is maximized where marginal revenue equals marginal cost. Part (a) of the figure shows a short-run profit-maximizing situation. The quantity produced is Q_S, the price is P_S, average total cost is C_S, and profit is represented by the blue rectangle.

Profit encourages new entrants, and so the firm's demand curve

begins to shift to the left, as shown in part (b). As the demand curve shifts to the left, so too does the firm's marginal revenue curve (only the new marginal revenue curve is shown). When the demand curve has shifted all the way from D to D', the marginal revenue curve is MR' and the firm is in long-run equilibrium. The output that maximizes profit is Q_L, and the price is P_L. Profit, in long-run equilibrium, is zero. There is no further entry into the industry.

---

tity. The key difference between monopoly and monopolistic competition lies in what happens next.

There is no restriction on entry in monopolistic competition, so with economic profit being earned, new firms enter the industry and take some of the market away from the existing firms. As they do so, the firm's demand curve starts to shift to the left. The marginal revenue curve also starts to shift to the left. At each point in time, the firm will seek to maximize its short-run profit. That is, it chooses its output so that marginal revenue equals marginal cost, and it charges the highest possible price for the good. But as the demand curve shifts to the left, the profit-maximizing quantity and price fall. In long-run equilibrium, shown in Fig. 13.3(b), the firm produces Q_L and sells it at a price of P_L. In this situation, the firm is making a zero economic profit.

Average total cost exactly equals price. There is no incentive for firms to enter or exit.

A process similar to the one that we've just described seems to be going on in the video game industry at the present time, as you can see by studying Reading Between the Lines on pp. 348–349.

Excess Capacity

Recall that a firm's capacity output is the output produced when average total cost is at its minimum point—the output at the bottom of the U-shaped *ATC* curve. In monopolistic competition, in the long run, firms always have excess capacity. That is, they produce a lower output than that which minimizes average total cost. As a consequence, the consumer pays more than the minimum average total cost.

Monopolistic Competition in Action

The Wall Street Journal, September 18, 1990

Nintendo Tries to Zap Game Rentals by Video Stores

by Michael W. Miller

Nintendo Co. is trying to stomp a new enemy that's sprouting up faster than the dread Micro-Goombas in Super Mario Brothers 3: video stores that rent Nintendo games.

With game prices in the range of $40 to $50, rental has become an increasingly popular way for Nintendo addicts to get a quick fix. Game rentals make up an estimated 5% to 15% of the revenue of the nation's roughly 25,000 video stores, up from virtually nothing three years ago.

Nintendo, based in Kyoto, Japan, and the companies that make games for the Nintendo system are lobbying Congress for a law to ban game rental, which the House Judiciary Committee is scheduled to vote on today. They argue that the rental boom is cutting into Nintendo game sales, which they project will total 70 million units this year.

Both sides can claim legal precedent thanks to the patchwork of federal regulations covering rental of published works. For instance, videos can be rented whereas records cannot. Congress seems likely to pass a bill that would ban the rental of personal-computer software. Game makers point out that some titles are available both for PCs and Nintendo machines, and say it makes no sense to ban rental of one format and not the other.

The video-store industry argues that movie rentals haven't damaged the movie business, despite Hollywood's anguished predictions that they would. Even though video stores typically don't pay royalties on rentals, the movie industry makes huge revenue from sales to the stores.

In fact, some video-store owners say they ultimately help Nintendo and the game-makers, who also don't earn royalties from rentals. "I sell games mainly through rentals—people come in here, try a game, like it, and buy it," says Franklin Sellars, owner of Videotape Home Systems Inc., a Pasadena, Texas, store.

Nintendo and its allies deride this argument: They say kids are renting games over and over again, not just once to try them out. "Consumers can obtain complete use and enjoyment of many video games through rental without purchasing them, creating lost sales to the copyright owner," said Bruce Davis, chairman of game-maker Mediagenic, in testimony to Congress this summer.

The video-store lobby argues that the rationale for anti-rental laws should be to prevent copying. It is easy for consumers to copy records and PC software, but there is no simple way to duplicate a Nintendo game (although Nintendo has been circulating advertisements for a game-copying device marketed overseas by a Taiwanese concern, Baelih Co.). . . .

The Essence of the Story

Nintendo games cost from $40 to $50, and renting has become increasingly popular—making up an estimated 5% to 15% of the revenue of the nation's roughly 25,000 video stores.

Nintendo Co., based in Kyoto, Japan, wants a law to ban video game rentals, which, it argues, cut into game sales.

The video-store industry says that it helps Nintendo and the game-makers—much as video rentals help the movie industry—because people try games, like them, and then buy them.

Nintendo disagrees, arguing that people are renting games over and over again, not just once to try them out.

Both sides can claim legal precedent for a rental ban: videos can be rented, but records cannot. There is also support for a ban on the rental of personal-computer software.

The video-store lobby argues that the rationale for anti-rental laws should be to prevent copying. Records and PC software are easily copied, but Nintendo games are not—although a game-copying device apparently does exist.

Background and Analysis

If Nintendo could get a ban on game rentals and if it could keep other competitors out of the business, it would have a monopoly as shown in Fig. 1.

In that figure, the demand curve for Nintendo games is D, the marginal revenue curve is MR, the average total cost curve is ATC, and the marginal cost curve is MC. Profit is maximized by producing Q_M games per week at a price of P_M per game. Economic profit is shown by the blue rectangle.

Profit leads to entry. Video stores get into the game rental business, and other game-makers such as Camerica and Game Genie compete for business with Nintendo.

Video games for rent and games made by other producers are substitutes for Nintendo games, and their availability decreases the demand for Nintendo games.

The demand for Nintendo games falls, and the demand curve and marginal revenue curves shift to those shown in Fig. 2. Nintendo is in the position shown in that figure. The price of video games has fallen to P_C, and Nintendo is sharing the market with other firms producing Q_C games a week.

It is likely that the situation in the real-world video-games market lies between the two shown in Figs. 1 and 2. Nintendo is certainly not a monopolist, but it is making an economic profit, and entry into the industry continues.

It clearly pays Nintendo to try to get a ban on game rentals, since such a ban pushes the market toward that shown in Fig. 1 and away from that of Fig. 2.

It pays consumers of games to support rentals, since rentals lower the cost of games and increase their availability.

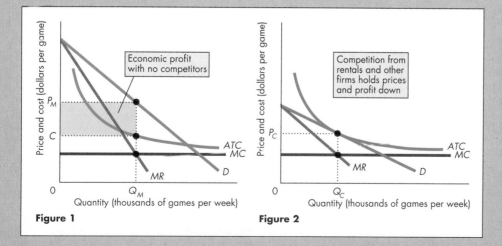

Figure 1

Figure 2

This result arises from the fact that the firm faces a downward-sloping demand curve. Only if the demand curve facing the firm is perfectly elastic is the long-run equilibrium at the point of minimum average total cost. The demand curve slopes down because of product differentiation. If each firm produces an identical product, each firm's output will be a perfect substitute for the outputs of all other firms and so the demand curve will be perfectly elastic. Thus it is product differentiation that produces excess capacity.

Efficiency of Monopolistic Competition

When we studied a perfectly competitive industry, we discovered that in some circumstances, such an industry achieves allocative efficiency. A key feature of allocative efficiency is that price equals marginal cost. Recall that price measures the value placed on the last unit bought by the consumer and marginal cost measures the opportunity cost of producing the last unit. We also discovered that monopoly is allocatively inefficient because it restricts output below the level at which price equals marginal cost. As we have just discovered, monopolistic competition shares this feature with monopoly. Even though there is zero economic profit in long-run equilibrium, the monopolistically competitive industry produces an output at which price equals average total cost and exceeds marginal cost.

Does this feature of monopolistic competition mean that this market structure, like monopoly, is allocatively inefficient? It does not. It is true that if the firms in a monopolistically competitive industry all produce identical products, products that are perfect substitutes, then each firm will face a perfectly elastic demand curve. In the long run, such firms will produce at the point of minimum average total cost and charge a price equal to marginal cost. But achieving that outcome will itself have a cost. The cost is the absence of product differentiation. Variety is valued by consumers, but variety is achievable only if firms make differentiated products. The loss in allocative efficiency that occurs in monopolistic competition has to be weighed against the gain of greater product variety.

Product Innovation

Another source of gain from monopolistically competitive industries is product innovation. Monopo-

listically competitive firms are constantly seeking out new products that will provide them with a competitive edge, even if only temporarily. A firm that manages to introduce a new and differentiated variety will temporarily face a steeper demand curve than before and will be able to temporarily increase its price. Entry of new firms will eventually compete away the profit arising from this initial advantage.

Advertising

Monopolistically competitive firms seek to differentiate their products partly by designing and introducing products that actually are different from those of the other firms in the industry. But they also attempt to differentiate the consumer's perception of the product. Advertising is the principal means whereby firms seek to achieve this end. But advertising increases the monopolistically competitive firm's costs above those of a competitive firm or a monopoly that does not advertise.

To the extent that advertising provides consumers with information about the precise nature of the differentiation of products, it serves a valuable purpose to the consumer, enabling a better product choice to be made. But the opportunity cost of the additional information provided through advertising has to be offset against the gain to the consumer from making a better choice.

The bottom line on the question of allocative efficiency of monopolistic competition is ambiguous. In some cases, the gains from extra product variety unquestionably offset the costs in the form of advertising and excess capacity. The tremendous varieties of books and magazines, clothing, food, and drink are examples of such gains. It is less easy to see the gains from being able to buy brand name drugs that have a chemical composition identical to that of a generic alternative. But some people do willingly pay more for the brand name alternative.

REVIEW

A firm in a monopolistically competitive industry faces a downward-sloping demand curve and so has to choose its price as well as the quantity to produce. Such firms also compete on product variety and by advertising. A lack of barriers to entry into such industry ensures that economic profit is competed away. In long-run equilibrium, firms make zero economic profit, charging a price equal to average total cost. But price exceeds marginal cost, and the quantity produced is below that which minimizes average total cost. The cost of monopolistic competition is excess capacity and high advertising expenditure; the gain is a wide product variety. ◆

Oligopoly

W e have defined oligopoly as a market in which a small number of producers compete with each other. In such a market, each producer is interdependent. The sales of any one producer depend upon that producer's price and the prices charged by the other producers. To see this interplay between prices and sales, suppose that you run one of the three gas stations in a small town. If you lower your price and your two competitors don't lower theirs, your sales increase but the sales of the other two firms decrease. In such a situation, the other firms will, most likely, lower their prices too. If they do cut their prices, your sales and profits will take a tumble. So, before deciding to cut your price, you try to predict how the other firms will react and you attempt to calculate the effects of those reactions on your own profit.

A variety of models have been developed to explain the determination of price and quantity in oligopoly markets, and no one theory has been found that can explain all the different types of behavior that we observe in such markets. The models fall into two broad groups: traditional models and game theory models. We'll look at examples of both types, starting with the traditional models.

Traditional Models of Oligopoly

E conomists have studied oligopoly and duopoly since the time of

Cournot in the 1830s. The earliest models were based on assumptions about the beliefs of each firm concerning the reactions of another firm (or firms) to its own actions. A particularly influential model was proposed in the 1930s by Paul M. Sweezy (editor of the *Monthly Review* for the past 40 years). It is known as the kinked demand curve model.

The Kinked Demand Curve Model

Sweezy's concern was to explain why prices did not fall more quickly during the years of the Great Depression—why prices were sticky. He proposed a theory based on the following propositions about the beliefs held by firms:

◆ If I increase my price, I will be on my own—others will not follow me.

◆ If I decrease my price, so will everyone else.

If these beliefs are correct, a firm faces a demand curve for its product that has a kink occurring at the current price, P, as shown in Fig. 13.4. At prices above P, the demand curve is relatively elastic. It reflects the belief that if the firm increases its price, it will be out of line with all other firms and so will experience a large fall in the quantity demanded. At prices below P, the demand curve is less elastic. It reflects the belief that if the firm cuts its price, all other firms will match the price cut and so will experience a small increase in the quantity demanded. This increase in the quantity demanded will not be as large as the decrease in the quantity demanded resulting from a price rise.

The kink in demand curve D creates a break in the marginal revenue curve (MR). To maximize profit, the firm produces the quantity that makes marginal cost and marginal revenue equal. But that output, Q, is where the marginal cost curve passes through the discontinuity in the marginal revenue curve—the gap ab. If marginal cost fluctuates between a and b, an example of which is shown in the figure with the marginal cost curves MC_0 and MC_1, the firm will change neither its price nor its quantity of output. Only if marginal cost fluctuates outside the range ab will the firm change its price and quantity produced.

Thus the kinked demand curve model predicts that price and quantity will be insensitive to small cost changes but will respond if cost changes are large enough. But there are two problems with the

FIGURE **13.4**

The Kinked Demand Curve Model

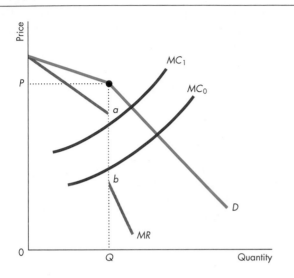

The price in an oligopoly market is *P*. Each firm believes that it faces the demand curve *D*. At prices above *P*, demand is highly elastic because the firm believes that its price increases will not be matched by other firms. At prices below *P*, demand is less elastic because the firm believes that its price cuts will be matched. Because the demand curve is kinked, the marginal revenue curve, *MR*, has a break, *ab*. Profit is maximized by producing *Q*. The marginal cost curve passes through the break in the marginal revenue curve. Marginal cost changes inside the range *ab* leave the price and quantity unchanged.

kinked demand curve model:

◆ It does not tell us how the price, *P*, is determined.

◆ It does not tell us what happens if firms discover that their belief about the demand curve is incorrect.

Suppose, for example, that marginal cost increases by enough to cause the firm to increase its price and that all firms experience the same increase in marginal cost so they all increase their prices together. Each firm bases its action on the belief that other firms will not match its price increase, but that belief is incorrect. The firm's beliefs are inconsistent with reality, and the demand and marginal revenue curves that summarize those beliefs are not the correct ones for the purpose of calculating the new profit-maxi-

mizing price and output. A firm that bases its actions on beliefs that are wrong does not maximize profit and might well end up incurring a loss leading to its eventual exit from the industry.

The kinked demand curve model is an attempt to understand price and output determination in an oligopoly in which the firms are of similar size. Another traditional model deals with the case in which firms differ in size and one firm dominates the industry.

Dominant Firm Oligopoly

Suppose there are eleven firms operating gas stations in a city. Big-G is huge and controls 50 percent of all the city's gas sales. The others are small, accounting for only 5 percent of the city's gas sales each. The market for gas in this city is a type of oligopoly, but one with a dominant firm.

To see how the price and quantity of gas sales are determined, look at Fig. 13.5. Here, in part (a), the demand curve *D* tells us how the total quantity of gas demanded in the city is influenced by its price. The supply curve S_{10} is the supply curve of the ten small price-taking suppliers all added together.

Part (b) shows the situation facing Big-G, the dominant firm. Big-G's marginal cost curve is *MC*. The demand curve for gasoline facing Big-G is *XD*. This curve is found by working out the amount of excess demand arising from the rest of the market. It graphs the difference between the quantity demanded and the quantity supplied in the rest of the market at each price. Thus, for example, at a price of $1 a gallon, there is an excess demand in the rest of the market measured by the distance *ab* in part (a). That same distance *ab* at the price $1 a gallon, in part (b), provides us with one point, point *b*, on Big-G's demand curve, *XD*.

If Big-G sold gasoline in a perfectly competitive city gas market, it would be willing to supply the gas at the prices indicated by its marginal cost curve. The city market would operate at the point of intersection of Big-G's marginal cost curve and its demand curve. But Big-G can do better for itself than that. Because it controls 50 percent of the city's gas market, it can restrict its sales, decreasing the amount of gas available and increasing its price.

To maximize its profit, Big-G operates like a monopoly. It calculates the extra revenue obtained from selling one more gallon of gas—its marginal

FIGURE **13.5**

A Dominant Firm Oligopoly

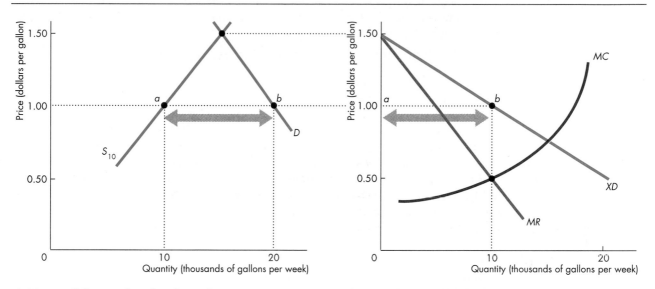

(a) Ten small firms and market demand

(b) Big–G's price and output decision

The demand curve for gas in a city is *D* in part (a). There are ten small firms that (taking all ten together) have a supply curve of S_{10} in part (a). In addition there is one large firm, Big-G, shown in part (b). Big-G faces the demand curve, *XD*, determined as market demand *D* minus the supply of the other firms, S_{10}— the excess demand not satisfied by the small

firms. Big-G's marginal revenue is *MR* and marginal cost is *MC*. Big-G sets the price to maximize profit by equating marginal cost, *MC*, and marginal revenue, *MR*. The price is $1 a gallon. Big-G sells 10 thousand gallons, and the other 10 firms sell 1 thousand gallons each.

revenue curve. It then sells the quantity that makes its marginal revenue equal to its marginal cost. Thus it sells 10 thousand gallons of gas for $1 a gallon. This combination of price and quantity of sales gives Big-G the biggest possible profit. The quantity of gas demanded in the entire city at $1 a gallon is 20 thousand gallons, as shown in part (a). The additional 10 thousand gallons are sold by 10 small firms that sell 1 thousand gallons each.

R E V I E W

Oligopoly is a market in which a small number of interdependent producers compete with each other. The profit of any one producer depends on the prices charged by that producer and all the

other producers. So any theory of oligopoly must contain an account of how firms react to each other's price changes. One traditional theory is based on the kinked demand curve model. This model assumes that if a firm increases its price, no other firm will follow, while if a firm decreases its price, so will all the other firms. Given these assumptions, each firm faces a kinked demand curve for its product and the kink occurs at the current price and quantity. The kink creates a break in the marginal revenue curve and a range over which marginal cost can vary without causing a change in the profit-maximizing price. Hence prices are sticky. Another traditional oligopoly model deals with an industry in which one firm dominates. The dominant firm acts like a monopoly and sets its profit-maximizing price. The other firms take this price as given and act like competitive firms. ◆

The dominant firm model of oligopoly works for some markets in which there really is a dominant producer. But even in such markets, it does not explain why sometimes the dominant firm tries to drive the smaller firms out of business rather than just putting up with their competition. Also it is of no help in predicting prices and quantities in markets in which firms are of similar size. The kinked demand curve model is an attempt to deal with this alternative case. But, as we've seen, that model has some weaknesses.

The weaknesses of traditional theories and a widespread dissatisfaction with them are the main forces leading to the development of new oligopoly models based on game theory.

The situation faced by firms in an oligopolistic industry is not unlike that faced by military planners. For example, in deciding whether to launch an attack on Iraq in the winter of 1991, U.S. military planners had to take into account the effects of U.S. actions on the behavior of Iraq. Would Iraq counter with chemical-laden SCUD missiles against Israel? Similarly, in making its plans, Iraq had to take into account the reactions of the United States—and in this case Israel. Neither side can assume that its rival's behavior will be independent of its own actions.

Whether we're studying price wars or star wars, we need a method of analyzing choices that takes into account the interactions between agents. Such a method has been developed and is called game theory.

Oligopoly and Game Theory

A **game theory** is a method of analyzing strategic behavior. Acting in a way that takes into account the expected behavior of others and the mutual recognition of interdependence is called **strategic behavior**. Game theory was invented by John von Neumann in 1937 and extended by von Neumann and Oskar Morgenstern in 1944. It is the topic of a massive amount of current research in economics.

Game theory seeks to understand oligopoly as well as political and social rivalries by using a method of analysis specifically designed to understand games of all types, including the familiar games of everyday life. We will begin our study of game theory, and its application to the behavior of firms, by considering those familiar games.

Familiar Games: What They Have in Common

What is a game? At first thought, the question seems silly. After all, there are many different games. There are ball games and parlor games, games of chance and games of skill. What do games of such diversity and variety have in common? In answering this question, we will focus on those features of games that are relevant and important for game theory and for analyzing oligopoly as a game. All games have three things in common:

◆ Rules
◆ Strategies
◆ Payoffs

Let's see how these common features of ordinary games apply to oligopoly.

Rules of the Oligopoly Game

The rules of the oligopoly game have not been written down by the "National Oligopoly League." They arise from the economic, social, and political environment in which the oligopolists operate.

One rule of the oligopoly game is the number of players—the number of firms in the market. Another rule is the method of calculating the score. This rule states that the score of each player is the player's economic profit or loss. The goal of each player of the oligopoly game is to make the largest possible profit. The remaining rules of the oligopoly game are determined by the framework of laws within which the oligopolists are operating. Oligopolists' actions are restricted only by the legal code.

Strategies in the Oligopoly Game

In game theory as in ordinary games, **strategies** are all the possible actions of each player. A comprehensive list of strategies in the oligopoly game would be very long, but it would include, for each player, such actions as:

◆ Raise price, lower price, hold price constant

- Raise output, lower output, hold output constant
- Increase advertising, cut advertising, hold advertising constant
- Enhance features of product, simplify product, leave product unchanged

Payoffs in the Oligopoly Game

In game theory, the score of each player is called the **payoff**. In the oligopoly game, the payoffs are the profits and losses of the players. These payoffs are determined by the oligopolists' strategies and by the constraints that they face. Constraints come from customers who determine the demand curve for the product of the oligopoly industry, from the technology available, and from the prices of the resources used by the oligopolists.

To understand how an oligopoly game works, it is revealing to study a special case of oligopoly called duopoly. **Duopoly** is a market structure in which there are two producers of a commodity competing with each other. There are few cases of duopoly on a national and international scale but many cases of local duopolies. For example, in some communities, there are two suppliers of milk, two local newspapers, two taxi companies, or two car rental firms. But the main reason for studying duopoly is not its "realism" but the fact that it captures all the essential features of oligopoly and yet is more manageable to analyze and understand. Furthermore, there is a well-known game called "the prisoners' dilemma" that captures some of the essential features of duopoly. It provides a good illustration of how game theory works and how it leads to predictions about the behavior of the players. Let's now turn our attention to studying a duopoly game, beginning with the prisoners' dilemma.

The Prisoners' Dilemma

Abe and Bob have been caught red-handed stealing a car. Facing airtight cases, they will receive a sentence of 2 years each for their crime. During his interviews with the two prisoners, the district attorney begins to suspect that he has stumbled on the two people who were responsible for a multimillion-dollar bank robbery some months earlier. The district attorney also knows, however, that this is just a suspicion. He has no evidence on which he can con-

vict them of the greater crime unless he can get each of them to confess. The district attorney comes up with the following idea.

He places the prisoners in separate rooms so that they cannot communicate with each other. Each prisoner is told that he is suspected of having carried out the bank robbery and that if he and his accomplice both confess to that crime, each will receive a sentence of 3 years. Each is also told that if he alone confesses and his accomplice does not, he will receive an even shorter sentence of 1 year while his accomplice will receive a 10-year sentence. The prisoners know that if neither of them confesses, then they will be tried for and convicted of only the lesser offense of car theft, which carries a 2-year prison term. How do the prisoners respond to the district attorney?

First, notice that the prisoners' dilemma is a game with two players. Each player has two strategies: to confess to the multimillion-dollar bank robbery or to deny the charge. Because there are two players, each with two strategies, there are four possible outcomes:

1. Neither player confesses.
2. Both players confess.
3. Abe confesses but Bob does not.
4. Bob confesses but Abe does not.

Each prisoner can work out exactly what will happen to him—his payoff—in each of these four situations. We can tabulate the four possible payoffs for each of the prisoners in what is called a payoff matrix for the game.

The Payoff Matrix A **payoff matrix** is a table that shows the payoffs for every possible action by each player for every possible action by each other player.

Table 13.3 shows a payoff matrix for Abe and Bob. The squares show the payoffs for each prisoner—the red triangle in each square shows Abe's and the blue triangle shows Bob's. If both prisoners confess (top left), each gets a prison term of 3 years. If Bob confesses but Abe denies (top right), Abe gets a 10-year sentence and Bob gets a 1-year sentence. If Abe confesses and Bob denies (bottom left), Abe gets a 1-year sentence and Bob gets a 10-year sentence. Finally, if both of them deny (bottom right), neither can be convicted of the bank robbery charge but both are sentenced for the car theft—a 2-year sentence.

TABLE 13.3

Prisoners' Dilemma Payoff Matrix

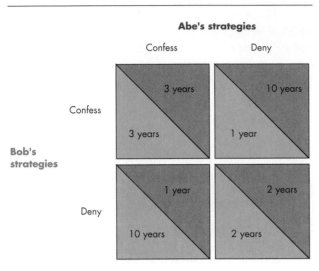

Each square shows the payoffs for the two players, Abe and Bob, for each possible pair of actions. In each square, Abe's payoff is shown in the red triangle and Bob's in the blue triangle. For example, if both confess, the payoffs are in the top left square. Abe reasons as follows: If Bob confesses, it pays me to confess because then I get 3 years rather than 10. If Bob denies, it pays me to confess because then I get 1 year rather than 2. Regardless of what Bob does, it pays me to confess. Thus Abe's dominant strategy is to confess. Bob reasons similarly: If Abe confesses, it pays me to confess and get 3 years rather than 10. If Abe denies, it pays me to confess and get 1 year rather than 2. Thus Bob's dominant strategy is to confess. Since each player's dominant strategy is to confess, the equilibrium of the game is for both players to confess and to get 3 years each.

The Dilemma The dilemma is seen by considering the consequences of confessing and not confessing. Each prisoner knows that if he and his accomplice remain silent about the bank robbery, they will be sentenced to only 2 years for stealing the car. Neither prisoner, however, has any way of knowing that his accomplice will remain silent and refuse to confess. Each knows that if the other confesses and he denies, the other will receive only a 1-year sentence while the one denying will receive a 10-year sentence. Each poses the following questions: Should I deny and rely on my accomplice to deny so that we may both get only 2 years? Or should I confess in the hope of getting just 1 year (provided that my accomplice denies) but knowing that if my accom-

plice does confess, we will both get 3 years in prison? Resolving the dilemma involves finding the equilibrium for the game.

Equilibrium The equilibrium of a game is called a Nash equilibrium; it is so named because it was first proposed by John Nash. A **Nash equilibrium** occurs when player A takes the best possible action given the action of player B and player B takes the best possible action given the action of player A. In the case of the prisoners' dilemma, the equilibrium occurs when Abe makes his best choice given Bob's choice and when Bob makes his best choice given Abe's choice.

The prisoners' dilemma is a game that has a special kind of Nash equilibrium called a dominant strategy equilibrium. A **dominant strategy** is a strategy that is the same regardless of the action taken by the other player. In other words, there is a unique best action regardless of what the other player does. A **dominant strategy equilibrium** occurs when there is a dominant strategy for each player. In the prisoners' dilemma, no matter what Bob does, Abe's best strategy is to confess; and no matter what Abe does, Bob's best strategy is to confess. Thus the equilibrium of the prisoners' dilemma is that each player confesses.

If each prisoner plays the prisoners' dilemma game in his own individual best interest, the outcome of the game will be that each confesses. To see why each player confesses, let's consider again their strategies and the payoffs from the alternative courses of action.

Strategies and Payoffs Look at the situation from Abe's point of view. Abe realizes that his outcome depends on the action Bob takes. If Bob confesses, it pays Abe to confess also, because in that case, he will be sentenced to 3 years rather than 10 years. But if Bob does not confess, it still pays Abe to confess, because in that case he will receive 1 year rather than 2 years. Abe reasons that regardless of Bob's action, his own best action is to confess.

The dilemma from Bob's point of view is identical to Abe's. Bob knows that if Abe confesses, he will receive 10 years if he does not confess or 3 years if he does. Therefore, if Abe confesses, it pays Bob to confess. Similarly, if Abe does not confess, Bob will receive 2 years for not confessing and 1 year if he confesses. Again, it pays Bob to confess. Bob's best action, regardless of Abe's action, is to confess.

Each prisoner sees that regardless of what the other prisoner does, his own best action is to confess. Since each player's best action is to confess, each confesses, each gets a 3-year prison term, and the district attorney has solved the bank robbery. This is the equilibrium of the game.

A Bad Outcome   For the prisoners, the equilibrium of the game, with each confessing, is not the best outcome. If neither of them confesses, each will get only 2 years for the lesser crime. Isn't there some way in which this better outcome can be achieved? It seems that there is not, because the players cannot communicate with each other. Each player can put himself in the other player's place, and so each player can figure out that there is a dominant strategy for each of them. The prisoners are indeed in a dilemma. Each knows that he can serve 2 years only if he can trust the other not to confess. Each prisoner also knows, however, that it is not in the best interest of the other to not confess. Thus each prisoner knows that he has to confess, thereby delivering a bad outcome for both.

Let's now see how we can use the ideas we've just developed to understand price fixing, price wars, and the behavior of duopolists.

A Duopoly Game

To study a duopoly game, we're going to build a model of a duopoly industry.[1] Suppose that only two firms, Trick and Gear, make a particular kind of electric switchgear. Our goal is to make predictions about the prices charged and the outputs produced by each of the two firms. We are going to pursue that goal by constructing a duopoly game that the two firms will play. To set out the game, we need to specify the strategies of the players and the payoff matrix.

We will suppose that the two firms enter into a collusive agreement. A **collusive agreement** is an

agreement between two (or more) producers to restrict output in order to raise prices and profits. Such an agreement is illegal and is undertaken in secret. A group of firms that has entered into a collusive agreement to restrict output and increase prices and profits is called a **cartel**. The strategies that firms in a cartel can pursue are to:

♦ Comply
♦ Cheat

Complying simply means sticking to the agreement. Cheating means breaking the agreement in a manner designed to benefit the cheating firm and harm the other firm.

Since each firm has two strategies, there are four possible combinations of actions for the two firms:

♦ Both firms comply.
♦ Both firms cheat.
♦ Trick complies and Gear cheats.
♦ Gear complies and Trick cheats.

We need to work out the payoffs to each firm from each of these four possible sets of actions. To do that, we need to explore the costs and demand conditions in the industry.

Cost and Demand Conditions

The cost of producing switchgears is the same for both Trick and Gear. The average total cost curve (*ATC*) and the marginal cost curve (*MC*) for each firm are shown in Fig. 13.6(a). The market demand curve for switchgears (*D*) is shown in Fig. 13.6(b). Each firm produces an identical switchgear product, so one firm's switchgear is a perfect substitute for the other's. The market price of each firm's product, therefore, is identical. The quantity demanded depends on that price—the higher the price, the lower is the quantity demanded.

Notice that in this industry, there is room for only two firms. For each firm, the *minimum efficient scale* of production is 3,000 switchgear units a week. When the price equals the average total cost of production at the minimum efficient scale, total industry demand is 6,000 switchgear units a week. Thus there is no room for three firms in this industry. If there were only one firm in the industry, it would make an enormous profit and invite competition. If there were three firms, at least one of them would make a loss. Thus the number of firms that an

FIGURE **13.6**

Costs and Demand

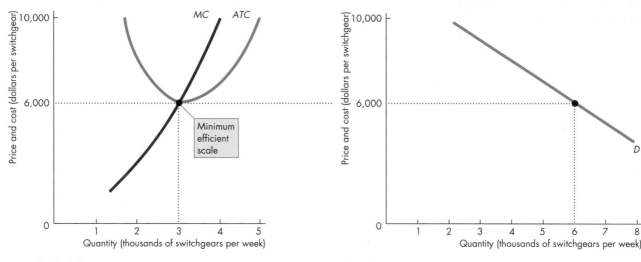

(a) Individual firm

(b) Industry

Part (a) shows the costs facing Trick and Gear, two duopolists that make switchgears. Each firm faces identical costs. The average total cost curve for each firm is *ATC*, and the marginal cost curve is *MC*. For each firm, the minimum efficient scale of production is 3,000 units per

week and the average total cost of producing that output is $6,000 a unit. Part (b) shows the industry demand curve. At a price of $6,000, the quantity demanded is 6,000 units per week. There is room for only two firms in this industry.

industry can sustain depends on the relationship between cost and the industry's demand conditions.

In the model industry that we're studying here, the particular cost and demand conditions assumed are designed to generate an industry in which two firms can survive in the long run. In real-world oligopoly and duopoly, barriers to entry may arise from economies of scale of the type featured in our model industry, but there are other possible barriers as well (as discussed in Chapter 12, p. 314).

Colluding to Maximize Profits

Let's begin by working out the payoffs to the two firms if they collude to make the maximum industry profit—the profit that would be made by a single monopoly. The calculations that the two firms will perform are exactly the same calculations that a monopoly performs. (You have already studied such calculations in Chapter 12, pp. 314–315.) The only additional thing that the duopolists have to do is to

agree on how much of the total output each of them will produce.

The price and quantity that maximize industry profit for the duopolists are shown in Fig. 13.7. Part (a) shows the situation for each firm, and part (b) for the industry as a whole. The curve labeled *MR* is the industry marginal revenue curve. The curve labeled MC_I is the industry marginal cost curve if each firm produces the same level of output. That curve is constructed by adding together the outputs of the two firms at each level of marginal cost. That is, at each level of marginal cost, industry output is twice as much as the output of each individual firm. Thus the curve MC_I in part (b) is twice as far to the right as the curve *MC* in part (a).

To maximize industry profit, the duopolists agree to restrict output to the rate that makes the industry marginal cost and marginal revenue equal. That output rate, as shown in part (b), is 4,000 switchgear units a week. The highest price for which the 4,000 units can be sold is $9,000 each. Let's suppose that

Colluding to Make Monopoly Profits

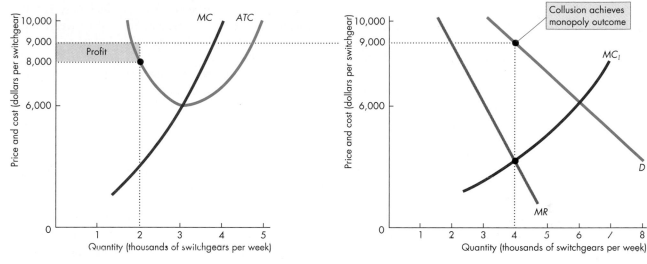

(a) Individual firm

(b) Industry

If Trick and Gear come to a collusive agreement, they can act as a single monopolist and maximize profit. Part (a) shows the consequences of reaching such an agreement for each firm, and part (b) shows the situation in the industry as a whole.

To maximize profit, the firms first calculate the industry marginal cost curve (*MC₁*) shown in part (b)—the horizontal sum of the two firms' marginal cost curves (*MC*) in part (a). Next they calculate the industry marginal revenue, *MR* in part (b). They then choose the output

rate that makes marginal revenue equal to marginal cost (4,000 units per week). They agree to sell that output for a price of $9,000, the price at which 4,000 switchgear units are demanded.

The costs and profit of each firm are seen in part (a). Each firm produces half the total output—2,000 units per week. Average total cost is $8,000 per unit, so each firm makes a profit of $2 million (blue rectangle)—2,000 units multiplied by $1,000 profit per unit.

Trick and Gear agree to split the market equally so that each firm produces 2,000 switchgear units a week. The average total cost (*ATC*) of producing 2,000 units a week is $8,000, so the profit per unit is $1,000 and the total profit is $2 million (2,000 units × $1,000 per unit). The profit of each firm is represented by the blue rectangle in Fig. 13.7(a).

We have just described one possible outcome for the duopoly game: the two firms collude to produce the monopoly profit-maximizing output and divide that output equally between themselves. From the industry point of view, this solution is identical to a monopoly. A duopoly that operates in this way is indistinguishable from a monopoly. The profit that is made by a monopoly is the maximum profit that can be made by colluding duopolists.

Cheating on a Collusive Agreement

Under a collusive agreement, the colluding firms restrict output to make their joint marginal revenue equal to their joint marginal cost. They set the highest price for which the quantity produced can be sold—a price higher than marginal cost. In such a situation, each firm recognizes that if it cheats on the agreement and raises its output, even though the price will fall below that agreed to, more will be added to revenue than to cost, so its profit will increase. Since each firm recognizes this fact, there is a temptation for each firm to cheat. There are two possible cheating situations: one in which one firm cheats and one in which both firms cheat. What happens if one of the firms cheats on the agreement?

One Firm Cheats What is the effect of one firm cheating on a collusive agreement? How much extra profit does the cheating firm make? What happens to the profit of the firm that sticks to the agreement in the face of cheating by the other firm? Let's work out the answers to these questions.

There are many different ways for a firm to cheat. We will work out just one possibility. Suppose that Trick convinces Gear that there has been a fall in industry demand and that it cannot sell its share of the output at the agreed price. It tells Gear that it plans to cut its price in order to sell the agreed 2,000 switchgear units each week. Since the two firms produce a virtually identical product, Gear has no alternative but to match the price cut of Trick.

In fact, there has been no fall in demand, and the lower price has been calculated by Trick to be exactly the price needed to sell the additional output that it plans to produce. Gear, though lowering its price in line with that of Trick, restricts its output to the previously agreed level.

Figure 13.8 illustrates the consequences of Trick cheating in this way: part (a) shows what happens to Gear (the complier), part (b) shows what happens to Trick (the cheat), and part (c) shows what is happening in the industry as a whole.

Suppose that Trick decides to raise output from 2,000 to 3,000 units a week. It recognizes that if Gear sticks to the agreement to produce only 2,000 units a week, total output will be 5,000 a week and, given demand in part (c), the price will have to be cut to $7,500 a unit.

Gear continues to produce 2,000 units a week at a cost of $8,000 a unit and incurs a loss of $500 a unit, or $1 million a week. This loss is represented by the red rectangle in part (a). Trick produces 3,000 units a week at an average total cost of $6,000 each. With a price of $7,500, Trick makes a profit of $1,500 a unit and therefore a total profit of $4.5 million. This profit is the blue rectangle in part (b).

We have now described a second possible outcome for the duopoly game—one of the firms cheats on the collusive agreement. In this case, the industry output is larger than the monopoly output and the industry price is lower than the monopoly price. The

---

FIGURE **13.8**

Cheating on a Collusive Agreement

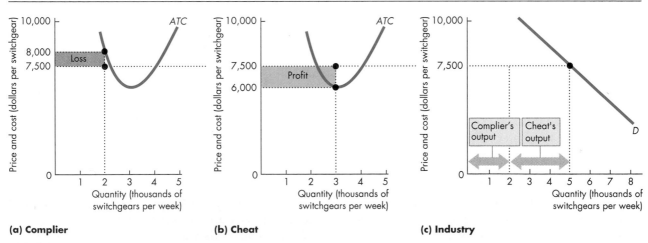

(a) Complier **(b) Cheat** **(c) Industry**

In part (a), one firm complies with the agreement. In part (b), the other firm cheats by raising output above the agreed limit to 3,000 switchgears per week. Either firm can be the complier and the other the cheat. In part (c), the effect on the industry price of the actions of the cheat is shown. As a result of cheating, industry output rises to 5,000 units a week and the market price falls to $7,500—the price at which 5,000 switchgear units can be sold.

Part (a) describes the complier's situation. Output remains at 2,000 units, and average total cost remains at $8,000 per unit. The firm loses $500 per switchgear and makes a total loss of $1 million (red rectangle). Part (b) describes the cheat's situation. Average total cost is $6,000 per unit, and profit per switchgear is $1,500, so the cheat's total profit is $4.5 million (blue rectangle).

total profit made by the industry is also smaller than the monopoly's profit. Trick (the cheat) makes a profit of $4.5 million, and Gear (the complier) incurs a loss of $1 million. The industry makes a profit of $3.5 million. Thus the industry profit is $0.5 million less than the maximum profit would be with a monopoly outcome. But that profit is distributed unevenly. Trick makes an even bigger profit than it would under the collusive agreement, while Gear makes a loss.

We have just worked out what happens if Trick cheats and Gear complies with the collusive agreement. There is another similar outcome that would arise if Gear cheated and Trick complied with the agreement. The industry profit and price would be the same, but in this case, Gear (the cheat) would make a profit of $4.5 million and Trick (the complier) would incur a loss of $1 million.

There is yet another possible outcome—both firms cheat on the agreement.

Both Firms Cheat   Suppose that instead of just one firm cheating on the collusive agreement, both firms cheat. In particular, suppose that each firm behaves in exactly the same way as the cheating firm that we have just analyzed. Each firm tells the other that it is unable to sell its output at the going price and that it plans to cut its price. But since both firms cheat, each will propose a successively lower price. They will stop proposing lower prices only when the price has reached $6,000. That is the price that equals minimum average cost. At a price of less than $6,000, each firm will make a loss. At a price of $6,000, each firm will cover all its costs and make zero economic profit. Also, at a price of $6,000, each firm will want to produce 3,000 units a week, so the industry output will be 6,000 units a week. Given the demand conditions, 6,000 units can be sold at a price of $6,000 each.

The situation just described is illustrated in Fig. 13.9. Each firm, shown in part (a) of the figure, is

FIGURE **13.9**

Both Firms Cheat

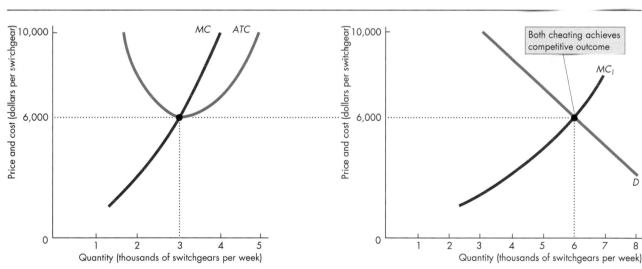

(a) Individual firm

If both firms cheat by raising their output and lowering the price, the collusive agreement completely breaks down. The limit to the breakdown of the agreement is the competitive equilibrium. Neither firm will want to cut the price below $6,000 (minimum average total cost), because to do so will result in losses. Part (a) shows the situation facing each firm. At a price of $6,000, the firm's profit-maximizing output is 3,000 units per week. At that output rate, price equals marginal cost,

(b) Industry

and it also equals average total cost. Economic profit is zero. Part (b) describes the situation in the industry as a whole. The industry marginal cost curve (MC_I)—the horizontal sum of the individual firms' marginal cost curves (MC)—intersects the demand curve at 6,000 switchgear units per week and at a price of $6,000. This output and price are the ones that would prevail in a competitive industry.

producing 3,000 units a week, and this output level occurs at the point of minimum average total cost ($6,000 per unit). The market as a whole, shown in part (b), operates at the point at which the demand curve (*D*) intersects the industry marginal cost curve. This marginal cost curve is constructed as the horizontal sum of the marginal cost curves of the two firms. Each firm has lowered its price and increased its output in order to try to gain an advantage over the other firm. They have pushed this process as far as they can without incurring losses.

We have now described a third possible outcome of this duopoly game—both firms cheat. If both firms cheat on the collusive agreement, the output of each firm is 3,000 units a week and the price is $6,000. Each firm makes zero profit.

The Payoff Matrix and Equilibrium

Now that we have described the strategies and the payoffs in the duopoly game, let's summarize the strategies and the payoffs in the form of the game's payoff matrix and then calculate the equilibrium.

Table 13.4 sets out the payoff matrix for this game. It is constructed in exactly the same way as the payoff matrix for the prisoners' dilemma in Table 13.3. The squares show the payoffs for the two firms—Gear and Trick. In this case, the payoffs are profits. (In the case of the prisoners' dilemma, the payoffs were losses.)

The table shows that if both firms cheat (top left), they achieve the perfectly competitive outcome—each firm makes zero economic profit. If both firms comply (bottom right), the industry makes the monopoly profit and each firm earns a profit of $2 million. The top right and bottom left squares show what happens if one firm cheats while the other complies. The firm that cheats collects a profit of $4.5 million, and the one that complies makes a loss of $1 million.

This duopoly game is, in fact, the same as the prisoners' dilemma that we examined earlier in this chapter; it is a duopolist's dilemma. You will see this once you have determined what the equilibrium of this game is.

To find the equilibrium, let's look at things from the point of view of Gear. Gear reasons as follows: Suppose that Trick cheats. If we comply with the agreement, we make a loss of $1 million. If we also cheat, we make a zero profit. Zero profit is better than a $1 million loss, so it will pay us to cheat. But

TABLE 13.4

Duopoly Payoff Matrix

Each square shows the payoffs from a pair of actions. For example, if both firms comply with the collusive agreement, the payoffs are recorded in the square at the bottom right corner of the table. Gear's payoff is shown in the red triangle and Trick's in the blue triangle. Gear reasons as follows: If Trick cheats, it pays me to cheat and make a zero economic profit rather than a $1 million loss. If Trick complies, it pays me to cheat and make a $4.5 million profit rather than a $2 million profit. Thus cheating is Gear's dominant strategy. Trick reasons similarly: If Gear cheats, it pays me to cheat and make a zero profit rather than a $1 million loss. If Gear complies, it pays me to cheat and make a $4.5 million profit rather than a $2 million profit. The equilibrium is a Nash equilibrium in which both firms cheat.

suppose Trick complies with the agreement. If we cheat, we will make a profit of $4.5 million, and if we comply, we will make a profit of $2 million. A $4.5 million profit is better than a $2 million profit, so it would again pay us to cheat. Thus, regardless of whether Trick cheats or complies, it pays us to cheat. Gear's dominant strategy is to cheat.

Trick comes to the same conclusion as Gear. Therefore both firms will cheat. The equilibrium of this game, then, is that both firms cheat on the agreement. Although there are only two firms in the industry, the price and quantity are the same as in a competitive industry. Each firm makes zero profit.

Although we have done this analysis for only two firms, it would not make any difference (other than to increase the amount of arithmetic) if we were to play the game with three, four, or more firms. In other words, though we have analyzed duopoly, the game theory approach can also be used to analyze oligopoly. The analysis of oligopoly is much harder, but the essential ideas that we have learned apply to oligopoly.

Repeated Games

The first game that we studied, the prisoners' dilemma, was played just once. The prisoners did not have an opportunity to observe the outcome of the game and then play it again. The duopolist game just described was also played only once. But real-world duopolists do get opportunities to play repeatedly against each other. This fact suggests that real-world duopolists might find some way of learning to cooperate so that their efforts to collude are more effective.

If a game is played repeatedly, one player always has the opportunity to penalize the other player for previous "bad" behavior. If Trick refuses to cooperate this week, then Gear can refuse to cooperate next week (and vice versa). If Gear cheats this week, won't Trick cheat next week? Before Gear cheats this week, shouldn't it take account of the possibility of Trick cheating next week?

What is the equilibrium of this more complicated prisoners' dilemma game when it is repeated indefinitely? Actually, there is more than one possibility. One is the Nash equilibrium that we have just analyzed. Both players cheat, and each makes zero profit forever. In such a situation, it will never pay one of the players to start complying unilaterally, because to do so would result in a loss for that player and a profit for the other. The price and quantity will remain at the competitive levels forever.

But another equilibrium is possible—one in which the players make and share the monopoly profit. How might this equilibrium come about? Why wouldn't it always pay each firm to try to get away with cheating? The key to answering this question is the fact that when a prisoners' dilemma game is played repeatedly, the players have an increased array of strategies. Each player can punish the other player for previous actions.

There are two extremes of punishment. The smallest penalty that one player can impose on the other is what is called "tit for tat." A **tit-for-tat strategy** is one in which a player cooperates in the current period if the other player cooperated in the previous

period but cheats in the current period if the other player cheated in the previous period. The most severe form of punishment that one player can impose on the other arises in what is called a trigger strategy. A **trigger strategy** is one in which a player cooperates if the other player cooperates but plays the Nash equilibrium strategy forever thereafter if the other player cheats. Since a tit-for-tat strategy and a trigger strategy are the extremes of punishment—the most mild and most severe—there are evidently other intermediate degrees of punishment. For example, if one player cheats on the agreement, the other player could punish by refusing to cooperate for a certain number of periods. In the duopoly game between Gear and Trick, it turns out that a tit-for-tat strategy keeps both players cooperating and earning monopoly profits. Let's see why.

Table 13.5 sets out the profits that each firm will make in each period of play under two sets of condi-

TABLE 13.5

Repeated Duopoly Game

Period of play	Collude		Cheat with tit-for-tat strategy	
	Trick's profit	Gear's profit	Trick's profit	Gear's profit
	(millions of dollars)		(millions of dollars)	
1	2	2	2.0	2.0
2	2	2	4.5	−1.0
3	2	2	−1.0	4.5
4	2	2	2.0	2.0
.	.	.	.	.
.	.	.	.	.

If duopolists repeatedly play the "cooperate" strategy, each makes $2 million in each period. If one player cheats in one period, the other player cheats in the following period—tit for tat. The profit from cheating can be made only for a single period. In the following period, the other player cheats and the first player must cooperate if the cooperative agreement is to be restored in period 4. The profit from cheating, calculated over four periods of play, is lower than that from colluding. Under collusion, each player makes $8 million; with a single cheat responded to with a tit for tat, each makes a profit of $7.5 million. It pays each player to cooperate, so cooperation is an equilibrium.

tions: first, if they cooperate, and second, if cheating is responded to with a tit-for-tat strategy. As you can see, as long as both firms stick to the collusive agreement, they make the monopoly profit ($2 million per period each). Suppose that Trick contemplates cheating in period 2. The cheating produces a quick $4.5 million profit and inflicts a $1 million loss on Gear. The next period, Gear will hit Trick with its tit-for-tat response and cheat. If Trick reverts to cooperating (to induce Gear to cooperate in period 4), Gear now makes a profit of $4.5 million and Trick makes a loss of $1 million. Adding up the profits over two periods of play, Trick comes out ahead by cheating ($6.5 million compared with $4 million). But if we run the game forward for four periods, Trick would be better off having cooperated. In that case, it would have made $8 million in profit compared with $7.5 million from cheating and generating Gear's tit-for-tat response.

Though we have just worked out what happens if Trick cheats, we can turn the tables and perform the same thought experiment for Gear cheating. We will come up with the same conclusion—it pays Gear to collude. Since it pays both firms to stick with the collusive agreement, both firms will do so and the monopoly price, quantity, and profit will prevail in the industry. This equilibrium is called a **cooperative equilibrium**—an equilibrium resulting from each player responding rationally to the credible threat of the other player to inflict heavy damage if the agreement is broken. But in order for this strategy to work, the threat must be credible—that is, each player must recognize that it is in the interest of the other player to respond with a "tit for tat." The tit-for-tat strategy is credible because if one player cheats, it clearly does not pay the other player to continue complying. So the threat of cheating next period is credible and sufficient to support the monopoly equilibrium outcome.

Two firms form a cartel to charge the same price as a monopoly would charge and share the monopoly profit. Each firm may either comply with the agreement or break it. If the game is played just once, both firms break the agreement. The price is competed down to the competitive level and profits are competed away. If the game is played repeatedly, cheating can be punished and this threat enables the duopolists to make the monopoly price stick and share the monopoly profit. ◆

Uncertainty

In reality, there are random fluctuations in demand and in costs that make it impossible for one firm to detect whether the other firm is cheating. For example, a fall in demand can lower the industry price. One firm increasing its output can also lower the industry price. If a firm observes only that the industry price has fallen, it cannot tell which of these forces caused it. If it knows that the price has fallen because of a fall in demand, its profit-maximizing action will be to continue cooperating with the other firm to maintain the monopoly agreement. But if the price fall resulted from the other firm cheating and increasing its output, the profit-maximizing response will be to hit the other firm with a tit for tat in the next period. Yet by observing only the price fall, neither firm can tell whether the other firm has cheated. What can the firms do in a situation such as this one?

If each always *assumes* that whenever the price falls it is because the other firm has cheated, the monopoly agreement will repeatedly break down and the firms will fail to realize the potentially available monopoly profits. If, on the other hand, one firm assumes that the other firm is always cooperating and that any price falls have resulted from market forces beyond the control of either firm, then that other firm will have an incentive to cheat. (Recall that with one firm cheating and the other cooperating, the cheat makes even bigger profits than when they both cooperate.) To remove that incentive to cheat, each firm will assume that the other is cooperating, provided that the price does not fall by more than a certain amount. If the price does fall below that predetermined amount, each firm will react as if the other firm had cheated. When market forces take the price back up above the critical level, the firms will cooperate again.

R E V I E W

G ame theory, a method of analyzing actions that takes into account the expected reactions of others, is a tool that can be used to explain the behavior of oligopolists. A classic game, the prisoners' dilemma, explains the behavior of duopolists.

Games and Price Wars

Let's see whether the theory of price and output determination under duopoly can help us understand real-world behavior and, in particular, price wars. Suppose that two (or more) producers reach a collusive agreement and set their prices at the monopoly profit-maximizing level. Let's also suppose that the agreement is enforced by each firm pursuing a strategy that involves cooperating unless the price falls below a certain critical level, as described above. Fluctuations in demand will lead to fluctuations in the industry price and output. Most of the time, these fluctuations are small, and the price does not fall far enough to make either firm depart from the agreement. When the price falls below the critical level, each firm responds by abandoning the agreement. What happens looks exactly like a price war. It is extremely unlikely that each firm abandons the agreement and lowers its price at exactly the same moment. But it appears as if one firm abandons the agreement and then the other abandons it in retaliation. But what is actually happening is that each firm is reacting to the large price fall in a manner that maintains the credibility of the threat to the other firm and that preserves the monopoly cooperative equilibrium in normal demand conditions. When demand increases again and market forces increase the price, the firms revert to their cooperative behavior, reaping the monopoly profit.

Thus there will be cycles of price wars and the restoration of collusive agreements. The behavior of prices and outputs in the oil industry can be explained by the type of game that you have just studied. The market for crude oil is dominated by the OPEC cartel. From time to time, to increase the price of oil, the cartel has agreed to production limits for each member. But also, from time to time, the agreements have broken down. Members of the cartel have exceeded their agreed production levels, and prices have fallen.

The Incredible Electrical Conspiracy

Price-fixing arrangements such as those we've just studied are illegal in the United States. This means that any conspiracies by firms to fix prices have to be undertaken in secrecy. As a result, we get to know about such agreements only after they have been cracked by the Justice Department.

One famous price-fixing arrangement, involving almost 30 firms, has been called "the incredible electrical conspiracy."[2] For most of the 1950s, 30 producers of electrical equipment, including such giants as General Electric and Westinghouse, fixed prices "on items ranging from $2 insulators to huge turbine generators costing several million dollars."[3]

Although the electrical equipment pricing conspiracy operated throughout the entire decade of the 1950s, the individual firms conspiring often changed. In particular, General Electric sometimes participated in the price-fixing agreement and sometimes dropped out, undercutting the agreed price and dragging down the industry price and profit in much the way that the model we've studied predicts.

Preserving Secrecy

Because collusion is illegal, one special problem that colluding firms face is hiding the fact of their collusion and preserving secrecy. "The incredible electrical conspiracy" provides a fascinating view of one way in which this problem has been solved. The particular device used in this conspiracy was called the "phases of the moon" pricing formula.

> [These pricing formulas were listed on] sheets of paper, each containing a half dozen columns of figures. . . . One group of columns established the bidding order of the seven switchgear manufacturers—a different company, each with its own code number, phasing into the priority position every two weeks (hence "phases of the moon"). A second group of columns, keyed into the company code numbers, established how much each company was to knock off the agreed-upon book price. For example, if it were No 1's (G.E.'s) turn to be low bidder at a certain number of dollars off book, then all Westinghouse (No 2), or Allis-Chalmers (No 3) had to do was look for their code number in the second group of columns to find how many dollars they were to bid *above* No 1. These bids would then

[2]Richard A. Smith, "The Incredible Electrical Conspiracy," Part I, *Fortune* (April 1961): 132; Part II, (May 1961): 161.

[3]James V. Koch, *Industrial Organization and Prices,* 2nd ed. (Englewood Cliffs, N.J.: Prentice-Hall, 1980): 423.

be fuzzed up by having a little added to them or taken away by companies 2, 3, etc. Thus, there was not even a hint that the winning bid had been collusively arrived at.[4]

Before stumbling on the "phases of the moon" papers, the Justice Department was having a very hard time proving conspiracy, but, with the formula in hand, it was able to put the conspiracy under the spotlight and end it.

Other Strategic Variables

We have focused here on firms that play a simple game and consider only two possible strategies (complying and cheating) concerning two variables (price and quantity produced). However, the approach that we have used can be extended to deal with a much wider range of choices facing firms. For example, a firm has to decide whether to enter or leave an industry; whether to mount an expensive advertising campaign; whether to modify its product; how reliable to make its product (the more reliable a product, usually, the more expensive it is to produce); whether to price discriminate and, if so, among which groups of customers and to what degree; and whether to undertake a large research and development (R&D) effort aimed at lowering production costs. All of these choices that firms make can be analyzed by using game theory. The basic method of analysis that you have studied can be applied to these problems by working out the payoff for each of the alternative strategies and then finding the equilibrium of the game. Let's look at an example—based on an important real-world case—of an R&D game.

An R&D Game in the Disposable Diaper Industry

Disposable diapers were first marketed in 1966. The two market leaders from the start of this industry

---

[4]Richard A. Smith, "The Incredible Electrical Conspiracy," Part II, *Fortune* (May 1961): 210.

have been Procter & Gamble (makers of Pampers) and Kimberly-Clark (makers of Huggies). Procter & Gamble has 60 to 70 percent of the total market, while Kimberly-Clark has 25 percent. The disposable diaper industry is fiercely competitive. When the product was first introduced in 1966, it had to be cost-effective in competition against reusable, laundered diapers. A massive research and development effort resulted in the development of machines that could make disposable diapers at a low enough cost to achieve that initial competitive edge. But, as the industry has matured, a large number of firms have tried to get into the business and take market share away from the two industry leaders, and the industry leaders themselves have battled against each other to maintain or increase their own market share.

The disposable diaper industry is one in which technological advances that result in small decreases in the average total cost of production can provide an individual firm with an enormous competitive advantage. The current machines can produce disposable diapers at a rate of 3,000 an hour—a rate that represents a tenfold increase on the output rate of just a decade earlier. The firm that develops and uses the least-cost technology gains a competitive edge, undercutting the rest of the market, increasing its market share, and increasing its profit. But the research and development effort that has to be undertaken to achieve even small cost reductions is itself very costly. This cost of research and development has to be deducted from the profit resulting from the increased market share that lower costs achieve. If no firm does R&D, every firm can be better off, but if one firm initiates the R&D activity, all must.

Each firm is in a research and development dilemma situation. Table 13.6 illustrates the dilemma (with hypothetical numbers) for the R&D game that Kimberly-Clark and Procter & Gamble are playing. Each firm has two strategies: to spend $25 million a year on R&D or to spend nothing on R&D. If neither firm spends on R&D, they make a joint profit of $100 million, $30 million for Kimberly-Clark and $70 million for Procter & Gamble (bottom right square in payoff matrix). If each firm conducts R&D, market shares are maintained but each firm's profit is lower, by the amount spent on R&D (top right square of payoff matrix). If Kimberly-Clark pays for R&D but Procter & Gamble does not, Kimberly-Clark gains a large part of Procter &

TABLE 13.6

Pampers versus Huggies: An R&D Game

Procter & Gamble's strategies

If both firms undertake R&D, their payoffs are those shown in the top left square. If neither firm undertakes R&D, their payoffs are in the bottom right square. When one firm undertakes R&D and the other one does not, their payoffs are in the top right and bottom left squares. The dominant strategy equilibrium for this game is for both firms to undertake R&D. The structure of this game is the same as that of the prisoners' dilemma.

Gamble's market. Kimberly-Clark profits, and Procter & Gamble loses (top right square of payoff matrix). Finally, if Procter & Gamble invests in R&D and Kimberly-Clark does not, Procter & Gamble gains market share from Kimberly-Clark, increasing its profit while Kimberly-Clark makes a loss.

Confronted with the payoff matrix in Table 13.6, the two firms calculate their best strategies. Kimberly-Clark reasons as follows: If Procter & Gamble does not undertake R&D, we make $85 million if we do and $30 million if we do not; therefore it pays to conduct R&D. If Procter & Gamble conducts R&D, we lose $10 million if we don't and make $5 million if we do. Again, R&D pays off. Thus conducting R&D is a dominant strategy for Kimberly-Clark. Doing it pays regardless of Procter & Gamble's decision.

Procter & Gamble reasons similarly: If Kimberly-Clark does not undertake R&D, we make $70 mil-

lion if we follow suit and $85 million if we conduct R&D. It therefore pays to conduct R&D. If Kimberly-Clark does undertake R&D, we make $45 million by doing the same and lose $10 million by not doing R&D. Again, it pays to conduct R&D. So, for Procter & Gamble, R&D is also a dominant strategy.

Since R&D is a dominant strategy for both players, it is the Nash equilibrium. The outcome of this game is that both firms conduct R&D. They make lower profits than they would if they could collude to achieve the cooperative outcome of no R&D.

The real-world situation has more players than Kimberly-Clark and Procter & Gamble. There are a large number of other firms sharing a small portion of the market, all of them ready to eat into the market share of Procter & Gamble and Kimberly-Clark. So the R&D effort by these two firms not only serves the purpose of maintaining shares in their own battle, but also helps to keep barriers to entry high enough to preserve their joint market share.

◆ ◆ ◆ ◆ We have now studied the four main market types—perfect competition, monopolistic competition, oligopoly, and monopoly—and discovered how prices and outputs, revenue, cost, and profit are determined in these industries. We have used the various models to make predictions about behavior and to assess the efficiency of alternative market structures. ◆ ◆ A key element in our analysis of the markets for goods and services is the behavior of costs. Costs are determined partly by technology and partly by the prices of factors of production. We have treated those factor prices as given. We are now going to see how factor prices are themselves determined. Factor prices interact with the goods market that we have just studied in two ways. First, they determine the firm's production costs. Second, they determine household incomes and therefore influence the demand for goods and services. Factor prices also have an important effect upon the distribution of income. The firms that we've been studying in the past four chapters decide *how* to produce; the interactions of households and firms in the markets for goods and services decide *what* will be produced. But the factor prices determined in the markets for factors of production determine *for whom* the various goods and services are produced.

Varieties of Market Structure

Most real-world industries lie between the extremes of perfect competition and monopoly. The degree of competition is sometimes measured by the four-firm concentration ratio—the percentage of the value of the sales of an industry accounted for by its four largest firms—or by the Herfindahl-Hirschman Index. High concentration ratios indicate a relatively low degree of competition, and vice versa, with some important qualifications. Three problems with concentration ratios are: (1) they refer to the national market, but some industries are local while others are international; (2) they do not tell us about the degree of turnover of firms and the ease of entry; and (3) some firms classified in one particular industry operate in several others. In the United States, most industries are effectively competitive, but there are important non-competitive elements.

Two models of industries that lie between monopoly and perfect competition are monopolistic competition and oligopoly. Monopolistic competition is a market type in which a large number of firms compete, each making a slightly differentiated product from the others by competing on price, quality, and advertising. Oligopoly is a market type in which a small number of firms compete with each other and in which the actions of any one firm have an important impact on the profit of the others. (pp. 342–346)

Monopolistic Competition

Monopolistic competition occurs when a large number of firms compete with each other by making slightly different products. Under monopolistic competition, each firm faces a downward-sloping demand curve and so has to choose its price as well as its output level. Because there is free entry, in long-run equilibrium zero economic profit is earned. When profit is maximized, with marginal cost equal to marginal revenue, average cost also equals price in the long run. But average cost is not at its minimum point. That is, in monopolistic competition, firms operate with excess capacity. (pp. 346–351)

Oligopoly

Oligopoly is a situation in which a small number of producers compete with each other. The key feature of oligopoly is that the firms strategically interact. Each firm has to take into account the effects of its own actions on the behavior of other firms and the effects of the actions of other firms on its own profit. (p. 351)

Traditional Models of Oligopoly

The kinked demand curve model of oligopoly is based on the assumption that each firm believes that its price cuts will be matched by its rivals but its price increases will not be matched. If these beliefs are correct, each firm faces a kinked demand curve for its product, the kink occurring at the current price, and has a break in its marginal revenue curve. To maximize profit, the firm produces the quantity that makes marginal cost and marginal revenue equal, an output level such that the marginal cost curve passes through the break in the marginal revenue curve. Fluctuations in marginal cost inside the range of the break in marginal revenue have no effects on either price or output.

The dominant firm model of oligopoly assumes that an industry consists of one large firm and a large number of small firms. The large firm acts like a monopoly and sets a profit-maximizing price. The small firms take this price as given and act like perfectly competitive firms. (pp. 351–354)

Oligopoly and Game Theory

Game theory is a method of analyzing strategic behavior. Game theory focuses on three aspects of a game:

◆ Rules
◆ Strategies
◆ Payoffs

The rules of the oligopoly game specify the permissible actions by the players. These actions are limited only by the legal code and involve such things as raising or lowering prices, raising or lowering output, increasing or cutting advertising, and enhancing or not enhancing the product. The strategies in the oligopoly game are all the possible actions that each player can take given the action of the other player. The payoff of the oligopoly game is the player's profit or loss. It depends on the actions of each player and on the constraints imposed by the market, technology, and input costs.

Duopoly is a market structure in which there are two producers of a good competing against each other. Duopoly is a special case of oligopoly. The duopoly game is similar to the prisoners' dilemma game. Two prisoners are faced with the problem of deciding whether or not to confess to a crime. If neither confesses, they are tried for a lesser crime and receive a light penalty. If both confess, they receive a higher penalty. If one confesses and the other does not confess, the one confessing receives the lightest of all penalties and the one not confessing receives a very heavy penalty.

The prisoners' dilemma has a dominant strategy Nash equilibrium. That is, regardless of the action of the other player, there is a unique best action for each player—to confess. (pp. 354–357)

A Duopoly Game

A duopoly game can be constructed in which two firms contemplate the consequences of colluding to achieve a monopoly profit or of cheating on the collusive agreement to make a bigger profit at the expense of the other firm. Such a game is identical to the prisoners' dilemma. The equilibrium of the game is one in which both firms cheat on the agreement. The industry output is the same in this case as it would be if the industry were perfectly competitive. The industry price is also the competitive price, and firms make zero economic profit. If the firms are able to enforce the collusive agreement, the industry looks exactly like a monopoly industry. Price, output, and profit are the same as in a monopoly.

If a game is repeated indefinitely, there is an opportunity for one player to punish another player for previous "bad" behavior. In such a situation, a tit-for-tat strategy can produce an equilibrium in which both firms stick to the agreement. A tit-for-tat strategy is one in which the players begin by colluding. If one player cheats, the other player responds

at the next play by also cheating. Since each knows that it pays the other to respond in this manner, no one cheats. This equilibrium is a cooperative equilibrium—one in which each player cooperates because such behavior is a rational response to the credible threat of the other to inflict damage if the agreement is broken. Uncertainty makes it possible for such an equilibrium to break down from time to time. (pp. 357–364)

Games and Price Wars

Price wars can be interpreted as the outcome of a repeated duopoly game. The competing firms comply with the agreement unless market forces bring about a sufficiently large fall in price. A large fall in price is responded to as if it had resulted from the other firm cheating. Only by responding in this manner can each firm maintain the credible threat that it will punish a cheat and thereby ensure that the ever-present temptation to cheat is held in check and the monopoly agreement is maintained. When market conditions bring about an increase in price, the firms revert to their cooperative behavior. Industries will go through cycles, starting with a monopoly price and output and occasionally, when demand falls by enough, temporarily pursuing noncooperative actions. At these times, the industry price and output will be the competitive ones. (pp. 365–366)

Other Strategic Variables

Firms in oligopolistic industries have to make a large range of decisions: whether to enter or leave an industry; how much to spend on advertising; whether to modify its product; whether to price discriminate; whether to undertake research and development. All these choices result in payoffs for the firm and the other firms in the industry, and a game can be constructed to predict the outcome of such choices.

An interesting real-world example is the research and development game played between producers of disposable diapers. The equilibrium of that game results in a large amount of research and development being undertaken and lower profits than would emerge if the firms could collude somehow to keep out new entrants and undertake less research and development. Thus that game is similar to the prisoners' dilemma. (pp. 366–367)

K E Y   E L E M E N T S

Key Terms

Cartel, 357
Collusive agreement, 357
Cooperative equilibrium, 364
Dominant strategy, 356
Dominant strategy equilibrium, 356
Duopoly, 355
Four-firm concentration ratio, 342
Game theory, 354
Herfindahl-Hirschman Index, 343
Monopolistic competition, 344
Nash equilibrium, 356
Oligopoly, 345
Payoff, 355
Payoff matrix, 355

Product differentiation, 344
Strategic behavior, 354
Strategies, 354
Tit-for-tat strategy, 363
Trigger strategy, 363

Key Figures and Tables

Figure 13.3   Monopolistic Competition, 347
Figure 13.6   Costs and Demand, 358
Figure 13.7   Colluding to Make Monopoly Profits, 359
Figure 13.9   Both Firms Cheat, 361
Table 13.2   Market Structure, 345
Table 13.4   Duopoly Payoff Matrix, 362

R E V I E W   Q U E S T I O N S

1 What are the main varieties of market structure? What are the main characteristics of each of those market structures?

2 What is a four-firm concentration ratio? If the four-firm concentration ratio is 90 percent, what does that mean?

3 Give some examples of U.S. industries that have a high concentration ratio and of U.S. industries that have a low concentration ratio.

4 What is the Herfindahl-Hirschman Index, and what does a large value of that index indicate?

5 What are barriers to entry? Give some examples of barriers to entry that exist in the U.S. economy.

6 Explain how a firm can differentiate its product.

7 What is the difference between monopolistic competition and perfect competition?

8 Is monopolistic competition more efficient or less efficient than perfect competition?

9 What is the difference between duopoly and oligopoly?

10 Why might the demand curve facing an oligopolist be kinked, and what happens to a firm's marginal revenue curve if its demand curve is kinked?

11 In what circumstances might the dominant firm model of oligopoly be relevant?

12 What is the essential feature of both duopoly and oligopoly?

13 List the key features that all games have in common.

14 What are the features of duopoly that make it reasonable to treat duopoly as a game between two firms?

15 What is the prisoners' dilemma?

16 What is a dominant strategy equilibrium?

17 What is meant by a repeated game?

18 Explain what a tit-for-tat strategy is.

19 What is a price war? What is the effect of a price war on the profit of the firms in the industry and on the profitability of the industry itself?

PROBLEMS

1 A monopolistically competitive industry is in long-run equilibrium as illustrated in Fig. 13.3(b). Demand for the industry's product increases, increasing the demand for each firm's output. Using diagrams similar to those in Fig. 13.3, analyze the short-run and long-run effects of this increase in demand on price, output, and profit.

2 Another monopolistically competitive industry is in long-run equilibrium, as illustrated in Fig. 13.3(b), when it experiences a large increase in wages. Using diagrams similar to those in Fig. 13.3, analyze the short-run and long-run effects of this increase in wages on price, output, and profit.

3 A firm with a kinked demand curve experiences an increase in its fixed cost. Explain the effects on the firm's price, output, and profit/loss.

4 An industry with one very large firm and a hundred very small firms experiences an increase in the demand for its product. Explain the effects on:

a The price, output, and profit of the large firm

b The price, output, and profit of a typical small firm

5 Describe the game known as the prisoners' dilemma. In describing the game:

a Make up a story that motivates the game.

b Work out a payoff matrix.

c Describe how the equilibrium of the game is arrived at.

6 Consider the following game. There are two players, each isolated from the other. They are asked a question. They can answer the question honestly, or they can lie. If both answer honestly, each receives a payoff of $100. If one answers honestly and the other lies, the liar gains at the expense of the honest player. In that event, the liar receives a profit

of $500 and the honest player gets nothing. If both lie, then each receives a payoff of $50.

a Describe this game in terms of its players, strategies, and payoffs.

b Construct the payoff matrix.

c What is the equilibrium for this game?

7 Explain the behavior of world oil prices since 1973 by using a repeated prisoners' dilemma game. Describe the types of strategy that individual countries of OPEC have adopted.

8 Two firms, Soapy and Suddies Inc., are the only two producers of laundry detergent. They collude and agree to share the market equally. If neither firm cheats on the agreement, each can make $1 million profit. If either firm cheats, the cheater can increase its profit to $1.5 million, while the firm that abides by the agreement makes a loss of $0.5 million. Neither firm has any way of policing the actions of the other.

a Describe the best strategy for each firm in a game that is played once.

b What is the payoff matrix and what is the equilibrium of a game that is played just once?

c If the buyers of laundry detergent lobby successfully for government regulation of the laundry detergent industry, explain what happens to the price and the profits made by the industry.

d If this duopolist game can be played many times, describe some of the strategies that each firm may adopt.

9 Use the model of oligopoly to explain why, in the disposable diaper industry, Procter & Gamble and Kimberly-Clark spend so much on R&D.

PART 6

MARKETS FOR FACTORS OF PRODUCTION

Talking with Claudia Goldin

Born in New York City, Claudia Goldin was an undergraduate at Cornell University and a graduate student at the University of Chicago, where she obtained her Ph.D. in 1972. Now Professor of Economics at Harvard University and Program Director at the National Bureau of Economic Research, Claudia Goldin has made important contributions to our understanding of the evolution of modern labor markets. Michael Parkin talked with Professor Goldin about some of the problems facing U.S. labor markets in the 1990s.

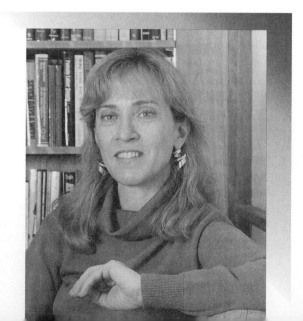

Professor Goldin, why and how did you get into economics?

I entered Cornell University from the Bronx High School of Science intending to be a microbiologist, but I first wanted to acquire a strong liberal arts education. Economics appealed to me because of its rigor, its internal consistency, and, most of all, its relevance. But only after I took economics from Fred Kahn (who later, as head of the Civil Aeronautics Board, deregulated the airline industry) did I decide to major in the subject. I traded the laboratory of the scientist for that of the social scientist. Ours, I should add, is more challenging because we have to devise controlled experiments from already existing data.

In 1890, 18 percent of women were in the labor force; in 1990, 58 percent were in the labor force. What have been the driving forces behind this substantial change?

In 1890, most of the 18 percent were young, single, foreign-born, and black. Women generally worked for pay only before they married, although black women and poor women worked regardless of their marital status and age. Less than 5 percent of all married women in 1890 were in the paid labor force. Thus the question is why married and adult women entered the labor force in such large numbers in the past 100 years. Contrary to popular opinion, the first large increase in married women's employment did not occur during the resurgence of feminism in the late 1960s, nor did it occur among the younger age groups. The large initial movement into the labor force occurred during the 1940s and 1950s among women older than 40 years. A host of long-run factors had been operating to reduce the time demands of women in their homes. These include the markedly reduced birth rate and the appearance of market goods substituting for those produced within the home, such as factory-made bread and clothing.

How do you explain the timing and the extent of the explosion in women's employment?

It was rooted in two changes earlier in the century. Between 1915 and 1930, the proportion of all Americans graduating from high school vastly increased, and at the same time there was a surge in the demand for educated labor in the burgeoning clerical and sales sectors. Young women entered these jobs in droves in the 1920s but generally exited when they married. After World War II, rising wages and an increased demand for labor drew these women back into the labor force. Younger married women were raising the baby boom of the 1950s and were less willing to trade the household for the marketplace. The shift of employment from manufacturing to office and sales work from

1920 to 1950 was an important factor in enabling adult and married women to work for pay. And the generation of older women in the 1950s, who had the requisite education for these jobs, was ripe for this monumental change in employment. They, not the young women of their era, were the real pioneers in women's employment. But the trailblazers did not view these changes as part of a larger social movement.

In the 1970s and 1980s, younger women greatly increased their participation in the labor force, and in the 1980s, even women with infants expanded their employment. In short, rising real wages, falling relative prices of market substitutes for home-produced goods, a declining demand for goods within the home, and a shift of jobs from blue collar to white collar led women to enter the labor force. But the timing of the changes suggests that various norms and institutional rigidities had to be broken down for the long-run forces to operate. These were accomplished first during the 1940s and 1950s.

What have we learned from your work and the work of other labor economists about the sources of persistent wage differences between men and women?

From the mid-1950s to 1980, the ratio of female to male full-time, year-round earnings was constant at about 0.60. Women as a group made little if any noticeable progress relative to men. But from 1981 to the present, the ratio increased by approximately 10 percentage points to 0.70. The analysis of the period of stability and the subsequent period of a

narrowing gap reveals much about the sources of gender differences in earnings.

The factors that economists group under the heading of "human capital" are most relevant. When working women's job experience and education advanced on those of men, their relative earnings increased, and when these factors remained constant compared with those of men, women's relative earnings were stable. The aspirations and expectations of teenaged girls are another factor. These young women formed far more realistic expectations in the 1970s than in the 1960s, when they severely underestimated their future participation in the labor force. Young women today are in a much better position to prepare themselves for a lifetime of labor market work than were their elders.

We also know that in the 1980s the returns to education and job experience increased for women relative to men. We aren't certain why this has been the case. Some of the increase could be due to better education or women's greater willingness to undertake more demanding jobs. But we cannot dismiss the notion that the labor market became more gender-neutral in the 1980s, and we also cannot dismiss the role of policy interventions in making it so.

What trend do we observe in the wage differences between blacks and whites?

Similar forces have operated over the long run to narrow differences in earnings between white and black males and between white and black females. In 1940, the ratio of the earnings of black men to white men was astoundingly low—0.43—but by 1980 it was 0.73. Among college graduate men about 35 years old, the increase was even greater—from 0.45 in 1940 to 0.81 in 1980. On average, black women have made greater progress relative to white women than have black men relative to white men.

What caused these extraordinary changes?

There were two compelling factors—educational changes, including advances in the quality of the education of black Americans, and the movement of blacks from the low-wage South to the higher-wage North. But there were critical junctures in this history. Two occurred during World Wars I and II and led to the greater integration of blacks into the white-dominated manufacturing sector and to an enormous migration to the North. The third occurred during the mid-1960s, when the Civil Rights Act led to further inroads by blacks into the higher-wage manufacturing sector. Unfortunately, some of the gains made since World War I were reversed in the 1980s. I don't mean that we have turned the clock back with regard to education and prejudice. The 1980s were a period a widening inequality in which the lower-educated and the manufacturing sector in particular lost a tremendous amount of ground, and black Americans are still disproportionately represented in these two groups.

What do minimum wage laws do?

The minimum wage sets a floor for covered workers below which the hourly wage cannot fall. If the minimum wage is set very high, as it is, for example, in Puerto Rico, which is covered by the U.S. minimum wage, it can create substantial unemployment. In the United States, the current minimum wage, which was recently increased after nine years, is about 38 percent of the average wage in manufacturing. But in Puerto Rico it was 70 to 90 percent of the average at its inception and has remained extremely high by Puerto Rican standards. Not surprisingly, the unemployment rate in Puerto Rico, particularly among young and inexperienced workers, is enormous, running in the double-digit range for some time. Surely we do not want a minimum wage that is so much higher than the average wage that the supply of labor greatly exceeds the demand. If the demand for labor is very inelastic, there will be an increase in income from a minimum wage, but the decrease in employment will be small. Many researchers believe that the U.S. minimum wage is currently in this range. The employment effects appear to be small while the income effects appear moderate.

What is your view of comparable-worth laws?

Comparable worth is a doctrine that says jobs that use comparable skills should get paid the same amount per unit time. Therefore if a nurse uses 10 units of skill and a truck driver also uses 10 units of skill, there should be no difference in their earnings per

hour if the jobs don't differ in other important dimensions, such as benefits or intensity of work.

The first question is why a competitive labor market doesn't produce such an outcome. If identical levels of skill are used in two jobs that do not differ in any other manner (except that one is nursing and one is truck driving), then workers should be indifferent between the two. If workers are indifferent between the two, firms would be forced to pay nurses and truck drivers the same wage. If truck drivers received more than nurses, the nurses would become truck drivers. The champions of comparable worth claim that women are segregated into particular jobs. Because they were denied access to various higher-paying jobs, like being a physician, they "crowd" into nursing, thereby depressing the wages of nurses. Because they were denied access to becoming a truck driver, they cannot equalize wages between the two occupations. The result is lower wages for nurses than for truck drivers. The proponents of comparable worth see it as a means of increasing the wages of nurses relative to, say, truck drivers and bringing about the free market solution that would exist had there been no discrimination.

The question is how the researcher can evaluate whether two occupations use comparable skills and thus ought to have the same wages in a competitive and discrimination-free labor market. The answer is that the researcher cannot. None of us is so all-knowing that we can assess all the skills required in a job and all the attributes of a job that are valued or devalued by workers. I would much rather see the energies of legislatures channeled into ensuring that women and minorities are afforded equal access to positions such as truck driver and physician, among others. We can try to guarantee equality of opportunity, and we can try to remedy past inequities through affirmative action. But we cannot easily dictate market prices.

What have been the main effects of affirmative action programs? Have they helped or hindered the progress of women and minorities?

Affirmative action is a complex doctrine under which federal contractors, that is, firms that sell goods or services to the federal government, have target levels for the hiring and promotion of women and minorities. There are direct effects from affirmative action programs and, possibly, indirect effects. Most scholarly work has been focused on the direct effects and finds that affirmative action programs have increased the employment and earnings of minorities. There is little evidence, however, that the programs have served to increase the employment and earnings of women. The indirect effects are more difficult to quantify.

Let's look at the economics profession, for example. Far fewer women than men major in economics, so it isn't surprising that women are vastly underrepresented as teachers and researchers in the field. If we want to know whether having more women economics professors would encourage more female undergraduates to major in economics—that is, if there is a "role model effect"—we could test whether female enrollments increase when women teach the basic economics courses, such as

principles. If so, we can make a case for affirmative action as a means of increasing the pool of candidates for a field and thus increasing the future employment of the group even in the absence of further affirmative action. Another possible indirect effect has been the subject of considerable controversy and forms the conservative attack on the programs. It is that women and minorities get hired or promoted under affirmative action when they should not have been. Such actions will then reinforce discriminatory views of women and minorities as being incompetent at particular jobs and can, in addition, make both groups more complacent and less competitive. I know of no hard evidence to substantiate such claims.

What are the most important labor market problems that we don't understand and that the next generation of economists will work on and possibly solve?

A pressing problem today is why the wage structure and distribution of earnings widened so substantially during the past 10 or 15 years. We need to know more about the interaction among education, inherent ability, and new technologies, such as the computer revolution. What makes some individuals more able to adapt while others are left behind? What types of educational and training interventions will help workers make the transition?

Returning to gender differences in the workplace, I wonder whether the gap in earnings can ever be eliminated, given the structure of jobs and the division of labor in the home. If women are still expected to raise children

"**E**ven if individual husbands and wives would like to create the egalitarian home, the husband is likely to confront considerable problems . . ."

and do a disproportionate share of household work, they will not advance with men in the labor market. Even if individual husbands and wives would like to create the egalitarian home, the husband is likely to confront considerable problems if he asks his employer for family leave, shorter hours, or a flexible schedule, even at greatly reduced pay. The labor market isn't yet structured or ready for the egalitarian family. I see this restructuring of the workplace as a major issue facing the next generation of labor economists.

CHAPTER 14

PRICING
AND
ALLOCATING
FACTORS
OF
PRODUCTION

After studying this chapter, you will be able to:

◆ Explain how firms choose the quantities of labor, capital, and land to employ in their production activities

◆ Explain how households choose the quantities of labor, capital, and land to supply

◆ Explain how wages, interest, and rent are determined in competitive factor markets

◆ Explain the concept of economic rent

◆ Distinguish between economic rent and transfer earnings

T MIGHT NOT BE YOUR BIRTHDAY, AND EVEN IF IT IS, chances are you are spending most of it working. But at the end of the week or month (or, if you're devoting all your time to college, when you graduate), you will receive the *returns* from your labor. Those returns vary a lot. Pedro Lopez, who spends his chilly winter days in a small container suspended from the top of Chicago's John Hancock Tower cleaning windows, makes a happy return of $12 an hour. Dan Rather, who puts on a 30-minute news show each weekday evening, makes a very happy return of $3.6 million a year. Students working at McDonald's and in the fields of southern California labor away for just a few dollars an hour. What determines the jobs we do and the wages we are paid? ◆ ◆ Most of us have little trouble spending our pay. But most of us do manage to save some of what we earn. What determines the amount of saving that people do and the returns that

Many Happy Returns

they make on that saving? How do the returns on saving influence the allocation of savings across the many industries and activities that use our capital resources? ◆ ◆ Some people receive income from renting land, but the amount earned varies enormously with its location and quality. For example, an acre of farmland in Iowa rents for about $1,000 a year, while a block on Chicago's Magnificent Mile rents for several million dollars a year. What determines the rent that people are willing to pay for different blocks of land? Why are rents so enormously high in big cities and so relatively low in the great farming regions of the country?

◆ ◆ ◆ ◆ In this chapter we deal with the kinds of questions that we have just posed. We study markets for factors of production—labor, capital, and land—and learn how their prices and people's incomes are determined.

Factor Prices and Incomes

Factors of production are the inputs into production. They are divided into three broad categories: *labor, capital,* and *land*. (We defined these factors of production in Chapter 1, p. 14.) The owners of factors of production receive an income from the firms that use those factors as inputs into their production activities. These incomes are *wages* paid for labor, *interest* paid for capital, and *rent* paid for land. Wages include all labor income including salaries, commissions, bonuses, and benefits paid in compensation for labor. Interest includes all forms of capital income including dividends paid by firms. Rent is the income paid for the use of land and natural resources. Apartment rents include an element of rent and also an element of interest—a payment for the use of capital.

Labor is by far the most important factor of production and generates about 70 percent of all income, and that percentage has been steadily increasing over the years.

In the rest of this chapter, we're going to build a model of a factor market, a model that determines factor prices, the quantities of factors used, and the incomes that factors of production earn.

An Overview

Factor prices are determined in factor markets, and we can understand those prices by using the model of demand and supply. The quantity of a factor of production demanded depends on the factor's price. That is, the quantity of labor demanded depends on the wage rate, the quantity of capital demanded depends on the interest rate, and the quantity of land demanded depends on the rent. The law of

demand applies to factors of production just as it applies to all other economic entities. Thus as the price of a factor of production decreases, the quantity of the factor demanded increases. The demand curve for a factor of production is shown in Fig. 14.1 as the curve labeled *D*.

The quantity supplied of a factor of production depends on its price. With some exceptions that we'll identify later in this chapter, the law of supply applies to factors of production: as the price of a factor of production increases, the quantity of the factor supplied increases. The supply of a factor of production is shown in Fig. 14.1 as the curve labeled *S*.

The equilibrium factor price is determined at the point of intersection of the factor demand and factor supply curves. Figure 14.1 shows such an equilibrium—*QF* is the quantity of the factor of production used and *PF* is the factor price.

FIGURE **14.1**

Demand and Supply in a Factor Market

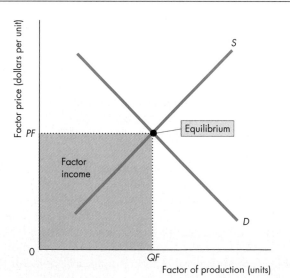

The demand curve for a factor of production (*D*) slopes downward, and the supply curve (*S*) slopes upward. Where the demand and supply curves intersect, the factor price (*PF*) and the quantity of a factor used (*QF*) are determined. The factor income is the product of the factor price and the quantity of the factor, as represented by the blue rectangle.

The income earned by a factor of production is its price multiplied by the quantity used. In Fig. 14.1, the price is measured by the distance from the origin to PF, and the quantity used is measured by the distance from the origin to QF. The factor income is the product of these two distances and is equivalent to the blue area in the figure.

All the influences on the quantity of a factor bought other than its price result in a shift in the factor demand curve. We'll study what those influences are in the next section. For now, let's simply work out the effects of a change in the demand for a factor of production. An increase in demand for a factor of production, as illustrated in Fig. 14.2(a), shifts the demand curve to the right, leading to an increase in the quantity of the factor used and an increase in its price. Thus when the demand curve shifts from D_0 to D_1, the quantity used increases from QF_0 to QF_1 and the price increases from PF_0 to PF_1. An increase in the demand for a factor of production increases that factor's income. The dark blue area in Fig. 14.2(a) illustrates the increase in income.

When the demand for a factor of production decreases, its demand curve shifts to the left. Figure 14.2(b) illustrates the effects of a decrease in demand. The demand curve shifts to the left from D_0 to D_2, the quantity used decreases from QF_0 to QF_2, and the price decreases from PF_0 to PF_2. When the demand for a factor of production decreases, the income of that factor also decreases. The light blue area in Fig. 14.2(b) illustrates the decrease in income.

The extent to which a change in the demand for a factor of production changes the factor price and the quantity used depends on the elasticity of supply. If the supply curve is very flat (supply is elastic), the change in the quantity used is large and the change in price is small. If the supply curve is very steep (supply is inelastic), the change in the price is large and the change in the quantity used is small.

A change in the supply of a factor of production also changes the price and quantity used as well as the income earned by those supplying the factor. An increase in supply results in an increase in the quantity used and a decrease in the factor price. A decrease in supply results in a decrease in the quantity used and an increase in the factor price. But whether a change in supply increases or decreases income depends on the elasticity of demand for the factor.

FIGURE 14.2

Changes in Demand

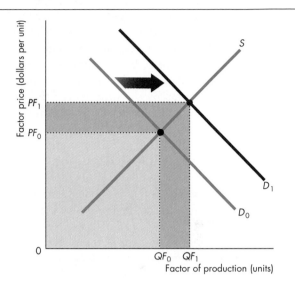

(a) An increase in demand

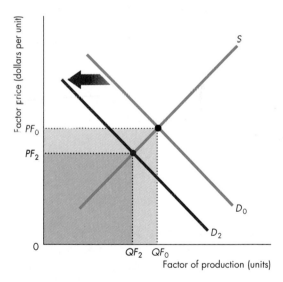

(b) A decrease in demand

An increase in the demand for a factor of production (part a) shifts its demand curve to the right—from D_0 to D_1. The quantity used increases from QF_0 to QF_1, and the price increases from PF_0 to PF_1. The factor income increases, and that income increase is shown by the dark blue area. A decrease in the demand for a factor of production from D_0 to D_2 results in a decrease in the quantity used from QF_0 to QF_2, and a decrease in the factor price from PF_0 to PF_2. The decrease in demand results in a decrease in the factor income. That decrease in income is illustrated by the light blue area.

Suppose that the quantity used of the factor of production illustrated in Fig. 14.3 decreases from 3 units to 2 units. Initially, the price is $10 a unit. If the demand curve is D_0, the decrease in supply results in an increase in the price of the factor but a decrease in the income of the suppliers of this factor of production. You can see that income decreases by multiplying the factor price by the quantity used. Initially, when the quantity is 3 units and the price is $10, the income earned by the suppliers of this factor of production is $30 (the $20 light blue area plus the $10 red area). When the quantity decreases to 2 units and the price increases to $14, income decreases by the $10 red area but increases by the $8 dark blue area for a net decrease to $28. Over the range of the price change that we've just considered, the demand curve D_0 is elastic—its elasticity is greater than 1.

Conversely, suppose that the demand curve is D_1. In this case, when the quantity decreases to 2 units,

the price increases to $20 a unit. Income increases to $40. The smaller quantity lowers income by $10 (red area), but the higher factor price increases income by $20 (dark blue plus green areas). Over the range of the price change that we've just considered, the demand curve D_1 is inelastic—its elasticity is less than 1.

The markets for factors of production determine factor prices in much the same way as goods markets determine the prices of goods and services. Factor markets also determine factor incomes. Factor income is the factor price multiplied by the quantity of the factor used. Thus to work out the influences on factor incomes, we have to pay attention simultaneously to the determination of the prices and the quantities used of the factors of production.

We're going to spend the rest of this chapter exploring more closely the influences on the demand for and supply of factors of production. We're also going to discover what determines the elasticities of supply of and demand for factors. These elasticities are important because of their effects on factor prices and the incomes earned. Let's begin by studying the demand for inputs.

FIGURE **14.3**

Factor Income and Demand Elasticity

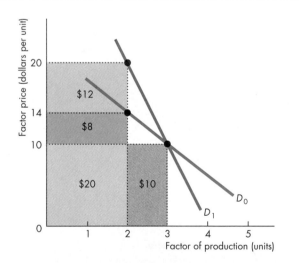

A decrease in the quantity used of a factor of production may result in a decrease or an increase in the factor's income. If the demand curve is D_0 (an elastic demand curve over the relevant range), a decrease in the quantity from 3 to 2 results in a decrease in the factor income from $30 to $28. If the demand curve is D_1 (an inelastic demand curve over the relevant range), a decrease in the quantity from 3 to 2 results in an increase in the factor's income from $30 to $40.

Demand for Factors

The demand for any factor of production is a derived demand. A **derived demand** is a demand for an input not for its own sake but in order to use it in the production of goods and services. A firm's derived demand for inputs depends on the constraints the firm faces—its technology constraint and its market constraint. It also depends on the firm's objective. The objective of the model firms that we have studied is to maximize profit. We'll continue to study the behavior of such firms.

A firm's demand for factors stems from its profit-maximization decision. *What* to produce and *how* to produce it are the questions that the firm must answer in order to make maximum profit. Those choices have implications for the firm's demand for inputs, which we'll now investigate.

Profit Maximization

A firm's inputs fall into two categories: fixed and variable. In most industries, the fixed inputs are capital (plant, machinery, and buildings) and land, and the variable input is labor. A firm meets permanent changes in output by changing the scale of its inputs of capital and land. It meets short-run variations in output by varying its input of labor.

Profit-maximizing firms produce the output at which marginal cost equals marginal revenue. This principle holds true whether the firm is in a perfectly competitive industry, in monopolistic competition, in oligopoly, or in a monopoly. If one more unit of output adds less to total cost than it adds to total revenue, the firm can increase its profit by producing more. A firm maximizes profit by producing the output at which the additional cost of producing one more unit of output equals the additional revenue from selling it. If we shift our perspective slightly, we can also state the condition for maximum profit in terms of the marginal cost of an input and the marginal revenue that input generates. Let's see how.

Marginal Revenue Product and Factor Price

The change in total revenue resulting from employing one more unit of any factor is called the factor's **marginal revenue product**. The concept of marginal revenue product sounds a bit like the concept of marginal revenue that you have met before. These concepts are indeed related, but there is an important distinction between the two. *Marginal revenue product* is the extra revenue generated as a result of employing one extra unit of a factor; *marginal revenue* is the extra revenue generated as a result of selling one additional unit of output.

A profit-maximizing firm hires the quantity of a factor that makes the marginal revenue product of the factor equal to the marginal cost of the factor. For a firm that buys its factors of production in competitive factor markets, the marginal cost of a factor is the factor's price. That is, in a competitive factor market, each firm is such a small demander of the factor that the firm has no influence on the factor's price. The firm simply has to pay the going factor price—market wage rate for labor, interest rate for capital, and rent for land.

Factor Price as Opportunity Cost You might be wondering why the interest rate is the factor price for capital. It looks different from the other two factor prices. Why isn't the factor price for capital the price of a piece of machinery—the price of a knitting machine for Swanky's sweater factory, the price of a computer for a tax consultant, or the price of an automobile assembly line for GM? The answer is that these prices do not represent the opportunity cost of *using* capital equipment. They are the prices at which a piece of capital can be bought. A firm can buy or sell a piece of capital equipment at its going market price. The opportunity cost of *using* the equipment is the interest rate that has to be paid on the funds tied up in its purchase. These funds may be borrowed, in which case there is an explicit payment of interest to the bank or other lender. Or the funds may be owned by the firm, in which case there is an implicit interest cost—the interest that could have been earned by using those funds in some other way.

Quantity of Factor Demanded We have defined the additional revenue resulting from employing one more unit of a factor as the factor's marginal revenue product. We have seen that in competitive factor markets, the marginal cost of a factor equals its price. Therefore a profit-maximizing firm—a firm that makes the marginal revenue product equal to the marginal cost of each input—hires each factor up to the point at which its marginal revenue product equals the factor's price. As the price of a factor varies, the quantity demanded of it also varies. The lower the price of a factor, the larger is the quantity demanded of that factor. Let's illustrate this proposition by working through an example—that of labor.[1]

The Firm's Demand for Labor

Labor is a variable input. A firm can change the quantity of labor it employs in both the short run

---

[1] The principles governing the demand for factors of production are the same for all factors—labor, capital, and land. There are some interesting special features concerning the demand for capital, however, that are explained in greater detail in Chapter 16. That part of Chapter 16 is relatively self-contained and may be studied at the same time as the material that you are now studying in this chapter.

and the long run. Let's focus first on a firm's short-run demand for labor.

A firm's short-run technology constraint is described by its *total product schedule*. Table 14.1 sets out the total product schedule for a car wash operated by Max's Wash 'n' Wax. (This total product schedule is similar to the one we studied in Chapter 10, Fig. 10.1.) The numbers in the first two columns of the table tell us how the maximum number of car washes each hour varies as the amount of labor employed varies. The third column shows the *marginal product of labor*—the change in output resulting from a one-unit increase in labor input.

Max's market constraint is the demand curve for his product. If, in the goods market, a firm is a monopoly or engaged in monopolistic competition or oligopoly, it faces a downward-sloping demand curve for its product. If a firm is perfectly competitive, it faces a fixed price for its product regardless

of its output level and therefore faces a horizontal demand curve for its product. We will assume that Max operates his car wash in a perfectly competitive market and can sell as many washes as he chooses at a constant price of $4 a wash. Given this information, we can calculate Max's total revenue (fourth column) by multiplying the number of cars washed per hour by $4. For example, if 9 cars are washed each hour (row *c*), total revenue is $36.

The fifth column of Table 14.1 shows the calculation of the marginal revenue product of labor—the change in total revenue per unit change in labor input. For example, if Max hires a second worker (row *c*), total revenue increases from $20 to $36, so the marginal revenue product is $16. There is an alternative way of calculating the marginal revenue product of labor—multiply marginal product by marginal revenue. To see that this method gives the same answer, multiply the marginal product of hiring a second worker—4 cars an hour—by marginal

---

TABLE **14.1**

Marginal Revenue Product and Average Revenue Product at Max's Wash 'n' Wax

	Quantity of labor (L) (workers)	Output (Q) (cars washed per hour)	Marginal product (MP = ΔQ/ΔL) (washes per worker)	Total revenue (TR = P x Q) (dollars)	Marginal revenue product (MRP = ΔTR/ΔL) (dollars per worker)	Average revenue product (ARP = TR/L) (dollars per worker)
a	0	0		0		
			 5		 20	
b	1	5		20		20
			 4		 16	
c	2	9		36		18
			 3		 12	
d	3	12		48		16
			 2		 8	
e	4	14		56		14
			 1		 4	
f	5	15		60		12

The marginal revenue product of labor is the change in total revenue that results from a one-unit increase in labor input. To calculate marginal revenue product, first work out total revenue. If Max hires 1 worker (row *b*), output is 5 washes an hour and total revenue, at $4 a wash, is $20. If he hires 2 workers (row *c*), output is 9 washes an hour and

total revenue is $36. By hiring the second worker, total revenue rises by $16—the marginal revenue product of labor is $16. The average revenue product of labor is total revenue per unit of labor employed. For example, when Max employs 2 workers, total revenue is $36 and average revenue product is $18 ($36 divided by 2).

revenue—$4 a car—and notice that the answer is the same ($16).

Total revenue divided by the quantity of the factor hired is called the **average revenue product** of the factor. Thus average revenue product is the average contribution of each unit of an input to the firm's total revenue. The last column of Table 14.1 shows the average revenue product of labor. For example, when Max employs 3 workers (row *d*), total revenue is $48. Thus the average revenue product of labor is $48 divided by 3 workers, which is $16 per worker.

Notice that as the quantity of labor rises, the marginal revenue product of labor falls. When Max hires the first worker, the marginal revenue product of labor is $20. If Max hires a second worker, the marginal revenue product of labor is $16. Marginal revenue product of labor continues to decline as Max hires more workers.

Marginal revenue product diminishes as Max hires more workers because of the principle of diminishing returns that we first studied in Chapter 10. With each additional worker hired, the marginal product of labor falls and so brings in a smaller marginal revenue product. Because Max's Wash 'n' Wax is a perfectly competitive firm, the price of each additional car wash is the same and brings in the same marginal revenue. If instead Max had a monopoly, he would have to lower his price to sell more washes. In such a case, the marginal revenue product of labor diminishes even more quickly than in perfectly competitive conditions. Marginal revenue product diminishes because of diminishing marginal product of labor and also because of diminishing marginal revenue. Table 14.2 provides a compact glossary of factor market terms.

We can illustrate the average revenue product and marginal revenue product of labor as curves. The **average revenue product curve** shows the average revenue product of a factor at each quantity of the factor hired. The **marginal revenue product curve** shows the marginal revenue product of a factor at each quantity of the factor hired.

Figure 14.4(a) shows the marginal revenue product and average revenue product curves for workers employed by Max. The horizontal axis measures the number of workers that Max hires, and the vertical axis measures the average and marginal revenue product of labor. The curve labeled *ARP* is the average revenue product curve and is based on the num-

---

TABLE 14.2

A Compact Glossary of Factor Market Terms

Factors of production	Labor, capital, and land (including raw materials)
Factor prices	Wages—price of labor; interest—price of capital; rent—price of land
Marginal product	Output produced by last unit of input hired; for example, the marginal product of labor is additional output produced by employing one more person
Average product	Output per unit of input; for example, average product of labor is output divided by labor input
Marginal revenue	Revenue resulting from selling one additional unit of output
Marginal revenue product	Revenue resulting from hiring one additional unit of a factor of production; for example, marginal revenue product of labor is the additional revenue resulting from selling the output produced by employing one more person
Average revenue product	Total revenue per unit of input; calculated as total revenue divided by labor input

---

bers in Table 14.1. For example, point *d* on the *ARP* curve represents row *d* in the table. Max employs 3 workers, and the average revenue product of labor is $16 a worker. The blue bars show the marginal revenue product of labor as Max employs more workers. These bars correspond to the numbers in Table 14.1. The curve *MRP* is the marginal revenue product curve.

The firm's demand for labor curve is based on its marginal revenue product curve. You can see Max's demand for labor curve (*D*) in Fig. 14.4(b). The horizontal axis measures the number of workers hired—the same as part (a). The vertical axis measures the wage rate in dollars per hour. The demand for labor curve is exactly the same as the firm's marginal revenue product curve. For example, when Max employs 3 workers an hour, his marginal revenue product is $10 an hour, as in Fig. 14.4(a); and

FIGURE **14.4**

The Demand for Labor at Max's Wash 'n' Wax

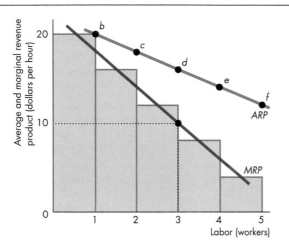

(a) **Average and marginal revenue product**

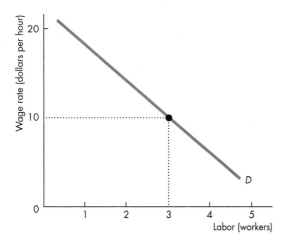

(b) **Demand for labor**

Part (a) shows the average and marginal revenue product curves for Max's Wash 'n' Wax. Points *b* through *f* on the average revenue product curve correspond to the rows of Table 14.1. The blue bars representing marginal revenue product are also based on the numbers in that table. (Each point is plotted midway between the labor inputs used in its calculation.) Average revenue product and marginal revenue product decline, and the marginal revenue product curve is always below the average revenue product curve. Part (b) shows Max's demand for labor curve. It is identical to his marginal revenue product curve. Max demands labor up to the point at which the wage rate (the worker's marginal cost) equals marginal revenue product.

at a wage rate of $10 an hour, Max hires 3 workers an hour, as in Fig. 14.4(b).

But why is the demand for labor curve identical to the marginal revenue product curve? Because the firm hires the profit-maximizing quantity of labor. If the cost of hiring one more worker—the wage rate—is less than the additional revenue that worker will bring in—the marginal revenue product of labor—then it pays the firm to employ one more worker. Conversely, if the cost of hiring one more worker is greater than the additional revenue that worker will bring in—the wage rate exceeds the marginal revenue product—then it does not pay the firm to employ one more worker. When the cost of the last worker hired equals the revenue brought in by that worker, the firm is making the maximum possible profit. Such a situation occurs when the wage rate equals the marginal revenue product. Thus the quantity of labor demanded by the firm is such that the wage rate equals the marginal revenue product of labor.

R E V I E W

A firm chooses the quantity of labor to hire so that its profit is maximized. The additional total revenue generated by hiring one additional worker is called the marginal revenue product of labor. It is the change in total revenue generated by a one-unit change in labor input. In a competitive labor market, the marginal cost of labor is the wage rate. Profit is maximized when the marginal revenue product of labor equals the wage rate. The marginal revenue product of labor curve is the firm's demand for labor curve. The lower the wage rate, the higher is the quantity of labor demanded. ◆

Two Conditions for Profit Maximization   When we studied firms' output decisions, we discovered that a condition for maximum profit is that marginal revenue equals marginal cost. We've now discovered another condition for maximum profit—marginal revenue product of a factor equals the factor's price. How can there be two conditions for a maximum profit? It is because they are equivalent to each other. When marginal revenue equals marginal cost,

TABLE 14.3

Two Conditions for Maximum Profit

Symbols

Marginal product	*MP*
Marginal revenue	*MR*
Marginal cost	*MC*
Marginal revenue product	*MRP*
Factor price	*PF*

Two conditions for maximum profit

1. *MR* = *MC*	2. *MRP* = *PF*

Equivalence of conditions

1.　　*MRP/MP* = **MR**　　=　　**MC** = *PF/MP*

Multiply by
MP
to give

MRP = *MR* x *MP*

Flipping the
equation over

Multiply by
MP
to give

MC x *MP* = *PF*

Flipping the
equation over

2.　　*MR* x *MP* = **MRP**　　=　　**PF** = *MC* x *MP*

Marginal revenue (*MR*) equals marginal cost (*MC*), and marginal revenue product (*MRP*) equals the price of the factor (*PF*). The two conditions for maximum profit are equivalent because marginal revenue product (*MRP*) equals marginal revenue (*MR*) multiplied by marginal product (*MP*) and the factor price (*PF*) equals marginal cost (*MC*) multiplied by marginal product (*MP*).

the marginal revenue product of a factor equals the factor's price. The equivalence of these two conditions is set out in Table 14.3.

We have just derived the law of demand as it applies to the labor market. And we've discovered that the same principles that apply to the demand

for goods and services apply here as well. The demand for labor curve slopes downward. Other things being equal, the lower the wage rate (the price of labor), the greater is the quantity of labor demanded. Let's now study the influences that result in a change in the demand for labor and therefore in a shift in the demand for labor curve.

Shifts in the Firm's Demand for Labor Curve　The position of the demand for labor curve depends on three factors:

◆ The price of the firm's output
◆ The prices of other inputs
◆ Technology

The higher the price of a firm's output, the greater is the quantity of labor demanded by the firm, other things being equal. The price of output affects the demand for labor through its influence on marginal revenue product. A higher price for the firm's output increases marginal revenue, which, in turn, increases the marginal revenue product of labor. A change in the price of a firm's output leads to a shift in the firm's demand for labor curve. If the output price increases, the demand for labor increases.

The other two influences on the demand for labor have their main effects not in the short run but in the long run. The **short-run demand for labor** is the relationship between the wage rate and the quantity of labor demanded when the firm's capital is fixed and labor is the only variable input. The **long-run demand for labor** is the relationship between the wage rate and the quantity of labor demanded when all inputs can be varied. A change in the relative price of inputs—such as the relative price of labor and capital—leads to a substitution away from the input whose relative price has increased and toward the input whose relative price has decreased. Thus, if the price of using capital decreases relative to that of using labor, the firm substitutes capital for labor, increasing the quantity of capital demanded and decreasing its demand for labor.

Finally, a technological change that influences the marginal product of labor also affects the demand for labor. For example, the development of electronic telephones with memories and a host of clever features decreased the marginal product of and the demand for telephone operators. At the same time, it increased the marginal product of and the demand for telephone engineers trained in the installation and maintenance of the new telephones. Again, these effects are felt in the long run when the firm adjusts all its inputs and incorporates new technologies into its production process. Table 14.4 summarizes the influences on a firm's demand for labor.

As we saw earlier, Fig. 14.2 illustrates the effects of a change in the demand for a factor. If that factor is labor, then Fig. 14.2 shows the effects of a change in the demand for labor on the wage rate and the quantity of labor hired. But we can now say why the demand for labor curve shifts. For example, an increase in the price of the firm's output, an increase in the price of capital, or a technological change that increases the marginal product of labor shifts the demand for labor curve from D_0 to D_1 in Fig. 14.2(a). Conversely, a decrease in the price of the firm's output, a decrease in the price of capital, or a technological change that lowers the marginal product of labor shifts the demand curve for labor from D_0 to D_2 in Fig. 14.2(b).

TABLE **14.4**

A Firm's Demand for Labor

The law of demand

The quantity of labor demanded by a firm

Decreases if:	*Increases if:*
◆ The wage rate increases	◆ The wage rate decreases

Changes in demand

A firm's demand for labor

Decreases if:	*Increases if:*
◆ The firm's output price decreases	◆ The firm's output price increases
◆ The prices of other inputs decrease	◆ The prices of other inputs increase
◆ A technological change decreases the marginal product of labor	◆ A technological change increases the marginal product of labor

Market Demand

So far, we've studied only the demand for labor by an individual firm. Let's now look at the market demand. The market demand for a factor of production is the total demand for that factor by all firms. The market demand curve for a given factor is obtained by adding up the quantities demanded of that factor by each firm at each given factor price. Thus the concept of the market demand for labor curve is exactly like the concept of the market demand curve for a good or service. The market demand curve for a good or service is obtained by adding together the quantities demanded of that good by all households at each price. The market demand curve for labor is obtained by adding together the quantities of labor demanded by all firms at each wage rate.

Elasticity of Demand for Labor

The elasticity of demand for labor measures the responsiveness of the quantity of labor demanded to the wage rate. We calculate this elasticity in the same way that we calculate a price elasticity. The elasticity of demand for labor equals the percentage change in the quantity of labor demanded divided by the percentage change in the wage rate. The elasticity of demand for labor depends on the elasticity of demand for the good that the firm is producing and on the properties of the firm's total product curve—on how rapidly the marginal product of labor diminishes. There is, however, a slight difference in the things that affect the elasticity of demand for labor in the short run and in the long run.

Short-Run Elasticity   The **short-run elasticity of demand for labor** is the magnitude of the percentage change in the quantity of labor demanded divided by the percentage change in the wage rate when labor is the only variable input. The short-run elasticity of demand for labor depends on three things:

1. *Labor intensity.* The proportion of labor in the production of a good—the labor intensity of the production process—also affects the elasticity of demand for labor. Suppose that the cost of labor is 90 percent of the total cost of producing a good. In such a situation, a 10 percent change in the cost of labor generates a 9 percent change in

total cost. Conversely, if the cost of labor is only 10 percent of the total cost, then a 10 percent change in the cost of labor produces only a 1 percent change in total cost. The larger the percentage change in total cost, the larger is the percentage change in price and, for a given elasticity of demand for the product, the larger is the percentage change in output. The larger the change in output, the larger is the change in labor input. So the larger the proportion of total cost coming from labor (labor intensity), the more elastic is the demand for labor, other things being equal.

2. *The slope of the marginal product of labor curve.* The slope of the marginal product of labor curve depends on the production technology. In some activities marginal product diminishes quickly. For example, the marginal product of one bus driver is high, but the marginal product of a second driver on the same bus is close to zero. In other activities marginal product is fairly constant. For example, hiring a second window cleaner on a team almost doubles the amount of glass that can be cleaned in an hour—the marginal product of the second window cleaner is almost the same as the first. The steeper the slope of the marginal product curve, the more responsive is marginal revenue product to a change in labor input and the less responsive is the quantity of labor demanded to a change in the wage rate—the less elastic is the firm's demand for labor.

3. *The short-run elasticity of demand for the product.* If a wage rate changes, so does the supply of the good produced by the labor whose wage has changed. A change in supply changes the price of the good and changes the quantity of the good demanded. The greater the elasticity of demand for the good, the larger is the change in the quantity demanded of both the good and the labor used to produce it.

Long-Run Elasticity The **long-run elasticity of demand for labor** is the magnitude of the percentage change in the quantity of labor demanded divided by the percentage change in the wage rate when all inputs are varied. The long-run elasticity of demand for labor depends on *labor intensity* and on the long-run elasticity of demand for the product. In addition, it depends on the *substitutability of capital for labor*. The more easily capital can be substituted

for labor in production, the more elastic is the long-run demand for labor. For example, it is fairly easy to substitute robots for assembly line workers in car factories and to substitute automatic picking machines for labor in vineyards and orchards. At the other extreme, it is difficult (though not impossible) to substitute robots for newspaper reporters, bank loan officers, and stockbrokers. The more readily capital can be substituted for labor, the more elastic is the firm's demand for labor in the long run.

R E V I E W

T he short-run elasticity of demand for labor depends on three factors:

♦ Labor intensity of the production process
♦ The slope of the marginal product of labor curve
♦ The short-run elasticity of demand for the product

The long-run elasticity of demand for labor also depends on three factors:

♦ Labor intensity of the production process
♦ Substitutability of capital for labor
♦ The long-run elasticity of demand for the product ♦

Supply of Factors

T he supply of factors is determined by the decisions of households. Households allocate the factors of production they own to their most rewarding uses. The quantity supplied of any factor of production depends on its price. Usually, the higher the price of a factor of production, the larger is the quantity supplied. There is an important possible exception to this general law of supply concerning the supply of labor. It arises from the fact that labor is the single most important factor of production and the source of the largest portion of household income.

Let's examine household factor supply decisions, beginning with the supply of labor.

Supply of Labor

A household chooses how much labor to supply as part of its time allocation decision. Time is allocated between two broad activities:

◆ Market activity
◆ Nonmarket activity

Market activity is the same thing as supplying labor. **Nonmarket activity** consists of leisure and nonmarket production activities including housework, education, and training. The household obtains an immediate return from market activities in the form of an income. Nonmarket activities generate a return in the form of goods and services produced in the home, in the form of a higher future income, or in the form of leisure, which is valued for its own sake and which is classified as a good.

In deciding how to allocate its time between market activity and nonmarket activity, a household weighs the returns that it can get from the different activities. We are interested in the effects of the wage rate on the household's allocation of its time and on how much labor it supplies.

Wages and Quantity of Labor Supplied To induce a household to supply labor, it must be offered a high enough wage rate. Nonmarket activities are valued by households either because the time is used in some productive activity or because of the value they attach to leisure. In order for it to be worthwhile to supply labor, a household has to be offered a wage rate that is at least equal to the value it places on the last hour it spends in nonmarket activities. This wage rate—the lowest one for which a household will supply labor to the market—is called its **reservation wage**. At wage rates below the reservation wage, the household supplies no labor. Once the wage rate reaches the reservation wage, the household begins to supply labor. As the wage rate rises above the reservation wage, the household varies the quantity of labor that it supplies. But a higher wage rate has two offsetting effects on the quantity of labor supplied—a *substitution effect* and an *income effect*.

Substitution Effect Other things being equal, the higher the wage rate, the more will people economize on their nonmarket activities and increase the time they spend working. As the wage rate rises, the household will discontinue any nonmarket activity that yields a return that is less than the wage rate; instead, the household will switch to market activity. For example, a household might use some of its time to cook meals and do laundry—nonmarket activities—that can, alternatively, be bought for $10 an hour. If the wage rate available to the household is less than $10 an hour, the household will cook and wash for itself. If the household's wage rate rises above $10 an hour, it will be worthwhile for the household to work more hours and use part of its income ($10) to buy laundry services and to eat out. The higher wage rate induces a switch of time from nonmarket activities to market activities.

Income Effect The higher the household's wage rate, the higher is its income. A higher income, other things being equal, induces an increase in demand for most goods. Leisure, a component of nonmarket activity, is one of those goods. Since an increase in income creates an increase in the demand for leisure, it also creates a decrease in the amount of time allocated to market activities and therefore a fall in the quantity of labor supplied.

Backward-Bending Household Supply of Labor Curve The substitution effect and the income effect work in opposite directions. The higher the wage rate, the higher is the quantity of labor supplied via the substitution effect but the lower is the quantity of labor supplied via the income effect. At low wage rates, the substitution effect is larger than the income effect. As the wage rate rises, the household supplies more labor. But as the wage rate continues to rise, there comes a point at which the substitution effect and the income effect just offset each other. At that point, a change in the wage rate has no effect on the quantity of labor supplied. If the wage rate continues to rise, the income effect begins to dominate the substitution effect and the quantity of labor supplied declines. The household's supply of labor curve does not slope upward throughout its entire length but begins to bend back on itself. It is called a backward-bending supply curve.

Three individual household labor supply curves are shown in Fig. 14.5(a). Each household has a

F I G U R E 14.5

The Supply of Labor

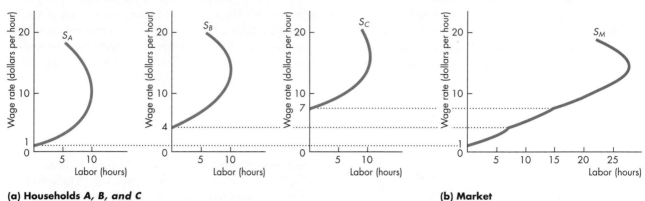

(a) Households A, B, and C

(b) Market

Part (a) shows the labor supply curves of three households (S_A, S_B, and S_C). Each household has a reservation wage below which it will supply no labor. As the wage rises above the reservation wage, the quantity of labor supplied rises to a maximum. If the wage continues to rise, the quantity of labor supplied begins to decline. Each household's supply curve eventually bends backward. When the quantity of labor supplied increases as the wage increases, the substitution effect dominates the income effect. When the quantity of labor supplied begins to fall as the wage rate increases, the income effect (which leads people to demand more leisure) dominates the substitution effect.

Part (b) shows how, by adding together the quantities of labor supplied by the individual households at each wage rate, we derive the market supply curve of labor (S_M). The market supply curve also eventually bends backward but, in the real world, at a higher wage rate than that currently experienced. The upward-sloping part of the labor supply curve before it bends backward is the part along which the market operates.

different reservation wage. Household A has a reservation wage of $1 an hour, household B of $4 an hour, and household C of $7 an hour. Each household's labor supply curve is backward bending.

Market Supply The quantity of labor supplied to the entire market is the total quantity supplied by all households. The market supply of labor curve is the sum of the supply curves of all the individual households. Figure 14.5(b) shows the market supply curve (S_M) derived from the supply curves of the three households (S_A, S_B, and S_C) in Fig. 14.5(a). At wage rates of less than $1 an hour, the three households do laundry and cook but they do not supply any market labor. The household most eager to supply market labor has a reservation wage of $1 an hour. As the wage rate rises to $4 an hour, household A increases the quantity of labor that it supplies to the market. The reservation wage of household B is $4

an hour, so as the wage rate rises above $4 an hour, the quantity of labor supplied in the market is the sum of the labor supplied by households A and B. When the wage rate reaches $7 an hour, household C begins to supply some labor to the market. At wage rates above $7 an hour, the quantity supplied in the market is equal to the sum of the quantities supplied by the three households.

Notice that the market supply curve S_M, like the individual household supply curves, eventually bends backward. But the market supply curve has a long upward-sloping section. The reason why the market supply curve slopes up for such a long stretch is that the reservation wages of individual households are not equal and, at higher wage rates, additional households are confronted with their reservation wage and so begin to supply labor.

Although the market supply curve eventually bends backward, no real-world wage rate is so high that the economy operates on the backward-bending portion of its labor supply curve. But many individual households are on the backward-bending portion of their own labor supply curve. Thus as wage rates rise, some people work fewer hours. But higher wage rates induce those workers who are on the upward-sloping part of their labor supply curve to supply more hours and induce additional workers to enter the work force. The response of these workers to higher wage rates dominates that of the workers whose work hours decline as wage rates rise. Therefore, for the economy as a whole, the labor supply curve slopes upward. For this reason, we will restrict our attention to the upward-sloping part of the labor supply curve in Fig. 14.5(b).

Supply to Individual Firms   We've studied the labor supply decisions of individual households and seen how those decisions add up to the total market supply. But how is the supply of labor to each individual firm determined? The answer to this question depends on the degree of competitiveness in the labor market. In a perfectly competitive labor market, each firm faces a perfectly elastic supply of labor curve. This situation arises because the individual firm is such a small part of the total labor market that it has no influence on the wage rate.

Some labor markets are noncompetitive in the sense that firms can and do influence the price of the labor that they hire. In these cases, firms face an upward-sloping supply of labor curve. The more labor they wish to employ, the higher is the wage rate they have to offer. We examine how this type of labor market operates in Chapter 15. Here, we deal only with the case of perfectly competitive input markets.

REVIEW

At wage rates above the household's reservation wage, the household supplies labor to the market. An increase in the wage has two opposing effects on the quantity of labor supplied: a substitution effect (higher wage, more work) and an income effect (higher wage, less work). At low wages, the substitution effect is the more powerful and the labor supply curve slopes upward. At high wages, the income effect is the more powerful and the labor supply curve bends backward. The market supply of labor curve is the sum of the supply curves of individual households. Actual economies operate on the upward-sloping part of the market supply of labor curve. The supply of labor curve faced by each individual firm depends on the degree of competitiveness of the labor market. In a perfectly competitive labor market, each firm faces a perfectly elastic supply curve. ◆

Supply of Capital

Capital—the physical plant, buildings, and equipment used in production—is purchased by firms using funds borrowed from households. These funds are channeled through a complex network of financial institutions (banks, insurance companies, and others) and financial markets (bond and stock markets). But the amount of capital that firms can buy depends on the amount of saving that households undertake. Ultimately, households supply capital to firms by consuming less than their income. Thus the scale on which a household supplies capital depends on how much of its income the household saves.

The most important factors determining a household's saving are

◆ Its current income in relation to its expected future income
◆ The interest rate

Current and Future Income   A household with a current income that is low in comparison with its expected future income saves little and might even have negative saving. A household with a current income that is high in comparison with its expected future income saves a great deal in the present in order to be able to consume more in the future. The stage in the household's life cycle is the main factor influencing whether current income is high or low in comparison with expected future income. Young households typically have a current income that is low in comparison with their expected future income, while older households have a current income that is high relative to their expected future income. The consequence of this pattern in income over the life cycle is that young people have negative saving and older people have positive saving. Thus the young incur debts (such as mortgages and consumer credit) to acquire durable goods and to consume more than their income, while older people save and accumulate assets (often in the form of pension and life insurance arrangements) to provide for their later retirement years.

Interest Rate and Capital Supply Curve   A household's supply of capital is the stock of capital that it has accumulated as a result of its past saving. The household's supply curve of capital shows the relationship between the quantity of capital supplied and the interest rate. Other things being equal, a higher interest rate encourages people to economize on current consumption in order to take advantage of the higher return available from saving. Thus the higher the interest rate, the greater is the quantity of capital supplied.

Market Supply   The market supply of capital is the sum of the supplies of all the individual households. The market supply curve of capital shows how the quantity of capital supplied varies as the interest rate varies. In the short run, the supply of capital is inelastic and might even be perfectly inelastic. Such a case is illustrated in Fig. 14.6 by the vertical supply curve SS. The long-run supply of capital is elastic. Such a case is illustrated in Fig. 14.6 by the supply curve LS.

Supply to Individual Firms   In the short run, a firm can vary its labor input but not its capital. Thus in the short run, the firm's supply of capital is fixed. It has a specific set of capital assets. For example, an auto producer has a production assembly line; a laundromat operator has a number of washing machines and dryers; the campus print shop has a number of photocopying and other printing machines. These pieces of capital cannot be quickly disposed of or added to.

In the long run, a firm can vary all its inputs—capital as well as labor. A firm operating in a competitive capital market can obtain any amount of capital it chooses at the going market interest rate. Thus it faces a perfectly elastic supply of capital.

The fact that the short-run supply of capital is inelastic and the long-run supply is elastic has important implications for the returns obtained

FIGURE 14.6

The Short-Run and Long-Run Supply of Capital

The long-run supply of capital (*LS*) is highly elastic. If the interest rate is above *R*, households increase their saving and increase the total amount of capital supplied. If the interest rate is below *R*, households decrease their saving and reduce the amount of capital supplied. The short-run supply of capital (*SS*) is highly inelastic (perfectly inelastic in the figure). For the economy as a whole and for individual firms in the short run, once capital is put in place, it is difficult to vary its quantity easily and quickly. Thus no matter what the interest rate, at a given point in time there is a given amount of capital supplied.

from different types of capital. We'll explore those implications later in this chapter when we study equilibrium in the capital market. But before that, let's complete our analysis of the supply of factors of production by examining the supply of land.

Supply of Land

Land is the stock of natural resources, and its aggregate quantity supplied cannot be changed by any individual decisions. Individual households can vary the amount of land they own, but whatever land is acquired by one household is sold by another, so the aggregate quantity of land supplied of any particular type and in any particular location is fixed regardless of the decisions of any individual household. This fact means that the supply of each particular piece of land is perfectly inelastic. Figure 14.7 illustrates such a supply. Regardless of the rent available, the quantity of land supplied on Chicago's Magnificent Mile is a fixed number of square feet.

Expensive land can be, and is, used more intensively than inexpensive land. For example, high-rise buildings enable land to be used more intensively. However, to use land more intensively, it has to be combined with another factor of production—capital. Increasing the amount of capital per block of land does nothing to change the supply of land itself.

Although the supply of each type of land is fixed and its supply is inelastic, each individual firm, operating in competitive land markets, faces an elastic supply of land. That is, each firm can acquire the land that it demands at the going rent, as determined in the marketplace. Thus provided that land markets are highly competitive, firms are price takers in these markets, just as they are in the markets for other factors of production.

FIGURE 14.7

The Supply of Land

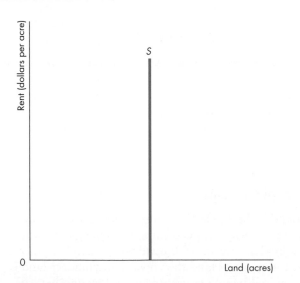

The supply of a given piece of land is perfectly inelastic. No matter what the rent, no more land than exists can be supplied.

REVIEW

The supply of capital is determined by households' saving decisions. Other things being equal, the higher the interest rate, the greater is the amount of capital supplied. The supply of capital to individual firms is highly inelastic in the short run but elastic in the long run. ◆ Individual households can vary the amount of land that they supply, but the aggregate supply of land is determined by the fact that there is a given, fixed quantity of it available. Thus the supply of each particular piece of land is perfectly inelastic. In a competitive land market, each firm faces an elastic supply of land at the going rent. ◆

Let's now see how factor prices and quantities are determined.

Competitive Equilibrium

The price of a factor of production and the quantity of it used are determined by the interaction of the demand for the factor and its supply. We'll illustrate competitive equilibrium by looking at the markets for labor, capital, and land and by looking at two examples of each.

Labor Market Equilibrium

Figure 14.8 shows two labor markets. That in part (a) is the labor market for national news anchors. Such people have a very high marginal revenue product, and this is reflected in the demand curve for their services, curve D_N. The supply of individuals with the required talents for this kind of job is low, and this fact is reflected in supply curve S_N. Equilibrium occurs at a high hourly wage rate ($500 in this example) and a low quantity employed, Q_N.

Figure 14.8(b) shows another market, that for babysitters. Although people value the output of

FIGURE **14.8**

Labor Market Equilibrium

(a) News anchors

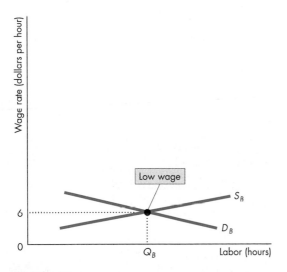

(b) Babysitters

News anchors (part a) have a high marginal revenue product, which is reflected in the high demand for their services—curve D_N. The number of people with the talents required for this job is few, and the supply curve is S_N. Equilibrium occurs at a high hourly wage rate of $500 and a low quantity employed, Q_N. The marginal revenue product of babysitters (part b) is low, so the demand curve is D_B. There is a huge supply of babysitters, and the supply curve is S_B. Equilibrium occurs at a low wage rate of $6 an hour and a high quantity employed, Q_B.

babysitters, the marginal revenue product of these services is low, a fact reflected in demand curve D_B. There are many households, typically those with high school students, willing to supply these services, and the supply curve is S_B. This market achieves an equilibrium at a low wage rate ($6 an hour in this example) and at a relatively high quantity employed, Q_B.

If there is an increase in the demand for news anchors, the demand curve D_N in Fig. 14.8(a) shifts to the right, increasing their wage rate and increasing the quantity employed. The higher wage rate will induce more households to offer their services in this activity. If there is an increase in demand for babysitters, the demand curve D_B in Fig. 14.8(b) shifts to the right, increasing their wage rate and increasing the quantity employed. Again, a higher wage rate will induce an increase in the quantity supplied. Movements in wage rates occur to achieve a balance between the quantities demanded and supplied in each individual labor market. Changes in demand result in changes in the wage rate that achieve a reallocation of the labor force.

There have been some important changes in recent years in the demand for a highly paid part of the labor force—senior executives. Reading Between the Lines on pp. 394–395 looks at this market.

Capital Market Equilibrium

Figure 14.9 shows capital market equilibrium. In Fig. 14.9(a), we illustrate that part of the capital market in the steel industry—the market for steel mills. The long-run supply of capital to the steel industry is shown as the perfectly elastic supply curve LS. But the actual quantity of steel mills in place is Q_1, and the short-run supply curve is SS_1. The demand curve for steel mills, determined by their marginal revenue product, is D_1. The interest rate earned by the owners of steel mills—the stockholders of USX and similar firms—is R_1.

Figure 14.9(b) shows that part of the capital market in the computer industry. Again, the long-run supply curve is LS, the same curve as in the steel industry. That is, in the long run, capital is supplied to each of these industries at an interest rate R. But the amount of computer-producing capital in place is Q_3, and the short-run supply curve is SS_3 in part (b). The demand curve for computer-producing capital, determined by its marginal revenue product, is

The Market for CEOs

The Wall Street Journal, April 17, 1991

Hard Times Trim CEO Pay Raises

by Amanda Bennett

For Barry F. Sullivan, chairman of First Chicago Corp., last year's hard times brought both good and bad pay news.

The bad news: a pay cut. Because of slumping profits at the Chicago-based bank-holding company, Mr. Sullivan did without a bonus last year, thus cutting his cash compensation by 50%, to $735,632. The good news: Last year, the company gave him 65,000 stock options, as well as 25,000 restricted shares valued at $662,500.

"Our senior people took a significant zap in terms of annual pay," says Paul Knuti, vice president of human-resources policy at First Chicago. But in bad times and good, he adds, "we want to provide them significant long-term opportunities. Then our shareholders will be happy, and we will create some nice wealth for our senior management."

As Mr. Sullivan and others are discovering, hard times cut into many executives' pay last year. Overall, chief executives' salary and bonuses still rose, but the rate of increase slid for the second year in a row, to its lowest rate in five years. Many executives saw annual bonuses slip away altogether as corporate profits faded.

But don't weep for anyone just yet. Behind the scenes, many companies continue to fatten executive stock plans. That may not have boosted pay for 1990, but it set the stage for huge pay gains in the future.

"It is very safe to predict that if the stock market remains strong, the gains reaped from [these] stock plans will yield dramatic numbers in the mid- to late-1990s," says Michael Halloran, head of the executive-compensation practice at compensation consultants Towers Perrin.

Of course, stock ownership implies risk, since stock prices go down as well as up. But most of these stock and option grants represent net additions to executives' compensation packages, and their sheer size means that even very small stock-price gains will translate into big paper profits. . . .

The Essence of the Story

Chief executives' salaries and bonuses increased in 1990 but at their lowest rate in five years, and many annual bonuses were eliminated entirely.

At the same time, many executives received increased compensation in the form of stock plans.

An example is Barry F. Sullivan, chairman of First Chicago Corp., who, because of slumping profits, took a cash pay cut of 50 percent in 1990. But he also received 65,000 stock options as well as 25,000 restricted shares valued at $662,500.

Paul Knuti, vice-president of human-resources policy at First Chicago, says that the company's senior executives took a significant cut in annual pay but the company wants to provide them with significant long-term rewards.

Stock ownership is risky, since stock prices go both down and up. But if the stock market remains strong, executives stand to make large gains later in the 1990s.

Background and Analysis

In 1989, the demand curve for top executives at First Chicago was D_{89} in part (a) of the figure. The short-run supply curve of senior executives was SS, and an executive's wage was $500,000 a year. (The numbers are hypothetical.)

In 1990, the marginal productivity of top executives declined and the demand curve for their services shifted to the left to D_{90} in part (a) of the figure. Their wages fell to $300,000.

First Chicago is a small buyer in the large nationwide market for senior executives, and in the long run, if it does not offer a compensation package comparable with those of other firms, it will lose its executives. It faces a long-run supply curve that is perfectly elastic, shown as LS in part (b) of the figure.

If the demand for executives at First Chicago remains at D_{90}, the company will decrease the number of executives employed to L_1 and pay that smaller number the going market rate of $500,000 a year.

But First Chicago wants its executives to become more productive, so it offers them stock in the company, the value of which depends on the effectiveness of the executives.

If the plan works, the marginal productivity of executives increases, and the demand curve shifts back to the right to D_{95}. First Chicago continues to employ the same number of executives as before—L—and an executive's pay package—wage plus income from stocks—returns to $500,000.

(a) The short run at First Chicago

(b) The long run at First Chicago

FIGURE **14.9**

Capital Market Equilibrium

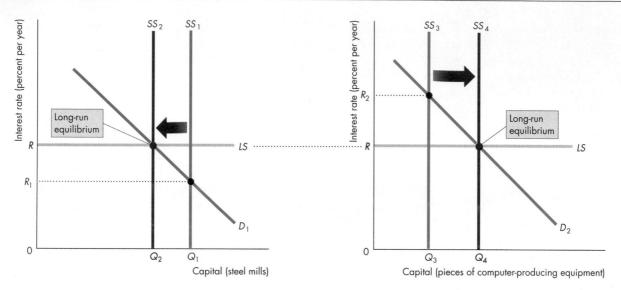

(a) Steel industry

(b) Computer industry

The long-run supply curve of capital (*LS*) in the steel industry (part a) and the computer industry (part b) is perfectly elastic. The number of steel mills in place is fixed at Q_1, so the short-run supply curve in the steel industry is SS_1. The demand curve for steel mills is D_1. The interest rate on capital invested in steel is R_1. The amount of computer-producing equipment in place is fixed at Q_3, so the short-run supply curve in the computer industry is SS_3. The demand curve for computer-producing equipment is D_2. The interest rate in the computer industry is R_2.

With a higher interest rate in the computer industry, capital leaves the steel industry and goes into the computer industry. The short-run supply curves shift. In the steel industry, the short-run supply curve shifts to the left, to SS_2, and the interest rate rises. In the computer industry, the short-run supply curve shifts to the right, to SS_4, and the interest rate falls. In long-run equilibrium, interest rates are the same in both industries.

D_2. The interest rate earned by the owners of computer production equipment—the stockholders of IBM and similar firms—is R_2.

You can see that the interest rate paid to owners of capital in the steel industry is lower than that in the computer industry. This inequality of interest rates on capital sets up an interesting dynamic adjustment process that gradually lowers the stock of capital in the steel industry and increases the stock of capital in the computer industry. With a low interest rate on capital in the steel industry and a high interest rate on capital in the computer industry, it pays people to take their investments out of the steel industry and to put them into the computer industry. But physical plant and equipment have been built in the steel industry and cannot be readily transformed into computer-making equipment. An individual steel producer could sell off its unwanted capital or operate it until it has worn out. Even if the producer does sell off the equipment, the firm that buys it will be willing to pay only a low price for it and that firm also will not replace the equipment when it is finally worn out. Whether the equipment is operated by its present owner or a new owner that buys it for a low price, the equipment continues to be operated. But it gradually wears out and is not replaced, so the capital stock in the steel industry declines. The short-run supply curve shifts to the left, to SS_2. Conversely, as additional saving is made, it is directed toward the computer industry, so the short-run supply curve in that industry shifts to the right, to SS_4. During this process, interest rates adjust in the two industries, increasing in the steel industry and decreasing in the computer industry.

Eventually, in long-run equilibrium, the interest rate on capital in the two industries will have equalized at R.

The Stock Market   In the story of a contracting steel industry and an expanding computer industry that we have just worked through, you might be wondering why people are willing to own shares in the steel industry when the rate of return on steel mills is below that on computer-producing equipment. The answer is that the stock market reacts by lowering the value of steel shares relative to computer shares. The fall in the price of steel shares increases the interest rate that people expect to earn on steel shares to equal that expected on computer shares. That is, during the period in which the steel industry is declining and its capital stock is decreasing, the stock market lowers the value of the steel industry to equalize the return expected on shares in that industry and in all other industries.

Next, let's see how rents are determined in the market for land.

Land Market Equilibrium

Equilibrium in the land market occurs at rents that allocate the fixed amounts of land available to their highest-value uses. Figure 14.10 illustrates two land markets. Part (a) shows the market for land on Chicago's Magnificent Mile. Its marginal revenue product gives rise to the demand curve D_M. There are a fixed number of square feet of land, Q_M, so the supply is inelastic, as shown by the curve S_M. Equilibrium occurs at a rent of $10,000 a square foot a year.

Figure 14.10(b) illustrates the market for farmland in Iowa. Here, the marginal revenue product produces the demand curve D_I. There is a vast amount of land available but, again, only a fixed quantity—in this case Q_I. Thus the supply curve lies a long way to the right but is vertical—perfectly inelastic—at S_I. Here, the equilibrium rent occurs at $1,000 an acre a year.

The explanation of land rents given here can be extended to the rents and prices of all natural resources, and a discussion of some of these broader issues is found in Our Advancing Knowledge on pp. 398–399.

We've now studied the markets for the three factors of production and seen how wages, interest, and rent are determined. We now turn to our final task in this chapter—defining and distinguishing between economic rent and transfer earnings.

FIGURE **14.10**

Land Market Equilibrium

(a) Magnificent Mile

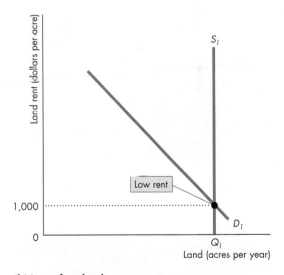

(b) Iowa farmland

The marginal revenue product of land on Chicago's Magnificent Mile gives rise to the demand curve D_M (part a). The quantity of land on the Magnificent Mile is fixed at Q_M, so the supply curve is S_M. Equilibrium occurs at an annual rent of $10,000 a square foot. The marginal revenue product of farmland in Iowa (part b) gives rise to a demand curve D_I. The quantity of farmland in Iowa is fixed at Q_I, and the supply curve is S_I. Equilibrium occurs at an annual rent of $1,000 an acre.

RUNNING out of SPACE?

Is there a limit to economic growth, or can we expand production and population without effective limit? One of the most influential answers to these questions was given by Thomas Malthus in 1798. He reasoned that population, unchecked, would grow at a geometric rate—1, 2, 4, 8, 16, . . .—while the food supply would grow at an arithmetic rate—1, 2, 3, 4, 5, ... To prevent the population from outstripping the available food supply, there would be periodic wars, famines, and plagues. In Malthus's view, only "moral restraint" could prevent such periodic disasters.

As industrialization proceeded through the nineteenth century, Malthus's idea came to be applied to all natural resources, especially those that are exhaustible. A modern day Malthusian, ecologist Paul Ehrlich, believes that we are sitting on a "population bomb" and that the government must limit both population growth and the resources that may be used each year.

In 1931, Harold Hotelling developed a theory of natural resources with different predictions from those of Malthus. The Hotelling Principle is that the relative price of an exhaustible natural resource will rise steadily, bringing a decline in the quantity used and an increase in the use of substitute resources.

Julian Simon, a contemporary economist, has challenged both the Malthusian gloom and the Hotelling Principle. He believes that *people* are the "ultimate resource" and predicts that a rising population *lessens* the pressure on natural resources. A bigger population provides a larger number of resourceful people who can work out more efficient ways of using scarce resources. As these solutions are found, the prices of exhaustible resources actually fall. To demonstrate his point, in 1980 Simon bet Ehrlich that the prices of five metals—copper, chrome, nickel, tin, and tungsten—would fall during the 1980s. Simon won the bet!

> "Men, like all animals, naturally multiply in proportion to the means of their subsistence."
>
> ADAM SMITH
> *The Wealth of Nations*

No matter whether it is agricultural land, an exhaustible natural resource, or the space in the center of Chicago and no matter whether it is 1992 or, as shown here, 1909, there is a limit to what is available, and we persistently push against that limit. Economists see urban congestion as a consequence of the value of doing business in the city center relative to the cost. They see the price mechanism, bringing ever higher rents and prices of raw materials, as the means of allocating and rationing scarce natural resources. Malthusians, in contrast, explain congestion as the consequence of population pressure, and they see the solution as population control.

HUNT.

A PARSON & A MATHEMATICIAN

PROBE the Pressure on Resources

Thomas Robert Malthus (1766–1834), pictured right, an English parson and professor, was an extremely influential social scientist. In his best-selling *Essay on the Principle of Population,* published in 1798, he argued that population growth would outstrip food production. Modern-day Malthusians believe that his basic idea was right and that it applies to all natural resources.

The most profound work on the economics of natural resources is that of Harold Hotelling (1895–1973), pictured left. Hotelling worked as a journalist, schoolteacher, and mathematical consultant before becoming an economics professor at Columbia University. He explained how the price mechanism allocates exhaustible resources, making them progressively more expensive. Their higher price encourages the development of new technologies, the discovery of new sources of supply, and the development of substitutes.

Economic Rent and Transfer Earnings

The total income of a factor of production is made up of its economic rent and its transfer earnings. **Economic rent** is an income received by the owner of a factor over and above the amount required to induce that owner to offer the factor for use. The income required to induce the owner to offer the factor for use is called **transfer earnings**.

These concepts of economic rent and transfer earnings are illustrated in Fig. 14.11. The figure shows the market for a factor of production. It could be *any* factor of production—labor, capital, or land. The demand curve for the factor of production is *D*, and its supply curve is *S*. The factor price is *PF* and the quantity of the factor used is *QF*. The

FIGURE **14.11**

Economic Rent and Transfer Earnings

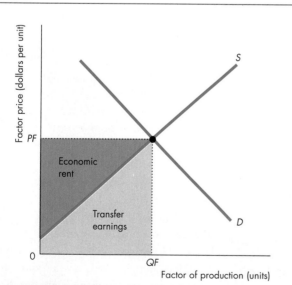

The total income of a factor of production is made up of its economic rent and its transfer earnings. Transfer earnings are measured by the yellow area under the supply curve, and economic rent is measured by the green area above the supply curve and below the factor price.

income of the factor is the sum of the yellow and green areas. The yellow area below the supply curve measures transfer earnings, and the green area below the factor price but above the supply curve measures economic rent.

To see why the area below the supply curve measures transfer earnings, recall that a supply curve can be interpreted in two different ways. The standard interpretation is that a supply curve indicates the quantity supplied at a given price. But the alternative interpretation of a supply curve is that it shows the minimum price at which a given quantity is willingly supplied. If suppliers receive only the minimum amount required to induce them to supply each unit of the factor of production, they will be paid a different price for each unit. The prices will trace the supply curve, and the income received is entirely transfer earnings—the yellow area in Fig. 14.11.

The concept of economic rent is similar to the concept of consumer surplus that you met in Chapter 7, p. 171. Consumer surplus, recall, is the difference between the price the household pays for a good and the maximum price it would be willing to pay, as indicated by the demand curve. In a parallel sense, economic rent is the difference between the factor price a household actually receives and the minimum factor price at which it would be willing to supply a given amount of a factor of production.

It is important to distinguish between *economic rent* and *rent*. Rent is the price paid to the factor of production land. Economic rent is a component of the income received by every factor of production.

The portion of the income of a factor of production that consists of economic rent depends on the elasticity of the supply of the factor of production. When the supply of a factor of production is inelastic, its entire income is economic rent. Most of Peter Jennings's and Joe Montana's incomes are economic rent. When the supply of a factor of production is perfectly elastic, none of its income is economic rent. Most of the income of a babysitter is transfer earnings. In general, when the supply curve is neither perfectly elastic nor perfectly inelastic (like that illustrated in Fig. 14.11), some part of the factor income is economic rent and the other part is transfer earnings.

Figure 14.12 illustrates the three possibilities. Part (a) of the figure shows the market for a particular parcel of land in New York City. The land is fixed in size at *L* square yards. Therefore the supply

FIGURE **14.12**

Economic Rent and Supply Elasticity

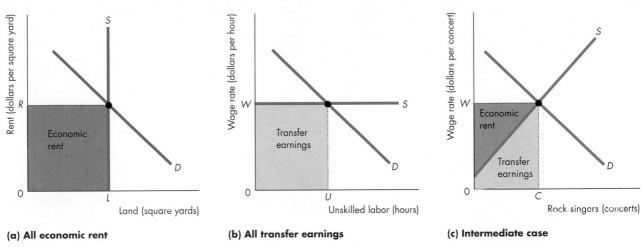

(a) All economic rent

(b) All transfer earnings

(c) Intermediate case

When the supply of the factor of production is perfectly inelastic (the supply curve is vertical), as in part (a), the entire factor income is economic rent. When the supply of the factor of production is perfectly elastic, as in part (b), the factor's entire income is transfer earnings.

When a factor supply curve slopes upward, as in part (c), part of the factor income is economic rent and part is transfer earnings. Land is the example shown in part (a); unskilled labor in poor countries such as India and China in part (b); and rock singers in part (c).

curve of the land is vertical—perfectly inelastic. No matter what the rent on the land is, there is no way of increasing the quantity that can be supplied.

The demand for that block of land is determined by its marginal revenue product. The marginal revenue product in turn depends on the uses to which the land can be put. In a central business district such as Manhattan, the marginal revenue product is high because a large number of people are concentrated in that area, making it a prime place for conducting valuable business. Suppose that the marginal revenue product of this block of land is shown by the demand curve in Fig. 14.12(a). Then it commands a rent of R. The entire income accruing to the owner of the land is the green area in the figure. This income is *economic rent*. The rent charged for this piece of land depends entirely on its marginal revenue product—on the demand curve. If the demand curve shifts to the right, the rent rises. If the demand curve shifts to the left, the rent falls. The quantity of land supplied remains constant at L.

Is coffee expensive in New York City because rents are high, or are rents high because people in New York City are willing to pay a high price for

coffee? The conclusion we've just reached answers this question. We've seen that the rent of a New York City block is determined entirely by the demand for it and that the demand, in turn, is determined by the marginal revenue product. Land has a high marginal revenue product only if people are willing to pay a high price to use the land. Of course, from the point of view of McDonald's, it feels that it has to charge a high price for coffee at its 57th Street restaurant because of the high rent it pays there. But the rent wouldn't be high if McDonald's (and other potential users) did not have a high marginal revenue product "attached" to that land, making it willing to pay those high rents.

Figure 14.12(b) shows the market for a factor of production that is in perfectly elastic supply. An example of such a market might be that for unskilled labor in a poor country such as India or China. In those countries, large amounts of labor flock to the cities and are available for work at the going wage rate (in this case, W). Thus in these situations, the supply of labor is almost perfectly elastic. The entire income earned by this labor is transfer earnings. It receives no economic rent.

Figure 14.12(c) shows the market for rock singers. To induce a rock singer to sing at a larger number of concerts, a higher income has to be offered—the rock singer's supply curve is upward sloping. The demand curve—measuring the marginal revenue product of the rock singer—is labeled D in the figure. Equilibrium occurs where the rock singer receives a wage of W and sings in C concerts. The green area above the rock singer's supply curve is economic rent, and the yellow area below the supply curve is the rock singer's transfer earnings. If the rock singer is not offered at least the amount of the transfer earnings, then the singer will withdraw from the rock concert market and perform an alternative activity.

◆ ◆ ◆ ◆ We've now studied the market for the three factors of production—labor, capital, and land—and we've seen how the returns to these factors of production—wages, interest, and rent—are determined. We've seen the crucial role played in determining the demand for a factor of production by the factor's marginal revenue product. We've seen how the interaction of demand and supply determines factor prices and factor incomes. We've also seen how changes in these prices and incomes come about from changes in demand and supply. Finally, we've distinguished between economic rent and transfer earnings. ◆ ◆ In the next chapter, we're going to examine some detailed features of the labor market more closely, explaining differences in wage rates among the skilled and the unskilled, males and females, and racial and ethnic minorities.

SUMMARY

Factor Prices and Incomes

The factors of production—labor, capital, and land—earn a return—wages, interest, and rent. Labor is the most important source of income. Factor prices are determined by the demand for and supply of factors of production. Incomes are determined by the prices of factors of production and the quantities used. An increase in the demand for a factor of production increases the factor's price and income; a decrease in the demand for a factor of production decreases its price and income. An increase in supply increases the quantity used of a factor of production but decreases its price. A decrease in supply decreases the quantity used and increases the factor's price. Whether an increase in supply leads to an increase or a decrease in the income of a factor of production depends on the elasticity of demand for the factor. When elasticity of demand is greater than 1, an increase in supply leads to an increase in the factor's income. When the elasticity of demand for a factor is less than 1, an increase in supply leads to a decrease in the factor's income. (pp. 378–380)

Demand for Factors

A firm's demand for a factor stems from its desire to maximize profit. The extra revenue generated by hir-

ing one more unit of a factor is called the marginal revenue product of the factor. A firm's demand curve for a factor is derived from that factor's marginal revenue product curve. A firm demands an input up to the point at which the marginal revenue product of the factor equals the factor's price.

A firm's labor input is variable in both the short run and the long run. The firm's capital input may be varied only in the long run. The elasticity of the demand for labor in the short run depends on the short-run elasticity of demand for the firm's product, on the labor intensity of the production process, and on the slope of the marginal product of labor curve. The long-run elasticity of a firm's demand for labor depends on the long-run elasticity of demand for the product, on labor intensity, and on the ease with which capital can be substituted for labor.

The market demand for labor is the sum of the demands by each individual firm. (pp. 380–387)

Supply of Factors

The supply of factors is determined by households' decisions on the allocation of their time and the division of their income between consumption and saving. In choosing how much time to allocate to market activities, each household compares the wage rate that can be earned with the value of its time in other nonmarket activities. The household will supply no market labor at wage rates below its reservation wage. At wage rates above the household's reservation wage, the quantity of labor supplied rises as long as the substitution effect of the higher wage rate is larger than the income effect. As the wage rate continues to rise, the income effect, which leads to more time taken for leisure, becomes larger than the substitution effect, and the quantity of labor supplied by the household falls.

The market supply curve of labor is the sum of the supply curves of all households. Like the household's labor supply curve, the market supply curve of labor eventually bends backward. However, the response to higher wage rates of households on the upward-sloping part of their labor supply curve dominates the response of those on the backward-bending part, and the market supply curve slopes upward over the range of wage rates that we experience.

Households supply capital by saving. Saving increases as the interest rate increases. The supply of capital to an individual firm is highly inelastic in the short run but highly elastic in the long run.

The supply of land is fixed and independent of its rent. (pp. 387–392)

Competitive Equilibrium

In a competitive factor market, the factor price and quantity used are determined at the point of intersection of the demand and supply curves. High factor prices occur for factors of production that have a high marginal revenue product and a low supply. Low factor prices occur for factors of production with a low marginal revenue product and a high supply. (pp. 392–399)

Economic Rent and Transfer Earnings

Economic rent is that part of the income received by a factor owner over and above the amount needed to induce the owner to supply the factor of production for use. The rest of a factor's income is transfer earnings. When the supply of a factor is perfectly inelastic, its entire income is made up of economic rent. Factors that have a perfectly elastic supply receive only transfer earnings. In general the supply curve of a factor is upward sloping, and part of its income received is transfer earnings (below the supply curve) and part is economic rent (above the supply curve but below the factor price). (pp. 400–402)

KEY ELEMENTS

Key Terms

Average revenue product, 383
Average revenue product curve, 383
Derived demand, 380
Economic rent, 400
Long-run demand for labor, 385
Long-run elasticity of demand for labor, 387
Marginal revenue product, 381
Marginal revenue product curve, 383
Market activity, 388
Nonmarket activity, 388
Reservation wage, 388
Short-run demand for labor, 385
Short-run elasticity of demand for labor, 386
Transfer earnings, 400

Key Figures and Tables

Figure 14.1   Demand and Supply in a Factor Market, 378
Figure 14.4   The Demand for Labor at Max's Wash 'n' Wax, 384
Figure 14.8   Labor Market Equilibrium, 393
Figure 14.9   Capital Market Equilibrium, 393
Figure 14.10   Land Market Equilibrium, 397
Figure 14.11   Economic Rent and Transfer Earnings, 400
Table 14.2   A Compact Glossary of Factor Market Terms, 383
Table 14.3   Two Conditions for Maximum Profit, 385
Table 14.4   A Firm's Demand for Labor, 386

REVIEW QUESTIONS

1 Explain what happens to the price of a factor of production and its income if the following occurs:

a There is an increase in demand for the factor.
b There is an increase in supply of the factor.
c There is a decrease in demand for the factor.
d There is a decrease in supply of the factor.

2 Explain why the effect of a change in supply of a factor on a factor's income depends on the elasticity of demand for the factor.

3 Define marginal revenue product and distinguish between marginal revenue product and marginal revenue.

4 Why does marginal revenue product decline as the quantity of a factor employed increases?

5 What is the relationship between the demand curve for a factor of production and its marginal revenue product curve? Why?

6 Show that the condition for maximum profit in the product market—marginal cost equals marginal revenue—is equivalent to the condition for maximum profit in the factor market—marginal revenue product equals marginal cost of factor (equals factor price in a competitive factor market).

7 Review the main influences on the demand for a factor of production—the influences that shift the demand curve for a factor.

8 What determines the short-run and long-run elasticity of demand for labor?

9 What determines the supply of labor?

10 Why might the supply of labor curve bend backward at a high enough wage rate?

11 What determines the supply of capital?

12 Define economic rent and transfer earnings and distinguish between these two components of income.

13 Suppose that a factor of production is in perfectly inelastic supply. If the marginal revenue product of the factor decreases, what happens to the price, quantity used, income, transfer earnings, and rent of the factor?

PROBLEMS

1 Wanda owns a fish shop. She employs students to sort and pack the fish. Students can pack the following amounts of fish in an hour:

Number of students	Quantity of fish (pounds)
1	20
2	50
3	90
4	120
5	145
6	165
7	180
8	190

a Draw the average and marginal product curves of these students.

b If Wanda can sell her fish for 50¢ a pound, draw the average and marginal revenue product curves.
c Draw Wanda's demand for labor curve.
d If all fish packers in Wanda's area pay their packers $7.50 an hour, how many students will Wanda hire?

2 The price of fish falls to 33.33¢ a pound, and fish packers' wages remain at $7.50 an hour.
a What happens to Wanda's average and marginal product curves?
b What happens to her average and marginal revenue product curves?
c What happens to her demand for labor curve?
d What happens to the number of students that she hires?

3 Fish packers' wages increase to $10 an hour, but the price of fish remains at 50¢ a pound.

a   What happens to the average and marginal revenue product curves?
b   What happens to Wanda's demand curve?
c   How many packers does Wanda hire?

4 Using the information provided in problem 1, calculate Wanda's marginal revenue and marginal cost, marginal revenue product, and marginal cost of labor. Show that when Wanda is making maximum profit, marginal cost equals marginal revenue and marginal revenue product equals the marginal cost of labor.

5 You are given the following information about the labor market in an isolated town in the Amazon rainforest. Everyone works for logging companies, but there are many logging companies in the town. The market for logging workers is perfectly competitive. The town's labor supply is given as follows:

Wage rate (cruzados per hour)	Quantity of labor supplied (hours)
2	120
4	160
6	200
8	240
10	280
12	320
14	360

The market demand for labor from all the logging firms in the town is as follows:

Wage rate (cruzados per hour)	Quantity of labor demanded (hours)
2	400
4	360
6	320
8	280
10	240
12	200
14	160

a   What is the competitive equilibrium wage rate?
b   What is the quantity of labor employed?
c   What is total labor income?
d   How much of that labor income is economic rent and how much is transfer earnings? (You might find it easier to answer this question by drawing graphs of the demand and supply curves and then finding the economic rent and transfer earnings as areas on the graph in a manner similar to what was done in Fig. 14.11.)

CHAPTER 15

LABOR MARKETS

After studying this chapter, you will be able to:

♦ Explain why skilled workers earn more, on. the average, than unskilled workers

♦ Explain why college graduates earn more, on the average, than high school graduates

♦ Explain why union workers earn higher wages than nonunion workers

♦ Explain why, on the average, men earn more than women and whites earn more than minorities

♦ Predict the effects of a comparable-worth program

AS YOU WELL KNOW, COLLEGE IS NOT JUST A BALL. THOSE exams and problem sets require a lot of hard work. Are they worth the effort that goes into them? What is the payoff? Is it sufficient to make up for the years of tuition, room and board, and lost wages? (You could, after all, be washing dishes now instead of slogging through this economics course.) ◆ ◆ Many workers belong to labor unions. Usually, union workers earn a higher wage than nonunion workers in comparable jobs. Why? How are unions able to get higher wages for their members than the wages that nonunion workers are paid? ◆ ◆ Among the most visible and persistent differences in earnings are those between men and women and between whites and minorities. White men, on the average, earn incomes that are one third higher than the incomes earned by black men. Black men earn more, in descending order, than Hispanic men, white women, black women, and Hispanic women, who

The Sweat of Our Brows

earn only 56 cents for each dollar earned by the average white man. Certainly a lot of individuals defy the averages. But why do minorities and women so consistently earn less than white men? Is it because of discrimination and exploitation? Or is it because of economic factors? Or is it a combination of the two? ◆ ◆ Equal pay legislation has resulted in comparable-worth programs, which try to ensure that jobs of equivalent value receive the same pay regardless of the pay set by the market. Can comparable-worth programs bring economic help to women and minorities?

◆ ◆ ◆ ◆ In this chapter, we study the way labor markets work and answer questions such as these. We begin by using the competitive labor market model developed in Chapter 14 to analyze the effects on wages of differences in education and training. We then extend the model to explain differences in union and nonunion wages, to explain differences in pay among men, women, and minorities, and to analyze the effects of comparable-worth laws.

Skill Differentials

D ifferences in earnings between workers with varying levels of education and training can be explained by using a model of competitive labor markets. In the real world, there are many different levels and varieties of education and training. To keep our analysis as clear as possible, we'll study a model economy in which there are just two different levels that result in two types of labor, what we will call skilled labor and unskilled labor. We'll study the demand for and supply of these two types of labor and see why there is a difference in their wages and what determines that difference. Let's begin by looking at the demand for the two types of labor.

The Demand for Skilled and Unskilled Labor

Skilled workers can perform a wide variety of tasks that unskilled workers would perform badly or perhaps could not even perform at all. Imagine an untrained, inexperienced person performing surgery or piloting an airplane. Because skilled workers perform complex tasks, they have a higher marginal revenue product than unskilled labor. As we learned in Chapter 14, the demand for labor curve is derived from the marginal revenue product curve. The higher the marginal revenue product of labor, the higher is the demand for labor.

Figure 15.1(a) shows the demand curves for skilled and unskilled labor. At any given level of employment, firms are willing to pay a higher wage

to a skilled worker than to an unskilled worker. The gap between the two wages is the difference between the marginal revenue products of a given number of skilled and unskilled workers. This difference is the marginal revenue product of skill. For example, at an employment level of 2,000 hours, firms are willing to pay $12.50 for a skilled worker and only $5 for an unskilled worker. The difference in the marginal revenue product of the two workers is $7.50 an hour. Thus the marginal revenue product of skill is $7.50 an hour.

The Supply of Skilled and Unskilled Labor

Skills are costly to acquire. Furthermore, a worker pays the cost of acquiring a skill before benefiting from a higher wage. For example, attending college usually leads to a higher income, but the higher income is not earned until after graduation. These facts make the acquisition of skills similar to investment. To emphasize the investment nature of acquiring a skill, we call that activity an investment in human capital. **Human capital** is the accumulated skill and knowledge of human beings. The value of a person's human capital is the present value of the extra earnings received as a result of acquiring skill and knowledge. (The concept of present value is explained in Chapter 9.) It is equivalent to a sum of money that, if invested today at the average interest rate, will yield a stream of income equivalent to the extra earnings resulting from a person's acquired knowledge and skills.

The cost of acquiring a skill includes actual expenditures on such things as tuition and room and board and also includes costs in the form of lost or reduced earnings while the skill is being acquired. When a person goes to school full-time, that cost is the total earnings forgone. However, some people acquire skills on the job. Such skill acquisition is called on-the-job training. Usually, a worker undergoing on-the-job training is paid a lower wage than one doing a comparable job but not undergoing training. In such a case, the cost of acquiring the skill is the difference between the wage paid to a person not being trained and that paid to a person being trained.

Supply Curves of Skilled and Unskilled Labor   The position of the supply curve of skilled workers

FIGURE **15.1**

Skill Differentials

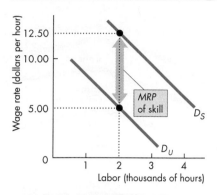

**(a) Demand for skilled
and unskilled labor**

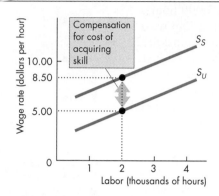

**(b) Supply of skilled
and unskilled labor**

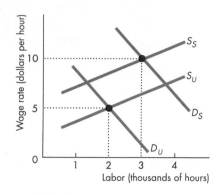

**(c) Markets for skilled
and unskilled labor**

Part (a) illustrates the marginal revenue product of skill. Unskilled workers have a marginal revenue product that gives rise to the demand curve marked D_U. Skilled workers have a higher marginal revenue product than unskilled workers. Therefore the demand curve for skilled workers, D_S, lies to the right of D_U. The vertical distance between these two curves is the marginal revenue product of the skill.

Part (b) shows the effects of the cost of acquiring skills on the supply curves of labor. The supply curve for unskilled workers is S_U. Skilled workers have to incur costs in order to acquire their skills. Therefore they would supply labor services only at a wage rate that exceeds that of unskilled labor. The supply curve for skilled workers is S_S. The verti-

cal distance between these two curves is the required compensation for the cost of acquiring a skill.

Part (c) shows the determination of the equilibrium levels of employment and the skilled-unskilled wage differential. Unskilled workers earn the wage rate $5 an hour where the quantities demanded and supplied of unskilled workers are equal. The employment level of unskilled workers is 2,000 hours. Skilled workers earn the wage rate $10 an hour, where the quantities demanded and supplied of skilled workers are equal. The employment level of skilled workers is 3,000 hours. Wages for skilled workers are always greater than those for unskilled workers.

reflects the cost of acquiring the skill. Figure 15.1(b) shows two supply curves, one for skilled workers and the other for unskilled workers. The supply curve for skilled workers is S_S, and that for unskilled workers is S_U.

The skilled worker's supply curve lies above the unskilled worker's supply curve. The vertical distance between the two supply curves is the compensation for the cost of acquiring the skill. (The difference is the amount that has a present value equal to the cost of acquiring the skill.) For example, suppose that the quantity of unskilled labor supplied is 2,000 hours at a wage rate of $5 an hour. This wage rate compensates the unskilled workers purely for their time on the job. Consider next the supply of skilled workers. To induce 2,000 hours of skilled labor to be supplied, firms have to pay a wage rate of $8.50 an hour. This wage rate for skilled labor is higher

than that for unskilled labor, since skilled labor must be compensated not only for the time on the job but also for the time and other costs of acquiring the skill.

Wage Rates of Skilled and Unskilled Labor

To work out the wage rates of skilled and unskilled labor, all we have to do is bring together the effects of skill on the demand for and supply of labor. Figure 15.1(c) shows the demand curves and the supply curves for skilled and unskilled labor. These curves are exactly the same as those plotted in parts (a) and (b). Equilibrium occurs in the market for unskilled labor where the supply and demand curves for unskilled labor intersect. The equilibrium wage rate is $5 an hour, and the quantity of unskilled labor employed is 2,000 hours. Equilibrium in the market for skilled workers occurs where the supply and demand curves for skilled workers intersect. The equilibrium wage rate is $10 an hour, and the quantity of skilled labor employed is 3,000 hours.

As you can see in part (c), the equilibrium wage rate of skilled labor is higher than that of unskilled labor. There are two reasons why this occurs: first, skilled labor has a higher marginal revenue product than unskilled labor, so at a given wage rate the demand for skilled labor is greater than the demand for unskilled labor; second, skills are costly to acquire, so at a given wage rate the supply of skilled labor is less than the supply of unskilled labor. The wage differential (in this case $5 an hour) depends on both the marginal revenue product of the skill and the cost of acquiring it. The higher the marginal revenue product of the skill, the larger is the vertical distance between the demand curves for skilled and unskilled labor. The more costly it is to acquire a skill, the larger is the vertical distance between the supplies of skilled and unskilled labor. The higher the marginal revenue product of the skill and the more costly it is to acquire, the larger is the wage differential between skilled and unskilled workers.

Do Education and Training Pay?

There are large and persistent differences in earnings based on the degree of education and training. An indication of those differences can be seen in Fig. 15.2. This figure highlights two important sources of earnings differences. The first is the degree of education itself. The higher the level of education, other things being equal, the higher are a person's earnings. The second source of earnings differences apparent in Fig. 15.2 is age. Age is strongly correlated with experience and the degree of on-the-job training a person has had. Thus as a person gets older, up to middle age, earnings increase.

We can see, from Fig. 15.2, that going through high school, college, and postgraduate education leads to higher incomes. But does education pay in the sense of yielding a higher income that compensates for its cost and for the delay in the start of earnings? For most people, education does indeed pay. Rates of return have been calculated suggesting that a college degree is a better investment than almost any other that a person can undertake. Rates of return as high as 15 percent, after allowing for inflation, are not uncommon.

FIGURE 15.2

Education and Earnings

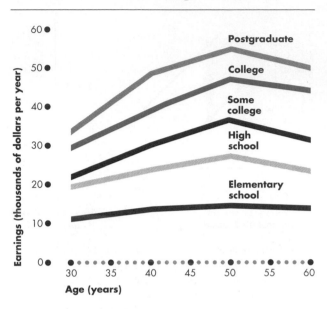

Earnings of male employees at various ages and with varying school levels are shown. Earnings increase with length of education and also with age, but only up to the middle forties. Beyond that age, earnings decrease. These differences show the importance of experience and education in influencing skill differentials.

Source: U.S. Bureau of the Census, *Money Income in 1981 of Families and Persons in the United States,* Current Population Reports, Series P-60, No. 137 (1983), Table 48.

Differences in education and training are an important source of differences in earnings. But they are not the only source. Another is the activities of labor unions. Let's see how unions affect wages and why, on the average, union wages exceed nonunion wages.

Union-Nonunion Wage Differentials

A **labor union** is an organized group of workers whose purpose is to increase wages and influence other job conditions. A labor union acts in the labor market like a monopo-

TABLE **15.1**
A Compact Glossary on Unions

Labor union	An organized group of workers that attempts to increase wages and improve other conditions of employment
AFL-CIO	A federation of unions formed in 1955 by a merger of the American Federation of Labor (AFL) and the Congress of Industrial Organizations (CIO); acts as the voice of organized labor in media and political arenas
Craft union	A union in which workers have a similar range of skills but work for many firms and in many different industries
Industrial union	A union in which workers have a variety of skills and job types but work in the same industry
Local	A subunit of a union that organizes individual workers; in craft unions, the local is geographical, and in industrial unions, the local is based on a plant or a company
Open shop	A place of work that has no union restriction on who can work in the shop; here, the union bargains for its members but not for nonmembers
Closed shop	A place of work where only union members may be employed; illegal since 1947, when Congress passed the Labor-Management Relations Act (the Taft-Hartley Act)
Union shop	A place of work that may hire nonunion workers but only if they join the union within a specified period; illegal in the 20 states where "right-to-work" legislation has been passed
Right-to-work law	A law that protects the right of an individual to work without joining a union
Collective bargaining	Negotiations between representatives of employers and unions on wages and other employment conditions
Strike	A group decision to refuse to work under prevailing conditions
Lockout	A firm's refusal to allow its labor force to work
Binding arbitration	Determination of wages and other employment conditions by a third party (an arbitrator) acceptable to both parties

list in the product market. The union seeks to restrict competition and, as a result, raises the price at which labor is traded. A compact glossary on unions can be found in Table 15.1.

There are two main types of union: craft unions and industrial unions. A **craft union** is a group of workers who have a similar range of skills but work for many different firms in many different industries and regions. Examples are the carpenters' union and the electrical workers' union (IBEW). An **industrial union** is a group of workers who have a variety of skills and job types but work for the same firm or industry. The United Auto Workers (UAW) and the United Steelworkers of America are examples of industrial unions.

Most unions are members of the AFL-CIO. The AFL-CIO was created in 1955 when two labor organizations combined: the American Federation of Labor (AFL), which was founded in 1886 to organize craft unions, and the Congress of Industrial Organizations (CIO), founded in 1938 to organize industrial unions. The AFL-CIO acts as the national voice of organized labor in the media and in politics.

Unions vary enormously in size. Craft unions are the smallest, and industrial unions are the biggest. The 12 largest unions in the United States—measured by number of members—are shown in Fig. 15.3.

Union strength peaked in the 1950s, when 35 percent of the work force belonged to unions. That percentage has declined steadily since 1955 and is now less than 20 percent. Changes in union membership, however, have been uneven. Some unions have declined dramatically, while others, especially those in the government sector, such as the American Federation of State, County, and Municipal Employees, have increased in strength.

Union organization is based on a subdivision known as the local. The **local** is a subunit of a union that organizes the individual workers. In craft unions the local is based on a geographical area, while in industrial unions the local is based on a plant or an individual firm.

There are three possible forms of organization for a local: an open shop, a closed shop, or a union shop. An **open shop** is an arrangement in which

FIGURE **15.3**

Unions with the Largest Membership

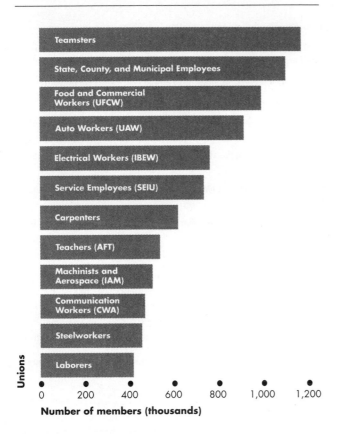

Each of the 12 largest labor unions in the United States, shown here, have more than 400,000 members.

Source: U.S. Bureau of the Census, *Statistical Abstract of the United States: 1991,* 111th edition, 424–425.

workers have a right to be employed without joining the union—there is no union restriction on who can work in the "shop." A **closed shop** is an arrangement in which only union members may be employed by a firm. Closed shops have been illegal since the passage of the Taft-Hartley Act in 1947. A **union shop** is an arrangement in which a firm may hire nonunion workers, but in order for such workers to remain employed they must join the union within a brief period specified by the union. Union shops are illegal in the 20 states that have passed "right-to-work"

laws. A **right-to-work law** allows an individual to work at any firm without joining a union.

Unions negotiate with employers or their representatives in a process called **collective bargaining**. The main weapons available to the union and the employer in collective bargaining are the strike and the lockout. A **strike** is a group decision to refuse to work under prevailing conditions. A **lockout** is a firm's refusal to operate its plant and employ its workers. Each party uses the threat of a strike or a lockout to try to get an agreement in its own favor. Sometimes, when the two parties in the collective bargaining process cannot agree on wages and other conditions of employment, they agree to put their disagreement to binding arbitration. **Binding arbitration** is a process in which a third party—an arbitrator—determines wages and other employment conditions on behalf of the negotiating parties and the decision is final.

Though not labor unions in a legal sense, professional associations act, in many ways, like labor unions. A **professional association** is an organized group of professional workers such as lawyers, dentists, or doctors (an example of which is the American Medical Association—AMA). Professional associations control entry into the professions and license practitioners, ensuring the adherence to minimum standards of competence. But they also influence the compensation and other labor market conditions of their members.

Unions' Objectives and Constraints

A union has three broad objectives:

◆ Increasing compensation
◆ Improving working conditions
◆ Expanding job opportunities

Each of these objectives contains a series of more detailed goals. For example, in seeking to increase its members' compensation, a union operates on a variety of fronts: wages, fringe benefits, retirement pay, and such things as vacation allowances. In seeking to improve working conditions, a union is concerned with occupational health and safety as well as the environmental quality of the workplace. In seeking to expand job opportunities, a union tries to obtain greater job security for existing union members and to find ways of creating additional jobs for existing and new members.

A union's ability to pursue its objectives is restricted by two sets of constraints—one on the supply side and the other on the demand side of the labor market. On the supply side, the union's activities are limited by how well it can restrict nonunion workers from offering their labor. The larger the fraction of the work force controlled by the union, the more effective the union can be. For example, unions find it difficult to be effective in markets for unskilled farm labor in southern California because of their inability to control the flow of nonunion, often illegal, labor from Mexico. At the other extreme, unions in the construction industry can better pursue their goals because they can influence the number of people obtaining skills as electricians, plasterers, and carpenters. The unions that are best able to restrict supply are the professional associations for such groups as lawyers, dentists, and doctors. These groups control the number of qualified workers by controlling the examinations that new entrants must pass.

On the demand side of the labor market, the constraint facing a union is the fact that it cannot force firms to hire more labor than they demand. Anything that raises wages or other employment costs decreases the quantity of labor demanded. Unless the union can take actions that shift the demand curve for the labor that it represents, it has to accept the fact that a higher wage can be obtained only at the price of lower employment. Recognizing the importance of the demand for labor curve, unions try to make the demand for their labor inelastic and to increase the demand for union labor. Here are some of the methods that they employ:

◆ Encouraging import restrictions
◆ Supporting minimum wage laws
◆ Supporting immigration restrictions
◆ Increasing product demand
◆ Increasing the marginal product of union members

One of the best examples of import restrictions is the support by the United Auto Workers union (UAW) for import restrictions on foreign cars. Unions support minimum wage laws in order to increase the cost of unskilled labor. An increase in the wage rate of unskilled labor leads to a decrease in the quantity demanded of unskilled labor and to an increase in demand for skilled union labor, a sub-

stitute for unskilled labor. Restrictive immigration laws decrease the supply and increase the wage rate of unskilled workers. As a result, the demand for skilled union labor increases. Increasing product demand indirectly increases the demand for union labor. The best examples of attempts by unions in this activity are in the textile and auto industries. The garment workers union urges us to buy union-made clothes, and the UAW urges us to buy only American cars made by union workers. Increasing the marginal product of union members directly shifts the demand curve for their services. Unions use apprenticeship, training, and professional certification to increase the marginal product of their members.

Unions in a Competitive Labor Market

When a union operates in an otherwise competitive labor market, it seeks to raise wages and other compensation and to limit employment reductions by increasing demand for the labor of its members.

Figure 15.4 illustrates a labor market. The demand curve is D_C, and the supply curve is S_C. If the market is a competitive one with no union, the wage rate is $4 an hour and 100 hours of labor will be employed. Suppose that a union is formed to organize the workers in this market and that the union has sufficient control over the supply of labor to be able to artificially restrict that supply below its competitive level—to S_U. If that is all the union does, employment will fall to 62.5 hours of labor and the wage rate will rise to $10 an hour. If the union can also take steps that increase the demand for labor to D_U, it can achieve an even bigger rise in the wage rate with a smaller fall in employment. By maintaining the restricted labor supply at S_U, the union raises the wage rate to $16 an hour and achieves an employment level of 75 hours of labor.

Because they restrict the supply of labor in the markets in which they operate, labor unions increase the supply of labor in nonunion markets. Workers who can't get union jobs must look elsewhere for work. This increase in supply in nonunion markets lowers the wage rate in those markets and further widens the union-nonunion differential. But low nonunion wages decrease the demand for union labor and limit the increase in wages that unions can achieve. For this reason, unions are strong supporters of minimum wage laws that keep nonunion

FIGURE **15.4**

A Union in a Competitive Labor Market

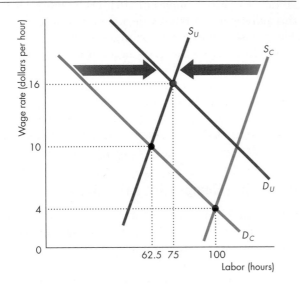

In a competitive labor market, the demand curve is D_C and the supply curve is S_C. Competitive equilibrium occurs at a wage rate of $4 an hour with 100 hours employed. By restricting employment below its competitive level, the union shifts the supply of labor to S_U. If the union can do no more than that, the wage rate will rise to $10 an hour, but employment will fall to 62.5 hours. If the union can increase the demand for labor (by increasing the demand for the good produced by the union members or by raising the price of substitute labor) and shift the demand curve to D_U, then it can raise the wage rate still higher, to $16 an hour, and achieve employment of 75 hours.

wages high and limit the incentive to use nonunion labor (see Reading Between the Lines, pp. 416–417).

We next turn our attention to the case in which employers have considerable influence in the labor market.

Monopsony

A **monopsony** is a market structure in which there is just a single buyer. With the growth of large-scale production over the last century, large manufacturing plants such as coal mines, steel and textile mills, and car manufacturers became the major employer of labor in some regions, and in some places a single firm employed almost all the labor. Such a firm is a monopsonist in the labor market.

A monopsonist can make a bigger profit than a group of firms that have to compete with each other for their labor. Figure 15.5 illustrates how a monopsonist operates. The monopsonist's marginal revenue product curve is *MRP*. This curve tells us the extra revenue from selling the output produced by the last hour of labor hired. The curve labeled *S* is the supply curve of labor. This curve tells us how many hours are supplied at each wage rate. It also tells us the minimum wage that is acceptable at each level of labor supplied.

In deciding how much labor to hire, the monopsonist recognizes that to hire more labor it must pay a higher wage, or, equivalently, by hiring less labor the monopsonist can get away with paying a lower wage. The monopsonist takes account of this fact when calculating its marginal cost of labor. The marginal cost of labor is shown by the curve *MCL*. The relationship between the marginal cost of labor curve and the supply curve is similar to the relationship between the marginal cost and average total cost curves that you studied in Chapter 10. The supply curve is like the average total cost of labor curve.

FIGURE **15.5**

A Monopsony Labor Market

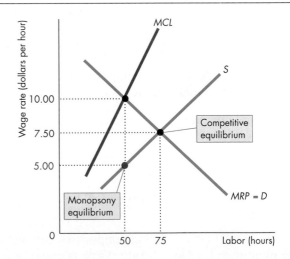

A monopsony is a market structure in which there is a single buyer. A monopsonist who has marginal revenue product curve *MRP* faces a labor supply curve *S*. The marginal cost of labor curve is *MCL*. Profit is maximized by making the marginal cost of labor equal to marginal revenue product. The monopsonist hires 50 hours of labor and pays the lowest wage for which that labor will work, $5 an hour.

For example, in Fig. 15.5 the firm can hire 50 hours of labor at $5 an hour, so its average total cost is $5 an hour. The total cost of labor is $5 an hour multiplied by 50 hours, which equals $250. But suppose that the firm hires slightly less than 50 hours of labor, say 49 hours. The wage rate at which 49 hours of labor can be hired is $4.90 an hour. The firm's total labor cost is 49 multiplied by $4.90, which equals $240.10. Hiring the 50th hour of labor raises the total cost of labor from $240.10 to $250, which is almost $10. The curve *MCL* shows the $10 marginal cost of hiring the 50th hour of labor.

To calculate the profit-maximizing quantity of labor to hire, the firm sets the marginal cost of labor equal to the marginal revenue product of labor. That is, the firm wants the cost of the last worker hired to equal the extra revenue brought in. In Fig. 15.5, this outcome occurs when the monopsony employs 50 hours of labor. To hire 50 hours of labor, the firm has to pay $5 an hour. The marginal revenue product of labor, however, is $10 an hour, which means that the firm makes an economic profit of $5 on the last hour of labor that it hires. Each worker gets paid $5, and marginal revenue product is $10. So the firm gets an extra $5 economic profit out of the last hour of labor hired.

The ability of a monopsonist to make an economic profit depends on the elasticity of labor supply. The more elastic the supply of labor, the less opportunity a monopsonist has to make an economic profit. If this labor market is competitive, the wage rate will be $7.50 and the level of employment will be 75 hours. Compared with a competitive labor market, employment and the wage rate are lower under monopsony.

Monopsony Tendencies   With today's low costs of transportation, it is unlikely that many pure monopsonists remain. Workers can easily commute long distances to a job, and so for most people there is not just one potential employer. Nevertheless, many firms face an upward-sloping supply of labor curve and so have a problem similar to that of a monopsonist. To attract more workers, they must offer higher wages. Firms compete with each other for labor by offering wages that compensate their workers not only for time on the job but also for commuting time. The more workers a firm hires, the larger is the area from which it must recruit and the longer is the commute for the marginal worker.

Therefore, as a firm hires more workers, the higher is the wage it must pay to attract that worker. How strong such a monopsony tendency is depends on the size and density of the urban area in which the labor market is situated.

Next, let's see the effects of minimum wage laws and unions in a monopsonistic labor market.

Monopsony, Minimum Wage, and Unions

In Chapter 6, we saw how a minimum wage usually decreases employment. However, if a firm is a monopsonist, minimum wage regulations can actually raise both the wage rate and employment. A union can also raise the wage rate and employment. Let's see how.

Minimum Wages and Monopsony   Suppose that the labor market is that shown in Fig. 15.6 and that the wage rate is $5 an hour with 50 hours of labor

FIGURE **15.6**

Minimum Wage in Monopsony

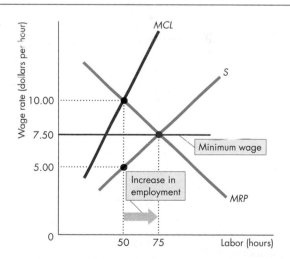

In a monopsony labor market the wage rate is $5 an hour. If a minimum wage law raises the wage rate to $7.50 an hour, employment rises to 75 hours. Equivalently, if a union enters the market, it will attempt to increase the wage rate to above $5 an hour. If the union is all powerful, the highest wage rate it can achieve is $10 an hour. If the union and the firm are equally powerful, they will bargain and agree to a wage rate of $7.50 an hour—the wage rate that splits in half the difference between marginal revenue product and the lowest wage for which labor will work.

Wage Laws versus Laws of Supply and Demand

The Essence of the Story

The New York Times, February 5, 1991

Business Groups Fight Laws in California on Wage Scales

BY ANDREW POLLACK

Several communities in the San Francisco Bay area have enacted what labor lawyers say are the nation's first local laws that specify the wages to be paid to employees of private businesses.

The ordinances require that workers on private construction projects be paid what is called the prevailing wage. That wage, determined by a state agency, is usually close to union wages.

Prevailing-wage laws have been applied to Federal and some state public works projects, starting with the Federal Davis-Bacon Act in 1931. But the ordinances in the Bay Area are the first in the nation to cover private construction projects.

The difference in wages can be striking. A study commissioned by construction unions showed that on one project nonunion workers were paid an average of $12.39 an hour, including benefits, while the average prevailing wage would have been $27.97. And in an affidavit filed in one of the lawsuits challenging the laws, the president of a company that provides maintenance and repair service for industry said that under prevailing wages he would have to pay $25.03 an hour, including benefits, to workers who now receive $11.27.

Supporters of the laws argue that they prevent businesses from using low-paid, poorly trained workers who pose a workplace safety hazard and do construction of poor quality.

"If someone thinks that all you do is hire someone off the street and they know what they are doing, that's not the way it works," said Robert Gilmore, business manager for the Building and Construction Trades Council in San Mateo County, which is immediately south of San Francisco.

Often, he and other supporters say, such workers are brought in from other parts of the country in migrations reminiscent of *The Grapes of Wrath,* overloading local schools and hospitals and hurting the local economy.

Union officials concede that the laws help the unions. While the ordinances do not require union labor, the fact that high wages must be paid removes a big incentive for private businesses to use nonunion workers. . . .

The Essence of the Story

Some San Francisco Bay area communities have enacted laws that require that workers on private construction projects be paid the "prevailing wage."

The prevailing wage is determined by a state agency and is usually close to the union wage.

Prevailing-wage laws have been applied to federal and state public works projects, but the Bay Area laws are the first in the nation to cover private construction projects.

The laws will increase wages (including benefits) from $11 and $12 an hour to $25 to $27 an hour.

Unions agree that the laws benefit them because they decrease the incentive to hire nonunion labor.

Background and Analysis

With no unions, all workers (of a given ability) receive the same wage—illustrated in Fig. 1. In both part (a) and part (b), the demand for labor is D_0, the supply of labor is S_0, the quantity of labor employed is L_0, and the wage rate is W_0.

A union restricts the supply of labor in the union sector, and the supply curve in part (b) shifts to S_1.

Workers who can't get a union job supply their labor to the nonunion sector. The supply curve in part (a) shifts to the right to S_1. The nonunion wage falls to $12 an hour. L_N workers are employed in nonunion jobs.

The low nonunion wage decreases the demand for union workers—the demand curve in part (b) shifts to D_1. With the decreased demand for union workers but a larger decrease in supply, the union wage rises and is $28 an hour.

The prevailing-wage law increases the nonunion wage—in Fig. 2(a) to $25 an hour. The quantity of nonunion labor employed falls to L_D, and the quantity supplied increases to L_S. Unemployment arises—illustrated in part (a).

With a higher nonunion wage, the demand for union labor increases to D_2 in part (b). The union wage increases to W_U, and the number of union workers employed increases to L_U.

Union workers benefit from the prevailing-wage law. Nonunion workers who get jobs also benefit. But the law creates unemployment.

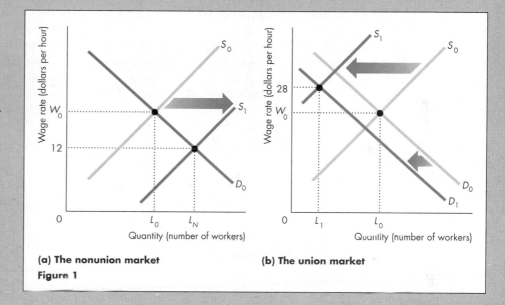

(a) The nonunion market

(b) The union market

Figure 1

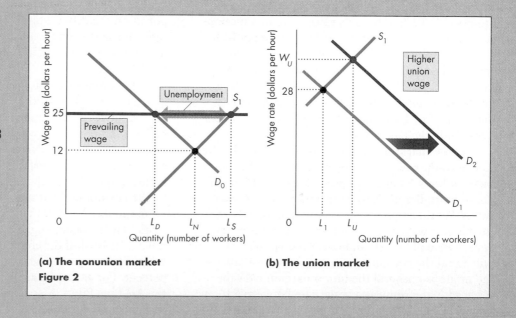

(a) The nonunion market

(b) The union market

Figure 2

being employed. The government now passes a minimum wage law that prohibits anyone from hiring labor for less than $7.50 an hour. Firms can hire labor for $7.50 an hour or more but not for less than that wage. The monopsonist in Fig. 15.6 now faces a perfectly elastic supply of labor at $7.50 an hour up to 75 hours. Above 75 hours, a higher wage than $7.50 an hour has to be paid to hire additional hours of labor. Since the wage rate is a fixed $7.50 an hour up to 75 hours, the marginal cost of labor is also constant at $7.50 up to 75 hours. Beyond 75 hours, the marginal cost of labor rises above $7.50 an hour. To maximize profit, the monopsonist sets the marginal cost of labor equal to its marginal revenue product. That is, the monopsonist hires 75 hours of labor at $7.50 an hour. The minimum wage law has made the supply of labor perfectly elastic and made the marginal cost of labor the same as the wage rate up to 75 hours. The law has not affected the supply of labor curve or the marginal cost of labor at employment levels above 75 hours. The minimum wage law has succeeded in raising wages by $2.50 an hour and raising the amount of labor employed by 25 hours.

Monopsony and Unions   When we studied monopoly in Chapter 12, we discovered that a single seller in a market is able to determine the price in that market. We have just studied monopsony—a market with a single buyer—and discovered that in such a market the buyer is able to determine the price. Suppose that a union starts to operate in a monopsony labor market. A union is like a monopoly. It controls the supply of labor and acts like a single seller of labor. If the union (monopoly seller) faces a monopsony buyer, the situation is one of **bilateral monopoly**. In bilateral monopoly, the wage rate is determined by bargaining between the two traders. Let's study the bargaining process.

We saw that if the monopsony in Fig. 15.5 is free to determine the wage rate and the level of employment, it hires 50 hours of labor for a wage rate of $5 an hour. If a union that represents the workers can maintain employment at 50 hours but charge the highest wage rate acceptable to the employer, the wage rate will be $10 an hour. That is, the wage rate will equal the marginal revenue product of labor. If the monopsonist and the union bargain over the wage rate, the result is a wage rate between $10 an hour (the maximum that the union can get) and $5 an hour (the minimum that the firm can pay).

The actual outcome of the bargaining depends on the costs that each party can inflict on the other as a result of a failure to agree on the wage rate. The firm can shut down the plant and lock out its workers, and the workers can shut down the plant by striking. Each party knows the strength of the other and knows what it has to lose if it does not agree to the demands of the other. If the two parties are equally strong, and they realize it, they will split the difference and agree to a wage rate of $7.50 an hour. If one party is stronger than the other—and both parties know that—the agreed wage will favor the stronger party. Usually, an agreement is reached without a strike or a lockout. The threat—the knowledge that such an event can occur—is usually enough to bring the bargaining parties to an agreement. When strikes or lockouts do occur, it is because one party has misjudged the situation.

The Scale of Union-Nonunion Wage Differentials

We have seen that unions can influence the wages of their members partly by restricting the supply of labor and partly by increasing the demand for labor. How much of a difference to wage rates do unions make in practice?

Union wage rates are, on the average, 33 percent higher than nonunion wage rates. In mining and financial services, union and nonunion wages are similar, and in services, manufacturing, and transportation the differential is between 11 and 19 percent. But in the wholesale and retail trades the differential is 42 percent, and in construction it is 77 percent.

These union-nonunion wage differentials do not give a true measure of the effects of unions on wages, however. In some industries, union wages are higher than nonunion wages because union members do jobs that involve greater skill. Even without a union, those who perform such tasks receive a higher wage. To calculate the effects of unions, we have to examine the wages of unionized and nonunionized workers who do nearly identical work. The evidence suggests that after allowing for the effects of skill differentials, the union-nonunion wage differential lies between 10 percent and 25 percent. For example, airline pilots who belong to the Air Line Pilots Association earn about 25 percent more than nonunion pilots with the same level of skill.

Differences in earnings based on skill or education level arise because skilled labor has a higher marginal revenue product than unskilled labor and because skills are costly to acquire. Union workers have higher wages than nonunion workers because unions are able to control the supply of labor and, indirectly, influence the marginal revenue product of their members. ◆

Wage Differentials Between Sexes and Races

There are persistent earnings differences between the sexes and the races. Figure 15.7 provides a snapshot of these differences in 1989. The wages of each race and sex group are expressed as a percentage of the wages of white men. By definition, then, the wages of white

FIGURE 15.7

Sex and Race Differentials

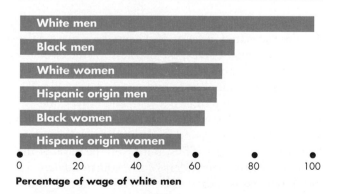

Wages of different race and sex groups in the labor market are shown as percentages of white male wages. These differentials have persisted over many years.

Source: U.S. Bureau of the Census, *Statistical Abstract of the United States: 1991,* 111th edition, 415.

men are 100. As you can see, the wages of each group fall progressively from 72 percent for black men down to 56 percent for women of Hispanic origin.

Why do the differentials shown in Fig. 15.7 exist, and why do they persist? Do they arise because there is discrimination against women and members of minority races, or is there some other explanation? These controversial questions generate an enormous amount of passion. It is not my intention to make you angry, but that might happen as an unintended consequence of this discussion. The objective of this section is to show you how to use economic analysis to address controversial and emotionally charged issues.

We are going to examine three possible explanations for these earnings differences:

◆ Discrimination
◆ Differences in human capital
◆ Differences in degree of specialization

Discrimination

To see how discrimination can affect earnings, let's look at an example—the market for investment advisors. Suppose that there are two groups of investment advisors who are identical in terms of picking good investments. One group consists of black females, and the other of white males. The supply curve of black females, S_{BF}, is shown in Fig. 15.8(a). The supply curve of white males, S_{WM}, is shown in Fig. 15.8(b). These supply curves are identical. The marginal revenue product of investment advisors, whether they are black female or white male, is also identical and is shown by the two curves labeled *MRP* in parts (a) and (b). (Their revenues are the fees their customers pay for investment advice.)

Suppose that everyone in this society is free of prejudice about color and sex. The market for black female investment advisors determines a wage rate of $40,000 a year, and there are 2,000 black female investment advisors. The white male investment advisor market also clears at a wage rate of $40,000 a year, and there are 2,000 white male investment advisors.

In contrast to the previous situation, suppose that the customers of investment houses are prejudiced against women and against members of racial

FIGURE **15.8**

Discrimination

(a) Black females

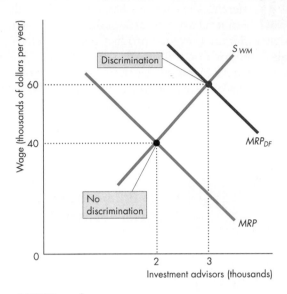

(b) White males

The supply curve for black female investment advisors is S_{BF} in part (a), and the supply curve for white male investment advisors is S_{WM} in part (b). If the marginal revenue product of both groups of investment advisors is *MRP* (the same curve in each part), then the equilibrium wage rate for each group is $40,000 a year and 2,000 of each type of advisor are employed. If there is discrimination against blacks and women, the marginal revenue product curve is to the left of the original curve. It is the curve labeled MRP_{DA}—*DA* standing for discriminated against. There is discrimination in favor of white males, so their marginal revenue product curve is MRP_{DF}—*DF* standing for discriminated in favor of. The wage rate for black women falls to $20,000 a year, and only 1,000 are employed. The wage rate for white males rises to $60,000 a year, and 3,000 are employed.

minorities. The two groups are equally able, as before, but the degree of prejudice is so strong that the customers are not willing to pay as much for investment advice given by a black female as they will pay for advice from a white male. Because of the differences in the amounts that people are willing to pay, based purely on their prejudices, the marginal revenue products of the two groups are different. The ability of the two groups is the same, but the value that prejudiced consumers place on their outputs is not the same. Suppose that the marginal revenue product of the black females, when discriminated against, is the line labeled MRP_{DA}—*DA* standing for discriminated against. Suppose that the marginal revenue product for white males, the group discriminated in favor of, is MRP_{DF}—*DF* standing

for discriminated in favor of. Given these marginal revenue product curves, the markets for the two groups of investment advisors will now determine very different wages and employment levels. Black females will earn $20,000 a year, and only 1,000 will work as investment advisors. White males will earn $60,000 a year, and 3,000 of them will work as investment advisors. Thus, purely on the basis of the prejudice of the demanders of investment advice, black women will earn one third the wages of white men, and three quarters of all investment advisors will be white men and only one quarter will be black women.

The case that we have just examined is a hypothetical example of how prejudice can produce differences in earnings. But economists disagree about whether or not prejudice actually causes wage differentials for a simple but difficult reason: you can recognize prejudice when you see it, but you cannot easily measure it. Our model shows that sex and race differentials might come from prejudice. But without a way of measuring prejudice in the real world, we cannot easily test that model to see whether it is true.

We need to make another point as well. Our model of prejudice, like all economic models, is in an equilibrium, albeit an unhappy one. But simply because a model is in equilibrium does not mean that such a real situation is either desirable or inevitable. Economic theory makes predictions about the way things will be, not moral statements about the way things ought to be. Policies designed to bring equal wages and employment prospects to women and minorities can be devised. But to be successful, such policies must be based on careful economic analysis. Good intentions are not enough to bring about equality.

Human Capital Differences

As we saw above (pp. 408–410), wages are compensation, in part for time spent on the job and in part for the cost incurred in acquiring skill— in acquiring human capital. The more human capital a person supplies, the higher is that person's earnings, other things being equal. Measuring human capital with any precision is difficult. But there are some rough indicators. One such indicator is the number of years of schooling that a person has had. A second indicator is the number of years of work experience. The most recent figures indicate that the median years in school for all races and both sexes are almost equal at about 12½ years. But this equality in median years of schooling is recent. In 1960, whites, on the average, spent about 11 years in school, while blacks, on the average, had about 8 years of schooling. By 1970, that differential had been cut to 2 years, and today it has virtually disappeared.

A third possible indicator of human capital is the number of job interruptions. Interruptions to a career disrupt and reduce the effectiveness of job experience and slow down the accumulation of human capital. Also, during a job interruption, it is possible that human capital depreciates through lack of use. Traditionally, women's careers have been

interrupted more frequently than men's, usually for bearing and rearing children. This factor is a possible source of lower wages, on the average, for women. Just as education differences are virtually disappearing, so career interruptions for women are becoming less severe. Maternity leave and day-care facilities are providing an increasing number of women with uninterrupted employment that makes their human capital accumulation indistinguishable from that of men.

Thus it seems that human capital differences possibly can account for earnings differentials among races and sexes in the past and some of the differentials that still remain. The trends, however, suggest that wage differentials from this source will eventually disappear.

Degrees of Specialization

People undertake two kinds of production activities: they supply labor services to the market (market activities), and they undertake household production (nonmarket activities). **Household production** creates goods and services to be consumed within the household rather than to be supplied to the market. Such activities include cooking, cleaning, minor repair work, education, and various organizational services such as arranging vacations and other leisure activities. Bearing and rearing children are other important nonmarket activities.

In Chapter 3, we discovered that people can gain from specializing in particular activities and trading their output with each other. Specialization and the gains from trade do not operate exclusively in the marketplace. They also operate within the household and among its members. It is not uncommon for one member of a household to specialize in shopping, another in cleaning, another in laundry, and so on. Specialization in bearing children is a biological necessity, although rearing them is not.

Consider, for example, a household that has two members—Bob and Sue. Bob and Sue have to decide how they will allocate their time between various nonmarket household production activities and market activity. One solution is for Bob to specialize in market activity and Sue to specialize in nonmarket activity. Another solution is to reverse the roles and have Sue specialize in market activity and Bob in nonmarket activity. Alternatively, one or both of them can become diversified, doing some market and some nonmarket activity. A completely egalitari-an allocation will have them share the nonmarket tasks equally and each devote the same amount of time and energy to market activity. But unequal allo-cations of time are also possible, with one of the household members specializing in market activity and the other being diversified.

In deciding which of the many alternative time allocations to choose, Bob and Sue will take into consideration their future plans for having children. The particular allocation chosen by Bob and Sue will depend on their preferences and on the market earning potential of each of them. An increasing number of households are choosing the egalitarian allocation with each person diversified between non-market household production and market activity. Most households, however, still choose an allocation that would have Bob almost fully specialized in mar-ket activity and Sue covering a greater diversity of tasks in both the job market and the household. What are the effects of this more common assign-ment of market and nonmarket tasks? Though there will always be exceptions, on the average, it seems likely that if Bob specializes in market production and Sue diversifies between market and nonmarket production, Bob will have higher earning potential in the marketplace than Sue. If Sue is devoting a great deal of productive effort to ensuring Bob's mental and physical well-being, the quality of Bob's market labor will be higher than if he were under-taking his household production tasks on his own. If the roles were reversed, Sue would be able to supply market labor capable of earning more than Bob.

Economists have attempted to test whether the degree of specialization can account for earnings dif-ferentials between the sexes by examining the wages of men and women where, as far as possible, the degree of specialization is held constant. For exam-ple, if the degree of specialization is an important factor influencing a person's wage, then men and women of identical ages and educational back-grounds in identical occupations will be paid differ-ent wages depending on whether they are single, married to a spouse who specializes in household production, or married to a spouse who works. Single men and women who live alone and who are equally specialized in household and market produc-tion and who have the same amounts of human cap-ital and who do similar jobs will be paid the same wage. To make nonmarket factors as similar as pos-

sible, two groups have been chosen for analysis. They are "never married" men and women. The available evidence suggests that, on the average, when they have the same amount of human capi-tal—measured by years of schooling, work experi-ence, and career interruptions—the wages of these two groups are not identical but are much closer than the difference between *average* wages for men and women. The average wage differential between women and men exceeds 30 percent. But, when allowance is made for degree of specialization and human capital, this wage differential comes down to between 5 and 10 percent, by some estimates. Some economists suspect that the remaining discrepancy stems from discrimination against women, although the difficulty of measuring such discrimination makes this hypothesis hard to test.

Most of the difference in men's and women's wages arises from the fact that men and women do different jobs, and, for the most part, men's jobs are better paid than women's jobs. There are, however, an increasing number of women entering areas that were traditionally the preserve of men. This trend is particularly clear in professions such as architecture, medicine, economics, law, accounting, and pharma-cology. The percentage of total enrollments in uni-versity courses in these subjects for women has increased from less than 20 percent in 1970 to approaching, and in some cases exceeding, 50 per-cent today.

Comparable-Worth Laws

In 1963, Congress passed the Equal Pay Act, and in 1964 it passed the Civil Rights Act. These acts require equal pay for equal work. They are attempts to remove the most blatant forms of discrimination between men and women and between whites and minorities. But many people believe that these acts do not go far enough. In their view, getting paid the *same* wage for doing the *same* job is just the first tiny step that has to be taken. What's important is that *compara-ble* jobs receive the *same* wages regardless of whether they are done by men or women or by blacks or whites. Paying the same wage for different jobs that are judged to be comparable is called **comparable worth.**

Advocates of comparable-worth laws argue that wages should be determined by analyzing the characteristics of jobs and determining their worth on objective grounds. However, such a method of determining wage rates does not achieve the objectives sought by supporters of wage equality. Let's see why.

Figure 15.9 shows two markets: that for oil rig operators in part (a) and that for school teachers in part (b). The marginal revenue product curves (MRP_R and MRP_T) and the supply curves (S_R and S_T) are shown for each type of labor. Competitive equilibrium generates a wage rate W_R for oil rig operators and W_T for teachers.

Suppose that the knowledge and skills required in those two occupations—the mental and physical demands, the responsibilities, and the working conditions—result in a judgment that these two jobs are

of comparable worth. The wage rate that is judged to apply to each of them is W_C, and the courts enforce this wage rate. What happens? First, there is a shortage of oil rig operators. Oil rig companies are able to hire only S_r workers at the wage rate W_C. They cut back their production or build more expensive labor-saving oil rigs. There is also a decrease in the number of teachers employed. But this decrease occurs because school boards demand fewer teachers. At the higher wage W_C, school boards demand only D_t teachers. The quantity of teachers supplied is S_t and the difference between S_t and D_t is the number of unemployed teachers looking for jobs. These teachers eventually accept non-teaching jobs (which they don't like as much as teaching jobs) at a lower rate of pay than that of teachers.

Thus legislated comparable wages for comparable work may have serious and costly unintended consequences.

FIGURE 15.9

The Problem with Comparable Worth

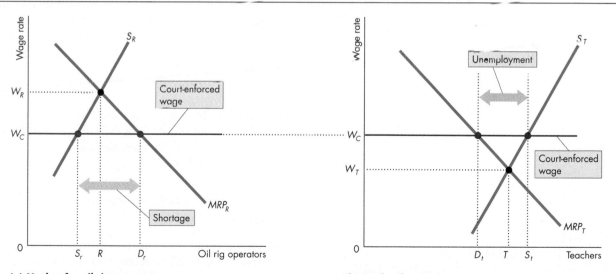

(a) Market for oil rig operators

(b) Market for teachers

The demand for and supply of oil rig operators, MRP_R and S_R, are shown in part (a), and those for schoolteachers, MRP_T and S_T, in part (b). The competitive equilibrium wage rate for oil rig operators is W_R and for teachers is W_T. If an evaluation of the two jobs finds that they have comparable worth and rules that the wage rate W_C be paid to both types of workers, there is an excess of demand for oil rig opera-

tors and an excess supply of teachers. There are $S_t - D_t$ teachers unemployed and a shortage of $D_r - S_r$ oil rig operators. Oil producers have to find other labor-saving ways of producing oil (that are more expensive), and teachers have to find other jobs (that are less desirable to them and less well paid).

| R E V I E W |

Wage differences between the sexes and the races may arise from discrimination and from differences in human capital. Sex differentials may also in part arise from differences in the degree of specialization. Comparable-worth law cannot, on its own, eliminate wage differentials. Differentials will be reduced only if differences in marginal revenue product are reduced. The process of equalization of human capital and of the degree of specialization will lead to lower differentials and possibly will eliminate them. ◆

◆ ◆ ◆ ◆ In this chapter, we extended and applied the factor markets model to understand a variety of phenomena in labor markets, such as wage differentials. In the next chapter, we apply and extend the factor markets model to deal with markets for capital and for natural resources.

| S U M M A R Y |

Skill Differentials

Skill differentials arise partly because skilled labor has a higher marginal product than unskilled labor and partly because skills are costly to acquire. The higher marginal product of skilled workers results in a higher marginal revenue product. Since the demand for labor curve is derived from the marginal revenue product curve, the higher the marginal revenue product of skilled labor, the greater is the demand for skilled labor.

Skills are costly to acquire because households have to invest in human capital to become skilled. Investment sometimes means direct payments such as tuition and other training fees and sometimes means working for a lower wage during on-the-job training. Because skills are costly to acquire, households supply skilled labor on terms that compensate them for both the time spent on the job and the costs of acquiring the skills. Thus the supply curve of skilled labor lies above the supply curve of unskilled labor.

Wage rates of skilled and unskilled labor are determined by demand and supply in the two labor markets. The equilibrium wage rate for skilled labor exceeds that for unskilled labor. The difference in wages reflects the higher marginal product of skill and the cost to acquire skill. (pp. 408–410)

Union-Nonunion Wage Differentials

Labor unions influence wages by controlling the supply of labor. In competitive labor markets, unions obtain higher wages only at the expense of lower employment. Unions in competitive industries also attempt to influence the marginal revenue product of their members—and the demand for their members' labor—by restricting imports, raising minimum wages, supporting immigration restrictions, increasing demand for their product, and increasing the marginal product of their members.

In a monopsony—a market in which there is a single buyer—unions increase wages without sacrificing employment. Bilateral monopoly occurs when the union is a monopoly seller of labor, the firm is a monopsony buyer of labor, and the wage rate is determined by bargaining between the two parties.

In practice, union workers earn an estimated 10–25 percent more than comparable nonunion workers. (pp. 410–419)

Wage Differentials Between Sexes and Races

There are persistent differentials in earnings between men and women and between whites and minorities. Three possible explanations for these differentials are discrimination, differences in human capital, and differences in degree of specialization.

Discrimination results in lower wage rates and lower employment for workers who are discriminated against and higher wage rates and higher employment levels for those discriminated in favor of. Human capital differences result from differences in schooling and work experience. Differentials based on schooling have been falling and have almost been eliminated. Differentials based on work experience have kept women's pay below that for men because women's careers have traditionally been interrupted more frequently than those of men, resulting, on the average, in a smaller accumulation of human capital. This difference is less important today than in the past. Differentials arising from different degrees of specialization are probably important and may persist. Men have traditionally been more specialized in market activity, on the average, than women. Women have traditionally undertaken both nonmarket (household production) activities and market activities. Attempts to test for the importance of the degree of specialization suggest that it is an impor-

tant source of the difference between the earnings of men and women. (pp. 419–422)

Comparable-Worth Laws

Comparable-worth laws determine wages by assessing the value of different types of jobs according to objective characteristics rather than what the market will pay. Determining wages through comparable worth results in a decrease in the number of people employed in those jobs on which the market places a lower value and shortages of those workers that the market values more highly. Thus the attempt to achieve comparable wages for comparable work has costly, unintended consequences. (pp. 422–424)

KEY ELEMENTS

Key Terms

Bilateral monopoly, 418
Binding arbitration, 412
Closed shop, 412
Collective bargaining, 412
Comparable worth, 423
Craft union, 411
Household production, 421
Human capital, 408
Industrial union, 411
Labor union, 410
Local, 411
Lockout, 412

Monopsony, 414
Open shop, 411
Professional association, 412
Right-to-work law, 412
Strike, 412
Union shop, 412

Key Figures and Tables

Figure 15.1   Skill Differentials, 409
Figure 15.4   A Union in a Competitive Labor Market, 414
Figure 15.8   Discrimination, 420
Table 15.1   A Compact Glossary on Unions, 411

REVIEW QUESTIONS

1 Explain why skilled workers are paid more than unskilled workers.

2 What are the main types of labor union?

3 How does a labor union try to influence wages?

4 What can a union do in a competitive labor market?

5 How might a union increase the demand for its members' labor?

6 Under what circumstances will the introduction of a minimum wage increase employment?

7 How big are the union-nonunion wage differentials in the United States today?

8 What are the three main reasons why sex and race differentials in earnings exist?

9 How do comparable-worth laws work, and what are their predicted effects?

P R O B L E M S

1 The demand for and supply of unskilled laborers are given by the following schedules:

Hourly wage rate (dollars per hour)	Quantity supplied (hours)	Quantity demanded (hours)
9	9,000	1,000
8	8,000	2,000
7	7,000	3,000
6	6,000	4,000
5	5,000	5,000
4	4,000	6,000
3	3,000	7,000
2	2,000	8,000

a What is the wage rate of unskilled labor?
b What is the quantity of unskilled labor employed?

2 The workers in problem 1 can be trained—can obtain a skill—and their marginal productivity doubles. (The marginal product at each employment level is twice the marginal product of an unskilled worker.) But the compensation for the cost of acquiring a skill adds $2 an hour to the wage that must be offered to attract skilled labor.

a What is the wage rate of skilled labor?
b What is the quantity of skilled labor employed?

3 Suppose that skilled workers become unionized and the union restricts entry into skilled work to 1,000 workers. What is the wage rate of skilled workers? How do unskilled workers react to the new situation?

4 In a small, isolated town in the Rocky Mountains, the only firm hiring workers is a logging company. The firm's demand for labor and the town's supply of labor are as follows:

Wage rate (dollars per hour)	Quantity supplied (hours per day)	Quantity demanded (hours per day)
1	20	220
2	40	200
3	60	180
4	80	160
5	100	140
6	120	120
7	140	100
8	160	80
9	180	60
10	200	40

a What is the wage rate?
b How much labor does the firm hire?

5 The townspeople in problem 4 form a union. The union and the firm agree that the level of employment will not change and the union gets the highest wage rate acceptable to the firm. What is that wage rate?

6 A nationwide investigation determines that on the basis of comparable worth, a logger should be paid $7 an hour. In the logging village in problem 4 before the union described in problem 5 is formed:
a What is the actual hourly wage rate paid?
b How much labor does the logging company hire at this wage?
c How much labor is unemployed?

CHAPTER 16

CAPITAL
AND
NATURAL
RESOURCE
MARKETS

After studying this chapter, you will be able to:

- ◆ Define and distinguish among financial and physical assets, capital, and investment
- ◆ Define and distinguish between saving and portfolio choice
- ◆ Describe the structure of capital markets in the United States today
- ◆ Explain how interest rates and stock prices are determined and why the stock market fluctuates
- ◆ Define natural resources and explain how their prices are determined
- ◆ Explain how markets regulate the pace at which we use exhaustible resources such as oil

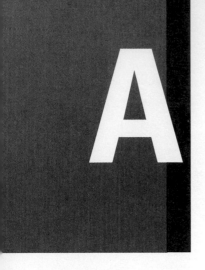

AN AIR OF PANIC FILLED THE CAVERNOUS NEW YORK Stock Exchange on Monday, October 19, 1987. It had taken five years, from August 1982, for the average price of a common stock to climb 200 percent. But on that single day, stock prices fell an unheard of 22 percent—knocking billions of dollars off the value of people's investments. The crash touched off other stock market plunges from Tokyo to London. Why does the stock market boom for several years and then crash suddenly and spectacularly? ◆ ◆ The New York Stock Exchange, large as it is, is only a part of the enormous capital market of the United States and the even more enormous worldwide capital market. Every year, billions of dollars are saved and flow into these capital markets. Savings flow through banks, insurance companies, and stock exchanges and end up financing the purchases of machinery, factory and office buildings, cars, and homes. How does a dollar saved and placed

Boom and Bust

on deposit in a bank enable Pepsi-Cola to open a new bottling plant? ◆ ◆ Many of our natural resources are exhaustible, yet we are using them up at a rapid rate. Every year we burn billions of cubic feet of natural gas, billions of gallons of petroleum, and millions of tons of coal. We extract bauxite to make aluminum and iron ore to make steel. Aren't we one day going to run out of these and other natural resources? And long before that day, aren't they going to become too expensive to use? How are the prices of natural resources determined? And do their prices adjust to encourage conservation, or does the market need help to ensure that we do not pillage nature's exhaustible endowments?

◆ ◆ ◆ ◆ In this chapter, we study capital and natural resource markets. We'll find out what determines the amount of saving and purchases of new capital equipment and how interest rates and stock values are determined. In our study of natural resource markets, we'll discover how market forces encourage conservation.

Capital, Investment, and Saving

L et's begin with some capital market vocabulary and define three key terms:

◆ Asset

◆ Liability

◆ Balance sheet

An **asset** is anything of value that a household, firm, or government *owns*. A **liability** is a debt—something that a household, firm, or government *owes*. A **balance sheet** is a list of assets and liabilities.

Table 16.1 shows an example of a balance sheet—that for Rocky's Mountain Bikes. It lists three assets—cash in the bank, an inventory of bikes, and fixtures and fittings—that add up to $243,000. The balance sheet contains two liabilities—a bank loan of $120,000 and Rocky's equity of $123,000. Rocky's equity is his personal stake in the company—equivalently, it is the amount the company owes to Rocky.

Financial Assets and Physical Assets

Assets fall into two broad classes: financial and physical. **Financial assets** are sophisticated IOUs—pieces of paper that represent a claim against another household, firm, or government. When you hold an IOU, it means that somebody else owes you money. Similarly, if you own a financial asset, someone else has a financial liability—owes you money. For example, the savings deposit that you own (your asset) is a liability of your bank. The difference between financial assets and financial liabilities is called **net financial assets**. Net financial assets are the

net value of the paper claims that one household, firm, or government has against everyone else.

Physical assets are buildings, plant and equipment, inventories, and consumer durable goods. Physical assets are also called capital. **Capital** is the physical assets owned by a household, firm, or government.

Table 16.2 illustrates the distinction between financial assets and physical assets by again presenting the information contained in the balance sheet of Rocky's Mountain Bikes. But this time the informa-

TABLE 16.1

Balance Sheet of Rocky's Mountain Bikes

Assets		Liabilities	
Cash in bank	$ 18,000	**Bank loan**	$120,000
Inventory of bikes	15,000	**Rocky's equity**	123,000
Fixtures and fittings	210,000		
Total assets	$243,000	**Total liabilities**	$243,000

TABLE 16.2

Financial Assets and Physical Assets of Rocky's Mountain Bikes

Financial assets	
Cash in bank	$ 18,000
Bank loan	−120,000
Rocky's equity	−123,000
Net financial assets	−$225,000

Physical assets	
Inventory of bikes	$ 15,000
Fixtures and fittings	210,000
Capital	$225,000

tion is sorted into financial and physical items. The financial items in the balance sheet are the cash in bank (an asset) and the bank loan (a liability). To calculate net financial assets, we have to subtract financial liabilities from financial assets, so the bank loan and Rocky's equity appear with negative signs. The net financial assets of Rocky's Mountain Bikes are –$225,000. The physical assets are the inventory of bikes and the fixtures and fittings—the firm's capital—which add up to $225,000.

Capital and Investment

Capital is the value of buildings, plant and equipment, and inventories in existence at a given point in time. **Investment** is the value of new capital equipment purchased in a given time period. **Depreciation** is the decrease in the value of capital resulting from its use in a given time period. Investment is an addition to capital; depreciation is a subtraction from capital. The net change in capital is investment minus depreciation. To emphasize this fact, we distinguish between **gross investment,** the value of all the new capital purchased in a given time period, and **net investment,** which equals gross investment minus depreciation.

Capital, gross investment, and depreciation are similar to the water in Lake Powell and the San Juan and Colorado Rivers. Capital is like the water in Lake Powell at a given point in time. Gross investment is like the water flowing from the San Juan and Colorado Rivers into Lake Powell. It adds to the water in the lake. Depreciation is like the water flowing out of Lake Powell into the Colorado River. That flow lowers the water in the lake. The lake level (the amount of capital) rises by an amount equal to the inflow (gross investment) minus the outflow (depreciation).

Saving and Portfolio Choice

The quantity of capital supplied results from people's saving decisions. Saving is the opposite of consuming. **Saving** is income minus consumption. The current market value of a household's past saving, together with any inheritances it has received, is the household's **wealth.** Wealth is allocated across a variety of financial assets such as stocks, bonds, and bank deposits and physical assets such as houses,

cars, and other consumer durable goods. These assets together with the household's liabilities are described by its balance sheet.

A household's choice regarding how much to hold in various assets and how much to owe in various liabilities is called a **portfolio choice**. For example, if a household decides to borrow $100,000 from a bank and to use that $100,000 to buy stock in a corporation, the household is making a portfolio choice. It is choosing the amount of an asset (the equity in a corporation) and the amount of a liability (the bank loan).

In everyday language, we often refer to the purchase of stocks and bonds as investment. That everyday use of the word *investment* can cause confusion in economic analysis. It is to avoid that confusion that we use the term *portfolio choice* to refer to the choices that households make in allocating their wealth across the various assets available to them. *Investment* is the purchases of new physical assets by firms and households.

We can illustrate the concepts of saving, wealth, and portfolio choice by looking at Rocky's *personal* situation—at Rocky's household balance sheet. Rocky has an initial wealth of $150,000 (see Table 16.3). During year 1, Rocky earns an income of $58,000, consumes $50,000, and saves $8,000. His wealth rises to $158,000.

How has Rocky allocated his wealth among the various assets and liabilities? Table 16.4 separates out Rocky's financial assets and liabilities from his physical assets. His financial assets include, first of all, his equity in Rocky's Mountain Bikes. Second, Rocky has some cash in the bank. This is his own personal bank account and is completely separate

TABLE 16.3

Rocky's Income, Consumption, Saving, and Wealth

	Income	Consumption	Saving	Wealth
Initial net worth				150,000
Year 1	58,000	50,000	8,000	158,000

TABLE 16.4

Rocky's Financial Assets and Physical Assets at End of Year 1

Financial assets

Equity in Rocky's Mountain Bikes	$123,000
Cash in bank	10,000
Mortgage	−140,000
Car loan	−10,000
Net financial assets	−$17,000

Physical assets

House	$160,000
Car	15,000
Capital	$175,000
Wealth	$158,000

from the cash in the bike business. Third, Rocky has a mortgage on his home of $140,000 and a bank loan of $10,000 secured by the value of his car. Rocky's personal net financial assets are −$17,000. Note the minus sign. It tells us that, ignoring his physical assets, Rocky *owes* $17,000 more than he owns—his net *financial* assets are negative.

Rocky's physical assets are his house (valued at $160,000) and his car (valued at $15,000), so his capital stock is $175,000. Rocky's wealth is the sum of his capital stock and his net financial assets. Since Rocky's net financial assets are negative (he owes more than he owns), his wealth is his capital stock minus what he owes—$158,000.

With exactly the same saving, investment, and wealth, Rocky could have chosen a different portfolio allocation. For example, he could have used his bank deposit to pay off part of his bank loan or part of his mortgage. Alternatively, he could have taken a bigger mortgage and a smaller bank loan. Saving and investment decisions determine how much wealth a person has. Portfolio decisions determine how that wealth is held and financed.

REVIEW

There are two kinds of assets: financial and physical. Financial assets are the claims that lenders have on borrowers. One person's financial asset is another person's financial liability. Physical assets are buildings, plant and equipment, and inventories. Physical capital is the value of physical assets in existence at a point in time. Additions to capital are called investment. Capital wears out over time. This process is called depreciation. The quantity of capital supplied results from people's saving decisions. Saving is income minus consumption. The accumulated value of past saving is wealth. The allocation of wealth among the different assets is called portfolio choice. ◆

Capital Markets in the United States Today

Capital markets are the channels through which savings flow into firms to finance investment—the purchase of new capital. Figure 16.1 illustrates the structure of the capital markets and the financing of investment.

The actors in the capital markets are households, firms, and financial intermediaries.[1] You've met *households* and *firms* before. **Financial intermediaries** are institutions whose principal business is taking deposits, making loans, and buying securities. The best-known type of financial intermediary is a commercial bank. Other important types of financial intermediaries are insurance companies and savings and loan associations.

---

[1]Other actors in capital markets are governments and foreigners. We ignore these actors so that we can concentrate on the links between households' saving and firms' investment. These additional actors change the details of the story but not its main point.

Capital Market Flows

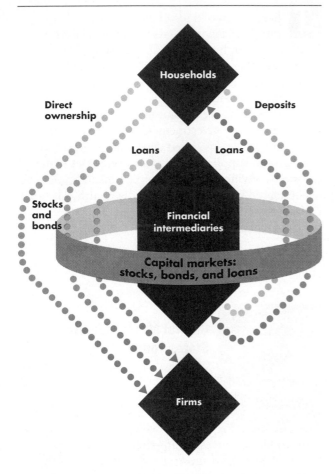

Households, firms, and financial intermediaries have extensive interactions in capital markets. Households purchase stocks and bonds, make deposits in financial intermediaries, and own firms directly. These flows are shown by the green dotted lines. Financial intermediaries lend to both households and firms.

The main types of capital market are

◆ The **stock market,** in which the equities of firms are traded

◆ The **bond market,** in which the bonds issued by firms are traded[2]

[2]The distinction between stocks and bonds is explained in Chapter 9, pp. 213–214.

◆ The **loans market,** in which households and firms borrow and lend

These markets coordinate the decisions of households, firms, and financial intermediaries. Investment takes place as a result of:

◆ Households buying capital directly and financing it either with their own resources or by borrowing from financial intermediaries

◆ Firms buying capital and financing it by selling stocks and bonds to households

◆ Firms buying capital and financing it by loans from financial intermediaries who in turn borrow from households

These financial transactions are illustrated by the green dotted lines in Fig. 16.1. Households use their savings to buy capital for their own firms (proprietorships and partnerships), to buy stocks or bonds issued by firms, and to make deposits with financial intermediaries. Financial intermediaries make loans to households and firms.

The Nation's Balance Sheet

How large are the U.S. capital markets? How big a role do the various elements play? The borrowing and lending pictured in Fig. 16.1 can be measured in the nation's balance sheet. This balance sheet lists the assets and liabilities of each of the major groups of agents in the economy—households, financial intermediaries, firms, and governments. Figure 16.2 provides a picture of those balance sheets. The data, in trillions of dollars, are from December 31, 1989 and are the most recent available. Assets are shown in blue and liabilities in red. The green arrows show the direction of the flow of funds.

First look at the households. They have financial assets in the form of deposits with financial intermediaries, savings in life insurance and pension funds, and holdings of equity and bonds. The total of these items is $10.3 trillion. Households have financial liabilities in the form of mortgages and consumer credit, totaling $3.3 trillion. Total financial assets of households exceed their liabilities by $7 trillion, that is, $10.3 trillion minus $3.3 trillion. Households own physical assets in the form of houses and consumer durable goods valued at a total of $6.4 trillion ($4.5 trillion houses plus $1.9 trillion consumer durables). Total household wealth is the sum of financial and physical assets and is $13.4 trillion.

FIGURE **16.2**
The Nation's Balance Sheet

The nation's balance sheet records the indebtedness between the sectors of the economy—households, financial intermediaries, firms, and governments. The financial assets (blue) and liabilities (red) are shown in the top part of the figure, and capital (physical assets—purple) appears in the bottom part. All numbers are in trillions of dollars.

Households' financial assets are deposits with financial intermediaries, life insurance and pension funds, equity, and bonds. These assets are the liabilities of financial intermediaries, firms, and governments. Financial intermediaries take deposits and life insurance and pension fund contributions from households. Then they lend some of these funds back to households as mortgages and consumer credit;

the remainder is lent to firms and governments in the form of bonds and mortgages. Both firms and governments borrow from financial intermediaries and households.

Capital (physical assets) consists of houses and consumer durables owned by households and of plant and equipment and buildings owned by firms and governments.

Source: Statistical Abstract of the United States: 1991, 111th edition, U.S. Bureau of the Census, Washington, D.C., p. 496; *Survey of Current Business,* 70 (9), September 1990, pp. 99–106; and my calculations.

Next look at the financial intermediaries. Their liabilities are the deposits and life insurance and pension funds, which we have just seen as the assets of households. They are liabilities of financial intermediaries because the financial intermediaries "owe" them to households. The assets of financial intermediaries represent loans by these institutions to households, firms, and governments. Financial intermediaries make loans to households in the form of mortgages and consumer credit. The financial intermediaries make loans to firms and governments as a result of purchasing bonds issued by these institutions. Financial intermediaries also make mortgage loans to firms. These bond sales provide firms and governments with funds to buy physical assets. The financial assets and liabilities of financial intermediaries are each $6.6 trillion.

The financial liabilities of firms—bonds ($1.2 trillion), mortgages ($1.1 trillion), and equity ($2.4 trillion)—totaling $4.7 trillion, are matched by their capital—plant and equipment ($2.3 trillion) and buildings ($2.4 trillion).

Government financial liabilities (bonds) generate funds to finance the purchase of plant and equipment and buildings. The value of the government sector's physical assets exceeds the value of its liabilities, and the difference is the wealth of the government sector.

The numbers in Fig. 16.2 give you an idea of the scale of the operations of the various elements in the capital markets. But they do not provide a flavor of the huge volume of transactions that take place—the flow of activity each day—or of the dynamic change over time in the scale of capital market transactions. The daily turnover in the ownership of stocks and bonds is enormous. On a typical day more than 200 million individual stocks change hands on the New York Stock Exchange. On what has come to be called Black Monday—October 19, 1987—a record 605 million shares were traded.

Demand for Capital

The demand for capital, like the demand for any other input,

stems from firms' profit-maximization choices. As a firm increases the quantity of capital employed, other things being equal, the marginal revenue product of capital eventually diminishes. To maximize profit, a firm uses additional amounts of capital until the marginal revenue product of capital equals the opportunity cost of a unit of capital. That is, the firm increases its capital stock until the additional total revenue generated by one extra unit of capital equals the opportunity cost of one unit of capital. When a firm rents capital equipment, its calculations are identical to those made to choose its labor input. The firm faces an hourly rate for renting a machine, and it calculates the marginal revenue product of the machine per hour and compares that number with the hourly rental rate. Many machines are rented—for example, earth-moving equipment, cars, and airplanes—so these calculations are relevant in such cases.

But most capital is not rented. Firms *buy* buildings, plant, and equipment and operate them for several years. To decide how much capital equipment to buy, the firm has to compare the price of the equipment to be paid, here and now, with the returns—the marginal revenue products—that the equipment will generate over its entire life. To see how a firm decides how much capital to buy, we need to convert the future stream of marginal revenue products into its present value so that it can be directly compared with the price of buying a new piece of capital equipment. You have already met the concept of present value in Chapter 9 (pp. 214–217), and you might like to flip back to it to refresh your memory before moving on.

Net Present Value of Investment

Let's calculate the present value of the marginal revenue product of a capital input and see how we can use the result to make an investment decision. Table 16.5(a) summarizes the data that we'll use.

Tina runs a firm called Taxfile, Inc. The firm sells advice to taxpayers designed to minimize the taxes that they have to pay. Tina is considering buying a new computer that will cost $10,000. The computer has a life of two years, after which it will be worthless. Although Tina works hard all year studying tax law and writing sophisticated computer programs that will enable her to corner a good share of the

TABLE 16.5

Net Present Value of an
Investment—Taxfile, Inc.

(a) Data

Price of computer	$10,000
Life of computer	2 years
Marginal revenue product	$5,900 at end of each year
Interest rate	4% a year

(b) Present value of the flow of marginal revenue product

$$PV = \frac{MRP}{1+r} + \frac{MRP}{(1+r)^2}$$

$$= \frac{\$5,900}{1.04} + \frac{\$5,900}{(1.04)^2}$$

$$= \$5,673 + \$5,455$$

$$= \$11,128$$

(c) Net present value of investment

$$NPV = PV \text{ of Marginal revenue product} - \text{Cost of computer}$$

$$= \$11,128 - \$10,000$$

$$= \$1,128$$

market, she generates an income only once each year—at tax filing time. If she buys the computer that she is now evaluating, Tina expects to be able to sell tax advice in each of the next two years that will bring in $5,900 at the end of each year. The interest rate that she has to pay is 4 percent a year.

We can calculate the present value of the marginal revenue product of Taxfile's computer by using a formula similar to the one that you met on p. 215. The formula is set out in Table 16.5(b). The present value (PV) of $5,900 one year in the future is $5900 divided by 1.04 (1 plus the interest rate expressed as a proportion—4 percent as a proportion is 0.04). The present value of $5,900 two years in the future is $5,900 divided by $(1.04)^2$. Working out those two present values and then adding them gives the pres-

ent value of the flow of marginal revenue product from the machine as $11,128.

To decide whether or not to buy the computer, Tina compares the present value of its stream of marginal revenue products with its price. She makes this comparison by calculating the net present value (NPV) of the investment. The **net present value of an investment** is the present value of the stream of marginal revenue products generated by the investment minus the cost of the investment. If the net present value of the investment is positive, it pays her to buy the computer. If the net present value of the investment is negative, it does not pay her to buy the computer. In such a case, the cost of the computer exceeds the present value of the stream of income that it generates. Table 16.5(c) shows the calculation of the net present value of Tina's investment in a computer. The net present value is $1,128. Therefore Tina buys the computer.

Whenever the net present value of an investment is positive, a firm will increase its net worth by making the investment. Like all other inputs, capital is subject to diminishing marginal returns. The more capital is added, the lower is its marginal product and the lower is its marginal revenue product. We have seen in the above example that it pays the firm to buy one machine because that investment yields a positive net present value. Should Tina invest in two computers or three? To answer this question, she must do more calculations similar to those summarized in Table 16.5.

Suppose, in particular, that Taxfile's investment opportunities are as set out in Table 16.6. Tina can buy any number of computers. Each computer costs $10,000 and has a life of two years. The marginal revenue product generated by each computer depends on how many computers Taxfile operates. If it operates just one computer, it has a marginal revenue product of $5,900 a year (the case just reviewed). If Taxfile uses a second computer, marginal revenue product falls to $5,600 a year, and in the case of a third computer it falls to $5,300 a year. Part (b) of the table calculates the present value of the marginal revenue product of each of these three levels of investment in computers.

We have seen that with an interest rate of 4 percent it pays to invest in the first computer—the net present value of that computer is positive. It also pays to invest in a second computer. The present value of the marginal revenue product resulting

---

TABLE **16.6**

Taxfile's Investment Decision

(a) Data

Price of computer	$10,000
Life of computer	2 years
Marginal revenue product:	
Using one computer	$5,900 a year
Using two computers	$5,600 a year
Using three computers	$5,300 a year

(b) Present value of the stream of marginal revenue products

If r = 0.04 (4% a year):

Using one computer, $PV = \dfrac{\$5,900}{1.04} + \dfrac{\$5,900}{(1.04)^2} = \$11,128$

Using two computers, $PV = \dfrac{\$5,600}{1.04} + \dfrac{\$5,600}{(1.04)^2} = \$10,562$

Using three computers, $PV = \dfrac{\$5,300}{1.04} + \dfrac{\$5,300}{(1.04)^2} = \$9,996$

If r = 0.08 (8% a year):

Using one computer, $PV = \dfrac{\$5,900}{1.08} + \dfrac{\$5,900}{(1.08)^2} = \$10,521$

Using two computers, $PV = \dfrac{\$5,600}{1.08} + \dfrac{\$5,600}{(1.08)^2} = \$9,986$

If r = 0.12 (12% a year):

Using one computer, $PV = \dfrac{\$5,900}{1.12} + \dfrac{\$5,900}{(1.12)^2} = \$9,971$

---

from using two computers, $10,562, exceeds the cost of the second machine by $562. You can also see that it does not pay to invest in a third computer. The present value of the marginal revenue product resulting from using three computers is $9,996. But the computer costs $10,000, so the net present value of the third computer is –$4. Tina buys a second computer but does not buy a third one. If she does, the net worth of Taxfile will fall by $4.

We have just discovered that at an interest rate of 4 percent a year it pays Tina to buy two computers but not three. Suppose that the interest rate is higher than 4 percent a year—say, 8 percent a year. In this case, the present value of one machine (see the calculations in Table 16.6b) is $10,521. Therefore it still pays to buy the first machine. But its net present

value is smaller when the interest rate is 8 percent than at the lower rate of 4 percent. At an 8 percent interest rate, the net present value resulting from using two machines is negative. The present value of the marginal revenue product, $9,986, is less than the $10,000 that the second computer costs. Therefore at an interest rate of 8 percent it pays Tina to buy one computer but not two.

Suppose that the interest rate is even higher, say, 12 percent a year. In this case the present value of the marginal revenue product of one computer is $9,971 (see Table 16.6b). At this interest rate, it does not pay to buy even one computer.

The calculations that you have just reviewed trace out Taxfile's demand schedule for capital. The demand schedule for capital shows the value of computers demanded by Taxfile at each interest rate. As the interest rate falls, the value of capital demanded increases. At an interest rate of 12 percent a year, the firm demands no computers. At an interest rate of 8 percent a year, one computer or $10,000 of capital is demanded; at 4 percent a year, $20,000 of capital is demanded (two computers). (Although we have stopped our calculations at two computers, at lower interest rates Tina would buy yet more machines and demand more capital.)

Demand Curve for Capital

A firm's demand curve for capital relates the quantity of capital demanded to the interest rate. Figure 16.3 illustrates the demand for computers (D_F) by Tina's firm. The horizontal axis measures the value of computers that Taxfile owns, and the vertical axis measures the interest rate. Points a, b, and c correspond to the example that we have just worked through. At an interest rate of 12 percent a year, it does not pay Tina to buy any computers—point a. At an interest rate of 8 percent, it pays to buy 1 computer worth $10,000—point b. At an interest rate of 4 percent, it pays to buy 2 computers worth $20,000—point c.

In our example, we've only considered one type of computer—that which costs exactly $10,000. In practice, Tina could consider buying a different type of computer, the power of which could be expressed as a multiple or fraction of one of the $10,000 computers that we've been considering here. For example, there might be a $5,000 computer that has half

FIGURE 16.3

A Firm's Demand for Capital

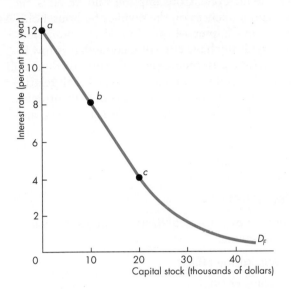

Taxfile demands capital (computers) until the present value of the stream of marginal revenue products of computers equals the price of a computer. The present value depends on the interest rate. The lower the interest rate, the higher is the number of computers demanded. At an interest rate of 12 percent a year, Taxfile demands no computers (point *a*). At an interest rate of 8 percent, the firm demands 1 computer worth $10,000 (point *b*). At an interest rate of 4 percent, the firm demands 2 computers worth $20,000 (point *c*). If computers of different types (fractions of a $10,000 computer) can be bought, a demand curve that passes through points *a*, *b*, and *c* is generated.

FIGURE 16.4

The Market Demand for Capital

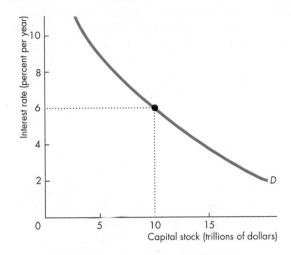

The market demand curve for capital is obtained by adding together the demand curves for capital of all the firms in the economy. An example of a market demand curve is *D*. On this demand curve, quantity of capital demanded is $10 trillion when the interest rate is 6 percent a year and the quantity of capital demanded falls as the interest rate rises, other things being equal.

Changes in the Demand for Capital

The demand for capital is constantly changing, and the demand curve for capital is constantly shifting. Also, the composition of the demand for capital is constantly changing; the demand for some types of capital increases, while the demand for other types decreases. Technological change is the main force generating these changes in the demand for capital. For example, the development of diesel engines for railroad transportation resulted in a decrease in demand for steam engines, an increase in demand for diesel engines, and not much change in the overall demand for capital in the railroad industry. In contrast, the development of desktop computers has led to a large increase in demand for office and research computing equipment.

The general trend resulting from the development of new technology and its exploitation through innovation is for the demand for capital to steadily increase over time with a steady rightward shift of the demand curve for capital.

the power of a $10,000 machine or a bigger machine costing $12,500 that has one and a quarter times the power of a $10,000 machine. If we consider all the different types of computers that Tina can buy, we will generate not just the three points, *a*, *b*, and *c*, but an entire demand curve like that shown in the figure.

The market demand curve for capital is shown in Fig. 16.4. It measures the total quantity of capital demanded (in trillions of dollars) on the horizontal axis and the interest rate on the vertical axis. On that curve, at an interest rate of 6 percent per year the quantity of capital demanded is $10 trillion. Like the firm's demand curve, the market demand curve slopes down.

REVIEW

The demand for capital is determined by firms' profit-maximization choices. The marginal product of capital declines as the amount of capital used rises. As a consequence, the marginal revenue product of capital declines as more capital is used. Capital is demanded up to the point where the present value of its stream of marginal revenue products equals its price. The interest rate is an important factor in the present value calculation. The higher the interest rate, the lower is the present value of the stream of marginal revenue products. ◆ ◆ The demand curve for capital is the relationship between the quantity of capital demanded and the interest rate. The higher the interest rate, the lower is the present value of the stream of marginal products and the smaller is the quantity of capital demanded by a firm. The demand curve for capital slopes downward. The demand for capital changes as a result of technological change. There is a general tendency for the demand for capital to increase over time with the demand curve for capital shifting to the right. ◆

The Supply of Capital

The quantity of capital supplied results from the saving decisions of households.[3] The most important factors determining a household's saving are

◆ The household's current income in relation to its expected future income

◆ The interest rate

_____

[3]We ignore the government and foreign sectors so that we can focus on essentials without making things too complicated. The basic story is not changed by the existence of foreign and government sources of saving.

The stage in the household's life cycle is the major factor influencing whether current income is high or low in comparison with expected future income. Households typically smooth their consumption over the life cycle. Consumption smoothing is one of the main influences on the saving of a household. As we saw in Chapter 14 (pp. 390–391), young households typically have current income that is low in comparison with their expected future income, and older households have income that is high relative to expected future income; young people incur debts, while older people save, pay off earlier debts, and accumulate assets. A household's saving depends on how much it smooths its consumption over the life cycle.

Interest Rate

There are two distinct effects of interest rates on the level of saving:

◆ Substitution effect
◆ Income effect

Substitution Effect   A higher interest rate increases the future payoff from today's saving. It therefore increases the opportunity cost of current consumption. Thus a higher interest rate encourages people to economize on current consumption and take advantage of the higher interest rate available on savings. As the interest rate rises, people substitute higher future consumption for current consumption, and saving increases.

Income Effect   A change in the interest rate changes people's incomes. Other things being equal, the higher a person's income, the higher is the level of current consumption and the higher are the levels of future consumption and of saving.

The effect of a change in the interest rate on income depends on whether a person is a borrower or a lender. For a lender—a person with positive net financial assets—an increase in interest rates increases income, so the income effect is positive. The income effect reinforces the substitution effect, and a higher interest rate results in higher saving.

For a borrower—a person with negative net financial assets—an increase in interest rates decreases the income available for consumption. In this case, the income effect is negative—higher interest rates lower consumption and saving. The income effect works in a direction opposite to that of the substitution effect, and saving may decrease.

Supply Curve of Capital

The quantity of capital supplied is the total value of accumulated savings. The supply curve of capital shows the relationship between the quantity of capital supplied and the interest rate. We've seen that this relationship depends on the relative strengths of the income effect and the substitution effect and, for an individual household, may be either positive or negative. For the economy as a whole, however, the substitution effect is stronger than the income effect, so a higher interest rate encourages saving and the supply curve of capital is upward sloping. Figure 16.5 illustrates the supply curve of capital. On that curve, at an interest rate of 6 percent per year, the quantity of capital supplied is $10 trillion.

Changes in the Supply of Capital

The supply of capital changes constantly. The main influences on the supply of capital are demographic. As the population changes and as its age distribution changes, so does the supply of capital. A population with a larger proportion of young people has a smaller supply of capital than a population with a larger proportion of middle-aged people. The age distribution of the population affects the supply of capital as a result of the life-cycle consumption smoothing described above.

Another influence on the supply of capital is the average income level. The higher the level of income, the larger is the supply of capital. A growing population and steadily rising income result in the supply of capital curve shifting to the right over time.

REVIEW

The quantity of capital supplied is determined by households' saving decisions. Saving depends on the amount of consumption smoothing the household undertakes over its life cycle and the interest rate. The more the household smooths its consumption and the higher the interest rate, the larger is the amount people save. The supply curve of capital is the relationship between the interest rate and the quantity of capital supplied. It slopes upward—the higher the interest rate, the larger is the quantity of capital supplied, other things being equal. The supply of capital changes as a result of changes in the population and its age composition and the level of income. Increasing population and increasing income result in a steady increase in the supply of capital—with the supply curve shifting steadily to the right. ◆

Now that we have studied the demand for and supply of capital, we can bring these two sides of the capital market together and study the determination of interest rates and asset prices. We'll then be able to answer some of the questions posed at the beginning of this chapter about the stock market and understand the forces that produce stock market booms and crashes.

FIGURE **16.5**
The Supply of Capital

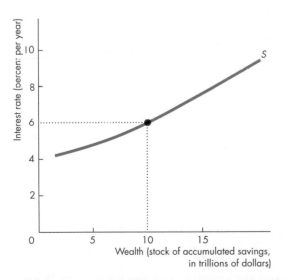

The higher the interest rate, the more capital households supply—the supply curve of capital slopes upward. At an interest rate of 6 percent a year, the quantity of capital supplied is $10 trillion.

Interest Rates and Asset Prices

Households' saving plans and firms' investment plans are coordinated through capital markets. Asset prices and interest rates adjust to make these plans compatible. We are now going to study the way in which these market forces work. And we are going to discover what determines the stock market value of a firm.

Two Sides of the Same Coin

Interest rates and asset prices can be viewed as two sides of the same coin. We'll look first at interest rates, then at asset prices, and finally at the connection between them. Some assets, such as bank deposits, earn a guaranteed interest rate. Other assets, such as bonds and shares in the stocks of firms, do not. The interest rates on these assets are usually called bond yields and stock yields. A **bond yield** is the interest on a bond, expressed as a percentage of the price of the bond. A **stock yield** is the income from a share in the stock of a firm, expressed as a percentage of the price of the share—the stock market price. A bond earns a guaranteed dollar income, but its market price fluctuates and hence its yield also fluctuates. A share in the stock of a firm earns a dividend based on the profitability of the firm. Also the stock market value of the share fluctuates. Thus a stock yield fluctuates for two reasons—fluctuations in the dividend and fluctuations in its stock market price.

Let's now look at the two sides of the same coin—the price of an asset and its yield or interest rate. To calculate a bond yield or stock yield, we divide the earnings of the asset by the price paid for it. For example, if Taxfile, Inc. pays a dividend of $5 a share and if a share can be bought for $50, the stock yield will be 10 percent ($5 divided by $50, expressed as a percentage). It follows from this calculation that for a given amount of earnings, the higher the price of an asset, the lower is its yield. For example, if the price of a share in Taxfile is $100 but its dividend remains constant at $5, its yield falls to 5 percent. This connection between the price of an asset and its yield or interest rate means that we can study the market forces in capital markets as simultaneously determining asset yields (interest rates) and asset prices. We will look at capital market equilibrium first in terms of interest rate (or yield) determination and then in terms of the stock market value of a particular firm.

Equilibrium Interest Rate

Figure 16.6 brings together the relevant parts of the previous analysis of the demand for and supply of capital. The diagram shows the entire capital market. The horizontal axis measures the total quantity of capital. Notice that the axis is labeled "Capital stock and wealth." This label emphasizes the fact that the value of the capital stock and wealth are equivalent. The vertical axis measures the interest rate. The demand curve (D) is the market demand for capital that you met in Fig. 16.4. The supply curve (S) is the market supply of capital shown in Fig. 16.5.

FIGURE **16.6**

Capital Market Equilibrium

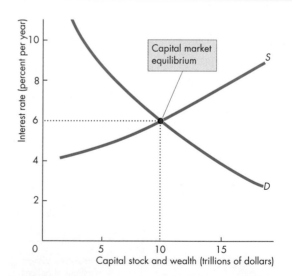

Capital market equilibrium occurs when the interest rate is such that the quantity of capital demanded equals the quantity of capital supplied. The demand curve is *D*, and the supply curve is *S*. These curves intersect at an interest rate of 6 percent a year and a capital stock of $10 trillion.

Capital market equilibrium occurs where the quantity of capital supplied equals the quantity of capital demanded. In Fig. 16.6, this equilibrium is at an interest rate of 6 percent a year and $10 trillion of capital is supplied and demanded. The market forces that bring about the equilibrium are exactly the same as those that we studied in the markets for goods and services.

If the interest rate exceeds 6 percent, the quantity of capital demanded is less than the quantity supplied. There is an excess supply of funds in the capital markets. In such a situation, financial intermediaries, anxious to increase their loans, lower the interest rates. The quantity demanded increases as firms increase their borrowing and buy additional capital. The interest rate continues to fall until financial institutions are able to lend all they wish to at the going rate. Conversely, if the interest rate is below 6 percent, the quantity of capital supplied is less than the quantity demanded. Financial intermediaries, unable to find enough funds to lend, increase interest rates. Rates increase until there are no unsatisfied borrowers. The end point of either of these situations is an interest rate of 6 percent, the equilibrium interest rate. The institutions that trade most heavily in capital markets—banks, insurance companies, and specialized dealers—handle millions of dollars of business every day and maintain a near continuous equality between the quantity of capital demanded and the quantity supplied.

These same competitive forces ensure that the interest rate is the same in all parts of the capital market, both across the regions of the nation and around the world. A further description of how these forces work to keep interest rates the same in all parts of the world can be seen in Reading Between the Lines on pp. 442–443.

The interest rate determined in Fig. 16.6 (and in Reading Between the Lines) is the *average* interest rate. Interest rates on individual assets will be distributed around that average, based on the relative degree of riskiness of individual assets. An asset with a high degree of risk will earn an interest rate that exceeds the average, and a very safe asset will earn an interest rate that is below the average. For example, if the average interest rate is 6 percent a year as shown in Fig. 16.6, the interest rate on a safe asset, such as a bank deposit, might be 4 percent a year and that on a riskier asset, such as a stock, could be 8 percent a year.

We've now seen how asset yields or interest rates are determined. Let's look at the other side of the coin—asset prices. To determine asset prices, we will change our focus and look not at the capital market in aggregate but at the stock market value of an individual firm.

Stock Market Value of a Firm

We've seen that there is a connection between an asset's yield (or interest rate) and that asset's price. The yield is the earnings on the asset divided by its price (expressed as a percentage). Let's use this fact to work out the stock market value of a firm. Suppose that a firm finances its purchases of capital by selling shares of its stock. What determines the price of a share? What determines the total value of all the shares sold?

The value of a share depends on the total value of the firm and on the number of shares sold. The value of one share is equal to the value of a firm divided by the number of shares sold, or, equivalently, the value of the firm is equal to the value of one share multiplied by the number of shares sold. So for a firm with a given number of shares, asking what determines the price of a share is the same as asking what determines the value of the firm.

When a person buys a share in the stock of a firm, that person becomes entitled to receive a profit each year. The price of a share depends on the expected future profit to be paid out by the firm. As we discovered in Chapter 9 (pp. 214–217) when we looked at the value of a share in Wisconsin Toy, the price of a share is the present value of its expected future profit. If a firm is expected to pay out no profits at all in the future, its shares will be worthless. If it is expected to pay out $10 a year on a share and if the interest rate is 10 percent a year, its shares will be worth $100 each. If it is expected to pay out $20 a year on a share and the interest rate is 10 percent, its shares will be worth $200 each.

Price-Earnings Ratio

A commonly used measure to describe the performance of a firm's stock is its price-earnings ratio. A *price-earnings ratio* is the current price of a share in a firm's stock divided by the most recent year's profit per share. In 1982, the average price-earnings ratio of the stocks that formed the Dow Jones Industrial

The Global Capital Market

THE ECONOMIST, NOVEMBER 16, 1991

The Surprising Emergence of Distant Shares

"Emerging markets" once seemed an optimistic term. Now it is really happening. The stock markets of Asia and Latin America, plus a handful of others classified as "emerging" by the International Finance Corporation (IFC, the private-sector arm of the World Bank), have collectively grown fourfold since 1985. Last year they provided $22 billion of fresh money for companies. . . . The IFC reckons that foreigners' stake in the young markets has grown from next to nothing a decade ago to around $17 billion.

By the end of the decade, this sum may seem paltry. For reasons unconnected with the individual charms of these markets, the world's biggest savings institutions—pension and mutual funds, insurance companies—are keener to spread their assets internationally; Salomon Brothers, an American investment bank, reckons that the value of cross-border equity flows increased 20 times during the 1980s. As they diversify, fund managers establish benchmarks to guide their asset allocation. A popular solution is to allocate money in proportion to the capitalisation of each market. If this were applied to the developing world, the result would be a deluge of foreign capital.

Each year the rich world's savers invest something like $1 trillion of new money in equities. Together the emerging markets represent 5% of world stockmarket capitalisation, so the benchmark would imply an annual transfer of $50 billion. If the savings institutions also began to shift existing funds to reflect that proportion, the transfers could be even bigger—perhaps amounting to $100 billion a year. . . .

Next consider the scope for issuing international equity. The new rival to the growth of cross-border equity flows is "cross-exchange" trading. . . . Salomon Brothers calculates that the volume of cross-exchange equity trading jumped from $583 billion in 1989 to $874 billion last year.

Developing countries have recently begun to exploit investors' appetite for international listings. The most noted example is Telmex, Mexico's telephone company, whose listing on the New York Stock Exchange in May [1991] raised $2.2 billion; on October 28th [1991] Telmex was the exchange's most actively traded stock. South Korean, Indonesian and Thai companies issued $1.6 billion of international equity and convertible bonds between them during the 18 months from January 1990. Indian and Brazilian rivals are tipped to join in next.

The Essence of the Story

The stock markets of Asia and Latin America (plus a few others) have grown fourfold since 1985. In 1990, $22 billion of savings were channeled through these markets, $17 billion of which were foreign savings.

The world's pension and mutual funds and insurance companies have spread their assets internationally, resulting in a twenty-fold increase in the value of cross-border equity flows during the 1980s.

If these institutions also shift existing funds in proportion to market size, the transfers will be $100 billion a year.

An alternative to allocating funds to foreign stock markets is for investors to buy foreign shares in their own countries—cross-exchange trading—which increased from $583 billion in 1989 to $874 billion in 1990.

Developing countries are taking advantage of cross-exchange equities. Telmex, Mexico's telephone company, raised $2.2 billion on the New York Stock Exchange, and South Korean, Indonesian, and Thai companies raised $1.6 billion. Indian and Brazilian companies are expected to be next.

Background and Analysis

The world capital market is made up of thousands of local markets, but it is a single integrated market. People with funds to lend supply them where they can get the highest interest rate. People borrowing funds to buy capital demand them where they can get the lowest interest rate. As a result, each local capital market has the same interest rate.

The figure shows how the world capital market for equity capital—shares in companies—works. Part (a) illustrates the Asian and Latin American "emerging" markets, and part (b) illustrates the New York market. Initially, the demand and supply curves are D_0 and S_0. The interest rate is r_N, and the quantities of equity capital are K_N in New York and zero in the emerging markets.

Then the demand for equity capital increases in Asia and Latin America, and the demand curve for capital shifts to the right, to D_1. (Such an increase occurred in Asia and Latin America during the 1980s partly because the number of profitable business opportunities increased and partly because banks stopped lending to companies in these regions.)

Other things remaining equal, the interest rate rises in the emerging markets to r_E and the quantity of equity capital increases to K_E.

But other things do not remain equal. With the interest rate in the emerging markets higher than that in New York, U.S. institutions with funds to lend move them from the New York market to the emerging markets. The supply curves shift to S_2 (in both markets). These are the "cross-border equity flows" in the story.

Also, borrowers in Asia and Latin America switch their borrowing from their local market to the New York market. The demand curves shift to D_2 in both markets. This is the "cross-exchange trading" in the story.

As a consequence of these changes in supply and demand, the interest rate rises in the New York market and falls in the emerging markets. When the two rates are equal at r_W, the demand and supply curves stop shifting and a single interest rate prevails in both markets.

The capital markets of Asia and Latin America are "emerging" and "cross-exchange" trading is expanding because, if they did not, interest rates in the two markets would diverge and profits could be made simply by borrowing in the market that has the low interest rate and lending in the other market.

(a) Emerging markets

(b) New York market

Average was 8.1. By 1987, the price-earnings ratio had risen to 20.5, but that was a peak year. The ratio then fell off and, at the beginning of 1989, stood at about 12.

What determines a price-earnings ratio? Why, at the beginning of 1989, was Ford's price-earnings ratio only 5 while Sony's was 33?

We have seen that the price of a share of stock is determined by the present value of the expected future profit of the firm. The higher the *expected future* profit, the higher is *today's* price. The price-earnings ratio of a firm depends on its current profit in relation to its expected future profit. When expected future profit is high relative to current profit, the price-earnings ratio is high. When expected future profit is low relative to current profit, the price-earnings ratio is low. Fluctuations in the price-earnings ratio arise from fluctuations in expected future profit relative to current profit.

Stock Market Volume and Prices

Sometimes the prices quoted on the stock market rise or fall with little trading taking place. At other times, stock market prices rise or fall with an enormous volume of trading. On yet other occasions, there is little change in the stock prices but there is an enormous volume of trading. Why do stock prices rise or fall, and what determines the volume of trading on the stock market?

Stock prices rise and fall because of changes in expectations of future profit. Consider the firm whose profit per share is $1. Suppose that the interest rate on assets that are as risky as a share of this firm's stock is 8 percent a year. Further suppose that the firm's profit in each future year is expected to be exactly the same as this year's. The price of the firm's stock will adjust until a share can be bought for the price that makes the stock yield equal to 8 percent a year. That price is $12.50. People will buy shares in this company for $12.50 and expect, on the average, to make $1 a share each year, or a stock yield of 8 percent ($1 is 8 percent of $12.50). The price-earnings ratio will be 12.5—today's price ($12.50) divided by last year's profit ($1 per share).

Suppose that market conditions change and people now expect the firm's profit to double to $2 per share starting next year. With an expected profit of $2 a share the stock market price jumps to $25. It's true that at $25 a share this year's profit ($1 per share) represents only a 4 percent stock yield ($1 is

4 percent of $25), but with profit expected to be $2 per share next year and every year thereafter, the expected yield is 8 percent a year—the interest rate available on other assets of similar risk. This price jump to $25 occurs with no change in the current year's profitability of the firm. It occurs entirely because people observe some event today that leads them to expect higher profit in the future.

Suppose that the change in market conditions leading to expected higher future profit is so obvious that everyone can see it and everyone agrees that this firm's earnings are indeed going to double next year. In such a situation, the market value of the firm's shares rises to $25 but no one buys or sells shares. Stockholders are happy with the shares that they already hold. If the price does not rise to $25, everyone will want to buy some shares. If the price rises to more than $25, everyone will want to sell some shares. If the price rises to exactly $25, everyone will be indifferent between hanging onto those shares or buying some other shares that are currently yielding 8 percent a year.

On the other hand, suppose that the event that changed expectations about this firm's profitability is difficult to interpret. Some people think the event will lead to a rise in the firm's profit, and others think it will not have any effect on profit. Let's call the first group optimists and the second group pessimists. The optimists will want to buy the stock and will be willing to do so as long as its price is less than $25. The pessimists will sell the stock as long as its price is above $12.50. In such a situation, the pessimists will sell out and the optimists will buy in. The price will not necessarily change, but there will be a large volume of trading activity. What causes the trading activity is the disagreement, not the event that triggered the change in expected profitability. High volume of trading on the stock market implies a large amount of disagreement. Large price changes with low volume of trading imply a great deal of agreement that something fundamental has changed. A large volume of trading with hardly any price change means that the underlying changes are difficult to interpret: some people predict that things will move in one direction, while others predict the opposite.

Takeovers and Mergers

The theory of capital markets that you've now studied can be used to explain why takeovers and mergers occur. A **takeover** is the purchase of the stock of one firm by another firm. A takeover occurs when the stock market value of a firm is lower than the present value of the expected future profits from operating the firm. For example, suppose that Taxfile, Inc. has a stock market value of $120,000. But suppose also that the present value of the future profit of the firm is $150,000. It will pay for someone to try to take over the firm. Takeover activity affects the price of a firm, and often the threat of a takeover drives the price to the point at which the takeover is no longer profitable.

There are other takeover situations in which the expected future profit of a firm depends on the firm taking it over. A recent example illustrates this point very well. The Atari Computer Company was having difficulty in breaking into the retail computer market on the scale that it desired. To overcome its problems, Atari searched out, surprisingly, a retail chain that was losing money. The present value of a firm that is making a loss is less than the value of its plant and equipment. So Atari was able to buy retail outlets for a lower price from their current owners than it could have done by starting afresh. Atari believed that by buying the firm and using its retail stores to sell Atari computers, Atari could convert that firm's loss into a profit.

A **merger** is the combining of the assets of two firms to form a single new firm. Mergers take place when two firms perceive that by combining their assets, they can increase their combined stock market values. For example, the merger of Piedmont and USAir enabled the resulting firm to increase its profit by integrating their routes and schedules.

REVIEW

S aving plans and investment plans are coordinated through capital markets. Adjustments in asset prices and interest rates make the saving plans and investment plans compatible. Interest rates and asset prices are two sides of the same coin. The interest rate on an asset is the income on the asset divided by its price. The average interest rate makes the quantity of capital demanded equal to the quantity of savings supplied. ◆ ◆ The value of a share of a firm's stock is determined by the firm's current and expected future profit. Expected future profit is based on expectations of future prices, costs, and technologies that the firm will face. The stock market value of a firm is often expressed as a ratio of the firm's current profit per share—the price-earnings ratio. The price-earnings ratio depends on expected profit growth. ◆ ◆ Stock market prices sometimes move dramatically, and the volume of trading on the stock market is sometimes high and sometimes low. Prices change quickly when everyone expects changes in future profitability. The volume of stock market trading rises when people disagree about the future. ◆ ◆ Mergers and takeovers occur when the stock market value of a firm is lower than the present value of the future profit stream that another firm believes it could generate with the first firm's assets. ◆

The lessons that we've just learned about capital markets have wider application than explaining fluctuations in the stock market. They also help us to understand how natural resource markets work. Let's now examine these important markets.

Natural Resource Markets

N atural resources are the nonproduced factors of production with which we are endowed. Natural resources fall into two categories: exhaustible and nonexhaustible. **Exhaustible natural resources** are natural resources that can be used only once and that cannot be replaced once used. Examples of exhaustible natural resources are coal, natural gas, and oil—the so-called hydrocarbon fuels. **Nonexhaustible natural resources** are natural resources that can be used repeatedly without depleting what's available for future use. Examples of nonexhaustible natural resources are land, sea, rivers and lakes, rain, and sunshine. Plants and animals are also examples of nonexhaustible natural resources. By careful cultivation and husbandry, more of these natural resources can be produced to replace those used up in production and consumption activities.

Natural resources have two important economic dimensions—a stock dimension and a flow dimension. There is a stock of each natural resource determined by nature and by the previous rate of use of the resource. The flow of a natural resource is the rate at which it is being used. This flow is determined by human choices, and those choices determine whether a given stock of natural resources is used up quickly, slowly, or not at all. In studying the operation of natural resource markets, we'll begin by considering the stock dimension of a natural resource.

Supply and Demand in a Natural Resource Market

The stock of a natural resource supplied is the amount of the resource in existence. For example, the stock of oil supplied is the total volume of oil lying beneath the earth's surface. This amount is fixed independently of the price of the resource. Its supply is perfectly inelastic, and the position of its supply curve depends on the amount of the resource available initially and on the rate at which it has been used up in the past.[4] The smaller the initial stock and the faster the rate of use, the smaller is the stock of a resource available.

Demand for a Stock   The demand for a stock of a natural resource is one aspect of portfolio choice. People own stocks of natural resources as an alternative to owning equities in corporations, other financial assets such as bonds, or other physical assets such as plant, equipment, and buildings.

The demand for a stock of a natural resource is determined in the same way as the demand for any other asset—by the income that it is expected to earn, expressed as a percentage yield or interest rate.

But what is the interest rate on a natural resource? It is the rate of change in the price of the resource. If you buy a stock of a natural resource,

you buy it at today's price. If you sell your natural resource stock a year later, you sell it at the price prevailing at that time. The percentage change in the price of the resource over the year is the interest rate you make from holding the stock of the natural resource over the year. Thus the more rapid the increase in the price of a natural resource, other things being equal, the larger is the interest rate on that natural resource.

If the expected interest rate on a stock of a natural resource exceeds that on other assets (with comparable risk), people allocate more of their net worth to owning the natural resource and less to other assets. Conversely, if the expected interest rate on a natural resource falls short of that on other assets (with comparable risk), portfolios are reallocated by selling the stock of a natural resource and buying other assets.

Stock Equilibrium   Equilibrium occurs in the market for a stock of a natural resource when the interest rate on owning a natural resource stock equals that on other comparably risky assets. In such a situation, there is no tendency for people to either buy or sell stocks of natural resources or other assets. They are satisfied with their existing portfolio allocation and with the quantity of the stock of the natural resource that they are holding.

Since the interest rate on a natural resource stock is the rate at which the price of the natural resource rises, the expected interest rate is the rate at which the price of the resource is *expected* to rise over time. That rate equals the interest rate on other assets. This proposition is known as the **Hotelling Principle**.[5]

Why is the price of a natural resource expected to grow at a rate equal to the interest rate on other assets? It is to make the expected interest rate on the natural resource equal to the interest rate on other comparably risky assets.

The supply of and demand for the stock of a natural resource determine the interest rate from owning that stock. But the supply of and demand for the stock of the resource do not determine the current *level* of the price—only its future expected rate of

---

[4]The actual quantity is not the same as the *known* (or proven) quantity. The known quantity of a natural resource in existence is larger the higher its price, other things being equal. For example, the known reserves of oil in 1973, when the price of oil was $3 a barrel, were 580 billion barrels. By 1990, after we had consumed 350 billion barrels but by which time the price of oil had increased to $30 a barrel, known reserves had *increased* to more than 1 trillion barrels.

[5]The Hotelling Principle, discovered by Harold Hotelling, first appeared in "Economics of Exhaustible Resources," *Journal of Political Economy* 39 (April 1931): 137–175.

change. To determine the level of the price of a natural resource, we have to consider not only the supply of and demand for the stock of the resource but also the demand for its flow.

Price of a Natural Resource

To determine the price of a natural resource, we first consider the influences on the demand for the flow of the natural resource and then we study the equilibrium that emerges from the interaction of the demand for the flow with the available stock.

Demand for a Flow   The demand for a flow of a natural resource is determined in the same way as the demand for any other input. It arises from firms' profit-maximization decisions. A firm maximizes profit when the marginal revenue product of an input equals the marginal cost of the input. In a perfectly competitive market, the marginal cost of an input equals the factor price. The quantity demanded of a flow of a natural resource is the amount that makes the marginal revenue product of that flow equal to the price of the resource. As in the case of all other inputs, the marginal revenue product of a natural resource diminishes as the quantity of the resource used increases. Thus the lower the price of a resource, the greater is the quantity demanded of the flow of the natural resource—as illustrated in Fig. 16.7.

For any resource, there is a price that is so high that it does not pay anyone to use the resource. The price at which it no longer pays to use a natural resource is called the **choke price**. Figure 16.7 shows a choke price of P_C. Everything has substitutes, and at a high enough price, a substitute is used. For example, we do not have to use aluminum to make cans for soft drinks; we can use plastic instead. We do not have to use oil as the fuel for cars; we can use alcohol or electric cars instead. We do not have to use gas and electric power to heat our homes; we can use solar energy instead. The natural resources that we *do* use are the least expensive resources available. They cost us less than the next best alternatives would.

Equilibrium Stock and Flow

The price and the flow of a natural resource depend on three things:

- The interest rate

FIGURE **16.7**

Demand for a Flow of a Natural Resource

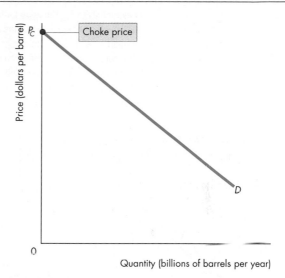

Natural resources have substitutes. If the price of a natural resource is too high, then a substitute will be used. At a price below P_C, the quantity demanded is positive, and the lower the price, the larger is the quantity demanded. The price P_C is called the choke price. At P_C, none of this resource is demanded and a substitute will be used.

- The demand for the flow
- The stock of the resource remaining

Figure 16.8 shows how these three factors combine to determine the price of a natural resource: the expected path of that price, the rate at which the resource is used up, and the stock of the resource remaining. Let's take the figure one part at a time.

In part (a), you can see the expected price path of the natural resource. That path is determined by the interest rate r. The line with a slope of $1 + r$ shows the relationship between the price in the current year and the price next year if the price rises at a rate equal to the interest rate. Suppose that initially the price is P_0. Next year, the price will rise to P_1, the price that is r percent higher than P_0. You can see the rise in price by following the steps between the 45° line and the line with a slope of $1 + r$. Each step represents a price increase. The steps become larger,

FIGURE 16.8

The Market for an Exhaustible Natural Resource

The expected rate of increase in the price of a natural resource equals the interest rate. Starting at P_0, in part (a), the price increases at first to P_1 and eventually to P_C. The price path follows the steps shown, with each step bigger than the previous one. Part (b) shows the rate at which the resource is used up. Its demand curve (D) determines the quantity demanded for use (a flow) at each price. Initially, when the price is P_0, that flow is Q_0. As the price increases, the flow decreases. When the price reaches P_C, the choke price, the flow is zero. Part (c) illustrates the remaining stock after each year. The initial stock is used up in decreasing amounts until, after six years, the stock is exhausted. The price P_0 is the equilibrium price because it achieves equality between the sum of the flows in each year and the initial stock.

(a) Expected price path   **(b) Rate of use**   **(c) Remaining stock**

but the height of each step is a constant percentage of the previous year's price. Since the price keeps rising, eventually it reaches the choke price, identified as P_C in the figure.

Next, consider Fig. 16.8(b), which shows the rate at which the resource is used up. The demand for the flow, based on the marginal revenue product of the natural resource, is illustrated by the curve D. In the initial year, at a price of P_0, the quantity Q_0 is used. In the following year, we know from part (a) that the price increases to P_1. At this price, the quantity used up is Q_1. As the price increases each year, the quantity used each year decreases.

Figure 16.8(c) shows the remaining stock. The initial stock is identified in the figure, and the stock remaining after each year is also identified. For example, the stock after one year is the initial stock

minus Q_0, the amount used up in the first year. In this example, after six years there is no stock left. The price has increased from P_0 to the choke price P_C, and the quantity used in each year has declined until, in the final year, it has become zero—the quantity of the flow of natural resources demanded at the choke price.

How do we know that P_0 is the current price? It is because it is the price that achieves an equilibrium between the remaining stock and the current year's flow and the future years' expected flows. That is, it is the only current price that leads to a sequence of future prices (growing at the interest rate) that generate a sequence of flows such that the stock is exhausted in the same year that the choke price is reached. If the current price is higher than P_0 and if the future prices are expected to rise at the interest rate, the choke price will be reached before the stock is exhausted. If the current price is below P_0 and, again, if the future prices are expected to rise at the interest rate, the stock will be exhausted before the choke price is reached.

We can now see how the current price is determined by the three factors that we identified above. First, the higher the interest rate, the lower is the current price of a natural resource. The higher interest rate means that the price is going to increase more quickly. Thus starting from the same initial price, the choke price will be reached sooner. But if the choke price is reached sooner, the stock available will not be used up at that point in time. Thus the initial price has to be lower when the interest rate is higher to ensure that by the time the price does reach the choke price, the total stock available has been used.

Second, the higher the marginal revenue product of the natural resource—the higher the demand for the flow of the natural resource—the higher is the current price of the resource. You can see why this relationship exists by looking again at Fig. 16.8(b). If the demand for the flow of the resource were higher than that shown in this figure, the demand curve would lie to the right of the demand curve shown. In this case, the current price would be higher than P_0.

Third, the larger the initial stock of the natural resource, the lower is the current price. You can also see why this relationship holds by considering Fig. 16.8(c). If the initial stock is larger than that shown in the figure, P_0 cannot be the equilibrium price, because it leads to a sequence of prices that generate a sequence of quantities demanded that do not exhaust the stock by the time the choke price is reached. Thus the initial price would have to be below P_0 to ensure that the larger stock is exhausted by the time that the choke price is reached.

Equilibrium in the market for a natural resource determines the current price of the natural resource and the expected path of future prices. But the price path actually followed is rarely the same as its expected path. For example, in 1984, expectations about the future price of oil were that it would rise at a rate equal to the interest rate. Opinions differed about the long-term average interest rate, so projections ranged from a low growth rate of 1.8 percent a year to a high growth rate of 7.1 percent a year. But, as events have turned out, the price of oil fell after 1984 (see Fig. 16.9).

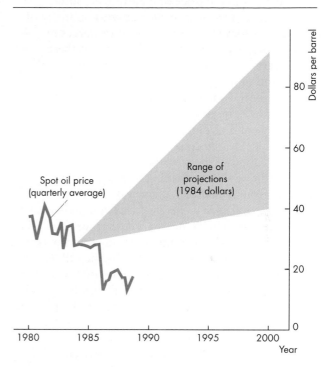

FIGURE **16.9**
Unfulfilled Expectations

In 1984, the price of oil was expected to increase at a rate equal to the interest rate. There were different views of the future interest rate, so there was a range of expected price increases. The events of the 1980s unfolded in a way that was different from what had been expected in 1984. Higher interest rates, the discovery of increased reserves, and new energy-saving technologies all contributed to a falling price of oil. The breakup of the OPEC cartel also contributed significantly to falling oil prices.

Source: "Future Imperfect," *The Economist:* Feb. 4, 1989, p. 67. © 1989, The Economist Newspaper Limited. Reprinted with permission.

Why do natural resource prices change unexpectedly, sometimes even falling rather than following their expected path?

Unexpected Price Changes

The price of a natural resource depends on expectations about future events. It depends on expectations about the interest rate, the future demand for the flow of the resource, and the size of the remaining stock. Natural resource markets are constantly being bombarded by new information that leads to new expectations. For example, new information about the stock of a resource or the technologies available for its use can lead to sudden and perhaps quite large changes in the price of a natural resource.

All of these forces have been at work in many of the markets for exhaustible natural resources in recent years. The market for oil illustrates these effects very well. The discovery of new sources of supply and of new extraction technologies has resulted in previously unforeseen increases in the supply of oil. The development of energy-efficient automobile and airplane engines has decreased the demand for oil. The combination of these factors has led to a fall in the price of oil.

An additional force leading to price changes in natural resource markets in general and in the oil market in particular is the degree of competitiveness in the markets. The model market that we have been studying is a perfectly competitive one. But the real-world market for oil is dominated by the OPEC cartel, an oligopoly similar to that analyzed in Chapter 14 (pp. 351–354). The breakup of the OPEC cartel contributed significantly to the decline in the price of oil during the 1980s.

In forecasting the future price of a natural resource, it is necessary to forecast future changes in market structure. Adding this complication to an already complex forecasting problem makes it clear that the fluctuations in prices of natural resources such as oil are, for the most part, unforecastable.

Conservation and Doomsday

The analysis that you have just reviewed concerning the price of a natural resource and its expected change over time has important implications for the popular debate concerning natural resources and their use. Many people fear that we are using the earth's exhaustible natural resources at such a rapid pace that we shall eventually (and perhaps in the not very distant future) run out of important sources of energy and of other crucial raw materials. Such people urge a slowing down in the rate of use of exhaustible natural resources so that the limited stocks available will last longer.

This topic is an emotional one and generates passionate debate. It is also a matter that involves economic issues that can be understood by using the economic model of a depletable natural resource that you have just studied.

The economic analysis of an exhaustible natural resource market predicts that doomsday—the using up of the entire stock of a natural resource—will eventually arise if our use of natural resources is organized in competitive markets. The economic model also implies that a competitive market will provide an automatic conservation program arising from a steadily rising price. As a natural resource gets closer and closer to being depleted, its price gets closer to the choke price—the price at which no one wants to use the resource anymore. Each year, as the price rises, the quantity demanded of the flow declines.

But what if the resource gets completely used up? Don't we have a real problem then? We have the problem of scarcity but in no more acute a form than we had it before. The resource that is no longer available was used because to use it was more efficient than to use some alternative. Once that resource is completely used up, then and only then does it pay to turn to using a more expensive substitute. So the market economy handles the depleting stocks of natural resources by persistently forcing up their prices. Higher prices cause us to ration our use and eventually drive the quantity demanded of the flow to zero when the supply of the stock disappears.

There is an important economic issue as to whether or not a competitive market leads us to use our scarce exhaustible natural resources at an efficient rate. Recall that we studied the allocative efficiency of a perfectly competitive market in Chapter 11 (pp. 305–308). There we discovered that perfectly competitive markets achieve allocative efficiency if there are no external costs and benefits. The same conclusion applies to markets for natural resources. If there are no external costs or benefits impinging upon these markets, then the rate of use determined in a perfectly competitive exhaustible natural resource market is the allocatively efficient rate of use. But if there are external costs associated with the use of the natural resource, allocative efficiency will result from a slowdown in the rate of use of the resource compared with that arising in the competitive market. For example, if burning hydrocarbon fuels increases the carbon dioxide in the atmosphere and a warming of the earth's atmosphere results—the so-called greenhouse effect—the costs associated with this atmospheric change have to be added to the costs of using oil and coal as fuels. When these costs are taken into account, the allocatively efficient rate of use of these fuels is lower than that resulting from a perfectly competitive market. We examine ways in which government intervention can achieve allocative efficiency in such a situation in Chapter 19 (pp. 519–520).

◆ ◆ ◆ ◆ We have now studied the way in which factor markets allocate scarce productive resources —labor, capital, and land—and the determination of factor prices and factor incomes. The outcome of the operation of the factor markets is the distribu-

tion of income among individuals and families that determines *for whom* goods and services are produced. But that outcome is uncertain. People decide what type of work to do, how much to save, and what to do with their savings with no sure knowledge of the payoffs from their decisions. In the next part we study uncertainty and its consequences in a more systematic way. And we examine the distribution of income that emerges from our choices about work, saving, and investment. We discover the ways in which we cope with uncertainty and the main sources of income and wealth inequality in our economy.

SUMMARY

Capital, Investment, and Saving

There are two kinds of assets: financial and physical. Financial assets are all the paper claims of one economic agent against another. Physical assets, or capital, are the stock of all the productive assets owned by households and firms. Investment is the flow of additions to the stock of capital. Depreciation is the flow reduction in the stock of capital through use or the passage of time.

The quantity of capital supplied results from people's saving decisions. Saving equals income minus consumption. People allocate their savings to a variety of alternative financial and physical assets. (pp. 429–431)

Capital Markets in the United States Today

Capital markets provide the link between the saving decisions of households and the investment decisions of firms and governments. Households finance firms' investment by buying equity and bonds or by making deposits in financial intermediaries that in turn make loans to firms. Households also make loans to governments by buying bonds and indirectly through deposits with financial intermediaries. (pp. 431–434)

Demand for Capital

The demand for capital is determined—like the demand for factors—by firms' profit-maximization

choices. The quantity of capital demanded by a firm is such that the marginal revenue product of capital equals its opportunity cost. A firm can make the comparison between marginal revenue product and cost by calculating the present value of marginal revenue product and comparing that present value with the price of a new piece of capital.

The quantity of capital demanded by a firm depends on the interest rate. The higher the interest rate, the lower is the present value of the future stream of marginal revenue products and the smaller is the quantity of capital equipment a firm buys. The lower the interest rate, the greater is the quantity of capital demanded—the demand curve for capital is downward sloping. The demand curve for capital shifts steadily to the right as a result of technological change and the general tendency to exploit innovations over time. (pp. 434–438)

The Supply of Capital

The quantity of capital supplied results from the saving decisions of households. Savings depend on how much households smooth their consumption over the life cycle and on the interest rate. The supply curve for capital is upward sloping—as interest rates rise, the quantity of capital supplied increases. The supply curve of capital shifts over time as a result of changes in the population and its age composition and the level of income. (pp. 438–439)

Interest Rates and Asset Prices

Interest rates and asset prices can be viewed as two sides of the same coin. Interest rates and asset prices adjust to achieve equality between the quantity of capital demanded and the quantity supplied. Interest rates on particular assets are distributed around the average rate according to the degree of riskiness of different types of assets.

The stock market value of a firm depends on the firm's current profit and expectations of its future profit. The higher the expected growth rate of a firm's profit, the higher is the price of a share of its stock. The price-earnings ratio is the ratio of the price of a share in a firm's stock to its profit per share. That ratio depends on the expected growth rate of profit.

The volume of trading on the stock market is determined by the extent of the divergence of expectations of the future. When everyone agrees about the future, volume of trading is low. When there is widespread disagreement, volume of trading is high. There can be large changes in prices with low or high volume of trading. Price changes occur when there is a change in expectations about profit growth.

Mergers and takeovers occur as part of the process of maximizing profit. If a firm's stock market value is lower than the value of its assets when used by another firm, it will pay that other firm to take over the first firm. Mergers occur when there is a mutually agreed benefit from combining the assets of two (or more) firms. (pp. 440–445)

Natural Resource Markets

Natural resources are the nonproduced factors of production with which we are endowed. The price of a natural resource is determined by the interest rate, its marginal revenue product (which determines the demand for its flow), and the quantity remaining of the natural resource (the supply of its stock). The price of a natural resource is such that its future price is expected to rise at a rate equal to the interest rate and to reach the choke price at the time at which the resource is exhausted. The actual price is constantly changing to take into account new information. Even though the future price is expected to increase, the actual price often decreases as a result of new information leading to an increase in the estimate of the remaining stock or to a decrease in the demand for the flow of the resource. (pp. 445–451)

K E Y   E L E M E N T S

Key Terms

Asset, 429
Balance sheet, 429
Bond market, 432
Bond yield, 440
Capital, 429
Choke price, 447
Depreciation, 430
Exhaustible natural resources, 445
Financial assets, 429
Financial intermediary, 431
Gross investment, 430
Hotelling Principle, 446
Investment, 430
Liability, 429

Loans market, 432
Merger, 445
Natural resources, 445
Net financial assets, 429
Net investment, 430
Net present value of an investment, 435
Nonexhaustible natural resources, 445
Physical assets, 429
Portfolio choice, 430
Saving, 430
Stock market, 432
Stock yield, 440
Takeover, 445
Wealth, 430

Key Figures and Tables

Figure 16.1   Capital Market Flows, 432
Figure 16.2   The Nation's Balance Sheet, 433
Figure 16.6   Capital Market Equilibrium, 440
Table 16.1   Balance Sheet of Rocky's Mountain
              Bikes, 429

Table 16.2   Financial Assets and Physical Assets of
              Rocky's Mountain Bikes, 429
Table 16.5   Net Present Value of an Investment—
              Taxfile, Inc., 435

R E V I E W   Q U E S T I O N S

1 Why does the quantity of capital demanded by a firm rise as the interest rate falls?

2 Set out the key reasons for differences in interest rates on different types of assets.

3 What is the relationship between interest rates and asset prices?

4 Explain how the stock market value of a firm is determined.

5 Define the price-earnings ratio and explain how it is determined.

6 Why are there some occasions when stock market prices change a lot but with little trading and other times when prices are stable but trading volumes are high?

7 Why do mergers and takeovers occur?

8 Distinguish between the stock and the flow of an exhaustible natural resource.

9 Explain why the price of an exhaustible natural resource is expected to rise at a rate equal to the interest rate.

10 What determines the price of a natural resource?

11 Why are most of the fluctuations in the price of a natural resource unforecastable?

P R O B L E M S

1 At the end of 1991 a firm had a production plant worth $1,000,000. The plant depreciated during 1992 by 10 percent. During the same year, the firm also bought new capital equipment for $250,000. What is the value of the firm's stock of capital at the end of 1992? What was the firm's gross investment during 1992? What was the firm's net investment during 1992?

2 You earn $20,000 per year (after paying your taxes) for three years, and you spend $16,000 each year. How much do you save each year? What happens to your wealth during this three-year period?

3 What are the different ways in which a holder of wealth can channel capital into firms?

4 Why is a deposit in a financial intermediary less risky than buying equity or bonds?

5 A firm is considering buying a new machine. It is estimated that the marginal revenue product of the machine will be $10,000 a year for five years. The machine will have a scrap value at the end of five years of $10,000. The interest rate is 10 percent a year.

a   What is the maximum price that the firm will pay for the machine?

b   If the machine costs $40,000, would the firm buy the machine at an interest rate of 10 percent?

c   What is the highest interest rate at which the firm would buy the machine?

PART **7**

MARKETS, UNCERTAINTY, AND DISTRIBUTION

Talking

with

Tony

Atkinson

Tony Atkinson was born in Caerleon, Wales, in 1944. He studied economics at Cambridge University, has been a professor at the University of Essex and the London School of Economics, and has recently returned to Cambridge. Professor Atkinson's major contributions have been in the area of taxation and the distribution of income.

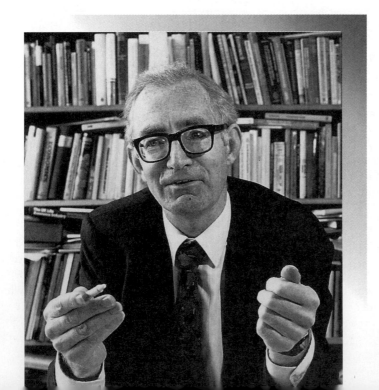

How did you get interested in economics?

Like many other economists, I began as a mathematics student and then became interested in social problems. In the 1960s, we believed that we could change the world for the better—and I am not sure that we were wrong.

What are the key principles of economics that you have repeatedly found useful in your work?

I should say that I am suspicious of "general principles" in economics. When I hear people say "economic theory tells us X," I am immediately on my guard. Increasingly, I have become impressed with the importance of blending economic theory with the institutional realities of particular countries and particular time periods. Historical, cultural, and social factors mean that an economic model that is applicable to the United States might not be equally relevant to Europe or Japan. Too often, economic theory is applied without regard to such institutional features. The standard economic treatment of unemployment insurance, for example, ignores important fea-

> "**W**hat I believe economics can teach is not a set of universally applicable tools, like a wrench that will always undo a nut, but an *approach*."

tures of real-world unemployment insurance schemes, which may change its economic impact.

Why is a background in economics useful today?

What I believe economics can teach is not a set of universally applicable tools, like a wrench that will always undo a nut, but an *approach*. After receiving an economics degree, a student should not expect to have the answers but to be able to ask the right questions. When considering a particular policy change, for example, an economist will ask how the new policy might affect the behavior of different groups and will ask who gains and who loses from its introduction.

One particular question that I have found useful to ask is "What is the quantitative importance of different phenomena? Is the effect under discussion large or small?" One major contribution that economists can make is in evaluating and providing statistical information. I was once a member of a multidisciplinary group investigating the transmission of deprivation from generation to generation. It turned out that there was, at the time, no information at all about the propor-

tion of children from poor families who went on to create poor families themselves. This led to a fascinating piece of research in which we traced the children of families who had been poor when studied a generation earlier. From this detective work, we were able to quantify the extent to which these children faced a greater risk of poverty.

Of course, everyone knows that statistics can be misused, and one should certainly not treat numbers in statistical yearbooks with undue reverence. At the same time, one cannot discuss applied economic problems without a view of their quantitative importance. A first reaction of the good economist should be to reach for some numbers.

What drew you to work on problems of poverty and the distribution of income?

There were two important influences that affected the direction of my first research. The first were the lectures and writing of James Meade, who later won the Nobel Prize. From him, I learned both that economic analysis could contribute to understanding issues of inequality and that explaining the distribution of income was an

intellectual challenge. The second was reading *The Poor and the Poorest* by Brian Abel-Smith and Peter Townsend, two British experts on social policy. Published in 1965, the book described the poverty in Britain despite the welfare state and despite—at that time—full employment. It also demonstrated the potential impact of careful empirical research, just as the writing of economists in the United States was at the same time influential in leading to the launching of Lyndon Johnson's War on Poverty.

How does the study of income distribution relate to the main body of economics?

For classical economists, such as Adam Smith or David Ricardo, the distribution of income was central to the study of economics. Today, on the other hand, the distribution of income is often treated as a special subject—one that sits uneasily between macroeconomics and microeconomics.

This seems to me a great pity, since distributional issues are at the heart of economics. Aggregate objectives, such as the growth of GDP, are only a means of achieving the more fundamental goal of improving the welfare of individuals. The welfare of individuals in turn depends on how total GDP is distributed. By this, I do not just mean the distribution of money income, but also the provision of public goods and the quality of the environment. It is paradoxical that Western democratic societies, with their emphasis on individual liberty, should be preoccupied with macroeconomic aggregates and show much less interest in measuring individual welfare.

Which economic systems stand out as having achieved the greatest measure of equality and which as having determined the greatest inequity?

I recently finished a research project with John Micklewright of the European University Institute at Florence in which we looked at the distribution of income under communism in Eastern Europe and the former Soviet Union. When we started work on this, we found that opinion was sharply divided. Some people pointed to the absence of property income and to the compression of wage differentials and concluded that Communist governments had succeeded in reducing income inequality. Others argued that inequality was in fact no different under communism than under capitalism, citing the privileged

position of the political elite, the so-called *nomenklatura*, and suggesting that old inequalities had simply been replaced by new ones.

In the case of the former Soviet Union, it used to be very difficult to obtain firm evidence about income inequality, which appeared on the list of censored subjects along with alcoholism and drug addiction. With *glasnost*, however, much information has been made available. It now appears that under Khrushchev, wage dispersion was indeed reduced below that in Britain, particularly because of the minimum wage. But in the 1980s, there was little difference, and Gorbachev's wage reform actually widened differentials. On the other hand, the distribution of *income*, taking into account transfer payments and capital income and including those not in the labor force, did appear to be significantly less unequal in the USSR than in Britain in the mid-1980s. This conclusion might be modified if a value could be placed on the nonmonetary advantages of the elite, but, on the other hand, fringe benefits for executives add to inequality in Western countries.

However, these conclusions cannot be attributed simply to the differences in economic systems, since the situation in the Central European communist countries appears to be distinctly different from that in the former Soviet Union. In particular, Czechoslovakia has a much lower recorded degree of earnings dispersion and of income inequality than Western countries. From our research, I conclude that the degree of inequality is influenced by the particular traditions and history of the country and that it can be affected by government policy.

A grand solution to the redistribution problem is the negative income tax. What are its major attractions to economists? And what are the major impediments in the political arena to its introduction?

A negative income tax means different things to different people. In its least radical form, it would involve the Internal Revenue Service paying to people below the tax threshold a proportion of the extent to which their income falls below that amount. As such, it appears to some economists as a better targeted form of redistribution, being directly related to income, rather than paid on the basis of unemployment, sickness, family size, or other criteria. The effectiveness of such a proposal depends on the level of the tax threshold and on the proportion of the gap filled, but it does not seem realistic to suppose that it would allow existing social security programs to be dismantled.

A more radical proposal, which has attracted more support in Europe, is for a *basic income policy*. In its pure form, this would replace all income tax exemptions and social security and welfare benefits by a basic income payable at so many dollars a week to every citizen. This

would provide a comprehensive guaranteed minimum income and would greatly simplify the benefit system. The problem is that the abolition of tax exemptions means that income tax would be due on every dollar of income. Moreover, to finance an adequate basic income, the tax rate would have to be set at a level that frightens politicians. The electorate has not been asked whether it would support such a plan, but politically it might be easier to redistribute by other means.

If you could start from scratch to write the tax code for a large country like the United States, or an emerging political grouping such as the European Community, what would the code contain?

I have difficulty answering this question, since I do not believe in immutable principles of economic policy. Economists have, for example, stongly advocated an expenditure tax in place of the income tax, and I can see the attractions. However, I do not believe that an expenditure tax is necessarily better in all circumstances. Similarly, economists have objected to the use of earmarked taxes, but again there may be occasions when they are desirable.

My conception of the proper role of the public finance economist is that of illuminating the choices open to democratically elected governments and to the voters who elect them. To this end, I would be happy to draw up a menu of choices—to draft two or three alternative tax codes—as the basis for political discussion and to advise on their possible implications.

This gives the central role to

the political authority, which is where it belongs in a democratic country. But one has to recognize that governments change, and one general principle that I will accept is that any tax code should ideally be sustainable in the face of changes in public opinion. No doubt rates of tax will be different with different governments, but a hallmark of a successful tax code is one that can accommodate different political preferences.

> "**A**ny tax code should ideally be sustainable in the face of changes in public opinion."

CHAPTER 17

UNCERTAINTY AND INFORMATION

After studying this chapter, you will be able to:

◆ Explain how people make decisions when they are uncertain about the consequences

◆ Explain why people buy insurance and how insurance companies make a profit

◆ Explain why buyers search and sellers advertise

◆ Explain why private information can limit the gains from exchange and how markets attempt to overcome these problems with warranties and other devices

◆ Explain how people use financial markets to lower risk

L IFE IS LIKE A LOTTERY. YOU WORK HARD IN SCHOOL, but what will the payoff be? Will you get an interesting, well-paying job or a miserable, low-paying one? You set up a small summer business and work hard at it. But will you make enough profit to keep you in school next year, or will you get wiped out? How do people make a decision when they don't know its consequences? ◆ ◆ As you cross an intersection on a green light, you see a car on your left that's still moving. Will it stop, or will it run the red light? You buy insurance against such a risk, and insurance companies profit from your business. Why are we willing to buy insurance at prices that leave insurance companies with a profit? ◆ ◆ Buying a new car—or a used car—is fun, but it's also scary. You could get stuck with a lemon. And cars are not unique. Just about every complicated product you buy could be defective. How do car dealers and retailers induce us to buy what might turn out to be a

Lotteries and Lemons

lemon? ◆ ◆ People keep some of their wealth in the bank, some in bonds, and some in stocks; and they hold a diversity of stocks. Some of these ways of holding wealth have a high return, and some a low return. Why don't people put all their wealth in the place that has the highest return? Why does it pay to diversify?

◆ ◆ ◆ ◆ In this chapter we answer questions such as these. We'll begin by explaining how people make decisions when they're uncertain about the consequences. We'll see how it pays to buy insurance, even if its price leaves the insurance company with a profit. We'll explain why we use scarce resources to generate and disseminate information. And we'll look at transactions in a wide variety of markets in which uncertainty and the cost of acquiring information play important roles.

Coping with Uncertainty

Although we live in an uncertain world, it rarely occurs to us to ask what uncertainty is. Yet to explain how we make decisions and do business with each other in an uncertain world, we need to think a bit more deeply about uncertainty. What exactly is uncertainty? We also live in a risky world. Is risk the same as uncertainty? Let's begin by defining uncertainty and risk and distinguishing between them.

Uncertainty and Risk

Uncertainty is a state in which more than one event may occur but we don't know which one. Usually, the event that does occur affects our economic well-being. For example, when farmers plant their crops, they are uncertain about the weather during the growing season, but their profits depend on the weather.

To describe uncertainty, we use the concepts of probability and risk. A **probability** is a number between zero and 1 that measures the chance of some possible event occurring. A zero probability means the event will not happen. A probability of 1 means the event will occur for sure—with certainty. A probability of 0.5 means that half the time the event will occur and half the time it will not. An example is the probability of a tossed coin falling heads. In a large number of tosses, half of them will most likely be heads and the other half tails.

In ordinary speech, risk is the probability of incurring a loss (or some other misfortune). In economics, **risk** is a state in which more than one outcome may occur and the *probability* of each possible outcome can be estimated. Sometimes the probabilities can be measured. For example, the probability that a tossed coin will come down heads is based on the fact that, in a large number of tosses, half are heads and half are tails; the probability that a

woman will give birth to twins is determined from the records of births in previous years; the probability of an automobile in Chicago in 1992 being involved in an accident is based on police and insurance records of previous accidents.

Some situations cannot be described by using probabilities based on observed events. These situations may be unique events, such as the introduction of a new product. How much will sell and at what price? This question cannot be answered by looking at the previous occasions on which *this particular* new product was introduced. But it can be answered by looking at past experience with *similar* new products, supported by some judgments. Such judgments are called *subjective probabilities*.

Regardless of whether the probability of some event occurring is based on actual data or judgments—or even guesses—we can use probability to study the way in which people make decisions in the face of uncertainty. The first step in doing this is to describe how people assess the cost of risk.

Utility of Wealth

Some people are more willing to take chances than others, but everyone prefers less risk to more, other things being equal. We measure people's attitudes toward risk by using their utility of wealth schedules and curves. A **utility of wealth schedule (or curve)** describes how much utility a person attaches to each level of wealth. The greater a person's wealth, other things being equal, the higher is the person's utility. The utility of wealth is based on the same concept of utility that you studied in Chapter 7. Not only does greater wealth bring higher utility, but as wealth increases, each additional unit of wealth increases utility by a smaller amount. That is, the *marginal utility of wealth diminishes*.

Figure 17.1 sets out Tania's utility of wealth schedule and curve. Each point *a* through *e* on Tania's utility of wealth curve corresponds to the row of the table identified by the same letter. You can see that as her wealth increases, her utility of wealth also increases. You can also see that her marginal utility of wealth diminishes. When wealth increases from $3,000 to $6,000, utility increases by 20 units and her marginal utility is 6.7. But when wealth increases by a further $3,000, to $9,000, utility increases by only 10 units and her marginal utility falls to 3.3.

FIGURE 17.1

The Utility of Wealth Curve

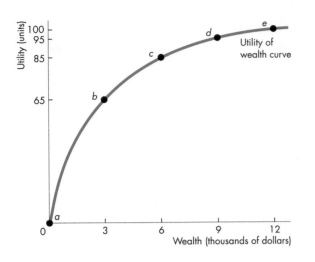

	Wealth (thousands of dollars)	Utility (units)	Marginal utility (units: change in utility ÷ change in wealth)
a	0	0	
b	3	65	. . . . 21.7
c	6	85	. . . . 6.7
d	9	95	. . . . 3.3
e	12	100	. . . . 1.7

The level of utility increases as wealth increases, but there is diminishing marginal utility of wealth—each increment in wealth brings a smaller increment in utility. Tania's utility of wealth schedule is set out in the table and shown in the figure. Each row of the table corresponds to a point in the figure.

Measuring the Cost of Risk

We can use Tania's utility of wealth curve to measure the cost of risk. The bigger the risk Tania faces, the worse off she is and the less she likes it. To measure the cost of risk to Tania, let's see how she evaluates two alternative summer jobs that involve different amounts of risk.

One job, working as a painter, pays enough for her to save $5,000 by the end of the summer. There is no uncertainty about the income from this job. If Tania takes this job, by the end of the summer her wealth will be $5,000. The other job, as a telemarketer selling subscriptions to a magazine, is risky. If she takes this job, her wealth at the end of the summer depends entirely on her success at selling. She might be a good salesperson or a poor one. A good salesperson makes $9,000 in a summer, and a poor one makes $3,000. Tania has never tried this line of business before, and she doesn't know how successful she'll be. She assumes that there is an equal chance—a probability of 0.5—of making either $3,000 or $9,000. Which outcome does Tania prefer, $5,000 for sure from the painting job or a 50 percent chance of either $3,000 or $9,000 from the telemarketing job?

When there is uncertainty, people do not know how much utility they will end up with from taking a particular action. The amount of utility they get is called *actual* utility. But it is possible to calculate the utility they expect to get. And they take the action that gives them the highest expected utility. **Expected utility** is the average utility arising from all the possible outcomes. Equivalently, it is the average utility the person would get if the action could be repeated a large number of times. So, to choose her summer job, Tania must calculate the expected utility arising from painting and telemarketing. Figure 17.2 shows how she does this.

If Tania takes the painting job, she has $5,000 of wealth and 80 units of utility, as shown in Fig. 17.2(a). There is only one possible outcome in this case. Her expected utility, which also equals her actual utility, is 80 units. Figure 17.2(b) shows the value to Tania of the risky alternative. If she makes $9,000, her utility is 95 units. If she makes only $3,000, her utility is 65 units. Her *expected utility* is the average of these two possible outcomes and is 80 units—calculated as $(95 \times 0.5) + (65 \times 0.5)$.

Tania does the best she can by maximizing expected utility. In this case, the two alternatives give the same expected utility—80 units—so she is indifferent between them. She is equally likely to take either job. The difference between Tania's expected wealth of $6,000 from the risky job and $5,000 from the no-risk job—$1,000—is just large enough to offset the additional risk that Tania faces.

FIGURE **17.2**

Choice in a Risky Situation

(a) No risk

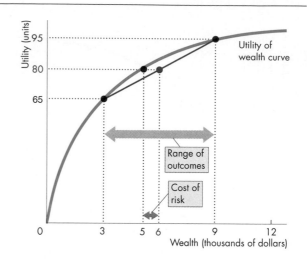

(b) Risk

To make a choice in the face of uncertainty, a person maximizes expected utility. In part (a), Tania's wealth is $5,000 and her utility is 80 units. In part (b), she faces an equal probability of having $9,000 with a utility of 95 units or $3,000 with a utility of 65 units. Her expected wealth

is $6,000—$1,000 more than in part (a)—but her expected utility is 80 units, the same as in part (a). Tania is indifferent between these two alternatives. The extra $1,000 of expected wealth is just sufficient to offset the risk associated with it.

The calculations that we've just done enable us to measure Tania's cost of risk. The cost of risk is the amount by which expected wealth must be increased to give the same expected utility as a no-risk situation. In Tania's case, the cost of the risk arising from an uncertain income is $1,000.

If the amount Tania can make from painting falls to only $3,000, the extra income from the risky job will be more than sufficient to cover her cost of the risk, and she will take the risky alternative of telemarketing. An income of $3,000 for sure gives only 65 units of utility, an amount less than the 80 units expected from the telemarketing job.

If the amount Tania can make from painting remains at $5,000 and the expected income from telemarketing also remains constant while its range of uncertainty increases, Tania will take the painting job. To see this conclusion, suppose that good telemarketers make $12,000, and poor ones make nothing. The average income from telemarketing is unchanged at $6,000, but the range of uncertainty

has increased. Looking at the table in Fig. 17.1 you can see that Tania gets 100 units of utility from a wealth of $12,000 and zero units of utility from a wealth of zero. Thus in this case Tania's expected utility from telemarketing is 50 units—calculated as $(100 \times 0.5) + (0 \times 0.5)$. Since the expected utility from telemarketing is now less than that from painting, she chooses painting.

Risk Aversion and Risk Neutrality

There is an enormous difference between Bill Parcells, former coach of the New York Giants, who favors a cautious running game, and Jim Kelley, quarterback of the Buffalo Bills, who favors a risky passing game. They have different attitudes toward risk. Bill is much more *risk averse* than is Jim. Tania is also *risk averse*—other things being equal, she prefers situations with less risk. The shape of a person's utility of wealth curve tells us about his or her attitude toward risk—about the person's degree of *risk aversion.* The more rapidly a person's marginal utility of wealth diminishes, the more the person dislikes risk—the more risk-averse the person is. You can see this fact best by considering an extreme case, that of *risk neutrality.* A risk-neutral person is one for whom risk is costless. Such a person cares only about *expected wealth* and does not mind how much uncertainty there is.

Figure 17.3 shows the utility of wealth curve of a risk-neutral person. It is a straight line, and the marginal utility of wealth is constant. If this person has an expected wealth of $6,000, expected utility is 50 units regardless of the range of uncertainty around that average. An equal probability of having $3,000 or $9,000 gives the same expected utility as an equal probability of having $0 or $12,000, which is also the expected utility of a certain $6,000. Real people are risk averse, and their utility of wealth curves look like Tania's. But the extreme case of risk neutrality illustrates the importance and the consequences of the shape of the utility of wealth curve for a person's degree of risk aversion.

FIGURE 17.3

Risk Neutrality

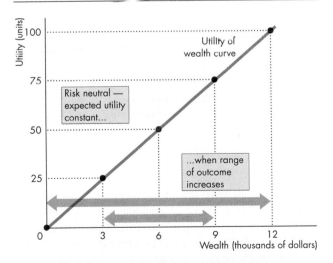

People dislike risk because they have diminishing marginal utility of wealth. A (hypothetical) risk-neutral person has a linear utility of wealth curve. Expected utility is constant, regardless of the range of uncertainty.

REVIEW

Uncertainty, a state in which the outcome is unknown, is described by using the concepts of probability and risk. Risk is a state of uncertainty in which the probability of each possible outcome can be estimated. The probability of each outcome may be estimated by using data or making judgments—called a subjective probability. Faced with uncertainty, people make decisions to maximize *expected utility.* Greater wealth gives higher utility, but the marginal utility of wealth diminishes. Because the marginal utility of wealth diminishes, greater risk with constant expected wealth gives smaller expected utility. To choose a riskier action, a person must expect a sufficiently higher expected wealth to compensate for bearing the higher risk. ◆

Insurance

One way of reducing the risk we face is to buy insurance. How does insurance reduce risk? Why does it pay people to insure? And how much of our incomes do we spend on insurance? Let's answer this last question first and take a look at the insurance industry in the United States today.

Insurance Industry in the United States

We spend close to 15 percent of our income, on the average, on insurance. That's as much as we spend on housing and more than we spend on cars and food. When we buy insurance, we enter into an agreement with an insurance company to pay an agreed price—called a *premium*—in exchange for benefits to be paid to us if some specified event occurs. There are three main types of insurance:

◆ Life insurance
◆ Health insurance
◆ Property and casualty insurance

Life Insurance   Life insurance reduces the risk of financial loss in the event of death. More than 80 percent of households in the United States have life insurance, and the average amount of coverage is $110,000 per household. More than 2,400 companies supply life insurance, and the total premiums paid in a year are around $300 billion. As you can see in Fig. 17.4, life insurance has been the greatest source of the insurance industry's business in recent years and has generated most of the industry's profit.

Health Insurance   Health insurance reduces the risk of financial loss in the event of illness. It can provide funds to cover both lost earnings and the cost of medical care. This type of insurance is growing rapidly, but in recent years it has not been highly profitable. Figure 17.4 illustrates its scale and relative importance.

Property and Casualty Insurance   Property and casualty insurance reduces the risk of financial loss in the event of an accident involving damage to per

sons or property. It includes auto insurance—its biggest component—workers' compensation, fire, earthquake, professional malpractice, and a host of other, smaller items. Figure 17.4 shows that we spend more on this type of insurance than on health insurance but not as much as on life insurance.

How Insurance Works

Insurance works by pooling risks. It is possible and profitable because people are risk averse. The probability of any one person having a serious auto accident is small, but the cost to that person in the event of an accident is enormous. For a large population, the probability of one person having an accident is the proportion of the population that does have an accident. Since this probability can be estimated, the total cost of accidents can be predicted. An insurance company can pool the risks of a large population and share the costs. It does so by collecting premiums from everyone and paying out benefits to those who suffer a loss. If the insurance company does its calculations right, it collects at least as much in premiums as it pays out in benefits and operating costs.

Why It Pays to Insure

To see why insurance pays and why it is profitable, let's consider an example. Dan has the utility of wealth curve shown in Fig. 17.5. He owns a car worth $10,000, and that is his only wealth. If there is no risk of his having an accident, his utility will be 100 units. But there is a 10 percent chance (a probability of 0.1) that he will have an accident within a year. Suppose Dan does not buy insurance. If he does have an accident, his car is worthless, and with no insurance, he has no wealth and no utility. Because the probability of an accident is 0.1, the probability of *not* having an accident is 0.9. Dan's expected wealth, therefore, is $9,000—calculated as ($10,000 × 0.9) + ($0 × 0.1)—and his expected utility is 90 units—calculated as (100 × 0.9) + (0 × 0.1).

Given his utility of wealth curve, Dan has 90 units of utility if his wealth is $7,000 and he faces no uncertainty. That is, Dan is just as well off, in his own opinion, if he has a guaranteed wealth of $7,000 as he is with a 90 percent chance of having wealth of $10,000 and a 10 percent chance of hav-

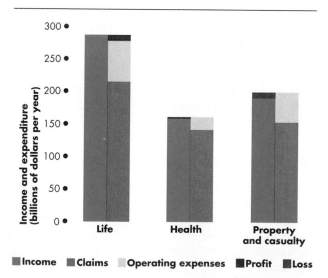

FIGURE 17.4

The Insurance Industry

Income and expenditure (billions of dollars per year)

300
250
200
150
100
50
0

Life   Health   Property and casualty

■ Income ■ Claims ■ Operating expenses ■ Profit ■ Loss

Total expenditure on insurance is more than $600 billion a year. Most is spent on life insurance, and in recent years this type of insurance has also been the most profitable.

Source: U.S. Bureau of the Census, *Statistical Abstract of the United States: 1991,* 111th edition (1991), 518–521.

FIGURE **17.5**

Insurance

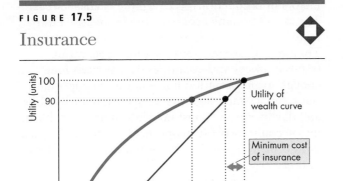

Dan has a car valued at $10,000, which gives him a utility of 100 units, but there is a 0.1 probability that he will have an accident, making his car worthless (wealth and utility equal to zero). With no insurance, his expected utility is 90 units and he is willing to pay up to $3,000 for insurance. An insurance company (with no operating expenses) can offer insurance to Dan and the rest of the community for $1,000. Hence there is a gain from insurance for both Dan and the insurance company.

ing nothing. If Dan can buy, for less than $3,000 ($10,000 minus $7,000), insurance that pays out in the event of an accident, he will be better off. Thus Dan has a demand for insurance at premiums less than $3,000.

Suppose there are lots of people like Dan, each with a $10,000 car and each with a 10 percent chance of having an accident within the year. If an insurance company agrees to pay each person who has an accident $10,000, the company will pay out $10,000 to one tenth of the population, or an average of $1,000 per person. This amount is the insurance company's minimum premium for such insurance. It is a smaller amount than the value of insurance to Dan because Dan is risk averse. He is willing to pay something to reduce the risk he faces.

Suppose the insurance company's operating expenses are a further $1,000 and that it offers insurance for $2,000. The company now covers all its costs—the amounts paid out to policyholders for their losses plus the company's operating expenses. But Dan—and all the other people who are similar to Dan—are better off with this insurance deal than without it. The calculations in Table 17.1 summarize the gain each makes. With no insurance, expected utility is 90 units. But with insurance costing $2,000, expected utility is 95 units, a gain of 5 units.

TABLE **17.1**

Risk Taking versus Insurance

(a) Possible outcomes	No accident Probability 0.9		Accident Probability 0.1	
	Wealth	Utility	Wealth	Utility
No insurance	$10,000	100	$ 0	0
Insurance	$ 8,000	95	$8,000	95

(b) Expected outcomes	Expected wealth	Expected utility
No insurance	($10,000 x 0.9) + ($0 x 0.1) = $9,000	(100 x 0.9) + (0 x 0.1) = 90
Insurance	($8,000 x 0.9) + ($8,000 x 0.1) = $8,000	(95 x 0.9) + (95 x 0.1) = 95

With no insurance, Dan's expected wealth is $9,000 and his expected utility is 90 units. By buying insurance for $2,000, Dan's expected wealth falls to $8,000, but he has no uncertainty and his expected utility increases to 95 units.

REVIEW

Americans spend 15 percent of their income, on the average, on life, health, and property and casualty insurance. Insurance works by pooling risks. Every insured person pays in, but only those who suffer a loss are compensated. Insurance pays and insurance is profitable because people are risk averse and are willing to pay for lower risk. ◆

Much of the uncertainty we face arises from ignorance. We just don't know all the things we could benefit from knowing. But knowledge or information is not free. We must make decisions about how much information to acquire. Let's now study the choices we make about obtaining information and see how incomplete information affects some of our economic transactions.

Information

We spend a huge quantity of our scarce resources on economic information. **Economic information** includes data on the prices, quantities, and qualities of goods and services and factors of production.

In the models of perfect competition, monopoly, and monopolistic competition, information is free. Everyone has all the information they need. Households are completely informed about the prices of the goods and services they buy and the factors of production they sell. Similarly, firms are completely informed.

In contrast, information is scarce in the real world. If it were not, we wouldn't need *The Wall Street Journal* and CNN. And we wouldn't need to shop around for bargains or spend time looking for a job. The opportunity cost of economic information—the cost of acquiring information on prices, quantities, and qualities of goods and services and

factors of production—is called the **information cost.** The fact that many economic models ignore information costs does not make those models useless. They give us insights into the forces generating trends in prices and quantities over periods long enough for information limits not to be important. But to understand how markets work hour by hour and day by day, we must take information problems into account, because people economize on their use of information just like they economize on their use of other productive resources.

We'll look at some examples, starting with a buyer's problem of searching for the lowest available price.

Searching for Price Information

In real-world markets, when many firms offer an identical good for sale, it is unusual for their prices to be identical. Usually, there is a range of prices and buyers want to find the lowest price. But searching takes time and is costly, so the buyer must balance the expected gain from further search against its additional cost. Let's see how buyers perform this balancing act, deciding when to buy and at what price.

You've decided to buy a used Mazda Miata, but you want to pay the lowest possible price. How will you find it? You can't just look at the advertisements in the Friday newspaper. They tell you the prices but not the qualities of the cars available at those prices. You're looking for a car in mint condition, so you need to check the dealers and do some test driving. It takes half a day to visit a dealer and check out a car. And you don't know enough about cars to trust your own judgment, so you take an expert along. The value of your time plus the cost of your expert's time is your opportunity cost. Let's call it $C per visit.

Thirty dealers are offering used Miatas at prices that range between $6,000 and $9,000. You know this is the range of prices, but you don't know which dealer is offering the lowest price for a car in mint condition. You are about to start your search, but how will you know when it's time to stop looking and to buy?

You need a decision rule. The *optimal-search rule*—also called the *optimal-stopping rule*—is to search for a lower price until the expected marginal benefit of search equals the marginal cost of search.

FIGURE **17.6**

Optimal-Search Rule

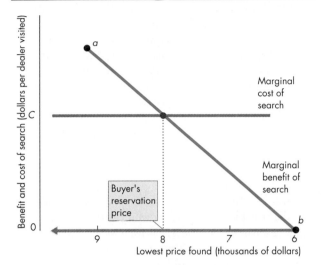

The marginal cost of search is constant at $C. As a lowest price found (measured from right to left on the horizontal axis) declines, the expected marginal utility of further search diminishes. The lowest price found at which the marginal cost equals the expected marginal benefit is the reservation price. The optimal-search rule is to search until the reservation price (or lower) is found and then buy at that lowest found price.

When the expected marginal benefit equals the marginal cost, stop searching and buy.

Your marginal cost is constant, $C, and is illustrated in Fig. 17.6 as the horizontal line. Your expected marginal benefit is not constant; it depends on the lowest price that you've found. Let's see how the marginal benefit curve is constructed. To do this, we'll go on an imaginary car shopping trip, not a real one. We'll do the real trip after we've discovered the stopping rule.

An Imaginary Car Shopping Trip   Suppose the lowest price that you've found for a used car in top condition is $9,000. You know that this is the highest price dealers are offering and that if you visit another dealer, there is a good chance that you'll find a lower price. If you do find a lower price, you will gain the difference between $9,000 and the price found. This amount is your marginal benefit. You won't find a lower price for sure. So you must multiply this marginal benefit by the probability of

obtaining it to calculate your *expected* marginal benefit. We'll suppose that this expected marginal benefit is greater than your marginal cost of search, as shown by point *a* in Fig. 17.6.

Next, suppose that the lowest price you've found is $6,000. You know that $6,000 is the lowest price at which cars are being offered, and since you've now found such a car, you can't do any better. Your expected marginal benefit from further search is zero. This fact is shown by point *b* on the marginal benefit curve in Fig. 17.6.

Lying between these two prices are all the other possible prices that dealers are offering. For any given price found, except for the lowest ($6,000), there is some chance that you'll find an even lower one. But the lower the price you've found, the less likely it is that you'll find an even lower price. Because it is less likely that you'll find a lower price, the *expected* marginal benefit from additional search diminishes as the lowest price found declines. That is, the marginal benefit curve slopes downward as shown in Fig. 17.6 when the lowest price found measured on the horizontal axis runs from *right to left*.

There is a particular lowest price found that makes the expected marginal benefit equal to the marginal cost of visiting one more dealer. It is called the buyer's reservation price. The **buyer's reservation price** is the highest price that the buyer is willing to pay for a good. The buyer will happily buy for a lower price than the reservation price but will continue to search for a lower price if the lowest price found exceeds the reservation price. At the buyer's reservation price, the expected marginal benefit of search equals the marginal cost of search.

We can now state the **optimal-search rule**: search until an item is found at or below the buyer's reservation price and then stop searching and buy.

A Real Car Shopping Trip   Real car shoppers are confronted with a much bigger problem than the one we've just studied. They probably don't even know the range of prices being offered. Also, there are many more dimensions of the car they are looking for than its price. They could spend almost forever gathering information about the alternatives. But at some point in their search, they decide they've done enough looking and make a decision to buy. The imaginary shopping trip rationalizes their decision. Real shoppers are saying, the benefits I expect from further search are insufficient to make it worth going on with the process. They don't do the calculations we've just done—at least, not explicitly—but their actions can be explained by those calculations.

Real shoppers differ in their marginal cost of search and so have different buyer's reservation prices. As a result, similar items can be found selling for a wide range of prices. Such a case is described in Reading Between the Lines on pp. 470–471.

Buyers are not alone in creating information. Sellers do a lot of it too—in the form of advertising. Let's see what the effects of advertising are.

Advertising

Advertising constantly surrounds us—on television, radio, or billboards and in newspapers or magazines—and costs billions of dollars. How do firms decide how much to spend on advertising? And what are the effects of advertising? Does it create information, or does it just persuade us to buy things that we don't really want? What does it do to prices?

Advertising for Profit Maximization   A firm's advertising decision is part of its overall profit maximization strategy. Firms in perfect competition don't advertise, because everyone has all the information there is. But firms selling differentiated products in monopolistic competition and firms locked in the struggle of survival in oligopoly advertise a great deal.

The amount of advertising undertaken by firms in monopolistic competition is such that the marginal revenue from advertising equals the marginal cost of advertising. The amount of advertising undertaken by firms in oligopoly is determined by the game they are each playing. If that game is a *prisoners' dilemma,* they might end up spending amounts that lower their combined profits but that they can't avoid spending without being wiped out by other firms in the industry.

Persuasion or Information   Much advertising is designed to persuade us that the product being advertised is the best in its class. For example, the Pepsi advertisement tells us that Pepsi is really better than Coke. The Coca-Cola advertisement tells us that Coke is really better than Pepsi. But advertising also informs. It provides information about the quality and price of a good or service.

Does advertising mainly persuade or mainly inform? The answer varies for different goods and different types of markets. Goods whose quality can be assessed *before* they are bought are called *search goods.* Typically, the advertising of search goods mainly informs—gives information about price, quality, and location of suppliers. Examples of such goods are gasoline, basic foods, and household goods. Goods whose quality can be assessed only *after* they are bought are called *experience goods.* Typically, the advertising of experience goods is light on information and mainly persuades—is designed to encourage the consumer to buy now and make a judgment later about quality, based on experience with the good. Cigarettes and alcoholic beverages are in this category.

Because most advertising involves experience goods, it is likely that advertising is more often persuasive rather than merely informative. But persuasive advertising doesn't necessarily harm the consumer. It might result in lower prices.

Advertising and Prices   Advertising is costly, but does it increase the price of the good advertised? Since firms advertise to increase their profits, it makes sense for them to do so only if the consumer is willing to pick up the advertising tab.

But two lines of reasoning tell us that advertising can actually lower prices. The first is that to the extent that advertising is informative, it *increases* competition. By informing potential buyers about alternative sources of supply, informative advertising forces firms to keep their prices and profit margins low. There is evidence of such effects, especially in retailing. The second is that if advertising—even persuasive advertising—enables firms to increase their output and reap economies of scale, it is possible that the price of the good will be lower with advertising than without it, provided that competition prevents monopoly pricing. There are certainly economies of scale in advertising itself. That is, the effect of advertising on sales is much larger for large firms than for small firms. So, provided that a large firm does not become so large that it is able to extract monopoly profits, consumers will benefit from the greater preponderance of large firms made possible by advertising.

The final cost-benefit calculation on advertising is not yet available, and whether these pro-consumer aspects of advertising are the largest ones is not known.

REVIEW

Information on the prices, quantities, and qualities of goods and services and factors of production—economic information—is scarce, and people economize on its use. Buyers searching for price information stop when they find their reservation price, the price that makes the expected marginal benefit of search equal to the marginal cost of search. Sellers advertise to inform potential buyers of the good or to persuade them to buy it. Informative advertising can increase competition. If advertising enables economies of scale to be reaped, it is possible that it lowers the price of the advertised good. ◆

Private Information

So far we have looked at situations in which information is available to everyone and can be obtained with an expenditure of resources. But not all situations are like this. For example, it might be the case that one person has information that is too costly for anyone else to obtain. Such information is called private information. **Private information** is information that is available to one person but is too costly for anyone else to obtain.

There are many examples of private information that affects economic transactions. One is your knowledge about your driving. You know much more than your auto insurance company does about how carefully and defensively you drive. Another is your knowledge about your work effort. You know far more than your employer about how hard you work. Yet another is your knowledge about the quality of your car. You know whether it's a lemon. But the person to whom you are about to sell it does not and can't find out until after he or she has purchased it from you, and then it's too late.

Private information creates two problems:

◆ Moral hazard
◆ Adverse selection

Moral hazard exists when one of the parties to an agreement has an incentive, *after the agreement is made,* to act in a manner that brings additional benefits to himself or herself at the expense of the other party. It arises because it is too costly for the injured party to monitor the actions of the advantaged party. For example, Jackie hires Mitch as a salesperson and pays him a fixed wage regardless of the level of sales. Mitch faces a moral hazard. He has an incentive to put in the least possible effort, benefiting himself and lowering Jackie's profits. For this reason, salespeople are not paid a fixed wage. Instead, they receive an income that depends in some way on the volume (or value) of their sales.

Adverse selection is the tendency for the people who accept contracts to be those with private information that they plan to use to their own advantage and to the disadvantage of the less informed party. For example, if Jackie really offers the type of contract we've just described, it will attract lazy salespeople. Hardworking salespeople will prefer *not* to work for Jackie because they can do better working for someone who pays by results. The fixed wage contract adversely selects those with private information (knowledge about their work habits) who can use that knowledge to their own advantage and to the disadvantage of the other party.

A variety of devices have evolved that enable markets to function in the face of moral hazard and adverse selection. We've just seen one, the use of incentive payments for salespeople. Let's look at some more and also see how moral hazard and adverse selection influence three real-world markets:

◆ Markets for cars
◆ Markets for credit
◆ Markets for insurance

Markets for Cars

When a person buys a new car, it might turn out to be a lemon. If the car is a lemon, it is worth less to the person who bought it and to everyone else than if it has no defects. Does the used car market have two prices reflecting these two values—a low price for lemons and a higher price for cars without defects? It does not. To see why, let's look at a used car market, first with no dealer warranties and second with warranties.

Cars Without Warranties   To make the points as clearly as possible, we'll make some extreme

Profiting from Information

FORTUNE, DECEMBER 2, 1991

Reading the Customer Right

BY SUSAN CAMINITI

We're at Galeries Lafayette, a chic new Parisian clothing store in midtown Manhattan. A stylish woman in her 30s is speaking rapid French to a friend in front of a display of denim jeans. Spotting a pricetag, she turns to her companion and says in pristine English: "Are they kidding—$110 for a pair of *jeans*? I'm sticking with the Gap."

So are legions of other shoppers, which is why analysts who follow the Gap's stock closely are estimating the San Francisco retailer's earnings will grow around 20% a year during each of the next several years. Says Joseph Ellis of Goldman Sachs: "The Gap continues to be *the* apparel specialty-store leader in terms of product integrity and quality and fastidious attention to color, style, and detail."

The company has floated above the general misery in retailing by offering reasonably priced casual clothing that doesn't go out of style in a season but changes enough to keep shoppers interested. For example, fans of the Gap's popular $10.50 cotton T-shirt might find it in a dozen bright colors one month and pastels the next. Explains Millard—everyone

calls him Mickey—Drexler, 47, the Gap's Bronx-born, fast-talking president: "We just keep trying to figure out what people wear on a regular basis. Our business is reading signals from the customer day in and day out."

The merchandise, all with a Gap label, draws customers back again and again. Plenty of retailers offer private-label goods, but few have elevated their name to the dignity of a brand the way the Gap has. Tight cost controls help pump up profits: The company has goods made exclusively for it, mainly in the U.S. and Hong Kong, and large production runs keep unit costs low.

Drexler likes to boast that almost anybody can wear the Gap's clothes. That's because the company has wisely realized that those anybodies' bodies are changing. The Gap division now has four cuts of jeans for women and three for men. With names like Relaxed Fit ("loose-fitting, very relaxed leg") and Reverse Fit ("full at the top, tapered at the bottom"), the sizes recognize that baby-boom customers can no longer squeeze into the slim-cut jeans they wore to Woodstock. But they still want to wear jeans.

Drexler & Co. also understand that customers' lifestyles are changing with their figures. So there are now 213 GapKids stores, some with babyGap boutiques in them, selling tiny T-shirts, jeans, and sweaters for the under-12 set. While the Gap doesn't break out results for its divisions, Edward Weller, a retail analyst at Montgomery Securities in San Francisco, estimates GapKids made $13 million on sales of $125 million last year. To attract working moms and other shoppers too tired to trek out to the mall after work or on the weekends, new Gap stores are opening in busy downtown locations.

If imitation is the sincerest form of you-know-what, then the Gap is in the middle of an outright lovefest. Superfashionable—and superexpensive—designers such as Donna Karan and Giorgio Armani are selling their versions of the Gap's T-shirts, khakis, and jeans, priced mostly under $100. Is Drexler worried? "Sure," he says, "but, hey look, there aren't too many secrets in this business. It's just going to make us run a little harder." Talk like that makes the Gap's competitors worried too.

The Essence of the Story

The Gap is expanding quickly, and its earnings are forecast to grow by 20 percent a year during each of the next several years.

The Gap sells only its own label and has a big reputation for quality; attention to color, style, and detail; and reasonable prices.

The company keeps sales high by "reading signals from the customer day in and day out," making clothes that fit most people and locating downtown as well as in suburban malls.

The Gap keeps unit costs low by having goods made for it in the United States and Hong Kong in large production runs.

Fashionable and expensive designers such as Donna Karan and Giorgio Armani are copying the Gap's product range but offering their versions at higher prices—sometimes as high as $110 for a pair of jeans.

The Gap's president, Mickey Drexler, says there are no secrets in clothes retailing and competition just makes the Gap run harder.

Background and Analysis

Clothes retailing is a highly competitive industry, but many different types of firms compete.

Some jeans sell for very high prices (at designer boutiques); some sell for average prices (at the Gap); and some sell for very low prices (at discount chains).

A key reason for the diversity of prices is that buyers lack complete information on quality, and to get information, valuable time must be spent searching.

But the cost of searching for information is not the same for everyone. A person's opportunity cost of time spent searching depends on his or her wage rate. For people with very high wage rates, the opportunity cost is high. For people with low wage rates, the opportunity cost is low.

Suppose that everyone gets the same benefit from finding a pair of jeans of given quality, color, fit, and price. To find the "best buy," time must be spent searching. Other things being equal, the longer the time spent searching (shopping), the better is the buy found. But the marginal benefit from finding a better pair of jeans diminishes as shown in the figure by the marginal benefit of search curve MB.

The figure illustrates how differences in the marginal cost of search can lead to a variety of types and prices of the same product.

For high wage earners, the marginal cost of search is MC_H, for average wage earners it is MC_A, and for low wage earners it is MC_L.

High wage earners confine their search to the boutiques that sell expensive designer items, average wage earners go to the Gap, and low wage earners check out all the discount stores and keep looking until they've found the best buy in town.

The Gap is profitable and growing quickly because it incurs the cost of identifying the preferences of mid-range wage earners and produces the items demanded by this group at the least possible cost.

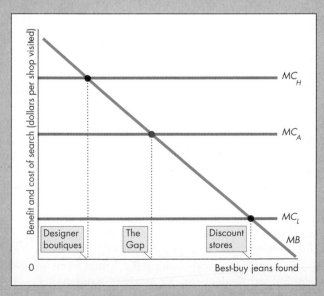

assumptions. There are just two kinds of cars, lemons and those without defects. A lemon is worth $1,000 both to its current owner and to anyone who buys it. A car without defects is worth $5,000 to its current and potential future owners. Whether a car is a lemon is private information to the person who owns it and has spent enough time driving it to discover its quality. Buyers of used cars can't tell whether they are buying a lemon until *after* they have bought the car and learned as much about it as its current owner knows. There are no dealer warranties.

The first thing to notice is that because buyers can't tell the difference between a lemon and a good car, they are willing to pay only one price for a used car. What is that price? Are they willing to pay $5,000, the value of a good car? They are not, because there is at least some probability that they are buying a lemon worth only $1,000. If buyers are not willing to pay $5,000 for a used car, are the owners of good cars willing to sell? They are not because a good car is worth $5,000 to them, so they hang onto their cars. Only the owners of lemons are willing to sell—as long as the price is $1,000 or higher. But, reason the buyers, if only the owners of lemons are selling, all the used cars available are lemons, so the maximum price worth paying is $1,000. Thus the market for used cars is a market for lemons, and the price is $1,000.

Moral hazard exists in the car market because sellers have an incentive to claim that lemons are good cars. But, given the assumptions in the above description of the car market, no one believes such claims. Adverse selection exists, resulting in only lemons actually being traded.

The market for used cars is not working well. Good used cars just don't get bought and sold, but people want to be able to exchange good used cars. How can they do so? The answer is by introducing warranties into the market.

Cars with Warranties   Car dealers perform two economic functions: they are intermediaries between buyers and sellers, and they do auto maintenance work (usually on the cars they have sold). The information they get from their auto maintenance business is useful in helping them make the market for used cars operate more efficiently than the market for lemons that we've just described.

Buyers of used cars can't tell a lemon from a good car, but car dealers can. From their maintenance

records, they have as much information about a car's quality as its owner has. They know, therefore, whether they are buying a lemon or a good car and can offer $1,000 for lemons and $5,000 for good cars.[1] But how can they convince buyers that it is worth paying $5,000 for what might be a lemon? The answer is by giving a guarantee in the form of a warranty. The dealer *signals* which cars are good ones and which are lemons. A **signal** is an action taken outside a market that conveys information that can be used by that market. In this case, the dealer takes an action in the market for car repairs that can be used by the market for cars. For each good car sold, the dealer agrees to pay the costs of repairing the car if it turns out to have a defect. Cars with a warranty are good; cars without a warranty are lemons.

Why do buyers believe the signal? It is because the cost of sending a false signal is high. A dealer who gives a warranty on a lemon ends up paying the high cost of repairs—and risks gaining a bad reputation. A dealer who gives a warranty only on good cars has no repair costs and a reputation that gets better and better. It pays the dealer to send an accurate signal. It is rational, therefore, for buyers to believe the signal. Warranties break the lemon problem and enable the used car market to function with two prices, one for lemons and one for good cars.

Markets for Credit

When a bank or other financial institution makes a loan, it is uncertain about whether the loan will be repaid. Some people always repay their debts and are better risks than others. But the lender has no way of knowing who is a good risk and who is a bad risk until after the loan has been repaid, and by then it is too late. Lending to low-risk people is much less costly than lending to high-risk people.

Faced with this situation, banks and other financial institutions use a variety of devices to minimize the risk they face. They check the credit worthiness of borrowers. And for large loans, they monitor the borrower's activities. They also often require the borrower to pledge assets that are valued more high-

---

[1]In this example, to keep the numbers simple, we'll ignore dealers' profit margins and other costs of doing business and suppose that dealers buy cars for the same price as they sell them. The principles are the same with dealers' profit margins.

ly than the loan to secure a loan. A secured loan, in effect, puts the risk back on the borrower. But many loans are unsecured. They are made to people on the basis of a promise to repay, and their ultimate worth depends on the value of that promise.

What determines the interest rate paid on unsecured loans? To see the problem, look at Fig. 17.7. "No-risk borrowers" in part (a) are those who always repay their loans and "risky borrowers" in part (b) are those who attempt to evade loan repayments and impose higher costs on the lender. The demand curves in the two markets are D_n and D_r. If the bank can sort borrowers into no-risk borrowers and risky ones, its supply curve of loans to no-risk borrowers is S_n and its supply curve to risky borrowers is S_r. The high interest rate at which loans are offered to risky borrowers reflects the high cost of lending to them. The bank lends Q_n to no-risk borrowers at an interest rate r_n and Q_r to risky borrowers at an interest rate of r_r.

But the problem is that the bank has no way of knowing who is risky when a loan is made, so the arrangement just described can't be implemented. Instead, the bank must charge the same interest rate to all borrowers. If it lends to all borrowers at r_n, no-risk borrowers borrow Q_n. The opportunity cost of these loans is reflected in the supply curve of no-risk loans, so the bank just covers its opportunity cost on these loans and makes no profit on them. Risky customers borrow Q'_r (in part b). But to get their money back from risky borrowers, banks incur a great deal of expense chasing borrowers, bringing lawsuits, and enforcing their claims. These costs are built into the supply curve for risky loans, so the banks incur a loss recovering these loans equal to the red rectangle in part (b). It's clear that banks would not be in business for long if this is how they operated.

Suppose the banks make loans available to everyone at the interest rate that covers the cost of lend-

F I G U R E **17.7**

Low- and High-Risk Borrowers

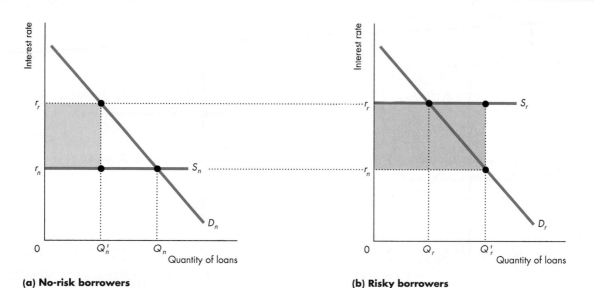

(a) No-risk borrowers

(b) Risky borrowers

Banks can't distinguish between borrowers with differing risk characteristics. If they could, they would lend to "no-risk borrowers" at interest rate r_n (part a) and to "risky borrowers" at interest rate r_r (part b). If they lend to all borrowers at r_n, they incur a loss on "risky borrowers"

(part b) equal to the red area. If they lend to all borrowers at interest rate r_r, they make a profit equal to the blue area in part (a). But they have an incentive to find ways of lending more to "no-risk borrowers," and competition among banks forces interest rates down below r_r.

ing to risky borrowers—r_r. In this case, the quantity of loans to risky borrowers is Q_r (part b), and the banks break even on these loans. No-risk customers borrow Q'_n at the interest rate r_r, and banks make a profit on these loans equal to the blue rectangle in part (a). If this is how banks operate, they will make huge profits and there will be a scramble to get into the banking business. Banks will also have an incentive to find ways of identifying no-risk customers and do even more business with them at lower interest rates.

Figure 17.8 shows what happens to resolve these problems. First, competition among banks for loan business forces interest rates down below the rate on risky loans. In the absence of any further changes, the interest rate will fall until the banks are incurring losses on risky loans and making profits on no-risk loans that balance out to a zero economic profit. At such a point there is no further entry into the loan business.

But banks use *signals* to discriminate between borrowers, and they ration or limit loans to

amounts below those demanded. Using signals such as length of time in a job, ownership of a home (even if mortgaged), marital status, and age, banks restrict the amounts they are willing to lend to each type of borrower. These loan limits are shown in each part of Fig. 17.8. The factors used to determine loan limits have a bigger impact on risky borrowers than on no-risk borrowers, so the amounts that the two groups can borrow based on these rationing devices are L_n and L_r. Competition between banks lowers the interest rate to r and shifts the supply curve to S. The profit on loans made to no-risk borrowers (the blue rectangle in part a) equals the loss made on loans to risky borrowers (the red rectangle in part b). Both no-risk borrowers and risky borrowers would like to borrow more. Both types of borrowers have an excess demand for loans. But these amounts of excess demand are efficient as far as the banks are concerned. They cannot increase their profits made on loans because they can't identify the type of borrower taking out the loan. And because far more risky borrowers are unsatisfied

FIGURE **17.8**

The Market for Loans

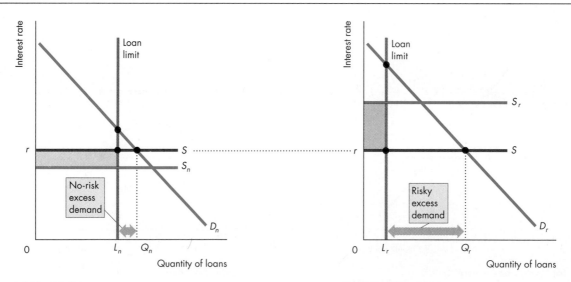

(a) No-risk borrowers

(b) Risky borrowers

Competition among banks forces the interest rate down until the profit on loans to "no-risk borrowers"—the blue area in part (a)—is equal to the losses on loans to "risky borrowers"—the red area in part (b). In an attempt to discriminate in favor of "no-risk borrowers" the banks use

signals and ration loans, imposing limits on the amounts that may be borrowed based on characteristics of their borrowers. The excess demand does not force interest rates up because banks can't tell the quality of potential borrowers.

than no-risk borrowers, it is likely that any new business will be biased toward high-risk lending.

Markets for Insurance

When we studied Dan's auto insurance, earlier in this chapter, we looked at problems that can arise from private information. People who buy insurance face a moral hazard problem, and insurance companies face an adverse selection problem.

The moral hazard problem is that a person with insurance coverage for a loss has less of an incentive to avoid such a loss than an uninsured person. While nobody goes out looking for an accident, the risk of an auto accident certainly depends on how carefully and defensively a person drives. Similarly, the risk of poor health and large medical bills depends on a person's decisions about exercise and diet.

In the absence of some means of overcoming moral hazard problems, insurance premiums are higher than they would otherwise be. Thus safe, defensive drivers and people who pursue healthy exercise and diets contribute more to the insurance fund than they receive from it, while the less careful drivers and less health-conscious individuals receive more than they pay in. As a result there is an adverse selection problem. Insurance companies attract high-risk people rather than low-risk people. That is, high-risk people tend to buy insurance, and low-risk people tend not to buy insurance but to self-insure—to bear more of the risk themselves.

Real-world insurance markets have developed a variety of devices for overcoming or at least moderating these private information problems. One device is that of using signals, much like banks do and based on similar criteria.

One of the clearest signals a person can give an auto insurance company is her or his accident record. Suppose that Dan is a good driver and rarely has an accident. If he can demonstrate to the insurance company that his driving record is impeccable over a long enough period, then the insurance company will recognize him as a good driver. It reasons that there is only a slim chance that a bad driver could have such a good accident record. If Dan has established a long and unblemished driving record, then he is most likely a good driver. It pays Dan to work at establishing a reputation as a good driver because he will be able to get his insurance at a lower price.

If all drivers, good and bad alike, can establish good records, then simply having a good record will not convey any information. For the signal to be informative, it must be the case that the cost of sending the signal increases with increasing risk. Thus it must be difficult for bad drivers to fake low risk by having a good record. These types of signals are used in car insurance in the form of "no-claim" bonuses that drivers accumulate the more years they go without making an insurance claim.

Another device used by insurance companies is the deductible. A deductible is the amount of a loss that the insured person agrees to bear. For example, most auto insurance policies have the insurer paying the first few hundred dollars worth of damage. The size of the premium varies with the size of the deductible and in a significant way. That is, the decrease in the premium is more than proportionate to the increase in the size of the deductible. By offering insurance with full coverage on terms attractive only to the highest-risk people and then by offering coverage with a deductible on more favorable terms, insurance companies can do profitable business with everyone. High-risk people fully cover at the full cost of their risk, and lower-risk people cover partially at a cost commensurate with their risk.

REVIEW

P rivate information, a situation in which one party to an exchange has information that is not available to the other party, creates moral hazard and adverse selection. In many markets, such as those for cars, loans, and insurance, methods have been devised to limit the problems caused by private information. Warranties, loan limits, no-claim bonuses, and deductibles are examples. ◆

Managing Risk in Financial Markets

R isk is a dominant feature of markets for stocks and bonds—indeed for any asset whose price fluctuates and is determined by demand and supply in a market. One thing people do to cope with risky asset prices is diversify their asset holdings.

Diversification to Lower Risk

The idea that diversification lowers risk is very natural. It is just an application of not putting all one's eggs into the same basket. How exactly does diversification reduce risk? The best way to answer this question is to consider an example.

Suppose there are two risky projects that you can undertake. Each involves investing $100,000. The two projects are independent of each other, but both promise the same degree of risk and return.

Project 1 will either lose $25,000 or make $50,000, and the chance that either of these things will happen is 50 percent. The expected return is (−$25,000 × 0.5) + ($50,000 × 0.5), which is $12,500.

Project 2 also holds out the same promise of return—a 50 percent chance of losing $25,000 and a 50 percent chance of making $50,000. But the two

projects are completely independent. The outcome of one project in no way influences or is related to the outcome of the other.

Undiversified Suppose you put all your eggs in one basket—investing the $100,000 in either project 1 or project 2. Your returns are illustrated in the frequency distribution shown in Fig. 17.9(a). You expect to make $12,500, which is an expected return of 12.5 percent. But there is no chance that you will actually make a return of 12.5 percent. You will either lose $25,000, a return of −25 percent, or make $50,000, a return of 50 percent, and the probability of each of these outcomes is 50 percent.

Diversified Suppose instead that you diversify by putting 50 percent of your money into project 1 and 50 percent into project 2. (Someone else is putting up the other money in these two projects.) What now are your possible returns? If both projects lose, your loss is $12,500 on each project, or a total loss of $25,000. Your return is −25 percent. If project 1 turns out to be a winner and project 2 a loser, you

FIGURE **17.9**

The Gains from Diversification

(a) Not diversified

(b) Diversified

With no diversification (part a), returns are equally likely to be −25 percent and +50 percent with an expected return of 12.5 percent. But with diversification (part b), the probability of the extremes falls and the

probability of the expected return increases. Diversification lowers risk.

lose $12,500 on project 1 and make $25,000 on project 2, or in total you make $12,500. Your return is 12.5 percent. Also if project 1 turns out to be a loser and project 2 a winner, you make $12,500—a 12.5 percent return. If both projects turn out to be winners, you make $50,000—a 50 percent return. There are now four possible outcomes, and each is equally probable. Each outcome has a 25 percent chance of occurring. The frequency distribution for your returns is now that shown in Fig. 17.9(b). Your expected return is still 12.5 percent, and there is now an excellent chance—a 50 percent chance, in fact—that your return will be 12.5 percent. There is now only a 25 percent chance that you will lose $25,000 and make a –25 percent return. Also there is now only a 25 percent chance that you will make $50,000, or a 50 percent return. By diversifying portfolio assets you have reduced its riskiness while maintaining an expected return of 12.5 percent.

If you are risk averse—that is, if your utility of wealth curve looks like Tania's, which you studied earlier in this chapter—you'll prefer the diversified portfolio to the one that is not diversified. That is, your *expected utility* with a diversified set of assets is greater.

A further consequence of risk in asset markets is the development of market institutions that enable people to avoid risk. One of these is the establishment of forward and futures markets.

Forward and Futures Markets

Producers are especially concerned about two uncertainties: the price at which they will be able to sell their product and the conditions affecting how much of their product will be produced. Farmers provide a clear illustration of the importance of these two uncertainties. First, when farmers decide how many acres of corn to plant, they do not know the price at which the corn will be sold. Knowing the price of corn today does not help them make decisions about how much seed to sow today. Today's planting becomes tomorrow's crop, and so tomorrow's price determines how much revenue farmers get from today's sowing decisions. Second, when farmers plant corn, they do not know what the growing conditions will turn out to be. Conditions might be excellent, producing a high yield and a bumper crop, or conditions such as drought and inadequate sunshine might lead to a low crop yield and disaster.

Uncertainty about the future price of a good can arise from uncertainty about its future demand or its future supply. We have just considered some uncertainties about supply. There are also many uncertainties about demand. We know that demand for a good depends on the prices of its substitutes and complements, income, population, and preferences. Demand varies as a result of fluctuations in all these influences on buyers' plans. Since these influences *do* fluctuate and are impossible to predict exactly, the level of future demand is always uncertain.

Forward Markets   Uncertainties about future supply and demand make future prices uncertain. But producers must make decisions today even though they do not know the price at which their output will be sold. In making such decisions, farmers are able to take advantage of special types of markets—forward markets. A **forward market** is a market in which a commitment is made at a price agreed here and now to exchange a specified quantity of a particular commodity at a specified future date.

Forward markets are very useful for farmers and others whose production decisions yield an output with a time lag. By engaging in a forward transaction it is possible to know the price at which the output will be sold even though the output is not yet available.

Futures Markets   Forward contracts enable farmers and others engaging in transactions for the future to reduce their risk arising from price variations. But they don't eliminate risk altogether. The person holding the contract has to stand ready to deliver or make delivery at the agreed price. In some situations it might not be convenient to actually deliver goods. In such a case the person holding a promise to deliver might want to sell that promise. To facilitate such exchanges, futures markets have been developed. A **futures market** is an organized market operated on a futures exchange in which large-scale contracts for the future delivery of goods can be exchanged. Rarely do futures contracts result in an actual delivery taking place. All futures contracts are liquidated through subsequent resale of the future promise before the delivery date becomes due. The existence of futures markets enables people to diversify risk in much the same way as holding a range of assets in a portfolio enables risks to be diversified.

Rational Expectations

To decide whether to engage in a forward or futures transaction, traders and producers must make forecasts of future prices. How do they do that?

Making Forecasts   The amount of time and effort devoted to making forecasts varies considerably from one individual to another. Most people devote hardly any time to this activity at all. Instead, they follow rules of thumb that, most of the time, seem to work well. But in important matters that directly affect their incomes, people will try to do better than that. One way of doing better is to simply imitate the actions of others who have a track record of success. Another way of doing better is to buy forecasts from specialists. A large number of forecasting agencies exist—from investment advisors and stock and commodity brokers to professional economic forecasting agencies. Such agencies have a strong incentive to make their forecasts correct, at least on the average.

The particular methods used to make forecasts are, of course, highly diverse, but our task is not to describe all of the actual methods used to make forecasts. Instead, our task is to build a model of forecasting. To build such a model, we use the fundamental assumption of economics—the assumption that people are seeking to get the most they can out of their scarce resources. In pursuit of that goal, forecasts will be correct on the average, and forecasting errors will be as small as possible. If any information is available that can improve a forecast, that information will be used. The forecast that uses all of the relevant information available about past and present events and that has the least possible error is called a **rational expectation.**

How does an economist go about calculating a rational expectation? The answer is by using an economic model. The economic model that explains prices is the model of demand and supply. Therefore, we use the demand and supply model to forecast prices—to calculate a rational expectation of a future price. We know that the point at which next year's demand curve intersects next year's supply curve determines next year's price. Until next year arrives, we don't know where those demand and supply curves will be located. However, we do know the factors that determine their position, and by

forecasting those factors we can forecast next year's demand and supply curves and forecast their point of intersection—next year's price. Let's work out a rational expectation of the future price of corn.

Expected Demand and Expected Supply   Our goal is to make the best forecast we can of the future price of corn. To make that forecast, we must forecast the positions of next year's demand and supply curves for corn. We learned earlier that the position of the demand curve for a good depends on the prices of its substitutes and complements, income, population, and preferences. The expected position of a demand curve, therefore, depends on the expected values of all these variables. In order to form an expectation about the future position of the demand curve of corn, it is necessary to forecast the future prices of corn's substitutes and complements, income, population, and current trends that might influence tastes. By taking into account every conceivable piece of available information that helps forecast such variables, farmers—or the specialists from whom farmers buy forecasts—can form a rational expectation of next year's demand for corn.

We also learned earlier that the position of the supply curve of a good depends on the prices of its substitutes and complements in production, the prices of the resources used to produce the good, and technology. An important part of the technology of farming is the biological process that converts seed to crop. That process, of course, depends in an important way on the temperature, the amount of sunshine, and the amount of rain. Expected supply depends on the expected values of all these variables. In order to form an expectation about the future supply of corn, it is necessary to forecast the future prices of corn's substitutes and complements in production, the prices of the resources used to produce the corn (the wages of farm workers and the prices of seed and fertilizers), and any current trends in weather patterns that might influence growing conditions. By taking into account every available piece of information that helps forecast such variables, people can form a rational expectation of the next year's corn supply.

Calculating a Rational Expectation   A rational expectation of next year's price of corn can be

FIGURE **17.10**

A Rational Expectation of Price

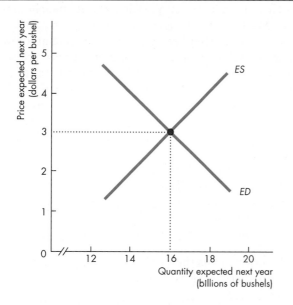

Since actual price is determined by actual supply and demand, expected price is determined by expected supply and expected demand. The point where expected demand, *ED*, cuts expected supply, *ES*, determines the rational expectation of the price ($3 a bushel) and quantity traded (16 billion bushels).

formed by bringing together expectations about next year's demand and supply. Figure 17.10 illustrates how to accomplish this. The quantities measured on the two axes are expectations of next year's price and quantity. The curve labeled *ED* is the best forecast available of next year's demand for corn. The curve labeled *ES* is the best forecast available of next year's supply of corn.

What do people expect the price of corn to be next year? They expect it to be $3 a bushel. That is the price at which expected quantity demanded equals the expected quantity supplied. People also can forecast next year's quantity traded. That forecast is 16 billion bushels. The price of $3 a bushel is the rational expectation of next year's price of corn. It is the forecasted price based on all the available relevant information. Producers use that forecast of the price to decide how many acres of corn to plant.

R E V I E W

Risk can be lowered by diversifying asset holdings. Diversification works by combining the returns on projects that are independent of each other. Risk can also be lowered by trading in forward markets. Such trading enables producers to know the future price at which their output will be sold. The existence of futures markets provides even greater opportunities for risk reduction. They enable people to take positions in forward markets without necessarily having to take delivery of goods. Decisions to engage in a forward or futures transaction are based on rational expectation of future prices. All organized asset markets determine a price that embodies all the available information about the future price. ◆

What are the implications of rational expectations for the way in which competitive asset markets work? Let's answer this question by looking at the stock market.

The Stock Market   The stock market is the market on which the stocks of corporations are traded. Figure 17.11 illustrates how a stock price is determined. The horizontal axis measures the quantity expected next period. The vertical axis measures the price expected next period and the actual price this period. This period's expectations of next period's demand and supply curves are shown as *ED* and *ES*. The intersection point of those curves determines the rational expectation of next period's price, *EP*. If the actual price rises above the expected price, people sell stocks. If the price falls below the expected price, people buy stocks. Thus the *current period supply curve* is the perfectly elastic supply curve *S* at the price level that is rationally expected for next period. The actual price (*P*) is equal to the expected price (*EP*).

We have seen that a rational expectation is an expectation that uses all the available information that is relevant for forecasting a future price. Since the actual stock price is equal to the rational expectation of the future stock price, that stock price also

FIGURE **17.11**

The Stock Market

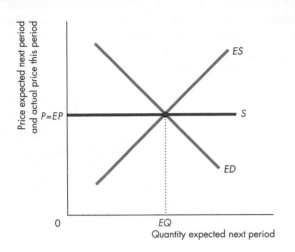

Holders of stocks form a rational expectation of the future price of a stock, *EP*, at the point of intersection of the expected demand curve (*ED*) and the expected supply curve (*ES*). If the price is above their expectation of the future price, stockholders sell. If the price is below their expectation of the future price, they buy. As a consequence, the current supply curve (*S*) is horizontal at the expected price (*EP*). These transactions keep the actual price (*P*) equal to the expected future price. Such a market is called an efficient market. In an efficient market, it is not possible to forecast a future price change and profit from that forecast. A foreseen price change is acted on immediately, and the actual price adjusts to eliminate the profit opportunity.

embodies all the relevant information that is available. A market in which the actual price embodies all currently available relevant information is called an **efficient market**. In an efficient market, it is impossible to forecast changes in price. Why? If your forecast is that the price is going to rise next period, you will buy now (since the price is low today in comparison with what you predict it is going to be in the future). Your action of buying today acts like an increase in demand today and increases today's price. It's true that your action—the action of a single trader—is not going to make much difference to a huge market like the New York Stock Exchange. But if traders in general expect a higher price next period and they all act today on the basis of that

expectation, then today's price will rise. It will keep on rising until it reaches the expected future price. Only at that price do traders see no profit in buying more stock today.

There is an apparent paradox about efficient markets. Markets are efficient because people try to make a profit. They seek a profit by buying at a low price and selling at a high price. But the very act of buying and selling to make a profit means that the market price moves to its expected future value. Having done that, no one, not even those who are seeking to profit, can *predictably* make a profit. Every profit opportunity seen by a trader leads to an action that produces a price change that removes the profit opportunity for others. Even the possibility of an intergalactic attack on New York City is taken into account in determining stock market prices— see the cartoon.

Thus an efficient market has two features:

◆ Its price equals the expected future price and embodies all the available information.

◆ There are no forecastable profit opportunities available.

The key thing to understand about an efficient market such as the stock market is that if something can be anticipated, it will be, and the anticipation will be acted upon.

Volatility in Stock Prices If the price of a stock is always equal to its expected future price, why is the stock market so volatile? The answer must be that expectations themselves are subject to fluctuation. Expectations depend on the information available. As new information becomes available, stock traders form new expectations about the future state of the economy and, in turn, new expectations of future stock prices. Expectations about the economy are of crucial importance: Is the economy going to enjoy sustained rapid expansion? Or is it going to suffer a recession? Macroeconomic events, such as expansion and recession, influence stock prices. Individual stock prices are influenced by technological change, which in turn influences the supply of and demand for particular goods and services. Since new information is being accumulated daily about all these matters, expectations about the future price of a stock are constantly being re-evaluated. It is this process of re-evaluation that leads to high volatility in the stock market. As expectations change from being optimistic to pessimistic, the stock market can plunge many percentage points—as it did dramatically on October 19, 1987. On the other hand, a sustained period of increasing optimism can produce a long upswing in stock prices. The five-year run from mid-1982 to mid-1987 is an example of such stock market behavior.

◆ ◆ ◆ ◆ We've studied the way people cope with uncertainty and how markets work when there are important information problems. In the next chapter we're going to see how the market economy solves one of its biggest problems—determining the distribution of the gains from economic activity. We'll also see how government programs modify the outcome of a pure market economy.

"Drat! I suppose the market has already discounted this, too."

Drawing by Lorenz; © 1986 The New Yorker Magazine, Inc.

SUMMARY

Coping with Uncertainty

Uncertainty is a state in which more than one event may occur but we don't know which one. To describe uncertainty, we use concepts of probability and risk. A probability is a number between zero and 1 that measures the chance of some possible event occurring. Risk is a state of uncertainty in which the probability of each possible outcome can be estimated. Sometimes the probabilities can be measured, and sometimes they cannot. When they cannot be measured, they are subjective probabilities.

People's attitudes toward risk are described by their utility of wealth schedules and curves. Greater wealth brings higher utility, but as wealth increases, the marginal utility of wealth diminishes. The cost of risk is measured as the dollar change in expected wealth necessary to keep expected utility constant in the face of a given increase in risk. Faced with uncertainty, people choose the action that gives them the greatest expected utility. (pp. 460–463)

Insurance

We spend 15 percent of our income on insurance, one of the most important ways in which we reduce risk. The three main types of insurance are life, health, and property and casualty. Insurance works by pooling risks, and it pays people to insure because they are risk averse—they value risk reduction. By pooling risks, insurance companies can eliminate the risks people face (from insured activities) and at a low cost in terms of reduced expected wealth. The lower risk is valued much more highly than the lower expected wealth. (pp. 463–466)

Information

Economic information is data on the prices, quantities, and qualities of goods and services and factors of production. Information is scarce, and people economize on their use of information just like they economize on their use of other productive resources.

Buyers search for price information—looking for the source of supply with the lowest cost. In doing so, they use the optimal-search rule of searching for a lower price until the expected marginal benefit of search equals the marginal cost of search. When the expected marginal benefit equals the marginal cost, stop searching and buy. There is a reservation price at which the expected marginal benefit of search equals the marginal cost of search. When a price equal to (or less than) the reservation price is found, the search ends and the item is bought.

Sellers advertise, sometimes to persuade and sometimes to inform. Advertising is part of a firm's profit maximization strategy. The general presumption is that advertising increases prices. But advertising can increase competition and enable economies of scale to be experienced, in which case it is possible that some prices are lower because of advertising. (pp. 466–469)

Private Information

Private information is the knowledge that one person has that is just too costly for anyone else to discover. Private information creates the problems of moral hazard—the use of private information to the advantage of the informed and the disadvantage of the uninformed—and adverse selection—the tendency for the people who accept contracts to be those

with private information that can be used to their own advantage and to the disadvantage of the uninformed person or firm. Devices that enable markets to function in the face of moral hazard and adverse selection are incentive payments, guarantees and warranties, and signals. (pp. 469–475)

Managing Risk in Financial Markets

Risk can be lowered by diversifying asset holdings, thereby combining the returns on projects that are independent. Risk can also be lowered by trading in forward markets, which enables producers to know the future price at which their output will be sold. Futures markets provide yet further opportunities for risk reduction, enabling people to take positions in forward markets without necessarily taking delivery of goods. Decisions to engage in a forward or futures transaction are based on rational expectation of future prices. A rational expectation is one that uses all the available and relevant information. It is correct on the average and has the smallest possible range of forecast error. Asset markets determine a price that embodies a rational expectation of the future price and are efficient. The stock market is an example of such a market. In such markets there are no forecastable price changes or profit opportunities. (pp. 475–481)

K E Y   E L E M E N T S

Key Terms

Adverse selection, 469
Buyer's reservation price, 467
Economic information, 466
Efficient market, 480
Expected utility, 461
Forward market, 477
Futures market, 477
Information cost, 466
Moral hazard, 469
Optimal-search rule, 467
Private information, 469
Probability, 460

Rational expectation, 478
Risk, 460
Signal, 472
Uncertainty, 460
Utility of wealth schedule (or curve), 460

Key Figures

Figure 17.1   The Utility of Wealth Curve, 461
Figure 17.2   Choice in a Risky Situation, 462
Figure 17.5   Insurance, 465
Figure 17.6   Optimal-Search Rule, 467
Figure 17.10 A Rational Expectation of Price, 479

REVIEW QUESTIONS

1 What is the difference between uncertainty and risk?

2 How do we measure a person's attitude toward risk? How do these attitudes vary from one person to another?

3 Why do people buy insurance, and why do insurance companies make a profit?

4 Why is information valuable?

5 What determines the amount of searching you do for a bargain?

6 Why do firms advertise?

7 What are moral hazard and adverse selection, and how do they influence the way credit and insurance markets work?

8 Explain how the used car market works.

9 Why do firms give warranties and guarantees?

10 How do deductibles make insurance more efficient and enable insurance companies to discriminate between high-risk and low-risk customers?

11 How does diversification lower risk?

12 What is the difference between a forward market and a futures market?

13 What is a rational expectation? How is such an expectation arrived at?

14 What is an efficient market? What types of markets are efficient?

PROBLEMS

1 Jimmy and Zenda have the following utility of wealth schedules:

Wealth	Jimmy's utility	Zenda's utility
0	0	0
100	200	512
200	300	640
300	350	672
400	375	678
500	387	681
600	393	683
700	396	684

Who is more risk averse, Jimmy or Zenda?

2 Suppose that Jimmy and Zenda have $400 each and that each sees a business project that involves committing the entire $400 to the project. They reckon that the project could return $600 (a profit of $200) with a probability of 0.85 or $200 (a loss of $200) with a probability of 0.15. Who goes for the project and who hangs onto the initial $400?

3 Who is more likely to buy insurance, Jimmy or Zenda, and why?

4 There are two independent investment projects: Project 1 is expected to give the investor a wealth of $200 with a probability of 0.5 and a wealth of zero with a probability of 0.5. Project 2 is expected to give a wealth of $300 with a probability of 0.5 and a wealth of zero with a probability of 0.5.

a Which project would a risk-neutral person invest in?

b How much would Jimmy (from problem 1) be willing to invest in project 1? In project 2?

c How much would Zenda (from problem 1) be willing to invest in project 1? In project 2?

d Draw a diagram similar to Fig. 17.9 illustrating the wealth resulting from investing in project 1, investing in project 2, and investing equal amounts in both projects.

5 Explain how the rational expectation of next year's wheat price is arrived at.

CHAPTER 18

THE DISTRIBUTION OF INCOME AND WEALTH

After studying this chapter, you will be able to:

◆ Describe the distribution of income and wealth in the United States today

◆ Explain the effects of income redistribution policies

◆ Explain why the wealth distribution shows greater inequality than the income distribution

◆ Explain how the distribution of income arises from the prices of productive resources and the distribution of endowments

◆ Explain how the distribution of income and wealth is affected by individual choices

◆ Explain the different views about fairness in the distribution of income and wealth

IFTY-THREE STORIES ABOVE MANHATTAN IS A PENTHOUSE with unobstructed views of Central Park, the Hudson River, and the city skyline: its price? $4 million. "Now, you can be one of the enviable few to fly Around the World by Supersonic Concorde . . . for just $26,800 per person," trumpets an advertisement in the *New Yorker*. Obviously, only the very richest Americans can afford homes and vacations as costly as these. Not quite within view of the $4 million penthouse, but not far from it, is Fort Washington Armory in Upper Manhattan. What was opened as a temporary shelter in 1981 permanently houses 850 men sleeping in one huge room. "As the men at Fort Washington stretch out on cots on the coarse wooden drill floor in a room the size of a football field, there is pervasive fear—fear of AIDS and tuberculosis, fear for physical survival. And there is widespread despair over the future. . . . There, side by side, are predators and their prey, the mental-

Riches and Rags

ly ill, alcoholics, men with limbs thinned by disease and malnutrition, others with muscles trained through exercise in prison."[1] ◆ ◆ Why are some people exceedingly rich while others earn very little and own almost nothing? Are the rich getting richer and the poor getting poorer? Is it fair that some people are incredibly rich while others live in miserable poverty? And what do we mean by fairness?

---

[1]*New York Times* (February 18, 1988): 1, 42.

◆ ◆ ◆ ◆ In this chapter, we study the sources of income and wealth inequality. We'll also study the connection between income and wealth and discover why the distribution of wealth is much more uneven than that of income. We'll see how factor prices and the quantities of factors hired, as determined in factor markets, result in unequal incomes. We'll also see how inequality results in part from the choices that people make. ◆ ◆ Most of the chapter deals with positive issues—with trying to understand the world as it is—and not normative matters—commenting on or making judgments about what is desirable. Nevertheless, the final section reviews some of the key contributions to the unending search for a widely acceptable concept of fairness. ◆ ◆ Let's begin by looking at some facts about the distributions of income and wealth.

Distributions of Income and Wealth in the United States Today

The incomes earned by the factors of production are the wages (including salaries and other forms of compensation) paid to labor, the interest (and dividend) income paid to the owners of capital, and the rental incomes received by the owners of land and minerals. Labor earns the largest share of total income, and that share has increased slightly over the years.

The distribution of income among individuals and families depends on the amount of labor, capital, and natural resources that they supply and on the wage rates, interest and dividend rates, and rental rates that they receive. The resource that everyone has in identical amounts is time. But the price at which a person can sell his or her time, the wage rate, depends on the individual's marginal product. That marginal product in turn depends partly on natural ability, partly on luck or chance, and partly on the amount of human capital that the individual has built up. The income from working is a mixture of a return on human capital and a compensation for forgoing leisure.

There is a great deal of inequality in the distribution of ownership of all other factors of production. We will more closely examine that inequality shortly. For now, let's just note that the total income of a

family depends on its labor income (including its returns on human capital) as well as its income from other assets.

In 1989, the average U.S. family income was $41,506. But there was considerable inequality around that average. Figure 18.1 shows the percentage of total income received by each of five equal-sized groups from the poorest 20 percent to the richest 20 percent of families in 1989. The 20 percent of families with the lowest incomes received less than 5 percent of total income. The second lowest 20 percent received less than 11 percent of total income. You can continue reading across the figure to see the percentages of income received by families that are increasingly better off. The 20 percent of families with the highest incomes received almost 45 percent of total income.

Although the distribution of income shows considerable inequality, the distribution of wealth shows even greater inequality. Wealth and income are

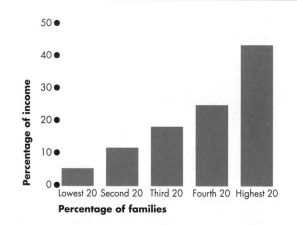

FIGURE **18.1**

Family Income Shares

One way of measuring income inequality is to calculate the percentage of total income earned by a given percentage of families, starting with the poorest. The figure shows us that in 1989, the poorest 20 percent of families earned only 5 percent of total income while the richest 20 percent earned 44 percent of total income. On the average, the incomes of the richest 20 percent of families were almost nine times the incomes of the poorest 20 percent of families.

Source: Current Population Reports, Consumer Income, Series P-60, Nos. 167 and 168 (1990) (Washington, D.C.: U.S. Department of Commerce, Bureau of the Census).

linked in a way that we will examine shortly, but it's important to remember the distinction: income is what you earn, wealth is what you own. Wealth is measured as the value of an individual's or family's holdings of real estate and financial assets. Average family wealth in 1988 was $36,000. The range about that average was enormous. The poorest 90 percent of families owned about one third of total wealth. The next 9 percent owned another third of total wealth. And the wealthiest 1 percent of families owned the remaining one third of total wealth.

Lorenz Curves

Another way of describing the distributions of income and wealth is presented in Fig. 18.2. The table divides families into five groups arranged from the lowest income (row *a*) to highest income (row *e*) and shows the percentages of income of each of these groups. For example, row *a* tells us that the lowest 20 percent of families receives 5 percent of total income; row *e* tells us that the highest 20 percent of families receives 44 percent of total income. The table also shows the cumulative percentages of families and income. For example, row *b* tells us that the lowest 40 percent of families receives 16 percent of total income.

The data on cumulative income shares are illustrated in the figure by a Lorenz curve. A **Lorenz curve** graphs the cumulative percentage of income (or wealth) against the cumulative percentage of families. The horizontal axis of the figure measures the cumulative percentages of families ranked from the lowest to the highest income. For example, the point marked 40 on the horizontal axis represents the 40 percent of families with the lowest income. The vertical axis measures the cumulative percentages of income. For example, the point marked 40 indicates 40 percent of total income.

If each family had the same amount of income, the cumulative percentages of income received by the cumulative percentages of families would fall along the straight line labeled "Line of equality." The actual distribution of income is shown by the curve labeled "Income." The points on the income distribution curve labeled *a* through *e* correspond to the family income shares shown in the table.

The horizontal axis of the figure also measures the cumulative percentage of families ranked from the lowest to the highest wealth, and the vertical axis also measures the cumulative percentage of

FIGURE **18.2**

Lorenz Curves for Income and Wealth

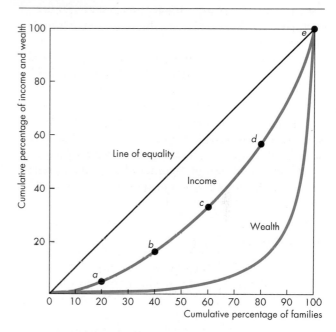

	Families		Income	
	Percentage	Cumulative percentage	Percentage	Cumulative percentage
a	Lowest 20	20	5	5
b	Second 20	40	11	16
c	Third 20	60	16	32
d	Fourth 20	80	24	56
e	Highest 20	100	44	100

The cumulative percentages of income and wealth are graphed against the cumulative percentage of families. If income and wealth were distributed equally, each 20 percent of families would have 20 percent of the income and wealth—the line of equality. Points *a* through *e* on the Lorenz curve for income correspond to the rows of the table showing family income. The Lorenz curve for wealth is based on the fact that the top 1 percent, the next 9 percent, and the bottom 90 percent of families each own about one third of total wealth.

Source: Income: *Current Population Reports, Consumer Income,* Series P-60, Nos. 167 and 168 (1990) (Washington, D.C.: U.S. Department of Commerce, Bureau of the Census). Wealth: Robert D. Avery and Arthur B. Kennickell, "Measurement of Household Saving Obtained from First Differencing Wealth Estimates" (Washington, D.C.: Federal Reserve Board, February 1990).

wealth. Plotting the cumulative percentage of wealth against the cumulative percentage of families gives the Lorenz curve for wealth—the curve labeled "Wealth." This curve is based on the distribution described above in which total wealth is divided approximately equally between the bottom 90 percent, the next 9 percent, and the top 1 percent of families.

The advantage of using Lorenz curves to describe the distributions of income and wealth is that they provide a graphic illustration of the degree of inequality. The closer the Lorenz curve is to the line of equality, the more equal is the distribution. As you can see from the two Lorenz curves in Fig. 18.2, the distribution of wealth is much more unequal than the distribution of income. That is, the Lorenz curve for the wealth distribution is much farther away from the line of equality.

Inequality over Time

Figure 18.3 shows how the distribution of income has changed over the years. The first impression gained from this figure is that the distribution has been remarkably constant. But a closer look reveals that from 1950 to about 1967 the distribution was becoming more equal—the richest 20 percent were becoming slightly less rich, the poorest 20 percent were becoming slightly less poor, and the three middle groups were not changing much. Since 1967, the trends have been reversed and the distribution of income has become less equal. All three of the lower groups have lost ground, and the two richest groups have gained. We do not have a good explanation for these trends at the present time.

These trends are apparent in other data and apply not only to the population in total but also to each major group. Reading Between the Lines on pp. 490–491 examines these trends for black families during the 1980s.

Who Are the Rich and the Poor?

We have seen that there is a great deal of inequality in income and wealth. But *who* are the rich and *who* are the poor? What are the key characteristics of rich and poor families?

The poorest person in the United States today is most likely to be a black woman living on her own, probably widowed, who is over 65 years of age, has

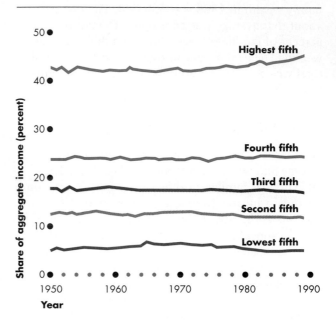

FIGURE **18.3**

Trends in the Distribution of Income: 1950–1990

The distribution of income in the United States became more equal between 1950 and 1967 and less equal after 1967. The main change was in the percentage of income earned by the highest fifth.

Source: Current Population Reports, Consumer Income, Series P-60, Nos. 162 (1989), 167, and 168 (1990) (Washington, D.C.: U.S. Department of Commerce, Bureau of the Census).

had less than eight years of elementary school, and lives in the South. The highest-income family in the United States today is likely to be a married couple, between ages 45 and 54, with two children. The adult household members in this family have had four years or more of college education, are white, and live in the Northeast. These snapshot profiles are the extremes in Fig. 18.4. That figure illustrates the importance of education, marital status, size of household, age of householder, race, and region of residence in influencing the size of a family's income.

Education is the single most important factor. On the average, people with eight years or less of elementary school earn $13,523 a year, while those with four years or more of college earn over $50,000 a year. Marital status is also important.

FIGURE **18.4**

Distribution of Income by Selected Family Characteristics in 1990

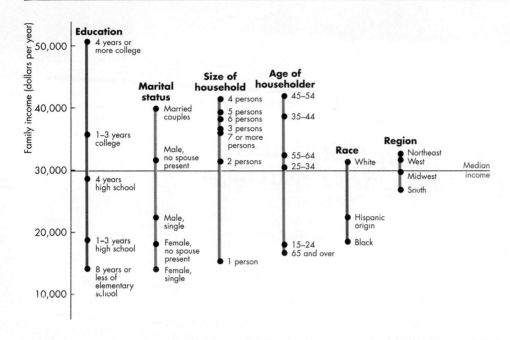

Education is the single biggest factor affecting family income distribution, but marital status, size of household, and age of householder are also important. Race and region of residence also play a role.

Source: Statistical Abstract of the United States: 1992, 112th edition (Washington D.C.: 1992), 446.

Single females, on the average, have incomes of only about $14,000 a year, while married couples earn an average income of $40,000 a year. Household size has an obvious effect on household income, but the household size at which income is highest is four persons. Age also is important, with the oldest and youngest households having the lowest incomes and middle-aged households the highest. Race and region of residence also influence the income distribution but on a smaller scale than the other characteristics that we have just examined. Black families have a median income of $18,700, while white families have a median income of slightly more than $31,000. The family with the median income is located in the middle of the income distribution—50 percent of families have higher incomes and 50 percent have lower incomes than the median income. Incomes are lowest in the South and highest in the Northeast, with those in the West fairly close to those in the Northeast and incomes in the Midwest lying midway between these two.

Poverty

Families at the bottom end of the income distribution are so poor that they are considered to be living in poverty. **Poverty** is an income level measured by a poverty index first calculated by the Social Security Administration in 1964. The index is based on Department of Agriculture assessments of the minimum consumption requirements of families based on their size and composition. In 1989, the poverty level for a two-person family was an income of $8,076. For a four-person family, it was $12,675. In 1989, 28 million Americans, 11.4 percent of the population, had incomes below the poverty level. The distribution of poverty is very unequal by race, with 6.8 percent of white families, 20.9 percent of Hispanic origin families, and 25.4 percent of black families being below the poverty level. Poverty is also heavily influenced by family status. More than 30 percent of families in which the householder is a female and no husband is present are below the

Black Inequality

THE SAN FRANCISCO CHRONICLE, AUGUST 9, 1991

Income Gap Widens Among U.S. Blacks, New Report Says

As the income gap widens between rich and poor in the black community, blacks may define themselves more by economic status than by race, demographic researchers reported yesterday.

"The middle-class blacks of the future may feel little in common with poor blacks because their experiences will have been dramatically different in so many ways," said the report, "African Americans in the 1990s." The study is the work of the Population Reference Bureau, a non-profit educational organization that reports on demographic trends.

Researchers found two black communities: "one of middle-class and affluent blacks who took advantage of the increased opportunities provided by the civil rights movement; the other poor, largely urban blacks who remain socially and economically isolated from the American mainstream."

The study documents the plight of the so-called black underclass but also shows that the number of black families with annual incomes of more than $50,000 doubled during the 1980s.

"In families headed by younger blacks, especially those with a college degree, average income is almost as high for blacks as it is for whites," said the report. "Among married-couple families where the head of household is 25 to 44 years old and a college graduate, the median income of blacks ($54,400) is 93 percent that of whites ($58,800)."

Dismal Findings

Overall, however, the report's findings are dismal.

"Economically, blacks fare poorly compared to whites," said Taynia Mann, one of four researchers who prepared the profile of black society in the 1990s from federal and academic statistics.

"They are more than twice as likely to be unemployed, much less likely to work in managerial and professional jobs, and earn 56 percent of whites' incomes. They are three times more likely to live in poverty and have an average net worth only 10 percent that of whites."

Single Parents Hit Hard

The report says that economic problems among black families can be linked "foremost" to the growth in households headed by women. In 1989, the average female-headed black family had only one-third the annual income ($11,600) of the average black family with both a husband and wife ($30,700).

"While most of the 10 million African households are family households, only half of them are headed by a married couple, compared to four-fifths of white families," Mann said.

Mann warned that African Americans cannot be sterotyped as a "monolithic" group.

"The report indicates in general that the black population is changing," said Mann. "In fact, there's an increasing amount of social and economic diversity within the African American population." . . .

The Essence
of the Story

A report, "African Americans in the 1990s," identified two black communities, an affluent middle class and a poor "black underclass."

The number of black families with annual incomes of more than $50,000 doubled during the 1980s, and young, college-educated, black married couples earned a median income of $54,400, 93 percent of that of similar white couples.

But compared to white families, poor black families are more than twice as likely to be unemployed, less likely to have managerial and professional jobs, and three times more likely to live in poverty. These families earn 56 percent of whites' incomes and have an average net worth only 10 percent that of whites.

Black families headed by women are among the poorest. They earn one third of the income of the average black married couple, and while four fifths of white families are married couples, only half of black families are.

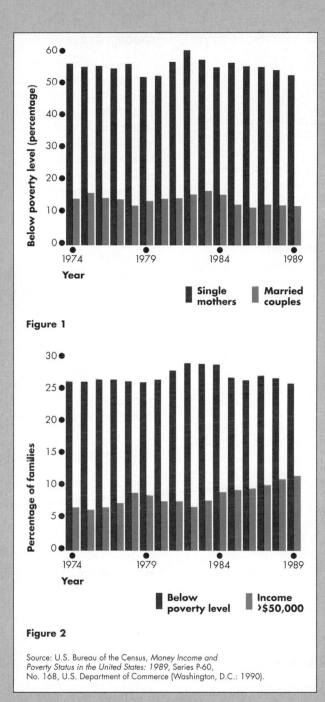

Figure 1

Figure 2

Source: U.S. Bureau of the Census, *Money Income and Poverty Status in the United States: 1989,* Series P-60, No. 168, U.S. Department of Commerce (Washington, D.C.: 1990).

Background
and Analysis

The findings of the report "African Americans in the 1990s" are similar to the official U.S. Department of Commerce current population reports.

But the Commerce Department's numbers reveal no simple trends during the 1980s.

Figure 1 shows the percentage of black families living below the poverty level. That percentage increased sharply between 1979 and 1982. After 1983, the percentage declined for both married couples and single mothers.

Figure 2 shows the percentages of all black families at the two ends of the income distribution. The percentage living below the poverty level increased through 1982 and then declined, and the percentage earning an annual income in excess of $50,000 (1989 dollars) declined through 1982 and then steadily increased.

poverty level, while fewer than 5 percent of other families are.

Extreme Wealth

We've seen that there are a large number of very poor families—families living in poverty. Are there a similarly large number of extremely rich families? The answer is no. Extremely rich families are rare in comparison with extremely poor families. For example, in 1985 there were only 32,000 families in the United States whose wealth exceeded $5 million, and those families had an average wealth of $10 million each. There were, in that same year, only 375,000 families with wealth of more than $1 million but less than $5 million. These families have an average wealth of almost $2 million.

R E V I E W

There is a great deal of inequality of income and wealth. The degree of inequality is illustrated by the Lorenz curve. The closer the Lorenz curve is to the line of equality, the more equal is the distribution. From 1950 to 1967, the distribution of income became more equal, and after 1967 it became less equal. The main influences on a family's income (in decreasing order of importance) are education, marital status, family size, age of householder, race, and region of residence. ◆

Income Redistribution

There are three main ways in which governments redistribute income in the United States today:

◆ Income taxes
◆ Income maintenance programs
◆ Provision of goods and services below cost

Income Taxes

The scale of redistribution of income achieved through income taxes depends on the form that the income taxes take. Income taxes may be progressive, regressive, or proportional. A **progressive income tax** is one that taxes income at a marginal rate that rises with the level of income. The term *marginal,* applied to income tax rates, refers to the fraction of the last dollar earned that is paid in taxes. A **regressive income tax** is one that taxes income at a marginal rate that falls with the level of income. A **proportional income tax** (also called a *flat-rate income tax*) is one that taxes income at a constant rate regardless of the level of income.

The income tax rates that apply in the United States are composed of two parts: federal and state taxes. Some cities also have an income tax—for example, New York City. There is variety in the detailed tax arrangements in the individual states, but the tax system, at both the federal and state levels, is progressive. The poorest families pay no federal income tax, the middle-income families pay 15 percent of their taxable income, and successively richer families pay 28 percent and 33 percent.

Income Maintenance Programs

Three main types of programs redistribute income by making direct payments (in cash, services, or vouchers) to people in the lower part of the income distribution. They are

◆ Social security programs
◆ Unemployment compensation
◆ Welfare programs

Social Security   The main social security program is OASDHI—Old Age, Survivors, and Disability Health Insurance. Monthly cash payments to retired or disabled workers or their surviving spouses are paid for by compulsory payroll taxes on both employers and employees. In 1990, total social security expenditure was $236 billion, and 39 million people received an average monthly social security check of $550.

The other component of social security is Medicare, which provides hospital and health insurance for the elderly and disabled.

Unemployment Compensation   To provide an income to unemployed workers, every state has established an unemployment compensation program. Under these programs, a tax is paid based on the income of each covered worker and a benefit is received by such a worker when he or she becomes unemployed. The details of the benefits vary from state to state. In 1990, more than 2 million people benefited from unemployment compensation programs and received a total of $15 billion.

Welfare Programs   Four state-administered federal welfare programs provide income maintenance for families and persons who do not qualify for social security or unemployment compensation. They are

◆ Supplementary Security Income (SSI) program, designed to help the neediest elderly, disabled, and blind people
◆ Aid to Families with Dependent Children (AFDC) program, designed to help families in which a single parent (usually a mother) has no other source of financial support
◆ Food Stamp program, designed to help the poorest families obtain a basic diet
◆ Medicaid, designed to cover the costs of medical care for families receiving help under the SSI or AFDC programs

Provision of Goods and Services below Cost

A great deal of redistribution takes place in the United States through the provision of goods and services by the government that the consumer pays for through taxes rather than as a fee-for-service. One of the most important of these services is education, especially college and university education. For example, in 1991, students enrolled in the University of California system who were state residents paid annual tuition fees of around $3,000. The cost of a year's education at Berkeley or San Diego in 1991 was close to $15,000. Thus California families with a member enrolled in these institutions received a benefit from the state government of $12,000 a year. Those with several college or university students received proportionately higher benefits.

The Scale of Income Redistribution

A person's income in the absence of government redistribution is called **market income**. One way of

measuring the scale of income redistribution is to calculate the percentage of market income paid in taxes and the percentage received in benefits at each income level. Making such a calculation in a way that takes into account the value of government-provided services is almost impossible. The only calculations available ignore this aspect of redistribution and focus on taxes and cash benefits.

The most recent year for which such a calculation has been done is 1980, and the results are shown in Fig. 18.5. This figure shows that the poorest 32 percent of the population receive more benefits than they pay in taxes—they receive net benefits. For example, people at the tenth percentile point (the

FIGURE **18.5**

The Effect of Taxes and Income Maintenance Programs on the Distribution of Income in 1980

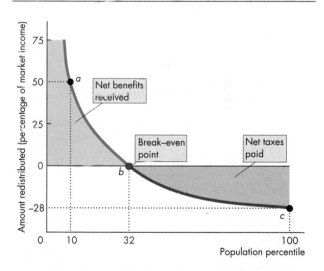

Taxes and income maintenance programs reduce the degree of inequality that the market generates. In 1980, the 32 percent of families with the lowest incomes received net benefits and the 68 percent of families with the highest incomes paid net taxes. Families at the 10th percentile received 50 percent of their income from income maintenance programs, those at the 32nd percentile broke even, and those at the top of the income distribution paid 28 percent of their incomes in taxes.

Source: Joseph A. Pechman, *Who Paid the Taxes, 1966–85?* (Washington, D.C.: Brookings Institution, 1985), 54.

point at which 10 percent are poorer and 90 percent are richer) receive benefits equal to 50 percent of their market incomes, on the average (point *a* in the figure). In contrast, the richest 68 percent of the population pay more in taxes than they receive in benefits—they pay net taxes. For example, the very richest people, on the average, pay 28 percent of their market incomes to the government in net taxes (point *c* in the figure). Those at the dividing line between these two groups break even, paying as much in taxes as they receive in benefits, on the average (point *b* in the figure).

Another measure of the scale of redistribution is provided by an examination of the sources of income of families at different points on the income distribution scale. The poorest 20 percent of families receive almost two thirds of their income in the form of payments from the government—called transfer income. Even the second 20 percent receive a third of their income in government transfers. In contrast, the richest 20 percent receive hardly anything from the government but receive a third of their income from capital—interest and dividends from financial assets. The fraction of income from that source for the other 80 percent of families is remarkably constant at about 8 percent.

Problems and Reform Proposals

Our complex and piecemeal income maintenance programs create several important problems and have led to a variety of reform proposals.

Problems

1. *Discourage work.* For many families, the income from not working and receiving benefits under programs such as Supplementary Security Income and Aid to Families with Dependent Children is larger than the income they can earn from working. In such a family, when a person gets a job and benefits are withdrawn, the family in effect pays a tax of more than 100 percent on the earnings. This marginal tax rate is higher than that paid by the wealthiest Americans, and it locks poor families in a welfare trap.

2. *Break up families and increase number of illegitimate children.* For many families, benefits are larger if the family breaks up or if a young mother is unmarried. The result is a kind of poverty trap—the limited opportunities for the children in

such families increase the probability that they will become low-income earners and join the next generation of welfare recipients.

3. *Create social tensions and unfairness.* Social tensions arise because the poor often believe they should receive larger benefits, and some people, especially those who work for low incomes, resent the payment of benefits to those who don't work. Unfairness arises because, ignorant of their entitlements, some poor families miss out on benefits.

4. *Create a costly administrative superstructure.* The cost of administering welfare programs is large, there being close to half a million people employed in the public welfare departments of federal, state, and local governments.

Reform Proposals   Several proposals have been made for the reform of income maintenance programs. One of these is the negative income tax. A **negative income tax** gives every family a *guaranteed annual income* and decreases the family's benefit at a specified *benefit-loss rate* as its market income increases. For example, suppose the guaranteed annual income is $10,000 and the benefit-loss rate is 25 percent. A family with no earnings receives the $10,000 guaranteed income. A family with earnings of $8,000 loses 25 percent of that amount—$2,000—and receives a total income of $16,000 ($8,000 earnings plus $10,000 guaranteed income minus $2,000 benefit loss). A family earning $40,000 receives an income of $40,000 ($40,000 earnings plus $10,000 guaranteed income minus $10,000 benefit loss). Such a family is at the break-even income level. Families with earnings exceeding $40,000 pay more in taxes than they receive in benefits.

A negative income tax is illustrated and compared with our current arrangements in Fig. 18.6. In both parts of the figure, the horizontal axis measures *market income*—that is, income *before* taxes are paid and benefits received—and the vertical axis measures income *after* taxes are paid and benefits received. The 45° line shows the hypothetical case of "no redistribution."

Part (a) shows the current redistribution arrangements—the blue line. Benefits of G are paid to families with no income. As incomes increase from zero to A, benefits are withdrawn, lowering income after redistribution below G. This arrangement creates a *welfare trap*—it does not pay a person to work if the

Comparing Current Income Maintenance Programs and a Negative Income Tax

(a) Current redistribution arrangements

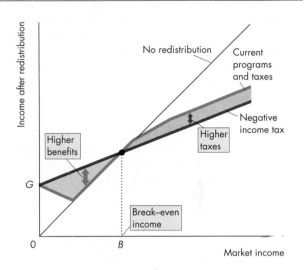

(b) A negative income tax

The 45° line shows the hypothetical case of no redistribution. Part (a) shows the current redistribution arrangements —the blue line. Benefits of G are paid to people with no income. As incomes increase from zero to A, benefits are withdrawn, *lowering* income after redistribution below G and creating a welfare trap—the gray triangle in the figure. In the range A to C, there is no redistribution. As incomes rise above C, income taxes are paid at successively higher rates.

In part (b), a negative income tax gives a guaranteed annual income of G and decreases benefits at the same rate as the tax rate on incomes. The red line shows how market incomes translate into income after redistribution. Families with market incomes below B, the break-even income, receive benefits. Those with market incomes above B pay taxes.

---

income he or she can earn is less than A. The welfare trap is shown as the gray triangle in the figure. Over the income range A to C, each additional dollar of market income increases income after redistribution by a dollar. At incomes greater than C, income taxes are paid, at successively higher rates, and income after redistribution is smaller than market income.

Part (b) shows the negative income tax. The guaranteed annual income is G, and the break-even income is B. Families with market incomes below B receive a net benefit (blue area), and those with incomes above B pay taxes (red area). You can see why such a scheme is called a negative income tax. Every family receives a guaranteed minimum income, and every family pays a tax on its earnings—losing benefits is like paying a tax—but fami-

lies below the break-even income level receive more than they pay and so, in total, pay a negative amount of tax.

A negative income tax removes the welfare trap (the gray triangle) and gives greater encouragement to low-income families to seek additional employment, even at a low wage. It also overcomes many of the other problems arising from existing income maintenance programs.

So why don't we have a negative income tax scheme? The main reason is cost. The guaranteed annual income that puts a family of four on the official *poverty* level is $12,675. With a benefit-loss rate equal to 20 percent—a rate similar to the income tax rate for most families—the break-even income level is $63,375. This income level is much higher than the average income, and the taxes on families with incomes above this level would increase substantially (as shown in Fig. 18.6b). Less generous negative income tax schemes are feasible, but most welfare experts believe that a better job can be done by a more piecemeal approach to reform.

The critical aspect of welfare that is receiving attention is the removal of disincentives to work and the encouragement of people on welfare to find jobs. The Family Support Act of 1988 is an attempt to do just this. Its Job Opportunities and Basic Skills (JOBS) program provides education and training; it provides incentives for young people to complete high school education; it provides benefits to two-parent families to discourage family breakups; and it requires unpaid work—*workfare*—by one member of a two-parent welfare family. It is too early to know whether the 1988 act is achieving its objectives.

R E V I E W

Governments redistribute income in the United States using income taxes, income maintenance programs, and provision of goods and services below cost. The income maintenance programs are social security, unemployment compensation, and welfare. The poorest 20 percent of families receive almost two thirds of their income from the government. Existing programs tend to discourage work, encourage family breakup and illegitimacy, create social tensions, and are costly to administer. Proposals for reform include a negative income tax that gives every family a guaranteed annual income but that lowers the disincentives faced by the poor and encourages them to seek work, even if it is low paid. Removing disincentives to work and encouraging people on welfare to find jobs is also the main focus of the Family Support Act of 1988. ◆

Comparing Like with Like

In order to determine just how much inequality there is, it is

necessary to compare one person's economic situation with another's. But what is the correct comparison? Should we be looking at income, or should we be looking at wealth? And should we, as we have so far, look at *annual* income, or should we look at income over some other time period—for example, over a family's lifetime?

Wealth versus Income

The main reason wealth is distributed much more unequally than income is that the data on wealth and income measure different things. The wealth data refer only to nonhuman capital—tangible assets that are traded on capital markets (such as those items analyzed in Chapter 16). The data on income distribution refer to income from all sources, not only from nonhuman capital but also from human capital. Let's explore the sources of these differences a bit more closely by looking at an example. We will begin, however, by refreshing our memory of the distinction between *income* and *wealth*.

Income and Wealth: Flow and Stock   Income and wealth can be considered different ways of looking at precisely the same thing. *Wealth* is the *stock* of assets owned by an individual. *Income* is the *flow* of earnings received by an individual. It is the *flow of earnings* that results from the *stock of wealth*. It is easiest to see the relationship between income and wealth by considering an example. Suppose that Lee owns assets worth $1 million. Thus Lee's wealth is $1 million. If the rate of return on assets is 5 percent a year, then Lee will receive an income of $50,000 a year from his assets of $1 million. We can describe Lee's economic condition by saying that he has either wealth of $1 million or an income of $50,000. If the rate of return is 5 percent, these two statements are equivalent to each other.

In order to talk about the distribution of income and wealth, let's consider two individuals: Lee, who has wealth of $1 million and income of $50,000, and Peter, who has assets of $500,000. Peter and Lee have the same investment opportunities, and they invest their assets at the same rate of return—5 percent a year. Peter has an income of $25,000 (5 percent of $500,000). We can now talk about the distribution of wealth and income between Peter and Lee. Lee has wealth of $1 million compared with Peter's wealth of $500,000. Thus Lee has twice as much wealth as Peter. Lee has an income of $50,000, and Peter has an income of $25,000.

Again, Lee's income is twice as much as Peter's. Regardless of whether we compare Peter and Lee on the basis of their wealth or their income, we reach the same conclusion: Lee is twice as rich as Peter, in terms of both wealth and income.

Human Capital

So far, we have discussed only the earnings that Peter and Lee receive from their nonhuman wealth. We sometimes refer to physical and financial assets as *tangible assets* or, to contrast them with human capital, as *nonhuman capital*. What about their work effort? The earnings received from work are partly a compensation for giving up leisure time and partly a return on *human capital*. Although human capital represents intangible things like skills, we can put a value on it. We value human capital by looking at the earnings that a person can make from working over and above what would be earned by someone who has had no education or training. The extra earnings are the income from human capital. The value of human capital is the amount of money that a person would have to be given today so that, if invested, it would generate an interest income equal to the income from that individual's human capital.

Consider Peter and Lee again. Suppose now that each of them has no assets other than their productive skills. Lee earns $50,000 a year, and if the interest rate is 5 percent a year, then Lee has $1 million of human capital. A million dollars invested at an interest rate of 5 percent a year will earn $50,000 a year. Peter earns $25,000 a year, and, again, if the interest rate is 5 percent a year, Peter has human capital of $500,000. Lee earns twice as much income as does Peter, and Lee has twice as much human capital.

Human and Nonhuman Capital

We have now considered the distributions of income and wealth in two extreme cases. In the first case, Lee and Peter owned no human capital, so their entire income was generated by their financial and real assets. In the second case, Lee and Peter had only human capital—their productive skills. Most people have both nonhuman and human capital. Wealth, correctly measured, includes both of these types of capital.

No matter what the source of income—whether human capital or nonhuman capital—the distribu-

tion of wealth and income is the same when we count both human and nonhuman capital. In both the cases that we have just examined, Lee has twice the wealth and twice the income of Peter. So the distribution of wealth between Lee and Peter is identical to the distribution of income between them.

Let's finally examine the case in which Peter and Lee have both human capital and nonhuman capital. For a reason that will become apparent shortly, however, let's suppose that Peter has much more human capital than does Lee and that Lee has more nonhuman capital than does Peter. Table 18.1 sets out some hypothetical numbers to illustrate this case. As before, Lee has twice the total wealth and twice the total income of Peter. Lee's human capital is only $200,000, so Lee's labor income is just $10,000. But Lee has nonhuman capital of $800,000, which generates an income of $40,000. In contrast, Peter's wealth is almost exclusively human capital. Peter earns $24,950 of income from $499,000 worth of human capital. Peter has only $1,000 worth of tangible assets (nonhuman capital), which generates an annual income of $50.

Suppose that a national wealth and income surveyor is examining this economy comprised of Peter and Lee and observes their incomes of $25,000 and $50,000, respectively. The surveyor concludes that on the basis of income, Lee is twice as rich as Peter. The surveyor then measures their assets. The only assets that are measured are tangible assets. The surveyor observes that Lee owns $800,000 worth of such assets and Peter has $1,000 worth. The assets are listed in a distribution of wealth table, and the

TABLE **18.1**

Capital, Wealth, and Income

	Lee		Peter	
	Wealth	Income	Wealth	Income
Human capital	$ 200,000	$10,000	$499,000	$24,950
Nonhuman capital	800,000	40,000	1,000	50
Total	$1,000,000	$50,000	$500,000	$25,000

When wealth is measured to include the value of human capital as well as nonhuman capital, the distribution of income and the distribution of wealth display the same degree of inequality.

national surveyor concludes that, in terms of assets, Lee is 800 times as wealthy as Peter. The national survey concludes that wealth is much more unevenly distributed than income.

You can see that the national survey techniques measure the distribution of wealth in a way that does not include human capital. The distribution of income takes into account human capital and is the correct measure of the distribution of economic resources. Measured wealth distributions that ignore the distribution of human capital overstate the inequality among individuals.

Annual or Lifetime Income and Wealth

The income distributions that we examined earlier in this chapter are based on annual incomes. And the wealth distributions are based on measuring family wealth in a given year. There are many sources of inequality in annual income and in wealth in a given year, but these do not imply inequality over a family's entire lifetime. For example, young people earn less, on the average, than middle-aged people. Thus in a given year, a young family has a lower income than a middle-aged family. But when the young family becomes middle-aged itself, its income on the average will not differ from the current middle-aged family's income. This is an example of an inequality in annual income that does not reflect an inequality across families over their entire lifetimes. The case of wealth is more extreme. Most young families have few assets and often have debts that exceed those assets. Families with people between middle age and retirement age are at a stage in life when they're building up their assets to provide for a retirement income. Again, the older family looks wealthier than the younger family, but by the time the younger family reaches that same later stage in the life cycle, it will have accumulated assets similar in scale to those of the existing older family.

In order to compare the income and wealth situation of one family with another, it is important that we take into account the family's stage in the life cycle and not be misled by differences arising purely from that factor. To illustrate the importance of this source of inequality, we'll work through an example.

Figure 18.7 shows a family's income, consumption, and wealth over its entire life cycle. The horizontal axis in both parts measures age. The vertical axis measures thousands of dollars of income and consumption in part (a) and of wealth in part (b).

FIGURE **18.7**

Life-Cycle Income, Consumption, and Wealth

(a) Income and consumption

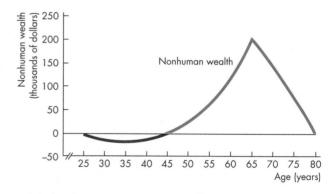

(b) Nonhuman wealth

Part (a) of the figure shows the consumption and income of a household. Consumption is constant at $20,000 a year throughout the lifetime. Labor income starts at $18,000 and gradually increases to $30,000 at retirement. After retirement, the household has no labor income. Total income is labor income plus interest on capital (on nonhuman wealth). Part (b) shows the household's nonhuman wealth. In its early years, the household is consuming more than its income and going into debt. At age 35, the household is at its maximum debt. After that time, the household gradually gets out of debt and begins to accumulate nonhuman wealth up to retirement age. After retirement the household spends its nonhuman wealth throughout the rest of its life. An economy populated by households like this one but with each household at a different stage in its life cycle will have highly unequal distributions of annual income and wealth. The small fraction of the population close to (both before and after) retirement will own almost all the economy's nonhuman wealth.

Part (a) shows the pattern of income and consumption. This family consumes at a steady rate of $20,000 a year throughout its life. The family's income from employment starts out at $18,000 a year. It gradually rises until, just before retirement, the family is earning $30,000 a year. After retirement the family's income from work is zero, but it continues to receive an income in the form of interest on the capital that it has accumulated in the years before retirement. (Some of the transactions of this hypothetical family are being ignored—for example, the purchase of a house, an automobile, and other consumer durable goods. For the purpose of this example, let's imagine that when the family bought these items, it financed their purchase by borrowing. Thus any real assets owned by the family had offsetting financial liabilities and therefore did not change the family's wealth.)

Part (b) shows the family's nonhuman wealth. At first, the family has to borrow to sustain its consumption level. As it does so, it incurs debt and also has to pay interest on the debt. The family is at its deepest point of debt at age 35. After that age, the family gradually gets out of debt and, through its sixties, starts accumulating a great deal of nonhuman wealth. After retirement, that nonhuman wealth is spent on post-retirement consumption.

Now suppose that there are two families identical to the one that we've looked at here but at different stages of the life cycle. One of these families is 25 years old, and the other is 66. If all we look at is income, we will conclude that the 25-year-old family is almost twice as well off as the 66-year-old family. If all we look at is nonhuman wealth, we will conclude that the 66-year-old family, which has accumulated assets worth $200,000, is much better off than the 25-year-old family. Yet from the point of view of consumption, these two families are identical.

If the entire population of this imaginary economy is made up of families that are identical except for their stage of the life cycle, and if there are an equal number of people at each age, we discover some startling facts about the distributions of wealth and annual income. First, let's look at the distribution of nonhuman wealth in this imaginary economy. That distribution is illustrated in Fig. 18.8. For comparison, the wealth distribution in the United States is also shown. As you can see, the Lorenz curve for the imaginary economy's wealth distribution lies inside that for the actual U.S. economy, so

FIGURE **18.8**

Lorenz Curves for Imaginary and Actual Economies

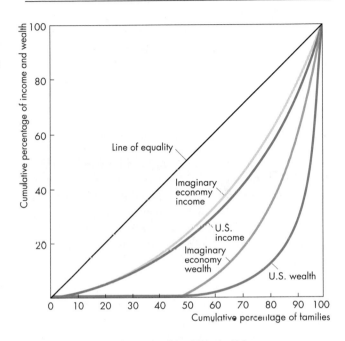

The Lorenz curves for income and wealth in the U.S. economy are shown alongside those for an imaginary economy in which everyone has the same lifetime income and consumption. The degree of lifetime inequality is exaggerated by looking only at the distribution of annual income and the distribution of nonhuman wealth.

wealth in the United States is more unequally distributed than wealth in the imaginary economy. This means that although inequality in wealth arising from measuring different families at different points in the life cycle accounts for some of the inequality in the real world, it does not account for it all.

Second, let's consider the distribution of annual income. The Lorenz curve for the imaginary economy is plotted against that for the U.S. economy, again in Fig. 18.8. As you can see, there is more inequality in the United States than in the imaginary economy, but the difference is smaller than it appears when we do not take account of the differences in the stage of the life cycle.

This example shows that some of the measured inequality in income and wealth arises purely from the fact that different families are at different stages in the life cycle. It also shows, however, that there are important remaining inequalities in income and wealth in the United States today. In the next two sections, we're going to explore the sources of those inequalities.

R E V I E W

The distribution of wealth is more unequal than the distribution of income because wealth data measure only nonhuman capital—tangible assets—while income data measure income from all sources—nonhuman capital and human capital. The distributions of annual income and wealth in a given year are much more unequal than the distributions of lifetime income and average lifetime wealth. But there remains a great deal of inequality, even when comparisons are made on a lifetime basis. ◆

Factor Prices and Endowments

Each individual owns factors of production and sells the services of those factors to provide an income. A person's income is the price paid for the use of each factor multiplied by the quantity supplied. Factor prices are determined by the forces that we analyzed in Chapters 14 through 16. The amount of each factor service that an individual supplies depends partly on the endowment of the factor owned by the individual and partly on the choices that the individual makes. Let's now examine the extent to which differences in income arise from differences in factor prices and from differences in the quantity of factors that people supply.

Labor Market and Wages

We've seen that the biggest single source of income is labor. To what extent do variations in wage rates account for the unequal distribution of income? Table 18.2 helps answer this question. It sets out the average hourly earnings of private sector employees in seven industry groups in the United States in 1991. Average hourly earnings for all industries is $10.34. As a group, people working in construction earn $14.01, substantially more than the average. Those working in the retail trades earn $7.00, substantially less than the average. Within the seven

---

TABLE 18.2

Average Hourly Earnings in 1991

Industry	Average hourly earnings (dollars)	
Mining		14.21
Coal mining	17.11	
Non-metallic minerals	11.88	
Manufacturing		11.18
Flat glass making	15.80	
Children's outerwear	6.15	
Construction		14.01
Transportation		13.23
Pipeline transport	17.61	
Local transit	9.46	
Retail trade		7.00
Auto dealers	9.08	
Eating and drinking places	5.18	
Finance, insurance, and real estate		10.42
Services		10.24
Computer and data processing	15.53	
Laundry and cleaning	7.06	
Average, all industries (private sector)		10.34

There is considerable inequality in average hourly earnings across different occupations. But the range of inequality is much lower than the inequality of income. For example, the highest-paid group, pipeline transport workers, earn only 3.4 times the income of the lowest-paid group, those who work in eating and drinking places.

Source: Statistical Abstract of the United States: 1992, 112th edition, 405–408.

groups, there is a large variation in individual wage rates. For example, in the mining group the highest-paid work is in coal mining ($17.11 an hour) and the lowest-paid work is in non-metallic minerals ($11.88 an hour). In the lowest-paid industry, retail trade, the highest-paid work is for auto dealers ($9.08 an hour), while the lowest-paid work is in eating and drinking places ($5.18 an hour).

We can measure the spread between the highest- and lowest-paid workers in these employment categories. Take the highest-paid group of workers, pipeline transport workers, who earn $17.61 an hour on the average, and divide that wage by the wage of the lowest-paid group, those working in eating and drinking places, who earn $5.18 an hour. That calculation, which we call a wage differential, is 17.61 divided by 5.18, which is (approximately) 3.4. This differential says that the highest-paid group of workers earns 3.4 times as much as the lowest-paid group.

One of the things that wage differentials reflect is differences in skills or human capital. For example, the most highly paid people in manufacturing are the makers of flat glass (glass for windows and mirrors), while the least-paid workers make children's outerwear. The wage differential between those two categories probably reflects, to some degree, differences in training and skill. Similarly, in transportation, operating highly sophisticated pipeline-transport networks requires more skill than driving a local train or bus. Again, the wage differential reflects this difference in human capital. You can see other examples in the table.

Differences in wages are one source of income inequality. Differences in endowments of factors of production are another.

Distribution of Endowments

Although we are all endowed with equal amounts of time, we are not endowed with equal abilities. Physical and mental differences (some inherited, some learned) are such an obvious feature of human life that they hardly need mentioning. But these differences produce differences in earnings and, therefore, differences in income and wealth.

A person's earnings potential is influenced by many physical attributes such as height, weight, strength, and endurance and mental attributes such as memory, vocabulary, mathematical and logical

capacity, patience, and motivation. All of these attributes appear to have what is called a normal distribution in the population, and so the distribution of ability and earnings potential is also normally distributed. An example of a normal distribution—the distribution of heights of male students—is shown in Fig. 18.9. The horizontal axis measures those heights in inches. The average height is 70 inches (5'10"). The vertical axis measures the number of students at each height. The curve in the figure traces the percentage of students at each height. The distribution is symmetric. That is, for each person above the average height, there is another person who is below the average by the same amount, so the two are like a mirror image of each other. There are more people at the average and clustered around the average than there are at the two extremes.

The range of individual ability is a major source of differences in income and wealth. But it is not the only source. If it were, the distributions of income and wealth would look like the bell-shaped curve that describes the distribution of heights in Fig. 18.9. In fact, the distribution of income in the

FIGURE 18.9

A Normal Distribution

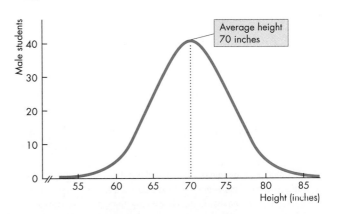

A normal distribution is shaped like a bell and is symmetric around the average. The distribution shown here is the height of a group of male students. The average height is 70 inches. For every person with a height above 70 inches, there is a mirror-image person with a height an equal distance below 70 inches. A symmetric, bell-shaped distribution describes a large number of human characteristics.

United States looks like Fig. 18.10. Figure 18.10 shows different levels of income on the horizontal axis and the percentage of families on the vertical axis. The median income is shown as $34,200. There are many more people with below-average incomes than with above-average incomes, and a relatively small number of people receive extremely high incomes. Because of this, the most common income, $29,000, is below the median, and the average income, $41,500, is above the median.

The distribution of income is skewed. A skewed distribution is one in which there are a larger number of people on one side of the average than on the other. In the case of income distribution, more people have below-average income than above-average income. The asymmetric shape of the distribution of income and wealth has to be explained by something more than the distribution of individual abilities.

FIGURE **18.10**

The Distribution of Income

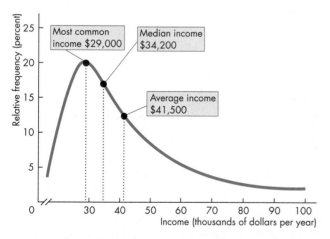

The distribution of income is unequal and is not symmetric around the average. There are many more people below the average than above the average. Also, the distribution has a long, thin upper tail representing a small number of people earning very large incomes. The particular distribution shown here is for 1989, but the features just described are persistent.

Source: *Current Population Reports, Consumer Income*, Series P-60, Nos. 167 and 168 (1990) and *Money Income and Poverty Status in the United States 1989*, Series P-60, No. 168 (1990) (Washington, D.C.: U.S. Department of Commerce, Bureau of the Census). The mode is my estimate.

Choices and the Distribution of Income and Wealth

A person's income and wealth depend in part on the choices that he or she makes. Households get paid for supplying factors of production—labor services, capital, and natural resources. The income received depends partly on the price of those factors of production and partly on the quantities that the household chooses to supply. In most cases, people can't influence the prices of the factors of production. They can't go to a bank and demand that it pay a higher interest rate or to the New York Stock Exchange and demand that stocks improve their performance. People can't demand higher wages than the equilibrium wage rate for their babysitting, truck driving, car washing, or taxation advice work. An investment banker earns more than a parking lot attendant because of differences in human capital, but the market still determines the wages at which labor is traded.

In contrast, people can and do choose how much of each factor to supply. They also choose whether to babysit or to work in a bank, whether to put their savings in the bank or in stocks. Each individual chooses how much of each factor to supply. So the distribution of income depends not only on factor prices but also on people's choices about supplying factors.

We are going to discover that the choices that people make exaggerate the differences among individuals. Their choices make the distribution of income more unequal than the distribution of abilities and thus make the distribution of income more skewed.

Wages and the Supply of Labor

A family's supply curve of labor shows the relationship between the quantity of labor the household supplies and the wage rate. Suppose that a family has a labor supply curve like the one shown in Fig. 18.11. At a wage rate at or below $1 an hour, the household supplies no labor. As the wage rate increases, the quantity of labor supplied increases, and at a wage rate of $9 an hour, 40 hours a week of labor are supplied. The fact that the quantity of

FIGURE **18.11**
The Supply of Labor

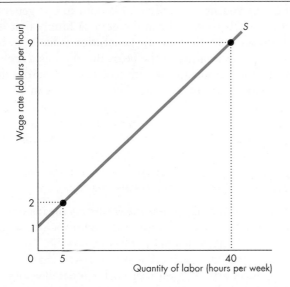

As the wage rate increases, so does the quantity of labor supplied. A person facing a wage rate of $2 an hour works for 5 hours and so earns $10 a week. A person facing a wage rate of $9 an hour works for 40 hours and earns $360 a week. The wage rate of the second person is 4.5 times that of the first, but the second person's income is 36 times larger.

labor supplied increases as the wage rate increases results in the distribution of income being more unequal than the distribution of hourly wages. It also results in the distribution of income being skewed even if the distribution of wages is symmetric. To see why these features of the income distribution occur, let's imagine a population of 1,000 people, each one of whom has a labor supply curve like the one shown in Fig. 18.11.

Although everyone has the same labor supply curve, suppose that each person has a different marginal revenue product of labor and so is paid a different wage rate (see pp. 408–410). Figure 18.12 describes this artificial economy. Part (a) shows the distribution of marginal revenue products—and hourly wage rates—for the 1,000 people. This distribution is a normal curve—bell-shaped, like the distribution of students' heights. The average wage rate is $5 an hour, and the wage rate ranges from $1 an hour to $9 an hour.

FIGURE **18.12**
The Distribution of Wages, Hours, and Income

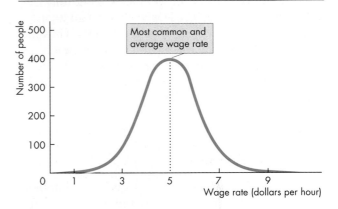

(a) Distribution of wage rates

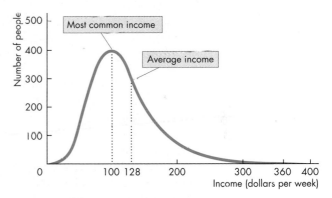

(b) Distribution of weekly incomes

Economic choices create a skewed income distribution. Part (a) graphs the distribution of wages. It is symmetric around the average wage rate of $5 an hour. Part (b) graphs the distribution of weekly income. A majority of the people earn less than the average income. The higher the wage rate, the more labor is a person willing to supply; therefore the distribution of income is more unequal and not symmetric around the average. The range of inequality in wage rates—$1 to $9— is accentuated in the inequality of weekly income—$0 to $360.

Choices Skew the Distribution of Income

Choices make the distribution of income skewed. You can see how by looking at Fig. 18.12(b), which shows the distribution of weekly income. Since people who earn a higher hourly wage work longer hours, their weekly income is disproportionately larger than that of people with low hourly wages who work shorter hours. As you can see from Fig. 18.12(b), the most common income is $100 a week, but the average income is $128 a week. People who earn $2 an hour work only 5 hours a week for a weekly wage of $10. Those who earn $9 an hour work 40 hours a week for a wage of $360. Thus the range of income from the highest to the lowest is 36 to 1. In contrast, the wage rate of the highest paid is only 4.5 times that of the lowest paid. This example is artificial, but the point that it illustrates applies in the real world.

Savings and Bequests

Another choice that results in unequal distributions in income and wealth is savings and bequests. A **bequest** is a gift from one generation to the next. The wealthier the family, the more that family tends to save and bequeath to later generations. By making a bequest, a family can spread good and bad luck across the generations.

Savings and bequests are not inevitably a source of increased inequality. Savings that merely redistribute uneven income over the life cycle to enable consumption to be constant are an example of savings having no effect on inequality. A generation that is lucky might make a bequest to a generation that is unlucky, in which case the bequest would be a source of equality, not inequality. But there are two important features of bequests that do make intergenerational transfers of wealth a source of increased inequality:

◆ Debts cannot be bequeathed.
◆ Mating is assortative.

Debts Cannot Be Bequeathed Though a person may die with debts in excess of assets, those debts cannot be forced onto the remaining members of the family of the deceased debtor. Also, as a rule, it is difficult to incur debts in excess of assets. It is hard to find anyone willing to lend if there is not some kind of security either in the form of assets that could be seized and sold or in the form of a future earnings potential.

Because a zero inheritance is the smallest inheritance that anyone can receive, savings and bequests can only add to future generations' wealth and income potential. The vast majority of people inherit nothing or a very small amount from the previous generation. A tiny number of people inherit enormous fortunes. As a result of bequests, the distribution of income and wealth is not only more unequal than the distribution of ability and job skills but also more persistent. A family that is poor in one generation is likely to be poor in the next. A family that is enormously wealthy in one generation is likely to be enormously wealthy in the next. But there is a tendency for income and wealth to converge, across the generations, to the average. Though there can be long runs of good luck or bad luck or of good judgment or bad judgment, such long runs are uncommon across the generations. However, one additional feature of human behavior slows down convergence to the average and makes wealth and income inequalities persist—assortative mating.

Assortative Mating **Assortative mating** means that people tend to marry within their own socioeconomic class. In the vernacular, "like attracts like." Although there is a good deal of folklore that "opposites attract," perhaps such Cinderella tales appeal to us because they are so rare in reality. Marriage partners tend to have similar socioeconomic characteristics. Wealthy individuals seek wealthy partners. The consequence of assortative mating is that inherited wealth becomes more unequally distributed. (A further, and in some ways deeper, look at the evolution of the distribution of wealth across the generations is found in Our Advancing Knowledge on pp. 506–507).

R E V I E W

The unequal distribution of income arises from unequal wage rates, an unequal distribution of endowments, and the choices that people make. Wage rates are unequal mainly because of differences in skills or human capital. Endowments are unequal for a variety of environmental and biological reasons and are likely to be distributed "normally." The distribution of income is skewed—more people have below-average incomes than above-average incomes—because of the choices people make. Those with greater ability and higher wages choose to work longer hours and make a disproportionately larger income. With higher incomes they save more and bequeath more to the next generation. Marriage among groups with similar wealth reinforces these effects. ◆

We've now completed our positive analysis of inequality in the distribution of income and wealth. We've described the extent of inequality and have identified some of the reasons that it exists. But we have not attempted to make any assessment about fairness or justice in the distribution of income and wealth. Is it fair that some people can be so incredibly rich and others so abjectly poor? In the final section of this chapter, we examine the way in which economists and philosophers have tried to wrestle with this type of question.

Ideas about Fairness

We all have views about fairness and what constitutes a "fair" distribution of income and wealth. These views are diverse, and they are a source of political and philosophical debate. Throughout the ages, moral philosophers have tried to find a satisfactory theory of distributive justice. A **theory of distributive justice** is a set of principles against which we can test whether a particular distribution of economic well-being is fair. There are two broad classes of theories of distributive justice: end-state theories and process theories.

An **end-state theory of distributive justice** focuses on the justice or fairness of the outcomes or ends of economic activity. A **process theory of distributive justice** focuses on the justice or fairness of the *mechanisms* or *means* whereby the ends are achieved. For example, the belief that everyone should have exactly the same income and wealth is an end-state theory. The belief that everyone should have the same *opportunity* to earn and accumulate wealth is a process theory. Equality of income and wealth requires an equality of outcomes or ends. That is, when the process is over, everyone has to have the same income and wealth. Requiring that people have equal opportunity does not imply that they will have equal income and wealth because people will use their opportunities in different ways. Depending on how they use their opportunities and on a variety of chance events (good and bad luck), unequal income and wealth will emerge.

End-State Theories

The two leading end-state theories of distributive justice are the utilitarian and Rawlsian theories.

The **utilitarian theory** is that the fairest outcome is the one that makes the sum of the utilities of all the individuals in a society as large as possible. If Rob gets less utility than does Ian from the last dollar spent, then fairness requires that a dollar be taken from Rob and given to Ian. The reduction in Rob's utility is less than the gain in Ian's utility, so society is better off. Redistribution should take place until the marginal utility of the last dollar spent by each individual is the same. Utilitarian theories of fairness were developed in the eighteenth and nineteenth centuries by such economists as David Hume, Adam Smith, Jeremy Bentham, and John Stuart Mill.

The **Rawlsian theory of fairness** is that the fairest distribution is that which gives the least well-off person the biggest possible income. In the Rawlsian view, if the poorest person can be made better off by taking income from any other person, justice requires that such redistribution take place. The fairest distribution—according to Rawls's criterion—might be one of complete equality but not necessarily so. Because redistribution creates disincentives, too much equality could result in lower average income and a lower income for the least well-off person. The Rawlsian theory of fairness was developed in the 1960s by John Rawls, a contemporary philosopher at Harvard University, and published in his classic work, *A Theory of Justice*, in 1971.[2]

As you can see, the two end-state theories of justice differ in what they regard as the desirable end-state or desirable outcome: for the utilitarian, it is the average or sum of all the individuals that counts; for Rawls, it is the least well-off individual or individuals that count.

How Much Inequality Is Consistent with End-State Theories?

It used to be thought that an end-state theory of justice implied that complete equality in the distribution of income was the best outcome. This conclusion was reached by reasoning along the following lines: First, people are much alike in their capacity for enjoyment. (In the technical language of eco-

---

[2]John Rawls, *A Theory of Justice* (Cambridge, Mass.: Harvard University Press, 1971).

UNCERTAINTY
and the Distribution
OF INCOME
AND WEALTH

Why is there such vast inequality in income and wealth? The apparently obvious answer is that there is vast inequality in luck. As Simon Kuznets saw it, a major source of good and bad luck is economic growth and the technological change that accompanies it. As technology advances, people who can move to the advancing sectors experience rising incomes, while those who remain in traditional sectors experience low income growth.

But there are many examples of bad luck that do *not* translate into poverty. We *insure* against such misfortunes as fire, earthquake, flood, and sickness. So why don't companies with names like Safety Net, Inc. spring up and do profitable business selling insurance against misfortunes such as an advance in mining technology that wipes out hundreds of jobs in the coalfields of West Virginia?

The main reason is that most poor people are poor for their entire lives and can't afford such insurance. When an advance in mining technology destroys a job, an already poor family becomes even poorer. For poverty insurance to work, the mining family's relatively lucky ancestors—say in seventeenth-century England—would have had to have bought insurance for their less fortunate heirs. With no knowledge of future technological changes and with no guarantee that insurance companies would pay up, those ancestors made no demand for such insurance.

Because we can't buy insurance against poverty, we make other arrangements that act as substitutes. One substitute is redistribution through political institutions. Another substitute is wealth. According to Robert E. Lucas, Jr., the absence of poverty insurance is the key reason why there is so much inequality. By accumulating and bequeathing assets, people spread the effects of good and bad luck across the generations. This response to the risk of poverty decreases inequality within a family but increases inequality across families.

> "If the children of Noah had been able and willing to pool risks . . . among themselves and their descendants, then the vast inequality we see today . . . would not exist."
>
> ROBERT E. LUCAS, JR.
> *"On Efficiency and Distribution"*

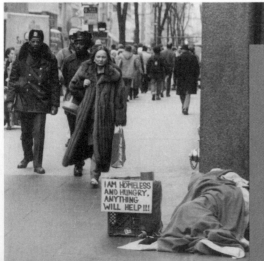

Social insurance, welfare programs, progressive income taxes and subsidizing of health care, education, and declining industries are some ways in which we pool the risks of poverty. Despite these programs designed to lessen the severity of poverty and bring everyone's living standard up to some minimum level, people fall through the net. And despite advances in knowledge and a great deal of experience with alternative redistribution arrangements—in both the United States and other countries—we have not yet been able to devise and implement programs that help the truly needy, maintain strong incentives to work, and are politically acceptable.

In Western European cities such as Frankfurt, Germany, poverty is virtually invisible. There is a smaller degree of economic inequality in Germany and in other Western European countries than in the United States. Top income tax rates of more than 50 percent pay for generous benefits to the sick and unemployed. How would economic life in the United States change if a redistribution system similar to that of Germany was adopted here? What would be the effect on employment, productivity, and average incomes? Although we have learned a great deal about the effects of alternative tax and redistribution arrangements, we have not yet discovered the answers to questions such as these with sufficient certainty to allow general agreement.

UNDERSTANDING
THE
Sources
of
Inequality

Born in Kharkov, Russia, in 1901, Simon Kuznets had his first taste of the subjects that were to dominate the rest of his life when he was the teenaged head of the Ukraine government's economic statistics department. Kuznets arrived in the United States in 1922 and immediately enrolled in economics and statistics courses at Columbia University. He went on to a life of relentless work carefully collecting, organizing, and interpreting facts about economic growth and the distribution of income. For this work, in 1971, he became the third recipient of the Nobel Prize in economics.

From his measurements of income distribution, Kuznets discovered that the ravages of the Great Depression of the 1930s took the largest toll, surprisingly, on the richest 5 percent of the population, whose share in the income pie fell. Arguing the case for better economic data, Kuznets once said that the data available during the 1930s "were neither fish nor flesh nor even red herring."

nomics, they have the same marginal utility of income schedule.) Second, marginal utility declines with income. Therefore if a dollar is taken from a rich person and given to a poorer person, the marginal utility lost by the rich person is less than the marginal utility gained by the poorer person. Thus taking from the rich and giving to the poor increases total utility. Maximum utility occurs when each individual has the same marginal utility, a point that is reached only when incomes—after redistribution—are equal. When incomes have been equalized, total utility of the society has been maximized and "fair shares" have been achieved.

The Big Tradeoff

Although it used to be thought that justice implied complete equality, it is now recognized that there exists what has been called a "big tradeoff" between fairness and economic efficiency. The term comes from the title of a book by Arthur Okun, chairman of the Council of Economic Advisors to President Lyndon Johnson.[3]

The big tradeoff is based on the following idea. Greater equality can be achieved only by taxing productive activities. Taxing people's income from their work and savings lowers the after-tax income they receive. This lower income makes them work and save less. In economic terms, lower after-tax factor prices result in reduced factor supplies. Lower factor supplies result in smaller output, and the smaller output results in less consumption not only for the rich but also, possibly, for the poor. According to this line of reasoning, the correct amount of redistribution to undertake depends on the balance between greater equality and lower average level of consumption.

It also must be recognized that taking resources from the rich to give to the poor cannot be achieved without using resources to administer the redistribution. Tax-collecting agencies such as the Internal Revenue Service as well as all the tax accountants, auditors, and lawyers together with the welfare-administering agencies use massive quantities of skilled labor and capital equipment, such as computers, to do their work. A dollar collected from a rich person does not translate into a dollar received by a

poor person. The bigger the scale of redistribution, the greater are the costs of administering the process.

When these aspects of redistribution are taken into account, it is not obvious that taking a dollar from a rich person to give to a poor person increases the welfare of the poor person. The wealth available for redistribution could be reduced to the point at which everyone is worse off. Taking account of the disincentive effects of redistribution and the resource costs of administering the redistribution is what produces the "big tradeoff." A more equally shared pie results in a smaller pie.

The Process View of Justice

The process view of distributive justice was given its most recent statement by Harvard philosopher Robert Nozick in his book *Anarchy, State, and Utopia*.[4] Nozick argues that no end-state theory of justice can be valid and that a theory of justice must be based on the justice of the mechanisms through which the distribution of income and wealth arises. Nozick argues for the justice of a system based on private property rights, in which private property can be acquired and transferred only through voluntary exchange. His argument can be illustrated with the following story.

We start out with a distribution of income that you personally regard as the best possible. Now suppose that your favorite rock singer enters into a contract with a recording company and a rock concert organizer. The deal is that she will get 5¢ on every record sold and 50¢ for every ticket sold to her rock concerts. In a given year, she sells 5 million records and 500,000 people attend her concerts. Her total income is half a million dollars. This income is much larger than the average and much larger than she had under the original "ideal" distribution.

Is she entitled to this income? Is the new distribution unfair? The original distribution was fair. You and 5 million other fans contributed 5-cent and 50-cent pieces to the income of this successful singer. Was there something illegitimate about you buying a record and attending a rock concert? Nozick believes that the rock singer is entitled to the income and that there is nothing illegitimate about you and

[3]Arthur Okun, *Equality and Efficiency: The Big Tradeoff* (Washington, D.C.: Brookings Institution, 1975).

[4]Robert Nozick, *Anarchy, State, and Utopia* (New York: Basic Books, 1974).

your friends buying records and attending rock concerts. According to Nozick's definition of fairness, the new distribution is also fair.

The philosophical debate continues and will perhaps never be settled. But this state of affairs is no deterrent to people in the practical world of politics. While moral philosophers continue their disagreement about fairness, federal, state, and local legislators create and implement laws that change the distribution of income in response to the political pressures they face.

◆ ◆ ◆ ◆ We've examined the distributions of income and wealth in the United States and seen that there is a large amount of inequality across families and individuals. Some of that inequality arises from comparing families at different stages in the life cycle. But even taking a lifetime view, there remains a great deal of inequality. Some of that inequality arises from differences in rates of pay. But economic choices accentuate those differences. Also, savings and bequests result in the growth of huge wealth concentrations over the generations. ◆ ◆ The topic of this chapter is highly political, and, as we've seen, governments attempt to redistribute income to alleviate the worst aspects of poverty. In the next three chapters, we're going to undertake a systematic study of a broad range of political economic issues and of the economic behavior of government. We'll return to questions concerning the distribution of income and wealth as part of that broader study.

S U M M A R Y

Distributions of Income and Wealth in the United States Today

Labor's share in income is the largest, and it has grown slightly over the years. It is approximately three quarters of total income. The distribution of wealth and income among individuals is uneven. The richest 1 percent of Americans own one third of the total wealth in the country. The next 9 percent own another one third, and the remaining 90 percent also own one third. Income is distributed less unevenly than wealth. The income distribution has changed only slightly over time. In the 1960s, inequality declined, and in the 1980s it increased. The poorest people in the United States are most likely to be older, single, black women, with less than eight years of schooling, living in the South. The richest are mostly likely to live in the Northeast and to be college-educated, middle-aged, white families with husband and wife living together. (pp. 486–492)

Income Redistribution

Governments redistribute income in the United States today through income taxes, income maintenance programs, and provision of goods and services below cost. Income taxes are progressive. The poorest families pay no federal income tax, the middle-income families pay 15 percent of their taxable income, and the richest families pay 28 or 33 percent. The income maintenance programs are social security, unemployment compensation, and welfare. The social security programs are OASDHI—Old Age, Survivors, and Disability Health Insurance—and Medicare. Welfare programs provide income maintenance for families and persons who do not qualify for social security or unemployment compensation. The poorest 32 percent of the population receive more benefits than they pay in taxes—they receive net benefits—and the richest 68 percent of the population pay more in taxes than they receive in benefits—they pay net taxes.

The main problems created by the income maintenance programs are the discouragement of work, the encouragement of family breakup, and a high rate of birth of illegitimate children, all of which create a welfare trap. Other problems are social tensions and costly welfare bureaucracy. Reform of income maintenance programs includes the provisions of the Family Support Act of 1988 and the negative income tax proposal. These reforms seek to strengthen the incentives for people on welfare to find work. (pp. 492–496)

Comparing Like with Like

In order to judge the extent of inequality, it is important that we make valid comparisons. The measured distribution of wealth exaggerates the degree of inequality because it fails to take into account the distribution of human capital. The distributions of annual income and wealth exaggerate the degree of lifetime inequality because they do not take into account the family's stage in the life cycle. (pp. 496–500)

Factor Prices and Endowments

Differences in income and wealth arise partly from differences in individual endowments and partly from differences in factor prices. Wage rates vary considerably, depending on skill and other factors. But these differences, on their own, are not enough to account for differences in the distribution of income and wealth. Those differences get exaggerated by the economic choices that people make. (pp. 500–502)

Choices and the Distribution of Income and Wealth

The economic choices that people make have an important influence on income and wealth. Attitudes toward work result in some people taking a larger amount of leisure, earning a smaller income than others, and consuming a smaller amount of goods. Also, savings and bequests affect wealth across the generations. Because of assortative mating, bequests accentuate inequality. (pp. 502–505)

Ideas about Fairness

People disagree on what constitutes a fair distribution of income. Moral philosophers have tried to resolve the issue by finding principles on which we can all agree, but agreement still has not been reached. Two broad groups of theories have been developed: end-state theories and process theories. End-state theories of fairness assert that it is the outcome that matters. Process theories assert that it is equality of opportunity that matters. (pp. 505–509)

K E Y   E L E M E N T S

Key Terms

Assortative mating, 504
Bequest, 504
End-state theory of distributive justice, 505
Lorenz curve, 487
Market income, 493
Negative income tax, 494
Poverty, 489
Process theory of distributive justice, 505
Progressive income tax, 492
Proportional income tax, 492
Rawlsian theory of fairness, 505

Regressive income tax, 492
Theory of distributive justice, 505
Utilitarian theory, 505

Key Figures

Figure 18.2   Lorenz Curves for Income and Wealth, 487
Figure 18.4   Distribution of Income by Selected Family Characteristics in 1990, 489
Figure 18.6   Comparing Current Income Maintenance Programs and a Negative Income Tax, 495

R E V I E W   Q U E S T I O N S

1 Which of the following statements describe the distributions of personal income and wealth in the United States today?

a The distributions of income and wealth are best represented by normal or bell-shaped curves.

b The richest people are more than 800 times as wealthy as the poorest people, but there is the same percentage of people at each different level of wealth.

c More than 50 percent of the population are wealthier than the average.

d More than 50 percent of the population are poorer than the average.

2 Which is more unequally distributed, income or wealth? In answering this question, pay careful attention both to the way in which income and wealth are measured by official statistics and to the fundamental concepts of income and wealth.

3 How has the distribution of income in the United States changed over the past 20 years? Which groups have gained and which have lost?

4 What is wrong with the way in which the official statistics measure the distribution of wealth?

5 Explain why the work/leisure choices made by individuals can result in a distribution of income and consumption that is more unequal than the distribution of ability. If ability is distributed normally (bell-shaped), will the resulting distribution of income also be bell-shaped?

6 Explain how the distribution of income and wealth is influenced by bequests and assortative mating.

7 What is a Lorenz curve? How does a Lorenz curve illustrate inequality? Explain how the Lorenz curves for the distributions of income and wealth in the United States economy differ from each other.

PROBLEMS

1 Imagine an economy in which there are five people who are identical in all respects. Each lives for 70 years. For the first 14 of those years, they earn no income. For the next 35 years, they work and earn $30,000 a year from their work. For their remaining years, they are retired and have no income from labor. To make the arithmetic easy, let's suppose that the interest rate in this economy is zero; the individuals consume all their income during their lifetime and at a constant annual rate. What are the distributions of income and wealth in this economy if the individuals have the following ages?

a All are 45.

b Their ages are 25, 35, 45, 55, and 65.

Is case (a) one of greater inequality than case (b)?

2 You are given the following information about income and wealth shares:

	Income shares (percent)	Wealth shares (percent)
Lowest 20%	5	0
Second 20%	11	1
Third 20%	17	3
Fourth 20%	24	11
Highest 20%	43	85

Draw the Lorenz curves for income and wealth for this economy. Explain which of the two variables—income or wealth—is more unequally distributed.

3 An economy consists of 10 people, each of whom has the following labor supply schedule:

Hourly wage rate (dollars per hour)	1	2	3	4	5
Hours worked per day	0	1	2	3	4

The people differ in ability and earn different wage rates. The distribution of *wage rates* is as follows:

Wage rate (dollars per hour)	1	2	3	4	5
Number of people	1	2	4	2	1

a Calculate the average wage rate.

b Calculate the ratio of the highest to the lowest wage rate.

c Calculate the average daily income.

d Calculate the ratio of the highest to the lowest daily income.

e Sketch the distribution of hourly wage rates.

f Sketch the distribution of daily incomes.

g What important lesson is illustrated by this problem?

PART 8

MARKETS AND GOVERNMENT

Born in Philadelphia in 1938, Ann Friedlaender was an undergraduate at Radcliffe College and a graduate student at MIT, from which she obtained her Ph.D. in 1964. Professor Friedlaender is a distinguished teacher, researcher, and university administrator and is a prominent contributor to the public policy debate, especially in the area of transportation policy.

Talking

with

Ann

Friedlaender

Professor Friedlander, what brought you to the study of economics?

My parents were deeply affected by the Great Depression. I consequently grew up in a family in which economic and social issues were very much in the forefront of discussion and concern. As a freshman in college, I took a course in economic principles and was hooked. I liked the combination of analytical rigor and elegance on the one hand and the focus on important social problems on the other. As an economist, I have been primarily interested in normative issues and believe that the discipline provides a powerful analytic framework to address social questions related to distributional equity and economic efficiency.

You are well-known for your work on transportation policy. What is your report card on the deregulation of the trucking and airline industries?

I would give trucking deregulation an A+ and air deregulation a C–. Prior to deregulation, economists argued that both industries were inherently competitive with few barriers to entry or economies of scale. To the extent that rates were propped up by regulatory protection, economists believed that rates would fall and service would improve in a deregulated environment. They were right about the trucking industry. Rates have fallen, service has improved, and shippers have received benefits on the order of several billions of dollars. In the case of airlines, however, economists appear to have been wrong. Not only are there scale economies related to the hub-and-spoke networks that the airlines have adopted, but there also appear to be substantial scale economies associated with passenger reservation systems. The result has been a dramatic increase in the degree of concentration in the industry and in the number of routes served by only one or two carriers, with noncompetitive pricing on these routes as a consequence. Thus while passengers initially benefited from lower rates and increased service competition, as the industry has evolved, it has become relatively noncompetitive.

Have we done all the deregulation that needs doing?

Probably, at least for the time being. During the past 15 years, there has been substantial deregulation of the transportation industries—namely, air, truck, and rail—as well as the telecommunications, cable TV, banking and financial, natural gas, and petroleum industries, to mention just a few. For the most part, the deregulation has been successful, although it has not brought forth all of the benefits expected in the air transportation and financial industries. Although there is some evidence that state-by-state regulation of the insurance industry is

not very efficient, we should probably fully digest the deregulation of the past decade before we enter into large-scale deregulation in other areas.

You mentioned cable TV, which has become a highly profitable business in recent years. Does this industry need reregulating?

There are admittedly some troubling aspects of cable TV. For example, most cities are served by a single supplier; cable rates have risen substantially above the rate of inflation; and the industry as a whole is relatively concentrated, raising questions about monopsony power with respect to the programmers. Nevertheless, I think it would be a mistake to reregulate the industry, which was deregulated in 1984. In the last few years, the number of cities with two competing cable carriers has risen substantially, and there is potential for further competition from direct broadcast satellites and microwave television. The best way to ensure that consumers get what they want is to encourage competition rather than to reregulate the industry.

Several economists over the years, including the 1991 Nobel laureate, Ronald Coase, have suggested that the frequency spectrum—the airwaves over which broadcasts and other communications are transmitted—should be allocated to the highest bidder by auction rather than allocated by committee or lottery as they are today. What is your view on this?

I agree. The frequency spectrum has enormous economic value, which will increase as it gets more

> " I would give trucking deregulation an A+ and air deregulation a C−."

> " The best way to ensure that consumers get what they want is to encourage competition rather than regulate the industry."

crowded. Since this is a fixed resource, there is a large economic rent associated with its allocation, which some have estimated to be as large as $50 billion. For the government to give this away freely, either by lottery or by committee allocation, seems to make little sense. An auction not only would ensure that a given slot on the spectrum would go to the use that generated the highest value, but would also ensure that the potential economic rent would be utilized by society rather than accrue to a few lucky firms and their shareholders.

What are the major economic problems in urban transportation today?

The major economic problems in urban transportation are related to congestion and the underutilization of mass transit. Both of these are essentially pricing problems. During peak commuting hours, highways become congested. My use of the roads imposes an additional cost on you, and vice versa. However, other than the additional congestion costs that I incur while driving, the costs of peak and nonpeak travel are the same. Thus the costs of peak travel are too low relative to nonpeak travel, and the costs of driving are too low relative to the

costs of mass transit. Consequently, during peak hours, the highway network is overutilized and the mass transit systems are underutilized.

What role can economics and economists play in designing solutions to such problems?

Economics has developed the concept of "externalities" to describe situations in which the private costs of using resources differ from the social costs. Congestion is a classic example of an externality, since in using a highway during peak hours, a given driver imposes additional time and usage costs on all other drivers that he or she does not take into account in personal cost calculations. In such a case, economics indicates that the solution is to impose a congestion charge that would equate an individual's private driving costs with the social costs that he or she imposes on all other drivers. Economists have done considerable work in estimating the difference between private marginal travel costs and social marginal travel costs. The technology is now being developed to install sensors in automobiles that would measure peak travel in congested zones and bill drivers for their congestion costs.

Do you think that the next 30 years are going to provide a set of challenges for the next generation of economists as exciting as those of the past 30 years? What will those challenges be?

During the last 30 years, much of the focus on the interactions between markets and government has been on issues related to regulation. For the most part, economists have successfully argued that markets can do a better job of allocating resources than can government or administrative agencies, and deregulation has occurred in a host of industries that had previously been tightly regulated. With a few notable exceptions, the effects of deregulation have been that rates or prices have fallen, service has improved, and consumers have gained.

Over the next 30 years, I believe that environmental issues will become increasingly important. One of the major challenges facing economists will be to devise marketlike solutions in the environmental and natural resource areas instead of the command and control regulatory solutions that have tended to dominate the debate in the past. Examples of this already exist. The recent acid rain legislation established tradable permits for pollution that can be exchanged between utilities. This seems to be an idea that is long overdue and has clear applications to a whole host of problems related to air and water pollution, hazardous waste disposal, and greenhouse gas emissions. Similarly, market solutions could be applied to fisheries and forests, which are increasingly being subject to excessive exploitation.

Another important area in which the next generation of economists could have a significant impact has to do with competitiveness and growth. Currently, there is a major debate concerning the proper role of government in stimulating research, development, and innovation. The whole question of industrial policy is really one of whether the private market can allocate resources in such a way as to sustain the growth and productivity changes needed to enable the United States to compete in world markets, and thus whether the private gains from investment and innovation fail to reflect their full social gains.

What advice would you give to a student today who is interested in pursuing a career that combines economics with public policy issues?

If you are a student interested in economics and public policy, I would urge you to get a Ph.D. in economics. This would give you a strong analytical framework that could be applied to a host of important policy questions. While a professional degree in law, management, or public policy is certainly useful, on balance, I believe that a Ph.D. in economics would give you the greatest flexibility to pursue a career in government, business, or academia. The potential impact of a career in academic economics on public policy should not be underestimated, since academics often take leaves from their universities and play central policy roles, for example as members of the Council of Economic Advisors or as senior members in the Treasury or Justice Department.

CHAPTER 19

MARKET FAILURE

After studying this chapter, you will be able to:

◆ Describe the range of economic actions governments undertake

◆ Outline the structure of the government sector of the U.S. economy

◆ Distinguish between a normative and a positive analysis of government economic behavior

◆ Define market failure and explain how it might be overcome by government action

◆ Distinguish between private goods and public goods

◆ Explain the free-rider problem

◆ Explain how government provision of public goods avoids the free-rider problem

◆ Explain how property rights and taxes and subsidies may be used to achieve a more efficient allocation of resources when externalities are present

GOVERNMENT IS BIG BUSINESS—ONE OF THE BIGGEST. IN 1990, the U.S. federal government employed more than 5 million people and spent more than $1 trillion. State and local governments employed a further 14 million people, spending $0.8 trillion between them. Independent government agencies employed yet another million people. What do all these people and all these dollars do for us? Is the government sector of our economy simply too big? Is government, as conservatives often suggest, "the problem"? Or, despite its enormous size, is government too small? Is more government intervention the solution to many outstanding problems? ◆ ◆ Governments provide an enormous array of goods and services. Some are intangibles like laws and their enforcement; others are tangibles like schools and highways. Why does government supply some goods and not others? You've probably seen a Wells Fargo security truck delivering cash to your local bank.

Government—The Solution or the Problem?

Why does Wells Fargo, a private company, supply security services to banks, while the local police department provides similar services to residential neighborhoods, streets, and highways? What is so special about roads and highways, nuclear weapons, and judicial services that results in such services always being provided by government and never by private firms? ◆ ◆ We've heard a lot recently about our endangered planet. The massive quantities in which we burn fossil fuels—coal, natural gas, and oil—have immediate effects on the atmosphere that result in acid rain. And there are harder to measure but potentially more serious effects on the chemical balance of the earth's atmosphere, increasing the proportion of carbon dioxide and reducing the proportion of other elements. It is predicted that the continuation of this process will result in a gradual warming of the planet—the so-called greenhouse effect. It is also predicted that the persistent and large-scale use of chlorofluorocarbons (CFCs) will cause irreparable damage to the earth's ozone layer, thereby exposing us to an increased amount of radiation. These environmental issues are simultaneously everybody's problem and nobody's problem. Everyone is put at risk by the continued damage to our atmosphere, and yet no one individual can take the necessary action to protect the environment. What, if anything, might government do to protect our environment? How can the government help us to take account of the damage that we cause others every time we turn on our heating or air conditioning systems?

◆ ◆ ◆ ◆ We've seen that households' and firms' choices are influenced by actions taken by government. For example, rent controls and minimum wage laws influence the way competitive markets operate. We've also seen that many markets are not competitive. They have monopoly elements, and those elements often arise from legal restrictions imposed by government. In this chapter and the next two, we turn our attention to the economic choices that governments make and to the effects of those choices on the economy. ◆ ◆ In this chapter, our main concern is to describe the government sector and explain how the market economy, in the absence of a government, would fail to achieve an efficient allocation of resources. We also provide a brief sketch of the economic theory of government behavior that will be elaborated and applied in the next two chapters.

The Government Sector

We'll begin by describing the anatomy of the government sector.

The Structure and Scale of Government

The government sector of the U.S. economy consists of more than 80,000 separate organizations, some

tiny like the Yuma, Arizona, School District and some enormous like the U.S. federal government. The total government sector of the U.S. economy accounts for 35 percent of spending on goods and services and 36 percent of total employment.

There are three levels of government in the United States: federal, state, and local. The federal government spends more than the state and local governments do—about $1 trillion a year—but local government has the highest number of employees—close to 10 million. Each level of government is organized into branches and departments. The branches of government are the legislative, judicial, and executive branches, and the departments are the bureaucracies that take care of the day-to-day business of government. The bulk of the federal government's economic activity takes place in the Departments of Defense, Health and Human Services, and Treasury. Including military personnel, the Defense Department employs almost two thirds of total government-sector employees and spends almost one third of the budget. The Department of Health and Human Services, which administers welfare programs (including social security), spends more than one third of the total budget. Even the Treasury Department spends close to one fifth of the budget (mainly on debt interest and tax collection).

The Scale and Growth of Government

The scale of government has changed dramatically over the years. In 1940, for example, government-sector expenditure accounted for less than 20 percent of the economy's total expenditure, while in 1992 it had reached 35 percent. But the growth of government expenditure over the past 50 years probably understates the growth of the importance of government in economic life. That importance stems partly from the government's expenditure and partly from the extent of the laws and regulations passed by government that affect the economic actions of individual households and firms. We look at this aspect of government in Chapter 21, where we study regulation and antitrust.

Our main task in this chapter is not to describe the anatomy of government and the pace at which it has grown but to analyze the failure of markets to achieve *allocative efficiency* and to explore the role of government in coping with market failure. Before we embark on that main task, we're going to take an overview of the alternative approaches that economists use to study the economic behavior of government.

Economic Theory of Government

We all have opinions on political matters, and some of those opinions are strongly held. As students of economics, our task is to understand, explain, and predict the economic choices that the government sector makes. Although we cannot suppress our political views, it is important, if we are to make progress in studying political behavior, to continually remind ourselves of the important distinction between positive and normative analysis. We first reviewed that distinction in Chapter 1 (pp. 17–18). But because the distinction is so important for the economic study of political behavior, let's remind ourselves of what that distinction is.

Positive and Normative Analysis   An economic analysis of government choices may be either *positive* or *normative*. The positive analysis of government seeks to explain the reasons for and effects of government economic choices. A normative analysis seeks to evaluate the desirability of a government action and argues for or against some particular proposal. Positive analysis seeks to understand what *is*; normative analysis seeks to reach conclusions on what *ought* to be. The economic analysis used in both of these activities is similar. But the use to which the analysis is put differs.

Here we undertake a positive study of government action; that is, we seek to understand the reasons for and the effects of the actions that we see being undertaken by governments in the United States today. We do not seek to establish the desirability of any particular course of action or to argue for or against any particular policy.

All government economic action stems from two aspects of economic life:

◆ Market failure
◆ Redistribution

Market Failure

One explanation for government intervention in the economy is market failure. **Market failure** is the inability of an unregulated market to achieve, in all circumstances, allocative efficiency. There are three types of situations in which market failure arises:

◆ The provision of goods and services that we consume in common with everyone else

◆ The production of goods and services that give rise to *external costs* or *external benefits*
◆ The restriction of output by monopolies and cartels

In all three cases, the unregulated market produces waste in the sense that a different allocation would result in producing more of some goods without producing less of others and could make someone better off without making anyone worse off. It is important not to take this last statement as being normative. The presence or absence of waste is a positive matter. It is a statement about what *is*. A prediction that government action will (or will not) occur to eliminate such waste is also a positive statement. The proposition that government *ought* (or ought not) to intervene to eliminate waste is normative. In dealing with market failure, it is its positive aspects that will be our concern.

Redistribution

Another explanation for government intervention in the economy is to redistribute income and wealth. Such redistribution is usually justified on the basis of some notion of equity or distributive justice, which we discussed in Chapter 18. But not all redistribution is explained in this way. The creation of monopoly and government protection of cartels also result in the redistribution of income and wealth. And the *rent-seeking* activities that we described in Chapter 12 have an important political dimension.

Again, it is important to keep the distinction between positive and normative aspects of the redistributive role of government clear. The proposition that most people believe that the market distributions of income and wealth are unfair is positive. The proposition that government intervention can redistribute income from the rich to the poor is also positive. The statement that the government *ought* to redistribute income and wealth is normative. We have described the scale of income redistribution in Chapter 18, and we will study it further in Chapter 20. When we do so, our focus will be entirely on its positive aspect.

Public Interest and Public Choice

There are two broad classes of economic theories of government behavior:

◆ Public interest theories
◆ Public choice theories

A **public interest theory** of government behavior predicts that government action will take place to eliminate waste and achieve an efficient allocation of resources. A **public choice theory** predicts that the behavior of the government sector is the outcome of individual choices made by voters, politicians, and bureaucrats interacting with each other in a political marketplace. According to public interest theories of government, whenever there is market failure, government action can be designed to eliminate the consequences of that failure and to achieve allocative efficiency. According to public choice theories, matters are not that simple. Not only is there the possibility of market failure (arising in the situations that we have outlined above), but there is also the possibility of "government failure." That is, it is possible that when each voter, politician, and bureaucrat pursues his or her own best interests and interacts in the political "marketplace," the resulting "public choice" no more achieves the elimination of waste and the attainment of allocative efficiency than does an unregulated market. Understanding why not is the main topic of Chapter 20.

In the next section, we're going to explain more fully the economic role of the government arising from two of the sources of market failure—the provision of goods and services that we consume in common with everyone else and the production of goods and services that create external costs or external benefits. The other source of market failure, arising from monopoly and cartels and from the government regulation of such industries, is dealt with in Chapter 21.

Public Goods

Why does the government provide certain goods and services, such as a legal system, a system of national defense, schools and highways, and public health services? Why don't we simply leave the provision of these goods and services to private firms that sell their output in markets? How much national defense would we have if a private firm, Star Wars, Inc., had

to compete for our dollars in the marketplace in the same way that McDonald's and Coca-Cola do?

Most of the answers to the above questions lie in the distinction between private goods and public goods.

Private Goods and Public Goods

A **private good** is a good or service each unit of which is consumed by only one individual. An example of a private good is a can of soda. There are two important features of a private good. The first feature is called *rivalry*. Rivalry emphasizes the idea that one person's consumption can take place only at the expense of another person's. If you increase your consumption of soda by one can, other things being equal, someone else has to consume one can less. The second feature of a private good is called *excludability*. Once you have bought a can of soda, the soda is yours to do with as you choose. You can exclude others from using it.

A **pure public good** is a good or service each unit of which is consumed by everyone and from which no one can be excluded. An example of a pure public good is the national defense system. There are two important features of a pure public good that parallel the two features that we identified concerning a private good. The first feature is called *nonrivalry*. One person's consumption of a pure public good does not reduce the amount available for someone else. For example, your consumption of the security provided by a national defense system does not decrease the security of anyone else. The second feature is called *nonexcludability*. No one can be excluded from the additional security that every citizen enjoys from the national defense system.

Many goods lie in between a pure public good and a private good. Such goods are called **mixed goods**. An example of a mixed good is a city street. A city street is like a pure public good until it becomes congested. One more car or truck on a street with plenty of space on it does not reduce the consumption of transportation services of anyone else. But once the street becomes congested, the addition of one more user lowers the quality of the service available for everyone else—it becomes like a private good.

Pure public goods and mixed goods with a large public element—referred to as public goods—give rise to what is called the free-rider problem.

Free Riding

A **free rider** is someone who consumes a good without paying for it. The **free-rider problem** is the tendency for the scale of provision of a public good to be too small if it is produced and sold privately. The free-rider problem arises because there is no incentive for a person to pay for a good if the payment makes no difference to the quantity of the good that the person is able to consume. Public goods are such goods. To see why, let's look at an example.

Imagine that an effective antimissile laser weapon has been developed. One of these new weapons can attack and destroy 400 intercontinental ballistic missiles within seconds of their being launched. The larger the number of antimissile laser weapons deployed, the larger is the number of missiles destroyed. Potential enemies have 1,500 missile launchers, and four of the new weapons can eliminate all of them. Three can do a pretty good job, and even two can severely limit the amount of damage done by missiles that get through the laser defense.

But the new weapons system is very expensive. To build it, resources have to be diverted from peaceful space programs and from the development of other productive uses of lasers in medicine. As a result, the larger the number of weapons installed, the greater is their marginal cost.

Our task is to work out the scale on which to install this new defense system to achieve allocative efficiency. We'll then examine whether private provision can achieve allocative efficiency, and we'll discover that it cannot—that there is a free-rider problem.

Benefits and Costs

The benefits provided by a weapons system are based on the preferences and beliefs of the consumers of the services of that system. The costs are based on technology and the prices of the factors of production used to produce the system. When studying private goods, we observed that the value of a good to an individual is the maximum amount that the person is willing to pay for one more unit of the good. We worked out this value from the individual's demand curve. That is, the demand curve tells us the quantity demanded at a given price or, for a given quantity, the maximum price that is willingly

paid for the last unit bought. We can work out the value a person places on a public good in a similar manner. That is, the value that a person places on a public good is the maximum amount willingly paid for one additional unit of the good.

To calculate the maximum amount that a person is willing to pay for one more unit of a public good, we first need to establish that person's total benefit schedule. **Total benefit** is the total dollar value that a person places on a given level of provision of a public good. The greater the scale of provision, the larger is the total benefit. The table in Fig. 19.1 sets out an example of the total benefits to Lisa and Max of different scales of provision of the proposed antimissile lasers. Lisa and Max believe that the weapons system reduces the chance of a nuclear war occurring and, if it does occur, increases the chance of preventing nuclear warheads from reaching their targets. The more lasers there are in place, the greater is the degree of security, but up to a maximum level. Each additional laser is believed to provide less additional security than the previous one. The increase in total benefit resulting from a unit increase in the scale of provision of a public good is called its **marginal benefit**. The marginal benefits to Lisa and Max are calculated in the table in Fig. 19.1. As you can see, the greater the scale of provision, the smaller is the marginal benefit. By the time 4 lasers are deployed, Lisa perceives no additional benefits, and Max perceives only $10 worth. Lisa's and Max's marginal benefits are graphed as MB_L and MB_M, respectively, in parts (a) and (b) of the figure.

The marginal benefit of a public good is the maximum amount that a person is willing to pay for one more unit of the good. This maximum amount varies with the quantity of the good consumed. The greater the quantity, the smaller is the maximum amount that will be paid for one more unit.

Part (c) of the figure shows the economy's marginal benefit curve, MB (where the economy has only two people, Lisa and Max). The marginal benefit curve of a public good for an individual is similar to the demand curve for a private good. But there is an important difference between the economy's marginal benefit curve for a public good and the market demand curve for a private good. To obtain the market demand curve for a private good, we add up the quantities demanded by each individual at each price. In other words, we sum the individual

FIGURE **19.1**

Benefits of a Public Good

(a) Lisa's marginal benefit curve

(b) Max's marginal benefit curve

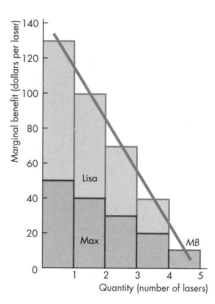

(c) Economy's marginal benefit curve

Quantity (number of antimissile lasers)	Lisa		Max		Economy	
	Total benefit (dollars)	Marginal benefit (dollars per laser)	Total benefit (dollars)	Marginal benefit (dollars per laser)	Total benefit (dollars)	Marginal benefit (dollars per laser)
0	0		0		0	
		80		50		130
1	80		50		130	
		60		40		100
2	140		90		230	
		40		30		70
3	180		120		300	
		20		20		40
4	200		140		340	
		0		10		10
5	200		150		350	

The table shows various scales of provision of an antimissile laser defense system. It also lists the total benefits accruing to Lisa, Max, and the economy (comprised of only Lisa and Max) from different scales of provision. The table also calculates the marginal benefit—the change in the total benefit resulting from a unit increase in the scale of provi-

sion to Lisa, Max, and the economy. The marginal benefits are graphed in the figure, for Lisa in part (a) and for Max in part (b). The marginal benefit to the economy at each level of provision is the sum of the marginal benefits to each individual and is shown in part (c). The marginal benefit curves are MB_L for Lisa, MB_M for Max, and MB for the economy.

demand curves horizontally (see Fig. 7.1, p. 158). In contrast, to find the economy's marginal benefit curve of a public good, we sum the marginal benefit of each individual at each quantity of provision. That is, we sum the individual marginal benefit curves vertically. The resulting marginal benefit for the economy comprised of just Lisa and Max is calculated in the table, and the economy's marginal benefit curve is graphed in part (c)—the curve labeled *MB*.

An economy with just two people would not buy any antimissile lasers—their total benefits fall far short of their cost. But an economy with 250 million people might. To determine the efficient scale of provision, consider the example set out in Fig. 19.2. The second and third columns of the table show the total and marginal benefits to an entire economy consisting of 250 million people. The next two columns show the total and marginal cost of producing antimissile lasers. These costs are opportunity costs and are derived in exactly the same way as the costs associated with the production of sweaters that we studied in Chapter 10. The final column of the table shows net benefit. **Net benefit** is total benefit minus total cost. The efficient scale of provision is the one that maximizes net benefit.

Total benefit and total cost are graphed as the total benefit curve, *TB*, and total cost curve, *TC*, in part (a). Net benefit is also visible in that part of the figure as the vertical distance between the two curves. Net benefit is maximized when that distance is at its largest, a situation that occurs at a scale of provision of 2 lasers. This is the efficient scale of provision.

Another way of describing the efficient scale of provision is in terms of marginal benefit and marginal cost. The marginal benefit and marginal cost of lasers are graphed as the marginal benefit curve, *MB*, and marginal cost curve, *MC*, in part (b). When marginal benefit exceeds marginal cost, net benefit increases if the quantity produced increases. When marginal cost exceeds marginal benefit, net benefit increases if the quantity produced decreases. When marginal benefit equals marginal cost, net benefit cannot be increased—it is at its maximum possible level. Thus when marginal benefit equals marginal cost, allocative efficiency has been achieved.

Now that we have worked out the efficient scale of provision of a public good, let's go on to see how much of such a good would be provided by a private producer.

Private Provision

We have now worked out the scale of provision of a national defense system that maximizes net benefit. Would a private firm—Star Wars, Inc.—deliver that scale of provision? It would not. To do so, it would have to collect $15 billion to cover its costs—or $60 from each of the 250 million people in the economy. But no one would have any incentive to buy his or her "share" of the laser weapon system. Each person would reason as follows: The number of antimissile lasers provided by Star Wars, Inc. is not going to be affected by my $60. But my own private consumption is going to be affected by whether or not I pay. If I do not pay, I will enjoy the same level of security from the laser weapons and more of other goods. Therefore it pays me to keep my $60 and spend it on other goods, my consumption of which is affected by my spending on them. In other words, it pays me to free ride on the public good and buy private goods.

Since everyone reasons in the same manner, no one pays for a share in the output of Star Wars, Inc. The firm has zero revenue and has no incentive to produce anything. The output of antimissile lasers is zero.

Public Provision

Suppose that the people in this economy have instituted a government that makes the following proposition: the government will collect $60 from each person and will spend the resulting $15 billion to provide 2 antimissile lasers. Will the people vote for this proposition? Clearly, they will. If there is no antimissile system (the output of Star Wars, Inc.), the marginal benefit of installing 1 laser greatly exceeds its marginal cost. By proposing to provide 2 antimissile lasers, the government is offering each voter a level of security that maximizes net benefit. The voters obtain a benefit of $35 billion—$140 each—for a total cost of $15 billion—$60 each. Since the voters recognize this as an improvement over the zero provision by Star Wars, Inc., they will vote for it.

Whether or not actual governments produce public goods on a scale that maximizes net benefit is something that we examine in Chapter 20. But we have established a key proposition: a government is able to provide any public good on a scale larger than that provided by a private producer.

FIGURE 19.2

The Efficient Scale of Provision of a Public Good

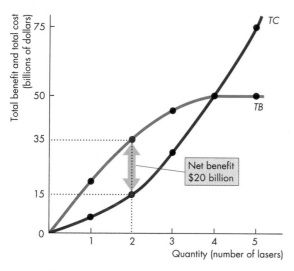

(a) Total benefit and total cost curves

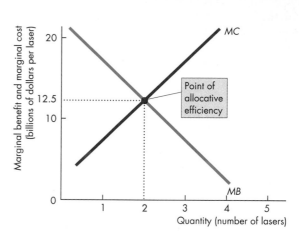

(b) Marginal benefit and marginal cost curves

Quantity (number of antimissile lasers)	Total benefit (billions of dollars)	Marginal benefit (billions of dollars per laser)	Total cost (billions of dollars)	Marginal cost (billions of dollars per laser)	Net benefit (billions of dollars)
0	0		0		0
		20		5	
1	20		5		15
		15		10	
2	35		15		20
		10		15	
3	45		30		15
		5		20	
4	50		50		0
		0		25	
5	50		75		−25

The table shows the total benefit and marginal benefit to the entire economy of various scales of provision of a laser weapons system. It also shows the total cost and marginal cost of the various scales of provision. Total benefit and total cost are graphed in part (a) as the total benefit curve, *TB*, and the total cost curve, *TC*. Net benefit is visi-ble as the vertical distance between these two curves and is maximized when 2 lasers are installed. Part (b) shows the marginal benefit curve, *MB*, and marginal cost curve, *MC*. When marginal cost equals marginal benefit, net benefit is maximized and allocative efficiency is achieved.

R E V I E W

I f people make their own decisions about the provision of public goods and buy those goods in private markets, there is a free-rider problem. It is in everyone's individual interest to free ride, with the result that the scale of provision of the goods is smaller than that required for allocative efficiency. A government that balances marginal cost and marginal benefit provides the public good on a scale that achieves allocative efficiency. ◆

Externalities

A n **externality** is a cost or a benefit arising from an economic transaction that falls on a third party and that is not taken into account by those who undertake the transaction. For example, when a chemical factory dumps its waste products into a river and kills the fish, it imposes an externality—in this case, an external cost—on the fisherman who lives downstream. Since these costs are not borne by the chemical factory, they are not taken into account in deciding whether to dump waste into the river and, if so, how much. When a person drives a car that burns leaded gasoline and does not have a catalytic converter, an externality—again, an external cost—is imposed on everyone who tries to breathe the unbreathable air. When a homeowner fills her garden with beautiful spring bulbs, she generates an externality—in this case an external benefit—for all the joggers and walkers who pass by. In deciding how much to spend on this lavish display, she takes into account only the benefits accruing to herself.

Two particularly dramatic externalities have received a lot of attention in recent years. The first arises from the use of chlorofluorocarbons (CFCs). These manufactured chemicals are used in a wide variety of products—from coolants in refrigerators and air conditioners to plastic phones to cleaning

solvents for computer circuits. Though the precise chemistry of the process is not understood and is even the subject of dispute, many atmospheric physicists believe that CFCs damage the atmosphere's protective ozone layer. Discoveries of depleted ozone over Antarctica in 1983 have heightened fears of extended ozone depletion.

The second externality arises from burning fossil fuels that add carbon dioxide and other gases to the atmosphere, which prevent infrared radiation from escaping, resulting in what has been called the "greenhouse effect." If the greenhouse scenario turns out to be correct, it is predicted that much of the Midwest will become a dustbowl and many eastern and Gulf Coast regions will disappear under an expanded Atlantic Ocean (see Reading Between the Lines, pp. 526–527).

When you take a cold drink from the refrigerator or switch on the air conditioner on a steamy August evening, you do not take into account the consequences of your actions on global atmospheric matters. You compare the private benefits to yourself of drinking the cold can of soda or having a comfortable night's sleep with the cost that *you* have to incur. You do not count the costs of an increase in the incidence of skin cancer as part of the price that has to be paid for the cold soda.

Externalities are not always negative—they are not always external costs. In fact, many activities bring external benefits. Education is a good example. Not only do more highly educated people derive benefits for themselves in the form of higher incomes and the enjoyment of a wider range of artistic and cultural activities, but they also bring benefits to others through social interaction. But in deciding how much schooling to undertake, we make our calculations on the basis of the costs borne by us and the benefits accruing to us as individuals. We do not take into account the extra benefits that we're creating for others.

Health services also create external benefits. The pursuit of good health and personal hygiene reduces the risk that people with whom we come into contact will be infected by transmitted diseases. Again, in making economic choices about the scale of resources to devote to health and hygiene, we take account of the costs borne by ourselves and the benefits accruing to ourselves and not the greater benefit that our actions bring to others.

A Global
Externality

TIME, JANUARY 2, 1989

Feeling the Heat

BY MICHAEL D. LEMONICK

For more than a decade, many scientists have warned that cars and factories are spewing enough gases into the atmosphere to heat up the earth in a greenhouse effect that could eventually produce disastrous climatic changes.

Carbon dioxide is released in large quantities when wood and such fossil fuels as coal, oil and natural gas are burned. As society industrialized, coal-burning factories began releasing CO_2 faster than plants and oceans, which absorb the gas, could handle it. In the early 1900s, people began burning oil and gas at prodigious rates. And increasing population led to the widespread cutting of trees in less developed countries. These trees are no longer available to soak up excess CO_2, and whether they are burned or left to rot, they instead release the gas. By the late 1800s atmospheric CO_2 had risen to between 280 and 290 parts per million. Today it stands at 350 p.p.m., and by 2050 it could reach 500 to 700 p.p.m., higher than it has been in millions of years.

By far the most efficient and effective way to spur conservation is to raise the cost of fossil fuels. Current prices fail to reflect the very real environmental costs of pumping carbon dioxide into the air. The answer is a tax on CO_2 emissions—or a CO_2 user fee, if that is a more palatable term. The fee need not raise a country's overall tax burden; it could be offset by reductions in income taxes or other levies.

Imposing a CO_2 fee would not be as difficult as it sounds. It is easy to quantify how much CO_2 comes from burning a gallon of gasoline, a ton of coal or a cubic yard of natural gas. Most countries already have gasoline taxes; similar fees, set according to the amount of CO_2 produced, could be put on all fossil-fuel sources. At the same time, companies could be given credits against their CO_2 taxes if they planted trees to take some of the CO_2 out of the air.

A user fee would have benefits beyond forcing a cutback in CO_2 emissions. The fuels that generate carbon dioxide also generate other pollutants, like soot, along with nitrogen oxides and sulfur dioxide, the primary causes of acid rain. The CO_2 tax would be a powerful incentive for consumers to switch from high-CO_2 fuels, such as coal and oil, to power sources that produce less CO_2, notably natural gas. When burned, methane generates only half as much CO_2 as coal, for example, in producing the same amount of energy. . . .

The Essence
of the Story

The amount of carbon dioxide (CO_2) in the earth's atmosphere has been increasing and continues to do so.

In the late nineteenth century, atmospheric carbon dioxide was between 280 and 290 p.p.m.; in the late 1980s, it was 350 p.p.m.; by 2050, it could reach 500 to 700 p.p.m.

The most effective method for controlling the greenhouse effect is to impose a tax on carbon dioxide emissions.

Background and Analysis

The marginal private cost of generating electricity by using fossil fuels is the curve MPC in Figs. 1(a) and 2(a). The marginal cost of generating electricity using solar power is the curve MC in Figs. 1(b) and 2(b). The supply curve of electricity is S and the demand curve is D in Figs. 1(c) and 2(c).

The power generated by solar energy has no externalities.

Generating power by using fossil fuel creates a carbon dioxide buildup with a possible greenhouse effect that imposes potentially large social costs. The marginal social cost of generating electricity using fossil fuels, including the external costs of the greenhouse effect, is the curve MSC in Figs. 1(a) and 2(a).

With no intervention (Fig. 1), equilibrium occurs at price P_0 and quantity Q_0; only fossil fuels are used; the marginal social cost is MSC_0, which exceeds the price P_0; there is allocative inefficiency—too much electricity is generated.

If a CO_2 tax is imposed equal to the external costs (Fig. 2), fossil fuel producers of electricity face costs shown by the curve labeled $MPC + tax = MSC$.

The market supply curve becomes the curve labeled $S + tax$.

Equilibrium occurs at price P_1 and quantity Q_1; Q_F is produced by fossil fuels and Q_S by solar energy; marginal social cost is MSC_1, which equals the price P_1; allocative efficiency is achieved.

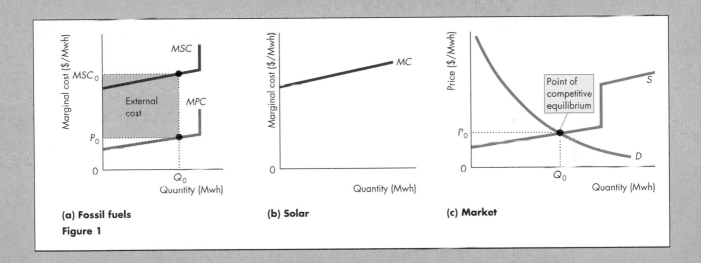

(a) Fossil fuels   (b) Solar   (c) Market

Figure 1

(a) Fossil fuels   (b) Solar   (c) Market

Figure 2

The existence of externalities—both costs and benefits—is another source of market failure. There are two possible types of action that governments can take to achieve a more efficient allocation of resources in the face of externalities:

♦ Establish and enforce private property rights
♦ Tax activities that produce external costs and subsidize those that bring external benefits

The evolution of our understanding of externalities and of the alternative ways of dealing with them is dealt with in Our Advancing Knowledge on pp. 530–531. Let's next consider the use of private property rights for dealing with externalities.

Private Property Rights and Externalities

There are some cases in which externalities arise because of an absence of private property rights. A **private property right** is a legally established title to the sole ownership of a scarce resource. A private property right is enforceable in the courts. The creation of externalities in the absence of private property rights is illustrated well by the example of the chemical factory and a private fishing club. Members of a private fishing club use a particular stretch of a stream that is well stocked with excellent fish. A typical factory opens upstream from the fishing club. It has to make a decision about how it will dispose of some of its waste products.

Consider two different legal situations. In the first, no one owns the stream. If the chemical factory dumps its waste products in the stream, its cost of waste disposal is zero. But the waste kills the fish, and the fishing club goes out of business.

In the second situation, there are property rights established in the stream. The fishing club owns its stretch of the stream and the fish that swim in it. The chemical factory might still dump its waste into the stream, but if it does so, and if it kills the fish, the fishing club will successfully bring a lawsuit against the chemical plant for damages. The damages paid to the fishing club are the cost to the chemical company of disposing of the chemical waste by dumping it in the river. If some other method of waste disposal is available that has a lower cost than killing the fish, the chemical factory will choose that alternative.

Whenever externalities arise from the absence of property rights that can easily be established and enforced, this method of dealing with externalities is

a natural one for governments to contemplate. But there are many situations in which private property rights simply cannot be established and enforced. In these cases, governments resort to the alternative method of coping with externalities—using taxes and subsidies. Let's see how these government tools work.

Taxes and External Costs

As we've just noted, every time you burn fossil fuel, you release carbon dioxide into the atmosphere. These carbon dioxide emissions impose unintended costs on others. Let's see how the government might modify your choices and encourage you to take account of the potential costs that you're imposing on others.

FIGURE **19.3**

Taxing and Regulating an Externality

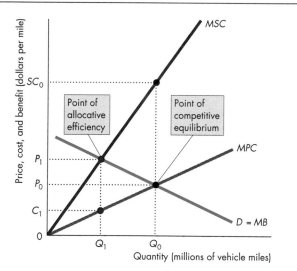

The demand curve for transportation services is also the marginal benefit curve ($D = MB$). The marginal private cost curve is MPC. Because of congestion and environmental pollution, the marginal cost of providing transportation services exceeds the marginal private cost. A marginal social cost is shown by curve MSC. If the market is competitive, output is Q_0 and the price is P_0. Marginal social cost is SC_0. If a tax is imposed to confront producers of transportation services with their full marginal social cost, the MSC curve becomes the relevant marginal cost curve for suppliers' decisions. The price increases to P_1, and the quantity decreases to Q_1. Allocative efficiency is achieved.

One activity that creates carbon dioxide is driving a gasoline-fueled vehicle. To study the demand for this activity, we'll examine the market for transportation services. Figure 19.3 illustrates this market. The demand curve is also the marginal benefit curve, the curve $D = MB$. It tells us how much consumers value each different level of output. Curve MPC measures the marginal private cost of producing transportation services. **Marginal private cost** is the marginal cost directly incurred by the producer of a good. Thus the MPC curve shows the marginal cost directly incurred by the producers of transportation services. But there are externalities in transportation. The fact that fossil fuels are burned creates atmospheric pollution and contributes to the greenhouse effect. It also causes other, more immediate health problems. Furthermore, one person's decision to use a highway imposes congestion costs on others. These costs are also external costs. When all the external marginal costs are added to the marginal private cost, we obtain the marginal social cost of transportation services. **Marginal social cost** is the marginal cost incurred by the producer of a good together with the marginal cost imposed as an externality on others. Marginal social cost is illustrated by the curve MSC in the figure.

Suppose that the transportation market is competitive and unregulated. People will balance the marginal private cost against the marginal benefit and travel Q_0 million miles at a price of P_0 per mile. At this scale of travel, a large amount of external costs will be borne. The marginal social cost is SC_0. The difference between P_0 and SC_0 represents the marginal cost imposed on others—the external marginal cost.

Suppose that the government taxes transportation and that it sets the tax equal to the external marginal cost. By imposing such a tax, the government raises the marginal private cost—the original marginal private cost *plus* the tax—to equal the marginal social cost. The MSC curve is now the relevant marginal cost curve for each person's decision, since each person now faces a marginal cost of transportation equal to its marginal social cost. The market supply curve shifts upward to become the MSC curve. The price rises to P_1, and the amount of travel falls to Q_1. The marginal cost of the resources used in producing Q_1 million miles of travel is C_1, but the marginal external cost generated is P_1 minus C_1. That external marginal cost is paid by the consumer through the tax.

The situation depicted at the price P_1 and the quantity Q_1 is allocatively efficient. At an output rate above Q_1, marginal social cost exceeds marginal benefit, so net benefit increases by producing less. At an output rate below Q_1, marginal benefit exceeds marginal social cost, so net benefit increases by producing more.

Subsidies and External Benefits

Some goods bring external benefits—benefits to people who do not directly consume the good. In some cases, the government induces additional consumption of such goods by subsidizing them. A **subsidy** is a payment made by the government to producers that depends on the level of output. Figure 19.4 shows how subsidizing education can increase the

FIGURE **19.4**

Subsidizing an External Benefit

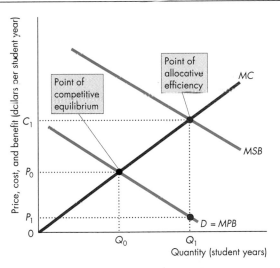

The demand curve for education also measures the marginal private benefit of education ($D = MPB$). The curve MC shows the marginal cost of education. If education is provided in a competitive market with no government intervention, the price of education is P_0 and the quantity bought is Q_0. But education produces a social benefit, and the marginal social benefit is shown by the curve MSB. Allocative efficiency is achieved if the government provides education services on a scale such that marginal social cost equals marginal social benefit. This scale of provision is Q_1, which is achieved if the government subsidizes education, making it available for a price of P_1. The quantity demanded at price P_1 is Q_1, and at that quantity marginal cost equals marginal social benefit at a level of C_1.

UNDERSTANDING
EXTERNALTIES

Whether it's dead fish caused by DDT, acid rain caused by smokestacks, or global warming caused by burning carbon fuels, externalities are easy to see. But solutions have been slow to evolve. Fifty years ago, none of these problems was high on anyone's agenda. Why?

There are two main reasons: as incomes grow, people value the environment more highly; and as technology advances, we discover external effects that were previously unknown. In combination, these two factors have increased the demand (and willingness to pay) for a cleaner and safer environment. And as demand has grown, so has our understanding of alternative economic solutions.

One solution is regulation. For example, DDT was banned and farmers had to substitute more expensive insecticides that were easier on the environment. Were the additional costs of such insecticides lower or higher than the value of reduced toxicity of our rivers and lakes? When regulation is used to control externalities, it is regulators and lawmakers who make judgments about value.

Another solution is taxation. For example, electric power companies could be charged a tax proportional to the volume of pollution they create. Again, lawmakers and bureaucrats make the decisions about comparative values. But given those decisions, firms decide how much pollution to create.

A third solution is establishing property rights over the resources being damaged by external factors. For example, the fishing companies of Lake Erie could be assigned property rights over the lake. They would decide the value of avoiding pollution and charge polluters a price sufficiently high to compensate for lost or lowered incomes resulting from pollution.

Finally, an externality can simply be endured. This is our current "solution" to the problem of global warming. In this case, no one has been able to implement an arrangement at a cost that is sufficiently low to result in a net social gain.

> "The question to be decided is: is the value of the fish lost greater or less than the value of the product which contamination of the stream makes possible."
>
> R. H. COASE
> *The Problem of Social Cost*

Chester Jackson, a Lake Erie fisherman, recalls that when he began fishing on the lake, boats didn't carry drinking water. Fishermen drank from the lake. Speaking after World War II, Jackson observed, "Can't do that today. Those chemicals in there would kill you." Ignorant of their external effects, farmers used chemicals such as the insecticide DDT that got carried into the lake by runoff. Industrial waste and trash were also dumped in the lake in large quantities. As a result, Lake Erie became badly polluted during the 1940s and became incapable of sustaining a viable fish stock.

Today, Lake Erie supports a fishing industry, just as it did in the 1930s. No longer treated as a garbage dump for chemicals, the lake is regenerating its ecosystem. Fertilizers and insecticides are now recognized as products that have potential externalities, and their external effects are assessed by the Department of the Environment before new versions are put into widespread use. Dumping industrial waste into rivers and lakes is now subject to much more stringent regulations and penalties. Lake Erie's externalities problems have been solved by one of the methods available: government regulation.

Externalities are solved by *public choices*. But for a time, economists lost sight of this fact. During the 1920s, Arthur Cecil Pigou (1877–1959), pictured left, of Cambridge, England, pioneered a branch of economics designed to guide public choices—*welfare economics*. Pigou devised rules which, if followed, ensured that decisions about externalities were in the *public interest*. But the rules were not followed.

Not until the 1950s did economists develop *public choice theory* and explain the choices *actually* made by politicians and bureaucrats. Among the leaders in this field was the 1986 Nobel laureate James Buchanan (1919–), pictured right, of George Mason University. Because of the

THE *Public Interest and Public Choices*

FROM PIGOU TO BUCHANAN

work of Buchanan and others, we now understand that the solutions adopted for externalities depend not on the public interest, but on private interests—on private costs and benefits. We also now appreciate, as a result of the work of Ronald H. Coase, that the transactions costs of organizing alternative solutions are crucial in determining which, if any, of those solutions is pursued.

amount of education and achieve allocative efficiency. Suppose that the marginal cost of producing education is shown by the curve *MC* (assuming there is no difference between marginal private cost and marginal social cost). The demand curve for education tells us the quantity of education demanded at each price when people are free to choose the amount of education that they undertake and pay for it themselves. It also measures the marginal private benefit—the benefit perceived by the individuals undertaking education. That curve is $D = MPB$. A competitive market in private education produces an output of Q_0 at a price of P_0.

Suppose that the external benefit—the benefit derived by people other than those undertaking education—results in marginal social benefits described by the curve *MSB*. Allocative efficiency occurs when marginal cost equals marginal social benefit. The quantity of education at which this equality occurs is Q_1. By providing the quantity of education Q_1 and making it available at the price P_1, the government can achieve allocative efficiency in the education sector. In this case, by producing education at a low price, the government encourages people to undertake the amount of education that makes its marginal social benefit equal to its marginal cost.

We've now looked at two examples of the way in which government action can help market participants take account of external costs and benefits.

REVIEW

When externalities are present, the market allocation is not efficient. Sometimes an efficient allocation can be achieved by establishing private property rights. But in many cases, private property rights simply cannot be established and enforced. In such cases, if the government confronts people with taxes equivalent to the external marginal costs or subsidies equivalent to external marginal benefits, it induces people to produce goods on a scale that achieves allocative efficiency, even in the face of externalities. ◆

◆ ◆ ◆ ◆ We've seen that markets do not always achieve allocative efficiency. When the market fails, we can describe an allocation that is efficient. But showing an efficient allocation is not the same thing as designing institutions to achieve one. Do governments in fact achieve allocative efficiency? Or are there economic problems arising from the functioning of a political system leading to "government failure" and preventing the attainment of an efficient allocation of resources? These questions are dealt with in the next chapter.

SUMMARY

The Government Sector

The government sector of the U.S. economy accounts for 35 percent of all expenditure on goods and services and 36 percent of total employment. The biggest departments of government deal with the provision of defense and health services. The Treasury Department is also a large one. The government share of the economy has grown over the years, increasing from less than 20 percent in 1940 to more than 35 percent in 1990.

But when economists study political behavior, they are careful to maintain the distinction between positive and normative analysis. Their main focus is on positive matters—on what *is* and on how the political system works rather than on what *ought* to be and how the political system *ought* to function.

All government economic actions stem from either market failure or the redistribution of income and wealth. Market failure arises from the provision of public goods and services, from externalities, and from monopolies and cartels. The redistribution of income and wealth arises partly from notions of equity and justice and partly from rent-seeking activities.

There are two broad approaches to the economic analysis of government—public interest theories and public choice theories. Public interest theories emphasize the idea of government as an institution able to eliminate waste and achieve allocative efficiency—an agent that operates with public interest. Public choice theories emphasize the idea that government operates in a political marketplace in which politicians, bureaucrats, and voters interact with each other. According to the public choice view, government failure to achieve allocative efficiency is as real as the possible failure of the market. (pp. 518–520)

Public Goods

Pure public goods have two features: nonrivalry and nonexcludability. One person's consumption does not reduce the amount available for someone else (nonrivalry), and no one can be kept from sharing the consumption of such a good (nonexcludability). An example of a pure public good is the national defense system.

The existence of public goods gives rise to the free-rider problem. This problem is the tendency for the scale of provision of a public good to be too small if it is produced and sold privately. The free-rider problem arises because there is insufficient incentive for a person to pay for a good if that payment has no effect on the quantity of the good the person consumes. Thus it pays everyone to free ride;

so with private provision, no revenue can be raised from the sale of a public good. In such a situation, no public goods are produced. In contrast, the government can produce a public good, paying for it out of taxation. People will vote for taxes and a public good provided that the net benefits are positive. The government is able to provide any public good on a scale larger than that provided by a private producer, but it does not necessarily produce an allocatively efficient amount of a public good. (pp. 520–525)

Externalities

An externality is a cost or a benefit arising from an economic transaction that falls on a third party and that is not taken into account by the parties undertaking the transaction. When external costs are present, allocative efficiency requires a reduction in the scale of output below what the market will produce. When external benefits are present, allocative efficiency requires an increase in output. There are two ways in which government can deal with externalities: establishing and enforcing private property rights or using taxes and subsidies. If the government uses taxes and subsidies, it imposes taxes where there are external costs and gives subsidies where there are external benefits. (pp. 525–532)

Key Terms

Externality, 525
Free rider, 521
Free-rider problem, 521
Marginal benefit, 521
Marginal private cost, 529
Marginal social cost, 529
Market failure, 519
Mixed good, 520
Net benefit, 523
Private good, 520
Private property right, 528
Public choice theory, 520

Public interest theory, 520
Pure public good, 520
Subsidy, 529
Total benefit, 521

Key Figures

Figure 19.1   Benefits of a Public Good, 522
Figure 19.2   The Efficient Scale of Provision of a Public Good, 524
Figure 19.3   Taxing and Regulating an Externality, 528
Figure 19.4   Subsidizing an External Benefit, 529

REVIEW QUESTIONS

1 How big is the government sector of the U.S. economy today?

2 Set out the main economic functions of government.

3 Provide an example of each function of government.

4 What is a pure public good?

5 Name examples of three goods: a pure public good, a private good, and a mixed good.

6 What is the free-rider problem, and how does government help overcome it?

7 What is an externality?

8 Give three examples of externalities.

PROBLEMS

1 You are given the following information about a sewage disposal system that a city of 1 million people is considering installing:

Capacity (thousands of gallons a day)	Marginal private benefit to one person (dollars)	Total cost (millions of dollars)
0		0
	100	
1		10
	80	
2		30
	60	
3		60
	40	
4		100
	20	
5		150

a What is the capacity that achieves the maximum net benefit?

b How much will each person have to be taxed to pay for the efficient capacity level?

c What are the total and net benefits?

2 A chemical factory dumps waste in a river. Damage is done to the local fish stock, and membership fees at a nearby fishing club are lowered by the following amounts:

Output of chemical plant (gallons per hour)	Lost fees to fishing club (dollars)
0	0
100	10
200	30
300	70
400	210

a The local government plans to tax the chemical factory. Devise a tax that will achieve allocative efficiency.

b How might private property rights be used in this situation?

3 The demand schedule for education in Brightland is as follows:

Number of students (thousands)	Tuition fee (dollars per year)
0	5,000
100	4,000
200	3,000
300	2,000
400	1,000
500	500
600	250

The marginal cost of providing education is $3,000 per year. There are external benefits of $2,000 per student.

a If the market for education in Brightland is private with no government intervention, how many students enroll in school, and what is the tuition fee?

b If the government wants to achieve allocative efficiency, how many student school places does it make available, and how big is the subsidy per student?

4 Two countries, Greenhaven and Smokehole, have identical marginal private benefit and marginal private cost schedules for electric power generated by burning coal. These schedules are as follows:

Quantity (millions of megawatts a day)	Marginal private benefit (dollars)	Marginal private cost (dollars)
0	14	1
1	12	1
2	10	1
3	8	2
4	6	3
5	5	5
6	4	6
7	3	7
8	2	8
9	1	9
10	0	10

The people of Greenhaven believe that each megawatt generated has a marginal social cost equal to twice its marginal private cost, and the government of Greenhaven imposes an electricity tax that achieves allocative efficiency. The people of Smokehole believe there are no social costs of producing electric power, and there is no government intervention in the market for electricity.

a How much electricity is generated in Greenhaven?

b What is the price of electricity in Greenhaven?

c How much tax revenue does the government of Greenhaven collect on the generation of electricity?

d How much electricity is generated in Smokehole?

e What is the price of electricity in Smokehole?

CHAPTER 20

PUBLIC CHOICE

After studying this chapter, you will be able to:

- ◆ Describe the components of the political marketplace
- ◆ Define a political equilibrium
- ◆ Explain how the main political parties choose their economic policy platforms
- ◆ Explain how governments determine the scale of provision of public goods and services
- ◆ Explain why we vote for redistributions of income and wealth
- ◆ Explain why governments tax some goods at much higher rates than others
- ◆ Predict the effects of taxes on prices, production, and profits
- ◆ Explain why governments subsidize the producers of some goods
- ◆ Predict the effects of subsidies on prices, production, and profits

DEMOCRATS AND REPUBLICANS BATTLE TO DOMINATE politics. The Democrats usually advocate increased government spending and intervention. The Republicans generally take the opposite side, promising lower spending and less intervention. Yet when they are in office, the two parties behave in remarkably similar ways. It was Jimmy Carter the Democrat who most effectively kept government spending in check. And it was Ronald Reagan the Republican who allowed spending—especially defense spending—to grow extremely quickly. Voters recognize these patterns. They hear the dramatic differences in the political rhetoric and complain that there really aren't all that many differences in the policies of opposing parties. Why do the two political parties take strongly different positions in what they say and yet deliver such similar policies? ◆ ◆

Rhetoric and Reality

Government pervades many aspects of our lives. It is present at our birth, supporting the hospitals in which we are born and training the doctors and nurses who deliver us. It is present throughout our education, supporting schools and colleges and training our teachers. It is present throughout our working lives, taxing our incomes, regulating our work environment, and paying us benefits when we are unemployed. It is present throughout our retirement, paying us a small income, and when we die, taxing our bequests. But the government does not make all our economic choices. We decide for ourselves what work to do, how much to save, and what to spend our income on. Why does the government intervene in some aspects of our lives but not others? Why doesn't the government provide more of our health services? Why doesn't it provide less of our education services? ◆ ◆ Almost everyone, from the poor single mother to the wealthy taxpayer, grumbles about government bureaucracy. Even presidents, senators, and representatives complain that the bureaucracy is too big, too slow, and inefficient. Why is the bureaucracy so unpopular and the target of so much scorn? How do government agencies and departments operate to deliver the many public services for which they are responsible? ◆ ◆ Government taxes almost all the goods and services that we buy. Some goods such as gasoline, alcohol, and tobacco products are taxed heavily. A few items are not taxed at all, and their producers even get subsidies from the government. Examples are milk and wheat. Why does government impose heavy taxes on some goods and subsidies on others? What are the effects of taxes on the amount of revenue raised by the government?

◆ ◆ ◆ ◆ In this chapter, we study the economic interactions of voters, politicians, and bureaucrats and discover how the scale and variety of government economic activity are determined. Our focus here is the provision of public goods and services, the taxes levied to pay for those services, the control of externalities, and the redistribution of income.

The Political Marketplace

Government is not a huge computer that grinds out solutions to resource allocation problems plagued with free riders and externalities. It does not simply calculate and balance marginal social costs and benefits, automatically achieving allocative efficiency. Rather, it is a complex organization made up of thousands of individuals. These individuals have their *own* economic objectives, and government policy choices are the outcomes of the choices made by these individuals. To analyze these choices, economists have developed a theory of the political marketplace that parallels theories of ordinary markets—*public choice theory*.

There are three types of actors in the political marketplace:

◆ Voters
◆ Politicians
◆ Bureaucrats

Voters are the consumers of the outcome of the political process. In ordinary markets for goods and services, people express their demands by their willingness to pay. In the political marketplace, voters express their demands in three principal ways. First, they express them by a willingness to vote, either in an election or on a referendum issue. Second, and less formally, they express their demands through campaign contributions. Third, they express their demands by lobbying. **Lobbying** is the activity of bringing pressure to bear on government agencies or institutions through a variety of informal mechanisms. The pro-life and pro-choice lobbies are two of the most prominent examples of such organizations in the United States today.

Politicians are the elected officials in federal, state, and local government—from the chief executives (the president, state governors, and mayors) to members of the legislatures (state and federal senators and representatives and city councilors). Politicians are chosen by voters.

Bureaucrats are the appointed officials who work at various levels in the many government departments, again at the federal, state, and local levels. The most senior bureaucrats are appointed by politicians. Junior bureaucrats are appointed by senior ones.

Voters, politicians, and bureaucrats make their economic choices in a way that best furthers their own objectives, but each group faces two types of constraints. First, each group is constrained by the preferences of the others. Bureaucrats are constrained by the preferences of politicians; politicians are constrained by the preferences of bureaucrats and voters; and voters are constrained by the preferences of bureaucrats and politicians. Second, voters, bureaucrats, and politicians cannot ignore technological constraints. They can do only things that are technologically feasible. We are going to examine the objectives of voters, politicians, and bureaucrats and the constraints they face when making their choices. We're also going to study the interactions among the three types of actors. In so doing, we are going to discover how the political system actually works.

The predictions of an economic model of voter, politician, and bureaucrat behavior are the equilibrium of the political process—the political equilibrium. A **political equilibrium** is a situation in which the choices of voters, politicians, and bureaucrats are all compatible and in which no one group of agents will be better off by making a different choice. Thus a political equilibrium has the same characteristics as an equilibrium in the markets for goods and services and factors of production.

The theory of public choice that we are about to study is a relatively new branch of economics that has grown rapidly in the past 30 years. It was recently recognized by the awarding of the Nobel Prize for economics to one of its principal architects, James Buchanan.

Let's begin our study of public choice theory by looking at the behavior of politicians and voters.

The Behavior of Politicians and Voters

All kinds of people go into politics. Some have noble ideals and want to make a lasting contribution to improving the conditions of their fellow citizens. Others are single-minded in pursuit of their own self-interest and profit. Most politicians, no doubt, blend these two extremes. Economic models of public choice are based on the assumption that in a democratic political system politicians' central objective is to get enough votes to be elected and to keep enough support to remain in office. Votes, to a politician, are similar to dollars to a private firm. In order to obtain enough votes, politicians form coalitions with each other; we call these coalitions political parties. A political party is simply a collection of politicians who have banded together for the purpose of achieving and maintaining office. A political party attempts to develop policies that appeal to a majority of the voters.

Public choice theory assumes that voters support policies that they believe make them better off and oppose policies that they believe make them worse off. They neither oppose nor support—they are indifferent among—policies that they believe have no effect on them. Voters' *perceptions* rather than reality are what guide their choices.

To obtain the support of voters, a politician (or political party) must offer a package of policies that voters believe will make them better off than the policies proposed by the opposing political parties.

There are two ways in which a political program can seek to make a voter better off. One way is to implement policies that make *everyone* better off. Providing national defense and protecting the environment are examples of such policies. Another way is to implement policies that make some voters worse off but at least 50 percent of the voters better off. Redistributing income in such a way that at least one half of the electorate reaps net benefits is one example. Supporting or opposing abortion is another, and supporting or opposing gun control yet another.

Political programs that make everyone better off feature in the platforms of all parties. Policies that favor one group over another differ from party to party and depend on which segment of the population or particular interest group a political party wants to appeal to. Let's see how politicians and voters interact and how the policy platforms of political parties emerge by examining how the political process handles the provision of public goods and external costs and benefits.

Public Goods   In Chapter 19, we compared the scale of provision of public goods that achieves allocative efficiency with the scale that would be provided through the private marketplace. Now we want to work out the scale of provision of public goods that a political system will actually deliver.

For the moment, let's ignore differences among individual voters and suppose that people have identical views about the benefits of public goods and externalities. Later we'll consider what happens when people disagree and have different preferences. To be concrete, let's stick with the example of national defense that we studied in Chapter 19.

Suppose that the total costs and total benefits of producing antimissile lasers are the ones shown in Fig. 20.1. (These are the same costs and benefits that we used in Chapter 19, pp. 521–524.) Suppose also that there are two political parties. Let's call one the Hawks and the other the Doves. Suppose that the Hawks and the Doves propose exactly the same policy platform in all respects except for national defense. The Hawks offer a high level of national defense. They propose to provide 4 antimissile lasers at a cost of $50 billion, with benefits of $50 billion and a net benefit of zero. The Doves propose to provide just 1 laser at a cost of $5 billion, with a benefit of $20 billion and a net benefit of $15 billion ($20

FIGURE **20.1**

Provision of a Public Good in a Political System

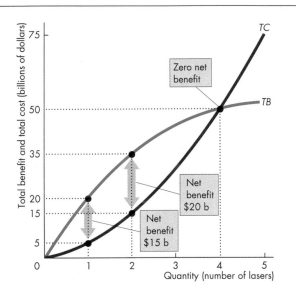

The total benefit curve for an antimissile laser weapon is *TB*, and the total cost curve is *TC*. Net benefit is maximized if 2 antimissile lasers are installed, with a total benefit of $35 billion and a total cost of $15 billion. There are two political parties offering platforms on this defense system: the Doves and the Hawks. Their platforms are identical on all matters except defense. The Doves propose to install 1 antimissile laser, and the Hawks propose 4. In an election, the Doves would win, since their proposal generates a larger net benefit than the Hawks' proposal. But if the Hawks propose to install 2 lasers, they would beat the Doves, since the net benefit resulting from 2 lasers exceeds that from 1. To get even, the Doves would have to match the Hawks. If voters are well informed and in general agreement about the value of a public good, competition between political parties for their votes can achieve an efficient scale of provision.

billion total benefit minus $5 billion total cost).

In an election in which voters are presented with the two platforms just described, the Doves will win. Recall that we assume that both parties are offering identical programs in every respect except for defense. The defense program of the Doves provides the voters with a net benefit of $15 billion over and above the taxes that they are asked to pay, while the Hawks are offering no net benefit; so the Doves will get all the votes.

Now suppose that the Hawks, contemplating the election outcome that we have just described, realize

that their party is being too hawkish. It is offering too high a level of defense to get elected. It figures that it has to offer net benefits in excess of $15 billion if it is to beat the Doves. It therefore scales back its plans and proposes to build 2 antimissile lasers. At this level of provision, the total cost is $15 billion and total benefit is $35 billion, so net benefit is $20 billion. The Hawks are now offering a package that the voters prefer to the one offered by the Doves. Now in an election, the Hawks will win.

The Doves, contemplating this outcome, realize that the best they can do is to match the Hawks. They too propose to provide 2 lasers on exactly the same terms as the Hawks. The voters are now indifferent between the proposals of the two parties and are indifferent about which one they vote for.

Competition for votes among political parties, even when there are only two of them, produces a political platform that maximizes the perceived net benefit accruing to the voters. For this outcome to occur, it is necessary that the voters be able to evaluate the alternatives. We'll see below that this condition is not necessarily going to be satisfied.

Externalities

The example that we have just worked through deals with a situation in which the voters are in agreement about and can calculate the benefits arising from different proposals. The same line of reasoning applies to policies concerning the control of externalities. Provided that the voters are in agreement about the benefits and can evaluate them, the political party that offers the level of control of externalities that maximizes net benefits will be the one that wins an election. The political party that proposes a total ban on the production of CFCs or sulfur dioxide emission will lose an election to a party that proposes more limited controls. A party that proposes a free-for-all on CFCs and sulfur dioxide emissions will lose an election to a party that proposes restraint in the production of goods that generate these external costs. Competition for votes will force each party to find the degree of control that maximizes net benefit.

In the examples of public goods and externalities that we have just worked out, we have ignored differences of opinion among the voters. We'll now go on to consider cases in which the preferences of voters differ and in which these differences are crucial in determining the outcome of the political process.

Interest Groups and Redistribution

Most matters decided in the political arena are ones on which people have different opinions. Some people favor a large national defense program while others urge disarmament; some favor a large scale of income redistribution while others urge tax cuts; some want massive government intervention to protect the environment while others want more limited environmental controls. Faced with this diversity of opinion, no political party can propose a platform that pleases everyone. But to attain office, a party must put together a package that attracts a majority of the votes. To do so, each party has to deliver a package that makes a majority of the voters better off (as the voters perceive it) than under the policies proposed by the opposing party (or parties). This search for a majority results in each political party offering policies that are very close to the policies of the others. This tendency toward similar policies is known as the principle of minimum differentiation.

The Principle of Minimum Differentiation   The **principle of minimum differentiation** is the tendency for competitors to make themselves almost identical in order to appeal to the maximum number of clients or voters. Let's study the principle of minimum differentiation by looking at a problem that is more familiar and concrete than that faced by political parties.

There are two ice cream vendors on a beach. The beach is one mile long, and it is illustrated in Fig. 20.2 as the distance from A to B. Sunbathers lounge at equal intervals over the entire beach. One of the ice cream vendors comes along and sets up a stand. Where will she locate? The answer is at position C— exactly halfway between A and B. With the ice cream stand in this position, the farthest that anyone has to walk to buy ice cream is a mile (half a mile to the ice cream stand and half a mile back to the beach towel).

Now suppose that a second ice cream vendor comes along. Where will he place his ice cream stand? The answer is right next to the original one at point C. To understand why, imagine that the second vendor locates his stand at point D—halfway between C and B. How many customers will he attract, and how many will go to the stand at C? The stand at D will pick up all the customers on the beach between B and D, because this stand is closer for them. It will also pick up all the customers

FIGURE 20.2

The Principle of Minimum Differentiation

A beach stretches from A to B. Sunbathers are distributed at even intervals along the whole beach. An ice cream seller sets up a stand at point C. The distance that people have to walk for ice cream is the same no matter on which side of the ice cream stand they are located. If a second ice cream seller sets up a stand, it will pay to place it exactly next to C in the middle of the beach. If the second stand is placed at D, only the customers on the beach between E and B will buy ice cream at D. Those between A and E will go to C. By moving as close to C as possible, the second ice cream vendor picks up half the ice cream customers.

between D and E (the point halfway between C and D), because they too will have a shorter trip for an ice cream by going to D than by going to C. All the people between A and C and all those between C and E will go to stand C. So the ice cream stand located at C will pick up all the people on the beach between A and E, and the stand located at D will pick up all the people located between E and B.

Now suppose that the vendor with a stand at D moves to C. There are now two stands at C. Half the customers will go to the first vendor and the other half to the second vendor. Only by locating bang in the center of the beach can each pick up half the customers. If either of them moves slightly away from the center, then that vendor picks up less than half the customers and the one remaining at the center picks up a majority of the customers.

This example illustrates the principle of minimum differentiation. By having no differentiation in location, both ice cream vendors do as well as they can and share the market evenly.

The principle of minimum differentiation has been applied to explain a wide variety of choices—how supermarkets choose their locations, how the makers of automobiles and microwave popcorn design their products, and how political parties choose their platforms.

The principle of minimum differentiation predicts that political parties will be similar to each other. But it does not tell us which policies they will favor, only that they will favor similar ones. In the case of the ice cream vendor, the location is determined by technological considerations—minimizing the distance that the bathers have to walk. But what determines a political party's choice of platform? Let's now address this question.

The Median Voter Theorem   An interesting proposition about a political party's choice of platform is provided by the median voter theorem. The **median voter theorem** states that political parties will pursue policies that maximize the net benefit of the median voter. (The median of a distribution of, say, student heights is the height of the student in the middle. One half of the students are taller and one half of the students are shorter than the median.) Let's see how the median voter theorem applies to the question of how large a tax to impose on sulfur dioxide emissions that cause acid rain.

Imagine arranging all the voters along a line running from *A* to *B*, as shown in Fig. 20.3. The voter wanting the highest tax is at *A*, the one wanting no tax is at *B*, and all the other voters are arranged along the line based on the level of the tax that they favor. The curve in the figure shows the tax rate favored by each voter between *A* and *B*. As shown, the median voter favors a tax rate of 30 percent.

Suppose that two political parties propose similar but not quite identical taxes on emissions of sulfur dioxide. One party proposes a tax of 61 percent, and the other proposes a tax of 59 percent. All the voters lying between *A* and *C* prefer the higher tax and will vote for it. All the voters lying between *C* and *B* prefer the lower tax and will vote for it. The lower tax party will win the election.

Alternatively, suppose that the two political parties offer a low tax rate—and, again, slightly different rates. One party offers a rate of 11 percent, and the other offers a rate of 9 percent. The voters between *A* and *D* will vote for the higher tax rate and those between *D* and *B* for the lower rate. This time, the higher tax party will win.

FIGURE **20.3**
The Median Voter Theorem

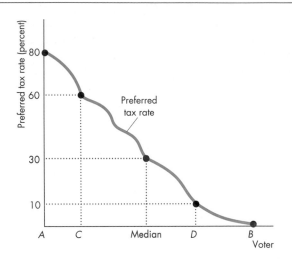

A political party can win an election by proposing policies that appeal to the median voter and to all the other voters on one side of the median. If the median voter mildly favors a policy, that policy will be proposed. In the figure, voters have different preferences concerning the rate at which to tax an externality. They are ranked from *A* to *B* in descending order of their preferred tax. There are two political parties. If one proposes a 61 percent tax and the other a 59 percent tax, the lower tax party will win the election—voters between *A* and *C* will vote for the high tax, and those between *C* and *B* will vote for the low tax. If both parties propose low taxes—11 percent and 9 percent—the party proposing the higher tax will win. It will pick up the votes between *A* and *D*, leaving only the votes between *D* and *B* for the lower tax party. Each party will have an incentive to move toward the tax rate preferred by the median voter, 30 percent. At that point, each party picks up half the votes and neither can improve its share.

But each party, in either of these situations, will see that it can win the election by moving closer to the tax rate preferred by the median voter. Once the two parties are offering that tax rate, however, neither will be able to increase its share of the vote by changing its proposal. One party will get the votes between *A* and the median, and the other the votes between the median and *B*. All the voters except the median will be dissatisfied—for those between *A* and the median the tax rate is too low, and for those between *B* and the median the tax is too high. But no political party can propose a tax other than 30 percent and expect to win the election. Of course, if the two parties propose exactly 30 percent, the voters will be indifferent and either will not bother to vote or will flip a coin to decide which party to vote for.

The principle of minimum differentiation and the median voter theorem seem to imply that all political parties will be identical in all respects. If that is so, it is too bad for the principle and the theorem. The world that we live in has political parties that certainly do differ. Many of us are heated in our support for and opposition to particular parties and policy proposals. It is in the area of the redistribution of income and wealth that one of the major differences in political parties arises. Let's use the principle of minimum differentiation and the median voter theorem to see if we can understand why all political parties favor some redistribution but why, also, there are differences in the parties in this respect.

Voting for Income Redistribution

The first model of redistribution that we'll consider is one that results in voting cycles. Imagine a society with 100 voters. These voters are divided into four different income groups, as set out in Table 20.1. Twenty-five of the voters earn $10,000 a year, another 25 earn $20,000 a year, another 25 earn $40,000 a year, and the richest 25 earn $90,000 a year. The average income in this community is $40,000 a year.

Suppose that a political party proposes to tax the richest 25 people $5,000 and the second richest

$3,000. It proposes to make transfers of $5,000 to the poorest 25 people and $3,000 to the next poorest 25. The incomes resulting from the tax and transfers in this proposal are set out in the third column of Table 20.1. The average income is still $40,000. The final column of the table shows the gains and losses to each income group. The poorest gain and the richest lose.

Suppose that there is a second political party in this society that opposes the redistribution scheme just described. Which party will win the election? The answer is that it will be a tie. The party proposing the redistribution scheme will pick up 50 percent of the votes—those of the poorer half of the electorate. The party opposing the redistribution scheme will pick up the other half of the votes (those at the wealthier end of the income distribution).

Now suppose that one of the parties offers the modified scheme set out in Table 20.2. The proposal is to tax the richest quarter of the people not $5,000 but $8,000 and not to tax the second richest quarter at all. Under this scheme, the two poorest groups of people will receive benefits of $5,000 and $3,000, respectively. One party supports these measures, and the other opposes them and proposes no redistribution at all. Which party will win? The answer is the party supporting redistribution. All the people with original incomes of $10,000 and $20,000 will vote for the scheme. Those with incomes of $40,000 will be indifferent between the two parties, so we may suppose that half will vote for one party and half for the other. The party opposing the redistribution

---

TABLE 20.1

Voting for Income Redistribution: A Tie

Number of voters		Income before redistribution (thousands of dollars)	Income after redistribution (thousands of dollars)	Gain (+) or loss (−) (thousands of dollars)
25		10	15	+5
25		20	23	+3
25		40	37	−3
25		90	85	−5
Total: 100	Averages:	40	40	0

TABLE 20.2

Voting for Income Redistribution: The Rich Lose

Number of voters		Income before redistribution (thousands of dollars)	Income after redistribution (thousands of dollars)	Gain (+) or loss (−) (thousands of dollars)
25		10	15	+5
25		20	23	+3
25		40	40	0
25		90	82	−8
Total: 100	Averages:	40	40	0

scheme will collect the votes of the richest quarter of the people plus half of those in the second richest group.

This example shows one particular redistribution proposal that could gain the support of the majority of voters. But there will be many other proposals that could also gain majority support (but with different people making up the majority in each case). There is no end to the different proposals that could win a majority. As these different schemes are proposed, there are cycles in the voting.

Why do we not observe voting cycles in reality? Why do we see a tendency for redistribution policies to remain in place for very long periods of time? The answer is suggested by a second model of redistribution—a median voter model. A key feature of this model is what has been called the "big tradeoff" (see Chapter 18, p. 508). The greater the amount of income that is redistributed, the smaller is the incentive to work and the lower is the average level of income. As a consequence, redistributive taxes have two effects on the median voter: they raise the median voter's income by taking from those above the median and redistributing to those at and below the median; they also lower the median voter's income by reducing the incentive to work, which lowers average income. Which of these two opposing effects is stronger depends on the scale of redistribution. At low tax rates, the disincentive effects are small, so an increase in taxes makes the median voter better off. The higher income resulting from transfers from the rich is more than enough to offset

the lower income resulting from disincentive effects. If tax rates are set too high, a cut in taxes will make the median voter better off. In this case, the lower income resulting from smaller transfers from the rich is more than made up for by the higher average income resulting from improved incentives. But there is a scale of redistribution—level of taxes and transfers—that is exactly right from the point of view of the median voter. This scale of redistribution is the one that balances these two considerations and maximizes the median voter's income. This amount of redistribution is a possible political equilibrium.

Model and Reality

We've now looked at two models of equilibrium redistribution—a voting cycles model and a median voter model. In the voting cycles model, there is a never-ending sequence of different majorities for different directions of redistribution. In the median voter model, there is a unique equilibrium that maximizes the net benefit to the median voter.

Which of these models best fits the facts about income redistribution? The median voter model comes closest. Its strengths lie in its predictions that the political parties will differ in their rhetoric but be very close to each other in the actual redistribution measures for which they vote. In contrast, the voting cycles model predicts a sequence of difference majorities for different directions of redistribution that we do not observe in reality.

REVIEW

Politicians seek to obtain enough votes to achieve and maintain power. They do this by appealing to slightly more than half of the electorate. The key voter is the median voter. To appeal to the median voter, political parties offer programs that favor a majority of the electorate. Each party tries to outdo the other by appealing to the median voter. In part, that appeal results from the political parties proposing income-increasing policies. It also, in part, results from the redistribution of income to the point where no one can invent a way of raising the income of the median voter. ◆

We have analyzed the behavior of politicians but not that of the bureaucrats who translate the choices of the politicians into programs. Let's now turn to an examination of the economic choices of bureaucrats.

The Behavior of Bureaucrats

An interesting model of the behavior of bureaucrats has been suggested by William Niskanen. In that model, bureaucrats aim to maximize the budget of the agency in which they work. The bigger the budget of the agency, the greater is the prestige of the agency chief and the larger is the opportunity for promotion for people farther down the bureaucratic ladder. Thus all the members of an agency have an interest in maximizing the agency's budget. In seeking to obtain the largest budget it can, each government agency and department marshals its best arguments for why it should have more funds to spend. Since each agency does its best to obtain more funds, the net result is upward pressure for expenditure on all publicly provided goods and services.

The constraints on maximizing the budget of a government department or agency are the taxes that politicians have to levy and the implications of those taxes for the politicians' ability to win votes. But government departments and agencies recognize and appreciate the interplay between their own objectives and those of politicians and so do their best to help the politicians appreciate the vote-winning consequences of spending more on their own particular department or agency. Thus budget maximization,

to some degree, translates itself into political campaigns designed to explain to voters why they need more defense, more health services, and so on.

Let's examine the consequences of bureaucratic budget maximization for the provision of public goods and their cost by looking again at the example of national defense. We've studied this example twice before. The first time (in Chapter 19, pp. 521–524), our concern was to establish that a government could overcome the free-rider problem and produce a larger quantity of a public good than would be produced by the private market. In this chapter (on pp. 539–540), we examined the way in which political parties competing for votes determine the scale of provision of a public good in a situation in which the voters are in agreement about the benefits of the public good and in which they are able to assess the costs and benefits of different scales of provision. In that example, no bureaucrats intervene in the process.

But the creation and operation of weapons and defense systems require the establishment of a large and complex government bureaucracy. How does the defense bureaucracy influence the scale and cost of the defense program? Let's answer this question by returning to the example of the installation of an antimissile laser defense system.

Take a look at Fig. 20.4. You will recognize it as being similar to Fig. 20.1. The horizontal axis shows the number of antimissile lasers, and the vertical axis shows their total benefit and total cost. The curve labeled *TB* shows the total benefit as perceived by all the individuals in the economy, and the curve labeled *TC* shows the total cost.

We saw earlier that the level of provision that maximizes net benefit is 2 lasers. This level of defense costs $15 billion, and it yields a total benefit of $35 billion and a net benefit of $20 billion. A political party that proposes installing 2 lasers will win an election because there is no higher net benefit possible. But will the Pentagon press Congress to vote for 2 lasers? According to Niskanen's model of bureaucracy, it will not. The Pentagon will push to expand the scale of provision and budget for national defense to the largest possible level. If it is able to increase the number of antimissile lasers to 4, for example, it can increase the budget to $50 billion. In this situation, total benefit equals total cost and net benefit is zero. If the Pentagon is able to increase defense to an even higher level, its budget increases yet further and net benefit becomes negative.

FIGURE 20.4

Bureaucratic Overprovision

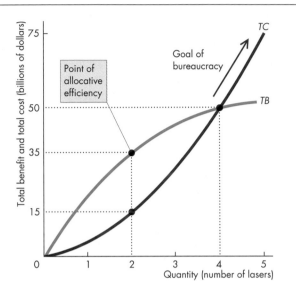

An agency that maximizes its budget will seek to expand output and expenditure as far as possible. For example, the Pentagon prefers 4 antimissile lasers at a cost of $50 billion to the allocatively efficient number—2 at a cost of $15 billion. The goal of the agency is to move as far up the total cost curve as possible, as shown in the figure. If voters are well informed, politicians will not be able to deliver the taxes that enable the agency to get beyond the point of allocative efficiency. But if some voters are rationally ignorant while others are well informed, it is possible that the agency will be able to raise its budget above the allocatively efficient level. In general, the agency will produce a higher quantity than the one that maximizes net benefit.

But how would it be possible for the Pentagon to get away with pressing the politicians for a scale of defense spending in excess of that which maximizes net benefit? Won't it always pay the politicians to take control of the Pentagon and cut back on the scale of military spending?

We've already seen that when there are two political parties competing for votes, the party that gets closest to maximizing net benefit is the one that picks up the most votes. Don't these forces of competition for votes dominate the wishes of the bureaucrats and ensure that the maximum budget allowed to them is that which maximizes net benefit?

If voters are well informed and if their perception of their self-interest is correct, the political party

that wins the election is the one that holds the Pentagon budget to the level that provides the efficient amount of defense. But there is another possible equilibrium. It is one based on the principle of voter ignorance and well-informed interest groups.

Voter Ignorance and Well-Informed Interest Groups

One of the major propositions of public choice theory is that it does not pay voters to be well informed about the issues on which they are voting unless those issues have an immediate and direct consequence for their own income. In other words, it pays voters to be rationally ignorant. **Rational ignorance** is the decision *not* to acquire information because the cost of acquiring the information is greater than the benefit derived from having it. For example, each voter knows that he or she can make virtually no difference to the actual defense policy pursued by the U.S. government. Each voter also knows that it would take an enormous amount of time and effort to become even moderately well-informed about alternative defense technologies and the most effective ways of achieving different levels of defense. As a result, voters see it as being in their best interests to remain relatively uninformed about the technicalities of national defense issues. (Though we are using national defense as an example, the same applies to all aspects of government economic activity.)

All voters are consumers of national defense. But not all voters produce it. Only a small number are in this latter category. Those voters who produce national defense, whether they be members of the military or firms and households that work in producing defense equipment, have a direct personal interest in defense because it affects their incomes. Unlike other voters, therefore, it pays these voters to become well informed about national defense issues and to operate a political lobby aimed at furthering their own interests. These voters, in collaboration with the bureaucracies that deliver national defense, will exert a larger influence through the voting process than the relatively uninformed general voters who only consume this public good.

If the rationality of the uninformed voter and the rationality of the informed special interest group are taken into account, a political equilibrium emerges in which the scale of provision of public goods exceeds the one that maximizes net benefit.

Bureaucrats seek the largest possible budgets, and politicians balance the demand for bigger budgets against the cost of losing votes through higher taxes. If voters are well informed, they vote for the budget size that maximizes net benefit. If the consumers of public goods are less well informed about their costs and benefits than are the producers of those goods, the scale of provision of public goods exceeds that which maximizes net benefit. ◆

We've now seen how voters, politicians, and bureaucrats interact to determine the scale of provision of public goods and services and the scale of redistribution and how they deal with external costs and benefits. But public goods and services have to be paid for with taxes. How does the political marketplace determine the scale and variety of taxes that we pay? And why does the government not tax some goods and services, but instead subsidizes them? We've seen one partial answer to some of these questions already—taxes and subsidies might be used as a part of the government's attempt to deal with externalities. But that is not the entire story, as we'll now see.

Taxes and Subsidies

The bulk of the government's revenue arises from income taxes. But more than one fifth of the revenue of the federal, state, and local governments comes from taxes on expenditure. The highest tax rates are levied on such commodities as gasoline, alcoholic beverages, tobacco products, and some imported goods. Why are some goods taxed very highly and others hardly at all? Why are some goods even subsidized?

Excise Taxes

An **excise tax** is a tax on the sale of a particular commodity. The tax may be set as a fixed dollar amount per unit of the commodity, in which case it is called

a *specific tax*. Alternatively, the tax may be set as a fixed percentage of the value of the commodity, in which case it is called an *ad valorem tax*. The taxes on gasoline, alcoholic beverages, and tobacco products are all examples of excise taxes.

Let's study the effects of an excise tax by considering the tax on gasoline. We'll assume that the market for gasoline is competitive. The presence of monopolistic elements does affect the answer to the question that we're now examining, and we'll consider what that effect is when we've worked through the competitive case.

Figure 20.5 illustrates the market for gasoline. The quantity of gasoline, measured in millions of gallons a day, is shown on the horizontal axis, and the price of gasoline (measured in cents per gallon) is on the vertical axis. The demand curve for gasoline is *D*, and the supply curve is *S*. If there is no tax on gasoline, its price is 60¢ a gallon and 400 million gallons of gasoline a day are bought and sold.

FIGURE 20.5

An Excise Tax ◆

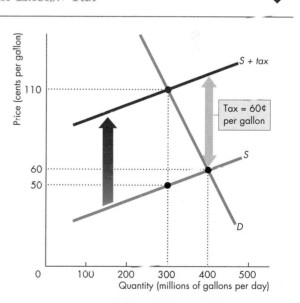

The demand curve for gasoline is *D*, and the supply curve is *S*. In the absence of any taxes, gasoline will sell for 60¢ a gallon and 400 million gallons a day will be bought and sold. When a tax of 60¢ a gallon is imposed, the supply curve shifts upward to become the curve *S* + *tax*. The new equilibrium price is $1.10 a gallon, and 300 million gallons a day are traded.

Let's suppose that a tax is imposed on gasoline at the rate of 60¢ a gallon. If producers are willing to supply 400 million gallons a day for 60¢ when there is no tax, then they will be willing to supply that same quantity in the face of a 60¢ tax only if the price increases to $1.20 a gallon. That is, they will want to get the 60¢ a gallon they received before, plus the additional 60¢ that they now have to hand over to the government in the form of a gasoline tax. As a result of the tax, the supply curve shifts upward by the amount of the tax and becomes the red curve labeled *S + tax*. The new supply curve intersects the demand curve at a quantity of 300 million gallons a day and at a price of $1.10 a gallon. This situation is the new equilibrium after the imposition of the tax.

Although we have just examined the effects of an excise tax on gasoline, the same basic analysis has widespread application. Taxes on alcohol and tobacco, sales taxes, and even taxes imposed in the labor market—for example, personal income taxes and social security taxes—can be analyzed in the same manner. The imposition of a tax shifts the supply curve upward by the amount of the tax. The new equilibrium is determined at a higher price and a lower quantity.

Monopoly Markets   A monopoly industry has a higher price and smaller quantity than the same industry would have in competitive conditions. The monopoly determines its profit-maximizing price by making marginal revenue and marginal cost equal. The imposition of a sales tax or excise tax on a monopoly works in a manner similar to the way it works in a competitive industry. The tax represents an increase in the monopoly's marginal cost. Its marginal cost curve shifts upward by the amount of the tax. Monopoly profit is maximized by producing the output at which marginal cost plus tax equals marginal revenue. Thus the imposition of a sales tax or an excise tax on a monopoly industry has the effect of raising the price and lowering output in the same way that it does in a competitive industry.

Why Do Tax Rates Vary?

Why is the structure of taxes the way it is? Why do we tax alcohol, tobacco, and gasoline at a very high rate and some goods not at all? There are two main reasons why some commodities are taxed very high-

ly and others hardly at all. First, the consumption of some goods, as we saw in Chapter 19, imposes external costs. By placing taxes on the purchase and consumption of such goods, people can be made to take into account the external costs they are imposing on others when they make their own consumption choices. Second, taxes create *deadweight losses,* and levying taxes at different rates on different commodities can minimize the deadweight loss arising from raising a given amount of revenue. Let's look at these two explanations for variable tax rates a bit more closely.

External Costs   External costs are associated with many goods that are taxed at a high rate. For example, the high tax on gasoline in part enables road users to be confronted with the marginal social cost of the congestion that they impose on others. The high taxes on alcohol and tobacco products in part serve to confront drinkers and smokers with the external costs that their consumption habits impose on others. The impairment of long-term health that results from using these products and the subsequent health-care costs may lead to costs that are borne by others. These costs are not taken into account when a person is deciding whether or not to drink or smoke.

Some goods that have high external costs associated with their consumption are not taxed. Instead, they are made illegal. Marijuana and cocaine are important examples of such goods. Large amounts of these goods are consumed every day in the United States, and the illegal markets in which they are traded generate large external costs. An alternative way of organizing these markets would be to make these drugs legal but to impose heavy taxes on them. Sufficiently high taxes would leave the quantities consumed similar to (and perhaps even smaller than) what they currently are and would confront the users of these drugs with the marginal social cost of their actions. Such taxes would also result in a source of revenue (perhaps a large one) for the government. (Of course, matters relating to drugs have dimensions that go beyond a narrow economic calculation. Some people believe that the consumption of these drugs is so immoral that it would be equally immoral for the government, or anyone else, to legally profit from their production and consumption. These considerations, important though they are, go beyond the scope of economics.)

Let's now look at the deadweight loss that arises from taxes and the way in which this loss can be minimized.

Minimizing the Deadweight Loss of Taxes   By returning to the example of the gasoline tax that you studied in Fig. 20.5, it's easy to see that taxes create deadweight loss. The deadweight loss associated with the gasoline tax is illustrated in Fig. 20.6. Without a tax, 400 million gallons of gasoline a day are consumed at a price of 60¢ a gallon. With a 60¢ tax, the price paid by the consumer rises to $1.10 a gallon and the quantity consumed declines to 300 million gallons a day. There is a loss of consumer surplus arising from this price increase and quantity decrease. There is also a loss of producer surplus. Producers now receive 50¢ a gallon for 300 million gallons compared with 60¢ a gallon for 400 million gallons in the absence of taxes. The deadweight

loss—the sum of the loss of consumer surplus and the loss of producer surplus—is indicated by the gray triangle in Fig. 20.6. The dollar value of that triangle is 30 million dollars a day.[1] But how much revenue is raised by this tax? Since 300 million gallons of gasoline are sold each day and since the tax is 60¢ a gallon, total revenue from the gasoline tax is $180 million a day (300 million gallons multiplied by 60¢ a gallon). Thus to raise tax revenue of $180 million dollars a day using the gasoline tax, a deadweight loss of $30 million a day—one sixth of the tax revenue—is incurred.

One of the main influences on the deadweight loss arising from a tax is the elasticity of demand for the product. The demand for gasoline is fairly inelastic. As a consequence, when a tax is imposed, the quantity demanded falls by a smaller percentage than the percentage rise in price. In the example that we've just studied, the quantity demanded falls by 25 percent but the price increases by 83.33 percent.

To see the importance of the elasticity of demand, let's consider a different commodity—orange juice. So that we can make a quick and direct comparison, let's assume that the orange juice market is exactly as big as the market for gasoline. Figure 20.7 illustrates this market. The demand curve for orange juice is D, and the supply curve is S. Orange juice is not taxed, and so the price of orange juice is 60¢ a gallon—where the supply curve and the demand curve intersect—and the quantity of orange juice traded is 400 million gallons a day.

Now suppose that the government contemplates abolishing the gasoline tax and taxing orange juice instead. The demand for orange juice is more elastic than the demand for gasoline. It has many more good substitutes in the form of other fruit juices. The government wants to raise $180 million a day so that its total revenue is not affected by this tax change. The government's economists, armed with their statistical estimates of the demand and supply curves for orange juice that appear in Fig. 20.7, work out that a tax of 90¢ a gallon will do the job. With such a tax, the supply curve shifts upward to

FIGURE 20.6

The Deadweight Loss from an Excise Tax

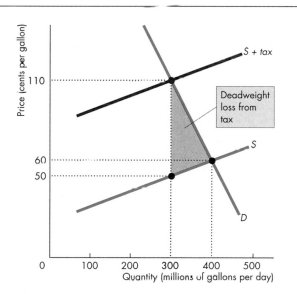

An excise tax creates a deadweight loss represented by the gray triangle. The tax revenue collected is 60¢ a gallon on 300 million gallons, $180 million a day. The deadweight loss from the tax is $30 million a day. That is, to raise tax revenue of $180 million a day, a deadweight loss of $30 million a day is incurred.

---

[1]You can calculate the area of that triangle by using the formula (base × height)/2. Turn the triangle on its side so that its base is 60¢, the size of the tax. Its height then becomes the reduction in the quantity sold—100 million gallons a day. Multiplying 60¢ by 100 million gallons and then dividing by 2 gives $30 million a day.

FIGURE **20.7**

Why We Don't Tax Orange Juice

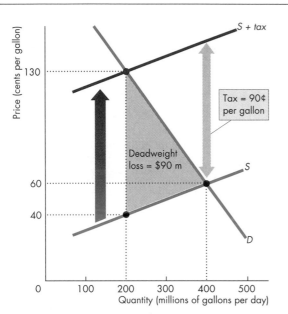

The demand curve for orange juice is *D*, and the supply curve is *S*. The equilibrium price is 60¢ a gallon, and 400 million gallons of juice a day are traded. To raise $180 million of tax revenue, a tax of 90¢ a gallon will have to be imposed. The introduction of this tax shifts the supply curve to *S + tax*. The price rises to $1.30 a gallon, and the quantity traded falls to 200 million gallons a day. The deadweight loss is represented by the gray triangle and equals $90 million a day. The deadweight loss from taxing orange juice is much larger than that from taxing gasoline (Fig. 20.6) because the demand for orange juice is more elastic than the demand for gasoline. Items that have a low elasticity of demand are taxed more heavily than items that have a high elasticity of demand.

the curve labeled *S + tax*. This new supply curve intersects the demand curve at a price of $1.30 a gallon and at a quantity of 200 million gallons a day. The price at which suppliers are willing to produce 200 million gallons a day is 40¢ a gallon. The government collects a tax of 90¢ a gallon on 200 million gallons a day, so it collects a total revenue of $180 million dollars a day—exactly the amount that it requires.

But what is the deadweight loss in this case? The answer can be seen by looking at the gray triangle in Fig. 20.7. The magnitude of the deadweight loss is

$90 million.[2] Notice how much bigger the deadweight loss is from taxing orange juice than that from taxing gasoline. In the case of orange juice, the deadweight loss is one half the revenue raised, while in the case of gasoline it is only one sixth. The difference between these two markets is the elasticity of demand. The supply curves are identical in each case, and the examples were also set up to ensure that the initial no-tax prices and quantities were identical. The difference between the two cases is the elasticity of demand: In the case of gasoline, the quantity demanded falls by only 25 percent when the price almost doubles. In the case of orange juice, the quantity demanded falls by 50 percent when the price only slightly more than doubles.

You can see why taxing orange juice is not on the political agenda of any of the major parties. Vote-seeking politicians seek out taxes that benefit the median voter. Other things being equal, this means that they try to minimize the deadweight loss of raising a given amount of revenue. Equivalently, they tax items with an inelastic demand more heavily than items with an elastic demand.

Let's now turn to an examination of subsidies.

Subsidies Subsidies do not constitute a large percentage of government expenditure at the federal, state, or local level. Nevertheless, subsidies are important for many individual industries and are particularly important in agriculture. Even goat farmers receive subsidies on the production of mohair—see Reading Between the Lines, pp. 552–553. But the big subsidies are paid to the grain and dairy industries. For grain producers, subsidies bring in more than 10 percent of their total receipts. We'll study subsidies by looking at the market for wheat.

Suppose that the wheat market is as illustrated in Fig. 20.8. The demand curve is *D*, and the supply curve is *S*. Two billion bushels a year are produced at a price of $3.50 a bushel. Now suppose that the government offers wheat growers a subsidy of $1 a

---

[2]This deadweight loss is calculated in exactly the same way as the deadweight loss from the gasoline tax. If we turn the deadweight loss triangle on its side, the base is 90¢ and the height is 200 million gallons. Using the formula for the area of the triangle—base multiplied by height divided by 2—we calculate the deadweight loss as 90¢ multiplied by 200 million and then divided by 2, which equals $90 million a day.

FIGURE **20.8**
Subsidies

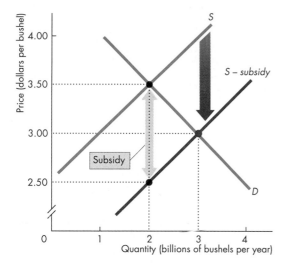

The demand curve for wheat is *D*, and the supply curve is *S*. A competitive market with no taxes or subsidies produces 2 billion bushels of wheat a year at a price of $3.50 a bushel. If the government subsidizes wheat production by $1 a bushel, the supply curve shifts downward to the curve labeled *S – subsidy*. The price of wheat falls to $3 a bushel, and the quantity produced increases to 3 billion bushels a year. Wheat growers receive just enough revenue from the market, along with the subsidy, to cover their costs.

FIGURE **20.9**
Subsidies with Quotas

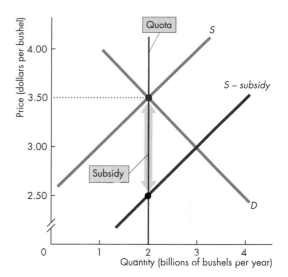

A competitive wheat market with no taxes or subsidies produces 2 billion bushels a year at a price of $3.50 a bushel—the point of intersection of the curves *D* and *S*. A subsidy of $1 a bushel shifts the supply curve to *S – subsidy*. But if a quota is introduced, at the same time as the subsidy, the output of each producer is restricted so that total output stays at 2 billion bushels a year, and the price remains $3.50 a bushel. With the quota, producers receive $3.50 from the market plus $1 from the government. Producers gain from the quota. The revenue from the market covers costs, so the subsidy is like a monopoly profit.

bushel. If suppliers are willing to supply 2 billion bushels a year for $3.50 without a subsidy, then they will be willing to supply that same quantity for $2.50 with a $1 subsidy. The supply curve for wheat, therefore, shifts downward by the amount of the subsidy and becomes the curve that is labeled *S – subsidy*. The equilibrium occurs where the new supply curve intersects the demand curve at a price of $3 a bushel and at a quantity of 3 billion bushels a year. The price of wheat falls by 50¢ a bushel. Consumers pay 50¢ a bushel less, and producers' costs rise by 50¢ a bushel. The 50¢ cost increase and the 50¢ price cut are made up by the $1 subsidy to the producer.

Subsidies with Quotas In the United States, in addition to subsidies on production in the farm sector, there are also quotas. A **quota** is a limit on the

quantity that a firm is permitted to produce. When a group of producers can enforce quotas, it is possible to restrict output and thereby obtain monopoly profit. We can see the effects of quotas and subsidies in Fig. 20.9. Suppose that the government establishes and enforces quotas for each producer that result in total output being 2 billion bushels a year (shown by the vertical line marked "Quota" in the figure). At this output level, consumers are willing to pay $3.50 a bushel for the wheat, and so that will be its market price. Producers also get a subsidy of a dollar a bushel on everything they produce, so the supply curve becomes *S – subsidy*. With the subsidy and a market price of $3.50, producers would like to supply 4 billion bushels a year—the quantity on the new (red) supply curve at a price of $3.50. But they're prevented from doing so by the quota.

The Political Market in Subsidies

The New York Times, February 26, 1993

'Strategic' Goats Gobble Up Trade Subsidy

BY KEITH BRADSHER

MENARD, Tex.—Here on a stony meadow in West Texas, at the end of 10 miles of unpaved road through mesquite-covered, coyote-infested scrub land, several hundred bearers of a strategic commodity of the United States of America are gathered.

They are goats.

"Woody, woody, woody, yip!" cries Bob Rieck, a rancher, as he calls the milling herd of angora goats to a feeding of high-protein cottonseed while his border collie, Traveler, chases after strays.

Of all the disputes that President Clinton faces with the end of the cold war, perhaps none is as strange as the plight of the nation's mohair ranchers.

'Strategic' Goods for Soviets

At the end of the Korean War, the ranchers persuaded Congress to include them in a strategic commodity program for sheep wool. But because the military has had dwindling use for mohair, the ranchers ended up sending three-fifths of their subsidized annual production by 1990 to the Soviet Union through intermediaries who produced scarves, caps and overcoats.

The demise of the Soviet Union the next year has cut sales and led, in an odd reversal of the peace dividend, to increases in the Federal subsidies for owners of the greasy, inbred herds.

Payments to ranchers have soared to an estimated $3.60 for every $1 of mohair sold to manufacturers last year from 88.2 cents in 1987. The nation's 10,000 mohair ranchers collected $50 million in subsidies in 1991, and falling market prices last year have sent the subsidy cost even higher.

As part of the economic plan he announced on Feb. 17, President Clinton proposed to reduce their Federal wool and mohair subsidies to a maximum of $50,000 per producer, from $150,000 now. . . .

Mr. Rieck, who receives about $30,000 a year in Federal payments, said President Clinton's reduction in payment caps to $50,000 would actually save the Federal Government very little money. He said large ranchers would break up their herds among their families to collect several payments, or would sell the goats to smaller ranchers who could continue to collect payments on them.

The Essence of the Story

The federal government subsidizes the production of mohair—the wool of angora goats. In 1991, 10,000 U.S. mohair ranchers collected $50 million in subsidies.

The subsidy program began after the Korean War (in 1953), when the government was persuaded that mohair had strategic value and when the military had a large demand for it.

The military's demand for mohair fell, and 60 percent of U.S. production in 1990 was sold to the Soviet Union.

After 1991, sales to the Soviet Union collapsed. By 1992, the subsidy had soared to $3.60 for every $1.00 of mohair sold to manufacturers (up from 88¢ in 1987).

President Clinton has proposed reducing the subsidy to a maximum of $50,000 per producer, from the current maximum of $150,000.

One rancher says that the reduction in the subsidy cap will not decrease the subsidy payments because large ranchers will break up their herds to collect several payments or sell goats to smaller ranchers who will continue to collect subsidies.

Background and Analysis

Mohair is an internationally traded commodity, so its price is determined by world demand and world supply.

The United States is such a small producer of mohair that its output has a negligible effect on the world price.

The situation facing U.S. mohair producers in 1987 is shown in Fig. 1. In that year, the world price of mohair was $2.63 a pound and the demand curve facing domestic producers was D_{87}. The marginal cost curve (of an average producer) was MC_{87}. With a subsidy of 88¢ a pound, the total subsidy payment made by the federal government is shown by the red area.

By 1991, the world price had fallen to 75¢ a pound, but costs had increased to MC_{91} as shown in Fig. 2. The subsidy per pound increased to $3.60, increasing the total subsidy paid by the federal government.

As rancher Bob Rieck points out, putting a cap on the total subsidy that any one producer can receive will limit the size of a producer. In the conditions of 1991, a cap of $50,000 would have limited the size of a herd to one that could produce 13,889 pounds of mohair ($13,889 \times $3.60 = $50,000$). Herds larger than this size would be more valuable broken into smaller herds.

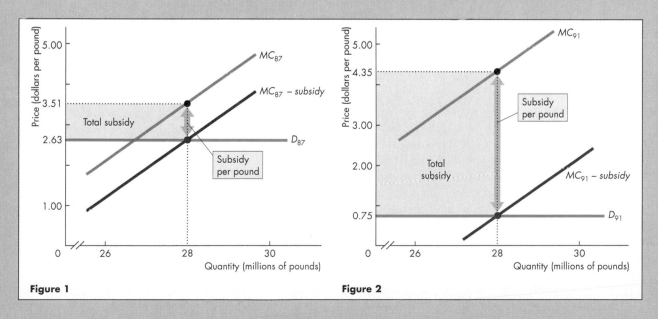

Figure 1

Figure 2

With output restricted to 2 billion bushels of wheat, producers' costs are $3.50 a bushel. They are also selling their wheat for $3.50 a bushel. In addition, they are receiving $1 a bushel in subsidies from the government. The subsidy is like a monopoly profit.

It is interesting to contrast this situation with the one in which there is a subsidy but no quota. Without a quota, output is 3 billion bushels and marginal cost is $4 a bushel. The market price is $3 a bushel, so the subsidy of $1 a bushel makes up the difference between the market price and marginal cost. Without a quota, the price plus the subsidy just covers marginal cost. With a quota, price covers marginal cost and the subsidy is a surplus for the producer—an excess revenue over cost.

Subsidies with quotas are clearly a good thing from the point of view of producers. But they are a bad thing from the point of view of consumers. To pay a subsidy, the government has to raise taxes that create deadweight loss. So why do we have subsidies with quotas?

Why Subsidies and Quotas?   The existence of quotas and subsidies is explained by the fact that the people who stand to gain from a system of quotas and subsidies are relatively well-defined and easily organized into a political force. Those who stand to lose are highly diffuse and much more difficult and costly to organize. As a result, the political equilibrium that prevails is one in which a relatively small number of people gain a significant per person amount while a relatively large number of people lose an unnoticeable amount each.

◆ ◆ ◆ ◆ We have now reviewed the structure of the government sector, market failure, and the theory of public choice that explains how politicians, bureaucrats, and voters interact to determine the scale of provision of public goods, the extent to which taxes and subsidies are used to cope with externalities, the amount of income redistribution, and the levels of taxes and subsidies. ◆ ◆ We have seen that a political equilibrium emerges in which no individual can improve his or her own situation by proposing or implementing a different policy. Each political party devises a program that appeals as closely as possible to half of the electorate. The parties differ in their rhetoric because of differences in the particular half of the electorate to which they appeal, but their actions are similar to each other. Bureaucrats increase their budgets to the point at which politicians perceive the votes gained from additional public goods and services to be matched by the votes lost from higher taxes. Voters are as well informed as it pays them to be—they are rationally ignorant. ◆ ◆ In the next chapter, we're going to study a further range of government actions—their interventions in markets for goods and services in which there are monopoly and cartel elements.

S U M M A R Y

The Political Marketplace

There are three types of actors in the political marketplace: voters, politicians, and bureaucrats. Voters are the consumers of the outcome of the political process. They express their demands through their votes, campaign contributions, and lobbying. Public choices are made by politicians and implemented by bureaucrats. The objective of politicians is to win enough votes to be elected and then to remain in office. They do so by offering policies that are likely to appeal to a majority of voters. To appeal to a majority of voters, politicians have to appeal to the median voter. Since politicians aim for the vote of the median voter, their policies will resemble each other—they will be minimally differentiated. For example, in designing income redistribution policies, politicians transfer from the rich not only to the poor but to everyone with incomes at or below the median. Redistribution will be aimed at making the median voter as rich as possible.

Bureaucrats, in pursuing their own objectives, seek to maximize the budget of their own bureau. If voters are well informed, politicians will not be able to collect taxes to enable bureaucrats to achieve budgets in excess of those that maximize net benefit. But if voters are rationally ignorant, producer interests may result in voting to support taxes that in turn support a level of provision of public goods in excess of that which maximizes net benefit. (pp. 538–547)

Taxes and Subsidies

The imposition of a tax on a good shifts the supply curve upward, raises the price of the good, lowers the quantity bought and sold, and creates a deadweight loss. The size of the deadweight loss depends on the elasticity of demand. Taxing goods that have a low elasticity of demand minimizes the deadweight loss of raising a given amount of tax revenue. The highest tax rates are applied to goods with a low elasticity of demand.

Subsidizing a good shifts the supply curve downward, lowers the price of the good, and increases the quantity traded. Subsidies combined with quotas generate additional income for producers at the expense of consumers. (pp. 547–554)

K E Y   E L E M E N T S

Key Terms

Bureaucrats, 538
Excise tax, 547
Lobbying, 538
Median voter theorem, 542
Political equilibrium, 539
Politicians, 538
Principle of minimum differentiation, 541
Quota, 551
Rational ignorance, 546
Voters, 538

Key Figures

Figure 20.1	Provision of a Public Good in a Political System, 540
Figure 20.2	The Principle of Minimum Differentiation, 541
Figure 20.3	The Median Voter Theorem, 542
Figure 20.4	Bureaucratic Overprovision, 546
Figure 20.5	An Excise Tax, 547
Figure 20.8	Subsidies, 551
Figure 20.9	Subsidies with Quotas, 551

R E V I E W   Q U E S T I O N S

1 What are the three types of actors in the political marketplace?

2 Describe the economic functions of voters, and explain how voters make their economic choices.

3 Describe the economic functions of politicians, and explain how politicians make their economic choices.

4 What is meant by "political equilibrium"?

5 What is the principle of minimum differentiation?

6 How does the principle of minimum differentiation explain political parties' policy platforms?

7 What is the median voter theorem?

8 What features of political choices does the median voter theorem explain?

9 What are the economic functions of bureaucrats, and how do bureaucrats make their economic choices?

10 Describe the ways in which government redistributes income.

11 Why is it rational for voters to be ignorant?

12 Explain why it is likely that the scale of provision of public goods will exceed the allocatively efficient scale.

P R O B L E M S

1 Your local city council is contemplating upgrading its system for controlling traffic signals. It reckons that by installing a sophisticated computer with sensing mechanisms at all the major intersections, it can better adjust the timing of the changes in signals and improve the speed of the traffic flow. The bigger the computer the council buys, the better the job it can do, and the more sensors it installs, the more intersections it can monitor and the faster the overall traffic flow that will result. The mayor and the other elected officials who are working on the proposal want to determine the scale and sophistication of the system that will win them the most votes. The city bureaucrats in the traffic department want to maximize the budget. Suppose that you are an economist who is observing this public choice. Your job is to calculate the scale of provision of this public good that maximizes net benefit—that achieves allocative efficiency.

a   What data would you need in order to reach your own conclusions?

b   What does the public choice theory predict will be the scale of provision chosen?

c   How could you, as an informed voter, attempt to influence the choice?

2 Three people—Jan, Jill, and Joyce—have incomes of $10,000, $5,000, and $2,500, respectively. Set up a proposed redistribution of income among these three people that will achieve majority support. Once you've determined the new distribution (after implementing your proposal), set up another scheme that will also command a majority support. Show that you can find a voting cycle.

3 A community of nine people, identified by letters *A* through *I*, have strong views about a local factory that is polluting the atmosphere. Some of them work at the factory and don't want the government to take any action against it, while others want to see the imposition of a huge tax based on the scale of pollution. The preferences of the nine people concerning the scale of the tax that should be imposed are as follows:

A	B	C	D	E	F	G	H	I
90	80	70	60	50	0	0	0	0

Suppose there are two political parties competing for office in this community. What tax rate would the parties propose?

4 You are given the following information about a perfectly competitive market for cookies:

Price (dollars per pound)	Quantity demanded (pounds per month)	Quantity supplied (pounds per month)
10	0	36
8	3	30
6	6	24
4	9	18
2	12	12
0	15	0

a   What are the competitive equilibrium price and quantity?

b   Suppose that a 10 percent tax is imposed on cookies.

(1)   What is the new price of cookies?

(2)   What is the new quantity bought and sold?

(3)   What is the total amount of tax revenue raised by the government?

(4)   What is the deadweight loss?

c   Now suppose that cookies are not taxed but are instead subsidized by 10 percent.

(1)   What happens to the price of cookies?

(2)   What happens to the quantity bought and sold?

(3)   How much is the subsidy paid out by the government?

(4)   Suppose that along with the 10 percent subsidy, a quota of 12 pounds per month is imposed on cookie producers. What is the level of profit for the producer?

CHAPTER **21**

REGULATION AND ANTITRUST LAW

After studying this chapter, you will be able to:

- ◆ Define regulation

- ◆ Describe the main elements of antitrust law

- ◆ Distinguish between the public interest theory and the capture theory of regulation

- ◆ State which parts of the economy are subject to regulation

- ◆ Describe the main trends in regulation and deregulation

- ◆ Explain how regulation of natural monopolies affects prices, outputs, profits, and the gains from trade for consumers and producers

- ◆ Explain how regulation of cartels affects prices, outputs, profits, and the gains from trade for consumers and producers

- ◆ Explain how antitrust law has been applied in a number of landmark cases

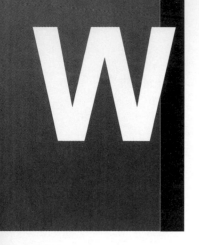

WHEN YOU CONSUME WATER, ELECTRIC POWER, GAS, cable TV, or local telephone services, you are buying from regulated natural monopolies. Why are the industries that produce these goods and services regulated? How are they regulated? And do the regulations work in the interests of consumers—the public interest—or do they serve the interests of the producer—special interests? ◆ ◆ Regulation extends beyond natural monopoly to cartels. For example, until 1978, the price of air transportation in the United States and the routes that airlines could fly were regulated by the Civil Aeronautics Board (CAB). But in 1978, domestic air travel was deregulated and the CAB was disbanded, leaving the airlines free to choose their own routes and fares. Interstate trucking and financial services were regulated in the past but in recent years have been deregulated. Why do governments sometimes regulate an industry and at other times deregulate that same industry? Whose interest is served by regulation and deregulation—the consumers' or the producers'? ◆ ◆ Government also influences the economy with its antitrust laws—laws that block mergers and that result in companies being broken up. For example, until a few years ago, to make a long-distance phone call, you had no choice but to use the American Telephone and Telegraph Company (AT&T). Our antitrust laws were used to break up AT&T and to create a number of independent producers of long-distance telephone service such as MCI and U.S. Sprint. ◆ ◆ What are the antitrust laws? How have they evolved over the years? How are they used today? Do antitrust laws serve consumer interests or the special interests of producer groups?

Public Interest or Special Interests?

◆ ◆ ◆ ◆ This chapter studies the actions taken by government to influence trading in markets for goods and services. The chapter draws on your earlier study of how markets work and on your knowledge of the gains from trade—of consumer surplus and producer surplus. It shows how consumers and producers might redistribute those gains and identifies who stands to gain and who stands to lose from various types of government intervention. Since such intervention is supplied by politicians and bureaucrats, the chapter also looks at the economic behavior of these groups in the "political marketplace."

Market Intervention

There are two main ways in which the government intervenes in monopolistic and oligopolistic markets to influence *what, how,* and *for whom* various goods and services are produced:

◆ Regulation
◆ Antitrust law

Regulation

Regulation consists of rules administered by a government agency to restrict economic activity by determining prices, product standards and types, and the conditions under which new firms may enter an industry. In order to implement its regulations, the government establishes agencies to oversee the regulations and ensure their enforcement. The first such agency to be set up in the United States was the Interstate Commerce Commission (ICC), established in 1887. Over the years since then and up to the late 1970s, regulation of the economy grew until, at its peak, almost a quarter of the nation's output was produced by regulated industries. Regulation applied to banking and financial services, telecommunications, gas and electric utilities, railroads, trucking, airlines and buses, and many agricultural products. Since the late 1970s, there has been a tendency to deregulate the U.S. economy.

Deregulation is the process of removing restrictions on prices, product standards and types, and entry conditions. In recent years, deregulation has occurred in domestic air transportation, telephone service, interstate trucking, and banking and financial services.

Antitrust Law

An **antitrust law** is a law that regulates and prohibits certain kinds of market behavior, such as monopoly and monopolistic practices. Antitrust law is enacted by Congress and enforced through the judicial system. Lawsuits under the antitrust laws may be initiated either by government agencies or by privately injured parties.

The main thrust of the antitrust law is the prohibition of monopoly practices and of restricting output in order to achieve higher prices and profits. The first antitrust law—the Sherman Act—was enacted in 1890. Successive acts and amendments have strengthened and refined the body of antitrust law. Antitrust law (like all law) depends as much on decisions of the courts and of the Supreme Court as on the statutes passed by Congress. Over the hundred years since the passage of the Sherman Act, there have been some interesting turns of direction in how the courts have interpreted the law and how vigorously it has been enforced. We'll study these later in this chapter.

To understand why the government intervenes in markets for goods and services and to work out the effects of its interventions, we need to identify the gains and losses that government actions can create. These gains and losses are the consumer surplus and producer surplus associated with different output levels and prices. You've already met these concepts in Chapters 7 (pp. 171–174) and 12 (pp. 330–331). All we need to do here, therefore, is refresh our understanding of these concepts and of the way in which their magnitudes are affected by the price at which a good is sold and the quantity bought.

Surpluses and Their Distribution

Consumer surplus is the difference between the maximum amount that consumers are willing to pay and the amount that they actually do pay for a given quantity of a good. Consumer surplus is the gain from trade accruing to consumers. *Producer surplus* is the difference between the producer's revenue and the opportunity cost of production. Producer surplus is the gain from trade accruing to producers. **Total surplus** is the sum of consumer surplus and producer surplus.

The lower the price and the larger the quantity bought and sold, the larger is consumer surplus. The closer the price and quantity bought to their monopoly profit-maximizing levels, the larger is producer surplus. Total surplus is maximized (in the absence of external costs and benefits) when marginal cost equals price. In this situation, allocative efficiency is achieved.

There is a conflict between maximizing producer surplus and maximizing total surplus. Monopoly firms have an incentive to restrict output below the competitive level, increasing producer surplus but reducing consumer surplus and creating deadweight loss. Thus there is a tension between the public interest of maximization of total surplus and the producer's interest of maximizing monopoly profit and producer surplus. This tension is of central importance in the economic theory of regulation. Let's now examine that theory.

Economic Theory of Regulation

The economic theory of regulation is part of the broader theory of public choice. You have already met that theory in Chapter 20 and seen the main components of a public choice model. We're going to reexamine the main features of such a model but with an emphasis on the regulatory aspects of government behavior. We'll examine the demand for government actions, the supply of those actions, and the political equilibrium—the balancing of demands and supplies.

Demand for Regulation

The demand for regulation is expressed through political institutions. Both consumers and producers vote, lobby, and campaign for regulations that best further their own interests. None of these activities are costless. Voters incur costs in order to acquire information on the basis of which to decide their vote. Lobbying and campaigning cost time, effort, and contributions to the campaign funds of political parties. Individual consumers and producers demand political action only if the benefit that they individually receive from such action exceeds the

costs incurred by them in obtaining the action. There are four main factors that affect the demand for regulation:

◆ Consumer surplus per buyer
◆ Number of buyers
◆ Producer surplus per firm
◆ Number of firms

The larger the consumer surplus per buyer resulting from regulation, the greater is the demand for regulation by buyers. Also, as the number of buyers increases, so does the demand for regulation. But numbers alone do not necessarily translate into an effective political force. The larger the number of buyers, the greater is the cost of organizing them, so the demand for regulation does not increase proportionately with the number of buyers.

The larger the producer surplus per firm arising from a particular regulation, the larger is the demand by firms for that regulation. Also, as the number of firms that might benefit from some regulation increases, so does the demand for that regulation. But again, as in the case of consumers, large numbers do not necessarily mean an effective political force. The larger the number of firms, the greater is the cost of organizing them.

For a given surplus, consumer or producer, the smaller the number of households or firms that share the surplus, the larger is the demand for the regulation that creates it.

The Supply of Regulation

Regulation is supplied by politicians and bureaucrats. As we saw in Chapter 20, politicians choose policies that appeal to a majority of voters, thereby enabling themselves to achieve and maintain office. Bureaucrats support policies that maximize their budgets. Given these objectives of politicians and bureaucrats, the supply of regulation depends on the following factors:

◆ Consumer surplus per buyer
◆ Producer surplus per firm
◆ The number of people affected

The larger the consumer surplus per buyer or producer surplus per firm generated, and the larger the number of people affected by a regulation, the greater is the tendency for politicians to supply that regulation. If regulation benefits a large number of people significantly enough for it to be noticed and if the recipients know who is the source of the benefits, that regulation appeals to politicians and it is supplied. If regulation affects markets that benefit a large number of people but by a small amount per person, and if such benefits do not attract notice, that regulation does not appeal to politicians and it is not supplied. Regulation that bestows clear and large benefits on a small number of people may be attractive to politicians provided that some of those benefits flow back and thus enable the politicians to fight more effective election campaigns.

Equilibrium

In equilibrium, the regulation that exists is such that no interest group feels it is worthwhile to use additional resources to press for changes and no group of politicians feels it is worthwhile to offer different regulations. Being in a political equilibrium is not the same thing as everyone being in agreement. Lobby groups will devote resources to trying to change regulations that are already in place. And others will devote resources to maintaining the existing regulations. But no one will feel it is worthwhile to *increase* the resources they are devoting to such activities. Also, political parties will not agree with each other. Some will support the existing regulations, and others will propose different regulations. In equilibrium, no one wants to change the proposals that they are making.

What will a political equilibrium look like? There are two theories of political equilibrium: one is called the public interest theory, and the other is called the capture theory. Let's look at these two theories.

Public Interest Theory
The **public interest theory of regulation** states that regulations are supplied to satisfy the demand of consumers and producers for the maximization of total surplus—or the attainment of allocative efficiency. Public interest theory predicts that the political process will relentlessly seek out deadweight loss and introduce regulations that eliminate it. For example, where monopoly or monopolistic practices by collusive oligopoly exist, the political process will introduce price regulation to ensure that output and price are close to their competitive levels.

Capture Theory
The **capture theory of regulation** states that the regulations that exist are those that maximize producer surplus. The key idea of capture theory is that only those regulations that increase the surpluses of small, easily identified groups that have low organization costs will be supplied by the political process. Such regulations will be supplied even if they impose costs on others, provided that those costs are spread thinly and widely enough that they do not have negative effects on votes.

Whichever theory of regulation is correct, the political system delivers regulations that best further the electoral success of politicians. Since we have seen that producer-oriented and consumer-oriented regulation are in direct conflict with each other, it is clear that the political process cannot satisfy both groups in any particular industry. Only one group can win. This makes the regulatory actions of government a bit like a unique product—for example, a painting by Rembrandt. There is only one original, and it will be sold to just one buyer. Normally, a unique commodity is sold through an auction: the highest bidder takes the prize. Equilibrium in the regulatory process can be thought of in much the same way: the suppliers of regulation will satisfy the demands of the higher bidder. If the producer demand offers a bigger return to the politicians, either directly through votes or indirectly through campaign contributions, then the producers' interests will be served. If the consumer demand translates into a larger number of votes, then the consumer interest will be served by regulation.

R E V I E W

The demand for regulation is expressed by both consumers and producers who spend scarce resources voting, lobbying, and campaigning for regulations that best further their own interests. Regulation is supplied by politicians and bureaucrats. Politicians choose actions that appeal to a majority of voters, and bureaucrats choose actions that maximize their budgets. The regulation that exists is the equilibrium that balances the opposing demand and supply forces. One possible political equilibrium is regulation that achieves allocative efficiency—the public interest theory of regulation. Another possible equilibrium is regulation that maximizes producer surplus—the capture theory of regulation. ◆

Regulation and Deregulation

T he past 20 years have seen dramatic changes in the way in which the U.S. economy is regulated by government. We're going to examine some of the more important changes. To begin, we'll look at what is regulated and also at the scope of regulation. Then we'll turn to the regulatory process itself and examine how regulators control prices and other aspects of market behavior. Finally, we'll tackle the more difficult and controversial questions: Why do we regulate some things but not others? Who benefits from the regulation that we have?

The Scope of Regulation

The first federal regulatory agency, the Interstate Commerce Commission (ICC), was set up in 1887 to control prices, routes, and the quality of service of interstate transportation companies—railroads, trucking lines, bus lines, water carriers, and, in more recent years, oil pipelines. Following the establishment of the ICC, the regulatory environment remained static until the years of the Great Depression. Then, in the 1930s, more agencies were established—the Federal Power Commission, the Federal Communications Commission, the Federal Maritime Commission, and, in 1938, the Civil Aeronautical Agency, which was replaced in 1940 by the Civil Aeronautics Board. There was a further lull until the establishment in the 1970s of the Postal Rate Commission, the Copyright Royalty Tribunal, and finally, the Federal Energy Regulatory Com-

TABLE 21.1

Regulation at Its Peak in 1977

Organization	Year established	Controls and regulates
Interstate Commerce Commission	1887	Prices, routes, and services of railroads, trucks, bus lines, oil pipelines, and domestic water carriers
Federal Power Commission	1930	Wellhead gas prices and wholesale prices of natural gas and electricity sold for resale in interstate commerce
Federal Communications Commission	1934	Prices for telephone and telegraph service; entry into telecommunications and broadcasting
Federal Maritime Commission	1936	Fares and schedules of transoceanic freight shipments
Civil Aeronautics Board	1938	Airline passenger fares; entry of airlines into city-to-city air routes
Postal Rate Commission	1970	Classes of mail and rates for those classes; sets fees for other services
Copyright Royalty Tribunal	1976	Fees and charges on copyright materials
Federal Energy Regulatory Commission	1977	Wellhead crude-oil prices and refinery, wholesale, and retail prices of petroleum products; allocation levels for wholesalers and retailers of crude oil, residual fuel oil, and most refined petroleum products produced in or imported into the United States during a period of energy emergency

Source: The Federal Regulatory Directory (Washington, D.C.: Congressional Quarterly, 1991).

mission. Table 21.1 provides a summary of the federal regulatory agencies at the peak of regulation in 1977 and describes their functions.

In the mid-1970s, almost one quarter of the economy was subject to some form of regulation, as seen in Table 21.2(a). The most heavily regulated industries—those subject both to price regulation and to regulation of entry of new firms—were electricity, natural gas, telephones, airlines, highway freight services, and railroads (see Table 21.2b).

Regulation reached its peak in 1977. Since then, there has been a gradual and important deregulation process. Deregulation has had the most significant impact in the telecommunication, banking and finance, railroad, bus, trucking, and airline industries.

What exactly do regulatory agencies do? How do they regulate?

The Regulatory Process

Though regulatory agencies vary in size and scope and in the detailed aspects of economic life that they control, there are certain features common to all agencies.

First, the senior bureaucrats who are the key decision makers in a regulatory agency are appointed by the administration or Congress. In addition, all agencies have a permanent bureaucracy made up of experts in the industry being regulated. These experts are often recruited from the regulated firms. Agencies have financial resources, voted by Congress, to cover the costs of their operations.

Second, each agency adopts a set of practices or operating rules for controlling prices and other aspects of economic performance. These rules and practices are based on well-defined physical and financial accounting procedures that are relatively easy to administer and to monitor.

In a regulated industry, individual firms are free to determine the technology that they will use in production. But they are not free to determine the prices at which they will sell their output, the quantities that they will sell, or the markets that they will serve. The regulatory agency grants certification to a company to serve a particular market with a particular line of products, and it determines the level and structure of prices that will be charged. In some cases, the agency also determines the scale of output permitted.

TABLE 21.2

How Much Regulation?

(a) Regulation as a percentage of total output

	Year	
	1965	1975
Price regulation	5.5	8.8
Financial regulation	2.7	3.0
Health and safety regulation	—	11.9
Total	8.2	23.7

(b) Industries subject to price and entry regulation

Industry	Jurisdiction and extent of regulation
Electricity	Federal Energy Regulatory Commission and 49 state agencies certify service.
Natural gas	Federal Energy Regulatory Commission controls interstate transportation, and 49 state agencies set rates for distribution.
Telephones	Federal Communications Commission and 50 state agencies set rates, entry, and service conditions.
Airlines	Civil Aeronautics Board regulations set fares and entry conditions before the Airline Deregulation Act of 1978; 21 state agencies set fare and entry conditions interstate.
Highway freight	Interstate Commerce Commission and 47 state agencies regulate rates; the ICC and 45 state agencies control entry into common-carrier services.
Railroads	Interstate Commerce Commission and 44 state agencies set freight rates; the ICC and 26 state agencies certify entry into the provision of rail services.

Source: Paul W. MacAvoy, *The Regulated Industries and the Economy* (New York: W.W. Norton, 1979), 18, 25.

To analyze the way in which regulation works, it is convenient to distinguish between the regulation of natural monopoly and the regulation of cartels. Let's begin with natural monopoly.

Regulation of Natural Monopoly

Natural monopoly was defined in Chapter 12 (p. 314) as an industry in which one firm can supply the entire market at a lower price than two or more firms can. As a consequence, a natural monopoly experiences economies of scale, no matter how large an output it produces. Examples of natural monopolies include local distribution of gas and electricity and subway services. It is much more expensive to have two or more competing sets of pipes, wires and train lines serving every neighborhood than it is to have a single set.

Let's consider the example of a subway train service. The demand for the subway service and the subway's cost curves are illustrated in Fig. 21.1. The demand curve is *D*. The marginal cost curve is *MC*. Notice that the marginal cost curve is horizontal at 20¢ a ride—that is, the cost of each additional ride is a constant 20¢. The subway company has a heavy investment in track, trains, and control equipment and so has high fixed costs. These fixed costs feature in the company's average total cost curve, shown as *ATC*. The average total cost curve slopes downward because as the number of rides increases, the fixed cost is spread over a larger number of rides. (If you need to refresh your memory on how the average total cost curve is calculated, take a quick look back at pp. 240–245.)

Regulation in the Public Interest How will this industry be regulated according to the public interest theory? Recall that, in the public interest theory, regulation maximizes total surplus—achieves allocative efficiency. Allocative efficiency occurs when marginal cost equals price. Equivalently, it occurs when total surplus is maximized—when the area above the marginal cost curve and below the demand curve is at a maximum. As you can see in the example in Fig. 21.1, that outcome occurs if the price is regulated at 20¢ a ride and if 8,000 rides an hour are produced. Such a regulation is called a marginal cost pricing rule. A **marginal cost pricing rule** sets price equal to marginal cost. It maximizes total surplus in the regulated industry.

A natural monopoly that is regulated to set price equal to marginal cost makes an economic loss. Because its average total cost curve is falling, marginal cost is below average total cost. Because price equals marginal cost, price is below average total cost. The difference between price and average total cost is the loss per unit produced. It's pretty obvious

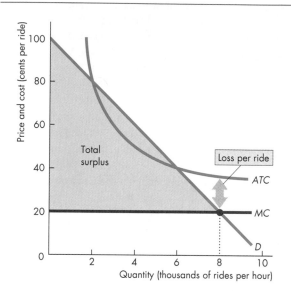

FIGURE 21.1

Natural Monopoly: Marginal Cost Pricing

A natural monopoly is an industry in which average total cost is falling even when the entire market demand is satisfied. A natural monopoly for subway rides has a demand curve *D*. Marginal costs are constant at 20¢ a ride, as shown by the curve *MC*. Fixed costs are heavy, and the average total cost curve, which includes average fixed cost, is shown as *ATC*. A marginal cost pricing rule that maximizes total surplus sets the price of a ride at 20¢, with 8,000 rides an hour being taken. The resulting consumer surplus is shown as the green area. The producer makes a loss on each ride, indicated by the arrow. In order to remain in business, the producer must either price discriminate or receive a subsidy.

that a private subway company that is required to use a marginal cost pricing rule will not stay in business for long. How can a company cover its costs and, at the same time, obey a marginal cost pricing rule?

One possibility is price discrimination. Some natural monopolies can fairly easily price discriminate. For example, local telephone companies can charge consumers a monthly fee for being connected to the telephone system and then charge a low price (perhaps even zero) for each local call. A subway company can price discriminate by offering discounts on weekly or monthly season tickets.

But a natural monopoly cannot always price discriminate. When a natural monopoly cannot price discriminate, it can cover its total cost and follow a marginal cost pricing rule only if it receives a subsidy from the government. In such a case, the government would have to raise the revenue for the subsidy by taxing some other activity. But as we saw in Chapter 20, taxes themselves generate deadweight loss. Thus the deadweight loss resulting from additional taxes has to be offset against the allocative efficiency gained by forcing the natural monopoly to adopt a marginal cost pricing rule.

It is possible that deadweight loss will be minimized by permitting the natural monopoly to charge a higher price than marginal cost rather than by taxing some other sector of the economy in order to subsidize the natural monopoly. Such a pricing arrangement is called an average cost pricing rule. An **average cost pricing rule** sets price equal to average total cost. The average cost pricing solution is shown in Fig. 21.2. The subway company charges 40¢ for each ride and sells 6,000 rides an hour. Deadweight loss arises, represented by the gray triangle in the figure. Even though there is a deadweight loss, this situation might well be allocatively efficient. Recall that the subway company goes out of business if it doesn't cover its costs. If a subsidy is required to cover costs and if the subsidy requires a tax that has a deadweight loss larger than the one shown in the figure, then the average cost pricing rule is the best available.

Capturing the Regulator What does the capture theory predict about the regulation of this industry? Recall that according to the capture theory, regulation serves the interests of the producer. The interests of the producer, in this case, are best satisfied by maximizing profit. To work out the price that achieves this goal, we need to look at the relationship between marginal revenue and marginal cost. As you know, a monopoly maximizes profit by producing the output at which marginal revenue equals marginal cost. The monopoly's marginal revenue curve in Fig. 21.3 is the curve MR. Marginal revenue equals marginal cost when output is 4,000 rides an hour and the price is 60¢ a ride. Thus a regulation that best serves the interest of the producer will set the price at 60¢ a ride.

But how can a producer go about obtaining regulation that results in this monopoly profit-maximizing outcome? To answer this question, we need to look at the way in which agencies determine the

FIGURE **21.2**

Natural Monopoly: Average Cost Pricing

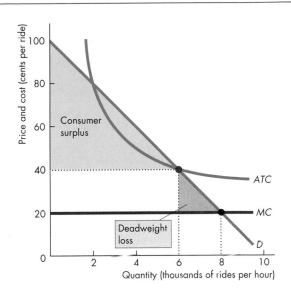

Average cost pricing sets price equal to average total cost. The subway company charges 40¢ a ride and sells 6,000 rides an hour. In this situation the subway company will break even—average total cost equals price. Deadweight loss, shown by the gray triangle, is generated. Consumer surplus is reduced to the green area.

level at which to set a regulated price. The key method used is called rate of return regulation.

Rate of Return Regulation **Rate of return regulation** determines a regulated price by setting the price at a level that enables the regulated firm to earn a specified target percent return on its capital. The target rate of return is determined with reference to what is normal in competitive industries. This rate of return is part of the opportunity cost of the natural monopolist and is included in the firm's average total cost. By examining the firm's total cost, including the normal rate of return on capital, the regulator attempts to determine the price at which average total cost is covered. Thus rate of return regulation is equivalent to average cost pricing.

In the example that we have just been examining—in Fig. 21.2—average cost pricing results in a regulated price of 40¢ a ride with 6,000 rides an hour being sold. Thus rate of return regulation,

FIGURE **21.3**

Natural Monopoly: Profit Maximization

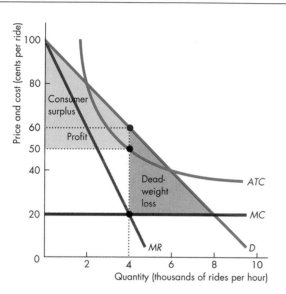

The subway company would like to maximize profit. To do so, marginal revenue (*MR*) is made equal to marginal cost. At a price of 60¢ a ride, 4,000 rides an hour are sold. Consumer surplus is reduced to the green triangle. The deadweight loss increases to the gray triangle. The monopoly makes the profit shown by the blue rectangle. If the producer can capture the regulator, the outcome will be the situation shown here.

FIGURE **21.4**

Natural Monopoly: Inflating Costs

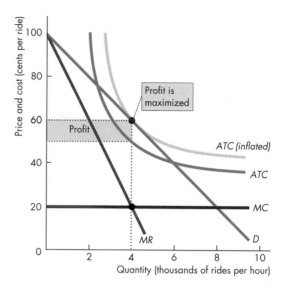

If the subway company is able to inflate its costs to *ATC(inflated)* and persuade the regulator that these are genuine minimum costs of production, rate of return regulation will result in a price of 60¢ a ride—the profit-maximizing price. To the extent that the producer can inflate costs above average total cost, the price will rise, output will fall, and deadweight loss will increase.

based on a correct assessment of the producer's average total cost curve, results in a price and quantity that favors the consumer and does not enable the producer to maximize monopoly profit. The special interest group will have failed to capture the regulator, and the outcome will be closer to that predicted by the public interest theory of regulation.

But there is an important feature of many real-world situations that the above analysis does not take into account—the ability of the monopoly firm to mislead the regulator about its true costs.

Inflating Costs The senior managers of a firm might be able to inflate the firm's costs by spending part of the firm's revenue on inputs that are not strictly required for the production of the good. By this device, the firm's apparent cost curves exceed

the true cost curves. The main way in which managers inflate costs is by providing themselves with on-the-job luxury in the form of sumptuous office suites, limousines, free baseball tickets (disguised as public relations expenses), company jets, lavish international travel, and entertainment.

If the subway company manages to inflate its costs and persuade the regulatory agency that its true cost curve is that shown as *ATC(inflated)* in Fig. 21.4, then the regulator, applying the normal rate of return principle, will regulate the price at 60¢ a ride. In this example, the price and quantity will be the same as those under unregulated monopoly. It might be impossible for firms to inflate their costs by as much as the amount shown in the figure. But to the extent that costs can be inflated, the apparent average total cost curve lies somewhere between the true *ATC* curve and *ATC(inflated)*. The greater the ability of the firm to pad its costs in this way, the more closely its profit (measured in economic terms) approaches the maximum possible. The shareholders of this firm don't receive this economic profit. It gets used up by the managers of the firm on the self-serving activities that they have used to inflate the company's costs.

Public Interest or Capture?

It is not clear whether actual regulation produces prices and quantities that correspond more closely with the predictions of capture theory or with those of public interest theory. One thing is clear, however. Price regulation does not require natural monopolies to use the marginal cost pricing rule. If it did, most natural monopolies would make losses and receive hefty government subsidies to enable them to remain in business. But there are even exceptions to this conclusion. For example, many local telephone companies do appear to use marginal cost pricing for local telephone calls. They cover their total cost by charging a flat fee each month for being connected to their telephone system but then permitting each call to be made at its marginal cost—zero or something very close to it.

A test of whether natural monopoly regulation is in the public interest or the interest of the producer is to examine the rates of return earned by regulated natural monopolies. If those rates of return are significantly higher than those in the rest of the economy, then, to some degree, the regulator may have been captured by the producer. If the rates of return in the regulated monopoly industries are similar to those in the rest of the economy, then we cannot tell for sure whether the regulator has been captured or not, since we cannot know the extent to which costs have been inflated by the managers of the regulated firms.

Table 21.3 shows the rates of return in regulated natural monopolies as well as the economy's average rate of return. In the 1960s, rates of return in regulated natural monopolies were somewhat below the economy average; in the 1970s, those returns exceeded the economy average. Overall, the rates of return achieved by regulated natural monopolies were not very different from those in the rest of the economy. We can conclude from these data either that natural monopoly regulation does, to some degree, serve the public interest or that natural monopoly managers inflate their costs by amounts sufficiently large to disguise the fact that they have

TABLE 21.3

Rates of Return in Regulated Monopolies

	Years	
	1962–1969	1970–1977
Electricity	3.2	6.1
Gas	3.3	8.2
Railroad	5.1	7.2
Average of above	3.9	7.2
Economy average	6.6	5.1

Source: Paul W. MacAvoy, *The Regulated Industries and the Economy* (New York, W.W. Norton, 1979), 49–60.

captured the regulator and that the public interest is not being served.

We've now examined the regulation of natural monopoly. Let's next turn to regulation in oligopolistic industries—to the regulation of cartels.

Regulation of Cartels

A *cartel* is a collusive agreement among a number of firms designed to restrict output and achieve a higher profit for the members of the cartel. Cartels arise in oligopolistic industries. An oligopoly is an industry in which a small number of firms compete with each other. We studied oligopoly and duopoly in Chapter 14. There we saw that if firms manage to collude and behave like a monopoly, they can set the same price and sell the same total quantity as a monopoly firm would. But we also discovered that in such a situation, each firm will be tempted to "cheat," increasing its own output and profit at the expense of the other firms. The result of such "cheating" on the collusive agreement is the unraveling of the monopoly equilibrium and the emergence of a competitive outcome with zero profit for producers. Such an outcome benefits consumers at the expense of producers.

How is oligopoly regulated? Does regulation prevent monopoly practices, or does it encourage those practices?

According to the public interest theory, oligopoly is regulated to ensure a competitive outcome. Consider, for example, the market for trucking tomatoes from the San Joaquin Valley to Los Angeles, illustrated in Fig. 21.5. The demand curve for trips is D. The industry marginal cost curve—and the competitive supply curve—is MC. Public interest regulation will regulate the price of a trip at $20, and there will be 300 trips a week.

How would this industry be regulated according to the capture theory? Regulation that is in the producer interest will set the price at $30 a trip and, to ensure that that price is maintained, will restrict the number of trips to 200 a week. Each producer will

make a maximum profit, and the industry marginal revenue will be equal to the industry marginal cost. If there are 10 trucking companies, this outcome can be achieved by issuing a production quota to each trucking company restricting it to 20 trips a week so that the total number of trips in a week is 200. Penalties can be imposed to ensure that no single producer violates its quota.

What does regulation of oligopoly do in practice? Though there is disagreement about the matter, the consensus view is that regulation tends to favor the producer. Trucking (when it was regulated by the Interstate Commerce Commission), taxicabs (regulated by cities), and airlines (when they were regulated by the Civil Aeronautics Board) are specific examples of industries in which profits of producers increased as a result of regulation. In some cases—and trucking is one of these—the work force, through unionization, also manages to take a large part of the total surplus.

Some further evidence in support of the conclusion that regulation sometimes increases profit is presented in Table 21.4. If regulation ensures a competitive outcome, rates of return in a regulated oligopoly will be no higher than those in the economy as a whole. As the numbers in Table 21.4 show, rates of return in airlines and trucking exceeded twice the economy average rate of return in the 1960s. In the 1970s, the rate of return in trucking remained higher than the economy average (although by a smaller margin than had prevailed in the 1960s). Airline rates of return in the 1970s fell to below the economy average. The overall picture that emerges from examining data on rates of return is mixed. The regulation of oligopoly does not always result in higher profit, but there are many situations in which it does.

Further evidence on cartel and oligopoly regulation can be obtained from the performance of prices and profit following deregulation. If, following deregulation, prices and profit fall, then, to some degree, the regulation must have been serving the interest of the producer. In contrast, if, following deregulation, prices and profits remain constant or increase, then the regulation may be presumed to have been serving the public interest. Since there has been a substantial amount of deregulation in recent years, we may use this test of oligopoly regulation to see which of the two theories better fits the facts. The evidence is mixed, but there are many cases in which deregulation has been accompanied by falling

FIGURE **21.5**

Collusive Oligopoly

Ten trucking firms transport tomatoes from the San Joaquin Valley to Los Angeles. The demand curve is *D,* and the industry marginal cost curve is *MC.* Under competition, the *MC* curve is the industry supply curve. If the industry is competitive, the price of a trip will be $20 and 300 trips will be made each week. Producers will demand regulation that restricts entry and restricts the output of producers to 200 trips a week. This regulation will raise the price to $30 a trip and result in each producer making maximum profit—as if it is a monopoly. The industry marginal revenue will be equal to industry marginal cost.

TABLE 21.4

Rates of Return in Regulated Oligopolies

	Years	
	1962–1969	1970–1977
Airlines	12.8	3.0
Trucking	13.6	8.1
Economy average	6.6	5.1

Source: Paul W. MacAvoy, *The Regulated Industries and the Economy* (New York: W.W. Norton, 1978), 49–60.

prices. Airlines, trucking, railroads, long-distance telephones, and banking and financial services are all industries in which deregulation was, initially at least, associated with more competition, lower prices, and a large increase in the volume of transactions.

Interpreting the deregulation evidence, however, is made difficult by the possibility that firms in oligopolistic industries will find other ways of restricting competition in a deregulated environment. There is evidence, for example, that the big airlines managed to do this in the 1980s through the creation of regional monopolies based on routes that radiate like the spokes of a wheel from hub airports and through their control of computerized reservation systems.

Making Predictions

Most industries have a few producers and many consumers. In these cases, public choice theory predicts that regulation will protect producer interests because a small number of people stand to gain a large amount and so they will be fairly easy to organize as a cohesive lobby. Under such circumstances, politicians will be rewarded with campaign contributions rather than votes. But there are situations in which the consumer interest is sufficiently strong and well organized and thus able to prevail. There are also cases in which the balance switches from

producer to consumer, as seen in the deregulation process that began in the late 1970s.

Deregulation raises some hard questions for economists seeking to understand and make predictions about regulation. Why were the transportation and telecommunication sectors deregulated? If producers gained from regulation and if the producer lobby was strong enough to achieve regulation, what happened in the 1970s to change the equilibrium to one in which the consumer interest prevailed? We do not have a complete answer to this question at the present time. But regulation had become so costly to consumers, and the potential benefits to them from deregulation so great, that the cost of organizing the consumer voice became a price worth paying.

An important factor that increased the cost of regulation borne by consumers and brought deregulation in the transportation sector was the large increase in energy prices in the 1970s. These price hikes made route regulation by the ICC extremely costly and changed the balance in favor of consumers in the political equilibrium. Technological change was the main factor at work in the telecommunication sector. New satellite-based, computer-controlled long-distance technologies enabled smaller producers to offer low-cost services. These producers wanted a share of the business—and profit—of AT&T. Furthermore, as communication technology improved, the cost of communication fell and the cost of organizing larger groups of consumers also fell. If this line of reasoning is correct, we can expect to see more consumer-oriented regulation in the future. In practice, more consumer-oriented regulation means deregulation—removing the regulations that are already in place to serve the interests of producer groups.

REVIEW

A gencies regulate natural monopolies by setting their prices at levels that enable them to earn a target percent return on their capital. Such regulation gives firms an incentive to inflate costs and move as closely as possible to maximizing profit instead of producing the output that maximizes total surplus—the sum of consumer surplus and producer surplus. ◆ ◆ Cartels—collusive agreements among firms to restrict output and increase profit—

are unstable because each firm faces the temptation to increase its own output and profit at the expense of the other firms. The end result of this process is zero profit. Regulation of cartels, by establishing output levels for each firm, can help perpetuate the cartel and work against the public interest. The evidence suggests that cartel regulation tends to operate in the producer's interest. ◆

Let's now leave regulation and turn to the other main method of intervention in markets—antitrust law.

Antitrust Law

Antitrust law provides an alternative way in which the government may influence the marketplace. As in the case of regulation, antitrust law can be formulated in the public interest, to maximize total surplus, or in private interests, to maximize the surpluses of particular special interest groups such as producers.

Landmark Antitrust Cases

The antitrust laws themselves are brief and easily summarized. The first antitrust law, the Sherman Act, was passed in 1890 in an atmosphere of outrage and disgust at the actions and practices of J. P. Morgan, John D. Rockefeller, and W. H. Vanderbilt —the so-called "robber barons."[1] (See Our Advancing Knowledge on pp. 322–323.) The most lurid stories of the actions of these great American capitalists are not of their monopolization and exploitation of consumers but of their sharp practices against each other. Nevertheless, monopolies did emerge—for example, the spectacular control of the oil industry by John D. Rockefeller, Sr. The Sherman Act had little effect until the early part of this century, and by 1914 it was augmented by the more powerful Clayton Act and the creation of the Federal Trade Commission, an agency charged with

[1]Business practices of this era are discussed by Matthew Josephson, *The Robber Barons: The Great American Capitalists, 1861–1901* (New York: Harcourt, Brace & Co., 1934).

TABLE 21.5

Antitrust Laws

Name of law	Year passed	What the law prohibits
Sherman Act	1890	◆ Combination, trust, or conspiracy to restrict interstate or international trade ◆ Monopolization or attempt to monopolize interstate or international trade
Clayton Act Robinson-Patman Amendment Cellar-Kefauver Amendment	1914 1936 1950	◆ Price discrimination if the effect is to substantially lessen competition or create monopoly and if such discrimination is not justified by cost differences ◆ Contracts that force other goods to be bought from same firm ◆ Acquisition of competitors' shares or assets if the effect is to reduce competition ◆ Interlocking directorships among competing firms
Federal Trade Commission Act	1914	◆ Unfair methods of competition and unfair or deceptive business practices

---

enforcing the antitrust laws. Table 21.5 gives a summary of the main antitrust laws.

The real force of any law arises from its interpretation. Interpretation of the antitrust laws has ebbed and flowed. At times, it has appeared to favor producers, and at other times, consumers. Let's see how.

Table 21.6 summarizes the landmark antitrust cases. The first important cases were those against the American Tobacco Company and Standard Oil Company, decided in 1911. These two companies were found guilty of violations under the Sherman Act and ordered to divest themselves of large holdings in other companies. The breakup of John D. Rockefeller's Standard Oil Company resulted in the creation of the oil companies that today are household names—such as Exxon.

TABLE **21.6**

Landmark Antitrust Cases

Case(s)	Year	Verdict and consequence
American Tobacco Co. and *Standard Oil Co.*	1911	*Guilty:* Ordered to divest themselves of large holdings in other companies; "rule of reason" enunciated—only *unreasonable* combinations guilty under Sherman Act.
U.S. Steel Co.	1920	*Not guilty:* Although U.S Steel had a very large market share (near monopoly), mere "size alone is not an offense"; application of the "rule of reason."
Socony-Vacuum Oil Co.	1940	*Guilty:* Combination was formed for purpose of price fixing; no consideration of "reasonableness" applied.
ALCOA	1945	*Guilty:* Too big—had too large a share of the market; end of "rule of reason."
General Electric, Westinghouse, and others	1961	*Guilty:* Price-fixing conspiracy; executives fined and jailed.
Brown Shoe	1962	*Guilty:* Ownership of Kinney, a retail chain, reduced competition; ordered to sell Kinney (Brown supplied 8% of Kinney's shoes, and Kinney sold 2% of nation's shoes).
Von's Grocery	1965	*Guilty:* Merger of two supermarkets in Los Angeles would restrain competition (the merged firm would have had 7½% of the L.A. market).
IBM	1982	*Case dismissed* as being "without merit."
AT&T	1983	*Agreement* between AT&T and government that company would divest itself of all local telephone operating companies—80% of its assets.

In finding American Tobacco and Standard Oil to be in violation of the provisions of the Sherman Act, the Supreme Court enunciated the "rule of reason." The rule of reason states that monopoly arising from mergers and agreements among firms is not necessarily illegal. Only if there is an unreasonable restraint of trade does the arrangement violate the provisions of the Sherman Act. The rule of reason was widely regarded as removing the force of the Sherman Act itself. This view was reinforced in 1920 when U.S. Steel Company was acquitted of violations under the act even though it had a very large (more than 50 percent) share of the U.S. steel market. Applying the "rule of reason," the court declared that "size alone is not an offense."

Matters remained much as they were in 1920 until 1940, when the *Socony-Vacuum Oil Company* case resulted in the first chink in the armor of the "rule of reason." The court found Socony-Vacuum Oil Company guilty because a combination had been formed for the purpose of price fixing. The court ruled that no consideration of reasonableness should be applied to such a case. But if the purpose

of the agreement was price fixing, the automatic interpretation was to be that the agreement was unreasonable.

The "rule of reason" received its death blow in the *ALCOA* case, decided in 1945. ALCOA was judged to be in violation of the law because it was too big. It had too large a share of the aluminum market. A relatively tough interpretation of the law continued through the late 1960s. In 1961, General Electric, Westinghouse, and other electrical component manufacturers were found guilty of a price-fixing conspiracy. This case was the first one in which the executives (as opposed to the company itself) were fined and also jailed.

Tough antimerger decisions were taken in 1962 against Brown Shoe and in 1965 against Von's Grocery. In the first of these cases, Brown Shoe was required to divest itself of ownership of Kinney's shoe retail chain. This case is an example of the court ruling that a vertically integrated firm is capable of restraining competition. **Vertical integration** is the merger of two or more firms operating at different stages in a production process of a single good

Limiting

Competition

in Chips

The Wall Street Journal, July 1, 1991

FTC Inquiry on Intel's Business Tactics Signals Increased Scrutiny of Industry

by Stephen Kreider Yoder

Intel Corp.'s admission that the Federal Trade Commission is looking into its business tactics hangs a cloud of doubt over the strategies that made Intel one of Silicon Valley's biggest success stories. . . .

Intel's critics have long charged that the chip maker abuses its powerful monopoly of the chips called microprocessors that are the "brains" of popular personal computers. They say the Santa Clara, Calif., chip maker divvies out scarce chips improperly and unfairly crowds competition out of the market. Now, apparently, the FTC plans to test those charges.

Intel last week said it received a letter from the FTC saying the commission was carrying out the "nonpublic" investigation of Intel's business practices to determine whether they violate antitrust laws. . . .

The FTC's initial probe of Intel appears [to be] broad, covering customers and competitors. Intel says the commission's lawyers approached at least one of Intel's PC-making customers for information on Intel. Some PC makers are disgruntled with the way Intel allocates its microprocessors, which are often in short supply, charging that Intel unfairly sells its chips to big customers such as Compaq Computer Corp. while snubbing small newcomers.

"Competitors and customers have been concerned about Intel's ability to allocate market share," says analyst William Tai of Alex. Brown & Sons Inc. Intel's allocation of sought-after chips, in effect, decides which customers gain market share, he says. "Intel's allocations policy creates clear winners and losers, and the non-winners are sure to take issue with Intel's practices," he says. . . .

FTC officials over the past month have also grilled executives and lawyers from at least two companies that have filed antitrust complaints against Intel: chip maker Cyrix Corp. of Richardson, Texas, and Tokyo Cobra Corp., a chip distributor in Irvine, Calif.

Cyrix, which makes chips that mimic the functions of certain Intel chips called "math co-processors," filed suit last year charging that Intel was conspiring to keep Cyrix out of the business by intimidating Cyrix's customers. Tokyo Cobra sued Intel after Intel cut off the distributor's chip supplies.

Intel's [general counsel, Thomas] Dunlap calls the lawsuits "knee-jerk reactions" to Intel's own suits against both companies. Intel sued Cyrix for alleged patent infringements and charged Tokyo Cobra with not paying bills.

Still, some antitrust lawyers speculate that the FTC may be concerned about what Intel's critics say is the company's pattern of using the courts to batter down potential competitors. Rivals such as Cyrix and Tokyo's NEC Corp. charge that Intel uses drawn-out court proceedings to cast clouds over competing products for years, until the market is gone. Intel denies that it unfairly uses the courts. . . .

The Essence of the Story

The Federal Trade Commission (FTC) is investigating Intel Corp., the profitable maker of the microprocessors used in personal computers.

Critics of Intel charge that the company improperly allocates its chips to big customers while snubbing small newcomers and that it improperly uses court proceedings to discourage competition.

Intel has sued Cyrix Corp., a maker of a math coprocessor that performs a similar function to an Intel chip, for alleged patent infringements.

Cyrix has responded that Intel conspired to keep Cyrix out of the chip market by intimidating Cyrix's customers.

Intel has charged Tokyo Cobra, a chip distributor, with not paying its bills.

Tokyo Cobra has sued Intel for cutting off the distributor's chip supplies.

Background and Analysis

Intel makes the microprocessor (chip) that powers IBM and IBM-compatible personal computers, and its market is protected to some degree by patents. But other firms are attempting to enter the profitable chip market.

With limited competition, Intel maximizes profit as illustrated in Fig. 1. The quantity of chips produced, Q_0, is that at which marginal cost, MC, equals marginal revenue, MR. The price is P_0, and Intel's economic profit is shown by the blue rectangle.

Economic profit encourages entry, which, if unchecked, will eventually put Intel in the situation shown in Fig. 2. Intel still maximizes its profit, but that profit will be zero. The quantity produced will fall to Q_1, and the price will fall to P_1.

It pays Intel to incur costs—such as the costs of establishing and enforcing patents—that create barriers to entry and limit the decrease in the demand for its chips that results from entry.

It pays potential entrants to find ways around Intel's barriers to entry, including using all the available legal moves, such as showing a violation of the antitrust laws.

There is a fine line between legitimate protection of a firm's interests and illegal restriction of competition. The job of the FTC is to investigate cases in which there are allegations or suspicions that the line has been crossed. This is what was happening in the computer chip industry in 1991.

Figure 1

Figure 2

or service. For example, the merger of a firm that produces raw materials, a firm that converts those raw materials into a manufactured good, and a firm that retails the finished product will be a vertically integrated firm. The vertically integrated Brown Shoe and Kinney retail chain was ordered to be broken up even though Brown supplied only 8 percent of Kinney's shoes and Kinney sold only 2 percent of the nation's shoes.

Von's Grocery is an example of a horizontally integrated firm. **Horizontal integration** is a merger of two or more firms providing essentially the same product or service. In the *Von's Grocery* case, the court ruled that the combination of two supermarkets in Los Angeles would restrict competition even though the combined sales of the two firms would have been only 7½ percent of total supermarket sales in the Los Angeles area.

The two most visible recent antitrust cases are those involving AT&T and IBM. Though important and highly visible cases, neither of the two was decided by the courts. The *AT&T* case was resolved by an agreement between AT&T and the Department of Justice, and the *IBM* case, after 13 years of litigation, was dismissed by the government as being "without merit."

The present attitude toward monopoly is pragmatic. AT&T's monopoly on telephone services has gone. IBM's position in the computer industry is much less secure and looks much less like a monopoly today than it did in 1967 when the Justice Department began its proceedings against that firm. Also, increased international competition has reduced monopoly power in the computer industry.

Nevertheless, many practices of firms in that industry continue to draw the interest and attention of the FTC, as you can see in Reading Between the Lines on pp. 572–573.

Public or Special Interest?

It is clear from the historical contexts in which antitrust law has evolved that its intent has been to protect and pursue the public interest and restrain the profit-seeking and anticompetitive actions of producers. But it is also clear from the above brief history of antitrust legislation and cases that from time to time the interest of the producer has had an influence on the way in which the law has been interpreted and applied. Nevertheless, the overall thrust of antitrust law appears to have been directed toward achieving allocative efficiency and, therefore, toward serving the public interest.

◆ ◆ ◆ ◆ In this chapter, we've seen how the government intervenes in markets to affect prices, quantities, the gains from trade, and the division of those gains between consumers and producers when there is monopoly or oligopoly. We've seen that there is a conflict between the pursuit of the public interest—achieving allocative efficiency—and the pursuit of the special interests of producers—maximizing monopoly profit. The political and legal arenas are the places in which these conflicts are resolved. We've reviewed the two theories—public interest and capture—concerning the type and scope of government intervention.

S U M M A R Y

Market Intervention

There are two ways in which the government intervenes to regulate monopolistic and oligopolistic markets: regulation and antitrust law. In the United States, both of these methods are widely used. We seek to understand the reasons for and the effects of regulation.

Government action can influence consumer surplus, producer surplus, and total surplus. Consumer surplus is the difference between what consumers are willing to pay for a given consumption level and what they actually pay. Producer surplus is the difference between a producer's revenue from its sales and the opportunity cost of production. Total surplus is the sum of consumer surplus and producer surplus. Total surplus is maximized under competition. Under monopoly, producer surplus is increased and consumer surplus is decreased, and a deadweight loss is created. (pp. 559–560)

Economic Theory of Regulation

Consumers and producers express their demand for the regulation that influences their surpluses by voting, lobbying, and making campaign contributions. The larger the surplus that can be generated by a particular regulation, and the smaller the number of people affected, the larger is the demand for the regulation. A smaller number of people are easier to organize into an effective political lobby. Regulation is supplied by politicians, who pursue their own best interest. The larger the surplus per head generated and the larger the number of people affected by it, the larger is the supply of regulation. In equilibrium, the regulation that exists is such that no interest group feels it is worthwhile to employ scarce resources to press for further changes. There are two theories of political equilibrium: public interest theory and capture theory. Public interest theory predicts that total surplus will be maximized; capture theory predicts that producer surplus will be maximized. (pp. 560–561)

Regulation and Deregulation

Regulation began with the establishment of the Interstate Commerce Commission in 1887. A further expansion of regulation occurred in the 1930s. There was further steady growth of regulatory activity to the mid-1970s. Since 1978, the transportation, telecommunication, and financial sectors have been deregulated.

Regulation is conducted by regulatory agencies controlled by politically appointed bureaucrats and staffed by a permanent bureaucracy of experts. Regulated firms are required to comply with rules about price, product quality, and output levels. Two types of industries are regulated: natural monopolies and cartels. In both cases, regulation has enabled firms in the regulated industries to achieve profit levels equal to or greater than those attained on the average in the rest of the economy. This outcome is closer to the predictions of the capture theory of regulation than to the predictions of the public interest theory. (pp. 562–570)

Antitrust Law

Antitrust law provides an alternative way in which the government can control monopoly and monopolistic practices. The law itself is brief, and its interpretation has fluctuated between favoring the consumer and favoring the producer.

But the overall thrust of the law has been directed toward serving the public interest. In recent years, increased international competition has reduced the monopoly power. (pp. 570–574)

K E Y   E L E M E N T S

Key Terms

Antitrust law, 559
Average cost pricing rule, 565
Capture theory of regulation, 561
Deregulation, 559
Horizontal integration, 574
Marginal cost pricing rule, 564
Public interest theory of regulation, 561
Rate of return regulation, 565
Regulation, 559
Total surplus, 559
Vertical integration, 571

Key Figures and Tables

Figure 21.1   Natural Monopoly: Marginal Cost Pricing, 564
Figure 21.2   Natural Monopoly: Average Cost Pricing, 565
Figure 21.3   Natural Monopoly: Profit Maximization, 566
Figure 21.5   Collusive Oligopoly, 568
Table 21.1   Regulation at Its Peak in 1977, 562
Table 21.5   Antitrust Laws, 570
Table 21.6   Landmark Antitrust Cases, 571

REVIEW QUESTIONS

1 What are the two main ways in which the government can intervene in the marketplace?

2 What is consumer surplus? How is it calculated, and how is it represented in a diagram?

3 What is producer surplus? How is it calculated, and how is it represented in a diagram?

4 What is total surplus? How is it calculated, and how is it represented in a diagram?

5 Why do consumers demand regulation? In what kinds of industries are their demands for regulation greatest?

6 Why do producers demand regulation? In what kinds of industries would their demands for regulation be greatest?

7 Explain the public interest and capture theories of the supply of regulation. What does each theory imply about the behavior of politicians?

8 How is oligopoly regulated in the United States? In whose interest is it regulated?

9 What are the main antitrust laws in force in the United States today?

10 What is the "rule of reason"? When was this rule formulated? How has it been applied? When was it abandoned?

PROBLEMS

1 Cascade Springs, Inc. is an unregulated natural monopoly that bottles water from a natural spring high in the Grand Tetons. The total fixed cost incurred by Cascade Springs is $160,000, and its marginal cost is 10¢ a bottle. The demand for bottled water from Cascade Springs is as follows:

Price (cents per bottle)	Quantity demanded (thousands of bottles per year)
100	0
90	200
80	400
70	600
60	800
50	1,000
40	1,200
30	1,400
20	1,600
10	1,800
0	2,000

a What is the price of a bottle of water?

b How many bottles does Cascade Springs sell?

c Does Cascade Springs maximize total surplus or producer surplus?

2 The government regulates Cascade Springs in problem 1 by imposing a marginal cost pricing rule.

a What is the price of a bottle of water?

b How many bottles does Cascade Springs sell?

c What is Cascade Springs' producer surplus?

d What is the consumer surplus?

e Is the regulation in the public interest or in the private interest?

3 The government regulates Cascade Springs in problem 1 by imposing an average cost pricing rule.

a What is the price of a bottle of water?

b How many bottles does Cascade Springs sell?

c What is Cascade Springs' producer surplus?

d What is the consumer surplus?

e Is the regulation in the public interest or in the private interest?

4 The value of the capital invested in Cascade Springs in problem 1 is $2 million. The government introduces a rate of return regulation requiring the firm to sell its water for a price that gives it a rate of return of 5 percent on its capital.

a What is the price of a bottle of water?

b How many bottles does Cascade Springs sell?

c What is Cascade Springs' producer surplus?

d What is the consumer surplus?

e Is the regulation in the public interest or in the private interest?

PART 9

INTERNATIONAL ECONOMICS AND REFORM

Talking

with

Jeffrey

Sachs

Jeffrey Sachs was born in Detroit in 1954 and has spent his entire university career at Harvard, first as an undergraduate and eventually as a professor. Today, however, Professor Sachs spends most of his time on airplanes or in Eastern Europe. He first began advising foreign governments on economic policy by helping Bolivia with hyperinflation in 1985. His name burst before the public with his work on Poland, but now he is increasingly associated with the economic reforms of Boris Yeltsin and the Russian Federation.

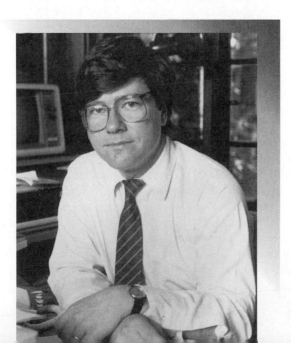

How did you get drawn into the Eastern European reform area?

I started my work in Eastern Europe in Poland at the time that Solidarity was legalized in the spring of 1989. I had been invited by the Communist government to give advice to them about their financial troubles. Events obviously went very fast because soon after legalization there was an election, which Solidarity won overwhelmingly. From that point on, I became an economic advisor to believers in Solidarity and helped them draft an outline of a radical economic reform program. Soon after that, a Solidarity government actually came to power, and I began to work on the implementation of economic reforms, which were widely viewed as the first and most comprehensive reforms in Eastern Europe. From there, I got to know reformers in all of the countries in the region and began to work closely with some Russian economists who are now senior members of the Yeltsin government. As democratization proceeded in Russia, these people invited me to help them develop their reform strategy.

Your name has been associated with the "big bang" or "cold turkey" approach to reform. Can you describe that approach and explain why you favor it over a more gradual and tentative one?

The basic idea is to start with the goal of the reform, such as to put in place a working capitalist system. Of course, it'll be a capitalist system that reflects the particular culture, history, tradition, and resources of the country. It is an attempt not to find a so-called "third way in" between the old system and the new system but to go fully toward the working capitalist model. In the case of Eastern Europe, the goal is even more explicit: to implement reforms that will make these countries harmonize with the economies of Western Europe so that in a short period of time—within a decade is their hope—they can actually become members of the European Community.

The essence of "big bang" is that it's important to move comprehensively and quickly toward the goal of a working capitalist economy because various aspects of the market economy are all interrelated. If one does just a piece of the reform but leaves much of the old system intact, the conflicts of the old and the new are likely to make things considerably worse rather than better.

What are the major pieces of the radical reform strategy that you're recommending to governments in Eastern Europe?

The reform strategy comes down to four components. The first is macroeconomic stabilization, because usually these countries start out in a deep macroeconomic crisis characterized by high inflation and intense shortages. Second is economic liberalization, which means ending central planning, trade quotas, and other barriers that cut the country off from the world market. The third part of the reform is privatization, which is the transfer of state property back to private owners. Those private owners could be individuals or they could be, as in the West, financial intermediaries like mutual funds or banks or pension funds that are in turn owned by individuals. When I say privatization, I use the word "transfer" rather than "sell" because selling state property is only one way to privatize. There are other ways, such as giving away the state property to workers, managers, or the public. The Eastern European countries are privatizing through a mix of sales and direct giveaways. The fourth part of the radical reform is the introduction of social safety nets, which provide protection for the most vulnerable parts of the society that are perhaps hardest hit by the reform or are already suffering even irrespective of the reform. That means putting in place unemployment benefits, an adequate retirement system and health care system, job training, public works spending, and so forth. Those are the four main pillars.

It's called "big bang" because you must move quickly on this. Probably the most dramatic part of all is the stabilization and liberalization phase, where subsidies are cut very quickly and price controls are eliminated. The result is usually a very dramatic one-time jump in prices. That starts off the reform.

How long does the reform process generally take?

Certain things can be done quickly, and others take more time. Stabilization and liberalization can be accomplished fast, or most parts of them. Freeing price controls, eliminating trade barriers, and cutting subsidies, for example, can all be done on the first day of the program, which is why it's sometimes called "shock therapy" or "cold turkey." Privatization, though, takes much longer. Some aspects of the fourth component of the reform strategy, the social safety net, can be done quickly. For example, pensions of retirees can be protected through budgetary allocation. An unemployment insurance system was started up very quickly in Poland, and it has worked adequately. Other parts of the social safety net, for instance, real reform of the health care system, are very complex and take a considerable amount of time to effect.

Even if the reforms go very quickly, the process of change that those reforms set loose will take years or even decades to work themselves out. What do I mean? The socialist system wasn't just messed up in terms of the organization of production and the ways that prices were set. It was also systematically misusing resources by putting tremendous overemphasis on heavy industrial production while neglecting other important parts of the economy, such as services and wholesale and retail trade. When you free up market forces, the market doesn't demand all the heavy industrial production that was built up in the past. This leads to unemployment, a drop in demand, and people voluntarily quitting those industries to move into areas that were starved for people, resources, and capital in the past. You get a great boom in retail trade, for example, with tens of thousands of new shops opening up. The reforms set loose that process, but the corresponding shift of resources could take five, ten, fifteen, even twenty years to adjust.

Even within a big bang approach, presumably you can't literally do everything at once. What are the highest priorities?

The highest priority is to avoid real financial chaos. Poland, Yugoslavia, and Russia all fell into hyperinflation at the end of the Communist system. That meant that the new democratic governments' highest priority was to end the underlying conditions that were feeding the hyperinflation. If you can accomplish the financial stability, then I think the next highest priority is to have the rudiments of the private property system in place, such as a commercial code and laws for corporate enterprises, contracts, and protection of private property. Then the next priority is rapid privatization because until the enterprises are with real owners facing proper incentives, one has to be skeptical that they'll be managed in an efficient and sensible way.

What are the earliest indicators of whether the reforms are beginning to take hold?

Of course, different things happen at different times. The first thing one looks for if an economy is trying to emerge from hyperinflation is stability of prices. After freeing prices and experiencing a significant one-time jump in the price level, this should not turn into ongoing high inflation but rather be followed by price stability.

Can the countries of Eastern Europe and the former Soviet Union evolve into democratic nations with market economies without economic aid from the West?

The whole history of radical economic change underscores the importance of financial assistance during the first critical years of reform. It takes many years for the real fruits of the reform to be widely evident in the society. Certain costs of the reform, however, such as closing down old inefficient enterprises, can become evident very quickly. It's during that crucial period between the introduction of the reforms and the time when they really are bearing fruit that lie the greatest dangers and also the greatest need for international assistance to help provide a cushion to living standards and a bolstering of the reform effort until the reforms really take hold.

The foreign assistance does not actually pay for the reconstruction of the country. It's never big enough. The Marshall Plan was not enough to really rebuild Europe, but what the Marshall Plan did was to give the new democratic postwar governments time to put in place market-based policies so that they could take hold.

Whether it's postwar Germany or Japan, Mexico's turnaround in the 1980s, or Poland at the beginning of the 1990s, countries on the path to economic and political reform need help at the begin-

ning. For Russia and the other states of the former Soviet Union, it will be the same. They will definitely need some years of Western and foreign help to keep their reforms on track and to make the living conditions tolerable.

What form will that aid take? Free-trading opportunities? Private investment? Government loans?

The form of aid has to be linked to the timetable of the reform process. At the beginning, say in the first year, the aid is inevitably of two sorts. First, humanitarian emergency assistance to make sure that food is getting to the table and that medical supplies are available. Second, stabilization assistance, or various kinds of financial support to help make the currency strong and to increase the flow of basic imports, which are needed just to keep the economy functioning. Russia has suffered a sharp decline in its own capacity to buy imports because its export earnings have fallen sharply in the past few years. They need help just to keep basic imports going, and by doing that you help strengthen the currency.

In later years, you want to get away from that kind of emergency stabilization support and put much more attention on project financing to get new enterprises going. One hopes these will become the major engine of economic growth in the future. Private investment, of course, is to be desired, but it will take many years to attract. Private investors first want to know the market, and then they wait to see signs that the reforms are working and that political stability is being achieved. The official support from government has to come first. Then the private money will flow in.

What are the economic principles that you find most valuable in dealing with the acute problems of Russia today?

The starting point for me is to recognize that all of the successful economies in the world have a shared core set of institutions. There are, of course, major differences across countries, but all of the advanced industrial economies share certain features—such as a currency that trades, that can be used to buy goods without facing fixed prices or shortages, and that is convertible internationally; an open trading system in which, with some exceptions, goods can be bought and sold from abroad on normal market terms; an economy based on private ownership not state ownership; a legal infrastructure that supports private ownership so that property rights are clearly defined and defensible. Things like that. It's that core of institutions that is so important to put into place.

What are the undergraduates studying economics in Russia today actually studying? Are they learning about demand and supply, competition and monopoly, aggregate demand and aggregate supply, and the role of money in creating inflation?

Of course, things are changing very fast. It was only a few years ago that ideas like market economy and private property were unfamiliar. What one sees now is incredible hunger to study and analyze the basic properties of market economies. There is no doubt, I think, in the minds of virtually everybody that the old system was a terrible failure and that what Russia should have is a normal economy like that which is in place in Western Europe, the United States, and Japan. The curricula are being revised with incredible speed to teach the standard economics that we also learn. Of course, students' attention is focused not just on the well-functioning system but also on the problems of transitions.

What do you see as the major obstacles to economic development in Eastern Europe?

The major obstacle is that this is a time of great upheaval. The collapse of communism occurred, in part, because the old system had failed so thoroughly and people were in economic misery. So all this transformation is starting in the midst of a real economic crisis—a crisis that breeds confusion, fear, and anxiety. That confusion, fear, and anxiety can lead a whole country astray from its basic path of building up democratic market institutions. There are politicians waiting with messages attacking democracy, trying to take advantage of the anxieties of the people to win power. This could derail the reforms. If the new governments cannot deliver economic improvement, then I think risks to democracy will certainly exist. And once there is doubt about the basic

direction of these changes, then things become unpredictable, but very hazardous results are possible. I don't think that's the likely outcome, but it's one of the reasons why I underscored the need for support, understanding, and a financial cushion from the West during this very critical and complicated stage of implementing the reforms.

Assuming that Russia does develop rapidly and solves its economic problems in the decade ahead, what are the major implications for the United States?

The overwhelming implication is that the chance for us to live in a peaceful world is enormously improved. We should not underestimate the difference that will mean to our own quality of life. The success of Russian democracy will make a huge difference to our security and, in financial terms, to our ability to divert our own resources from military spending to civilian use. Now, Russia's success with democracy depends a great deal on its success in overcoming this economic crisis. We know all too well that economic instability is one of the great dangers to a young democracy.

There are many, many other implications. The whole world will change, and I think vastly for the better. There will be a huge trading and investment opportunity when a country that covers one sixth of the world's land mass, spanning over eleven time zones, becomes closely integrated with the rest of the world economy after having been cut off for seventy-five years. There will be important changes in trade patterns, investment opportunities, and global cooperation.

CHAPTER **22**

TRADING
WITH
THE
WORLD

After studying this chapter, you will be able to:

◆ Describe the patterns and trends in international trade

◆ Explain comparative advantage

◆ Explain why all countries can gain from international trade

◆ Explain how prices adjust to bring about balanced trade

◆ Explain how economies of scale and diversity of taste lead to gains from international trade

◆ Explain why trade restrictions lower the volume of imports and exports and lower our consumption possibilities

◆ Explain why we have trade restrictions even though they lower our consumption possibilities

SINCE ANCIENT TIMES, PEOPLE HAVE STRIVEN TO EXPAND their trading as far as technology allowed. Roman coins have been found in the ruins of ancient Indian cities, and Marco Polo opened up the silk route between Europe and China in the thirteenth century. Today, container ships laden with cars and machines and Boeing 747s stuffed with farm-fresh foods ply sea and air routes, carrying billions of dollars worth of goods. Why do people go to such great lengths to trade with those in other nations? ◆ ◆ In recent years, a massive increase in the penetration of the foreign car industry into the United States has brought about a severe contraction of our own car industry. Jobs in Detroit and other car-producing cities have disappeared, creating what has come to be called the Rust Belt. Do the benefits of international trade make up for the cost of jobs displaced by foreign competition? Could we, as politicians often claim, improve our economy by restricting imports?

Silk Routes and Rust Belts

◆ ◆ The wages earned by the workers in the textile and electronics factories of Singapore, Taiwan, and Hong Kong are low compared with wages in the United States. Obviously, these countries can make manufactured goods much more cheaply than we can. How can we possibly compete with countries that pay their workers a fraction of U.S. wages? Are there any industries, besides perhaps the Hollywood movie industry, in which we have an advantage? ◆ ◆ In the 1930s, Congress passed the Smoot-Hawley Act, an act that increased taxes on imports to 60 percent, provoking widespread retaliation from the world's major trading countries. In contrast, after World War II, a process of trade liberalization brought about the creation of the General Agreement on Tariffs and Trade

(GATT) and a gradual reduction of taxes on imports. What are the effects of taxes on international trade? Why don't we have completely unrestricted international trade?

◆ ◆ ◆ ◆ In this chapter, we're going to learn about international trade. We'll discover how *all* nations can gain by specializing in producing the goods and services at which they have an advantage compared with other countries and by exchanging some of their output with each other. We'll discover that all countries can compete, no matter how high their wages. We will also explain why, despite the fact that international trade brings benefits to all, countries restrict trade. We'll discover who suffers and who benefits when international trade is restricted.

Patterns and Trends in International Trade

The goods and services that we buy from people in other countries are called **imports**. The goods and services that we sell to people in other countries are called **exports**. What are the most important things that we import and export? Most people would probably guess that a rich nation such as the United States imports raw materials and exports manufactured goods. While that is one feature of U.S. international trade, it is not its most important feature. The vast bulk of our exports *and* imports is manufactured goods. We sell earth-moving equipment, airplanes, supercomputers, and scientific equipment, and we buy TVs, VCRs, blue jeans, and T-shirts. Also, we are a major exporter and importer of agricultural products and raw materials. We also import and export a huge volume of services. Let's look at the international trade of the United States in a recent year.

U.S. International Trade

Table 22.1 classifies U.S. international trade in four major categories of goods—agricultural products,

TABLE 22.1

U.S. Exports and Imports in 1992

Category	Exports	Imports	Balance
	(billions of dollars)		
Agricultural products	43.9	27.9	16.0
Industrial supplies and materials (excluding agricultural)	109.6	139.8	−30.2
Manufactured goods	285.8	367.8	−82.0
Services	178.5	123.4	55.1
Total	617.8	658.9	−41.1

Source: Survey of Current Business (May 1993), vol. 73.

industrial supplies and materials, manufactured goods, and services. The second column gives the value of U.S. exports, and the third column gives the value of U.S. imports. The fourth column tells us the balance of trade in the various categories. The **balance of trade** is the value of exports minus the value of imports. If the balance is positive, then the value of exports exceeds the value of imports and the United States is a **net exporter**. But if the balance is negative, the value of imports exceeds the value of exports and the United States is a **net importer**.

Trade in Goods   About 80 percent of U.S. international trade is trade in goods, and 20 percent is trade in services. Of the categories of goods traded, by far the most important is manufactured goods. But the total value of exports of manufactured goods is less than that of imports—the United States is a net importer of manufactured goods. The United States is also a net importer of industrial supplies. It is a net exporter of agricultural products and services.

Table 22.2 highlights some of the major items of U.S. imports and exports of goods. The country's biggest net exports are aircraft, machinery, grains, and chemicals. The country's largest net imports are manufactured consumer goods, fuel, and automobiles (including auto parts).

TABLE 22.2

U.S. Exports and Imports of Goods in 1990: Some Large Individual Items

Item	Exports	Imports	Balance
	(billions of dollars)		
Aircraft	32.3	10.7	21.6
Machinery	119.8	104.6	15.2
Grains	14.9	—	14.9
Chemicals	28.4	14.3	14.1
Automobiles	37.4	87.3	−49.9
Fuels	14.0	65.7	−51.7
Manufactured consumer goods	43.3	105.7	−62.4

Source: Survey of Current Business (December 1991), vol. 71.

TABLE 22.3

U.S. Trade in Services in 1990

Category	Exports	Imports	Balance
	(billions of dollars)		
Travel and transportation	75.2	71.1	4.1
Other services	48.2	18.7	29.5
Military services	9.9	17.1	−7.2
Total	133.3	106.9	26.4

Source: Survey of Current Business (December 1991), vol. 71.

Trade in Services   One fifth of U.S. international trade is not of goods but of services. You might be wondering how a country can "export" and "import" services. Let's look at some examples.

Suppose that you decided to vacation in France, traveling there on an Air France flight from New York. What you buy from Air France is not a good, but a transportation service. Although the concept might sound odd at first, in economic terms you are importing that service from France. Since you pay U.S. money to a French company in exchange for a service, it doesn't matter that most of your flight time is over the Atlantic Ocean. For that matter, the money you spend in France on hotel bills, restaurant meals, and other things is also classified as the import of services. Similarly, the vacation taken by a French student in the United States counts as an export of services to France.

When we import TV sets from South Korea, the owner of the ship that carries those TV sets might be Greek and the company that insures the cargo might be British. The payments that we make for the transportation and insurance to the Greek and British companies are also payments for the import of services. Similarly, when an American shipping compa-

ny transports California wine to Tokyo, the transportation cost is an export of a service to Japan.

The importance of the various components of trade in services is set out in Table 22.3. As you can see, transportation and travel are the largest items—accounting for more than 50 percent of exports and almost 70 percent of imports.

Geographical Patterns   The United States has important trading links with almost every part of the world except for Eastern Europe, where trade is almost nonexistent. As you can see from Table 22.4, our biggest trading partners are Canada and the European Community. Our *imports* from Japan and the newly industrializing countries of Asia such as Hong Kong, Singapore, South Korea, and Taiwan are also very large. Our international trade deficit is almost exclusively with this group of countries.

Trends in Trade

International trade has become an increasingly important part of our economic life. In 1950, we exported less than 5 percent of total output and imported only 4 percent of the goods and services that we consumed ourselves. Over the years since then, that percentage has steadily increased, and today it is more than double its level of 1950.

On the export side, all the major commodity categories have shared in the increased volume of international trade. Machinery, food, and raw materials have remained the most important components of

TABLE 22.4

U.S. Exports and Imports of Goods in 1992: Geographical Patterns

Country or region	Exports	Imports	Balance
	(billions of dollars)		
Canada	90.4	100.7	−10.3
Japan	46.9	96.9	−50.0
European Community	100.6	94.0	6.6
Latin America	75.3	69.1	6.2
Other Western Europe	13.8	17.4	−3.6
Eastern Europe	5.6	2.0	3.6
Other Asia and Africa	98.0	151.7	−53.7
Australia, New Zealand, and South Africa	8.7	3.7	5.0
Total	439.3	535.5	−96.2

Source. Survey of Current Business (March 1993), vol. 73.

FIGURE 22.1

The U.S. Balance of Trade

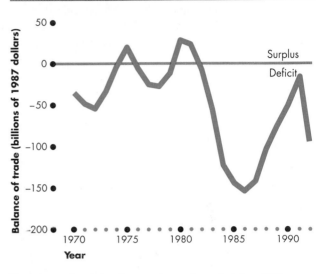

The balance of trade has fluctuated around zero, but since 1982, imports have been higher than exports and a deficit has emerged.

Source: Economic Report of the President, 1993.

exports and have roughly maintained their share in total exports.

But there have been dramatic changes in the composition of imports. Food and raw material imports have declined steadily. Imports of fuel increased dramatically in the 1970s but declined in the 1980s. Imports of machinery of all kinds, after being a fairly stable percentage of total imports until the middle 1980s, now approach 50 percent of total imports.

There have been important trends in the overall balance in U.S. international trade in recent years. That overall *balance of trade* (of goods and services) is shown in Fig. 22.1. As you can see, the balance fluctuates around zero, but in the years since 1982 there has been a large excess of imports over exports (a negative balance of trade).

Balance of Trade and International Borrowing

When people buy more than they sell, they have to finance the difference by borrowing. When they sell more than they buy, they can use the surplus to make loans to others. This simple principle that governs the income and expenditure and borrowing and lending of individuals and firms is also a feature of our balance of trade. If we import more than we export, we have to finance the difference by borrowing from foreigners. When we export more than we import, we make loans to foreigners to enable them to buy goods in excess of the value of the goods they have sold to us.

This chapter does *not* cover the factors that determine the balance of trade and the scale of the international borrowing and lending that finance that balance. It is concerned with understanding the volume, pattern, and directions of international trade rather than its balance. So that we can keep our focus on these topics, we'll build a model in which there is no international borrowing and lending— just international trade in goods and services. We'll find that we are able to understand what determines the volume, pattern, and direction of international trade and also establish its benefits and the costs of trade restrictions within this framework. This model can be expanded to include international borrowing and lending, but such an extension does not change the conclusions that we'll reach here about the factors that determine the volume, pattern, and directions of international trade.

Let's now begin to study those factors.

Opportunity Cost and Comparative Advantage

L et's apply the lessons that we learned in Chapter 3 about the gains from trade between Jane and Joe to the trade between nations. We'll begin by recalling how we can use the production possibility frontier to measure opportunity cost.

Opportunity Cost in Pioneerland

Pioneerland (a fictitious country) can produce grain and cars at any point inside or along the production possibility frontier shown in Fig. 22.2. (We're holding constant the output of all the other goods that Pioneerland produces.) The Pioneers (the people of Pioneerland) are consuming all the grain and cars that they produce, and they are operating at point *a* in the figure. That is, Pioneerland is producing and consuming 15 billion bushels of grain and 8 million cars each year. What is the opportunity cost of a car in Pioneerland?

We can answer that question by calculating the slope of the production possibility frontier at point *a*. As we discovered in Chapter 3 (pp. 54–56), the slope of the frontier measures the opportunity cost of one good in terms of the other. To measure the slope of the frontier at point *a*, place a straight line tangential to the frontier at point *a* and calculate the slope of that straight line. Recall that the formula for the slope of a line is the change in the value of the variable measured on the *y*-axis divided by change in the value of the variable measured on the *x*-axis as we move along the line. Here, the variable measured on the *y*-axis is billions of bushels of grain, and the variable measured on the *x*-axis is millions of cars. So the slope (opportunity cost) is

FIGURE **22.2**

Opportunity Cost in Pioneerland

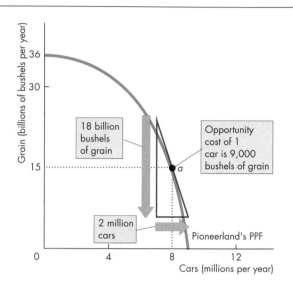

Pioneerland produces and consumes 15 billion bushels of grain and 8 million cars a year. That is, it produces and consumes at point *a* on its production possibility frontier. Opportunity cost is measured as the slope of the production possibility frontier. At point *a*, 2 million cars cost 18 billion bushels of grain. Equivalently, 1 car costs 9,000 bushels of grain or 9,000 bushels cost 1 car.

the change in the number of bushels of grain divided by the change in the number of cars. As you can see from the red triangle at point *a* in the figure, if the number of cars produced increases by 2 million, grain production decreases by 18 billion bushels. Therefore the slope is 18 billion divided by 2 million, which equals 9,000. To get one more car, the people of Pioneerland must give up 9,000 bushels of grain. Thus the opportunity cost of 1 car is 9,000 bushels of grain. Equivalently, 9,000 bushels of grain cost 1 car.

Opportunity Cost in Magic Empire

Now consider the production possibility frontier in Magic Empire (another fictitious country and the only other country in our model world). Figure 22.3 illustrates its production possibility frontier. Like the Pioneers, the Magicians (the people in Magic Empire) consume all the grain and cars that they produce. Magic Empire consumes 18 billion bushels of grain a year and 4 million cars, at point *a'*.

FIGURE **22.3**

Opportunity Cost in Magic Empire

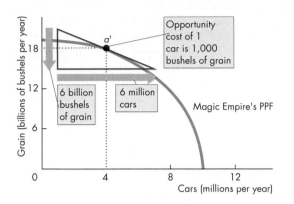

Magic Empire produces and consumes 18 billion bushels of grain and 4 million cars a year. That is, it produces and consumes at point *a'* on its production possibility frontier. Opportunity cost is measured as the slope of the production possibility frontier. At point *a'*, 6 million cars cost 6 billion bushels of grain. Equivalently, 1 car costs 1,000 bushels of grain or 1,000 bushels cost 1 car.

We can do the same kind of calculation of opportunity cost for Magic Empire as we have just done for Pioneerland. At point *a'*, 1 car costs 1,000 bushels of grain, or, equivalently, 1,000 bushels of grain costs 1 car.

Comparative Advantage

Cars are cheaper in Magic Empire than in Pioneerland. One car costs 9,000 bushels of grain in Pioneerland but only 1,000 bushels of grain in Magic Empire. But grain is cheaper in Pioneerland than in Magic Empire—9,000 bushels of grain cost only 1 car in Pioneerland, while that same amount of grain costs 9 cars in Magic Empire.

Magic Empire has a comparative advantage in car production. Pioneerland has a comparative advantage in grain production. A country has a **comparative advantage** in producing a good if it can produce that good at a lower opportunity cost than any other country can. Let's see how opportunity cost differences and comparative advantage generate gains from international trade.

The Gains from Trade

I f Magic Empire bought grain for what it costs Pioneerland to produce it, then Magic Empire could buy 9,000 bushels of grain for 1 car. That is much lower than the cost of growing grain in Magic Empire, since there it costs 9 cars to produce 9,000 bushels of grain. If the Magicians buy at the low Pioneerland price, they will reap some gains.

If the Pioneers buy cars for what it costs Magic Empire to produce them, they will be able to obtain a car for 1,000 bushels of grain. Since it costs 9,000 bushels of grain to produce a car in Pioneerland, the Pioneers would gain from such an activity.

In this situation, it makes sense for Magicians to buy their grain from Pioneers and for Pioneers to buy their cars from Magicians. Let's see how such profitable international trade comes about.

Reaping the Gains from Trade

We've seen that the Pioneers would like to buy their cars from the Magicians and that the Magicians would like to buy their grain from the Pioneers. Let's see how the two groups do business with each other, concentrating attention on the international market for cars.

Figure 22.4 illustrates such a market. The quantity of cars traded internationally is measured on the horizontal axis. On the vertical axis we measure the price of a car, but it is expressed as its opportunity cost—the number of bushels of grain that a car costs. If no international trade takes place, that price in Pioneerland is 9,000 bushels of grain, indicated by point *a* in the figure. Again, if no trade takes place, that price is 1,000 bushels of grain in Magic Empire, indicated by point *a'* in the figure.

The points *a* and *a'* in Fig. 22.4 correspond to the points identified by those same letters in Figs. 22.2 and 22.3. The lower the price of a car (in terms of bushels of grain), the greater is the quantity of cars that the Pioneers import from the Magicians. This fact is illustrated in the downward-sloping curve that shows Pioneerland's import demand for cars.

FIGURE **22.4**

International Trade in Cars

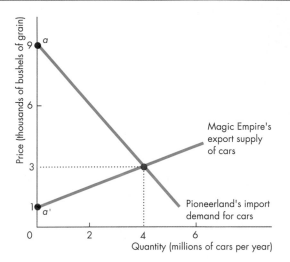

As the price of a car decreases, the quantity of imports demanded by Pioneerland increases—Pioneerland's import demand curve for cars is downward-sloping. As the price of a car increases, the quantity of cars supplied by Magic Empire for export increases—Magic Empire's export supply curve of cars is upward-sloping. Without international trade, the price of a car is 9,000 bushels of grain in Pioneerland (point *a*) and 1,000 bushels of grain in Magic Empire (point *a'*). With free international trade, the price of a car is determined where the export supply curve intersects the import demand curve—a price of 3,000 bushels of grain. At that price, 4 million cars a year are imported by Pioneerland and exported by Magic Empire. The value of grain exported by Pioneerland and imported by Magic Empire is 12 billion bushels a year, the quantity required to pay for the cars imported.

The Magicians respond in the opposite direction. The higher the price of cars (in terms of bushels of grain), the greater is the quantity of cars that Magicians export to Pioneers. This fact is reflected in Magic Empire's export supply of cars—the upward-sloping line in the figure.

The international market in cars determines the equilibrium price and quantity traded. This equilibrium occurs where the import demand curve intersects the export supply curve. In this case, the equilibrium price of a car is 3,000 bushels of grain. Four million cars a year are exported by Magic Empire and imported by Pioneerland. Notice that the price at which cars are traded is lower than the initial price in Pioneerland but higher than the initial price in Magic Empire.

Balanced Trade

Notice that the number of cars exported by Magic Empire—4 million a year—is exactly equal to the number of cars imported by Pioneerland. How does Pioneerland pay for its cars? By exporting grain. How much grain does Pioneerland export? You can find the answer by noticing that for 1 car, Pioneerland has to pay 3,000 bushels of grain. Hence for 4 million cars they have to pay 12 billion bushels of grain. Thus Pioneerland's exports of grain are 12 billion bushels a year. Magic Empire imports this same quantity of grain.

Magic Empire is exchanging 4 million cars for 12 billion bushels of grain each year, and Pioneerland is doing the opposite, exchanging 12 billion bushels of grain for 4 million cars. Trade is balanced between these two countries. The value received from exports equals the value paid out for imports.

Changes in Production and Consumption

We've seen that international trade makes it possible for Pioneers to buy cars at a lower price than that at which they can produce them for themselves. It also enables Magicians to sell their cars for a higher price, which is equivalent to saying that Magicians can buy grain for a lower price. Thus everybody seems to gain. Magicians buy grain at a lower price, and Pioneers buy cars at a lower price. How is it possible for everyone to gain? What are the changes in production and consumption that accompany these gains?

An economy that does not trade with other economies has identical production and consumption possibilities. Without trade, the economy can consume only what it produces. But with international trade, an economy can consume different quantities of goods from those that it produces. The production possibility frontier describes the limit of what a country can produce, but it does not describe the limits to what it can consume. Figure 22.5 will help you to see the distinction between production possibilities and consumption possibilities when a country trades with other countries.

First of all, notice that the figure has two parts, part (a) for Pioneerland and part (b) for Magic Empire. The production possibility frontiers that you saw in Figs. 22.2 and 22.3 are reproduced here. The slopes of the two black lines in the figure represent the opportunity costs in the two countries when

FIGURE 22.5

Expanding Consumption Possibilities

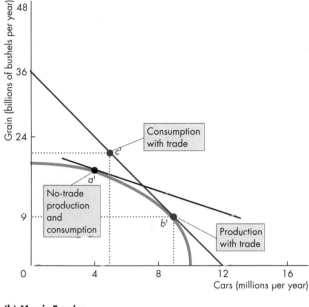

(a) Pioneerland

(b) Magic Empire

With no international trade, the Pioneers produce and consume at point *a* and the opportunity cost of a car is 9,000 bushels of grain (the slope of the black line in part a). Also, with no international trade, the Magicians produce and consume at point *a'* and the opportunity cost of 1,000 bushels of grain is 1 car (the slope of the black line in part b).

Goods can be exchanged internationally at a price of 3,000 bushels of grain for 1 car along the red line. In part (a), Pioneerland decreases its production of cars and increases its production of grain, moving

from *a* to *b*. It exports grain and imports cars, and it consumes at point *c*. The Pioneers have more of both cars and grain than they would if they produced all their own consumption goods—at point *a*. In part (b), Magic Empire increases car production and decreases grain production, moving from *a'* to *b'*. Magic Empire exports cars and imports grain, and it consumes at point *c'*. The Magicians have more of both cars and grain than they would if they produced all their own consumption goods—at point *a'*.

there is no international trade. Pioneerland produces and consumes at point *a*, and Magic Empire produces and consumes at *a'*. Cars cost 9,000 bushels of grain in Pioneerland and 1,000 bushels of grain in Magic Empire.

Consumption Possibilities The countries' consumption possibilities with international trade are shown by the two red lines in Fig. 22.5. These lines in both parts of the figure have the same slope, and that slope is the opportunity cost of a car in terms of grain on the world market—3,000 bushels per car. The *slope* of the consumption possibilities line is common to both countries because it is determined by the *world* price. But the position of a country's

consumption possibilities line depends on its production possibilities. A country cannot produce outside its production possibility curve, so its consumption possibilities curve touches its production possibility curve. Thus Pioneerland could choose to consume what it produces, at point *b*, and not trade internationally or to trade internationally and consume at a point on its red consumption possibilities line.

Free Trade Equilibrium With international trade, the producers of cars in Magic Empire can get a higher price for their output. As a result, they increase the quantity of car production. At the same time, grain producers in Magic Empire are getting a lower price for their grain and so they reduce production. Producers in Magic Empire adjust their output until the opportunity cost in Magic Empire equals the opportunity cost in the world market. This situation arises when Magic Empire is producing at point b' in Fig. 22.5(b).

But the Magicians do not consume at point b'. That is, they do not increase their consumption of cars and decrease their consumption of grain. They sell some of the cars they produce to Pioneerland in exchange for some of Pioneerland's grain. But to see how that works out, we first need to check in with Pioneerland to see what's happening there.

In Pioneerland, cars are now less expensive and grain more expensive than before. As a consequence, producers in Pioneerland decrease car production and increase grain production. They do so until the opportunity cost of a car in terms of grain equals the cost on the world market. They move to point b in part (a). But the Pioneers do not consume at point b. They exchange some of the additional grain they produce for the now cheaper cars from Magic Empire.

The figure shows us the quantities consumed in the two countries. We saw in Fig. 22.4 that Magic Empire exports 4 million cars a year and Pioneerland imports those cars. We also saw that Pioneerland exports 12 billion bushels of grain a year and Magic Empire imports that grain. Thus Pioneerland's consumption of grain is 12 billion bushels a year less than it produces, and its consumption of cars is 4 million a year more than it produces. Pioneerland consumes at point c in Fig. 22.5(a).

Similarly, we know that Magic Empire consumes 12 billion bushels of grain more than it produces and 4 million cars fewer than it produces. Thus Magic Empire consumes at c' in Fig. 22.5(b).

Calculating the Gains from Trade

You can now literally "see" the gains from trade in Fig. 22.5. Without trade, Pioneers produce and consume at a (part a)—a point on Pioneerland's production possibility frontier. With international trade, Pioneers consume at point c in part (a)—a point *outside* the production possibility frontier. At point c, Pioneers are consuming 3 billion bushels of grain a year and 1 million cars a year more than before. These increases in consumption of cars and grain, beyond the limits of the production possibility frontier, are the gains from international trade.

But Magicians also gain. Without trade, they consume at point a' in part (b)—a point on Magic Empire's production possibility frontier. With international trade, they consume at point c'—a point outside the production possibility frontier. With international trade, Magic Empire consumes 3 billion bushels of grain a year and 1 million cars a year more than without trade. These are the gains from international trade for Magic Empire.

Gains for All

When Pioneers and Magicians trade with each other, potentially everyone can gain. Domestic sellers add the net demand of foreigners to their domestic demand, and so their market expands. Buyers are faced with domestic supply plus net foreign supply and so have a larger total supply available to them. As you know, prices increase when there is an increase in demand and they decrease when there is an increase in supply. Thus the increased demand (from foreigners) for exports increases their price and the increased supply (from foreigners) of imports decreases their price. Gains in one country do not bring losses in another. Everyone, in this example, gains from international trade.

Absolute Advantage

Suppose that in Magic Empire, fewer workers are needed to produce any given output of either grain or cars than in Pioneerland—productivity is higher in Magic Empire than in Pioneerland. In this situation, Magic Empire has an *absolute advantage* over Pioneerland. We defined absolute advantage in Chapter 3 in terms of an individual. If one person has greater productivity than another in the production of all goods, that person is said to have an absolute advantage. A country has an absolute advantage if it has greater productivity than another country in the production of all goods. With an absolute advantage, isn't it the case that Magic Empire can outsell Pioneerland in all markets? Why, if Magic Kingdom has greater productivity than Pioneerland, does it pay Magic Empire to buy *anything* from Pioneerland?

The answer is that the cost of production in terms of the factors of production employed is irrelevant for determining the gains from trade. It does not matter how much labor, land, and capital are required to produce 1,000 bushels of grain or a car.

What matters is how many cars must be given up to produce more grain or how much grain must be given up to produce more cars. That is, what matters is the opportunity cost of one good in terms of the other good. Magic Empire may have an absolute advantage in the production of all things, but it cannot have a comparative advantage in the production of all goods. The statement that the opportunity cost of cars in Magic Empire is lower than in Pioneerland is identical to the statement that the opportunity cost of grain is higher in Magic Empire than that in Pioneerland. Thus *whenever opportunity costs diverge, everyone has a comparative advantage in something.* All countries can potentially gain from international trade.

The story of the discovery of the logic of the gains from international trade is presented in Our Advancing Knowledge on pp. 592–593.

REVIEW

When countries have divergent opportunity costs, they can gain from international trade. Each country can buy goods and services from another country at a lower opportunity cost than that at which it can produce them for itself. Gains arise when each country increases its production of those goods and services in which it has a comparative advantage (of goods and services that it can produce at an opportunity cost that is lower than that of other countries) and exchanges some of its production for that of other countries. All countries gain from international trade. Everyone has a comparative advantage at something. ◆

Gains from Trade in Reality

The gains from trade that we have just studied between Pioneerland and Magic Empire in grain and cars are taking place in a model economy—in an economy that we have imagined. But these same phenomena are occurring every minute of every day in real-world economies. We buy cars made in Japan, and American producers of grain and lumber sell large parts of their output to Japanese households and firms. We buy cars and machinery from European producers and sell airplanes and comput-

ers to Europeans in return. We buy shirts and fashion goods from the people of Hong Kong and sell them machinery in return. We buy TV sets and VCRs from South Korea and Taiwan and sell them financial and other services as well as manufactured goods in return.

Thus much of the international trade that we see in the real world takes precisely the form of the trade that we have studied in our model of the world economy. But as we discovered earlier in this chapter, a great deal of world trade is heavily concentrated among industrial countries and primarily involves the international exchange of manufactured goods. Thus the type of trade that we have just analyzed—exchanging cars for grain—although an important and clearly profitable type of trade, is not the most prominent type. Why do countries exchange manufactured goods with each other? Can our model of international trade explain such exchange?

Trade in Similar Goods

At first thought, it seems puzzling that countries would trade manufactured goods. Consider, for example, America's trade in automobiles and auto parts. Why does it make sense for the United States to produce automobiles for export and at the same time to import large quantities of them from Canada, Japan, Korea, and Western Europe? Wouldn't it make more sense to produce all the cars that we buy here in the United States? After all, we have access to the best technology available for producing cars. Auto workers in the United States are surely as productive as their fellow workers in Canada, Western Europe, and the Pacific countries. Capital equipment, production lines, robots, and the like used in the manufacture of cars are as available to American car producers as they are to any others. This line of reasoning leaves a puzzle concerning the sources of international exchange of similar commodities produced by similar people using similar equipment. Why does it happen?

Diversity of Taste   The first part of the answer to the puzzle is that people have a tremendous diversity of taste. Let's stick with the example of cars. Some people prefer a sports car, some prefer a limousine, some prefer a regular, full-size car, and some prefer a compact. In addition to size and type of car, there are many other dimensions on which cars vary.

UNDERSTANDING
the Gains from
INTERNATIONAL
TRADE

Until the mid-eighteenth century, it was generally believed that the purpose of international trade was to keep exports above imports and pile up gold. If gold was accumulated, it was believed, the nation would prosper; and if gold was lost through an international deficit, the nation would be drained of money and be impoverished. These beliefs are called *mercantilism,* and the *mercantilists* were pamphleteers who advocated with missionary fervor the pursuit of an international surplus. If exports did not exceed imports, the mercantilists wanted imports restricted.

In the 1740s, David Hume explained that as the quantity of money (gold) changes, so also does the price level, and the nation's *real* wealth is unaffected. In the 1770s, Adam Smith explained that restricting imports lowers the gains from specialization and makes a nation poorer. Mercantilism was intellectually bankrupt.

Gradually, through the nineteenth century, the mercantilists' influence waned, and North America and Western Europe prospered in an environment of increasingly free international trade. But despite remarkable advances in economic understanding, mercantilism never quite died. It had a brief and devastating revival in the 1920s and 1930s, when tariff hikes brought about the collapse of international trade and accentuated the Great Depression. It subsided again after World War II with the establishment of the General Agreement on Tariffs and Trade (GATT).

But mercantilism lingers on. The often expressed view that the United States should restrict Japanese imports and reduce its deficit with Japan is a modern manifestation of mercantilism. It would be interesting to have Hume and Smith commenting on these views. But we know what they would say—the same things that they said to the eighteenth-century mercantilists. And they would still be right.

> "Free trade, one of the greatest blessings which a government can confer on a people, is in almost every country unpopular."
>
> THOMAS MACAULAY
> *Essay on Mitford's History of Greece*

In the eighteenth century, when mercantilists and economists were debating the pros and cons of free international exchange, the transportation technology available severely limited the gains from international trade. Sailing ships with tiny cargo holds took close to a month to cross the Atlantic Ocean. But the potential gains were large and so was the incentive to cut shipping costs. By the 1850s, the clipper ship had been developed, cutting the time for the journey from Boston to Liverpool to only 12¼ days. Half a century later, 10,000-ton steamships were sailing between America and England in just 4 days. As sailing times and costs declined, the gains from international trade increased and the volume of trade expanded.

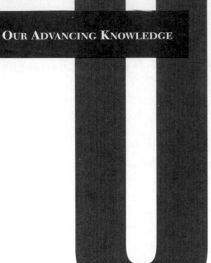

Merchants' Express Line of Clipper Ships for San Francisco.
Despatching the greatest number of vessels, and only those standing in the first-class in all respects.

THE SPLENDID A 1 CLIPPER SHIP
W. B. DINSMORE
FOSTER Commander,
IS LOADING AT PIER 13 EAST RIVER.

As this very fine vessel was BUILT for the trade, it is scarcely necessary to say that she combines all of the necessary qualifications, viz.:—strength, speed and good ventilation. Early despatch may be relied upon.

D. S. STETSON & CO.,
112 North Wharves, Philadelphia.

Agents in San Francisco,
Messrs. De Witt, Kittle & Co.

The container ship and the Boeing 747 have revolutionized international trade and contributed to its continued expansion. Today, most goods cross the oceans in containers—metal boxes—packed into and piled on top of ships like the one shown here. Container technology has cut the cost of ocean shipping by economizing on handling and by making cargoes harder to steal, which lowers insurance costs. It is unlikely that there would be much international trade in goods such as television sets and VCRs without this technology. High-value and perishable cargoes such as flowers and fresh foods, as well as urgently needed items, travel by air. Every day, dozens of cargo-laden 747s fly between all major U.S. cities and destinations across the Atlantic and Pacific Oceans.

FROM SMITH & RICARDO TO GATT

David Ricardo (1772–1832) was a highly successful 27-year-old stockbroker when he stumbled on a copy of Adam Smith's *Wealth of Nations* on a weekend visit to the country. He was immediately hooked and went on to become the most celebrated economist of his age and one of the greatest economists of all time. One of his many contributions was to develop the principle of comparative advantage, the foundation on which the modern theory of international trade is built. The example he used to illustrate this principle was the trade between England and Portugal in cloth and wine.

The General Agreement on Tariffs and Trade (GATT) was established as a reaction against the devastation wrought by beggar-my-neighbor tariffs imposed during the 1920s. But it is also a triumph for the logic first worked out by Smith and Ricardo.

Some have low fuel consumption, some have high performance, some are spacious and comfortable, some have a large trunk, some have four-wheel drive, some have front-wheel drive, some have manual transmission, some have automatic transmission, some are durable, some are flashy, some have a radiator grill that looks like a Greek temple, others look like a wedge. People's preferences across these many dimensions vary.

The tremendous diversity in tastes for cars means that people would be dissatisfied if they were forced to consume from a limited range of standardized cars. People value variety and are willing to pay for it in the marketplace.

Economies of Scale   The second part of the answer to the puzzle is economies of scale. *Economies of scale* are the tendency, present in many production processes, for the average cost of production to be lower, the larger the scale of production. In such situations, larger and larger production runs lead to ever lower average production costs. Many manufactured goods, including cars, experience economies of scale. For example, if a car producer makes only a few hundred (or perhaps a few thousand) cars of a particular type and design, the producer has to use production techniques that are much more labor-intensive and much less automated than those actually employed to make hundreds of thousands of cars in a particular model. With low production runs and labor-intensive production techniques, costs are high. With very large production runs and automated assembly lines, production costs are much lower. But to obtain lower costs, the automated assembly lines have to produce a large number of cars.

It is the combination of diversity of taste and economies of scale that produces such a large amount of international trade in similar commodities. Diversity of taste and the willingness to pay for variety do not guarantee that variety will be available. It could simply be too expensive to provide a highly diversified range of different types of cars, for example. If every car bought in the United States today was made in the United States and if the present range of diversity and variety was available, production runs would be remarkably short. Car producers would not be able to reap economies of scale. Although the current variety of cars could be made

available, it would be at a very high price, perhaps at a price that no one would be willing to pay.

But with international trade, each manufacturer of cars has the whole world market to serve. Each producer specializes in a limited range of products and then sells its output to the entire world market. This arrangement enables large production runs on the most popular cars and feasible production runs even on the most customized cars demanded by only a handful of people.

The situation in the market for cars is also present in many other industries, especially those producing specialized machinery and specialized machine tools. Thus international exchange of similar but slightly differentiated manufactured products is a highly profitable activity.

This type of trade can be understood with exactly the same model of international trade that we studied earlier. Although we normally think of cars as a single commodity, we simply have to think of sports cars, sedans, and so on as different goods. Different countries, by specializing in a few of these "goods," are able to enjoy economies of scale and, therefore, a comparative advantage in their production.

You can see that comparative advantage and international trade bring gains regardless of the goods being traded. When the rich countries of the European Community, Japan, and the United States import raw materials from the Third World and from Australia and Canada, the rich importing countries gain and so do the exporting countries. When we buy cheap TV sets, VCRs, shirts, and other goods from low-wage countries, both we and the exporters gain from the exchange. It's true that if we increase our imports of cars and produce fewer cars ourselves, jobs in our car industry disappear. But jobs in other industries, industries in which we have a comparative advantage and supply to other nations, expand. After the adjustment is completed, people whose jobs have been lost find employment in the expanding industries. They buy goods produced in other countries at even lower prices than those at which the goods were available before. The gains from international trade are not gains for some at the expense of losses for others.

But changes in comparative advantage that lead to changes in international trade patterns can take a long time to adjust to. For example, the increase in automobile imports and the corresponding relative decline in domestic car production have not brought increased wealth for displaced auto workers. Good new jobs take time to find, and often people go through a period of prolonged search, putting up with inferior jobs and lower wages than they had before. Thus only in the long run does everyone potentially gain from international specialization and exchange. Short-run adjustment costs that can be large and relatively prolonged are borne by the people who have lost their comparative advantage. Some of the people who lose their jobs may be too old for it to be worth their while to make the move to another region of the country or industry, and so they never share in the gains.

Partly because of the costs of adjustment to changing international trade patterns, but partly also for other reasons, governments intervene in international trade, restricting its volume. Let's examine what happens when governments restrict international trade. We'll contrast restricted trade with free trade. We'll see that free trade brings the greatest possible benefits. We'll also see why, in spite of the benefits of free trade, governments sometimes restrict trade.

Trade Restrictions

Governments restrict international trade in order to protect domestic industries from foreign competition. The restriction of international trade is called **protectionism.** There are two main protectionist methods employed by governments:

◆ Tariffs
◆ Nontariff barriers

A **tariff** is a tax that is imposed by the importing country when a good crosses an international boundary. A **nontariff barrier** is any action other than a tariff that restricts international trade. Examples of nontariff barriers are quantitative restrictions and licensing regulations limiting imports. We'll consider nontariff barriers in more detail below. First, let's look at tariffs.

The History of Tariffs

Average tariff levels in the United States today are quite modest compared with their historical levels. As you can see from Fig. 22.6, tariff levels averaged around 40 percent before World War II. During the 1930s, with the passage of the Smoot-Hawley Act, they reached 60 percent. Today, average tariffs are only 4 percent of total imports and 6 percent of the value of those imports that are subject to a tariff.

The reduction in tariffs followed the establishment of the General Agreement on Tariffs and Trade (GATT). The **General Agreement on Tariffs and Trade** is an international agreement designed to limit government intervention to restrict international trade. It was negotiated immediately following World War II and was signed in October 1947. Its goal is to liberalize trading activity and to provide an organization to administer more liberal trading arrangements. GATT itself is a small organization located in Geneva, Switzerland.

Since the formation of GATT, several rounds of negotiations have taken place that have resulted in general tariff reductions. One of these, the Kennedy Round, which began in the early 1960s, resulted in large tariff cuts in the late 1960s. Yet further tariff cuts resulted from the Tokyo Round, which took place between 1973 and 1979, and the Uruguay Round of the late 1980s and early 1990s.

In addition to the agreements under the GATT, the United States is a party to several important trade agreements with individual countries. One of these is the Canada–United States free trade agreement that became effective on January 1, 1989. Under this agreement, barriers to international trade between Canada and the United States will be virtually eliminated after a ten-year phasing-in period. Another important development is an attempt to work out a free trade deal with Mexico that could create a large North American free trade area embracing Mexico, Canada, and the United States. Within Western Europe, trade barriers among the member countries of the European Community were virtually eliminated by 1992, creating the largest unified tariff-free market in the world.

The benefits of free trade, both in theory and in the recent experience of the countries of the European Community, have given impetus to a series of talks among the countries of Central and South America aimed at creating a series of free-trade

FIGURE **22.6**

U.S. Tariffs: 1900–1990

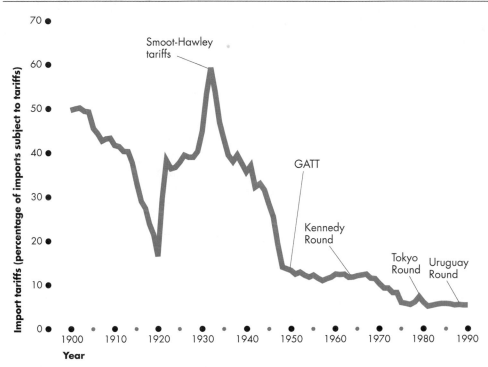

Tariffs in the United States averaged around 40 percent before World War II. In the early 1930s, they increased to 60 percent with the passage of the Smoot-Hawley Act. Since the establishment of GATT following World War II, tariffs have steadily declined in a series of negotiating rounds and are now at the lowest level they have ever been.

Sources: U.S. Bureau of the Census, *Historical Statistics of the United States, Colonial Times to 1970, Bicentennial Edition, Part 1* (Washington D.C.: 1975); Series U-212: *Statistical Abstract of the United States: 1986*, 106th edition (Washington, D.C.: 1985); and *Statistical Abstract of the United States: 1992*, 112th edition (Washington, D.C.: 1992).

agreements among these countries and, even more ambitiously, free-trade American continents. This movement is discussed in Reading Between the Lines on pp. 598–599.

The talks taking place among the countries of North and South America underline the fact that despite a steady process of tariff reductions, trade among some countries and trade in some goods are still subject to extremely high tariffs. The highest tariffs faced by U.S. buyers are those on textiles and footwear. A tariff of more than 10 percent (on the average) is imposed on almost all our imports of textiles and footwear. For example, when you buy a pair of blue jeans for $20, you pay about $5 more than you would if there were no tariffs on textiles. Other goods protected by tariffs are agricultural products, automobiles, energy and chemicals, minerals, and metals. Almost all the meat and cheese that you consume costs significantly more because of protection than it would with free international trade.

The temptation for governments to impose tariffs is a strong one. First, tariffs provide revenue to the government. Second, they enable the government to satisfy special interest groups in import-competing industries. But, as we'll see, free international trade brings enormous benefits that are reduced when tariffs are imposed. Let's see how.

How Tariffs Work

To analyze how tariffs work, let's return to the example of trade between Pioneerland and Magic Empire. Suppose that these two countries are trading cars and grain in exactly the same way that we analyzed before. Magic Empire exports cars, and Pioneerland exports grain. The volume of car imports into Pioneerland is 4 million a year, and cars are selling on the world market for 3,000 bushels of grain. Let's suppose that grain costs $1 a bushel, so, equivalently, cars are selling for $3,000. Figure 22.7 illustrates this situation. The volume of trade in cars and their price are determined at the point of inter-section of Magic Empire's export supply curve of cars and Pioneerland's import demand curve for cars.

Now suppose that the government of Pioneer-land, perhaps under pressure from car producers, decides to impose a tariff on imported cars. In par-ticular, suppose that a tariff of $4,000 per car is imposed. (This is a huge tariff, but the car producers of Pioneerland are pretty fed up with competition from Magic Empire.) What happens?

The first part of the answer is obtained by study-ing the effects on the supply of cars in Pioneerland. Cars are no longer going to be available at the Magic Empire export supply price. The tariff of $4,000 must be added to that price—the amount paid to the government of Pioneerland on each car imported. As a consequence, the supply curve in Pioneerland shifts upward as shown in Fig. 22.7. The new supply curve becomes that labeled "Magic Empire's export supply of cars plus tariff." The ver-tical distance between Magic Empire's export supply curve and the new supply curve is the tariff imposed by the government of Pioneerland.

The next part of the answer is found by determin-ing the new equilibrium. Imposing a tariff has no effect on the demand for cars in Pioneerland and so has no effect on Pioneerland's import demand for cars. The new equilibrium occurs where the new supply curve intersects Pioneerland's import demand curve for cars. That equilibrium is at a price of $6,000 a car with 2 million cars a year being imported. Imports fall from 4 million to 2 million cars a year. At the higher price of $6,000 a car, domestic car producers increase their production. Domestic grain production decreases to free up the resources for the expanded car industry.

The total expenditure on imported cars by the Pioneers is $6,000 a car multiplied by the 2 million cars imported ($12 billion). But not all of that money goes to the Magicians. They receive $2,000 a car, or $4 billion for the 2 million cars. The differ-ence—$4,000 a car, or a total of $8 billion for the 2 million cars—is collected by the government of Pioneerland as tariff revenue.

Obviously, the government of Pioneerland is happy with this situation. It is now collecting $8 bil-lion that it didn't have before. But what about the Pioneers? How do they view the new situation? The demand curve tells us the maximum price that a

FIGURE 22.7
The Effects of a Tariff

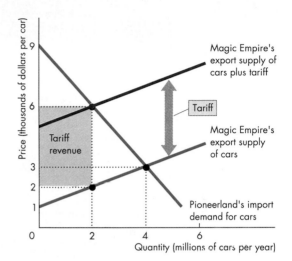

Pioneerland imposes a tariff on car imports from Magic Empire. The tariff increases the price that Pioneers have to pay for cars. It shifts the supply curve of cars in Pioneerland upward. The distance between the original supply curve and the new one is the amount of the tariff. The price of cars in Pioneerland increases, and the quantity of cars import-ed decreases. The government of Pioneerland collects a tariff revenue of $4,000 per car—a total of $8 billion on the 2 million cars imported. Pioneerland's exports of grain decrease, since Magic Empire now has a lower income from its exports of cars.

buyer is willing to pay for one more unit of a good. As you can see from Pioneerland's import demand curve for cars, if one more car could be imported, someone would be willing to pay almost $6,000 for it. Magic Empire's export supply curve of cars tells us the minimum price at which additional cars are available. As you can see, one additional car would be supplied by Magic Empire for a price only slight-ly more than $2,000. Thus, since someone is willing to pay almost $6,000 for a car and someone is will-ing to supply one for little more than $2,000, there is obviously a gain to be had from trading an extra car. In fact, there are gains to be had—willingness to pay exceeds the minimum supply price—all the way up to 4 million cars a year. Only when 4 million cars are being traded is the maximum price that a Pioneer is willing to pay equal to the minimum price that is acceptable to a Magician. Thus restricting

The Gains from Trade in Action

THE ECONOMIST, JANUARY 4, 1992

Free-trade free-for-all

Having spent the 1950s and 1960s building the non-communist world's most impenetrable trade barriers, Latin America is pulling them down as fast as it can . . ., preparing the way for a single Latin American trade block. In fact the dream of most Latin American countries is to join, together or alone, with a North American Free-Trade Area of Mexico, Canada and the United States. . . .

The first pillar in this ambitious and hurried edifice is this month's free-trade pact between Venezuela, Colombia and Bolivia. Peru and Ecuador will join the pact in six months' time. . . .

[A] . . . free-trade agreement [is] being forged by Argentina, Brazil, Uruguay and Paraguay. Called Mercosur, it originated in 1988 as a free-trade pact between Brazil and Argentina and was expanded to embrace Uruguay and Paraguay last March. By the end of 1994 it is supposed to enshrine a completely free market in goods, services and labour for Argentina and Brazil, with Uruguay and Paraguay following a year later. . . .

Two other pacts are in the offing. Central America is trying to revive its common market, which

was set up in the 1960s. It collapsed in 1969, when war broke out between Honduras and El Salvador. . . .

Lastly, there is the customs union that . . . the English-speaking Caribbean countries under the auspices of the Caribbean Community (Caricom) [are attempting to establish]. . . .

The real prize is . . . the establishment of a pan-American free-trade area. . . . Since 1987 the United States has signed 16 "framework" agreements with Latin American countries. In theory these are agreements merely to talk about trade. In practice, they are paving the way for a trade block embracing all the Americas.

Achieving such a goal depends almost entirely upon success of the free-trade agreement that the United States is negotiating with Mexico. Once this is approved by Congress, other Latin American governments might accede to it, just as new members join the EC. A stampede to join is expected. . . .

The Essence of the Story

Among Latin American countries, trade barriers are high, but a movement is underway to lower them.

Four agreements are being forged:

◆ The Andean Pact between Bolivia, Colombia, Ecuador, Peru, and Venezuela

◆ Mercosur, a free-trade area embracing Argentina, Brazil, Uruguay, and Paraguay

◆ The Central American common market embracing Costa Rica, El Salvador, Guatemala, Honduras, and Nicaragua

◆ Caricom, a customs union among the English-speaking Caribbean countries

Since 1987 the United States has signed 16 "framework" agreements to talk about trade with Latin American countries. These agreements are paving the way for a trade block embracing all the Americas.

Achieving such a goal depends crucially on the success of the United States–Mexico free-trade agreement. Once this agreement is approved by Congress, there could be a stampede of other Latin American governments seeking to join the group— just like countries joining the European Community.

Background and Analysis

With the exception of the Caricom countries, international trade plays a much smaller part in the nations of North and South America than it does in Western Europe—see Fig. 1.

The move to open up the countries of the Americas to greater international competition will bring increased specialization as countries seek to gain from exporting the goods and services in which they have a comparative advantage.

The evidence from Western Europe is that lower trade barriers bring a larger amount of international trade and more rapidly growing real incomes—see Fig. 2.

Figure 1

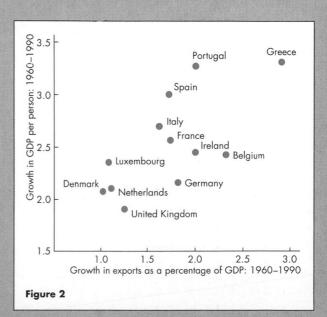

Figure 2

international trade reduces the gains from international trade.

It is easy to see that the tariff has lowered Pioneerland's total import bill. With free trade, Pioneerland was paying $3,000 a car and buying 4 million cars a year from Magic Empire. Thus the total import bill was $12 billion a year. With a tariff, Pioneerland's imports have been cut to 2 million cars a year and the price paid to Magic Empire has also been cut to only $2,000 a car. Thus the import bill has been cut to $4 billion a year. Doesn't this fact mean that Pioneerland's balance of trade has changed? Is Pioneerland now importing less than it is exporting?

To answer that question, we need to figure out what's happening in Magic Empire. We've just seen that the price that Magic Empire receives for cars has fallen from $3,000 to $2,000 a car. Thus the price of cars in Magic Empire has fallen. But if the price of cars has fallen, the price of grain has increased. With free trade, the Magicians could buy 3,000 bushels of grain for one car. Now they can buy only 2,000 bushels for a car. With a higher price of grain, the quantity demanded by the Magicians decreases. As a result, Magic Empire's import of grain declines. But so does Pioneerland's export of grain. In fact, Pioneerland's grain industry suffers from two sources. First, there is a decrease in the quantity of grain sold to Magic Empire. Second, there is increased competition for inputs from the now expanded car industry. Thus the tariff leads to a contraction in the scale of the grain industry in Pioneerland.

It seems paradoxical at first that a country imposing a tariff on cars would hurt its own export industry, lowering its exports of grain. It might help to think of it this way: Foreigners buy grain with the money they make from exporting cars. If they export fewer cars, they cannot afford to buy as much grain. In fact, in the absence of any international borrowing and lending, Magic Empire has to cut its imports of grain by exactly the same amount as the loss in revenue from its export of cars. Grain imports into Magic Empire will be cut back to a value of $4 billion, the amount that can be paid for by the new lower revenue from Magic Empire's car exports. Thus trade is still balanced in this post-tariff situation. Although the tariff has cut imports, it has also cut exports, and the cut in the value of exports is exactly equal to the cut in the value of imports. The tariff, therefore, has no effect on the balance of trade—it reduces the volume of trade.

The result that we have just derived is perhaps one of the most misunderstood aspects of international economics. On countless occasions, politicians and others have called for tariffs in order to remove a balance of trade deficit or have argued that lowering tariffs would produce a balance of trade deficit. They reach this conclusion by failing to work out all the implications of a tariff. Because a tariff raises the price of imports and cuts imports, the easy conclusion is that the tariff strengthens the balance of trade. But the tariff also changes the *volume* of exports. The equilibrium effects of a tariff are to reduce the volume of trade in both directions and by the same value on each side of the equation. The balance of trade itself is left unaffected.

Learning the Hard Way   Although the analysis that we have just worked through leads to the clear conclusion that tariffs cut both imports and exports and make everyone worse off, we have not found that conclusion easy to accept. Time and again in our history, we have imposed high tariff barriers on international trade (as Fig. 22.6 illustrates). Whenever tariff barriers are increased, trade collapses. The most vivid historical example of this interaction of tariffs and trade occurred during the Great Depression years of the early 1930s when, in the wake of the Smoot-Hawley tariff increases and the retaliatory tariff changes that other countries introduced as a consequence, world trade almost dried up.

Let's now turn our attention to the other range of protectionist weapons—nontariff barriers.

Nontariff Barriers

There are two important forms of nontariff barriers:

◆ Quotas
◆ Voluntary export restraints

A **quota** is a quantitative restriction on the import of a particular good. It specifies the maximum amount of the good that may be imported in a given period of time. A **voluntary export restraint** is an agreement between two governments in which the government of the exporting country agrees to restrain the volume of its own exports. Voluntary export restraints are often called VERs.

Nontariff barriers have become important features of international trading arrangements in the period since World War II, and there is now general agreement that nontariff barriers are a more severe impediment to international trade than tariffs.

It is difficult to quantify the effects of nontariff barriers in a way that makes them easy to compare with tariffs, but some studies have attempted to do just that. Such studies attempt to assess the tariff rate that would restrict trade by the same amount as the nontariff barriers do. With such calculations, nontariff barriers and tariffs can be added together to assess the total amount of protection. When we add nontariff barriers to tariffs for the United States, the overall amount of protection increases more than threefold. Even so, the United States is the least protectionist country in the world. Total protection is higher in the European Community and higher still in other developed countries and Japan. The less developed countries and the so-called newly industrializing countries have the highest protection rates.

Quotas are especially important in the textile industries, in which there exists an international agreement called the Multifiber Agreement, which establishes quotas on a wide range of textile products. Agriculture is also subject to extensive quotas. Voluntary export restraints are particularly important in regulating the international trade in cars between Japan and the United States.

How Quotas and VERs Work

To understand how nontariff barriers affect international trade, let's return to the example of trade between Pioneerland and Magic Empire. Suppose that Pioneerland imposes a quota on car imports. Specifically, suppose that the quota restricts imports to not more than 2 million cars a year. What are the effects of this action?

The answer is found in Fig. 22.8. The quota is shown by the vertical red line at 2 million cars a year. Since it is illegal to import more than that number of cars, car importers buy only that quantity from Magic Empire producers. They pay $2,000 a car to the Magic Empire producer. But what do they sell their cars for? The answer is $6,000 each. Since the import supply of cars is restricted to 2 million

FIGURE **22.8**
The Effects of a Quota

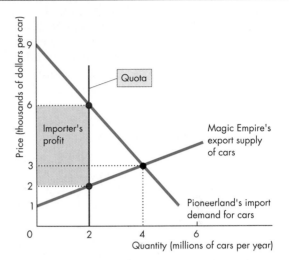

Pioneerland imposes a quota of 2 million cars a year on car imports from Magic Empire. That quantity appears as the vertical line labeled "Quota." Since the quantity of cars supplied by Magic Empire is restricted to 2 million, the price at which those cars will be traded increases to $6,000. Importing cars is profitable, since Magic Empire is willing to supply cars at $2,000 each. There is competition for import quotas—rent seeking.

cars a year, people with cars for sale will be able to get $6,000 each for them. The quantity of cars imported equals the quantity determined by the quota.

Importing cars is now obviously a profitable business. An importer gets $6,000 for an item that costs only $2,000. Thus there is severe competition among car importers for the available quotas. The pursuit of the profits from quotas is called "rent seeking."

The value of imports—the amount paid to Magic Empire—declines to $4 billion, exactly the same as in the case of the tariff. Thus with lower incomes from car exports and with a higher price of grain, Magicians cut back on their imports of grain in exactly the same way they did under a tariff.

The key difference between a quota and a tariff lies in who gets the profit represented by the difference between the import supply price and the domestic selling price. In the case of a tariff, that difference goes to the government. In the case of a quota, that difference goes to the person who has the right to import under the import-quota regulations.

A voluntary export restraint is like a quota arrangement in which quotas are allocated to each exporting country. The effects of voluntary export restraints are similar to those of quotas but differ from them in that the gap between the domestic price and the export price is captured not by domestic importers but by the foreign exporter. The government of the exporting country has to establish procedures for allocating the restricted volume of exports among its producers.

Paying with Your Shirt!   Two of the most heavily protected industries in the United States today are apparel and textiles. It has been estimated that the total protection on these industries, most of which takes the form of quotas, costs the average American family between $200 and $400 a year. Despite this fact, the House of Representatives passed a new act (the Textile and Apparel Trade Act) in 1975 that, if it had become law, would have increased protection in those industries even further, adding $300 to $400 a year in additional costs for the average household.[1] Taking all protection together, it has been estimated that the cost per year to an individual U.S. family is more than $1,000.[2]

Another way of looking at the cost of protection is to calculate the cost per job saved. It has been estimated, for example, that to protect one job in the textile industry costs $46,000 a year; one job in the footwear industry costs close to $80,000 a year; and one job in the carbon, steel, and auto industries costs more than $80,000 a year. In all these cases, it costs many times more to save a job through international trade barriers than the wages of the workers involved.[3]

---

[1]For more on this topic, see "Expanding Trade and Avoiding Protectionism," *Economic Report of the President* (1988), pp. 127–162.

[2]Murray Weidenbaum and N. Munger, "Protection at Any Price?" *Regulation* (July/August 1983): 14–18.

[3]Keith E. Maskus, "Rising Protectionism and U.S. International Trade Policy," *Economic Review of the Federal Reserve Bank of Kansas City* (July/August 1984): 3–17.

REVIEW

W hen a country opens itself up to international trade and trades freely at world market prices, it expands its consumption possibilities. When trade is restricted, some of the gains from trade are lost. A country may be better off with restricted trade than with no trade but not as well off as it could be if it engaged in free trade. A tariff reduces the volume of imports, but it also reduces the volume of exports. Under both free trade and restricted trade (and without international borrowing and lending), the value of imports equals the value of exports. With restricted trade, both the total value of exports and the total value of imports are lower than under free trade, but trade is still balanced. ◆

Why Quotas and VERs Might Be Preferred to Tariffs

At first sight, it seems puzzling that countries would ever want to use quotas and even more puzzling that they would want to use voluntary export restraints. We have seen that the same domestic price and the same quantity of imports can be achieved by using any of the three devices for restricting trade. However, a tariff provides the government with a source of revenue; a quota provides domestic importers with a profit; and a voluntary export restraint provides the foreigner with a profit. Why, then, would a country use a quota or a voluntary export restraint rather than a tariff?

There are three possible reasons. First, a government can use quotas to reward its political supporters. Under a quota, licenses to import become tremendously profitable. So the government bestows riches on the people to whom it gives licenses to import.

Second, quotas are more precise instruments for holding down imports. As demand fluctuates, the domestic price of the good fluctuates but not the quantity of imports. You can see this implication of a quota by going back to Fig. 22.8. Suppose that the demand for imports fluctuates. With a quota, these demand fluctuations simply produce fluctuations in the domestic price of the import but no change in the volume of imports. With a tariff, fluctuations in demand lead to no change in the domestic price but to large changes in the volume of imports. Thus if for some reason the government wants to control the quantity of imports and does not care about fluctuations in the domestic price, it will use a quota.

Third, different branches of government have jurisdiction over different aspects of international trade restriction. Congress has the power to impose tariffs. The administration has the power to impose nontariff barriers. Thus changing tariffs is a slow and cumbersome matter requiring the passage of an act of Congress. In contrast, nontariff barriers can be changed quickly, provided that the administration is persuaded of the need for the change.

Why would a government use voluntary export restraints rather than a tariff or quota? The government might want to avoid a tariff or quota war with another country. If one country imposes a tariff or a quota, that might encourage another country to impose a similar tariff or quota on the exports of the first country. Such a tariff or quota war would result in a much smaller volume of trade and a much worse outcome for both countries. A voluntary export restraint can be viewed as a way of achieving trade restrictions to protect domestic industries but with some kind of compensation to encourage the foreign country to accept that situation and not retaliate with its own restrictions. Finally, VERs are often the only form of trade restriction that can be legally entered into under the terms of the General Agreement on Tariffs and Trade.

Dumping and Countervailing Duties

Dumping is the selling of a good in a foreign market for a lower price than in the domestic market or for a lower price than its cost of production. Such a practice can arise from a discriminating monopoly seeking to maximize profit. An example of alleged dumping has occurred with Japanese sales of pickup trucks to the United States. Under current U.S. law and under GATT, dumping is illegal and antidumping duties may be imposed on foreign producers if U.S. producers can show that they have been injured by dumping.

Countervailing duties are tariffs that are imposed to enable domestic producers to compete with subsidized foreign producers. Often, foreign governments subsidize some of their domestic industries. Two examples are the Canadian pork and lumber industries. Under current U.S. law, if American producers can show that a foreign subsidy has damaged their market, a countervailing duty may be imposed.

Why Is International Trade Restricted?

There are many reasons why international trade is restricted. We've just seen two reasons—to offset the effects of dumping and of foreign subsidies. Even in these cases, it does not obviously benefit a country to protect itself from cheap foreign imports. However, more generally, we've seen that international trade benefits a country by raising its consumption possibilities. Why do we restrict international trade when such restrictions lower our consumption possibilities?

The key reason is that consumption possibilities increase *on the average* but not everyone shares in the gain and some people even lose. Free trade brings benefits to some and costs to others, with total benefits exceeding total costs. It is the uneven distribution of costs and benefits that is the principal source of impediment to achieving more liberal international trade.

Returning to our example of international trade in cars and grain between Pioneerland and Magic Empire, the benefits from free trade accrue to all the producers of grain and to those producers of cars who would not have to bear the costs of adjusting to a smaller car industry. The costs of free trade are borne by those car producers and their employees who have to move and become grain producers. The number of people who gain will, in general, be enormous compared with the number who lose. The gain per person will, therefore, be rather small. The loss per person to those who bear the loss will be large. Since the loss that falls on those who bear it is large, it will pay those people to incur considerable expense in order to lobby against free trade. On the other hand, it will not pay those who gain to organize to achieve free trade. The gain from trade for any one individual is too small for that individual to spend much time or money on a political organization to achieve free trade. The loss from free trade will be seen as being so great by those bearing that loss that they *will* find it profitable to join a political organization to prevent free trade. Each group is optimizing—weighing benefits against costs and choosing the best action for themselves. The anti–free-trade group will, however, undertake a larger quantity of political lobbying than the pro–free-trade group.

Compensating Losers

If, in total, the gains from free international trade exceed the losses, why don't those who gain compensate those who lose so that everyone is in favor of free trade? To some degree, such compensation does take place. It also takes place indirectly as a consequence of unemployment compensation arrangements. But, as a rule, only limited attempts are made to compensate those who lose from free international trade. The main reason why full compensation is not attempted is that the costs of identifying the losers would be enormous. Also, it would never be clear whether a person who has fallen on hard times is suffering because of free trade or for other reasons, perhaps reasons largely under the control of the individual. Furthermore, some people who look like losers at one point in time may, in fact, wind up gaining. The young auto worker who loses his job in Michigan and becomes an insurance salesperson in Chicago resents the loss of work and the need to move. But a year or two later, looking back on events, he counts himself fortunate. He's made a move that has increased his income and given him greater job security.

It is because we do not, in general, compensate the losers from free international trade that protectionism is such a popular and permanent feature of our national economic and political life.

Political Outcome

The political outcome that emerges from this activity is one in which a modest amount of restriction on international trade occurs and is maintained. Politicians react to constituencies pressing for protection and find it necessary, in order to get re-elected, to support legislative programs that protect those constituencies. The producers of protected goods are far more vocal and much more sensitive swing-voters than the consumers of those goods. The political outcome, therefore, leans in the direction of maintaining protection.

The politics of trade can be seen easily today. The United States restricts imports of sugar by quota. Who profits from the quotas? Not the foreign exporters. Whereas voluntary export restraints give exporters like Toyota and Honda big profits, quotas do not help foreign producers. In this case, the quotas have brought real economic and political suffering to Central American and Caribbean countries that produce sugar. The U.S. sugar growers, on the other hand, who benefit from the quotas, are extremely active in their support for politicians who can see their point of view. Similarly, the auto producers and unions are extremely active in their attempts to further limit the intrusion of Japanese imports.

◆ ◆ ◆ ◆ You've now seen how free international trade enables everyone to gain from increased specialization and exchange. By producing goods in which we have a comparative advantage and exchanging some of our own production for that of others, we expand our consumption possibilities. Placing impediments on that exchange when it crosses national borders restricts the extent to which we can gain from specialization and exchange. When we open our country up to free international trade, the market for the things that we sell expands and the price rises. The market for the things that we buy also expands, and the price falls. All countries gain from free international trade. As a consequence of price adjustments, and in the absence of international borrowing and lending, the value of imports adjusts to equal the value of exports. ◆ ◆ In the next chapter, we're going to study the ways in which international trade is financed and also learn why the international borrowing and lending that permits unbalanced international trade arises. We'll discover the forces that determine the U.S. balance of payments and the value, in terms of foreign currency, of our dollar.

S U M M A R Y

Patterns and Trends in International Trade

Large flows of trade take place between rich and poor countries. Resource-rich countries exchange natural resources for manufactured goods, and resource-poor countries import their resources in exchange for their own manufactured goods. However, by far the biggest volume of trade is in manufactured goods exchanged among the rich industrialized countries. The biggest single U.S. export item is machinery. However, the biggest single U.S. net export is grain. Trade in services has grown in recent years. Total trade has also grown over the years. The U.S. balance of trade fluctuates around zero, but since 1982 the United States has had a balance of trade deficit. (pp. 583–586)

Opportunity Cost and Comparative Advantage

When opportunity costs differ between countries, the country with the lowest opportunity cost of producing a good is said to have a comparative advantage in that good. Comparative advantage is the source of the gains from international trade. A country can have an absolute advantage, but not a comparative advantage, in the production of all goods. Every country has a comparative advantage in something. (pp. 586–587)

The Gains from Trade

Countries can gain from trade if their opportunity costs differ. Through trade, each country can obtain goods at a lower opportunity cost than it could if it produced all goods at home. International trade allows a country to consume outside its production possibilities. By specializing in producing the good in which it has a comparative advantage and then trading some of that good for imports, a country can consume at points outside its production possibility frontier. Each country can consume at such a point.

In the absence of international borrowing and lending, trade is balanced as prices adjust to reflect the international supply of and demand for goods. The world price is established at the level that bal-ances the production and consumption plans of the trading parties. At the equilibrium price, trade is balanced and domestic consumption plans exactly match a combination of domestic production and international trade.

Comparative advantage explains the enormous volume and diversity of international trade that takes place in the world. But much trade takes the form of exchanging similar goods for each other— one type of car for another. Such trade arises because of economies of scale in the face of diversified tastes. By specializing in producing a few goods, having long production runs, and then trading those goods internationally, consumers in all countries can enjoy greater diversity of products at lower prices. (pp. 587–595)

Trade Restrictions

A country can restrict international trade by imposing tariffs or nontariff barriers—quotas and voluntary export restraints. All trade restrictions raise the domestic price of imported goods, lower the volume of imports, and reduce the total value of imports. They also reduce the total value of exports by the same amount as the reduction in the value of imports.

All trade restrictions create a gap between the domestic price and the foreign supply price of an import. In the case of a tariff, that gap is the tariff revenue collected by the government. But the government raises no revenue from a quota. Instead, domestic importers who have a license to import increase their profit. A voluntary export restraint resembles a quota except that a higher price is received by the foreign exporter.

Governments restrict trade because restrictions help the producers of the protected commodity and the workers employed by those producers. Because their gain is sufficiently large and the loss per consumer is sufficiently small, the political equilibrium favors restricted trade. Politicians pay more attention to the vocal concerns of the few who stand to lose than to the less strongly expressed views of the many who stand to gain. (pp. 595–604)

KEY ELEMENTS

Key Terms

Balance of trade, 583
Comparative advantage, 587
Countervailing duties, 603
Dumping, 603
Exports, 583
General Agreement on Tariffs and Trade, 595
Imports, 583
Net exporter, 583
Net importer, 583
Nontariff barrier, 595
Protectionism, 595
Quota, 600
Tariff, 595
Voluntary export restraint, 600

Key Figures

Figure 22.2   Opportunity Cost in Pioneerland, 586
Figure 22.3   Opportunity Cost in Magic Empire, 587
Figure 22.4   International Trade in Cars, 588
Figure 22.5   Expanding Consumption Possibilities, 589
Figure 22.7   The Effects of a Tariff, 597
Figure 22.8   The Effects of a Quota, 601

REVIEW QUESTIONS

1 What are the main exports and imports of the United States?

2 How does the United States trade services internationally?

3 Which items of international trade have been growing the most quickly in recent years?

4 What is comparative advantage? Why does it lead to gains from international trade?

5 Explain why international trade brings gains to all countries.

6 Distinguish between comparative advantage and absolute advantage.

7 Explain why all countries have a comparative advantage in something.

8 Explain why we import and export such large quantities of certain goods that are similar—for example, cars.

9 What are the main ways in which we restrict international trade?

10 What are the effects of a tariff?

11 What are the effects of a quota?

12 What are the effects of a voluntary export restraint?

13 Describe the main trends in tariffs and nontariff barriers.

14 Which countries have the largest restrictions on their international trade?

15 Why do countries restrict international trade?

PROBLEMS

1 Using Fig. 22.2, calculate the opportunity cost of cars in Pioneerland at the point on the production possibility frontier at which 4 million cars are produced.

2 Using Fig. 22.3, calculate the opportunity cost of a car in Magic Empire when it produces 8 million cars.

3 With no trade, Pioneerland produces 4 million cars and Magic Empire produces 8 million cars. Which country has a comparative advantage in the production of cars?

4 If there is no trade between Pioneerland and Magic Empire, how much grain is consumed and how many cars are bought in each country?

5 Suppose that the two countries in problems 1–4 trade freely.

a Which country exports grain?

b What adjustments will be made to the amount of each good produced by each country?

c What adjustment will be made to the amount of each good consumed by each country?

d What can you say about the price of a car under free trade?

6 Compare the total production of each good produced in problems 1–5.

7 Compare the situation in problems 1–5 with that analyzed in this chapter (pp. 586–590). Why does Magic Empire export cars in the chapter but import them in problem 5?

8 The following figure depicts the international market for soybeans (there are only two countries in the world).

a What is the world price of soybeans if there is free trade between these countries?

b If the country that imports soybeans imposes a tariff of $2 per bushel, what is the world price of soybeans and what quantity of soybeans gets traded internationally? What is the price of soybeans in the importing country? Calculate the tariff revenue.

9 If the importing country in problem 8(a) imposes a quota of 300 million bushels, what is the price of soybeans in the importing country? What is the revenue from the quota, and who gets this revenue?

10 If the exporting country in problem 8(a) imposes a VER of 300 million bushels of soybeans, what is the world price of soybeans? What is the revenue of soybean growers in the exporting country? Which country gains from the VER?

11 Suppose that the exporting country in problem 8(a) subsidizes production by paying its farmers $1 a bushel for soybeans harvested.

a What is the price of soybeans in the importing country?

b What action might soybean growers in the importing country take? Why?

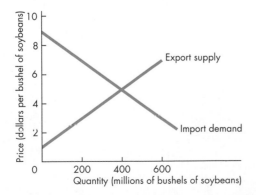

CHAPTER 23

ECONOMIC SYSTEMS IN TRANSITION

After studying this chapter, you will be able to:

- ◆ Describe the fundamental economic problem that confronts all nations

- ◆ Describe the alternative systems that have been used to solve the economic problem

- ◆ Describe the Soviet-style system of central planning

- ◆ Describe the economic problems confronting the former Soviet Union

- ◆ Describe the economic problems of Eastern European countries

- ◆ Describe the process of economic change in China

- ◆ Describe and evaluate the alternative strategies for making the transition from a centrally planned economy to a market economy

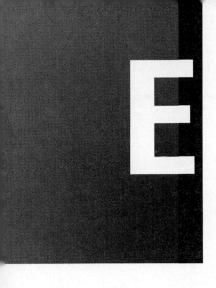

EXTRAORDINARY EVENTS HAVE TAKEN PLACE IN EASTERN Europe. The Berlin Wall has fallen, and Germany is reunited. The centrally planned economy of East Germany has been replaced by the market economic system of West Germany. Poland, Hungary, the Czech Republic, Slovakia, Bulgaria, and Rumania have embraced democratic political institutions and are creating market economies. The Soviet Union has disintegrated. Some of its former republics are now independent nations, and the others are loosely linked in a Commonwealth of Independent States. These nations have abandoned central economic planning and are moving toward a market economy. And the process of adopting the market economic system does not end with Eastern Europe. The People's Republic of China, although remaining a communist dictatorship, is undergoing massive economic change, gradually replacing its system of central planning with the market. ◆ ◆ Why are so many countries abandoning central economic planning and jumping on the market bandwagon? What are the problems that a country faces as it makes the transition to a market economy?

The Market Bandwagon

◆ ◆ ◆ ◆ This chapter brings you full circle. In Chapter 1 you studied the fundamental economic problem of scarcity and considered the alternative ways in which people attempt to solve that problem. In the rest of the book you studied the way in which our own economy (and the similar economies of Western Europe, Japan, and most of the world) solves the economic problem. But a significant number of countries, in which more than a quarter of the human population lives, have employed an economic system that relies on the state to direct the economy through a central planning system. We are going to look at this alternative system and also at the extraordinary—perhaps revolutionary—process of change that is taking place during the 1990s as the centrally planned economies make the transition toward market economies.

The Economic Problem and Its Alternative Solutions

The economic problem is the universal fact of scarcity—we want to consume more goods and services than the available resources make possible. The economic problem is illustrated in Fig. 23.1. People have preferences about the goods and services they would like to consume and about how they would like to use the factors of production that they own or control. Techniques of production—technologies—convert factors of production into goods and services. The economic problem is to choose the quantities of goods and services to produce—*what*—the ways to produce them—*how*—and the distribution of goods and services to each individual—*for whom*.

The production of goods and services is the objective of the economic system. But *what, how,* and *for whom* goods and services are produced depend on the way the economy is organized—on who makes which decisions. Different systems deliver different outcomes. Let's look at the main alternatives that have been used.

Alternative Economic Systems

Economic systems vary in two dimensions:

◆ Ownership of capital and land
◆ Incentive structure

Ownership of Capital and Land   Capital and land may be owned entirely by individuals, entirely by the state, or by a mixture of the two. The private ownership of capital and land enables individuals to create and operate their own firms. It also enables them to buy and sell capital, land, and firms freely at their going market prices. State ownership of capital

The Fundamental Economic Problem

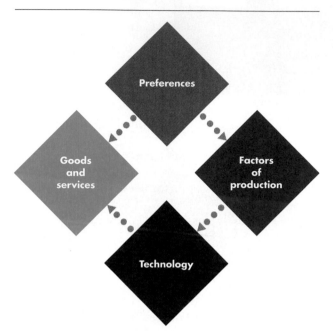

People have preferences about goods and services and the use of factors of production. Technologies are available for transforming factors of production into goods and services. People want to consume more goods and services than can be produced with the available factors of production and technology. The fundamental economic problem is to choose *what* goods and services to produce, *how* to produce them, and *for whom* to produce them. Different economic systems deliver different solutions to this problem.

and land enables individuals to control the use of these resources in state-owned firms but does not permit this control to be passed to others in a market transaction.

In practice, no economy has pure private ownership or pure and exclusive state ownership. For example, in an economy with widespread private ownership, the freedom to buy and sell firms is modified by the antitrust laws. Also, national defense or the public interest may be invoked to limit private ownership. Such limitations operate to restrict the private ownership of beaches and areas of natural scenic beauty.

In an economy that has predominantly state ownership, individuals sometimes own small plots of land and their homes. Also, in many economies, private ownership and state ownership exist side by side. In such cases, the state acts like a private individual and buys capital, land, or even a production enterprise from its existing owner.

Incentive Structure   An **incentive structure** is a set of arrangements that induce people to take certain actions. Incentives may be created by market prices, by administered prices and administrative sanctions, or by a mixture of the two.

An incentive system based on market prices is one in which people respond to the price signals they receive and the price signals themselves respond to people's actions. For example, suppose a severe frost wipes out the Florida orange crop one year. The supply of orange juice falls. As a result, the price of orange juice rises. Faced with the higher price, people have an *incentive* to economize on orange juice and they decrease the quantity demanded. At the same time, the higher price of orange juice induces an increase in the demand for apple juice, a substitute for orange juice. As a result, the price of apple juice also rises. With higher prices for orange juice and apple juice, orange and apple growers in other parts of the country and in other countries have an *incentive* to increase the quantity supplied.

An incentive system based on administered prices is one in which administrators set prices to achieve their own objectives. For example, a government might want everyone to have access to low-cost bread. As a result, bread might be priced at, say, a penny a loaf. Under these circumstances, people have an *incentive* to buy lots of bread. Poor children might even use stale loaves as footballs! (This use of bread apparently did actually occur in the former Soviet Union.) An incentive system based on administrative sanctions is one in which people are rewarded or punished in a variety of non-monetary ways to induce them to take particular actions. For example, a manager might reward a salesperson for achieving a sales goal with more rapid promotion or with a bigger office. Alternatively, a salesperson might be punished for failing to achieve a sales goal by being moved to a less desirable sales district. When an entire economy is operated on administrative incentives, everyone, from the highest political authority to the lowest rank of workers, faces non-monetary rewards and punishments from immediate superiors.

Types of Economic System   Economic systems differ in the ways in which they combine ownership and incentive arrangements. The range of alternatives is illustrated in Fig. 23.2. One type of economic

---

FIGURE 23.2

Alternative Economic Systems

Incentives created by	Capital and land owned by		
	Individuals	Mixed	State
Market prices	Capitalism USA Japan		Market socialism
Mixed		Great Britain Sweden	Yugoslavia Hungary
Administrators	Welfare state capitalism		China Former USSR Socialism

Under capitalism, individuals own capital—farms and factories, plant and equipment—and incentives are created by market prices. Under socialism, the state owns capital, and incentives are created by administrated prices and administrative sanctions. Market socialism combines state ownership of capital with incentives based on market prices. Welfare state capitalism combines private capital ownership with a high degree of state intervention in the incentive structure.

system is **capitalism,** a system based on the private
ownership of capital and land and on an incentive
system based on market prices. Another type of economic system is **socialism,** a system based on state
ownership of capital and land and on an incentive
system based on administered prices or sanctions
arising from a central economic plan. **Central planning**
is a method of allocating resources *by command.* A
central plan for action is drawn up, and the plan is
implemented by creating a set of sanctions and
rewards that ensure that the commands are carried
out.

No country has used an economic system that
precisely corresponds to one of these extreme types,
but the United States and Japan come closest to
being capitalist economies and the former Soviet
Union and China before the 1980s came closest to
being socialist economies. Socialism evolved from
the ideas of Karl Marx (see Our Advancing
Knowledge on pp. 616–617).

Some countries combine private ownership with
state ownership, and some combine market price
incentives with administrative incentives and central
planning. **Market socialism** (also called **decentralized
planning**) is an economic system that combines state
ownership of capital and land with incentives based
on a mixture of market and administered prices.
Hungary and Yugoslavia have had market socialist
economies. In such economies, planners set the
prices at which the various production and distribution organizations are able to buy and sell and then
leave those organizations free to choose the quantities of inputs and outputs. But the prices set by the
planners responded to the forces of demand and
supply.

Another combination is welfare state capitalism.
Welfare state capitalism combines the private ownership of capital and land with state intervention in
markets that change the price signals that people
respond to. Sweden, Great Britain, and other
Western European countries are examples of such
economies.

Alternative Systems Compared

Since all economic systems are made up of a combination of the two extreme special cases—capitalism
and socialism—let's examine these two extreme
types a bit more closely.

Capitalism   Figure 23.3 shows how capitalism
solves the economic problem of scarcity. Households

FIGURE **23.3**

Capitalism's Solution to the Economic Problem

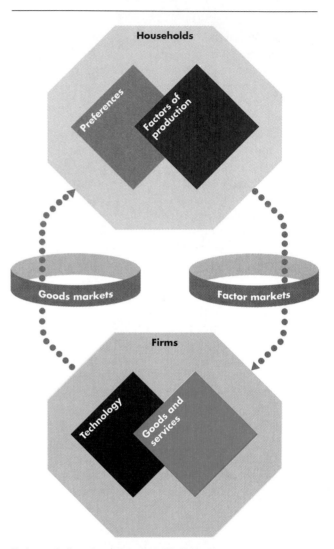

Under capitalism, the preferences of individual households dictate the
choices that are made. Households own all the factors of production
and sell the services of those factors in factor markets. Households
decide which goods and services to consume and buy them in markets
for goods and services. Firms decide which goods and services to produce and which factors of production to employ, selling their output
and buying their inputs in the goods and factor markets. The markets
determine the prices that bring the quantities demanded and quantities
supplied into equality for each factor of production and good or service. Capitalism economizes on information because households and
firms need to know only the prices of various goods and factors that
they buy and sell.

own the factors of production and are free to use those factors, and the incomes they receive from the sale of their services, in any way they choose. These choices are governed by their preferences. The preferences of households are all-powerful in a capitalist economy.

Households choose the quantity of each factor of production to sell, and firms, which organize production, choose the quantity of each factor to buy. These choices respond to the prices prevailing in the factor markets. An increase in a factor price gives households an incentive to increase the quantity supplied and gives firms an incentive to decrease the quantity demanded. Factor prices adjust to bring the quantity of each factor supplied into equality with the quantity of each factor demanded.

Households choose the quantity of each good or service to buy, and firms choose the quantity of each to produce and sell. These choices respond to the prices confronting households and firms in the goods markets. An increase in the price of a good gives firms an incentive to increase the quantity supplied of that good and gives households an incentive to decrease the quantity demanded. Prices adjust to bring the quantities demanded and supplied into equality with each other.

Resources and goods and services flow in a clockwise direction from households to firms and back to households through the factors and goods markets. *What* is produced, *how* it is produced, and *for whom* it is produced are determined by the preferences of the households, the resources that they own, and the technologies available to the firms.

Nobody *plans* the capitalist economy. Doctors perform nearly miraculous life-saving surgery by using sophisticated computer-controlled equipment. The equipment is designed by medical and electronic engineers, programmed by mathematicians, financed by insurance companies and banks, and bought and installed by hospital administrators. Each individual household and firm involved in this process allocates the resources that it controls in the way that seems best for it. The firms try to maximize profit, and the households try to maximize utility. And these plans are coordinated in the markets for health care equipment, computers, engineers, computer programmers, insurance, hospital services, nurses, doctors, and hundreds of other items that range from anaesthetic chemicals to apple juice.

When a surgeon performs an operation, an incredible amount of information is used. Yet no one possesses this information. It is not centralized in one place. The capitalist economic system economizes on information. Each household or firm needs to know very little about the other households and firms with which it does business. The reason is that *prices convey most of the information it needs.* By comparing the prices of factors of production, households choose the quantity of each factor to supply. And by comparing the prices of goods and services, they choose the quantity of each to buy. Similarly, by comparing the prices of factors of production, firms choose the quantity of each factor to use, and by comparing the prices of goods and services, they choose the quantity of each to supply.

Socialism   Figure 23.4 shows how socialism solves the economic problem of scarcity. In this case the planners' preferences carry the most weight. Those preferences dictate the activities of the production enterprises. The planners control capital and natural resources, directing them to the uses that satisfy their priorities. The planners also decide what types of jobs will be available, and the state plays a large role in the allocation of the only factor of production owned by households—labor.

The central plan is communicated to state-owned enterprises, which use the factors of production and the available technologies to produce goods and services. These goods and services are supplied to households in accordance with the central plan. The purchases by each household are determined by household preferences, but the total amount available is determined by the central planners.

A centrally planned economy has prices, but prices do not adjust to make quantity demanded and quantity supplied equal. Instead, they are set to achieve social objectives. For example, the prices of staple food products are set at low levels so that even the poorest families can afford an adequate basic diet. The effect of setting such prices at low levels is chronic shortages. The incentives that people respond to are the penalties and rewards that superiors can impose on and give to their subordinates.

R E V I E W

The economic problem—*what, how,* and *for whom* to produce the various goods and

FIGURE **23.4**

Socialism's Solution to the Economic Problem

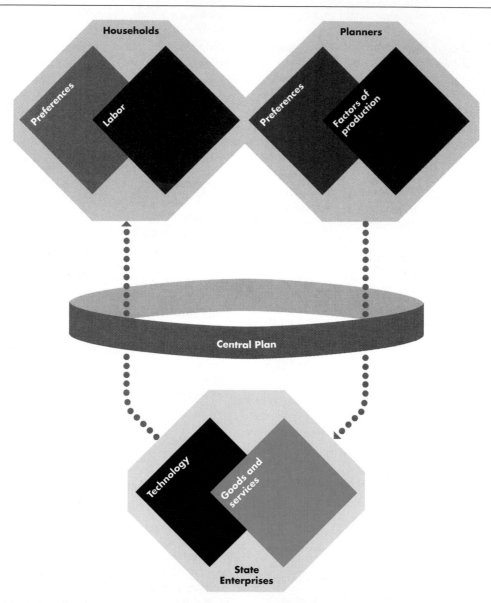

Under socialism, the preferences of the planners dictate the choices that are made. The planners control all the capital and natural resources owned by the state. They draw up plans and issue orders that determine how these resources will be used in the production of goods and services. Households decide which goods and services to consume and buy them from state-owned shops. State enterprises produce the goods and services and employ the factors of production required by the central plan. The output of state enterprises is shipped to other enterprises in accordance with the plan or sold in the state-owned shops. Prices are set by the planners to achieve social objectives and bear no relation to the quantities demanded and quantities supplied. Prices set at low levels for social reasons—as in the case of basic food products—result in chronic shortages.

services—is solved in different ways by different economic systems. Capitalism solves it by permitting households and firms to exchange factors of production and goods and services in markets. Firms produce the items that maximize their profits, households buy the goods that maximize their utility, and markets adjust prices to make buying and selling plans compatible. Socialism solves the economic problem by setting up a central planning system. The planners decide what will be produced and communicate their plans to state-owned enterprises. Incentives to fulfill the plan are created by a series of non-monetary rewards and sanctions. Each household decides what it wants to buy, but the total amount available is determined by the planners. Shortages, especially of basic staple food products, frequently arise. ◆

Let's now take a closer look at some socialist economies. We'll begin with the country that invented central planning and "exported" its system to the other socialist countries, the former Soviet Union.

Economic Change in the Former Soviet Union

The Soviet Union, or the Union of Soviet Socialist Republics (USSR), was founded in 1917 following the Bolshevik revolution led by Vladimir Ilyich Lenin. The union collapsed and was replaced by the Commonwealth of Independent States (CIS) in 1991. The republics that make up the Commonwealth are resource-rich and diverse. Their land area is three times that of the United States; their population is approaching 300 million, 20 percent larger than the United States; they have vast reserves of coal, oil, iron ore, natural gas, timber, and almost every other mineral resource. They are republics of enormous ethnic diversity with Russians making up 50 percent of the population and many European, Asian, and Arabic ethnic groups making up the other 50 percent.

Economic History of the Soviet Union

A compact economic history of the Soviet Union appears in Table 23.1. Although the nation was founded in 1917, its economic management system was not put in place until the 1930s. The architect of this system was Joseph Stalin. The financial,

TABLE 23.1

A Compact Summary of Key Periods in the Economic History of the Soviet Union

Period	Main economic events/characteristics
1917–1921 (Lenin)	◆ **Bolshevik Revolution**
	◆ **Nationalization of banking, industry, and transportation**
	◆ **Forced requisitioning of agricultural output**
1921–1924 (Lenin)	◆ **New Economic Policy (NEP), 1921**
	◆ **Market allocation of most resources**
1928–1953 (Stalin)	◆ **Abolition of market**
	◆ **Introduction of command planning and five-year plans**
	◆ **Collectivization of farms**
	◆ **Emphasis on capital goods and economic growth**
	◆ **Harsh conditions**
1953–1970 (Khrushchev to Brezhnev)	◆ **Steady growth**
	◆ **Increased emphasis on consumer goods**
1970–1985 (Brezhnev to Chernenko)	◆ **Deteriorating productivity in agriculture and industry**
	◆ **Slowdown in growth**
1985–1991 (Gorbachev)	◆ **Perestroika—reforms based on increased accountability**
1991	◆ **Breakup of the Soviet Union**
1992	◆ **Creation of the Commonwealth of Independent States**

UNDERSTANDING
the Limits of
CENTRAL PLANNING

Our economy is a highly planned one. But it is not *centrally* planned. The planning takes place inside corporations—some of them huge. General Motors, for example, is bigger than many countries. If it makes sense to plan GM's economy, why doesn't it make sense to plan a national economy?

This question has puzzled and divided economists for many years. The answer given by Friedrich von Hayek is that an economy produces billions of different goods and services, while a corporation, even a very large one, produces only a limited range of items. As a consequence, central planning requires the centralization of vast amounts of information that it is extremely costly to collect. The market economizes on this information. Each household or firm needs to know only the prices of the range of goods and services that it buys and sells. No household or firm needs to know every price. And none needs to know the technologies for producing anything beyond its area of specialization. Markets find the prices that make the plans of producers and consumers consistent.

But Hayek's answer leaves open another question. Why does GM plan? Why isn't the market used to allocate resources inside GM? This question was answered by Ronald H. Coase. Planning, he explained, economizes on transactions costs, while the market economizes on information costs. There is an optimal size of the planning unit (firm) and an optimal extent of the market for each activity.

"The more complicated the whole, the more dependent we become on that division of knowledge between individuals whose separate efforts are coordinated by the impersonal . . . price system."

FRIEDRICH VON HAYEK
The Road to Serfdom

The poor economic performance of the former Soviet Union, the communist countries of Eastern Europe, and China before 1978 suggests that planning was taken too far in those countries and that the scope of the market was too restricted. These countries were run like big firms, but the firms were too big.

Before 1978, the farms of China were operated as part of the national economic plan. The planners decided what would be produced and how the food would be distributed. Peasant farmers received an allocation of food, but their rewards were unrelated to their efforts. Food production and living standards were low. In 1978, Deng Xiaoping reformed the farms. Families were permitted to take long-term leases on their land and to decide what to produce and where to sell it. The result was a massive increase in food production and a rapid increase in the standard of living. By 1984, the farms had become so productive that China became an *exporter* of grain.

Deng Xiaoping's 1978 economic reforms have had dramatic effects on China's large cities and urban population. New laws that permitted the creation of private firms resulted in massive numbers of new private enterprises springing up—manufacturing a wide range of consumer goods and providing employment for people who were no longer needed on the increasingly efficient farms. By 1990, real income per person had increased to 2½ times its 1978 level. Between 1982 and 1988, real income per person grew at a staggering 9.7 percent a year, almost doubling in six years. Many of the new private firms sell on world markets, and China's exports grew at a much faster rate than GDP during the 1980s. By 1990, they stood at 17 percent of GDP.

KARL MARX: An *Alternative Economic Vision*

Karl Marx (1818–1883) was a social scientist (political scientist, sociologist, and economist) of extraordinary breadth and influence. Born in Germany, he spend most of his adult life in London, using the British Museum as his workplace. With little income, life was harsh for Marx and his wife (his childhood sweetheart to whom he was devoted). Marx's major work in economics was *Das Kapital*, in which he argued that capitalism was self-destructive and would be replaced by a system in which private property was abolished and a central plan replaced the market—a system he called "communism." Events have rejected Marx's theory, and his lasting contribution to modern economics is negligible. But his contribution to modern politics is substantial. Marxism, a political creed based on his ideas, thrives throughout much of the world today.

manufacturing, and transportation sectors of the economy had been taken under state ownership and control by Lenin. Stalin added the farms to this list. He abolished the market and introduced a command planning mechanism, initiating a series of five-year plans that placed their major emphasis on setting and attaining goals for the production of capital goods. The production of consumer goods was given a secondary place, and personal economic conditions were harsh. With emphasis on the production of capital goods, the Soviet economy grew quickly.

By the 1950s, after Stalin's death, steady economic growth continued, but the emphasis in economic planning gradually shifted away from capital goods production toward consumer goods production. In the 1960s, the growth rate began to sag, and by the 1970s and early 1980s, the Soviet economy was running into serious problems. Productivity was actually declining, especially in agriculture but also in industry. Growth slowed, and, by some estimates, per capita income in the Soviet Union began to fall. It was in this situation that Mikhail Gorbachev came to power with plans to restructure the Soviet economy, based on the idea of increased individual accountability and rewards based on performance.

As a unified political entity, the Soviet Union effectively disintegrated following an unsuccessful coup to topple former President Gorbachev in August 1991. What emerged from that coup in 1992 was a more loosely federated Commonwealth of Independent States. Political freedoms began to be enjoyed in the late 1980s under President Gorbachev's programs of *perestroika* (restructuring) and *glasnost* (openness). These political freedoms released nationalist and ethnic feelings that had been held in check for 50 years and created a virtual explosion of political activity. At the same time, the economies of the now independent republics underwent tumultuous change.

We are going to look at that change. But you will better appreciate the severity and nature of the problems posed by economic change if we first look at the way the Soviet Union operated before it abandoned its central planning system.

Soviet-Style Central Planning

Soviet-style central planning is a method of economic planning and control that has four key elements:

◆ Administrative hierarchy

◆ Iterative planning process
◆ Legally binding commands
◆ Taut and inflexible plans

Administrative Hierarchy   A large and complex hierarchy implements and controls the central economic plan that determines almost every aspect of economic activity. A **hierarchy** is an organization arranged in ranks, each rank being subordinate to the one above it. At the top of an economic planning hierarchy is the highest *political* authority. Immediately below it is the economic planning ministry, the senior of a large number of ministries. Below the planning ministry are a large number of ministries that are responsible for the detailed aspects of production. For example, one ministry deals with engineering production, another with fruit and vegetables, and another with railroad transportation. Responsibility for production processes is divided and subdivided yet further down to the level of the individual factories that carry out the production processes. For example, engineering is divided into light, heavy, electrical, and civil divisions. Light engineering is divided into departments that deal with individual product groups, such as ball bearings. And finally, ball bearings are manufactured in a number of factories. At each level of the hierarchy, there are superiors and subordinates. Superiors have absolute and arbitrary power over their subordinates.

Iterative Planning Process   Central planning is an iterative planning process. An iterative process is a repetitive series of calculations that get closer and closer to a solution. A plan is proposed, and adjustments are repeatedly made until all the elements of the plan are consistent with each other. But a plan is not arrived at as the result of a set of neat calculations performed on a computer. Rather, the process involves a repeated sequence of communications of proposals and reactions down and up the administrative hierarchy.

The process begins with the issue of a big picture set of objectives or directives by the highest political authority. These directives are translated into targets by the planning ministry and retranslated into ever more detailed targets as they are passed down the hierarchy. Tens of millions of raw materials and intermediate goods featured in the detailed plans of the Soviet Union, which filled 70 volumes, or 12,000 pages, each year.

When the targets are specified as production plans for individual products, the factories react with their own assessments of what is feasible. Reactions as to feasibility are passed back up the hierarchy, and the central planning ministry makes the targets and reports of feasibility consistent. A good deal of bargaining takes place in this process, the superiors demanding the impossible and subordinates claiming requests to be infeasible.

Legally Binding Commands   Once a consistent (even if infeasible) plan has been determined by the planning ministry, the plan is given the force of law in a set of binding commands from the political authority. The commands are translated into increasing detail as they pass down the chain of command and are implemented by the production units in a way that most nearly satisfies the superiors of each level.

Taut and Inflexible Plans   In the Soviet Union, the targets set by superiors for their subordinates were infeasible. The idea was that in the attempt to do the impossible, more would be achieved than if an easily attained task was set. The outcome of this planning process was a set of taut and inflexible plans. A taut plan is one that has no slack built into it. If one unit fails to meet its planned targets, all the other units that rely on the output of the first unit will fail to meet their targets also. An inflexible plan is one that has no capacity for reactions to changing circumstances.

Faced with impossible targets, factories produced a combination of products that enabled their superiors to report plan fulfillment, but the individual items produced did not meet the needs of the other parts of the economy. No factory received exactly the quantity and types of inputs needed, and the economy was unable to respond to changes in circumstances. In practice, the plan for the current year was the outcome of the previous year plus a wished for but unattainable increment.

The Market Sector

Although the economy of the Soviet Union was a planned one, a substantial amount of economic activity took place outside the planning and com-mand economy. The most important component of the market sector was in agriculture. It has been estimated that during the 1980s there were 35 million private plots worked by rural households in the Soviet Union. These private plots constituted less than 3 percent of the agricultural land of the Soviet Union but produced close to 25 percent of total agricultural output and a third of all the meat and milk. Some estimates suggested that the productivity on private plots was 40 times that of state enterprise farms and collective farms. Other economic activities undertaken by Soviet citizens outside the planning system were illegal.

Money in the Soviet Union

Money played a minor role in the economy of the Soviet Union. It was used in the market sector and in the state sector to pay wages and buy consumer goods and services. But all the transactions among state enterprises and between state enterprises and government took place as part of the *physical* plan, and money was used only as a means of keeping records. International trade was undertaken by the direct exchange of goods for goods— barter.

Soviet Economic Decline

Table 23.2 describes the growth performance of the Soviet economy between 1928 and 1990. The economy performed extraordinarily well before 1970. Growth rates of output in excess of 5 percent a year were achieved on the average for the entire period between 1928 and 1970, bringing an eightfold increase in aggregate output over these years. Then the growth rate began to fall. During the 1970s, output expanded by 3.2 percent a year, and in the 1980s, growth collapsed to 2 percent a year between 1980 and 1986 and then to only 1 percent a year between 1986 and 1990. In 1990, the economy shrank by 4 percent.

Why did the economy perform well before 1970 and then begin to deliver successively slower growth rates? What brought the decline of the Soviet economy during the 1980s? The combination and interaction of three features were responsible. They are

◆ Transition from investment to consumption economy
◆ External shocks
◆ Taut and inflexible plans

TABLE **23.2**

Economic Growth Rates in the Soviet Union

Years	Growth rates (percent per year)
1928–1937	5.4
1940–1960	5.7
1960–1970	5.1
1970–1979	3.2
1980–1986	2.0
1987	1.6
1988	4.4
1989	2.5
1990	−4.0

Economic growth in the Soviet Union was rapid between 1928 and 1970. During the 1970s, growth began to slow down, and the growth rate became successively lower until the early 1990s, when the economy began to contract.

Sources: Paul R. Gregory and Robert C. Stuart, *Soviet Economic Structure and Performance,* 2nd edition (New York: Harper and Row, 1981); U.S. Central Intelligence Agency, *USSR: Measures of Economic Growth and Development, 1950–1980,* U.S. Congress, Joint Economic Committee (Washington, D.C.: U.S. Government Printing Office, 1982); U.S. Central Intelligence Agency, "Gorbachev's Economic Program," Report to U.S. Congress, Subcommittee on National Security Economics, April 13, 1989 (Washington, D.C.: U.S. Government Printing Office, 1989); and The World Bank, *The Economy of the USSR* (Washington, D.C.: 1990).

Transition from Investment to Consumption Economy

Before 1960, the Soviet economic planners concentrated on producing capital goods and maintaining a rapid rate of investment in new buildings, plant, and equipment. They ran the Soviet economy like a large corporation intent on rapid growth that puts all its profits into yet more growth. The central planning system is at its best when implementing such a strategy. The planners know exactly which types of capital they need to remove or reduce bottlenecks and can achieve a high rate of growth.

During the 1960s, the orientation of the Soviet economy began to change with a relative increase in the production of consumer goods and services. By the 1970s and 1980s, this process had gone much further. A centrally planned economy does a very bad job of handling the complexities of producing a large variety of types, sizes, colors, designs, and styles of consumer goods. The planners need to collect and take into account more information than their computers can handle.

As a result, the planners order the wrong goods to be produced, creating surpluses of some and chronic shortages of others. Easy-to-produce plain white bread is available in excessive quantities at give-away prices, and hard-to-produce blueberry muffins can't be found at any price. Surplus goods get wasted or used inefficiently, and increasing amounts of the resources that could be used to add to the economy's productive capital get diverted to meeting ever more desperate consumer demands. Gradually, economic growth vanishes.

External Shocks   As the world's largest producer of crude oil, the Soviet Union benefited enormously, during the 1970s, from the massive oil price increases. The extra revenue obtained from oil exports helped, during those years, to mask the problems just described. But the 1980s brought *falling* oil prices and exposed the problems of the Soviet Union in a sharp light.

During the late 1980s, the countries of Eastern Europe that had been the Soviet Union's traditional trading partners embarked on their own transitions to market economies and began to look to the West for trading opportunities. As a consequence, the Soviet Union's sources of international trade collapsed.

Taut and Inflexible Plans   A flexible economic system might have been able to deal with the switch to consumption goods production and the consequences of a changing world economic environment. But the Soviet economy was not flexible. On the contrary, with its system of taut planning and its unresponsive command structure, it was only able to attempt to produce the same bundle of goods as it had produced in the previous year. With less revenue from oil and other raw material exports, fewer imported inputs could be obtained. Imbalances in the central plan rippled through the entire economy, disrupting the production of all goods and putting the system itself under enormous strain.

Living Standards in the Late 1980s

The problems of the Soviet economy are put in sharp focus in Fig. 23.5. In this figure, the productivity and consumption levels of the Soviet Union in the mid-1980s are compared with those of the United States, Western Europe (Germany, France, and Italy), Japan, and Portugal. As you can see from the figure, average worker productivity in the Soviet Union, measured by GDP per worker, was less than 40 percent of real GDP per worker in the United States and lagged considerably behind that in the other Western European countries and Japan. A similar picture is painted by comparing consumption per worker and consumption per person. The capitalist country whose level of productivity and consumption was most similar to that of the Soviet Union was Portugal.

FIGURE **23.5**

GDP and Consumption in the Soviet Union and Other Countries

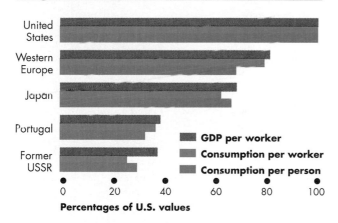

GDP per worker in the Soviet Union in the mid-1980s was less than 40 percent of its level in the United States and similar to the level in Portugal. Consumption per worker and consumption per person were even lower at less than 30 percent of the U.S. level. The Soviet Union lagged considerably behind Western Europe and Japan in GDP and consumption level.

Source: Abram Bergson, "The USSR Before the Fall: How Poor and Why," *Journal of Economic Perspectives* 5, 4 (Fall 1991): 29–44.

Market Economy Reforms

By the end of the 1980s, there was widespread dissatisfaction throughout the Soviet Union with the economic planning system, and a process of transition toward a market economy began. This process had three main elements:

1. Relaxing central plan enforcement
2. Deregulating prices
3. Permitting limited private ownership of firms

The transition in all three areas was one of gradual change. But the relaxation of central plan enforcement was the fastest and most far-reaching element of the transition. The idea was that by relaxing central control over the annual plan and permitting the managers of state enterprises greater freedom to act like the managers of private firms, enterprises would be able to respond to changing circumstances without having to wait for orders from the center.

Price deregulation was gradual and covered a limited range of products. Here, the idea was that with the removal of price controls, the price mechanism would allocate scarce resources to their highest-value uses. Shortages would disappear and be replaced by available but sometimes expensive goods and services. High prices would strengthen the inducement for producers to increase the quantities supplied. The move toward private ownership of firms was extremely gradual. The idea here was that enterprising individuals would move quickly to seize profit opportunities by responding to price signals much more rapidly than the replaced planning system could respond to shortages and bottlenecks.

But the transition process ran into problems. One of these problems was that of unlearning the old methods of the centrally planned economy. Reading Between the Lines on pp. 622–623 looks at an example of this problem in the Moscow market for bread. But deeper transition problems arose from the nature of the system being replaced.

Transition Problems

There are three major problems confronting the republics of the former Soviet Union that complicate

The Market Comes to Moscow

The Essence of the Story

In Russia, the prices of many items, including bread, were deregulated on January 2, 1992.

In December 1991, in preparation for this event, the executives of Moscow's bread factories attended a meeting at the Moscow Bread Consortium (the de facto ministry of bread).

The consortium suggested that producers increase the price of bread to 3½ times the old price. This "suggestion" did not, as in the formerly planned economy, have the force of law.

The bread producers were confused, anxious, nervous, and suspicious.

For two days the factory directors discussed their fears by telephone and eventually decided to jointly fix the price of bread.

There was a rumor that one bread factory (No. 26) was charging a lower price.

The Wall Street Journal, January 21, 1992

Moscow's 'Capitalists' Decide the Best Price Is a Firmly Fixed One

by Laurie Hays and Adi Ignatius

Late last month, on the eve of Russia's historic plunge into a market economy, Vladimir Grechanik, the top financial planner of Moscow's Bread Factory No. 14, went into a panic.

After 70 years of government control of everything from the cost of raw materials to salaries, the factory suddenly would be able to set its own prices. He and his fellow producers anxiously tried to calculate how much flour would cost, how much transportation might rise and what consumers would be willing to pay.

Just before prices were freed Jan. 2, Mr. Grechanik and executives from Moscow's other bread factories were called to a meeting at the Moscow Bread Consortium, the de facto ministry of bread. They eyed one another nervously, suspicious that, after years of mandated equality, the system might make rivals of former comrades. The bread consortium suggested raising the free-market bread price to 3½ times the old price, but not a kopeck more. The factory men were confused. In the old days, such a "suggestion" carried the full weight of a decree. But there were no certainties anymore. The new freedom was unbearable.

An Old Reflex

Left to his own devices, Mr. Grechanik returned to his office and got on the phone. For the next two days he and the other factory directors discussed their fears. Finally, they came to a decision: If the state was no longer to set prices, the factories themselves would jointly fix them—to ensure their mutual survival.

"We all agreed on a single price," says Mr. Grechanik, as he walks past huge vats of flour on the factory floor. Lowering his voice, he confides, "I've heard that Bread Factory No. 26 is charging a little less, but I hope it's just a rumor." . . .

Background and Analysis

When the central planning system operated, the price and quantity of bread were determined by the planners.

Figure 1 illustrates this situation. The plan quantity is Q_0, and the plan price is 0.50 ruble (50 kopecks). The average cost of producing bread was higher than this price, and bread factories were subsidized. In this example (the numbers are hypothetical) the subsidy is 50 kopecks per loaf.

The move toward the market economy that began in January 1992 resulted in:

◆ The removal of the subsidy to bread producers
◆ Increased cost of flour and other raw materials and salaries

Increases in incomes (increases in ruble incomes, not increases in real incomes) and increases in other prices also led to an increase in the demand for bread.

The combination of these changes is illustrated in Fig. 2. There was uncertainty in the minds of the executives of the bread factories about the magnitude of these changes.

Figure 1

Figure 2

Adding to these uncertainties, each producer was uncertain about the prices that the other producers would charge for bread.

To remove the last-mentioned uncertainty, the producers pooled their information and fixed a single price. This price is based on the assumption that the costs of production—the opportunity cost of bread—would increase to 1.75 rubles a loaf.

If the demand for bread increased to D_1, the quantity produced would remain at its previous level of Q_0.

If the bread producers overestimated the opportunity cost of producing bread, the free market would result in new firms entering to compete with them and the price would fall below the level they had fixed.

If the bread producers underestimated the opportunity cost of bread, some of them would begin to incur losses and might eventually go out of business. In this event, the supply of bread would decrease and its price would rise until it covered its opportunity cost.

their transition to the capitalist market economic system. They are

◆ Value and legal systems alien to capitalism
◆ Collapse of traditional trade flows
◆ Fiscal crisis

Value and Legal Systems   More than 60 years of socialist dictatorship have left a legacy of values and memories alien to the rapid and successful establishment of a capitalist, market economy. The political leaders and people of the former Soviet Union have no personal memories of free political institutions and markets. And they have been educated, both formally and informally, to believe in a political creed in which traders and speculators are not just shady characters, but criminals. Unlearning these values will be a slow and perhaps painful process.

The legal system is also unsuited to the needs of a market economy in two ways. First, there are no well-established property rights and methods of protecting those rights. Second, and more important, there is no tradition of government behaving like individuals and firms before the rule of law. In the Soviet system, the government *was* the law. Its economic plan and the arbitrary decisions made by superiors at each level in the hierarchy were the only law that counted. Rational, self-promoting actions taken outside the plan were illegal. It will take a long time to establish a legal system based on private property rights and the rule of law.

Collapse of Traditional Trade Flows   A centrally administered empire has collapsed, and its constituent republics have decided to create a loose federation. Such a political reorganization can have devastating economic consequences. The most serious of these is the collapse of traditional trade flows. The Soviet Union was a highly interdependent grouping of republics organized on a wheel-hub basis with Moscow (and to a lesser degree Leningrad—now St. Petersburg) at its center. This view of the Soviet economy is shown in Fig. 23.6. The figure also shows the magnitude of the flows of goods from the republics through the Moscow hub.

The most heavily dependent republic, Belorussia, delivered 70 percent of its output to other republics and received a similar value of goods from the other republics. Even the least dependent republic, Kazakhstan, traded 30 percent of its production

FIGURE **23.6**

The Wheel-Hub Economy of the Soviet Union

■ **Percentage of republic output exported to other republics**
▫ **Percentage of republic output consumed within republic**

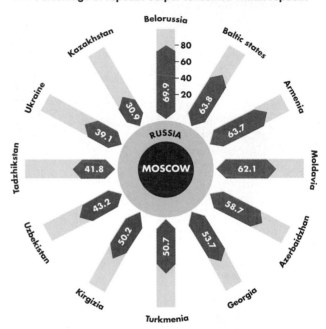

The Soviet economy was organized on a wheel-hub model. Vast amounts of goods and services were traded among the republics but mainly through the Moscow hub. The percentages of production in each republic exported to other republics are shown along the spokes of the wheel.

Source: The World Bank, *The Economy of the USSR* (Washington, D.C.: 1990), p. 51.

Note: The names of the republics in this figure are the ones used in the former Soviet Union. With the breakup of the Soviet Union, Belorussia became Belarus, Moldavia became Moldova, Turkmenia became Turkmenistan, Kirgizia became Kyrgyzstan, and Talzhikstan became Tajikistan.

with the other republics. The vast amount of interrepublic trade, managed by the central planners and channeled through the Moscow hub, meant that individual enterprise managers had (and still have) little knowledge of where their products end up being used or their inputs originate.

With the collapse of the central plan, managers must search for supplies and for markets. Until they have built new networks of information, shortages of raw materials and other material inputs will be common and a lack of markets will stunt production. This problem can be solved by the activities of specialist traders and speculators, but the emergence of this class of economic agent is likely to be slow because of political attitudes toward this activity.

The collapse of an economic empire does not inevitably lead to a collapse of traditional trade flows and an associated decline in production. But it usually has done so. The most similar collapse this century was that of the Austro-Hungarian Empire in 1919. Like the Soviet Union, the Austro-Hungarian Empire was a centralized economic system organized with Vienna and Budapest as its hubs with a single currency and free trade. The empire was a great economic success, achieving rapid improvements in living standards for its people. Following the collapse of the empire, tariffs were introduced, each country established its own currency, trade flows dried up, and economic growth declined.

Fiscal Crisis   Under the central planning system of the Soviet Union, the central government collected taxes in an arbitrary way. One source of revenue was a tax on consumer goods. But the major source of revenue was the profits of the state enterprises. Since the state owned these enterprises, it also received the profits. Money played virtually no role in the centrally planned system. Workers received their wages in currency and used it to purchase consumer goods and services. But for the state enterprises and the government, money was just a unit for keeping records.

With the collapse of central planning, money has become more important, especially for the government. With the loss of its traditional sources of revenue and with little change in its spending, the government has a large budget deficit. It covers this deficit by printing money, and the result is inflation. The inflation rate during the final six months of the life of the Soviet Union—the first half of 1991—reached close to 200 percent and was on a rising path.

Inflation is not an inevitable accompaniment of the collapse of an economic empire, but like the collapse of trade flows, it has happened before. The rates of growth of the newly created currencies of Austria, Hungary, Poland, Rumania, and Yugoslavia following the disintegration of the Austro-Hungarian Empire were extremely rapid and led to hyperinflation. In Poland, the hyperinflation reached an annual rate of 250 million percent.

REVIEW

T he Soviet Union's system of central economic planning and state ownership was established in the 1930s. Under this system, a hierarchical administrative structure engaged in an iterative planning process to arrive at a consistent economic plan. The plan was implemented by the political authority issuing legally binding commands that were translated into ever greater detail as they were passed down the chain of command. In practice, the plans were infeasible and inflexible. The system performed well before 1970 but became steadily less effective during the 1970s and 1980s. The system's inflexibility could not cope with the transition from an investment to a consumption economy and with a series of external shocks. As a result, its growth rate slowed, and eventually output began to decrease. A market reform process was begun that deregulated prices, permitted limited private ownership of firms, and relaxed the enforcement of the central plan. But the value and legal systems, the collapse of traditional trade flows, the loss of tax revenue, and inflation are making the transition extremely costly. ◆

Economic Transition in Eastern Europe

T he formerly planned economies of Eastern Europe—Czechoslovakia, East Germany, Hungary, and Poland—are also making transitions to market economies. The processes being followed and the problems faced are similar to those of the former Soviet Union. But their problems, although severe, take different forms from those of the Soviet Union. The major differences arise from political factors. Let's take a brief look at the transition process in these countries.

East Germany

For East Germany, the transition from a centrally planned economy has been the most dramatic and the most complete. On October 3, 1990, East

Germany united with West Germany. East Germany was a country with 16 million people, 26 percent of the population of West Germany, and with a GDP per person of less than 80 percent of that of West Germany. Even before the formal reunification of the two parts of Germany, East Germany had begun to dismantle its Soviet-style planning system and replace it with a market economy.

The former East Germany adopted the monetary system of West Germany, deregulated its prices, and opened itself up to free trade with its western partner. State enterprises were permitted to fail in the competition with western private firms, private firms were permitted to open up in the former East Germany, and a massive sell-off of state enterprises was embarked upon.

The process of selling state enterprises began by the creation of a state corporation called Treuhandanstalt (which roughly translates as "Trust Corporation") that took over the assets of the almost 11,000 state enterprises. The idea was to then sell off these enterprises in an orderly way over a few years. By November 1991, Treuhandanstalt had disposed of more than 4,000 firms. Most of these firms had been sold to the private sector, but about 900 firms were closed down or merged with other firms.

The loss of jobs resulting from this rapid shake-out of state enterprises was large. Even by July 1990, before the two Germanies were reunited, unemployment in East Germany had reached one third of the labor force. The unemployment rate in the east will remain high for some years, but the safety net of the West German social security system will cushion the blow to individual workers and their families.

East Germany has no fiscal policy crisis and no inflation problem. It has adopted the West German taxation and monetary systems and has assured financial stability. But the transition for East Germany will last for several years, even though it will be the most rapid transition imaginable.

Czech Republic, Slovakia, Hungary, and Poland

The problems facing the Czech Republic, Slovakia, Hungary, and Poland differ in important ways but share some common features. And these common features are similar to some of the problems faced by the former Soviet Union that we've already seen. The most severe of these are the collapse of tradi-

tional trade flows and the loss of traditional sources of government revenue.

Czech Republic and Slovakia   The Czech Republic and Slovakia (formerly Czechoslovakia) removed their communist government in what has been called the "Velvet Revolution" in November 1989 and almost immediately embarked on a program of economic reforms aimed at replacing a centrally planned economy with a market system.

The first step in the transition was the freeing of wages, prices, and interest rates. This step was accomplished quickly, but the emergence of well-functioning markets did not immediately follow. Financial markets were especially nervous, and a shortage of liquidity created a financial crisis.

The second step in the transition was privatization. Czechoslovakia pursued a so-called two-track policy of "little privatization" and "big privatization." "Little privatization" is the sale or, where possible, the return to their former owners of small businesses and shops. "Big privatization" is the sale of shares in the large industrial enterprises. One feature of this privatization process is the issue of vouchers to citizens that may be used to buy shares in formerly state-owned enterprises.

Czechoslovakia's transition was slowed down by the decision of its people to divide the country into two parts. It has not yet reached the point of a positive economic payoff.

Hungary   Hungary has been in a long transition toward a capitalist, market economy. The process began in the 1960s when central planning was replaced by decentralized planning based on a price system. Hungary has also established a taxation system similar to that in the market economies. But the privatization of large-scale industry began only in the 1990s and is proceeding slowly.

Because of its extreme gradualism, Hungary's transition is much less disruptive than those in the other countries. But it is feeling the repercussions of the economic restructuring of the other Eastern European countries with which it has traditionally had the strongest trade links, so its rate of economic expansion has slowed substantially in recent years.

Poland   Severe shortages, black markets, and inflation were the jumping off point for Poland's journey toward a market economy. This journey began in September 1989 when a non-communist government that included members of the trade union Solidarity took office. The new government has deregulated prices, and black markets have disappeared. It has also pursued a policy of extreme financial restraint, bringing the state budget and inflation under control.

Privatization has also been put on a fast track in Poland. In mid-1991, the government announced its Mass Privatization Scheme. Under this scheme, the shares of 400 state enterprises were to be transferred to a Privatization Fund, the shares in which were to be distributed freely to the entire adult population. This method of privatization is like creating a giant insurance company that owns most of the production enterprises and that is in turn owned by private shareholders.

Although the transition to the market economy is the most dynamic in Eastern Europe and the former Soviet Union, it has been going on for longer and has had more dramatic effects on living standards in China. Let's now look at this country.

Economic Transition in China

China is the world's largest nation. In 1990, its population was 1.2 billion—almost a quarter of the world's population. Chinese civilization is ancient and has a splendid history, but the modern nation—the People's Republic of China—dates only from 1949. A compact summary of key periods in the economic history of the People's Republic is presented in Table 23.3.

Modern China began when a revolutionary Communist movement, led by Mao Zedong, captured control of China, forcing the country's previous leader, Chiang Kai-shek (Jiang Jie-shi) onto the island of Formosa—now Taiwan. Like the Soviet Union, China is a socialist country. But unlike the Soviet Union, China is largely nonindustrialized—it is a developing country.

During the early years of the People's Republic, the country followed the Soviet model of economic planning and command. Urban manufacturing industry was taken over and operated by the state, and the farms were collectivized. Also, following the Stalin model of the 1930s, primary emphasis was placed on the production of capital equipment.

TABLE 23.3

A Compact Summary of Key Periods in the Economic History of the People's Republic of China

Period	Main economic events/characteristics
1949	◆ People's Republic of China established under Mao Zedong
1949–1952	◆ Economy centralized under a new communist government
	◆ Emphasis on heavy industry and "socialist transformation"
1952–1957	◆ First five-year plan
1958–1960	◆ The Great Leap Forward: an economic reform plan based on labor-intensive production methods
	◆ Massive failure
1966	◆ Cultural Revolution: revolutionary zealots
1976	◆ Death of Mao Zedong
1978	◆ Deng's reforms: under leadership of Deng Xiaoping, liberalization of agriculture and introduction of individual incentives
	◆ Growth rates accelerated
1989	◆ Democracy movement, government crackdown

The Great Leap Forward

In 1958, Mao Zedong set the Chinese economy on a sharply divergent path from that which the Soviet Union had followed. Mao called his new path the Great Leap Forward. The **Great Leap Forward** was an economic plan based on small-scale, labor-intensive production. The Great Leap Forward paid little or no attention to linking individual pay to individual effort. Instead, a revolutionary commitment to the success of collective plans was relied upon. The Great Leap Forward was an economic failure. Productivity increased, but so slowly that living standards hardly changed. In the agricultural sector, massive injections of modern high-yield seeds, improved irrigation, and chemical fertilizers were insufficient to enable China to feed its population. The country became the largest importer of grains, edible vegetable oils, and even raw cotton.

The popular explanation within China for poor performance, especially in agriculture, was that the country had reached the limits of its arable land and that its population explosion was so enormous that agriculture was being forced to use substandard areas for farming. But the key problem was that the revolutionary and ideological motivation for the Great Leap Forward degenerated into what came to be called the Cultural Revolution. Revolutionary zealots denounced productive managers, engineers, scientists, and scholars and banished them to the life of the peasant. Schools and universities were closed, and the accumulation of human capital was severely disrupted.

The 1978 Reforms

By 1978, two years after the death of Mao Zedong, the new Chinese leader, Deng Xiaoping, proclaimed major economic reforms. Collectivized agriculture was abolished. Agricultural land was distributed among households on long-term leases. In exchange for a lease, a household agreed to pay a fixed tax and contracted to sell part of its output to the state. But the household made its own decisions on cropping patterns and the quantity and types of fertilizers and other inputs to use, and it also hired its own workers. Private farm markets were liberalized, and farmers received a higher price for their produce. Also, the state increased the price that it paid to farmers, especially for cotton and other nongrain crops.

The results of the reforms of Deng Xiaoping were astounding. Annual growth rates of output of cotton and oil-bearing crops increased a staggering fourteenfold. Soybean production, which had been declining at an annual rate of 1 percent between 1957 and 1978, started to grow at 4 percent a year. Growth rates of yields per acre also increased dramatically. By 1984, a country that six years earlier had been the world's largest importer of agricultural products became a food exporter!

The reforms led to more than a massive expansion in the agricultural sector. Increased rural incomes brought an expanding rural industrial sec-

tor that, by the mid-1980s, was employing a fifth of the rural population.

China has gone even further and is encouraging foreign investment and joint ventures. In addition, China is experimenting with formal capital markets and now has a stock market.

Motivated partly by political considerations, China is proclaiming the virtues of what it calls the "one country, two systems" approach to economic management. The political source of this movement is the existence of two capitalist enclaves in which China has a close interest—Taiwan and Hong Kong. China claims sovereignty over Taiwan and wants to create an atmosphere in which it becomes possible for China to be "reunified" at some future date. Hong Kong, a British crown colony, is currently leased by Britain from China, and that lease terminates in 1997. When the lease expires, Hong Kong will become part of China. Anxious not to damage the economic prosperity of Hong Kong, China is proposing to continue operating Hong Kong as a capitalist economy. With Hong Kong and Taiwan as part of the People's Republic of China, the stage will be set for the creation of other capitalist "islands" in such dynamic cities as Shanghai.

The results of this move toward capitalism in China are dramatically summarized in the country's real GDP growth statistics. Between 1978 and 1990, real GDP per person grew at an average rate of 7.2 percent a year—a 2.3-fold increase in income per person over the twelve-year period. Between 1982 and 1988, real GDP per person grew at a staggering 9.7 percent a year, almost doubling in a six-year period. To see how staggering these growth rates are, look at Fig. 23.7. It shows the consequences of China and the United States maintaining their post-1978 average growth rates of real GDP per person. For the United States, that growth rate was a little over 1 percent a year, and for China it was almost 8 percent a year. If they maintain these growth rates, China will catch up with the United States in a single generation, by 2010. Even if China's growth slackens off to 5 percent a year, with no change in the U.S. growth rate, China will catch up by 2030.

China is not only experiencing rapid growth of real income per person but is also increasing its international competitiveness. Its exports have grown during the 1980s at a much faster rate than GDP and, by 1990, stood at 17 percent of GDP.

How has China achieved this dramatic success?

FIGURE 23.7

Economic Growth in China

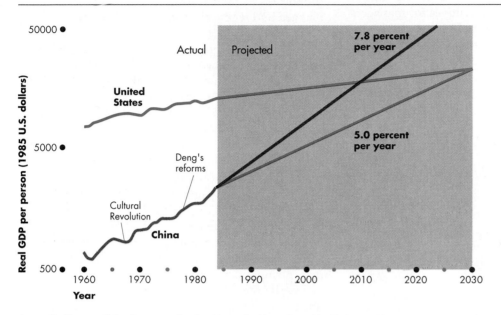

The growth of per capita income in China has been strongly influenced by the economic system. During the Cultural Revolution, per capita income fell. Under a central planning and command mechanism in the early 1970s, per capita income grew at a moderate pace. Under capitalist methods of production in agriculture following the 1978 reforms, per capita income growth increased dramatically. If China continues to grow at the pace it has achieved since 1978, and if the United States also maintains its post-1978 growth rate, China will catch up with the United States in 2010. Even if China slows to a 5 percent growth rate, it will catch up with the United States in 2030.

Source: Alan Heston and Robert Summers, "A New Set of International Comparisons of Real Product and Price Levels: Estimates for 130 Countries, 1950–1985," *Review of Income and Wealth,* series 34, vol. 1, 1988, pp. 1–25, Appendix B.

China's Success

China's success in achieving a high rate of economic growth has resulted from four features of its reforms.[1] They are

◆ Massive rate of entry of new non-state firms

◆ Increases in the productivity and profitability of state firms

◆ An efficient taxation system

◆ Gradual price deregulation

Entry of Non-State Firms   The most rapidly growing sector of the Chinese economy during the 1980s was non-state industrial firms located typically in rural areas. This sector grew at an annual rate of 17½ percent between 1978 and 1990. In 1978 this sector produced 22 percent of the nation's industrial output. By 1990 it was producing 45 percent of total industrial output. By contrast, the state-owned firms—the firms organized by the state under its national plan—shrank (relatively) from producing 78 percent of total output in 1978 to 55 percent in 1990.

The entry of new firms created a dramatic increase in competition both among the new firms and between the new firms and the state firms. This competition spurred both non-state and state firms into greater efficiency and productivity.

Increases in the Productivity and Profitability of State Firms   China has not privatized its economy by selling off state firms. Instead, privatization has come from the entry of new firms. The state firms have continued to operate. But the government has a strong incentive to ensure that the state firms are profitable. If state firms make no profit, the government collects no taxes from them.

To achieve the greatest possible level of profit and tax revenue, the Chinese economic planners have changed the incentives faced by the managers of

---

[1]This section is based on John McMillan and Barry Naughton, *How to Reform a Planned Economy: Lessons from China,* Graduate School of International Relations and Pacific Studies, University of California, San Diego, 1991.

state enterprises to resemble those of the market incentives faced by the non-state sector. Managers of state-owned firms are paid according to the firm's performance—similar to managers in private firms.

The Chinese system gives incentives for managers of state enterprises to be extremely enterprising and productive. As a result of this new system the Chinese government is now able to auction off top management jobs. Potential managers bid for the right to be manager. The manager offering the best promise of performance is the one who gets the job.

Efficient Taxation System   Firms (both private and state firms) are taxed, but the tax system is unusual and different from that in our own economy. Firms are required to pay a fixed amount of profit to the government. Once that fixed amount of tax has been paid, the firm keeps any additional profit beyond that point. In contrast, the U.S. corporate tax system requires firms to pay a fixed percentage of their profits in tax. Thus in the United States, more profit means higher taxes, while in China, taxes are set independently of a firm's profit level. The Chinese system creates much stronger incentives than does our own system for firms to seek out and pursue profitable ventures.

Gradual Price Deregulation   China has not abandoned planning its prices. The socialist planning system keeps the prices of manufactured goods fairly high and keeps domestic prices higher than world prices. This pricing arrangement makes private enterprise production in China extremely profitable. In 1978, when the non-state sector was small, the profit rate in that sector was almost 40 percent—for every dollar invested, 40¢ a year was earned. With such high profits there was a tremendous incentive for enterprising people to find niches and engage in creative and productive activity. The forces of competition have gradually lowered prices; by 1990, rates of return had fallen to 10 percent. But the price movements were gradual. There was no "big bang" adjustment of prices—no abandonment of the planning mechanism and introduction of a rip-roaring free market system.

Growing Out of the Plan

As a result of the reforms adopted in the 1970s and pursued vigorously since that time, the Chinese economy has gradually become a much more market-oriented economy and is, in effect, growing out of its central plan.[2] The proportion of the economy accounted for by private enterprise and market-influenced prices has gradually increased, and the proportion accounted for by state enterprises and planned and regulated prices has gradually decreased.

To sustain this process, changes in fiscal policy and monetary policy have been necessary. The reform of the economy has entailed the redesigning of the tax system. In a centrally planned economy the government's tax revenues come directly through its pricing policy. Also, the government, as the controller of all financial institutions, receives all of the nation's saving. When the central planning system is replaced by the market, the government must establish a tax collection agency similar to the Internal Revenue Service of the United States. Also, it must establish financial markets so that the savings of households can be channeled into the growing private firms to finance their investment in new buildings, plant, and equipment.

Despite the reform of its tax system, the government of China spends more than it receives in tax revenue and covers its deficit by the creation of money. The result is a steady rate of inflation. But the inflation in China is not out of control, as it is in the former Soviet Union, because the rapidly growing level of economic activity absorbs a great deal of the new money.

Whether China has found a way of making the transition from socialism to capitalism in a relatively painless way is a controversial issue. The violent suppression of the democracy movement in Tiananmen Square in the summer of 1989 suggests that China might have bought economic gains at the expense of political freedoms. Because China has retained a strong central government and only gradually changed its system, its experience is not directly useful to the struggling countries of Eastern Europe. But the experiment in comparative *economic* systems currently going on in China is one of the most exciting that the world has seen. Economists of all political shades of opinion will closely watch its outcome, and its lessons will be of enormous value for future generations—whatever those lessons turn out to be.

---

[2]Barry Naughton, *Growing Out of the Plan: Chinese Economic Reform, 1978–90,* Graduate School of International Relations and Pacific Studies, University of California, San Diego, 1992.

The Transition from Central Plan to Market

As the countries of Eastern Europe and China abandon their central planning systems, they must make a series of important choices. The key ones are these:

◆ The style of market economy to adopt
◆ The sequencing of reforms
◆ The speed of reforms

Styles of Market Economy

There is no unique type of market economy, and countries that formerly relied on central planning must choose from an array of possible models. The three main ones are

1. U.S.-style capitalism
2. Japanese-style capitalism
3. Welfare state capitalism

U.S.-Style Capitalism   No country relies on a pure, unregulated market mechanism to solve its economic problem. But the United States comes closer than any other country to doing so. In this country, individuals own the factors of production and decide how to use their factors to earn an income. They decide how much of their incomes to save to add to their capital resources and how much to spend, and on which goods and services. These decisions by more than 250 million individuals are coordinated in markets. Governments (federal, state, and local) regulate these markets, provide public goods and services, and tax income and expenditure. Command mechanisms similar in kind to those used in the centrally planned economies are used in the government sector and by firms in their internal planning processes.

The other types of capitalism depart from the U.S. model mainly in the degree and nature of state intervention in the economy. But there are two distinct styles.

Japanese-Style Capitalism   Japan's economic performance since World War II has been called the "Japanese economic miracle." Emerging from war

with an average income per person that was less than one fifth of that in the United States, Japan has transformed itself into an economic giant whose income per person now approaches our own. The most spectacular growth period occurred in the 25 years from 1945 to 1970, when per capita income increased eightfold. Today, Japan has a dominant position in world markets for cars and computers, audio and video equipment, and a whole range of high-tech commodities. The Japanese tourist is now as common a sight in London, Paris, and Rome as the U.S. tourist. And there are more Japanese visitors to the United States than U.S. visitors to Japan. What has led to this transformation of Japan into one of the world's most powerful and richest economies?

Three features of the Japanese economy have contributed to its dramatic success: reliance on free-market, capitalist methods; the small scale of government; and pro-business government intervention.

The economic system in Japan is like that in the United States. People are free to pursue their ideas, to own firms, to hire labor and other inputs, and to sell their outputs in relatively free markets.

The Japanese government is the smallest in the capitalist world. Average taxes and government spending account for slightly less than one fifth of GDP. This contrasts with close to 30 percent in the United States and more than 40 percent in some Western European capitalist countries. A small scale of government means that taxes are low and therefore do not constitute a discouragement to work and to saving and accumulating capital.

But the Japanese government does intervene in the economy, and its intervention is pro-business. The main vehicle for intervention is the Ministry of International Trade and Industry (MITI)—a government agency responsible for stimulating Japanese industrial development and international trade. In the years immediately following World War II, MITI encouraged the development of basic industries such as coal, electric power, shipbuilding, and steel. It used tariffs and quotas to protect these industries in their early stages of development, subsidized them, and ensured that capital resources were abundantly available for them. MITI is almost entrepreneurial in its activities. During the 1960s, with the basic industries in place, MITI turned its attention to helping the chemical and lighter manufacturing industries. In the 1980s, it helped Japanese industry dominate the world computer market.

MITI not only fosters the growth and development of industries. It also helps speed the decline of those industries that are not contributing to rapid income growth. For example, in the mid-1970s, when the price of oil increased dramatically, the smelting of bauxite to create aluminum became inefficient in Japan. Within two years, Japan's bauxite-smelting industry had been closed down, and Japan was importing all its aluminum from Australia. By identifying industries for profitable growth and those for profitable decline, MITI helps speed the adjustment process in reallocating resources to take maximum advantage of technological change and trends in prices.

The result of Japan's economic system and government economic intervention has been a high rate of capital accumulation. There has also been a high rate of accumulation of human capital, especially in the applied sciences. Going along with a high rate of capital accumulation—both physical and human—has been a high rate of technological advance with no inhibitions about using the best technologies available, wherever in the world they might have been developed.

Welfare State Capitalism   Capitalism in Western Europe is more heavily tinged with socialism than in either the United States or Japan. It is welfare state capitalism. The countries of Western Europe, many of which now belong to the European Community, are basically capitalist market economies in the sense that most productive resources are owned by private individuals and most resources are allocated by individuals trading freely in markets for both goods and services and factors of production. But the scale of government and the degree and direction of government intervention are much larger in these countries than in the United States and Japan.

Government expenditure and taxes range between 40 and 50 percent of GDP in European countries. Tax rates this high create disincentives that result, other things being equal, in less effort and lower saving rates than in countries with lower taxes. The European countries also have a large, nationalized industry sector. A **nationalized industry** is an industry owned and operated by a publicly owned authority that is directly responsible to the government. Railways, airlines, gas, electricity, telephones, radio and television broadcasting, coal, steel, banking and finance, and even automobiles are

among the industries that are either wholly or partly publicly owned in some European countries. Nationalized industries are often managed on a command rather than a market principle and usually are less efficient than privately owned, competitive firms.

Increasingly in recent years, European governments have been selling state-owned enterprises. The process of selling state-owned enterprises is called **privatization**. There has also been a retreat, in some countries, from very high tax rates. European countries, impressed by the economic success of Japan and the United States, have reached the conclusion that the greater reliance on capitalism in those economies is, in part, responsible for their economic success, and they are seeking to emulate the more successful economies.

The Sequence of Reform

We've seen that socialism and capitalism differ along two dimensions: the ownership of capital and land and the incentive structure. The features of a capitalist economy that must be adopted by a socialist economy if it is to make the transition are

◆ Private ownership of capital and natural resources
◆ Market-determined prices

In making the transition from socialism to capitalism, a country must choose the order in which to adopt these capitalist features.

By placing firms in private ownership, a formerly socialist economy gets the benefits of strengthened incentives to put resources to work at their most profitable uses. Also, by permitting the free entry of new firms, the economy is able to reap the benefits of increased competition. Both the existing firms and new firms become more efficient. At the same time, the state loses its major source of revenue—the profits of state enterprises. Thus, as industry is privatized, a taxation system must be set up to enable the state to raise the revenue needed to provide public goods and services.

By freeing markets and allowing prices to be determined by supply and demand, a formerly socialist economy gets the benefits of price signals that reflect the relative scarcity of different goods and services. These signals get translated into changes in production. Those items whose prices rise most become highly profitable, so their production increases fastest.

But often, the prices that rise the fastest are those on such basic staples as bread and milk. Because food items such as these are a very important part of the budget of the poorest families, when their prices increase sharply, there is great hardship. There is also likely to be political opposition to the reform process.

The Speed of Reform

Since reform brings turmoil, there is a case for doing it slowly—gradualism—and a case for doing it quickly—in a "big bang." The case for gradualism is that the adverse effects of reform are minimized and the transition can be managed and made smooth. The case for a big bang is that the socialist economy is a complete organism and that it cannot function unless it is left intact. Remove one piece of the system and the rest ceases to function.

◆ ◆ ◆ The countries that we've studied in this chapter—the former Soviet Union, the countries of Eastern Europe, and China—are undergoing enormous political and economic change. These changes will have repercussions throughout the world economy of the 1990s of historical proportions. No one can foresee what the world economy of the mid-1990s will look like. ◆ ◆ But the world has seen change of historical proportions before. The transformation of the economies of formerly war-torn Germany and Japan into the economic powerhouses of today is one example. Throughout all this change—past and present—our knowledge and understanding of the economic forces that produce the change and are unleashed by it have been gradually getting better. There remains a great deal that we do not understand. But we have made a great deal of progress. The economic principles presented in this book summarize this progress and the current state of knowledge. As the world continues to change, you will need a compass to guide you into unknown terrain. The principles of economics are that compass!

S U M M A R Y

The Economic Problem and Its Alternative Solutions

The economic problem is the universal fact of scarcity. Different economic systems deliver different solutions to the economic problem of determining *what, how,* and *for whom* goods and services are produced. Alternative economic systems vary in two dimensions: ownership of capital and land and the incentives people face. Capital and land may be owned by individuals, by the state, or by a mixture of the two. Incentives may be created by market prices, by administered prices and administrative sanctions, or by a mixture of the two. Economic systems differ in the ways in which they combine ownership and incentive arrangements. Capitalism is based on the private ownership of capital and land and on market price incentives. Socialism is based on state ownership of capital and land and on administrative incentives and a central economic

plan. Market socialism combines state ownership of capital and land with incentives based on a mixture of market and administered prices. Welfare state capitalism combines the private ownership of capital and land with state intervention in markets that change the price signals that people respond to. (pp. 610–615)

Economic Change in the Former Soviet Union

The Soviet Union was founded in 1917 and collapsed in 1991. The economy of the Soviet Union was based on a system of central planning that had four key elements: an administrative hierarchy, an iterative planning process, legally binding commands, and taut and inflexible plans. The Soviet Union had a market sector in which a substantial amount of economic activity took place, especially in agriculture. Money played only a minor role in the economy of the Soviet Union.

The Soviet economy grew extraordinarily quickly before 1970—in excess of 5 percent a year—but during the 1970s, and more especially during the 1980s, output growth declined. By the early 1990s, the economy was shrinking. A combination of three features of the Soviet economy caused this deterioration in economic performance: the economy made a transition from being an investment economy to being a consumption economy; the economy was hit by serious external shocks; and its taut and inflexible planning system was incapable of coping with these events.

By the end of the 1980s, the Soviet Union began a process of transition toward a market economy. This process had three main elements: the relaxation of central plan enforcement, the deregulation of prices, and the introduction of limited private ownership of firms. The transition was a process of gradual change, but it ran into severe problems. The most important were value and legal systems alien to capitalism, the collapse of traditional trade flows, and the emergence of a large state budget deficit and inflation. (pp. 615–625)

Economic Transition in Eastern Europe

The formerly planned economies of East Germany, Czechoslovakia, Hungary, and Poland are also making transitions to market economies. East Germany's transition has been the most dramatic and the most complete. It has taken the form of a reunification of the two Germanies and the adoption by the former East Germany of West Germany's monetary and taxation system. Price deregulation and privatization have been rapid. Czechoslovakia has deregulated wages, prices, and interest rates and is privatizing its industry by returning small businesses and shops to their former owners and by issuing vouchers to its citizens that they may use to buy shares in formerly state-owned enterprises. Hungary began the process of moving toward a market economy during the 1960s when central planning was replaced by decentralized planning. Hungary has established a taxation system similar to that in the market economies. But the privatization of large-scale industry began only in the 1990s and is proceeding slowly. Poland has deregulated prices, pursued a policy of financial restraint that has brought inflation under control, and put privatization on a fast track. (pp. 625–627)

Economic Transition in China

Since the foundation of the People's Republic of China, economic management has been through turbulent changes. At first, China used the Soviet system of central planning. It then introduced the Great Leap Forward, which in turn degenerated into the Cultural Revolution. China at first grew quickly with heavy reliance on state planning and capital accumulation, but growth slowed, and, at times, per capita income actually fell. In 1978, China revolutionized its economic management, placing greater emphasis on private incentives and markets. As a consequence, productivity grew at a rapid rate and per capita income increased.

China's success in achieving a high rate of economic growth has resulted from four features of its reforms: a massive rate of entry of new non-state firms, large increases in the productivity and profitability of state firms, an efficient taxation system, and gradual price deregulation. Whether China has found a way of making the transition from socialism to capitalism in a relatively painless way is a controversial issue. (pp. 627–630)

The Transition from Central Plan to Market

In the transition from central planning to the market economy, three important choices must be made: the style of market economy to adopt, the sequencing of reforms, and the speed of reforms.

There are three main types of market economy to choose from: U.S.-style capitalism, Japanese-style capitalism, and welfare state capitalism. Two features of Japanese capitalism distinguish it from U.S. capitalism: its smaller scale of government and its pro-business government intervention. The capitalism of Western Europe, welfare state capitalism, is more heavily tinged with socialism than is that of either the United States or Japan. Government expenditure and taxes are much higher there—between 40 and 50 percent of GDP—and more of the manufacturing sector is state-owned, or nationalized.

The main issue in the sequencing of reform is the order in which to privatize the ownership of capital and land and to deregulate prices. The main issue concerning the speed of reform is whether to go slowly—gradualism—or quickly—in a "big bang." (pp. 631–633)

KEY ELEMENTS

Key Terms

Capitalism, 612
Central planning, 612
Decentralized planning, 612
Great Leap Forward, 627
Hierarchy, 618
Incentive structure, 611
Market socialism, 612
Nationalized industry, 632
Privatization, 632
Socialism, 612
Welfare state capitalism, 612

Key Figures and Tables

Figure 23.1 The Fundamental Economic
            Problem, 610
Figure 23.2 Alternative Economic Systems, 611
Figure 23.3 Capitalism's Solution to the Economic
            Problem, 612
Figure 23.4 Socialism's Solution to the Economic
            Problem, 614
Table 23.1   A Compact Summary of Key Periods
            in the Economic History of the Soviet
            Union, 615
Table 23.3   A Compact Summary of Key Periods
            in the Economic History of the
            People's Republic of China, 627

REVIEW QUESTIONS

1 What is the fundamental economic problem that any economic system must solve?

2 What are the main economic systems? Set out the key features of each.

3 Give examples of countries that are capitalist, socialist, market socialist, and welfare state capitalist. (Name some countries other than those in Fig. 23.2.)

4 How does capitalism solve the economic problem? What determines how much of each good to produce?

5 How does socialism solve the economic problem? What determines how much of each good to produce?

6 How does market socialism determine the price and quantity of each good?

7 Why did the Soviet economy begin to fail in the 1980s?

8 What are the main features of the transition program in the former Soviet Union?

9 What are the main problems faced by the republics of the former Soviet Union?

10 What are the problems faced by the Eastern European countries as they make the transition to a market economy?

11 Review the main episodes in China's economic management since 1949.

12 Compare the economic growth performance of the United States and China. What do we learn from this comparison?

13 What are the lessons of the economic experiment that is going on in China?

GLOSSARY

Absolute advantage   A person has an absolute advantage in production if that person has greater productivity than anyone else in the production of all goods. A country has an absolute advantage if its output per unit of inputs of all goods is larger than that of another country.

Adverse selection   The tendency for the people who accept contracts to be those with private information that they plan to use to their own advantage and to the disadvantage of the less informed party.

Agency relationship   The relationship between a firm and its owners, managers, and workers and between a firm and other firms.

Agent   A person (or firm) hired by a firm (or another person) to do a specific job.

Allocative efficiency   The situation that occurs when no resources are wasted—when no one can be made better off without someone else being made worse off.

Antitrust law   A law that regulates and prohibits certain kinds of market behavior, such as monopoly and monopolistic practices.

Asset   Anything of value that a household, firm, or government owns.

Assortative mating   Marrying within one's own socioeconomic group.

Assumptions   The foundation on which a model is built.

Average cost pricing rule   A rule that sets the price equal to average total cost.

Average fixed cost   Total fixed cost per unit of output—total fixed cost divided by output.

Average product   Total product per unit of variable input.

Average revenue   Total revenue divided by the quantity sold. Average revenue also equals price.

Average revenue product   Total revenue divided by the quantity of the factor hired.

Average revenue product curve   A curve that shows the average revenue product of a factor at each quantity of the factor hired.

Average total cost   Total cost per unit of output—total cost divided by output.

Average variable cost   Total variable cost per unit of output—total variable cost divided by output.

Axes   The scale lines on a graph.

Balance of trade   The value of exports minus the value of imports.

Balance sheet   A list of assets and liabilities.

Barriers to entry   Legal or natural impediments protecting a firm from competition from potential new entrants.

Barter   The direct exchange of goods and services for other goods and services.

Bequest   A gift from one generation to the next.

Bilateral monopoly   A market structure in which a single buyer and a single seller confront each other.

Binding arbitration   A process in which a third party—an arbitrator—determines wages and other employment conditions on behalf of the negotiating parties and the decision is final.

Black market   An illegal trading arrangement in which buyers and sellers do business at a price that is higher than the legally imposed price ceiling.

Bond   A legally enforceable obligation to pay specified sums of money at specified future dates.

Bond market   The market in which the bonds issued by firms and governments are traded.

Bond yield   The interest on a bond expressed as a percentage of the price of the bond.

Break-even point   The output at which total revenue equals total cost (and at which profit is zero).

Budget equation   An equation that states the limits to consumption for a given income and given prices.

Budget line   The limits to a household's consumption choices.

Bureaucrats   Appointed officials who work at various levels in government departments.

Buyer's reservation price   The highest price that the buyer is willing to pay for the good.

Capacity   The output rate at which a plant's average total cost is at a minimum.

Capital   The real assets—the equipment, buildings, tools, and other manufactured goods used in production—owned by a household, firm, or government.

Capital accumulation   The growth of capital resources.

Capital goods   Goods that are added to our capital resources.

Capital-intensive technique   A method of production that uses a relatively large amount of capital and a relatively small amount of labor to produce a given quantity of output.

Capitalism   An economic system that permits private ownership of capital and land used in production and market allocation of resources.

Capture theory of regulation   A theory of regulation that states that the regulations that exist are those that maximize producer surplus.

Cartel   A group of producers that enter into a collusive agreement to restrict output in order to raise prices and profits.

Central planning   A method of allocating resources by command.

Ceteris paribus   Other things being equal, or other things remaining constant.

Change in demand   A shift of the entire demand curve that occurs when some influence on buyers' plans, other than the price of the good, changes.

Change in quantity demanded   A movement along a demand curve that results from a change in the price of the good.

Change in quantity supplied   A movement along the supply curve that results from a change in the price of the good.

Change in supply   A shift in the entire supply curve that occurs when some influence on producers' plans, other than the price of the good, changes.

Choke price   The price at which it no longer pays to use a natural resource.

Closed economy   An economy that has no links with any other economy.

Closed shop   An arrangement (illegal since the passage of the Taft-Hartley Act in 1947) in which only union members may be hired.

Collective bargaining   A process of negotiation between representatives of employers and unions.

Collusive agreement   An agreement between two or more producers to restrict output in order to raise prices and profits.

Command economy   An economy that relies on a command mechanism.

Command mechanism   A method of determining *what*, *how*, and *for whom* goods and services are produced, based on the authority of a ruler or ruling body.

Commercial bank   A private firm, chartered either by the Comptroller of the Currency (in the U.S. Treasury) or by a state agency to receive deposits and make loans.

Comparable worth   The payment of equal wages for different jobs that are judged to be comparable.

Comparative advantage   A person has a comparative advantage in producing a good if he or she can produce that good at a lower opportunity cost than anyone else. A country has a comparative advantage in producing a good if it can produce that good at a lower opportunity cost

than any other country.

Competition   A contest for command over scarce resources.

Complement   A good that is used in conjunction with another good.

Constant returns to scale   Technological conditions under which the percentage increase in a firm's output is equal to the percentage increase in its inputs.

Consumer equilibrium   A situation in which a consumer has allocated his or her income in the way that maximizes utility.

Consumer surplus   The difference between the value of a good and its price.

Consumption   The process of using up goods and services.

Consumption goods   Goods that are used up as soon as they are produced.

Cooperation   People working with others to achieve a common end.

Cooperative equilibrium   An equilibrium resulting from each player responding rationally to the credible threat of the other player to inflict heavy damage if the agreement is broken.

Coordinates   Lines running from a point on a graph perpendicularly to the axes.

Coordination mechanism   A mechanism that makes the choices of one individual compatible with the choices of others.

Corporation   A firm owned by one or more limited liability stockholders.

Countervailing duty   A tariff that is imposed to enable domestic producers to compete with subsidized foreign producers.

Craft union   A group of workers who have a similar range of skills but work for different firms and industries.

Cross elasticity of demand   The percentage change in the quantity demanded of a good divided by the percentage change in the price of another good (a substitute or complement).

Curve   Any relationship between two variables plotted on a graph, even a linear relationship.

Deadweight loss   A measure of allocative inefficiency as the reduction in consumer and producer surplus resulting from a restriction of output below its efficient level.

Decentralized planning   An economic system that combines state ownership of capital and land with incentives based on a mixture of market and administered prices.

Decreasing returns to scale   Technological conditions under which the percentage change in a firm's output is less than the percentage change in the scale of inputs; sometimes called diseconomies of scale.

Demand   The entire relationship between the quantity demanded of a good and its price.

Demand curve   A graph showing the relationship between the quantity demanded of a good and its price, holding everything else constant.

Demand schedule   A list of the quantities demanded at different prices, holding everything else constant.

Depreciation   The decrease in the value of capital stock or the value of a durable input that results from wear and tear and from the passage of time.

Deregulation   The process of removing restrictions on prices, product standards and types, and entry conditions.

Derived demand   Demand for an input not for its own sake but in order to use it in the production of goods and services.

Diminishing marginal rate of substitution   The general tendency for the marginal rate of substitution to diminish as the consumer moves along an indifference curve, increasing the con-sumption of good x and decreasing the consumption of good y.

Diminishing marginal returns   A situation in which the marginal product of the last worker hired falls short of the marginal product of the second last worker hired.

Diminishing marginal utility   The decline in marginal utility that occurs as more and more of the good is consumed.

Discounting The conversion of a future amount of money to its present value.

Diseconomies of scale Technological conditions under which the percentage change in a firm's output is less than the percentage change in the scale of inputs; sometimes called decreasing returns to scale.

Dominant strategy A strategy in a game that is the unique best action regardless of the action taken by the other player.

Dominant strategy equilibrium A Nash equilibrium in which there is a dominant strategy for each player in a game.

Double coincidence of wants A situation that occurs when person A wants to buy what person B is selling and person B wants to buy what person A is selling.

Dumping The sale of a good in a foreign market for a lower price than in the domestic market or for a lower price than its cost of production.

Duopoly A market structure in which two producers of a commodity compete with each other.

Durable input A factor of production that is not entirely used up in a single production period.

Economic activity What people do to cope with scarcity.

Economic depreciation The change in the market price of a durable input over a given period.

Economic efficiency A state in which the cost of producing a given output is as low as possible.

Economic growth The expansion of our production possibilities.

Economic information Data on prices, quantities, and qualities of goods and services and factors of production.

Economic profit Revenue minus cost when the opportunity costs of production are included in cost.

Economic rent An income received by the owner of a factor over and above the amount required to induce that owner to offer the factor for use.

Economic theory A rule or principle that enables us to understand and predict economic choices.

Economics The study of how people use their limited resources to try to satisfy unlimited wants.

Economies of scale Technological conditions under which the percentage increase in a firm's output exceeds the percentage increase in its inputs; sometimes called increasing returns to scale.

Economies of scope Decreases in average total cost made possible by increasing the number of different goods produced.

Economizing Making the best use of scarce resources.

Economy A mechanism that allocates scarce resources among competing uses.

Efficient market A market in which the actual price embodies all currently available relevant information.

Elastic demand Elasticity of demand is greater than 1; the quantity demanded of a good decreases by a larger percentage than its price increases.

Elasticity of demand The absolute value of the price elasticity of demand.

Elasticity of supply The percentage change in the quantity supplied of a good divided by the percentage change in its price.

Endowment The resources that people have.

End-state theory of distributive justice A theory of distributive justice that examines the fairness of the outcome of economic activity.

Entry The act of setting up a new firm in an industry.

Equilibrium A situation in which everyone has economized—that is, all individuals have made the best possible choices in the light of their own preferences and given their endowments, technologies, and information—and in which those choices have been coordinated and made compatible with the choices of everyone else. Equilibrium is the solution or outcome of an economic model.

Equilibrium price The price at which the quantity demanded equals the quantity supplied.

Equilibrium quantity The quantity bought and sold at the equilibrium price.

Equity or equity capital The owner's stake in a business.

Excess capacity A state in which output is below that at which average total cost is a minimum.

Excise tax A tax on the sale of a particular commodity.

Exhaustible natural resources Natural resources that can be used only once and that cannot be replaced once used.

Exit The act of closing down a firm and leaving an industry.

Expected utility The average utility arising from all possible outcomes.

Exports The goods and services that we sell to people in other countries.

External benefits Those benefits accruing to people other than the buyer of a good.

External costs Those costs not borne by the producer but borne by other members of society.

External diseconomies Factors outside the control of a firm that raise its average total cost as industry output rises.

External economies Factors beyond the control of a firm that lower its average total cost as industry output rises.

Externality A cost or a benefit arising from an economic transaction that falls on a third party and that is not taken into account by those who undertake the transaction.

Factor market A market in which the factors of production are bought and sold.

Factors of production The economy's productive resources—land, labor, and capital.

Fair Labor Standards Act An act making it illegal to hire an adult worker for less than $4.25 an hour.

Financial assets Paper claims of the holder against another household or firm.

Financial intermediary A firm that takes deposits from households and firms and makes loans to other households and firms.

Firm An institution that buys or hires factors of production and organizes them to produce and sell goods and services.

Fixed cost A cost that is independent of the output level.

Fixed inputs Those inputs whose quantity used cannot be varied in the short run.

Forward market A market in which a commitment is made at a price agreed here and now to exchange a specified quantity of a particular commodity at a specified future date.

Four-firm concentration ratio The percentage of the value of sales accounted for by the largest four firms in an industry.

Free rider Someone who consumes a good without paying for it.

Free-rider problem The tendency for the scale of provision of a public good to be too small—to be allocatively inefficient—if it is produced and sold privately.

Futures market An organized market operated on a futures exchange in which large-scale contracts for the future delivery of goods can be exchanged.

Game theory A method of analyzing strategic behavior.

General Agreement on Tariffs and Trade An international agreement that limits government intervention to restrict international trade.

Goods and services All the valuable things that people produce. Goods are tangible, and services are intangible.

Goods market A market in which goods and services are bought and sold.

Government An organization that provides goods and services to households and firms and redistributes income and wealth.

Government license A license that controls entry into particular occupations, professions, or industries.

Great Leap Forward An economic plan for postrevolutionary China based on small-scale, labor-,intensive production.

Gross investment The amount spent on replacing depreciated capital and on net additions to the capital stock.

Herfindahl-Hirschman Index An index calculated as the square of the market share (percentage) of each firm summed over the largest 50 firms (or all firms if there are fewer than 50 firms) in the market.

Hierachy An organization arranged in ranks, each rank being subordinate to the one above.

Historical cost Cost that values factors of production at the prices actually paid for them.

Horizontal integration The merger of two or more firms providing essentially the same product or service.

Hotelling Principle The proposition that the market for a stock of a natural resource is in equilibrium when the price of the resource is expected to rise at a rate equal to the interest rate.

Household Any group of people living together as a decision-making unit.

Household production The production of goods and services for consumption within the household.

Human capital The accumulated skill and knowledge of human beings; the value of a person's education and acquired skills.

Implications The outcome of a model that follows logically from its assumptions.

Implicit rental rate The rent that a firm implicitly pays to itself for the use of the durable inputs that it owns.

Imports The goods and services that we buy from people in other countries.

Imputed cost An opportunity cost that does not require an actual expenditure of cash.

Incentive structure A set of arrangements that induce people to take certain actions.

Income effect The effect of a change in income on consumption.

Income elasticity of demand The percentage change in the quantity demanded divided by the percentage change in income.

Increasing marginal returns A situation in which the marginal product of the last worker hired exceeds the marginal product of the second last worker hired.

Increasing returns to scale Technological conditions under which the percentage increase in a firm's output exceeds the percentage increase in its inputs; sometimes called economies of scale.

Indifference curve A line showing all possible combinations of two goods that give the consumer equal satisfaction.

Individual demand The relationship between the quantity of a good demanded by a single individual and its price.

Industrial union A group of workers who have a variety of skills and job types but who work for the same firm or industry.

Inelastic demand Elasticity of demand is between 0 and 1; the quantity demanded of a good decreases by a smaller percentage than its price increases.

Inferior good A good the demand for which decreases when income increases.

Information costs The cost of acquiring information on prices, quantities, and qualities of goods and services and factors of production—the opportunity cost of economic information received.

Intellectual property The intangible product of creative effort, protected by copyrights and patents. This type of property includes books, music, computer programs, and inventions of all kinds.

Inventories The stocks of raw materials, semifinished products, and unsold final goods held by firms.

Investment The purchase of new plant, equipment, and buildings and additions to inventories.

Labor The brain power and muscle power of human beings.

Labor-intensive technique A method of production that uses a relatively large amount of labor and a relatively small amount of capital to produce a given quantity of output.

Labor union An organized group of

workers whose purpose is to increase wages and influence other job conditions.

Land   Natural resources of all kinds.

Law of diminishing marginal rate of substitution   A law stating that the marginal rate of substitution of capital for labor falls as the amount of capital decreases and the amount of labor in-creases.

Law of diminishing returns   The general tendency for marginal product to eventually diminish as more of the variable input is employed, holding the quantity of fixed inputs constant.

Legal monopoly   A monopoly that occurs when a law, license, or patent restricts competition by preventing entry.

Liability   A debt—something that a household, firm, or government owes.

Linear relationship   The relationship between two variables depicted by a straight line on a graph.

Loans market   The market in which households and firms borrow and lend.

Lobbying   The activity of bringing pressure to bear on government agencies or institutions through a variety of informal mechanisms.

Local   A subunit of a union that organizes individual workers.

Lockout   The refusal by a firm to operate its plant and employ its workers.

Long run   A period of time in which the quantities of all inputs can be varied.

Long-run average cost curve   A curve that traces the relationship between the lowest attainable average total cost and output when all inputs can be varied.

Long-run cost   The cost of production when a firm uses the economically efficient plant size.

Long-run demand curve   The demand curve that describes the response of buyers to a change in price after all possible adjustments have been made.

Long-run demand for labor   The relationship between the wage rate and the quantity of labor demanded

when all inputs can be varied.

Long-run elasticity of demand for labor   The magnitude of the percentage change in the quantity of labor demanded divided by the percentage change in the wage rate when all inputs are varied.

Long-run supply curve   The supply curve that describes the response of the quantity supplied to a change in price after all technologically possible adjustments to supply have been exploited.

Lorenz curve   A curve that shows the cumulative percentage of income or wealth against the cumulative percentage of families or population.

Macroeconomics   The branch of economics that studies the economy as a whole. Macroeconomics is concerned with the overall level of economic activity rather than with detailed individual choices.

Marginal benefit   The increase in total benefit resulting from a one-unit increase in the scale of provision of a public good.

Marginal cost   The increase in total cost resulting from a one-unit increase in output.

Marginal cost pricing rule   The rule that sets price equal to marginal cost.

Marginal private cost   The marginal cost directly incurred by the producer of a good.

Marginal product   The increase in total product resulting from a one-unit increase in a variable input.

Marginal product of capital   The change in total product resulting from a one-unit increase in the quantity of capital employed, holding the quantity of labor constant.

Marginal product of labor   The change in total product (output) resulting from a one-unit increase in the quantity of labor employed, holding the quantity of all other inputs constant.

Marginal rate of substitution   The rate at which a person will give up one good in order to get more of another good and at the same time remain indifferent.

Marginal revenue   The change in total revenue resulting from a one-

unit increase in the quantity sold.

Marginal revenue product   The change in total revenue resulting from employing one more unit of a factor.

Marginal revenue product curve   A curve that shows the marginal revenue product of a factor at each quantity of the factor hired.

Marginal social benefit   The dollar value of the benefit from one additional unit of consumption, including the benefit to the buyer and any indirect benefits accruing to other members of society.

Marginal social cost   The cost of producing one additional unit of output, including the costs borne by the producer and any other costs indirectly incurred by any other member of society; the marginal cost incurred by the producer of a good together with the marginal cost imposed as an externality on others.

Marginal utility   The change in total utility resulting from a one-unit increase in the quantity of a good consumed.

Marginal utility per dollar spent   The marginal utility obtained from the last unit of a good consumed divided by the price of the good.

Market   Any arrangement that facilitates buying and selling of a good, service, factor of production, or future commitment.

Market activity   The supplying of labor through the market.

Market constraints   The conditions under which a firm can buy its inputs and sell its output.

Market demand   The relationship between the total quantity of a good demanded and its price.

Market economy   An economy that determines *what*, *how*, and *for whom* goods and services are produced by coordinating individual choices through markets.

Market failure   The inability of an unregulated market to achieve, in all circumstances, allocative efficiency.

Market income   A person's income in the absence of government redistribution.

Market socialism   An economic system that combines state ownership of capital and land with incentives based on a mixture of market and administered prices.

Median voter theorem The proposition that political parties will pursue policies that maximize the net benefit of the median voter.

Medium of exchange Anything that is generally acceptable in exchange for goods and services.

Merger The combining of the assets of two firms to form a single, new firm.

Microeconomics The branch of economics that studies the decisions of individual households and firms and the way in which individual markets work. Microeconomics also studies the way in which taxes and government regulation affect our economic choices.

Minimum wage law A regulation that makes trading labor below a specified wage illegal.

Mixed economy An economy that relies partly on markets and partly on a command mechanism to coordinate economic activity.

Mixed good A good that lies between a private good and a pure public good.

Momentary supply curve The supply curve that describes the immediate response of the quantity supplied to a change in price.

Monetary exchange A system in which some commodity or token serves as the medium of exchange.

Money Any commodity or token that is generally acceptable as a means of payment for goods and services.

Monopolistic competition A market type in which a large number of firms compete with each other by making similar but slightly different products.

Monopoly The sole supplier of a good, service, or resource that has no close substitutes and in which there is a barrier preventing the entry of new firms.

Monopsony A market structure in which there is just a single buyer.

Moral hazard When one of the parties to an agreement has an incentive, after the agreement is made, to act in a manner that benefits himself or herself at the expense of the other party.

Nash equilibrium The outcome of a game in which player A takes the best possible action given the action of player B and player B takes the best possible action given the action of player A.

Nationalized industry An industry owned and operated by a publicly owned authority that is directly responsible to the government.

Natural monopoly A monopoly that occurs when there is a unique source of supply of a raw material or when one firm can supply the entire market at a lower price than two or more firms can.

Natural resources The nonproduced factors of production with which we are endowed—all the gifts of nature, including land, water, air, and all the minerals that they contain.

Negative income tax A redistribution scheme that gives every family a *guaranteed annual income* and decreases the family's benefit at a specified *benefit loss rate* as its market income increases.

Negative relationship A relationship between two variables that move in opposite directions.

Net benefit Total benefit minus total cost.

Net exporter A country whose value of exports exceeds its value of imports—its balance of trade is positive.

Net financial assets Financial assets minus financial liabilities.

Net importer A country whose value of imports exceeds its value of exports—its balance trade is negative.

Net investment Net additions to the capital stock—gross investment minus depreciation.

Net present value The sum of the present values of payments spread over several years.

Net present value of an investment The present value of a stream of marginal revenue product generated by the investment minus the cost of the investment.

Nonexhaustible natural resources Natural resources that can be used repeatedly without depleting what is available for future use.

Nonmarket activity Leisure and nonmarket production activities, including housework, education, and training.

Nontariff barriers Any action other than a tariff that restricts international trade.

Normal good A good the demand for which increases when income increases.

Normative statement A statement about what *ought* to be. An expression of an opinion that cannot be verified by observation.

Oligopoly A market type in which a small number of producers compete with each other.

Open economy An economy that has economic links with other economies.

Open shop An arrangement in which no requirement is placed on an individual worker to join a union.

Opportunity cost The best forgone alternative.

Optimal search rule A rule that says that the buyer searches until an item is found at or below the buyer's reservation price and then stops searching and buys.

Optimizing The process of balancing benefits against costs and doing the best within the limits of what is possible.

Origin The zero point that is common to both axes on a graph.

Overutilized capacity When a plant produces more than the output at which average total cost is a minimum.

Partnership A firm with two or more owners who have unlimited liability.

Patent An exclusive right granted by the government to the inventor of a product or service.

Payoff The score of each player in a game.

Payoff matrix A table that shows the payoffs resulting from every possible action by each player for every possible action by each other player.

Perfect competition A state that occurs in markets in which a large number of firms sell an identical product; there are many buyers; there are no restrictions on entry; firms have no advantage over potential new entrants; and all firms and buyers are fully informed about the prices of each and every firm.

Perfect price discrimination The practice of charging a different price for each unit sold and of charging each consumer the maximum price that he or she is willing to pay for each unit bought.

Perfectly competitive firm's supply curve A curve that shows how a perfectly competitive firm's output varies as the market price varies, other things remaining constant.

Perfectly elastic demand Elasticity of demand is infinite; the quantity demanded becomes zero if the price rises by the smallest amount, and the quantity demanded becomes infinite if the price falls by the smallest amount.

Perfectly inelastic demand Elasticity of demand is zero; the quantity demanded does not change as the price rises.

Physical assets Buildings, plant and equipment, inventories, and consumer durable goods.

Physical limits The maximum output that a plant can produce.

Political equilibrium A situation in which the choices of voters, politicians, and bureaucrats are all compatible and in which no one group of agents will be better off by making a different choice.

Politicians Elected officials in federal, state, and local government—from chief executives (the president, state governors, and mayors) to members of the legislature (state and federal senators and repr-esentatives and city councilors).

Portfolio choice A choice concerning which assets and liabilities to hold.

Positive relationship A relationship between two variables that move in the same direction.

Positive statement A statement about what *is*. Something that can be verified by careful observation.

Poverty An income level measured by a poverty index first calculated by the Social Security Administration in 1964.

Preferences People's likes and dislikes and the intensity of those likes and dislikes.

Present value The value in the present of a future amount of money; equal to the amount that, if invested today, will grow as large as that future amount, taking into account the interest that it will earn.

Price discrimination The practice of charging some customers a higher price than others for an identical good or of charging an individual customer a higher price on a small purchase than on a large one.

Price effect The effect of a change in the price on the quantity of a good consumed.

Price elasticity of demand The responsiveness of the quantity demand of a good to a change in its price. It is measured by the percentage change in the quantity demanded of a good divided by the percentage change in its price.

Price taker A firm that cannot influence the price of its product.

Principal A firm (or person) that hires a person (or firm) to undertake a specific job.

Principle of minimum differentiation The tendency for competitors to make themselves almost identical in order to appeal to the maximum number of clients or voters.

Private enterprise An economic system that permits individuals to decide on their own economic activities.

Private good A good or service, each unit of which is consumed by only one individual.

Private information Information that is available to one person but is too costly for anyone else to obtain.

Private property right A legally established title to the sole ownership of a scarce resource.

Privatization The process of selling state-owned enterprises to private individuals and firms.

Probability A number between 0 and 1 that measures the chance of some possible event occurring.

Process theory of distributive justice A theory of distributive justice that examines the fairness of the *mechanism* or *process* that results in a given distribution.

Producer surplus The difference between a producer's revenue and the opportunity cost of production.

Product differentiation Making a product slightly different from that of a competing firm.

Production The conversion of natural, human, and capital resources into goods and services.

Production function A relationship showing how output varies as the employment of inputs is varied.

Production possibility frontier The boundary between attainable and unattainable levels of production.

Productivity The amount of output produced per unit of inputs used to produce it.

Professional association An organized group of professional workers such as lawyers, dentists, or doctors that seeks to influence the compensation and other labor market conditions affecting its members.

Profit maximization Making the largest possible profit.

Progressive income tax An income tax at a marginal rate that rises with the level of income.

Property Anything of value that is owned.

Property rights Social arrangements that govern the ownership, use, and disposal of economic resources.

Proportional income tax An income tax that is at a constant rate regardless of the level of income.

Proprietorship A firm with a single owner who has unlimited liability.

Protectionism The restriction of international trade.

Public choice theory A theory predicting the behavior of the government sector of the economy as the outcome of the individual choices made by voters, politicians, and bureaucrats interacting with each other in a political marketplace.

Public franchise An exclusive right granted to a firm to supply a good or service.

Public interest theory   A theory predicting that government action will take place to eliminate waste and achieve an efficient allocation of resources.

Public interest theory of regulation   A theory of regulation that states that regulations are supplied to satisfy the demand of consumers and producers for the maximization of total surplus—or the attainment of allocative efficiency.

Pure public good   A good each unit of which is consumed by everyone and from which no one can be excluded.

Quantity demanded   The amount of a good or service that consumers plan to buy in a given period of time at a particular price.

Quantity supplied   The amount of a good or service that producers plan to sell in a given period of time at a particular price.

Quota   A restriction on the quantity of a good that a firm is permitted to produce or that a country is permitted to import.

Rate of return regulation   A regulation that sets the price at a level that enables the regulated firm to earn a specified target percent return on its capital.

Rational choice   The choice that, among all possible choices, best achieves the goals.

Rational expectation   A forecast that uses all of the relevant information available about past and present events and that has the least possible error.

Rational ignorance   The decision not to acquire information because the cost of acquiring the information is greater than the benefit derived from having it.

Rawlsian theory of fairness   A theory of distributive justice that gives the biggest income possible to the least well-off.

Real income   Income expressed in units of goods. Real income in terms of a particular good is income divided by the price of that good.

Regressive income tax   An income tax at a marginal rate that falls with the level of income.

Regulation   Rules administered by a government agency to restrict economic activity by determining prices, product standards and types, and the conditions under which new firms may enter an industry.

Relative price   The ratio of the price of one good to the price of another.

Rent ceiling   A regulation making it illegal to charge a rent higher than a specified level.

Rent seeking   The activity of attempting to create a monopoly.

Reservation wage   The lowest wage rate at which a person or household will supply labor to the market. Below that wage, a person will not work.

Returns to scale   Increases in output that result from increasing all the inputs by the same percentage.

Right-to-work law   A law allowing an individual to work at any firm without joining a union.

Risk   A state in which more than one outcome may occur and the probability of each possible outcome can be estimated.

Saving   Income minus consumption. Saving is measured in the national income accounts as disposable income (income less taxes) minus consumption expenditure.

Scarcity   The universal state in which wants exceed resources.

Scatter diagram   A diagram that plots the value of one economic variable associated with the value of another.

Search activity   The time and effort spent in searching for someone with whom to do business.

Self-sufficiency   A state that occurs when people produce only enough for their own consumption.

Short run   A period of time in which the quantity of at least one input is fixed and the quantities of the other input can be varied.

Short-run demand curve   The demand curve that describes the initial response of buyers to a change in the price of a good.

Short-run demand for labor   The relationship between the wage rate and the quantity of labor demanded when the firm's capital input is fixed and labor is the only variable input.

Short-run elasticity of demand for labor   The magnitude of the percentage change in the quantity of labor demanded divided by the percentage change in the wage rate when labor is the only variable input.

Short-run industry supply curve   A curve that shows how the total quantity supplied in the short run by all firms in an industry varies as the market price varies.

Short-run supply curve   The supply curve that describes the response of the quantity supplied to a change in price when only *some* of the technologically possible adjustments have been made.

Shutdown point   The quantity and price at which the firm is just covering its total variable cost.

Signal   An action taken outside a market that conveys information that can be used by that market.

Single-price monopoly   A monopoly that charges the same price for each and every unit of output.

Slope   The change in the value of the variable measured on the y-axis divided by the change in the value of the variable measured on the x-axis.

Socialism   An economic system based on state ownership of capital and land and on an incentive system based on administered prices or sanctions arising from a central economic plan.

Specialization   The production of only one good or a few goods.

Stock exchange   An organized market for trading in stock.

Stock market   The market in which the equities of firms are traded.

Stock yield   The income from a share in the stock of a firm expressed as a percentage of the price of the share.

Strategic behavior   Acting in a way that takes into account the expected behavior of others and the mutual recognition of interdependence.

Strategies   All the possible actions of each player.

Strike   The refusal of a group of workers to work under the prevailing conditions.

Subsidy   A payment made by the government to producers that depends on the level of output.

Substitute   A good that may be used in place of another good.

Substitution effect   The effect of a change in price on the quantities consumed when the consumer remains indifferent between the original and the new combinations of goods consumed.

Sunk costs   The historical cost of buying plant and machinery that have no current resale value.

Supply   The entire relationship between the quantity supplied of a good and its price.

Supply curve   A graph showing the relationship between the quantity supplied and the price of a good, holding everything else constant.

Supply schedule   A list of quantities supplied at different prices, holding everything else constant.

Takeover   The purchase of the stock of one firm by another firm.

Tariff   A tax on an import by the government of the importing country.

Team production   A production process in which individuals work in a group and each individual specializes in mutually supportive tasks.

Technique   Any feasible way of converting inputs into output.

Technological efficiency   A state in which it is not possible to increase output without increasing inputs.

Technological progress   The development of new and better ways of producing goods and services.

Technology   The method for converting resources into goods and services.

Theory of distributive justice   A set of principles against which we can test whether a particular distribution of economic well-being is fair.

Time-series graph   A graph showing the value of a variable on the y-axis plotted against time on the x-axis.

Tit-for-tat strategy   A strategy in which a player cooperates in the current period if the other player cooper-ated in the previous period but cheats in the current period if the other player cheated in the previous period.

Total benefit   The total dollar value that a person places on a given level of provision of a public good.

Total cost   The sum of the costs of all the inputs used in production.

Total fixed cost   The cost of all the fixed inputs.

Total product   The total quantity produced by a firm in a given period of time.

Total product curve   A graph showing the maximum output attainable with a given amount of capital as the amount of labor employed is varied.

Total surplus   The sum of consumer surplus and producer surplus.

Total utility   The total benefit or satisfaction that a person gets from the consumption of goods and services.

Total variable cost   The cost of variable inputs.

Transactions costs   The costs arising from finding someone with whom to do business, reaching an agreement about the price and other aspects of the exchange, and ensuring that the terms of the agreement are fulfilled.

Transfer earnings   The income required to induce the owner to offer the factor of production for use.

Trend   A general tendency for a variable to rise or fall.

Trigger strategy   A strategy in which a player cooperates if the other player cooperates but plays the Nash equilibrium strategy forever thereafter if the other player cheats.

Uncertainty   A state in which more than one event may occur but we don't know which one.

Union shop   An arrangement in which a firm may hire nonunion workers but, in order for such workers to remain employed, they must join the union within a brief period specified by the union.

Unit elastic demand   An elasticity of demand of 1; the quantity demanded of a good and its price change in equal proportions.

Utilitarian theory   The theory that the fairest outcome is the one that maximizes the sum of the utilities of all individuals in a society.

Utility   The benefit or satisfaction that a person obtains from the consumption of a good or service.

Utility of wealth schedule (or curve)   A schedule or curve that describes how much utility a person attaches to each level of wealth.

Utility maximization   The attainment of the greatest possible utility.

Value   The maximum amount that a person is willing to pay for a good.

Variable cost   A cost that varies with the output level.

Variable inputs   Those inputs whose quantity used can be varied in the short run.

Vertical integration   The merger of two or more firms operating at different stages in the production process of a single good or service.

Voluntary export restraint   A self-imposed restriction by an exporting country on the volume of its exports of a particular good. Voluntary export restraints are often called VERs.

Voters   The consumers of the outcome of the political process.

Wants   The unlimited desires or wishes that people have for goods and services.

Wealth   Total assets of a household, firm, or government minus its total liabilities.

Welfare state capitalism   An economic system that combines the private ownership of capital and land with state interventions in markets that change the price signals that people respond to.

x-axis   The horizontal scale on a graph.

x-coordinate   A line running from a point on a graph horizontally to the y-axis. It is called the x-coordinate because its length is the same as the value marked off on the x-axis.

y-axis   The vertical scale on a graph.

y-coordinate   A line running from a point on a graph vertically to the x-axis. It is called the y-coordinate because its length is the same as the value marked off on the y-axis.

INDEX

Key concepts and pages on which they are defined appear in boldface.

Absolute advantage, **62**, 590–591
Ad valorem tax, 547
Advantage
  absolute, 62, 590–591
  comparative, 60–61, 64–65, 587
Adverse selection, 469
Advertising
  in monopolistic competition, 350
  for persuasion or information, 468
  prices and, 468
  for profit maximization, 468
AFC. *See* Average fixed cost
AFDC. *See* Aid to Families with
  Dependent Children
AFL. *See* American Federation of Labor
AFL-CIO, 411
Agency relationships, 209
Agent, 209, 210
Aid to Families with Dependent Children
  (AFDC), 493
Air Line Pilots Association, 418
Airline industry
  external diseconomies and, 299, 301
  regulation of, 558
  rent seeking and, 334
Alchian, Armen, 225
ALCOA, 571
Allis-Chalmers, 365–366
Allocative efficiency, 305, 305–308
  government and, 518
  of monopolistic competition, 350
  monopoly and competition compared
  and, 330–331
AMA. *See* American Medical Association
American Airlines Inc., 328
American Federation of Labor (AFL), 411
American Federation of State, County, and
  Municipal Employees, 411
American Medical Association (AMA),
  412
American Stock Exchange (ASE), 213
American Telephone and Telegraph
  Company (AT&T), 558, 571, 574
American Tobacco Company, 570, 571
Andean Pact, 598, 599
Antitrust laws, 559, 570–574
  landmark cases and, 570–571, 574
  public and special interests and, 574
Apparel industry, trade restrictions and,
  602
Apple Computer, 208
Arrow, Kenneth, interview with, 274–277
ASE. *See* American Stock Exchange
Asia, stock markets in, 442–443
Assets, 429
  financial, 429–431
  net financial, 429, 431
  physical, 429–430, 431
  prices of, interest rates and, 440–445
  tangible, 497
Assortative mating, 504

Assumptions, 19, 19–20
AT&T. *See* American Telephone and
  Telegraph Company
Atari Computer Company, 445
ATC. *See* Average total cost
Atkinson, Tony, interview with, 454–457
Austro-Hungarian Empire, 625
Automobile industry, cost curves for,
  246–247
AVC. *See* Average variable cost
Average cost curve, long-run, 251–255
Average cost pricing rule, 565
Average fixed cost (AFC), 242, 243
Average product, 237, 237–238, 240
  marginal product and, 238
Average product curve, shape of, 238–239
Average revenue, 282
Average revenue product, 382, 383
Average revenue product curve, 383
Average total cost (ATC), 242, 243
Average variable cost (AVC), 242, 243
Axes, 29
  breaks in, 31

Balance of trade, 583, 585–586
Balance sheet, 429
  for United States, 432–434
Barriers to entry, 314
  concentration ratios and, 344
  legal, 314
  natural, 314–315
Barter, 66
Becker, Gary, 173
Benefit(s)
  cost-benefit analysis and, 86
  external, 306, 307, 519, 529, 532. *See*
  also Externalities
  marginal, 521
  net, 523
  public goods and, 521–523, 524
  social, 306
  total, 521
Benefit-loss rate, 494
Bentham, Jeremy, 173
Bequests, 504
Best affordable point, 190
"Big tradeoff," between fairness and eco-
  nomic efficiency, 508
Bilateral monopoly, 418
Binding arbitration, 411, 412
Black market, 130. *See also* Illegal drugs
Bond(s), 213
  present value of, 215–217
  selling, 213, 214
Bond market, 432
Bond yield, 440
Boulding, Kenneth E., 256
Braniff, 289
Break-even point, 282
Brown Shoe, 571, 574

Buchanan, James, 507
Budget equation, 181, 181–182
Budget line, 180, 180–181
  best affordable point on, 190
Bureaucrats, 538, 538–539
  behavior of, 545–546
Business finance, 212–221
  cost and profit and, 218–221
  financing decisions and stock prices
  and, 214–217
  how firms raise capital and, 212–214
Business names, 220
Buyer's reservation price, 467

CAB. *See* Civil Aeronautics Board
Canada, U.S. trade with, 584, 595
Canada–United States free trade agreement, 595
Capacity, 248
  capacity utilization puzzle and, 248
  excess, 248, 258
  overutilized, 248
Capital, 14, 429
  demand for, 434–438
  equity, 212, 213
  how firms raise, 212–214
  human, 51, 408, 421, 497–498
  investment and, 430
  marginal product of, 250
  nonhuman, 497–498
  private and state ownership of,
  610–611
  substitutability of labor and, 264–265,
  387
  supply of, 390–391, 438–439
Capital accumulation, 57, 57–59
Capital goods, 51
Capital-intensive technique, 233
Capital markets
  equilibrium in, 393, 396–397
  in United States, 431–434
Capitalism, 63, 611, 612, 612–613, 615,
  617
  Japanese-style, 631–632
  private enterprise, property rights in,
  63, 66
  transition to, 632–633
  U.S.-style, 631
  welfare state, 611, 612, 632
Capture theory of regulation, 561, 565,
  567
Caribbean Community (Caricom), 598
Cartels, 357. *See also* Organization of
  Petroleum Exporting Countries
  regulation of, 567–569
Carter, Jimmy, 537
Cellar-Kefauver Amendment (1950), 570
Central American common market, 598,
  599
Central planning, 612

Centrally planned economies, 7, 612, 613, 614, 615, 616–617
  administrative hierarchy and, 618
  iterative planning process and, 615, 618–619
  legally binding commands and, 619
  Soviet, 618–619
  taut and inflexible plans and, 619
  transition to market economy from, 631–632
Ceteris paribus, 44, 44–45
  law of demand and, 73
CFCs. *See* Chlorofluorocarbons
Change in demand, 75–76, 77
  for capital, 437
  change in quantity demanded versus, 77–78
  expected future prices and, 75–76
  income and, 75
  population and, 76
  predicting changes in price and quantity traded and, 85, 88, 89, 92–93
  preferences and, 76
  prices of related goods and, 75
Change in supply, 79–80, 81
  of capital, 439
  change in quantity demanded versus, 81–82
  number of suppliers and, 80
  predicting changes in price and quantity traded and, 88–93
  prices and, 80
  technology and, 80
Change in the quantity demanded, 77
  change in demand versus, 77–78
Change in the quantity supplied, 81
  change in supply versus, 81–82
Cheating, on collusive agreements, 359–362
Chiang Kai-shek (Jiang Jie-shi), 627
Chicago's "Magnificent Mile," 377, 392, 397
China. *See* People's Republic of China; Taiwan
Chlorofluorocarbons (CFCs), 7, 518, 525
Choice, 189–199. *See also* Public choice; Public choice theory
  best affordable point and, 190
  coordination of, 19–20
  income and wealth distribution and, 502–505
  model of, 195–196
  portfolio, 430
  rational, 19
  saving and, 197
  scarcity and, 10
  utility-maximizing, 162
  work hours and labor supply and, 196–197, 198–199
Choke price, 447
CIO. *See* Congress of Industrial Organizations
CIS. *See* Commonwealth of Independent States
Civil Aeronautics Board (CAB), 558, 562
Civil Rights Act (1964), 422
Clayton Act (1914), 570
Closed economy, 16
Closed shop, 411, 412
Coase, Ronald H., 225, 256, 257, 507, 616

interview with, 203–206
Collective bargaining, 411, 412
Collusive agreement, 357, 357–364
  cheating on, 359–362
  cost and demand conditions and, 357–358
  payoff matrix and equilibrium and, 362–363
  price wars and, 365–366
  profit maximization and, 358–359
  regulation of cartels and, 567–569
  repeated games and, 363–364
  uncertainty and, 364
Command economy, 15, 15–16
Command mechanisms, 15, 15–16
Common stock, 213
Commonwealth of Independent States (CIS), 615–625, 616. *See also* Soviet Union
  command economy of, 16
  economic system in, 609
  economic system of, 7
  transition problems in, 621, 624–625
Communism, 617
Comparable worth, 422–424, 423
Comparative advantage, 60, 60–61, 64–65, 587
Competition, 11, 278–309
  allocative efficiency and, 330–331
  monopolistic. *See* Monopolistic competition
  monopoly compared with, 328–336
  perfect. *See* Perfect competition
  price and output and, 329–330
  redistribution and, 330, 331, 332–333
  rent seeking and, 331, 334
Complements, 75, 80
  elasticity of demand and, 115
  preferences and, 188–189
Computers, 18
Concentration ratios, 342–345
  four-firm, 342–343
  limitations of, 344–345
  in U.S. economy, 343–344
Congress of Industrial Organizations (CIO), 411
Conservation, 450–451
Constant returns to scale, 250
Constraints
  consumption and, 180–181
  on firm, 233–240
  household consumption choices and, 159
  market, 233
  technology. *See* Technology constraint of unions, 413
Consumer behavior, 191–195
  demand curve and, 191, 192
  income effect and, 192–193, 194
  price effect and, 191, 194, 195
  substitution effect and, 192, 193, 195
Consumer choice. *See* Choice
Consumer equilibrium, 162
Consumer surplus, 171, 559–560
  calculating, 171, 174
  marginal utility and, 171, 174
  monopoly and competition compared and, 330
  price discrimination and, 324–325
Consumption, 51
  changes in, gains from trade and, 589–590

income related to, 31
  Soviet transition from investment to, 620
Consumption goods, 51
Consumption possibilities, 180–184
  budget equation and, 181–182
  change in income and, 184
  changes in prices and, 182–184
  constraints on, 180–181
  divisible and indivisible goods and, 181
Convertible stock, 213
Cooperation, 11
Cooperative equilibrium, 364
Coordinates, 30
Coordination mechanisms, 14–16, 19–20
  command, 15–16
  firm, 224–227
  market, 15, 224
Copyright Royalty Tribunal, 562
Corporation, 210, 210–212
  methods of raising capital, 212–214
Cost(s), 209–210, 220–221
  average, 242, 243, 251–255
  collusive agreements and, 357–358
  dollar, 10
  of economic growth, 57
  external, 10, 306, 307, 519, 528–529, 548–549. *See also* Externalities
  fixed, 240, 243
  historical, 218, 220
  imputed, 219
  inflating, regulation and, 566–567
  information, 466
  of interest, 219
  of inventory, 220
  long-run, 248–249, 251–255
  marginal, 242, 243, 272–273, 284–286, 529
  opportunity. *See* Opportunity cost
  private, marginal, 529
  public goods and, 521–523, 524
  of risk, 461–462
  short-run, 240–248, 256
  social, 306, 529
  sunk, 219
  time, 10
  total, 240–242, 243, 255, 282
  transaction, 224–225
  variable, 240, 243, 287
Cost-benefit analysis, 86
Cost curves
  for auto plant, 246–247
  long-run average, 251–255, 256
  shifts in, 255
  short-run, 242–243
  short-run average, 256
  technology constraint and, 244
Countervailing duties, 603
Coupon payment, 213
Cournot, Antoine-Augustin, 87, 322
Craft union, 411
Credit. *See also* Loans
  markets for, private information and, 472–475
Cross elasticity of demand, 114, 115, 118
Cultural Revolution, 628
Current period supply curve, 479
Curve, 38
Czechoslovakia, economic transition in, 626

De Beers, 314
Deadweight losses, 331, 548
  minimizing, 549–550
Decentralized planning, 612
Decision(s), 14
  financing, 214–217
  of firm, 209–210
Decision makers. *See* Firm(s);
  Government; Household(s)
Decreasing returns to scale, 250
Demand, 73–78, 75
  buying plans and, 73
  for capital, 434–438
  change in. *See* Change in demand
  collusive agreements and, 357–358
  derived, 380
  elastic, 106, 115, 316, 318
  elasticity of. *See* Elasticity of demand
  expected, 478
  for factors, 378–387. *See also* Labor
    demand
  individual, 158–159
  inelastic, 106, 115, 316, 318
  for labor. *See* Labor demand
  law of, 73–74, 86–87
  market, 158–159
  for natural resources, 446, 447
  perfectly elastic, 106, 115, 138–139
  perfectly inelastic, 106, 115, 138
  permanent decrease in, 296–297
  permanent increase in, 297–299
  quantity demanded and, 73
  for regulation, 560
  single-price monopoly and, 315–316,
    317
  unit elastic, 106–107, 115, 316, 318
Demand curve, 74
  for capital, 436–437
  constant elasticity, 108
  consumer behavior and, 191, 192
  kinked, 351–352
  long-run, 110–111, 112
  movement along, 76, 77
  shifts in, 76–77, 385–386
  short-run, 110, 111, 112
  straight-line, elasticity along, 107–108
  willingness to pay and, 74–75, 84
Demand schedule, 74
Demsetz, Harold, 225
Deng Xiaoping, 628
Depreciation, 218, 430
  economic, 219
Deregulation, 559
Derived demand, 380
**Diminishing marginal rate of substitution,
  187**
  law of, 264–265
Diminishing marginal returns, 239, 242
Diminishing marginal utility, 160,
  160–161
Diminishing returns, 250
  law of, 239, 263–264
  marginal, 239
Discounting, 215
Discrimination, wage differentials and,
  419–421
Diseconomies of scale, 250, 250–251
  external, 299, 302
Disposable diaper industry, R&D game in,
  366–367
Disraeli, Benjamin, 28
Diversification, to lower risk, 476–477

Dollar cost, 10
Dominant strategy, 356
Dominant strategy equilibrium, 356
Domino's Pizza, Inc., 300–301
Double coincidence of wants, 66
Drugs, illegal. *See* Illegal drugs
Dumping, 603
Duopoly, 355. *See also* Collusive agree-
  ment; Oligopoly
Dupuit, Jules, 86, 87
Durable inputs, 218
Duties. *See* Tariffs

Earnings. *See also* Income; Wage(s)
  economic questions and, 7
  ratio of price to, 216, 441, 444
  transfer, 400–402
East Germany
  economic system in, 609
  economic transition in, 625–626
Easterlin, Richard, interview with,
  152–155
Eastern European countries, 616
  economic systems in, 7, 16, 609
  economic transition in, 625–627
  Soviet trade with, 620
Economic activity, 9, 9–10
Economic depreciation, 219
Economic efficiency, 222, 223, 268–271
  tradeoff between fairness and, 508
Economic growth, 57, 57–60
  capital accumulation and technological
    change and, 57–59
  cost of, 57
  in real world, 59–60
Economic information, 466, 466–469
  advertising and, 468
  searching for price information and,
    466–468, 470–471
Economic models, 18–21
  assumptions of, 19–20
  graphs used in, 38–41
  implications of, 20
  microeconomic and macroeconomic,
    20–21
  production possibilities frontier and,
    51–53
  theory and reality and, 21, 24
Economic problem, 12
  alternative economic systems and,
    610–615
  command coordination and, 15–16
  market coordination and, 15
  technology and, 7–9
Economic profit, 220
Economic rent, 400, 400–402
Economic systems, 608–634. *See also*
  Capitalism; Centrally planned
  economies; Market economy;
  Socialism
  in China, 609, 627–630
  in Eastern European countries, 609,
    625–627
  economic problem and, 7, 610–615
  in former Soviet Union, 609, 615–625
  sequence of reform in, 632–633
  transition from centrally planned econo-
    my to market economy and,
    631–632
  types of, 611–612

Economic theory, 18
  models and reality and, 21, 24
Economically efficient technique, 268–271
Economics, 9, 9–10, 17–24
  limits of, 142
  models and. *See* Economic models
  observation and measurement and, 18
  positive and normative analysis and,
    519
  positive and normative statements and,
    17–18
  theory and, 18, 21, 24
  welfare, 507
Economies of scale, 225, 250, 250–251
  external, 299, 302
  gains from trade and, 594–595
  monopoly and, 335
Economies of scope, 335
  monopoly and, 335–336
Economizing, 10
Economy, 12, 12–17
  closed, 16
  command, 15–16. *See also* Centrally
    planned economies
  coordination mechanisms and, 14–16
  decision makers and, 13–14
  decisions and, 14
  definition of, 12–13
  global, 16–17
  market. *See* market economy
  markets and, 14. *See also* Market(s)
  mixed, 16
  open, 16–17
Education
  income distribution and, 488–489
  wages and, 410
Efficiency, 305–308
  allocative, 305–308, 330–331, 350, 518
  economic, 222, 223, 268–271, 508
  obstacles to, 307–308
  technological, 222–223
Efficient market, 480
Ehrlich, Paul, 398
Einstein, Albert, 24
Elastic demand, 106, 115, 316, 318
Elasticity of demand, 103–118, 105
  along straight-line demand curve, 107
  average prices and quantity and,
    105–106
  calculating, 104–105
  constant demand curves and, 108
  cross, 114, 115, 118
  elastic and inelastic demand and,
    106–107
  farm revenue and, 145–146
  income, 112–114, 115
  for industry and firm, 280–281
  for labor, 386–387
  long-run demand curve and, 110–111
  at lower prices, 107–108
  minus sign and, 105
  percentages and proportions and, 106
  price, 104–105
  proportion of income spent on a good
    and, 109–110
  in real world, 108–109, 114
  revenue and expenditures and, 111–112
  sales tax and, 135–138
  short-run demand curve and, 110, 111
  single-price monopoly and, 316–318
  slope of demand curve and, 104
  substitutability and, 109

Elasticity of supply, 118, 118–119
  long-run supply curve and, 119
  momentary supply curve and, 118–119
  sales tax and, 135, 138–139
  short-run supply curve and, 119
  technology and, 118
End-state theory of distributive justice,
    505, 508
Endowments, 19, 501–502
Entry, 293, 293–295
  barriers to, 314–315, 344
  long-run equilibrium and, 294–295
  in monopolistic competition, 346
  profits and losses and, 293–294
Environment, economic questions and, 7
Equal Pay Act (1963), 422
Equilibrium, 20
  in capital market, 393, 396–397
  collusive agreements and, 362–363
  consumer, 162
  cooperative, 364
  dominant strategy, 356
  free trade, 589–590
  of game (Nash), 356
  interest rate at, 440–441
  in labor market, 392–393, 394–395,
    409–410
  in land market, 397–399
  long-run, entry and exit and, 294–295
  in natural resource market, 446–449
  political, 539
  regulation at, 561
  short-run competitive, 292
  in stock market, 397
Equilibrium price, 83, 83–84
Equilibrium quantity, 84
Equity, 212
Equity capital, 212, 213
Ethiopia, poverty in, 8
European Community, 595
  U.S. trade with, 584
Excess capacity, 248, 258
  in monopolistic competition, 347, 350
Excise tax, 547, 547–548
Excludability, private goods and, 520
Exhaustible natural resources, 445
Exit, 293, 293–295
  long-run equilibrium and, 294–295
  in monopolistic competition, 346
  profits and losses and, 293–294
Expectations, rational, 478–481
Expected demand, 478
Expected utility, 461
Expenditures, elasticity of demand and,
    111–112
Experience goods, 468
Exports, 583. See also International trade
External benefits, 306, 307, 519. See also
    Externalities
  subsidies and, 529, 532
External costs, 10, 306, 307, 519. See also
    Externalities
  taxes and, 528–529, 548–549
External diseconomies, 299, 302
External economies, 299, 302
Externalities, 10, 306, 307, 519, 525–532
  private property rights and, 528
  public choice and, 540
  subsidies and external benefits and, 529,
    532
  taxes and external costs and, 528–529,
    530

Factor income, 378–380
Factor markets, 14
Factor prices, 378–380, 500–501
  labor market and wages and, 500–501
  marginal revenue product and, 381
  as opportunity cost, 381
Factors of production, 14. See also
    Capital; Inputs; Labor; Land
  competitive equilibrium and, 392–397
  demand for, 378–387. See also Labor
    demand
  distribution of endowments of,
    501–502
  economic rent and transfer earnings
    and, 400–402
  prices of. See Factor prices; Price(s)
  supply of, 378–380, 387–392
Fair Labor Standards Act, 133
Fairness, of income and wealth distribu-
    tion, 505, 508–509
Family Support Act (1988), 496
Farm distress, 304–305
Farm revenue, 144–147
  bumper harvest and, 145
  elasticity of demand and, 145–146
  poor harvest and, 144–145
  speculative markets in inventories and,
    146–147
  without stabilization program, 144–146
  stabilizing, 147
Federal Communications Commission,
    562
Federal Energy Regulatory Commission,
    562–563
Federal Maritime Commission, 562
Federal Power Commission, 562
Federal Trade Commission, 570, 572–573
Federal Trade Commission Act (1914),
    570
FIFO (First In, First Out) inventory
    method, 220
Finance. See Business finance
Financial assets, 429, 429–431
  net, 429
Financial intermediaries, 431, 434
Financial markets, managing risk in,
    475–481
Firm(s), 14, 209, 209–212. See also
    Capacity; Corporation; Output;
    Partnership; Plant; Plant size;
    Production; Proprietorship
  constraints of, 233–240
  decisions of, 209–210
  definition of, 209
  demand for labor, 381–384
  elasticity of demand for, 280–281
  financial liabilities of, 434
  forms of, 210–212
  importance of different types of, 211
  labor supply to, 390
  objectives of, 233
  in perfect competition, 280–281,
    282–290
  plant size, cost, and capacity and,
    248–251
  plant size and cost and, 251–255,
    256–257
  principal-agent relations and, 209
  returns to scale and, 255, 258–259
  short-run costs and, 240–248
  stock market value of, 441
  supply curve of, 289–291

  supply of capital to, 391
  supply of land and, 392
  takeovers and mergers and, 444–445
Firm coordination, 224–227
First In, First Out (FIFO) inventory
    method, 220
Fixed cost, 240, 243
Fixed inputs, 234, 240
Flat-rate income tax, 492
Food stamp program, 493
Forecasts, rational expectations and, 478
Formosa. See Taiwan
Forward market, 477
Four-firm concentration ratio, 342,
    342–343
Franchise, public, 314
Free rider, 521
Free-rider problem, 521
Friedlaender, Ann, interview with, 512–515
Futures market, 477

Gains from monopoly, 335–336
Gains from trade, 587–595. See
    also Consumer surplus; Producer
    surplus
  absolute advantage and, 590–591
  achieving, 61–62, 587–588
  balanced trade and, 588
  calculating, 590
  changes in production and consumption
    and, 588–590
  comparative advantage and, 60–61
  consumer surplus and, 171
  Latin American free trade and, 598–599
  productivity and, 62
  in real world, 591
  specialization and, 64–65
  trade in similar goods and, 591,
    594–595
Game theory, 354. See also Collusive
    agreement
  equilibrium and, 356
  payoff matrix and, 355–356
  payoffs and, 356–357
  prisoners' dilemma and, 355–357
  rules and, 354
  strategies and, 354–355, 356–357, 363,
    364, 366–367
  tit-for-tat strategy and, 363, 364
  trigger strategy and, 363
Gap, The, 470–471
General Agreement on Tariffs and Trade
    (GATT), 582–583, 592, 593, 595
General Cinema, 214–217
General Electric, 365, 571
General Motors, 246–247
Glasnost, 618
Global economy, 16–17
Goldin, Claudia, interview with, 372–375
Goods
  capital, 51
  complementary, 75, 80, 115, 188–189
  consumption, 51
  divisible and indivisible, 181
  experience, 468
  illegal, 142–144. See also Illegal drugs
  inferior, 75, 114, 115, 192
  mixed, 520
  normal, 75, 114, 115, 192
  prices of. See Price(s)
  private, 520
  public, 539–540. See Public goods

search, 468
substitute, 75, 80, 109, 115, 188
trade in, 591, 594–595
U.S. trade in, 583–584
Goods and services, 51. *See also* Goods; Services
Goods markets, 14
Gorbachev, Mikhail, 618
Government, 14, 518–520
antitrust laws and. *See* Antitrust laws
economic questions and, 7
economic theory of, 519
financial liabilities of, 434
market failure and, 519–520
public interest and public choice and, 519–520
redistribution and, 519
scale and growth of, 518–519
structure and scale of, 518
Government license, 314
Graphs, 27–46
in economic models, 38–41
independent variables and, 41
linear relationships and, 38
maximum and minimum points, 40–41
with more than two variables, 44–45
negative relationships and, 38, 39, 40
positive relationships and, 38, 39
scatter diagrams, 30–32
slope and, 42–44
time-series, 32–38
two-variable, 29–30
Great Depression, 507
unemployment during, 7
Great Leap Forward, 627, 627–628
"Greenhouse effect," 7, 525, 526–527
Gross investment, 430
Guaranteed annual income, 494

Health insurance, 464, 493
Hierarchy, 618
administrative, in Soviet Union, 618
Hirfindahl-Hirschmann (H-H) index, 343
Historical cost, 218, 220
Hong Kong, 628
U.S. trade with, 584
wealth of, 8
Horizontal integration, 574
Hotelling, Harold, 398, 399
Hotelling Principle, 398, **446**
Household(s), 14
backward-bending supply of labor curve and, 388–389
capital markets and, 432
capital supply and, 390–391
choice of. *See* Choice
labor supply and, 388–389
supply of land and, 391–392
Household production, 421
Housing market, 126–131
black market and, 130
rent ceilings and, 128–129, 130–131
search activity and, 129–130
Human behavior, economic analysis of, 172
Human capital, 51, 408. *See also* Labor
income distribution and, 497–498
wage differentials and, 421
Hume, David, 592
Hungary
economic transition in, 626
inflation in, 8

IBM, 226–227, 571, 574
ICC. *See* Interstate Commerce Commission
Illegal drugs, 142–144
external costs and, 548
free market for, 142
legalizing and taxing, 143–144
penalties and, 143
prohibition on, 142–143
Immigration laws, unions and, 413
Implications, 19, 20
Implicit rental rate, 219
Imports, 583. *See also* International trade
Imputed cost, 219
Incentive structure, 611
Income
annual or lifetime, 498–500
change in demand and, 75
consumption related to, 31
elasticity of demand and, 109–110
factor, 378–380
guaranteed annual, 494
market, 493, 494
real, 182
wealth versus, 496–497
Income and wealth distribution, 486–492, 496–500. *See also* Income redistribution
across generations, 506–507
annual or lifetime income and wealth and, 498–500
choices and, 502–505
demographics of, 488–489
fairness and, 505, 508–509
human and nonhuman capital and, 497–498
inequality over time and, 488, 490–491
Lorenz curves and, 487–488
poverty and, 489, 492
savings and bequests and, 504
uncertainty and, 506–507
in United States, 486–489, 490–491
wages and supply of labor and, 502–503
wealth versus income and, 496–497
Income changes
consumer behavior and, 192, 194
consumption and, 184
marginal utility and, 167
Income effect, 192, 194
consumer behavior and, 192–193, 194
interest rate and, 438–439
labor supply and, 388
Income elasticity of demand, 112, 114, 115
Income maintenance programs, 492–494
Income redistribution, 492–496
government and, 519
income maintenance programs and, 492–493
income taxes and, 492
interest groups and, 541–543
model of, 544
problems and reform proposals for, 494–496
provision of goods and services below cost and, 493
scale of, 493–494
voting for, 543–544
Income taxes. *See also* Taxes
flat-rate, 492
income redistribution and, 492

negative, 494–496
progressive, 492
proportional, 492
regressive, 492
Increasing marginal returns, 239
Increasing returns to scale, 250
Incredible electrical conspiracy, 365–366
Independent variables, 41
Indifference curves, 185–187, 186
best affordable point on, 190
Individual demand, 158, 158–159
constraints and, 159
preferences and, 159
Industrial union, 411
Industry(ies)
concentration ratios and, 344–345
elasticity of demand for, 280–281
nationalized, 632
short-run supply curve for, 290–291
Inelastic demand, 106, 115, 316, 318
Inferior goods, 75, 115
elasticity of demand and, 114
income effect and, 192
Inflation, 219
in Commonwealth of Independent States, 625
economic questions and, 8
Information
advertising for, 468
economic. *See* Economic information
private. *See* Private information
Information cost, 466
Innovation, 314
in monopolistic competition, 350
monopoly and, 336
Inputs. *See also* Capital; Factors of production; Labor; Land
durable, 218
fixed, 234, 240
least-cost technique and, 268–271
prices of, 267, 270–271
substitution of, 263–265
variable, 234, 240
Insecticides, 530
Insurance, 463–466, 506
health, 464, 493
life, 464
markets for, private information and, 475
property and casualty, 464
reasons for insuring and, 464–465
in United States, 463–464
Intel Corp., 572–573
Intellectual property, 63
Interest, 219, 378
cost of, 219
Interest groups
redistribution and, 541–543
well-informed, 546
Interest rate
asset prices and, 440–445
capital supply curve and, 391
equilibrium, 440–441
saving and, 438–439
International Harvester, 294
International trade, 581–605. *See also* Gains from trade
of Commonwealth of Independent States, 624–625
comparative advantage and, 60–61, 64–65, 587
economic questions and, 8

International trade *(cont.)*
  gains from, 60–63, 64–65, 171
  General Agreement on Tariffs and Trade
    and, 582–583, 592, 593, 595
  money and, 66–67
  open economy and, 16–17
  opportunity cost and, 586–587
  productivity and absolute advantage
    and, 62
  property rights and, 63, 66
  in real world, 63–67
  of Soviet Union, 620
  trade restrictions and, 595–604
  trends in, 584–586
  of United States, 583–584
Interstate Commerce Commission (ICC),
    559, 562
Inventories, 220
  costs of, 220
  speculative markets in, 146–147
Investment, 430, 432
  capital and, 430
  gross, 430
  net, 430
  net present value of, 434–436
  Soviet transition to consumption from,
    620
Invisible hand, 22, 307
Isocost equation, 266, 266–267
Isocost lines, 266, 266–268
  input prices and, 267
  isocost equation and, 266–267
  isocost map and, 268
Isocost map, 268
Isoquant, 265, 265–266
  marginal rate of substitution and,
    265–266
Isoquant map, 265

Japan
  capitalism in, 631–632
  economic growth of, 59–60
  U.S. trade with, 584
Jenkin, Fleeming, 137
Jevons, William Stanley, 173
Job Opportunities and Basic Skills (JOBS)
    program, 496

Kimberly-Clark, 366–367
Kinked demand curve model, 351–352
Kinney's, 571, 574
Kuznets, Simon, 506, 507

Labor, 14
  demand for. *See* Labor demand
  marginal product of, 263, 382–383
  substitutability of capital and, 264–265,
    387
  supply of. *See* Labor supply
Labor demand, 381–384
  elasticity of, 386–387
  of firm, 381–384
  long-run, 385
  market, 386
  short-run, 385
  skill differentials and, 408, 409
Labor intensity, elasticity of demand for
    labor and, 386–387
Labor-intensive technique, 233
Labor market, 131, 132–134, 406–425
  equilibrium in, 392–393, 394–395,
    409–410

  minimum wage and, 132–133
  skill differentials in, 408–410
  unions in, 413–414, 416–417
  wages and. *See* Wage(s); Wage differen-
    tials
Labor supply, 388–390
  backward-bending household supply of
    labor curve and, 388–389
  household choice and, 196–197,
    198–199
  income effect and, 388
  to individual firms, 390
  market, 389–390
  skill differentials and, 408–409
  substitution effect and, 388
  wages and, 502–503
Labor unions, 410, 410–411
Land, 14
  equilibrium in market for, 397–399
  private and state ownership of,
    610–611
Lardner, Dionysius, 86, 87
Latin America
  free trade in, 595–596, 598–599
  stock markets in, 442–443
Law(s). *See also* regulation
  antitrust, 559, 570–574
  in Commonwealth of Independent
    States, 624
  comparable-worth, 422–424
  minimum wage, 132–133, 415, 418
  right-to-work, 411, 412
  wage, 132–133, 415, 416–417, 418
Law of demand, 73–74, 86–87
**Law of diminishing marginal rate of sub-
    stitution, 264,** 264–265
Law of diminishing marginal returns, 242
Law of diminishing returns, 239, 263–264
Law of supply, 78–79, 86–87
Least-cost technique, 268, 268–271, 272
Legal monopoly, 314
Lenin, Vladimir Ilyich, 615, 618
Liability, 429
  limited, of corporation, 210
  unlimited, 210
License, government, 314
Life insurance, 464
LIFO (Last In, First Out) inventory
    method, 220
Limited liability, of corporation, 210
Linear relationship, 38
Little Caesar's Pizza, 300–301
Living standards, Soviet, 621
Loans. *See also* Credit
  international, 16, 585–586
Loans market, 432
Lobbying, 538
Local, 411
Lockout, 411, 412
Long run, 234
  output, price, and profit in, 292–296
  profit maximization in, 284–285
Long-run average cost curve (LRAC), 251,
    251–255, 256
Long-run cost, 248–249, 251–255
  returns to scale and, 254–255
  as total costs, 255
Long-run demand curve, 112
Long-run demand for labor, 385
**Long-run elasticity of demand for labor,
    387**
Long-run supply curve, 119

Lorenz curves, 487, 487–488
Loss, 209–210
  benefit-loss rate and, 494
  deadweight, 331, 548, 549–550
LRAC. *See* Long-run average cost curve
Lucas, Robert E., Jr., 506

Macroeconomics, 20, 20–21
Malthus, Thomas Robert, 398, 399
Mao Zedong, 627
Marginal benefit, 521
Marginal cost, 242, 243
  profit and, 284–286
Marginal cost pricing rule, 564
Marginal private cost, 529
Marginal product, 235, 235–236, 240
  average product and, 238
  marginal rate of substitution and,
    271–272
Marginal product curve, 235, 235–236
  shape of, 238–239
Marginal product of capital, 250
Marginal product of labor, 263, 382–383
  short-run elasticity of demand for labor
    and, 387
Marginal rate of substitution (MRS), 186,
    186–187
  diminishing, 187, 264–265
  isoquants and, 265–266
  marginal products and, 271–272
  relative input price and, 270
**Marginal rate of substitution of labor for
    capital, 264,** 264–265
Marginal returns
  diminishing, 239, 242
  increasing, 239
Marginal revenue, 282, 381
  profit and, 284–286
Marginal revenue product, 381, 382, 383
Marginal revenue product curve, 383
Marginal social benefit, 306
Marginal social cost, 306, 529
Marginal tax rates, 492
Marginal utility, 160, 160–161, 164–170
  consumer surplus and gains from trade
    and, 171, 174
  criticisms of, 170–171
  diminishing, 160–161
  fall in prices and, 164–165
  paradox of value and, 174
  in real world, 167–170
  rise in income and, 167
  rise in prices and, 165–166
  of wealth, 460
Marginal utility per dollar spent, 162
  equalizing, 162–164
Market(s), 14, 123–149
  black, 130
  bond, 432
  capital. *See* Capital markets
  for cars, private information and, 469,
    472
  as coordination mechanism, 15
  for credit, private information and,
    472–475
  efficient, 480
  entry into. *See* Entry
  exit from. *See* Exit
  factor, 14
  for farm products, 144–147
  financial, managing risk in, 475–481
  forward, 477

futures, 477
geographic scope of, 344
goods, 14
housing, 126–131
for illegal goods, 142–144. *See also*
  Illegal drugs
for insurance, private information and,
  475
labor. *See* Labor market
loans, 432
natural resources, 445–451
sales tax and. *See* Sales tax
Soviet, 619
speculative, in inventories, 146–147
stock, 432
supply and. *See* Market supply
Market activity, 388
Market constraints, 233
Market coordination, 15, 224
Market demand, 158, 158–159
for labor, 386
Market economy, 16, 631–633
sequence of transition to, 632–633
speed of transition to, 633
styles of, 631–632
transition from centrally planned economy to, 621–625, 631–632
Market failure, 516–533, 519
externalities and, 525–529, 532
in government sector, 518–520
public goods and, 520–525
Market income, 493, 494
Market intervention. *See* Antitrust laws;
  Regulation
Market socialism, 611, 612
Market structure, 342–345. *See also*
  Competition; Monopolistic competition; Monopoly; Monopsony;
  Oligopoly; Perfect competition
concentration measures and, 342–343,
  344–345
in U.S. economy, 343–344, 345–346
Market supply
of capital, 391
of labor, 389–390
Marshall, Alfred, 86, 87
Marx, Karl, 617
Maturity date, of bonds, 213
Maximum, graphing, 40–41
McDonald's, 335, 377
Measurement, 18
of inventories, 220
of opportunity cost, 54
units of, slope of demand curve and,
  104
of utility, 170
Median voter theorem, 542, 542–543
Medicaid, 493
Medium of exchange, 67
Mercantilism, 592
Mercantilists, 592
Mercosur, 598, 599
Mergers, 444–445, 445
Mexico, free trade agreement with, 595
Microeconomics, 20
Minimum, graphing, 40–41
Minimum differentiation
principle of, 541–542, 543
Minimum efficient scale, 357
Minimum wage law, 132–133
monopsony and, 415, 418
in real world, 135

Ministry of International Trade and
  Industry (MITI), 631–632
Mixed economy, 16
Mixed goods, 520
Momentary supply curve, 118, 118–119
Monetary exchange, 66, 67
Money, 66–67, 67
in Commonwealth of Independent
  States, 625
as medium of exchange, 66–67
Soviet, 619
Monopolistic competition, 344, 344–345,
  346–351
advertising in, 350
efficiency of, 350
excess capacity in, 347, 350
market structure and, 345
price and output in, 346–347, 348–349
product innovation in, 350
Monopoly, 308, 311–338, 314
allocative efficiency and, 330–331
barriers to entry and, 314–315
bilateral, 418
competition compared with, 328–336
demand and revenue and, 315–316,
  317
excise taxes and, 548
gains from, 335–336
lack of supply curve for, 321
legal, 314
market structure and, 345
natural, 314, 564–567
price and output and, 318–321,
  329–330
price discrimination and, 321, 324–328
redistribution and, 330, 331, 332–333
rent seeking and, 331, 334
revenue and elasticity and, 316–318
single-price, 315–321
unregulated, 315
Monopoly power, 322–323
Monopsony, 414, 414–415, 418
minimum wages and, 415, 418
tendencies in, 415
unions and, 418
Moral hazard, 469
Morgan, J.P., 570
Morgenstern, Oskar, 354
MRS. *See* Marginal rate of substitution

Nash, John, 356
Nash equilibrium, 356
Nationalized industry, 632
Natural monopoly, 314
regulation of, 564–567
Natural resource(s), 445, 445–451
exhaustible, 445
nonexhaustible, 445
Natural resource markets, 445–451
conservation and, 450–451
equilibrium in, 446–449
prices in, 447, 449–450
supply and demand in, 446–447
Navistar International, 294
Negative income tax, 494, 494–496
Negative relationship, 38, 39, 40
NEPOOL. *See* New England Power Pool
Net benefit, 523
Net exporter, 583
Net financial assets, 429, 431
Net importer, 583

Net investment, 430
Net present value (NPV), 216
Net present value of an investment,
  434–436, **435**
New England Power Pool (NEPOOL),
  245, 248, 258–259
New York Stock Exchange (NYSE), 213,
  428
Nintendo Co., 348–349
Niskanen, William, 545
Nonexcludability, public goods and,
  520
Nonexhaustible natural resources, 445
Nonhuman capital, income distribution
  and, 497–498
Nonmarket activity, 388
Nontariff barriers, 595, 600–603
Normal goods, 75, 115
elasticity of demand and, 114
income effect and, 192
Normative analysis, 519
Normative statements, 17, 17–18
Nozick, Robert, 508
NPV. *See* Net present value
NutraSweet Co., 332–333
NYSE. *See* New York Stock Exchange

Objectives
of firm, 233
of unions, 412
Observation, 18
of utility, 170
Oil industry
OPEC and, 102, 108–109, 341
Soviet, 620
Okun, Arthur, 508
Oligopoly, 345, 351–357
collusion and. *See* Collusive agreement
dominant firm, 352–353
game theory and, 354–367
kinked demand curve model of,
  351–352
market structure and, 345
regulation of cartels and, 567–569
OPEC. *See* Organization of Petroleum
  Exporting Countries
Open economy, 16, 16–17
Open shop, 411–412
Opportunity cost, 10, 10–11, 218, 220
best alternative foregone and, 10, 54
dollar cost and, 10
of economic information, 466
external cost and, 10
factor price as, 381
increasing, 54–56
international trade and, 586–587
inventories and, 220
measuring, 54
production possibility frontier and,
  54–56
time cost and, 10
Optimal-search rule, 466–468, 467
Optimal-stopping rule, 466–468
Optimizing, 10
graphs and, 40–41
Organization of Petroleum Exporting
  Countries (OPEC), 102, 108–109,
  341
Origin, 29
Other things being equal. *See* Ceteris
  paribus

Output. *See also* Production
  in monopolistic competition, 346–347,
    348–349
  monopoly and, 318–321
  monopoly and competition compared
    and, 329–330
  price discrimination and, 325–326
  profit-maximizing, 284–285
Overutilized capacity, 248
Owner's wages, 220
Ownership, private and state, 610–611

Pan American Airlines, 334
Paradox of value, 174
Partnership, 210, 211, 212
  methods of raising capital, 212
Patents, 220, 314
Payoff, 355
  in prisoners' dilemma, 356–357
Payoff matrix, 355, 355–356
  collusive agreements and, 362–363
Penalties, in markets for illegal goods, 143
People's Republic of China, 616, 627–630
  decreasing central planning in, 630
  economic system in, 609
  Great Leap Forward in, 627–628
  1978 reforms in, 628–629
  success of, 629–630
Perestroika, 618
Perfect competition, 280, 280–308
  allocative efficiency in, 305–307
  changing tastes and advancing technolo-
    gy and, 296–305
  elasticity of industry and firm demand
    and, 280–281
  entry and exit in, 293–295
  in everyday life, 281–282
  external economies and diseconomies
    in, 299, 302
  farm distress and, 304–305
  firm's choices in, 282–290
  firm's supply curve and, 289–290
  influence of single firm and, 280
  invisible hand and, 307
  market structure and, 345
  obstacles to efficiency in, 307–308
  permanent decrease in demand in,
    296–297
  permanent increase in demand in,
    297–299, 300–301
  plant size changes in, 295
  profit and revenue in, 282–283
  profit in short run and, 285–289
  profit-maximizing input and, 284–285
  short-run competitive equilibrium in,
    292
  short-run industry supply curve in,
    290–291
Perfect price discrimination, 321, 327
**Perfectly competitive firm's supply curve,
  289**, 289–290
Perfectly elastic demand, 106, 115
  sales tax and, 138–139
Perfectly elastic supply, sales tax and, 138
Perfectly inelastic demand, 106, 115
  sales tax and, 138
Perfectly inelastic supply, sales tax and,
  135–138
Persuasion, advertising for, 468
Physical assets, 429, 429–430, 431
Physical limits, 248
Pigou, Arthur Cecil, 507

Pizza Hut, Inc., 300–301
Planning
  central, 612. *See also* Centrally planned
    economies
  decentralized, 612
Plant
  capacity of. *See* Capacity
  temporary shutdown of, 287–289
Plant size
  cost and, 251–255
  cost and capacity and, 248–251
  profit and, 295
Poland, economic transition in, 626–627
Political equilibrium, 539
Politicians, 538, 538–539
  behavior of, 539–540
Politics, trade restrictions and, 604
Polo, Marco, 582
Population
  change in demand and, 76
  Malthus' ideas about, 398, 399
Portfolio choice, 430, 430–431
Positive analysis, 519
Positive relationship, 38, 39
Positive statements, 17
Postal Rate Commission, 562
Poverty, 489, 492, 506. *See also* Income
    and wealth distribution; Income redis-
    tribution
  economic questions and, 8
PPF. *See* Production possibility frontier
Preferences, 19, 184–189
  change in demand and, 76
  household consumption choices and,
    159
  indifference curves and, 185–187
  production possibilities frontier and, 53
  substitutability and, 188–189
  trade in similar goods and, 591, 594
Preferred stock, 213
Premium, insurance, 463
Present value, 214, 214–217
  of bonds, 215–217
  net, 216, 434–436
Price(s). *See also* Factor prices
  advertising and, 468
  average cost pricing rule and, 565
  best deal for buyers and sellers and, 84
  change in demand and, 75–76
  changes in. *See* Price changes
  choke, 447
  in Commonwealth of Independent
    States, 622–623
  deregulation of, in China, 630
  determination of. *See* Price determina-
    tion
  elasticity of demand and, 104–105,
    107–108
  entry and exit and, 293–294
  equilibrium, 83–84
  expected, 75–76, 80
  of inputs, 270–271
  interest rates and, 440–445
  isocost lines and, 267
  marginal cost pricing rule and, 564
  marginal utility and, 164–167
  market-determined, transition to capi-
    talism and, 632–633
  minimum, supply and, 79, 84
  in monopolistic competition, 346–347,
    348–349
  monopoly and, 318–321

monopoly and competition compared
    and, 329–330
  of natural resources, 447, 449–450
  under perfect competition, 280
  price discrimination and, 325–326
  of related goods, 75, 80
  relative, 182
  reservation, of buyer, 467
  searching for information about,
    466–468, 470–471
  sticky, 351
  of stock, 217, 444
Price changes
  consumer behavior and, 191, 192–195,
    194, 195
  consumption and, 182–184
  marginal utility and, 164–165
  in natural resource markets, 449–450
  stock and, 480–481
Price determination, 82–85
  equilibrium and, 83–84
  price as regulator and, 82–83
Price discrimination, 321, 321, 324–328
  consumer surplus and, 324–325
  among groups, 328
  among individuals, 325
  limits to, 328
  perfect, 321, 327
  price and output decisions with,
    325–326
  total revenue and, 324
  among units of a good, 325
Price-earnings ratio, 216, 441, 444
Price effect, 191, 194, 195
Price elasticity of demand, 104, 104–105
Price taker, 280
Price wars, 365–366
  secrecy and, 365–366
Principal, 209, 210
Principle of minimum differentiation, 541,
    541–542, 543
Prisoners' dilemma, 355–357
Private cost, marginal, 529
Private enterprise, 63
  property rights and, 63, 66
Private good, 520
Private information, 469, 469, 472–475
  markets for cars and, 469, 472
  markets for credit and, 472–475
  markets for insurance and, 475
Private ownership, transition to capitalism
    and, 632
Private property rights, 528
Privatization, 632
  in China, 629
  in Eastern European countries, 626, 627
Probability, 460
  subjective, 460
Process theory of distributive justice, 505,
    508–509
Procter & Gamble, 366–367
Producer surplus, 331
Product
  average, 237–239, 240
  marginal, 235–236, 238, 240, 250, 263,
    271–272
  total, 234–235, 240
Product differentiation, 344, 344–345
Production, 51, 206–228. *See also* Output
  business finance and, 212–218
  changes in, gains from trade and,
    588–590

complements in, 80
cost and profit and, 218–221
economic efficiency and, 222–223
factors of. *See* Capital; Factors of production; Inputs; Labor; Land
firms and, 209–212, 224–227
fluctuations in, speculative markets in inventories and, 146–147
household, 421
least-cost, 263–273
markets and, 224–225
minimum efficient scale of, 357
substitutes in, 80
Production function, 249
Production possibility frontier (PPF), 51, 51–53
model economy and, 51–52
opportunity cost and, 54–56
preferences and, 53
in real world, 56, 59–60
shape of, 54
Productivity, 62
in China, 629–630
Professional association, 412
Profit(s), 209–210, 220–221
in China, 629–630
of different types of firms, 210, 211
economic, 220
entry and exit and, 293–294
under perfect competition, 282
plant size and, 295
profit-maximizing output and, 284–285
in short run, 285–289
total revenue and total cost and, 282
Profit maximization, 233
advertising for, 468
collusive agreements and, 358–359
conditions for, 384–385
demand for factors and, 381
Progressive income tax, 492
Property, 63
intellectual, 63
ownership of, private and state, 610–611
Property and casualty insurance, 464
Property rights, 63, 66
externalities and, 530
private, 528
in private enterprise capitalism, 63, 66
regulation and, 66
taxes and, 66
Proportional income tax, 492
Proprietorship, 210, 211, 212
methods of raising capital, 212
Protectionism, 595. *See also* Trade restrictions
Public choice, 536–555
externalities and, 531
political marketplace and, 538–547
taxes and subsidies and, 547–554
Public choice theory, 519–520, **520,** 538
externalities and, 507
Public franchise, 314
Public goods, 520–525
benefits and costs and, 521–523, 524
free riding and, 521
private goods and, 520
private provision of, 523
public choice and, 539–540
public provision of, 523
pure, 520

Public interest
antitrust laws and, 574
externalities and, 507
Public interest theory (of government behavior), 519–520, **520**
Public interest theory of regulation, 561, 564–565, 567
Pure public good, 520

Quantity, equilibrium, 84
Quantity demanded, 73
change in, 77–78
of factors, 381
Quantity supplied, 78
change in, 81–82
of labor, wages and, **388**
Quotas, 551, 600, 600–603
subsidies with, 551, 554
tariffs versus, 602–603

Race
income distribution and, 488, 489, 490–491
wage differentials and, 419–422
Rate of return regulation, 565, 565–566
Rather, Dan, 377
Rational choice, 19
Rational expectations, 478, 478–481
calculating, 478–479
stock market and, 479–481
Rational ignorance, 546
Rawlsian theory of fairness, 505
Reagan, Ronald, 537
Real income, 182
Redemption value, of bonds, 213
Redistribution
of income. *See* Income redistribution
monopoly and competition compared and, 330, 331, 332–333
Regressive income tax, 492
Regulation, 314, 559
capture theory of, 561, 565, 567
of cartels, 567–569
demand for, 560
deregulation and, 559
equilibrium and, 561
of housing market, 128–129, 130–131
of natural monopoly, 564–567
predictions and, 569
prices and, 82–83
process of, 563
property rights and, 66
public interest theory of, 561, 564–565, 567
rate of return, 565–566
scope of, 562–563
supply of, 560–561
Relative price, 182
Rent, 334, 378. *See also* Consumer surplus; Producer surplus
economic, 400–402
Rent ceilings, 128–129, 130–131
Rent seeking, 334
income redistribution and, 519
monopoly and competition compared and, 331, 334
Rental rate, implicit, 219
Reservation price, of buyer, 467
Reservation wage, 388
Residual claimant, 210

Resource(s)
endowment and, 19
natural, 445–451
scarcity of. *See* Scarcity
Returns, diminishing, 250
law of, 263–264
Returns to scale, 250
constant, 250
decreasing, 250
increasing, 250
long-run costs and, 254–255
in real world, 255, 258–259
Revenue(s), 209–210, 220–221
average, 282
elasticity of demand and, 111–112
farm, 144–147
marginal, 282, 284–286
under perfect competition, 282–283
single-price monopoly and, 315–318
total, 282, 324
Ricardo, David, 593
Right-to-work law, 411, 412
Risk, 460, 475–481
diversification to lower, 476–477
forward and futures markets and, 477
measuring cost of, 461–462
rational expectations and, 478–479
risk aversion and neutrality and, 462–463
uncertainty and, 460
Rivalry, private goods and, 520
Robinson, Joan, 323
Robinson-Patman Amendment (1936), 570
Rockefeller, John D., Sr., 570
Rules, of oligopoly game, 354

Sachs, Jeffrey, interview with, 577–580
Sales tax,
burden of, 134–139
elasticity of demand and, 138–139
elasticity of supply and, 135–138
Samuelson, Paul, 323
San Francisco earthquake, 124, 126–131
Saving, 430
household choice and, 197
income distribution and, 504
interest rate and, 438–439
portfolio choice and, 430–431
supply of capital and, 438–439
Scale
diseconomies of, 250–251, 299, 302
economies of. *See* Economies of scale
minimum efficient, 357
returns to. *See* Returns to scale
Scarcity, 9, 9–12
choice and, 10
competition and cooperation and, 11
economic activity and, 9–10
human behavior and, 172
opportunity cost and, 10–11
Scatter diagrams, 30, 30–32
Scholastic Aptitude Test, declining scores on, 36–37
Scope, economies of, 335–336
Search activity, 129, 129–130
Search goods, 468
Secrecy, collusive agreements and, 365–366
Self-sufficiency, 60, 61–62

Services, 51
  U.S. trade in, 584
Sex, wage differentials and, 419–422
Share of stock, 210
Sherman Act (1890), 559, 570, 571
Short run, 234
  competitive equilibrium in, 292
  profit in, 285–289
  profit maximization in, 284–285
  technology constraint in, 234–240
Short-run average cost curve (SRAC), 256
Short-run cost(s), 240–248, 256
  in real world, 245–248
Short-run cost curves, 242–243
Short-run demand curve, 112
Short-run demand for labor, 385
Short-run elasticity of demand for labor, 386, 386–387
Short-run industry supply curve, 290, 290–291
Short-run supply curve, 119
Shutdown point, 287, 287–289
Signals, 472
  in markets for credit, 474
  profits and losses as, 293
Simon, Julian, 398
Singapore, U.S. trade with, 584
Singer, 294
Single-price monopoly, 315, 315–321
  demand and revenue and, 315–316, 317
  price and output decision and, 318–321
  revenue and elasticity and, 316–318
Skill differentials, 408–410
  demand and, 408, 409
  education and training and, 410
  supply and, 408–409
  wage rates and, 409–410
Slope, 42, 42–44
  across arc, 44
  of curved line, calculating, 43–44
  of demand curve, units of measurement and, 104
  at point, 43–44
  of straight line, calculating, 42–43
Smith, Adam, 21, 22–23, 174, 307, 322, 592, 593
Smoot-Hawley Act, 582, 595
Social benefit, marginal, 306
Social cost, marginal, 306, 529
Social Security, 492
Socialism, 611, 612, 613, 614, 615
  market, 611, 612
Socony-Vacuum Oil Co., 571
Solow, Robert M., interview with, 1–4
Sony, 72
South Korea, U.S. trade with, 584
Soviet Union. See also Commonwealth of
    Independent States
  central planning in, 618–619
  economic decline of, 619–620
  economic history of, 615, 618
  living standards in, 621
  market economy reforms in, 621, 622–623
  market sector of, 619
  money in, 619
Special interest, antitrust laws and, 574
Specialization, 60, 61–62, 64–65
  wage differentials and, 421–422
Specific tax, 547
SRAC. See Short-run average cost curve
SSI. See Supplemental Security Income

Stabilization program, farm revenues and, 144–146, 147
Stalin, Joseph, 615, 618
Standard Oil Company, 570, 571
Stein, Herbert, interview with, 97–100
Stigler, George J., 256
Stock, 210
  common, 213
  convertible, 213
  issuing, 213–214
  preferred, 213
  price-earnings ratio and, 216, 441, 444
  prices of, 217, 480–481
Stock exchange, 213
Stock market, 432
  in Asia and Latin America, 442–443
  crash of 10/19/87, 428
  equilibrium in, 397
  rational expectations and, 479–481
  volume of, prices and, 444
Stock market value, of firms, 441
Stock of wealth, 496
Stock yield, 440
Stockholders, 210–211
Strategic behavior, 354
Strategies, 354
  in oligopoly game, 354–355
  in prisoners' dilemma, 356–357
  tit-for-tat, 363, 364
  trigger, 363
Strike, 411, 412
Subjective probabilities, 460
Subsidies, 529, 550–553
  external benefits and, 529, 532
  with quotas, 551, 554
Substitutes, 75, 80
  preferences and, 188
Substitution
  elasticity of demand and, 109, 115
  of inputs, 263–265
  marginal rate of. See Marginal rate of
      substitution
  preferences and, 188–189
Substitution effect, 192, 193, 194
  consumer behavior and, 192, 193, 195
  interest rate and, 438
  labor supply and, 388
Sunk cost, 219
Supplemental Security Income (SSI), 493
Suppliers, number of, change in supply
    and, 80
Supply, 78–82, 79
  of capital, 390–391, 438–439
  change in. See Change in supply
  elasticity of, 118–119, 135–138
  expected, 478
  of factors, 378–380, 387–392. See also
      Labor supply
  of labor, 196–197, 198–199. See Labor
      supply
  of land, 391
  law of, 78–79, 86–87
  market. See Market supply
  perfectly elastic, 138
  perfectly inelastic, 135–138
  quantity supplied and, 78
  of regulation, 560–561
  selling plans and, 78
Supply curve, 79
  of capital, 439
  current period, 479
  of firm, 289–291

  for industry, short-run, 290–291
  for labor, backward-bending, 388–389
  long-run, 119
  minimum supply price and, 79, 84
  momentary, 118–119
  monopoly and, 321
  movement along, 81
  shift in, 81
  short-run, 119
  of skilled and unskilled labor, 408–409
Supply schedule, 79
Surplus
  consumer, 171, 174, 324–325, 330, 559–560
  distribution of, 559–560
  producer, 559–560
  total, 559
Sweezy, Paul M., 351

Taft Hartley Act (1947), 412
Taiwan, 627, 628
  U.S. trade with, 584
Takeovers, 444–445, 445
Tangible assets, 497
Tariffs, 595, 595–597, 600
  countervailing duties and, 603
  General Agreement on Tariffs and Trade
      and, 582–583, 592, 593, 595
  quotas and voluntary export restraints
      versus, 602–603
Tastes. See Preferences
Tax rates
  marginal, 492
  variation in, 548–550
Taxes, 547–550. See also Income taxes
  ad valorem, 547
  in China, 630
  in Commonwealth of Independent
      States, 625
  deadweight loss of, 548, 549–550
  of different types of firms, 210, 211
  on drugs, 143–144
  excise, 547–548
  external costs and, 528–529, 530, 548–549
  property rights and, 66
  specific, 547
Team production, 225
Technique, 233, 233–234
  capital-intensive, 233
  labor-intensive, 233
  least-cost, 268–271, 272
Technological efficiency, 222, 222–223
Technological progress, 57, 57–59, 506
  competition and, 302–303
  demand for labor and, 385–386
  human behavior and, 172
  monopoly and, 336
Technology, 19
  change in supply and, 80
  economic questions and, 7–9
  elasticity of supply and, 118
Technology constraint
  average product and, 237–238
  cost curves and, 244
  marginal product and, 235–236
  relationship between marginal and aver-
      age values and, 238
  shapes of product curves and, 238–239
  short-run, 234–240
  total product and, 234–235

Textile and Apparel Trade Act (1975), 602
Textile industry, trade restrictions and, 602
Theory of distributive justice, 505, 505, 508–509
Timber industry, elasticity of demand and, 116–117
Time allocation, household choices about, 196–197, 198–199
Time cost, 10
Time-series graphs, 32, 32–38
  comparing, 35, 38
  misleading, 33–35
Tit-for-tat strategy, 363, 364
Total benefit, 521
Total cost, 240, 240–242
  long-run cost as, 255
  profit and, 282
Total fixed cost, 240, 243
Total product, 234, 234–235, 240
Total product curve, 234, 234–235
  shape of, 238–239
Total product schedule, 382
Total revenue, 282
  price discrimination and, 324
  profit and, 282
Total surplus, 559
Total utility, 160, 161
Total variable cost, 240, 243
Trade. *See also* International trade
  balance of, 583, 585–586
  gains from. *See* Consumer surplus;
    Gains from trade; Producer surplus
Trade deficit, 16
Trade restrictions, 595–604
  compensating losers and, 604
  dumping and countervailing duties and, 603
  nontariff, 595, 600–603
  political outcome of, 604
  reasons for, 603–604
  tariffs and, 595–597, 600
  unions and, 413
Trade surplus, 16, 17
Trademarks, 220
Training, wages and, 410
Transactions costs, 224–225, 225
Transfer earnings, 400, 400–402
Trend, 33
Treuhandanstalt, 626
Trigger strategy, 363
Turnover, concentration ratios and, 344

UAW. *See* United Auto Workers
Uncertainty, 460, 460–463
  collusive agreements and, 364
  income and wealth distribution and, 506–507
  risk and, 460, 461–463
  utility of wealth and, 460
Unemployment
  economic questions and, 7–8
  minimum wage and, 133
Unemployment compensation, 492–493
Union(s), 410–414
  in competitive labor market, 413–414, 416–417

craft, 411
industrial, 411
labor, 410–411
local and, 411
monopsony and, 418
objectives and constraints of, 412–413
Union of Soviet Socialist Republics. *See* Commonwealth of Independent States; Soviet Union
Union shop, 411, 412
Unit elastic demand, 106, 106–107, 115, 316, 318
United Airlines, 334
United Auto Workers (UAW), 411, 413
United States
  capital markets in, 431–434
  capitalism in, 631
  concentration ratios in, 343–344
  economic growth of, 59–60
  economic system of, 7, 631
  farm distress in, 304–305
  inflation in, 8
  insurance industry in, 463–464
  international trade of, 583–584
  market types in, 345–346
  mixed economy of, 16
  open economy of, 16–17
  trade agreements of, 595
  unemployment in, 7–8
University of California, 493
Unlimited liability
  of partnership, 210
  of proprietorship, 210
U.S. Postal Service, 314
USSR. *See* Commonwealth of Independent States; Soviet Union
U.S. Steel Company, 571
Utilitarian theory, 505
Utility, 159, 159–174
  equalizing per dollar spent, 162–164
  expected, 461
  lack of observability of measurement of, 170
  marginal. *See* Marginal utility
  maximization of, 162
  total, 160, 161
  units of, 164
Utility maximization, 162
Utility of wealth schedule (curve), 460

Value, 171
  paradox of, 174
  present, 214–217
  redemption, 213
  stock market, of firms, 441
Value system, in Commonwealth of Independent States, 624
Vanderbilt, W. H., 570
Variable(s)
  independent, 41
  linear relationship between, 38
  multiple, graphing relationship among, 44–45
  negative relationship between, 38, 39, 40
  positive relationship between, 38, 39

Variable cost, 240, 243
  plant shutdown and, 287
Variable inputs, 234, 240
"Velvet Revolution," 626
Vertical integration, 571, 574
Viner, Jacob, 256, 257
Voluntary export restraints (VERs), 600, 600–603
  tariffs versus, 602–603
von Hayek, Friedrich, 616
von Neumann, John, 354
Von's Grocery, 571, 574
Voters, 538, 538–539
  behavior of, 539–540
  ignorance of, 546
  median voter theorem and, 542–543
Voting, for income redistribution, 543–544

Wage(s), 378. *See also* Earnings; Income
  comparable-worth laws and, 422–424
  economic questions and, 7
  education and training and, 410
  labor market and, 500–501
  minimum, 132–133, 415, 418
  of owner, 220
  quantity of labor supplied and, 388
  reservation, 388
  skill differentials and, 409–410
  supply of labor and, 502–503
Wage differentials, 410–422
  monopsony and, 414–415, 418
  scale of, 418
  between sexes and races, 419–422
  unions and, 410–414, 416–417
Wage laws, 132-133, 415, 416–417, 418
Wants, 73
  double coincidence of, 66
Wealth, 430
  annual or lifetime, 498–500
  distribution of. *See* Income and wealth distribution; Income redistribution
  economic questions and, 8
  expected, 463
  extreme, 492
  income versus, 496–497
  sources of, 22–23
  utility of, 460
Welfare economics, 507
Welfare programs, 493
Welfare state capitalism, 611, 612, 632
Welfare trap, 494–495
Wells Fargo, 517
Westinghouse, 344, 365, 571
Wisconsin Toy Company, Inc., 214, **216**
Women, allocation of time by, 172
Work hours, household choice and, 196–197, 198–199

x-axis, 29
x-coordinate, 30

y-axis, 29
y-coordinate, 30

Federal, state, and local government receipts and expenditures

Bond yields and interest rates

Year	Receipts	Expenditures	Surplus or deficit (–)	U.S. treasury bills	Corporate bonds
		(billions of dollars)		(percent per year)	
1959	128.8	131.9	–3.1	3.4	4.4
1960	138.8	135.2	3.6	2.9	4.4
1961	144.1	147.1	–3.0	2.4	4.4
1962	155.8	158.7	–2.9	2.8	4.3
1963	167.5	165.9	1.6	3.2	4.3
1964	172.9	174.5	–1.6	3.5	4.4
1965	187.0	185.8	1.2	4.0	4.5
1966	210.7	211.6	–1.0	4.9	5.1
1967	226.4	240.2	–13.7	4.3	5.5
1968	260.9	265.5	–4.6	5.3	6.2
1969	294.0	284.0	10.0	6.7	7.0
1970	299.8	311.2	–11.5	6.5	8.0
1971	318.9	338.1	–19.2	4.3	7.4
1972	364.2	368.1	–3.9	4.1	7.2
1973	408.5	401.6	6.9	7.0	7.4
1974	450.7	455.2	–4.5	7.9	8.6
1975	465.8	530.6	–64.8	5.8	8.8
1976	532.6	570.9	–38.3	5.0	8.4
1977	598.4	615.2	–16.8	5.3	8.0
1978	673.2	670.3	2.9	7.2	8.7
1979	754.7	745.3	9.4	10.0	9.6
1980	825.7	861.0	–35.3	11.5	11.9
1981	941.9	972.3	–30.3	14.0	14.2
1982	960.5	1,069.1	–108.6	10.7	13.8
1983	1,016.4	1,156.2	–139.8	8.6	12.0
1984	1,123.6	1,232.4	–108.8	9.6	12.7
1985	1,217.0	1,342.2	–125.3	7.5	11.4
1986	1,290.8	1,437.5	–146.8	6.0	9.0
1987	1,405.2	1,516.9	–111.7	5.8	9.4
1988	1,492.4	1,590.7	–98.3	6.7	9.7
1989	1,622.6	1,700.1	–77.5	8.1	9.3
1990	1,704.4	1,840.5	–136.1	7.5	9.3
1991	1,746.8	1,940.1	–193.3	5.4	8.8
1992	1,809.6	2,094.9	–285.2	3.5	8.1

Sources: *Economic Report of the President*, 1993, Tables B-69 and B-77.